HUDSON^s

Historic Houses & Gardens
Castles and Heritage Sites

'Hudson's ...
not just excellent, it is indispensable'

Simon Jenkins, *The Times*

2 0 0 4

Published by:

NORMAN HUDSON & COMPANY

High Wardington House, Upper Wardington, Banbury, Oxfordshire OX17 1SP, United Kingdom

Tel: +44 (0) 1295 750750 • Fax: +44 (0) 1295 750800 • e-mail: enquiries@hudsons.co.uk

www.hudsonsguide.co.uk

THE GLOBE PEQUOT PRESS
246 Goose Lane, Guilford, Connecticut 06437, USA

REGIONS ... REGIONS ... REGIONS ... REGIONS ... REGIONS ... REGIONS

N IRELAND

THE OUTER ISLANDS

SHETLAND ISLANDS

JOHN O' GROATS

ORKNEY ISLANDS

JOHN O' GROATS

GRAMPIAN HIGHLANDS

& SKYE

PERTHSHIRE/FIFE

GREATER GLASGOW

EDINBURGH

BORDERS

SOUTH WEST SCOTLAND

NORTHUMBERLAND

TYNE & WEAR

CUMBRIA

DURHAM

YORKSHIRE

LANCASHIRE

MERSEYSIDE

CHESHIRE

CONWY

DENBIGHSHIRE

WREXHAM

GWYNEDD

DERBY-SHIRE

NOTTING-HAMSHIRE

LINCOLNSHIRE

STAFFORD-SHIRE

LEICESTER-SHIRE

RUTLAND

NORFOLK

SHROP-SHIRE

WEST MIDLANDS

POWYS

WORCESTER-SHIRE

WARWICK-SHIRE

NORTHAMPTON-SHIRE

CAMBRIDGE-SHIRE

SUFFOLK

CEREDIGION

HEREFORD-SHIRE

BEDFORDSHIRE

CARMARTHEN-SHIRE

MONMOUTH-SHIRE

GLOUCESTER-SHIRE

BUCKINGHAM-SHIRE

HERTFORD-SHIRE

ESSEX

SWANSEA

CAERPHILLY

NEWPORT

OXFORD-SHIRE

LONDON

BRIDGEND

CARDIFF

BERKSHIRE

SURREY

KENT

WILTSHIRE

HAMPSHIRE

W. SUSSEX

E. SUSSEX

SOMERSET

DEVON

DORSET

ISLE OF WIGHT

CHANNEL ISLANDS
Guernsey
Jersey
Alderney
Sark

Special Events Index

see pages 22 - 26

Historical re-enactments, gardening festivals, country & craft fairs, concerts, fireworks, car and steam rallies.

Accommodation Index

see page 31

Historic properties which offer accommodation - from basic comfort to ultimate luxury.

Civil Wedding Venues

see pages 32 - 33

Places where the ceremony itself can take place and may also provide facilities for receptions.

Corporate Hospitality

see pages 34 - 37

Properties able to accommodate corporate functions, wedding receptions and events.

Plant Sales Index

see pages 39 - 40

Properties and gardens offering collections of rare and unusual plants not generally available.

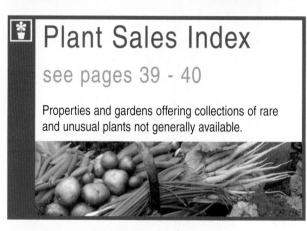

Website Information

see page 42

Access property and related heritage websites quickly and easily by using the direct links found at **www.hudsonsguide.co.uk**

Open All Year Index

see pages 43 - 47

Properties and/or their grounds included in this list are open all or most of the year.

Education Index

see pages 48 - 53

Properties providing facilities for schools/educational groups.

Access to Grant Aided Properties - page 541

English Heritage, as well as managing land opening properties in its care gives grants towards the cost of repairing outstanding buildings in private, National Trust and other ownerships, subject to appropriate public access being given.

1

Historic properties, such as those featured in *Hudson's*, are now used in a variety of ways. They make an enormous cultural, economic and social contribution to the nation.

Their cultural value is well recognised. The economic benefits from tourism, only a small proportion of which accrue to the property itself, fall mainly to other associated businesses and the wider community. The social contribution is gathering speed – providing wonderful resources for education, not just history but also the natural environment and as a means of including minority groups in what is also their heritage. With the growing number of weddings taking place at historic properties, they are also becoming milestone features in our personal lives.

This guide provides information that can be accessed speedily, with ease, and on the move. Further, more extensive information may be available on an individual property's website. That is why we give prominence to web addresses – most of which you can reach rapidly through our own much used portal site **www.hudsonsguide.co.uk**.

Norman Hudson

Norman Hudson OBE

Packwood House, Warwickshire. © NTPL /Stephen Robson

Hudson's Historic Houses & Gardens

Publisher and Editor-in-Chief	Norman Hudson
Editorial	Edwina Brash
Production Co-ordinator	Adrian Baggett
Administration	Jennie Carwithen
Graphic Design	KC Graphics
Maps	Taurus Graphics
Scanning & Pre-press	Spot-On Reprographics
Sales	Fiona Rolt
Printed by	Wyndeham Heron Ltd
UK & European Distribution	Portfolio - tel: 020 8997 9000
USA Distribution	The Globe Pequot Press - tel: 001 203 458 4505

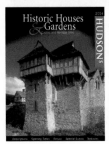

Published by:
Norman Hudson & Company
High Wardington House,
Upper Wardington, Banbury,
Oxfordshire OX17 1SP, UK
Tel: 01295 750750
Fax: 01295 750800
enquiries@hudsonsguide.co.uk
www.hudsonsguide.co.uk
ISBN: 1 904387 01 2

Co-published in the USA by:
The Globe Pequot Press
246 Goose Lane, Guilford,
Connecticut 06437, USA

**Library of Congress
Cataloging-in-Publication
data is available.**

ISBN: 0-7627-2526-5

UK Cover: Stokesay Castle © English Heritage Photo Library/Nigel Corrie
US Cover: Lodge Park © National Trust Photo Library/Nadia Mackenzie
Frontispiece: Flete, Devon © CHA Images

BEN

Black Environment Network

Our historic houses and gardens, castles and heritage sites can touch all of us through giving us an astonishing range of experiences. Yet not everyone is aware of this. Every school and community group should have a copy of *Hudson's* to open their eyes to unforgettable beauty and cultural richness.

The present movement for opening out our treasures to new audiences is very welcome. One example is the work that the Historic Houses Association (HHA) is doing in partnership with the Black Environment Network (BEN). Many features and artefacts in our historic properties point to our historical connections with the world. "Linking People and Places" is an innovative project which aims to bring together historic houses and ethnic minority communities to explore ways of designing programmes of activities in a culturally relevant way. BEN uses the word Black symbolically, working to increase access by black, white and other ethnic minority communities. Eight HHA member houses across Britain have come forward enthusiastically to pioneer the introduction of members of ethnic community groups to what is for them a new form of social activity. Others are ready to follow.

One of the participating houses is Arley Hall in Cheshire. Elderly members of the Wai Yin Chinese Women's Society were personally welcomed by Lord Ashbrook. At the sight of so many Chinese porcelain objects in Arley Hall, there were cries of delight "These are from our country !" Through the interpreter, they found common ground with Lord Ashbrook in his stories of the time he spent in China. They took immense interest in the interior design and wanted to learn about the care of items of furniture. They enjoyed seeing the ingredients of their traditional cooking growing in the herb garden. It was a lovely day out.

This significant pilot initiative has been marked by generosity and enjoyment. We look forward to future developments across the sector. For the many different social groups which are yet to experience our historic properties, such access programmes will ultimately release their vast missing contribution to the care and protection of our invaluable shared heritage. All of us care about what we are privileged to love and enjoy.

Judy Ling Wong   FRSA OBE
Director UK
Black Environment Network

Cottesbrooke Hall & Gardens, Nothamptonshire

The HHA Friends scheme provides amazing value for the interested house and gardens visitor

Athelhampton, Dorset

Eyam Hall, Derbyshire

The HHA is a group of highly individualistic and diverse properties most of which are still lived-in family houses. They range from the great palaces to small manor houses.

Many HHA member properties are open to the public and offer free admission to Friends of the HHA.

Southside House, London

Forde Abbey & Gardens, Dorset

Castle Howard, Yorkshire

Duart Castle, West Highlands & Islands

Minterne Gardens, Dorset

HISTORIC HOUSES ASSOCIATION

Become a Friend of the HHA and visit nearly 300 privately owned houses and gardens for FREE.

join on line
www.hha.org.uk

HISTORIC
HOUSES
ASSOCIATION

KINGSTON BAGPUIZE HOUSE, OXFORDSHIRE

Other benefits:

- Receive the quarterly magazine of the HHA which gives news and features about the Association, its members and our heritage

- Take advantage of organised tours in the UK and overseas

- Join the specially arranged visits to houses, some of which are not usually open to the public

LEVENS HALL GARDENS,
CUMBRIA

Richard Wilkin, Director General of the HHA, explains . . .

"It is not generally realised that two-thirds of Britain's built heritage remains in private ownership. There are more privately-owned houses, castles and gardens open to the public than are opened by the National Trust, English Heritage and their equivalents in Scotland and Wales put together.

Successive Governments have recognised the private owner as the most economic and effective guardian of this heritage. But the cost of maintaining these properties is colossal, and the task is daunting. The owners work enormously hard and take a pride in preserving and presenting this element of Britain's heritage.

The HHA helps them do this by:

- *representing their interests in Government*
- *providing an advisory service for houses – taxation, conservation, security, regulations, etc.*
- *running charities assisting disabled visitors, conserving works of art and helping promote educational facilities*

There is a fascinating diversity of properties to visit free with a Friends of the HHA card – from the great treasure houses such as Blenheim and Castle Howard through to small manor houses. What makes these places so special is their individuality and the fact that they are generally still lived in – often by the same family that has owned them through centuries of British history. As well as the stunning gardens which surround the houses, there are over 60 additional wonderful gardens to visit.

The subscription rate remains outstanding value for money. Individual Friend: £32. Double Friends living at the same address: £50 (each additional Friend living at same address, £15 – only available to holders of a Double Membership). If you wish to become a Friend of the HHA, and I very much hope you will, then you can join, using your credit/debit card by calling 01462 896688 or simply fill in the form below."

HOLKHAM HALL,
NORFOLK

Membership: Single £32, Double £50, £15 additional Friend at same address. Members of NADFAS, CLA and NACF are offered special rates of £29 Individual and £47 Double (at same address).

FRIENDS APPLICATION FORM   HHHG/04

PLEASE USE BLOCK CAPITALS   *DELETE AS APPROPRIATE

MR/MRS/MS or MR & MRS* INITIALS _____

SURNAME _____

ADDRESS _____

_____

_____ POST CODE _____

ADDITIONAL FRIENDS AT SAME ADDRESS

_____

_____

I/We* are members of NADFAS/NACF/CLA (please circle name of organisation to which you belong) our membership number is: _____

☐ I/We* enclose remittance of £_____ payable to the Historic Houses Association.

☐ I/We* have completed the direct debit adjacent.

Please return to: Historic Houses Association, Friends Membership Department, Heritage House, PO Box 21, Baldock, Hertfordshire SG7 5SH. **Tel: (01462) 896688**

PHOTOCOPIES OF THIS FORM ARE ACCEPTABLE

INSTRUCTION TO YOUR BANK TO PAY DIRECT DEBITS

Please complete Parts 1 to 5 to instruct your Bank to make payments directly from your account. Then return the form to: Historic Houses Association, Membership Department, Heritage House, PO Box 21, Baldock, Herts, SG7 5SH.
1. Name and full postal address of your Bank

_____

_____

_____

Your Bank may decline to accept instructions to pay Direct Debits from some types of accounts.

2. Account holder name _____

3. Account number ☐☐☐☐☐☐☐☐

4. Bank sort code ☐☐ ☐☐ ☐☐

Originator's identification No. |9|3|0|5|8|7|

Originator's reference (office use only) ☐☐☐☐☐☐

IF COMPLETING THE DIRECT DEBIT FORM, YOU MUST ALSO COMPLETE THE APPLICATION FORM.

5. Your instructions to the Bank and signature.

■ I instruct you to pay Direct Debits for my annual subscription from my account at the request of the Historic Houses Association.
■ The amounts are variable and may be debited on various dates.
■ I understand that the Historic Houses Association may change the amounts and dates only after giving me prior notice of not less than 21 days.
■ Please cancel all previous Standing Order and Direct Debiting instructions in favour of the Historic Houses Association.
■ I will inform the Bank in writing if I wish to cancel this instruction.
■ I understand that if any Direct Debit is paid which breaks the terms of the instruction, the Bank will make a refund.

Signature(s) _____

_____

_____

_____ Date _____

DIRECT Debit Completion of the form above ensures that your subscription will be paid automatically on the date that it is due. You may cancel the order at any time. The Association guarantees that it will only use this authority to deduct annually from your account an amount equal to the annual subscription then current for your class of membership.

'Years spent as an archaeologist working on ruins cannot equal the pleasure of living in the real thing.'

When did you last stay in a pineapple?

The Landmark Trust is a charity that rescues and restores worthwhile historic buildings and gives them a new life by offering them for holidays.

By sleeping, eating and living in a building you can study it at leisure, be there early and late and in all lights and weather. You will come to know it and its habits and understand why and how its builders made it as they did.

Beamsley Hospital, North Yorkshire, a circular stone Almshouse built in the 16th century.

Sleeps 5 people.

The Pineapple is just one of the buildings featured in the Landmark Trust Handbook, your first step to staying at some of the country's finest buildings.

Browsing through its 212 pages, you will find details of 175 buildings from the humblest of cottages to the most ornamental of banqueting houses, each one is remarkable in some way for its architecture, history or setting. The Handbook is far more than a holiday guide with a description of each building, local maps showing places of interest and detailed plans of the accommodation.

The 20th Edition of the Landmark Trust Handbook currently costs £9.50 when sent to a UK address, which is refundable on your first booking. Payment can be made online **www.landmarktrust.co.uk** or by telephoning our Booking Office on **01628 825925** using MasterCard, Visa, Switch, Delta, sterling cheque.

Stogursey Castle, Somerset, a thatched gatehouse on the site of a ruined 13th century castle.

Sleeps 4 people.

The Landmark Trust

Shottesbrooke, Maidenhead, Berkshire, SL6 3SW

Registered Charity 243312

THE NATIONAL TRUST

Miles of coastline and big stately houses…

For many people, that's what the National Trust is all about. And it's partly true, for the Trust has an excellent track record saving country houses and their collections, and protecting vast swathes of beautiful countryside and coastline. But this is not the whole story. Indeed, much of the Trust's work and resources are focused on smaller properties, which although sometimes undersung and overlooked, make as vital a contribution to our national heritage as any large country house or landscape park.

Souter Lighthouse, Tyne and Wear.
NTPL/Matthew Antrobus

The National Trust welcomes visitors to over 300 historic buildings and gardens in total, ranging from industrial sites such as Quarry Bank Mill in Cheshire to epic country estates like that at Cragside in Northumberland.

Some of these properties are huge – like Lanhydrock in Cornwall, with over 50 rooms on show – but size is not everything! Small can be beautiful, too. In an age when we are increasingly aware of the importance of local distinctiveness – of what makes one part of the country different from another – the more modest buildings really come into their own. Built and furnished using local materials and in styles that reflect their immediate environment, these smaller properties can speak to us on a direct and intimate level. They offer a different type of visit, and the

chance to connect with our own past.

In the heart of the Snowdonia National Park are two wonderful examples. Ty Mawr Wybrnant, set delightfully in a small valley, is a classic Welsh hill farmhouse, with thick stone walls and a heavy slate roof. In the next valley is Ty'n-y-Coed Uchaf, a typical small-holding surrounded by traditionally managed fields. Once commonplace across upland Wales, these types of dwelling are increasingly scarce in such an unaltered state. Oakhurst Cottage in Surrey offers an equally rare glimpse into a way of rural life that is all but gone today. Once a labourer's house on the edge of the heath, this delightful timber-framed building has a cottage garden full of flowers and vegetables. The unchanged interior reflects the often cramped nature

of domestic life in the past, with the whole family gathering round the hearth in the evenings and the cooking done in a pot over the fire.

Although many of the National Trust's smaller properties are important for their ability to tell the story of ordinary folk, some are notable for their association with a famous figure. These include Shaw's Corner, a typical Edwardian family house in which the celebrated playwright George Bernard Shaw lived and wrote, and Hardy's Cottage, the childhood home of Thomas Hardy. Built in cob, brick and thatch, this modest but charming house is set in the heart of the dramatic landscape that Hardy came to describe so evocatively. In later life he lived in more exalted circumstances at Max Gate, a classic red-brick villa in Dorchester which he designed

World War soldiers, these touching scenes show the men making their beds, picking berries and cooking breakfast in an oasis of calm and normality amid the wider nightmare around them.

Daily life has changed so much in recent decades that reminders of how things used to be are often little short of revelatory. This is especially so with buildings designed for a particular purpose or function and which may now be virtually redundant. Buildings like Finch Foundry in Devon, for example. This water-powered ironworks dates from the early nineteenth century and specialised in the production of agricultural and mining tools. With demand for these falling away dramatically during the second half of the twentieth century, the foundry closed in 1960. However, the Trust has maintained the machinery in good working order and the huge tilt hammers and grindstone can still be seen in action.

The demise of such small-scale industrial enterprises, once vital to village life, was mirrored across Britain in the last century. Whole industries came and went. For example, in the 1850s there were 28 linen mills in Belfast alone, part of the lucrative Irish linen industry. Today Wellbrook Beetling Mill, rescued by the National Trust in 1969, survives as one of the last working examples of its type. The original machinery has been restored, and regular demonstrations show how 'beetling' (the final part of the linen-

making process, in which the cloth was pounded repeatedly by hammers to give it a characteristic sheen) was carried out.

The National Trust has always championed the cause of vernacular buildings and indeed it was this concern that helped lead to the creation of the organisation in 1895. Over a century later, the Trust's commitment continues with the recent acquisition of Court 15 Inge Street, in the heart of Birmingham. Built in 1789, this terrace of several houses is one of the last surviving 'Back to Backs' in the city and was somehow spared in the large-scale slum clearances that took place after World War II. As an insight into the past it is unparalleled, a powerful reminder of Birmingham's industrial heyday and of the harsh social conditions of that time. The 'Back to Backs' is opening to the public for the first time in 2004; further details are available on 0121 753 7757.

himself and where he wrote some of his most successful novels.

For sheer atmosphere it is difficult to beat Clouds Hill, where T.E.Lawrence – 'of Arabia' – lived until his untimely death in a motorcycle accident. Set on a slope deep in the woods and containing tiny rooms, this stark yet intimate cottage encapsulates the spartan, spiritual life that Lawrence retired to after his desert adventures. A similarly atmospheric quality can be found at Sandham Memorial Chapel, perched on the downs near Newbury and built to house Stanley Spencer's superb murals. Depicting the everyday lives of First

Chartwell, Kent.

Ickworth, Suffolk.

Belton House, Lincolnshire.

Knightshayes Court, Devon.

Kingston Lacy, Dorset.

So next time you are planning a visit to an historic property, why not seek out one of these little gems? Many of them hold events and demonstrations explaining their history and the lives of the people who lived or worked there. And if big country houses are still your first choice, remember that many of the large estates also have a variety of fascinating smaller buildings to explore. Take Killerton in Devon, where the elegant country house is complemented by a water-powered grain mill, a medieval cob house, a 1950s post office room, an ice house, a summer house called 'The Bear's Hut' and a range of vernacular farm-buildings, not to mention a superb garden and miles of estate walks. More than enough for a day out!

Corfe Castle Estate, Dorset.
© NTPL/David Levenson

THE NATIONAL TRUST

To find out more about National Trust properties near you visit www.nationaltrust.org.uk or call 0870 458 4000

Florence Court, Ireland.
© NTPL/Matthew Antrobus

Belton House, Lincolnshire.
© NTPL/Ian Shaw

Red House, London.
© NTPL/Andrew Butler

Llanerchaeron, Wales.
© NTPL/Andrew Butler

The Workhouse, Nottinghamshire.
© NTPL/Andrew Butler

ENGLISH HERITAGE

Exquisite historic venues and stunning locations for memorable events

kenwood house

wellington arch

kenwood house

Special occasions for both business and pleasure become unforgettable when they are staged in the stylish surroundings of an English Heritage historic property.

osborne house

Whether in London, town or country, English Heritage's prestigious properties are well-known for their stunning architecture and unique historic pedigree. Now they can be hired as venues for exclusive events. Grand houses where royalty and nobility lived and entertained, romantic coastal castles where the course of history was changed and London locations that will impress the most sophisticated guests can be hired for private and corporate events that offer discreet novelty and unarguable cachet.

Dedicated hospitality managers at each venue offer expertise – and the personal touch – helping to plan and fine-tune all arrangements. By choosing English Heritage, clients are also assured that carefully selected top class caterers, florists, entertainers and other essential suppliers will be dedicated to providing the finest service.

eltham palace

chiswick house

venue hire and hospitality

Venues available for hire	Location	Hospitality Manager Contact Telephone Numbers
Audley End House and Gardens	Essex	020 7973 3675
Bolsover Castle	Derbyshire	01246 856456
Chiswick House	London	020 7973 3292
Deal Castle	Kent	01304 211067
Dover Castle	Kent	01304 211067
Eltham Palace	London	020 8294 2577
Kenwood House	London	020 7973 3507
Marble Hill House	London	020 7973 3534
Osborne House	Isle of Wight	01983 200022
Pendennis Castle	Cornwall	01326 310106
St Mawes Castle	Cornwall	01326 310106
Walmer Castle and Gardens	Kent	01304 211067
Wellington Arch	London	020 7973 3292

st mawes castle

pendennis castle

walmer castle and gardens

ENGLISH HERITAGE

kenwood house

chiswick house

ENGLISH HERITAGE

bolsover castle

eltham palace

13

All venues are suitable for wedding receptions, parties and corporate hospitality

London
Chiswick House
Eltham Palace
Kenwood House
Marble Hill House
Wellington Arch

South East
Deal Castle, Kent
Dover Castle, Kent
Osborne House, Isle of Wight
Walmer Castle & Gardens, Kent

South West
Pendennis Castle, Cornwall
St Mawes Castle, Cornwall

Eastern
Audley End House & Gardens, Essex

East Midlands
Bolsover Castle, Derbyshire

also licensed for civil wedding ceremonies

London
Chiswick House
Eltham Palace

South West
Pendennis Castle, Cornwall

East Midlands
Bolsover Castle, Derbyshire

bolsover castle

eltham palace

chiswick house

osborne house

eltham palace

eltham palace

dover castle

ENGLISH HERITAGE
www.english-heritage.org.uk/hospitality

14

The Churches Conservation Trust cares for over 330 churches in England of exceptional historic, architectural, or archaeological importance which are no longer needed for regular parish use.

The Trust encourages public appreciation and enjoyment of these churches. Our website, **www.visitchurches.org.uk** provides everything you need to know to visit a church, including background, directions, opening arrangements and images. The Lumley Chapel, Cheam, Surrey, pictured here, is just one of our outstanding churches, however all have something special to offer – and can be visited *free* throughout the year.

Overleaf you will find a taster of some of the exceptional churches in our care. For further information visit our website. Alternatively, send off for our free county guides and Your Starter for 50 using the tear off slip on the back page.

Caring for historic churches throughout England for all to enjoy

THE CHURCHES
CONSERVATION TRUST

www.visitchurches.org.uk

DEVON

Torbryan, Holy Trinity

The approach to this church, through typical narrow Devon lanes to an isolated and wooded valley, does not prepare visitors for a building of such size and grandeur. The fine Perpendicular tower rises in three stages and the central stair turret on the south wall is a dramatic feature. Unusually, the church was constructed in one 20-year building campaign, from about 1450 to 1470. The south porch has an exquisite fan-vaulted ceiling. A magnificent carved mediaeval rood-screen spans the church from wall to wall, with graceful arches and tracery, and panels below, each containing a painting of a saint. The delicacy of the woodcarving is echoed by the elegant tracery of the windows, many of which contain mediaeval stained glass.

4m SW of Newton Abbot, off A381
SX 820 669
Open daily

SHROPSHIRE

Shrewsbury, St Mary the Virgin

Standing on high ground in the heart of the town, St Mary's is now the only complete mediaeval church in Shrewsbury. The spire, said to be the third highest in England, dominates the skyline. St Mary's most famous treasure is the wonderful collection of stained glass, with examples of different styles from the 14th to the 19th centuries, all of the highest quality. Much of the glass was brought from Europe in the 18th and 19th centuries. Most spectacular is the huge 14th-century east window depicting the Tree of Jesse. Warmth and richness are also provided by superb coloured Victorian floor tiles. The wonderful 15th-century carved oak ceiling of the nave has a profusion of animals, birds and angels.

St Mary's Street, opposite the main Post Office
SJ 494 126
Open Mon–Fri 10am–5pm, Sat 10am–4pm
and occasional Sundays
Custodian 01743 357 006

CUMBRIA

Brougham, St Ninian

Known locally as Ninekirks, St Ninian's stands remote down a long track, above a bend in the River Eamont, and with views of the Pennines and the Lake District. The original Norman church was completely rebuilt in the 17th century by Lady Anne Clifford, who inherited Brougham Castle. Her restoration work is recorded in the plasterwork above the altar with her initials and the date 1660. The long, low, sandstone building is almost unaltered since, and its simplicity, combined with excellent workmanship, make it enchanting and memorable. The interior is whitewashed, with clear glass in the windows and a stone-flagged floor. The fine oak fittings include box pews, and family pews with canopies, an elegant screen, and a three-decker pulpit.

3m E of Penrith off A66
NY 559 299
Open daily

WORCESTERSHIRE

Croome d'Abitot, St Mary Magdalene

The present church, set on a low hill in Croome Park, was designed as an 'eye-catcher' by Lancelot 'Capability' Brown for the 6th Earl of Coventry as part of a mid-18th-century scheme to replace his adjacent Jacobean House and redesign the parkland. The interiors of both house and church are attributed to Robert Adam and were completed in 1763. The church is in the Gothick style with elegant windows, and interior features designed by Adam include plasterwork, the hexagonal pulpit, communion rails, an intricate classical mahogany font and floors of limestone slabs with patterned insets of black slate. The chancel is a mausoleum to the Coventry family with splendid monuments brought from the old church demolished by the 6th Earl.

4m W of Pershore off A38 and A4104;
follow National Trust signs to Croome
Landscape Park
SO 886 450
Open Mar–Dec, Thu–Mon 11am–5pm
Other times by arrangement 01905 371 006

NORTH YORKSHIRE

York, Holy Trinity Goodramgate

Approached through a gateway off Goodramgate, Holy Trinity hides in a small, secluded, leafy churchyard, with the Minster towering behind. Dating mostly from the 15th century, it is an unpretentious building, with uneven floors and the arcades slightly askew. The colour of the stone and the gentle light from the stained glass enrich the interior. The east window has marvellous stained glass donated in the early 1470s by the Revd John Walker, rector of the church. The furnishings date mostly from the 17th and 18th centuries. The box pews, unique in York, are exceptionally fine, and there is an interesting collection of monuments and memorials. Two boards record the names of Lord Mayors of the city, including George Hudson 'The Railway King'.

Off Goodramgate in city centre
SE 605 522
Open Mon–Sat, 10am–5pm, Sun, 12pm–5pm
(summer), Tue–Sat, 10am–4pm (winter)
Custodian 01904 613 451

SHROPSHIRE

Wroxeter, St Andrew

St Andrew's is built on the site of the Roman town of *Viroconium*. The gateway to the churchyard is formed by a pair of Roman columns, massive Roman stones are built into the walls of the nave, and the huge font is made from the capital of a Roman column. The church is an archaeologist's delight. Dating from before the Domesday Book (1086), the building has been altered and enlarged throughout the centuries. The mostly 17th- and 18th-century interior has excellent woodwork in the box pews, pulpit and altar rails. There are splendid 16th-century monuments. The earliest and finest, carved in alabaster, commemorates Lord Chief Justice Sir Thomas Bromley and his wife Mabel. There is a fine Royal Arms of 1765.

5m SE of Shrewsbury off B4380 next to
English Heritage Roman site
SJ 564 083
Open daily

GLOUCESTERSHIRE

Gloucester, St Nicholas

The truncated and coronetted spire of St Nicholas to the west of the cathedral is a familiar landmark in the city. Dating in part from the 12th century, the church was extensively rebuilt and enlarged in the 13th century, with Perpendicular windows added in the 14th and 15th centuries. The splendid tower with a fine decorated vault was built around 1450. Formerly one of Gloucester's most prosperous parish churches, many of its monuments commemorate significant citizens. Most notable is the altar tomb of Alderman John Wallton, sheriff in 1613 (d.1626) and his wife Alice. 16th-century squints on either side of the chancel gave the congregation a view of the sanctuary. Above the south door is a Royal Arms of Charles II.

Westgate Street in city centre
SO 829 188
Open 1 Apr–30 Sep, Thu & Fri
10.30am–2.30pm, Sat 10.30am–3.30pm
Other times keyholder nearby

WEST YORKSHIRE

Leeds, St John the Evangelist

St John's, built in 1632–34, is the oldest church in Leeds city centre. The glory of the church lies in its Jacobean fittings, particularly the superb carved wooden screen, with lovely carving on the wall panels, pews and pulpit. The ceiling panels have pretty plaster reliefs, and the corbels supporting the beams have curiously carved creatures, including angels with musical instruments. The 19th-century stained glass includes a memorial window to the church's founder, John Harrison, a wealthy local wool merchant. Monuments commemorating the citizens of Leeds emphasise the importance of the wool industry to the city's prosperity. A mid-19th-century restoration by Norman Shaw, after the church was saved from demolition, is very much in the original style of the building.

New Briggate in central Leeds
SE 302 338
Open Tue–Sat, 9.30am–5.30pm
Custodian 0113 244 1689

NORFOLK

Little Witchingham, St Faith

This outwardly modest 12th-century church with 14th-century additions and a 15th-century tower, set among trees in a country lane, conceals a great treasure within. The north wall of the nave, tower arch, south side of the arcade and south wall contain a remarkable sequence of 14th-century wall paintings, only discovered in 1967, when the unrestored church was near to ruin, and subsequently conserved by Eve Baker. Designs feature the symbols of the Evangelists shown in cusped roundels – which are among the finest paintings of this period in the country, the story of the Passion and Resurrection, St George and delightful vine leaf decoration. Today the interior of St Faith's enables visitors to imagine what an ordinary church looked like in the early 14th century.

9m W of Norwich and 3m S of Reepham off A1067
TG 115 203
Open daily

BUCKINGHAMSHIRE

Edlesborough, St Mary the Virgin

Situated on an isolated chalk hillock with fine views from its churchyard, St Mary's is a prominent landmark in the Vale of Aylesbury. The building dates from the 13th century, with 14th- and 15th-century additions, including the massive limestone tower. The interior was restored in the 19th and 20th centuries, and contains a wealth of furnishings and decorations, including the fine mediaeval woodwork of the chancel screen, pulpit, choir desks, stalls with carved misericords, and the nave and chancel roofs. Above the chancel arch is a striking scheme of mid-Victorian wall painting by Daniel Bell. Mediaeval and Victorian floor tiles and a fine stained glass window of 1898 by Kempe in the chancel are also notable. There are excellent brasses in the sanctuary and north transept.

11m ENE of Aylesbury on A4146
TL 970 191
Keyholder nearby

CAMBRIDGESHIRE

Cambridge, All Saints

This imposing Victorian church, opposite the gates of Jesus College, was designed by G F Bodley, and built between 1863 and 1870 in the Decorated style of the early 14th century. The soaring spire is a prominent landmark in the city. The majestic interior displays great unity of design, colour and ornament, largely following Bodley's original specification. The painted wall and ceiling decorations of remarkable scale and beauty were executed by Kempe and others. The east window contains fine stained glass by Morris & Co., to designs by Burne-Jones, Ford Madox Brown and William Morris, and there are other windows by Kempe and Morris. Fittings designed by Bodley include the alabaster font, pulpit with painted panels and oak aisle screen.

Jesus Lane
TL 452 587
Open 31 Mar–31 Oct, Wed–Sun
10.30am–3.30pm
Other times keyholder nearby

SURREY

Cheam, Lumley Chapel

Situated within the churchyard of 19th-century St Dunstan's, Lumley Chapel is the former chancel and only surviving portion of the original late-11th-century church demolished in 1864 when the present building was constructed. John, Lord Lumley refurnished the chapel in the 1590s as a burial place for himself and his two wives. Memorials to the Lumley family and other local residents display carving and craftsmanship of the highest order. The most elaborately designed and detailed is the marble monument to Lumley's first wife Jane, through whom he inherited nearby Nonsuch Palace. The chapel also contains a collection of late mediaeval brasses from the former Fromond Chapel. 20th-century stained glass in the east window includes the arms of the Lumley family.

Off A2043 Malden Road (next to Cheam Library)
TQ 243 638
Keyholder nearby

Churches in the care of The Churches Conservation Trust

All churches on the map are opened regularly or have keyholders nearby*.
For further information on our churches visit www.visitchurches.org.uk

*Please remember that emergency building work may mean that we need to close a church temporarily for safety reasons.

Complete and send to The Churches Conservation Trust, 1 West Smithfield, London, EC1A 9EE

Name.. Title ....

Address .... Postcode ....

Please send me: *Your Starter for 50* booklet ☐

Full List of Churches in the care of The Churches Conservation Trust ☐

County leaflets, please specify county(ies) ....

Why not visit our website? www.visitchurches.org.uk

HHH5

THE CHURCHES
CONSERVATION TRUST

CADW
WELSH HISTORIC MONUMENTS

The National Assembly for Wales
Cathays Park
Cardiff CF10 3NQ
Telephone: 029 2050 0200   Fax: 029 2082 6375
E-mail: cadw@wales.gsi.gov.uk

Cadw is the executive agency of the Welsh Assembly Government exercising the **National Assembly for Wales's** statutory responsibilities to protect, conserve and promote an appreciation of the built heritage of Wales.

Cadw gives grant aid for the repair or restoration of outstanding historic buildings. Usually it is a condition of grant that the owner or occupier should allow some degree of public access to the property. Conditions of grant remain in force for ten years.

Details of properties grant aided by Cadw and to which the public currently enjoys a right of access can be found on Cadw's website: **www.cadw.wales.gov.uk**

This contains a wide range of information, including details of buildings and monuments in its care. If you experience any difficulty in exercising the rights of access indicated, please write to Cadw at the above address or contact us via telephone, fax or e-mail.

Cadw encourages you to visit these properties, as well as buildings and monuments in its care.

Celebrate the

RHS Bicentenary and Year of Gardening

The British love of gardening will be celebrated next year as the Royal Horticultural Society (RHS) - the UK's leading gardening charity – marks its bicentenary with a year of special events and activities.

Exhibitions, lectures and shows will be held around the country, with a birthday flavour to the RHS's 18 annual flower shows including those at Chelsea, Hampton Court Palace and Tatton Park. To share its celebrations with gardening enthusiasts of all abilities, in this the 'Year of Gardening', the RHS's programme of events will be launched officially at the Horticultural Halls in London on February 16. Other events planned include:

❦ a series of six inspirational evening lectures, "The World in Our Gardens – Two Centuries of Plant Introductions" – hosted by the Royal Geographical Society with the Institute of British Geographers (January to December);

❦ an exhibition at London's Tate Britain, "Art of the Garden" (June 3 - August 30) celebrating British paintings of plants and gardens;

❦ an International Lily Show and Conference at RHS Horticultural Halls (June 29 - July 3);

❦ a series of exhibitions at the RHS Lindley Library, 80 Vincent Square, London SW1 – the world's finest gardening library – the subjects including Mediterranean plants in Britain (May 15 - 29) and Frederick Warne's "Flower Fairies" paintings and drawings (September 14 - October 30);

❦ a special bicentenary exhibit at the Chelsea Flower Show (May 25 - 28);

❦ the Hampton Court Flower Show (July 6 - 11) – the world's largest annual flower show;

❦ more than 80 museums, gardening organisations and community groups around Britain will take part in the 'Year of Gardening' by holding exhibitions, displays and other events.

Founded by seven friends in March 1804 as the Horticultural Society of London, the RHS now has more than 330,000 members around the world. There are hundreds of gardens open to the public in Britain, many of them the grounds of stately homes, castles and historic houses featured in *Hudson's*. For those properties in *Hudson's* that offer free access to RHS members, please refer to the listing on page 41.

For full details of the anniversary programme click on the link from www.hudsonsguide.co.uk to www.rhs.org.uk

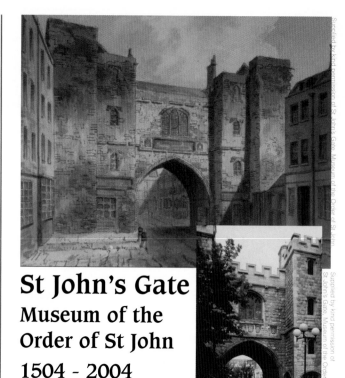

St John's Gate
Museum of the Order of St John
1504 - 2004

Take time in 2004 to visit the fascinating Museum of the Order of St John in London.

The Museum and Library of the Order of St John is situated in St John's Gate, which was built in 1504. It served as the entrance to the Priory of Clerkenwell, which was the British headquarters of the Knights Hospitaller during and after the Crusades.

After the dissolution of the monasteries by Henry VIII in 1540 it became the palace of Mary Tudor, the Revels Office, a coffee house run by Richard Hogarth (father of the painter William), and a public house called the Old Jerusalem Tavern. In the 18th century the Gate was the home and printing works of the *Gentleman's Magazine*, playing host to Dr Johnson and David Garrick. In 1874 the British Order of St John obtained the building.

The Gate houses the historic collections of the Order, including Maltese silver and furniture, pharmacy jars, paintings, prints, drawings and arms and armour. The Museum illustrates the history of the Knights Hospitaller from the time of the Crusades to the present day, including a recently built section devoted to St John Ambulance.

To celebrate the 500th anniversary, the Museum will be holding various family events through the year. The Gate will also play host to the launch in May of a book on the archaeological excavations of the Priory site entitled 'A Lost Palace of London' published by English Heritage and the Museum of London Archaeological Service. A temporary exhibition on the history of the Priory featuring material found in the excavations has been planned.

For further details about St John's Gate, London please see page 84.

Centenaries
2004

Dispatches from Blenheim!

Visit Blenheim Palace and discover how one man changed the history of England, Europe and the world.

2004 is the 300th anniversary of one of the most important battles in English military history. On August 13th 1704 at Blindheim in Bavaria, the Allied troops under John Churchill, the first Duke of Marlborough, defeated the forces of Louis XIV in the War of the Spanish Succession. In doing so Churchill saved Vienna – and ultimately England – from French invasion.

So important was the battle that Queen Anne bestowed on Churchill Blenheim and the means to build the Palace in recognition of his victory and as a gift 'from a grateful nation'.

Many historians rank John Churchill's military achievements as comparable with those of Montgomery or Wellington, for if he had failed in his mission against the French in 1704 the world today could be a very different place. French could have come to be the dominant language in the majority of what is today a largely English-speaking Western world, and the role of the British in exploring the New World, together with the political and religious make-up of Europe as a whole, could have been very different.

To mark the 300th anniversary of this historic victory, the Palace will play host to a number of excellent special events:

❧ Costumed characters and historical re-enactments will bring history to life at the Palace from 14-29 February, Bank Holiday weekend 1-3 May, the weekend of August 13 (anniversary of the Battle of Blenheim) and half term, October 23-31.

❧ Visit the inaugural three day music festival held in the stunning courtyard of the Palace from July 1-3. Guests will enjoy a variety of music over the course of the festival including pop, jazz and classical.

For a listing of other special events at Blenheim, refer to the *Hudson's* Special Events Index, and see the entry for Blenheim Palace, Oxfordshire on page 142.

Blenheim Palace © Skyscan Photolibrary

Right: Battle of Blenheim Tapestry © By the kind permission of His Grace The Duke of Marlborough and Jarrold Publishing 1993, 1996, 1999, 2000, 2002.

Left: Detail from the Schellenburg Tapestry: Marlborough prepares to storm the fortress. © By the kind permission of His Grace The Duke of Marlborough and Jarrold Publishing 1993, 1996, 1999, 2000, 2002.

This information is intended only as a guide, please check with individual properties before travelling. More information on Special Events can be obtained from individual property websites – for quick access to these sites visit: www.hudsonsguide.co.uk

JANUARY

31
Hatfield House & Gardens, Hertfordshire
Rock 'n' Gem Show.

FEBRUARY

1
Hatfield House & Gardens, Hertfordshire
Rock 'n' Gem Show.

8
Hatfield House & Gardens, Hertfordshire
Snowdrop Sunday.

8
Kelmarsh Hall, Northamptonshire
Snowdrop Day.

11 - 12
Hatfield House & Gardens, Hertfordshire
Living History Days (for school groups).

15
Hatfield House & Gardens, Hertfordshire
Snowdrop Sunday.

20 - 22
Stowe House, Buckinghamshire
Homes & Gardens Exhibition.

22
Hatfield House & Gardens, Hertfordshire
Snowdrop Sunday.

27 - 29
Hatfield House & Gardens, Hertfordshire
Bailey Antiques Fair.

MARCH

1 - 31
Exbury Gardens & Steam Railway, Hampshire
'Drawn from Nature' Sculpture Exhibition in grounds.

1 - 31
Fairfax House, Yorkshire
Gilray & Gout – an 18th century view of men behaving badly.

5 - 7
Wilton House, Wiltshire
27th Annual Antiques Fair.

6
Blenheim Palace, Oxfordshire
Winston Churchill Memorial Concert, Palace (separate admission) tel Rosie Lewis 01869 350049.

6 - 7
RHS Garden Wisley, Surrey
Hellebore Weekend.

7
Hatfield House & Gardens, Hertfordshire
Dolls Houses & Miniatures Fair.

17 - 18
Hatfield House & Gardens, Hertfordshire
Living History Days (for school groups).

21
Hatfield House & Gardens, Hertfordshire
Book Fair.

26
Blair Castle, Perthshire
Perthshire Tourism Fair.

28
Kelmarsh Hall, Northamptonshire
Daffodil Day.

APRIL

1 - 30
Exbury Gardens & Steam Railway, Hampshire
'Drawn from Nature' Sculpture Exhibition in grounds.

1 - 30
Fairfax House, Yorkshire
Gilray & Gout – an 18th century view of men behaving badly.

3
Hatfield House & Gardens, Hertfordshire
British Model Soldiers Society Annual Show.

3 - 4
Boconnoc, Cornwall
Cornwall Spring Flower Show.

9 - 12
Blenheim Palace, Oxfordshire
Tercentenary Event – Easter Egg Challenge.

11
Cobham Hall, Kent
National Garden Scheme (+ House open 2-5pm).

11
Floors Castle, Borders
Easter Eggstravaganza.

11
Newby Hall & Gardens, Yorkshire
Easter Fun Day.

11
Traquair, Borders
Easter Egg Extravaganza.

11 - 12
Boughton Monchelsea Place, Kent
Classic Car & Transport Show.

11 - 12
Eastnor Castle, Herefordshire
Easter Treasure Hunt.

11 - 12
Holdenby House Gardens & Falconry Centre, Northamptonshire
Victorian Easter.

11 - 12
Milton Manor House, Oxfordshire
Easter Egg Hunt

16 - 18
Wilton House, Wiltshire
Flower Show.

17 - 18
Hatfield House & Gardens, Hertfordshire
Shakespeare Sonnet Walks.

18
RHS Garden Rosemoor, Devon
NCCPG Plant Sale.

18
Stowe House, Buckinghamshire
Plant Fair.

23 - 25
Blair Castle, Perthshire
Tartan Exhibition (9.30am - 4.30pm).

25
Beaulieu, Hampshire
Boat Jumble & Boatworld.

27 - 28
RHS Garden Wisley, Surrey
Late Daffodil Competition.

1 - 3
Blenheim Palace, Oxfordshire
Tercentenary Event – Re-enactment Battles.

1 - 3
Constable Burton Hall Gardens, Yorkshire
Tulip Festival (groups tours of the house and gardens by arrangement).

1 - 3
Exbury Gardens & Steam Railway, Hampshire
Hampshire's Beautiful Craft & Garden Show.

1 - 3
Harewood House, Yorkshire
Noddy & Friends.

1 - 3
Leonardslee Lakes & Gardens, Sussex
Bonsai Weekend.

1 - 3
Raby Castle, Co Durham
Orchid Show.

1 - 30
Fairfax House, Yorkshire
Gilray & Gout – an 18th century view of men behaving badly.

1 - 31
Exbury Gardens & Steam Railway, Hampshire
'Drawn from Nature' Sculpture Exhibition in grounds.

2
Hatfield House & Gardens, Hertfordshire
Packard Automobile Club of GB Rally.

2
RHS Garden Harlow Carr, Yorkshire
NCCPG Plant Fair.

2 - 3
Eastnor Castle, Herefordshire
Spring Crafts Festival.

7 - 9
Blenheim Palace, Oxfordshire
Home and Interior Design Show (separate admission).

11 - 12
Holdenby House Gardens & Falconry Centre, Northamptonshire
Medieval Weekend.

6 - 9
Hatfield House & Gardens, Hertfordshire
Living Crafts.

9
Newby Hall & Gardens, Yorkshire
Spring Plant Fair.

9 - 31
Exbury Gardens & Steam Railway, Hampshire
SBA Exhibition in Five Arrows.

12 - 13
Hatfield House & Gardens, Hertfordshire
Living History Days (for school groups).

15
Hatfield House & Gardens, Hertfordshire
Model Soldiers Day.

15 - 16
Beaulieu, Hampshire
Spring Autojumble.

15 - 16
Parham House & Gardens
'Stitches in Time' – needlework event based on ecclesiastical theme.

19 - 23
Harewood House, Yorkshire
Spirit of the Horse.

20 - 26
Tissington Hall, Derbyshire
Well Dressings.

21 - 23
Blair Castle, Perthshire
Galloway Antiques Fair.

22 - 23
Floors Castle, Borders
Floors Castle Horse Trials.

22 - 23
Hatfield House & Gardens, Hertfordshire
An Exhibition of Exquisite Furniture.

23
Browsholme Hall, Lancashire
Garden and Craft Fair.

23
Traquair, Borders
Garden Lovers' Fair.

29
Blair Castle, Perthshire
Atholl Highlanders Parade (2.30pm).

29 - 30
Traquair, Borders
Medieval Fayre.

29 - 31
Blenheim Palace, Oxfordshire
Battle of Blenheim Exhibition, Stable Courtyard (included in admission price).

29 - 31
Blenheim Palace, Oxfordshire
Living Heritage Oxfordshire Craft Fair, Blenheim Park (included in admission price), tel 01283 820548.

29 - 31
Exbury Gardens & Steam Railway, Hampshire
The Exbury Festival of Art, Crafts & Gardens.

30
Blair Castle, Perthshire
Atholl Gathering and Highland Games (1.15pm).

30
Raby Castle, Co Durham
Raby Castle 10K Race (Teesdale Athletics Club).

30 - 31
Eastnor Castle, Herefordshire
Steam & Woodland Fair.

30 - 31
Lamport Hall & Gardens, Northamptonshire
17th Lamport Steam & Country Festival.

30 - 31
Finchcocks, Kent
Garden Fair & Flower Festival.

30 - 31
Holdenby House Gardens & Falconry Centre, Northamptonshire
Plant Fair.

30 - 31
RHS Garden Hyde Hall, Essex
Guild of Essex Craftsmen Craft Fair.

1 - 6
Exbury Gardens & Steam Railway, Hampshire
SBA Exhibition in Five Arrows.

1 - 30
Blenheim Palace, Oxfordshire
Battle of Blenheim Exhibition, Stable Courtyard (included in admission price).

1 - 30
Exbury Gardens & Steam Railway, Hampshire
'Drawn from Nature' Sculpture Exhibition in grounds.

4 - 6
Newby Hall & Gardens, Yorkshire
Craft Fair (Free Spirit, tel 01777 701177).

5 - 6
Cawdor Castle, Highlands & Skye
Special Gardens Weekend – guided tours of gardens.

6
Raby Castle, Co Durham
Spring Plant Fair.

7 - 30
Fairfax House, Yorkshire
The Glory of Glass 1700-1850.

10 - 13
Blenheim Palace, Oxfordshire
Blenheim Palace Flower Show, Blenheim Park (separate admission), tel 01737 379911 Event Innovations Ltd.

10 - 13
Bramham Park, Yorkshire
Bramham International 3 Day Event.

10 - 13
Ripley Castle, Yorkshire
Grand Summer Sale.

11 - 13
Hatfield House & Gardens, Hertfordshire
Flower Festival.

12 - 13
RHS Garden Hyde Hall, Essex
Rose Weekend.

12 - 27
Groombridge Place & Gardens, Kent
Midsummer Garden Celebration.

13
Boughton Monchelsea Place, Kent
Gardens Open – NGS.

15
Harewood House, Yorkshire
Classic Car Rally.

16 - 17
Hatfield House & Gardens, Hertfordshire
Living History Days (for school groups).

20
Hatfield House & Gardens, Hertfordshire
Shakespeare in the Park: 'The Merry Wives of Windsor' by Theatre Set-Up.

20
RHS Garden Rosemoor, Devon
Rose Sunday.

23

22 - 24
RHS Garden Wisley, Surrey
Wisley Flower Show.

25 - 27
Harewood House, Yorkshire
Live Crafts.

26
Hatfield House & Gardens, Hertfordshire
Bentley Drivers Club National Rally.

26
Lamport Hall & Gardens, Northamptonshire
Shakespeare in the Garden.

26 - 27
Leonardslee Lakes & Gardens, Sussex
West Sussex Country Craft Fair.

26 - 30
Eyam Hall, Derbyshire
Eyam Hall Open Air Music & Drama Festival with 'Love's Labours Lost' by the Rain or Shine Theatre Company and 'Summer Serenade' by Baslow Choir.

27
Lamport Hall & Gardens, Northamptonshire
Traditional Jazz in the Garden.

27
Raby Castle, Co Durham
Vintage Car Rally.

J U L Y

1 - 3
Blenheim Palace, Oxfordshire
Tercentenary Event – Blenheim Music Festival (separate admission).

1 - 4
Eyam Hall, Derbyshire
Eyam Hall Open Air Music & Drama Festival with 'Love's Labours Lost' by the Rain or Shine Theatre Company and 'Summer Serenade' by Baslow Choir.

1 - 31
Blenheim Palace, Oxfordshire
Battle of Blenheim Exhibition, Stable Courtyard (included in admission price).

1 - 31
Fairfax House, Yorkshire
The Glory of Glass 1700-1850.

3
Exbury Gardens & Steam Railway, Hampshire
Bournemouth Symphony Orchestra Evening Concert.

3
Hatfield House & Gardens, Hertfordshire
Children's Folk Dance Festival.

3 - 4
Floors Castle, Borders
Gardeners' Festival – Herbaceous Perennials.

3 - 4
RHS Garden Harlow Carr, Yorkshire
Herb Event.

4
Harewood House, Yorkshire
Teddy Bears' Picnic.

6 - 7
RHS Garden Harlow Carr, Yorkshire
Shakespeare in the Gardens.

7
RHS Garden Wisley, Surrey
Summer Fruit & Vegetable Competition.

7 - 8
Hatfield House & Gardens, Hertfordshire
Living History Days (for school groups).

8
Harewood House, Yorkshire
Midsummer's Night Dream.

10 - 11
Beaulieu, Hampshire
4 x 4 Show.

10 - 11
Parham House & Gardens
'Garden Weekend' annual event.

10 - 11
Powderham Castle, Devon
30th Annual Historic Vehicle Rally.

11
Burton Constable Hall, Yorkshire
Burton Constable Country Fair.

11
Groombridge Place & Gardens, Kent
Hot Air Balloons & Ferraris.

11
Harewood House, Yorkshire
Jaguar Rally.

16 - 18
Boconnoc, Cornwall
Boconnoc Steam Fair.

17
Wilton House, Wiltshire
Classical Firework Concert.

17 - 18
Dalemain, Cumbria
Dalemain Craft Fair.

18
Cobham Hall, Kent
National Garden Scheme (+ House open 2-5pm).

21
Blair Castle, Perthshire
Blair Castle Highland Night (7.45pm - 9.15pm).

22
Floors Castle, Borders
As You Like It – Shakespeare open air theatre.

23 - 25
Blenheim Palace, Oxfordshire
CLA Game Fair, Blenheim Park (separate admission), tel 01256 389767.

23 - 25
Stourhead, Wiltshire
Fete Champetre.

24
Hatfield House & Gardens, Hertfordshire
Battle Proms Concert.

24
Raby Castle, Co Durham
As You Like It – outdoor theatre in the gardens.

24 - 26
Harewood House, Yorkshire
Leeds Championship Dog Show.

24 - 31
RHS Garden Hyde Hall, Essex
Festival Fortnight.

25 - 31
RHS Garden Harlow Carr, Yorkshire
Textile Exhibition.

28
Cobham Hall, Kent
Summer Stroll (guidebook tour and glass of wine, £5 pp – please telephone to book).

30
Eastnor Castle, Herefordshire
The Big Chill Festival (Deer Park) – info line 020 7684 2020.

31
Lamport Hall & Gardens, Northamptonshire
Shakespeare in the Garden.

31
Stowe House, Buckinghamshire
Stowe Opera.

31
Traquair, Borders
Traquair Fair.

A U G U S T

1
Boughton Monchelsea Place, Kent
Gardens Open – NGS.

1
Eastnor Castle, Herefordshire
The Big Chill Festival (Deer Park) – info line 020 7684 2020.

1
Lamport Hall & Gardens, Northamptonshire
Traditional Jazz in the Garden.

1
Powderham Castle, Devon
'Last Night of the Powderham Proms' Bournemouth Symphony Orchestra Open Air Firework Concert.

1
Traquair, Borders
Traquair Fair.

1 - 7
RHS Garden Hyde Hall, Essex
Festival Fortnight.

1 - 8
Stowe House, Buckinghamshire
Stowe Opera.

1 - 16
RHS Garden Harlow Carr, Yorkshire
Textile Exhibition.

1 - 31
Blenheim Palace, Oxfordshire
Battle of Blenheim Exhibition, Stable Courtyard (included in admission price).

1 - 31
Fairfax House, Yorkshire
The Glory of Glass 1700-1850.

2
Powderham Castle, Devon
Open Air Pop Concert.

6 - 8
Hatfield House & Gardens, Hertfordshire
Art in Clay (National Pottery & Ceramics Festival).

7 - 8
RHS Garden Rosemoor, Devon
Family Weekend.

8
Great Comp Garden, Kent
Annual Garden Show.

10 - 15
Boughton Monchelsea Place, Kent
Open Air Shakespeare – 'Romeo & Juliet'.

13
Blenheim Palace, Oxfordshire
SSAFA (separate admission).

14
Stowe House, Buckinghamshire
Battleproms Concert.

14 - 15
Raby Castle, Co Durham
High Force Kite Festival (the highest kite festival in England).

15
Cobham Hall, Kent
British Red Cross (+ House open 2-5pm).

16 - 20
Eastnor Castle, Herefordshire
Children's Fun Week.

17 - 19
RHS Garden Wisley, Surrey
Wisley Flower Show.

18
RHS Garden Harlow Carr, Yorkshire
Children's Day.

21 - 22
Bosworth Battlefield, Leicestershire
Medieval Spectacular.

22
Dalemain, Cumbria
Cumbria Classic Car Show.

26 - 29
Blair Castle, Perthshire
Bowmore International Horse Trials and Country Fair.

27
Blenheim Palace, Oxfordshire
Classic Proms with Fireworks, Performing Arts, Blenheim Park
(separate admission), tel 0845 644 2355.

27 - 30
Bramham Park, Yorkshire
Leeds Festival.

28 - 30
Blenheim Palace, Oxfordshire
Living Heritage Oxfordshire Craft Fair, Blenheim Park
(included in admission price), tel 01283 820548.

28 - 30
Milton Manor House, Oxfordshire
Georgian/Stuart weekend.

29
Floors Castle, Borders
Massed Pipe Bands Family Day.

29 - 30
Eastnor Castle, Herefordshire
Medieval Treasure Hunt.

29 - 30
Finchcocks, Kent
18th Century Gala.

S E P T E M B E R

1 - 30
Blenheim Palace, Oxfordshire
Battle of Blenheim Exhibition, Stable Courtyard (included in
admission price).

---

3 - 5
Hatfield House & Gardens, Hertfordshire
Country Homes, Gardens & Rare Breeds Show.

4 - 5
Parham House & Gardens
'Autumn Flowers at Parham House' – a celebration of flower
arranging, Parham style.

4 - 22
RHS Garden Rosemoor, Devon
Autumn Festival.

5
RHS Garden Rosemoor, Devon
NCCPG Plant Sale.

5
Raby Castle, Co Durham
Autumn Plant Fair.

8 - 30
Fairfax House, Yorkshire
Tales from the Teatable 1700-1850 – the English obsession
with tea explained.

9 - 12
Blenheim Palace, Oxfordshire
The Blenheim International Horse Trials, Blenheim Park
(separate admission), tel 01993 813335/0870 830 0209.

10 - 12
Blair Castle, Perthshire
Galloway Antiques Fair.

10 - 12
Newby Hall & Gardens, Yorkshire
Craft Fair (Free Spirit, tel 01777 701177).

11 - 12
Beaulieu, Hampshire
International Autojumble.

12
Dalemain, Cumbria
Plant Fair.

22 - 23
Hatfield House & Gardens, Hertfordshire
Living History Days (for school groups).

25 - 26
Blenheim Palace, Oxfordshire
The British Cheese Awards, Blenheim Park (separate
admission), tel 01608 659325/01993 823590.

O C T O B E R

1 - 31
Blenheim Palace, Oxfordshire
Battle of Blenheim Exhibition, Stable Courtyard (included in
admission price).

1 - 31
Fairfax House, Yorkshire
Tales from the Teatable 1700-1850 – the English obsession
with tea explained.

2 - 3
Eastnor Castle, Herefordshire
Festival of Fine Food & Drink.

2 - 3
Hatfield House & Gardens, Hertfordshire
Rock 'n' Gem Show.

8 - 9
Ripley Castle, Yorkshire
Fashion Sale.

8 - 10
Finchcocks, Kent
Autumn Fair.

10
RHS Garden Rosemoor, Devon
Apple Day.

13 - 14
Hatfield House & Gardens, Hertfordshire
Living History Days (for school groups).

16 - 17
Lamport Hall & Gardens, Northamptonshire
Craft & Gift Fair.

17
Harewood House, Yorkshire
Great Trees & Birds of Harewood.

17
Hatfield House & Gardens, Hertfordshire
Book Fair.

23 - 24
RHS Garden Harlow Carr, Yorkshire
Apple Event.

23 - 24
RHS Garden Hyde Hall, Essex
Apple Festival.

23 - 24
RHS Garden Wisley, Surrey
Apple Tasting Weekend.

23 - 24
Stowe House, Buckinghamshire
Christmas Fayre.

30
Beaulieu, Hampshire
Fireworks Fair.

30
Blair Castle, Perthshire
Glenfiddich Piping Championships.

31
Blair Castle, Perthshire
Glenfiddich Fiddling Championships.

N O V E M B E R

1 - 30
Blenheim Palace, Oxfordshire
Battle of Blenheim Exhibition, Stable Courtyard (included in
admission price).

1 - 30
Blenheim Palace, Oxfordshire
Living Crafts for Christmas, Palace Courtyard (inclusive
admission), tel 023 9242 6523/08700 111912.

1 - 30
Fairfax House, Yorkshire
Tales from the Teatable 1700-1850 – the English obsession
with tea explained.

5 - 7
Hatfield House & Gardens, Hertfordshire
Bailey Antiques Fair.

6
Groombridge Place & Gardens, Kent
Fireworks Spectacular.

6
RHS Garden Harlow Carr, Yorkshire
Pumpkin Day.

12 - 14
Hatfield House & Gardens, Hertfordshire
Gifts for Christmas Fair.

17 - 18
Hatfield House & Gardens, Hertfordshire
Living History Days (for school groups).

20

Hatfield House & Gardens, Hertfordshire
A Christmas Market.

26 - 28

Harewood House, Yorkshire
Christmas Craft Fair.

28

Hatfield House & Gardens, Hertfordshire
Book Fair.

28

RHS Garden Hyde Hall, Essex
Christmas Craft Fair.

D E C E M B E R

1 - 12

Blenheim Palace, Oxfordshire
Battle of Blenheim Exhibition, Stable Courtyard (included in admission price).

1 - 23

Hatfield House & Gardens, Hertfordshire
Christmas Tree Sales.

1 - 31

Fairfax House, Yorkshire
Tales from the Teatable 1700-1850 – the English obsession with tea explained.

3 - 31

Fairfax House, Yorkshire
The Keeping of Christmas.

4 - 5

Exbury Gardens & Steam Railway, Hampshire
Santa Steam Special.

5

Hatfield House & Gardens, Hertfordshire
Dolls Houses & Miniatures Fair.

5

RHS Garden Rosemoor, Devon
Christmas Food Fair.

11 - 12

Exbury Gardens & Steam Railway, Hampshire
Santa Steam Special.

18 - 19

Exbury Gardens & Steam Railway, Hampshire
Santa Steam Special.

This information is intended only as a guide, please check with individual properties before travelling.

More information on Special Events can be obtained by visiting individual property websites, see www.hudsonsguide.co.uk for quick access.

© All images kindly supplied by NTPL.

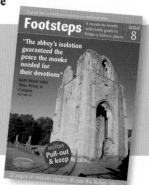

Walpole Old Chapel

The Dissenters' Chapel

Farfield Friends Meeting House

The Historic Chapels Trust – Preserving places of worship in England

Established to take into ownership redundant chapels and other places of worship in England which are of outstanding architectural and historic interest. Securing for public benefit the preservation, repair and maintenance of these buildings and their contents.

Listed below are 14 of the chapels the Trust has in its care which can be visited on application to the keyholder.

Biddlestone RC Chapel, Northumberland 01665 574420

Coanwood Friends Meeting House, Northumberland 01434 320256

Cote Baptist Chapel, Oxfordshire 01993 850421

Farfield Friends Meeting House, West Yorkshire 01756 710225

The Dissenters' Chapel, Kensal Green Cemetery, London..... 020 7402 2749

Penrose Methodist Chapel, St Ervan, Cornwall................... 01841 540737

Salem Chapel, East Budleigh, Devon 01395 445236

Shrine of Our Lady, Blackpool, Lancashire 020 7584 6072

St Benet's Chapel, Netherton, Merseyside 0151 520 2600

St George's German Lutheran Church,

Tower Hamlets, London 020 8302 3437

Todmorden Unitarian Church, West Yorkshire 01706 815648

Umberslade Baptist Church, Warwickshire 01564 783362

Wallasey Unitarian Church, Merseyside 0151 639 9707

Walpole Old Chapel, Suffolk 01986 798308

For further information please ring the Director at the office address or visit our website: www.hct.org.uk

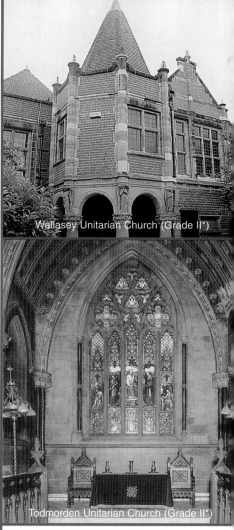

Wallasey Unitarian Church (Grade II*)

Todmorden Unitarian Church (Grade II*)

HISTORIC TRUST

CHAPELS

CHAIRMAN
Rt Hon Alan Beith MP

DIRECTOR
Dr Jennifer M Freeman

PRESIDENT
Sir Hugh Rossi

MAIDS & MISTRESSES

Celebrating 300 years of Women and the Yorkshire Country House

A county-wide special exhibitions project 2004

Where did the *real* power and influence lie in the great houses of Yorkshire?

Contrary to popular opinion, maintaining these huge households was never exclusively a male preserve. Very often the social, domestic and artistic identity of these houses was determined by the women who lived and worked in them.

In 2004 a series of linked exhibitions across some of Yorkshire's greatest country houses will highlight the lives and achievements of the female occupants of these establishments.

The exhibitions will draw on a wealth of new research and offer a chance for many previously unseen objects and documents to be displayed. Mistresses, cooks, scullery-maids and governesses all played vital rôles in the daily routine of a great house. *Maids & Mistresses* will explore life above and below stairs, examining the role of women as both decision-makers and workhorses. This is a unique opportunity to present the country house in an entirely new guise, allowing the female occupants to be heard and understood fully for the first time.

The complementary exhibitions will reveal all manner of links between these Yorshire houses, with attractions ranging from their great art collections to the more prosaic items of everyday life, such as recipe books, linen and undergarments, as well as letters and journals that reveal the inner lives of these great women.

The participating houses include: Brodsworth Hall, Doncaster, Burton Constable, East Riding of Yorkshire, Castle Howard, near York, Harewood House, Leeds, Nostell Priory, Wakefield, Lotherton Hall and Temple Newsam House, Leeds. Accompanying the exhibitions at each house will be a full educational programme aimed at schools, as well as various activities and events throughout the year. The exhibitions will open on Saturday 3 April 2004, running until the end of October.

For further information visit:
www.ychp.org.uk

Brodsworth Hall was built as a Victorian home for the Thellusson family and their many staff. By the 1980s it was lived in by only Sylvia Grant-Dalton, her cook and her butler. Learn how women's rôles in the country house changed through time.

Tel: 01302 722598
www.english-heritage.org.uk/yorkshire

Doncaster
BRODSWORTH HALL ⊞

▶ The entry for Brodsworth Hall is on page 383 of *Hudson's*.

Grand images of women at Harewood are renowned, but you can discover their 'secret lives' through a new trail, audio guide, and special exhibition of previously unseen diaries, paintings and correspondence. Find out about life 'below stairs' and visit the Servants' Hall and Housekeeper's Room to discover how servants lived, what they wore and what they did.

Tel: 0113 2181010
midway between Leeds & Harrogate   www.harewood.org

HAREWOOD HOUSE

▶ The entry for Harewood House is on page 387 of *Hudson's*.

At Castle Howard meet the mistresses of the house, liberated at last from the silent confines of their glamorous portraits. Mothers, wives and daughters mingle with cooks, maids and governesses … visit this exhibition with costumed enactments and educational activites and find out who really ran Castle Howard over the centuries!

Tel: 01653 648333
www.castlehoward.co.uk

nr York
CASTLE HOWARD

▶ The entry for Castle Howard is on page 384 of *Hudson's*.

At Burton Contstable's exhibition enjoy the rich colourful and varied lives of its women from the Elizabethan to the Edwardian era.

Tel: 01964 562400
www.burtonconstable.com

East Riding of Yorkshire
BURTON CONSTABLE HALL

▶ The entry for Burton Constable Hall is on page 394 of *Hudson's*.

A journey through the British countryside and heritage

DAVID J OSBORN
ENGLISH LANDSCAPE PHOTOGRAPHER

As you look through this year's Hudson's guide you will see a selection of hauntingly beautiful photographs, used to illustrate the different regions of the United Kingdom. The majority of these images have been supplied by David Osborn, an accomplished photographer, who has used his considerable skills to produce some very beautiful landscape images.

David J Osborn was born in London in 1961 and studied graphic design at the Camberwell School of Art. While there he discovered that photography was more suited to his personality and, though he graduated with a first class degree in graphic design, he emerged from Camberwell a photographer.

After a year in the photography department at Shell Oil, David Osborn joined Reuter News Pictures in Fleet Street, one of the world's largest and oldest news agencies. There he began his intensive, on-the-job training as a photojournalist. During that time, he photographed Presidents Reagan, Gorbachev and Bhutto, the presidents of Turkey, Portugal, Germany, and ex-President Jimmy Carter. He photographed the Kings of Norway and of Spain, King Hussein and ex-King Constantine. He took numerous photographs of Margaret Thatcher and of the Royal Family.

David also covered hundreds of assignments for national and foreign newspapers and magazines. Today, much of his time is dedicated to his landscape work.

Further information may be obtained from his award-winning website:

www.BritishPanoramics.com

David J. Osborn
120 Dalrymple Close, Southgate,
London N14 4LQ

TEL: +44 (0)208 882 8958
FAX: +44 (0)208 882 7048
MOB: +44 (0)771 204 5126
E-MAIL: osborndjo@aol.com

Prints may be purchased directly from David J. Osborn or from:
The Afterimage Gallery, Dallas, Texas, USA
Tel: 001 (214) 871 9140
www.AfterimageGallery.com

CPRE Houses and Gardens Scheme 2004

The Campaign to Protect Rural England offers members half-price entry to 200 properties listed in *Hudson's Historic Houses & Gardens*. Membership also means you will be part of an organisation dedicated to the protection of the beauty, tranquillity and diversity of our countryside. Some of our members wish to help protect the English countryside for future generations. **Legacy donations are valuable to our work and we'll be happy to send you information.**

If you wish to join CPRE by credit card or would like more information please call freephone 0800 163680 quoting HHG, or fill in the membership form opposite. Members receive our magazine *Countryside Voice*, access to our members' website, and membership of a local branch.

Attention all Property Managers and Owners
If boosting visitor numbers and encouraging them to spend more freely is important to you, CPRE is looking for houses and gardens to join its membership privilege scheme. The scheme is completely free to join.
Please call **020 7981 2853** for an information pack and an application form or email **chrisb@cpre.org.uk**.

Places Offering **Accommodation**

The historic properties listed below are not hotels. Their inclusion indicates that accommodation can be arranged, often for groups only. The type and standard of rooms offered vary widely – from the luxurious to the utilitarian.

Full details can be obtained from each individual property.

Eastnor Castle.

ENGLAND

Quenby Hall.

accommodation

Civil Wedding Venues

Places at which the marriage ceremony itself can take place – many will also be able to provide facilities for wedding receptions.

Full details about each property are available in the regional listings. There are numerous other properties included within *Hudson's* which do not have a Civil Wedding Licence but which can accommodate wedding receptions. In Scotland religious wedding ceremonies can take place anywhere, subject to the Minister being prepared to perform them.

ENGLAND

WALES

NORTHERN IRELAND

Corporate Hospitality Venues

Properties which are able to accommodate corporate functions, wedding receptions and events. Some properties specialise in corporate hospitality and are open, only rarely, if ever, to day visitors. Others do both. See entry for details.

Goodwood House. © Goodwood Photo Collection.

corporate hospitality venues

Chavenage.

Imagine having your own key to hundreds of Britain's greatest historic houses, castles and garden.

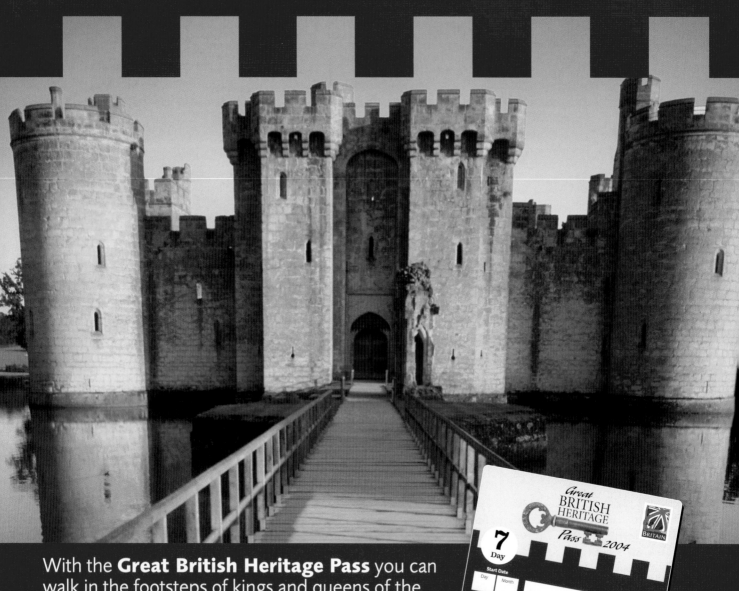

With the **Great British Heritage Pass** you can walk in the footsteps of kings and queens of the past or experience how heroes and heroines lived.

How much does it cost?

Pay just once, and get free* entry to a great range of castles, stately homes and gardens. Choose from 4 types of pass, designed to suit the length of your visit.

4-day pass	7-day pass	15-day pass	1-month pass
(£22)	(£35)	(£46)	(£60)

To obtain your own pass to Britain's past, contact your local VisitBritain office, or you can purchase the Great British Heritage Pass after arrival in Britain at selected Tourist Information Centres.
Please view our website on **www.visitbritain.com/heritagepass** for details.

*Tower of London, half price. Prices quoted in sterling or local equivalent.

🌼 Plant Sales

Properties where plants are offered for sale

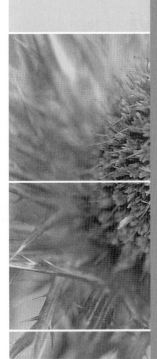

plants for sale

Trerice, Cornwall 204
Trewithen, Cornwall 204
Trull House, Gloucestershire 238

SCOTLAND

WALES

NORTHERN IRELAND

This list is merely intended to draw attention to properties which have plant sales, it is intended only as a guide.

RHS Partner Gardens

Properties in *Hudson's* that offer free garden access at specified times to RHS Members.

PROPERTY	OPENING DATES AND TIMES	FREE ACCESS DATES
Abbotsbury Sub-Tropical Gardens	All year, daily, 10am - 6pm (dusk in winter). Closed over Christmas and New Year	Oct - Feb
Adlington Hall & Gardens	2 Jun - 25Aug: Weds, 2 - 5pm	When open
Arley Hall & Gardens	9 Apr - 28 Sept: Tue - Sun & BHs, 11am - 5pm. Oct: w/ends only	When open, (not special event days)
Bedgebury National Pinetum	All year, daily, 10am - 5pm	When open
Belvoir Castle	Apr - Sept: Tue - Thur, w/e & BH Mons, 11am - 5pm	Mar: Sat - Sun, Jun: when open
Benington Lordship Gardens	Contact garden for opening times	7 - 22 Feb: 12 noon - 4pm
Bicton Park Botanical Gardens	All year, daily, 10am - 6pm (5pm winter). Closed 25 & 26 Dec	Mar & Nov
Blenheim Palace Park & Gardens	14 Feb - 12 Dec: daily. Nov - Dec: Wed - Sun. All 10.30am - 5.30pm	14 Feb - 28 May (excl. Easter) & 13 Sept - Oct: Mon - Fri. Gardens only
Bodnant Garden	13 Mar - 31 Oct: daily, 10am - 5pm	When open
Borde Hill Garden	All year, daily, 10am - 6pm (or dusk if earlier)	Jan - Feb & Nov - Dec
Burton Agnes Hall	1 Apr - 31 Oct: daily, 11am - 5pm	When open
Caerhays Castle & Garden	16 Feb - 31 May: daily, 10am - 5.30pm (Gardens only)	16 Feb - 16 Mar
Cawdor Castle & Gardens	1 May - 10 Oct: daily, 10am - 5.30pm	May - Jun & Sept - Oct (Gardens only)
Cholmondeley Castle Garden	Apr - Sept: Wed, Thu, Sun & BHs, 11.30am - 5pm	June
Coleton Fishacre House & Garden	6 - 28 Mar: Sat & Sun, 11am - 5pm. 31 Mar - 31 Oct: Wed - Sun & BHs, 10.30am - 5.30pm	When open
Corsham Court Gardens	20 Mar - 30 Sept: Tues - Thur, Sat & Sun, 2 - 5pm. 1 Oct - 19 Mar: w/e only, 2 - 4pm. Closed Dec	When open (Gardens only)
Cottesbrooke Hall & Gardens	3 May - end June : Wed, Thur & BH Mon, 2 - 5pm. Jul - Sept: Thur & BH Mon, 2 - 5pm	When open (Gardens only)
Coughton Court	Mar & Oct: w/e. Apr - Jun & Sept: Wed - Sun. Jul - Aug: Tues - Sun. All 11am - 5.30pm	When open (Gardens only)
Dalemain	28 Mar - 21 Oct: Sun - Thur, 10.30am - 5pm	20 Apr - 16 May
Docton Mill & Garden	Mar - Oct: daily, 10am - 6pm	Mar - Apr & Sept - Oct. Sats, May - Sept
The Dorothy Clive Garden	13 Mar - 31 Oct: daily, 10am - 5.30pm	Jul - Aug
Duncombe Park	13 Apr - 24 Oct: Sun - Thurs (please telephone for opening times)	When open
Dunrobin Castle Gardens	Apr - Sept & 1 - 15 Oct: daily, 10.30am - 4.30pm (5.30pm, Jun - Sept)	When open
Exbury Gardens	28 Feb - 2 Nov: daily, 10am - 5.30pm. Please call for winter opening dates	Mar & Oct
Fairhaven Woodland & Water Garden	All year, daily, 10am - 5pm. May - Aug: Wed & Thur, 10am - 9pm. Closed 25 Dec	Feb - Apr & Oct
Floors Castle Gardens	3 Apr - 31 Oct: daily, 10am - 5pm	When open
Forde Abbey & Gardens	Daily, 10am - 4.30pm	Oct - Feb (Gardens only)
Furzey Gardens	All year: daily, 10am - 5pm (dusk in winter). Closed 25 & 26 Dec	Mar & Oct
Goodnestone Park Gardens	31 Mar - 28 Sept: Mon & Wed - Fri, 11am - 5pm. 6 Apr - 28 Sept: also Sun, 12 noon - 6pm	Apr - May & Sept (not special event days)
Harewood House	11 Feb - 31 Oct: daily, 10am - 6pm	Mar - Jun (not w/e, BHs & special event days)
Harmony Garden	9 Apr - 12 Apr & Jun - Sept: Mon - Sat, 10am - 5pm, Sun, 1 - 5pm	When open
Hatfield House & Gardens	Easter Sat - 30 Sept: daily, 11am - 5.30pm	When open (not major event days)
Hill of Tarvit Mansionhouse & Garden	All year: daily, 9.30am - sunset	When open (Gardens only)
Holker Hall Garden	28 Mar - 31 Oct: Sun - Fri, 10am - 6pm	Apr - Oct (not special event days)
Houghton Hall	Easter Sun - Sept: Wed - Thurs, Sun & BH Mons, 1 - 5.30pm	June
Kellie Castle & Garden	All year, daily, 9.30am - sunset	When open
Kingston Maurward Garden	5 Jan - 19 Dec: daily, 10am - 5.30pm	When open
Knoll Gardens & Nursery	Jan - Dec: Wed - Sun, 10am - 5pm (or dusk). Closed 25 Dec - New Year	Apr - Oct
Loseley Park	3 May - 30 Sept: Wed - Sun, 11am - 5pm	May & Sept (not special event days)
Mapperton Gardens	Mar - Oct: daily, 2 - 6pm	When open
Muncaster Castle Garden	All year, daily, 10.30am - 5pm	Jul - 7 Nov
Middleton, The National Botanic Garden of Wales	Please contact the garden for current opening times	Jan - Mar & Oct - Dec
Newby Hall & Gardens	1 Apr - 26 Sept: Tue - Sun & BHs Mon, 11am - 5.30pm	When open (not special event days)
Normanby Hall	All year: daily, 10.30am - 5pm (4.30pm in winter). Closed 25/26 Dec & 1 Jan	When open
Nymans Garden	18 Feb - 31 Oct: Wed - Sun & BH Mon, 11am - 6pm (or dusk). Nov - Feb: w/e only, 11am - 4pm	When open
Parcevall Hall Gardens	1 Apr - 31 Oct: daily, 10am - 6pm	May - Aug
Penshurst Place & Gardens	6 - 27 Mar: w/e, 10.30am - 6pm. 27 Mar - 31 Oct: daily, 10.30am - 6pm	Apr & Sept - Oct
Picton Castle	Apr - Oct: Tue - Sun & BHs, 10.30am - 5pm	Apr - Sept (not event days). Gardens only
Raby Castle	Jun - Aug: Sun - Fri. May & Sept: Wed & Sun. BHs: Sat - following Wed. All 11am - 5.30pm.	When open (not special event days)
Ripley Castle	All year: daily, 9am - 5pm (4.30pm during winter)	When open
Rode Hall	7 - 22 Feb: daily, 12 noon - 4pm. 1 Apr - 30 Sept: Tue - Thur & BHs, 2 - 5pm	When open
Rodmarton Manor	3 May - 30 Aug: Wed, Sat & BHs. Jun & Jul: Mon. All 2 - 5pm	May and Aug (Gardens only)
Ryton Organic Gardens	All year, daily, 9am - 5pm. Closed 25 & 26 Dec	When open
Sandringham	10 Apr - 23 Jul & Aug - Oct: daily, 10.30am - 5pm (4pm, Oct)	When open
Scone Palace & Grounds	Apr - Oct: daily, 9.30am - 5.45pm	Sept - Oct
Seaforde Gardens	All year: Mon - Sat, 10am - 5pm, Sun, 1 - 6pm (Nov - Feb, closed Sat & Sun). Closed 24 Dec - 2 Jan	Apr - May (Gardens only)
Sheffield Park Garden	Jan - Feb: w/e, 10.30am - 4pm. Mar - Dec: Tue - Sun & BHs, 10.30am - 6pm (4pm, Nov - Dec)	When open
Tapeley Park	18 Mar - 1 Nov: Sun - Fri, 10am - 5pm	3 Jun - 9 Jul
Tatton Park	27 Mar - 3 Oct: Tue - Sun, 10am - 6pm. 4 Oct - 25 Mar: Tue - Sun, 11am - 4pm	When open
Thorp Perrow Arboretum	Mar - mid - Nov: daily, dawn - dusk	Mon - Fri (not BHs) when open
Threave Castle	All year: daily, 9.30am - sunset	Apr - May & Sept - Oct
Torosay Castle & Gardens	All year: daily, 9am - sunset	Apr - Jun & Sept - Oct
Trebah Garden	All year, daily, 10.30am - 5pm	When open
Trewithen Gardens	Mar - Sept: daily (closed Sun, Mar & Jun - Sept), 10am - 4.30pm.	Jul - Sept
Waddesdon Manor	3 Mar - Oct: Wed - Sun & BH Mon, 10am - 5pm. 3 Nov - 23 Dec: Wed - Sun & 20/21 Dec, 11am - 5pm	Mar & Sept - Oct
Wartnaby Gardens	Apr - Jul: Tue, 9.30am - 12.30pm	When open
Wentworth Castle Gardens	Access to the gardens is mainly by guided tour (contact garden directly)	When open
Westonbirt Arboretum	All year, daily, 10am - 8pm (or dusk if earlier)	When open
Wollerton Old Hall Garden	Good Fri - Aug: Fri, Sun & BHs, 12 noon - 5pm	Apr - May & Sept

The above information has been supplied by the RHS.

41

Visit www.hudsonsguide.co.uk

Gateway to Britain's heritage properties

- Live links to hundreds of sites
- Special Event Listings
- Corporate Hospitality Venues
- Romantic properties for Civil Weddings

Direct links to hundreds of properties – no need to type in long web addresses. Let *Hudson's* be your guide.

Useful Web Addresses

Hudson's	www.hudsonsguide.co.uk
Historic Houses Association	www.hha.org.uk
The National Trust	www.nationaltrust.org.uk
English Heritage	www.english-heritage.org.uk
The National Trust for Scotland	www.nts.org.uk
Historic Scotland	www.historic-scotland.gov.uk
CADW	www.cadw.wales.gov.uk
VisitBritain (formerly British Tourist Authority)	www.visitbritain.com
Royal Horticultural Society	www.rhs.org.uk
The Churches Conservation Trust	www.visitchurches.org.uk
Country Houses Association	www.cha.org.uk
Heritage Venues	www.heritagevenues.co.uk
Historic Chapels Trust	www.hct.org.uk
CPRE	www.cpre.org.uk

PLACES TO STAY

Landmark Trust	www.landmarktrust.co.uk
National Trust	www.nationaltrustcottages.co.uk

Open **All Year**

Properties included in this list are open to some extent for all or most of the year. See individual entries for details.

Chatsworth - the Serpentine Hedge.

Blenheim Palace

ENGLAND

Kenwood House. © English Heritage Photo Library.

Capel Manor Gardens.

open all year

WALES

IRELAND

Wellington Arch. © English Heritage Photo Library.

Beaulieu.

Educational Venues

The properties listed below provide special facilities for schools/educational groups. The range of these services varies, so it is vital that you contact the property directly when preparing to arrange a trip.

ENGLISH HERITAGE

English Heritage offers free admission for pre-booked educational groups.
For a free teacher's information pack please contact:
Tel: 020 7973 3385 Email: education@english-heritage.org.uk
www.english-heritage.org.uk/education

ENGLAND

EASTERN REGION

EAST MIDLANDS

SCOTLAND

WALES

NORTH WALES

SOUTH WALES

NORTHERN IRELAND

Hudson's helpful terms...

AMAZING ARCHITECTS

"Have you told your teacher about Hudson's new Education/ Schools Index?"

FAMOUS GARDENERS & LANDSCAPE DESIGNERS

GARDEN JARGON AND TECHNICAL TERMS

VERY CLEVER &
CREATIVE CRAFTSMEN

DO YOU KNOW
YOUR DATES?

HUDSON'S

HISTORIC FAMILY
HOMES & GARDENS

FROM THE AIR

WITH AERIALS PHOTOGRAPHS BY SKYSCAN

Dunvegan Castle

For those, like myself, never quite at ease abroad, Historic Family Homes and Gardens from the Air provides comfort and reassurance. Despite the strange absence of God's Own County of Lincolnshire, this is an original and impressive coverage of Great Britain".

Hugh Massingberd, The Spectator, 6th September 2003.

"... a glorious new book on Britain's historic houses provides plenty of holiday sightseeing ideas".

Jane Barry, Evening Standard 9th July 2003

This remarkable collection of aerial photographs affords new and unique perspectives of some of Britain's greatest houses, their gardens and parkland settings. It provides a record of how they are at the beginning of the 21st century, a testament to the resilience and achievements of the mainly private owners who have maintained and enhanced these houses and opened them to the public.

The aerial pictures of 84 featured properties are accompanied by further photographs and a description of the property by the owners – often an intriguing combination of historic and architectural fact, with personal comment.

The special relationship between house, garden and ancillary buildings and its setting in parkland, by river, lake or sea, can only be appreciated fully from a bird's eye view. Clearly seen from the air more vividly than is possible from the ground are the exciting new garden developments at Alnwick Castle, Belmont, Coughton Court, Deene Park, Hever Castle, Holker Hall, Leeds Castle and Stanway; also the Mazes at Burton Agnes Hall, Cawdor Castle, Somerleyton Hall, Traquair, Kentwell Hall, Longleat and Scone Palace.

"Britain's greatest contribution to European culture is the country house, together with art objects, gardens and parks", says the Earl of Leicester, President of the Historic Houses Association, in his foreword to the book.

Hoghton Tower

HISTORIC FAMILY HOMES & GARDENS – FROM THE AIR
Photographs by Skyscan

Published by Norman Hudson & Co
192pp   Hardback   £25

ISBN 0-9531426-8-X
available from all good bookshops.

Somerleyton Hall

Eastnor Castle

Beaulieu, Hampshire from the book *Historic Family Homes and Gardens from the Air*, see page 54.

ENGLAND

london

© David Osborn

elthampalace
london

Tucked away behind a suburban shopping street in south east London is one of England's architectural treasures. There is no other place quite like Eltham Palace – the stunning remains of one of the country's largest medieval palaces joined to the largest surviving Art Deco house and all set within delightful moated gardens.

The house is a fascinating example of state-of-the-art design from its era, built in 1936 by the millionaire Stephen Courtauld and his wife Virginia. Stephen Courtauld was, notably, a director of Ealing Studios, and Eltham provided the perfect setting for entertaining and their love of gardening.

The couple's home movies reveal that their social life was largely given over to house parties, with swimming, squash and tennis held in the splendid moated gardens by day and sumptuous dinners and soirées enjoyed by their friends at night.

Characterised by a 1930s ocean-liner-meets-Hollywood style, the house includes many unusual and innovative design features – from a central vacuum system to concealed lighting, electric clocks and a loud-speaker system. Its principal rooms are undeniably luxurious: Virginia Courtauld's onyx and gold mosaic-lined vaulted bathroom; the breathtaking domed entrance hall with its amazing marquetry; the dining room with its silver ceiling, pink leather-covered dining chairs and exquisite black and silver doors decorated with reliefs of exotic animals, are all exemplars of their period.

Only a sliding Chinese screen separates the Art Deco House from the medieval Great Hall, all that remains intact of the original Eltham Palace – the boyhood home of Henry VIII. The Great Hall, with its fine oak hammerbeam roof, was built for Edward IV in the 1470s as a dining hall for the Court and is a fine example of late Gothic architecture.

The Courtaulds only enjoyed Eltham for eight short years. Eventually the war made it impractical for the couple to continue living there and in 1944 they moved first to Scotland and then Rhodesia. The house subsequently became the headquarters of the Royal Army Educational Corps.

Outside, the 19 acres of parkland and gardens are being restored and the South Moat area was developed as a Contemporary Heritage Garden. Visitors can enjoy areas devoted to unusual shade-tolerant shrubs and perennials, and a short border devoted to old roses.

▸ For further details about Eltham Palace see entry on page 67.

Images courtesy of: © English Heritage Photo Library
Jeremy Richards / Jonathan Bailey

Map 3

Owner:
Historic Royal Palaces

THE BANQUETING HOUSE

WHITEHALL

www.banqueting-house.org.uk

The magnificent Banqueting House is all that survives of the great Palace of Whitehall which was destroyed by fire in 1698. It was completed in 1622, commissioned by King James I, and designed by Inigo Jones, the noted classical architect. In 1635 the main hall was further enhanced with the installation of 9 magnificent ceiling paintings by Sir Peter Paul Rubens, which survive to this day. The Banqueting House was also the site of the only royal execution in England's history, with the beheading of Charles I in 1649.

The Banqueting House is open to visitors, as well as playing host to many of society's most glittering occasions.

▶ **CONTACT**

The Banqueting House
Whitehall
London SW1A 2ER

General Enquiries:
0870 751 5178
Functions:
0870 751 5185 / 5186

▶ **LOCATION**

OS Ref. TQ302 801

Underground:
Westminster,
Embankment and
Charing Cross.

Rail: Charing Cross.

▶ **OPENING TIMES**

All Year
Mon - Sat
10am - 5pm
Last admission 4.30pm.

Closed
24 December - 1 January,
Good Friday and other
public holidays.

NB. Liable to close at short
notice for Government
functions.

▶ **ADMISSION**

Enquiry line for
admission prices:
0870 751 5178

 Concerts.
No photography in house.

 Banquets.

Undercroft suitable.

Video and audio guide.

P None.

Welcome.

CONFERENCE/FUNCTION		
ROOM	SIZE	MAX CAPACITY
Main Hall	110' x 55'	400
Undercroft	64' x 55'	350

Andrew Holt / The Royal Collection © 2004 HM Queen Elizabeth II

BUCKINGHAM PALACE
THE STATE ROOMS
THE QUEEN'S GALLERY
THE ROYAL MEWS

LONDON

www.royal.gov.uk

Map 3

Owner:
Official Residence of
Her Majesty The Queen

▶ **CONTACT**

Ticket Sales &
Information Office
Buckingham Palace
London SW1A 1AA

Tel: 020 7766 7300
Groups (15+):
020 7766 7321
Fax: 020 7930 9625

e-mail: information@
royalcollection.org.uk

▶ **LOCATION**
OS Ref. TQ291 796

Underground:
Green Park, Victoria,
St James's Park.

Rail: Victoria.

Sightseeing tours
A number of tour
companies include a
visit to Buckingham
Palace in their
sightseeing tours. Ask
your concierge or hotel
porter for details.

Buckingham Palace is the official London residence of Her Majesty The Queen and serves as both home and office. Its nineteen State Rooms, which open for eight weeks a year, form the heart of the working palace. They are used extensively by The Queen and members of the Royal Family to receive and entertain their guests on State, ceremonial and official occasions. The State Rooms are lavishly furnished with some of the finest treasures from the Royal Collection – paintings by Rembrandt, Rubens, Van Dyck; sculpture by Canova; exquisite examples of Sèvres porcelain, and some of the most magnificent English and French furniture in the world. The garden walk offers superb views of the Garden Front of the Palace and the 19th-century lake.

Adjacent to Buckingham Palace are the Royal Mews and The Queen's Gallery. The Royal Mews is one of the finest working stables in existence and houses both the horse-drawn carriages and motor cars used for coronations, State visits, royal weddings and the State Opening of Parliament.

The Queen's Gallery hosts a programme of changing exhibitions from the Royal Collection. Exhibitions in 2004 include *Fabergé* (open until 7 March 2004), which brings together more than 300 of Carl Fabergé's finest works. *George III and Queen Charlotte: Patronage, Collecting and Court Taste,* (26 March 2004 - early 2005), is one of the largest and finest groups of Georgian material ever assembled.

Johan Zoffany (1733 - 1810) George III, 1771 The Royal Collection © 2004 Her Majesty Queen Elizabeth II.

David Cripps/The Royal Collection © 2004 HM Queen Elizabeth II

🛍 ℹ No photography inside.
♿ Wheelchair users are required to pre-book.

✗ None. 🎧 The State Rooms and some exhibitions.
🅿 None 📷 🐕 Guide dogs only.

▶ **OPENING TIMES**

As Buckingham Palace is a working royal palace, opening arrangements may change at short notice. Please check before planning a visit.

The State Rooms
August - September
Daily: 9.30am - 4.30pm.

Tickets available during Aug & Sept from the Ticket Office in Green Park.
To pre-book your tickets telephone the Ticket Sales & Information Office or visit the website.

The Queen's Gallery
All year except
25/26 Dec & 9 Apr and between exhibitions.
10am - 5.30pm
Last admission 4.30pm.
Entry by timed ticket.
To pre-book your tickets telephone the Ticket Sales & Information Office or visit the website.

The Royal Mews
26 Mar - 31 October except 9 April & 12 June
Daily: 11am - 4pm
Last admission 3.15pm.
Extended opening hours during August & September.
To pre-book your tickets telephone the Ticket Sales & Information Office or visit the website.

▶ **ADMISSION**

**The State Rooms,
The Queen's Gallery,
The Royal Mews**
For admission prices please call the Ticket Sales & Information Office.
Group (15+) discounts available, ask for details.

English Heritage Photo Library

Map 3

CHISWICK HOUSE ⊞

CHISWICK

www.english-heritage.org.uk/visits

Owner:
English Heritage

▶ **CONTACT**
Visits:
House Manager
Chiswick House
Burlington Lane
London W4 2RP

Tel: 020 8995 0508

Venue Hire and Hospitality:
Hospitality Manager
Tel: 020 7973 3292

▶ **LOCATION**
OS Ref: TQ210 775

Burlington Lane
London W4.

Rail: 1/4 mile NE of Chiswick Station.

Tube: Turnham Green, 3/4 mile

Bus: 190, E3.

Chiswick House is internationally renowned as one of the first and finest English Palladian villas. Lord Burlington, who built the villa from 1725 - 1729, was inspired by the architecture and gardens of ancient Rome and this house is his masterpiece. His aim was to create a fit setting to show his friends his fine collection of art and his library. The opulent interior features gilded decoration, velvet walls and painted ceilings. The important 18th century gardens surrounding Chiswick House have, at every turn, something to surprise and delight the visitor from the magnificent cedar trees to the beautiful Italianate gardens with their cascade, statues, temples, urns and obelisks.

Venue Hire and Hospitality

English Heritage offers exclusive use of Chiswick House in the evenings and Saturday afternoons for dinners, receptions and weddings.

▶ **OPENING TIMES***

Summer
1 April - 30 September
Wed - Sun & BHs,
10am - 6pm.
Closed from 2pm on Sats.

Autumn
October
Wed - Sun, 10am - 5pm.
Closed from 2pm on Sats.

Winter
1 Nov - 31 March
Closed but available for exclusive groups visits.

▶ **ADMISSION***

Adult £3.50
Child (5-15yrs)....... £2.00
Conc £3.00
Groups
(11+) ....15% discount

Tour leader & coach driver have free entry. 1 extra place for every 20 additional people.

* Times & prices subject to change from April 2004.

English Heritage Photo Library

WCs. Filming, plays, photographic shoots.

Café in grounds not managed by English Heritage.

Private & corporate hospitality.

Please call in advance. WC.

Personal guided tours must be booked in advance. Colour guide book £2.50.

Free audio tours in English, French & German.

Free if booked in advance. Tel: 020 7973 3485.

Guide dogs in grounds.

Civil Wedding Licence.

Tel for details.

CONFERENCE/FUNCTION

ROOM	MAX CAPACITY
Domed Saloon	100 standing 48 dining
Red Velvet Room	24 dining
Green Velvet Room	24 dining
Whole House	150 standing 80 dining

English Heritage Photo Library/Jonathan Bailey

Map 3

ELTHAM PALACE

ELTHAM

www.english-heritage.org.uk/visits

The epitome of 1930s chic, Eltham Palace dramatically demonstrates the glamour and allure of the period.

Bathe in the light flooding from a spectacular glazed dome in the Entrance Hall as it highlights beautiful blackbeam veneer and figurative marquetry. It is a *tour de force* only rivalled by the adjacent Dining Room – where an Art Deco aluminium-leafed ceiling is a perfect complement to the bird's-eye maple walls. Step into Virginia Courtauld's magnificent gold-leaf and onyx bathroom and throughout the house discover lacquered, 'ocean liner' style veneered walls and built-in furniture.

A Chinese sliding screen is all that separates chic '30s Art Deco from the medieval Great Hall. You will find concealed electric lighting, centralised vacuum cleaning and a loud-speaker system that allowed music to waft around the house. Authentic interiors have been recreated by the finest contemporary craftsmen. Their appearance was painstakingly researched from archive photographs, documents and interviews with friends and relatives of the Courtaulds.

Outside you will find a delightful mixture of formal and informal gardens including a rose garden, pergola and loggia, all nestled around the extensive remains of the medieval palace.

Owner:
English Heritage

▶ **CONTACT**

Eltham Palace
Court Yard
Eltham
SE9 5QE

Visits:
Property Secretary
Tel: 020 8294 2548

Venue Hire and Hospitality:
Hospitality Manager
Tel: 020 8294 2577

▶ **LOCATION**

OS Ref. TQ425 740

M25/J3, then A20 towards Eltham. The Palace is signposted from A20 and from Eltham High Street. A2 from Central London.

Rail: 20 mins from Victoria or London Bridge Stations to Eltham or Mottingham, then 15 min walk.

CONFERENCE/FUNCTION	
ROOM	MAX CAPACITY
Great Hall	300 standing 200 dining
Entrance Hall	100 seated
Drawing Room	120 standing 80 theatre-style
Dining Room	50 dining

English Heritage Photo Library/Jonathan Bailey

 WCs. Filming, plays and photographic shoots.

Exclusive private and corporate hospitality.

 WC.

Guided tours on request.

Free. English, German & French.

Coaches must book.

 Tel for details.

▶ **OPENING TIMES***

1 April - 31 October:
Wed - Fri, Sun & BHs
10am - 5pm.

1 November - 31 March:
Wed - Fri & Sun,
10am - 4pm.

Closed for a few weeks in the winter, please call for details.

Groups visits must be booked two weeks in advance.

Venue Hire and Hospitality

English Heritage offers exclusive use of the Palace on Mon, Tue or Sat for daytime conferences, meetings and weddings and in the evenings for dinners, concerts and receptions.

▶ **ADMISSION***

House and Grounds

Adult £6.50
Child £3.50
Conc. £5.00
Family (2+3) £16.50

Grounds only

Adult £4.00
Child £2.00
Conc. £3.00

* Times & prices subject to change from April 2004.

London - England

Crown Copyright: Historic Royal Palaces

Crown Copyright: Historic Royal Palaces

KENSINGTON PALACE
STATE APARTMENTS

KENSINGTON

www.kensington-palace.org.uk

Map 3

Managed by:
Historic Royal Palaces

▶ **CONTACT**
Kensington Palace
London W8 4PX

**Recorded
Information:**
0870 751 5170

All Other Enquiries:
0870 751 5176

▶ **LOCATION**
OS Ref. TQ258 801

In Kensington Gardens.

Underground:
Queensway on
Central Line,
High Street Kensington
on Circle & District Line.

Dating back to 1689, Kensington Palace has seen such momentous events as the death of George II and the birth of the future Queen Victoria. Today it provides an oasis of tranquillity from the hustle and bustle of London. Originally known as Nottingham House, the Palace has been a royal residence for over 300 years and remains so, in part, to date.

Multi-language sound guides lead visitors around the magnificent State Apartments, including the lavishly decorated Cupola Room, where Queen Victoria was baptised. Visitors are also presented with a vivid glimpse of characters from the court of King George I, depicted in the decorative wall paintings of the King's Grand Staircase. Whilst exploring the Palace, visitors can take pleasure from the impressive display of paintings from the Royal Collection, located within the beautifully restored King's Gallery, and enjoy splendid interiors designed by Sir Christopher Wren.

The Royal Court and Ceremonial Dress collection dates from the 18th century, and audio tours allow visitors to participate in the excitement of dressing for Court, from invitation to presentation. There are also selections of dresses owned and worn by HM Queen Elizabeth II, and Diana, Princess of Wales, with other special exhibitions throughout the year.

▶ **OPENING TIMES**
March - October
Daily, 10am - 5pm

Nov - Feb
Daily, 10am - 4pm

Last admission 1 hr
before closing.

Closed 24 - 26 Dec.

▶ **ADMISSION**
Telephone Information
Line for admission prices:
0870 751 5170

Advance Ticket Sales:
0870 751 5180

Crown Copyright, HRP

No photography indoors.

The Orangery (located nearby) serves light refreshments.

Partial.

Sound guides for Dress Collection and State Apartments.

Nearby.

Welcome, please book.

In grounds, on leads. Guide dogs only in Palace.

FUNCTIONS

ROOM	SIZE	MAX CAPACITY
Orangery	7.1 x 34m	250 receptions 150 dinners

English Heritage Photo Library

KENWOOD HOUSE ⊞

HAMPSTEAD

www.english-heritage.org.uk/visits

Kenwood, one of the treasures of London, is an idyllic country retreat close to the popular villages of Hampstead and Highgate.

The house was remodelled in the 1760s by Robert Adam, the fashionable neo-classical architect. The breathtaking library or 'Great Room' is one of his finest achievements.

Kenwood is famous for the internationally important collection of paintings bequeathed to the nation by Edward Guinness, 1st Earl of Iveagh. Some of the world's finest artists are represented by works such as a Rembrandt *Self Portrait*, Vermeer's *The Guitar Player; Mary, Countess*

Howe by Gainsborough and paintings by Turner, Reynolds and many others.

As if the house and its contents were not riches enough, Kenwood stands in 112 acres of landscaped grounds on the edge of Hampstead Heath, commanding a fine prospect towards central London. The meadow walks and ornamental lake of the park, designed by Humphry Repton, contrast with the wilder Heath below. The open air concerts held in the summer at Kenwood have become part of London life, combining the charms of music with the serenity of the lakeside setting.

Owner:
English Heritage

▶ **CONTACT**

Kenwood House
Hampstead Lane
London   NW3 7JR

Visits:
The House Manager
Tel: 020 8348 1286

Venue Hire and Hospitality:
Hospitality Manager
Tel: 020 7973 3507

▶ **LOCATION**

OS Ref. TQ271 874

M1/J2. Signed off A1, on leaving A1 turn right at junction with Bishop's Ave, turn left into Hampstead Lane. Visitor car park on left.

Bus: London Transport 210.

Rail: Hampstead Heath.

Underground:
Archway or Golders Green Northern Line then bus 210.

English Heritage Photo Library

English Heritage Photo Library

▶ **OPENING TIMES***

Summer
1 April - 30 September
Daily: 10am - 6pm.
Open 10.30am Wed & Fri.

Autumn
1 - 31 October
Daily: 10am - 5pm.
Open 10.30am Wed & Fri.

Winter
1 November - 31 March
Daily: 10am - 4pm.
Open 10.30am Wed & Fri.

Closed 24 - 26 &
31 December & 1 January.

Venue Hire and Hospitality
English Heritage offers exclusive use of Kenwood House in the evenings for dinners, concerts and receptions, and the lecture room for daytime events.

▶ **ADMISSION**

House & Grounds: Free.
Donations welcome.

* Times & prices subject to change from April 2004.

CONFERENCE/FUNCTION	
ROOM	MAX CAPACITY
Orangery	80 dining
Music Room	40 dining
Dining Room	50 dining
Lecture Room	80 theatre-style
Whole House	150 dining

ℹ WCs. Concerts, exhibitions, filming. No photography in house.

🍽 Exclusive private and corporate hospitality.

♿ Ground floor access. WC.

☕ Available in the Brew House.

🚶 Available on request (in English). Please call for details.

🎧 English, French, Italian & German.

🅿 West Lodge car park on Hampstead Lane. Parking for the disabled.

Free when booked in advance on 020 7973 3485.

❄

Tel for details.

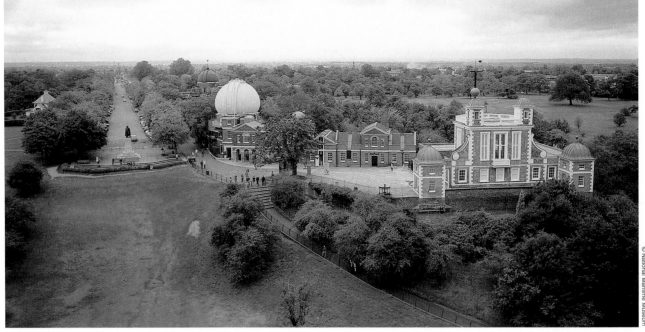

© National Maritime Museum

Map 3

ROYAL OBSERVATORY, NATIONAL MARITIME MUSEUM & QUEEN'S HOUSE

GREENWICH PARK

www.nmm.ac.uk

Owner: National Maritime Museum

▶ **CONTACT**

Groups: Robin Scates
Events: Eleanor Goody
Park Row, Greenwich
London SE10 9NF

Tel: 020 8858 4422
Fax: 020 8312 6632

Visit Bookings:
Tel: 020 8312 6608
Fax: 020 8312 6522
e-mail:
bookings@nmm.ac.uk
Functions:
Tel: 020 8312 6644/6693
Fax: 020 8312 6572

▶ **LOCATION**
OS Ref. TQ388 773

Within Greenwich Park
on the S bank of the
Thames at Greenwich.
Travel by river cruise or
Docklands Light Railway
(Cutty Sark station).
M25 (S) via A2. From
M25 (N) M11, A12 and
Blackwall Tunnel.

The Maritime Greenwich World Heritage Site encompasses Wren's imposing Royal Observatory (1675), the National Maritime Museum and the Queen's House (Inigo Jones c1635).

The Royal Observatory defines the Prime Meridian of the world – Longitude 0°. Visitors will see the Astronomer Royal's apartments, the 1833 time ball and admire Harrison's intricate marine timekeepers. There is an extensive collection of clocks, the original transit instruments and displays on modern astronomy. Wren's fine Octagon Room is available for small dinners. The Observatory has fine views over London, the Thames and modern Docklands.

The National Maritime Museum's 20 modern galleries chart Britain's history of seafaring and Empire. The story of Nelson and Trafalgar, exploration, immigration and environmental issues are covered. Books and manuscripts are accessed through a traditional reference library with a Lutyen's entrance hall as well as a new e-library and resource centre.

The Queen's House, designed for Anne of Denmark and used by the Stuarts as a place of entertainment, is Inigo Jones's first classical house in England. The Great Hall, Orangery and 'Tulip' Stairs are elegant examples of his work. The House is used to display selections from the fine art collection of the museum with superb portraits and seacapes by many famous artists.

▶ **OPENING TIMES**

Daily, 10am - 5pm (later opening in summer). Last admission 30 mins prior. Varies at New Year and Marathon Day (18 Apr).

Closed 24 - 26 December.

Gallery talks and drama (see notices on arrival).

Planetarium shows (not Sundays).

Special Exhibitions
• **Dodds exhibition:**
24 Nov '03 - 12 Apr '04.

• **Tintin's Adventures at Sea**
31 Mar - 5 Sept '04.

• **William Hodges**
6 July - mid-November

▶ **ADMISSION**

Free admission except for Special Exhibitions:
Dodds ....Free
Tintin
   Adult £5.00
   Child .... Free
   Conc £4.00

Hodges ....TBA

Planetarium Show
   Adult £4.00
   Child/Conc. £2.00

 No photography.

Partial. WC.

Licensed.

P Limited for coaches.

Guide dogs only.

CONFERENCE/FUNCTION

ROOM	SIZE	MAX CAPACITY
Queen's House	40' x 40'	Dining 120 Standing 200 Conference 120
Observatory, Octagon Rm	25' x 25'	Dining 60 Standing 150
NMM Upper Court	140' x 70'	Dining 500 Standing 1000
NMM Lecture Theatre		Conference 120

Easter Island (Rapanui) 1775 by William Hodges.
© National Maritime Museum London, Ministry of Defence Art Collection.

Sampson Lloyd

Map 3

ST PAUL'S CATHEDRAL

LONDON

www.stpauls.co.uk

Owner: Dean & Chapter of St Paul's Cathedral

▶ **CONTACT**

Mark McVay
The Chapter House
St Paul's Churchyard
London   EC4M 8AD

Tel: 020 7246 8348
020 7246 8346

Fax: 020 7248 3104

e-mail: chapterhouse@
stpaulscathedral.org.uk

▶ **LOCATION**

OS Ref. TQ321 812

Central London.

Underground:
St Paul's,
Mansion House,
Blackfriars, Bank.

Rail: Blackfriars,
City Thameslink.

Air: London Airports.

A Cathedral dedicated to St Paul has stood at the heart of the City of London for 1400 years, a constant reminder of the spiritual life in this busy commercial centre.

The present St Paul's, the fourth to occupy the site, was built between 1675 - 1710. Sir Christopher Wren's masterpiece rose from the ashes of the previous Cathedral, which had been destroyed in the Great Fire of London.

Over the centuries, the Cathedral has been the setting for royal weddings, state funerals and thanksgivings. Admiral Nelson and the Duke of Wellington are buried here, Queen Victoria celebrated her gold and diamond jubilees and Charles, Prince of Wales married Lady Diana Spencer. Most recently, St Paul's hosted the

thanksgiving service for the 100th birthday of HM Queen Elizabeth the Queen Mother. On 4 June 2002 the Cathedral hosted the National Service of Thanksgiving for the Golden Jubilee of HM The Queen.

Hundreds of memorials pay tribute to famous statesmen, soldiers, artists, doctors and writers and mark the valuable contributions to national life made by many ordinary men and women.

The soaring dome, one of the largest in the world, offers panoramic views across London from the exterior galleries. Inside, a whisper in the Whispering Gallery can be heard on the opposite side.

Far more than a beautiful landmark, St Paul's Cathedral is a living symbol of the city and nation it serves.

Sampson Lloyd

🚫📷ℹ️ No photography, video or mobile phones.

♿ Partial.

☕🍴 Licensed.

🚶♿

🅿️ None for cars, limited for coaches.

🐕 Guide dogs only.

❄️

▶ **OPENING TIMES**

Mon - Sat, 8.30am - 4.30pm, last admission 4pm.

Guided tours: daily, 11.30am, 1.30pm and 2pm.

Tours of the Triforium: Mon & Thur, 11.30am & 2.30pm.

All tours are subject to an additional charge.

Cathedral Shop & Café:
9am - 5.30pm,
Sun, 10.30am - 5pm.

Restaurant:
11am - 5.30pm.

Service Times
Mon - Sat
7.30am Mattins (Sat 8.30am)
8am Holy Communion (said)
12.30pm Holy Communion (said)
5pm Choral Evensong

Sun: 8am Holy Communion (said)
10.15am Choral Mattins & sermon
11.30am Choral Eucharist & sermon
3.15pm Choral Evensong & sermon
6pm Evening service

The Cathedral may be closed to tourists on certain days of the year. It is advisable to phone or check our website for up-to-date information.

▶ **ADMISSION**

Adult £7.00
Child £3.00
Student £6.00
OAP £6.00
Groups (10+)
Adult £6.50
Child £2.50
Student £5.50
OAP £5.50

CONFERENCE/FUNCTION

ROOM	MAX CAPACITY
Conference Suite	100 (standing)

Map 3

**Somerset House
Owner:** Somerset
House Trust, Strand,
London WC2R 1LA

Tel: 020 7845 4600
Fax: 020 7836 7613
e-mail: info@
somerset-house.org.uk

**Courtauld Institute
of Art Gallery**
Courtauld Institute of Art
Tel: 020 7848 2526
e-mail: galleryinfo@
courtauld.ac.uk

**Gilbert Collection
Tel:** 020 7420 9400
e-mail: info@
gilbert-collection.org.uk

**Hermitage Rooms
Tel:** 020 7845 4630

▶ **LOCATION**
OS Ref. TQ308 809

Entrances Victoria
Embankment or Strand.

Underground: Temple
or Covent Garden.

Air: London airports.

FUNCTION/RECEPTION

ROOM	MAX CAPACITY
Silver Gallery	350
Fine Rooms	250
Great Room	200
Fine & Gt Rm.	400
Seamen's Hall	200
Hermitage Rooms	60
Lecture Theatre	60
Navy Boardroom	60
Introductory Gallery	120
Courtyard	2,000

SOMERSET HOUSE
LONDON
www.somerset-house.org.uk
including
Courtauld Institute of Art Gallery ~ www.courtauld.ac.uk
Gilbert Collection ~ www.gilbert-collection.org.uk
Hermitage Rooms ~ www.hermitagerooms.org.uk

Somerset House, Sir William Chambers' 18th century architectural masterpiece, is situated between Covent Garden and the South Bank. It takes its place as one of Europe's great centres for art and culture, and is noted for its classical interiors and architectural vistas.

The Courtauld Institute of Art Gallery has one of the greatest small collections of paintings in the world, including world famous Old Masters, Impressionist paintings and 20th century paintings, as well as sculpture and decorative arts.

The Gilbert Collection is an outstanding collection of the decorative arts. Given to the nation by Sir

Arthur Gilbert, the magnificent collections of European silver, gold snuffboxes and Italian mosaics are pre-eminent in the world. The vaulted spaces of Somerset House provide an inspirational setting for these works of great historical and artistic importance.

The Hermitage Rooms at Somerset House recreate, in miniature, the imperial splendour of the Winter Palace and its various wings, which now make up The State Hermitage Museum in St Petersburg. The beautifully furnished galleries provide a backdrop for a programme of changing exhibitions, offering a privileged glimpse of some of the museum's magnificent treasures.

🛇 Apply at desk for permission
for photography/filming.

🍴 Licensed.

♿ By arrangement.

🎧 Gilbert Collection and
Hermitage Rooms.

🅿 None.

🐕 Guide dogs only.

❄

▶ **OPENING TIMES**

**Courtauld Institute
of Art Gallery,
Gilbert Collection &
Hermitage Rooms**
Daily, 10am - 6pm.
Last admission 5.15pm.
Closed 25/26 December.

▶ **ADMISSION**

Somerset House
Free except special
exhibitions.

**Courtauld Institute
of Art Gallery**
Adult £5.00
Child (under 18yrs) .... Free
Student (UK full) ....Free
OAP £4.00
Pre-booked Groups
Adult £4.00
Disabled Person's Carer Free

Mon, 10am - 2pm ...... Free
(excluding BHs)

Gilbert Collection
Adult £5.00
Child (under 18yrs) .... Free
Student (UK full) ....Free
OAP £4.00
Pre-booked Groups
Adult £4.00
Disabled Person's Carer Free

Hermitage Rooms
Adult £5.00
Child (under 18yrs) .... Free
Student (UK full)......Free
Conc. £4.00
Pre-booked Groups
Adult £4.00
Disabled Person's Carer Free

Triple Ticket
(all 3 collections)
Adult £12.00
Conc.....................£11.00
Double Ticket
(any 2 collections)
Adult £8.00
Conc......................£7.00

Map 3

SPENCER HOUSE

ST JAMES'S PLACE

www.spencerhouse.co.uk

Spencer House, built 1756 - 66 for the 1st Earl Spencer, an ancestor of Diana, Princess of Wales (1961-97), is London's finest surviving 18th century town house. The magnificent private palace has regained the full splendour of its late 18th century appearance, after a painstaking ten-year restoration programme.

Designed by John Vardy and James 'Athenian' Stuart, the nine state rooms are amongst the first neo-classical interiors in Europe. Vardy's Palm Room, with its spectacular screen of gilded palm trees and arched fronds, is a unique Palladian setpiece, while the elegant mural decorations of Stuart's Painted Room reflect the 18th century passion for classical Greece and Rome. Stuart's superb gilded furniture has been returned to its original location in the Painted Room by courtesy of the V&A and English Heritage. Visitors can also see a fine collection of 18th century paintings and furniture, specially assembled for the house, including five major Benjamin West paintings, graciously lent by Her Majesty The Queen.

The state rooms are open to the public for viewing on Sundays. They are also available on a limited number of occasions each year for private and corporate entertaining during the rest of the week.

▶ CONTACT

Jane Rick
Director
Spencer House
27 St James's Place
London SW1A 1NR

Tel: 020 7514 1958
Fax: 020 7409 2952

Info Line: 020 7499 8620

▶ LOCATION
OS Ref. TQ293 803

Central London:
off St James's Street,
overlooking
Green Park.

Underground:
Green Park.

▶ OPENING TIMES

All Year
(except January & August)
Suns, 10.30am - 5.30pm.

Last tour 4.45pm.

Tours begin approximately every 20 mins and last 1hr 10 mins. Maximum number on each tour is 20.

Mon mornings for pre-booked groups only.

Open for corporate hospitality except during January & August.

▶ ADMISSION

Adult	£6.00
Conc.*	£5.00

* Students, Friends of V&A, Tate Gallery and Royal Academy (all with cards), children under 16 (no under 10s admitted). Group size: min 15 - 60.

Prices include guided tour.

ℹ️ No photography inside House or Garden.

🍸

♿ House only ramps and lifts. WC.

🚶 Obligatory. Comprehensive colour guidebook £3.50.

🅿️ None. Coaches can drop off at door.

🚫

🔔

▶ SPECIAL EVENTS

SPECIFIC SUNDAYS
The authentically restored garden of this 18th century London palace will be open to the public on specific Sundays during Spring and Summer.

For updated information telephone 020 7499 8620 or see our website.

CONFERENCE/FUNCTION

ROOM	MAX CAPACITY
Receptions	400
Lunches & Dinners	130
Board Meetings	40
Theatre Style Meetings	100

London - England

Map 3

Owner: The Duke of Northumberland

▶ CONTACT

Pamela Brightey
Syon House
Syon Park
Brentford
TW8 8JF

Tel: 020 8560 0882
Fax: 020 8568 0936

e-mail: info@
syonpark.co.uk

▶ LOCATION

OS Ref. TQ173 767

Between Brentford and Twickenham, off the A4, A310 in SW London.

Rail: Kew Bridge or Gunnersbury Underground then Bus 237 or 267.

Air: Heathrow 8m.

SYON PARK 🏛

BRENTFORD

www.syonpark.co.uk

Described by John Betjeman as 'the Grand Architectural Walk', Syon House and its 200 acre park is the London home of the Duke of Northumberland, whose family, the Percys, have lived here for 400 years.

Originally the site of a late medieval monastery, recently excavated by Channel 4's *Time Team*, Syon Park has a fascinating history. The present house has Tudor origins but contains some of Robert Adam's finest interiors, which were commissioned by the 1st Duke in the 1760s. The private apartments and State bedrooms are available to view. The house is regularly used for feature films and productions.

Within the 'Capability' Brown landscaped park

are 40 acres of gardens which contain the spectacular Great Conservatory designed by Charles Fowler in the 1820s. The House and Great Conservatory are available for corporate and private hire.

Syon House is an excellent venue for small meetings, lunches and dinners in the Duke's private dining room (max 22). The State Apartments make a sumptuous setting for dinners, concerts, receptions, launches and wedding ceremonies (max 120). Marquees can be erected on the lawn adjacent to the house for balls and corporate events. The Great Conservatory is available for summer parties, launches and wedding receptions.

▶ OPENING TIMES

House
24 March - 31 October
Wed, Thur, Sun & BHs
11am - 5pm
(open Good Fri &
Easter Sat).

Other times by
appointment for groups.

Gardens
Daily (except 25 & 26 Dec)
10.30am - 5.30pm or dusk
if earlier.

▶ ADMISSION

House and Gardens
Adult £7.25
Child/Conc. £5.95
Family (2+2) £16.00

Gardens only
Adult £3.75
Child/Conc £2.50
Family (2+2) £8.00
Groups (15 - 50 persons)

House & Gardens
(Group bookings)
Adult £6.50
Child/Conc £5.50

Gardens only
Adult £3.50
Child/Conc £2.50

 No photography in house. Indoor adventure playground.

  Garden centre.

Partial.

Licensed.

By arrangement.

 Guide dogs only.

CONFERENCE/FUNCTION

ROOM	SIZE	MAX CAPACITY
Great Hall	50' x 30'	120
Great Conservatory	60' x 40'	150
Marquee		1000

Crown Copyright: Historic Royal Palaces 2002

ENTRY TO THE TRAITORS GATE

THE TOWER OF LONDON

LONDON

www.tower-of-london.org.uk

Map 3

Managed by:
Historic Royal Palaces

▶ **CONTACT**

The Tower of London
London   EC3N 4AB

**Recorded
Information Line:**
0870 756 6060

All Other Enquiries:
0870 751 5177

▶ **LOCATION**
OS Ref. TQ336 806

Underground:
Tower Hill on
Circle/District Line.

**Docklands Light
Railway:**
Tower Gateway Station.

Rail: Fenchurch Street
Station and
London Bridge Station.

Bus: 15, 25, 42,
78, 100, D1.

Riverboat: From
Charing Cross,
Westminster or
Greenwich to
Tower Pier.

William the Conqueror began building the Tower of London in 1078 as a royal residence and to control the volatile City of London. Over the ensuing 900 years the Tower has served as a royal fortress, mint, armoury and more infamously as a prison and place of execution.

The Tower of London has been home to the Crown Jewels for the last 600 years and today visitors can see them in all their glory in the magnificent new Jewel House. They are still used by HM The Queen for ceremonies such as the State Opening of Parliament.

Visit the White Tower, the original Tower of London, which features new displays by the Royal Armouries including the Block and Axe, Tudor arms and armour and the Instruments of Torture.

Once inside, the Yeoman Warder 'Beefeaters' give free guided tours providing an unrivalled insight into the darker secrets of over 900 years of royal history. Above the notorious Traitors' Gate, costumed guides evoke life at the court of King Edward I in the recently restored rooms of his Medieval Palace.

See the execution site where many famous prisoners, such as two of Henry VIII's wives, were put to death and visit the Chapel Royal where they are buried. Special events take place throughout the year, including events during every school holiday, with costumed interpreters.

▶ **OPENING TIMES**

Summer
1 March - 31 October
Daily
Mon - Sat: 9am - 5pm
(last admission)
Suns: 10am - 5pm.

Winter
1 November - 28 February
Tues - Sat: 9am - 4pm
(last admission)
Mons & Suns: 10am - 4pm.

Closed 24 - 26 December
and 1 January.

Buildings close 30 minutes
after last admission.
Tower closes 1 hour after
last admission.

▶ **ADMISSION**

Telephone Information
Line for admission prices:
0870 756 6060

Advance Ticket Sales:
0870 756 7070

Groups are advised to book,
telephone: 020 7488 5681.

No photography in
Jewel House.

020 7488 5762.

Partial. WC.

Obligatory. Yeoman Warder
tours are free and leave front
entrance every 1/2 hr.

None.

Welcome. Group rates on
request.

Tel for details.

Copyright HRP 2002

Copyright HRP 2002

Crown Copyright: Historic Royal Palaces 2002

© V&A Images.

2 WILLOW ROAD

HAMPSTEAD, LONDON NW3 1TH

Tel: 020 7435 6166   **e-mail:** 2willowroad@nationaltrust.org.uk

Owner: The National Trust   **Contact:** The Custodian

The former home of Erno Goldfinger, designed and built by him in 1939. A three-storey brick and concrete rectangle, it is one of Britain's most important examples of modernist architecture and is filled with furniture also designed by Goldfinger. The interesting art collection includes works by Henry Moore and Max Ernst.

Location: OS Ref. TQ270 858. Hampstead, London.

Open: 6 - 27 Mar, 6 - 27 Nov: Sat, 12 noon - 5pm. 1 Apr - 30 Oct: Thurs - Sat, 12 noon - 5pm. Open Good Fri. Last admission 4.30pm. Tours: 12 noon, 1 & 2 pm. Unrestricted access for unguided visits 3 - 5pm.

Admission: Adult £4.60, Child £2.30, Family £11.50. Joint ticket with Fenton House £6.40. Private groups are welcome throughout the year outside public afternoon opening times. Groups must be 5+, booking essential.

Small ground floor area accessible, filmed tour of whole house available.

APSLEY HOUSE

HYDE PARK CORNER, LONDON W1J 7NT

www.apsleyhouse.org.uk

Tel: 020 7499 5676   **Fax:** 020 7493 6576

Owner: V & A Museum & DCMS   **Contact:** The Administrator

Apsley House (No.1, London) was originally designed by Robert Adam in 1771-8. In 1817 it was bought by the Duke of Wellington and enlarged. His London palace houses his magnificent collection: paintings by Velazquez, Goya, Rubens, Lawrence, Wilkie, Steen, de Hooch and other masters; sculpture, silver, porcelain, furniture, caricatures, medals and memorabilia.

Location: OS Ref. TQ284 799. N side of Hyde Park Corner. Nearest tube station: Hyde Park Corner exit 1 Piccadilly Line.

Open: Tue - Sun, 11am - 5pm. Closed Mon, (except BHs), Good Fri, May Day BH, 24 - 26 Dec and New Year's Day. Current arrangements may be subject to change from 1 April 2004, contact us before you visit.

Admission: Adult £4.50. Groups: £2.50pp. Under 18yrs & OAPs Free.

No photography in house. Partial. By arrangement. In Park Lane. Guide dogs only. Tel for details.

---

18 FOLGATE STREET

Spitalfields, East London E1 6BX

Tel: 020 7247 4013   **Fax:** 020 7377 5548   **www.**dennissevershouse.co.uk

Owner: Spitalfields Historic Buildings Trust   **Contact:** Mick Pedroli

A time capsule furnished and decorated to tell the story of the Jervis family, Huguenot silk weavers from 1724 - 1919.

Location: OS Ref. TQ335 820. ¹/₂ m NE of Liverpool St. Station. E of Bishopsgate (A10), just N of Spitalfields Market.

Open: "Silent Night" every Mon evening. Booking required. 1st & 3rd Sun each month: 2 - 5pm. Mons following these Suns 12 noon - 2pm.

Admission: "Silent Night" Mons £12, Suns £8. Monday afternoons £5.

Partial. Obligatory by private bookings. Tel for details.

ALBERT MEMORIAL

Princes Gate, Kensington Gore SW7

Tel: 020 7495 0916 (Booking Agency)

Managed by/Contact: The Royal Parks Agency

An elaborate memorial by George Gilbert Scott to commemorate the Prince Consort.

Location: OS Ref. TQ266 798. Victoria Station 1¹/₂ m, South Kensington Tube ¹/₂ m.

Open: All visits by booked guided tours; Sunday afternoons only. Tours last 45 mins and are weather dependent so please ring for confirmation. Times and prices subject to change from April 2004.

Admission: Adult £3.80, Child/Conc. £3.

THE BANQUETING HOUSE   *See page 64 for full page entry.*

BLEWCOAT SCHOOL

23 Caxton Street, Westminster, London SW1H 0PY

Tel: 020 7222 2877

Owner: The National Trust   **Contact:** Janet Bowden

Built in 1709 at the expense of William Green, a local brewer, to provide an education for poor children. Used as a school until 1926, it is now the NT London Gift Shop and Information Centre.

Location: OS Ref. TQ295 794. Near the junction with Buckingham Gate.

Open: All year: Mon - Fri, 10am - 5.30pm (Thurs 7pm). Also Sat 13 Nov - 18 Dec: 10am - 4pm. Closed BHs.

BOSTON MANOR HOUSE

Boston Manor Road, Brentford TW8 9JX

Tel: 020 8560 5441

Owner: Hounslow Cultural & Community Services   **Contact:** Jerome Farrell

A fine Jacobean house built in 1623.

Location: OS Ref. TQ168 784. 10 mins walk S of Boston Manor Station (Piccadilly Line) and 250yds N of Boston Manor Road junction with A4 - Great West Road, Brentford.

Open: Apr - end Oct: Sat, Sun & BHs, 2.30 - 5pm. Due to structural works during 2003/04 please check times prior to your visit. Park open daily.

Admission: Free.

BRUCE CASTLE MUSEUM

Haringey Libraries, Archives & Museum Service, Lordship Lane, London N17 8NU

Tel: 020 8808 8772   **Fax:** 020 8808 4118   **e-mail:** museum.services@haringey.gov.uk

Owner: London Borough of Haringey

A Tudor building. Sir Rowland Hill (inventor of the Penny Post) ran a progressive school at Bruce Castle from 1827.

Location: OS Ref. TQ335 906. Corner of Bruce Grove (A10) and Lordship Lane, 600yds NW of Bruce Grove Station.

Open: All year: Wed - Sun & Summer BHs (except Good Fri), 1 - 5pm. Organised groups by appointment.

Admission: Free.

BUCKINGHAM PALACE

See page 65 for full page entry.

BURGH HOUSE

New End Square, Hampstead, London NW3 1LT
Tel: 020 7431 0144 **Buttery:** 020 7431 2516 **Fax:** 020 7435 8817
e-mail: burghhouse@talk21.com **www.**burghhouse.org.uk
Owner: London Borough of Camden **Contact:** Ms Helen Wilton
A Grade I listed building of 1703 in the heart of old Hampstead with original panelled rooms, "barley sugar" staircase banisters and a music room. Home of the Hampstead Museum, permanent and changing exhibitions. Prize-winning terraced garden. Regular programme of concerts, art exhibitions, and meetings. Receptions, seminars and conferences. Rooms for hire. Special facilities for schools visits. Wedding receptions.
Location: OS Ref. TQ266 859. New End Square, E of Hampstead underground station.
Open: All year: Wed - Sun, 12 noon - 5pm. Sats by appointment only. BH Mons, 2 - 5pm. Closed Christmas fortnight, Good Fri & Easter Mon. Groups by arrangement. Buttery: Wed - Sun, 11am - 5.30pm. BHs, 1 - 5.00pm.
Admission: Free.
🅿 🎦 🚹 Ground floor & grounds. WC. 🍴 Licensed buttery. 🍴 📷 By arrangement. 🅿 None. 🚗 By arrangement. 🐕 Guide dogs only. 🔼 ❄

🔔 Civil Wedding Venues *see front section*

CARLYLE'S HOUSE 🦋

24 Cheyne Row, Chelsea, London SW3 5HL
Tel: 020 7352 7087 **Fax:** 020 7352 5108 **e-mail:** carlyleshouse@nationaltrust.org.uk
Owner: The National Trust **Contact:** The Custodian
This Queen Anne house was the home of Thomas Carlyle for some 47 years until his death in 1881.
Location: OS Ref. TQ272 777. Off Cheyne Walk, between Battersea and Albert Bridges on Chelsea Embankment, or off the King's Road and Oakley Street.
Open: 31 Mar - 31 Oct: Wed - Fri, 2 - 5pm; Sat, Sun & BH Mons, 11am - 5pm. Good Fri 2 - 5pm. Last admission 4.30pm.
Admission: Adult £3.80, Child £1.80.
📷 By arrangement for groups. 🎦 Send SAE for details.

CHAPTER HOUSE ⚏

East Cloisters, Westminster Abbey, London SW1P 3PE
Tel: 020 7222 5897 **www.**english-heritage.org.uk/visits
Owner: English Heritage **Contact:** Head Custodian
The Chapter House, built by the Royal masons c1250 and faithfully restored in the 19th century, contains some of the finest medieval sculpture to be seen and spectacular wall paintings. The building is octagonal, with a central column, and still has its original floor of glazed tiles, which have been newly conserved. Its uses have varied and in the 14th century it was used as a meeting place for the Benedictine monks of the Abbey and as well as for Members of Parliament.
Location: OS Ref. TQ301 795. Approach either through the Abbey or through Dean's Yard and the cloister.
Open: 1 Apr - 30 Sept: daily, 9.30am - 5pm. 1 - 31 Oct: daily, 10am - 5pm.1 Nov - 31 Mar: daily, 10am - 4pm. Liable to be closed at short notice on State & Holy occasions. Closed Good Fri, 24 - 26 Dec & 1 Jan. Times subject to change from April 2004.
Admission: Adult £1, Child 50p, Conc. 80p. Prices subject to change from April 2004.
📷 🅿 Small charge. ❄ 🎦 Tel for details.

CAPEL MANOR GARDENS

BULLSMOOR LANE, ENFIELD EN1 4RQ

www.capel.ac.uk

Tel: 020 8366 4442 **Fax:** 01992 717544
Owner: Capel Manor Charitable Organisation **Contact:** Miss Julie Ryan
These extensive, richly planted gardens are delightful throughout the year offering inspiration, information and relaxation. The gardens include various themes - historical, modern, walled, rock, water, sensory and disabled and an Italianate Maze, Japanese Garden and 'Gardening Which?' demonstration and model gardens. Capel Manor is a College of Horticulture and runs a training scheme for professional gardeners originally devised in conjunction with the Historic Houses Association.
Location: OS Ref. TQ344 997. Minutes from M25/J25. Tourist Board signs posted.
Open: Daily in summer: 10am - 5.30pm. Last ticket 4.30pm. Check for winter times.
Admission: Adult £5, Child £2, Conc. £4, Family £12. Charges alter for special show weekends and winter months.
📷 🅿 Grounds. WC. 🍴 🅿 🐕 In grounds, on leads. ❄ 🎦 Tel for details.

CHELSEA PHYSIC GARDEN

66 ROYAL HOSPITAL ROAD, LONDON SW3 4HS

Tel: 020 7352 5646 **Fax:** 020 7376 3910
Owner: Chelsea Physic Garden Company **Contact:** The Curator
The second oldest botanic garden in Britain, founded in 1673. For many years these 4 acres of peace and quiet, with many rare and unusual plants, were known only to a few. Specialists in medicinal plants, tender species and the history of plant introductions.
Location: OS Ref. TQ277 778. Off Embankment, between Chelsea & Albert Bridges. Entrance - Swan Walk.
Open: 4 Apr - 31 Oct: Weds, 12 noon - 5pm & Suns, 2 - 6pm. Special winter openings: 8 & 15 Feb: 11am - 3pm.
Admission: Adult £5, Child £3, OAP £5, Conc. £3. Carers for disabled: Free.
📷 🅿 🚹 🐕 🎦 Tel for details.

CHISWICK HOUSE ⌗
See page 66 for full page entry.

COLLEGE OF ARMS
Queen Victoria Street, London EC4V 4BT
Tel: 020 7248 2762 **Fax:** 020 7248 6448 **e-mail:** enquiries@college-of-arms.gov.uk
Owner: Corp. of Kings, Heralds & Pursuivants of Arms
Contact: The Officer in Waiting
Mansion built in 1670s to house the English Officers of Arms and their records.
Location: OS Ref. TQ320 810. On N side of Queen Victoria Street, S of St Paul's Cathedral.
Open: Earl Marshal's Court only; open all year (except BHs, State and special occasions) Mon - Fri, 10am - 4pm. Group visits (up to 10) by arrangement only. Record Room: open for tours (groups of up to 20) by special arrangement in advance with the Officer in Waiting.
Admission: Free (groups by negotiation).

COURTALD INSTTITUE OF ART GALLERY
See page 72 for full page entry.

EASTBURY MANOR HOUSE ⚘
Eastbury Square, Barking, Essex IG11 9SN
Tel: 020 8724 1002 **Fax:** 020 8724 1003 **e-mail:** sarahwillis@lbbd.gov.uk
Owner: The National Trust **Contact:** Sarah Willis
Eastbury Manor is a unique example of a medium sized Elizabethan Manor House with attractive grounds. Leased to the London Borough of Barking and Dagenham and used for a variety of events and arts and heritage activites. In addition Eastubury can be hired for business conferences, wedding ceremonies and education days.
Location: OS TQ457 838. In Eastbury Square off Ripple Road off A13, 10 mins S from Upney Station. Buses 287, 368 or 62.
Open: Mar - Dec: Mons & Tues and 1st & 2nd Sat of the month, 10am - 4pm.
Admission: Adult £2.50, Child 65p, OAP £1.25, Student £1.20, Family £5. Groups (15+) by arrangement. Rates on application.
⬚ ⬚ ⬚ **P** None. ⬛ ⬛ In grounds only. ⬚ ⬚ Tel for details.

ELTHAM PALACE ⌗
See page 67 for full page entry.

THE CHARLES DICKENS MUSEUM
48 DOUGHTY STREET, LONDON WC1N 2LX

www.dickensmuseum.com

Tel: 020 7405 2127 **Fax:** 020 7831 5175 **e-mail:** info@dickensmuseum.com
Owner: Dickens House Museum Trust **Contact:** Mr Andrew Xavier – Curator
House occupied by Charles Dickens and his family from 1837 - 1839 where he produced *Pickwick Papers, Oliver Twist, Nicholas Nickleby* and *Barnaby Rudge.* Contains the most comprehensive Dickens library in the world as well as portraits, illustrations and rooms laid out exactly as they were in Dickens's time.
Location: OS Ref. TQ308 822. W of Grays Inn Road.
Open: All year: Mon - Sat, 10am - 5pm, Sun, 11am - 5pm (last admission 4.30pm).
Admission: Adult £5, Child £3, Conc. £4. Booked groups (10+): Adult £4.
⬚ ⬚ ⬚ By arrangement. **P** Limited. No coaches. ⬛ ⬛ Guide dogs only. ⬚ ⬚ Tel for details.

FENTON HOUSE ✦

WINDMILL HILL, HAMPSTEAD, LONDON NW3 6RT

Tel/Fax: 020 7435 3471   **Infoline:** 01494 755563

e-mail: fentonhouse@nationaltrust.org.uk

Owner: The National Trust   **Contact:** The Custodian

A delightful late 17th century merchant's house, set among the winding streets of Old Hampstead. The charming interior contains an outstanding collection of Oriental and European porcelain, needlework and furniture. The Benton Fletcher Collection of beautiful early keyboard instruments is also housed at Fenton and the instruments are sometimes played by music scholars during opening hours. The walled garden has a formal lawn and walks, an orchard and vegetable garden and fine wrought-iron gates. Telephone for details of demonstrations and porcelain tours.

Location: OS Ref. TQ262 860. Visitors' entrance on W side of Hampstead Grove. Hampstead Underground station 300 yds.

Open: 6 - 28 Mar: Sat & Sun, 2 - 5pm. 3 Apr - 31 Oct: Wed - Fri, 2 - 5pm, Sat, Sun & BHs & Good Fri, 11am - 5pm. Groups at other times by appointment.

Admission: Adult £4.60, Child £2.30, Family £11.50. Groups (15+) £3.90. Joint ticket with 2 Willow Road, £6.40.

♿Ground floor. Braille guide. No picnics in grounds.

⚕Demonstration tours. 🅿None. ✖ 🛈Send SAE for details.

FREUD MUSEUM

20 MARESFIELD GARDENS, LONDON NW3 5SX

www.freud.org.uk

Tel: 020 7435 2002   **Fax:** 020 7431 5452   **e-mail:** freud@gn.apc.org

Contact: The Director

The Freud Museum was the home of Sigmund Freud after he escaped the Nazi annexation of Austria. The house retains its domestic atmosphere and has the character of turn of the century Vienna. The centrepiece is Freud's study which has been preserved intact, containing his remarkable collection of antiquities: Egyptian, Greek, Roman, Oriental and his large library. The Freuds brought all their furniture and household effects to London; fine Biedermeier and 19th century Austrian painted furniture. The most famous item is Freud's psychoanalytic couch, where his patients reclined. Fine Oriental rugs cover the floor and tables. Videos are shown of the Freud family in Vienna, Paris and London.

Location: OS Ref. TQ265 850. Between Swiss Cottage and Hampstead. Nearest Underground: Finchley Road on the Jubilee and Metropolitan lines.

Open: Wed - Sun (inc) 12 noon - 5pm.

Admission: Adult £5, Child under 12 Free, Conc. £2. Coach groups by appointment.

📷 ♿Ground floor. 🅿Limited. ✖Guide dogs only. ✱

FULHAM PALACE & MUSEUM

Bishop's Avenue, Fulham, London SW6 6EA

Tel: 020 7736 5821   **Fax:** 020 7736 3233

Owner: London Borough of Hammersmith & Fulham & Fulham Palace Trust

Former home of the Bishops of London (Tudor with Georgian additions and Victorian Chapel). The gardens, famous in the 17th century, now contain specimen trees and a knot garden of herbs.

Location: OS Ref. TQ240 761.

Open: Closed for restoration works from approx July 2004 - August 2005. Please tel for further details.

Admission: Gardens: Free.

❄ **Open All Year Index** see front section

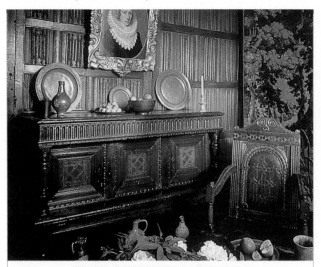

NTPL

HAM HOUSE 🌿

HAM, RICHMOND, SURREY TW10 7RS

www.nationaltrust.org.uk/hamhouse

Tel: 020 8940 1950 **Fax:** 020 8332 6903 **e-mail:** hamhouse@nationaltrust.org.uk

Owner: The National Trust   **Contact:** The Property Manager

Ham House, set on the banks of the Thames near Richmond, is perhaps the most remarkable Stuart house in the country. Formerly the home of the influential Duke and Duchess of Lauderdale, Ham was a centre for Court intrigue throughout the 17th century. In its time, the house was at the forefront of fashion and retains much of its interior decoration from that period. The sumptuous textiles, furniture and paintings collected by the couple are shown in 26 rooms. The gardens are a remarkable survival of English formal gardening and are being gradually restored to their former glory. Statues of *Venus Marina* and *Mercury* have recently returned to the garden. The 18th century dairy, decorated with cast iron cows' legs supporting marble work surfaces and hand-painted Wedgwood tiles, is now on view as is the 17th century still house, used for distilling alcohol and perfumes.

Location: OS Ref. TQ172 732. 1¹/₂ m from Richmond and 2m from Kingston. On the S bank of the River Thames, W of A307 at Petersham.

Open: House: 3 Apr - 31 Oct: daily except Thurs & Fri (open Good Fri) 1 - 5pm. Gardens: All year, daily except Thurs & Fri, 11am - 6pm/dusk if earlier. Closed 24, 26 Dec & 1 Jan. Special Christmas shop. Christmas lunches Dec. Some evening opening for Christmas for Gardens/shop/café.

Admission: House & Garden: Adult £7, Child £3.50, Family £17.50. Garden only: Adult £3, Child £1.50, Family £7.50. Booked groups (15+): Adult £6.

⬜ 🏵 🍴 🔍 Partial. WC. 🐕 🚫 🅿 🔊 🚌 Guide dogs. ▲ 🖥 Tel for details.

THE GEFFRYE MUSEUM

KINGSLAND ROAD, LONDON E2 8EA

Tel: 020 7739 9893 **Fax:** 020 7729 5647 **e-mail:** info@geffrye-museum.org.uk

Owner: Independent Charitable Trust

The Geffrye presents the changing style of the English domestic interior from 1600 to the present day through a series of period rooms. The displays lead the visitor on a walk through time, from the 17th century with oak furniture and panelling, past the refined splendour of the Georgian period and the high style of the Victorians, to 20th century modernity. The museum's displays are complemented by a walled herb garden and a series of period gardens.

Location: OS Ref. TQ335 833. 1m N of Liverpool St. Buses: 242, 149, 243, 67 & 394. Underground: Liverpool St. or Old St.

Open: Museum: Tue - Sat, 10am - 5pm. Sun & BH Mon, 12 noon - 5pm. Closed Mon (except BHs) Good Fri, Christmas Eve, Christmas Day, Boxing Day & New Year's Day. Gardens: Apr - Oct.

Admission: Free.

⬜ 🍴 🔍 🔊 🍴 🔊 ❄ 🖥 Tel for details

GILBERT COLLECTION   *See page 72 for full page entry.*

GUNNERSBURY PARK & MUSEUM

Gunnersbury Park, London W3 8LQ

Tel: 020 8992 1612 **Fax:** 020 8752 0686 **e-mail:** gp-museum@cip.org.uk

Owner: Hounslow and Ealing Councils   **Contact:** Lynn Acum

Built in 1802 and refurbished by Sydney Smirke for the Rothschild family.

Location: OS Ref. TQ190 792. Acton Town Underground station. ¹/₄ m N of the junction of A4, M4 North Circular.

Open: Apr - Oct: daily: 1 - 5pm. Nov - Mar: daily: 1 - 4pm. Victorian kitchens summer weekends only. Closed Christmas Day and Boxing Day. Park: open dawn - dusk.

Admission: Free. Donations welcome.

The Handel House Trust Ltd © 2001

HANDEL HOUSE MUSEUM

25 BROOK STREET, LONDON W1K 4HB

www.handelhouse.org

Tel: 020 7495 1685 **Fax:** 020 7495 1759 **e-mail:** mail@handelhouse.org

Owner: The Handel House Trust Ltd   **Contact:** Antonia Perkins

The only composer museum in London is located in 25 Brook Street W1, where G F Handel lived for 36 years, composed masterpieces such as *Messiah*, and died in 1759. It includes refurbished interiors, fine and decorative arts and instruments, temporary exhibitions, live music and educational programmes to bring enjoyment and understanding of Handel, his time and his music to the Museum visitor. Public recitals are held every Thursday between 6pm and 8pm.

Location: OS Ref. TQ286 809. Central London, between New Bond St and Grosvener Square. Bond Street Tube.

Open: Tue - Sat, 10am - 6pm (Thur until 8pm). Suns, 12 noon - 6pm. Closed Mons. Groups by arrangement.

Admission: Adult £4.50, Child £2, Conc. £3.50.

ℹ No inside photography. ⬜ 🔍 🚫 By arrangement. 🎧 🔊 ❄

HERMITAGE ROOMS

See page 72 for full page entry.

HOGARTH'S HOUSE

Hogarth Lane, Great West Road, Chiswick, London W4 2QN
Tel: 020 8994 6757
Owner: Hogarth House Foundation   **Contact:** Jerome Farrell
This late 17th century house was the country home of William Hogarth, the famous painter, engraver, satirist and social reformer between 1749 and his death in 1764.
Location: OS Ref. TQ213 778. 100 yds W of Hogarth roundabout on the Great West Road - junction of Burlington Lane. Car park in named spaces in Hogarth Business Centre behind house and Chiswick House grounds.
Open: Tue - Fri, 1 - 5pm (Nov - Mar: 1 - 4pm). Sat, Sun & BH Mons, 1 - 6pm (Nov - Mar: 1 - 5pm). Closed Mon (except BHs), Good Fri, Christmas Day, Boxing Day & Jan.
Admission: Free.

JEWEL TOWER ⌗

Abingdon Street, Westminster, London SW1P 3JY
Tel: 020 7222 2219 www.english-heritage.org.uk/visits
Owner: English Heritage   **Contact:** Head Custodian
Built c1365 to house the personal treasure of Edward III. One of two surviving parts of the original Palace of Westminster. Now houses an exhibition on 'Parliament Past and Present'.
Location: OS Ref. TQ302 794. Opposite S end of Houses of Parliament (Victoria Tower).
Open: 1 Apr - 31 Mar: daily, 10am - 6pm (closes 5pm in Oct, & 4pm Nov - Mar). Closed 24 - 26 Dec & 1 Jan. Times subject to change from April 2004.
Admission: Adult £2, Child £1, Conc. £1.50. Prices subject to change from April 2004.
⬚ 🔲 ✳ ♿ Tel for details.

DR JOHNSON'S HOUSE

17 Gough Square, London EC4A 3DE
Tel: 020 7353 3745 **e-mail:** curator@drjohnsonshouse.org
Owner: The Trustees
Fine 18th century house, once home to Dr Samuel Johnson, the celebrated literary figure, famous for his English dictionary.
Location: OS Ref. TQ314 813. N of Fleet Street.
Open: Oct - Apr: Mon - Sat, 11am - 5pm. May - Sept: Mon - Sat, 11am - 5.30pm. Closed BHs.
Admission: Adult £4, Child £1 (under 10yrs Free), Conc. £3. Family Ticket £9. Groups: £3.

KEATS HOUSE

Keats Grove, Hampstead, London NW3 2RR
Tel: 020 7435 2062 **Fax:** 020 7431 9293
e-mail: keatshouse@corpoflondon.gov.uk
www.keatshouse.org.uk www.cityoflondon.gov.uk/keats
Owner: Corporation of London   **Contact:** The Manager
Regency home of the poet John Keats (1795 - 1821).
Location: OS Ref. TQ272 856. Hampstead, NW3. Nearest Underground: Belsize Park & Hampstead.
Open: Apr - end Nov: Tue - Sun & BHs, 12 noon - 5pm. Visits by appointment: Tue - Sun, 10am - 12 noon. Nov - end Mar: Tue - Sun & BHs, 12 noon - 4pm. Visits by appointment, Tue - Sat, 10am - 12 noon. Closed until 4 Jan 2004.
Admission: Adult £3, Under 16s Free, Conc. £1.50.
⬚ ♿Ground floor & garden. 🅿None. 🐕Guide dogs only. ✳

KENSINGTON PALACE STATE APARTMENTS

See page 68 for full page entry.

KENWOOD HOUSE ⌗

See page 69 for full page entry.

LSO ST LUKE'S, THE UBS AND LSO MUSIC EDUCATION CENTRE

161 Old Street, London EC1V 9NG
Tel: 020 7490 3939 **Minicom:** 020 7490 8299 **Fax:** 020 7566 2881
e-mail: alaw@lso.co.uk
www.lso.co.uk/lsostlukes   **Contact:** Alison Law, Events Manager
Formerly St Luke's Church, a Grade I listed Hawksmoor church built in 1728. LSO St Luke's is the new home for the London Symphony Orchestra's music education and community programme, LSO Discovery. The church was derelict for 40 years, but has been rebuilt and opened in early 2003 with state-of-the-art facilities.
Location: OS Ref. TQ325 824. On corner of Old Street and Helmet Row, 5mins walk from Old Street Station (Northern Line, National Rail).
Open: By appointment only. Contact the Events Manager.
Admission: Free.
♿ 🏫By arrangement. 🅿No cars, limited for coaches. 🔲 🐕Guide dogs only.

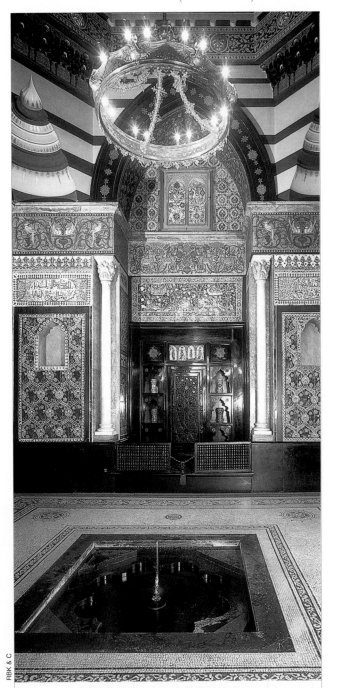

RBK & C

LEIGHTON HOUSE MUSEUM

12 HOLLAND PARK ROAD, KENSINGTON, LONDON W14 8LZ

www.rbkc.gov.uk/leightonhousemuseum

Tel: 020 7602 3316 **Fax:** 020 7371 2467
e-mail: museums@rbkc.gov.uk
Owner: Royal Borough of Kensington & Chelsea   **Contact:** Curator
Leighton House was the home of Frederic, Lord Leighton 1830 - 1896, painter and President of the Royal Academy, built between 1864 - 1879. It was a palace of art designed for entertaining and to provide a magnificent working space in the studio, with great north windows and a gilded apse. The Arab Hall is the centrepiece of the house, containing Leighton's collection of Persian tiles, a gilt mosaic frieze and a fountain. Victorian paintings by Leighton, Millais and Burne-Jones are on display.
Location: OS Ref. TQ247 793. Nearest underground: High Street Kensington (exit staircase turn left, take first right for Melbury Road after Commonwealth Institute. Leighton House is located in Holland Park Road, the first left. Bus: 9, 10, 27, 28, 33, 49, 328 (to Commonwealth Institute).
Open: Daily, except Tues, 11am - 5.30pm. Also open Spring/Summer BHs. Guided tours on Wed & Thur, 2.30pm. Closed 25/26 Dec.
Admission: Adult £3, Conc £1. Family £6. Guided tours free on Weds & Thurs. Joint group guided tour with Linley Sambourne House £10pp.

⬚ ℹ️No photography. 🔝 ♿Unsuitable. 🏫Wed & Thurs at 2.30pm. 🎧 🅿None. 🔲 ✳ ♿ Tel for details.

London - England

LINDSEY HOUSE ❧

100 Cheyne Walk, London SW10 0DQ

Tel: 020 7447 6605 **Fax:** 01494 463310

Owner: The National Trust   **Contact:** Area Manager

Part of Lindsey House was built in 1674 on the site of Sir Thomas More's garden, overlooking the River Thames. It has one of the finest 17th century exteriors in London.

Location: OS Ref. TQ268 775. On Cheyne Walk, W of Battersea Bridge near junction with Milman's Street on Chelsea Embankment.

Open: 12 May, 16 Jun, 8 Sept & 6 Oct: 2 - 4pm.

Admission: Free.

MARBLE HILL HOUSE ⊞

RICHMOND ROAD, TWICKENHAM TW1 2NL

www.english-heritage.org.uk/visits

Tel: 020 8892 5115 **Venue Hire and Hospitality:** 020 973 3534

Owner: English Heritage   **Contact:** House Manager

This beautiful villa beside the Thames was built in 1724 - 29 for Henrietta Howard, mistress of George II. Here she entertained many of the poets and wits of the Augustan age including Alexander Pope and later Horace Walpole. The perfect proportions of the villa were inspired by the work of the 16th century Italian architect, Palladio. Today this beautifully presented house contains an important collection of paintings and furniture, including some pieces commissioned for the villa when it was built. Summer concerts.

Location: OS Ref. TQ174 736. A305, 600yds E of Orleans House.

Open: 1 Apr - 30 Sept: Wed - Sun & BHs, 10am - 6pm. 1 Oct - 31 Oct: Wed - Sun, 10am - 5pm. Closed Nov - Mar, but exclusive group tours available on request. Times subject to change from April 2004.

Admission: Adult £3.50, Child £2, Conc. £3. Prices subject to change from April 2004.

⬚ ⊤ ⬚Ground floor. WC. ⬛Summer only. ⬚ ⵏ ⬚ ⬚Tel for details.

LINLEY SAMBOURNE HOUSE

18 STAFFORD TERRACE, LONDON W8 7BH

www.rbkc.gov.uk/linleysambournehouse

Info: 020 7602 3316 (ext 305 Mon - Fri) **or** 07976 060160 (Sats & Suns)

Fax: 020 7371 2467 **e-mail:** museums@rbkc.gov.uk

Owner: The Royal Borough of Kensington & Chelsea   **Contact:** Curatorial staff

Reopening after 2 years of restoration and refurbishment, Linley Sambourne House is the former home of the Punch cartoonist Edward Linley Sambourne and his family. Almost unchanged over the course of the last century, the house provides a unique insight into the life of an artistic middle-class family. The majority of the original decoration and furnishings remain in situ exactly as left by the Sambournes. All visits are by guided tour with special dramatic tours available and an introductory video. Larger groups can visit jointly with Leighton House Museum just 10 minutes walk away.

Location: OS Ref. TQ252 794. Parallel to Kensington High St, between Phillimore Gardens & Argyll Rd. Bus: 9, 10, 27, 28, 31, 49, 52, 70 & C1. Underground: Kensington High St. Parking on Sun in nearby streets.

Open: 17 Jan - 14 Mar, Sats & Suns; tours leaving at 10am, 11.15am, 1pm, 2.15pm and 3.30pm. Pre-booking is advised. At other times for booked groups (10+), by appointment. Larger groups (12+) will be divided for tours of the House. Access for Group tours: Mon - Fri.

Admission: Adult £6, Child (under 18yrs) £1, Conc £4. Groups (12+): Min £48.00. Joint group (10+) guided tour with Leighton House Museum £10pp.

⬚ ⒤No photography. ⬚Unsuitable. ⵏ Obligatory. ⵎNone. ⬛ ⬚Guide dogs only.

MORDEN HALL PARK ✹

Morden Hall Road, Morden SM4 5JD
Tel: 020 8545 6850   **Fax:** 020 8687 0094
e-mail: mordenhallpark@nationaltrust.org.uk
Owner: The National Trust   **Contact:** The Property Manager
Former deer park has an extensive network of waterways, ancient hay meadows and
wetlands. Workshops now house local craftworkers.
Location: OS Ref. TQ261 684. Off A24 and A297 S of Wimbledon, N of Sutton.
Open: All year: daily. NT shop & tea shop: 10am - 5pm. Car park closes 6pm.
Admission: Free.

WILLIAM MORRIS GALLERY

Lloyd Park, Forest Road, Walthamstow, London E17 4PP
Tel: 020 8527 3782   **Fax:** 020 8527 7070
Owner: London Borough of Waltham Forest   **Contact:** The Keeper
Location: OS Ref. SQ372 899. 15 mins walk from Walthamstow tube (Victoria line).
5 - 10 mins from M11/A406.
Open: Tue - Sat and first Sun each month, 10am - 1pm and 2 - 5pm.
Admission: Free for all visitors but a charge is made for guided tours which must
be booked in advance.

MUSEUM OF GARDEN HISTORY

LAMBETH PALACE ROAD, LONDON SE1 7LB

www.museumgardenhistory.org

Tel: 020 7401 8865 **Fax:** 020 7401 8869 **e-mail:** info@museumgardenhistory.org
Owner: Museum of Garden History
Fascinating permanent exhibition of the history of gardens, collection of ancient
tools and recreated 17th century garden displaying flowers and shrubs of the
period – seeds of which may be purchased in the garden shop. Visit the tombs of
the Tradescants and Captain Bligh of the Bounty. They have knowledgeable staff
and lectures, concerts and art exhibitions are held regularly. The Knot Garden,
part of the churchyard, is shown above.
Location: OS Ref. TQ306 791. At Lambeth Parish Church, next to Lambeth Palace,
at E end of Lambeth Bridge. Buses: 3, 77, 344, C10. Tube: Westminster or Waterloo.
Open: 2nd Sun in Feb - mid Dec: daily, 10.30am - 5pm.
Admission: Voluntary: Adult £3, Conc. £2.50.
⬜ 🌣 🚻 ♿ Partial. 🍴 🅿 None. 🎫 By arrangement (charge). 🔦 ❄
🐕 Tel for details.

MYDDELTON HOUSE GARDENS

Bulls Cross, Enfield, Middlesex EN2 9HG
Tel: 01992 702200   **Owner:** Lee Valley Regional Park Authority
Created by the famous plantsman F. A Bowles.
Location: OS Ref. TQ342 992. ¼ m W of A10 via Turkey St. ¾ m S M25/J25.
Open: Apr - Sept: Mon - Fri, 10am - 4.30pm, Suns & BH Mons, 12 noon - 4pm. Oct -
Mar: Mon - Fri, 10am - 3pm.
Admission: Adult £2.10, Conc. £1.50 until April 2004, then Adult £2.30, Conc. £1.80.

NT Photographic Library

OSTERLEY PARK ✹

JERSEY ROAD, ISLEWORTH, MIDDLESEX TW7 4RB

Tel: 020 8232 5050   **Fax:** 020 8232 5080   **Infoline:** 01494 755566
e-mail: osterley@nationaltrust.org.uk **www**.nationaltrust.org.uk/osterley/
Owner: The National Trust   **Contact:** Visitor Services Manager
Osterley's four turrets look out across one of the last great landscaped parks in
suburban London, its trees and lakes an unexpected haven of green. Originally
built in 1575, the mansion was transformed in the 18th century into an elegant villa
by architect Robert Adam. The classical interior, designed for entertaining on a
grand scale, still impresses with its specially made tapestries, furniture and
plasterwork. The magnificent 16th century stables (below) survive largely intact
and are still in use.

NT Photographic Library: Dennis Gilbert

Location: OS Ref. TQ146 780. Access via Thornbury Road on N side of A4.
Open: House: 6 - 28 Mar: Sat & Sun; 31 Mar - 31 Oct: Wed - Sun, 1 - 4.30pm. Park
& Pleasure Grounds: All year: daily, 9am - 7.30pm. Open BH Mons & Good Fri.
Park & Pleasure Grounds close dusk if earlier than 7.30pm. Park closes early
before major events. Car park closed: 25 & 26 Dec.
Admission: Adult £4.70, Child £2.30, Family £11.70, Groups £3.80.
Park & Pleasure Grounds: Free. Car Park: £3.
⬜ 🚻 ♿ Suitable, tel for details. 🍴 🅿 🔦 On leads in park. 🔦 ❄ 🐕 Tel for details.

London - England

THE OCTAGON, ORLEANS HOUSE GALLERY

Riverside, Twickenham, Middlesex TW1 3DJ
Tel: 020 8831 6000 **Fax:** 020 8744 0501 **e-mail:** galleryinfo@richmond.gov.uk
Owner: London Borough of Richmond-upon-Thames   **Contact:** Rachel Tranter
Outstanding example of baroque architecture by James Gibbs c1720. Art gallery.
Location: OS Ref. TQ168 734. On N side of Riverside, 700yds E of Twickenham town
centre, 400yds S of Richmond Road. Vehicle access via Orleans Rd only.
Open: Tue - Sat, 1 - 5.30pm, Sun & BHs, 2 - 5.30pm (Oct - Mar closes 4.30pm). Closed
Mons. Garden: open daily, 9am - sunset.
Admission: Free.

PALACE OF WESTMINSTER

London SW1A 0AA
Tel: 020 7219 3000   **First Call:** 0870 906 3773   **Info:** 020 7219 4272
                                                        Contact: Information Office
The first Palace of Westminster was erected on this site by Edward the Confessor in
1042 and the building was a royal residence until a devastating fire in 1512.
After this, the palace became the two-chamber Parliament for government - the House of Lords
(largely hereditary until the reforms of the present Government) and the elected
House of Commons. Following a further fire in 1834, the palace was rebuilt by Sir
Charles Barry and decorated by A W Pugin.
Location: OS Ref. TQ303 795. Central London, W bank of River Thames. 1km S of
Trafalgar Square. Underground: Westminster.
Open: Aug - Oct (exact dates TBA, please ring for details). At other times by
appointment. Ring Infoline.
Admission: Adult £7, Child/Conc. £5. 3 Big Ben: Free. (2003 prices.)

PITZHANGER MANOR HOUSE

Walpole Park, Mattock Lane, Ealing W5 5EQ
Tel: 020 8567 1227 **Fax:** 020 8567 0595
e-mail: pmgallery&house@ealing.gov.uk **www.**ealing.gov.uk/pmgallery&house
Owner: London Borough of Ealing   **Contact:** Gill Bohee
Pitzhanger Manor House is a restored Georgian villa, once owned and designed by the
architect Sir John Soane (1753 - 1837). Rooms in the house continue to be restored using
Soane's highly individual ideas in design and decoration. Exhibitions of contemporary
art are programmed year-round and sited in both the adjacent Gallery and the House.
Location: OS Ref. TQ176 805. Ealing, London.
Open: All year: Tue - Fri, 1 - 5pm. Sat, 11am - 5pm. Summer Sunday Openings, please
ring for details. Closed Christmas, Easter, New Year and BHs.
Admission: Free.
🆃 ♿By arrangement. 🎧 🅿Limited. ▉ 🐕In grounds, on leads. ▲ ✳

RED HOUSE 🦡

Red House Lane, Bexleyheath DA6 8JF
Tel: 01494 755588 (Booking line)
Owner: The National Trust
Commissioned by William Morris in 1859 and designed by Philip Webb, Red House is
of enormous international significance in the history of domestic architecture and
garden design. The garden was designed to "clothe" the house with a series of sub-
divided areas that still clearly exist today. Inside, the house retains many of the original
features and fixed items of furniture designed by Morris and Webb, as well as
wall paintings and stained glass by Burne-Jones.
Location: OS Ref. TQ48 1750. Off A221 Bexleyheath. Visitors will be advised on how
to reach the property when booking. Nearest rail station Bexleyheath, 15 mins' walk.
Open: Mar - Sep: Wed - Sun, 11am - 5pm; Oct - Feb: Wed - Sun, 11am - 4.15pm.
Closed Christmas Day, Boxing Day, New Year's Day. Open Easter Sun, Good Fri, BH
Mons. Admission by pre-booked guided tour only. Telephone booking line 01494
755588.
Admission: Adult £5, Child £2.50, Family £12.50.
ℹNo WC. ♿Ground floor only. ▣Limited.
🅿No Parking on site. Parking at Danson Park (15 min walk). 90p parking charge at
weekends and BHs. Disabled drivers can pre-book (limited parking).

ROYAL OBSERVATORY   *See page 70 for full page entry.*
NATIONAL MARITIME MUSEUM
& QUEEN'S HOUSE

ST GEORGE'S CATHEDRAL, SOUTHWARK

Westminster Bridge Road, London SE1 7HY
Tel: 020 7928 5256 **Fax:** 020 7202 2189
e-mail: stgeorges@rc.net   **Contact:** Canon James Cronin
Neo-Gothic rebuilt Pugin Cathedral bombed during the last war and rebuilt by Romily
Craze in 1958.
Location: OS Ref. TQ315 794. Near Imperial War Museum. 1/2 m SE of Waterloo Stn.
Open: 8am - 6pm, every day, except BHs.
Admission: Free.

ST JOHN'S GATE
MUSEUM OF THE ORDER OF ST JOHN
ST JOHN'S GATE, LONDON EC1M 4DA
www.sja.org.uk/history

Tel: 020 7324 4070 **Fax:** 020 7336 0587 **e-mail:** museum@nhg.sja.org.uk
Owner: The Order of St John   **Contact:** Pamela Willis
Early 16 century Gatehouse (1504 - 2004), Priory Church and Norman Crypt. The
remarkable history of the Knights Hospitaller, dedicated to caring for the sick and
dating back to the 11th century, is revealed in collections including furniture, paintings,
armour, stained glass and other items. Notable associations with Shakespeare, Hogarth,
Edward Cave, Dr Johnson, Dickens, David Garrick and many others. In Victorian times,
St John Ambulance was founded here and a modern interactive gallery tells its story.
Location: OS Ref. TQ317 821. St. John's Lane, Clerkenwell. Nearest Underground:
Farringdon.
Open: Mon - Fri: 10am - 5pm. Sat: 10am - 4pm. Closed BHs & Sat of BH weekend.
Tours: Tue, Fri & Sat at 11am & 2.30pm. Reference Library: Open by appointment.
Admission: Museum Free. Tours of the building: £5, OAP £3.50 (donation).
🖼 ♿Ground floor. WC. 🎦 ▉ 🐕Guide dogs only. ✳   Reg. Charity No. 1077265

ST PAUL'S CATHEDRAL   *See page 71 for full page entry.*

SIR JOHN SOANE'S MUSEUM

13 Lincoln's Inn Fields, London WC2A 3BP
Tel: 020 7405 2107 **Fax:** 020 7831 3957 **www.**soane.org
Owner: Trustees of Sir John Soane's Museum   **Contact:** Julie Brock
The celebrated architect Sir John Soane built this in 1812 as his own house. It now
contains his collection of antiquities, sculpture and paintings.
Location: OS Ref. TQ308 816. E of Kingsway, S of High Holborn.
Open: Tue - Sat, 10am - 5pm. 6 - 9pm, first Tue of the month. Closed BHs & 24 Dec.
Admission: Free. Groups must book.

SOMERSET HOUSE   *See page 72 for full page entry.*

SOUTHSIDE HOUSE 🏛

3 WOODHAYES ROAD, WIMBLEDON, LONDON SW19 4RJ

Tel: 020 8946 7643

Owner: The Pennington-Mellor-Munthe Charity Trust   **Contact:** The Administrator
Built by Robert Pennington in 1665, the family befriended or were related to many
distinguished names - among others Ann Boleyn's descendents, Nelson, Hamilton,
the 'Hell Fire Duke of Wharton' and Natalie, Queen of Serbia. Family portraits and
possessions on show. Bedroom prepared for Prince of Wales in 1750. In 1907 the
heiress, Hilda Pennington Mellor married Axel Munthe the Swedish doctor and
philanthropist. After 1945 Hilda and her sons restored the house. Malcolm, who
had lived extraordinary adventures during the war, determined to make a cultural
ark of the family inheritance. Guided tours give reality and excitement to the old
family histories. Recently restored water gardens and orchard.

Location: OS Ref. TQ234 706. On S side of Wimbledon Common (B281),
opposite Crooked Billet Inn.

Open: Easter Saturday - first weekend in Oct. Otherwise by appointment
throughout the year with the Administrator.

Admission: Adult £5, Child £2.50 (must be accompanied by an adult), OAP £4,
Family £10.

🚫 Unsuitable. 🚶 Obligatory. 🅿 Limited. ▣ ✕

SOUTHWARK CATHEDRAL

London Bridge, London SE1 9DA
Tel: 020 7367 6700   **Fax:** 020 7367 6730   **Visitors' Officer:** 020 7367 6734
e-mail: cathedral@dswark.org.uk   **www.**dswark.org/cathedral
Owner: Church of England   **Contact:** Visitors' Officer
London's oldest gothic building and a place of worship for over 1,000 years,
Southwark Cathedral has connections with Chaucer, Shakespeare, Dickens and John
Harvard. Included in the new riverside Millennium buildings are: Interactive
Exhibition 'The Long View of London', the Cathedral Shop and The Refectory.

Location: OS Ref. TQ327 803. South side of London Bridge, near Shakespeare's
Globe and Tate Modern.

Open: Daily: 8.30am - 6pm. Weekday services: 8am, 12.30pm and 5.30pm. Sat
services, 9am and 4pm. Sun services: 9am, 11am, 3pm & 6.30pm. Visitor Centre: daily,
10am - 6pm, Sun, 11am - 5pm.

Admission: Recommended donation of £4 per person. Booked groups (min 10):
Adult £4, Child £2, Conc. £3.50. Exhibition: Adult £3, Child £1.50, Conc. £2.50. Trade
discounts available.

ℹ Indoor photography & video recording with permit. ▣ 🕓 🚫 Partial. WCs. ▣
🍴 Licensed. 🚶 By arrangement. 🔊 🅿 None. ▣ ✕ Guide dogs only. ✳

SPENCER HOUSE   *See page 73 for full page entry.*

STRAWBERRY HILL

ST MARY'S, STRAWBERRY HILL, WALDEGRAVE ROAD,
TWICKENHAM TW1 4SX

Tel: 020 8240 4224 /Appointments: 020 8240 4044

Contact: The Conference Office

Horace Walpole converted a modest house at Strawberry Hill into his own version
of a gothic fantasy. It is widely regarded as the first substantial building of the
Gothic Revival and as such is internationally known and admired. A century later
Lady Frances Waldegrave added a magnificent wing to Walpole's original
structure. Lady Waldegrave's suite of rooms can be hired for weddings, corporate
functions and conferences. Please telephone for details.

Location: OS Ref. TQ158 722. Off A310 between Twickenham & Teddington.

Open: 2 May - 26 Sept: Suns, 2 - 3.30pm. Tours commence between 2pm &
3.30pm, please tel: 020 8240 4224 for confirmation, or to make an appointment
020 8240 4044.

Admission: Adult £5, OAP £4.25. Group bookings: £4.25.

ℹ Conferences. ▣ ▣ 🚶 ✕

London - England

NT Photographic Library: Geoffrey Frosh

SUTTON HOUSE ❧

2 & 4 HOMERTON HIGH STREET, HACKNEY, LONDON E9 6JQ

Tel: 020 8986 2264   **e-mail:** suttonhouse@nationaltrust.org.uk

Owner: The National Trust   **Contact:** The Property Manager

A rare example of a Tudor red-brick house, built in 1535 by Sir Rafe Sadleir, Principal Secretary of State for Henry VIII, with 18th century alterations and later additions. Restoration revealed many 16th century details, even in rooms of later periods. Notable features include original linenfold panelling and 17th century wall paintings.

Location: OS Ref. TQ352 851. At the corner of Isabella Road and Homerton High St.

Open: Historic rooms: 23 Jan - 19 Dec: Fri & Sat, 1 - 5.30pm, Sun, 11.30am - 5.30pm. Café, Shop & Art Gallery: 21 Jan - 19 Dec: Wed - Sun, 11.30am - 5pm. Open BH Mons 11.30am - 5pm. Closed Good Fri.

Admission: Adult £2.20, Child 50p, Family £4.90. Group visits by prior arrangement.
⬛ 🅰 Ground floor only. WC. ▣ ℹ 🅿 None. 🅸 🔺 ♿ Tel for details.

English Heritage Photo Library

WELLINGTON ARCH ⌗

HYDE PARK CORNER, LONDON W1J 7JZ

www.english-heritage.org.uk/visits

Tel: 020 7930 2726   **Venue Hire and Hospitality:** 020 973 3292

Owner: English Heritage   **Contact:** The Site Manager

Newly restored and opened to the public for the first time in April 2001, Wellington Arch has had a chequered history. Originally designed in 1825 by Decimus Burton as a grand entrance to Buckingham Palace and gateway to Green Park, its lavish ornamentation was never finished. An equestrian statue of the Duke of Wellington, hoisted upon the Arch in 1846, was judged to be far too large, and caused public outcry. Plans to remove it were halted when the Duke himself announced that he would take such an action as a personal insult. The statue remained the scorn of London and beyond until 1882 when growing traffic congestion around Hyde Park Corner led to Wellington Arch being dismantled and moved to its current position. The equestrian statue was removed and the arch remained bare until 1912 when the magnificent 'Quadriga' that you see today took its place.

Location: OS Ref. TQ285 798. Hyde Park Corner Tube Station.

Open: All year: Wed - Sun & BHs. 1 Apr - 30 Sept: 10am - 5.30pm; Oct: 10am - 5pm; Nov - Mar: 10am - 4pm. Closed 24 - 26 Dec & 1 Jan. (Times subject to change from April 2004.)

Admission: Adult £2.50, Child £1.50, Conc. £2. Groups (11+) 15% discount. (Prices subject to change from April 2004.)
⬛ ⊤ 🅰 ℹ Mondays for groups only. ✳ ♿ Tel for details.

SYON PARK 🏛   *See page 74 for full page entry.*

THE TOWER BRIDGE EXHIBITION

Tower Bridge, London SE1 2UP

Tel: 020 7940 3985   **Fax:** 020 7357 7935

Owner: Corporation of London   **Contact:** Emma Parlow

One of London's most unusual and exciting exhibitions is situated inside Tower Bridge. Enjoy spectacular views from the high level walkways.

Location: OS Ref. TQ337 804. Adjacent to Tower of London, nearest Underground: Tower Hill.

Open: All year: 9.30am - 6pm. Last ticket sold at 5pm. Closed 25 Dec.

Admission: Adult £4.50, Child/Conc. £3, Family discounts apply. (Prices subject to Change from April 2004.)

THE TOWER OF LONDON   *See page 75 for full page entry.*

THE 'WERNHER COLLECTION' AT RANGER'S HOUSE ⌗

Chesterfield Walk, Blackheath, London SE10 8QX

Tel: 020 8853 0035   www.english-heritage.org.uk/visits

Owner: English Heritage   **Contact:** House Manager

This attractive red-brick villa built c1700 on the edge of Greenwich Park houses the 'Wernher Collection': the life-time collection of self-made millionaire, Julius Wernher. A superb display of fine and decorative arts with objects dating from 3BC to the 19th-century, and including a stunning array of Renaissance jewellery as well as paintings, sculpture, furniture, tapestries, enamels and ivories.

Location: OS Ref. TQ388 768. N of Shooters Hill Road.

Open: Wed - Sun & BHs. Apr - Sept: 10am - 6pm (5pm in Oct), Nov - Mar 10am - 4pm. Closed 22 Dec 2003 - 4 Mar 2004. (Times subject to change from April 2004.)

Admission: Adult £4.50, Child £2.50, Conc. £3.50. (Prices subject to change from April 2004.)
ℹ WC. ⬛ 🅰 Limited, lift available. 🅿 🖼 🐕 Guide dogs only. ♿ Tel for details.

WESTMINSTER CATHEDRAL

Victoria, London SW1P 1QW

Tel: 020 7798 9055   **Fax:** 020 7798 9090   www.westminstercathedral.org.uk

Owner: Diocese of Westminster   **Contact:** Revd Mgr Mark Langham

The Roman Catholic Cathedral of the Archbishop of Westminster. Spectacular building in the Byzantine style, designed by J F Bentley, opened in 1903, famous for its mosaics, marble and music. Westminster Cathedral celebrated the Centenary of its foundation in 1995.

Location: OS Ref. TQ293 791. Off Victoria Street, between Victoria Station and Westminster Abbey.

Open: All year: 7am - 7pm. Please telephone for times at Easter & Christmas.

Admission: Free. Lift charge: Adult £3. Child £1.50. Family (2+4) £7.
⬛ 🅰 Ground floor. ℹ Prior booking required. 🅿 None. 🖼 Worksheets & tours. 🐕 Guide dogs only. ✳

Syon House, London from the book *Historic Family Homes and Gardens from the Air*, see page 54.

southeast

Alfriston, Sussex. © David Osborn

The Cobbe Collection at
hatchlands
surrey

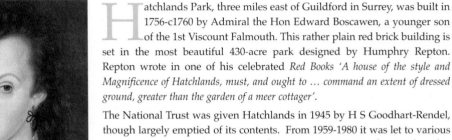

Hatchlands Park, three miles east of Guildford in Surrey, was built in 1756-c1760 by Admiral the Hon Edward Boscawen, a younger son of the 1st Viscount Falmouth. This rather plain red brick building is set in the most beautiful 430-acre park designed by Humphry Repton. Repton wrote in one of his celebrated *Red Books* '*A house of the style and Magnificence of Hatchlands, must, and ought to … command an extent of dressed ground, greater than the garden of a meer cottager*'.

The National Trust was given Hatchlands in 1945 by H S Goodhart-Rendel, though largely emptied of its contents. From 1959-1980 it was let to various tenants, and for a number of years housed a small girls' school. When this closed in 1980 it once again reverted to the National Trust, who redecorated some of the principal interiors and began to open the property to the public. It remained, though, a drab and somewhat depressing house to visit.

The man to breathe life back to Hatchlands has been Mr Alec Cobbe who, at the suggestion of Martin Drury, then the National Trust's Historic Buildings Secretary, took on the lease of Hatchlands as a setting for his collection of Old Master pictures and historic keyboard instruments (now vested in the Cobbe Collection Trust). Alec Cobbe comes from a distinguished Anglo-Irish family, seated at Newbridge House, Co Dublin which, before its restoration in 1985, he described as '*a romantic but decaying 18th century mansion, that still contains, virtually intact, the paintings, furniture and curiosities collected by generations of the Cobbe family.*' Having studied medicine, Mr Cobbe reverted to his childhood vocation of painter and musician, making a living painting *trompe l'oeil* murals, glass engraving and restoring pictures. It was his work at houses such as Burghley, Harewood, Powis and Nostell Priory that led to the suggestion that he take the lease of Hatchlands.

Few tenants would relish painting their own rooms, but this is exactly what Mr Cobbe and his assistants have done since 1987. The Saloon, Drawing Room and Library were the first rooms to be tackled, and were complete by April 1988. The Saloon, painted crimson, now acts as a spectacular picture gallery for The Cobbe Collection of Old Masters, a number brought from his old family home in Ireland and others collected more recently. The Robert Adam ceilings act as a superb delicate foil to the elaborate, ordered wall decorations below.

Scattered throughout these beautiful rooms are the celebrated collection of keyboard instruments once owned or played by composers such as Purcell, J C Bach, Mozart and Beethoven. Through the audio-guides and numerous musical events that are organised each year at Hatchlands, audiences can listen to the thrilling keyboard sounds that the composers themselves would have heard. A concert in the Music Room, designed by Sir Reginald Blomfield in 1903 – and surrounded by walls hung with Alec Cobbe's collection of prints of composers and musicians – is an experience quite magically different from any concert hall.

Hatchlands has been described as '*one of the most beautiful musical museums in the world*'. This is no exaggeration – but it is through the personality of Alec Cobbe and his family and their beautiful pictures, *objéts d'art* and furniture which clothe the house that make a visit to Hatchlands such an enriching and rewarding experience.

▸ For further details about the Cobbe Collection at Hatchlands see page 153.

Paul Procter, Chorley Handford

Map 3

Owner:
Official Residence of
Her Majesty The Queen

▶ **CONTACT**

Ticket Sales &
Information Office
Buckingham Palace
London SW1A 1AA

Tel: 020 7766 7304
Groups (15+):
020 7766 7321
Fax: 020 7930 9625

e-mail: information@
royalcollection.org.uk

▶ **LOCATION**
OS Ref. SU969 770

M4/J6, M3/J3.
20m from central
London.

Rail: Regular service
from London Waterloo.

Coach: Victoria Coach
Station - regular service.

Sightseeing tours:
Tour companies
operate a daily service
with collection from
many London hotels.
Ask your hotel
concierge or porter
for information.

WINDSOR CASTLE
& FROGMORE HOUSE
WINDSOR
www.royal.gov.uk

Whichever way you approach the town of Windsor, the view is dominated by the dramatic outline of Windsor Castle, the largest inhabited castle in the world and the oldest royal residence to have remained in continuous use by the monarchs of Britain. Today, along with Buckingham Palace and the Palace of Holyroodhouse in Edinburgh, it is one of the official residences of Her Majesty The Queen.

Windsor's rich history spans more than 900 years but, as a working royal palace, the Castle plays a large part in the official work of The Queen and members of the Royal Family today. The magnificent State Rooms are furnished with some of the finest works of art from the Royal Collection, including paintings by Rembrandt and

drawings by Leonardo da Vinci. Visitors also should not miss Queen Mary's Dolls' House, a masterpiece in miniature, the bullet that killed Lord Nelson and the last piece of armour made for Henry VIII.

Within the precincts is St George's Chapel, one of the most beautiful ecclesiastical buildings in England. Ten monarchs are buried here, including Henry VIII with his favourite wife, Jane Seymour.

Frogmore House has been a favourite royal retreat for over 300 years. It is open to visitors on a limited number of days during the year. Guided pre-booked group visits are available throughout August and September. Please contact the Ticket Sales and Information Office for details.

Derry Moore / The Royal Collection © 2002, HM Queen Elizabeth II

John Freeman / The Royal Collection © 2002, HM Queen Elizabeth II

▶ **OPENING TIMES**

March - October:
Daily except 9 April &
14 June: 9.45am - 5.15pm
(last adm 4pm).

November - February:
Daily except 25/26 Dec
9.45am - 4.15pm
(last admission 3pm).

**Opening arrangements
may change at short notice.**

St George's Chapel is
closed to visitors on
Sundays as services are
held throughout the day.
Worshippers are welcome.

The State Rooms
are closed during
Royal and State visits.

**Frogmore House &
Mausoleum**
Open on a limited number
of days during the year.
For times and prices
contact 020 7766 7305.

Private tours of the house
for pre-booked groups
(15+) during Aug & Sept.
Contact 020 7766 7321.

▶ **ADMISSION**
Windsor Castle
Adult £12.00
Child (up to 17yrs).... £6.00
Child (under 5yrs)...... Free
OAP/Student £10.00
Family (2+3).......... £30.00

Groups (15+)
Discounts available.

▣ **SPECIAL EVENTS**
With the exception of
Sundays, the Changing of
the Guard takes place at 11am
daily from April to the end of
June and on alternate days at
other times of the year.

ℹ No photography.   🛍 ♿ 🧑 August & September.   🎧 Audio Tours Windsor Castle.   🅿 None.

▣ 🐕 Guide dogs only.   ❄

BASILDON PARK

LOWER BASILDON, READING, BERKSHIRE RG8 9NR

www.nationaltrust.org.uk/basildonpark

Tel: 0118 984 3040   **Infoline:** 01494 755558   **Fax:** 0118 976 7370
e-mail: basildonpark@nationaltrust.org.uk

Owner: The National Trust   **Contact:** The Property Manager

An elegant, classical house designed in the 18th century by Carr of York and set in rolling parkland in the Thames Valley. The house has rich interiors with fine plasterwork, pictures and furniture, and includes an unusual Octagon Room and a decorative Shell Room. Basildon Park has connections with the East through its builder and was the home of a wealthy industrialist in the 19th century. It was rescued from dereliction in the mid 20th century. Small flower garden, pleasure grounds, 400 acres of parkland with woodland walks.

Location: OS Ref. SU611 782. 2¹/₂ m NW of Pangbourne on the west side of the A329, 7m from M4/J12.

Open: House: 31 Mar - 31 Oct: daily except Mon & Tue (open BH Mons), 1 -5.30pm. Park, Garden & Woodland Walk: as house 12 noon - 5.30pm. Property closes at 5pm 13 - 15 Aug.

Admission: House, Park & Garden: Adult £4.70, Child £2.30, Family £11.70. Park & Garden only: Adult £2.30, Child £1.10. Family £5.70. Groups (15+) by appointment: £3.50.

🔲 ♿ 🍴 𝑓 By appointment 🅿 In grounds. 🐕 On leads, in grounds only. 🔺 ♨ Tel for details.

DONNINGTON CASTLE ⌗

Newbury, Berkshire

Tel: 02392 581059   **www.**english-heritage.org.uk/visits

Owner: English Heritage   **Contact:** Area Manager

Built in the late 14th century, the twin towered gatehouse of this heroic castle survives amidst some impressive earthworks.

Location: OS Ref. SU463 691. 1m N of Newbury off B4494.

Open: Any reasonable time (exterior viewing only).

Admission: Free.

♿ Steep slopes within grounds. 🅿 🐕 On leads.

DORNEY COURT 🏠

WINDSOR, BERKSHIRE SL4 6QP

www.dorneycourt.co.uk

Tel: 01628 604638   **Fax:** 01628 665772   **e-mail:** palmer@dorneycourt.co.uk

Owner/Contact: Mrs Peregrine Palmer

Just a few miles from the heart of bustling Windsor lies "one of the finest Tudor Manor Houses in England", *Country Life*. Grade I listed with the added accolade of being of outstanding architectural and historical importance, the visitor can get a rare insight into the lifestyle of the squirearchy through 550 years, with the Palmer family, who still live there today, owning the house for 450 of these years. The house boasts a magnificent Great Hall, family portraits, oak and lacquer furniture, needlework and panelled rooms. A private tour on a 'non-open day' takes around 1¹/₂ hours, but when open to the public this is reduced to around 40 mins. The adjacent 13th century Church of St James, with Norman font and Tudor tower can also be visited, as well as the adjoining Plant Centre in our walled garden where light lunches and full English cream teas are served in a tranquil setting throughout the day.

Location: OS Ref. SU926 791. 5 mins off M4/J7, 10mins from Windsor, 2m W of Eton.

Open: May: BH Suns & Mons, 1.30 - 4.30pm. Aug: daily except Sat, 1.30 - 4pm (last admission).

Admission: Adult £5.50, Child (10yrs +) £3.50. Groups: By arrangement all year.

ℹ️ Film & photographic shoots. 🌱 Garden centre. 🍴 ♿ Garden centre. 🔲 𝑓 🅿 🐕 Guide dogs only. ❄

🌷 **Plant Sales Index** see front section

ETON COLLEGE

Windsor, Berkshire SL4 6DW

Tel: 01753 671177   **Fax:** 01753 671265   **e-mail:** visits@etoncollege.org.uk

Owner: Eton College   **Contact:** Rebecca Hunkin

Eton College, founded in 1440 by Henry VI, is one of the oldest and best known schools in the country. The original and subsequent historic buildings of the Foundation are a part of the heritage of the British Isles and visitors are invited to experience and share the beauty of the ancient precinct which includes the magnificent College Chapel, a masterpiece of the perpendicular style.

Location: OS Ref. SU967 779. Off M4/J5. Access from Windsor by footbridge only. Vehicle access from Slough 2m N.

Open: Mar - early Oct: Times vary, best to check with the Visits Office.

Admission: Ordinary admissions and daily guided tours. Groups by appointment only. Rates vary according to type of tour.

⬜ 🔲 ♿Ground floor. WC. 🔲 🅿Limited. 🦮Guide dogs only.

🍴 Corporate Hospitality see front section

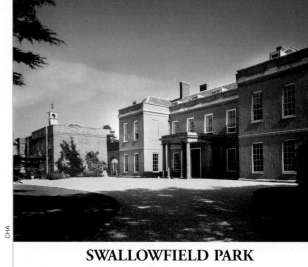

CHA

SWALLOWFIELD PARK

SWALLOWFIELD, READING, BERKSHIRE RG7 1TG

Tel: 0118 9883815   **Fax:** 0118 9883930

Owner: Country Houses Association   **Contact:** The Administrator

Built in 1678 by the second Earl of Clarendon. The arms of the Clarendons form part of the decorative plaster in the oval vestibule. The Talman Gate has been restored. Set in 25 acres, including a beautiful walled garden. Swallowfield Park has been converted into apartments for active retired people.

Location: OS Ref. SU730 655. In Swallowfield, 6 m SE of Reading. 4m S of M4/J11. Then via Spencers Wood.

Open: 1 May - 30 Sept: Wed & Thurs, 2 - 5pm by arrangement only.

Admission: Adult £3, Child £1.50 (Child under 12yrs Free). Groups by arrangement.

✖ 🛏1 single & 1 double w/bathroom. CHA members & Wolsey Lodge guests. 🔔

SAVILL GARDEN

WINDSOR GREAT PARK, BERKSHIRE SL4 2HT

www.savillgarden.co.uk

Tel: 01753 847518   **Fax:** 01753 847536   **e-mail:** savillgarden@crownestate.co.uk

Owner: Crown Estate Commissioners   **Contact:** Jan Bartholomew

World-renowned 35 acre woodland garden, providing a wealth of beauty and interest in all seasons. Spring is heralded by hosts of daffodils, masses of rhododendrons, azaleas, camellias, magnolias and much more. Roses, herbaceous borders and countless alpines are the great features of summer, and the leaf colours and fruits of autumn rival the other seasons with a great display.

Location: OS Ref. SU977 706. Wick Lane, Englefield Green. Clearly signposted from Ascot, Bagshot, Egham and Windsor. Nearest station: Egham.

Open: Mar - Oct: 10am - 6pm. Nov - Feb: 10am - 4pm.

Admission: Apr - May: Adult £5.50, Child (6-16) £2.50, Conc. £5. Jun - Oct: Adult £4.50, Child (6-16) £1.50, Conc. £4. Nov - Mar: Adult £3.50, Child (6-16) £1.25, Conc. £3.00. Child under 6 Free. Prices subject to change in 2005.

ℹ️Film & photographic shoots. ⬜ 🔲Plant centre. ♿Grounds. WC. 🍴Licensed. 🔲For groups, by appointment. 🦮Guide dogs only. ✳

TAPLOW COURT 🏛

BERRY HILL, TAPLOW, Nr MAIDENHEAD, BERKS SL6 0ER

www.sgi-uk.org

Tel: 01628 591209   **Fax:** 01628 773055

Owner: SGI-UK   **Contact:** Michael Yeadon

Set high above the Thames, affording spectacular views. Remodelled mid-19th century by William Burn. Earlier neo-Norman Hall. 18th century home of Earls of Orkney and more recently of Lord and Lady Desborough who entertained 'The Souls' here. Tranquil gardens & grounds. Anglo-Saxon burial mound. Permanent and temporary exhibitions.

Location: OS Ref. SU907 822. M4/J7 off Bath Road towards Maidenhead. 6m off M40/J2.

Open: House & Grounds: 30 May - 12 Sept: Sun & BH Mons, 2 - 5.30pm. Please telephone to confirm.

Admission: No charge. Free parking.

⬜ ♿ 🔲 🔲 🔲 🅿 🦮Guide dogs only.

WELFORD PARK

Newbury, Berkshire RG20 8HU
Tel: 01488 608203 / 608691
Owner/Contact: Mr J Puxley
A Queen Anne house, with attractive gardens and grounds. Riverside walks.
Location: OS Ref. SU409 731. On Lambourn Valley Road. 6m NW of Newbury.
Open: Mon 24 May, Mon 31 May; 5 - 30 Jun: 11am - 5pm. Home made cream teas available for groups (10+), must book 7 days in advance.
Admission: Booked House Tour: Adult £5, OAP & Child over 8yrs £3.50. Grounds: Free except when occasionally open in aid of charities.
⑤ Grounds. ⌘ On leads, in grounds.

WINDSOR CASTLE & FROGMORE HOUSE

See page 94 for full page entry.

Special Events Index see front section

Dorney Court, Berkshire from the book *Historic Family Homes and Gardens from the Air*, see page 54.

© Skyscan 2003.

STOWE HOUSE 🏛

BUCKINGHAM

www.stowe.co.uk

Map 5

Owner:
Stowe House
Preservation Trust

▶ **CONTACT**

The Commercial Office
Stowe School
Buckingham
MK18 5EH

Tel: 01280 818282
House only
or 01280 822850
Gardens

Fax: 01280 818186
House only

e-mail:
sses@stowe.co.uk
House only

▶ **LOCATION**

OS Ref. SP666 366

From London, M1 to
Milton Keynes, 1¹/₂ hrs
or Banbury 1¹/₄ hrs,
3m NW of Buckingham.

Bus: from
Buckingham 3m.

Rail: Milton Keynes 15m.

Air: Heathrow 50m.

Stowe owes its pre-eminence to the vision and wealth of two owners. From 1715 to 1749 Viscount Cobham, one of Marlborough's Generals, continuously improved his estate, calling in the leading designers of the day to lay out the gardens, and commissioning several leading architects – Vanbrugh, Gibbs, Kent and Leoni – to decorate them with garden temples. From 1750 to 1779 Earl Temple, his nephew and successor continued to expand and embellish both Gardens and House. The House is now a major public school. The magnificently restored North Front is well worth a visit. The Central Pavilion and South Front steps are due to be completed March 2005.

Around the mansion is one of Britain's most magnificent landscape gardens now in the ownership of the National Trust. Covering 325 acres and containing no fewer than 6 lakes and 32 garden temples, it is of the greatest historic importance. During the 1730s William Kent laid out in the Elysian Fields at Stowe, one of the first 'natural' landscapes and initiated the style known as 'the English Garden'. 'Capability' Brown worked there for 10 years, not as a consultant but as head gardener, and in 1744 was married in the little church hidden between the trees.

CONFERENCE/FUNCTION

ROOM	MAX CAPACITY
Roxburgh Hall	460
Music Room	120
Marble Hall	150
State Dining Rm	160
Garter Room	180
Memorial Theatre	120

ℹ Indoor swimming pool, sports hall, tennis court, squash courts, astroturf, parkland, cricket pitches and golf course. No photography in house.

🍴 International conferences, private functions, weddings, and prestige exhibitions. Catering on request.

♿ Visitors may alight at entrance. Allocated parking areas. WC in garden area. 'Batricars' available.

☕🍴 Morning coffee, lunch and afternoon tea available by pre-arrangement only, for up to 100.

🚶 For parties of 15 - 60 at additional cost. Tour time: house and garden 2¹/₂ - 4¹/₂ hrs, house only 1¹/₂ hrs.

🅿 Ample.

🐕 In grounds on leads.

🔔 Civil Wedding Licence.

♿ Available. ❄

▶ **OPENING TIMES**

House

24/25 Jan; 7/8 & 14/15 Feb; 13/14 Mar: Sat & Sun for guided tours only at 2pm.

27 Mar - 25 Apr: Wed - Sun, 12 noon - 5pm with guided tours at 2pm. Last admission 4pm.

30 May - 6 June: Wed - Sun for guided tours only at 2pm.

7 Jul - 29 Aug: Wed - Sun (open BH Mon), 12 noon - 5pm with guided tours at 2pm. Last admission 4pm.

2 Sep - 17 Oct: Wed - Sun for guided tours only at 2pm.

20/21 Nov; 11 - 19 Dec: Sat & Sun for guided tours only at 2pm.

Group visits to the House by arrangement throughout the year.

NB: House opening hours may vary. Please telephone 01280 818282 /280 to check latest information.

▶ **ADMISSION**

Adult £2.00
Child (under 16yrs)... £1.00
Guided Tours
Adult £3.00
Child (8 - 16yrs) £1.50

🎭 **SPECIAL EVENTS**

Feb 20 - 22: Homes & Garden Exhibition

Apr 18: Plant Fair

Jul 31 - Aug 8: Stowe Opera

Aug 14: Battleproms Concert

Oct 23/24: Christmas Fayre

South Front: John Bigelow Taylor

WADDESDON MANOR

NR AYLESBURY

www.waddesdon.org.uk

Map 5

Waddesdon Manor was built (1874-89), in the style of a 16th century French château, for Baron Ferdinand de Rothschild to entertain his guests and display his vast collection of art treasures. It houses one of the finest collections of French 18th century decorative arts in the world. The furniture, Savonnerie carpets, and Sèvres porcelain ranks in importance with the Metropolitan Museum in New York and the Louvre in Paris. There is also a fine collection of portraits by Gainsborough and Reynolds and works by Dutch and Flemish Masters of the 17th century.

Waddesdon has one of the finest Victorian gardens in Britain, renowned for its colourful parterre, specimen trees, shady walks and views, fountains and statuary. Carpet bedding designs are created each year. The rococo-style aviary houses a splendid collection of exotic birds and is known for breeding endangered species. Thousands of bottles of vintage Rothschild wines are found in the wine cellars.

There is an award-winning gift shop, a wine shop with a full selection of Rothschild wines and licensed restaurants. A full programme of events is organised throughout the year .

▶ CONTACT
Waddesdon
Nr Aylesbury
Buckinghamshire
HP18 0JH

Tel (24-hour recorded info):
01296 653211

Booking: 01296 653226

Fax: 01296 653208

▶ LOCATION
OS Ref. SP740 169

Between Aylesbury & Bicester, off A41.

Rail: Aylesbury 6m.

East Gallery: John Bigelow Taylor

▶ OPENING TIMES
Main Season House
(incl. Wine Cellars)
31 Mar - 31 Oct: Wed - Sun &
BH Mons, 11am - 4pm.
Last recommended
admission 2.30pm.

Bachelors' Wing
Wed - Fri, 11am - 4pm
(space is limited, entry
cannot be guaranteed).

Grounds*
3 Mar - 31 Oct: Wed - Sun &
BH Mons, 10am - 5pm.

Nov - pre Christmas House (part of House open)
17 Nov - 23 Dec: Wed - Sun
& 20/21 Dec, 1 - 5pm.

Grounds*
3 Nov - 23 Dec: Wed - Sun &
20/21 Dec, 11am - 5pm.

* Incl. Gardens, Aviary,
Restaurants, Gift & Wine Shops)

27 Dec - 2 Jan 2005:
Please tel 01296 653211 for
opening times.

▶ ADMISSION
- Main Season
House & Grounds
Adult £11.00
Child (5-16 yrs) £8.00
Groups (15+)
Adult £8.80
Child £6.40
Grounds only
Adult £4.00
Child (5-16 yrs) £2.00
Groups (15+)
Adult £3.20
Child £1.60
Bachelors' Wing £1.00

NT members free. HHA Members free entry to grounds. RHS members free to grounds in Mar, Sept & Oct.

A timed ticket system to the House is in operation. Tickets can be purchased up to 24 hours in advance for a fee of £3 per transaction from the Booking Office.

Children welcomed under parental supervision in the House. Babies must be carried in a front-sling.

Reservations can be made at the Manor Restaurant. Tel: 01296 653242.

ℹ️ No photography in house.

🏠 Gift and Wine Shops.

Ⓨ Conferences, corporate hospitality.

♿ WCs.

☕ Licensed.

🍴 Licensed.

🏃 By arrangement.

🎧

🅿️ Ample for coaches and cars.

🐕 Guide dogs only.

🎭 Civil Wedding Licence.

🦇 **SPECIAL EVENTS**

Wine Tasting, Special Interest Days, Family Events. Please telephone 01296 653226 for details.

ASCOTT ※

Wing, Leighton Buzzard, Bucks LU7 0PS

Tel: 01296 688242 **Fax:** 01296 681904

e-mail: info@ascottestate.co.uk **www**.ascottestate.co.uk

Owner: The National Trust **Contact:** Resident Agent

Originally a half-timbered Jacobean farmhouse, Ascott was bought in 1876 by the de Rothschild family and considerably transformed and enlarged. It now houses a quite exceptional collection of fine paintings, Oriental porcelain and English and French furniture. The extensive gardens are a mixture of the formal and natural, containing specimen trees and shrubs, as well as an herbaceous walk, lily pond, Dutch garden and remarkable topiary sundial.

Location: OS Ref. SP891 230. ½ m E of Wing, 2m SW of Leighton Buzzard, on A418.

Open: House & Garden: 16 Mar - 30 Apr: daily except Mon, 2 - 6pm. 4 May - 29 Jul: Tues - Thurs, 2 - 6pm. 1 - 31 Aug: daily except Mons, 2 - 6pm. Last admission 5pm.

Admission: Adult £6, Child £3. Garden only: £4. Child £2. No reduction for groups which must book. NT members charged on NGS days.

⬤Ground floor & grounds with assistance. 3 wheelchairs available. WCs.
🅿 220 metres. ⬤In car park only, on leads.

BOARSTALL DUCK DECOY ※

Boarstall, Aylesbury, Buckinghamshire HP18 9UX

Tel: 01844 237488/ 01296 381501 (Property Manager)

e-mail: boarstall@nationaltrust.org.uk

Owner: The National Trust **Contact:** Property Manager

A rare survival of a 17th century decoy in working order, set on a tree-fringed lake, with nature trail and exhibition hall.

Location: OS Ref. SP624 151. Midway between Bicester and Thame, 2m W of Brill.

Open: 20 Mar - 22 Aug: Sats, Suns & BH Mons, 10am - 5pm; 24 Mar - 25 Aug: Wed, 4 - 7pm. Talk/ demonstration: Sats, Suns & BH Mons if Warden available, tel for details. Please telephone for winter opening details.

Admission: Adult £2.20, Child £1.10. Family £5.50. Groups (6+) must book: £1.
⬤Partial. ⬤By arrangement. ⬤In car park only, on leads.

BOARSTALL TOWER ※

Boarstall, Aylesbury, Buckinghamshire HP18 9UX

Tel: 01296 381501 **e-mail:** Nick.Phillips@nationaltrust.org.uk

Owner: The National Trust **Contact:** Property Manager

The stone gatehouse of a fortified house long since demolished. It dates from the 14th century, and was altered in the 16th and 17th centuries, but retains its crossloops for bows. The gardens are surrounded by a moat on three sides.

Location: OS Ref. SP624 141. Midway between Bicester and Thame, 2m W of Brill.

Open: 31 Mar - 27 Oct: Wed & BH Mons, 2 - 6pm. Also Sats 10am - 4pm.

Admission: Adult £2.20, Child £1.10, Family £5.50.
ⓘNo WC. ⬤Ground floor & garden (steps to entrance). ⬤In car park only.

BUCKINGHAM CHANTRY CHAPEL ※

Market Hill, Buckingham

Tel: 01280 823020/01494 528051 (Regional Office) **Fax:** 01494 463310

Owner: The National Trust **Contact:** Buckingham Heritage Trust

Rebuilt in 1475 and retaining a fine Norman doorway. The chapel was restored by Gilbert Scott in 1875, at which time it was used as a Latin or Grammar School.

Location: OS Ref. SP693 340. In narrow lane, NW of Market Hill.

Open: Daily by written appointment with the Buckingham Heritage Trust, c/o Old Gaol Museum, Market Hill, Buckingham MK18 1JX.

Admission: Free. Donations welcome.
ⓘNo WCs. ⬤

CHENIES MANOR HOUSE 🏛

CHENIES, BUCKINGHAMSHIRE WD3 6ER

Tel/Fax: 01494 762888

Owners: Mrs MacLeod Matthews & Mr Charles MacLeod Matthews

Contact: Sue Brock

Home of the MacLeod Matthews family, this 15th and 16th century Manor House with fortified tower, is the original home of the Earls of Bedford. Visited by Henry VIII and Elizabeth I. She was a frequent visitor, first coming as an infant in 1534 and as Queen she visited on several occasions, one being for a six week period. The Bedford Mausoleum is in the adjacent church. The House contains tapestries and furniture mainly of the 16th and 17th centuries, hiding places, a collection of antique dolls, medieval undercroft and well. In the grounds stands the newly-restored 16th century pavilion which contains various exhibitions and most unusual cellars. The house is surrounded by beautiful gardens, famed for the spring display of tulips, which have featured in many publications and on TV. Tudor sunken garden, white garden, herbaceous borders, fountain court, physic garden containing a wide selection of medicinal and culinary herbs, parterre with an ancient oak, complicated yew maze and kitchen garden in Victorian style with unusual vegetables and fruit. Attractive dried and fresh flowers arrangements throughout the house. Our renowned annual Plant Fair will be held on 18 July with stalls from some of England's best nurseries. A Nature Trail consisting of woodlands, riverside and water meadow is suitable for childrens' groups. Delicious home-made teas.

Location: OS Ref TQ016 984. N of A404, between Amersham and Rickmansworth, M25/J18 3m.

Open: 1 April - 28 Oct, Wed, Thurs & BH Mons, 2-5pm. Last entry to house 4.15 p.m.

Admission: House & garden: Adult £5, Child £3. Garden only: Adult £3, Child £1.50. Groups (20+) by arrangement throughout the year.

🌱 Unusual plants for sale. ⬤⬤Grounds. ⬤ 🅿 Free nearby. ⬤⬤
⬤ Tel for details.

CHICHELEY HALL

Newport Pagnell, Buckinghamshire MK16 9JJ

Tel: 01234 391252   **Fax:** 01234 391388   **www**.chicheleyhall.co.uk

Owner: Trustees of Lord Beatty's Will Trust   **Contact:** Mrs V Child

Fine 18th century house. Naval museum, English sea paintings and furniture. The painting of two of Sir Francis Burdett's hunters held by groom waiting with three fox hounds to join the hunt; painted in 1817 by John Fernsley Senior can be viewed between 9am and 4pm Monday to Friday during June and the first week of July. Suitable for residential conferences up to 15 delegates.

Location: OS Ref. SP906 458. 2m from Milton Keynes, 5 mins from M1/J14. 10m W of Bedford.

Open: All year, by prior appointment. To view Sir Francis Burdett's painting contact the Administrator, Valerie Child prior to visit.

Admission: Groups (20+): Adult £7 with guided tour.

i Conferences. T By arrangement. Unsuitable. Obligatory.

CHILTERN OPEN AIR MUSEUM

Newland Park, Gorelands Lane, Chalfont St Giles, Buckinghamshire HB8 4AB

Tel: 01494 871117   **Fax:** 01494 872774

Owner: Chiltern Open Air Museum Ltd   **Contact:** Joanna Ruddock

A museum of historic buildings showing their original uses including a blacksmith's forge, stables, barns etc.

Location: OS Ref. TQ011 938. At Newland Park 1¹/₂ m E of Chalfont St Giles, 4¹/₂ m from Amersham. 3m from M25/J17.

Open: Apr - Oct: daily. Telephone 01494 872163 for details.

Admission: Adult £6, Child (5-16yrs) £3.50, Child under 5yrs Free, OAP £5, Family £16.50. Groups discount available on request.

COWPER & NEWTON MUSEUM

Home of Olney's Heritage, Orchard Side, Market Place, Olney MK46 4AJ

Tel: 01234 711516   **e-mail:** cnm@mkheritage.co.uk

www.cowperandnewtonmuseum.org

Owner: Board of Trustees   **Contact:** Mrs J McKillop

Once the home of 18th century poet and letter writer William Cowper and now containing furniture, paintings and belongings of both Cowper and his ex-slave trader friend, Rev John Newton (author of "Amazing Grace"). Attractions include re-creations of a Victorian country kitchen and wash-house, two peaceful gardens and Cowper's restored summerhouse. Costume gallery, important collections of dinosaur bones and bobbin lace, and local history displays.

Location: OS Ref. SP890 512. On A509, 6m N of Newport Pagnell, M1/J14.

Open: 1 Mar - 23 Dec: Tue - Sat & BH Mons, 10am - 1pm & 2 - 5pm. Closed on Good Fri. Open on Sundays in June, July & August, 2 - 5pm.

Admission: Adult £3, Conc. £2, Child & Students (with card) £1.50, Family £7.50.

i No photography. Gardens. By arrangement. Guide dogs only.

CLAYDON HOUSE

MIDDLE CLAYDON, Nr BUCKINGHAM MK18 2EY

Tel: 01296 730349   **Fax:** 01296 738511   **Infoline:** 01494 755561

e-mail: claydon@nationaltrust.org.uk

Owner: The National Trust   **Contact:** The Custodian

A fine 18th century house with some of the most perfect rococo decoration in England. A series of great rooms have wood carvings in Chinese and Gothic styles, and tall windows look out over parkland and a lake. The house has relics of the exploits of the Verney family in the English Civil War and also on show is the bedroom of Florence Nightingale, a relative of the Verneys and a regular visitor to this tranquil place.

NT Photographic Library: Andrew Butler

Location: OS Ref. SP720 253. In Middle Claydon, 13m NW of Aylesbury, signposted from A413 and A41. 3¹/₂ m SW of Winslow.

Open: 27 Mar - 25 Oct: daily except Thur & Fri; House, 1 - 5pm, last admission 4.30pm; 26 - 31 Oct: closes at 4pm; Grounds & Second-hand bookshop, 1 - 5pm.

Admission: Adult £4.70, Child £2.30, Family £11.70. Groups (15+) must book: Mon - Wed & Sat only. Adult £3.60, Child £1.80. Add 50p for guided tour.

i No photography. No pushchairs. No backpacks. No baby carriers. No large bags.

Ground floor only. WC. Braille guide. Photograph album. Ramp.

For groups only, by arrangement. P Limited for coaches.

In parkland only, on leads. Tel for details.

Sir Charles Bridgeman

d. 1738

A talented draughtsman and surveyor, little is known of his early life. Famous as the man who softened the formal 17th century gardens to create a natural romantic style of landscaping. Look for meandering woodland paths, and the ha-ha wall, which he used to bring the surrounding landscape into his design. **Little of his work now survives, but for the best examples visit Stowe Landscape Gardens and Cliveden, Buckinghamshire, Rousham House and Blenheim Palace, Oxfordshire and Claremont Landscape Garden, Surrey.**

Landscape Designer

NT Photographic Library

CLIVEDEN ✤
TAPLOW, MAIDENHEAD SL6 0JA

Tel: 01628 605069   **Infoline:** 01494 755562   **Fax:** 01628 669461
e-mail: cliveden@nationaltrust.org.uk
Owner: The National Trust   **Contact:** Property Manager

152 hectares of gardens and woodland. A water garden, 'secret' garden, herbaceous borders, topiary, a great formal parterre, and informal vistas provide endless variety. The garden statuary is one of the most important collections in the care of The National Trust and includes many Roman antiquities collected by 1st Viscount Astor. The Octagon Temple (Chapel) with its rich mosaic interior is open on certain days, as is part of the house (see below).

NT Photographic Library: Ian Shaw

© NTPL / Nick Meers

Cliveden, Buckinghamshire.

Location: OS Ref. SU915 851. 3m N of Maidenhead, M4/J7 onto A4 or M40/J4 onto A404 to Marlow and follow signs. From London by train take Thames Train service from Paddington to Burnham (taxi rank and office adjacent to station).

Open: Estate & Garden: 15 Mar - 31 Oct, daily, 11am - 6pm; 1 Nov - 23 Dec, daily, 11am - 4pm. House (part) & Octagon Temple: 1 Apr - 31 Oct: Thurs & Sun, 3 - 5.30pm. Admission to house by timed ticket, obtainable from information kiosk only. Restaurant: 15 Mar - 31 Oct, daily, 11am - 5pm; 5 Nov - 19 Dec, Fri - Sun, 11am - 2.30pm. Woodlands: 1 Apr - 31 Oct, daily, 11am - 5.30pm; 1 Nov - 23 Dec/ 3 Jan - 31 Mar, daily, 11am - 4pm. Shop: 15 Mar - 31 Oct, daily, 12 noon - 5.30pm; 1 Nov - 23 Dec, daily, 12 noon - 4pm. Some areas of formal garden may be roped off when ground conditions are bad.

Admission: Grounds: Adult £6.50, Child £3.20, Family £16.20, Groups (must book) £5.50. House: £1 extra, Child 50p. Note: Mooring charge on Cliveden Reach.

📷 ♿Partial. WC. 🍴Licensed. 🐕Specified woodlands only. ❋ ♿ Tel for details.

FORD END WATERMILL
Station Road, Ivinghoe, Buckinghamshire

Tel: 01582 600391   **Contact:** David Lindsey

The Watermill, a listed building, was recorded in 1767 but is probably much older.

Location: OS Ref. SP941 166. 600 metres from Ivinghoe Church along B488 (Station Road) to Leighton Buzzard.

Open: Easter Mon & 3 May - 26 Sept: 2nd & 4th Suns and BHs, 2.30 - 5.30pm. Milling Easter Mons & BHs and 2nd Sun in May, 2.30 - 5.30pm.

Admission: Adult £1.20, Child 40p. School Groups: Child 75p, Adults Free.

HUGHENDEN MANOR

HIGH WYCOMBE HP14 4LA

Tel: 01494 755573/ 755565 - Infoline   **Fax:** 01494 474284
e-mail: hughenden@nationaltrust.org.uk

Owner: The National Trust   **Contact:** The Property Manager

2004 Disraeli Bicentenary Year. Home of Prime Minister Benjamin Disraeli from 1847 - 1881, Hughenden has a red brick, 'gothic' exterior. The interior is a comfortable Victorian home and still holds many of Disraeli's pictures, books and furniture, as well as other fascinating mementoes of the life of the great statesman and writer. The surrounding park and woodland have lovely walks, and the formal garden has been recreated in the spirit of Mary Anne Disraeli's colourful designs.

Location: OS165 Ref. SU866 955. 1¹/₂ m N of High Wycombe on the W side of the A4128.

Open: House: 6 - 28 Mar: Sat & Sun, 1 - 5pm; 31 Mar - 31 Oct: Wed - Sun & BH Mons, 1 - 5pm (last admission 4.30pm). Open Good Fri. On BHs and busy days entry is by timed ticket. Gardens & Restaurant open same days as house, 12noon - 5pm. Park & Woodland: All year.

Admission: House & Garden: Adult £4.70, Child £2.30, Family £12. Groups: Adult £4.20, Child £2.10. Group visits outside normal hours £10. Garden only: Adult £1.70, Child 80p. Park & Woodland Free. Small groups only, no groups at weekends or BHs.

Ground floor only. WC. For booked groups.
In grounds, on leads. Guide dogs in house & formal gardens.
Tel for details.

JOHN MILTON'S COTTAGE

21 Deanway, Chalfont St. Giles, Buckinghamshire HP8 4JH

Tel: 01494 872313   **e-mail:** info@miltonscottage.org   **www**.miltonscottage.org

Owner: Milton Cottage Trust   **Contact:** Mr E A Dawson

Grade I listed 16th century cottage where John Milton lived and completed *Paradise Lost* and started *Paradise Regained*. Four ground floor museum rooms contain important first editions of John Milton's 17th century poetry and prose works. Amongst many unique items on display is the portrait of John Milton by Sir Godfrey Kneller. Well stocked, attractive cottage garden, listed by English Heritage.

Location: OS Ref. SU987 933. ¹/₂ m W of A413. 3m N of M40/J2. S side of street.

Open: 1 Mar - 31 Oct: Tue - Sun, 10am - 1pm & 2 - 6pm. Closed Mons (open BH Mons). Coach parking by prior arrangement only.

Admission: Adult £3, under 15s £1, Groups (20+) £2.

Ground floor. Talk followed by free tour.

NETHER WINCHENDON HOUSE

Aylesbury, Buckinghamshire HP18 ODY

Tel/Fax: 01844 290199   **Owner/Contact:** Mr Robert Spencer Bernard

Medieval and Tudor manor house. Great Hall. Dining Room with fine 16th century frieze, ceiling and linenfold panelling. Fine furniture and family portraits. Former home of Sir Francis Bernard, the last British Governor of Massachussetts Bay. Continuous family occupation since mid-16th century. House altered in late 18th century in the Strawberry Hill Gothick style. Interesting garden and specimen trees.

Location: OS Ref. SP734 121. 2m N of A418 equidistant between Thame & Aylesbury.

Open: 3 - 31 May & 30 Aug: 2.30 - 5.30pm (only conducted tours at ¹/₄ to each hour). Groups at any time by prior written agreement (minimum charge £50.00, no concessions)

Admission: Adult £5, OAP £4 (no concession at weekends or BHs), Child (under 12) £2. HHA members free (not on special groups).

By arrangement. Obligatory.

PITSTONE WINDMILL

Ivinghoe, Buckinghamshire

Tel: 01494 528051   Group organisers: 01582 872303   **Fax:** 01494 463310

Owner: The National Trust   **Contact:** David Goseltine

One of the oldest post mills in Britain; in view from Ivinghoe Beacon.

Location: OS Ref. SP946 158. ¹/₂ m S of Ivinghoe, 3m NE of Tring. Just W of B488.

Open: Jun - end Aug: Sun & BHs, 2.30 - 6pm.

Admission: Adult £1, Child 30p.

No WC. Difficult access.

PRINCES RISBOROUGH MANOR HOUSE

Princes Risborough, Aylesbury, Buckinghamshire HP17 9AW

Tel: 01494 528051/ 01296 381501   **Fax:** 01494 463310

Owner/Contact: The National Trust

A 17th century red-brick house with Jacobean oak staircase.

Location: OS Ref. SP806 035. Opposite church, off market square.

Open: House (hall, drawing room & staircase) and front garden by written appointment only with the owner. 31 Mar - 31 Oct: Weds, 2.30 - 4.30pm.

Admission: Adult £1.30, Child 60p, Family £3.20.

STOWE LANDSCAPE GARDENS & PARK ✤

Nr BUCKINGHAM MK18 5EH

www.nationaltrust.org.uk/.stowegardens

Tel: 01280 822850 **Infoline:** 01494 755568 **Fax:** 01280 822437
Group Visits: 01280 822850 **e-mail:** stowegarden@nationaltrust.org.uk
Owner: The National Trust   **Contact:** The Property Manager

Europe's most influential landscape garden. The scale, grandeur and beauty of Stowe has inspired writers, thinkers, artists, politicians and members of the public from the 18th century to the present day. 250 acres of landscape gardens lie beneath the House, designed with lakes, pasture, wooded valleys and open spaces adorned with over thirty temples and monuments. At the centre lies the House, a great ducal palace and now home to Stowe School, which is open to the public by Stowe House Preservation Trust. There is free public access to 750 acres of parkland surrounding the Gardens and House. Both Gardens and House are currently being magnificently restored to their former glory.

What's new in 2004: Light refreshment kiosk in Visitor Lodge. Introductory exhibition including audio-visual display about the development of the gardens. Newly restored monuments: Lakeside Pavilions, the Queen's Temple, the Doric Arch and the reconstruction of the Statue of King George II. Park features: three restored lakes in Stowe Park. Continuing restoration: Corinthian Arch and the House roof.

Location: OS Ref. SP665 366. Off A422 Buckingham - Banbury Rd. 3m NW of Buckingham.
Open: Gardens: 28 Feb - 31 Oct, Wed - Sun, 10am - 5.30pm; 6 Nov - 28 Feb, Sat & Sun, 10am - 4pm. Open BH Mons. Last admission 1 hr. before closing. Gardens closed 29 May, 24/25 Dec, may close in extreme weather conditions. House (not NT): call 01280 818282/280 for opening times.
Admission: Gardens: Adult £5.50, Child £2.70, Family £13.70. Groups (by arrangement, 15+) Adult £4.60, Child £2.30. House (incl. NT members): Adult £2, Child £1. House tours: Adult £3, Child £1.50. House admission payable at NT reception. House not NT.

⬚ ♿Pre-booked self-drive powered chairs available. WC. 🍴Licensed.
🦮By arrangement. 📷 ■ 🐕In grounds, on leads. ▲ ♿Call for details.

STOWE HOUSE 🏛

See page 98 for full page entry.

WADDESDON MANOR ✤

See page 99 for full page entry.

WEST WYCOMBE PARK ✤

West Wycombe, High Wycombe, Buckinghamshire HP14 3AJ
Tel: 01494 513569
Owner: The National Trust   **Contact:** The Head Guide

A perfectly preserved rococo landscape garden, created in the mid-18th century by Sir Francis Dashwood, founder of the Dilettanti Society and the Hellfire Club. The house is among the most theatrical and Italianate in England, its façades formed as classical temples. The interior has Palmyrene ceilings and decoration, with pictures, furniture and sculpture dating from the time of Sir Francis.

Location: OS Ref. SU828 947. At W end of West Wycombe S of the A40.
Open: House & Grounds: 1 Jun - 31 Aug: daily except Fri & Sat, 2 - 6pm. Weekday entry by guided tour every 20 mins (approx), last admission 5.15pm. Grounds only: 1 Apr - 31 May: daily except Fri & Sat, 2 - 6pm.
Admission: House & Grounds: Adult £5.20, Child £2.60, Family £13. Grounds only: Adult £2.70, Child £1.30. Groups by arrangement. Note: The West Wycombe Caves and adjacent café are privately owned and NT members must pay admission fees.
♿Grounds partly suitable. 🦮On weekdays. 🐕In car park only, on leads.

WOTTON HOUSE

Wotton Underwood, Aylesbury, Buckinghamshire HP18 0SB
Tel: 01844 238363 **Fax:** 01844 238380
e-mail: david.gladstone@which.net   **Owner/Contact:** David Gladstone

The Capability Brown Pleasure Grounds at Wotton, currently undergoing restoration, are related to the Stowe gardens, both belonging to the Grenville family when Brown laid out the Wotton grounds between 1750 and 1767. A series of man-made features on the 3 mile circuit include bridges, follies and statues.

Location: OS Ref. 468576, 216168. Either A41 turn off Kingswood, or M40/J7 via Thame. Rail: Haddenham & Thame 6m.
Open: 14 Apr - 15 Sep: Wed only, 2pm - 5pm. Also 24 Apr, 31 May, 3 Jul, 7 Aug, 4 Sep: 2pm - 5pm.
Admission: Adult £5, Child Free, Conc. £3. Groups (max 25).
🦮Obligatory. 🅿 Limited. 🐕.

WYCOMBE MUSEUM

Priory Avenue, High Wycombe, Buckinghamshire HP13 6PX
Tel: 01494 421895 **Fax:** 01494 421897
e-mail: museum@wycombe.gov.uk
Owner: Wycombe District Council   **Contact:** Grace Wilson

Set in historic Castle Hill House and surrounded by peaceful and attractive gardens.
Location: OS Ref. SU867 933. Signposted off the A404 High Wycombe/Amersham road. The Museum is about 5mins walk from the town centre and railway station.
Open: Mon - Sat, 10am - 5pm. Open Suns, 2 - 5pm. Closed BHs.
Admission: Free.

Accommodation Index see front section

Beaulieu, Hampshire from the book *Historic Family Homes and Gardens from the Air*, see page 54.

BEAULIEU 🏛

BEAULIEU

www.beaulieu.co.uk

Beaulieu is set in the heart of the New Forest and is a place that gives enormous pleasure to people with an interest in seeing history of all kinds.

Overlooking the Beaulieu River, Palace House has been the ancestral home of the Montagus since 1538. The House was once the Great Gatehouse of Beaulieu Abbey and its monastic origins are reflected in such features as the fan vaulted ceilings. Many treasures, which are reminders of travels all round the world by past generations of the Montagu family, can also be seen. Walks amongst the gardens and by the Beaulieu River can also be enjoyed.

Beaulieu Abbey was founded in 1204 and although most of the buildings have now been destroyed, much of the beauty and interest remains. The former Monks' Refectory is now the local Parish Church. The Domus, which houses an exhibition of monastic life, is home to beautiful wall hangings and 15th century beamed ceilings.

Beaulieu also houses the world famous National Motor Museum which traces the story of motoring from 1894 to the present day. 250 vehicles are on display including legendary world record breakers plus veteran, vintage and classic cars and motorcycles.

The modern Beaulieu is very much a family destination where there are various free and unlimited rides and drives on a transportation theme to be enjoyed by everyone, including a mile long monorail and replica 1912 London open-topped bus.

Map 3

Owner:
Lord Montagu

▶ **CONTACT**

Conference Office
John Montagu Building
Beaulieu
Brockenhurst
Hampshire SO42 7ZN

Tel: 01590 614605
Fax: 01590 612624

e-mail: conference@
beaulieu.co.uk

▶ **LOCATION**

OS Ref. SU387 025

From London, M3,
M27 W to J2,
A326, B3054 follow
brown signs.

Bus: Bus stops
within complex.

Rail: Stations at
Brockenhurst and
Beaulieu Rd
both 7m away.

CONFERENCE/FUNCTION

ROOM	SIZE	MAX CAPACITY
Brabazon (x3)	40'x40'	120 (x3)
Domus	69'x27'	140
Theatre		200
Hartford Suite	39'x17'	50
Palace House		60
Motor Museum		250

▶ **OPENING TIMES**

Summer
May - September
Daily, 10am - 6pm.

Winter
October - April
Daily, 10am - 5pm.

Closed Christmas Day.

▶ **ADMISSION**

All Year

Individual rates upon application.

Groups (15+)
Rates upon application.

🎭 **SPECIAL EVENTS**

Apr 25
Boat Jumble & Boat World

May 15/16
Spring Autojumble

Late June
Motorcycle World

July 10/11
4 x 4 Show

Late July
Summer Concerts Weekend

Sept 11/12
International Autojumble

Oct 30
Fireworks Fair

All enquiries should be made to our Special Events Booking Office where advance tickets can be purchased. The contact telephone is 01590 612888.

BEAULIEU...

CATERING AND FUNCTIONS

Beaulieu also offers a comprehensive range of facilities for conferences, company days out, product launches, management training, corporate hospitality, promotions, film locations, exhibitions and outdoor events.

The National Motor Museum is a unique venue for drinks receptions, evening product launches and dinners or the perfect complement to a conference as a relaxing visit.

The charming 13th century Domus banqueting hall with its beautiful wooden beams, stone walls and magnificent wall hangings, is the perfect setting for conferences, dinners, buffets or themed evenings.

Palace House, the ancestral home of Lord Montagu is an exclusive setting for smaller dinners, buffets and receptions. With a welcoming log fire in the winter and the coolness of the courtyard fountain in the summer, it offers a relaxing yet truly 'stately' atmosphere to ensure a memorable experience for your guests whatever the time of year

A purpose-built theatre, with tiered seating, can accommodate 200 people whilst additional meeting and syndicate rooms can accommodate from 5 to 200 delegates. With the nearby Beaulieu River offering waterborne activities and the Beaulieu Estate, with its purpose built off road course, giving you the opportunity of indulging in a variety of country pursuits and outdoor management training, Beaulieu provides a unique venue for your conference and corporate hospitality needs.

i Allow 3 hrs or more for visits. Last adm. 40 mins before closing. Helicopter landing point. When visiting Beaulieu arrangements can be made to view the Estate's vineyards. Visits, which can be arranged between Apr - Oct, must be pre-booked at least one week in advance with Beaulieu Estate Office.

Palace House Shop and Kitchen Shop plus Main Reception Shop.

Disabled visitors may be dropped off outside Visitor Reception before parking. WC. Wheelchairs can be provided free of charge in Visitor Reception by prior booking.

The self-service Brabazon restaurant seats 300. Prices range to £7 for lunch. Groups can book in advance. Further details and menus from Catering Manager 01590 612102.

Attendants on duty. Guided tours by prior arrangement for groups.

P 1,500 cars and 30 coaches. During the season the busy period is from 11.30am to 1.30pm. Coach drivers should sign in at Information Desk. Free admission for coach drivers plus voucher which can be exchanged for food, drink and souvenirs.

Professional staff available to assist in planning of visits. Services include introductory talks, films, guided tours, rôle play and extended projects. In general, educational services incur no additional charges and publications are sold at cost. Information available from Education at Beaulieu, John Montagu Building, Beaulieu, Hants SO42 7ZN.

In grounds, on leads only.

Map 3

HIGHCLERE CASTLE & GARDENS 🏛

NEWBURY

www.highclerecastle.co.uk

Designed by Charles Barry in the 1830s at the same time as he was building the Houses of Parliament, this soaring pinnacled mansion provided a perfect setting for the 3rd Earl of Carnarvon, one of the great hosts of Queen Victoria's reign. The extravagant interiors range from church Gothic through Moorish flamboyance and rococo revival to the solid masculinity in the long Library. Old Master paintings mix with portraits by Van Dyck and 18th century painters. Napoleon's desk and chair rescued from St. Helena sits with other 18th and 19th century furniture.

The 5th Earl of Carnarvon together with Howard Carter, discovered the Tomb of Tutankhamun and the Castle houses a unique exhibition of some of his discoveries. The 7th Earl of Carnarvon was the Queen's Racing Manager and in 1993, to celebrate his 50th year as a leading owner and breeder, the Racing Exhibition was opened offering a fascinating insight into a racing history which dates back four generations. The 8th Earl and his wife take a very personal interest in the Castle and they are often to be seen round and about the House and grounds.

GARDENS

The magnificent parkland with its massive cedars was designed by 'Capability' Brown. The walled gardens also date from an earlier house at Highclere but the dark yew walks are entirely Victorian in character. The glass Orangery and Fernery add an exotic flavour. The Secret Garden has a romance of its own with a beautiful curving lawn surrounded by densely planted herbaceous gardens. A place for poets and romantics.

Owner:
Earl of Carnarvon

▶ **CONTACT**

The Castle Office
Highclere Castle
Newbury
Berkshire RG20 9RN

Tel: 01635 253210
Infoline: 01635 253204
Fax: 01635 255315
e-mail: theoffice@
highclerecastle.co.uk

▶ **LOCATION**
OS Ref. SU445 587

Approx 7m out of Newbury on A34 towards Winchester. From London: M4/J13, A34 Bypass Newbury-Winchester 20 mins. M3/J5 approx 15m.

Air: Heathrow M4 45 mins.

Rail: Paddington - Newbury 45 mins.

Taxi: 4¹/₂ m 07778 156392.

CONFERENCE/FUNCTION

ROOM	SIZE	MAX CAPACITY
Library	43' x 21'	120
Saloon	42' x 29'	150
Dining Rm	37' x 18'	70
Library, Saloon, Drawing Rm, Music Rm, Smoking Rm		400

🛍 ℹ Conferences, exhibitions, filming, fairs, and concerts (cap. 8000). No photography in the house.

🍽 Receptions, dinners, corporate hospitality.

♿ Visitors may alight at the entrance. WC.

☕ Tearooms, licensed. Lunches for 20+ can be booked.

🅿 Ample.

🏛 Egyptian Exhibition: £3 per child. 1 adult free per every 10 children – includes playgroups, Brownie packs, Guides etc. Nature walks, beautiful old follies, Secret Garden.

🐕 In grounds, on leads.

💒 Civil Wedding Licence.

Please visit website.

▶ **OPENING TIMES**

6 July - 5 September
Tue - Fri & Sun,
11am - 5pm.
Also BHs: 11/12 Apr
2/3 & 30/31 May
& 30 Aug.
Last admission 1 hour before closing.

Mondays during this period - private groups by arrangement.

The house is occasionally closed during this period – please call our information line or visit our website.

▶ **ADMISSION**

Adult £7.00
Child (4-15yrs) £3.50
Conc. £5.50
Wheelchair Pusher . FOC
Family (2+2/1+3).... £17.00

Grounds & Gardens only
Adult £4.00
Child (4-15yrs) £1.50
Groups (15+)
Adult £5.50
Child (4-15yrs) £3.00
Conc. £4.50
Private guided tours at other times by arrangement.

School Groups (to visit Egyptian Exhibition only)
Child ... £3.00 (plus VAT)
1 adult Free for every 10 children

VIP Season Ticket*
(2+3) or (1+4) £25.00

*Runs for one year from date of joining. Free admission for 2 adults & 3 children to the House, Exhibitions & Gardens: 2 Jul - 1 Sept & when special events are taking place. 10% off shop, tearooms, free admission to daytime events. Discounted rate for evening concerts, free admission to 'Shakespeare in the Park', £2 off Newbury Racecourse Members' Enclosure badges when pre-booked, Newbury Hilton - Fri, Sat, Sun evenings - dinner for two for the price of one from chef's hot or cold table.

NT Photographic Library: Nick Carter

HINTON AMPNER GARDEN 🌿

BRAMDEAN

www.nationaltrust.org.uk

Map 3

Owner:
The National Trust

▶ **CONTACT**

The Property Manager
Hinton Ampner Garden
Bramdean
Alresford
Hampshire   SO24 0LA

Tel: 01962 771305
Fax: 01962 793101

e-mail: hintonampner@
nationaltrust.org.uk

▶ **LOCATION**

OS Ref. SU597 275

M3/J9 follow signs
to Petersfield.

On A272, 1m W of
Bramdean village, 8m E
of Winchester.

Rail: Winchester or
Petersfield.

Bus: Stagecoach 67
from Winchester
to Petersfield.

'I have learned during the past years what above all I want from a garden: this is tranquillity'. so said Ralph Dutton, 8th and last Lord Sherborne, of his garden at Hinton Ampner. He created one of the great gardens of the 20th century, a masterpiece of design based upon the bones of a Victorian garden, in which he united a formal layout with varied and informal planting in pastel shades. It is a garden of all year round interest with scented plants and magnificent vistas over the park and surrounding countryside.

The garden forms the link between the woodland and parkland planting, which he began in 1930, and the house, which he remodelled into a small neo-Georgian manor house in 1936. He made further alterations when the house was reconstructed after a fire in 1960. Today it contains his very fine collection of English furniture, Italian paintings and hard-stones. Both his collection and every aspect of the decoration at Hinton Ampner reflects Ralph Dutton's sure eye and fine aesthetic judgement.

He placed the whole within the rolling Hampshire landscape that he loved and understood so well.

NT Photographic Library: Stephen Robson

▶ **OPENING TIMES**

House
6 Apr - end Sept:
Tues & Weds,
also Sats & Suns in Aug,
1.30 - 5pm.

Garden
21 Mar & 28 Mar then
3 Apr - end Sept,
daily except Thur & Fri,
12 noon - 5pm.

▶ **ADMISSION**

House & Garden
Adult £5.80
Child (5-16yrs) £2.90
Child under 5yrs ......Free

Garden only
Adult £4.80
Child (5-16yrs) £2.40
Child under 5yrs ......Free

Please telephone for
group rates.

NT Members free.

Limited for coaches.
Guide dogs only.

SOMERLEY

RINGWOOD

www.somerley.com

Map 3

Sitting on the edge of the New Forest in the heart of Hampshire, Somerley, home of the 6th Earl of Normanton and his three children, is situated in 7,000 acres of meadows, woods and rolling parkland. Designed by Samuel Wyatt in the mid 1700s, the house became the property of the Normanton family in 1825 and has remained in the same family through the years. Housing a magnificent art and porcelain collection, the house itself, albeit impressively splendid, still retains the warmth and character of a family home.

Although never open to the public, Somerley is available for corporate events and its location, along with its seclusion and privacy, provide the perfect environment for conferences and meetings, product launches, lunches and dinners, activity and team building days (the estate boasts a hugely challenging off-road driving course) and film and photographic work. It is also available for a limited number of wedding receptions every year.

Somerley only ever hosts one event at a time so exclusivity in an outstanding setting is always guaranteed. From groups as small as eight to perhaps a large dinner for 150, the style of attention and personal service go hand in hand with the splendour of the house and the estate itself.

Owner:
The Earl of Normanton

▶ CONTACT

Richard Horridge
Somerley
Ringwood
Hampshire   BH24 3PL

Tel: 01425 480819
Fax: 01425 478613
e-mail:
info@somerley.com

▶ LOCATION
OS Ref. SU134 080

Off the A31 to Bournemouth 2m. London 1¾ hrs via M3, M27, A31. 2m NW of Ringwood.

Air: Bournemouth International Airport 5m.

Rail: Bournemouth Station 12m.

Taxi: A car can be arranged from the House if applicable.

▶ OPENING TIMES
Privately booked functions only.

▶ ADMISSION
Privately booked functions only.

CONFERENCE/FUNCTION

ROOM	SIZE	MAX CAPACITY
Picture Gall.	80' x 30'	200
Drawing Rm	38' x 30'	50
Dining Rm	39' x 19'	50
East Library	26' x 21'	30

ℹ️ No individual visits, ideal for all corporate events, activity days and filmwork.

🍽️ Dining Room and picture gallery available for private parties.

🅿️ Unlimited.

🛏️ 1 single & 9 double rooms (8 en-suite).

🔔

❄️

JANE AUSTEN'S HOUSE

CHAWTON, ALTON, HAMPSHIRE GU34 1SD

www.janeaustenmuseum.org.uk

Tel/Fax: 01420 83262 **e-mail:** museum@janeausten.demon.co.uk

Owner: Jane Austen Memorial Trust   **Contact:** The Curator

17th century house where Jane Austen wrote or revised her six great novels. Contains many items associated with her and her family, documents and letters, first editions of the novels, pictures, portraits and furniture. Pleasant garden, suitable for picnics, bakehouse with brick oven and wash tub, houses Jane's donkey carriage.

Location: OS Ref. SU708 376. Just S of A31, 1m SW of Alton, signposted Chawton.

Open: 1 Mar - 30 Nov: daily, 11am - 4.30pm; Dec, Jan & Feb: weekends only. Also open 27 Dec - 2 Jan. Closed 25 - 26 Dec.

Admission: Fee charged.

▣ Bookshop. ⬥ Ground floor & grounds. WC. ☻ Opposite house. ⊓ Opposite house. ⌖ Guide dogs only. ❋

BASING HOUSE

Redbridge Lane, Basing, Basingstoke RG24 7HB

Tel: 01256 467294

Owner: Hampshire County Council   **Contact:** Alan Turton

Ruins, covering 10 acres, of huge Tudor palace. Recent recreation of Tudor formal garden.

Location: OS Ref. SU665 526. 2m E from Basingstoke town centre. Signposted car parks are about 5 or 10 mins walk from entrance.

Open: 1 Apr - 3 Oct: Wed - Sun & BHs, 2 - 6pm.

Admission: Adult £2, Conc. £1.

BEAULIEU 🏛   *See pages 106/107 for double page entry.*

BISHOP'S WALTHAM PALACE ⌗

Bishop's Waltham, Hampshire SO32 1DH

Tel: 01489 892460 **www**.english-heritage.org.uk/visits

Owner: English Heritage   **Contact:** The Custodian

This medieval seat of the Bishops of Winchester once stood in an enormous park. There are still wooded grounds and the remains of the Great Hall and the three storey tower can still be seen. Dower House furnished as a 19th century farmhouse.

Location: OS Ref. SU552 173. In Bishop's Waltham, 5m NE from M27/J8.

Open: 1 Apr - 30 Sept: daily, 10am - 6pm. 1 Oct - 31 Oct: 10am - 5pm. Times subject to change April 2004.

Admission: Adult £2.50, Child £1.30, Conc. £1.90. Prices subject to change April 2004.

ℹ WCs. Exhibition. ▣ ⬥ Grounds. ⊓ ⌖ Grounds only, on leads. ⎚ Tel for details.

BOHUNT MANOR GARDENS

Liphook, Hampshire GU30 7DL

Tel/Fax: 01428 727936 **e-mail:** eddie@bohuntmanor.freeserve.co.uk

Owner: Lady Holman   **Contact:** Mr Edward Trotter

Woodland gardens with lakeside walk, collection of ornamental waterfowl, herbaceous borders and unusual trees and shrubs.

Location: OS Ref. SU839 310. W side of B2070 at S end of village.

Open: All year: daily, 10am - 5pm.

Admission: Adult £2, Child under 16yrs Free, Conc. £1. Group: 10% off.

AVINGTON PARK 🏛

WINCHESTER, HAMPSHIRE SO21 1DB

www.avingtonpark.co.uk

Tel: 01962 779260   **e-mail:** enquiries@avingtonpark.co.uk

Owner/Contact: Mrs S L Bullen

Avington Park, where Charles II and George IV both stayed at various times, dates back to the 11th century. The house was enlarged in 1670 by the addition of two wings and a classical Portico surmounted by three statues. The State rooms are magnificently painted and lead onto the unique pair of conservatories flanking the South Lawn. The Georgian church, St. Mary's, is in the grounds.

Avington Park is a privately owned stately home and is a most prestigious venue in peaceful surroundings. It is perfect for any event from seminars, conferences and exhibitions to wedding ceremonies and receptions, dinner dances and private parties.

The Conservatories and the Orangery make a delightful location for summer functions, whilst log fires offer a welcome during the winter. Excellent caterers provide for all types of occasion, ranging from breakfasts and light lunches to sumptuous dinners. All bookings at Avington are individually tailor-made and only exclusive use is offered. Several rooms available for Civil wedding ceremonies.

Location: OS Ref. SU534 324. 4m NE of Winchester ½ m S of B3047 in Itchen Abbas.

Open: May - Sept: Suns & BH Mons plus Mons in Aug, 2.30 - 5.30pm. Last tour 5pm. Other times by arrangement, coach parties welcome by appointment all year.

Admission: Adult £3.75, Child £2.

ℹ Conferences. ☂ ⬥ Partial. WC. ☻ 🖊 Obligatory. ⊓ ⌖ In grounds, on leads. Guide dogs only in house. ⬥ ❋

BREAMORE HOUSE & MUSEUM 🏠

BREAMORE, FORDINGBRIDGE, HAMPSHIRE SP6 2DF

Tel: 01725 512233 **Fax:** 01725 512858 **e-mail:** breamore@ukonline.co.uk

Owner/Contact: Sir Edward Hulse Bt

Elizabethan manor with fine collections of pictures and furniture. Countryside Museum takes visitors back to the time when a village was self-sufficient.

Location: OS Ref. SU152 191. W Off the A338, between Salisbury and Ringwood.

Open: Easter weekend; Apr: Tue & Sun; May, Jun, Jul & Sept: Tue, Wed, Thur, Sat, Sun & all hols. Aug: daily. House: 2 - 5.30pm. Countryside Museum: 1 - 5.30pm. Last admission 4.15pm.

Admission: Combined ticket for house and museum: Adult £6, Child £4, OAP £5, Family £15.

🔲 ♿ Ground floor & grounds. WC. ☕ ✕ €

CALSHOT CASTLE ⌗

Calshot, Fawley, Hampshire SO45 1BR

Tel: 023 8089 2023 www.english-heritage.org.uk/visits

Owner: English Heritage **Contact:** Hampshire County Council

Henry VIII built this coastal fort in an excellent position, commanding the sea passage to Southampton. The fort houses an exhibition and recreated pre-World War I barrack room.

Location: OS Ref. SU488 025. On spit 2m SE of Fawley off B3053.

Open: 29 Mar - 30 Sept: daily, 10am - 6pm. 1 Oct - 31 Oct: 10am - 5pm. Times subject to change April 2004.

Admission: Adult £2.50, Child £1.50, Conc. £1.80, Family £6. Prices subject to change April 2004.

ℹ️WCs. 🔲 🅿 ✕

ELING TIDE MILL

The Toll Bridge, Eling, Totton, Southampton, Hampshire SO40 9HF

Tel: 023 8086 9575 **e-mail:** info@elingtidemill.org.uk

Owner: Eling Tide Mill Trust Ltd & New Forest District Council

Contact: Mr David Blackwell-Eaton

Location: OS Ref. SU365 126. 4m W of Southampton. $^1/_2$ m S of the A35.

Open: Wed - Sun and BH Mons, 10am - 4pm.

Admission: Adult £1.90, Child £1, OAP £1.40, Family £5.20. Discounts for groups. Prices subject to change 1 April 2004.

BROADLANDS

ROMSEY, HAMPSHIRE SO51 9ZD

www.broadlands.net

Tel: 01794 505010 **Event Enquiry Line:** 01794 505020 **Fax:** 01794 518605

e-mail: admin@broadlands.net

Owner: Lord & Lady Romsey **Contact:** Estate Manager

Broadlands, the home of Viscount Palmerston and The Earl Mountbatten of Burma, is open to the public by guided tour only. The Mountbatten Exhibition depicts the life and times of Lord Mountbatten. Limited tours, which include items normally available by appointment, are offered on certain days.

Location: OS Ref. SU355 204. On A3090 at Romsey.

Open/Admission: Details of opening times and admission charges can be obtained from the website, or by telephone.

🖥 ♿ Ground floor.WC. 🚶 Obligatory. 🐕 Guide dogs only.

EXBURY GARDENS & STEAM RAILWAY 🏠

EXBURY, SOUTHAMPTON, HAMPSHIRE SO45 1AZ

www.exbury.co.uk

Tel: 023 8089 1203 **Fax:** 023 8089 9940

Owner: Edmund de Rothschild Esq **Contact:** Estate Office

HHA/Christie's Garden of the Year 2001. A spectacular 200-acre woodland garden showcasing the world famous Rothschild collection of rhododendrons, azaleas and camellias. Daffodil meadow, Rock Garden, Rose Garden and herbaceous borders ensure year-round interest. The Steam Railway enchants visitors of all ages, passing through a Summer Garden, and featuring a bridge, tunnel, viaduct and causeway.

Location: OS Ref. SU425 005. 11m SE of Totton (A35) via A326 & B3054 & minor road. In New Forest.

Open: 28 Feb - 31 Oct: daily, 10am - 5.30pm. Call for winter opening arrangements.

Admission: High Season (mid-March to mid-June, subject to alteration depending on flowering conditions): Adult £6, Child (5-15yrs) £1.50, OAP/Group £5.50 (OAPs £5, Tues - Thurs), Family (2+3) £15, Railway Fare £2.50, Rover Ticket not available. Low Season: Adult £4, Child (5-15yrs) £1, OAP/Group £3.50, Family (2+3) £10), Railway Fare £2, Rover Ticket £3. Child under 5yrs Free.

🔲 🍴 🖥 ♿ 🅿 🍴Licensed. 🚶 By arrangement. 🔲 🅿 🐕In grounds, on leads. 🎦

FORT BROCKHURST ⚌

Gunner's Way, Gosport, Hampshire PO12 4DS

Tel: 023 9258 1059 **www.**english-heritage.org.uk/visits

Owner: English Heritage   **Contact:** The Head Custodian

This 19th century fort was built to protect Portsmouth, today its parade ground, moated keep and sergeants' mess are available to hire as an exciting setting for functions and events of all types. The fort is also open to visitors at weekends when tours will explain the exciting history of the site and the legend behind the ghostly activity in cell no. 3.

Location: OS196, Ref. SU596 020. Off A32, in Gunner's Way, Elson on N side of Gosport.

Open: 1 Apr - 30 Sept: 10am - 6pm. 1 Oct - 31 Oct: 10am - 5pm. Weekends only. Times subject to change April 2004.

Admission: Adult £2.20, Child £1.10, Conc. £1.70. Prices subject to change April 2004.
ⓘWCs. ♿Grounds and ground floor only. 🐕Dogs on leads (restricted areas).

FURZEY GARDENS

Minstead, Lyndhurst, Hampshire SO43 7GL

Tel: 023 8081 2464 **Fax:** 023 8081 2297

Owner: Furzey Gardens Charitable Trust   **Contact:** Maureen Cole

Location: OS Ref. SU273 114. Minstead village ¹/₂ m N of M27/A31 junction off A337 to Lyndhurst.

Open: Please contact property for details.

GREAT HALL & QUEEN ELEANOR'S GARDEN

Winchester Castle, Winchester, Hampshire SO23 8PJ

Tel: 01962 846476 **Fax:** for bookings 01962 841326

www.hants.gov.uk

Owner: Hampshire County Council   **Contact:** Mrs Reading

The only surviving part of Henry III's medieval castle at Winchester, this 13th century hall was the centre of court and government life. The Round Table closely associated with the legend of King Arthur has hung here for over 700 years. Queen Eleanor's garden is a faithful representation of the medieval garden visited by Kings and Queens of England.

Location: OS Ref. SU477 295. Central Winchester. SE of Westgate archway.

Open: All year: daily, 10am - 5pm. Closed 25/26 Dec. Guided tours and children's quizzes availableGroup bookings essential.

Admission: Free. Donations are appreciated towards the upkeep of the Great Hall.
𝑖By arrangement. ✳

HIGHCLERE CASTLE 🏠 & GARDENS

See page 108 for full page entry.

THE HILLIER GARDENS

Jermyns Lane, Ampfield, Romsey SO51 0QA

Tel: 01794 368787 **Fax:** 01794 368027

Managed by: Hampshire County Council

Established in 1953 by the distinguished plantsman Sir Harold Hillier. Magnificent collection of over 40,000 plants from temperate regions around the world.

Location: OS Ref. SU380 236. 3m NE of Romsey. Follow brown tourist signs from the town centre on A3090 towards Winchester.

Open: Daily, 10.30am - 6pm or dusk if earlier. Closed Christmas Day & Boxing Day.

Admission: Contact property for details.

HINTON AMPNER GARDEN 🌿

See page 109 for full page entry.

Education Index see front section

GUILDHALL GALLERY

THE BROADWAY, WINCHESTER SO23 9LJ

www.winchester.gov.uk/heritage

Tel: 01962 848289 (gallery) 01962 848269 (office)   **Fax:** 01962 848299
e-mail: museums@winchester.gov.uk

Owner: Winchester City Council   **Contact:** Mr C Wardman Bradbury

A constantly changing programme of contemporary exhibitions including painting, sculpture, craft, photography and ceramics.

Location: OS Ref. SU485 293. Winchester - city centre. Situated above the Tourist Office in Winchester's 19th century Guildhall.

Open: Apr - Oct: Mon - Sat, 10am - 5pm; Sun, 12 noon - 5pm. Nov - Mar: Tue - Sat, 10am - 4pm; Sun, 12 noon - 4pm.

Admission: Free.
♿ ✳

© Andy Williams

HOUGHTON LODGE 🏠

STOCKBRIDGE, HAMPSHIRE, SO20 6LQ

www.houghtonlodge.co.uk

Tel: 01264 810502 **Fax:** 01264 810063 **e-mail:** info@houghtonlodge.co.uk

Owner/Contact: Captain M W Busk

A haven of peace beside the tranquil beauty of the River Test. Shady Shrubbery Walk reveals wonderful views from higher ground over the informal landscape (Grade II*) surrounding the 18th century Cottage Ornée (Grade II*). Rare chalk cob walls enclose ancient espaliers, greenhouses and herb garden. Formal topiary 'Peacock' Garden. Wild flowers. Snorting topiary dragon! Popular TV/film location.

Location: OS Ref. SU344 332. 1¹/₂ m S of Stockbridge (A30) on minor road to Houghton village.

Open: Garden: 1 Mar - 30 Sept: Sat, Sun & BHs, 10am - 5pm also Mon, Tue, Thur & Fri, 2 - 5pm. House: by appointment.

Admission: Adult £5, Child Free. Groups (35+) (booked): Adult £4.50.
🍴 ♿ 𝑖By arrangement. 🅿 🐕In grounds, on leads. 🔊

South East - England

HURST CASTLE

Keyhaven, Lymington, Hampshire PO41 0PB

Tel: 01590 642344   **www.**english-heritage.org.uk/visits

Owner: English Heritage   **Contact:** (Managed by) Hurst Castle Services

This was one of the most sophisticated fortresses built by Henry VIII, and later strengthened in the 19th and 20th centuries, to command the narrow entrance to the Solent. There is an exhibition in the Castle, and two huge 38-ton guns form the fort's armaments.

Location: OS196 Ref. SZ319 898. On Pebble Spit S of Keyhaven. Best approach by ferry from Keyhaven. 4m SW of Lymington.

Open: 1 Apr - 31 Oct: daily, 10am - 5.30pm. Café: open Apr - May weekends & Jun - Sept: daily. Times subject to change April 2004.

Admission: Adult £2.80, Child £1.60, Conc. £2.50. Prices subject to change April 2004.

ⓘWCs. ♿Unsuitable. ▣ 🐕Dogs on leads (restricted areas).

KING JOHN'S HOUSE
& HERITAGE CENTRE

CHURCH STREET, ROMSEY, HAMPSHIRE SO51 8BT

www.kingjohnshouse.org.uk

Tel/Fax: 01794 512200   **e-mail:** annerhc@aol.com

Owner: King John's House & Tudor Cottage Trust Ltd   **Contact:** Anne James

Three historic buildings on one site: Medieval King John's House, containing 14th century graffiti and rare bone floor, Tudor Cottage complete with traditional tea room and Victorian Heritage Centre with recreated shop and parlour. Beautiful period gardens, special events/exhibitions and children's activities. Gift shop and Tourist Information Centre. Receptions and private/corporate functions.

Location: OS Ref. SU353 212. M27/J3. Opposite Romsey Abbey, next to Post Office.

Open: Apr - Sept: Mon - Sat, 10am - 4pm. Oct - Mar: Heritage Centre only. Limited opening on Sundays. Evenings also for pre-booked groups.

Admission: Adult £2.50, Child 50p, Conc. £2. Heritage Centre only: Adult £1.50, Child 50p, Conc. £1. Discounted group booking by appointment.

▣ 🅣 ♿Partial. ▣ 🔔By arrangement.

🅿 Off Latimer St with direct access through King John's Garden.

▦ 🐕Guide dogs only. ✳ 🖁Tel for details.

MEDIEVAL MERCHANTS HOUSE

58 French Street, Southampton, Hampshire SO1 0AT

Tel: 02380 221503

Owner: English Heritage   **Contact:** The Custodian

The life of the prosperous merchant in the Middle Ages is vividly evoked in this recreated, faithfully restored 13th century townhouse.

Location: OS Ref. SU419 112. 58 French Street. ¼ m S of Bargate off Castle Way. 150yds SE of Tudor House.

Open: 1 Apr - 30 Sept: daily, 10am - 6pm. 1 - 31 Oct: daily, 10am - 5pm. Times subject to change April 2004.

Admission: Adult £2.50, Child £1.30, Conc. £1.90. Prices subject to change April 2004.

▣ ♿ ▣▦

MOTTISFONT ABBEY & GARDEN

MOTTISFONT, Nr ROMSEY, HAMPSHIRE SO51 0LP

www.nationaltrust.org.uk/regions/southern

Tel: 01794 340757   **Fax:** 01794 341492   **Recorded Message:** 01794 341220

e-mail: mottisfontabbey@nationaltrust.org.uk

Owner: The National Trust   **Contact:** The Property Manager

The Abbey and Garden form the central point of an 809 ha estate including most of the village of Mottisfont, farmland and woods. A tributary of the River Test flows through the garden forming a superb and tranquil setting for a 12th century Augustinian priory which, after the Dissolution, became a house. It contains the spring or "font" from which the place name is derived. The magnificent trees, walled gardens and the National Collection of Old-fashioned Roses combine to provide interest throughout the seasons. The Abbey contains a drawing room decorated by Rex Whistler and the cellarium of the old Priory. In 1996 the Trust acquired Derek Hill's 20th century picture collection.

Location: OS Ref. SU327 270. 4½ m NW of Romsey, 1m W of A3057.

Open: House & Garden: 6 - 21 Mar: Sat & Sun, 11am - 4pm; 22 Mar - 2 Jun: daily except Thur & Fri, 11am - 6pm; 5 - 27 Jun: daily 11am - 6pm (Garden only open until 8.30pm); 19 Jun - 31 Aug: daily except Fri, 11am - 6pm; 1 Sept - 31 Oct: daily except Thur & Fri, 11am - 6pm. Open Good Fri. Last adm. 1 hr before closing.

Admission: Adult £6.50, Child (5-18yrs) £3, Family £16. No reduction for groups. Coaches must book.

▣ ♿Partial. ▣ 🅣Licensed. 🅿🐕Guide dogs only. ▲ 🖁Tel for details.

NETLEY ABBEY

Netley, Southampton, Hampshire

Tel: 023 9258 1059

Owner: English Heritage   **Contact:** Area Manager

A peaceful and beautiful setting for the extensive ruins of this 13th century Cistercian abbey converted in Tudor times for use as a house.

Location: OS Ref. SU453 089. In Netley, 4m SE of Southampton, facing Southhampton Water.

Open: Any reasonable time.

Admission: Free.

♿ 🅿 🐕Dogs on leads

NORTHINGTON GRANGE

New Alresford, Hampshire

Tel: 023 9258 1059

Owner: English Heritage   **Contact:** Area Manager

Northington Grange and its landscaped park as you see it today, formed the core of the house as designed by William Wilkins in 1809. It is one of the earliest Greek Revival houses in Europe.

Location: OS 185, SU562 362. 4m N of New Alresford off B3046 along fram track - 450 metres.

Open: 11 Apr - 31 Oct: daily 10am - 6pm (closes 5pm in Oct, & 3pm in Jun & July for Opera evenings). 1 Nov - 31 Mar 2004: daily 10am - 4pm. Closed 24-26 Dec and 1 Jan 2004. Times subject to change April 2004.

Admission: Free.

♿ Wheelchair access (with assistance). 🅿 🐕Dogs on leads.

PORTCHESTER CASTLE

Portsmouth, Hampshire PO16 9QW

Tel/Fax: 023 9237 8291   **www.**english-heritage.org.uk/visits
Owner: English Heritage   **Contact:** The Custodian
The rallying point of Henry V's expedition to Agincourt and the ruined palace of King Richard II. This grand castle has a history going back nearly 2,000 years including the most complete Roman walls in Europe. Interactive exhibition telling the story of the castle and interactive audio tour.
Location: OS196, Ref. SU625 046. On S side of Portchester off A27, M27/J11.
Open: 1 Apr - 30 Sept: daily, 10am - 6pm. 1 - 31 Oct: 10am - 5pm. 1 Nov - 31 Mar: daily, 10am - 4pm. Closed 24 - 26 Dec & 1 Jan. Times subject to change April 2004.
Admission: Adult £3.50, Child £1.80, Conc. £2.60. 15% discount for groups (11+). One extra place free for every additional 20. Prices subject to change April 2004.
ℹ️WCs. Exhibition. 🅾️ ♿Partial. 🅾️ 🅿️ 🐕In grounds, on leads. ❄️ 🎦 Tel for details.

PORTSMOUTH CATHEDRAL

Portsmouth, Hampshire PO1 2HH

Tel: 023 9282 3300   **Fax:** 023 9229 5480   **Contact:** Rosemary Fairfax
Maritime Cathedral founded in 12th century and finally completed in 1991. A member of the ship's crew of Henry VIII's flagship Mary Rose is buried in Navy Aisle.
Location: OS Ref. SZ633 994. 1½ m from end of M275. Follow signs to Historic Ship and Old Portsmouth.
Open: 7.45am - 6pm all year. Sun service: 8am, 9.30am, 11am, 6pm. Weekday: 6pm (Choral on Tues and Fris in term time).
Admission: Donation appreciated.

SOMERLEY   *See page 110 for full page entry.*

STRATFIELD SAYE HOUSE 🏛️

Stratfield Saye, Basingstoke RG7 2BZ

Tel: 01256 882882   **Fax:** 01256 881466   **www.**stratfield-saye.co.uk
Owner: The Duke of Wellington   **Contact:** The Administrator
Family home of the Dukes of Wellington since 1817.
Location: OS Ref. SU700 615. Equidistant from Reading (M4/J11) & Basingstoke (M3/J6) 1½ m W of the A33.
Open: 9 - 12 Apr & 6 Jul - 1 Aug: daily, weekdays, 11.30am, weekends 10.30am - 3.30pm (last admission).
Admission: Adult £7, Child £3.50, OAP/Student £6. Groups (max 50): Adult £8, OAP £7.
🅾️ ♿ WC. 🎦 𝒾Obligatory. 🅿️ 🐕Guide dogs only.

TITCHFIELD ABBEY

Titchfield, Southampton, Hampshire

Tel: 01329 842133
Owner: English Heritage   **Contact:** Mr K E Groves
Remains of a 13th century abbey overshadowed by the grand Tudor gatehouse. Reputedly some of Shakespeare's plays were performed here for the first time. Under local management of Titchfield Abbey Society.
Location: OS Ref. SU544 067. ½ m N of Titchfield off A27.
Open: 1 Apr - 30 Sept: daily, 10am - 6pm (5pm in Oct). 1 Nov - 31 Mar: daily, 10am - 4pm. Times subject to change April 2004.
Admission: Free.
♿ 🅿️ 🐕Dogs on leads.

SANDHAM MEMORIAL CHAPEL 🌼

BURGHCLERE, Nr NEWBURY, HAMPSHIRE RG20 9JT

www.nationaltrust.org.uk/Sandham

Tel/Fax: 01635 278394   **e-mail:** sandham@nationaltrust.org.uk
Owner: The National Trust   **Contact:** The Custodian
This red brick chapel was built in the 1920s for the artist Stanley Spencer to fill with paintings inspired by his experiences of the First World War. Influenced by Giotto's Arena Chapel in Padua, Spencer took five years to complete what is arguably his finest achievement. The chapel is set amidst lawns and orchards with views across Watership Down. Pictures best viewed on a bright day.
Location: OS Ref. SU463 608. 4m S of Newbury, ½m E of A34, W end of Burghclere.
Open: 6 - 28 Mar & 6 - 28 Nov: Sat & Sun, 11am - 4pm. 31 Mar - 31 Oct: Wed - Sun, 11am - 5pm. Open BH Mons. Dec - Feb 2005: by appointment only.
Admission: Adult £3, Child £1.50. Groups by prior arrangement, no reduction.
♿Portable ramp for entrance. 𝒾By arrangement. ■ 🐕In grounds, on leads. ❄️

Lancelot 'Capability' Brown
1716-1783

Sketchy childhood details, but believed to have come from a poor family from Kirkhale in Northumberland. He trained as a gardener, and in 1739 got his first big break at Stowe Landscape Gardens in Buckinghamshire working for William Kent, the famous landscape gardener. Nicknamed 'Capability' because of the endless 'capabilities' he saw for improving the landscapes of his clients. Look for vast sweeping areas of grassland, which come right up to the house, the ha-ha which stops the cattle coming through the front door, large clumps and belts of trees, and lakes created by the rivers he dammed. He banished flowers and vegetables from his landscapes, so you will have to walk to the walled gardens he created to find these.

Visit in the

- **Eastern Region - Audley End, Essex, Holkham Hall, Norfolk, Wimpole Hall, Cambridgeshire, and Wrest Park Gardens, Bedfordshire**
- **West Midlands Region - Berrington Hall, Herefordshire, Warwick Castle, Warwickshire, and Weston Park, Shropshire.**
- **South East Region - Blenheim Palace, Oxfordshire, Broadlands and Highclere Castle, Hampshire, Claremont House, Surrey, Petworth House, and Sheffield Park Garden, Sussex.**
- **South West Region -Bowood House, Corsham Court, and Longleat in Wiltshire.**
- **East Midlands Region - Burghley House, Lincolnshire and Chatsworth, Derbyshire.**
- **Yorkshire & The Humber Region - Burton Constable Hall, Harewood House, Ripley Castle, and Sledmere House.**
- **London Region - Syon Park, London.**
- **North East Region – Alnwick Castle, Northumberland.**

NT Photographic Library: Andrea Jones

THE VYNE ❀

SHERBORNE ST JOHN, BASINGSTOKE RG24 9HL

www.nationaltrust.org.uk

Tel: 01256 883858 **Infoline:** 01256 881337 **Fax:** 01256 881720
e-mail: thevyne@nationaltrust.org.uk

Owner: The National Trust   **Contact:** The Property Manager

Built in the early 16th century for Lord Sandys, Henry VIII's Lord Chamberlain, the house acquired a classical portico in the mid-17th century (the first of its kind in England) and contains a fascinating Tudor chapel with Renaissance glass, a Palladian staircase and a wealth of old panelling and fine furniture. The attractive grounds feature herbaceous borders and a wild garden, with lawns, lakes and woodland walks. Weddings & Functions: Stone Gallery licensed for Civil Weddings. Receptions and private/corporate functions in Walled Garden or Brewhouse restaurant.

Location: OS Ref. SU639 576. 4m N of Basingstoke between Bramley & Sherborne St John.

Open: House: 20 Mar - 31 Oct: Sat & Sun, 11am - 5pm; Mon - Wed, 1 - 5pm. Grounds: 7 Feb - 14 Mar, Sat & Sun; 20 Mar - 31 Oct: daily except Thur & Fri, 11am - 5pm. Open BH Mons & Good Fri. Group visits: 20 Mar - 31 Oct: Mon - Wed, by appointment only.

Admission: House & Grounds: Adult £7, Child £3.50, Family £17.50. Groups £5.50. Grounds only: Adult £4, Child £2.

ℹ️No photography in house. 🄾 ♿ 🔽 🔄 🖥 🍴 🅿 ✖ 🔔 💺Tel for details.

GILBERT WHITE'S HOUSE & THE OATES MUSEUM

THE WAKES, HIGH STREET, SELBORNE, ALTON GU34 3JH

Tel: 01420 511275

Owner: Oates Memorial Trust   **Contact:** Mrs Anna Jackson

Charming refurbished 18th century house, home of Rev Gilbert White, author of *The Natural History of Selborne*. Lovely garden with many plants of the Georgian era. Tea parlour with fare based on 18th century recipes and excellent gift shop. Temporary exhibition on Captain Oates of Antarctic fame.

Location: OS Ref. SU741 336. On W side of B3006, in village of Selborne 4m NW of the A3.

Open: 1 Jan - 24 Dec: 11am - 5pm. Groups by prior arrangement.

Admission: Adult £4.50, Child £1, OAP £4.

ℹ️No photography in house. 🄾 ♿ 🔄Partial. 🖥 🎥By arrangement. 🅿
✖ Guide dogs only. 🌸 💺Tel for details.

WINCHESTER CATHEDRAL

Winchester, Hants SO23 9LS

Tel: 01962 857200 **Fax:** 01962 857201 **www.**winchester-cathedral.org.uk

The Cathedral was founded in 1079.

Location: OS Ref. SU483 293. Winchester city centre.

Open: 8.30am - 6pm. East end closes 5pm. Access may be restricted during services. Weekday services:7.40am, 8am, 5.30pm. Sun services: 8am, 10am, 11.15am, 3.30pm.

Admission: Recommended donations. Adult £3.50, Conc. £2.50. Photo permits £2, Video permits £3. Library & Triforium Gallery: £1, Tower & Roof tours: £3 (age restrictions 12 - 70). Groups (10+) must book, tel: 01962 857225. Special tours available.

WOLVESEY CASTLE ⌗

College Street, Wolvesey, Winchester, Hampshire SO23 8NB

Tel: 01962 854766 **www.**english-heritage.org.uk/visits

Owner: English Heritage   **Contact:** The Custodian

The fortified palace of Wolvesey was the chief residence of the Bishops of Winchester and one of the greatest of all medieval buildings in England. Its extensive ruins still reflect the importance and immense wealth of the Bishops of Winchester, occupants of the richest seat in medieval England. Wolvesey was frequently visited by medieval and Tudor monarchs and was the scene of the wedding feast of Philip of Spain and Mary Tudor in 1554.

Location: OS Ref. SU484 291. ¾ m SE of Winchester Cathedral, next to the Bishop's Palace; access from College Street.

Open: 1 Apr - 30 Sept: 10am - 6pm. 1 - 31 Oct: 10am - 5pm. Times subject to change April 2004.

Admission: Adult £2.20, Child £1.10, Conc. £1.70. Prices subject to change April 2004.
🄾 🔄Grounds. ✖ In grounds, on leads.

Website Information see front section

Map 4

Owner:
Mr & Mrs D Kendrick

▶ CONTACT

Mrs M Kendrick
Boughton
Monchelsea Place
Boughton Monchelsea
Nr Maidstone
Kent   ME17 4BU

Tel: 01622 743120
Fax: 01622 741168

e-mail: mk@
boughtonmonchelsea
place.co.uk

▶ LOCATION
OS Ref. TQ772 499

On B2163, 5$^{1}/_{2}$ m from
M20/J8 or 4$^{1}/_{2}$ m from
Maidstone via A229.

BOUGHTON MONCHELSEA PLACE

NR MAIDSTONE

www.boughtonmonchelseaplace.co.uk

Boughton Monchelsea Place is a battlemented manor house dating from the 16th century, set in its own country estate just outside Maidstone, within easy reach of London and the channel ports. This Grade I listed building has always been privately owned and is still lived in as a family home.

From the lawns surrounding the property there are spectacular views over unspoilt Kent countryside, with the historic deer park in the foreground. These views are shared by the 20 acre event site set back a little way from the house. A wicket gate leads from the grounds to the medieval church of St Peter, with its rose garden and ancient lych gate. At the rear of the house are to be found a pretty courtyard and walled gardens, together with an extensive range of Tudor barns and outbuildings.

Inside the house, rooms vary in character from Tudor through to Georgian Gothic; worthy of note are the fine Jacobean staircase and sundry examples of heraldic stained glass. Furnishings and paintings are mainly Victorian, with a few earlier pieces; the atmosphere is friendly and welcoming throughout.

The premises are licensed for Civil marriage ceremonies, although wedding receptions in the house may only be held on weekday afternoons. In addition we welcome conferences, group visits, location work and all types of corporate, private and public functions, but please note times of availability. Use outside these hours is sometimes possible, subject to negotiation. All clients are guaranteed exclusive use of this prestigious venue.

▶ OPENING TIMES

All year by prior arrangement only.

House & Garden
Not open to individual visitors.

Group visits/ house tours: (10-50),
Mon - Thur, 9am - 4pm.

Private functions:
Mon - Fri, 9am - 9pm.

Outdoor Event Site
365 days a year:
8am - 11.30pm.

▶ ADMISSION
**Gardens &
Guided House Tour**
Adult £5.00

Venue Hire
Prices on application.

Day Delegate Rate
From £40.

▶ SPECIAL EVENTS

Apr 11/12
Classic Car & Transport Show.

Jun 13 & Aug 1
Gardens Open - NGS.

Aug 10 - 15
Open Air Shakespeare 'Romeo and Juliet'.

By arrangement.
By arrangement.
By arrangement.

CONFERENCE/FUNCTION

ROOM	SIZE	MAX CAPACITY
Entrance Hall	25' x 19'	50 Theatre
Dining Room	31' x 19'	50 Dining
Drawing Room	28' x 19'	40 Reception
Courtyard Room	37' x 13'	60 Theatre

CANTERBURY CATHEDRAL

CANTERBURY

www.canterbury-cathedral.org

Map 4

▶ CONTACT
Visits Office
Canterbury Cathedral
The Precincts
Canterbury
Kent CT1 2EH

Tel: 01227 762862
Fax: 01227
865222/865250
e-mail: visits@
canterbury-
cathedral.org

▶ LOCATION
OS Ref. TR151 579

Canterbury city centre.
M2/M20, then A2.

Bus: Victoria Station
coach – regular service.

Rail: London Victoria
or London Bridge to
Canterbury East or
West.

Sightseeing Tours:
Tour operators operate a
daily service with
collection from most
London hotels. Ask
your hotel concierge or
porter for information.

Canterbury Cathedral has a tradition of visitor welcome that reaches back to the days of medieval pilgrimages. St Augustine, sent by Pope Gregory the Great, arrived in 597 AD and became the first Archbishop, establishing his seat (or 'Cathedra') in Canterbury. In 1170 Archbishop Thomas Becket was murdered in the Cathedral and ever since, the Cathedral has attracted thousands of pilgrims.

The saint is said to have worked miracles, and the Cathedral contains some rare stained glass depicting those events. The Cathedral is also noteworthy for its medieval tombs of royal personages, such as King Henry IV and Edward the Black Prince, as well as numerous archbishops. The Cathedral, together with St Augustine's Abbey and St Martin's Church, is a World Heritage Site.

The Cathedral's International Study Centre offers purpose-built conference facilities of the highest quality. Facilities range from small seminar rooms to two 60-seat lecture theatres and a 250-seat auditorium, equipped with the latest audio-visual technology and full theatre lighting, as well as first class accommodation for 40 people, two dining areas, common room with bar, library and private garden.

CONFERENCE/FUNCTION

ROOM	SIZE	MAX CAPACITY
Clagett Auditorium	10.5 x 15m	250
'The Barn'	14 x 5m	92
Lecture Theatre (x2)	7 x 7m	60
Seminar rms	vary	12 - 50

▶ OPENING TIMES
Summer
Mon - Sat, 9am - 7pm.

Winter
Mon - Sat, 9am - 5pm.

Crypt (all year):
10am - 7pm
(5pm in winter)

Sundays (all year):
12.30 - 2.30pm,
4.30 - 5.30pm.

Restrictions during services
or special events.
Arrangements may vary
at short notice, always
check opening times
before visiting.

Main Services
Evensong:
Mon - Fri, 5.30pm
Sats & Suns, 3.15pm.

Eucharist:
Suns, 11am.

▶ ADMISSION
Adult £4.00
Conc. £3.00

Pre-booked school
groups £2.00
(2003 prices)

 By arrangement.

NTPL / Rupert Truman

Map 4

Owner:
The National Trust

CHARTWELL 🌿

WESTERHAM

www.nationaltrust.org.uk/places/chartwell

The family home of Sir Winston Churchill from 1924 until the end of his life. He said of Chartwell, simply *'I love the place - a day away from Chartwell is a day wasted'*. With magnificent views over the Weald of Kent it is not difficult to see why.

The rooms are left as they were in Sir Winston & Lady Churchill's lifetime with daily papers, fresh flowers grown from the garden and his famous cigars. Photographs and books evoke his career, interests and happy family life. Museum and exhibition rooms contain displays and sound recordings and superb collections of memorabilia from Sir Winston's political career, including uniforms and a 'siren-suit'.

The garden studio contains Sir Winston's easel and paintbox, as well as many of his paintings. Terraced and water gardens descend to the lake, the gardens also include a golden rose walk, planted by Sir Winston and Lady Churchill's children on the occasion of their golden wedding anniversary, and the Marlborough Pavilion decorated with frescoes depicting the battle of Blenheim. Visitors can see the garden walls that Churchill built with his own hands, as well as the pond stocked with the golden orfe he loved to feed.

The Mulberry Room at the restaurant can be booked for meetings, conferences, lunches and dinners. Please telephone for details.

▶ **CONTACT**

The Property Manager
Chartwell
Westerham
Kent TN16 1PS

Tel: 01732 866368
01732 868381

Fax: 01732 868193

e-mail: chartwell@
nationaltrust.org.uk

▶ **LOCATION**

OS Ref. TQ455 515

2m S of Westerham,
forking left off B2026.

Bus: Metro bus 246
from Bromley South.
Please check times.

▶ **OPENING TIMES**

20 March - 30 June and
1 Sept - 7 November
Wed - Sun & BHs
11am - 5pm.

1 July - 31 August
Tue - Sun & BHs
11am - 5pm.

Last admission 4.15pm.

▶ **ADMISSION**

House, Garden & Studio
Adult £7.00
Child £3.50
Family £17.50

Garden & Studio only
Adult £3.50
Child £1.75
Family £8.75

NTPL / Andreas von Einsiedel

NTPL / Ian Shaw

▢ ⓘ Conference facilities. ⓣ ♿ Partial. WC. Please telephone before visit. ⧌ Licensed.

⚘ By arrangement. Ⓟ Parking. ⛬ In grounds, on leads. ⛨ Tel for details.

South East - England

Courtesy Ron Vernon

Owner:
Denys Eyre Bower
Bequest Reg.
Charity Trust

▶ **CONTACT**

Mrs R Vernon
Chiddingstone Castle
Edenbridge
Kent TN8 7AD

Tel: 01892 870347

▶ **LOCATION**
OS Ref. TQ497 452

B2027, turn to
Chiddingstone at Bough
Beech, 1m further on
to crossroads, then
straight to castle.

10m from Tonbridge,
Tunbridge Wells and
Sevenoaks. 4m
Edenbridge. Accessible
from A21 and M25/J5.

London 35m.

Bus: Enquiries:
Tunbridge Wells TIC
01892 515675.

Rail: Tonbridge,
Tunbridge Wells,
Edenbridge then taxi.
Penshurst then 2m walk.

Air: Gatwick 15m.

CHIDDINGSTONE CASTLE 🏛

EDENBRIDGE

www.chiddingstone-castle.org.uk

Henry Streatfeild, Squire of Chiddingstone, intoxicated by the current passion for medieval chivalry, embarked on the transformation of his ancient home into a fantasy castle in 1803, the first major commission of young William Atkinson, which a contemporary guidebook predicted would be the 'fairest house' in Kent. After five hectic years' work ceased, leaving a random mixture of old and new. The Establishment was not impressed: today, we find the place enchanting. In 1955 the now decrepit castle was bought by the distinguished collector Denys Bower – greater than Beckford or Burrell. They had wealth and expert agents –

he had neither. He died in 1977, leaving everything to the Nation, for the enjoyment of posterity, to be run as a living home, not a museum. The place is now administered by a registered private Charitable Trust. The restoration of the fabric being completed, the Trust is now improving the display of the collections, as contemplated by Denys Bower: Royal Stuart portraits and mementoes, Japanese lacquer (the finest private collection in the West), Egyptian and oriental antiquities. The 35-acre landscaped park (listed garden of Kent) has been restored – a haven for wild life, providing idyllic walks.

Great Hall

▶ **OPENING TIMES**

Summer
Easter Hol, All BHs.

June - September

Thur: 2 - 5.30pm

Sun & BHs:
11.30am - 5.30pm
Last admission 5pm.

Winter
Open only for specially
booked groups (20-80).
First Sun in Dec: Christmas
Fair, 10.30am - 4pm –
please enquire.

▶ **ADMISSION**

Adult	£5.00
Child*	£3.00
OAP	£5.00
Student	£5.00

Groups** (Booked 20-80)

Adult	£4.00
Child*	£3.00
OAP	£4.00
Student	£4.00

* Child under 16yrs
accompanied by paying adult.
Under 5 yrs Free.

** Usual hours, other times by
appointment. School groups
only by appointment.

ℹ Conferences, receptions, concerts. No photography in house; no smoking, prams/buggies, large bags or mobile phones.

▤ Available for special events. Wedding receptions.

♿ Partial (grounds unsuitable). WC.

🍽 Licensed.

🅿 Ample for cars. Limited for coaches, please book.

Teachers' pack. Educational programme.

🐕 In grounds, on leads.

🔔 ❄

Chiddingstone may be
closed without notice for
Special Events.

CONFERENCE/FUNCTION

ROOM	SIZE	MAX CAPACITY
Assembly Rm	14' x 35'	50
Seminar Rms	15' x 15'	
Stable Block	36' x 29'	

CHIDDINGSTONE CASTLE...

Stable Lecture Room

The Assembly Room

The Seminar Room

SMALL CONFERENCES AND FUNCTIONS:

The old domestic quarters, grouped around the courtyard, have been converted into a unique and elegant centre for various events. The self-contained Goodhugh Wing offers Assembly Room (capacity 50), three seminar rooms, and tea-kitchen. Meals can be provided in the refectory by our approved caterers. Additional lecture/meeting accommodation in the adjoining stable block, recently restored.

CIVIL MARRIAGES:

The Great Hall is licensed by Kent County Council, and is specially attractive to those who desire the dignity of a church ceremony without the religious aspect. We offer all features of wedding celebrations, including reception of guests and refreshments.

EDUCATION:

We welcome visits from schools who wish to use the collections in connection with classroom work. No anxiety for the teachers (admitted free). The children are safe here, can picnic and play in the grounds. Dr Nicholas Reevis F.S.A, Honorary Curator, is responsible for educational developments. Please enquire.

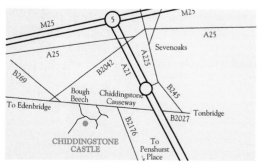

Map 4

COBHAM HALL 🏛

COBHAM

www.cobhamhall.com

Owner:
Cobham Hall
School

▶ **CONTACT**

Mr N Powell
Bursar
Cobham Hall, Cobham
Kent DA12 3BL

Tel: 01474 823371
Fax: 01474 825904
e-mail:
cobhamhall@aol.com

▶ **LOCATION**
OS Ref. TQ683 689

Situated adjacent to the
A2/M2. ¹/₂ m S of A2 4m
W of Strood. 8m E of
M25/J2 between
Gravesend & Rochester.

London 25m
Rochester 5m
Canterbury 30m

Rail: Meopham 3m
Gravesend 5m
Taxis at both stations.

Air: Gatwick 45 mins.
Heathrow 60 mins,
Stansted 50 mins.

Cobham Hall is now a leading Girls Boarding &
Day School, and has been visited by several
English monarchs from Elizabeth I to Edward VIII.
Charles Dickens used regularly to walk through
the grounds from his house in Higham to the
Leather Bottle Public House in Cobham Village.

Cobham Hall is one of the largest, finest and
most important houses in Kent, it is an
outstanding beautiful red brick mansion in
Elizabethan, Jacobean, Carolean and 18th
century styles, it yields much interest to the
students of art, architecture & history. The
Elizabethan Wings were begun in 1584, whilst
the central section, which contains the Gilt Hall,
was wonderfully decorated by John Webb.

Further rooms were decorated by James Wyatt in
the 18th century.

In 1883 the Hon Ivo Bligh, later the 8th Earl of
Darnley, led the victorious English cricket
team against Australia bringing the Ashes home
to Cobham.

GARDENS

The Park was landscaped for the 4th Earl by
Humphry Repton, and is now gradually being
restored. The Gothic Dairy, Aviary and the Pump
House are all being restored. The gardens are
beautiful at all times of the year but especially
delightful in the spring when the spring flowers
are out in full bloom.

ℹ️ Conferences, business or social
functions, 150 acres of parkland for sports,
corporate events, open air concerts, sports
centre, indoor swimming pool, art studios,
music wing, tennis courts, helicopter
landing area. Filming and photography.
No smoking.

🍴 In-house catering team for private,
corporate hospitality and wedding
receptions. (cap. 100).

♿ House tour involves 2 staircases,
ground floor access for w/chairs.

☕ Afternoon teas, other meals by
arrangement.

🎫 Obligatory guided tours; tour time 1¹/₂
hrs. Garden tours arranged outside standard
opening times.

🅿 Ample. Pre-booked coach groups are
welcome any time.

👥 Guide provided, Adult £4.50, Child /
OAP £3.50.

🐕 In grounds, on leads.

🛏 18 single and 18 double with
bathroom. 22 single and 22 double without
bathroom. Dormitory. Groups only.

🔔

CONFERENCE/FUNCTION

ROOM	SIZE	MAX CAPACITY
Gilt Hall	41' x 34'	180
Wyatt Dining Rm	49' x 23'	135
Clifton Dining Rm	24' x 23'	75
Activities Centre	119' x 106'	300

▶ **OPENING TIMES**
April:
7, 9 - 12, 14, 18, 21.

July:
7, 11, 14, 18, 21, 25, 28.

August:
1, 4, 8, 11, 15, 18, 22, 25,
29, 30.

September: 1.

House:
2 - 5pm. Last tour at 4pm.

Dates could change, please
telephone to confirm.

▶ **ADMISSION**

Adult £4.50
Child (4-14yrs.) £3.50
OAP £3.50

Gardens & Parkland
Self-guided tour
and booklet £1.50

**Historical/Conservation
tour of Grounds**
(by arrangement)

Per person £3.50

🎭 **SPECIAL EVENTS**

APR 11
National Garden Scheme Day
(+ House open 2 - 5pm).

APR 9 - 12
Easter Opening
(+ House open 2 - 5pm).

JUL 18
National Garden Scheme Day
(+ House open 2 - 5pm).

JUL 28
Summer Stroll Garden Tour.
Guidebook, tour & glass of
wine £5 per person. Tel to
book.

AUG 15
British Red Cross
(+ House open 2 - 5pm).

English Heritage Photo Library

Map 4

DOVER CASTLE ⬚
AND THE SECRET WARTIME TUNNELS
DOVER

www.english-heritage.org.uk/visits

Owner:
English Heritage

▶ **CONTACT**

The General Manager
Dover Castle
Dover
Kent   CT16 1HU

Tel: 01304 211067
Info Line: 01304 201628

**Venue Hire and
Hospitality:**
Hospitality Manager
Tel: 01304 211067

▶ **LOCATION**
OS Ref. TR326 416

Easy access from A2
and M20. Well signed
from Dover centre and
east side of Dover.
2 hrs from
central London.

Rail: London Charing
Cross or Victoria
1¹/₂ hrs.

Bus: Freephone
0870 6082608.

Journey deep into the White Cliffs of Dover and discover the top secret World War II tunnels. Through sight, sound and smells relive the wartime drama of the underground hospital as a wounded Battle of Britain pilot is taken to the operating theatre in a bid to save his life. Discover how life would have been during the planning days of the Dunkirk evacuation and Operation Dynamo as you are led around the network of tunnels and casements housing the communications centre.

Above ground you can explore the magnificent medieval keep and inner bailey of King Henry II. Visit the evocative Princess of Wales' Royal Regiment Museum. There is also the Roman Lighthouse and Anglo-Saxon church to see or take an audio tour of the intriguing 13th-century underground fortifications and medieval battlements. Enjoy magnificent views of the White Cliffs from Admiralty lookout.

See the exciting 'Life Under Siege' exhibition, and discover, through a dramatic light and sound presentation, how it must have felt to be a garrison soldier defending Dover Castle against the French King in 1216. In the Keep, see a reconstruction of the Castle in preparation for a visit from Henry VIII and visit the hands-on exhibition explaining the travelling Tudor court. The land train will help you around this huge site.

Throughout the summer there are many fun events taking place, bringing the Castle alive through colourful enactments and living history.

ℹ️ WCs. 📷 Two.

🍸 Exclusive private and corporate hire. Tel: 01034 211067.

♿ Lift for access to tunnels. Courtyard and grounds, some very steep slopes.

🍴 3 restaurants, hot and cold food and drinks.

🚶 Tour of tunnels approx. every 20 mins, more at peak times when a 30 min. wait can occur.

🅿️ Ample. Groups welcome, discounts available. Free entry for drivers. One extra place for each additional group of 20.

🏫 Free visits available for schools. Education centre. Pre-booking essential.

❄️ 🎭 Tel for details.

English Heritage Photo Library

▶ **OPENING TIMES***

Summer
1 Apr - 30 Sept
Daily: 10am - 6pm.

1 - 31 Oct:
Daily: 10am - 5pm.

Winter
1 November - 31 March
Daily: 10am - 4pm.

Closed 24 - 26 Dec &
1 Jan.

* Times subject to change
April 2004.

**Venue Hire and
Hospitality**

English Heritage offers
exclusive use of the Castle
Keep or Tunnels in the
evenings for receptions,
dinners, product launches
and themed banquets.

▶ **ADMISSION***

Adult	£8.00
Child	£4.00
Conc.	£6.00
Family (2+3)	£20.00

Groups: 15% discount for
groups (11+).

* Prices subject to change
April 2004.

CONFERENCE/FUNCTION

ROOM	MAX CAPACITY
The Castle Keep	standing 120 dining 90
Keep Yard Café	theatre-style 150
Secret Wartime Tunnels	standing 120 dining 80 theatre-style 80
Marquee on Palace Green	standing 400 dining 265

South East - England

English Heritage Photo Library / Jonathan Bailey

Map 4

DOWN HOUSE

DOWNE

www.english-heritage.org.uk/visits

Owner:
English Heritage

▶ **CONTACT**

The House Manager
Down House
Luxted Road
Downe
Kent   BR6 7JT

Tel: 01689 859119

▶ **LOCATION**

OS Ref, TQ431 611

In Luxted Road,
Downe, off A21 near
Biggin Hill.

Rail: From London
Victoria or
Charing Cross.

Bus: Orpington
(& Bus R2) or Bromley
South (& Bus 146).
Buses R2 & 146
do not run on Sunday.

A visit to Down House is a fascinating journey of discovery for all the family. This was the family home of Charles Darwin for over 40 years and now you can explore it to the full.

See the actual armchair in which Darwin wrote *'On the Origin of Species'*, which shocked and then revolutionised the way we think about the origins of mankind. His study is much the same as it was in his lifetime and is filled with belongings that give you an intimate glimpse into both his studies and everyday life.

At Down House you will discover both sides of Darwin - the great thinker and the family man.

Explore the family rooms where the furnishings have been painstakingly restored. An audio tour narrated by Sir David Attenborough will bring the house to life and increase your understanding of Darwin's revolutionary theory. Upstairs you will find state-of-the-art interpretation of the scientific significance of the house – especially designed to inspire a younger audience.

Outside, take the Sandwalk which he paced daily in search of inspiration, then stroll in lovely gardens. Complete your day by sampling the delicious selection of home-made cakes in the tea room.

▶ **OPENING TIMES***

Wed - Sun & BHs on
the following dates:

5 February - 31 March
10am - 4pm.

April - September
10am - 6pm.

October: 10am - 5pm.

November - 21 December
10am - 4pm.

Closed:
22 Dec 2004 - 3 Feb 2005

* Times subject to change
April 2004.

▶ **ADMISSION***

Adult	£6.00
Child	£3.00
Conc.	£4.50
Family (2+3)	£15.00

Groups (11+)
.... 15% discount

Tour leader and coach
driver have free entry.
1 extra place for every
20 additional people.

* Prices subject to change
April 2004.

 WCs.

 Free. English, French,
German, Japanese & for
visually impaired.

P Limited for coaches.

 Guide dogs only.

Tel for details.

English Heritage Photo Library / Jonathan Bailey

Map 4

GROOMBRIDGE PLACE GARDENS 🏛

TUNBRIDGE WELLS

www.groombridge.co.uk

There's magic and mystery, history and intrigue, romance and peace at this beautiful venue – which provides such an unusual combination of a traditional heritage garden with the excitement, challenge and contemporary landscaping of the ancient woodland – appealing to young and old alike.

First laid out in 1674 on a gentle, south-facing slope, the formal walled gardens are set against the romantic backdrop of a medieval moat, surrounding a classical Restoration manor house (not open to the public) and were designed as outside rooms. These award-winning gardens include magnificent herbaceous borders, the enchanting White Rose Garden with over 20 varieties of white roses, a Secret Garden with deep shade and cooling waters in a tiny hidden corner, Paradise Walk and Oriental Garden,

the Knot Garden and Nut Walk and the Drunken Garden with its crazy topiary. The gardens feature wonderful seasonal colour throughout spring, summer and autumn.

In complete contrast on a high hillside above the walled gardens and estate vineyard is the Enchanted Forest, where quirky and mysterious gardens have been developed in the ancient woodland by innovative designer, Ivan Hicks, to challenge the imagination. Children love the Dark Walk, Tree Fern Valley, Village of the Groms, the Serpent's Lair and the Mystic Pool, the Romany Camp, Double Spiral and the Giant Swings Walk. There are also Birds of Prey flying displays three times a day, a canal boat cruise to and from the Forest – plus a full programme of special events.

Owner:
Groombridge Asset Management

▶ CONTACT

The Estate Office
Groombridge Place
Groombridge
Tunbridge Wells
Kent TN3 9QG

Tel: 01892 863999
01892 861444

Fax: 01892 863996

e-mail: office@
groombridge.co.uk

▶ LOCATION
OS Ref. TQ534 375

Groombridge Place Gardens are located on the B2110 just off the A264. 4m SW of Tunbridge Wells and 9m E of East Grinstead.

Rail: London Charing Cross to Tunbridge Wells 55mins. (Taxis).

Air: Gatwick.

▶ OPENING TIMES

Summer
Gardens
1 April - 6 November
Daily, 9.30am - 6pm (or dusk if earlier).

The house is not open to visitors.

▶ ADMISSION

Adult	£8.50
Child (3-12yrs)	£7.00
Senior	£7.20
Family (2+2)	£28.50

Groups (20+)

Adult	£6.75
Child/School	£5.25
Senior	£5.00/£5.75
Student	£5.75

Children under 3yrs Free.

Partial. WCs.
Licensed.
By arrangement.
Limited for coaches.
Guide dogs only.

▶ SPECIAL EVENTS

JUN 12 - 27
Midsummer Garden Celebration

JUL 11
Hot Air Balloons & Ferraris.

NOV 6
Fireworks Spectacular

Map 4

HEVER CASTLE & GARDENS 🏛

EDENBRIDGE

www.hevercastle.co.uk

Owner:
Hever Castle Ltd

▸ **CONTACT**

Anne-Marie Pedley
Hever Castle
Hever, Edenbridge
Kent TN8 7NG

Infoline: 01732 865224
Fax: 01732 866796
e-mail:
mail@HeverCastle.co.uk

Hever Castle dates back to 1270, when the gatehouse, outer walls and the inner moat were first built. 200 years later the Bullen (or Boleyn) family added the comfortable Tudor manor house constructed within the walls. This was the childhood home of Anne Boleyn, Henry VIII's second wife and mother of Elizabeth I. There are many items relating to the Tudors, including two books of hours (prayer books) signed and inscribed by Anne Boleyn. The Castle was later given to Henry VIII's fourth wife, Anne of Cleves.

In 1903, the estate was bought by the American millionaire William Waldorf Astor, who became a British subject and the first Lord Astor of Hever. He invested an immense amount of time, money and imagination in restoring the castle and grounds. Master craftsmen were employed and the castle was filled with a magnificent collection of furniture, tapestries and other works of art.

'From Castles to Country Houses' the Miniature Model Houses exhibition, a collection of 1/12 scale model houses, room views and gardens, depicts life in English Country Houses.

GARDENS

Between 1904-8 over 30 acres of formal gardens were laid out and planted, these have now matured into one of the most beautiful gardens in England. The unique Italian garden is a four acre walled garden containing a superb collection of statuary and sculpture. The award-winning gardens include the Rose garden and Tudor garden, a traditional yew maze and a 110 metre herbaceous border. A water maze has been added to the other water features in the gardens. The Sunday Walk Garden has a stream meandering through a mature woodland with borders filled with specimen plants.

▸ **OPENING TIMES**

Summer
1 March - 30 November
Daily:
Grounds: 11am - 6pm.
Castle: 12 noon - 6pm.
Last admission 5pm.

Winter
March & November
Grounds: 11am - 4pm.

Castle: 12 noon - 4pm.

▸ **LOCATION**

OS Ref. TQ476 450

Exit M25/J5 & J6
M23/J10,
1¹/₂ m S of B2027 at
Bough Beech,
3m SE of Edenbridge.

Rail: Hever Station
1m (no taxis),
Edenbridge Town
3m (taxis).

ℹ ✿ Suitable for filming, conferences, corporate hospitality, weddings, product launches. Outdoor heated pool, tennis court and billiard room. No photography in house.

🎁 Gift, garden & book.

🍽 250 seat restaurant available for functions wedding receptions, etc.

♿ Access to gardens, ground floor only (no ramps into castle), restaurants, gift shop, book shop and water maze. Wheelchairs available. WC.

🍴 Two licensed restaurants. Supper provided during open air theatre season. Pre-booked lunches and teas for groups.

🚶 Pre-booked tours in mornings. 1 Mar - 30 Nov. Tour time 1 hr. Tours in French, German, Dutch, Italian and Spanish (min 20). Garden tours in English only (min 15).

P Free admission and refreshment voucher for driver and courier. Please book, group rates for 15+.

🚌 Welcome (min 15). Private guided tours available (min 25). 1:6 ratio (up to 8 year olds: 1:10 9yrs+. Free preparatory visits for teachers during opening hours. Please book.

🐕 In grounds, on leads.

✿ Tudor Village. 🎭 Call infoline: 01732 865224.

▸ **ADMISSION**

Castle & Gardens

Adult	£8.80
Child (5-14 yrs)	£4.80
OAP	£7.40
Family (2+2)	£22.40

Groups (15+)

Adult	£7.50
Child (5-14 yrs)	£4.60
OAP	£7.00
Student (15-19yrs)	£6.50

Gardens only

Adult	£7.00
Child (5-14 yrs)	£4.60
OAP	£6.00
Family (2+2)	£18.60

Groups (15+)

Adult	£6.10
Child (5-14 yrs)	£4.40
OAP	£5.80
Student (15-19yrs)	£5.70

Pre-booked private guided tours are available before opening, during season.

CONFERENCE/FUNCTION

ROOM	SIZE	MAX CAPACITY
Dining Hall	35' x 20'	70
Breakfast Rm	22' x 15'	12
Sitting Rm	24' x 20'	20
Pavilion	96' x 40'	250
Moat Restaurant	25 'x 60'	75

NTPL / Nadia MacKenzie

Map 4

IGHTHAM MOTE

SEVENOAKS

www.nationaltrust.org.uk/places/ighthammote

Beautiful moated manor house covering 650 years of history from medieval times to the 1960s. Discover the stories and characters associated with the house from the first owners in 1330 to Charles Henry Robinson, the American businessman who bequeathed Ightham Mote to the National Trust in 1985.

The visitor route includes the newly refurbished Great Hall and Jacobean staircase, along with the old chapel, crypt, Tudor chapel with painted ceiling, drawing room with Jacobean fireplace, frieze and 18th century hand-painted Chinese wallpaper and Victorian billiards room.

Conservation programme continues during 2004 which gives visitors a unique opportunity to see work in progress on the largest conservation project ever undertaken by the National Trust on a house of this age and fragility. Interpretation displays and a special exhibition 'Conservation in action' charts the progress of the project and gives insights into the techniques and skills used.

Extensive gardens with lakes and woodland walk. Surrounding 550 acre estate also provides many country walks including way-marked routes.

Free introductory talks and garden tours. Varied event programme including open air concerts and children's events throughout the season, for details please ring 01732 810378.

Owner:
The National Trust

▶ **CONTACT**

The Property Manager
Ightham Mote
Ivy Hatch
Sevenoaks
Kent   TN15 0NT

Tel: 01732 810378
Info: 01732 811145
Fax: 01732 811029

e-mail: ighthammote@
nationaltrust.org.uk

▶ **LOCATION**
OS Ref. TQ584 535

6m E of Sevenoaks off
A25. 2¹/₂ m S of
Ightham off A227.

▶ **OPENING TIMES**

28 March - 7 November:
Daily except Tues & Sats.

Gardens, Shop &
Restaurant: 10am - 5.30pm
(last admission 5pm).

House: 10.30am - 5.30pm
(last admission 5pm).

Restaurant & Shop evening
and winter opening times,
please call property.

▶ **ADMISSION**

Adult	£6.50
Child	£3.50
Family	£16.50

Groups (booked)
Adult	£5.50
Child	£3.00

NTPL / Nadia MacKenzie

 Ground floor. WC.

On leads, Estate only.

Tel for details.

LEEDS CASTLE & GARDENS

MAIDSTONE

www.leeds-castle.com

Map 4

Owner:
Leeds Castle
Foundation

▶ **CONTACT**

Sandra Matthews-Marsh
Leeds Castle
Maidstone
Kent ME17 1PL

Tel: 01622 765400
Fax: 01622 735616

▶ **LOCATION**

OS Ref. TQ835 533

From London to
A20/M20/J8, 40m, 1 hr.
7m E of Maidstone,
¼ m S of A20.

Rail: Combined ticket
available BR train
and admission.
London - Bearsted.

Coach: Nat Express/
Invictaway coach and
admission from Victoria.

Air: Gatwick 45m.
Heathrow 65m.

Channel Tunnel: 25m.

Channel Ports: 38m.

This "loveliest castle in the world", surrounded by 500 acres of magnificent parkland and gardens and set in the middle of a natural lake, is one of the country's finest historic properties. Leeds is also proud to be one of the Treasure Houses of England.

The site of a Saxon royal manor, a Norman fortress and a royal palace to the Kings and Queens of England, the chequered history of Leeds Castle continues well into the 20th century. The last private owner, the Honourable Olive, Lady Baillie, purchased the Castle in 1926. Her inheritance helped to restore the Castle and, prior to her death, she established the Leeds Castle Foundation which now preserves the Castle for the nation, hosts important international conferences and supports the arts.

The Castle has a fine collection of paintings, tapestries and furnishings and is also home to a unique collection of antique dog collars. The Park and Grounds include the colourful and quintessentially English Culpeper Garden, the delightful Wood Garden, and the terraced Lady Baillie Garden with its views over the tranquil Great Water. An Aviary houses rare and endangered species from around the world and, next to the traditional Greenhouses and Vineyard can be found a Maze with its secret underground grotto.

A highly popular and successful programme of Special Events is arranged throughout the year, details of which can be found on the website.

Culpeper Garden

CONFERENCE/FUNCTION

ROOM	SIZE	MAX CAPACITY
Fairfax Hall	19.8 x 1m	200
Gate Tower	9.8 x 5.2m	50
Culpeper	7.65 x 7.34m	40
Terrace	8.9 x 15.4m	80

▶ **OPENING TIMES**

Summer

1 April - 31 October
Daily: 10am - 5pm (last adm).

Winter

Times to be confirmed.

Special private tours for pre-booked groups by appointment.

Castle & Grounds closed 26 Jun & 3 July prior to open air concerts and 6 Nov prior to Grand Firework Spectacular.

▶ **ADMISSION**

Castle, Park & Gardens

15 Mar - 31 Oct
  Adult £12.50
  Child (4 -15yrs) £9.00
  OAP/Student £11.00
  Family (2+3) .... tbc

Group 15+ prices
from 15 Mar - 31 Oct
  Adult £9.00
  Child (4 -15yrs) £6.00
  OAP/Student £8.00

Call for rates for visitors with disabilities or visit our website.

A guidebook is published in English, French, German, Dutch, Spanish, Italian and Japanese.

Residential conferences, exhibitions, sporting days, clay shooting, falconry, field archery, golf, croquet and heli-pad. Talks can be arranged for horticultural, viticultural, historical and cultural groups. No radios.

Corporate hospitality, large scale marquee events, wedding receptions, buffets and dinners.

Land train for elderly/disabled, wheelchairs, wheelchair lift, special rates. WC.

Two restaurants and a tearoom, group lunch menus. Refreshment kiosks.

Guides in rooms. French, Spanish, Dutch, German, Italian and Russian speaking guides.

Free parking.

Welcome, outside normal opening hours, private tours. Teacher's resource pack and worksheets.

Tel for details. €

PENSHURST PLACE & GARDENS

NR TONBRIDGE

www.penshurstplace.com

Map 4

Owner:
Viscount De L'Isle

▶ **CONTACT**
Bonnie Vernon
Penshurst Place
Penshurst
Nr Tonbridge
Kent TN11 8DG

Tel: 01892 870307
Fax: 01892 870866

e-mail: enquiries
@penshurstplace.com

▶ **LOCATION**
OS Ref. TQ527 438

From London M25/J5
then A21 to
Hildenborough,
B2027 via Leigh;
from Tunbridge Wells
A26, B2176.

Visitors entrance at SE
end of village,
S of the church.

Bus: Maidstone &
District 231, 232, 233
from Tunbridge Wells.

Rail: Charing Cross/
Waterloo - Hildenborough,
Tonbridge or Tunbridge
Wells; then taxi.

Penshurst Place is one of England's greatest family-owned stately homes with a history going back six and a half centuries.

In some ways time has stood still at Penshurst; the great House is still very much a medieval building with improvements and additions made over the centuries but without any substantial rebuilding. Its highlight is undoubtedly the medieval Barons' Hall, built in 1341, with its impressive 60ft-high chestnut-beamed roof.

A marvellous mix of paintings, tapestries and furniture from the 15th, 16th and 17th centuries can be seen throughout the House, including the helm carried in the state funeral procession to St Paul's Cathedral for the Elizabethan courtier and poet, Sir Philip Sidney, in 1587. This is now the family crest.

GARDENS

The Gardens, first laid out in the 14th century, have been developed over successive years by the Sidney family who first came to Penshurst in 1552. A twenty-year restoration and re-planting programme undertaken by the late Viscount De L'Isle has ensured that they retain their historic splendour. He is commemorated with a new Arboretum, planted in 1991. The gardens are divided by a mile of yew hedges into "rooms", each planted to give a succession of colour as the seasons change. There is also a Venture Playground, Woodland Trail and Toy Museum together with a Gift Shop and Plant Centre.

A variety of events in the park and grounds take place throughout the season.

Product launches, garden parties, photography, filming, fashion shows, receptions, archery, clay pigeon shooting, falconry, parkland for hire, lectures on property, its contents and history. Conference facilities. Adventure playground & parkland & riverside walks. No photography in house.

Private banqueting, wedding receptions.

Limited, disabled and elderly may alight at entrance. WC.

Licensed tearoom (waitress service can be booked by groups of 20+).

Mornings only by arrangement, lunch/dinner can be arranged. Out of season tours by appointment. Guided tours of the gardens and house.

Ample. Double decker buses to park from village.

All year by appointment, discount rates, education room and packs.

Guide dogs only

  Tel for details.

CONFERENCE/FUNCTION

ROOM	SIZE	MAX CAPACITY
Sunderland Room	45' x 18'	100
Barons' Hall	64' x 39'	250
Buttery	20' x 23'	50

▶ **OPENING TIMES**
Summer
6 - 26 March:
Sats & Suns only.
27 March - 31 October
Daily.

House
Daily, 12 noon - 5.30pm
Last entry 5pm (Sat 4pm).

Grounds
Daily, 10.30am - 6pm.

Shop & Plant Centre
Open all year, 10.30am -
6pm.

Winter
Open to Groups by
appointment only
(see Guided Tours).

▶ **ADMISSION**
House & Gardens
Adult £7.00
Child* £5.00
Conc. £6.50
Family (2+2) £20.00
Groups (20+)
Adult £6.50

Garden only
Adult £5.50
Child* £4.50
Conc. £5.00
Family (2+2) £17.00

Garden Season
Ticket £35.00

House Tours (pre-booked)
Adult £7.50
Child £4.50

Garden Tours (pre-booked)
Adult £8.50
Child £5.00

House & Garden £11.00

* Aged 5-16yrs; under 5s Free.

Map 4

Owner:
John St A Warde Esq

▶ **CONTACT**

Mrs P A White
Administrator
Squerryes Court
Westerham
Kent   TN16 1SJ

Tel: 01959 562345
or 01959 563118

Fax: 01959 565949

e-mail: squerryes.court
@squerryes.co.uk

▶ **LOCATION**
OS Ref. TQ440 535

Off the M25/J6, 6m
E along A25 ¹/₂ m SW
of Westerham

London 1-1¹/₂ hrs.

Rail: Oxted Station 4m.
Sevenoaks 6m.

Air: Gatwick,
30 mins.

SQUERRYES COURT & GARDENS

WESTERHAM

www.squerryes.co.uk

Squerryes Court is a beautiful 17th century manor house which has been the Warde family home since 1731. It is surrounded by 10 acres of attractive and historic gardens which include a lake, restored parterres and an 18th century dovecote. Squerryes is 22 miles from London and easily accessible from the M25. There are lovely views and peaceful surroundings. Visitors from far and wide come to enjoy the atmosphere of a house which is still lived in as a family home.

There is a fine collection of Old Master paintings from the Italian, 17th century Dutch and 18th century English schools, furniture, porcelain and tapestries all acquired or commissioned by the family in the 18th century. General Wolfe of Quebec was a friend of the family and there are items connected with him in the Wolfe Room.

GARDENS

These were laid out in the formal style but were re-landscaped in the mid 18th century. Some of the original features in the 1719 Badeslade print survive. The family have restored the formal garden using this print as a guide. The garden is lovely all year round with bulbs, wild flowers and woodland walks, azaleas, summer flowering herbaceous borders and roses.

© Clive Boursnell

▶ **OPENING TIMES**

Summer
1 April - 30 September
Wed, Thu, Sun &
BH Mons.

Grounds:
12 noon - 5.30pm
House: 1.30 - 5.30pm
Last admission 5pm.

NB. Pre-booked groups welcome any day during season (except Sat).

Winter
October - 31 March
Closed.

▶ **ADMISSION**

House & Garden
Adult £5.00
Child (under 14yrs)... £2.70
Senior £4.40
Family (2+2).......... £12.50
Groups (20+)
Adult £4.30
Child (under 14yrs)... £2.70
Senior £4.30

Garden only
Adult £3.40
Child (under 14yrs)... £1.70
Senior £2.90
Family (2+2)........... £7.50
Groups (20+, booked)
Adult £2.90
Child (under 14yrs)... £1.70

CONFERENCE/FUNCTION		
ROOM	SIZE	MAX CAPACITY
Hall	32' x 32'	60
Old Library	20' x 25' 6"	40

Small. **i** Suitable for conferences, product launches, filming, photography, outside events, garden parties. No photography in house. Picnics permitted in grounds.

Exclusive entertaining & wedding receptions (marquee).

Limited access in house and garden, please telephone before visiting.

Teas and light refreshments on open days. Groups must book for lunch or tea. Menus upon request.

For pre-booked groups (max 55), small additional charge. Owner will meet groups by prior arrangement. Tour time 1 hr.

P Limited for coaches. Free teas for drivers and couriers.

Welcome, cost £1.50 per child, guide provided. Areas of interest: nature walk, ducks and geese.

On leads, in grounds.

BEDGEBURY NATIONAL PINETUM
Goudhurst, Cranbrook, Kent TN17 2SL
Tel: 01580 211781 **Fax:** 01580 212423
Owner: Forestry Commission   **Contact:** Mrs Elspeth Hill
Location: OS Ref. TQ714 337 (gate on B2079). 7m E of Tunbridge Wells on A21, turn N on B2079 for 1m.
Open: All year: daily, 10am - 5pm.
Admission: Adult £3.50, Child £1.20, OAP £3, Family £9.

BOUGHTON MONCHELSEA PLACE
See page 117 for full page entry.

BELMONT
BELMONT PARK, THROWLEY, FAVERSHAM ME13 0HH
www.belmont-house.org

Tel: 01795 890202 **Fax:** 01795 890042 **e-mail:** belmontadmin@btconnect.com
Owner: Harris (Belmont) Charity   **Contact:** Mr J R Farmer
Belmont is a charming late 18th century country mansion by Samuel Wyatt, set in delightful grounds, including a restored 2 acre kitchen garden and a greenhouse. The seat of the Harris family since 1801 it is beautifully furnished and contains interesting items from India and Trinidad as well as the unique clock collection formed by the 5th Lord.
Location: OS Ref. TQ986 564. 4¹/₂ m SSW of Faversham, off A251.
Open: 1 Apr - 30 Sept: Sats, Suns & BH Mons, 2 - 5pm. Last admission to house 4.15pm. Gardens: Sat - Thurs, 10am - 6pm. Groups (15+): Mon - Thurs, by appointment.
Admission: House & Garden: Adult £5.25, Child £2.50, Conc. £4.75. Groups (15+): Adult £4.75, Child £2.50. Garden: Adult £2.75, Child £1.
ℹ️ No photography in house. 🅾️ Partial. WC. Obligatory. 🅿️ On leads only.

CANTERBURY CATHEDRAL
See page 118 for full page entry.

CHART GUNPOWDER MILLS
Chart Mills, Faversham, Kent
Tel: 01795 534542 **e-mail:** faversham@btinternet.com
Owner: Swale Borough Council   **Contact:** John Breeze
Oldest gunpowder mill in the world. Supplied gunpowder to Nelson for the Battle of Trafalgar, and Wellington at Waterloo.
Location: OS Ref. TQ615 015. M2/J6. W of town centre, access from Stonebridge Way, off West Street.
Open: Apr - Oct: Sat, Sun & BHs, 2 - 5pm, or by arrangement.
Admission: Free.

CHARTWELL ✗
See page 119 for full page entry.

CHIDDINGSTONE CASTLE
See pages 120/121 for double page entry.

COBHAM HALL
See page 122 for full page entry.

DEAL CASTLE ⌗
VICTORIA ROAD, DEAL, KENT CT14 7BA
www.english-heritage.org.uk/visits

Tel: 01304 372762 **Venue hire and Hospitality:** 01304 211067
Owner: English Heritage   **Contact:** The Custodian
Crouching low and menacing, the huge, rounded bastions of this austere fort, built by Henry VIII, once carried 119 guns. A fascinating castle to explore, with long, dark passages, battlements and a huge basement. The interactive displays and exhibition give a fascinating insight into the Castle's history.
Location: OS Ref. TR378 521. SE of Deal town centre.
Open: 1 Apr - 30 Sept: daily, 10am - 6pm. 1 - 31 Oct: 10am - 5pm. 1 Nov - 31 Mar: Wed - Sun only, 10am - 4pm. Closed 24 - 26 Dec & 1 Jan. Times subject to change April 2004.
Admission: Adult £3.50, Child £1.80, Conc. £2.60. Prices subject to change April 2004.
ℹ️ WCs. 🅾️ Exclusive private & corporate hospitality. Restricted. 🅿️ Coach parking on main road. Guide dogs only. Tel for details.

DICKENS CENTRE - EASTGATE HOUSE
High Street, Rochester, Medway ME1 1EW
Tel: 01634 844176 **Fax:** 01634 844676 **e-mail:** Charlesdickenscentre@medway.gov.uk
Owner: Medway Council   **Contact:** Head Custodian
Much altered late 16th century brick house, now containing the Dickens Centre, with exhibits of his life and works, including his best known characters. At the rear is Dickens' prefabricated chalet, brought from Switzerland.
Location: OS Ref. TQ746 683. N side of Rochester High Street, close to the Eastern Road. 400yds SE of the Cathedral.
Open: 1 Apr - 30 Sept:, 10am - 5.30pm (last admission 4.45pm, Groups 3.30pm). 1 Oct - 31 Mar: 10am - 4pm (last admission 3.15pm, Groups 2pm). Groups please book in advance.
Admission: Adult £3.90, Conc £2.80, Family (2+2 or 1+3) £10.50. Groups (20+): Adult £3.30, Junior/School Parties (1 supervising adult Free per 10 children for educational visits) £2.20, OAP (60yrs+) £2.70. Prices valid until 31 Mar 2004.

DODDINGTON PLACE GARDENS 🏠
Doddington, Sittingbourne, Kent ME9 0BB
Tel: 01795 886101
Owner: Mr & Mrs Richard Oldfield   **Contact:** Mrs Richard Oldfield
10 acres of landscaped gardens in an area of outstanding natural beauty.
Location: OS Ref. TQ944 575. 4m N from A20 at Lenham or 5m SW from A2 at Ospringe, W of Faversham.
Open: Easter Day - June: Suns & BH Mons, also 1, 29/30 Aug & 19 Sept: 2 - 6pm. Groups at other times by appointment. Coaches by appointment.
Admission: Adult £3.50, Child 75p. Discount for groups.

DOVER CASTLE ⬦
and the Secret Wartime Tunnels

See page 123 for full page entry.

DOWN HOUSE ⬦

See page 124 for full page entry.

DYMCHURCH MARTELLO TOWER ⬦
Dymchurch, Kent
Tel: 01304 211067   **www.**english-heritage.org.uk/visits
Owner: English Heritage   **Contact:** Dover Castle Site Manager
Built as one of 74 such towers to counter the threat of invasion by Napoleon, Dymchurch is perhaps the best example in the country. Fully restored. You can climb to the roof which is dominated by an original 24-pounder gun complete with traversing carriage.
Location: OS189, Ref. TR102 294. In Dymchurch, access from High Street.
Open: Please telephone 01304 211067 for details. Times subject to change April 2004.
Admission: Adult £1.50, Child 80p, Conc. £1.10. Prices subject to change April 2004.
▣

EASTBRIDGE HOSPITAL OF ST THOMAS
High Street, Canterbury, Kent CT1 2BD
Tel: 01227 471688   **Fax:** 01227 781641   **e-mail:** eastbridge@freeuk.com
www.eastbridgehospital.co.uk   **Contact:** The Warden
Medieval pilgrims' hospital with 12th century undercroft, refectory and chapel.
Location: OS189, Ref. TR148 579. S side of Canterbury High Street.
Open: All year: (except Good Fri, Christmas Day & 29 Dec) Mon - Sat, 10am - 4.45pm. Includes Greyfriars Franciscan Chapel, House & Garden. Easter Mon - 27 Sept: Mon - Sat, 2 - 4pm.
Admission: Adult £1, Child 50p, Conc. 75p.

Chiddingstone, Kent from the book
Historic Family Homes and Gardens from the Air, see page 54.

EMMETTS GARDEN ❧
IDE HILL, SEVENOAKS, KENT TN14 6AY

www.nationaltrust.org.uk/places/emmetts

Tel: 01732 750367/868381 (Chartwell office)   **Info:** 01732 751509
e-mail: emmetts@nationaltrust.org.uk
Owner: The National Trust   **Contact:** The Property Manager
       (Chartwell & Emmetts Garden, Mapleton Road, Westerham, Kent TN16 1PS)
Influenced by William Robinson, this charming and informal garden was laid out in the late 19th century, with many exotic and rare trees and shrubs from across the world. Wonderful views across the Weald of Kent – with the highest treetop in Kent. There are glorious shows of daffodils, bluebells, azaleas and rhododendrons, then

acers and cornus in autumn, also a rose garden and rock garden.
Location: OS Ref. TQ477 524. 1¹/2 m N of Ide Hill off B2042. M25/J5, then 4m.
Open: 20 Mar - 27 Jun: Wed - Sun, 11am - 5pm; 30 Jun - 31 Oct: Wed, Sat & Sun, 11am - 5pm. Last admission 4.15pm. Open BH Mons.
Admission: Adult £4, Child £1, Family £9, Group £3.50.
▣ ♿ Steep in places. WC. Buggy from car park to garden entrance.
▣ ⬛ In grounds, on leads. ▣ Tel for details.

FINCHCOCKS
FINCHCOCKS, GOUDHURST, KENT TN17 1HH

www.finchcocks.co.uk

Tel: 01580 211702 **Fax:** 01580 211007 **e-mail:** katrina@finchcocks.co.uk

Owner: Mr Richard Burnett   **Contact:** Mrs Katrina Burnett

In 1970 Finchcocks was acquired by Richard Burnett, leading exponent of the early piano, and it now contains his magnificent collection of some eighty historical keyboard instruments: chamber organs, harpsichords, virginals, spinets and early pianos. About half of these are restored to full concert condition and are played whenever the house is open to the public. The house, with its high ceilings and oak panelling, provides the perfect setting for music performed on period instruments, and Finchcocks is now a music centre of international repute. Many musical events take place here.

There is a fascinating collection of pictures and prints, mainly on musical themes, and a special exhibition on the theme of the 18th century pleasure gardens, which includes costumes and tableaux.

Finchcocks is a fine Georgian baroque manor noted for its outstanding brickwork, with a dramatic front elevation attributed to Thomas Archer. The present house was built in 1725 for barrister Edward Bathurst. Despite having changed hands many times, it has undergone remarkably little alteration and retains most of its original features. The beautiful grounds, with their extensive views over parkland and hop gardens, include the newly restored walled garden, which provides a dramatic setting for special events.

Location: 1m S of A262, 2m W of Goudhurst. 5m from Cranbrook, 10m from Tunbridge Wells, 45m from London (1½ hrs). Rail: Marden 6m (no taxi), Paddock Wood 8m (taxi), Tunbridge Wells 10m (taxi).

Open: Easter Sun - end Sept: Sun & BH Mons, plus Wed & Thurs in Aug, 2 - 6pm. Groups & indivduals: Mid Mar - end Oct & Dec at other times by arrangement. Closed Nov, Jan - early Mar).

Admission: Adult £7.50, Child £4, Student £5. Garden only: Adult £2.50, Child 50p. Group (25+): Charge dependent on numbers and programme.

Music events, conferences, seminars, promotions, archery, ballooning, filming, television. Instruments for hire. No videos in house, photography by permission only. Private and corporate entertaining, weddings. Limited. WC. Suitable for visually handicapped. Licensed. Picnics permitted in grounds. Musical tours/recitals. Tour time: 2½ - 4 hrs. Pre-booked groups (25 - 100) welcome from Apr - Oct. Opportunity to play instruments. Can be linked to special projects and National Curriculum syllabus. Music a speciality.

GOODNESTONE PARK GARDENS

Goodnestone Park, Nr Wingham, Canterbury, Kent CT3 1PL

Tel/Fax: 01304 840107 **e-mail:** enquiries@goodnestoneparkgardens.co.uk

www.goodnestoneparkgardens.co.uk

Owner: The Lord & Lady FitzWalter   **Contact:** Lady FitzWalter

The garden is approximately 14 acres, set in 18th century parkland. There are many fine trees, a woodland area and a large walled garden with a collection of old-fashioned roses, clematis and herbaceous plants. Jane Austen was a frequent visitor, her brother Edward having married a daughter of the house.

Location: OS Ref. TR254 544. 8m ESE of Canterbury, 1½ m E of B2046, at S end of village. The B2046 runs from the A2 to Wingham, the gardens are signposted from this road.

Open: 22 Mar - 1 Oct: Weekdays (except Tue & Sat), 11am - 5pm. 28 Mar - 26 Sept: Suns, 12 noon - 6pm.

Admission: Adult £3.30, Child (under 12yrs) 50p, OAP £2.80, Student £1.50, Family (2+2) £5. Wheelchair users £1. Groups (20+): Adult £3. Guided garden tours: £5.50.

GREAT COMP GARDEN
COMP LANE, PLATT, BOROUGH GREEN, KENT TN15 8QS

www.greatcomp.co.uk

Tel: 01732 886154

Owner: R Cameron Esq   **Contact:** Mr W Dyson

One of the finest gardens in the country, comprising ruins, terraces, tranquil woodland walks and sweeping lawns with a breathtaking collection of trees, shrubs, heathers and perennials, many rarely seen elsewhere. The truly unique atmosphere of Great Comp is further complemented by its Festival of Chamber Music held in July/September.

Location: OS Ref. TQ635 567. 2m E of Borough Green, B2016 off A20. First right at Comp crossroads. ½ m on left.

Open: 1 Apr - 31 Oct: daily, 11am - 5.30pm.

Admission: Adult £4, Child £1. Groups (20+) £3.50, Annual ticket: Adult £12, OAP £8.

Teas daily. Guide dogs only.

Special Events Index see front section

CHA

GREAT MAYTHAM HALL

ROLVENDEN, CRANBROOK, KENT TN17 4NE

www.cha.org.uk

Tel: 01580 241346 **Fax:** 01580 241038

Managed by: Country Houses Association   **Contact:** The Administrators

Built in 1910 by Lutyens and set in 18 acres, the house has some fine features including an arched clock-house that frames the entrance. The walled garden inspired Frances Hodgson Burnett to write her children's classic 'The Secret Garden'. The house has been converted into apartments for active retired people.

Location: OS Ref. TQ848 306. 1/2 m S of Rolvenden village, on road to Rolvenden Layne. Stations: Headcorn 10m, Staplehurst 10m.

Open: 1 May - 30 Sept: Wed & Thur, 2 - 5pm.

Admission: Adult £4 Child £2. Garden only: Adult £2, Child £1. Groups by arrangement.

⊤ ✕ 🖼 2 twin w/bath, 1 single, w/bath. CHA members/Wolsey Lodge guests only.
▲

GROOMBRIDGE 🏠
PLACE GARDENS
See page 125 for full page entry.

HEVER CASTLE & GARDENS 🏠   *See page 126 for full page entry.*

THE HISTORIC DOCKYARD CHATHAM

Chatham, Kent   ME4 4TZ

Infoline: 01634 823807   **Admin:** 01634 823800   **Fax:** 01634 823801

e-mail: info@chdt.org.uk

Owner/Contact: Chatham Historic Dockyard Trust

An 80 acre site, in which the visitor can journey through 400 years of the history of Chatham and the Royal Navy, from its origins in the reign of Henry VII to the Falklands Crisis.

Location: OS Ref. TQ759 690. An hour's drive from London, Dover and the Channel Tunnel, and a short distance from M25. Signposted from M2/J1,3&4. From M2/J1&4 follow A289 to the Medway Tunnel, at the tunnel follow signs to Chatham and the brown tourist signs. From M2/J3 follow the signs to Chatham, A229 then A230 and A231 and the brown tourist signs. Brown Anchor signs lead to the Visitor Entrance.

Open: 14 Feb - 31 Oct: daily, 10am - 6pm (dusk if earlier). Last entry: 14 Feb - 27 Mar, 3pm; 28 Mar - 31 Oct, 4pm.

Admission: Adult £9.50, Child (5-15yrs) £6, Conc £7. Family (2+2) £25, Additional Family Child £3.

HALL PLACE & GARDENS

BOURNE ROAD, BEXLEY, KENT DA5 1PQ

www.hallplaceandgardens.com

Tel: 01322 526574   **Fax:** 01322 522921   **e-mail:** martin@hallplaceandgardens.com

Managed by: Bexley Heritage Trust   **Contact:** Mr Martin Purslow

A fine Grade I listed country house built c1537 for Lord Mayor of London, Sir John Champneys. The house stands at the centre of award winning gardens with magnificent topiary, a herb garden, a secret garden, Italianate garden and inspirational herbaceous borders on the banks of the River Cray at Bexley. In its former walled gardens is a plant nursery and sub-tropical plant house where you can see ripening bananas in mid-winter. The house boasts a panelled Tudor Great Hall and minstrels' gallery and many period rooms including a vaulted long gallery and splendid drawing room with a fine 17th century plaster ceiling. There is a shop and numerous exhibitions, including an opportunity to purchase artists' work throughout the year.

Various rooms including the Great Hall are available to hire for weddings and other events. Its close proximity to London makes it an ideal location for photographic, film and television use. Extensive Education & Outreach Service available.

Location: OS Ref. TQ502 743. On the A2 less than 5m from the M25/J2 (London bound).

Open: 1 Apr - 31 Oct: Mon - Sat, 10am - 5pm; Sun & BHs, 11am - 5pm. 1 Nov - 31 Mar: 10am - 4.15pm. Closed Sun & Mon,

Admission: Free. Pre-arranged tours (10+): Adult £3, Child (5 - 15yrs) £1.50.

🖾 🕸 ⊤ ♿House, lift & WC. ■ 🍴Licensed. 🅵By arrangement.
🅿 ▣ 🐕Guide dogs only. ▲ ✳ 🖵Tel for details.

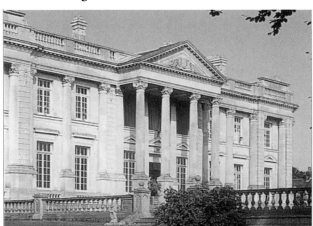

HIGHAM PARK, HOUSE & GARDENS

BRIDGE, NR CANTERBURY, KENT CT4 5BE

www.higham-park.co.uk

Tel/Fax: 01227 830830   **e-mail:** highampark@aol.com

Owner: Patricia P Gibb   **Contact:** Amanda Harris-Deans

"The Haunt of Ancient Peace" quotes Harold Peto in creating England's finest Italianate Gardens. Here two ladies' incredible DIY restoration of 24 acres and an 87 roomed Palladian Stately Home. Historical interest from 1320 Norman knights to Count Zborowski, creator of 1920s monster racing cars 'Chitty Bang Bangs' (inspiring Bond creator Fleming), Jane Austen and Dickens. Stunning Templed, Secret and Rose gardens. Colours and scents from spring to autumn; constantly changing borders. Contrast with unconquered yet charming Culpeper Walled Gardens. Home made teas.

Location: 3m S of Canterbury off the A2 at Bridge, entrance top of Bridge Hill. Rail: Victoria/Canterbury. Bus: Canterbury No.17.

Open: 21 Mar - end Sep: Sun - Thur. Gardens: 11am - 5pm. House Tours:12.30 & 2.30pm.

Admission: Garden: Adult £3.50, Child £1.50, Conc £3. House Tour: £2.50.
⬛ ⬛Home made teas. ⬛ ⬛ P ⬛ ⬛Tel for details.

IGHTHAM MOTE ⬛   *See page 127 for full page entry.*

KNOLE ⬛

Sevenoaks, Kent TN15 0RP

Tel: 01732 462100

Owner: The National Trust   **Contact:** The Property Manager

One of the great 'treasure houses' of England, home of the Sackville family since 1603. The largest private house in England.

Location: OS Ref. TQ532 543. M25/J5. 25m SE of London. S end of High St.

Open: House: 27 Mar - 31 Oct: Wed - Sun & BH Mons, 11am- 4pm. Garden: May - Sept: 1st Wed of month, 11am- 4pm. Last adm. 3pm. Shop/Tearoom: As house: 10.30am - 5pm. Christmas Shop: 3 Nov - 19 Dec, Wed - Sun, 11am - 4pm.

Admission: House: £6, Groups (15+): £5. Garden: £2.

LEEDS CASTLE & GARDENS   *See page 128 for full page entry.*

LESNES ABBEY

Abbey Road, Abbey Wood, London DA17 5DL

Tel: 01322 526574

Owner: Bexley Council   **Contact:** Mr Martin Purslow

The Abbey was founded in 1178 by Richard de Lucy as penance for his involvement in events leading to the murder of Thomas à Becket. Today only the ruins remain.

Location: OS Ref. TQ479 788. In public park on S side of Abbey Road (B213), 500yds E of Abbey Wood Station, ³/4 m N of A206 Woolwich - Erith Road.

Open: Any reasonable time.

Admission: Free.

LULLINGSTONE CASTLE ⬛

Lullingstone Castle, Eynsford, Kent DA4 0JA

Tel: 01322 862114   **Fax:** 01322 862115   **Owner/Contact:** Guy Hart Dyke Esq

Fine state rooms, family portraits and armour in beautiful grounds. The 15th century gatehouse was one of the first ever to be made of bricks.

Location: OS Ref. TQ530 644. 1m S Eynsford W side of A225. 600yds S of Roman Villa.

Open: May - Aug: Sats, Suns & BHs, 2 - 6pm. Booked groups by arrangement.

Admission: Adult £5, Child £2, Conc. £4, Family £10. Groups (25+) 10% discount.

ⓘNo interior photography. ⬛ ⬛Partial. ⬛Teas at visitor centre, 1km. ⬛By arrangement. P Limited. ⬛

HOLE PARK ⬛

ROLVENDEN, CRANBROOK, KENT TN17 4JB

Tel: 01580 241344/241386   **Fax:** 01580 241882

e-mail: barham@holepark.fsnet.co.uk

Owner/Contact: Edward Barham

A 15 acre garden with all year round interest, set in beautiful parkland with fine views. Trees, lawns and extensive yew hedges precisely cut are a feature. Walled garden with mixed borders, pools and water garden. Natural garden with bulbs, azaleas, rhododendrons and flowering shrubs. Bluebell walk and autumn colours a speciality.

Location: OS Ref. TQ830 325. 1m W of Rolvenden on B2086 Cranbrook road.

Open: 21 Mar - 30 Oct: Wed & Thur; 21 Mar, 25 Apr, 2 May (Bluebell weekend); 16 May (Rhododendron Sunday); 23 May, 13, 27 Jun, 4 Jul (Hardy Plant Society Fair); 17, 24 Oct: 2 - 6pm. Teas and plant stall on all Sun openings.

Admission: Adult £3.50, Child 50p. Groups welcome by appointment. Owner guided tours a speciality.

⬛Suns. ⬛ ⬛Groups and Sun only. ⬛By arrangement. P ⬛Car park only.

English Heritage Photo Library

LULLINGSTONE ROMAN VILLA ⬛

LULLINGSTONE LANE, EYNSFORD, KENT DA4 0JA

www.english-heritage.org.uk/visits

Tel: 01322 863467

Owner: English Heritage   **Contact:** The Custodian

Recognised as one of the most exciting archaeological finds of the century, the villa has splendid mosaic floors and one of the earliest private Christian chapels. Take the free audio tour and discover how the prosperous Romans lived, worked and entertained themselves.

Location: OS Ref. TQ529 651. ¹/2 m SW of Eynsford off A225, M25/J3. Follow A20 towards Brands Hatch. 600yds N of Castle.

Open: 1 Apr - 30 Sept: daily, 10am - 6pm. 1 - 31 Oct: 10am - 5pm. 1 Nov - 31 Mar: 10am - 4pm. Closed 24 - 26 Dec & 1 Jan. Times subject to change April 2004.

Admission: Adult £3, Child £1.50, Conc. £2.30. Prices subject to change April 2004.

⬛ ⬛Ground floor & grounds. WC. ⬛ ⬛ ⬛ ⬛Tel for details.

MAISON DIEU ⊞
Ospringe, Faversham, Kent
Tel: 01795 534542 **www.**english-heritage.org.uk/visits
Owner: English Heritage **Contact:** The Faversham Society
This forerunner of today's hospitals remains largely as it was in the 16th century with exposed beams and an overhanging upper storey.
Location: OS Ref. TR002 608. In Ospringe on A2, ¹/₂ m W of Faversham.
Open: 18 Apr - 26 Oct: Weekends & BHs, 2 - 5pm. Keykeeper in Winter. Times subject to change April 2004.
Admission: Adult £1, Child 50p, OAP 80p. Prices subject to change April 2004.
ℹ️WCs. 🐕 ❄️

MILTON CHANTRY ⊞
New Tavern Fort Gardens, Gravesend, Kent
Tel: 01474 321520 **www.**english-heritage.org.uk/visits
Owner: English Heritage **Contact:** Gravesend Borough Council
A small 14th century building which housed the chapel of the leper hospital and the chantry of the de Valence and Montechais families and later became a tavern.
Location: OS Ref.TQ652 743. In New Tavern Fort Gardens ¹/₄ m E of Gravesend off A226.
Open: 1 Apr - 30 Sept: Wed - Sat, 12 noon - 5pm; Sun & BH Mons, 10am - 5pm. 1 Oct - 23 Dec & 1 - 31 Mar: Sats, 12 noon - 4pm & Suns 10am - 4pm. Closed Jan & Feb. Times subject to change April 2004.
Admission: Adult £1, Child/Conc. 50p. Prices subject to change April 2004.
🐕

MOUNT EPHRAIM GARDENS 🏛
Hernhill, Faversham, Kent ME13 9TX
Tel: 01227 751496 **Fax:** 01227 750940
Owner: Mr & Mrs E S Dawes & Mrs M N Dawes **Contact:** Mrs L Dawes
8 acres of superb gardens set in the heart of family run orchards.
Location: OS Ref.TR065 598. In Hernhill village, 1m from end of M2. Signed from A2 & A299.
Open: Easter - end Sept: Weds, Thurs, Sats, Suns & BH Mons only, 1 - 6pm. Groups Mar - end Oct, by arrangement.
Admission: Adult £3.50, Child £1. Groups: £3.

NURSTEAD COURT
Nurstead Church Lane, Meopham, Nr Gravesend, Kent DA13 9AD
Tel: 01474 812368 (guided tours); 01474 812121 (weddings & functions)
Fax: 01474 815133 **e-mail:** info@nursteadcourt.co.uk **www.**nursteadcourt.co.uk
Owner/Contact: Mrs S Edmeades-Stearns
Nurstead Court is a Grade I listed manor house built in 1320 of timber-framed, crown-posted construction, set in extensive gardens and parkland. The additional front part of the house was built in 1825. Licensed weddings are now held in the house with receptions and other functions in the garden marquee.
Location: OS Ref. TQ642 685. Nurstead Church Lane is just off the A277 N of Meopham, 3m from Gravesend.
Open: Sep - 2 Oct: Wed & Thur, 2pm - 5pm. Open all the year round by arrangement.
Admission: Adult £5, Child £2.50, OAP/Student £4. Group (max 54): £4.
ℹ️Open by arrangement for guided tours. Weddings & functions also catered for. 🍽️ Licensed. 🎦By arrangement. 🅿️Limited for coaches. 🐕On leads, in grounds. 🛏3 doubles (2 ensuite). ♿ ❄️

OLD SOAR MANOR 🌿
Plaxtol, Borough Green, Kent TN15 0QX
Tel: 01732 810378 **Info Line:** 01732 811145
Owner: The National Trust **Contact:** The Property Manager
Location: OS Ref.TQ619 541. Plaxtol, Borough Green, Kent.
Open: 3 Apr - 30 Sept: daily except Fri, including BHs & Good Fri, 10am - 6pm.
Admission: Free.

Education Index see front section

OWL HOUSE GARDENS
LAMBERHURST, KENT TN3 8LY

Tel: 01892 890230 **Fax:** 01892 891222 **Contact:** Angela Kelso
The Owl House is a small timber-framed cottage, a former haunt of wool smugglers (not open to the public). Surrounding it are 13 acres of gardens, with spring flowers, azaleas, rhododendrons, roses, shrubs and ornamental fruit trees. The sweeping lawns lead to lovely woodlands of oak, elm and beech and sunken water gardens. Woodland walks.
Location: OS Ref. TQ665 372. 8m SE of Tunbridge Wells; 1m from Lamberhurst off A21.
Open: Gardens only: All year, daily, 11am - 6pm, except 25 Dec & 1 Jan.
Admission: Adult £4, Child £1. Coach parties welcome.
🖼 🚻 ♿ 🍽 🅿️Free. 🐕On leads. ❄️

PENSHURST PLACE & GARDENS
See page 129 for full page entry.

QUEBEC HOUSE 🌿
Westerham, Kent TN16 1TD
Tel: 01732 868381 (Chartwell Office)
Owner: The National Trust **Contact:** Chartwell Office
General Wolfe spent his early years in this gabled, red-brick 17th century house. Four rooms containing portraits, prints and memorabilia relating to Wolfe's family and career are on view. In the Tudor stable block is an exhibition about the Battle of Quebec (1759) and the parts played by Wolfe and his adversary, the Marquis de Montcalm.
Location: OS Ref. TQ449 541. At E end of village, on N side of A25, facing junction with B2026, Edenbridge Road.
Open: 4 Apr - 31 Oct: Sun & Tue, 2 - 5.30pm.
Admission: Adult £3, Child £1.50, Family (2+3) £7.50. Groups £2.50.

QUEX HOUSE & GARDEN & POWELL COTTON MUSEUM
Quex Park, Birchington, Kent CT7 0BH
Tel: 01843 842168 **e-mail:** powell-cotton-museum@virgin.net
Owner: Trustees of Powell Cotton Museum **Contact:** John Harrison
Regency/Victorian country residence, walled gardens and Victorian explorers' museum.
Location: OS Ref. TR308 683. ¹/₂ m from Birchington Church via Park Lane.
Open: Please contact Museum for details.
Admission: Summer: Adult £4, Child, OAP, Disabled & Carer £3, Student £2.50, Family (2+3) £12. Winter: Adult £3, Child, OAP, Disabled & Carer £2.50, Family (2+3) £8. (2003 prices.)

RECULVER TOWERS & ROMAN FORT ⊞
Reculver, Herne Bay, Kent
Tel: 01227 740676 **www.**english-heritage.org.uk/visits
Owner: English Heritage **Contact:** Reculver Country Park
This 12th century landmark of twin towers has guided sailors into the Thames estuary for seven centuries. Includes walls of a Roman fort, which were erected nearly 2,000 years ago.
Location: OS Ref. TR228 694. At Reculver 3m E of Herne Bay by the seashore.
Open: Any reasonable time. External viewing only.
Admission: Free.
ℹ️WCs. ♿Ground floor only. Long slope up from car park. 🅿️ 🐕Dogs on leads.

David Winston, Period Piano Company

RESTORATION HOUSE 🏠
17 – 19 CROW LANE, ROCHESTER, KENT ME1 1RF

www.restorationhouse.co.uk

Tel: 01634 848520 **Fax:** 01634 880058

Owner: R Tucker & J Wilmot   **Contact:** Robert Tucker

Unique survival of an ancient city mansion deriving its name from the stay of Charles II on the eve of The Restoration. Beautiful interiors with exceptional early paintwork related to decorative scheme 'run up' for Charles' visit. The house also inspired Dickens to situate 'Miss Havisham' here.

'Interiors of rare historical resonance and poetry', *Country Life*. Fine English furniture and pictures (Mytens, Kneller, Dahl, Reynolds and several Gainsboroughs). Charming interlinked walled gardens of ingenious plan in a classic English style. A private gem. 'There is no finer pre-Civil war town house in England than this' – Simon Jenkins, *The Times*.

Location: OS Ref, TQ744 683. Historic centre of Rochester, off High Street, opposite the Vines Park.

Open: 3 Jun - 1 Oct: Thurs & Fris also Sat 5 June, 10am - 5pm.

Admission: Adult £5.50 (includes 24 page illustrated guidebook), Child £2.75, Conc £4.50. Booked group (8+) tours: £6.50pp.

ℹ️ No stiletto heels. No photography in house. ♿Unsuitable. 🎭By arrangement. 🅿️None. 🐕Guide dogs only.

RICHBOROUGH ROMAN FORT ♯
Richborough, Sandwich, Kent CT13 9JW
Tel: 01304 612013 www.english-heritage.org.uk/visits
Owner: English Heritage   **Contact:** The Custodian
This fort and township date back to the Roman landing in AD43. The fortified walls and the massive foundations of a triumphal arch which stood 80 feet high still survive. The inclusive audio tour and the museum give an insight into life in Richborough's heyday as a busy township.
Location: OS Ref. TR324 602. 1¹/₂ m NW of Sandwich off A257.
Open: 1 Apr - 30 Sept: daily, 10am - 6pm. 1 - 31 Oct: daily, 10am - 5pm. 1 Nov - 28 Feb: Sat & Sun, 10am - 4pm; 1 - 31 Mar: Wed - Sun, 10am - 4pm. Closed 24 - 26 Dec & 1 Jan. Times subject to change April 2004.
Admission: Gardens: Adult £3, Child £1.50, Conc. £2.30. Prices subject to change April 2004.
ℹ️Museum. 🔲 ♿Ground floor. 🔲 🅿️ 🐕Guide dogs only. ❋ 🚻Tel for details.

RIVERHILL HOUSE 🏠
Sevenoaks, Kent TN15 0RR
Tel: 01732 458802/452557 **Fax:** 01732 458802
Owner: The Rogers Family   **Contact:** Mrs Rogers
Small country house built in 1714.
Location: OS Ref. TQ541 522. 2m S of Sevenoaks on E side of A225.
Open: Garden: 31 Mar - 13 June: Wed, Sun & BH weekends, 12 noon - 6pm. House: open only to pre-booked groups of adults (20+) on any day: Apr, May & Jun.
Admission: Adult £3, Child 50p. Pre-booked groups: £4.50.

ROCHESTER CASTLE ♯
The Lodge, Rochester-upon-Medway, Medway ME1 1SX
Tel: 01634 402276
Owner: English Heritage (Managed by Medway Council) **Contact:** Head Custodian
Built in the 11th century. The keep is over 100 feet high and with walls 12 feet thick.
Location: OS Ref. TQ743 685. By Rochester Bridge. Follow A2 eastwards from M2/J1 & M25/J2.
Open: 1 Apr - 30 Sept: daily, 10am - 6pm. 1 - 31 Mar: daily, 10am - 4pm. Closed 24 - 26 Dec & 1 Jan. Times subject to change April 2004.
Admission: Please telephone for details. Prices subject to change April 2004.
ℹ️WCs. 🔲 🔲 🐕

ROCHESTER CATHEDRAL
Garth House, The Precinct, Rochester, Kent ME1 1SX
Tel: 01634 401301 **Fax:** 01634 401410
e-mail: rochester_cathedral@yahoo.co.uk
Rochester Cathedral has been a place of Christian worship since its foundation in 604AD. It celebrates its 1400th anniversary in 2004. The present building is a blend of Norman and gothic architecture with a fine crypt and Romanesque façade. The first real fresco in an English Cathedral for 800 years is due for completion at the end of 2003.
Location: OS Ref. TQ742 686. Signposted from M20/J6 and on the A2/M2/J3. Best access from M2/J3.
Open: All year: 8.30am - 5pm. Visiting may be restricted during services.
Admission: Suggested donation. Adult £3. Guided groups: £3, please book on above number. Separate prices for schools.
ℹ️Photography permit £1. 🔲 ♿ 🚻 🎭By arrangement. 🅿️ 🔲 🐕 ❋

ROMAN PAINTED HOUSE
New Street, Dover, Kent CT17 9AJ
Tel: 01304 203279
Owner: Dover Roman Painted House Trust   **Contact:** Mr B Philp
Discovered in 1970. Built around 200AD as a hotel for official travellers. Impressive wall paintings, central heating systems and the Roman fort wall built through the house.
Location: OS Ref. TR318 414. Dover town centre. E of York St.
Open: Apr - Sept: 10am - 5pm, except Mons.
Admission: Adult £2, Child/OAP 80p.

ST AUGUSTINE'S ABBEY ♯
Longport, Canterbury, Kent CT1 1TF
Tel: 01227 767345 www.english-heritage.org.uk/visits
Owner: English Heritage   **Contact:** The Custodian
The Abbey, founded by St Augustine in 598, is a World Heritage Site. Take the free interactive audio tour which gives a fascinating insight into the Abbey's history and visit the museum displaying artifacts uncovered during archaeological excavations of the site.
Location: OS Ref. TR154 578. In Canterbury ¹/₂ m E of Cathedral Close.
Open: 1 Apr - 30 Sept: daily, 10am - 6pm. 1 - 31 Oct: 10am - 5pm. 1 Nov - 31 Mar: daily, 10am - 4pm. Closed 24 - 26 Dec & 1 Jan. Times subject to change April 2004.
Admission: Adult £3, Child £1.50, Conc. £2.30. 15% discount for groups (11+). One extra place for every additional 20. Prices subject to change April 2004.
🔲 ♿Grounds. 🔲Free. 🅿️Nearby. 🐕Guide dogs only. ❋ 🚻Tel for details.

NT Photographic Library / Jenny Harpur

SCOTNEY CASTLE GARDEN & ESTATE ❦

LAMBERHURST, TUNBRIDGE WELLS, KENT TN3 8JN

www.nationaltrust.org.uk/places/scotneycastle

Tel: 01892 891081 **Fax:** 01892 890110 **e-mail:** scotneycastle@nationaltrust.org.uk

Owner: The National Trust   **Contact:** Property Manager

One of England's most romantic gardens designed by Edward Hussey in the picturesque style. Dramatic vistas from the terrace of the new Scotney Castle, built in the 1830s, lead down to the ruins of a 14th century moated castle. Rhododendrons, kalmia, azaleas and wisteria flower in profusion. Roses and clematis scramble over the remains of the Old Castle, which is open for the summer. In autumn the garden's glowing colours merge with the surrounding woodlands

where there are many country walks to be explored all year round.

Location: OS Ref. TQ688 353. Signed off A21 1m S of Lamberhurst village.

Open: Castle: 1 May - 1 Oct. Garden: 20 Mar - 31 Oct: Wed - Sun & BHs (closed Good Fri), 11am - 6pm. Last admission 5pm or dusk. Car park: Free, all year for estate walks.

Admission: Adult £4.40, Child £2.20, Family (2+3) £11. Pre-booked groups weekdays £3.80.

🅿 ♿Grounds (but steep parts). 🐕Outside garden only, on leads. ❋

ST JOHN'S COMMANDERY ⌗

Densole, Swingfield, Kent

Tel: 01304 211067

Owner: English Heritage   **Contact:** The South East Regional Office

A medieval chapel built by the Knights Hospitallers. It has a moulded plaster ceiling and a remarkable timber roof and was converted into a farmhouse in the 16th century.

Location: OS Ref. TR232 440. 2m NE of Densole on minor road off A260.

Open: Any reasonable time for exterior viewing. Internal viewing by appointment only.

Admission: Free.

🐕 ❋

© NT Photographic Library / Eric Crichton

SISSINGHURST CASTLE GARDEN ❦

SISSINGHURST, CRANBROOK, KENT TN17 2AB

www.nationaltrust.org.uk/places/sissinghurst

Tel: 01580 710700 **Infoline:** 01580 710701

e-mail: sissinghurst@nationaltrust.org.uk

Owner: The National Trust   **Contact:** The Administration Assistant

One of the world's most celebrated gardens, the creation of Vita Sackville-West and her husband Sir Harold Nicolson. Developed around the surviving parts of an Elizabethan mansion with a central red-brick prospect tower, a series of small, enclosed compartments, intimate in scale and romantic in atmosphere, provide outstanding design and colour throughout the season. The study, where Vita worked, and library are also open to visitors.

Location: OS Ref. TQ807 383. 2m NE of Cranbrook, 1m E of Sissinghurst village (A262).

Open: 20 Mar - 31 Oct: Fri - Tues, including BHs & Good Fri, 11am - 6.30pm; Sat, Sun, BHs & Good Fri, 10am - 6.30pm. Last admission 1 hour before closing or dusk if earlier.

Admission: Adult £7, Child £3.50, Family (2+3) £17.50. Groups discounts (11-50) on Mons only. NT members Free.

🅿 ♿WCs. 🍴Licensed. 🅿Ample. Limited for coaches.
🐕Grounds only, on leads. Guide dogs only in Garden.

© NT Photographic Library / David Sellham

SMALLHYTHE PLACE 🍃

TENTERDEN, KENT TN30 7NG

www.nationaltrust.org.uk/places/smallhytheplace

Tel: 01580 762334   **Fax:** 01580 761960

e-mail: smallhytheplace@nationaltrust.org.uk

Owner: The National Trust   **Contact:** The House Manager

This early 16th century half-timbered house was home to Shakespearean actress Ellen Terry from 1899 to 1928. The house contains many personal and theatrical mementoes including many of her lavish costumes. The charming cottage grounds include her rose garden and the Barn Theatre, which is open most days by courtesy of the Barn Theatre Society.

Location: OS Ref. TQ893 300. 2m S of Tenterden on E side of the Rye road B2082.

Open: 6,7,13,14,20,21 Mar & 27 Mar - 3 Nov: daily except Thurs & Fris (open Good Fri), 11am - 5pm, last admission 4.30pm.

Admission: Adult £3.75, Child £1.80, Family £9.30.

ℹ️No photography in house. 🏷️ ♿Ground floor only. 🅿️Limited. 🐕On leads, in grounds. Tel for details.

Vita Sackville-West and Harold Nicolson

The husband and wife team, who designed Sissinghurst Castle Garden in Kent – today regarded as one of the world's most celebrated gardens. Inspired by the soft intimate cottage garden style of their friend, Lawrence Johnston, Harold Nicolson designed strong structural elements in the gardens – hedges, paths and walks, against which Vita created soft natural planting schemes which provide year around colour.

Garden Designers & Writers

SOUTH FORELAND LIGHTHOUSE 🍃 & GATEWAY TO THE WHITE CLIFFS

Langdon Cliffs, Nr Dover, Kent CT16 1HJ

Tel: 01304 202756   **Fax:** 01304 205295   **e-mail:** southforeland@nationaltrust.org.uk

Owner: The National Trust   **Contact:** Property Manager

The Gateway to the White Cliffs is a visitor centre with spectacular views across the English Channel.

Location: OS138 Ref. TR336 422. Follow White Cliffs brown signs from roundabout 1m NE of Dover at junction of A2/A258.

Open: 1 Mar - 31 Oct: Thur - Mon, 11am - 5.30pm (last adm. 5pm). Open school holidays.

Admission: Adult £2, Child £1, Family £5. Gateway car parking fee: £1.50 (NT free).

SPRIVERS GARDEN 🍃

Horsmonden, Kent TN12 8DR

Tel: 01892 891081

Owner: The National Trust   **Contact:** The Property Manager

A small formal garden with walled and hedged compartments, herbaceous borders and a rose garden.

Location: OS Ref. TQ6940. 3m N of Lamberhurst on B2162.

Open: 12, 16 & 20 Jun, 2 - 5pm, last admission 4.30pm.

Admission: Adult £2, Child £1, Family £5. Groups £1.50.

SQUERRYES COURT & GARDENS

See page 130 for full page entry.

STONEACRE 🍃

Otham, Maidstone, Kent ME15 8RS

Tel/Fax: 01622 862157

Owner: The National Trust   **Contact:** The Tenant

A half-timbered mainly late 15th century yeoman's house, with great hall and crownpost, and restored cottage-style garden.

Location: OS Ref. TQ800 535. In narrow lane at N end of Otham village, 3m SE of Maidstone, 1m S of A20.

Open: 20 Mar - 13 Oct: Weds, Sat & BH Mons 2 - 6pm (last admission 5pm).

Admission: Adult £2.60, Child £1.30, Family (2+3) £6.50. Groups £2.20.

TEMPLE MANOR

Strood, Rochester, Kent

Tel: 01634 827980   www.english-heritage.org.uk/visits

Owner: English Heritage   **Contact:** Medway Council

The 13th century manor house of the Knights Templar which mainly provided accommodation for members of the order travelling between London and the Continent.

Location: OS Ref. TQ733 686. In Strood (Rochester) off A228.

Open: 1 Apr - 30 Sept: weekends & BHs, 10am - 6pm. 1 - 31 Oct: weekends, 10am - 4pm. Times subject to change April 2004.

Admission: Free.

♿Grounds only. 🅿️ 🐕

TONBRIDGE CASTLE

Castle Street, Tonbridge, Kent TN9 1BG

Tel: 01732 770929   www.tonbridgecastle.org

Owner: Tonbridge & Malling Borough Council   **Contact:** The Administrator

Location: OS Ref. TQ588 466. 300 yds NW of the Medway Bridge at town centre.

Open: All year: Mon - Sat, 9am - 4pm. Suns & BHs, 10.30am - 4pm.

Admission: Gatehouse - Adult £4.50, Conc £2.50. Family £11 (max 2 adults). Admission includes audio tour. Last tour 1 hour before closing.

UPNOR CASTLE

Upnor, Kent

Tel: 01634 718742

Owner: English Heritage   **Contact:** Medway Council

Well-preserved 16th century gun fort built to protect Queen Elizabeth I's warships. However in 1667 it failed to prevent the Dutch Navy which stormed up the Medway destroying half the English fleet.

Location: OS Ref. TQ758 706. At Upnor, on unclassified road off A228. 2m NE of Strood.

Open: 1 Apr - 30 Sept: daily, 10am - 6pm. 1 - 31 Oct: daily, 10am - 4pm. Times subject to change April 2004.

Admission: Please telephone for details.

ℹ️WCs. ♿Grounds only. 🐕On leads in restricted areas.

English Heritage Photo Library

WALMER CASTLE & GARDENS ⚏
WALMER, DEAL, KENT CT14 7LJ

www.english-heritage.org.uk/visits

Tel: 01304 364288 **Venue Hire and Hospitality:** 01304 211067

Owner: English Heritage   **Contact:** The Custodian

A Tudor fort transformed into an elegant stately home. The residence of the Lords Warden of the Cinque Ports, who have included HM The Queen Mother, Sir Winston Churchill and the Duke of Wellington. Take the free audio tour and see the Duke's rooms where he died over 150 years ago. Beautiful gardens including the Queen Mother's Garden, The Broadwalk with its famous yew tree hedge, Kitchen Garden & Moat Garden. Lunches and cream teas available in the delightful Lord Warden's tearooms.

Location: OS Ref. TR378 501. S of Walmer on A258, M20/J13 or M2 to Deal.

Open: 1 Apr - 30 Sept: daily, 10am - 6pm. 1 - 31 Oct: daily, 10am - 5pm. 1 Nov - 31 Dec & 1 - 31 Mar: Wed - Sun only, 10am - 4pm. Jan & Feb: Sats & Suns, 10am - 4pm. Closed 24 - 26 Dec & 1 Jan and when Lord Warden is in residence. Times subject to change April 2004.

Admission: Adult £5.50, Child £2.80, Conc. £4.10, Family £13.80. 15% discount for groups (11+). One extra place for each additional 20. EH members free. Prices subject to change April 2004.

ⓘ WCs. 🅿 Ⓣ Private & corporate hire. ♿ Grounds. ● 🄰 🄿 ♿ Guide dogs only. ✳ 🔖 Tel for details.

WILLESBOROUGH WINDMILL
Mill Lane, Willesborough, Ashford, Kent TN24 0QG

Tel: 01233 661866

130 year old smock mill. Civil Wedding Licence.

Location: OS Ref. TR031 421. Off A292 close to M20/J10. At E end of Ashford.

Open: Apr - end Sept; Sats, Suns & BH Mons, also Weds in Jun, Jul & Aug, 2 - 5pm or dusk if earlier.

Admission: Adult £3, Conc. £1.50. Groups 10% reduction by arrangement only.

YALDING ORGANIC GARDENS
Benover Road, Yalding, Maidstone, Kent ME18 6EX

Tel: 01622 814650 **Fax:** 01622 814650 **e-mail:** enquiry@hdra.org.uk
www.hdra.org.uk

Owner: HDRA - The Organic Organisation   **Contact:** Tania Neumann

Five acres of stunning gardens tracing the history of gardening from medieval times to the present day. Described by the *Daily Telegraph* as 'among the most inspirational gardens anywhere, for everyone'. Kids will love the children's garden. Home cooking a speciality. Great shop. The gardens regularly appear on TV.

Location: OS Ref. TQ698 490. 6m SW of Maidstone, 1/2 m S of Yalding village on B2162. Rail 1 1/2 m. Bus from Maidstone - Yalding.

Open: Apr (Good Fri onwards) & Oct: weekends only. May - Sept: Wed - Sun, 10am - 5pm. Open BH Mons.

Admission: Adult £3, Child Free. Groups (14-55) £2.50. Guided tour £1.

🄰 🚻 ♿ ● 🍴 𝑓 By arrangement. ● 🄿 ♿ Guide dogs only.

🔖 **Accommodation Index** see front section

Belmont, Kent from the book
Historic Family Homes and Gardens from the Air, see page 54.

ARDINGTON HOUSE

WANTAGE

www.ardingtonhouse.com

Map 3

Owner:
The Baring Family

▶ CONTACT

Nigel Baring
Ardington House
Wantage
Oxfordshire OX12 8QA

Tel: 01235 821566
Fax: 01235 821151
e-mail: info@
ardingtonhouse.com

▶ LOCATION
OS Ref. SU432 883

12m S of Oxford, 12m
N of Newbury,
2¹/₂ m E of Wantage.

Just a few miles south of Oxford stands the hauntingly beautiful, gracefully symmetric Ardington House. Surrounded by well-kept lawns, terraced gardens and peaceful paddocks this baroque house is still the private home of the Baring family. You'll find it in the village of Ardington in the lee of the Berkshire Downs close to the Ridgeway, the historic path that runs along the top of the Downs linking the Thames Valley to the Kennet. Its rooms to the south look across the garden and grazing horses to the river, well known to enthusiastic fly fisherman. To the front is an immaculately tended lawn, ideal for croquet and enjoyed by different generations of the Baring family as they grew up in this beautiful setting. Sir John Betjeman, one of the best loved poets of recent times, thought highly of this gracious home. But it doesn't end there because one of the greatest joys in this impressive home is the wood panelled dining room with its large oil painting of the father of the founder of this famous banking family.

The astonishing mixture of history, warmth and style you'll find at Ardington truly does place it in a class of its own.

▶ OPENING TIMES

3 - 7, 10 - 14, 17 - 21 & 31
May: 2.30 - 4.30pm

2 - 6, 9 - 13, 16 - 20 & 30
Aug: 2.30 - 4.30pm.

Guided tours at 2.30pm.

▶ ADMISSION
House & Gardens

Adult £3.50

CONFERENCE/FUNCTION

ROOM	MAX CAPACITY
Imperial Hall	
Theatre Style	80
U shape	30
Cabaret	40
Oak Room	
Theatre Style	40
U shape	20
Cabaret	30
Music Room	
Theatre Style	40
U shape	20
Cabaret	30

ℹ️ Conferences, product launches, films.

🍴 Lunches and teas by arrangement for groups.

🚶 By members of the family.

🅿️ Free.

🐕 Guide dogs only.

🔔 Tel for details.

BLENHEIM PALACE 🏛

WOODSTOCK

www.blenheimpalace.com

Map 5

Owner:
The Duke of Marlborough

▶ **CONTACT**

Operations Director
Blenheim Palace
Woodstock   OX20 1PX

Tel: 01993 811091
Fax: 01993 813527
e-mail: administrator@
blenheimpalace.com

▶ **LOCATION**

OS Ref. SP441 161

From London, M40, A44
(1½ hrs), 8m NW of
Oxford. London 63m
Birmingham 54m.
Air: Heathrow 60m.
Birmingham 50m.
Coach: From London
(Victoria) to Oxford.
Rail: Oxford Station.
Bus: Oxford
(Cornmarket) -
Woodstock.

"I have not time to say more, but to beg you will give my duty to the Queen, and let her know her army has had a glorious victory."

This year Blenheim Palace celebrates 300 years since the 1704 "glorious victory" of the Battle of Blenheim. The Palace, home of the 11th Duke of Marlborough and birthplace of Sir Winston Churchill, was built for John Churchill, 1st Duke of Marlborough, by Sir John Vanbrugh between the years 1705 and 1722 after the land and a sum of £240,000 were given to the Duke by Queen Anne and a grateful nation in recognition of his great victory over the French and Bavarians. It is now considered a masterpiece of the English Baroque style.

The original gardens were designed by Queen Anne's gardener Henry Wise, with later alterations by Lancelot "Capability" Brown which included the creation of Blenheim's most outstanding feature, the lake. In more recent times the French architect, Achille Duchêne, built the formal gardens to the east and west of the Palace. The combination of house, gardens and park was recognised as uniquely important when Blenheim was listed as a World Heritage Site.

The Pleasure Gardens area includes the Marlborough Maze, the Butterfly House, the Herb and Lavender Garden and the Adventure Play Area, but still keeps the atmosphere of Vanbrugh's original walled kitchen garden. The restoration of the 10th Duke's "Lost Garden" close to the Palace is a new and very exciting project for 2003/2004.

CONFERENCE/FUNCTION

ROOM	SIZE	MAX CAPACITY
Orangery		200
Great Hall	70' x 40'	150
Saloon	50' x 30'	72
with Great Hall		450
with Great Hall & Library		750
Library	180' x 30'	300

🖼 Four Shops.

ℹ️ Filming, product launches, activity days. No photography in house.

🍽 Corporate hospitality, including dinners and receptions and team building events.

♿ Car park for the disabled. Adapted toilets.

📹🍴 1 Restaurant, 2 Cafés. Group enquiries welcome (up to 150). Menus on request.

🚶 In off peak season; guides in rooms in peak season. Private and language tours may be pre-booked.

🅿️ Unlimited for cars and coaches.

🏆 Sandford Award holder since 1982. Teacher pre-visits welcome.

🐕 Dogs on leads in Park. Registered assistance dogs only in house and garden.

❄️ 🎭 Full programme. Tel for details.

Park & Gardens

Peak Period: 9 -12 April & 29 May - 12 Sept.

Adult £7.50
Child £3.50
Senior/Student £5.50
Family £18.00
Groups (15+)
Adult £5.50
Child £2.80
Senior/Student....... £4.50

Off Peak Period: 14 Feb - 12 Dec except above dates

Adult £6.00
Child £2.00
Senior/Student....... £4.00
Family £14.00
Groups (15+)
Adult £4.50
Child £1.50
Senior/Student....... £3.50

Private tours by appointment only, from £375.00.

▶ **OPENING TIMES**

Summer - Palace
14 February - 31 October
Daily
1 Nov - 12 Dec:
Wed - Sun

10.30am - 4.45pm
Last admission 4.45pm.

Winter - Park only
13 Dec - Mid Feb
Daily, 9am - Dusk.

The Duke of Marlborough reserves the right to close the Palace or Park or to amend admission prices without notice.

▶ **ADMISSION**

House & Grounds

Peak Period: 9 -12 April & 29 May - 12 Sept.

Adult £12.50
Child £7.00
Senior/Student.... £10.00
Family £33.00
Groups (15+)
Adult £9.50
Child £5.00
OAP/Student £8.50

Off Peak Period: 14 Feb - 12 Dec except above dates

Adult £11.00
Child £5.50
Senior/Student....... £8.50
Family £28.00
Groups (15+)
Adult £8.50
Child £4.50
Senior/Student....... £7.50

Park only
Mid Decenber - mid February

Adult £2.00
Child £1.00

BROUGHTON CASTLE

BANBURY

www.broughtoncastle.demon.co.uk

Map 5

Owner:
Lord Saye & Sele

▶ **CONTACT**

Mrs J Moorhouse
Broughton Castle
Banbury OX15 5EB

Tel/Fax: 01295 276070
Tel: 01295 722547

e-mail:
admin@broughton
castle.demon.co.uk

▶ **LOCATION**
OS Ref. SP418 382

Broughton Castle is
2¹/₂ m SW of Banbury
Cross on the B4035,
Shipston-on-Stour -
Banbury Road.
Easily accessible from
Stratford-on-Avon,
Warwick, Oxford,
Burford and the
Cotswolds. M40/J11.

Rail: From London/
Birmingham to Banbury.

Broughton Castle is essentially a family home
lived in by Lord and Lady Saye & Sele and
their family.

The original medieval Manor House, of which
much remains today, was built in about 1300 by
Sir John de Broughton. It stands on an island site
surrounded by a 3-acre moat. The Castle was
greatly enlarged between 1550 and 1600, at which
time it was embellished with magnificent plaster
ceilings, splendid panelling and fine fireplaces.

In the 17th century William, 8th Lord Saye & Sele,
played a leading role in national affairs. He
opposed Charles I's efforts to rule without
Parliament and Broughton became a secret
meeting place for the King's opponents.

During the Civil War William raised a regiment
and he and his four sons all fought at the
nearby Battle of Edgehill. After the battle the
Castle was besieged and captured.

Arms and armour from the Civil War and other
periods are displayed in the Great Hall. Visitors
may also see the gatehouse, gardens and park
together with the nearby 14th century Church of
St Mary, in which there are many family tombs,
memorials and hatchments.

GARDENS

The garden area consists of mixed
herbaceous and shrub borders containing many
old roses. In addition, there is a formal walled
garden with beds of roses surrounded by box
hedging and lined by more mixed borders.

▶ **OPENING TIMES**
Summer
1 May - 15 September
Weds & Suns
2 - 5pm.

Also Thurs in July and
August and all Bank
Holiday Suns and Bank
Holiday Mons
(including Easter)
2 - 5pm.

Groups welcome on
any day and at any time
throughout the year
by appointment.

▶ **ADMISSION**
Adult £5.50
Child (5-15yrs)....... £2.50
OAP/Student £4.50
Groups*
Adult £5.00
Child (5-15yrs)....... £2.00
OAP/Student £5.00

* Min payment: adults £80,
children £50.

Filming,
product launches, advertising
features, corporate events in
park. Photography permitted
for personal use. Brief
guidance notes available in
French, Spanish, Dutch,
Japanese, German, Polish,
Greek & Russian.

Visitors allowed vehicle
access to main entrance.

Teas on Open Days.
Groups may book tea, coffee
or light lunches/supper.

Available to pre-booked
groups at no extra charge. Not
available on open days.

300 yards from the Castle.

Welcome.

Guide dogs only in
house.

26A EAST ST HELEN STREET
Abingdon, Oxfordshire
Tel: 01865 242918 **e-mail:** info@oxfordpreservation.org.uk
www.oxfordpreservation.org.uk
Owner: Oxford Preservation Trust   **Contact:** Ms Debbie Dance
One of best preserved examples of a 15th century dwelling in the area. Originally a Merchant's Hall House with later alterations, features include a remarkable domestic wall painting, an early oak ceiling, traceried windows and fireplaces. The remains of a 17th century boy's doublet found in the roof during restoration works is on display.
Location: OS Ref. SU497 969. 300 yards SSW of the market place and Town Hall.
Open: By prior appointment.
Admission: Free.

ARDINGTON HOUSE
See page 141 for full page entry.

ASHDOWN HOUSE
Lambourn, Newbury RG16 7RE
Tel: 01793 762209 **e-mail:** ashdownhouse@nationaltrust.org.uk
www.nationaltrust.org.uk
Owner: The National Trust   **Contact:** Coleshill Estate Office
Location: OS Ref. SU282 820. 3$^1/_2$ m N of Lambourn, on W side of B4000.
Open: House & Garden: 31 Mar - 30 Oct: Wed & Sat, 2 - 5pm. Admission by guided tour at 2.15, 3.15 & 4.15pm. Woodland: All Year: daily except Fri, daylight hours.
Admission: House & garden: £2.20. Woodland: Free.

BLENHEIM PALACE
See pages 142 for full page entry.

BROOK COTTAGE
Well Lane, Alkerton, Nr Banbury OX15 6NL
Tel: 01295 670303/670590   **Fax:** 01295 730362
Owner/Contact: Mrs David Hodges
4 acre hillside garden. Roses, clematis, water gardens, colour co-ordinated borders, trees, shrubs.
Location: OS Ref. SP378 428. 6m NW of Banbury, $^1/_2$m off A422 Banbury to Stratford-upon-Avon road.
Open: Easter Mon - end Oct: Mon - Fri, 9am - 6pm. Evenings, weekends and all group visits by appointment.
Admission: Adult £4, OAP £3, Child Free.

BROUGHTON CASTLE
See page 143 for full page entry.

BUSCOT OLD PARSONAGE
Buscot, Faringdon, Oxfordshire SN7 8DQ
Tel: 01793 762209   **e-mail:** buscot@nationaltrust.org.uk
Owner: The National Trust   **Contact:** Coleshill Estate Office
An early 18th century house of Cotswold stone on the bank of the Thames with a small garden.
Location: OS Ref. SU231 973. 2m from Lechlade, 4m N of Faringdon on A417.
Open: 31 Mar - 27 Oct, Weds, 2 - 6pm by written appointment with tenant.
Admission: Adult £1.30, Child £60p, Family £3.20. Not suitable for groups.
[i] No WCs. [&] Partial.

Part of the Harold Peto Water Garden.

NTPL / Thames and Chiltern

BUSCOT PARK
BUSCOT, FARINGDON, OXFORDSHIRE SN7 8BU

www.buscot-park.com

Tel: Infoline 0845 345 3387 / Office 01367 240786 **Fax:** 01367 241794
e-mail: estbuscot@aol.com
Owner: The National Trust (Administered on their behalf by Lord Faringdon)
Contact: Lord Faringdon
The 18th century Palladian house contains the Faringdon Collection of fine paintings (including works by Murillo, Reynolds, Rossetti and the famous Briar Rose series by Burne-Jones) and furniture, with important pieces by Adam, Thomas Hope and others. The House is set in parkland offering peaceful walks through water gardens and a well-stocked walled garden. The tearoom serves delicious home-made cream teas and cakes.
Location: OS Ref. SU239 973. Between Lechlade and Faringdon on A417.

Open: House & Grounds: 1 Apr - 30 Sep: Wed - Fri, 2 - 6pm; Grounds only: 1 Apr - 30 Sep: Mon & Tues, 2 - 6pm. Tearoom: as house, 2.30 - 5.30pm. Open BH Mons & Good Fri. House & Grounds: weekends 10/11 & 24/25 Apr: 1/2, 8/9, 22/23 & 29/30 May: 12/13 & 26/27 Jun: 10/11 & 24/25 Jul; 14/15 & 28/29 Aug: 11/12 & 25/26 Sep: 2 - 6pm (last adm. to house 5.30pm). Tearoom: 2.30 - 5.30pm.
Admission: House & Grounds: Adult £6.50, Child £3.25. Grounds only: Adult £4.50, Child £2.25. Groups must book in writing, or by fax or e-mail. Booking is advised for disabled visitors wishing to use powered mobility vehicle.
[i] No photography in house. [T] Fully equipped theatre. [&] Partial, tel for details.
[🍴] Light lunches for groups by arrangement. [P] Ample for cars, 2 coach spaces. [✖]

CHASTLETON HOUSE

Chastleton, nr Moreton-in-Marsh, Oxfordshire GL56 0SU
Tel/Fax: 01608 674355 **Infoline:** 01494 755560 **e-mail:** chastleton@nationaltrust.org.uk
Owner: The National Trust   **Contact:** The Custodian
One of England's finest and most complete Jacobean houses, dating from 1607. It is filled with a mixture of rare and everyday objects and the atmosphere of four hundred years of continuous occupation by one family. The gardens have a Jacobean layout and the rules of modern croquet were codified here.
Location: OS Ref. SP248 291. 6m ENE of Stow-on-the-Wold. 1¹/2 m NW of A436. Approach only from A436 between the A44 (W of Chipping Norton) and Stow.
Open: 31 Mar - 2 Oct: Wed - Sat, 1 - 5pm, last admission 4pm. 6 Oct - 30 Oct: Wed - Sat, 1 - 4pm, last admission 3pm. Admission for all visitors (including NT members) by timed tickets booked in advance. Bookings can be made by telephone (01494 755585) on weekdays between 9.30am - 4pm.
Admission: Adult £5.80, Child £2.90. Family £14.50. Groups (11-25) by appointment.
⟨Partial. **P** Coaches limited to 25 seat minibuses. Guide dogs only.

CHRIST CHURCH CATHEDRAL

The Sacristy, The Cathedral, Oxford OX1 1DP
Tel: 01865 276154   **Contact:** Mr Jim Godfrey
12th century Norman Church, formerly an Augustinian monastery, given Cathedral status in 16th century by Henry VIII.
Location: OS Ref. SP515 059. Just S of city centre, off St Aldates. Entry via Meadow Gate visitors' entrance on S side of college.
Open: Mon - Sat: 9am - 5pm. Suns: 1 - 5pm, closed Christmas Day. Services: weekdays 7.20am, 6pm. Suns: 8am, 10am, 11.15am & 6pm.
Admission: Adult £4, Child under 5 Free, Conc. £3, Family £6.

COGGES MANOR FARM MUSEUM

Church Lane, Witney, Oxfordshire OX28 3LA
Tel: 01993 772602 **Fax:** 01993 703056
e-mail: Victoria.beaumont@westoxon.gov.uk **WWW**.cogges.org
Administered by: West Oxfordshire District Council **Contact:** Victoria Beaumont
The Manor House dates from the 13th century, rooms are furnished to show life at the end of the 19th century. Daily cooking on the Victorian range. On the first floor, samples of original wallpapers and finds from under the floorboards accompany the story of the history of the house. In one of the rooms, rare 17th century painted panelling survives. Farm buildings, including two 18th century barns, stables and a thatched ox byre, display farm implements. Traditional breeds of farm animals, hand-milking demonstration each day. Seasonal produce from the walled kitchen garden sold in the museum shop.
Location: OS Ref. SP362 097. Off A40 Oxford - Burford Rd. Access by footbridge from centre of Witney, 600 yds. Vehicle access from S side of B4022 near E end of Witney.
Open: Apr - end Nov: Tue - Fri & BH Mons, 10.30am - 5.30pm; Sat & Sun, 12 noon - 5.30pm. Closed Good Fri. Early closing in Oct & Nov.
Admission: Adult £4.40, Child £2.30, Conc. £2.85, Family (2+2) £12.90.
⟨Ground floor. WCs. ⟨ **P** In grounds, on leads.

DEDDINGTON CASTLE ⊞

Deddington, Oxfordshire
Tel: 023 9258 1059
Owner: English Heritage   **Contact:** Area Manager
Extensive earthworks concealing the remains of a 12th century castle which was ruined as early as the 14th century.
Location: OS Ref. SP471 316. S of B4031 on E side of Deddington, 17m N of Oxford on A423. 5m S of Banbury.
Open: Any reasonable time.
Admission: Free.
On leads. ⟨

DITCHLEY PARK

Enstone, Oxfordshire OX7 4ER
Tel: 01608 677346 **www**.ditchley.co.uk
Owner: Ditchley Foundation   **Contact:** Brigadier Christopher Galloway
The most important house by James Gibbs with most distinguished interiors by Henry Flitcroft and William Kent.
Location: OS Ref. SP391 214. 2m NE from Charlbury. 13m NW of Oxford.
Open: Visits only by prior arrangement with the Bursar.
Admission: £5 per person (minimum charge £40).

FAWLEY COURT

HISTORIC HOUSE & MUSEUM, HENLEY-ON-THAMES RG9 3AE
www.marians-uk.org

Tel: 01491 574917 **Fax:** 01491 411587
e-mail: fcoffice@dircon.co.uk **e-mail:** marian-f@dircon.co.uk
Owner: Marian Fathers   **Contact:** The Secretary
Designed by Christopher Wren, built in 1684 for Col W Freeman, decorated by Grinling Gibbons and by James Wyatt. The Museum consists of a library, various documents of the Polish Kings, a very well-preserved collection of historical sabres and many memorable military objects of the Polish army. Paintings, early books, numismatic collections, arms and armour.
Location: OS Ref. SU765 842. 1m N of Henley-on-Thames E to A4155 to Marlow.
Open: May - Oct: Weds, Thurs & Suns, 2 - 5pm. Other dates by arrangement. Closed Whitsuntide and Nov - Apr inclusive.
Admission: House, Museum & Gardens: Adult £4, Child £1.50, Conc. £3. Groups (15+) £3.
⟨Ground floor & grounds. WC. ⟨ On open days at 2.30pm. Guide dogs only.

GREAT COXWELL BARN ⚘

Great Coxwell, Faringdon, Oxfordshire

Tel: 01793 762209   **e-mail:** greatcoxwellbarn@nationaltrust.org.uk

Owner: The National Trust   **Contact:** Coleshill Estate Office

A 13th century monastic barn, stone built with stone tiled roof, which has an interesting timber construction.

Location: OS Ref. SU269 940. 2m SW of Faringdon between A420 and B4019.

Open: All year: daily at reasonable hours.

Admission: 50p.

✳

🔔 Civil Wedding Venues see front section

GREYS COURT ⚘

ROTHERFIELD GREYS, HENLEY-ON-THAMES, OXFORDSHIRE RG9 4PG

Infoline: 01494 755564   **Tel:** 01491 628529   **e-mail:** greyscourt@nationaltrust.org.uk

Owner: The National Trust   **Contact:** The Custodian

Rebuilt in the 16th century and added to in the 17th, 18th and 19th centuries, the house is set amid the remains of the courtyard walls and towers of a 14th century fortified house. A Tudor donkey wheel, well-house and an ice house are still intact, and the garden contains Archbishop's Maze, inspired by Archbishop Runcie's enthronement speech in 1980.

Location: OS Ref. SU725 834. 3m W of Henley-on-Thames, E of B481.

Open: House: 7 Apr - 24 Sept: Wed - Fri & 1st Sat in Month, 2 - 5pm. Garden: 3 - 31 Mar & 6 - 27 Oct: Wed, 2 - 5.30pm. 1 Apr - 30 Sept: Tue - Sat, 2 - 5.30pm. Tearoom: 3 - 31 Mar & 29 Sept - 27 Oct: Wed, 2 - 5.30pm. 1 Apr - 25 Sept: Tues - Sat, 2 - 5.30pm. Closed Good Fri.

Admission: House & Garden: Adult £5, Child £2.50, Family £12.50. Garden only: £3.50, Child £1.70, Family £8.70. Coach parties must book in advance.

♿ Grounds partial. WCs. ⬛ 🐕 In car park only, on leads. 🎫 Contact Custodian.

KINGSTON BAGPUIZE HOUSE 🏛

ABINGDON, OXFORDSHIRE OX13 5AX

www.kingstonbagpuizehouse.org.uk

Tel: 01865 820259   **Fax:** 01865 821659   **e-mail:** virginiagrant@btinternet.com

Owner/Contact: Mrs Francis Grant

A family home, this beautiful house originally built in the 1660s was remodelled in the early 1700s in red brick with stone facings. It has a cantilevered staircase and panelled rooms with some good furniture and pictures. Set in mature parkland, the gardens, including shrub border and woodland garden, contain a notable collection of trees, shrubs, perennials and bulbs including snowdrops, planted for year round interest. A raised terrace walk leads to an 18th century panelled gazebo with views of the house and gardens, including a large herbaceous border and parkland. Available for wedding receptions, special events, corporate functions, product launches and filming. Facilities for small conferences.

Location: OS Ref. SU408 981. In Kingston Bagpuize village, off A415 Abingdon to Witney road S of A415/A420 intersection. Abingdon 5m, Oxford 9m.

Open: BH Sun & Mon. 2nd & 4th Suns Feb - Sept and some Sats. Feb 7/8, 21/22 & 29; Mar 14, 27/28; Apr 11/12, 25; May 2/3, 9, 23, 30/31; Jun 13 & 27; Jul 11, 24/25; Aug 8, 22, 29/30; Sept 11/12, 26; Oct 10: 2 - 5.30pm (last tour of house 4.10pm). House: guided tours only. Last entry to garden 5pm.

Admission: House & Garden: Adult £4.50, Child (5-15) £2.50, (admission to house not recommended for children under 5yrs), Conc. £4. Gardens: £2.50 (child under 16yrs Free). Groups (20-80) by appointment throughout the year, prices on request.

ℹ No photography in house. ⬛ 🎁 🍽 ♿ Grounds. WC.

🍰 Home-made cakes. Light meals for groups by appointment.

🅿 📖 Obligatory tours of house. 🚫 ✳

MAPLEDURHAM HOUSE & WATERMILL

MAPLEDURHAM, READING RG4 7TR

www.mapledurham.co.uk

Tel: 01189 723350 **Fax:** 01189 724016 **e-mail:** mtrust1997@aol.com

Owner: The Mapledurham Trust **Contact:** Mrs Lola Andrews

Late 16th century Elizabethan home of the Blount family. Original plaster ceilings, great oak staircase, fine collection of paintings and a private chapel in Strawberry Hill Gothick added in 1797. Interesting literary connections with Alexander Pope, Galsworthy's *Forsyte Saga* and Kenneth Grahame's *Wind in the Willows*. 15th century watermill fully restored producing flour and bran which is sold in the giftshop.

Location: OS Ref. SU670 767. N of River Thames. 4m NW of Reading, 1¹/2 m W of A4074.

Open: Easter - Sept: Sats, Suns & BHs, 2 - 5.30pm. Last admission 5pm. Midweek parties by arrangement only (Tue - Thur). Mapledurham Trust reserves the right to alter or amend opening times or prices without prior notification.

Admission: Please call 01189 723350 for details.

🖥 ♿Grounds. WCs. 🖤 🐕Guide dogs only. 🏠11 holiday cottages (all year).

Jacobean House Design 1603-1660

Jacobean house designs are essentially similar to the Elizabethan houses, but increasingly intricate in their decoration. During this period more and more foreign workers were employed, chiefly Flemish craftsmen, particularly carvers. Look for a slavish adherence to symmetrical form on the exterior of a Jacobean building, often with gabled projections on all four sides of the building.

Visit Hatfield House, Hertfordshire, Audley End, Essex, Knole, Kent, and Blickling Hall in Norfolk. For small houses visit Fountains Hall, Yorkshire, Chastleton House, Oxfordshire, Bateman's, Sussex and Quebec House in Kent.

MILTON MANOR HOUSE

MILTON, ABINGDON, OXFORDSHIRE OX14 4EN

Tel: 01488 71036

Owner: Anthony Mockler-Barrett Esq **Contact:** Helen Hall

Dreamily beautiful mellow brick house, traditionally designed by Inigo Jones, with a celebrated Gothick library (pictured on right) and a startling Catholic chapel. Lived in by the family; pleasant, relaxed and informal atmosphere. Park with fine old trees, stables (pony rides usually available); Treehouse in the garden, Stockade in the woods. Walled garden, woodland walk, two lakes, variety of charming annuals and unusual ornaments. Plenty to see and enjoy for all ages, picnickers welcome.

Location: OS Ref. SU485 924. Just off A34, village and house signposted, 9m S of Oxford, 15m N of Newbury. 3m from Abingdon and Didcot.

Open: 1 - 31 Aug: 12 noon - 5pm. Guided tours of house: 2pm, 3pm, 4pm. Also all BH weekends: Easter - end Aug: open 12 noon - 5pm. For weddings etc. please write to the Administrator.

Admission: House & Gardens: Adult £5, Child £2.50. House: Guided tours only. Garden, Woodland & Grounds only: Adult £3, Child £1.50. Easter Egg Hunt on Easter w/end. Georgian/Stuart weekend on Aug BH weekend. Groups by arrangement throughout the year. For group bookings only please fax or phone 01235 831287.

🍴Available. ♿Grounds. 🖤 ℹ️Obligatory. 🅿️Free. 🐕Guide dogs only. ❋

🏠1 holiday flat (Easter to September). ♿

MINSTER LOVELL HALL & DOVECOTE

Witney, Oxfordshire

Tel: 023 9258 1059

Owner: English Heritage **Contact:** Area Manager

The ruins of Lord Lovell's 15th century manor house stand in a lovely setting on the banks of the River Windrush.

Location: OS Ref. SP324 114. Adjacent to Minster Lovell Church, 1/2 m NE of village. 3m W of Witney off A40.

Open: Any reasonable time.

Admission: Free.

On leads.

PRIORY COTTAGES

1 Mill Street, Steventon, Abingdon, Oxfordshire OX13 6SP

Tel: 01793 762209

Owner: The National Trust **Contact:** Coleshill Estate Office

Former monastic buildings, converted into two houses. South Cottage contains the Great Hall of the original priory.

Location: OS Ref. SU466 914. 4m S of Abingdon, on B4017 off A34 at Abingdon West or Milton interchange on corner of The Causeway and Mill Street, entrance in Mill Street.

Open: The Great Hall in South Cottage only: 31 Mar - 29 Sept: Wed, 2 - 6pm, by written appointment with the tenant.

Admission: Adult £1.10, Child 50p, Family £2.70.

ROUSHAM HOUSE

Nr STEEPLE ASTON, BICESTER, OXFORDSHIRE OX25 4QX

www.rousham.org

Tel: 01869 347110/07860 360407

Owner/Contact: Charles Cottrell-Dormer Esq

Rousham represents the first stage of English landscape design and remains almost as William Kent (1685 - 1748) left it. One of the few gardens of this date to have escaped alteration. Includes Venus' Vale, Townesend's Building, seven-arched Praeneste, the Temple of the Mill and a sham ruin known as the 'Eyecatcher'. The house was built in 1635 by Sir Robert Dormer. Excellent location for fashion, advertising, photography etc.

Location: OS Ref. SP477 242. E of A4260, 12m N of Oxford, S of B4030, 7m W of Bicester.

Open: House: Apr - Sept: Wed, Sun and BH Mon 2 - 4.30pm. Garden: All year: daily, 10am - 4.30pm.

Admission: House: £3. Garden: Adult £3. No children under 15yrs.

Partial. Obligatory.

RYCOTE CHAPEL

Rycote, Oxfordshire

Tel: 023 9258 1059 **www**.english-heritage.org.uk/visits

Owner: English Heritage **Contact:** Area Manager

A 15th century chapel with exquisitely carved and painted woodwork. It has many intriguing features, including two roofed pews and a musicians' gallery.

Location: OS165 Ref. SP667 046. 3m SW of Thame, off A329. 1 1/2 m NE of M40/J7.

Open: 1 Apr - 30 Sept: Fri - Sun & BHs, 2 - 6pm. Times subject to change April 2004.

Admission: Adult £2, Child £1, Conc. £1.30. 15% discount for groups (11+). Prices subject to change April 2004.

STONOR 🏛

HENLEY-ON-THAMES, OXFORDSHIRE RG9 6HF

www.stonor.com

Tel: 01491 638587 **Fax:** 01491 639348 **e-mail:** jweaver@stonor.com

Owner: Lord & Lady Camoys   **Contact:** The Administrator - John Weaver

Family home of Lord and Lady Camoys and generations of their family for over 800 years. Stonor, surrounded by deer park, sits in a beautiful wooded valley. The House and Chapel date from the 12th century, with 14th and 18th century additions and changes. Internal features include rare furniture, artworks and family portraits. Mass has been celebrated continuously since medieval times in the Chapel, sited close by a pagan stone circle. St Edmund Campion sought refuge here during the Reformation. An exhibition celebrates his life and work. Enclosed hillside gardens at the rear offer outstanding views of the park. Springtime daffodils are a major attraction.

Location: OS Ref. SU743 893. 1 hr from London, M4/J8/9. A4130 to Henley-on-Thames. On B480 NW of Henley. A4130/B480 to Stonor. Rail: Henley-on-Thames Station 5m.

Open: Apr - Sept: Suns & BH Mons; July - Sep: Weds. House & Tearoom: 2 - 5.30pm; Garden: 1 - 5.30pm. Private groups by arrangement: Apr - Sept, Tues - Thurs.

Admission: House, Garden & Chapel: Adult £6, Child (under 14yrs) Free. Garden & Chapel: Adult £3.50. Schools £2.50 pp, 1 teacher for every 10 children admitted free. Private guided tours (20+): £7pp (one group payment). School groups £4pp, 1 teacher per 10 children admitted free.

📷 ℹ️ No photography in house. 🚻 ♿ Partial. 👥 For 20-60. 🍽 Licensed. 🅿️ 100yds away. 🐕 In grounds on leads. 📧 Tel for details.

SWALCLIFFE BARN

Swalcliffe Village, Banbury, Oxfordshire

Tel: 01295 788278   **Contact:** Jeffrey Demmar

15th century half cruck barn, houses agricultural and trade vehicles. Exhibition of 2500 years of Swalcliffe history.

Location: OS Ref. SP378 378. 6m W of Banbury Cross on B4035.

Open: Easter - end Oct: Suns & BHs, 2 - 5pm.

Admission: Free.

UNIVERSITY OF OXFORD BOTANIC GARDEN

Rose Lane, Oxford OX1 4AZ

Tel/Fax: 01865 286690   **e-mail:** postmaster@botanic-garden.ox.ac.uk

Owner: University of Oxford   **Contact:** The Administrator

Founded in 1621; oldest botanic garden in Britain; 8,000 plants from all over the world; original walled garden; many trees over 200 years old.

Location: OS Ref. SP520 061. E end of High Street.

Open: Apr - Sept: 9am - 5pm; Jun, Jul & Aug: open until 8pm (glasshouses: 10am - 4.30pm). Oct - Mar: 9am - 4.30pm (glasshouses: 10am - 4pm). Closed 25 Dec & Good Fri. Last admission 4.15pm. (2003 details.)

Admission: Adult £2.50, Child (under 12ys) Free. (2003 prices.)

WATERPERRY GARDENS

Waterperry, Nr Wheatley, Oxfordshire OX33 1LB

Tel: 01844 339226   **Fax:** 01844 339883

e-mail: office@waterperrygardens.fs.net.co.uk

Owner: School of Economic Science   **Contact:** P Maxwell

See one of Britain's finest herbaceous borders which flowers continually from May to October. Rose garden; alpine gardens, formal garden, shrub borders, perennial borders and river walk.

Location: OS Ref. SP630 063. Oxford 9m, London 52m M40/J8, Birmingham M40/J8A 42m. Well signposted locally.

Open: Apr - Oct: 9am - 5.30pm. Nov - Mar: 9am - 5pm. (2003 details.)

Admission: Adult £3.75, Child £2.25 (under 10yrs Free), OAP £3.25. Groups (20+) £3. (2003 prices.)

Website Information see front section

The Colleges of Oxford University

All Souls' College
High Street
Tel: 01865 279379
Founder: Archbishop Henry Chichele 1438
Open: Mon - Fri, 2 - 4pm

Balliol College
Broad Street
Tel: 01865 277777
Founder: John de Balliol 1263
Open: Daily, 2 - 5pm

Brasenose College
Radcliffe Square
Tel: 01865 277830
Founder: William Smythe, Bishop of Lincoln 1509
Open: Daily, 10 - 11.30am (tour groups only)
and 2 - 4pm (5pm in summer)

Christ Church
St. Aldates
Tel: 01865 276150
Founder: Cardinal Wolsey/ Henry VIII 1546
Open: Mon - Sat, 9am - 5pm; Sun, 1 - 5pm

Corpus Christi College
Merton Street
Tel: 01865 276700
Founder: Bishop Richard Fox 1517
Open: Daily, 1.30 - 4.30pm

Exeter College
Turl Street
Tel: 01865 279600
Founder: Bishop Stapleden of Exeter 1314
Open: Daily, Term time 2 - 5pm;

Green College
Woodstock Road
Tel: 01865 274770
Founder: Dr Cecil Green 1979

Harris Manchester College
Mansfield Road
Tel: 01865 271006
Founder: Lord Harris of Peckham 1996

Hertford College
Catte Street
Tel: 01865 279400
Founder: TC Baring MP 1740
Open: Daily, l0am - Noon and 2pm - dusk.

Jesus College
Turl Street
Tel: 01865 279700
Founder: Dr Hugh Price (Queen Elizabeth I) 1571
Open: Daily, 2 - 4.30pm

Keble College
Parks Road
Tel: 01865 272727
Founder: Public money 1870
Open: Daily, 2 - 5pm

Lady Margaret Hall
Norham Gardens
Tel: 01865 274300
Founder: Dame Elizabeth Wordsworth 1878
Open: Gardens: 10am - 5pm

Linacre College
St Cross Road
Tel: 01865 271650
Founder: Oxford University 1962

Lincoln College
Turl Street
Tel: 01865 279800
Founder: Bishop Richard Fleming of Lincoln 1427
Open: Mon - Sat, 2 - 5pm; Sun, 11am - 5pm

Magdalen College
High Street
Tel: 01865 276000
Founder: William of Waynefleete 1458
Open: 1 Oct - 24 June: 1pm - 6pm/dusk
(whichever is the earlier) and
25 June - 30 Sept: Noon - 6pm

Mansfield College
Mansfield Road
Tel: 01865 270999
Founder: Free Churches 1995

Merton College
Merton Street
Tel: 01865 276310
Founder: Walter de Merton l264
Open: Mon - Fri, 2 -4pm; Sat & Sun,
10am - 4pm

New College
Holywell Street
Tel: 01865 279555
Founder: William of Wykeham, Bishop of
Winchester 1379
Open: Daily, 11am - 5pm (summer); 2 - 4pm
(winter)

Nuffield College
New Road
Tel: 01865 278500
Founder: William Morris (Lord Nuffield) 1937

Oriel College
Oriel Square
Tel: 01865 276555
Founder: Edward II/Adam de Brome 1326
Open: Mon - Fri, 2 - 4pm

Pembroke College
St Aldates
Tel: 01865 276444
Founder: James I 1624
Open: Daily, 10am – 17pm

Queen's College
High Street
Tel: 01865 279120
Founder: Robert de Eglesfield 1341
Open: By prior appointment through the Tourist
Information Office.

Somerville College
Graduate House, Woodstock Road
Tel: 01865 270600
Founder: Association for the Education of Women
1879

St. Anne's College
56 Woodstock Road
Tel: 01865 274800
Founder: Association for the Education of Women
1878

St. Antony's College
62 Woodstock Road
Tel: 01865 284700
Founder: M. Antonin Bess 1948

St. Catherine's College
Manor Road
Tel: 01865 271700
Founder: Oxford University 1964

St. Cross College
St. Giles
Tel: 01865 278490
Founder: Oxford University 1965
Open: Not open to the public.

St. Edmund Hall
Queens Lane
Tel: 01865 279000
Founder: St. Edmund Riche of Abingdon c.l278
Open: Daily, daylight hours.

St. Hilda's College
Cowley Place
Tel: 01865 276884
Founder: Miss Dorothea Beale l893

St. Hugh's College
St. Margarets Road
Tel: 01865 274900
Founder: Dame Elizabeth Wordsworth 1886

St. John's College
St. Giles
Tel: 01865 277300
Founder: Sir Thomas White 1555

St. Peter's College
New Inn Hall Street
Tel: 01865 278900
Founder: Rev. Christopher Charvasse 1928

Trinity College
Broad Street
Tel: 01865 279900
Founder: Sir Thomas Pope 1554-5
Open: Mon - Fri 10am - Noon and 2 - 4pm. Sat
& Sun in term, 2 - 4pm; Sat & Sun in vacation
10am - Noon and 2 - 4pm.

University College
High Street
Tel: 01865 276602
Founder: Archdeacon William of Durham 1249
Open: Not open to the public.

Wadham College
Parks Road
Tel: 01865 277900
Founder: Nicholas & Dorothy Wadham 1610
Open: Term time: daily, 10am - 4.15pm.
Vacation: daily 10.30 - 11.45am and 1 - 4.15pm.

Wolfson College
Linton Road
Tel: 01865 274100
Founder: Oxford University 1966

Worcester College
Walton Street
Tel: 01865 278300
Founder: Sir Thomas Cookes 1714

© Adrian Baggett

This information is intended only as a guide. Times are subject to change due to functions, examinations, conferences, holidays, etc. You are advised to check in advance opening times and admission charges which may apply at some colleges, and at certain times of the year. Visitors wishing to gain admittance to the Colleges (meaning the Courts, not to the staircases & students' rooms) are advised to contact the Tourist Information Office. It should be noted that Halls normally close for lunch (12 - 2pm) and many are not open during the afternoon. Chapels may be closed during services. Libraries are not normally open, and Gardens do not usually include the Fellows' garden. Visitors, and especially guided groups, should always call on the Porters Lodge first. Groups should always book in advance. Dogs, except guide dogs are not allowed in any colleges.

For further details contact: Oxford Information Centre, The Old School, Gloucester Green, Oxford OX1 2DA.
Tel: +44 (0)1865 726871   Fax: +44 (0)1865 240261

National Trust Photographic Library, Clandon Park

National Trust Photographic Library, Hatchlands Park

CLANDON PARK/ HATCHLANDS PARK

GUILDFORD

www.nationaltrust.org.uk/clandonpark

Map 3

Owner:
The National Trust

▶ **CONTACT**

The Property Manager
Clandon Park/
Hatchlands Park
East Clandon
Guildford
Surrey GU4 7RT

Tel: 01483 222482
Fax: 01483 223176
e-mail: hatchlands@
nationaltrust.org.uk

▶ **LOCATION**
Clandon
OS Ref. TQ042 512
At West Clandon
on the A247,
3m E of Guildford.

Rail: Clandon BR 1m.

Hatchlands
OS Ref. TQ063 516
E of East Clandon
on the A246 Guildford -
Leatherhead road.

Rail: Clandon BR
2¹/₂ m, Horsley 3m.

Clandon Park & Hatchlands Park were built during the 18th century and are set amidst beautiful grounds. They are two of England's most outstanding country houses and are only five minutes' drive apart.

Clandon Park is a grand Palladian mansion, built c1730 by the Venetian architect, Leoni and notable for its magnificent two-storey marble hall. The house is rightly acclaimed for its remarkable collection of 18th century porcelain, textiles and furniture, which includes the Ivo Forde Meissen collection of Italian comedy figures and a series of Mortlake tapestries. The attractive gardens feature a parterre, grotto, Dutch garden and a Maori house with a fascinating history. Clandon is also

home to the Queen's Royal Surrey Regiment Museum. The excellent restaurant is renowned for its Sunday lunches - booking is advisable.

Hatchlands Park was built in 1756 for Admiral Boscawen and is set in a beautiful 430 acre Repton park offering a variety of park and woodland walks. There is also a small garden by Gertrude Jekyll flowering from late May to early July. Hatchlands contains splendid interiors by Robert Adam, decorated in appropriately nautical style. The rooms are hung with the Cobbe Collection of old master paintings and portraits, initially formed in the 18th century. It includes works by Bernini, Guercino, Poussin, Van Dyck, Gainsborough and Zoffany.

Hatchlands also houses the Cobbe Collection of keyboard instruments, the world's largest group of early keyboard instruments owned or played by famous composers such as Purcell, J C Bach, Mozart, Chopin, Liszt, Mahler and Elgar. Notable too are Marie Antoinette's piano and the instrument on which the world's most performed opera, Bizet's Carmen, was composed.

There are frequent concerts on instruments of the collection. For information contact: The Cobbe Collection Trust, tel. 01483 211474 or visit www.cobbecollection.co.uk.

Clive Barda, London

▶ **OPENING TIMES**

Clandon - House
28 March - 31 October
Tue - Thur, Suns &
BH Mons, Good Fri
& Easter Sat
11am - 5pm.

Garden
As house.

Museum
28 March - 31 October
Tue - Thur & Suns,
BH Mons, Good Fri
& Easter Sat
12 noon - 5pm.

Hatchlands - House
1 April - 31 October
Tue - Thur,
Suns & BH Mon,
Fris in August only.
2 - 5.30pm.

Park Walks
27 Mar - 31 Oct: Daily
11am - 6pm. Trail leaflets.

▶ **ADMISSION**

Clandon:
House/Grounds........ £6.00
   Child £3.00
   Family £15.00
Groups (Tue - Thur only)
   Adult £5.00

Hatchlands
House/Grounds........ £6.00
   Child £3.00
Park Walks only £2.50
   Child £1.25
   Family £15.00
Groups (Tue - Thur only)
   Adult £5.00

Combined ticket
Clandon/Hatchlands .£9.00
   Child £4.50
   Family £22.50

CONFERENCE/FUNCTION

ROOM	SIZE	MAX CAPACITY
Marble Hall Clandon Pk	40' x 40'	160 seated 200 standing

📷 ℹ️ Clandon Park. Tel: 01483 222482. No photography.

🍽️ For Clandon weddings and receptions tel: 01483 224912.

♿ Hatchlands suitable. Clandon partially suitable. WCs.

🍴 Licensed. Clandon: 01483 222502.

🚶 Clandon - by arrangement.

🎧 Hatchlands only.

📽️ Children's quizzes available.

🅿️ 🐕 Guide dogs only.

🔔 Clandon only. 😊 Tel: 1483 222482.

THE COBBE COLLECTION
AT HATCHLANDS
SURREY

www.cobbecollection.co.uk

Map 3

Owner:
The National Trust

▶ **CONTACT**

Cobbe Collection Trust
Hatchlands Park
East Clandon
Guildford
Surrey
GU4 7RT

Tel: 01483 211474
Fax: 01483 225922

e-mail: enquiries@
cobbecollection.co.uk

▶ **LOCATION**
OS Ref. TQ063 516

E of East Clandon, N of
A246 Guildford to
Leatherhead road.

The Cobbe Collections are set in sumptuous rooms designed by Robert Adam. The house, given to the National Trust with few contents, has been let to Mr & Mrs Alec Cobbe since 1987 and is lived in as a family home. The resulting arrangement of pictures, furniture, *objéts d'art* and the celebrated collection of keyboards, spanning 400 years and formerly belonging to some of the greatest names of classical music, has been called 'one of the most beautiful musical museums in the world'. The family art collection, formed initially in the 18th century, includes pictures by Allori, Bernini, Guercino, Poussin, Van Dyck, Gainsborough, Zoffany and many others.

World headlines were occasioned by the recent identification, among the family portraits, of the most youthful picture of Shakespeare's friend and patron, Henry Wriothesley, 3rd Earl of Southampton, formerly thought to have been of Lady Norton!

An audio-guide enables visitors to hear the sounds of instruments played by Purcell, J C Bach, Mozart, Beethoven, Chopin, Liszt and Mahler, which are all maintained in playing order. Leading musicians give concerts on the instruments throughout the year.

▶ **OPENING TIMES**

Hatchlands - House
1 April - 31 October
Tue - Thur,
Suns & BH Mon,
Fris in August only.
2 - 5.30pm.

Park Walks
27 Mar - 31 Oct: Daily
11am - 6pm. Trail leaflets.

▶ **ADMISSION**

Hatchlands

House/Grounds........ £6.00
   Child £3.00
   Park Walks only £2.50
   Child £1.25
   Family £15.00
Groups (Tue - Thur only)
   Adult £5.00

Combined ticket
Clandon/Hatchlands . £9.00
   Child £4.50
   Family £22.50

David Mees

 Suitable. WCs.

Licensed. No booking required, except for groups, tel: 01483 222502

Children's quizzes .

P

Guide dogs only.

 01483 222482.

153

Crown Copyright: Historic Royal Palaces

HAMPTON COURT PALACE

SURREY

www.hampton-court-palace.org.uk

Map 3

Managed by:
Historic Royal Palaces

▶ CONTACT

Hampton Court Palace
Surrey
KT8 9AU

Recorded info:
0870 752 7777

All other enquiries:
0870 751 5175

▶ LOCATION

OS Ref. TQ155 686

From M25/J15 and
A312, or M25/J12 and
A308, or M25/J10 and
A307.

Rail: From London
Waterloo direct to
Hampton Court
(32 mins).

Cardinal Wolsey transformed Hampton Court Palace into a lavish royal residence during the 16th century. Favoured home to Henry VIII, George II and William III, the palace was refashioned by Sir Christopher Wren in 1689, creating the beautiful Baroque style east front. With costume guided tours and multi-lingual audio guides, experience a magical journey back through 500 years of royal history.

The State Apartments of Henry VIII feature some of the most magnificent rooms in the palace, including the Chapel Royal and the Great Hall. Below, the vast Tudor Kitchens are alive with the smell of herbs, authentic dishes from the period

and the roaring real fire.

Ceremonial life of William III is revealed in the King's Apartments. The spectacular staircase leads to an ornate display of over 3,000 weapons in the King's Guard Chamber, whilst the private chambers offer a beautiful view of the Privy Garden. Nearby one of the finest collections of Renaissance paintings in Europe can also be viewed.

Other features of the palace include the oldest grapevine in Europe and the world famous maze. Hampton Court Palace, set in 60 acres of riverside gardens, brings you face to face with some of Britain's grandest history.

▶ OPENING TIMES

Summer
March - October
Tue - Sun:
9.30am - 5.15pm
Mon: 10.15am - 5.15pm.

Winter
November - February
Tue - Sun:
9.30am - 3.45pm
Mon: 10.15am - 3.45pm

Closed 24 - 26 December.

Last admission 45 mins before closing.

▶ ADMISSION

Telephone Information Line for admission prices:
0870 752 7777.

Advance Ticket Sales:
0870 753 7777.

Crown Copyright: Historic Royal Palaces

Information Centre. No photography indoors.

Available by arrangement.

Motorised buggies available at main entrance. WCs.

Licensed.

Ample for cars, coach parking nearby.

Rates on request.

In grounds, on leads. Guide dogs only in Palace.

For a full list of special events please telephone for details.

CONFERENCE/FUNCTION

ROOM	SIZE	MAX CAPACITY
Great Hall	88'6" x 35'6"	280/400
Cartoon Gallery	22'6" x 116'	220/350
Gt Watching Chamber	66'6" x 25'	120
Painted Room	33'3" x 21'3"	60/100
Ante Room	22' x 21'6"	60/100
King's Award Chamber	60'3" x 36'4"	120/150
Public Dining Room	31'6" x 55'6"	80/150

LOSELEY PARK

GUILDFORD

www.loseley-park.com

Loseley Park, built in 1562 by Sir William More, is a fine example of Elizabethan architecture, its mellow stone brought from the ruins of Waverley Abbey now over 850 years old. The house is set amid magnificent parkland grazed by the Loseley Jersey herd. Many visitors comment on the very friendly atmosphere of the house, it is a country house, the family home of descendants of the builder.

Furniture has been acquired by the family and includes an early 16th century Wrangelschrank beautifully inlaid with many different woods, a Queen Anne cabinet, Georgian armchairs and settee, a Hepplewhite four-poster bed and King George IV's coronation chair. The King's bedroom has Oudenarde tapestry and a carpet commemorating James I's visit.

The Christian pictures include the Henri Met de Bles triptych of the Nativity and modern mystical pictures of the living Christ, St Francis and St Bernadette. A Christian Cancer Help Centre meets twice monthly. Loseley House is available for dinners, functions and Civil weddings.

GARDEN

A magnificent Cedar of Lebanon presides over the front lawn. Parkland adjoins the lawn and a small lake adds to the beauty of Front Park. Walled Garden: Based on a Gertrude Jekyll design. Five gardens exist each with their own theme and character, making up the whole. These include the award-winning rose garden containing over 1,000 bushes, a magnificent vine walk, colourful fruit and flower garden and the serene fountain garden. Other features include a vegetable garden and moat walk.

Owner:
Mr Michael
More-Molyneux

▶ **CONTACT**

Nicky Rooney
Loseley Park
Guildford
Surrey   GU3 1HS

Tel: 01483 405120
Fax: 01483 302036

e-mail: enquiries@
loseley-park.com

▶ **LOCATION**

OS Ref. SU975 471

30m SW of London, leave A3 S of Guildford on to B3000. Signposted.

Bus: 1¼ m
from House.

Rail: Farncombe 1½ m, Guildford 2m, Godalming 3m.

Air: Heathrow 30m, Gatwick 30m.

CONFERENCE/FUNCTION

ROOM	SIZE	MAX CAPACITY
Tithe Barn	100' x 18'	200
Marquee	sites available	
Great Hall	70' x 40'	100
Drawing Rm	40' x 30'	50
Walled Gdn	Marquee	sites
Chestnut Ldg	18' x 38'	60

Chapel. New lakeside walk. Business launches & promotions. 10 - 12 acre field can be hired in addition to the lawns. Fashion shows, archery, garden parties, shows, rallies, filming, parkland, moat walk & terrace. Lectures can be arranged on the property, its contents, gardens & history. Loseley Christian Trust Exhibition, children's play area, picnic area, nature trail, home to Jersey herd since 1916; No unaccompanied children, no photography in house, no videos on estate. All group visits must be booked in advance.

Special functions, banquets and conference catering. Additional marquees for hire. Wedding receptions.

May alight at entrance to property. Access to all areas except house first floor. WCs.

Courtyard Tea Room.

Lunchtime restaurant.

Obligatory. Tour time for house, 40 mins.

150 cars, 6 coaches. Summer overflow car park.

Guide dogs only.

▶ **OPENING TIMES**

Summer
Garden, Shop, Tea Room & Lunchtime Restaurant
5 May - 30 September
Wed - Sun & BH Mons in May & Aug,
11am - 5pm.

Loseley House
2 Jun - 29 Aug:
Wed - Sun & BH Mons in May & Aug (guided tours),
1 - 5pm.

All Year
Tithe Barn, Chestnut Lodge, House, Walled Garden and Grounds available for private/ business functions, Civil weddings and receptions. Off-road 4 x 4 course.

▶ **ADMISSION**

House & Gardens
Adult £6.00
Child (5-16yrs) £3.00
Conc. £5.00
Child (under 5yrs) ...... Free

Booked Groups (10+)
Adult £5.50
Child (5-16yrs) £2.50
Conc. £4.50

Garden only
Adult £3.00
Child (5-16yrs) £1.50
Conc. £2.50

Booked Groups (10+)
Adult £2.75
Child (5-16yrs) £1.25
Conc. £2.25

▶ **SPECIAL EVENTS**
Please telephone for details.

CHA

ALBURY PARK
ALBURY, GUILDFORD, SURREY GU5 9BB

www.cha.org.uk

Tel: 01483 202964 **Fax:** 01483 205013 **e-mail:** alburypark@cha.org.uk
Owner: Country Houses Association **Contact:** The Administrator
Former home of the Percy family, dukes of Northumberland. Pugin was largely responsible for the outside including the unique chimneys. Inside the house there is a beautiful staircase and drawing room designed by Sir John Soane. Albury Park has been converted into apartments for active retired people.
Location: OS Ref. TQ058 479. 1¹/₂ m E of Albury off A25 Guildford to Dorking road. Stations: Guildford 5m, Gomshall 1m. Bus route: No. 21, 25 or 32 from Guildford.
Open: 1 May - 30 Sept: Wed & Thur, 2 - 5pm.
Admission: Adult £2.50, Child £1.50. Groups by arrangement.
⊤ ✗ 2 twin w/bathroom. CHA members & Wolsey Lodge guests only. ▲

BOX HILL ✿
The Old Fort, Box Hill Road, Box Hill, Tadworth KT20 7LB
Tel: 01306 885502 **Fax:** 01306 875030 **e-mail:** boxhill@nationaltrust.org.uk
www.nationaltrust.org.uk/northdowns
Owner: The National Trust **Contact:** The Property Manager
An outstanding area of woodland and chalk downland, long famous as a destination for day-trippers from London.
Location: OS Ref. TQ171 519. 1m N of Dorking, 1¹/₂ m S of Leatherhead on A24.
Open: Servery: All year, daily (except 25/26 Dec & 1 Jan), 11 - 5pm or dusk.
Admission: Countryside: Free. Car/coach park £2, NT members Free.

CAREW MANOR DOVECOTE
Church Road, Beddington, Surrey SM6 7NH
Tel: 020 8770 4781 **Fax:** 020 8770 4777 **e-mail:** sutton.museum@ukonline.co.uk
www.sutton.gov.uk
Owner: London Borough of Sutton **Contact:** Ms V Murphy
An early 18th century octagonal brick dovecote with around 1200 nesting boxes and the original potence (circular ladder). Opened for tours with the adjacent late medieval Grade I listed Great Hall of Carew Manor.
Location: OS Ref. TQ295 652. Just off A232 at entrance to Beddington Park.
Open: Tours: 23 May, 27 Jun, 18 Jul & 26 Sept: 2 & 3.30pm.
Admission: Adult £3.50, Children £2.
🌣 P ✗ Guide dogs only.

CLANDON PARK/ ✿
HATCHLANDS PARK
See page 152 for full page entry.

NTPL / John Bethall

NT Photographic Library

CLAREMONT LANDSCAPE GARDEN ✿
PORTSMOUTH ROAD, ESHER, SURREY KT10 9JG

www.nationaltrust.org.uk/claremont

Tel: 01372 467806 **Fax:** 01372 464394 **e-mail:** claremont@nationaltrust.org.uk
Owner: The National Trust **Contact:** The Property Manager
One of the earliest surviving English landscape gardens, restored to its former glory. Begun by Sir John Vanbrugh and Charles Bridgeman before 1720, the garden was extended and naturalised by William Kent. 'Capability' Brown also made improvements. Features include a lake, island with pavilion, grotto, turf amphitheatre, viewpoints and avenues.
Location: OS Ref. TQ128 632. On S edge of Esher, on E side of A307 (no access from Esher bypass).
Open: Jan - end Mar, Nov - end Dec: daily except Mons: 10am - 5pm or sunset if earlier. Apr - end Oct: daily: Mon - Fri, 10am - 6pm, Sats, Suns & BHs, 10am - 7pm. NB: Garden closes for major event days in July, please check in advance. Closed 25 Dec.
Admission: Adult £4, Child £2. Coach groups must book; no coach groups on Suns. Family (2+2) £10. Groups (15+), £3.50. Discount if using public transport.
🅿 ♿ Limited. WC. ✗ No dogs (Apr - Oct). ✆ Tel for details.

THE COBBE COLLECTION 🌿
AT HATCHLANDS

See page 153 for full page entry.

CROYDON PALACE

OLD PALACE ROAD, CROYDON, SURREY CR0 1AX

www.friendsofoldpalace.org

Tel: 020 8688 2027

Owner/Contact: The Whitgift Foundation

A residence of the Archbishops of Canterbury between the 12th and 18th centuries and now home of Old Palace School of John Whitgift which is a Whitgift Foundation School for girls from 4 - 18. 15th century Banqueting Hall (one of the outstanding great medieval halls of London); Norman Undercroft; 15th century Guard Room and Chapel; Tudor Long Gallery; Elizabeth I's bedroom. West wing contains some of the earliest medieval brickwork in England.

Location: OS Ref. TQ320 654. 200 yds S of Croydon parish church, 400 yds W of Croydon High St.

Open: 13 - 17 Apr; 1 - 5 Jun; 12 - 17 Jul; 25 - 30 Oct.

Admission: Adult £5, Child/OAP £4.

NT Photographic Library: Geoff Hamilton

DAPDUNE WHARF 🌿

RIVER WEY NAVIGATIONS, WHARF ROAD, GUILDFORD GU1 4RR

www.nationaltrust.org.uk/riverwey

Tel: 01483 561389   **Fax:** 01483 531667   **e-mail:** riverwey@nationaltrust.org.uk

Owner: The National Trust   **Contact:** Wharf Warden

Dapdune Wharf is the centrepiece of one of The National Trust's most unusual properties, the River Wey Navigations. Restored wharf buildings and a Wey barge can be seen. Interactive exhibits and displays tell the fascinating story of Surrey's secret waterway, one of the first British rivers to be made navigable.

Location: OS Ref. SU993 502. On Wharf Road to rear of Surrey County Cricket Ground, 1/2 m N of Guildford town centre off Woodbridge Road (A322).

Open: 27 Mar - 31 Oct: Thur - Mon, 11am - 5pm. River trips as for Wharf.

Admission: Adult £3, Child £1.50, Family £7.50. Groups (booked, min 15): Adult £2.50. NT members Free.

▢ ♿ ☕ 𝑓 By arrangement. ■ 🅿 Limited. 🐕 In grounds, on leads.

FARNHAM CASTLE

Farnham, Surrey GU9 0AG

Tel: 01252 721194   **Fax:** 01252 711283   **e-mail:** info@farnhamcastle.com

Owner: The Church Commissioners   **Contact:** Farnham Castle

Bishop's Palace built in Norman times by Henry of Blois. Tudor and Jacobean additions.

Location: OS Ref. SU839 474. 1/2 m N of Farnham town centre on A287.

Open: All year: Weds, 2 - 4pm except Christmas & New Year.

Admission: Adult £2.50, Child/Conc £1.50.

FARNHAM CASTLE KEEP ⌗

Castle Hill, Farnham, Surrey GU6 0AG

Tel: 01252 713393   www.english-heritage.org.uk/visits

Owner: English Heritage   **Contact:** The Head Custodian

Used as a fortified manor by the medieval Bishops of Winchester, this motte and bailey castle has been in continuous occupation since the 12th century. You can visit the large shell-keep enclosing a mound in which are massive foundations of a Norman tower.

Location: OS Ref. SU839 474. 1/2 m N of Farnham town centre on A287.

Open: 1 Apr - 30 Sept: 10am - 6pm. 1 - 31 Oct, 10am - 5pm. Times subject to change April 2004.

Admission: Adult £2.50, Child, £1.30, Conc. £1.90. Prices subject to change April 2004.

▢ ♿ Ground floor & grounds. ▢ Free. 🅿 🐕 In grounds, on leads.

GODDARDS

Abinger Common, Dorking, Surrey RH5 6TH

Tel: 01628 825920 or 01628 825925 (bookings) **www**.landmarktrust.co.uk

Owner: The Lutyens Trust, leased to The Landmark Trust **Contact:** The Landmark Trust
Built by Sir Edwin Lutyens in 1898 - 1900 and enlarged by him in 1910. Garden by
Gertrude Jekyll. Given to the Lutyens Trust in 1991 and now managed and
maintained by the Landmark Trust, which let buildings for self-catering holidays. The
whole house, apart from the library, is available for up to 12 people. Full details of
Goddards and 178 other historic buildings available for holidays are featured in The
Landmark Handbook (price £9.50 refundable against booking), from The Landmark
Trust, Shottesbrooke, Maidenhead, Berkshire SL6 3SW.

Location: OS Ref. TQ120 450. 4$^{1}/_{2}$ m SW of Dorking on the village green in Abinger
Common. Signposted Abinger Common, Friday Street and Leith Hill from A25.

Open: Strictly by appointment. Must be booked in advance, including parking, which is
very limited. Visits booked for Weds afternoons from the Wed after Easter until the last Wed
of Oct, between 2.30 - 5pm. Only those with pre-booked tickets will be admitted.

Admission: £3. Tickets available from Mrs Baker on 01306 730871, Mon - Fri, 9am &
6pm. Visitors will have access to part of the garden and house only.

GUILDFORD HOUSE GALLERY

155 High Street, Guildford, Surrey Gu1 3AJ

Tel/Fax: 01483 444742 (Guildford Borough Council)

www.guildfordhouse.co.uk

Owner/Contact: Guildford Borough Council

A beautifully restored 17th century town house with a number of original features
including a finely carved staircase, panelled rooms and decorative plaster ceilings. A
varied temporary exhibition programme including paintings, photography and craft
work. Exhibition and events leaflet available. Lecture and workshop programme.
Details on application.

Location: OS Ref. SU996 494. Central Guildford on High Street.

Open: Tue - Sat, 10am - 4.45pm.

Admission: Free.

Public car park nearby. P Guide dogs only. Tel for details.

HAMPTON COURT PALACE

See page 154 for full page entry.

HATCHLANDS PARK/ CLANDON PARK

See page 152 for full page entry.

HONEYWOOD HERITAGE CENTRE

Honeywood Walk, Carshalton, Surrey SM5 3NX

Tel: 020 8770 4297 **Fax:** 020 8770 4297

e-mail: lbshoneywood@ukonline.co.uk **www**.sutton.gov.uk

Owner: London Borough of Sutton **Contact:** The Curator
A 17th century listed building next to the picturesque Carshalton Ponds, containing
displays on many aspects of the history of the London Borough of Sutton plus a
changing programme of exhibitions and events on a wide range of subjects.
Attractive garden at rear.

Location: OS Ref. TQ279 646. On A232 approximately 4m W of Croydon.

Open: Wed - Fri, 11am - 5pm. Sat, Suns & BH Mons, 10am - 5pm. Free admission to
shop & tearooms.

Admission: Adult £1.20, Child 60p, under 5 Free. Groups by arrangement.
Ground floor. WC. P Limited. Guide dogs only.
Tel for details.

KEW GARDENS

Kew, Richmond, Surrey TW9 3AB

Tel: 020 8332 5655 **Fax:** 020 8332 5197 **Contact:** Enquiry Unit

Kew's 300 acres offer many special attractions: including the 65ft high Palm House.

Location: OS Ref. TQ188 776. A307. Junc. A307 & A205 (1m Chiswick roundabout M4).

Open: 9.30am, daily except 24/25 Dec. Closing time varies according to the season.
Please telephone for further information.

Admission: Adult £7.50, Child (under 16yrs) Free, Conc. £5.50.

LEITH HILL

Coldharbour, Surrey

Tel: 01306 711777 **Fax:** 01306 712153 **www**.nationaltrust.org.uk/northdowns

Owner: The National Trust **Contact:** The Property Manager
The highest point in south-east England, crowned by an 18th century Gothic tower, from
which there are magnificent views. The surrounding woodland contains ancient stands
of hazel and oak, and there is a colourful display of rhododendrons in May - Jun.

Location: OS Ref. TQ139 432. 1m SW of Coldharbour A29/B2126.

Open: Tower: 27 Apr - 31 Oct: Wed, Fri, Sat, Sun & BHs; 10am - 5pm. 1 Nov - 26 Mar:
Sat, Sun & BHs (closed 25 Dec), 10am - 3.30pm. Rhododendron Wood & Estate: All
year: daily.

Admission: Tower: £1, Child 50p. Rhododendron Wood: £2 per car.
No vehicular access to summit. Partial. When Tower open. Guided walks.
P Parking at foot of hill, $^{1}/_{2}$m walk from Tower. Not in picnic area or Tower.

LITTLE HOLLAND HOUSE

40 Beeches Avenue, Carshalton, Surrey SM5 3LW

Tel: 020 8770 4781 **Fax:** 020 8770 4777

e-mail: valary.murphy@sutton.gov.uk **www**.sutton.gov.uk

Owner: London Borough of Sutton **Contact:** Ms V Murphy
The home of Frank Dickinson (1874 - 1961) artist, designer and craftsman, who
dreamt of a house that would follow the philosophy and theories of William Morris
and John Ruskin. Dickinson designed, built and furnished the house himself from
1902 onwards. The Grade II* listed interior features handmade furniture, metal work,
carvings and paintings produced by Dickinson in the Arts and Crafts style.

Location: OS Ref. TQ275 634. On B278 1m S of junction with A232.

Open: First Sun of each month & BH Suns & Mons (excluding Christmas & New Year),
1.30 - 5.30pm.

Admission: Free. Groups by arrangement, £3pp (includes talk and guided tour).
No photography in house. Ground floor. By arrangement.
Guide dogs only.

LOSELEY PARK

See page 155 for full page entry.

OAKHURST COTTAGE

Hambledon, Godalming, Surrey GU8 4HF

Tel: 01428 684090 **e-mail:** oakhurstcottage@nationaltrust.org.uk

Owner: The National Trust **Contact:** The Witley Centre
A small 16th century timber-framed cottage, painted by both Helen Allingham and
Myles Birket Foster, containing furniture and artefacts reflecting two or more
centuries of continuing occupation. There is a delightful cottage garden and a small
barn containing agricultural implements.

Location: OS Ref. SU965 385. Hambledon, Surrey.

Open: 27 Mar - 31 Oct: Weds, Thurs, Sats, Suns & BH Mons. Strictly by appointment,
2 - 5pm.

Admission: Adult £3, Child £1.50 (including guided tour). No reduction for groups.
Unsuitable. Obligatory, by arrangement. P Limited.

Jerry Harpur

PAINSHILL PARK 🏛

PORTSMOUTH ROAD, COBHAM, SURREY KT11 1JE

www.painshill.co.uk

Tel: 01932 868113   **Fax:** 01932 868001   **e-mail:** info@painshill.co.uk

Owner: Painshill Park Trust   **Contact:** Visitor Management

A unique award winning restoration of England's 18th century Heritage. Within its 160 acres, its Hamilton Landscapes are a work of art that influenced the future of England's countryside and culture. Between 1738 and 1773 the Hon Charles Hamilton transformed barren heathland into a sequence of subtle and surprising vistas. Around the 14 acre serpentine lake, Hamilton assembled a series of carefully designed views known as the Hamilton Landscapes. The visitor moves from scene to scene; past the vineyard to an evergreen amphitheatre and on to the Gothic Temple, from the magical crystal grotto to a ruined Mausoleum, from a wild wood to the colourful flower beds that surround the site of the Temple of Bacchus.

Following years of dereliction the Landscapes have been restored to their original pre-eminence, winning the Europa Nostra Medal for exemplary restoration. Available for corporate and private hire, location filming, wedding receptions, etc.

Location: OS Ref. TQ099 605. M25/J10 to London. W of Cobham on A245. Entrance 200 yds E of A245/A307 roundabout.

Open: Mar - Oct: Tue - Sun and BH Mons, 10.30am - 6pm (last admission 4.30pm). Nov - Feb: Wed - Sun and BH Mons (closed Christmas Day), 11am - 4pm or dusk if earlier (last admission 3pm).

Admission: Adult £6, Child (5-16) £3.50, under 5 Free, Conc. £5.25. Pre-booked groups (10+) £5pp.

📷 🍴Marquee site. ♿ ▣Licensed. 🅕By arrangement. 🅿 ♿Guide dogs only. ✳

NTPL/Nick Meers

Gertrude Jekyll

1843-1932

Born in London and brought up in Surrey, Gertrude Jekyll is one of the great legends of British garden design. Initially trained as an artist, failing eyesight in her early 30s led her to give up her work as an artist and pursue a highly successful career as a landscape designer. Working with the architect Edwin Lutyens, she created nearly 70 house and garden schemes influenced by the Arts & Crafts Movement. Miss Jekyll banned the bright gaudy flowers loved by the Victorians. Look out for a 'natural' planting style that includes old fashioned cottage garden plants, rambling roses and soft, carefully blended colours planted in large drifts.

Visit Hestercombe Gardens, Somerset to see a garden restored and planted to Miss Jekyll's original plans. Visit also Barrington Court, Somerset, Castle Drogo, Devon, Goddards, Surrey, and Knebworth House, Hertfordshire.

Garden Designer, Writer & Artist

POLESDEN LACEY ❦

GREAT BOOKHAM, Nr DORKING, SURREY RH5 6BD

www.nationaltrust.org.uk/polesdenlacey

Tel: 01372 452048   **Infoline:** 01372 458203   **Fax:** 01372 452023
e-mail: polesdenlacey@nationaltrust.org.uk

Owner: The National Trust   **Contact:** The Property Manager

Originally an elegant 1820s Regency villa in a magnificent landscape setting. The house was remodelled after 1906 by the Hon Mrs Ronald Greville, a well-known Edwardian hostess. Her collection of fine paintings, furniture, porcelain and silver are still displayed in the reception rooms and galleries. Extensive grounds, walled rose garden, lawns and landscaped walks.

Location: OS Ref. TQ136 522. 5m NW of Dorking, 2m S of Great Bookham, off A246.

Open: House: 24 Mar - 7 Nov: Wed - Sun, 11am - 5pm also BH Mons starting with Easter. Grounds: All year: daily, 11am - 6pm/dusk. Last admission to house ½ hr before closing.

Admission: Garden, grounds & landscape walks: Adult £5, Child £2.50, Family £12.50. House: Adult £3 extra, Child £1.50 extra, Family £7.50 extra. All year, booked groups £6.50 (house, garden & walks).

📷 🍴 ♿ 🍴Licensed. 🅿 Limited for coaches. ♿In grounds on leads. ✳
📺Tel: 01372 452048 for info.

South East - England

RHS GARDEN WISLEY

Nr WOKING, SURREY GU23 6QB

www.rhs.org.uk

Tel: 01483 224234 **Fax:** 01483 211750

Owner/Contact: The Royal Horticultural Society

A garden to enjoy all year round with something to see for everyone. Wisley provides the visitor with ideas and inspiration and the benefit of experience from experts. The Wisley Plant Centre with plants for sale, The Wisley Shop with books and gifts and for refreshments the Café and Restaurant.

Location: OS Ref. TQ066 583. NW side of A3 ¹/₂ m SW of M25/J10. Brown Signs.

Open: All year: daily (except Christmas Day), Mon - Fri, 10am - 6pm (4.30pm Nov - Feb). Sat & Sun, 9am - 6pm (4.30pm Nov - Feb).

Admission: RHS Members: Free. Adult £7, Child (6-16yrs) £2, Child (under 6) Free. Groups (10+): Adult £5.50, Child £1.60.

⬜ ⬛ ♿ Wheelchairs available tel: 01483 211113 & special map. WC. ⬛ ⓣ Licensed. 🅵 By arrangement. ⬜ 🅿 ⬛ 🚗 Guide dogs only. ❄ ⬜

RAMSTER GARDENS

Ramster, Chiddingfold, Surrey GU8 4SN

Tel: 01428 654167 **Fax:** 01428 658345

Owner/Contact: Mrs M Gunn

20 acres of woodland and shrub garden.

Location: OS Ref. SU950 333. 1¹/₂ m S of Chiddingfold on A283.

Open: 24 Apr - 27 Jun: 11am - 5pm.

Admission: £4, Child Free.

RUNNYMEDE ⚜

Egham, Surrey

Tel: 01784 432891 **Fax:** 01784 479007 **e-mail:** runnymede@nationaltrust.org.uk
www.nationaltrust.org.uk

Owner: The National Trust   **Contact:** The Head Warden

Runnymede is an attractive area of riverside meadows, grassland and broadleaf woodland, rich in diversity of flora and fauna, and part-designated a Site of Special Scientific Interest. It was on this site, in 1215, that King John sealed Magna Carta.

Location: OS Ref. TQ007 720. 2m W of Runnymede Bridge, on S side of A308, M25/J13.

Open: All year. Riverside Car park (grass): Apr - 30 Sept: daily, 9am - 7pm. Tearoom Car park (hard standing): daily, all year, 8.30am - 5pm (later in Summer).

Admission: Fees payable for parking (NT members Free), fishing & mooring.

⬜ ♿ Partial. ⬛ 🅵 🅿 ❄ ⬜ Tel for details.

SHALFORD MILL ⚜

Shalford, Guildford, Surrey GU4 8BS

Tel: 01483 561389 **www.**nationaltrust.org.uk

Owner: The National Trust

18th century watermill on the Tillingbourne, given in 1932 by "Ferguson's Gang".

Location: OS Ref. TQ000 476. 1¹/₂ m S of Guildford on A281, opposite Sea Horse Inn.

Open: Daily, 10am - 5pm.

Admission: Free. No unaccompanied children.

❄

Jerry Harpur

TITSEY PLACE

TITSEY, OXTED, SURREY RH8 0SD

www.titsey.com

Tel: 01273 407056 **Fax:** 01273 478995
e-mail: kate.moisson@struttandparker.co.uk

Owner: Trustees of the Titsey Foundation   **Contact:** Kate Moisson

Stunning mansion house. Situated outside Limpsfield. Extensive formal and informal gardens containing Victorian walled garden, lakes, fountains and rose gardens. Outstanding features of this house include important paintings and *objéts d'art*. Home of the Gresham and Leveson Gower family since the 15th century. Infinite capacity in this magnificent garden, numbers unavoidably restricted on house tours.

Location: OS Ref. TQ406 553. A25 Oxted - Westerham, through Limpsfield and into Bluehouse Lane and Water Lane, follow blue signs.

Open: Mid May - end Sept: Wed & Sun, 1 - 5pm including Easter Mon (garden only) and all Summer BHs.

Admission: House & Garden: Adult/Child £5. Garden only: £2.50. Groups (20+): Adult £6.

ⓘ No photography in house. No barbecues. ♿ Unsuitable. 🅵 Obligatory.
🅿 Limited for coaches. ⬛

WHITEHALL

1 Malden Road, Cheam, Surrey SM3 8QD

Tel: 020 8643 1236   **Fax:** 020 8770 4777

e-mail: curators@whitehallcheam.fsnet.co.uk   **www**.sutton.gov.uk

Owner: London Borough of Sutton   **Contact:** The Curator

A Tudor timber-framed house, c1500 with later additions, in the heart of Cheam village conservation area. Displays on the history of the house and the people who lived here, plus nearby Nonsuch Palace, Cheam School and William Gilpin (Dr Syntax). Changing exhibition programme and special event days throughout the year. Attractive rear garden features medieval well from c1400.

Location: OS Ref. TQ242 638. Approx. 2m S of A3 on A2043 just N of junction with A232.

Open: Wed - Fri, 2 - 5pm; Sat, 10am - 5pm; Sun & BH Mons, 2 - 5pm.

Admission: Adult £1.20, Child (under 16yrs) 60p, Child under 5yrs Free. Groups by arrangement.

▢ ♿Ground floor. ▣ 🚫 🎧 ▣ 🐕Guide dogs only. ❄ ♛Tel for details.

NTPL / D Sellman

Polesden Lacey, Surrey.

NTPL / D Sellman

WINKWORTH ARBORETUM ❧

HASCOMBE ROAD, GODALMING, SURREY GU8 4AD

www.nationaltrust.org.uk/winkwortharboretum

Tel: 01483 208477   **Fax:** 01483 208252

e-mail: winkwortharboretum@nationaltrust.org.uk

Owner: The National Trust   **Contact:** The Head of Arboretum

Hillside woodland with two lakes, many rare trees and shrubs and fine views. The most impressive displays are in spring for bluebells and azaleas, autumn for colour and wildlife. Delightful 100 year old boathouse on Rowes Flashe lake. Seasonal opening.

Location: OS Ref. SU990 412. Near Hascombe, 2m SE of Godalming on E side of B2130.

Open: All year round: daily during daylight hours. May be closed due to high winds. Boathouse: 1 Apr - 31 Oct. Due to essential works to dams it will be necessary to limit access to lakeside during 2003.

Admission: Adult £4, Child (5-16yrs) £2, Family (2+2) £10 (additional family member £1.75). Discounts for 10 or more.

▢ ♿Limited. WC. ▣ 🐕In grounds, on leads. ❄

161

ARUNDEL CASTLE

ARUNDEL

www.arundelcastle.org

Map 3

Owner:
Arundel Castle
Trustees Ltd

▶ **CONTACT**

The Comptroller
Arundel Castle
Arundel
West Sussex
BN18 9AB

Tel: 01903 883136
or 01903 882173

Fax: 01903 884581

e-mail: info@
arundelcastle.org

A thousand years of history is waiting to be discovered at Arundel Castle in West Sussex. Dating from the 11th century, the Castle is both ancient fortification and stately home of the Dukes of Norfolk and their ancestors and is now the principal residence of the present 18th Duke and Duchess and their family.

Set high on a hill, this magnificent castle commands stunning views across the River Arun and out to sea. Climb the Keep, explore the battlements, wander in the grounds and recently restored Victorian gardens and relax in the Fitzalan Chapel garden.

The Castle suffered tremendous damage during the English Civil War and the process of structural restoration began in earnest in the 18th century and continued up until 1900. It was one of the first private residences to have electricity and central heating and has its own fire engine, which is still on view today.

Inside the Castle, 23 rooms are open to the public including the vast Baron's Hall with its fine collection of 16th century furniture, the Armoury with a unique assemblage of armour and weaponry, tapestries hang above the Grand Staircase leading to the renovated Victorian bedrooms and bathrooms, paintings by Van Dyck, Gainsborough, Canaletto and others, together with the personal possessions of Mary, Queen of Scots, including the gold and enamel rosary that she carried to her execution.

A full programme of events takes place on most Sundays during the season, most of which are included in the standard admission charge.

▶ **LOCATION**

OS Ref. TQ018 072

Central Arundel, N of A27
Brighton 40 mins,
Worthing 15 mins,
Chichester 15 mins.
From London A3 or
A24, 1½ hrs.
M25 motorway, 30m.

Bus: Bus stop 100 yds.

Rail: Station ½ m.

Air: Gatwick 25m.

ℹ️ No photography inside the Castle. Guidebooks in French & German.

♿ Most areas accessible. Visitors may alight at the entrance, before parking in the allocated areas. WCs.

🍴 Restaurant seats 140. Special rates for booked groups. Self-service restaurant in Castle serves home-made food. Groups must book in advance for morning coffee, lunch or afternoon tea.

🚶 Pre-booked groups only. Tour time 1½ hrs. Tours available in Japanese.

🅿️ Ample. Coaches can park free in town coach park.

📷 Items of particular interest include a Norman Motte & Keep, Armoury & Victorian bedrooms. Special rates for schoolchildren (aged 5-15) and teachers.

❄️

▶ **OPENING TIMES**

Summer

1 April - 31 October
Daily (except Sats)
Grounds, gardens, shop
and restaurant
11am - 5pm.

Castle Rooms
12 noon - 5pm.
Last admission 4pm.

Winter

1 November - 31 March
Pre-booked groups only.

▶ **ADMISSION**

Summer

Adult	£9.50
Child (5-16)	£6.00
Conc.	£7.50
Family (2+5max)	£26.50

Groups (20+)

Adult	£8.00
Child (5-16)	£4.50
Conc.	£6.00

Pre-booked Groups
(subject to minimum fee)

Mornings	£8.00
Evenings	£25.00
Saturdays	£25.00

Winter

Pre-booked groups
(subject to minimum fee)

All entries	£25.00

NTPL: Rupert Truman

Map 4

Owner:
The National Trust

▶ CONTACT

The Property Manager
Bateman's
Burwash
Etchingham
East Sussex   TN19 7DS

Tel: 01435 882302

Fax: 01435 882811

e-mail: batemans@
nationaltrust.org.uk

▶ LOCATION
OS Ref. TQ671 238

¹/₂ m S of Burwash
off A265.

Rail: Etchingham 3m,
then bus (twice daily).

Air: Gatwick 40m.

BATEMAN'S ❦

BURWASH

www.nationaltrust.org.uk/places/batemans

Built in 1634 and home to Rudyard Kipling for over 30 years, Bateman's lies in the richly wooded landscape of the Sussex Weald. Visit this Sussex sandstone manor house, built by a local ironmaster, where the famous writer lived from 1902 to 1936. See the rooms as they were in Kipling's day, including the study where the view inspired him to write some of his well-loved works including *Puck of Pook's Hill* and *Rewards and Fairies*. Find the mementoes of Kipling's time in India and illustrations from his famous *Jungle Book* tales of *Mowgli, Baloo and Shere Khan*.

Wander through the delightful Rose Garden with its pond and statues, with Mulberry and Herb gardens and discover the wild garden, through which flows the River Dudwell. Through the wild garden, you will find the Mill where you can watch corn being ground on most Saturday and Wednesday afternoons and one of the world's first water-driven turbines installed by Kipling to generate electricity for the house. In the garage, see a 1928 Rolls Royce, one of several owned by Kipling who was a keen early motorist.

Savour the peace and tranquillity of this beautiful property which Kipling described as *'A good and peaceable place'* and of which he said *'we have loved it, ever since our first sight of it…'*.

There is a picnic glade next to the car park, or you can enjoy morning coffee, a delicious lunch or afternoon tea in the licensed tearoom where there is special emphasis on using local produce. The well-stocked gift shop offers the largest collection of Kipling books in the area.

▶ OPENING TIMES

3 Apr - 31 Oct:
Sat - Wed, Good Fri &
BH Mons, 11am - 5.00pm.
Last admission 4.30pm.

▶ ADMISSION

House & Garden

Adult	£5.50
Child	£2.70
Family (2+3)	£13.70
Groups	£4.60

NTPL/ Geoffrey Frosh

Ground floor & grounds.
WC. Computerised virtual tour of upper floors.

Licensed.

Tel for details.

South East - England

GOODWOOD HOUSE 🏛

CHICHESTER

www.goodwood.co.uk

Map 3

Owner:
The Earl of March

▶ **CONTACT**

Curator's Secretary
Goodwood House
Goodwood
Chichester
West Sussex PO18 0PX

Tel: 01243 755048
01243 755042
(Weddings)
Fax: 01243 755005
Recorded info:
01243 755040
e-mail: curator
@goodwood.co.uk
or weddings@
goodwood.co.uk

▶ **LOCATION**

OS Ref. SU888 088

3¹/₂m NE of Chichester.
A3 from London then
A286 or A285. M27/A27
from Portsmouth or
Brighton.

Rail: Chichester 3¹/₂m
Arundel 9m.

Air: Heathrow 1¹/₂ hrs
Gatwick ³/₄ hr.

Nestling at the heart of one of the world's finest sporting estates, Goodwood House epitomises history, style and glamour. Today, Goodwood continues to encapsulate the flamboyance, innovation and generous party spirit that have been the signature of the Dukes of Richmond for three hundred years. Set in the strongly coloured, gilded, Regency interiors, the art collection comprises fine French furniture and tapestries, Sèvres porcelain, glorious views of London by Canaletto and sporting scenes on the estate by George Stubbs. There are also hundreds of other superb paintings. Special pieces are regularly rotated and displayed, and can also be seen in temporary exhibitions, which are advertised on the website: in 2004 the *Mistress of the House*

exhibition will be on show in the early part of the year. Items are also available for viewing by written appointment, and arrangements to see the books can be made by written application to the Curator (there is a charge for these viewings). Still inhabited by the family, Goodwood effortlessly exudes the glamour of a ducal seat. It is not only a beautiful house to visit on an Open Day, but is also renowned for its elegant entertaining, enjoying a worldwide reputation for excellence as a venue for unforgettable weddings, functions and corporate events. With horse racing, motorsport, aviation, a hotel and leisure centre and two golf courses also on offer, there is something for everyone at Goodwood; and at its heart lies the great historic house.

▶ **OPENING TIMES**

Summer

28 March - 4 October:
Most Sun & Mon
afternoons.

1 - 30 Aug:
Sun - Thur, 1 - 5pm.

The house is sometimes closed for Special Events, please ring Recorded Information on 01243 755040 to check these dates and any additional closures, namely on 25 Apr; 20/21 & 27/28 Jun and on 5 Sept.

Connoisseurs' Days

Group visits with special guided tours can be booked.

▶ **ADMISSION**

House

Adult	£7.00
Child (12 - 18yrs)	£3.00
Child (under 12 yrs)	Free
OAP	£6.00

Groups (20 - 200)

Open Day	£6.00
Morning	£8.50
Connoisseur	£9.00

▶ **SPECIAL EVENTS**

MISTRESS OF THE HOUSE EXHIBITION
Glorious Goodwood
Race Week.

Goodwood Festival of Speed & Historic Motor Sport Event:
Please visit the website.

CONFERENCE/FUNCTION

ROOM	SIZE	MAX CAPACITY
Ballroom	79' x 23'	200
11 other rooms also available		

Conference facilities. No photography. Highly trained guides in every room. Shell House optional extra on Connoisseurs' Days or by Group Appointment.

 Obligatory. **P** Ample.

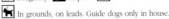 In grounds, on leads. Guide dogs only in house.

Civil Wedding Licence.

Map 3

LEONARDSLEE
LAKES & GARDENS

HORSHAM

www.leonardslee.com

Leonardslee represents one of the largest and most spectacular woodland gardens in England, in a most magnificent setting, only a few miles from the M23. Begun 200 years ago, and enlarged by Sir Edmund Loder since 1889, it is still maintained by the Loder family today. The 240 acre (100 hectare) valley is world famous for its spring display of azaleas and rhododendrons around the seven lakes, giving superb views and reflections.

The famous *rhododendron loderi*, was raised by Sir Edmund Loder in 1901. The original plants can still be seen in the garden. In May, the fragrance of their huge blooms pervades the air throughout the valley. The delightful Rock Garden, is a kaleidoscope of colour in May, then new plantings of *Hydrangeas*, *Cornus* and *Kalmias* give colour in the summer months.

A fine collection of Bonsai, including specimen Bonsai maples and choice group plantings show this living art-form to perfection. At Leonardslee, not only flora but fauna are welcome too! Wallabies (used as mowing machines!) have lived wild in parts of the valley for over 100 years, and deer, (Sika, Fallow and Axis) may be seen in the parklands. Ducks, geese and swans adorn the lakes where large carp glide.

Other attractions include the Loder family collection of Victorian motorcars (1889 - 1900), which provide a fascinating view of the different designs adopted by the first pioneers of the automobile industry, while the 'Behind the Dolls House' exhibition shows a country estate of 100 years ago, all in miniature $1/12$th scale, and has proved so popular that it has been extended.

Owner:
R Loder Esq

▶ CONTACT

R Loder Esq
Leonardslee Gardens
Lower Beeding
Horsham
West Sussex   RH13 6PP

Tel: 01403 891212
Fax: 01403 891305

e-mail: gardens@
leonardslee.com

▶ LOCATION

OS Ref. TQ222 260

M23 to Handcross then
B2110 (signposted
Cowfold) for 4m.
From London:
1 hr 15 mins.

Rail: Horsham
Station $4^{1}/_{2}$ m

Bus: No. 107 from
Horsham and Brighton

▶ OPENING TIMES

Summer
1 April - 31 October
Daily 9.30am - 6pm

Winter
1 November - 31 March
Closed to the general
public.

Available for functions.

▶ ADMISSION

April, June - October
Adult £6.00

May (Mon - Fri)
Adult £7.00

May (Sats, Suns & BH Mons)
Adult £8.00

Child (anytime) £4.00

Groups

April, June - October
Adult £5.00

May: (Mon - Fri) £6.00
Sat, Sun & BH Mons:. £7.00

Child (anytime) £3.50

▶ SPECIAL EVENTS

MAY 1 - 3
Bonsai Weekend.

JUN 26/27
West Sussex Country
Craft Fair.

AUG 7/8
Dolls' House Weekend

CONFERENCE/FUNCTION

ROOM	MAX CAPACITY
Clock Tower	100

📷 ✳ ℹ Photography - landscape & fashion, film location.

🍷 Restaurant available for private and corporate function in the evenings and out of season.

♿ Unsuitable.

☕ 🍴 Restaurant & café. Morning coffee, lunch and teas.

🅿 Ample. Refreshments free to coach drivers. Average length of visit 3 - 5 hours.

🐕

Geoff Hamilton/The National Trust

Map 3

Owner:
The National Trust

▶ **CONTACT**

The Administration
Office
Petworth House
Petworth
West Sussex GU28 0AE

Tel: 01798 342207

Info Line: 01798 343929

Fax: 01798 342963

e-mail: petworth@
nationaltrust.org.uk

▶ **LOCATION**

OS Ref. SU976 218

In the centre of
Petworth town
(approach roads
A272/A283/A285)
Car park signposted.

Rail: Pulborough
5¼ m.

PETWORTH HOUSE & PARK

PETWORTH

www.nationaltrust.org.uk/petworth

Petworth House is one of the finest houses in the care of the National Trust and is home to an art collection that rivals many London galleries. Assembled by one family over 350 years, it includes works by Turner, Van Dyck, Titian, Claude, Gainsborough, Bosch, Reynolds and William Blake.

The state rooms contain sculpture, furniture and porcelain of the highest quality and are complemented by the old kitchens in the Servants' Quarters. The Carved Room contains some of Grinling Gibbons' finest limewood carvings.

Petworth House is also the home of Lord and Lady Egremont and extra family rooms are open on weekdays by kind permission of the family (not Bank Holidays).

Petworth Park is a 700 acre park landscaped by 'Capability' Brown and is open to the public all year free of charge. Spring and autumn are particularly breathtaking and the summer sunsets over the lake are spectacular.

NTPL / Rupert Truman

[🖼][ℹ️] Events throughout the year. Large musical concerts in the park. Baby feeding and changing facilities, highchairs. Pushchairs admitted in house but no prams, please. No photography in house.

[🍽] Contact Retail & Catering Manager on 01798 344975.

[♿] Car park is 800 yards from house; there is a vehicle available to take less able visitors to House.

[🍴] Licensed. 11am-5pm.

[🚶] By arrangement with the Administration Office on variety of subjects.

[🎧] Audio House Tours.

[P] 800 yards from house. Coach parties alight at Church Lodge entrance, coaches then park in NT car park. Coaches must book in advance.

[📷] Welcome. Must book. Teachers' pack available.

[🐕] Guide dogs only in house. Dogs in park only.

[❄️][♥] Tel for details.

▶ **OPENING TIMES**

House
27 March - 31 October
Daily except Thurs & Fris
but open Good Fri,
11am - 5.30pm.

Last admission to House
5pm.

Extra rooms shown on
Mons, Tues & Weds,
not BH Mons.

Pleasure Ground
13 - 24 March for spring
bulbs and events,
12 noon - 4pm. Dates as
House, 11am - 6pm.

Park
All year: Daily, 8am - sunset.

Shop & Restaurant:
as House, 11am - 5pm.
Full programme of events
including lecture lunches,
family workshops and
Christmas lunches.

▶ **ADMISSION**

**House & Pleasure
Ground**
Adult £7.00
Child (5-17yrs) £4.00
Child (under 5 yrs) ..... Free
Family (2+3).......... £18.00

Groups (pre-booked 15+)
Adult £6.00

Park Only .... Free

Pleasure Ground
Adult £1.50
Children .... Free

NT Members Free.

THE ROYAL PAVILION

BRIGHTON

www.royalpavilion.org.uk

Map 3

Owner:
Brighton & Hove
City Council

▶ **CONTACT**

Visitor Services
The Royal Pavilion
Brighton
East Sussex BN1 1EE

Tel: 01273 290900

Fax: 01273 292871

▶ **LOCATION**

The Royal Pavilion is in
the centre of Brighton
easily reached by road
and rail. From London
M25, M23, A23 -
1 hr 30 mins.

Rail: Victoria to
Brighton station
50 mins.
15 mins walk from
Brighton station.

Air: Gatwick 20 mins.

Universally acclaimed as one of the most exotically beautiful buildings in the British Isles, the Royal Pavilion is the former seaside residence of King George IV.

Originally a simple farmhouse, in 1787 architect Henry Holland created a neo-classical villa on the site. It was later transformed into its current Indian style by John Nash between 1815 and 1822. With interiors decorated in the Chinese style and an astonishingly exotic exterior, this Regency Palace is quite breathtaking.

Magnificent decorations and fantastic furnishings have been re-created in the recent extensive restoration programme. From the opulence of the main state rooms to the charm of the first floor bedroom suites, the Royal Pavilion is filled with astonishing colours and superb craftsmanship.

Witness the magnificence of the Music Room with its domed ceiling of gilded scallop-shaped shells and hand-knotted carpet, and promenade through the Chinese bamboo grove of the Long Gallery.

Lavish menus were created in the Great Kitchen, with its cast iron palm trees and dazzling collection of copperware, and then served in the dramatic setting of the Banqueting Room, lit by a huge crystal chandelier held by a silvered dragon.

Set in restored Regency gardens replanted to John Nash's elegant 1820s design, the Royal Pavilion is an unforgettable experience.

Visitors can discover more about life behind the scenes at the Palace during the last 200 years with a specially commissioned interactive multimedia presentation. Public guided tours take place daily at 11.30am and 2.30pm for a small additional charge.

ℹ️ Location filming and photography, including feature films, fashion shoots and corporate videos.

🛍️ Gift shop with souvenirs unique to the Royal Pavilion.

🍽️ Spectacular rooms available for prestigious corporate and private entertaining and wedding receptions.

♿ Access to ground floor only. Tactile and signed tours can be booked in advance with Visitor Services Tel: 01273 292820/2.

☕ Tearooms with a balcony providing sweeping views across the restored Regency gardens.

🚶 Tours in English, French and German and other languages by prior arrangement. General introduction and specialist tours provided.

🅿️ Close to NCP car parks, town centre voucher parking. Coach drop-off point in Church Street, parking in Madeira Drive. Free entry for coach drivers.

📖 Specialist tours relating to all levels of National Curriculum, must be booked in advance with Visitor Services. Special winter student rates. Slide lecture presentations by arrangement.

💍 Civil Wedding Licence.

❄️

▶ **OPENING TIMES**

Summer
April - September
Daily: 9.30am - 5.45pm
Last admission at 5pm.

Winter
October - March
Daily: 10am - 5.15pm
Last admission at 4.30pm.

Closed 25/26 December.

▶ **ADMISSION**

Adult £5.80
Child £3.40
Conc. £4.00
Groups (20+)
Adult £4.90

Prices valid until 31.3.2004

🛡️ **SPECIAL EVENTS**

**AUTUMN, WINTER
& SPRING:**
Children's Events.

Please telephone for details
of other events throughout
the year.

CONFERENCE/FUNCTION

ROOM	MAX CAPACITY
Banqueting Room	200
Great Kitchen	90
Music Rm	180
Queen Adelaide Suite	100
Small Adelaide	40
William IV	80

SAINT HILL MANOR

EAST GRINSTEAD

Built 1792 by Gibbs Crawfurd. One of the finest Sussex sandstone buildings in existence and situated near the breathtaking Ashdown Forest. Subsequent owners included Edgar March Crookshank and the Maharajah of Jaipur. In 1959, Saint Hill Manor's final owner, acclaimed author and humanitarian L Ron Hubbard, acquired the Manor, where he lived for many years with his family. As a result of the work carried out under Mr Hubbard's direction, the Manor has been restored to its original beauty, including the uncovering of fine oak wood panelling, marble fireplaces and plasterwork ceilings. Other outstanding features of this lovely house include an impressive library of Mr Hubbard's works, elegant winter garden, and delightful Monkey Mural painted in 1945 by Winston Churchill's nephew John Spencer Churchill. This 100-foot mural depicts many famous personalities as monkeys, including Winston Churchill. Also open to the public are 59 acres of landscaped gardens, lake and woodlands. Ideal for corporate functions and also available as a film location. Annual events include open-air theatre, arts festivals, classical and jazz concerts.

Map 3

Owner:
Church of Scientology

▶ **CONTACT**

Mrs Liz Nyegaard
Saint Hill Manor
Saint Hill Road
East Grinstead
West Sussex   RH19 4JY

Tel: 01342 326711

Fax: 01342 317057

▶ **LOCATION**
OS Ref. TQ383 359

2m SW of East Grinstead. At Felbridge, turn off A22, down Imberhorne Lane and over crossroads into Saint Hill Road, 200yds on right.

Rail: East Grinstead station.

Air: 15 mins drive from Gatwick airport.

▶ **OPENING TIMES**
All year
Daily, 2 - 5pm, on the hour.

Groups welcome throughout the year.

▶ **ADMISSION**

Free.

 Ground floor.
Teas available.
Obligatory.
P

 SPECIAL EVENTS

Open Air Theatre in summer – please telephone for details.

NTPL

Map 4

SHEFFIELD PARK GARDEN

SHEFFIELD PARK

www.nationaltrust.org.uk/sheffieldpark

A magnificent 120 acre landscaped garden. The centrepiece of this internationally renowned, garden is the four lakes that mirror the unique planting and colour that each season brings. Displays of spring bulbs as the garden awakens, and a stunning exhibition of colour in May, of rhododendrons and the National Collection of Ghent Azaleas. Water lilies dress the lakes during the summer months. Visitors to the garden during the summer months can enjoy a leisurely walk perhaps pausing to sit on a seat to enjoy the tranquil ambience. In the autumn the garden is transformed by trees planted specifically for their autumn colour including *Nyssa sylvatica*, *Amelanchier* and *Acer palmatum*. These and other fine specimen trees, particularly North American varieties, produce displays of gold, orange and crimson. *Gentiana sino-ornata* offers two borders of amazing 'Gentian Blue' colour during the autumn months. The garden is open throughout the year and has something for all, whether a quiet stroll or a family gathering, allowing the children to participate in the many activities offered. Special Events run throughout the year – please call the property for details.

Owner:
The National Trust

▶ **CONTACT**

Jo Hopkins
Visitor Services &
Marketing Manager
Sheffield Park
East Sussex
TN22 3QX

Tel: 01825 790231
Fax: 01825 791264

e-mail: sheffieldpark@
nationaltrust.org.uk

▶ **LOCATION**
OS Ref. TQ415 240

Midway between East
Grinstead and Lewes,
5m NW of Uckfield on
E side of A275.

NTPL

▶ **OPENING TIMES**

3 Jan - 29 Feb:
Sat & Sun,
10.30am - 4pm.

2 Mar - 31 Oct:
Tue - Sun & BH Mons,
10.30am - 6pm.

2 Nov - 23 Dec:
Tue - Sun, 10.30am - 4pm.

Last admission to the
garden 1 hour before
closing or dusk if earlier.

▶ **ADMISSION**

Adult £5.20
Child £2.60
Family £13.00
Groups (15+)
Adult £4.50
Child £2.25

Joint Ticket available with
Bluebell Railway.

NT, RHS individual & Great
British Heritage members
Free.

Partial. WC.
(not NT).
By arrangement.
Guide dogs only.

▶ **SPECIAL EVENTS**

Tel for details.

NT Photographic Library: David Sellman

Map 3

Owner:
The National Trust

▶ **CONTACT**

The Property Manager
Uppark
South Harting
Petersfield   GU31 5QR

Tel: 01730 825415

Info Line: 01730 825857

Fax: 01730 825873

e-mail: uppark
@nationaltrust.org.uk

▶ **LOCATION**

OS Ref. 197 SU781 181

5m SE of Petersfield
on B2146, 1¹/₂ m S of
South Harting.

Bus: Stagecoach Sussex
Bus 54 (not Sun).

Rail: Petersfield 5¹/₂ m.

UPPARK ❧

SOUTH HARTING

www.nationaltrust.org.uk/uppark

A fine late 17th century house set high on the South Downs with magnificent sweeping views to the sea. The drama of the 1989 fire and restoration adds to the magic of this romantic house.

The elegant Georgian interior houses a famous Grand Tour collection that includes paintings by Pompeo Batoni, Luca Giordano, and Joseph Vernet, with furniture and ceramics of superb quality. The famous 18th century dolls' house with original contents is one of the star items in the collection, and provides a rare insight into life in a great house 300 years ago.

The restaurant in the Georgian kitchen in the East

Pavilion serves a delicious menu using local produce. The West Pavilion houses the beautiful stables and the atmospheric and romantic Dairy. The complete servants' quarters in the basement are shown as they were in Victorian days when H G Wells' mother was housekeeper. From the basement visitors leave the house via the subterranean passages.

The fine, peaceful, historic garden is now fully restored in the early 19th century 'Picturesque' style, with flowering shrubs and under-plantings of bulbs, perennials and herbaceous plants in a magical woodland and downland setting.

NT Photographic Library: Nadia MacKenzie

▶ **OPENING TIMES**

28 March - 28 October:
Daily except Fris & Sats.

House: 1 - 5pm
(opens 12 noon on Suns
in Aug, 11am on BH
Mons).

Last admission 4.15pm.

Print room open on 1st
Mon of each month.

Grounds & Garden
11am - 5.30pm.

Shop & Restaurant:
11.30am - 5.30pm.

▶ **ADMISSION**

**House, Garden &
Exhibition**

Adult	£5.50
Child	£2.75
Family	£13.75
Groups (15+)	
must book	£4.50

Booked group guided
tours: mornings by
arrangement.

Special group catering
arrangements: please
telephone for details.

NT members Free.

NB. To avoid congestion
timed tickets will be used
on BH Suns and Mons,
and on Suns in August.

ℹ️ Pushchairs on weekdays
only. No photography, large
bags or sharp heeled shoes in
the house.

📷 Tel for Xmas opening.

♿ Partial. WC. Wheelchairs
available.

🍴 Licensed.

🅿️ Coaches must pre-book.

🐕 On leads, in Car Park (no
shade) & woodland only.

Tel for details.

CONFERENCE/FUNCTION

ROOM	MAX CAPACITY
Restaurant	50
Lower Servants Hall	50

ALFRISTON CLERGY HOUSE

THE TYE, ALFRISTON, POLEGATE, EAST SUSSEX BN26 5TL

Tel: 01323 870001   **Fax:** 01323 871318   **e-mail:** alfriston@nationaltrust.org.uk

Owner: The National Trust   **Contact:** The Property Manager

Step back into the Middle Ages with a visit to this 14th century thatched Wealden 'Hall House'. Trace the history of this building which in 1896 was the first to be acquired by the National Trust. Discover what is used to make the floor in the Great Hall and visit the excellent shop with its local crafts. Explore the delightful cottage garden and savour the idyllic setting beside Alfriston's parish church, with stunning views across the meandering River Cuckmere. An intriguing variety of shops, pubs and restaurants in Alfriston village make this a wonderful day out.

Location: OS Ref. TQ521 029. 4m NE of Seaford, just E of B2108.

Open: 6 - 21 Mar: Sats & Suns, 11am - 4pm. 27 Mar - 31 Oct: daily, except Tue & Fri, 10am - 5pm. 3 Nov - 19 Dec: Wed - Sun, 11am - 4pm.

Admission: Adult £3, Child £1.50, Family (2+3) £7.50. Pre-booked groups £2.60.

ⓘ No WCs. 🖼 🅿 Parking in village car parks.

ANNE OF CLEVES HOUSE

52 Southover High Street, Lewes, Sussex BN7 1JA

Tel: 01273 474610   **Fax:** 01273 486990   **e-mail:** anne@sussexpast.co.uk
www.sussexpast.co.uk

Owner: Sussex Past   **Contact:** Mr Stephen Watts

This 16th century timber-frame Wealden hall-house was given to Anne of Cleves as part of her divorce settlement from Henry VIII in 1541, and contains wide-ranging collections of Sussex interest. Furnished rooms give an impression of life in the 17th and 18th centuries. Artefacts from Lewes Priory, Sussex pottery and Wealden ironwork.

Location: OS198 Ref. TQ410 096. S of Lewes town centre, off A27/A275/A26.

Open: 1 Jan - 28 Feb: Tue - Sat, 10am - 5pm. 1 Mar - 31 Oct: Tue - Sat, 10am - 5pm; Sun, Mon & BHs, 11am - 5pm. 1 Nov - 31 Dec: Tue - Sat, 10am - 5pm. Closed 24 - 28 Dec.

Admission: Adult £2.90, Child £1.45, Conc. £2.60, Family (2+2) £7.35 or (1+4) £5.90. Groups (15+): Adult £2.60, Child £1.25, Conc. £2.35. Combined ticket with Lewes Castle is also available.

🖼 🇮 By arrangement. 🅿 Limited (on road). 🔳 🖼 Guide dogs only. 🔺 ❋ 🅥 Tel for details.

ARUNDEL CASTLE   *See page 162 for full page entry.*

ARUNDEL CATHEDRAL

Parsons Hill, Arundel, Sussex BN18 9AY

Tel: 01903 882297   **Fax:** 01903 885335

e-mail: aruncath1@aol.com   **Contact:** Rev J Scott

French Gothic Cathedral, church of the RC Diocese of Arundel and Brighton built by Henry, 15th Duke of Norfolk and opened 1873.

Location: OS Ref. TQ015 072. Above junction of A27 and A284.

Open: Summer: 9am - 6pm. Winter: 9am - dusk. Mass at 10am each day. Sun Masses: 8am, 9.30am & 11am, Vigil Sat evening: 6.30pm. Shop opened after services and on special occasions and otherwise at request.

Admission: Free.

1066 BATTLE OF HASTINGS
BATTLEFIELD & ABBEY

BATTLE, SUSSEX TN33 0AD

www.english-heritage.org.uk/visits

Tel: 01424 773792   **Fax:** 01424 775059

Owner: English Heritage   **Contact:** The Custodian

Visit the site of the 1066 Battle of Hastings. A free interactive audio tour will lead you around the battlefield and to the exact spot where Harold fell. Explore the magnificent Abbey ruins and see the fascinating exhibition in the gate house and '1066 Prelude to Battle' exhibition. Children's themed play area.

Location: OS Ref. TQ749 157. Top of Battle High Street. Turn off A2100 to Battle.

Open: 1 Apr - 30 Sept: daily, 10am - 6pm. 1 - 31 Oct: 10am - 5pm. 1 Nov - 31 Mar: daily 10am - 4pm. Closed 24 - 26 Dec & 1 Jan. Times subject to change April 2004.

Admission: Adult £5, Child £2.50, Conc. £3.80, Family £12.50. 15% discount for groups (11+). EH members Free. Prices subject to change April 2004.

ⓘ WCs nearby. 🖼 🅖 Ground floor & grounds. 🅿 Charge payable. 🖼 Free. 🖼 In grounds, on leads. ❋ 🅥 Tel for details.

BATEMAN'S ❧

See page 163 for full page entry.

BAYHAM OLD ABBEY ⌗

Lamberhurst, Sussex

Tel/Fax: 01892 890381   www.english-heritage.org.uk/visits

Owner: English Heritage   **Contact:** The Custodian

These riverside ruins are of a house of 'White' Canons, founded c1208 and preserved in the 18th century, when its surroundings were landscaped to create its delightful setting. Two rooms in the Georgian Dower House are also open to the public.

Location: OS Ref. TQ651 366. 1¼ m W of Lamberhurst off B2169.

Open: 1 Apr - 30 Sept: daily, 10am - 6pm. 1 - 31 Oct: 10am - 5pm. 1 Nov - 31 Mar: w/ends only 10am - 4pm. Closed 24 - 26 Dec & 1 Jan. Times subject to change April 2004.

Admission: Adult £2.50, Child £1.30, Conc. £1.90, Family £6.30. Prices subject to change April 2004.

⬚ ⬚ Grounds. WC. 🅿 🐕 In grounds, on leads. ✳

BENTLEY HOUSE & MOTOR MUSEUM

Halland, Lewes, East Sussex BN8 5AF

Tel: 01825 840573   **Fax:** 01825 841322

e-mail: barrysutherland@pavilion.co.uk   www.bentley.org.uk

Owner: East Sussex County Council   **Contact:** Mr Barry Sutherland - Manager

Early 18th century farmhouse with a large reception room of Palladian proportions added on either end in the 1960s by the architect Raymond Erith, each lit by large Venetian windows. Furnished to form a grand 20th century evocation of a mid-Georgian house. Extensive Wildfowl Collection and Motor Museum.

Location: OS Ref. TQ485 160. 7m NE from Lewes, signposted off A22, A26 & B2192.

Open: Estate: 15 Mar - 31 Oct: daily, 10.30am - 4.30pm (last adm.). Nov, Feb - Mar: weekends only, 10.30am - 4pm (last adm.). House: 1 Apr - 31 Oct: daily 12 noon - 5pm. Estate closed Dec & Jan.

Admission: Adult £6, Child (4-15) £4, Conc. £5, Family (2+4) £19. Coach drivers free admission & refreshment ticket. 10% discount for groups of 11+. Special rates for the disabled.

⬚ ⓣ Wedding receptions. ⬚ 🍴 Licensed. ⓕ By arrangement. 🅿 ⬚ 🐕 Registered assistance dogs only. ⬚

BIGNOR ROMAN VILLA

Bignor Lane, Bignor, Nr Pulborough, West Sussex RH20 1PH

Tel/Fax: 01798 869259

Owner: Mr J R Tupper   **Contact:** Ging Allison – Curator

One of the largest villas to be open to the public in Great Britain, with some of the finest mosaics all *in situ* and all under cover, including Medusa, Venus & Cupid Gladiators and Ganymede. Discovered in 1811 and open to the public since 1814. See the longest mosaic on display in Great Britain at 24 metres. Walk on original floors dating back to circa 350 AD. We have a small café and picnic area available for Villa visitors only.

Location: OS Ref. SU987 146. 6m N of Arundel, 6m S of Pulborough A29. 7m S of Petworth A285.

Open: Mar & Apr: Tue - Sun & BHs, 10am - 5pm; May & Oct: daily: 10am - 5pm. Jun - Sept: daily, 10am - 6pm.

Admission: Adult £4, Child £1.70, OAP £2.85. Groups (10+): Adult £3.20, Child £1.30, OAP £2.30. Guided tours (max 30 per tour) £18.50.

⬚ ⬚ Partial. 🍴 ⓕ By arrangement. 🅿 ⬚ 🐕

Website Information see front section

BODIAM CASTLE ❧

BODIAM, Nr ROBERTSBRIDGE, EAST SUSSEX TN32 5UA

www.nationaltrust.org.uk/places/bodiamcastle

Tel: 01580 830436   **Fax:** 01580 830398   **e-mail:** bodiamcastle@nationaltrust.org.uk

Owner: The National Trust   **Contact:** The Property Manager

Built in 1385 to defend the surrounding countryside and as a comfortable dwelling for a rich nobleman, Bodiam Castle is one of the finest examples of medieval architecture. The virtual completeness of its exterior makes it popular with adults, children and film crews alike. Inside, although a ruin, floors have been replaced in some of the towers and visitors can climb the spiral staircase to enjoy superb views of the Rother Valley and local steam trains from the battlements. Discover more of its intriguing past in the Museum and Audio Visual Presentation, and wander in the peacefully romantic Castle grounds.

Location: OS Ref. TQ782 256. 3m S of Hawkhurst, 2m E of A21 Hurst Green.

Open: 3 Jan - 13 Feb: Sats & Suns, 10am - 4pm. 14 Feb - 31 Oct: daily including Good Fri, Easter Sat & Sun, 10am - 6pm. 6 Nov - 6 Feb 2005: Sats & Suns, 10am - 4pm. Last admission 1 hour before closing.

Admission: Adult £4.20, Child £2.10, Family (2+3) £10.50. Groups £3.60. Car parking £2 per car.

ⓘ Small museum. ⬚ ⬚ Ground floor & grounds. 🍴 🅿 ⬚ Teacher and student packs and education base. ✳

BORDE HILL GARDEN, PARK & WOODLAND 🏛

Haywards Heath, West Sussex RH16 1XP

Tel: 01444 450326   **www.**bordehill.co.uk

Owner: Border Hill Garden Ltd Reg Charity   **Contact:** Sarah Brook
Heritage and collector's Garden, listed Grade II*, set within 200 acres of spectacular parkland and woodland. Breathtaking botanical collection of rare trees, shrubs, rhododendrons, azaleas, roses and herbaceous borders. Intimate 'garden rooms' with stunning views and magical parkland and lakeside walks. Adventure playground and coarse fishing.
Location: OS Ref. TQ324 265. 1¹/₂m N of Haywards Heath on Balcombe Road, 3m from A23. 45mins from Victoria Station.
Open: Daily, all year: 10am – 6pm (or dusk if earlier).
Admission: Adult £6, Child £3.50, OAP £5. RHS members Free Nov - Feb.
✳

BOXGROVE PRIORY ⌘

Boxgrove, Chichester, Sussex

Tel: 01424 775705

Owner: English Heritage   **Contact:** Area Manager
Remains of the Guest House, Chapter House and Church of this 12th century priory, which was the cell of a French abbey until Richard II confirmed its independence in 1383.
Location: OS Ref. SU909 076. N of Boxgrove, 4m E of Chichester on minor road N of A27.
Open: Any reasonable time.
Admission: Free.
🅿 ♿ ✳

BRAMBER CASTLE ⌘

Bramber, Sussex

Tel: 01424 775705

Owner: English Heritage   **Contact:** Area Manager
The remains of a Norman castle gatehouse, walls and earthworks in a splendid setting overlooking the Adur valley.
Location: OS Ref. TQ187 107. On W side of Bramber village NE of A283.
Open: Any reasonable time.
Admission: Free.
🅿 Limited. 🐕 On leads. ✳

CAMBER CASTLE ⌘

Camber, Nr Rye, East Sussex

Tel: 01797 223862   **www.**english-heritage.org.uk/visits

Owner: English Heritage   **Contact:** Rye Harbour Nature Reserve
A fine example of one of many coastal fortresses built by Henry VIII to counter the threat of invasion during the 16th century. Monthly guided walks of Rye Nature Reserve including Camber Castle, telephone for details.
Location: OS189, Ref. TQ922 185. Across fields off A259, 1m S of Rye off harbour road.
Open: 1 Jul - 30 Sept: Sat & Sun, 2 - 5pm. Last admission 4.30pm. Times subject to change April 2004.
Admission: Adult £2, Child/Conc. £1. Accompanied Children Free. Friends of Rye Harbour Nature Reserve Free. Prices subject to change April 2004.
♿ Unsuitable. 𝒇 By arrangement. 🅿 None. 🐕 Guide dogs only. ✳

CHARLESTON

CHARLESTON, FIRLE, NR LEWES, EAST SUSSEX BN8 6LL

www.charleston.org.uk

Tel: 01323 811265   **Fax:** 01323 811628   **e-mail:** info@charleston.org.uk

Owner: The Charleston Trust   **Contact:** Visitor Manager
Charleston was discovered in 1916 by Virginia Woolf and became the country home of her sister, Vanessa Bell and her unconventional household, including fellow artist Duncan Grant. Charleston became a focal point for the group of artists, writers and intellectuals known as Bloomsbury. The artists decorated the walls, furniture and ceramics with their own designs inspired by Italian fresco painting and Post-impressionism. Creativity extended to the garden, with its mosaics and statues and the subtle masses of colour used in the planting. Charleston has been described as "one of the most difficult and imaginative feats of restoration current in Britain."
Location: OS Ref. TQ490 069. 7m E of Lewes on A27 between Firle & Selmeston.

Rail, bus, taxi & airport.

Open: 1 Apr - 31 Oct: Wed - Sun, 2 - 6pm (Last entry 5pm). Jul & Aug: Wed - Sat, 11.30am - 6pm; Sun, 2 - 6pm (Last entry 5pm). Nov & Dec Christmas Shopping: Sat & Sun, 1 - 4pm. Guided visits: Wed - Sat; Unguided on Suns. Open BH Mons. Just Friends and Lovers?' themed tour on Fris: Apr - Jun, Sep & Oct, special themed tour of the House, including Vanessa Bell's studio and the kitchen.

Admission: Adult £6, Conc. £4.50. Groups (10-50): Adult £5.50, Child £4, Student £4. Themed Fridays: £7.

ℹ Filming and photography by arrangement. 📷 🎁 🍴
♿ Partial.Access leaflet available. WC. 🍴 𝒇 Obligatory except Sun & BH Mons.
🅿 🚻 🐕 Guide dogs only.

CHICHESTER CATHEDRAL

Chichester, Sussex PO19 1PX

Tel: 01243 782595 **Fax:** 01243 812499 **e-mail:**
visitors@chichestercathedral.org.uk
www.chichestercathedral.org.uk **Contact:** Mrs P
Utting

In the heart of the city, this fine Cathedral has been a centre of Christian worship and community life for 900 years.

Location: OS Ref. SU860 047. West Street, Chichester.

Open: Summer: 7.15am - 7pm, Winter: 7.15am - 6pm. Choral Evensong daily (except Wed) during term time.

Admission: Donation.

❄

❄ Open All Year Index see front section

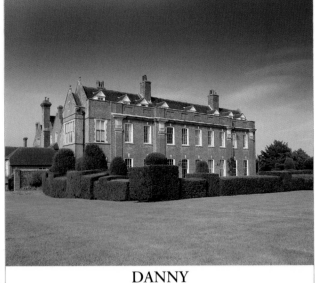

DANNY

HURSTPIERPOINT, SUSSEX BN6 9BB

www.cha.org.uk

Tel: 01273 833000 **Fax:** 01273 832436

Owner: Country Houses Association **Contact:** The Administrators

Built in 1595, Danny has many typical Elizabethan features and the house forms an 'E' shape. During WWI Danny was rented by Prime Minister Lloyd George as a secure location for Cabinet meetings. The Great Hall was their meeting place. Danny has been converted into apartments for active retired people.

Location: OS Ref. TQ285 149. 1m SE of Hurstpierpoint S of the Hassocks road.

Open: May - Sept: Wed & Thur, 2 - 5pm.

Admission: Adult £2.50, Child £1.50. Groups by arrangement.

⊤ ✖ 🖼1 twin with bathroom & 1 double with bathroom, CHA members & Wolsey Lodge guests. ▲

Jeremy Whitaker

FIRLE PLACE 🏛

FIRLE, LEWES, EAST SUSSEX BN8 6LP

www.firleplace.co.uk

Tel: 01273 858307 (Enquiries) **Events:** 01273 858567

Fax: 01273 858188 **Restaurant:** 01273 858307 **e-mail:** gage@firleplace.co.uk

Owner: The Rt Hon Viscount Gage

Firle Place is the home of the Gage family and has been for over 500 years. Set at the foot of the Sussex Downs within its own parkland, this unique house originally Tudor, was built of Caen stone, possibly from a monastery dissolved by Sir John Gage, friend of Henry VIII. Remodelled in the 18th century it is similar in appearance to that of a French château. The house contains a magnificent collection of Old Master paintings, fine English and European furniture and an impressive collection of Sèvres porcelain collected mainly by the 3rd Earl Cowper from Panshanger House, Hertfordshire.

Events: The Great Tudor Hall can, on occasion, be used for private dinners, with drinks on the Terrace or in the Billiard Room. A private tour of the house can be arranged. The paddock area is an ideal site for a marquee. The park can be used for larger events, using the house as a backdrop.

Restaurant: Enjoy the licensed restaurant and tea terrace with views over the garden for luncheon and cream teas.

Location: OS Ref. TQ473 071. 4m S of Lewes on A27 Brighton/Eastbourne Road.

Open: Easter & BH Sun/Mon. Jun - Sept: Wed, Thur, Sun & BHs, 2 - 4.30pm. Dates and times subject to change without prior notice.

Admission: Adult £5.50, Child £2.75, Conc. £5. Connoisseurs' Day (1st Thurs each month, Jun - Sept) £6.50.

ℹ️No photography in house. 🅟 ⊤ ♿ Ground floor & restaurant. 🍴 Licensed. ☕ Tea Terrace. 🐕 🅿 🖼 In grounds on leads. 🕿 Tel for details.

FISHBOURNE ROMAN PALACE

SALTHILL ROAD, FISHBOURNE, CHICHESTER, SUSSEX PO19 3QR

www.sussexpast.co.uk

Tel: 01243 785859 **Fax:** 01243 539266 **e-mail:** adminfish@sussexpast.co.uk

Owner: Sussex Past **Contact:** David Rudkin

A Roman site built around AD75. A modern building houses part of the extensive remains including a large number of Britain's finest *in situ* mosaics. The museum displays many objects discovered during excavations and an audio-visual programme tells Fishbourne's remarkable story. Roman gardens have been reconstructed and include a museum of Roman gardening.

Location: OS Ref. SU837 057. 1^1/2m W of Chichester in Fishbourne village off A27/A259.

Open: 1 Feb - 15 Dec: daily. Feb, Nov - Dec: 10am - 4pm. Mar - Jul & Sept - Oct: 10am - 5pm. Aug: 10am - 6pm. 16 Dec - 31 Jan (excluding Christmas): Sats & Suns, 10am - 4pm.

Admission: Adult £5.20, Child £2.70, Conc. £4.50, Family (2+2): £13.40, Registered disabled £4. Groups (20+): Adult £4.40, Child £2.50, Conc. £4.

🔲 🚻 ♿ 🖥 🎫 By arrangement. 🅿 🔲 🔓 Guide dogs only. ✳ 🔽 Tel for details.

GLYNDE PLACE 🏛

GLYNDE, LEWES, SUSSEX BN8 6SX

www.glyndeplace.com

Tel: 01273 858224 **Fax:** 01273 858224 **e-mail:** hampden@glyndeplace.co.uk

Owners: Viscount & Viscountess Hampden **Contact:** Viscount Hampden

Glynde Place is a magnificent example of Elizabethan architecture commanding exceptionally fine views of the South Downs. Amongst the collections of 400 years of family living can be seen a fine collection of 17th and 18th century portraits of the Trevors, a room dedicated to Sir Henry Brand, Speaker of the House of Commons 1872 - 1884 and furniture, embroidery and silver. Plus a collection of 18th century Italian masterpieces.

Location: OS Ref. TQ457 093. In Glynde village 4m SE of Lewes on A27.

Open: House & Garden: Jun - Sept: Weds & Suns also Aug BH Mon, 2 - 5pm. Last adm. 4.45pm.

Admission: Adult £5.50, Child £2.75.

🔲 🚻 🖥 🎫 🅿 Free. 🔓 Guide dogs only.

GOODWOOD HOUSE 🏛 *See page 164 for full page entry.*

Glynde Place, Sussex from the book
Historic Family Homes and Gardens from the Air, see page 54.

Jonathan Buckley

GREAT DIXTER HOUSE & GARDENS 🏛

NORTHIAM, RYE, EAST SUSSEX TN31 6PH

www.greatdixter.co.uk

Tel: 01797 252878 **Fax:** 01797 252879 **e-mail:** office@greatdixter.co.uk

Owner: Christopher Lloyd   **Contact:** Perry Rodriguez

Great Dixter, built c1450 is the birthplace of Christopher Lloyd, gardening author. The house boasts the largest surviving timber-framed hall in the country. The gardens feature a variety of topiary, pools, wild meadow areas and the famous Long Border and Exotic Garden.

Location: OS Ref. TQ817 251. Signposted off the A28 in Northiam.

Open: 1 Apr - 24 Oct: Tue - Sun, 2 - 5pm.

Admission: House & Garden: Adult £6.50, Child £2. Gardens only: Adult £5, Child £1.50. Groups (25+) by appointment.

ⓘNo photography in House. ⬜ ⬜ ⬜Obligatory. 🅿Limited for coaches. 🦮Guide dogs only.

HERSTMONCEUX CASTLE GARDENS

Hailsham, Sussex BN27 1RN

Tel: 01323 833816 **Fax:** 01323 834499 **e-mail:** c_dennett@isc.queensu.ac.uk **www.**herstmonceux-castle.com

Owner: Queen's University, Canada   **Contact:** C Dennett

This breathtaking 15th century moated Castle is within 500 acres of parkland and gardens (including Elizabethan Garden) and is ideal for picnics and woodland walks. At Herstmonceux there is something for all the family. For information on our attractions or forthcoming events tel: 01323 834457.

Location: OS Ref. TQ646 104. 2m S of Herstmonceux village (A271) by minor road. 10m WNW of Bexhill.

Open: 9 Apr - 24 Oct: daily, 10am - 6pm (last adm. 5pm) Closes 5pm from Oct.

Admission: Grounds & Gardens: Adults £4.50, Child under 15yrs & Students £3 (child under 5 Free), Conc. £3.50, Family £12. Group rates/bookings available.

ⓘVisitor Centre. ⬜ ♿Limited for Castle Tour. ⬜ ⬜ 🅿 ⬜On leads. ▲ 🛏Tel for details.

🖼 Accommodation Index see front section

HAMMERWOOD PARK

EAST GRINSTEAD, SUSSEX RH19 3QE

www.hammerwoodpark.com

Tel: 01342 850594 **Fax:** 01342 850864 **e-mail:** latrobe@mistral.co.uk

Owner/Contact: David Pinnegar

Built in 1792 as an Apollo's hunting lodge by Benjamin Latrobe, architect of the Capitol and the White House, Washington DC. Owned by Led Zepplin in the 1970s, rescued from dereliction in 1982. Teas in the Organ Room; mural by French artists in the hall; and a derelict dining room still shocks the unwary. Guided tours (said by many to be the most interesting in Sussex) by the family.

Location: OS Ref. TQ442 390. 3¹/2 m E of East Grinstead on A264 to Tunbridge Wells, 1m W of Holtye.

Open: 1 June - end Sept: Wed, Sat & BH Mon, 2 - 5pm. Guided tour starts 2.05pm. Private groups: Easter - Jun. Coaches strictly by appointment. Small groups any time throughout the year by appointment.

Admission: House & Park: Adult £6, Child £2. Private viewing by arrangement.

ⓘConferences. ⬜ ⬜ ⬜Obligatory. ⬜ 🦮In grounds. ⬜B&B. ❄ 🛏Tel for details. €

HIGH BEECHES GARDENS 🏛

HIGH BEECHES, HANDCROSS, SUSSEX RH17 6HQ

www.highbeeches.com

Tel: 01444 400589 **Fax:** 01444 401543 **e-mail:** office@highbeeches.com

Owner: High Beeches Gardens Conservation Trust (Reg. Charity)
                    Contact: Sarah Bray

Explore 25 acres of magically beautiful, peaceful woodland and water gardens. Daffodils, bluebells, azaleas, naturalised gentians, autumn colours. Rippling streams, enchanting vistas. Four acres of natural wildflower meadows. Rare plants. Marked trails. Recommended by Christopher Lloyd. Enjoy lunches and teas in the new tearoom and tea lawn in restored Victorian farm building.

Location: OS Ref. TQ275 308. S side of B2110. 1m NE of Handcross.

Open: 19 Mar - 30 Jun & 1 Sept - 31 Oct: Thur - Tue & Jul/Aug, daily except Weds & Sats, 1 - 5pm (last admission). Coaches/guided tours anytime, by appointment only.

Admission: Adult £5, Child (under 14) Free. Season ticket (12 months): £15. Concession for groups (30+). Guided tours for groups £8pp.

⬜ ♿Unsuitable. ⬜ Licensed. ⬜By arrangement. 🅿 🛏Tel for details. €

HIGHDOWN GARDENS

Littlehampton Road, Goring-by-Sea, Worthing, Sussex BN12 6PE

Tel: 01903 501054

Owner: Worthing Borough Council   **Contact:** C Beardsley Esq

Unique gardens in disused chalk pit, begun in 1909.

Location: OS Ref. TQ098 040. 3m WNW of Worthing on N side of A259, just W of the Goring roundabout.

Open: 1 Apr - 30 Sept: Mon - Fri, 10am - 6pm. W/ends & BHs, 10am - 6pm. 1 Oct - 30 Nov: Mon - Fri, 10am - 4.30pm. 1 Dec - 31 Jan: 10am - 4pm. 1 Feb - 31 Mar: Mon - Fri, 10am - 4.30pm.

Admission: Free.

LAMB HOUSE ⚜

West Street, Rye, Sussex TN31 7ES

Tel: 01797 229542   **Fax:** 01797 223492

Owner: The National Trust   **Contact:** Winchelsea Office

A delightful brick-fronted house dating from the early 18th century and typical of the attractive town of Rye. This was the home of writer Henry James from 1898 to 1916, and later of author E F Benson. There is a charming walled garden.

Location: OS Ref. TQ920 202. In West Street, facing W end of church.

Open: 27 Mar - 30 Oct: Weds & Sats only, 2 - 6pm. Last admission 5.30pm.

Admission: Adult £2.75, Child £1.30, Family (2+3) £6.90. Group: £2.35.

LEONARDSLEE LAKES & GARDENS

See page 165 for full page entry.

LEWES CASTLE & BARBICAN HOUSE MUSEUM

169 HIGH STREET, LEWES, SUSSEX BN7 1YE

www.sussexpast.co.uk

Tel: 01273 486290   **Fax:** 01273 486990   **e-mail:** castle@sussexpast.co.uk

Owner: Sussex Past   **Contact:** Alison Lawrence

Lewes's imposing Norman castle offers magnificent views across the town and surrounding downland. Barbican House, towered over by the Barbican Gate, is home to the Museum of Sussex Archaeology. A superb scale model of Victorian Lewes provides the centrepiece of a 25 minute audio-visual presentation telling the story of the county town of Sussex.

Location: OS198 Ref. TQ412 101. Lewes town centre off A27/A26/A275.

Open: Daily (except Mons in Jan & 24 - 28 Dec). Tue - Sat: 10am - 5.30pm; Sun, Mon & BHs, 11am - 5.30pm. Castle closes at dusk in winter.

Admission: Adult £4.30, Child £2.15, Conc. £3.80 Family (2+2) £11 or (1+4) £8.75. Groups (15+): Adult £3.80, Child £1.75, Conc. £3.20. Combined ticket with Anne of Cleves House available.

⬜ ♿Unsuitable. ▯By arrangement. ▮ 🐕Guide dogs only. ✲ ⬛Tel for details.

MARLIPINS MUSEUM

High Street, Shoreham-by-Sea, Sussex BN43 5DA

Tel: 01273 462994 or 01323 441279   **e-mail:** smomich@sussexpast.co.uk

www.sussexpast.co.uk

Owner: Sussex Past   **Contact:** Helen Poole

Shoreham's local and especially maritime history is explored at Marlipins, an important historic building of Norman origin.

Location: OS198 Ref. TQ214 051. Shoreham town centre on A259, W of Brighton.

Open: 1 May - 30 Sept: Tue - Sat, 10.30am - 4.30pm.

Admission: Adult £2, Child £1, Conc. £1.50. Groups: Adult £1.75, Child 80p, Conc. £1.25.

Robert Adam

1728-1792

Robert Adam was a Scot, one of four sons of the leading Scottish architect William Adam. Like his father, Adam trained as an architect but having done the Grand Tour to look at the ancient antiquities of Greece and Rome and the work of the Italian Renaissance architects, he was to turn all formal rules of the ancients upside down. Look at Adam's buildings and you will see that he frequently varied his proportions and handling of classical detail according to the individual needs of the building and the site. To Adam any idea of classical rigidity dictated by Palladio was to be challenged. His clients loved him and today, whether you like or loathe his style, he still has to be seen as one of the great innovators in English architecture. If his work as a builder wooed his clients, his abilities as an interior decorator wowed them … Adam was simply Polite Society's decorating darling! Look at an Adam interior and you will find delicate and intricate plasterwork ceilings and walls – soft shades of green, pink, lilac, blue, with gilding predominate. Look a little further and you find that Adam designed almost everything from the fenders, grates and fire-irons to most of the furniture and furnishings. Commissioning Adam to design your house or castle, you would know that you would get the very latest 'in' and 'must have' designs … all hopefully keeping you one up on your noble neighbour!

- **Visit in the London Region – Osterley Park, Syon Park and Kenwood House, London.**

- **Visit in the South West Region - Saltram House, Devon.**

- **Visit the Eastern Region - Audley End, Essex.**

- **Visit in the East Midlands Region - Kedleston Hall, Derbyshire.**

- **Visit in the North East Region - Alnwick Castle, Northumberland.**

- **Visit in the South West Region – Bowood, Wiltshire.**

- **Visit in the Yorkshire & The Humber Region - Newby Hall, Harewood House, Nostell Priory, Yorkshire.**

Architect and Decorator

MERRIMENTS GARDENS

HAWKHURST ROAD, HURST GREEN, EAST SUSSEX TN19 7RA

www.merriments.co.uk

Tel: 01580 860666   **Fax:** 01580 860324   **e-mail:** info@merriments.co.uk

Owner: Family owned   **Contact:** Alana Sharp

Set in 4 acres of gently sloping Weald farmland, a naturalistic garden which never fails to delight. The garden is planted according to the prevailing conditions and many areas are planted only using plants suited for naturalising and colonising their environment. This natural approach to gardening harks back to the days of William Robinson and is growing in popularity, especially in Northern Europe. Most of the garden however is crammed with deep curved borders, colour themed and planted in the great tradition of English gardening. These borders use a rich mix of trees, shrubs, perennials, grasses and many unusual annuals which ensure an arresting display of colour, freshness and vitality in the garden right through to its closing in autumn.

Location: OS198, Ref. TQ737 281. Signposted off A21 London - Hastings road, at Hurst Green.

Open: Apr - Sept: Mon - Sat, 10am - 5pm, Suns, 10.30am - 5pm.

Admission: Adult £3.50, Child £2. Groups (5+) by arrangement.

🖸 🚻 ♿ ▣ Licensed. 🍴 🐾 By arrangement. 🅿 🐕 In grounds, on leads.

MICHELHAM PRIORY 🏛

UPPER DICKER, HAILSHAM, SUSSEX BN27 3QS

www.sussexpast.co.uk

Tel: 01323 844224   **Fax:** 01323 844030   **e-mail:** adminmich@sussexpast.co.uk

Owner: Sussex Past   **Contact:** Mr Henry Warner

Set on a medieval moated island surrounded by superb gardens, the Priory was founded in 1229. The remains after the Dissolution were incorporated into a Tudor farm and country house that now contains a fascinating array of exhibits. Grounds include a 14th century gatehouse, working watermill, physic and cloister gardens and Elizabethan great barn.

Location: OS Ref. TQ557 093. 8m NW of Eastbourne off A22/A27. 2m W of Hailsham.

Open: 2 Mar - 31 Oct: Tue - Sun & BH Mons & daily in Aug. Mar & Oct: 10.30am - 4pm. Apr - Jul & Sept: 10.30am - 5pm. Aug: 10.30am - 5.30pm.

Admission: Adult £5.20, Child £2.70, Conc. £4.50, Family (2+2) £13.40, Registered disabled & carer £2.60 each. Groups (15+): Adult/Conc. £4.25, Child £2.45.

🖸 🚻 🇹 ♿ ▣ 🍴 Licensed. 🐾 By arrangement. 🅿 Ample for cars & coaches ▣ 🐕 Guide dogs only. ▣ 🖥 Tel for details.

MONK'S HOUSE 🌱

Rodmell, Lewes BN7 3HF

Tel: 01372 453401 (Regional Office)

Owner: The National Trust   **Contact:** Regional Office

A small weather-boarded house, the home of Leonard and Virginia Woolf until Leonard's death in 1969.

Location: OS Ref. TQ421 064. 4 m E of Lewes, off former A275 in Rodmell village, near church.

Open: 31 Mar - 30 Oct: Weds & Sats, 2 - 5.30pm. Last admission 5pm. Groups by arrangement with tenant.

Admission: Adult £2.80, Child £1.40, Family £7.

MOORLANDS

Friar's Gate, Crowborough, East Sussex TN6 1XF

Tel: 01892 652474

Owner: Dr & Mrs Steven Smith   **Contact:** Dr Steven Smith

This marvellously atmospheric garden is again open to the public after building alterations. The garden is on three levels. From a herbaceous border and Spring dell planted with pieris, camellias, rhododendrons and hellebores, go across a yew hedge lawn down to the river level with bridges across it to an area which, in late Summer, shows the bamboos and ornamental grasses at their best. Streams and ponds are at their best in Spring, planted with primulas, irises and other water loving plants. Many unusual trees, planted 20 years ago, have now reached maturity, particularly the Autumn colouring acers. It is a garden for every season.

Location: OS Ref. TQ498 329. 2m NW of Crowborough. From B2188 at Friar's Gate, take left fork signposted 'Crowborough Narrow Road', entrance 100yds on left. From Crowborough crossroads take St John's Road to Friar's Gate.

Open: For National Garden Scheme: 27 Jun, 2 - 6pm; 1 Apr - 1 Oct: Weds, 11am - 5pm. Tea on open day.

Admission: Adult £3, Child Free.

🚻 🐕 On leads.

NYMANS GARDEN

HANDCROSS, HAYWARDS HEATH, SUSSEX RH17 6EB

www.nationaltrust.org.uk/nymans

Tel: 01444 400321/405250 **Fax:** 01444 400253 **e-mail:** nymans@nationaltrust.org.uk

Owner: The National Trust   **Contact:** The Property Manager

One of the great gardens of the Sussex Weald, with rare and beautiful plants, shrubs and trees from all over the world. Wall garden, rose garden, pinetum, laurel walk and romantic ruins. Lady Rosse's library, drawing room and forecourt garden also open. Woodland walks and Wild Garden.

Location: OS Ref. TQ265 294. On B2114 at Handcross, 4¹/₂ m S of Crawley, just off London - Brighton M23/A23.

Open: 18 Feb - 31 Oct: daily except Mon & Tue (open BHs), 11am - 6pm (sunset if earlier). House: 24 Mar - 31 Oct: as garden, last entry at 4.30pm. Garden: 6 Nov - 20 Feb: Sats & Suns, 11am - 4pm. Christmas Shop 1-24 Dec, daily 11am - 4pm. For restaurant & other shop times contact property for details. Closed 25/26 Dec & 1/2 Jan.

Admission: Adult £6.50, Child £3.25, Family £16.25. Pre-booked Groups (15+) £5.50. Joint group ticket which includes same day entry to Standen £10, available Wed - Fri only. Winter weekends: Adult £3.25, Child £1.60, Family £8. Booked groups: £2.75. RHS members Free.

Grounds. WC. Licensed. Wed & Sat only. Tel for details.

PALLANT HOUSE GALLERY

9 North Pallant, Chichester, West Sussex PO19 1TJ

Tel: 01243 774557 **Fax:** 01243 536038

Owner: Pallant House Gallery Trust   **Contact:** Reception

The Gallery of Modern Art in the south. A Queen Anne townhouse and a contemporary extension showcasing the best of 20th century British Art.

Location: OS Ref. SU861 047. City centre, SE of the Cross.

Open: All year: Tue - Sat ,10am - 5pm. Suns & BHs 12.30 - 5pm. Last admission 4.45pm. Closed Mons.

Admission: Adult £4, OAP. £3, Student/Unemployed £2.50. West Sussex students and child under 16 Free.

Plant Sales Index see front section

PARHAM HOUSE & GARDENS

PARHAM PARK, Nr PULBOROUGH, WEST SUSSEX RH20 4HS

www.parhaminsussex.co.uk

Tel: 01903 744888 **Fax:** 01903 746557 **e-mail:** enquiries@parhaminsussex.co.uk

Owner: Parham Park Trust   **Contact:** Patricia Kennedy

Friendly staff give a warm welcome to this stunning Elizabethan house with award-winning gardens, set in the heart of a medieval deer park below the South Downs. The light, panelled rooms, from Great Hall to magnificent Long Gallery, house an important collection of contemporary paintings, furniture, needlework and working clocks, all complemented by informal arrangements of flowers, freshly cut twice a week from the four acre walled garden. Light lunches and cream teas are served in the 15th century Big Kitchen (licensed), and souvenirs and gifts can be purchased from the shop, with plants on sale from the garden shop.

"Stitches in Time" (needlework event based on ecclesiastical theme): 15/16 May.

"Garden Weekend" annual event: 10/11 July. "Autumn Flowers at Parham House", a celebration of flower arranging, Parham style: 4/5 September.

Location: OS Ref. TQ060 143. Midway between Pulborough & Storrington on A283.

Open: Easter Sun - end Sept: Wed, Thur, Sun & BH Mons (also Tue & Fri in Aug); 15 May, 10 Jul & 4 Sept. 28 Aug for NGS (evening). Groups by arrangement at other times. Picnic area, Big Kitchen & Gardens, 12 noon - 6pm. House: 2 - 6pm. Last entry 5pm.

Admission: House & Gardens: Adult £6.25, Child (5 - 15yrs) £2.50, OAP £5.50, Family (2+2) £15. Unguided booked groups (20+) £5. Gardens only: Adult/OAP £4.50, Child £1, Family (2+2) £10.

No photography in house. Partial. Licensed. In grounds, on leads. Special charges may apply.

PASHLEY MANOR GARDENS 🏛

TICEHURST, WADHURST, EAST SUSSEX TN5 7HE

www.pashleymanorgardens.com

Tel: 01580 200888 **Fax:** 01580 200102 **e-mail:** info@pashleymanorgardens.com
Owner: Mr & Mrs James A Sellick **Contact:** Claire Baker

HHA/Christie's Garden of the Year 1999. The gardens offer a sumptuous blend of romantic landscaping, imaginative plantings and fine old trees, fountains, springs and large ponds. This is a quintessentially English garden of a very individual character with exceptional views to the surrounding valleyed fields. Many eras of English history are reflected here, typifying the tradition of the English Country House and its garden.

Pashley prides itself on its delicious food. Home-made soups, ploughman's lunches with pickles and patés, fresh salad from the garden (whenever possible), home-made scones and delicious cakes, filter coffee, specialist teas, fine wines - served on the terrace or in the Old Stables café. The gift shop caters for every taste… from postcards and local honey to traditional hand-painted ceramics and tapestry cushions. A wide selection of plants and shrubs, many of which grow at Pashley, are available for purchase.

Location: OS Ref. TQ 707 291. On B2099 between A21 and Ticehurst village.
Open: 6 Apr - 30 Sept: Tues, Weds, Thurs, Sats & all BH Mons, 11am - 5pm. 1 - 31 Oct: Mon - Fri, 10am - 4pm Garden only (restaurant & shop closed).
Admission: £6. Groups (20+): £5.50. Coaches must book. Please telephone for details.

🖻 🎱 🖭 🔦 Partial. 🅿 Licensed. 🛠 By arrangement. 🅿 🔲 Guide dogs only. 🖵 Tel for details.

PETWORTH COTTAGE MUSEUM

346 High Street, Petworth, West Sussex GU28 0AU
Tel: 01798 342100
Owner: Petworth Cottage Trust **Contact:** Curator

Step into a Leconfield Estate Cottage furnished as if it were 1910. Lighting is by gas, heating by coal-fired range. The scullery has a stone sink and a copper for the weekly wash.
Open: Apr - Oct: Wed - Sun & BH Mons, 2 - 4.30pm.
Admission: Adult £2.50, Child (under 14yrs 50p. Group visits by arrangement.

PETWORTH HOUSE 🦌   *See page 166 for full page entry.*

PEVENSEY CASTLE ▯

Pevensey, Sussex BN24 5LE
Tel: 01323 762604 **www.**english-heritage.org.uk/visits
Owner: English Heritage **Contact:** The Custodian

Originally a 4th century Roman Fort, Pevensey was the place where William the Conqueror landed in 1066 and established his first stronghold. The Norman castle includes the remains of an unusual keep within the massive walls. Free audio tour tells the story of the Castle's 2,000 year history.
Location: OS Ref. TQ645 048. In Pevensey off A259.
Open: 1 Apr - 30 Sept: daily, 10am - 6pm. 1 - 31 Oct: 10am - 5pm. 1 Nov - 31 Mar: Wed - Sun only, 10am - 4pm. Closed 24 - 26 Dec & 1 Jan. Times subject to change April 2004.
Admission: Adult £3, Child £1.50, Conc. £2.30. 15% discount for groups of 11+. Prices subject to change April 2004.

ℹ️WC. 🖻 🔦 Grounds. 🅿 🔲 Free. 🅿 🔲 In grounds, on leads. ✳
🖵 Tel for details.

THE ROYAL PAVILION   *See page 167 for full page entry.*

PRESTON MANOR

PRESTON DROVE, BRIGHTON, EAST SUSSEX BN1 6SD

www.prestonmanor.virtualmuseum.info

Tel: 01273 292770 **Fax:** 01273 292771
Owner: Brighton & Hove City Council

A delightful Manor House which powerfully evokes the atmosphere of an Edwardian gentry home both 'upstairs' and 'downstairs'. Explore more than twenty rooms over four floors – from the servants' quarters, kitchens and butler's pantry in the basement to the attic bedrooms and nursery on the top floor. Plus charming walled gardens, pets' cemetery and 13th century parish church.
Location: OS Ref. TQ303 064. 2m N of Brighton on the A23 London road.
Open: All year: Tue - Sat 10am - 5pm, Suns 2 - 5pm, Mons 1 - 5pm (BHs 10am - 5pm). Closed Good Fri, 25/26 Dec.
Admission: Adult £3.70, Child £2.15, Conc. £3. Groups (20+) £3.15. Prices valid until 31 Mar 2004.

ℹ️No photography. 🖻 Gift kiosk. 🖭 🔦 Unsuitable. 🛠 By arrangement. 🅿
🅿 For coaches. 🐕 ✳ Spring, Summer & Autumn half-term. Easter, Summer & Christmas. Children's activities all year round. Tel for details.

THE PRIEST HOUSE

NORTH LANE, WEST HOATHLY, SUSSEX RH19 4PP

www.sussexpast.co.uk

Tel: 01342 810479   **e-mail:** priest@sussexpast.co.uk

Owner: Sussex Past   **Contact:** Antony Smith

Standing in the beautiful surroundings of a traditional cottage garden on the edge of Ashdown Forest, The Priest House is an early 15th century timber-framed hall-house. In Elizabethan times it was modernised into a substantial yeoman's dwelling. Its furnished rooms contain 17th and 18th century furniture, kitchen equipment, needlework and household items. A formal herb garden contains over 150 different herbs.

Location: OS187 Ref. TQ362 325. In triangle formed by Crawley, East Grinstead and Haywards Heath, 4m off A22, 6m off M23.

Open: 2 Mar - 31 Oct: Tue - Sat & BHs, 10.30am - 5.30pm; Sun, 12 noon - 5.30pm.

Admission: Adults £2.70, Child £1.35, Conc. £2.40. Groups (15+): Adult/Conc. £2.40, Child £1.25.

◻ ⛶ ♿ Partial. 🅕 By arrangement. 🅿 Limited (on street). ▣
🐾 In grounds, on leads.

SAINT HILL MANOR   *See page 168 for full page entry.*

ST MARY'S HOUSE & GARDENS 🏛

BRAMBER, WEST SUSSEX BN44 3WE

Tel/Fax: 01903 816205   **e-mail:** stmaryshouse@btopenworld.com

Owner: Mr Peter Thorogood

This enchanting, medieval timber-framed house is situated in the downland village of Bramber. The fine panelled interiors include the unique Elizabethan 'Painted Room' with its intriguing *trompe l'oeil* murals, give an air of tranquillity and timelessness. Once the home of the real Algernon and Gwendolen brilliantly portrayed in Oscar Wilde's comedy, *The Importance of Being Earnest*, St Mary's was more than likely the setting for the Sherlock Holmes story, *The Musgrave Ritual*, and has served as a location for a number of television series including the world-famous *Dr Who*. The formal gardens with amusing animal topiary include an exceptional example of the 'Living Fossil' tree, Gingko biloba, and a mysterious ivy-clad 'Monk's Walk'. In the 'Secret Garden' can still be seen the Victorian fruit-wall, potting shed, circular orchard,

and woodland walk. St Mary's is a house of fascination and mystery. Many thousands of visitors have admired its picturesque charm and enjoyed its atmosphere of friendliness and welcome, qualities which make it a visit to remember.

Location: OS Ref. TQ189 105. Bramber village off A283. From London 56m via M23/A23 or A24. Bus from Shoreham to Steyning, alight St Mary's, Bramber.

Open: Easter - Sept: Suns, Thurs & BH Mons, 2 - 6pm. Last entry 5pm. Groups at other times by arrangement. Secret Garden (3½ acres): May - Sept, 1st Sunday in every month.

Admission: House & Garden: Adult £5.50, Child £2.50, OAP £5. Groups (25+) £5. Secret Garden: Adult £3, Child Free.

ⓘ No photography in house. ◻ 🅣 ♿ Unsuitable. ▣
🅕 Obligatory for groups (max 60). Visit time 2½ hrs. 🅿 30 cars, 2 coaches.
▣ ✖ ♨ Tel for details.

NTPL/ Rupert Trueman

SACKVILLE COLLEGE

HIGH STREET, EAST GRINSTEAD, WEST SUSSEX RH19 3BX

www.sackville-college.co.uk

Tel: 01342 326561

Owner: Board of Trustees   **Contact:** College Co-ordinator

Built in 1609 for Richard Sackville, Earl of Dorset, as an almshouse and overnight accommodation for the Sackville family. Feel the Jacobean period come alive in the enchanting quadrangle, the chapel, banqueting hall with fine hammerbeam roof and minstrel's gallery, the old common room and warden's study where "Good King Wenceslas" was composed. Chapel weddings by arrangement.

Location: A22 to East Grinstead, College in High Street (town centre).

Open: 15 Jun - 15 Sep: Wed - Sun, 2 - 5pm. Groups all year by arrangement.

Admission: Adult £3, Child £1. Groups: (10 - 60) no discount.

ⓘ Large public car park adjacent to entrance. 🖼 ♿ ⓣ ☕ & Partial.
⚐ Obligatory. ⓟ Limited. ◼ Guide dogs only. ❋ By arrangement.
🏠 Tel for details.

STANDEN ❦

EAST GRINSTEAD, WEST SUSSEX RH19 4NE

www.nationaltrust.org.uk/standen

Tel: 01342 323029   **Fax:** 01342 316424   **e-mail:** standen@nationaltrust.org.uk

Owner: The National Trust   **Contact:** The Property Manager

Dating from the 1890s and containing original Morris & Co furnishings and decorations, Standen survives today as a remarkable testimony to the ideals of the Arts and Crafts Movement. The property was built as a family home by the influential architect Philip Webb and retains a warm, welcoming atmosphere. Details of Webb's designs can be found everywhere from the fireplaces to the original electric light fittings.

Location: OS Ref. TQ389 356. 2m S of East Grinstead, signposted from B2110.

Open: 27 Mar - 31 Oct: Wed - Sun & BHs. House: 11am - 5pm (last admission 4.30pm). Garden: As house, 11am - 6pm. Garden, Shop and Restaurant: 5 Nov - 19 Dec: Fri - Sun, 11am - 3pm.

Admission: House & Garden: £6, Family £15. Garden only: £3.20. Joint ticket with same day entry to Nymans Garden £10, available Wed - Fri. Groups: £5, Wed - Fri only, if booked in advance.

🖼 ♿ ⓣ & Partial. WC. ⓣ Licensed. ⓟ ◼
🐕 In woods on leads, not in garden. 🏠 Tel for details.

SHEFFIELD PARK GARDEN ❦   *See page 169 for full page entry.*

Borde Hill, Sussex from the book
Historic Family Homes and Gardens from the Air, see page 54.

STANSTED PARK 🏛

STANSTED PARK, ROWLANDS CASTLE, HAMPSHIRE   PO9 6DX

www.stanstedpark.co.uk

Tel: 023 9241 2265   **Fax:** 023 9241 3773   **e-mail:** events@stanstedpark.co.uk

Owner: Stansted Park Foundation   **Contact:** Visitor Services Manager

'One of the South's most beautiful stately homes' set amongst 1750 acres of glorious park and woodland, Stansted House gives an insight into the social history of an English Country House in its heyday. The State Rooms, containing Bessborough family furniture, portraits and colourful bird paintings, contrast with the Servants Quarters' equally interesting domestic artefacts. Visit the ancient Chapel which inspired Keats, the Bessborough Arboretum and the new maze. The beautiful walled garden contains a permanent exhibition of sculptures and the tearoom. The Garden Centre, working Glassblower and Potter make Stansted Park a fascinating and fun place to visit.

Location: OS Ref. SU761 103. Follow brown heritage signs from A3 Rowlands Castle or A27 Havant. Rail: Mainline station, Havant. Taxis: Rowlands Castle no taxis 30 minute walk.

Open: 11 Apr - 27 Sept: Sun & Mon, 1 - 5pm (last entry 4pm). Also Jul & Aug: Sun - Wed.

Admission: Adult £5.50, Child £3.50, OAP/Student £4.50. Groups and educational visits by arrangement only.

🚻 Ⓣ ♿ Partial. ☎ ✉ By arrangement. Ⓟ ☒ Guide dogs only. ▲ ❋ Grounds. ☷ Tel for details.

UPPARK ❧   *See page 170 for full page entry.*

WAKEHURST PLACE ❧

Ardingly, Haywards Heath, Sussex   RH17 6TN

Tel: 01444 894066   **Fax:** 01444 894069   **e-mail:** wakehurst@kew.org   **www.**kew.org

Owner: The National Trust (managed by Royal Botanic Gdns)   **Contact:** The Administrator

A superb collection of exotic trees, shrubs and other plants, many displayed in a geographic manner. Extensive water gardens, a winter garden, a rock walk and walled gardens. The Loder Valley Nature Reserve can be visited by prior arrangement.

Location: OS Ref. TQ339 314. 1¹/₂ m N of Ardingly, on B2028.

Open: Daily (not 25 Dec & 1 Jan). Feb & Oct: 10am - 5pm. Mar: 10am - 6pm. Apr - end Sept: 10am - 7pm. Nov - end Jan 2004: 10am - 4pm. Mansion, seed bank and restaurant closed 1hr before gardens.

Admission: Adult £7, Child (under 17) Free, Conc. £5.

▣ ♿ Ground floor & part of grounds. 🍴 ☷ Tel for details.

WEALD & DOWNLAND OPEN AIR MUSEUM

Singleton, Chichester, Sussex   PO18 0EU

Tel: 01243 811348   **www.**wealddown.co.uk

Over 45 original historic buildings. Interiors and gardens through the ages.

Location: OS Ref. SU876 127. 6m N of Chichester on A286. S of Singleton.

Open: 1 Mar - 31 Oct: daily, 10.30am - 6pm. Nov - Feb: weekends only. 10.30am - 4pm. 26 Dec - 2 Jan: daily, 10.30am - 4pm.

Admission: Adult £7, Child/Student £4, OAP £6.50. Family (2+3) £19. (2003 prices.) Group rates on request.

▣ 🚻 ♿ ☎ ✉ 🍴 ⚲ Ⓟ ☒ ◩ ▲ ❋ ☷ Tel for details.

WEST DEAN GARDENS 🏛

WEST DEAN, CHICHESTER, WEST SUSSEX   PO18 0QZ

www.westdean.org.uk

Tel: 01243 818210   **Fax:** 01243 811342   **e-mail:** gardens@westdean.org.uk

Owner: The Edward James Foundation   **Contact:** Jim Buckland, Gardens Manager

Visiting the Gardens you are immersed in a classic 19th century designed landscape with its 2¹/₂ acre walled kitchen garden, 13 original glasshouses dating from the 1890s, 35 acres of ornamental grounds, 240 acre landscaped park and the 49 acre St Roche's arboretum, all linked by a scenic 2¹/₄ mile parkland walk. Features of the grounds are a lavishly planted 300ft long Edwardian pergola terminated by a flint and stone gazebo and sunken garden. The Visitor Centre (free entry) houses a licensed restaurant and an imaginative garden shop.

Location: OS Ref. SU863 128. SE side of A286 Midhurst Road, 6m N of Chichester.

Open: 1 Mar - 31 October: daily. Mar, Apr & Oct: 11am - 5pm. May - Sept: 10.30am - 5pm.

Admission: Adult £5.50, Child £2.50, OAP £5. Groups (20+): Adult £5, Child £2.50

ⓘ No photography in house. ▣ 🚻 Ⓣ ♿ ☎ 🍴 Licensed. Ⓟ Limited for coaches. ✉ By arrangement. ☒ Guide dogs only. ☷ Tel for details.

WILMINGTON PRIORY

Wilmington, Nr Eastbourne, East Sussex BN26 5SW

Tel: 01628 825920 or 825925 (bookings) **www**.landmarktrust.co.uk

Owner: Leased to the Landmark Trust by Sussex Archaeological Society

Contact: The Landmark Trust

Founded by the Benedictines in the 11th century, the surviving, much altered buildings date largely from the 14th century. Managed and maintained by the Landmark Trust, which lets buildings for self-catering holidays. Full details of Wilmington Priory and 178 other historic buildings available for holidays are featured in The Landmark Handbook (price £9.50 refundable against booking), from The Landmark Trust, Shottesbrooke, Maidenhead, Berkshire, SL6 3SW.

Location: OS Ref. TQ543 042. 600yds S of A27. 6m NW of Eastbourne.

Open: Grounds, Ruins, Porch & Crypt: on 30 days between Apr - Oct. Whole property including interiors on 8 of these days, 17 - 20 May & 10 - 14 Sept. Telephone for details. Accommodation is available for up to 6 people for self-catering holidays.

Admission: Please contact Landmark Trust for details.

Glynde Place, Sussex from the book *Historic Family Homes and Gardens from the Air*, see page 54.

English Heritage Photo Library

Map 3

Owner:
English Heritage

▶ **CONTACT**

The House
Administrator
Osborne House
Royal Apartments
East Cowes
Isle of Wight
PO32 6JY

Tel: 01983 200022
Fax: 01983 297281

**Venue Hire and
Hospitality:**
Tel: 01983 200022

▶ **LOCATION**
OS Ref. SZ516 948

1m SE of East Cowes.

Ferry: Isle of Wight
ferry terminals .

East Cowes 1¹/2 m
Tel: 02380 334010.

Fishbourne 4m
Tel: 0870 582 7744.

CONFERENCE/FUNCTION

ROOM	MAX CAPACITY
Durbar Hall	standing 80 seated 50
Upper Terrace	standing 250
Walled Gardens	standing 100
Marquee	Large scale events possible

OSBORNE HOUSE ⌗

EAST COWES

Osborne House was the peaceful, rural retreat of Queen Victoria, Prince Albert and their family; they spent some of their happiest times here.

Many of the apartments have a very intimate association with the Queen who died here in 1901 and have been preserved almost unaltered ever since. The nursery bedroom remains just as it was in the 1870s when Queen Victoria's first grandchildren came to stay. Children were a constant feature of life at Osborne (Victoria and Albert had nine). Don't miss the Swiss Cottage, a charming chalet in the grounds built for the Royal children to play and entertain their parents in.

Enjoy the beautiful gardens with their stunning views over the Solent and the fruit and flower Victorian Walled Garden. The Durbar Wing has been refurbished. With interactive screens it displays the exquisite Indian gifts given by the Indian people to Queen Victoria.

English Heritage Photo Library

⬚ **i** WCs. Suitable for filming, concerts, drama. No photography in the House. Children's play area. WC.

T Private and corporate hire.

♿ Wheelchairs available, access to house via ramp, ground floor access only. WC.

☕ Teas, coffees and light snacks. Waitress service in Swiss Cottage tearoom.

P Ample. Coach drivers and tour leaders free, one extra place for every additional 20. Group rates.

▣ Visits free, please book. Education room available.

❋

▶ **OPENING TIMES***

House

1 April - 30 September
Daily: 10am - 6pm.
Last admission 4pm.

1 - 31 Oct
Daily: 10am - 5pm
Last admission 4pm.

May close earlier on concert days, please telephone for details.

Winter & Spring:
Telephone for details:
01983 200022.

* Times subject to change April 2004.

▶ **ADMISSION***

House & Grounds

Adult	£8.00
Child (5-15yrs)	£4.00
Child under 5yrs	Free
Conc.	£6.00
Family	£20.00

Grounds only

Adult	£4.50
Child (5-15yrs)	£2.30
Child under 5yrs	Free
Conc.	£3.40
Family	£11.30

Plus normal 15% discount for groups.

* Prices subject to change April 2004.

APPULDURCOMBE HOUSE ⚜

Wroxall, Shanklin, Isle of Wight

Tel: 01983 852484 **www.english-heritage.org.uk/visits**

Owner: English Heritage **Contact:** Mr & Mrs Owen

The bleached shell of a fine 18th century Baroque style house standing in grounds landscaped by 'Capability' Brown. An exhibition displays prints and photographs depicting the history of the house. Falconry Centre.

Location: OS Ref. SZ543 800. $^1/2$m W of Wroxall off B3327.

Open: 15 Feb - 15 Dec: daily, 10am - 4pm (last admission 3pm). 1 May - 30 Sept: daily, 10am - 5pm. Times subject to change from April 2004.

Admission: House: Adult £2.50, Child £1.50, Conc. £2.25. Falconry Centre from 1 Apr 2003: Adult £4.75, Child £2.75, Conc. £4.25, Family £12.50. Combined Ticket: Adult £5.75, Child £3.25, Conc. £5.25, Family £15. Prices subject to change from April 2004.

⬛ 🔄 **P** Limited. 🐕 In grounds, on leads. 🔱 Tel. for details.

BARTON MANOR GARDENS

Whippingham, East Cowes, Isle of Wight PO32 6LB

Tel: 01983 280676 **Fax:** 01983 293923

Owner: Robert Stigwood **Contact:** Julia Richards

Location: OS Ref. SZ519 944. Whippingham, East Cowes, Isle of Wight.

Open: Jun - Sept: 1st Sun in the month only, in aid of local hospice.

Admission: Adult £3, Child £1.

BEMBRIDGE WINDMILL ✿

Correspondence to: NT Office, Strawberry Lane, Mottistone, Isle of Wight PO30 4EA

Tel: 01983 873945 **www.nationaltrust.org.uk**

Owner: The National Trust **Contact:** The Custodian

Dating from around 1700, this is the only windmill to survive on the Island. Much of its original wooden machinery is still intact and there are spectacular views from the top.

Location: OS Ref. SZ639 874. $^1/2$m S of Bembridge off B3395.

Open: 29 Mar - 30 Jun & 1 Sept - 29 Oct: daily except Sat; 1 Jul - 31 Aug: daily, 10am - 5pm. Open Easter Sat.

Admission: Adult £1.90, Child 90p. All school groups are conducted by a NT guide; special charges apply.

⬛ ⬛ 🅘 By arrangement. **P** 100 yds. ⬛ 🐕 Guide dogs only.

BRIGHSTONE SHOP & MUSEUM ✿

North St, Brighstone, Isle of Wight PO30 4AX

Tel: 01983 740689

Owner: The National Trust **Contact:** The Manager

The vernacular cottages contain a National Trust shop and Village Museum (run by Brighstone Museum Trust) depicting village life in the late 19th century.

Location: OS Ref. SZ428 828. North Street, Brighstone, just off B3399.

Open: 2 Jan - 27 Mar: Mon - Sat, 10am - 1pm. 29 Mar - 22 May: Mon - Sat 10am - 4pm. 24 May - 23 Oct: Mon - Sat, 10am - 5pm. 25 Oct - 31 Dec: Mon - Sat, 10am - 4pm. Also Suns 23 May - 24 Oct: 12 noon - 5pm. Closed 25 - 27 Dec & 1 Jan.

Admission: Free.

🔄 Partial. 🔱

CARISBROOKE CASTLE ⚜

NEWPORT, ISLE OF WIGHT PO30 1XY

www.english-heritage.org.uk/visits

Tel: 01983 522107 **Fax:** 01983 528632

Owner: English Heritage **Contact:** The Custodian

The Island's Royal fortress and prison of King Charles I before his execution in London in 1648. See the famous Carisbrooke donkeys treading the wheel in the Well House or meet them in the donkey centre. Don't miss the castle story in the gatehouse, the museum in the great hall and the interactive coach house museum. Guided tours available in summer.

Location: OS196 Ref. SZ486 877. Off the B3401, 1$^1/4$m SW of Newport.

Open: 1 Apr - 30 Sept: daily, 10am - 6pm. 1 - 31 Oct: 10am - 5pm. 1 Nov - 31 Mar: daily, 10am - 4pm. Closed 24 - 26 Dec & 1 Jan. Times subject to change from April 2004.

Admission: Adult £5, Child £2.50, Conc. £3.80, Family (2+3) £12.50. 15% discount for groups (11+), extra place for additional groups of 20. Prices subject to change from April 2004.

🅘 WCs. ⬛ 🔄 ⬛ **P** 🐕 In grounds, on leads. 🔱 Tel. for details.

MORTON MANOR

Brading, Isle of Wight PO36 0EP

Tel/Fax: 01983 406168 **e-mail:** mortonmanor-iow@amserver.com

Owner/Contact: Mr J A J Trzebski

Refurbished in the Georgian period. Magnificent gardens and vineyard.

Location: OS Ref. SZ603 863 (approx.). $^1/4$m W of A3055 in Brading.

Open: Easter - end Oct: daily except Sats, 10am - 5.30pm. Last admission 4.30pm.

Admission: Adult £4.50, Child £2, Conc. £4, Group £3.50 (2003 prices, subject to alteration).

MOTTISTONE MANOR GARDEN ✿

Mottistone, Isle of Wight PO30 4ED

Tel: 01983 741302 **www.nationaltrust.org.uk**

Owner: The National Trust **Contact:** The Gardener

A haven of peace and tranquillity with colourful herbaceous borders and a backdrop of the sea making a perfect setting for the historic Manor House. An annual open air Jazz Concert is held in the grounds during Jul/Aug.

Location: OS Ref. SZ406 838. 2m W of Brighstone on B3399.

Open: 30 Mar - 27 Oct: Tue & Wed, 11am - 5.30pm. 28 Mar - 31 Oct: Sun 2 - 5.30pm. House: Aug BH Mon only: 2 - 5.30pm. Guided tours for NT members on that day 10am - 12 noon. Gardens also open Aug BH Mon 2 - 5.30pm.

Admission: Adult £2.90, Child £1.40, Family £7.20.

⬛ 🔄 Limited access for wheelchair users. ⬛ **P** ⬛ 🐕 In grounds, on leads.

NEEDLES OLD BATTERY ✿

West High Down, Totland, Isle of Wight PO39 0JH

Tel: 01983 754772 **www.nationaltrust.org.uk**

Owner: The National Trust **Contact:** The Property Manager

High above the sea, the Old Battery was built in the 1860s against the threat of French invasion. Exhibition of History of Battery. Stunning views.

Location: OS Ref. SZ300 848. Needles Headland W of Freshwater Bay & Alum Bay (B3322).

Open: 28 Mar - 30 Jun, 1 Sept - 31 Oct: daily except Fri (open Good Fri). Jul & Aug: daily, 10.30am - 5pm. Property closes in bad weather; please telephone on day of visit to check.

Admission: Adult £3.60, Child £1.80. Special charge for guided tours.

🔄 Partial. ⬛ 🅘 By appointment. ⬛ 🐕 In grounds, on leads.

Conservatory, Glasshouse, Stove House

– popular from the 17th century, conservatories in which to house exotic plants became all the rage in Victorian times. The most famous builder of Victorian conservatories was Sir Joseph Paxton who worked for much of his career for the wealthy 6th Duke of Devonshire at Chatsworth House, in Derbyshire.

Visit also Broughton Hall, Yorkshire and Somerleyton Hall & Gardens, Suffolk.

Garden Jargon

NUNWELL HOUSE & GARDENS
Coach Lane, Brading, Isle of Wight PO36 0JQ

Tel: 01983 407240

Owner: Col & Mrs J A Aylmer **Contact:** Mrs J A Aylmer

Nunwell has been a family home for five centuries and reflects much architectural and Island history. King Charles I spent his last night of freedom here. Jacobean and Georgian wings. Finely furnished rooms. Lovely setting with Channel views and five acres of tranquil gardens including walled garden. Family military collections.

Location: OS Ref. SZ595 874. 1m NW of Brading. 3m S of Ryde signed off A3055.

Open: 30/31 May. 5 Jul - 8 Sept: Mon - Wed, 1 - 5pm. House tours: 1.30, 2.30 & 3.30pm. Groups welcome by arrangement throughout the year.

Admission: Adult £4, Pair of Adults £7.50 (inc guide book), Child (under 10yrs) £1, OAP/Student £3.50. Garden only: Adult £2.50.

🗖 🖬 Obligatory. 🅿 🖬 Guide dogs only. ❀

OLD TOWN HALL 🖏
Newtown, Isle of Wight

Tel: 01983 531785 **www.**nationaltrust.org.uk

Owner: The National Trust **Contact:** The Custodian

A charming small 18th century building that was once the focal point of the 'rotten borough' of Newtown.

Location: OS Ref. SZ424 905. Between Newport and Yarmouth, 1m N of A3054.

Open: 29 Mar - 30 Jun, 1 Sept - 20 Oct: Mon, Wed & Sun, 2 - 5pm. Jul - Aug: Mon - Thur & Sun, 2 - 5pm.

Admission: Adult £1.70, Child 80p, Family £4.20. Special charge for guided tours (written application).

🅿 Limited. 🖬 Guide dogs only.

OSBORNE HOUSE ⌗
See page 185 for full page entry.

YARMOUTH CASTLE ⌗
Quay Street, Yarmouth, Isle of Wight PO41 0PB

Tel: 01983 760678 **www.**english-heritage.org.uk/visits

Owner: English Heritage **Contact:** The Custodian

This last addition to Henry VIII's coastal defences was completed in 1547 and is, unusually for its kind, square with a fine example of an angle bastion. It was garrisoned well into the 19th century. It houses exhibitions of paintings of the Isle of Wight and photographs of old Yarmouth.

Location: OS Ref. SZ354 898. In Yarmouth adjacent to car ferry terminal.

Open: 1 Apr - 30 Sept: daily, 10am - 6pm. 1 - 31 Oct: 10am - 5pm. Times subject to change from April 2004.

Admission: Adult £2.50, Child £1.30, Conc. £1.90. Prices subject to change from April 2004.

🗖 🖧 Ground floor. 🅿 None. 🖬 In grounds, on leads.

Osborne House, Isle of Wight.

southwest

Clovelly, Devon. © David Osborn.

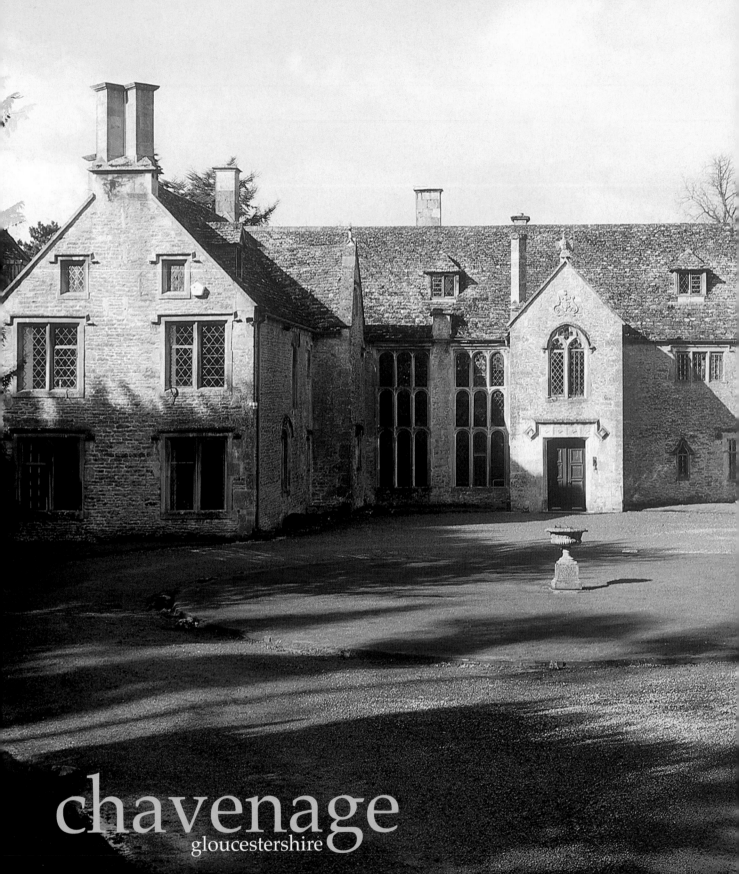

chavenage
gloucestershire

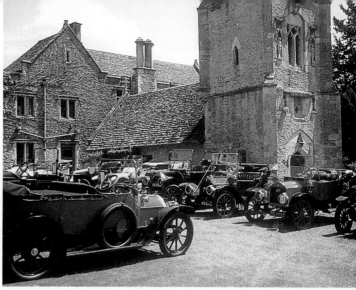

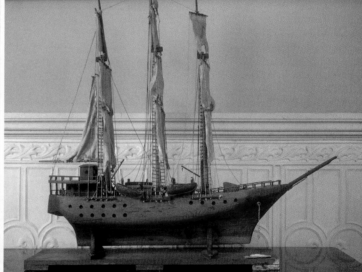

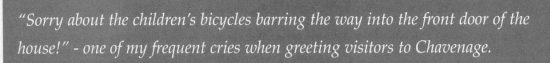

"Sorry about the children's bicycles barring the way into the front door of the house!" - one of my frequent cries when greeting visitors to Chavenage.

David Lowsley-Williams

C havenage House lies two miles north-west of Tetbury, Gloucestershire, set in the 1500 acre estate owned by David Lowsley-Williams. Drive down narrow sleepy lanes, and you arrive at an Elizabethan stone mullioned manor house dating from 1380 and reconstructed in 1576 by the Stephens family, who bought the monastic estate out of the profits from sheep farming. The house consists of a hall block with a central porch, flanked by two gabled wings – a classic example of the 16th century E-shaped building plan. The house and estate came into ownership of the present family in 1891 and, apart from the addition of the Edwardian ballroom modelled in the Arts and Craft style (used today for parties and wedding receptions) there have been few major changes.

But don't be deceived into thinking that Chavenage is a dusty time warp … far from it. Visit Chavenage and you will find a thriving community. For as David Lowsley-Williams says, the estate is a family run affair. His son George runs the farming enterprises, his wife oversees the dairy operation, Caroline, his elder daughter is the administrator of the house, and Joanna, her younger sister, runs the catering side of the business. This is what makes a visit to Chavenage so charming – whilst it is a house full of history, fine furniture, wonderful oak panelling, carved fireplaces and late-medieval glass, it is actually the family who inhabits it that makes the visit so memorable. Once you have negotiated the free-range bantams that roam the car park area and been greeted by the four family spaniels, you are then met by a member of the family to be taken on a tour of the house, and you cannot help but feel at your ease.

It might only be the ghosts, said to inhabit the house, that may not be quite so welcoming. You could just feel a small shiver down your spine when walking into the first floor tapestry-hung bedrooms named after Oliver Cromwell and Henry Ireton. The story goes that in 1648, Cromwell and his second in command, Henry Ireton, came to Chavenage to seek Colonel Nathaniel Stephens' support for King Charles I's impeachment. Stephens was related by marriage to Cromwell; a staunch Parliamentarian, he no doubt felt under intense pressure to agree to Cromwell's demands. Stephens apparently refused to give his assent, but when they returned on a second visit, Stephens agreed. On hearing this news, Stephens' daughter Abigail cried that the house would be cursed forever. Stephens died soon after, and the Colonel's ghost is to be seen being taken from the house in a carriage drawn by the headless King. … Well you never know, it might just be true and if you don't believe this one there is always the chance sighting of the spectral monk – who occasionally frequents the Chapel!

Enjoy the rich history of the place and imbibe the enthusiasm that the Lowsley-Williams feel towards their home. If you are an event organiser Chavenage offers the perfect venue for small conferences and functions. You can arrange anything from clay pigeon shoots, archery, fashion shoots, plays, concerts, and seminars – and Joanna's catering is superb. There is no better place to consider as a wedding reception venue, you will get the very best service, set in the most lovely of surroundings.

▸ For further details about Chavenage see page 230.

Map 2

SAUSMAREZ MANOR

GUERNSEY

www.artparks.co.uk   www.guernsey.org/sausmarez

The home of the Seigneurs de Sausmarez since c1220 with a façade built at the bequest of the first Governor of New York.

An entrancing and entertaining half day encompassing something to interest everyone. The family have been explorers, inventors, diplomats, prelates, generals, admirals, privateers, politicians and governors etc, most of whom left their mark on the house, garden or the furniture.

The sub-tropical woodland garden is crammed with such exotics as banana trees, tree ferns, ginger, 300 plus camellias, lilies, myriads of bamboos, as well as the more commonplace hydrangeas, hostas etc.

The sculpture in the art park with its 200 or so pieces by artists from a dozen countries is the most comprehensive in Britain. The dolls' house collection displays pieces from 1830 onwards and is the third largest dedicated collection in Britain. The pitch and put is a cruelly testing 500m 9 hole par 3. The ride-on-trains travel $1/4$ mile through part of the woodland. The two lakes are a haven for ornamental wildfowl and some of the sculpture.

Sausmarez Manor is available for corporate hospitality functions and Civil weddings. It also offers guided tours, welcomes schools (has education programmes), and has a tearoom, café and gift shop.

Owner:
The Seigneur de Sausmarez

▶ **CONTACT**

Peter de Sausmarez
Sausmarez Manor
Guernsey
Channel Islands
GY4 6SG

Tel: 01481
235571/235655
Fax: 01481 235572

e-mail:
peter@artparks.co.uk

▶ **LOCATION**

2m S of St Peter Port, clearly sign posted.

▶ **OPENING TIMES**

Easter - End Oct
Daily: 10am - 5pm

Guided tours of House
Mon - Thurs:
10.30 & 11.30am.
Additional 2pm tour
during high season.

▶ **ADMISSION**

There is no overall charge
for admission.

Dolls' Houses £2.50
Sub Tropical Garden . £4.00
Sculpture Trail £4.00
Pitch & Putt.............. £4.50
Putting...................... £1.00
House Tour * £5.40*
Train £1.50

Discounts for Children,
Students, OAPs &
Organised Groups.

 Partial.

 Guided tours of House.

 New holiday flat on the ground floor.

National Trust/ Jon Hicks

Map 1

Owner:
The National Trust

▶ **CONTACT**

Lewis Eynon
Property Manager
Cotehele
St Dominick
Saltash, Cornwall
PL12 6TA

Tel: 01579 351346
Fax: 01579 351222
e-mail:
cotehele@nationaltrust.
org.uk

▶ **LOCATION**

OS Ref. SX422 685
1m SW of Calstock by
foot. 8m S of Tavistock,
4m E of Callington,
15m from Plymouth
via the Tamar bridge
at Saltash

Trains: Limited service
from Plymouth to
Calstock (1¼ m uphill)

Boats: Limited (tidal)
service from Plymouth
to Calstock Quay
(Plymouth Boat
Cruises)
Tel: 01752 822797

River ferry: Privately
run from Calstock to
Cotehele Quay.
Tel: 01579 351346

Buses: Western
National (seasonal
variations)
Tel: 01752 222666

COTEHELE

SALTASH

www.nationaltrust.org.uk

Cotehele, owned by the Edgcumbe family for nearly 600 years, is a fascinating and enchanting estate set on the steep wooded slopes of the River Tamar. Exploring Cotehele's many and various charms provides a full day out for the family and leaves everyone longing to return.

The steep valley garden contains exotic and tender plants which thrive in the mild climate. Remnants of an earlier age include a mediaeval stewpond and domed dovecote, a 15th-century chapel and 18th-century tower with fine views over the surrounding countryside. A series of more formal gardens, terraces, an orchard and a daffodil meadow surround Cotehele House.

One of the least altered medieval houses in the country, Cotehele is built in local granite, slate and sandstone. Inside the ancient rooms, unlit by electricity, is a fine collection of textiles, tapestries, armour and early dark oak furniture.

National Trust /Tymn Lintell

The chapel contains the oldest working domestic clock in England, still in its original position.

A walk through the garden and along the river leads to the quay, a busy river port in Victorian times. The National Maritime Museum worked with the National Trust to set up a museum here which explains the vital role that the Tamar played in the local economy. As a living reminder, the restored Tamar sailing barge *Shamrock* (owned jointly by the Trust and the National Maritime Museum) is moored here.

A further walk through woodland along the Morden stream leads to the old estate corn mill which has been restored to working order.

This large estate with many footpaths offers a variety of woodland and countryside walks, opening up new views and hidden places. The Danescombe Valley, with its history of mining and milling, is of particular interest.

ℹ️ No photography in house. *NPI National Heritage Award winners 1996 & 1999.*

🛍️ National Trust shop.

🍽️ Available for up to 90 people.

♿ 2 wheelchairs at Reception. Hall & kitchen accessible. Ramps at house, restaurant and shop. Most of garden is very steep with loose gravel. Riverside walks are flatter (from Cotehele Quay) & Edgcumbe Arms is accessible. WCs near house and at Quay. Parking near house & mill by arrangement.

☕🍴 Barn restaurant daily (except Fri), 20 Mar - 31 Oct, plus limited opening from 14 Feb. At the Quay, Edgcumbe Arms offers light meals daily, 20 Mar - 31 Oct. Both licensed.

🅿️ Near house and garden and at Cotehele Quay. No parking at mill.

🚶 Groups (15+) must book with Property Office and receive a coach route (limited to two per day). No groups Suns & BH weekends. Visitors to house limited to 80 at any one time. Please arrive early and be prepared to queue. Avoid dull days. Allow a full day to see estate.

🐕 Under control welcome only on woodland walks.

❄️

▶ **OPENING TIMES**

House & Restaurant
20 Mar - 31 Oct: Daily
except Fris (but open
Good Fri), 11am - 5pm
(Oct: 11am - 4.30pm).
Last admission 30 mins
before closing time.

Mill
20 Mar - 31 Oct: Daily
except Fris (but open
Good Fri plus Fris in July
& August) 1 - 5.30pm
(closes 4.30pm during Oct,
6pm July & Aug).

Garden
All year: Daily,
10.30am - dusk.

▶ **ADMISSION**

House, Garden & Mill
Adult £7.00
Family Tickets £17.50
Pre-booked Groups .. £6.00

Garden & Mill only
Adult £4.00
Family £10.00

*Groups must book in
advance with the
Property Office.
No groups Suns or BHs.

NT members free.
You may join here.

NTPL / R Truman

Map 1

LANHYDROCK

BODMIN

Lanhydrock is the grandest and most welcoming house in Cornwall, set in a glorious landscape of gardens, parkland and woods overlooking the valley of the River Fowey.

The house dates back to the 17th century but much of it had to be rebuilt after a disastrous fire in 1881 destroyed all but the entrance porch and the north wing, which includes the magnificent Long Gallery with its extraordinary plaster ceiling depicting scenes from the Old Testament. A total of 50 rooms are on show today and together they reflect the entire spectrum of life in a rich and splendid Victorian household, from the many servants' bedrooms and the fascinating complex

of kitchens, sculleries and larders to the nursery suite where the Agar-Robartes children lived, learned and played, and the grandeur of the dining room with its table laid and ready.

Surrounding the house on all sides are gardens ranging from formal Victorian parterres to the wooded higher garden where magnificent displays of magnolias, rhododendrons and camellias climb the hillside to merge with the oak and beech woods all around. A famous avenue of ancient beech and sycamore trees, the original entrance drive to the house, runs from the pinnacled 17th-century gatehouse down towards the medieval bridge across the Fowey at Respryn.

Owner:
The National Trust

▶ **CONTACT**

Property Manager
Lanhydrock
Bodmin
Cornwall PL30 5AD

Tel: 01208 265950
Fax: 01208 265959

e-mail: lanhydrock@
nationaltrust.org.uk

▶ **LOCATION**
OS Ref. SX085 636

2½ m SE of Bodmin,
follow signposts from
either A30,
A38 or B3268.

NTPL: Andreas von Einsiedel

NT/Jon Hicks

No photography in house.

By arrangement.

Suitable. Braille guide. WC.

Licensed restaurant

In park, on leads. Guide dogs only in house.

Limited for coaches.

Please telephone for details.

▶ **OPENING TIMES**

House:
27 Mar - 31 Oct:
Daily except Mons
(but open BH Mons)
11am - 5.30pm.
Oct: 11am - 5pm.

Last admission ½ hr
before closing.

Garden:
All year: Daily.
10am - 6pm.
Charge levied from
14 Feb - 31 Oct.

Refreshments available
14 Feb - 31 Oct: Daily.
Nov - Jan: limited opening
(tel for details).

Plant Sales:
1 - 26 Mar: Daily
11am - 4pm
27 Mar - 30 Sept:
11am - 5.30pm.
Oct: 11am - 5pm.

Shop:
14 Feb - 26 Mar, 1 Nov -
23 Dec & 27 - 31 Dec:
Daily, 11am - 4pm.

27 Mar - 30 Sept: Daily
11am - 5.30pm

Oct: Daily
11am - 5pm.

▶ **ADMISSION**
House, Garden &
Grounds
Adult £7.50
Family £18.75
Groups................. £6.50

Garden &
Grounds only £4.20

National Trust/ Peter Cade

ANTONY HOUSE & GARDEN
& ANTONY WOODLAND GARDEN

TORPOINT, CORNWALL PL11 2QA

www.nationaltrust.org.uk

Antony House & Garden Tel: 01752 812191

Antony Woodland Garden Tel: 01752 812364

e-mail: antony@nationaltrust.org.uk

Antony House & Garden Owner: The National Trust

Antony Woodland Garden Owner: Carew Pole Garden Trust

Superb 18th-century house on the Lynher estuary, grounds landscaped by Repton. Formal garden with sculptures & National Collection of day lilies; woodland garden with magnolias, rhododendrons & National Collection of Camellia japonica.

Location: OS Ref. SX418 564. 5m W of Plymouth via Torpoint car ferry, 2m NW of Torpoint.

Open: House & Garden: 30 Mar - 28 Oct: Tue - Thur & BH Mons. Also Suns in June, July & Aug: 1.30pm - 5.30pm. Last adm. 4.45pm. Tearoom open from 12.30pm. Woodland Garden (not NT) 2 Mar - 31 Oct: daily except Mon & Fri (open BH Mons), 11am - 5.30pm.

Admission: House & Garden: £4.80, Family £12. Groups £4pp. NT Garden only: £2.50. Woodland Garden: Adult £3.50 (Free to NT members on days when the house is open). Joint Gardens-only tickets: Adult £4. Groups £3.30.

🔲 ♿ Braille guide. ⬛ 🅿 ♿

BOSVIGO 🏛

BOSVIGO LANE, TRURO, CORNWALL TR1 3NH

www.bosvigo.com

Tel/Fax: 01872 275774   **e-mail:** bosvigo.plants@virgin.net

Owner: Michael & Wendy Perry   **Contact:** Michael Perry

A series of small, densely planted 'rooms', each with its own colour theme, surround the Georgian house (not open). The Woodland Walk is crammed full of small spring treasures, whilst the herbaceous garden 'rooms' give non-stop colour from June to the end of September. Small specialist nursery attached.

Location: OS Ref. SW815 452. 3/4 m W of Truro city centre. Turn off A390 down Dobbs Lane just W of Sainsbury foodstore.

Open: Mar - end Sept: Thur & Fri, 11am - 6pm.

Admission: Adult £3, Child (5-15yrs) £1. No group concessions.

🔲 ♿ Partial. 🅿 Limited. ♿

BOCONNOC

ESTATE OFFICE, BOCONNOC, LOSTWITHIEL, CORNWALL PL22 0RG

Tel: 01208 872507   **Fax:** 01208 873836   **e-mail:** adgfortescue@btinternet.com

Owner/Contact: Anthony Fortescue Esq

Bought with the famous Pitt Diamond in 1717, Boconnoc remains one of Cornwall's best kept secrets. Home to three Prime Ministers, its unique combination of history, architecture, picturesque landscape and one of the great Cornish gardens created ideal film locations for *Poldark* and *The Three Musketeers*. King Charles I and the architect Sir John Soane played an influential part in Boconnoc's history. Groups visit the Boconnoc House restoration project, the gardens, church, Golden Jubilee lake walk and the Georgian Bath House. Ideal for private and corporate events, conferences,

activities; wedding receptions and holiday houses for long or short breaks.

Location: OS Ref. 148 605. A38 Plymouth, Liskeard or from Bodmin to Dobwalls, then A390 to Middle Taphouse.

Open: House & Garden: 18 & 25 Apr; 2, 9, 16 & 23 May. House also open 17 - 21 May. Groups (15-255) by appointment all year.

Admission: House: £3, Garden £3. Child under 12yrs Free.

🔲 ⬛ ♿Partial. ⬛ 📷By arrangement. 🅿 ⬛ ♿In grounds, on leads. 🛏8 doubles, 1 single, 3 ensuite. ✳ ⬛ 3 - 4 Apr: Cornwall Spring Flower Show. 16 - 18 Jul: Boconnoc Steam Fair.

BURNCOOSE NURSERIES & GARDEN

Gwennap, Redruth, Cornwall TR16 6BJ

Tel: 01209 860316 **Fax:** 01209 860011 **e-mail:** burncoose@eclipse.co.uk
www.burncoose.co.uk

Owner/Contact: C H Williams

The Nurseries are set in the 30 acre woodland gardens of Burncoose.

Location: OS Ref. SW742 395. 2m SE of Redruth on main A393 Redruth to Falmouth road between the villages of Lanner and Ponsanooth.

Open: Mon – Sat: 9am - 5pm, Suns, 11am - 5pm. Gardens and Tearooms open all year (except Christmas Day).

Admission: Nurseries: Free. Gardens: Adult/Conc. £2. Child Free. Group conducted tours: £2.50 by arrangement.

🖾 ♿ ♿Grounds. WCs. ● ⓘBy arrangement. 🅿 🖾In grounds, on leads. ✳

CAERHAYS CASTLE & GARDEN 🏛

CAERHAYS, GORRAN, ST AUSTELL, CORNWALL PL26 6LY

www.caerhays.co.uk

Tel: 01872 501310 **Fax:** 01872 501870 **e-mail:** estateoffice@caerhays.co.uk

Owner: F J Williams Esq **Contact:** The Estate Office

One of the very few Nash built castles still left standing – situated within approximately 60 acres of informal woodland gardens created by J C Williams, who sponsored plant hunting expeditions to China at the turn of the century. Noted for its camellias, magnolias, rhododendrons and oaks. English Heritage listing - Grade I: Outstanding.

Location: OS Ref. SW972 415. S coast of Cornwall – between Mevagissey and Portloe. 9m SW of St Austell.

Open: House: 15 Mar - 31 May: Mon - Fri only (incl BHs), 1 - 4pm, booking recommended. Gardens: 16 Feb - 31 May (including BHs): daily, 10am - 5.30pm (last admission 4.30pm).

Admission: House: £5.50. Gardens: £5.50. House & Gardens: £9.50. Guided group tours (15+) by Head Gardener, £6.50 - by arrangement.

♿ ♿Unsuitable. ● ⓘBy arrangement. 🖾In grounds, on leads.

CHYSAUSTER ANCIENT VILLAGE ⌗

Nr Newmill, Penzance, Cornwall TR20 8XA

Tel: 07831 757934 **e-mail:** customers@english-heritage.org.uk
www.english-heritage.org.uk/visits

Owner: English Heritage **Contact:** The Custodian

On a windy hillside, overlooking the wild and spectacular coast, is this deserted Romano-Cornish village with a 'street' of eight well preserved houses, each comprising a number of rooms around an open court.

Location: OS203 Ref. SW473 350. 2¹/₂ m NW of Gulval off B3311.

Open: 1 Apr - 31 Oct: daily, 10am - 6pm (5pm in Oct). Winter: closed. Times subject to change April 2004.

Admission: Adult £2, Child £1, Conc. £1.50. 15% discount for groups (11+). Prices subject to change April 2004.

🖾 🅿No coaches. 🖾On leads. 🔔 Tel for details.

COTEHELE 🌿 *See page 195 for full page entry.*

National Trust/ Andrew Besley

GLENDURGAN GARDEN 🌿

MAWNAN SMITH, FALMOUTH, CORNWALL TR11 5JZ

Tel: 01326 250906 (opening hours) or 01872 862090 **Fax:** 01872 865808
e-mail: trelissick@nationaltrust.org.uk

Owner: The National Trust

A valley of great beauty with fine trees, shrubs and water gardens. The laurel maze is an unusual and popular feature. The garden runs down to the tiny village of Durgan and its beach on the Helford River. Replica Victorian school room, rebuilt in 2002 in traditional thatch and cob to replace the 1876 original.

Location: OS Ref. SW772 277. 4m SW of Falmouth, ¹/₂ m SW of Mawnan Smith, on road to Helford Passage. 1m E of Trebah Garden.

Open: 14 Feb - 30 Oct: Tue - Sat & BH Mons, 10.30am - 5.30pm. Last admission 4.30pm. Closed Good Friday.

Admission: £4.20, Child £2.10, Family £10.50. Booked groups: £3.60/£1.80.

🖾 ♿ ♿Unsuitable. ● ⓘBy arrangement. 🅿 Limited for coaches.🖾

GODOLPHIN 🏛

GODOLPHIN CROSS, HELSTON, CORNWALL TR13 9RE

www.godolphinhouse.com

Tel/Fax: 01736 763194 **e-mail:** godo@euphony.net

Owner: Mrs L M P Schofield **Contact:** Mrs Joanne Schofield

A romantic Tudor and Stuart Grade I mansion commenced in c1475 with very early, formal Side Garden (c1300 and c1500) undergoing revival programme starting in 2004. Elizabethan stables displaying local wagons. English Heritage grant-aided programme of specialist repairs due to finish in 2004. The development of the Godolphin family's courtly ambition and taste is beautifully expressed in the evolving architecture of the house. Exploitation of tin provided the wealth for this family of entrepreneurs, poets and government officials. Birthplace of Queen Anne's Lord Treasurer. Pictures by American impressionist painter Elmer Schofield and exhibition of paintings in the newly repaired King's room. Traditional marquee in the orchard serving locally sourced food. Adjacent walks on the National Trust estate.

Location: OS Ref. SW602 318. Breage, Helston. On minor road from Godolphin Cross to Townshend. Follow brown signs.

Open: 1 Apr to 30 Sept. Tues, Thurs, Fri, 11am - 5pm. Suns, 2 - 5pm. BH Mons 11am - 5pm. Group bookings and tours all year by arrangement. Coaches welcome.

Admission: Adult £6, Child (5 - 15yrs) £1.50. Garden: £2.

🖾 ♿ ♿Partial. ● 🎁 Opens 11am Tues/Thurs/Fri. 12 noon on Suns.
ⓘBy arrangement. 🅿Limited for coaches. 🖾Guide dogs only. ✳

THE JAPANESE GARDEN & BONSAI NURSERY

St Mawgan, Nr Newquay, Cornwall TR8 4ET

Tel: 01637 860116   **Fax:** 01637 860887

Owner/Contact: Mr & Mrs Hore

Authentic Japanese Garden set in 1½ acres.

Location: OS Ref. SW873 660. Follow road signs from A3059 & B3276.

Open: Summer: Daily 10am - 6pm. WInter: 10am - 5.30pm. Closed Christmas Day - New Year's Day.

Admission: Adult £3.50, Child £1.50. Groups (10+): £2.50.

KEN CARO GARDENS

Bicton, Nr Liskeard PL14 5RF

Tel: 01579 362446

Owner/Contact: Mr and Mrs K R Willcock

4 acre plantsman's garden.

Location: OS Ref. SX313 692. 5m NE of of Liskeard. Follow brown sign off main A390 midway between Liskeard and Callington.

Open: 28 Mar - 30 Sept: Sun - Fri, 10am - 6pm.

Admission: Adult £3.50, Child £1.

LANHYDROCK ✿   *See page 196 for full page entry.*

LAUNCESTON CASTLE ⌘

Castle Lodge, Launceston, Cornwall PL15 7DR

Tel: 01566 772365   **Fax:** 01566 772396

e-mail: customers@english-heritage.org.uk **WWW.**english-heritage.org.uk/visits

Owner: English Heritage   **Contact:** The Custodian

Set on the motte of the original Norman castle and commanding the town and surrounding countryside. The shell keep and tower survive of this medieval castle which controlled the main route into Cornwall. An exhibition shows the early history.

Location: OS201 Ref. SX330 846. In Launceston.

Open: 1 Apr - 31 Oct: daily, 10am - 6pm (5pm in Oct). Winter: Fri - Sun, 10am - 4pm. Closed 24 - 26 Dec & 1 Jan. Times subject to change April 2004.

Admission: Adult £2.10, Child £1.10, Conc. £1.60. 15% discount for groups (11+). Prices subject to change April 2004.

▣ ♿Grounds. ☗ 🅿NCP adjacent. Limited. 🐕In grounds, on leads. ♛Tel for details.

LAWRENCE HOUSE ✿

9 Castle Street, Launceston, Cornwall PL15 8BA

Tel: 01566 773277

Owner: The National Trust   **Contact:** The Property Manager

A Georgian house given to the Trust to help preserve the character of the street, and now leased to Launceston Town Council as a museum and civic centre.

Location: OS Ref. SX330 848. Launceston.

Open: Apr - Oct, daily, except Sat & Sun, 10.30am - 4.30pm. Other times by appointment.

Admission: Free, but contributions welcome.

D Hastilow

THE LOST GARDENS OF HELIGAN

PENTEWAN, ST AUSTELL, CORNWALL PL26 6EN

www.heligan.com

Tel: 01726 845100   **Fax:** 01726 845101

e-mail: info@heligan.com   **Contact:** Mr H Cavender

Over 200 acres of superb working Victorian gardens and pleasure grounds together with a magnificent complex of walled gardens. Summerhouses, lawns, lakes and ponds, huge productive gardens and fruithouses, and 22 acre sub-tropical jungle, are just some of the delights of this 'sleeping beauty'. Heligan Home Farm and pioneering Horsemoor Hide invite visitors to witness the outer estate being brought back into 'good heart'.

Location: OS Ref. SX000 465. 5m SW of St Austell. 2m NW of Mevagissey. Take the B3273 to Mevagissey – follow tourist signs.

Open: Daily except 24 & 25 Dec: 10am - 6pm. (5pm in winter). Last admission 1½ hrs before closing.

Admission: Adult £7.50. Child (5-16yrs) £4, OAP £7. Family £20. Groups by arrangement.

▣ ♨ ♿ ☗ ✍By arrangement. ▧ ❈ ♛ Tel for details.

MOUNT EDGCUMBE HOUSE & COUNTRY PARK

CREMYLL, TORPOINT, CORNWALL PL10 IHZ

www.cornwalltouristboard.co.uk/mountedgcumbe

Tel: 01752 822236   **Fax:** 01752 822199 **e-mail:** mt.edgcumbe@plymouth.gov.uk

Owner: Cornwall County & Plymouth City Councils   **Contact:** Secretary

Former home of the Earls of Mount Edgcumbe. Miraculously the walls of the red stone Tudor House survived the bombs in 1941. Restored by the 6th Earl. Now beautifully furnished with family possessions. Set in historic 18th century gardens on the dramatic sea-girt Rame peninsula. Follies, forts; National camellia collection. Grade I listed. Exhibitions and events.

Location: OS Ref. SX452 527. 10m W of Plymouth via Torpoint.

Open: House & Earl's Garden: 4 Apr - 30 Sept: Sun - Thur, 11am - 4.30pm. Group bookings by arrangement. Country Park: All year, daily, 8am - dusk.

Admission: House & Earl's Garden: Adult £4.50, Child (5-15) £2.25, Conc. £3.50, Family (2+2 or 1+3) £10. Groups (10+): Adult £3.50, Child £2. Park: Free.

▣ ♨ ⊤ ♿ ☗ 🖪 Licensed. ✍By arrangement. 🅿 🐕In grounds, on leads. ⌂ ❈ ♛Tel for details.

Eye-catcher

– A building, column, tower, temple or obelisk set well away from the house or garden, and built purely to draw the eye to that point in the landscape.

Visit Blenheim Palace in Oxfordshire, Stowe Landscape Gardens in Buckinghamshire, Stourhead in Wiltshire and Mount Edgcumbe House & Country Park in Cornwall.

Garden Jargon

PENCARROW 🏛

BODMIN, CORNWALL PL30 3AG

www.pencarrow.co.uk

Tel: 01208 841369 **Fax:** 01208 841722 **e-mail:** pencarrow@aol.com

Owner: Molesworth-St Aubyn family · · · · · · · · · · · · · **Contact:** J Reynolds

Still owned and lived in by the family. Georgian house and Grade II* listed gardens. Superb collection of pictures, furniture and porcelain. Marked walks through 50 acres of beautiful formal and woodland gardens, Victorian rockery, Italian garden, over 700 different varieties of rhododendrons, lake and ice house.

Location: OS Ref. SX040 711. Between Bodmin and Wadebridge. 4m NW of Bodmin off A389 & B3266 at Washaway.

Open: 28 Mar - 28 Oct: Sun - Thur, 11am - 4pm (last tour). Gardens: 1 Mar - 31 Oct: daily.

Admission: House & Garden: Adult £7, Child £3.50. Family £20. Garden only: Adult £3.50, Child Free. Groups (throughout year by arrangement): House & Garden: Group 20 - 30, £6, 31+ £5. Gardens only: Group 20 - 30 £3, 31+ £2.50.

ⓘ Craft centre, small childrens' play area, self-pick soft fruit. ⬚ ⓣ By arrangement. ♿ ⬚ Licensed. 🍴 𝑓 Obligatory. 🅿 ⬚ ⬚ Grounds only. ⬚❄⬚ Tel for details.

PINE LODGE GARDENS & NURSERY

Holmbush, St Austell, Cornwall PL25 3RQ

Tel: 01726 73500 **Fax:** 01726 77370 **e-mail:** garden@pine-lodge.co.uk

www.pine-lodge.co.uk

Owner/Contact: Mr & Mrs R H J Clemo

30 acres with over 6,000 plants all labelled. Herbaceous and shrub borders. Many water features, pinetum, arboretum, Japanese garden, wild flower meadow, lake with waterfowl and black swans. Plant hunting expeditions every year to gather seeds for our nursery which contain very unusual plants, many rare. The gardens were given a Highly Commended Award by the Cornwall Tourist Board for 2002. Plenty of seats in the gardens.

Location: OS Ref. SX044 527. Signposted on A390.

Open: 1 Mar - 31 Oct: daily, 10am - 6pm, last ticket 5pm.

Admission: Adult £5, Child £3.

ⓘ WC. ⬚ ⬚ 🅿 ⬚

Education Index see front section

PENDENNIS CASTLE ⌗

FALMOUTH, CORNWALL TR11 4LP

www.english-heritage.org.uk/visits

Tel: 01326 316594 **Fax:** 01326 319911 **e-mail:** customers@english-heritage.org.uk

Venue and Hire Hospitality: 01326 310106

Owner: English Heritage · · · · · · · · · · · · · · **Contact:** The Head Custodian

Pendennis and its neighbour, St Mawes Castle, face each other across the mouth of the estuary of the River Fal. Built by Henry VIII in 16th century as protection against threat of attack and invasion from France. Extended and adapted over the years to meet the changing threats to national security from the French and Spanish and continued right through to World War II. It withstood five months of siege during the Civil War before becoming the penultimate Royalist Garrison to surrender on the mainland. Pendennis today stands as a landmark, with fine sea views and excellent site facilities including a hands-on discovery centre, exhibitions, a museum, guardhouse, shop and tearoom. Excellent special events venue.

Location: OS Ref. SW824 318. On Pendennis Head.

Open: 1 Apr - 31 Oct: daily, 10am - 6pm (5pm in Oct). 1 Nov - 31 Mar: daily, 10am - 4pm. Closed 24 - 26 Dec & 1 Jan. Times subject to change April 2004.

Admission: Adult £4, Child £2, Conc. £3, Family £10. 15% discount for groups (11+). Prices subject to change April 2004.

⬚ ♿ Partial. ⬚ ⬚ 𝑓 By arrangement. 🅿 ⬚ ⬚ In grounds only. ❄ ⬚ Tel for details.

PRIDEAUX PLACE 🏛
PADSTOW, CORNWALL PL28 8RP

Tel: 01841 532411 **Fax:** 01841 532945 **e-mail:** office@prideauxplace.fsnet.co.uk
Owner/Contact: Peter Prideaux-Brune Esq

Tucked away above the busy port of Padstow, the home of the Prideaux family for over 400 years, is surrounded by gardens and wooded grounds overlooking a deer park and the Camel estuary to the moors beyond. The house still retains its 'E' shape Elizabethan front and contains fine paintings and furniture as well as an exhibition reflecting its emergence as a major international film location. The impressive outbuildings have been restored in recent years and the 16th century plaster ceiling in the great chamber has been uncovered for the first time since 1760.

Location: OS Ref. SW913 756. 5m from A39 Newquay/Wadebridge link road. Signposted by Historic House signs.
Open: 11 (Easter Sun) - 15 Apr & 16 May - 7 Oct: Sun - Thur, 1.30 - 4pm (last tour 4pm). Grounds & Tearoom: 12.30 - 5pm. Open all year for groups (15+) by arrangement.
Admission: Adult £6, accompanied Child £2. Grounds only: Adult £2, Child £1. Groups from £4.50.

▢ ⊤ By arrangement. ♿ Ground floor & grounds. ▣ ⊠ Obligatory. ▣ By arrangement. ⊠ In grounds, on leads. ▣ ✲

RESTORMEL CASTLE ⌗
Lostwithiel, Cornwall PL22 0BD

Tel: 01208 872687 **e-mail:** customers@english-heritage.org.uk/visits
www.english-heritage.org.uk/visits

Owner: English Heritage   **Contact:** The Custodian

Perched on a high mound, surrounded by a deep moat, the huge circular keep of this splendid Norman castle survives in remarkably good condition. It is still possible to make out the ruins of Restormel's Keep Gate, Great Hall and even the kitchens and private rooms.

Location: OS200 Ref. SX104 614. 1¹/2 m N of Lostwithiel off A390.
Open: 1 Apr - 31 Oct: daily, 10am - 6pm (5pm in Oct). Winter: closed. Times subject to change April 2004.
Admission: Adult £2, Child £1, Conc. £1.50. 15% discount for groups (11+). Prices subject to change April 2004.

▢ ℙ Limited for coaches. ⊠ In grounds, on leads. ▣ Tel for details.

ST CATHERINE'S CASTLE ⌗
Fowey, Cornwall

Tel: 0117 9750700

Owner: English Heritage   **Contact:** The South West Regional Office

A small fort built by Henry VIII to defend Fowey harbour, with fine views of the coastline and river estuary.

Location: OS200 Ref. SX118 508. ³/4 m SW of Fowey along footpath off A3082.
Open: Any reasonable time, daylight only.
Admission: Free.

✲

Special Events Index see front section

ST MAWES CASTLE ⌗
ST MAWES, CORNWALL TR2 3AA

www.english-heritage.org.uk/visits

Tel/Fax: 01326 270526 **Venue Hire and Hospitality:** 01326 310106
e-mail: customers@english-heritage.org.uk/visits

Owner: English Heritage   **Contact:** The Head Custodian

The pretty fishing village of St Mawes is home to this castle. On the opposite headland to Pendennis Castle, St Mawes shares the task of watching over the mouth of the River Fal as it has done since Henry VIII built it as a defence against the French. With three huge circular bastions shaped like clover leaves, St Mawes was designed to cover every possible angle of approach. It is the finest example of Tudor military architecture. The castle offers views of St Mawes' little boat-filled harbour, the passenger ferry tracking across the Fal, and the splendid coastline which featured in the *Poldark* TV series. Also the start of some delightful walks along the coastal path.

Location: OS204 Ref. SW842 328. W of St Mawes on A3078.
Open: 1 Apr - 31 Oct: daily, 10am - 6pm (5pm in Oct). Winter: 1 Nov - 31 Mar: Wed - Sun, 10am - 4pm. Closed 1 - 2pm & 24 - 26 Dec & 1 Jan. Times subject to change April 2004.
Admission: Adult £3, Child £1.50, Conc. £2.30. 15% discount for groups (11+). Prices subject to change April 2004.

▢ ⊤ Private & corporate hire. ♿ Grounds. WC. ⌂ ℙ Limited. ⊠ Guide dogs only. ✲ ▣ Tel for details.

Rupert Tenison

ST MICHAEL'S MOUNT 🌿

MARAZION, Nr PENZANCE, CORNWALL TR17 0EF

Tel: 01736 710507 (710265 tide & ferry information) **Fax:** 01736 719930

e-mail: godolphin@manor-office.co.uk

Owner: The National Trust **Contact:** The Manor Office

This magical island is the jewel in Cornwall's crown. The great granite crag which rises from the waters of Mount's Bay is surmounted by an embattled medieval castle, home of the St Aubyn family for over 300 years. The Mount's flanks are softened by lush sub-tropical vegetation and on the water's edge there is a harbourside community which features shops and restaurants. There are spectacular coastal views from the castle's roof terraces.

Location: OS Ref. SW515 300. At Marazion there is access on foot over causeway at low tide. In summer months there is a ferry at high tide. 4m E of Penzance.

Open: Castle: 31 Mar - 20 June & 6 Sept - 31 Oct: Mon - Fri & Sun. 21 June - 5 Sept: Daily. Castle also open on Easter Sun. Last adm. 4.45pm on the island. Nov - end Mar: Mon, Wed & Fri, guided tours as tide, weather and circumstances permit. Garden (not NT): April & May: weekdays only. June - Oct: Thurs & Fri. All visits subject to weather and tides.

Admission: Adult £5.20 Child (under 16) £2.60, Family £13. Booked groups £4.70.
📷 🍴 ♿ Guide dogs only. ❋

SAUSMAREZ MANOR *See page 194 for full page entry.*

TATE ST IVES

Porthmeor Beach, St Ives, Cornwall TR26 1TG

Tel: 01736 796226 **Fax:** 01736 794480 **www.**tate.org.uk

Owner: Tate Gallery **Contact:** Ina Cole

Changing displays from the Tate Collection of British and modern art, focusing on the modern movement that St Ives is famous for. Also displays of new work by contemporary artists. Events programme, guided tours, gallery shop, rooftop café, with spectacular views over the beach. The Tate also manages the Barbara Hepworth Museum and Sculpture Garden in St Ives.

Location: OS Ref. SW515 407. Situated by Porthmeor Beach.

Open: Mar - Oct: daily, 10am - 5.30pm. Nov - Feb: Tue - Sun, 10am - 4.30pm.

Admission: Adult £4.75, Conc £2.50, Under 18s and Over 60s Free. Groups (10 - 30): Adult £2.50, Conc. £1.50.

📷 ♿ ♿ Licensed. 📷 Daily. 🅿 Nearby. ■ ♿ Guide dogs only. ❋ 📺 Tel for details.

© English Heritage Photo Library

TINTAGEL CASTLE ⌗

TINTAGEL, CORNWALL PL34 0HE

www.english-heritage.org.uk/visits

Tel/Fax: 01840 770328 **e-mail:** customers@english-heritage.org.uk/visits

Owner: English Heritage **Contact:** The Head Custodian

The spectacular setting for the legendary castle of King Arthur on the wild and windswept Cornish coast. Clinging precariously to the edge of the cliff face are the extensive ruins of a medieval royal castle, built by Richard, Earl of Cornwall, younger brother of Henry III. Also used as a Cornish stronghold by subsequent Earls of Cornwall. Despite extensive excavations since the 1930s, Tintagel Castle remains one of the most spectacular and romantic spots in the entire British Isles. Destined to remain a place of mystery and romance, Tintagel will always jealously guard its marvellous secrets.

Location: OS200 Ref. SX048 891. On Tintagel Head, ¹/₂ m along uneven track from Tintagel.

Open: 1 Apr - 31 Oct: daily, 11am - 6pm (5pm in Oct). 1 Nov - 31 Mar: daily, 10am - 4pm. Closed 24 - 26 Dec & 1 Jan. Times subject to change April 2004.

Admission: Adult £3.20, Child £1.60, Conc. £2.40. 15% discount for groups (11+). Prices subject to change April 2004.

ℹ️ No vehicles. 📷 ♿ ❋ 📺 Tel for details.

🍸 **Corporate Hospitality** see front section

TINTAGEL OLD POST OFFICE

Tintagel, Cornwall PL34 0DB

Tel: 01840 770024 or 01208 74281

Owner: The National Trust **Contact:** The Custodian

One of the most characterful buildings in Cornwall, and a house of great antiquity, this small 14th-century manor is full of charm and interest.

Location: OS Ref. SX056 884. In the centre of Tintagel.

Open: 29 Mar - 31 Oct: daily, 11am - 5.30pm (closes 4pm Oct). Last admission 15 mins before closing.

Admission: Adult £2.40, Family £6. Pre-arranged groups £1.90.

© Trebah Garden Trust

TREBAH GARDEN

MAWNAN SMITH, Nr FALMOUTH, CORNWALL TR11 5JZ

www.trebah-garden.co.uk

Tel: 01326 250448 **Fax:** 01326 250781 **e-mail:** mail@trebah-garden.co.uk

Owner: Trebah Garden Trust **Contact:** Vera Woodcroft

Steeply wooded 25 acre sub-tropical ravine garden falls 200 feet from 18th century house to private beach on Helford River. Stream cascading over waterfalls through ponds full of Koi Carp and exotic water plants winds through 2 acres of blue and white hydrangeas and spills out over beach. Huge Australian tree ferns and palms mingle with shrubs of ever-changing colours and scent beneath over-arching canopy of 100 year old rhododendrons and magnolias. A striking new Visitor Centre houses a selling art gallery and stylish catering.

Location: OS Ref. SW768 275. 4m SW of Falmouth, 1m SW of Mawnan Smith. Follow brown and white tourism signs from Treliever Cross roundabout at A39/A394 junction through Mawnan Smith to Trebah.

Open: All year: daily, 10.30am - 5pm (last admission).

Admission: 1 Mar - 31 Oct: Adult £5, Child (5-15yrs)/Disabled £3, Child under 5yrs Free, OAP £4.50. 1 Nov - 29 Feb: Adult £2.50, Child (5-15yrs)/Disabled £1.50, Child under 5yrs Free, OAP £2.25. NT members: free entry 1 Nov - end Feb.

⬛ ⬛ ♿Partial. ⬛ ⬛ ⬛ By arrangement. 🅿 ⬛ 🐕In grounds, on leads. ⬛

Pencarrow, Cornwall from the book
Historic Family Homes and Gardens from the Air, see page 54.

National Trust/ Giles Clotworthy

National Trust/ Tony Kent

TRELISSICK GARDEN

FEOCK, TRURO, CORNWALL TR3 6QL

Tel: 01872 862090 **Fax:** 01872 865808 **e-mail:** trelissick@nationaltrust.org.uk

Owner: The National Trust **Contact:** The Property Manager

A garden and estate of rare tranquil beauty with glorious maritime views over Carrick Roads to Falmouth Harbour. The tender and exotic shrubs make this garden attractive in all seasons. Extensive park and woodland walks beside the river. There is an Art and Craft Gallery.

Location: OS Ref. SW837 396. 4m S of Truro on B3289 above King Harry Ferry.

Open: Garden, Shop, Restaurant, Gallery and Plant Sales: 2 Jan - 13 Feb: Thurs - Sun, 11am - 4pm. 14 Feb - 31 October: Daily, 10.30am - 5.30pm. 1 Nov - 23 Dec: Daily, 11am - 4pm. 27 - 31 Dec: Daily 12 - 4pm. Woodland Walks: All year: Daily.

Admission: Adult £4.80, Family £12. Car Park £2. Pre-arranged groups £4.10pp.

⬛ ⬛ ⬛By arrangement. ♿ ⬛ ⬛By arrangement. 🅿 Limited for coaches. 🐕In park on leads; only guide dogs in garden. ⬛ ⬛Tel for details.

TRENGWAINTON GARDEN

PENZANCE, CORNWALL TR20 8RZ

Tel: 01736 363148 **Fax:** 01736 367762

Owner: The National Trust **Contact:** The Property Manager

This large shrub garden, with many plants brought back from 1920s' plant-gathering expeditions, is a beautiful place throughout the year and a plantsman's delight. Splendid views over Mount's Bay can be gained from summer-houses at either end of the restored terrace. The walled gardens have many tender plants which cannot be grown in the open anywhere else in England and restoration of the kitchen gardens is underway. The new tea-house serves a full range of snacks and meals.

Location: OS Ref. SW445 315. 2m NW of Penzance, 1/2m W of Heamoor on Penzance - Morvah road (B3312), 1/2m off St. Just road (A3071).

Open: 15 Feb - 31 Oct: Sun - Thur & Good Fri, 10am - 5.30pm (Feb, Mar & Oct: 10am - 5pm).

Admission: Adult £4.40, Child £2.20, Family £11. Booked groups: £3.80.

⬛ ⬛ ♿Partial. ⬛Tea-house. 🐕On leads.

National Trust/ Marcus Way

TRERICE ❧

KESTLE MILL, Nr NEWQUAY, CORNWALL TR8 4PG

Tel: 01637 875404   **Fax:** 01637 879300   **e-mail:** trerice@nationaltrust.org.uk

Owner: The National Trust   **Contact:** The Property Manager

Trerice is an architectural gem and something of a rarity – a small Elizabethan manor house hidden away in a web of narrow lanes and still somehow caught in the spirit of its age. An old Arundell house, it contains much fine furniture, ceramics, glasses and a wonderful clock collection. A small barn museum traces the development of the lawn mower.

Location: OS Ref. SW841 585. 3m SE of Newquay via the A392 & A3058 (right at Kestle Mill).

Open: 28 Mar - 31 Oct: Daily except Tues & Sat: (open Tues 20 Jul - 7 Sept). 11am - 5.30pm (5pm in Oct).

Admission: £4.70, Family £11.70. Pre-arranged groups £3.90.

⬚ ⬚ ⬚ ⬚ Braille & taped guides. WC. ⬚ Licensed. ⬚ Guide dogs only. ⬚

TREWITHEN ⛫

GRAMPOUND ROAD, TRURO, CORNWALL TR2 4DD

www.trewithengardens.co.uk

Tel: 01726 883647   **Fax:** 01726 882301
e-mail: gardens@trewithen-estate.demon.co.uk

Owner: A M J Galsworthy   **Contact:** The Estate Office

Trewithen means 'house of the trees' and the name truly describes this fine early Georgian House in its splendid setting of wood and parkland. Country Life described the house as *'one of the outstanding West Country houses of the 18th century'*. The gardens at Trewithen are outstanding and of international fame. 2004 is the 100th year since George Johnstone inherited and started developing the gardens which now contain a wide and rare collection of flowering shrubs. Some of the magnolias and rhododendron species in the garden are known throughout the world. They are one of two attractions in this country awarded three stars by Michelin. Viewing platforms and a *Camera Obscura* will be an additional interest to visitors.

TRESCO ABBEY GARDENS ⛫

ISLES OF SCILLY, CORNWALL TR24 0QQ

Tel: 01720 424105   **Tel/Fax:** 01720 422868   **e-mail:** mikenelhams@tresco.co.uk

Owner: Mr R A and Mrs L A Dorrien-Smith   **Contact:** Mr M.A Nelhams

Tresco Abbey, built by Augustus Smith, has been the family home since 1834. The garden here flourishes on the small island. Nowhere else in the British Isles does such an exotic collection of plants grow in the open. Agaves, aloes, proteas and acacias from such places as Australia, South Africa, Mexico and the Mediterranean grow within the secure embrace of massive Holm Oak hedges. Valhalla Ships Figurehead Museum.

Location: OS Ref. SV895 143. Isles of Scilly. Isles of Scilly Steamship 0345 105555. BIH Helicopters 01736 363871. Details of day trips on application.

Open: All year: 10am - 4pm.

Admission: Adult £8.50, (under 14yrs free). Guided group tours available.

⬚ ⬚ Grounds. ⬚ ⬚ ⬚ In grounds, on leads. ⬚

Location: OS Ref. SW914 476. S of A390 between Grampound and Probus villages. 7m WSW of St Austell.

Open: Gardens: 1 Mar - 30 Sept: Mon - Sat, 10am - 4.30pm. Suns in Apr & May only. House: Apr - Jul & Aug: BH Mons, Mons & Tues, 2 - 4pm.

Admission: Adult £4.25, Child Free. Pre booked groups (20+): Adult £4, Child Free. Combined gardens & house £6.

ⓘ No photography in house. ⬚ ⬚ Partial. WC. ⬚ ⬚ By arrangement. ⬚ Limited for coaches. ⬚ In grounds, on leads.

Map 2

BICTON PARK BOTANICAL GARDENS

BUDLEIGH SALTERTON

www.bictongardens.co.uk

Spanning three centuries of horticultural history, Bicton Park Botanical Gardens are set in the picturesque Otter Valley, near the coastal town of Budleigh Salterton and 10 miles south of Exeter.

The 63-acre park's oldest ornamental area is the Italian Garden, created in the axial style of Versailles landscaper Andre le Notre, c1735. By that time formal designs were becoming unfashionable in England, which may explain why the garden was located out of view of the manor house. Today, the full grandeur of the Italian Garden can be seen from the spacious restaurant in the classically styled Orangery, built at the beginning of the 19th century.

Bicton's high-domed Palm House, one of the world's most beautiful garden buildings, was the first of many developments between 1820 and 1850. Others included an important collection of conifers in the Pinetum, now the subject of a rare species conservation project, and St Mary's Church, where Queen Victoria worshipped.

A large museum reflects changes in agriculture and rural life generally over the past 200 years. The Grade I listed gardens, which are open all year, also feature a narrow-gauge railway which meanders through the garden on its 1½ mile track. Gift shop, garden centre, children's inside and outdoor play areas.

Owner:
Mr & Mrs S E Lister

▶ **CONTACT**

Mr Simon Lister
Bicton Park
Botanical Gardens
East Budleigh
Budleigh Salterton
Devon EX9 7BJ

Tel: 01395 568465

Fax: 01395 568374

e-mail: info@ bictongardens.co.uk

▶ **LOCATION**

OS Ref. SY074 856

2m N of Budleigh Salterton on B3178.

Follow the brown signs to Bicton Park from M5/J30 at Exeter.

Rail: Exmouth 5mins, Exeter St Davids 12m.

Air: Exeter Airport 5m.

▶ **OPENING TIMES**

Summer
10am - 6pm.

Winter
10am - 5pm.
Closed Christmas Day & Boxing Day.

▶ **ADMISSION**

Adult £4.95
Child £3.95
Conc £3.95
Family (2+2) £14.95

Groups (16-200)
Adult £3.60
Child £2.60
Conc. £3.60

Children under 3yrs Free

ℹ Children's inside & outdoor play areas.

🛍

❄ Garden Centre.

♿

☕ Licensed.

🍴

🚶 By arrangement.

🅿

🐕 In grounds, on leads.

CLOVELLY

DEVON

www.clovelly.co.uk

Map 1

Owner:
Hon John Rous

▶ **CONTACT**

Visitor Centre
Clovelly
Nr Bideford
N Devon EX39 5TA

Tel: 01237 431781

Fax: 01237 431288

▶ **LOCATION**
OS Ref. SS248 319

On A39 10 miles W of
Bideford, 15 miles E of
Bude. Turn off at
'Clovelly Cross
Roundabout' and follow
signs to car park.

Air: Exeter & Plymouth
Airport both 50 miles.

Rail: Barnstaple
19 miles.

Bus: from Bideford.

The ancient seaside village of Clovelly is mentioned in the Domesday Book (c1100 AD), and it is very probable that a settlement existed on the site well before that, in Saxon times. The privately owned village has been sympathetically restored to how it would have appeared in the 19th century and is now a visitor destination in its own right. Access is restricted to pedestrians only, via the Clovelly Visitor Centre.

(Land Rover taxi service for those unable to walk). Donkeys are used to transport goods into the village and down the steep lanes to the harbour. There are two museums in the village and an audio visual show in the Visitor Centre detailing the history of the village, as well as local craft workshops and two inns. Extensive coastal and woodland walks.

▶ **OPENING TIMES**

High season: 9am - 6pm.

Low season: 9am - 4.30pm.

▶ **ADMISSION**

The entrance fee covers parking and other facilities provided by Clovelly Estate, as well as admission to the audio-visual film, Fisherman's Cottage, and Kingsley Museum.

Adult	£4.00
Child (7 - 16yrs)	£2.75
Child (under 7yrs)	Free
Family (2+2)	£12.00

Group Rates (20+)
Adult	£3.50
Child	£2.50

ℹ️ Rubber soled, low heel shoes are recommended. 📷 ❀ ♿ Partial. Around the Visitor Centre. ☕ Licensed.
🍴 Licensed. 🅿️ 🚻 🐕 On leads. 🛏️ 18 double, 1 single, all en suite. ❄️

POWDERHAM CASTLE 🏛

EXETER

www.powderham.co.uk

The gardens and grounds have masses to occupy visitors of all ages. As well as informal areas, walks and the springtime Woodland Garden, there is a terraced Rose Garden overlooking an ancient deer park, home to a large herd of fallow deer. The Rose Garden is home to Timothy Tortoise, at 150+ the world's most senior family pet. A new tractor and trailer ride takes visitors around the grounds to the old estate yard where there is a working blacksmith and wheelwright. En-route the Victorian walled garden, known as the Children's Secret Garden, houses a collection of friendly birds and animals.

Powderham Country Store, comprising a Food Hall, butchers, delicatessen, House of Marbles Gift Centre and large licensed restaurant, specialises in the finest food and drink from the West Country and is open seven days a week, all year round. This makes Powderham a great destination in any season.

Winship's Medieval Jousting Tournament takes place in the grounds of Powderham. From mid July to mid September, The Knights of Powderham joust daily (except Saturday) at 3pm. Their fantastic displays make for great family entertainment and children and grown-ups alike will love the excitement, thrills and spills, action and comedy. From thundering hooves to tumbling knights and hilarious jesters there are two packed hours of entertainment, for which a separate charge applies.

Map 2

Owner:
The Earl of Devon

▶ **CONTACT**

Mr Tim Faulkner
General Manager
The Estate Office
Powderham Castle
Kenton, Exeter
Devon EX6 8JQ

Tel: 01626 890243
Functions:
01626 890243
(Virginia Bowman)
Fax: 01626 890729
e-mail: castle@
powderham.co.uk

▶ **LOCATION**

OS Ref. SX965 832

6m SW of Exeter,
4m S M5/J30.
Access from A379 in
Kenton village.

Air: Exeter Airport 9m.

Rail: Starcross
Station 2m.

Bus: Devon General
No: 85, 85A, 85B to
Castle Gate.

CONFERENCE/FUNCTION

ROOM	SIZE	MAX CAPACITY
Music Room	56' x 25'	170
Dining Room	42' x 22'	100
Ante Room	28' x 18'	25
Library 1	32' x 18'	85
Library 2	31"x18'	85

▶ **OPENING TIMES**

Summer

4 April - 2 October

Daily*: 10am - 5.30pm
*Except Sat: closed to public, but available for private hire. Gardens open Suns in March.

Powderham Country Store:
Daily, 9am - 5.30pm,
(Suns, 10am - 5.30pm).

Winter

Available for hire for conferences, receptions and functions and private tours.

▶ **ADMISSION**

Adult £6.90
OAP £6.40
Child £3.90

Group Rates available from Estate Office.

(2003 prices.)

🗄🏆ℹ️ Filming, car launches including 4WD, vehicle rallies, open air concerts, etc. Grand piano in Music Room, 3800 acre estate, cricket pitch, horse trials course. Deer park.

🍽 Conferences, dinners, corporate entertainment.

♿ Limited facilities. Some ramps. WC.

🍴 Fully licensed restaurant and coach room access.

🚶 Fully inclusive. Tour time: 1 hr.

🅿 Unlimited free parking. Commission and complimentary drinks for drivers. Advance warning of group bookings preferred but not essential.

🎓 Welcome. Fascinating tour and useful insight into the life of one of England's Great Houses over the centuries.

🐕 In part of grounds, on leads.

🔔 Civil Wedding Licence.

❄

▶ 🛡 **SPECIAL EVENTS**

JUL 10/11
The 30th Annual Historic Vehicle Rally.

AUG 1
'Last Night of the Powderham Proms' Bournemouth Symphony Orchestra Open Air Firework Concert.

AUG 2
Open Air Pop Concert.

NTPL / David Garner

A LA RONDE

SUMMER LANE, EXMOUTH, DEVON EX8 5BD

www.nationaltrust.org.uk

Tel: 01395 265514   **e-mail:** alaronde@nationaltrust.org.uk

Owner: The National Trust   **Contact:** John Rolfe – Custodian

A unique 16-sided house built on the instructions of two spinster cousins, Jane and Mary Parminter, on their return from a grand tour of Europe. Completed c1796, the house contains many 18th century contents and collections brought back by the Parminters. The fascinating interior decoration includes a feather frieze and shell-encrusted gallery which, due to its fragility, can only be viewed on closed circuit television.

Location: OS Ref. SY004 834. 2m N of Exmouth on A376.

Open: 31 Mar - 31 Oct: daily except Fri & Sat, 11am - 5.30pm. Last admission 1/2 hr before closing.

Admission: Adult £4.20, Child £2.10. No reduction for groups.

National Trust / Andreas Von Einsiedel

ARLINGTON COURT

Nr BARNSTAPLE, NORTH DEVON EX31 4LP

www.nationaltrust.org.uk

Tel: 01271 850296   **Fax:** 01271 851108

Owner: The National Trust   **Contact:** Ana Chylak - Property Manager

Nestling in the thickly wooded valley of the River Yeo, stands the 3000 acre Arlington estate. It comprises a delightful and intimate Victorian house full of treasures including collections of model ships, pewter, shells, extensive informal gardens, a formal terraced Victorian garden, a partially restored walled garden and historic parkland with breathtaking woodland and lakeside walks. The working stable yard houses the National Trust's museum of horse-drawn vehicles and offers carriage rides around the gardens.

Location: OS180 Ref. SS611 405. 7m NE of Barnstaple on A39.

Open: 28 Mar - 31 Oct: daily except Sat, 10.30am - 5pm. House & Carriage Collection open at 11am. Last admission 4.30pm. Gardens, shop, tearoom, sculpture trail & bat education room: 1 Jul - 31 Aug: Daily including Sats, 10.30am - 4.30pm. 1 Nov - Mar 2005: grounds open during daylight hours.

Admission: House, Gardens & Carriage Collection: Adult £6.20, Child £3, Family £15. Gardens & Carriage Collection only: Adult £4, Child £2. Sats during July & Aug: Adult £2.60, Child £1.30.

Ground floor & grounds. WC. Licensed. Teachers' pack. In grounds, on leads.

BAYARD'S COVE FORT

Dartmouth, Devon

Tel: 0117 9750700

Owner: English Heritage   **Contact:** South West Regional Office

Set among the picturesque gabled houses of Dartmouth, on the waterfront at the end of the quay, this is a small artillery fort built 1509 - 10 to defend the harbour entrance.

Location: OS Ref. SX879 510. In Dartmouth, on riverfront 200 yds, S of South ferry.

Open: Any reasonable time, daylight hours.

Admission: Free.

BERRY POMEROY CASTLE

Totnes, Devon TQ9 6NJ

Tel: 01803 866618   **e-mail:** customers@english-heritage.org.uk

www.english-heritage.org.uk/visits

Owner: The Duke of Somerset   **Contact:** English Heritage

A romantic late medieval castle, dramatically sited half-way up a wooded hillside, looking out over a deep ravine and stream. It is unusual in combining the remains of a large castle with a flamboyant courtier's mansion. Reputed to be one of the most haunted castles in the country.

Location: OS202 Ref. SX839 623. 2 1/2 m E of Totnes off A385. Entrance gate 1/2 m NE of Berry Pomeroy village, then 1/2 m drive. Narrow approach, unsuitable for coaches.

Open: 1 Apr - 31 Oct: daily, 10am - 6pm (5pm in Oct). Winter: closed. Times subject to change April 2004.

Admission: Adult £2.80, Child £1.40, Conc £2.10. 15% discount for groups (11+). Prices subject to change April 2004.

Ground floor & grounds. Not EH. No access for coaches. Tel for details.

BICTON PARK BOTANICAL GARDENS

See page 205 for full page entry.

BRADLEY MANOR

Newton Abbot, Devon TQ12 6BN

Tel: 01626 354513   www.nationaltrust.org.uk

Owner: The National Trust

A small medieval manor house set in woodland and meadows.

Location: OS Ref. SX848 709. On Totnes road A381. 3/4 m SW of Newton Abbot.

Open: 1 Apr - 30 Sept: Tue - Thur, 2 - 5 pm. Last admission 4.30pm.

Admission: £3, no reduction for groups.

BRANSCOMBE MANOR MILL, THE OLD BAKERY & FORGE

Branscombe, Seaton, Devon EX12 3DB

Tel: Manor Mill - 01392 881691   Old Bakery - 01297 680333   Forge - 01297 680481

www.nationaltrust.org.uk

Owner: The National Trust   **Contact:** NT Devon Office

Manor Mill, still in working order and recently restored, is a water-powered mill which probably supplied the flour for the bakery, regular working demonstrations. The Old Bakery was, until 1987, the last traditional working bakery in Devon. The old baking equipment has been preserved in the baking room and the rest of the building is now a tearoom. Information display in the outbuildings. The Forge opens regularly and ironwork is on sale - please telephone to check opening times.

Location: OS Ref. SY198 887. In Branscombe 1/2 m S off A3052 by steep, narrow lane.

Open: Manor Mill: 3 Apr - 31 Oct: Suns, 2 - 5pm; also Weds in Jul & Aug. The Old Bakery: 31 Mar - 31 Oct, Wed - Sun, 11am - 5pm.

Admission: £1.50 Manor Mill only.

BUCKFAST ABBEY

Buckfastleigh, Devon TQ11 0EE

Tel: 01364 645500   **Fax:** 01364 643891   **e-mail:** education@buckfast.org.uk

Owner: Buckfast Abbey Trust   **Contact:** The Warden

Location: OS Ref. SX741 674. 1/2 m from A38 Plymouth - Exeter route.

Open: Church & Grounds: All year: 5.30am - 7pm.

Admission: Free.

NTPL / Alec MacKenzie

NTPL / M Rattenbury

BUCKLAND ABBEY 🍃

YELVERTON, DEVON PL20 6EY

www.nationaltrust.org.uk

Tel: 01822 853607 **Fax:** 01822 855448 **e-mail:** bucklandabbey@nationaltrust.org.uk

Owner: The National Trust   **Contact:** Michael Coxson - Property Manager

The spirit of Sir Francis Drake is rekindled at his home with exhibitions of his courageous adventures and achievements throughout the world. One of the Trust's most interesting historical buildings and originally a 13th century monastery, the abbey was transformed into a family residence before Sir Francis bought it in 1581. Fascinating decorated plaster ceiling in Tudor Drake Chamber. Outside there are monastic farm buildings, herb garden, craft workshops and country walks. Introductory video presentation. Beautiful new Elizabethan garden now open. Exciting new gallery displays.

Location: OS201 Ref. SX487 667. 6m S of Tavistock; 11m N of Plymouth off A386. Bus: 55/56 from Yelverton (except Sun).

Open: 14 Feb - 26 Mar: Sat & Sun only, 2 - 5pm. 27 Mar - 31 Oct: daily except Thur, 10.30am - 5.30pm (last adm. 4.45pm). 6 Nov - 19 Dec: Sat & Sun only, 2 - 5pm.

Admission: Abbey & Grounds: Adult £5.30, Child £2.60. Group (15+): Adult £4.40, Child £2.20.

ℹ️No photography in house. 🖼️ 👶 🚹 ♿Ground floor & grounds. WC. 🍴Licensed. 🍽️ Licensed. 🎫By arrangement. 🏠 P 🦮Guide dogs only. ✳️

Sand, Devon from the book *Historic Family Homes and Gardens from the Air*, see page 54.

CLOVELLY   *See page 206 for full page entry.*

Orangery

– a building designed as a hot house, in which tender exotic plans (not just orange trees) are housed – very popular from the16th century.

Visit Tatton Park, Cheshire, Saltram House, Devon, Peckover House, Cambridgeshire, Hanbury Hall, Worcestershire, Wallington, Northumberland and Norton Conyers and Ripley Castle Yorkshire.

CADHAY 🏠
OTTERY ST MARY, DEVON EX11 1QT

Tel/Fax: 01404 812962

Contact: Mrs L Saunders

Cadhay is approached by an avenue of lime-trees, and stands in an extensive garden, with herbaceous borders and yew hedges, with excellent views over the original medieval fish ponds. The main part of the house was built about 1550 by John Haydon who had married the de Cadhay heiress. He retained the Great Hall of an earlier house, of which the fine timber roof (about 1420 - 1460) can be seen. An Elizabethan Long Gallery was added by John's successor at the end of the 16th century, thereby forming a unique and lovely courtyard with statues of Sovereigns on each side.

Location: OS Ref. SY090 962. 1m NW of Ottery St Mary. From W take A30 and exit at Pattersons Cross, follow signs for Fairmile and then Cadhay. From E, exit at the Iron Bridge and follow signs as above.

Open: Spring BH; July: Fri; August: Fri and BH Sun & Mon, 2 - 6pm. Last tour 5pm.

Admission: Guided tours: Adult £5, Child £2.

♿Ground floor & grounds. 🍴Gardens available. 📷 Obligatory.
🐕Guide dogs only. 📷

David Cripps

NTPL / David Garner

CASTLE DROGO 🍂
DREWSTEIGNTON, EXETER EX6 6PB

www.nationaltrust.org.uk

Tel: 01647 433306   **Fax:** 01647 433186

Owner: The National Trust   **Contact:** Mark Agnew, Property Manager

Extraordinary granite and oak castle, designed by Sir Edwin Lutyens, which combines the comforts of the 20th century with the grandeur of a Baronial castle. Elegant dining and drawing rooms and fascinating kitchen and scullery. Terraced formal garden with colourful herbaceous borders and rose beds. Panoramic views over Dartmoor and delightful walks in the dramatic Teign Gorge.

Location: OS191 Ref. SX721 900. 5m S of A30 Exeter – Okehampton road.

Open: Castle: 20 Mar - 7 Nov: daily except Tues, 11am - 5pm (last admission 4.30pm). 6, 7, 13 & 14 Mar: pre-season guided tours only. Garden: All year: daily, 10.30am - 5.30pm. Shop & tearoom: 20 Mar - 7 Nov: daily, 10.30am - 5.30pm; Nov & Dec: Wed - Sun, 11am - 4pm.

Admission: House & Garden: Adult £6.20, Child £3, Family £15. Group: £5.25. Garden only: Adult £3.15, Child £1.60, Group £2.85.

🏠 ♿ 2 rooms in castle & grounds. WCs. 🍴Licensed. 📷 By arrangement.
🐕 Guide dogs only in certain areas. ❋

NTPL / Alec MacKenzie

NTPL / Mark Rattenbury

COLETON FISHACRE HOUSE & GARDEN ❧

BROWNSTONE ROAD, KINGSWEAR, DARTMOUTH TQ6 0EQ

www.nationaltrust.org.uk

Tel: 01803 752466   **Fax:** 01803 753017   **e-mail:** coletonfishacre@nationaltrust.co.uk
Owner: The National Trust   **Contact:** David Mason, Property Manager

A 9 hectare property set in a stream-fed valley within the spectacular scenery of the South Devon coast. The Lutyensesque style house with art deco-influenced interior was built in the 1920s for Rupert and Lady Dorothy D'Oyly Carte who created the delightful garden, planted with a wide range of rare and exotic plants giving year round interest.

Location: OS202 Ref. SX910 508. 3m E of Kingswear, follow brown tourist signs.

Open: House: 31 Mar - 31 Oct: Weds - Suns & BH Mons, 11am - 4.30pm (last entry at 4pm). Garden: Mar: Sats & Suns only, 11am - 5pm. 31 Mar - 31 Oct: Weds - Suns & BH Mons, 10.30am - 5.30pm. Tearoom: Mar: Sats & Suns only, 11am - 5pm. 31 Mar - 31 Oct: Weds - Suns & BH Mons, 10.30am - 5pm..

Admission: House & Garden: Adult £5.25, Child £2.60. Family £13.00. Booked groups (15+): Adult £4.50, Child £2.25. Garden only: Adult £4.10, Child £2, Booked groups (15+) £3.50.

ℹ No photography in house. 📷 ⛲ ♿Limited access to grounds. WC. ▣
🅿Limited. Coaches must book. 🐕Guide dogs only in garden.

CULVER HOUSE

LONGDOWN, EXETER, DEVON EX6 7BD

www.culver.biz

Tel: 01392 811885   **Fax:** 01392 811817   **e-mail:** info@culver.biz
Owner/Contact: Charles Eden Esq

Culver was built in 1836, but redesigned by the great Victorian architect, Alfred Waterhouse in a mock Tudor style. The distinctive interior of the house makes it a favoured location for functions and Culver was featured in BBC1's 'Down to Earth' series in 2001. It has also been used by German and American filmcrews.

Location: OS Ref. SX848 901. 5m W of Exeter on B3212.

Open: Not open to the public. Available for corporate hospitality.

Admission: Please telephone for booking details.

🎦

COMPTON CASTLE ❧

Marldon, Paignton TQ3 1TA

Tel: 01803 875740 (answerphone) **www.**nationaltrust.org.uk

Owner/Contact: The National Trust

A fortified manor house with curtain wall, built at three periods: 1340, 1450 and 1520 by the Gilbert family.

Location: OS Ref. SX865 648. At Compton, 3m W of Torquay.

Open: 1 Apr - 28 Oct: Mons, Weds & Thurs, 10am - 12.15pm & 2 - 5pm. The courtyard, restored great hall, solar, chapel, rose garden and old kitchen are shown. Last admission ½ hr before closing.

Admission: £3.20, pre-arranged groups £2.60.

CUSTOM HOUSE

The Quay, Exeter EX2 4AN

Tel: 01392 265169 **Fax:** 01392 265165 **e-mail:** michael.carson@exeter.gov.uk

Owner: Exeter City Council   **Contact:** Michael Carson

The Custom House, located on Exeter's historic Quayside, was constructed from 1680 - 1682. It is the earliest substantial brick building in Exeter and was used by HM Customs and Excise until 1989. The building has an impressive sweeping staircase and spectacular ornamental plaster ceilings.

Location: OS Ref. SX919 921. Exeter's historic Quayside.

Open: 1 May - 30 Sept: Thurs & Sats, tours at 2pm outside Quay House Visitor Centre. Other times by prior arrangement with Exeter City Council.

Admission: Free.

♿Partial. 🎦Obligatory. ▣ 🐕Guide dogs only.

🌱 Plant Sales Index see front section

DARTMOUTH CASTLE ⌗

CASTLE ROAD, DARTMOUTH, DEVON TQ6 0JH

www.english-heritage.org.uk/visits

Tel: 01803 833588 **Fax:** 01803 834445
e-mail: customers@english-heritage.org.uk/visits

Owner: English Heritage **Contact:** The Custodian

This brilliantly positioned defensive castle juts out into the narrow entrance to the Dart estuary, with the sea lapping at its foot. When begun in 1480s it was one of the most advanced fortifications in England, and was the first castle designed specifically with artillery in mind. For nearly 500 years it kept its defences up-to-date in preparation for war. Today the castle is in a remarkably good state of repair, along with excellent exhibitions, the history of the castle comes to life. A picnic spot of exceptional beauty.

Location: OS202 Ref. SX887 503. 1m SE of Dartmouth off B3205, narrow approach road.

Open: 1 Apr - 31 Oct: daily, 10am - 6pm (5pm in Oct). 1 Nov - 31 Mar: Wed - Sun, 10am - 4pm. Closed 24 - 26 Dec & 1 Jan. Times subject to change from April 2004.

Admission: Adult £3.20, Child £1.60, Conc. £2.40. 15% discount for groups (11+). Prices subject to change from April 2004.

⬚ Ⓟ Limited (charged, not EH). ⊠ ❋ ⊡ Tel. for details.

THE ELIZABETHAN GARDENS

Plymouth Barbican Assoc. Ltd, New St, The Barbican, Plymouth

Tel/Fax: 01822 611027

Owner: Plymouth Barbican Association Limited **Contact:** Tony Golding Esq

Very small series of four enclosed gardens laid out in Elizabethan style in 1970.

Location: OS Ref. SX477 544. 3 mins walk from Dartington Glass (a landmark building) on the Barbican.

Open: Mon - Sat, 9am - 5pm. Closed Christmas.

Admission: Free.

ESCOT COUNTRY PARK & GARDENS

ESCOT, OTTERY ST MARY, DEVON EX11 1LU

www.escot-devon.co.uk

Tel: 01404 822188 **Fax:** 01404 822903 **e-mail:** escot@eclipse.co.uk

Owner/Contact: Mr J-M Kennaway

House: an idyllic setting for weddings, conferences and product launches. Gardens: 25 acres of gardens set within 220 acres of 'Capability' Brown parkland, featuring otters, wild boar, birds of prey displays in spring and summer, and including *'Ivan Hicks at Escot'* – a unique visit experience being created by BBC *Gardeners' World's* acclaimed gardener-artist. Estate: 1200 privately owned acres of glorious East Devon – ideal as a film location, for musical festivals and other special events.

Location: OS Ref. SY080 977 (gate). 9m E of Exeter on A30 at Fairmile.

Open: Gardens, Aquatic Centre, Devon Crafts Centre & Restaurant: open throughout the year as follows: Easter - 31 Oct: daily, 10am - 6pm. 1 Nov - Easter: daily, 10am - 5pm except 25, 26 Dec.

Admission: Adult £4.95, Child £3.50, Child (under 4yrs) Free, OAP £3.50, Family (2+2) £15. Booked groups (10+): Adult £4.50, Child/Conc. £3.25. Reduced rates apply in winter months.

⬚ 🏠 ⊤ ♿ Partial. ⬛ Licensed. 🍴 Licensed. 🎭 By arrangement. ⬛ Ⓟ ⬛ In grounds, on leads. ⬛ ❋ ⊡ Tel for details.

DOCTON MILL & GARDEN

Spekes Valley, Hartland, Devon EX39 6EA

Tel/Fax: 01237 441369

Owner/Contact: John Borrett

Garden for all seasons in 8 acres of sheltered wooded valley, plus working mill.

Location: OS Ref. SS235 226. 3m Hartland Quay. 15m N of Bude. 3m W of A39, 3m S of Hartland.

Open: 1 Mar - 31 Oct: 10am - 6pm. Coaches by appointment.

Admission: Adult £3.50, Child (under 14 yrs) £1, OAP £3.

DOWNES

Crediton, Devon EX17 3PL

Tel: 01392 439046 **Fax:** 01392 426183

Owner: Trustees of the Downes Estate Settlement **Contact:** Dianne Shirazian

Downes is a Palladian Mansion dating originally from 1692. As the former home of General Sir Redvers Buller, the house contains a large number of items relating to his military campaigns. The property is now predominantly a family home with elegant rooms hung with family portraits, and a striking main staircase.

Location: OS Ref. SX852 997. About a mile from Crediton town centre.

Open: Guided tours: Easter - mid Jul, plus Aug BH Mon & Tue: Mon - Tue, 2.15 & 3.30pm. Open to groups (15+) by prior arrangement.

Admission: Adult £4, Child (5 - 16yrs) £2, Child (under 5 yrs) Free, Group (20+) £3.50.

EXETER CATHEDRAL

Exeter, Devon EX1 1HS

Tel: 01392 255573/ 214219 (Visitors' Officer) **Fax:** 01392 498769

e-mail: admin@exeter-cathedral.org.uk

Owner: Dean & Chapter of Exeter **Contact:** Visitors' Officer

Fine example of decorated gothic architecture. Longest unbroken stretch of gothic vaulting in the world.

Location: OS Ref. SX921 925. Central to the City - between High Street and Southernhay. Groups may be set down in South Street.

Open: All year: Mon - Fri 7.30am - 6.30pm, Sats, 7.30am - 5pm, Suns, 8am - 7.30pm.

Admission: No entry charge – donation requested of £3.50 per person.

FINCH FOUNDRY ⌘

Sticklepath, Okehampton, Devon EX20 2NW

Tel: 01837 840046

Owner: The National Trust

19th-century water-powered forge, which produced agricultural and mining hand tools, holding regular demonstrations throughout the day.

Location: OS Ref. SX641 940. 4m E of Okehampton off the A30.

Open: 29 Mar - 31 Oct: Daily except Tue, 11am - 5.30pm.

Admission: Adult £3.30, Child £1.60.

⬚ ⬛ Ⓟ Not suitable for coaches. ⬛ ⬛ Except tearoom.

FLETE
ERMINGTON, IVYBRIDGE, DEVON PL21 9NZ

www.cha.org.uk

Tel: 01752 830308 **Fax:** 01752 830309

Leaseholder: Country Houses Association **Contact:** The Administrators

First mentioned in the Domesday Book, Flete became a manor house in Elizabethan times. A wing was added in 1800 and in 1876 Norman Shaw was appointed, adding the entire north front in Gothic style. Magnificent timber panelling and floors. Flete has been converted into apartments for active retired people.

Location: OS Ref. SX631 519. 11m E of Plymouth at junction of A379 & B3121. Stations: Plymouth 12m, Totnes 14m. Bus route: No 93 Plymouth - Dartmouth.

Open: 1 May - 30 Sept: Wed & Thur, 2 - 5pm. Groups by arrangement. Tours of the house: 2.30pm & 3.45pm.

Admission: Adult £4.50, Child Free. Groups by arrangement.

🅣 ⌷ 🅘 1 single & 2 doubles w/bathroom, CHA members & Wolsey Lodge guests.

FURSDON HOUSE 🏠
Cadbury, Nr Thorverton, Exeter, Devon EX5 5JS

Tel: 01392 860860 **Fax:** 01392 860126 **e-mail:** house@fursdon.co.uk
www.fursdon.co.uk

Owner: E D Fursdon Esq **Contact:** Mrs C Fursdon

The Fursdons have lived here since the 13th century and the house, which was greatly modified in the 18th century, is at the heart of a small farming estate within a wooded and hilly landscape. Family memorabilia is displayed including a letter to Grace Fursdon from King Charles during the Civil War and there are fine examples of costume and textiles. The garden to the south flows naturally into the parkland beyond; to the west it slopes up to a walled and terraced area with mixed borders, roses and herbs. There are two private wings of the house for self catering holiday accommodation.

Location: OS Ref. SS922 046. 1½ m S of A3072 between Tiverton & Crediton, 9m N of Exeter turning off A396 to Thorverton. Narrow lanes!

Open: 10 - 16 Apr, 1 - 8 May, 29 May - 5 Jun, 28 Aug - 3 Sep. Guided tours at 2.30 & 3.30pm. Garden: opens at 2pm.

Admission: Adult £4, Child (10-16yrs) £2, (under 10yrs Free). Groups (20+) £3.50. Gardens only: £2.

ℹ️ Conferences. No photography or video. 🅣 ♿Partial. 👣Obligatory. 🅟 🐕 Guide dogs only. 🛏 Self-catering.

THE GARDEN HOUSE
Buckland Monachorum, Yelverton, Devon PL20 7LQ

Tel: 01822 854769 **Fax:** 01822 855358 **e-mail:** office@thegardenhouse.org.uk
www.thegardenhouse.org.uk

Owner: Fortescue Garden Trust **Contact:** Stuart Fraser

'Is this the best garden in Britain?' *Sunday Express*: eight acres offer year-round colour and interest centred on an enchanting walled garden surrounding the romantic ruins of a 16th century vicarage. Modern garden planted in pioneering naturalistic style. Over 6,000 varieties feature in an idyllic valley on the edge of Dartmoor. 'You'd be mad to miss it' – Alan Titchmarsh.

Location: OS Ref. SX490 682. Signposted W off A386 Plymouth - Tavistock Road, 10m N of Plymouth.

Open: 1 Mar - 31 Oct: daily, 10.30am - 5pm. Last admission 4.30pm.

Admission: Adult £4.50, Child (5-16) £1, OAP £4, pre-booked groups (10+) £4.

🍴 ♿Partial. 🔲 👣 🅟 🛏

NTPL/Steve Bond

GREENWAY 🌿
GREENWAY ROAD, GALMPTON, CHURSTON FERRERS, DEVON TQ5 0ES

www.nationaltrust.org.uk

Tel: 01803 842382 **Riverlink:** 01803 834488

Owner: The National Trust **Contact:** Robyn Brown

A glorious woodland garden held on the edge of wildness that is set on the banks of the River Dart; Greenway is one of Devon's best kept secrets. Renowned for rare half-hardy trees and shrubs and underplanted by native wild flowers, this peaceful haven has magnificent views and some challenging paths. Riverlink provides 'Green' options for travel to Greenway, by ferry, hoppa bus or steam train from Dartmouth, Paignton and Totnes.

Location: OS Ref. SX876 254.

Open: 3 Mar - 9 Oct: Wed - Sat, 10.30am - 5pm (last admission 4.30pm)

Admission: Booked groups & visitors arriving on foot, bus or ferry: Adult £3.25, Child £1.65. Others: Adult £3.90, Child £1.95.

🔲 🍴 🅣 ♿Partial. WC. 🔲Licensed. 🍴Licensed. 👣By arrangement.

🅟All cars must pre-book their parking space before arrival - easily done on the day of visit. 1 midi size coach only. Please use green travel options. 🔲Tel for details.

HALDON BELVEDERE/LAWRENCE CASTLE

Higher Ashton, Nr Dunchideock, Exeter, Devon EX6 7QY

Tel: 01392 833846   **e-mail:** michaela.savage@talk21.com

www.haldonbelvedere.co.uk

Owner: Devon Historic Building Trust   **Contact:** Michaela Savage

18th century Grade II* listed triangular tower with circular turrets on each corner. Built in memory of Major General Stringer Lawrence, founder of the Indian Army. Recently restored to illustrate the magnificence of its fine plasterwork, gothic windows, mahogany flooring and marble fireplaces. Breathtaking views of the surrounding Devon countryside.

Location: OS Ref. SX875 861. 7m SW of Exeter. Exit A38 at Exeter racecourse for 2¹/₂m.

Open: Mar - Oct: Suns & BHs, 2 - 5pm.

Admission: Adult £1.75, Child Free.

⊤ 🔱Unsuitable. 🛠By arrangement. 🅿Limited. ▣ 🐾In grounds, on leads. 🏱 🔼

HEMERDON HOUSE 🏠

Sparkwell, Plympton, Plymouth, Devon PL7 5BZ

Tel: Business hours 01752 841410; other times 01752 337350   **Fax:** 01752 331477

e-mail: jim.woollcombe@btopenworld.com

Owner: J H G Woollcombe Esq   **Contact:** Paul Williams & Partners

Late 18th century family house, rich in local history.

Location: OS Ref. SX564 575. 3m E of Plympton off A38.

Open: 1 - 12 & 22 - 31 May; 22 - 30 Aug incl. BHs in May & Aug: 2 - 5.30pm. Last admission 5pm. Provisional dates, please telephone to confirm.

Admission: £4.

🔱Ground floor. 🛠Obligatory. 🅿

HEMYOCK CASTLE

Hemyock, Cullompton, Devon EX15 3RJ

Tel: 01823 680745

Owner/Contact: Mrs Sheppard

Former medieval moated castle, displays show site's history as fortified manor house, castle and farm.

Location: OS Ref. ST135 134. M5/J26, Wellington then 5m S over the Blackdown Hills.

Open: BH Mons 2 - 5pm. Other times by appointment. Groups and private parties welcome.

Admission: Adult £1, Child 50p. Group rates available.

HOUND TOR DESERTED MEDIEVAL VILLAGE ⌗

Ashburton Road, Manaton, Dartmoor, Devon

Tel: 01626 832093

Owner: English Heritage   **Contact:** Dartmoor National Park Authority

The remains of four bronze age to medieval dwellings.

Location: OS191 Ref. SX746 788. 1¹/₂ m S of Manaton off Ashburton road. 6m N of Ashburton.

Open: Any reasonable time, daylight only.

Admission: Free.

❊

Lady Stucley, Hartland Abbey

HARTLAND ABBEY 🏠

HARTLAND, BIDEFORD, DEVON EX39 6DT

www.hartlandabbey.com

Tel: 01237 441264/234 or 01884 860225   **Fax:** 01237 441264/01884 861134

Owner: Sir Hugh Stucley Bt   **Contact:** The Administrator

Founded as an Augustinian Monastery in 1157 in a beautiful valley only 1 mile's walk to a spectacular Atlantic Cove, the Abbey was given by Henry VIII in 1539 to the Sergeant of his Wine Cellar, whose descendants live here today. Remodelled in the 18th & 19th century, it contains spectacular architecture and murals. Important paintings, furniture, porcelain collected over generations. Documents from 1160. Victorian and Edwardian photographs. Museum. Dairy. Recently discovered Victorian fernery and paths by Jekyll. Extensive woodland gardens of camellias, rhododendrons etc. Bog Garden. 18th century Walled gardens of vegetables, summer borders, tender and rare plants including echium pininana. Peacocks, donkeys and Welsh Mountain sheep in the park. Location for BBC 'Hercules' in 2003. Newly restored Monks' Pond.

Location: OS Ref. SS240 249. 15m W of Bideford, 15m N of Bude off A39 between Hartland and Hartland Quay.

Open: 1 Apr - 3 Oct: Wed, Thur, Sun & BHs, plus Tues in Jul & Aug, 2 - 5.30pm. Gardens: 1 Apr - 3 Oct: daily except Sats, 2 - 5.30pm.

Admission: House, Gardens & Grounds: Adult £6, Child (9-15ys) £1.50, OAP £5.50. Groups (20+): Adult £5, Child £1.50. Gardens & Grounds: Adult £4, Child 50p.

🎪 ⊤Wedding receptions. 🔱Partial. WC. 🍽 🛠By arrangement. 🅿 🐾In grounds, on leads. 🔼

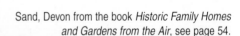

Sand, Devon from the book *Historic Family Homes and Gardens from the Air*, see page 54.

❊ **Open All Year Index** see front section

KILLERTON HOUSE & GARDEN ❧
BROADCLYST, EXETER EX5 3LE
www.nationaltrust.org.uk

Tel: 01392 881345

Owner: The National Trust **Contact:** Denise Melhuish - Property Manager

The spectacular hillside garden is beautiful throughout the year with spring flowering bulbs and shrubs, colourful herbaceous borders and fine trees. The garden is surrounded by parkland and woods offering lovely walks. The house is furnished as a family home and includes a costume collection dating from the 18th century in a series of period rooms and a Victorian laundry. Special costume exhibition for 2004: 'The Fair Equestrienne' – an exhibition of women's sporting dress, with stunning examples of tailored riding habits, illustrating women's leisure activities from the 1750s to early 20th century.

Location: OS Ref. SS977 001. Off Exeter – Cullompton Rd (B3181). M5 N'bound J30, M5 S'bound J28.

Open: House: 13 Mar - 31 Oct: daily except Tue (Mar & Oct also closed on Mon); Aug: daily, 11am - 5.30pm. Last entry ¹/₂ hour before closing. Garden: All year: daily, 10.30am - dusk.

Admission: House & Garden: Adult £5.80, Child £2.85, Family £14.30, Group £4.80. Garden only: Adult £4.20, Child £2.10.

Guide dogs only in house. Tel for details.

KNIGHTSHAYES COURT ❧
BOLHAM, TIVERTON, DEVON EX16 7RQ
www.nationaltrust.org.uk

Tel: 01884 254665 **Fax:** 01884 243050

Owner: The National Trust **Contact:** Penny Woollams – Property Manager

The striking Victorian gothic house is a rare survival of the work of William Burges with ornate patterns in many rooms. One of the finest gardens in Devon, mainly woodland and shrubs with something of interest throughout the seasons. Drifts of spring bulbs, summer flowering shrubs, pool garden and amusing animal topiary.

Location: OS Ref. SS960 151. 2m N of Tiverton (A396) at Bolham.

Open: House: 27 Mar - 31 Oct, daily except Fri, 11am - 5.30pm (Oct 4pm) last adm. ¹/₂ hr before closing. Garden: 27 Mar - 31 Oct, daily, 11am - 5.30pm.

Admission: House & Garden: Adult £6.20, Child £3.10, Family £14.80. Group £5.20. Garden only: Adult £4.80, Child £2.40, Group £4.10/£2.10.

Ground floor & grounds. WC. Guide dogs in park.

LOUGHWOOD MEETING HOUSE ✤

Dalwood, Axminster, Devon EX13 7DU

Tel: 01392 881691   **Fax:** 01392 881954

Owner: The National Trust   **Contact:** National Trust Regional Office

Around 1653 the Baptist congregation of the nearby village of Kilmington constructed this simple building dug into the hillside.

Location: OS Ref. SY253993. 4m W of Axminster.

Open: All year, daily.

Admission: Free

ⓘ Pushchairs and baby carriers admitted.

♿ Steep slope from the car park. Ground floor only.

🅿 Very narrow country lanes. No parking for coaches. ❋

LYDFORD CASTLES & SAXON TOWN ♯

Lydford, Okehampton, Devon

Tel: 01822 820320

Owner: English Heritage   **Contact:** The National Trust – 01822 820320

Standing above the lovely gorge of the River Lyd, this 12th century tower was notorious as a prison. The earthworks of the original Norman fort are to the south. A Saxon town once stood nearby and its layout is still discernible.

Location: OS191 Castle Ref. SX510 848, Fort Ref. SX509 847. In Lydford off A386 8m SW of Okehampton.

Open: Any reasonable time, daylight hours.

Admission: Free.

❋

MARKER'S COTTAGE ✤

Broadclyst, Exeter, Devon EX5 3HR

Tel: 01392 461546

Owner: The National Trust   **Contact:** The Custodian

Medieval cob house containing a cross-passage screen decorated with a painting of St Andrew and his attributes.

Location: OS Ref. SX985 973. ¼ E of B3181 in village of Broadclyst.

Open: 28 Mar - 31 Oct: Sun - Tue, 2 - 5pm.

Admission: £1.50.

MARWOOD HILL

Barnstaple, Devon EX31 4EB

Tel: 01271 342528   **Owner/Contact:** Dr J A Snowdon

20 acre garden with 3 small lakes. Extensive collection of camellias, bog garden. National collection of astilbes.

Location: OS Ref. SS545 375. 4m N of Barnstaple. ½ m W of B3230. Signs off A361 Barnstaple - Braunton road.

Open: Dawn to dusk throughout the year.

Admission: Adult £3, Child (under 12yrs) Free.

MORWELLHAM QUAY

Morwellham, Tavistock, Devon PL19 8JL

Tel: 01822 832766   **Fax:** 01822 833808

Owner: The Morwellham & Tamar Valley Trust   **Contact:** Anthony Power

Award-winning visitor centre at historic river port.

Location: OS Ref. SX446 697. Off A390 about 15 mins drive from Tavistock, Devon. 5m SW of Tavistock. 3m S of A390 at Gulworthy.

Open: Summer: daily, 10am - 5.30pm, last adm. 3.30pm. Winter: daily, 10am - 4.30pm, last adm. 2.30pm.

Admission: Adult £8.90, Child £6. Family (2+2) £26. Group rate please apply for details. Usual concessions.

OKEHAMPTON CASTLE ♯

Okehampton, Devon EX20 1JB

Tel: 01837 52844   **e-mail:** customers@english-heritage.org.uk

www.english-heritage.org.uk/visits

Owner: English Heritage   **Contact:** The Custodian

The ruins of the largest castle in Devon stand above a river surrounded by splendid woodland. There is still plenty to see, including the Norman motte and the jagged remains of the Keep. There is a picnic area and lovely woodland walks.

Location: OS Ref. SX584 942. 1m SW of Okehampton town centre off A30 bypass.

Open: 1 Apr - 31 Oct: daily, 10am - 6pm (5pm in Oct). Winter: Closed. Times subject to change April 2004.

Admission: Adult £2.60, Child £1.30, Conc. £2. 15% discount for groups (11+). Prices subject to change April 2004.

📷 ♿ Disabled access difficult for ambulant disabilities. Grounds. WC. 🎧 🅿
🐕 In grounds, on leads. 🎪 Tel. for details.

OLDWAY MANSION

Paignton, Devon

Tel: 01803 201201   **Fax:** 01803 207670

Owner: Torbay Council   **Contact:** Vanessa Merrifield

Built by sewing machine entrepreneur I M Singer in the 1870s.

Location: OS Ref. SX888 615. Off W side of A3022.

Open: All year: Mon - Sat, 9am - 5pm (except Christmas & New Year). Easter - Oct: Suns, 2 - 5pm. Visitors should note that not all rooms will always be open, access depends on other activities.

Admission: Free.

NTPL / Tony Murdoch

OVERBECK'S MUSEUM & GDN ✤

SHARPITOR, SALCOMBE, SOUTH DEVON TQ8 8LW

www.nationaltrust.org.uk

Tel: 01548 842893

Owner: The National Trust   **Contact:** Property Manager

A sub-tropical garden with rare and tender plants thriving in the mild climate and spectacular views over the Salcombe Estuary. In the Edwardian house are curios such as a polyphon and rejuvenating machine and displays on the maritime history and wildlife of the area. There is also a secret room for children, with dolls, tin soldiers, other toys and a ghost hunt.

Location: OS Ref. SX728 374. 1½ m SW of Salcombe. Signposted from Salcombe (single track lanes).

Open: Museum: 29 Mar - 30 July, Sept: Sun - Fri (open Easter Sat), 11am - 5.30pm. August, daily, 11am - 5.30pm. 3 - 31 Oct: Sun - Thur, 11am - 5pm. Garden: All year: daily, 10am - 7pm.

Admission: House & Garden: Adult £4.60, Child £2.30, Family £11.50. Garden only: Adult £3.40, Child £1.70.

ⓘ No photography in house. 📷 🎪 ♿ Partial. 🍴 🎫 By arrangement.
🅿 Limited. ▣ ⊠ ❋

POWDERHAM CASTLE 🏰   *See page 207 for full page entry.*

🔔 **Civil Wedding Venues** see front section

PUSLINCH
YEALMPTON, PLYMOUTH, DEVON PL8 2NN

Tel: 01752 880555 **Fax:** 01752 880909

Owner/Contact: Sebastian Fenwick

A perfect example of a medium sized early Georgian house in the Queen Anne tradition with fine contemporary interiors. Built in 1720 by the Yonge family.

Location: OS Ref. SX570 509. Yealmpton.

Open: Groups only (min charge £25). All year except Christmas & Boxing Day by prior appointment only.

Admission: Adult £5.

ℹ️No photography. 🎫Obligatory. 🅿️ ⊠ ❄️

RHS GARDEN ROSEMOOR
GREAT TORRINGTON, DEVON EX38 8PH
www.rhs.org.uk

Tel: 01805 624067 **Fax:** 01805 624717

Owner/Contact: The Royal Horticultural Society

A beautiful garden mixing new gardens with Lady Anne's original garden. Something for all interests and tastes whatever the season, from formal gardens to a lake and Arboretum. The Rosemoor Plant Centre stocks a variety of hardy plants, the shop has books and gifts and, for refreshments, there is a café and restaurant. Voted South West Visitor Attraction of the Year 2003.

Location: OS Ref. SS500 183. 1m S of Great Torrington on A3124.

Open: All year except Christmas Day; Apr - Sept: 10am - 6pm. Oct - Mar: 10am - 5pm.

Admission: Adult £5, Child (6 - 16yrs) £1, Child (under 6yrs) Free. Groups (10+) £4. Companion for disabled visitor Free. 2003 prices.

🅾️ 🔊 ♿ 🖥️ 🍴Licensed. 🎫By arrangement. 🅿️ 🐕Guide dogs only. ❄️ ♿

The National Trust

SALTRAM HOUSE 🌺
PLYMPTON, PLYMOUTH, DEVON PL7 1JH
www.nationaltrust.org.uk

Tel: 01752 333500 **Fax:** 01752 336474

Owner: The National Trust   **Contact:** Kevan Timms - Property Manager

A magnificent George II mansion set in beautiful gardens and surrounded by landscaped park overlooking the Plym estuary. Visitors can see the original contents including important work by Robert Adam, Chippendale, Wedgwood and Sir Joshua Reynolds. You can explore the garden follies including Fanny's Bower and the Castle, enjoy the garden trail and fascinating walks beside the river, through the parkland and in the woods. Saltram starred as Norland Park in the award winning film *Sense & Sensibility*. Children's activities and play area.

Location: OS Ref. SX520 557. 3¹/₂ m NE of Plymouth city centre. ³/₄ m S of A38.

Take Plympton turn at Marsh Mills/Sainsbury's roundabout.

Open: House: 29 Mar - 30 Sept: daily, except Fri, 12 noon - 4.30pm, last admission 4pm. 1 - 31 Oct: 11.30am - 3.30pm, last admission 3pm (due to viewing in natural light). House closed in winter. Garden, Chapel Art Gallery, Shop & Tearoom: As house, 11am - 5pm; 1 Nov - 21 Dec: 11am - 4pm.

Admission: House & Garden: Adult £6.60, Child £3.20, Family £16.30. Groups (15+): £5.80. Garden only: Adult £3.30, Child £1.60. Group discount available.

🅾️ ♿WC. Braille guide. 🍴Licensed. 🎧

🐕On signed perimeter paths only, on leads. Guide dogs only in house & garden.

SAND 📷
SIDBURY, SIDMOUTH EX10 0QN
www.eastdevon.net/sand

Tel: 01395 597230

Owner/Contact: Lt Col P Huyshe/Mrs Stella Huyshe-Shires

Sand is one of East Devon's hidden gems. The beautiful valley garden extends to 6 acres and is the setting for the lived-in house, the 15th century Hall House, and the 17th century Summer House. The family, under whose unbroken ownership the property has remained since 1560, provide guided house tours.

Location: OS Ref. SY146 925. Well signed, 250 yards off A375 between Honiton and Sidmouth.

Open: Garden: 4 Apr - 28 Sept: Sun - Tues. House: BH Suns & Mons, 11/12 Apr; 2/3, 30/31 May; 29/30 Aug: 2 - 6pm. Last admission to house & garden: 5pm.

Admission: House & Garden: Adult £4.50, Child/Student £1. Garden only: Adult £2.50, accompanied Child (under 16) Free.

ℹ️ No photography in house. 🅿️ Partial. 📷 🎫 Obligatory. 🅿️ Limited for coaches. 🔲 🐕 In grounds, on leads. ☎️ Tel. for details.

SHOBROOKE PARK
Crediton, Devon EX17 1DG

Tel: 01363 775153 **Fax:** 01363 775153 **e-mail:** admin@shobrookepark.com

Owner: Dr J R Shelley **Contact:** Clare Shelley

A classical English 180-acre park. The lime avenue dates from about 1800 and the cascade of four lakes was completed in the 1840s. Millennium amphitheatre built in the year 2000. The southern third of the Park is open to the public under the Countryside Commission Access Scheme. The 15 acre garden, created c1845 with Portland stone terraces, roses and rhododendrons is being restored.

Location: OS Ref. SS848 010. 1m E of Crediton. Access to park by kissing gate at SW end of park, just S of A3072. Garden access on A3072.

Open: South Park: daylight hours. Gardens: 17 Apr, 8 May & 5 Jun, 2 - 5pm.

Admission: Park: No charge. Gardens: NGS £3, accompanied child under 14 Free. 🅿️ Partial, wheelchairs in garden only. 🐕 Guide dogs only in garden. ❄️

SHUTE BARTON 🍂
Shute, Axminster, Devon EX13 7PT

Tel: 01297 34692 **www.**nationaltrust.org.uk

Owner: The National Trust

One of the most important surviving non-fortified manor houses of the Middle Ages.

Location: OS Ref. SY253 974. 3m SW of Axminster, 2m N of Colyton, 1m S of A35.

Open: 3 Apr - 30 Oct: Weds & Sats, 2 - 5.30pm. Last admission 5pm.

Admission: £2.10. No group reductions.

TAPELEY PARK 📷
Instow, Bideford, Devon EX39 4NT

Tel: 01271 342558 **Fax:** 01271 342371

Owner: Tapeley Park Trust

Much altered Queen Anne building with extensive gardens and park.

Location: OS Ref. SS478 291. Between Bideford and Barnstaple near Instow. Follow brown tourist signs from the A39 onto B3233.

Open: Good Fri - end Oct: daily except Sats, 10am - 5pm.

Admission: Adult £4, Child £2.50, OAP £3.50. Groups (5+): Adult £3.30, Child £2.10, OAP £2.90, under 5s Free. House tours (1 week notice required) £2.50 extra.

TIVERTON CASTLE 📷
Tiverton, Devon EX16 6RP

Tel: 01884 253200/255200 **Fax:** 01884 254200 **e-mail:** tiverton.castle@ukf.net
www.tivertoncastle.com

Owner: Mr and Mrs A K Gordon **Contact:** Mrs A Gordon

After nearly 900 years few buildings evoke such an immediate feeling of history as Tiverton Castle. Many ages of architecture can be seen, from medieval to modern. With continuing conservation there is always something new and interesting to see. Beautiful gardens. Civil War Armoury – try some on.

Location: OS Ref. SS954 130. Just N of Tiverton town centre.

Open: Easter - end of Jun, Sept: Sun, Thur, BH Mon, Jul & Aug, Sun - Thur, 2.30 - 5.30pm. Open to groups (12+) by prior arrangement at any time.

Admission: Adult £4, Child (7-16yrs) £2, Child under 7 Free. Garden only: £1.50. Groups (12+): Adult £5, Child £2.

🔲 🅿️ Partial. WC. 🎫 By arrangement. 🅿️ Limited. ✖️ 🛏️ 4 Apartments. 🔺 ❄️

TORRE ABBEY
THE KINGS DRIVE, TORQUAY, DEVON TQ2 5JE
www.torre-abbey.org.uk

Tel: 01803 293593 **e-mail:** torre-abbey@torbay.gov.uk

Owner: Torbay Council **Contact:** L Retallick

Torre Abbey was founded as a monastery in 1196. Later adapted as a country house and in 1741-3 remodelled by the Cary family. Bought by the Council in 1930 for an art gallery. Visitors can see monastic remains, historic rooms, family chapel, mementoes of Agatha Christie, Victorian paintings including Holman Hunt & Burne-Jones & Torquay terracotta. Torre Abbey overlooks the sea and is surrounded by parkland and gardens. Teas served in Victorian Kitchen.

Location: OS Ref. SX907 638. On Torquay sea front. Between station and town centre.

Open: Apr - 1 Nov: daily, 9.30am - 6pm, last adm. 5pm. Free access to members of the National Art Collections Fund.

Admission: Adult £3.50, Child £1.70, Conc. £3, Family £7.75. Groups (pre-booked, 10+): Adult £2.75, Child £1.50.

ℹ️ Conferences. 🔲 🚻 🅿️ Unsuitable. 📷 🍴 🎫 By arrangement. 🔲 Schools' programme, apply for details. 🐕 Guide dogs only. ☎️ Tel for details.

TOTNES CASTLE ⚜️
Castle Street, Totnes, Devon TQ9 5NU

Tel/Fax: 01803 864406 **e-mail:** customers@english-heritage.org.uk
www.english-heritage.org.uk/visits

Owner: English Heritage **Contact:** The Custodian

By the North Gate of the hill town of Totnes you will find a superb motte and bailey castle, with splendid views across the roof tops and down to the River Dart. It is a symbol of lordly feudal life and a fine example of Norman fortification.

Location: OS202 Ref. SX800 605. In Totnes, on hill overlooking the town. Access in Castle St off W end of High St.

Open: 1 Apr - 31 Oct: daily 10am - 6pm (5pm in Oct). Closed in winter. Times subject to change April 2004.

Admission: Adult £1.80, Child 90p, Conc. £1.40. 15% discount for groups (11+). Prices subject to change April 2004.

🔲 🅿️ Unsuitable. 🅿️ Charged parking 64 metres (70 yds). 🐕 In grounds, on leads. ☎️ Tel. for details.

Map 2

ATHELHAMPTON HOUSE & GARDENS

DORCHESTER

www.athelhampton.co.uk

Owner:
Patrick Cooke Esq

▶ CONTACT

Owen Davies
Athelhampton House
Dorchester   DT2 7LG

Tel: 01305 848363
Fax: 01305 848135

e-mail: enquiries@
athelhampton.co.uk

▶ LOCATION
OS Ref. SY771 942

Off A35 (T) at
Puddletown
Northbrook junction,
5m E of Dorchester.

Rail: Dorchester.

Athelhampton is one of the finest 15th century manor houses and is surrounded by one of the great architectural gardens of England. The Great Hall was built by Sir William Martyn in 1485. The West wing is Elizabethan in period and contains the Great Chamber, Library and Wine Cellar. Athelhampton houses a fine collection of English furniture starting in the Jacobean period leading on to late Victorian. There is also a collection relating to A W Pugin and The Palace of Westminster.

The glorious Grade I gardens, dating from 1891, contain the world-famous topiary pyramids, fountains and the River Piddle. Collections of tulips, magnolias, roses, clematis and lilies can be seen in season. Located in the gardens are a number of small buildings each with their own unique history. The two garden pavilions were used as water towers for the original fountain system. The Toll house was a collection point for the Wimborne turnpike trust between 1842 and 1878 and has now been restored along with its garden. The dovecote is one of the earliest in Dorset and with a capacity for 1200 birds would have supported a large household.

The Coach House contains all the facilities required for the comfort of daily visitors with private rooms available for visiting groups. The House and Gardens can be opened by appointment for evening visits and dinners. Friday late afternoons and Saturdays are available for wedding ceremonies and/or receptions.

▶ OPENING TIMES

March - October:
Daily (except Fridays & Saturdays).

November - February:
Sundays only,
10.30am - 5pm/dusk. Last admission 4pm.

Coach House Restaurant open as house & gardens.
Carvery on Suns.
Please book.

All facilities at Athelhampton are available for private hire outside our normal opening hours. We specialise in weddings on Fridays and Saturdays and dinners on any evening. Please contact Owen Davies, Manager.

▶ ADMISSION

House & Gardens

Adult	£7.75
Child	Free
Student	£4.95
Disabled	£4.95
OAP	£7.00
Groups (12+)	
Adult	£4.95

Gardens only

Adult	£5.50
Child	Free

Left: Great Hall   Below: Conservatory

CONFERENCE/FUNCTION

ROOM	SIZE	MAX CAPACITY
Coach House* Long Hall	13 x 6m	100
Conservatory*	16 x 11m	130
Main House* Great Hall	12 x 8m	70
Great* Chamber	10 x 6m	40
Garden Pavilions (2)	3 x 3m	6

*Licensed for Civil wedding ceremonies.

 By arrangement.
 Partial. WC.
 Licensed. Licensed.
 By arrangement.

 Guide dogs only.

FORDE ABBEY & GARDENS

DORSET

www.fordeabbey.co.uk

Map 2

Owner:
Mark Roper Esq

▶ **CONTACT**
Carolyn Clay
Forde Abbey
Chard
Somerset TA20 4LU

Tel: 01460 220231
Fax: 01460 220296

e-mail:
forde.abbey@virgin.net

▶ **LOCATION**
OS Ref. ST358 041

Just off the B3167
4m SE of Chard.

Forde Abbey is one of the oldest Abbeys still inhabited in England, founded by Cistercian monks in 1140. Over the next 400 years Forde became one of the most learned and wealthy monasteries in the land until Henry VIII dissolved it in 1539. In 1649 Sir Edmund Prideaux, Attorney General to Oliver Cromwell, bought the Abbey and transformed it into a beautiful country house, with immense charm and character, and it remains almost unchanged to this day.

The house contains a collection of elaborately decorated plaster ceilings, exquisite pictures and fine furniture. In the Grand Saloon are some spectacular tapestries, woven from cartoons painted for the Sistine Chapel in Rome by Raphael, depicting scenes from the lives of St Peter and St Paul.

The 30 acres of world-famous gardens that surround the house date from the early 18th century. However the majority of the garden has been developed by the present occupiers, to create a garden worthy of the great house it surrounds. Highlights of the garden include; spectacular carpets of crocus throughout the garden in the Spring, a magnificent Bog Garden, a unique living Beech House, sensational summer borders, and a large working kitchen garden. The garden has been described by Alan Titchmarsh as *"one of the greatest gardens of the West Country"*.

The Undercroft Restaurant serving morning coffee, lunches and cream teas, (using ingredients from the garden, estate, and local suppliers), together with the unique gift shop, plant centre, and pottery exhibition will complete a perfect day out.

▶ **OPENING TIMES**

House
1 April - 31 October
Tue - Fri, Sun & BH Mons
12 noon - 4pm.

Gardens
Daily
10am - 4.30pm.

▶ **ADMISSION**

House & Gardens

Adult	£7.00
Child (under 15yrs)	Free
Student	£7.00
OAP	£6.50

Groups (20+)

Adult	£5.10
Child (under 15yrs)	£2.50

(2003 prices)

i Available for wedding receptions. No photography in house.

Partial.

Licensed.

Licensed.

By arrangement.

P

 On leads, in grounds.

ABBOTSBURY SUB-TROPICAL GARDENS

ABBOTSBURY, WEYMOUTH, DORSET DT3 4LA

www.abbotsbury-tourism.co.uk   www.abbotsburyplantsales.co.uk

Tel: 01305 871387   **e-mail:** info@abbotsbury-tourism.co.uk

Owner: The Hon Mrs Townshend DL   **Contact:** Shop Manager

Established in 1765 by the first Countess of Ilchester. Developed since then into a 20-acre Grade I listed, magnificent woodland valley garden. World famous for its camellia groves, magnolias, rhododendron and hydrangea collections. In summer it is awash with colour. Since the restoration after the great storm of 1990 many new and exotic plants have been introduced. The garden is now a mixture of formal and informal, with charming walled garden and spectacular woodland valley views. Facilities include a Colonial Tea House for lunches, snacks and drinks, a plant centre

and quality gift shop. Events such as Shakespeare and concerts are presented during the year. The floodlighting of the garden at the end of October should not be missed.

Location: OS Ref. SY564 851. Off A35 nr Dorchester, on B3157 between Weymouth & Bridport.

Open: Mar - Nov: daily, 10am - 6pm. Winter: daily, 10am - 4pm. Last admission 1 hr before closing.

Admission: Adult £6.50, Child £3.75, OAP £5.80.

🖼 🗩 Plants also for sale online. 🔁 ♿ Partial. 🍷 Licensed. 🍴 𝒇 By arrangement. 🅿 Free. ⬛ 🐕 In grounds, on leads. ✳

ATHELHAMPTON HOUSE & GARDENS

See page 219 for full page entry.

BROWNSEA ISLAND

Poole Harbour, Dorset BH13 7EE

Tel: 01202 707744   **Fax:** 01202 701635   **e-mail:** brownseaisland@nationaltrust.org.uk
www.nationaltrust.org.uk/brownsea

Owner: The National Trust   **Contact:** The Property Manager

A wonderfully atmospheric island of heath and woodland. A haven for a rich variety of wildlife, including red squirrels and many species of bird. There are many fine walks and spectacular views of Poole Harbour. Visitors may land from own boats at Pottery Pier at west end of island, accessible at all stages of the tide. Please note that the island's paths are uneven in places.

Location: OS Ref. SZ032 878. In Poole Harbour. Boats run from Poole Quay and Sandbanks.

Open: 27 Mar - 31 Oct: daily, 10am - 5pm (closes at 6pm 24 Jul - 31 Aug, 4pm in Oct).

Admission: Adult £3.90, Child £1.90, Family (2+2) £9.70, (1+2) £5.80. Groups: Adult £3.60, Child £1.60.

🖼 ♿ Partial. 🗩 𝒇 ⬛ 🐕 Tel for details.

CHETTLE HOUSE

Chettle, Blandford Forum, Dorset DT11 8DB

Tel: 01258 830858

Owner/Contact: Mr & Mrs Peter Bourke

A fine Queen Anne manor house designed by Thomas Archer and a fine example of English baroque architecture. The house features a basement with the typical north-south passage set just off centre with barrel-vaulted ceilings and a magnificent stone staircase. The house is set in 5 acres of peaceful gardens.

Location: OS Ref. ST952 132. 6m NE of Blandford NW of A354.

Open: Easter - end Sept: 1st Sun in each month. Other times by appointment.

Admission: Adult £3.50, Child Free (under 16yrs).

🔁 Wedding receptions and special events. ♿ Grounds. 🗩 ✳

CHRISTCHURCH CASTLE & NORMAN HOUSE

Christchurch, Dorset

Tel: 0117 9750700

Owner: English Heritage   **Contact:** The South West Office

Early 12th century Norman keep and Constable's house, built c1160.

Location: OS Ref. SZ160 927. In Christchurch, near the Priory.

Open: Any reasonable time, daylight hours.

Admission: Free.

✳

CLOUDS HILL

Wareham, Dorset BH20 7NQ

Tel: 01929 405616   www.nationaltrust.org.uk

Owner: The National Trust   **Contact:** The Custodian

A tiny isolated brick and tile cottage, bought in 1925 by T E Lawrence (Lawrence of Arabia) as a retreat. The austere rooms inside are much as he left them and reflect his complex personality and close links with the Middle East. An exhibition details Lawrence's extraordinary life.

Location: OS Ref. SY824 909. 9m E of Dorchester, 1¹/₂ m E of Waddock crossroads B3390.

Open: 1 Apr - 31 Oct: Thurs - Sun & BH Mons, 12 noon - 5pm or dusk if earlier; no electric light. Groups wishing to visit at other times must telephone in advance.

Admission: £3.10, no reduction for children or groups.

ℹ No WC. ♿ Braille guide. 🅿 No coaches. ⬛

South West - England

NTPL/Joe Cornish

CORFE CASTLE

WAREHAM, DORSET BH20 5EZ

www.nationaltrust.org.uk

Tel: 01929 481294 **Fax:** 01929 477067 **e-mail:** corfecastle@nationaltrust.org.uk

Owner: The National Trust **Contact:** The Property Manager

One of Britain's most majestic ruins, the Castle controlled the gateway through the Purbeck Hills and had been an important stronghold since the time of William the Conqueror. Defended during the Civil War by the redoubtable Lady Bankes, the Castle fell to treachery from within and was heavily slighted afterwards by the Parliamentarians. Many fine Norman and early English features remain. Visitor Centre at Castle View. Seasonal regular Castle tours. New family guidebook. Improved on-sight interpretation.

Location: OS Ref. SY959 824. On A351 Wareham - Swanage Rd. NW of the village.

Open: All year: daily. Mar & Oct: 10am - 5pm; Apr - Sept: 10am - 6pm; Nov - Feb (Closed 25/26 Dec), 10am - 4pm.

Admission: Adult £4.70, Child £2.30, Family (2+3) £11.50, (1+3) £6.90. Groups: Adult £4.10, Child £2.

Limited. Braille guide. WC. On leads. Tel for details.

DEANS COURT

WIMBORNE, DORSET BH21 1EE

Tel: 01202 886116

Owner: Sir Michael & Lady Hanham **Contact:** Wimborne Tourist Info Centre

13 peaceful acres a few minutes walk south of the Minster. Specimen trees, lawns, borders, herb garden, kitchen garden with long serpentine wall and rose garden. Chemical-free produce usually for sale, also interesting herbaceous plants. Wholefood teas in garden or in Housekeeper's room (down steps).

Location: OS Ref. SZ010 997. 2 mins walk S from centre of Wimborne Minster. Entrance signed from Deans Court Lane.

Open: 11/12 Apr; 2/3 & 30/31 May; 7/8 & 29/30 Aug & 12 Sept: Suns, 2 - 6pm, Mons 10am - 6pm. Organic Gardening Weekend: 7/8 Aug: 2 - 6pm.

Admission: Adult £2, Child (5-15yrs) 50p, OAP £1.50. Groups by arrangement.

Garden produce sales. Guide dogs only.

EDMONDSHAM HOUSE & GARDENS

Cranborne, Wimborne, Dorset BH21 5RE

Tel: 01725 517207

Owner/Contact: Mrs Julia E Smith

Charming blend of Tudor and Georgian architecture with interesting contents. Organic walled garden, dower house garden, 6 acre garden with unusual trees and spring bulbs. 12th century church nearby.

Location: OS Ref. SU062 116. Off B3081 between Cranborne and Verwood, NW from Ringwood 9m, Wimborne 9m.

Open: House & Gardens: All BH Mons & Weds in Apr & Oct 2 - 5pm. Gardens: Apr - Oct, Suns & Weds 2 - 5pm.

Admission: House & Garden: Adult £3, Child £1 (under 5yrs Free). Garden only: Adult £1.50, Child 50p. Groups by arrangement, teas for groups.

Pre-booked (max 50). Obligatory. Car park only. (max 50).

FIDDLEFORD MANOR

Sturminster Newton, Dorset

Tel: 0117 9750700

Owner: English Heritage **Contact:** The South West Regional Office

Part of a medieval manor house, with a remarkable interior. The splendid roof structures in the hall and upper living room are the best in Dorset. (Adjacent buildings are private dwellings and not open for visits.)

Location: OS ST801 136. 1m E of Sturminster Newton off A357. No coach access.

Open: 1 Apr - 30 Sept: daily, 10am - 6pm. 1 Nov - 31 Mar: daily 10am - 4pm. Closed 24 - 26 Dec & 1 Jan. Times subject to change April 2004.

Admission: Free.

FORDE ABBEY & GARDENS

See page 220 for full page entry.

Sir Reginald Blomfield

1856-1942

Architect & Garden Designer

Famed for his book *The Formal Garden in England* published in 1892 in which he extolled the virtues of architectural, formal shapes when creating a garden. Look for yew topiary, hedges and the use of stonework, which he used to create his strong lines.

His work can be seen at Sulgrave Manor, Northamptonshire and his influence at Athelhampton House and Gardens, Dorset, designed by Inigo Thomas, his assistant, in the style of Blomfield.

HANFORD HOUSE
CHILDE OKEFORD, BLANDFORD, DORSET DT11 8HL

www.heritagevenues.co.uk

Tel/Fax: 01285 831417   **e-mail:** heritage.venues@virgin.net

Owner: The Canning Charitable Trust & Miss Sarah Canning

Contact: Hon Mrs G Bathurst

Described by Pevsner as *"a major Jacobean house"* and dated on rainwater heads 1623. Since 1947 The girls' prep school (of the same name), it is surrounded by its own much loved gardens with majestic trees and lawns. Ideal for parties, with some accommodation, it is available for selected events and receptions during school holidays.

Location: OS Ref. ST845 111. 1m W of A350 between Stourpaine & Iwerne Minster.

Open: Strictly by appointment only.

ⓘ No photography in house. 🅣 🅰 Partial. 🅕 By arrangement. 🔲

HARDY'S COTTAGE 🐾
Higher Bockhampton, Dorchester, Dorset DT2 8QJ
Tel: 01305 262366   www.nationaltrust.org.uk

Owner/Contact: The National Trust

A small thatched cottage where the novelist and poet Thomas Hardy was born in 1840, and from where he would walk to school every day in Dorchester, six miles away. It was built by his great-grandfather and is little altered since. The interior has been furnished by the Trust (see also Max Gate). His early novels *Under the Green Wood Tree* and *Far From the Madding Crowd* were written here. Charming cottage garden.

Location: OS Ref. SY728 925. 3m NE of Dorchester, 1/2 m S of A35. 10 mins walk through the woods from car park.

Open: 1 Apr - 1 Nov: daily except Tue & Wed, 11am - 5pm or dusk if earlier.

Admission: £3. No reduction for children or groups.

🔲 ⓘ No WC. 🅰 Partial. 🅿 No coach parking. 🔲 🐾

HIGHER MELCOMBE
Melcombe Bingham, Dorchester, Dorset DT2 7PB
Tel: 01258 880251

Owner/Contact: Mr M C Woodhouse

Consists of the surviving wing of a 16th century house with its attached domestic chapel. A fine plaster ceiling and linenfold panelling. Conducted tours by owner.

Location: OS Ref. ST749 024. 1km W of Melcombe Bingham.

Open: May - Sept by appointment.

Admission: Adult £2 (takings go to charity).

🅰 Unsuitable. 🅕 By written appointment only. 🅿 Limited. 🐾 Guide dogs only.

❄ Open All Year Index see front section

HIGHCLIFFE CASTLE 🏛
ROTHESAY DRIVE, HIGHCLIFFE-ON-SEA, CHRISTCHURCH BH23 4LE

www.highcliffecastle.co.uk

Tel: 01425 278807   **Fax:** 01425 280423   **e-mail:** castleman@christchurch.gov.uk

Owner: Christchurch Borough Council   **Contact:** The Manager

Built in 1830 in the Romantic and Picturesque style of architecture for Lord Stuart de Rothesay using his unique collection of French medieval stonework and stained glass. Recently repaired externally, it remains mostly unrepaired inside. Five rooms house a visitor centre, exhibitions, events and gift shop. Coastal grounds, village trail and nearby St Mark's church. Tea rooms in the Claretian's Wing.

Location: OS Ref. SZ200 930. Off the A337 Lymington Road, between Christchurch and Highcliffe-on-Sea.

Open: 1 Apr - Oct: daily, 11am - 5pm. Nov - Christmas: 11am - 4pm. Grounds/Tearooms: All year. Please ring to confirm exact dates. Access for coaches.

Admission: Adult £1.50, Child Free. Group guided tour (12+): Adult £3, Child £1. Grounds: Free.

🔲 🅣 🅰 Partial. WC. 🔲 10am - 5pm. 🅕 By arrangement. 🅿 Limited. Parking charge. 🔲 By arrangement. 🐾 In grounds, on leads. 🔲 ❄ 🔲 Tel for details.

THE KEEP MILITARY MUSEUM OF DEVON & DORSET

Bridport Rd, Dorchester, Dorset DT1 1RN

Tel: 01305 264066 **Fax:** 01305 250373

e-mail: keep.museum@talk21.com **www**.keepmilitarymuseum.org

Owner: Ministry of Defence (Museums Trustees) **Contact:** The Curator

The courage, humour, tradition and sacrifice of those who served in the Regiments of Devon and Dorset for over 300 years are brought to life using touch screen computers and creative displays in this modern museum situated in a Grade II listed building. View Hardy country from the battlements.

Location: OS Ref. SY687 906. In Dorchester at the top of High West Street.

Open: All year: Apr - Sept: Mon - Sat 9.30am - 5pm (last admission 1hr before closing time). Jul & Aug: Suns also, 10am - 4pm. Oct - Mar: Tue - Sat, 9.30am - 5pm.

Admission: Adult £3, Conc. £2, Family (2+3) £9. Groups (10-50): Adult £2.50, Conc. £1.50.

ⓘNo flash photography. 🅾 🚹 ♿ 🅵By arrangement. 🅿 Limited. ◼
🦮Guide dogs only. ✳ 🛏 Tel for details.

Dave Penman

KINGSTON MAURWARD GARDEN

DORCHESTER, DORSET DT2 8PY

www.kmc.ac.uk

Tel: 01305 215003 **Fax:** 01305 215001 **e-mail:** events@kmc.ac.uk

Contact: Wendy Cunningham

Classical 18th century parkland setting, with majestic lawns sweeping down from the Grade I listed Georgian house to the lake. The Rainbow beds and beautiful herbaceous borders complement the series of 'rooms' within the formal Edwardian garden. National Collections of Penstemons and Salvias. Lakeside walks, animal park, shop, plant centre and refreshments.

Location: OS Ref. SY713 911. 1m E of Dorchester. Roundabout off A35 by-pass.

Open: 5 Jan - 19 Dec: daily, 10am - 5.30pm or dusk if earlier.

Admission: Adult £4, Child £2.50 (under 3yrs Free), Family £12.50. Groups (10+): Adult £3.50. Guided tours (by arrangement) (12+): £5pp.

ⓘConferences. 🅾 🚹 🅃Wedding receptions. ♿Partial. ◖Licensed.
🅵By arrangement. 🅿 ◼ 🦮Guide dogs only. 🅰 ✳ 🛏Tel for details.

Rupert Truman

KINGSTON LACY ❧

WIMBORNE MINSTER, DORSET BH21 4EA

www.nationaltrust.org.uk

Tel: 01202 883402 / 01202 842913 (Sat & Sun 11am - 5pm)

Infoline: 01202 880413 **Fax:** 01202 882402

e-mail: kingstonlacy@nationaltrust.org.uk

Owner: The National Trust **Contact:** The Property Manager

A 17th century house altered by Sir Charles Barry in the 19th Century. The house contains an outstanding collection of paintings and other works of art and includes the famous and dramatic Spanish room, with walls hung in magnificent gilded leather. The house and garden are set in a wooded park with a find herd of Red Devon cattle. The surrounding estate is crossed by many paths and dominated by the Iron Age hill fort of Badbury Rings. Walk leaflets available from shop.

Location: OS Ref. ST980 019. On B3082 - Blandford / Wimborne road, 1¹/₂ m NW of Wimborne.

Open: House: 20 Mar - 31 Oct: Wed - Sun (open BH Suns & Mons), 11am - 5pm (last admission 4pm). Garden & Park: 20 Mar - 31 Oct: daily, 10.30am - 6pm; 5 Nov - 19 Dec: Fri - Sun; 5 Feb - 20 Mar: Sat & Sun, 10.30am - 4pm. Shop & Restaurant: as Garden but closes at 5.30pm during 20 Mar - 31 Oct. Special Snowdrop Days in Jan & Feb, tel infoline. 3 Jul: House & shop close at 4pm, restaurant & grounds at 4.30pm.

Admission: Adult £7.20, Child £3.60, Family £19. Pre-booked groups (15+): Adult £5.80, Child £2.90. Park & Garden only: Adult £3.60, Child £1.80, Family £9.50.

🅾 🚹 ♿Garden only. Braille guide. WC. ◖Licensed. 🅵By arrangement. 🅿 ◼
🦮On leads, in park only. 🛏Tel for details.

KNOLL GARDENS & NURSERY

Stapehill Road, Hampreston, Wimborne BH21 7ND

Tel: 01202 873931 **Fax:** 01202 870842

Owner: J & J Flude & N R Lucas **Contact:** Mr John Flude

Nationally acclaimed 6 acre gardens, with 6000+ named plants from the world over.

Location: OS Ref. SU059 001. Between Wimborne & Ferndown. Exit A31 Canford Bottom roundabout, B3073 Hampreston. Signposted 1¹/₂ m.

Open: All year: Wed - Sun, 10am - 5pm or dusk if earlier. Closed Christmas & New Year holiday period.

Admission: Adult £3.50, Child (5-15yrs) £2, OAP £3, Student £2.50. Groups: Adult £2.50, Child £1.75, Student £2.50. Family (2+2) £9.50.

Education Index see front section

LULWORTH CASTLE
WAREHAM, DORSET BH20 5QS

www.lulworth.com

Tel: 01929 400352 **Fax:** 01929 400563 **e-mail:** office@lulworth.com

Owner: The Weld Estate **Contact:** W J Weld Esq

Surrounded by beautiful parkland this 17th century hunting lodge was destroyed by fire in 1929 and has been restored by English Heritage. Steeped in history the Castle has remained in the same family since 1641. Features include a gallery on the Weld family, reconstructed kitchen, dairy and laundry rooms and a wine cellar. The Chapel is reputed to be one of the finest pieces of architecture in Dorset and houses an exhibition on vestments and recusant silver. **Lulworth Castle House:** Elegantly stands within the Park and has a stunning collection of pictures and furniture. The grounds also include the original kitchen garden to the Castle.

Location: OS Ref. SY853 822. In E Lulworth off B3070, 3m NE of Lulworth Cove.

Open: 11 Jan - 23 Dec: Sun - Fri (open Easter Sat). Summer: 10.30am - 6pm. Winter: 10.30am - 4pm. Lulworth Castle House: 12 May - 14 Jul: Wed, 2 - 5pm. Groups: Mon - Fri by appointment.

Admission: Castle: Adult £7, Child £4, OAP £5. Groups: Adult £5, Child £3, OAP £4. Lulworth Castle House: Adult £3, Child Free. Prices may vary for special events.

Partial. WC. Licensed. By arrangement. In ground, on leads. 5 holiday cottages, tel: 01929 400100. Tel for details.

MAPPERTON
BEAMINSTER, DORSET DT8 3NR

www.mapperton.com

Tel: 01308 862645 **Fax:** 01308 863348 **e-mail:** office@mapperton.com

Owner/Contact: The Earl & Countess of Sandwich

Jacobean 1660s manor with Tudor features and classical north front. Italianate upper garden with orangery, topiary and formal borders descending to fish ponds and shrub gardens. All Saints Church forms south wing opening to courtyard and stables. Area of outstanding natural beauty with fine views of Dorset hills and woodlands. House and Gardens featured in Restoration, Emma and Tom Jones.

Location: OS Ref. SY503 997. 1m S of B3163, 2m NE of B3066, 2m SE Beaminster, 5m NE Bridport.

Open: House: 28 Jun - 6 Aug: weekdays, 2 - 4.30pm, last admission 4pm. Other times by appointment. Garden & All Saints Church: 1 Mar - 31 Oct: daily, 2 - 6pm. Café: Mar - Sept: daily, 12.30 - 5.30pm, for lunch and tea.

Admission: Gardens: £4, House: £2.50. Child (under 18yrs) £2, under 5 Free. Groups tours by appointment.

Partial. Licensed. By arrangement. Limited for coaches. Guide dogs only. Tel for details.

MAX GATE
Alington Avenue, Dorchester, Dorset DT1 2AA

Tel: 01305 262538 **Fax:** 01305 250978 **www.**thomas-hardy.connectfree.co.uk

Owner: The National Trust **Contact:** The Tenant

Novelist and poet Thomas Hardy designed and lived in this house from 1885 until his death in 1928. Here he wrote *Tess of the d'Urbervilles*, *Jude the Obscure* and the *Mayor of Casterbridge*, as well as much of his poetry. The house contains several pieces of his furniture.

Location: OS Ref. SY704 899. 1m E of Dorchester just N of the A352 to Wareham. From Dorchester follow A352 signs to the roundabout named Max Gate (at Jct. of A35 Dorchester bypass). Turn left and left again into cul-de-sac outside Max Gate.

Open: 31 Mar - 29 Sept: Mons, Weds & Suns, 2 - 5pm. Only hall, dining, drawing rooms & garden open. Private visits, tours & seminars by schools, colleges and literary societies at other times by prior appointment with the tenants, Mr & Mrs Andrew Leah.

Admission: Adult £2.60, Child £1.40.

No WC. Partial. Braille guide.

MILTON ABBEY CHURCH
Milton Abbas, Blandford, Dorset DT11 0BZ

Tel: 01258 880215

Owner: Diocese of Salisbury **Contact:** Chris Fookes

Abbey church dating from 14th century.

Location: OS Ref. ST798 024. 3½ m N of A354. Between Dorchester/Blandford Road.

Open: Abbey Church: daily 10am - 6pm. Groups by arrangement please.

Admission: By donation except Easter & mid-Jul - end Aug. Adult £2, Child Free.

MINTERNE GARDENS

Minterne Magna, Nr Dorchester, Dorset DT2 7AU

Owner/Contact: The Lord Digby

Tel: 01300 341370   **Fax:** 01300 341747

If you want to visit a formal garden, do not go to Minterne, but if you want to wander peacefully through 20 wild woodland acres, where magnolias, rhododendrons, eucryphias, hydrangeas, water plants and water lilies, provide a new vista at each turn and where ducks enhance the small lakes and cascades, then you will be welcome at Minterne, the home of the Churchill and Digby families for 350 years. The house which contains magnificent Churchill tapestries and naval and other historical pictures is open for organised groups only which may be arranged by prior appointment.

Location: OS Ref. ST660 042. On A352 Dorchester/Sherborne Rd, 2m N of Cerne Abbas.

Open: 1 Mar - 10 Nov: daily, 10am - 7pm.

Admission: Adult £3, accompanied children Free.

Unsuitable. In grounds on leads.

ST CATHERINE'S CHAPEL

Abbotsbury, Dorset

Tel: 0117 9750700

Owner: English Heritage   **Contact:** The South West Regional Office

A small stone chapel, set on a hilltop, with an unusual roof and small turret used as a lighthouse.

Location: OS Ref. SY572 848. ½ m S of Abbotsbury by pedestrian track to the hilltop.

Open: Any reasonable time, daylight hours.

Admission: Free.

SANDFORD ORCAS MANOR HOUSE

Sandford Orcas, Sherborne, Dorset DT9 4SB

Tel: 01963 220206

Owner/Contact: Sir Mervyn Medlycott Bt

Tudor manor house with gatehouse, fine panelling, furniture, pictures. Terraced gardens with topiary and herb garden. Personal conducted tour by owner.

Location: OS Ref. ST623 210. 2½ m N of Sherborne, Dorset 4m S of A303 at Sparkford. Entrance next to church.

Open: Easter Mon, 10am - 5pm. May & Jul - Sept: Suns & Mons, 2 - 5pm.

Admission: Adult £3, Child £1.50. Groups (10+): Adult £2.50, Child £1.

Unsuitable. Obligatory. In grounds, on leads.

English Heritage Photo Library

PORTLAND CASTLE

CASTLETOWN, PORTLAND, WEYMOUTH, DORSET DT5 1AZ

www.english-heritage.org.uk/visits

Tel: 01305 820539   **Fax:** 01305 860853   **e-mail:** customers@english-heritage.org.uk

Owner: English Heritage   **Contact:** The Custodian

Discover one of Henry VIII's finest coastal fortresses. Perfectly preserved in a waterfront location overlooking Portland harbour, it is a marvellous place to visit for all the family whatever the weather. You can try on armour, explore the Tudor kitchen and gun platform, see ghostly sculptured figures from the past, enjoy the superb battlement views or picnic on the lawn in front of the Captain's House. An excellent new audio tour, included in the admission charge, brings the castle's history and characters to life. Visit the new 'Contemporary Heritage' Garden.

Location: OS Ref. SY684 743. Overlooking Portland harbour.

Open: 1 Apr - 31 Oct: daily, 10am - 6pm (5pm in Oct). 1 Nov - 31 Mar: Fri - Sun, 10am - 4pm. Closed 24/26 Dec & 1 Jan. Times subject to change April 2004.

Admission: Adult £3.50, Child £1.80, Conc. £2.60. 15% discount for groups (11+). Prices subject to change April 2004.

Captain's House & ground floor. WCs. Tel for details.

SHERBORNE CASTLE

SHERBORNE, DORSET DT9 5NR

www.sherbornecastle.com

Tel: 01935 813182   **Fax:** 01935 816727   **e-mail:** enquiries@sherbornecastle.com

Owner: Mr & Mrs John Wingfield Digby   **Contact:** Castle & Events Manager

Built by Sir Walter Raleigh in 1594, Sherborne Castle has been the home of the Digby family since 1617. Prince William of Orange was entertained here in 1688, and George III visited in 1789. Splendid collections of art, furniture and porcelain are on view in the Castle. Lancelot 'Capability' Brown created the lake in 1753 and gave Sherborne the very latest in landscape gardening.

Location: OS Ref. ST649 164. ¾ m SE of Sherborne town centre. Follow brown signs from A30 or A352. ½ m S of the Old Castle.

Open: 1 Apr - 31 Oct: Castle, Gardens, Shop & Tearoom: daily except Mon & Fri (open BH Mons) 11am - 4.30pm (last admission). Castle open Sats, 2.30 - 4.30pm (last admission). Groups (15+) by arrangement during normal opening hours. Private views on other days if possible.

Admission: Castle & Gardens: Adult £7, Child (0-15yrs) Free (max 4 accompanied by adult), OAP £6.50. Groups (15+): Adult/OAP £6.25, Child (0-15yrs) £3. Private View (15+): Adult/OAP £8, Child £4. Gardens only: Adult/OAP £3.50, Child (0-15yrs) Free (max 4 accompanied by adult), no concessions or group rates for gardens only. Discounted joint entry ticket available for Old & New Castles and grounds only.

Partial. By arrangement. In grounds, on leads. Tel for details.

SHERBORNE OLD CASTLE

Castleton, Sherborne, Dorset DT9 3SA

Tel/Fax: 01935 812730 **e-mail:** customers@english-heritage.org.uk
www.english-heritage.org.uk/visits

Owner: English Heritage **Contact:** The Custodian

The ruins of this early 12th century Castle are a testament to the 16 days it took Cromwell to capture it during the Civil War, after which it was abandoned. A gatehouse, some graceful arcading and decorative windows survive.

Location: OS Ref. ST647 167. ½ m E of Sherborne off B3145. ½ m N of the 1594 Castle.

Open: 1 Apr - 31 Oct: daily, 10am - 6pm (5pm in Oct). Closed in winter. Times subject to change April 2004.

Admission: Adult £2, Child £1, Conc. £1.50. 15% discount for groups of 11+. Prices subject to change April 2004.

⬜ ♿ Grounds. 🖰 P Limited for cars. No coach parking. ✖

SMEDMORE HOUSE

Smedmore, Kimmeridge, Wareham BH20 5PG

Tel/Fax: 01929 480719

Owner: Dr Philip Mansel **Contact:** Mr B Belsten

The home of the Mansel family for nearly 400 years nestles at the foot of the Purbeck hills looking across Kimmeridge Bay to Portland Bill.

Location: OS Ref. SY924 787. 15m SW of Poole.

Open: 30 May & 5 Sept: 2 - 5pm.

Admission: Adult £3.50, under 16s Free.

Athelhampton, Dorset from the book *Historic Family Homes and Gardens from the Air*, see page 54.

WHITE MILL

Sturminster Marshall, Nr Wimborne, Dorset BH21 4BX

Tel: 01258 858051 **www**.nationaltrust.org.uk

Owner: The National Trust **Contact:** The Custodian

Rebuilt in 1776 on a site marked as a mill in the Domesday Book, this substantial corn mill was extensively repaired in 1994 and still retains its original elm and applewood machinery (now too fragile to be operative). Peaceful setting with nearby riverside picnic area.

Location: OS Ref. ST958 006. On River Stour ½ m NE of Sturminster Marshall from the B3082 Blandford to Wimborne Rd, take road to SW signposted Sturminster Marshall. Mill is 1m on right. Car park nearby.

Open: 27 Mar - 24 Oct: Sats, Suns & BH Mons, 12 noon - 5pm. Admission by guided tour only.

Admission: Adult £2.80, Child £1.80. Groups by arrangement.

ⓘ No WC. ♿ Ground floor. 🎦 Obligatory. P
✖ Under close control in grounds and car park.

WOLFETON HOUSE

Nr Dorchester, Dorset DT2 9QN

Tel: 01305 263500 **Fax:** 01305 265090
e-mail: kthimbleby@wolfeton.freeserve.co.uk

Owner: Capt N T L L Thimbleby **Contact:** The Steward

A fine mediaeval and Elizabethan manor house lying in the water-meadows near the confluence of the rivers Cerne and Frome. It was much embellished around 1580 and has splendid plaster ceilings, fireplaces and panelling of that date. To be seen are the Great Hall, Stairs and Chamber, Parlour, Dining Room, Chapel and Cyder House. The mediaeval Gatehouse has two unmatched and older towers. There are good pictures and furniture.

Location: OS Ref. SY678 921. 1½ m from Dorchester on the A37 towards Yeovil. Indicated by Historic House signs.

Open: June - Sept: Mons, Weds & Thurs, 2 - 5.30pm. Groups by appointment throughout the year.

Admission: £4.

🍽 By arrangement. ♿ Ground floor. 🖰 By arrangement. 🎦 By arrangement. P
✖ ❄

Topiary

— where evergreen shrubs and trees such as box, privet, yew, and whitethorn are clipped into shapes such as pyramids, cones, balls, birds or animals. Used by the Elizabethans and Jacobeans in their planting schemes, topiary is still extremely popular with today's gardeners.
Visit Athelhampton House & Gardens, Dorset, Levens Hall, Cumbria, Haddon Hall, Derbyshire, Mapperton, Dorset, Danny, Sussex, Kimberley Hall, Norfolk, Sudeley Castle and Rodmarton Manor, Gloucestershire and Packwood, Warwickshire.

Athelhampton, Dorset from the book *Historic Family Homes and Gardens from the Air*, see page 54.

Map 2

Owner:
Mr R J G Berkeley

BERKELEY CASTLE 🏛

BERKELEY

Not many can boast of having their private house celebrated by Shakespeare nor of having held it in the possession of their family for nearly 850 years, nor having a King of England murdered within its walls, nor of having welcomed at their table the local vicar and Castle Chaplain, John Trevisa (1342-1402), reputed as one of the earliest translators of the Bible, nor of having a breach battered by Oliver Cromwell, which to this day it is forbidden by law to repair even if it was wished to do so. But such is the story of Berkeley.

This beautiful and historic Castle, begun in 1117, still remains the home of the famous family who gave their name to numerous locations all over the world, notably Berkeley Square in London, Berkeley Hundred in Virginia and Berkeley University in California. Scene of the brutal murder of Edward II in 1327 (visitors can see his cell and

nearby the dungeon) and besieged by Cromwell's troops in 1645, the Castle is steeped in history but twenty-four generations of Berkeleys have gradually transformed a Norman fortress into the lovely home it is today.

The State Apartments contain magnificent collections of furniture, rare paintings by primarily English and Dutch masters, and tapestries. Part of the world-famous Berkeley silver is on display in the Dining Room. Many other rooms are equally interesting including the Great Hall upon which site the Barons of the West Country met in 1215 before going to Runnymede to force King John to put his seal to the Magna Carta.

The Castle is surrounded by lovely terraced Elizabethan Gardens with a lily pond, Elizabeth I's bowling green, and sweeping lawns.

▶ CONTACT

The Custodian
Berkeley Castle
Gloucestershire
GL13 9BQ

Tel: 01453 810332
Fax: 01453 512995
e-mail: info@berkeley-castle.com

▶ LOCATION

OS Ref. ST685 990

SE side of Berkeley village. Midway between Bristol & Gloucester, 2m W off the A38.

From motorway M5/J14 (5m) or J13 (9m).

▶ OPENING TIMES

1 April - 2 October*
Tues - Sat & BH Mons,
11am - 4pm,
Sun, 2 - 5pm.

3 - 31 October
Sundays only, 2 - 5pm.

The Butterfly House
will be closed
throughout October.

* Except for weekends of 24/25 July and 31 July/1 August: entry via the mediaeval festival Joust event only.

NB. Groups must book.

▶ ADMISSION

Global Ticket including Castle, Gardens & Butterfly House

Adult	£7.00
Child	£4.00
OAP	£5.50
Family (2+2)	£18.50

Groups (25+ pre-booked)

Adult	£6.50
Child	£3.50
OAP	£5.00

Gardens & Butterfly House
(Tuesdays & Fridays only)

Adult	£4.00
Child	£2.00

Butterfly House

Adult	£2.00
Child	£1.00

Season Tickett

Adult	£20.00
Child	£10.00
OAP	£14.00
Family (2+2)	£45.00

CONFERENCE/FUNCTION

ROOM	MAX CAPACITY
Great Hall	150
Long Drawing Rm	100

Fashion shows and filming. Butterfly House. No photography inside the Castle.

Wedding receptions and corporate entertainment.

Visitors may alight in the Outer Bailey.

Licensed. Serving lunches and home-made teas.

Free. Max. 120 people. Tour time: One hour. Evening groups by arrangement. Group visits must be booked.

P Cars 150yds from Castle and 15 coaches 250yds away.

Welcome. General and social history and architecture.

CHAVENAGE

TETBURY

www.chavenage.com

Map 2

Owner:

Mr David Lowsley-Williams

▶ **CONTACT**

D Lowsley-Williams or Caroline Lowsley-Williams Chavenage Tetbury Gloucestershire GL8 8XP

Tel: 01666 502329
Fax: 01453 836778
e-mail: info@ chavenage.com

▶ **LOCATION**

OS Ref. ST872 952

Less than 20m from M4/J16/17 or 18. 1¾ m NW of Tetbury between the B4014 & A4135. Signed from Tetbury. Less than 15m from M5/J13 or 14. Signed from A46 (Stroud - Bath road)

Rail: Kemble Station 7m.

Taxi: Martin Cars 01666 503611.

Air: Bristol 35m. Birmingham 70m. Grass airstrip on farm.

Chavenage is a wonderful Elizabethan house of mellow grey Cotswold stone and tiles which contains much of interest for the discerning visitor.

The approach aspect of Chavenage is virtually as it was left by Edward Stephens in 1576. Only two families have owned Chavenage; the present owners since 1891 and the Stephens family before them. A Colonel Nathaniel Stephens, MP for Gloucestershire during the Civil War was cursed for supporting Cromwell, giving rise to legends of weird happenings at Chavenage since that time.

Inside Chavenage there are many interesting rooms housing tapestries, fine furniture, pictures and many relics of the Cromwellian period. Of particular note are the Main Hall, where a contemporary screen forms a minstrels' gallery and two tapestry rooms where it is said Cromwell was lodged.

Recently Chavenage has been used as a location for TV and film productions including a Hercule Poirot story *The Mysterious Affair at Styles*, many episodes of the sequel to *Are you Being Served* now called *Grace & Favour*, a *Gotcha* for *The Noel Edmonds' House Party*, episodes of *The House of Elliot* and *Casualty*, in 1997/98 *Berkeley Square* and *Cider with Rosie* and in 2002 the US series *Relic Hunter* III.

Chavenage is especially suitable for those wishing an intimate, personal tour, usually conducted by the owner, or for groups wanting a change from large establishments. Meals for pre-arranged groups have proved hugely popular. It also provides a charming venue for small conferences and functions.

▶ **OPENING TIMES**

Summer

May - September
Easter Sun, Mon
& BHs, 2 - 5pm.

Thurs & Suns
2 - 5pm.

NB. Will open on any day and at other times by prior arrangement for groups.

Winter

October - March
By appointment only for groups.

▶ **ADMISSION**

Tours are inclusive in the following prices.

Summer

Adult £5.00
Child (5 - 16 yrs)....... £2.50

CONCESSIONS

By prior arrangement, concessions may be given to groups of 40+ and also to disabled and to exceptional cases.

Winter

Groups only:
Rates by arrangement.

ℹ️ Clay pigeon shooting, archery, cross-bows, pistol shooting, ATV driving, small fashion shows, concerts, plays, seminars, filming, product launching, photography. No casual photography in house.

🍴 Corporate entertaining. In-house catering for drinks parties, dinners, wedding receptions. Telephone for details.

♿ Partial. WC.

☕ Lunches, teas, dinners and picnics by arrangement.

🚶 By owner. Large groups given a talk prior to viewing. Couriers/group leaders should arrange tour format prior to visit.

🅿️ Up to 100 cars. 2 - 3 coaches (by appointment). Coaches access from A46 (signposted) or from Tetbury via the B4014, enter the back gates for coach parking area.

🪑 Chairs can be arranged for lecturing. Tour of working farm, modern dairy and corn facilities can be arranged.

🐕 In grounds on leads. Guide dogs only in house. ❄️

CONFERENCE/FUNCTION

ROOM	SIZE	MAX CAPACITY
Ballroom	70' x 30'	120
Oak Room	25' x 20'	30

Sabina Rüber

SUDELEY CASTLE 🏛

WINCHCOMBE

www.sudeleycastle.co.uk

Owner:
Lady Ashcombe

CONTACT

The Secretary
Sudeley Castle
Winchcombe
Nr Cheltenham
Gloucestershire
GL54 5JD

Tel: 01242 602308
Fax: 01242 602959

e-mail: marketing@
sudeley.org.uk

LOCATION
OS Ref. SP032 277

8m NE of Cheltenham,
at Winchcombe
off B4632.

From Bristol or
Birmingham M5/J9.
Take A46 then B4077
towards Stow-on-the-Wold.

Bus: Castleways to
Winchcombe.

Rail: Cheltenham
Station 8m.

Air: Birmingham or
Bristol 45m.

Sudeley Castle, home of Lord and Lady Ashcombe and the Dent-Brocklehurst family, is one of England's great historic houses with royal connections stretching back 1000 years. Once the property of King Ethelred the Unready, Sudeley was later the magnificent palace of Queen Katherine Parr, Henry VIII's sixth wife, who is buried in St Mary's Church, in the grounds. Henry VIII, Anne Boleyn, Lady Jane Grey and Elizabeth I all visited Sudeley. King Charles I stayed here and his nephew, Prince Rupert established it as his headquarters during the Civil War.

During the 19th century a programme of reconstruction, under the aegis of Sir George Gilbert Scott, restored Sudeley for its new owners, the Dent brothers. The interiors were largely furnished with pieces bought by the Dents at the famous Strawberry Hill sale, when the contents of Horace Walpole's house were sold.

Surrounding the Castle are the enchanting award-winning gardens that have gained international recognition. Highlights include the Queens Garden, famous for its topiary and collection of old fashioned roses, the semi-Mediterranean planting in the Secret Garden, the intricate Tudor Knot Garden and the Tithe Barn. During 2004 visitors will be able to enjoy the tranquillity of the new East Garden.

The Castle Apartments house an impressive collection of furniture and paintings and some interesting Civil War memorabilia. A costume exhibition – 'Six Wives at Sudeley' – has recreated the elaborate, jewel-encrusted royal robes of Henry VIII and his Queens whilst the 'Lace and Times of Emma Dent' reflects the wide ranging interests of the Castle's Victorian chatelaine. A new exhibition based on Shackleton's expeditions is planned for 2004, along with a Pheasantry and Wildfowl area.

▶ **OPENING TIMES**

Summer

**Gardens, Shop &
Plant Centre**
6 March - 31 October
Daily: 10.30am - 5.30pm.

**Castle Apartments
& Church**
27 March - 31 October
Daily: 11am - 5pm.

Restaurant
27 March - 31 October
Daily: 10.30am - 5pm.

Winter
Groups by appointment.

▶ **ADMISSION**
Castle & Gardens
Adult £6.85
Child (5-15 yrs.) £3.85
Conc £5.85
Family (2+2)............ £18.50
Groups (20+)
Adult £5.85
Child (5-15 yrs.) £3.85
Conc £4.85

Gardens
Adult £5.50
Child (5-15 yrs.) £3.25
Conc £4.50

Adventure Playground
Child (5-15 yrs.)........... £1.50

Seasonal pricing will apply
on Suns and BHs between
2 May - 31 Aug.

ℹ️ Photography and filming by prior arrangement, concerts, corporate events and conferences. Product launches and activity days. Sudeley reserves the right to close part or all of the Castle, gardens and grounds and to amend information as necessary.

🍴 Corporate and private events, wedding receptions.

♿ Partial access to the grounds. WC.

🍽 Licensed restaurant.

👣 Special interest tours can be arranged.

🅿 1,000 cars. Meal vouchers, free access for coach drivers.

🏠 13 holiday cottages for 2 - 5 occupants.

🔔 Tel for details.

CONFERENCE/FUNCTION	
ROOM	MAX CAPACITY
Chandos Hall	80
Library	80
Banquet Hall & Pavilion	150

BERKELEY CASTLE 🏛

See page 229 for full page entry.

BLACKFRIARS PRIORY ⌗
Ladybellegate Street, Gloucester
Tel: 0117 9750700
Owner: English Heritage   **Contact:** The South West Regional Office
A small Dominican priory church converted into a rich merchant's house at the Dissolution. Most of the original 13th century church remains, including a rare scissor-braced roof.
Location: OS Ref. SO830 186. In Ladybellegate St, Gloucester, off Southgate Street and Blackfriars Walk.
Open: Restricted, access by guided tour only (Jul & Aug: weekends). Please contact the South West Regional Office.
Admission: Free.
🅿

Marianne Majerus

BOURTON HOUSE GARDEN 🏛
BOURTON-ON-THE-HILL GL56 9AE
www.bourtonhouse.com

Tel: 01386 700754   **Fax:** 01386 701081   **e-mail:** cd@bourtonhouse.com
Owner/Contact: Mr & Mrs Richard Paice

Exciting 3 acre garden surrounding a delightful 18th century Cotswold manor house and 16th century tithe barn. Featuring flamboyant borders, imaginative topiary, a unique shade house, a profusion of herbaceous and exotic plants and, not least, a myriad of magically planted pots.The mood is friendly and welcoming, the atmosphere tranquil yet inspiring. The garden... "positively fizzes with ideas". There are a further 7 of parkland where young trees progress apace. 'The Gallery' features contemporary art, craft and design in the tithe barn.
Location: OS Ref. SP180 324. 1¼ m W of Moreton-in-Marsh on A44.
Open: 26 May - 31 Aug: Wed - Fri; Sept - Oct: Thur & Fri. Also 30/31 May & 29/30 Aug (BH Sun & Mon). 10am - 5pm.
Admission: Adult £4.50, Child Free.
🖭 🚻 ♿Partial. 🖤 🅵By arrangement. 🅿Limited for coaches. 🐾

CHAVENAGE 🏛

See page 230 for full page entry.

NTPL / Ian Shaw

CHEDWORTH ROMAN VILLA 🦋
YANWORTH, CHELTENHAM, GLOS GL54 3JL
www.nationaltrust.org.uk

Tel: 01242 890256   **Fax:** 01242 890909   **e-mail:** chedworth@nationaltrust.org.uk
Owner: The National Trust   **Contact:** The Property Manager
The remains of one of the largest Romano-British villas in the country, set in a woodland Cotswold coombe. Over one mile of walls survives and there are several fine mosaics, two bath-houses, hypocausts, a water-shrine and latrine. Excavated in 1864, the site still has a Victorian atmosphere and the site museum houses objects from the villa. A 15 minute audio-visual presentation gives visitors an insight into the history of this fascinating place. What's new in 2004: Family activity packs.
Location: OS Ref. SP053 135. 3m NW of Fossebridge on Cirencester - Northleach road A429 via Yanworth or from A436 via Withington. Coaches must avoid Withington.
Open: 28 Feb - 26 Mar: Tues - Sun, 11am - 4pm. 27 Mar - 24 Oct: Tues - Sun, 10am - 5pm; 26 Oct - 14 Nov: Tues - Sun, 11am - 4pm. Open BH Mons. Shop open as Villa.
Admission: Adult £4.10, Child £2, Family(2+3) £10.20. Booked group tours (max 30 per guide): Schools £15, others £30.
🖭 ♿Partial. WC. 🅵By arrangement. 🅿 🖭Adult £1.20, Child 80p.
🖤 By arrangement. 🐾 ♿Tel for details.

NT Photographic Library: Ian Shaw

DYRHAM PARK 🦋
Nr CHIPPENHAM SN14 8ER
www.nationaltrust.org.uk

Tel: 01179 372501   **Fax:** 01179 371353   **e-mail:** dyrhampark@nationaltrust.org.uk
Owner: The National Trust   **Contact:** The Property Manager
Dyrham Park was built between 1691 and 1702 for William Blathwayt, William III's Secretary at War and Secretary of State. The rooms have changed little since they were furnished by Blathwayt and their contents are recorded in his housekeeper's inventory. Many fine textiles and paintings, as well as items of blue-and-white Delftware. Restored Victorian domestic rooms open, including kitchen, bells passage, bakehouse, larders, tenants' hall and Delft-tiled dairy.
Location: OS Ref. ST743 757. 8m N of Bath, 12m E of Bristol. Approached from Bath - Stroud road (A46), 2m S of Tormarton interchange with M4/J18.
Open: House: 26 Mar - 31 Oct: Fri - Tue, 12 noon - 5pm, last admission 4.15pm. Garden: as house, 11am - 5.30pm (dusk if earlier). Park: daily (closed 25 Dec), 11am - 5.30pm (dusk if earlier). Contact property for winter opening times.
Admission: Adult £8.30, Child £4.10, Family £20.50. Garden & Park only: Adult £3.20, Child £1.60, Family £7.30. Park only (on days when house & garden closed): Adult £2.10, Child £1.
🖭 ♿Partial. 🍴Licensed. 🅵Mons, 11.30am (max 20) 🖭House. 🅿 🖤
🐾 Only in dog-walking area. ✳ ♿Tel for details.

FRAMPTON COURT

FRAMPTON-ON-SEVERN, GLOUCESTERSHIRE GL2 7EU

www.framptoncourtestate.uk.com

Tel: 01452 740267 **Fax:** 01452 740698 **e-mail:** clifford.fce@farming.co.uk

Owner/Contact: Mr & Mrs P R H Clifford

Listed Grade I, school of Vanburgh. 1732. Stately family home of the Cliffords who have lived at Frampton since granted land by William the Conqueror, 1066. Panelled throughout. Period furniture. The famous botanical paintings of The Frampton Flora can be viewed. Fine views over parkland to extensive lake. A famous gothic orangery stands in the garden reflected in a Dutch ornamental canal. The Orangery is available for self-catering holidays.

Location: OS Ref. SO750 078. In Frampton, 1/4 m SW of B4071, 3m NW of M5/J13.

Open: By arrangement.

Admission: House & Garden: £4.50.

No photography in house. Unsuitable. Obligatory. Limited for coaches. In grounds, on leads. En suite. Bed & Breakfast £45 to £50. Tel for details.

FRAMPTON MANOR

Frampton-on-Severn, Gloucestershire GL2 7EU

Fax: 01452 740698

Owner: Mr & Mrs P R H Clifford **Contact:** Mrs P R H Clifford

Medieval/Elizabethan timber-framed manor house with walled garden. Reputed 12th century birthplace of 'Fair Rosamund' Clifford, mistress of King Henry II. Wool barn c1560 and 16th century dovecote.

Location: OS Ref. SO748 080. 3m M5/J13.

Open: House & Garden: open throughout the year by written appointment. Garden: 1 May - 17 Jul: Mons, 2 - 5pm.

Admission: House, Garden & Wool barn: £4.50. Garden only: £2. Wool barn only £1.

GLOUCESTER CATHEDRAL

Chapter Office, College Green, Gloucester GL1 2LR

Tel: 01452 508211 **Fax:** 01452 300469

e-mail: lin@gloucestercathedral.org.uk **www**.gloucestercathedral.org.uk

Contact: Mrs L Henderson

Daily worship and rich musical tradition continue in this abbey church founded 1300 years ago. It has a Norman nave with massive cylindrical pillars, a magnificent east window with medieval glass and glorious fan-vaulted cloisters. You can also find the tombs of King Edward II and Robert, Duke of Normandy.

Location: OS Ref. SO832 188. Off Westgate Street in central Gloucester.

Open: Daily, 8am until after Evensong. Groups must book via the Chapter Office.

Admission: £3 donation requested.

Partial. WC. Licensed. By arrangement. None. In grounds, on leads.

HAILES ABBEY

Nr Winchcombe, Cheltenham, Gloucestershire GL54 5PB

Tel/Fax: 01242 602398 **e-mail:** customers@english-heritage.org.uk

www.english-heritage.org.uk/visits

Owner: English Heritage & The National Trust **Contact:** The Custodian

Seventeen cloister arches and extensive excavated remains in lovely surroundings of an abbey founded by Richard, Earl of Cornwall, in 1246. There is a small museum and covered display area.

Location: OS Ref. SP050 300. 2m NE of Winchcombe off B4632. 1/2 m SE of B4632.

Open: 1 Apr - 31 Oct: daily, 10am - 6pm (5pm in Oct). Closed in winter. Times subject to change April 2004.

Admission: Adult £3, Child £1.50, Conc. £2.30. Prices subject to change April 2004.

Partial. WC. In grounds, on leads. Tel for details.

NTPL / Nick Meers

HIDCOTE MANOR GARDEN

CHIPPING CAMPDEN, GLOUCESTERSHIRE GL55 6LR

www.nationaltrust.org.uk/hidcote

Tel: 01386 438333 **Fax:** 01386 438817 **e-mail:** hidcote@nationaltrust.org.uk

Owner: The National Trust **Contact:** The Property Manager

One of the most delightful gardens in England, created in the early 20th century by the great horticulturist Major Lawrence Johnston; a series of small gardens within the whole, separated by walls and hedges of different species; famous for rare shrubs, trees, herbaceous borders, 'old' roses and interesting plant species.

Location: OS Ref. SP176 429. 4m NE of Chipping Campden, 1m E of B4632 off B4081. At Mickleton 1/4 m E of Kiftsgate Court.

Open: 27 Mar - 31 Oct: Sat - Wed, 10.30am - 6pm (from 4 Oct closes at 5pm), last admission 1hr before closing. Open Good Fri.

Admission: Adult £6.20, Child £3.10, Family (2+3) £15.20. Groups (15+) Adult £5.60, Child £2.50.

Limited. WC. Licensed. Send SAE for details.

HORTON COURT

Horton, Nr Chipping Sodbury, Bristol, South Gloucestershire BS37 6QR

Tel: 01179 372501 **www**.nationaltrust.org.uk

Owner: The National Trust **Contact:** Lacock Estate Office

A Norman Hall and an exceptionally fine detached ambulatory are all that remain of what is probably the oldest rectory in England.

Location: OS Ref. ST766 849. 3m NE of Chipping Sodbury, 3/4 m N of Horton, 1m W of A46 (Bath-Stroud road).

Open: 31 Mar - 30 Oct (closed 12 Jun): Wed & Sat, 2 - 6pm or dusk if earlier. Other times by written appointment with tenant. Unsuitable for coach tours.

Admission: Adult £2.20, Child £1.10, Family (2+2) £5.60.

No WC. Partial.

Nigel Fisher

KELMSCOTT MANOR
KELMSCOTT, Nr LECHLADE, GLOUCESTERSHIRE GL7 3HJ

www.kelmscottmanor.co.uk

Tel: 01367 252486 **Fax:** 01367 253754 **e-mail:** admin@kelmscottmanor.co.uk

Owner: Society of Antiquaries **Contact:** Property Manager

Kelmscott Manor, a Grade I listed Tudor farmhouse adjacent to the River Thames, was the summer house of William Morris from 1871 until his death in 1896. Morris loved the house as a work of true craftsmanship, totally unspoilt and unaltered, and in harmony with the village and the surrounding countryside. He considered it so natural in its setting as to be almost organic, it looked to him as if it had 'grown up out of the soil', and with 'quaint garrets amongst great timbers of the roof where of old times the tillers and herdsmen slept'. The house contains an outstanding collection of the possessions and work of Morris and his associates, including furniture, original textiles, carpets and ceramics. The Manor is surrounded by beautiful gardens with barns, dovecote, a meadow and a stream. The garden was a constant source of inspiration for Morris and the images are reflected in his textile and wallpaper designs. William Morris called the village of Kelmscott: 'a heaven on earth'. His delight in its discovery can still be felt by the visitor today. The Manor is the most evocative of all the houses associated with William Morris.

Location: OS Ref. SU252 988. At SE end of the village, 2m due E of Lechlade, off the Lechlade - Faringdon Road.

Open: Apr - Sept: Weds, 11am - 5pm. 3rd Sat in Apr, May, Jun & Sept, also 1st & 3rd Sat in July & Aug, 2 - 5pm. Last entry 30 min prior to closing. Private visits for groups on Thurs & Fris. Please note house only closed on Weds, 1 - 2pm.

Admission: Adult £8.50, Child/Student £4.25.

⬚ ⊤ ♿Grounds. WCs. ▶Licensed. ♿By arrangement. ℗Limited for coaches. ✖

KIFTSGATE COURT GARDENS
CHIPPING CAMPDEN, GLOUCESTERSHIRE GL55 6LN

www.kiftsgate.co.uk

Tel/Fax: 01386 438777 **e-mail:** kiftsgte@aol.com

Owner: Mr and Mrs J G Chambers **Contact:** Mr J G Chambers

Magnificently situated garden on the edge of the Cotswold escarpment with views towards the Malvern Hills. Many unusual shrubs and plants including tree peonies, abutilons, specie and old-fashioned roses.

Location: OS Ref. SP173 430. 4m NE of Chipping Campden. $\frac{1}{4}$ m W of Hidcote Garden.

Open: Apr, May, Aug, Sept: Wed, Thur & Sun, 2 - 6pm. Jun & Jul: Mon, Wed, Thur, Sat & Sun, 12 noon - 6pm. BH Mons, 2 - 6pm. Coaches by appointment.

Admission: Adult: £5, Child £1.50. Groups (20+) £4.50.

🖼 ▶

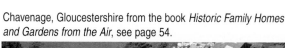

Chavenage, Gloucestershire from the book *Historic Family Homes and Gardens from the Air*, see page 54.

NTPL / Nadia MacKenzie

NTPL / Nadia MacKenzie

LODGE PARK & SHERBORNE ESTATE ❧

SHERBORNE, Nr CHELTENHAM, GLOUCESTERSHIRE GL54 3PP

www.nationaltrust.org.uk/lodgepark

Tel: 01451 844130 **Fax:** 01249 844131 **e-mail:** lodgepark@nationaltrust.org.uk

Owner: The National Trust **Contact:** The Visitor Services Manager

Situated on the picturesque Sherborne Estate in the Cotswolds, Lodge Park was created in 1634 by John 'Crump' Dutton. Inspired by his passion for gambling and banqueting, it is a unique survival of a Grandstand, Deer Course and Park. It was the home of Charles Dutton, 7th Lord Sherborne, until 1983 when he bequeathed his family's estate to The National Trust. The grandstand has been reconstructed to its original form and is the first project of its kind undertaken by the Trust that relies totally on archaeological evidence. The park behind was designed by Charles Bridgeman in 1725. The Sherborne Estate is 1650ha (4000 acres) of rolling Cotswold countryside with sweeping views down to the River Windrush. Much of the village of Sherborne is owned by the Trust, including the post office, shop, school and the social club. There are walks for all ages around the estate, which include the restored and working water meadows.

Location: OS Ref. SP146 123. 3m E of Northleach, approach only from A40. Bus: Swanbrook 53 Oxford-Gloucester, 1m walk from bus stop.

Open: 19 Mar - 31 Oct: Mon, Fri & Sun, 11am - 4pm; Sats, 11am - 3pm. Estate: All year: daily.

Admission: Adult £4.50, Child £2.20, Family £11. Estate: Free to pedestrians.

ℹ Video/slide shows during the day. 🆃 ♿ Partial. 🅿 📷
🐕 Dogs must be kept under close control. 🔺 ♨ Tel for details.

MISARDEN PARK GARDENS 🏛

Stroud, Gloucestershire GL6 7JA

Tel: 01285 821303 **Fax:** 01285 821530 **e-mail:** estate.office@miserdenestate.co.uk

Owner/Contact: Major M T N H Wills

Historic garden dating from 17th century, standing 250m above sea level overlooking the 'Golden Valley'. Terraced lawns, long double herbaceous borders – important yew topiary (some by Lutyens). Fine trees, parterre with roses. Summerhouse and rill. Blue border and scented border. Good nursery adjacent.

Location: OS Ref. SO941 088. 6m NW Cirencester. Follow signs to Miserden from A417 or B4070.

Open: 1 Apr - 30 Sept: Tue - Thur, 10am - 5pm.

Admission: Adult £3.50 (guided tours extra), Child Free, Student £1.75. 10% reduction for pre-arranged groups (20-55).

🆃 ♿ Partial. 🅕 By arrangement. 🅿 Limited for coaches. 🐕

OLD CAMPDEN HOUSE

Church St, Chipping Campden

Tel: 01628 825920/825925 (bookings) **e-mail:** bookings@landmarktrust.co.uk
www.landmarktrust.co.uk

Owner/Contact: The Landmark Trust

The site of Old Campden House, a Scheduled Ancient Monument, is owned and managed by the Landmark Trust, a building preservation charity. The main house was burnt to the ground during the Civil War but other buildings remain. The East and West Banqueting Houses and Almonry have been restored and are let for holidays throughout the year. Full details of Landmark's 178 historic buildings are featured in the Landmark Trust Handbook (price £9.50 refundable against first booking) from the Landmark Trust, Shottesbrooke, Maidenhead, Berkshire, SL6 3SW.

Location: OS Ref. SP156 394. Next to St James's Church in Church Street.

Open: Site open 30 days per year, with buildings open on 8 of these days. Contact the Landmark Trust for dates.

Admission: Free.

🅕 🐕 🛏 Self catering for 6 & 5.

David Brown/National Trust

NEWARK PARK ❧

OZLEWORTH, WOTTON-UNDER-EDGE, GLOUCESTERSHIRE GL12 7PZ

www.nationaltrust.org.uk

Tel/Fax: 01453 842644 **e-mail:** michael@newark98.freeserve.co.uk

Owner: The National Trust **Contact:** Michael Claydon

A Tudor hunting lodge converted into a castellated country house by James Wyatt. An atmospheric house, set in spectacular countryside with outstanding views. Spectacular snowdrop displays in early spring.

Location: OS Ref. GR078 932. 1¹/₂ m E of Wotton-under-Edge, 1³/₄ m S of Junction of A4135 & B4058, follow signs for Ozleworth, House signposted from main road.

Open: 31 Jan - 15 Feb: Sat & Sun, 11am - 5pm. 1 Apr - 27 May: Wed & Thurs, 11am - 5pm. 2 June - 31 Oct: Wed, Thurs, Sat & Sun, 11am - 5pm. Open BH Mons. Closes dusk if earlier.

Admission: Adult £4.50, Child £2.20, Family (2+3) £11. Groups by appointment. No reduction for groups.

ℹ No photography in house. ♿ Partial. 🅕 By arrangement. 🅿 📷
🐕 In grounds, on leads.

OWLPEN MANOR 🏠
Nr ULEY, GLOUCESTERSHIRE GL11 5BZ

www.owlpen.com

Tel: 01453 860261 **Fax:** 01453 860819 **Restaurant:** 01453 860816

e-mail: sales@owlpen.com

Owner: Mr & Mrs Nicholas Mander　　　　　　**Contact:** Julia Webb

Romantic Tudor manor house, 1450-1616, with Cotswold Arts & Crafts associations. Remote wooded valley setting, with 16th and 17th century formal terraced gardens and magnificent yews. Contains unique painted cloth wall hangings, family and Arts & Crafts collections. Mill (1726), Court House (1620); licensed restaurant in medieval Cyder House. Victorian church. "Owlpen - ah, what a dream is there!" - Vita Sackville-West.

Location: OS Ref. ST801 984. 3m E of Dursley, 1m E of Uley, off B4066, by Old Crown pub.

Open: Apr - Sept: Tue - Sun & BH Mons, 2 - 5pm. Restaurant 12 noon - 5pm.

Admission: Adult £4.80, Child (4-14yrs) £2, Family (2+4) £13.50. Gardens and Grounds: Adult £2.80, Child £1. Group rates available.

🆃 🔉Unsuitable. 🍴Licensed. 🅿 🛏Holiday cottages, all seasons, sleep 2 - 9.

PAINSWICK ROCOCO GARDEN 🏠
PAINSWICK, GLOUCESTERSHIRE GL6 6TH

www.rococogarden.co.uk

Tel: 01452 813204 **Fax:** 01452 814888 **e-mail:** paulmoir@rococogarden.co.uk

Owner: Painswick Rococo Garden Trust　　　　　**Contact:** P R Moir

Unique 18th century garden restoration situated in a hidden 6 acre Cotswold combe. Charming contemporary buildings are juxtaposed with winding woodland walks and formal vistas. Famous for its early spring show of snowdrops. Newly planted maze.

Location: OS Ref. SO864 106. 1/2 m NW of village of Painswick on B4073.

Open: 10 Jan - 31 Oct: daily, 11am - 5pm.

Admission: Adult £4, Child £2, OAP £3.50. Family (2+2) £10.50. Free introductory talk for pre-booked groups (20+).

🖼 ⬆ 🔉Partial. WC. 💺Licensed. 🍴 🅿 📷 🛏In grounds, on leads. 🅰 ❄ 💌 Tel for details.

RODMARTON MANOR 🏠
CIRENCESTER, GLOUCESTERSHIRE GL7 6PF

www.rodmarton-manor.co.uk

Tel: 01285 841253 **Fax:** 01285 841298 **e-mail:** simon.biddulph@farming.co.uk

Owner: Mr & Mrs Simon Biddulph　　　　　　**Contact:** Simon Biddulph

One of the last great country houses to be built in the traditional way and containing beautiful furniture, ironwork, china and needlework specially made for the house. The large garden complements the house and contains many areas of great beauty and character including the magnificent herbaceous borders, topiary, roses, rockery and kitchen garden. Rodmarton Manor is available as a film location and for functions.

Location: OS Ref. ST943 977. Off A433 between Cirencester and Tetbury.

Open: House & Garden: 3 May - 30 Aug: Weds, Sats & BHs, 2 - 5pm (Not guided tours). Garden only: Jun & Jul: Mons, 2 - 5pm. Groups please book. Individuals need not book. Guided tours of the house (last about 1hr) may be booked for groups (20+) at other times at any time of the year. Groups fewer than 20 please consider coming on open days as minimum charge (£140) applies. Groups (10+) can visit the garden at other times by appointment and a guided tour can be booked.

Admission: House & Garden: £7, Child (5 -15yrs) £3.50. Garden only: £4, Child (5 -15yrs) £1.

ℹ️Colour guidebook & postcards on sale. No photography in house. WCs in garden. 🔉Garden & ground floor. 💺Most open days and groups by appointment. 🎦By arrangement. 🅿 📷 🛏Guide dogs only.

ST MARY'S CHURCH ⌗

Kempley, Gloucestershire

Tel: 0117 9750700

Owner: English Heritage   **Contact:** The South West Regional Office

A delightful Norman church with superb wall paintings from the 12th - 14th centuries which were only discovered beneath whitewash in 1871.

Location: OS Ref. SO670 313. On minor road. 1½ m SE of Much Marcle, A449.

Open: 1 Apr - 31 Oct: daily, 10am - 6pm. Times subject to change April 2004.

Admission: Free.

SEZINCOTE 🏠

Moreton-in-Marsh, Gloucestershire   GL56 9AW

Tel: 01386 700444

Owner: Mr and Mrs D Peake   **Contact:** Mrs D Peake

Exotic oriental water garden by Repton and Daniell. Large semi-circular orangery. House by S P Cockerell in Indian style was the inspiration for Brighton Pavilion.

Location: OS Ref. SP183 324. 2½ m SW of Moreton-in-Marsh. Turn W along A44 to Broadway and left into gateway just before Bourton-on-the-Hill (opposite the gate to Batsford Park, then 1m drive.

Open: Garden: Thurs, Fris & BH Mons, 2 - 6pm (dusk if earlier) throughout the year except Dec. House: May, Jun, Jul & Sept, Thurs & Fris, 2.30 - 6pm. Groups by written appointment.

Admission: House & Garden £5 (no children in house). Garden: Adult £3.50, Child £1 (under 5yrs Free).

♿ Unsuitable. 🐕 Guide dogs only. ✲

NTPL/ Nick Meers

SNOWSHILL MANOR 🌿

SNOWSHILL, Nr BROADWAY, GLOUCESTERSHIRE   WR12 7JU

www.nationaltrust.org.uk

Tel: 01386 852410   **Fax:** 01386 842822

e-mail: snowshillmanor@nationaltrust.org.uk

Owner: The National Trust   **Contact:** The Property Manager

The terraces and ponds of this Arts and Crafts garden were laid out by Charles Paget Wade as a series of outdoor rooms to complement his Cotswold Manor house. The garden is a lively mix of architectural features, bright colours and delightful scents with stunning views across the Cotswold countryside. Mr Wade's cottage can also be viewed. The house will be closed in 2004 for essential reservicing work – the gardens will remain open.

The Snowshill Costume Collection can be viewed by appointment only at Berrington Hall, please tel: 01568 613720 on Thursdays or Fridays. What's new in 2004: 'Tracker' Activity Pack for children plus events throughout the season.

Location: OS Ref. SP096 339. 3m SW of Broadway, turning off the A44, by Broadway Green.

Open: Gardens, Shop & Restaurant: 19 Mar - 31 Oct: Wed - Sun & BH Mons, 11am - 5.30pm. Also Shop & Restaurant: 6 Nov - 12 Dec: 12 noon - 4pm.

Admission: Gardens, Shop & Restaurant: Adult £3.80, Child £1.90, Family £9.50. Coach & School groups by written appointment only.

📷 ♿Partial. 🍽Licensed. 🐕 📱 Tel for details.

STANWAY HOUSE

& WATER GARDEN 🏠

STANWAY, CHELTENHAM, GLOS   GL54 5PQ

Tel: 01386 584469   **Fax:** 01386 584688   **e-mail:** stanwayhouse@btinternet.com

Owner: Lord Neidpath   **Contact:** Debbie Lewis

"As perfect and pretty a Cotswold manor house as anyone is likely to see" (*Fodor's Great Britain 1998 guidebook*). Stanway's beautiful architecture, furniture, parkland and village are now complemented by the restored 18th century water garden and the magnificent fountain – 165 feet high in 2003, and expected to rise to over 300 feet in 2004, making it the tallest garden fountain and gravity fountain in the world. Tea at the Bakehouse, Beer for sale. Wedding reception venue.

Location: OS Ref. SP061 323. N of Winchcombe, just off B4077.

Open: House & Garden: Jul - Sept: Tue & Thur, 2 - 5pm. Garden: Jul - Sept, Sats only, 2 - 5pm. Private tours by arrangement at other times.

Admission: Adult £6, Child £1.50, OAP £4.50. Garden only: Adult £4, Child £1, OAP £3.

ℹ️ Film & photographic location. Wedding receptions. 📷 🖥 𝑓By arrangement. 🅿 🐕 In grounds on leads. ✲

SUDELEY CASTLE

See page 231 for full page entry.

TRULL HOUSE

nr Tetbury, Gloucestershire GL8 8SQ
Tel/Fax: 01285 841255   **e-mail:** simonmitchell@btconnect.com
Owner/Contact: Simon Mitchell
Trull House is magnificently set in rolling countryside and surrounded by gardens of many sorts amongst splendid trees and shrubs. Large lily pond, sunken garden, wilderness and behind the beautiful house are the walled gardens containing a series of spectacular herbaceous borders. An enormous variety of plants cleverly planted.
Location: OS Ref. ST924 966. Off A433, 3m E of Tetbury & 7m W of Cirencester. Follow signs.
Open: Easter - 1 Sept: Wed, Sat & BHs, 11am - 5pm. Jun: Tue & Fri evenings, 6 - 8pm.
Admission: Adult £3, Child Free. Groups (20+): Adult £2.50, Child Free.
ℹ No commercial photography without consent. 🖼 📷 📞 ♿ 💻
📷 By arrangement. 🅿 ♿

WESTBURY COURT GARDEN

Westbury-on-Severn, Gloucestershire GL14 1PD
Tel: 01452 760461   **e-mail:** westburycourt@nationaltrust.org.uk
www.nationaltrust.org.uk
Owner: The National Trust   **Contact:** The Head Gardener
A formal water garden with canals and yew hedges, laid out between 1696 and 1705; the earliest of its kind remaining in England. Restored in 1971 and planted with species dating from pre-1700 including apple, pear and plum trees.
Location: OS Ref. SO718 138. 9m SW of Gloucester on A48.
Open: 3 Mar - 30 Jun & 1 Sept - 31 Oct: Wed - Sun & BH Mons, 10am - 5pm. 1 Jul - 31 Aug: daily, 10am - 5pm. Other times by appointment. Garden tours: 12 May, 9 Jun, 14 Jul & 11 Aug.
Admission: Adult £3.50, Child £1.70.
🖼 ♿ Grounds largely accessible. WCs. 🅿 💻 Tel for details.

WESTONBIRT ARBORETUM

Tetbury, Gloucestershire GL8 8QS
Tel: 01666 880220   **Fax:** 01666 880559   **www.**forestry.gov.uk/westonbirt
Owner: The Forestry Commission   **Contact:** Mr P Morton
Westonbirt, The National Arboretum, has one of the world's finest collections of trees and shrubs. Over 18,000 specimens spread over 600 acres of beautiful countryside. A fascinating day out at any time of year.
Location: OS Ref. ST856 896. 3m S of Tetbury on the A433.
Open: 365 days a year, 10am - 8pm (or dusk if earlier).
Admission: Adult £6 - £7.50, Child £1, OAP £5 - £6.50.

WHITTINGTON COURT

Whittington, Cheltenham, Gloucestershire GL54 4HF
Tel: 01242 820556   **Fax:** 01242 820218
Owner: Mr & Mrs Jack Stringer   **Contact:** Mrs J Stringer
Elizabethan manor house. Family possessions including ceramics, antique and modern glass, fossils and fabrics.
Location: OS Ref. SP014 206. 4m E of Cheltenham on N side of A40.
Open: 10 - 25 Apr & 14 - 30 Aug: 2 - 5pm.
Admission: Adult £3, Child £1, OAP £2.50.
🖼 🅿

WOODCHESTER MANSION

Stroud, Gloucestershire GL10 3TS
Tel: 01453 750455   **Fax:** 01453 750457   **e-mail:** visitor@woodchestermansion.org.uk
www.woodchestermansion.org.uk
Owner: Woodchester Mansion Trust   **Contact:** David Price
Hidden in a wooded valley near Stroud is one of the most intriguing houses in the country. Woodchester Mansion was started in 1856 but abandoned incomplete in 1870. It offers a unique insight into traditional building techniques. The Trust's repair programme includes courses in stone masonry and building conservation.
Location: OS Ref. SO795 015 (gateway on B4066). 5m S of Stroud on B4066. NW of the village of Nympsfield, then 1m path E from gate.
Open: Easter - Sept: Suns & 1st Sat of every month & BH weekends including Mon. Jul & Aug: Sat & Sun.
Admission: Adult £5, Child (under 14yrs) Free, OAP/NT/Student £4. Groups (10+ people or £60): Adult £6pp. Free minibus service is provided.
🖼 💻 📷 🅿 ♿ Guide dogs only in Mansion.

Stanway House and Water Garden, Gloucestershire.

Norman Hudson

Lawrence Johnston
1871-1948

Born in Paris of American parents, Lawrence Johnston studied at Cambridge University and became a British subject in 1900. Having fought in the Boer War, he came back to England and bought the 280 acre estate of Hidcote. A shy and extremely self-effacing man, unlike many other great garden designers, Johnston did not write about his gardening passion.

Yet Johnston's Hidcote planting plans of breaking up the garden into a series of walks and intimate rooms, has become one of the great garden design schemes of the 20th and 21st centuries. Wander around the gardens at Chelsea Flower Show each year, and you will feel the influence of Johnston.

Visit Hidcote Manor Garden, Gloucestershire, given by Johnston to the National Trust in 1948 to see breathtaking small gardens, separated by walls and hedges of different species.

Garden Designer

MUSEUM OF COSTUME & ASSEMBLY ROOMS

BATH

www.museumofcostume.co.uk

Map 2

Owner:
The National Trust

▶ **CONTACT**

For Room Hire:
Mr Tom Deller
Room Hire Manager
Stall Street
Bath BA1 1LZ

Tel: 01225 477734
Fax: 01225 477476

e-mail: tom_deller@
bathnes.gov.uk

Museum Enquiries:
Tel: 01225 477785
Fax: 01225 477743

▶ **LOCATION**

OS Ref. ST750 648

Near centre of Bath,
10m from M4/J18.
Park & Ride or
public car park.

Rail: Great Western
from London Paddington
(regular service)
90 mins approx.

Air: Bristol airport
45 mins.

The Assembly Rooms in Bath are open to the public daily (free of charge) and are also popular for dinners, dances, concerts, conferences and Civil weddings.

Originally known as the Upper Rooms, they were designed by John Wood the Younger and opened in 1771. The magnificent interior consists of a splendid Ball Room, Tea Room and Card Room, connected by two fine octagonal rooms. This plan was perfect for 'assemblies', evening entertainments popular in the 18th century, which included dancing, music, card-playing and tea drinking. They are now owned by The National Trust and managed by Bath & North East Somerset Council, which runs a full conference service.

The building also houses one of the largest and most comprehensive collections of fashionable dress in the world, the Museum of Costume. Its extensive displays cover the history of fashion from the late 16th century to the present day. Hand-held audioguides allow visitors to learn about the fashions on display while the lighting is kept to levels suitable for fragile garments. The 'Dress of the Year' collection traces significant moments in modern fashion history from 1963. Special exhibition for 2004. *"Jane Austen – Film and Fashion"*. For the serious student of fashion, the reference library and study facilities are available by appointment.

The museum shops sell publications and gifts associated with the history of costume and are open daily to all visitors.

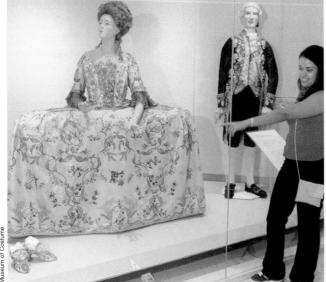

Museum of Costume

ℹ️	Conference facilities.
📖	Extensive book & gift shops.
🏵️	Corporate hospitality. Function facilities.
♿	Suitable. WC.
🚶	Hourly. Individual guided tours by arrangement.
🎧	English, Dutch, French, German, Italian, Japanese, Spanish.
🅿️	Charlotte Street car park.
▪️	Teachers' pack.
🐕	Guide dogs only.
💒	Civil Weddings/ Receptions.
❄️	

▶ **OPENING TIMES**

All Year
January/February &
November/December:
11am - 4pm.
March - October:
11am - 5pm.

Closed 25 & 26 December
Last exit 1hr after closing.

▶ **ADMISSION**

Assembly Rooms ... Free
Museum of Costume:
  Adult £6.00
  Child* £4.00
  OAP £5.00
Groups (20+)
  Adult £5.00
  Child* (summer).... £3.50
  Child* (winter)....... £3.00
  Family (2+4) £16.50
Combined ticket with Roman Baths
  Adult £12.00
  Child* £7.00
  OAP £10.50
  Family (2+4) £31.00
Groups (20+)
  Adult £8.00
  Child* (summer).... £5.00
  Child* (winter)....... £4.20

* Age 6 - 16yrs.
  Child under 6yrs Free

CONFERENCE/FUNCTION

ROOM	SIZE	MAX CAPACITY
Ballroom	103' x 40'	500/310
Octagon	47' x 47'	120/120
Tea Room	58' x 40'	260/170
Card Room	59' x 18'	80/60

Museum of Costume

Bath & North East Somerset Council

Map 2

THE ROMAN BATHS & PUMP ROOM

BATH

www.romanbaths.co.uk

The first stop for any visitor to Bath is the Roman Baths surrounding the hot springs where the city began and which are still its heart. Here you'll see one of the country's finest ancient monuments – the great Roman temple and bathing complex built almost 2000 years ago. Discover the everyday life of the Roman spa and see ancient treasures from the Temple of Sulis Minerva. A host of new interpretive methods bring these spectacular buildings vividly to life and help visitors to understand the extensive remains.

The Grand Pump Room, overlooking the Spring, is the social heart of Bath. The elegant interior of 1795 is something every visitor to Bath should see. You can enjoy a glass of spa water drawn from the fountain, perhaps as an appetiser to a traditional Pump Room tea, morning coffee or lunch. The Pump Room Trio and resident pianists provide live music daily. The Roman Baths shop sells publications and gifts related to the site.

In the evening, the Pump Room is available for banquets, dances and concerts. Nothing could be more magical than a meal on the terrace which overlooks the Great Bath, or a pre-dinner drinks reception by torchlight around the Great Bath itself.

Owner:
Bath & North East
Somerset Council

▶ **CONTACT**
For Room Hire:
Mr Tom Deller
Stall Street
Bath BA1 1LZ
Tel: 01225 477734
Fax: 01225 477476
e-mail: tom_deller@
bathnes.gov.uk

**For visits to
Roman Baths:**
Tel: 01225 477785
Fax: 01225 477743

▶ **LOCATION**
OS Ref. ST750 648

Centre of Bath,
10m from M4/J18. Park
& Ride recommended.

Rail: Great Western
from London
Paddington, half
hourly service,
1 hr 17 mins duration.

CONFERENCE/FUNCTION

ROOM	SIZE	MAX CAPACITY
Great Roman Bath		400 summer 200 winter
Pump Rm.	57' x 41'	180
Terrace overlooking Great Bath	83' x 11'	70
Reception Hall	56' x 44'	100
Smoking Rm & Drawing Rm	28' x 16'	40

Bath & North East Somerset Council

▶ **OPENING TIMES**

January - February:
9.30am - 4.30pm.
March - June: 9am - 5pm.
July - August: 9am - 9pm.
September - October:
9am - 5pm.
November - December:
9.30am - 4.30pm.
Last exit 1 hour after
closing.

Closed 25 & 26 December.

The Pump Room Trio
plays 10am - 12 noon Mon
- Sat and 3 - 5pm Sunday.
During the summer it also
plays from 3 - 5pm, Mon -
Sat. Resident pianists play
at lunch-time.

▶ **ADMISSION**

Adult	£9.00
Child*	£5.00
Family (2+4)	£24.00
OAP	£8.00
Groups (20+)	
Adult	£6.50
Child* (summer)	£3.70
Child* (winter)	£3.20

**Combined ticket with
Museum of Costume,
Bath**

Adult	£12.00
Child*	£7.00
OAP	£10.50
Family (2+4)	£31.00
Groups (20+)	
Adult	£8.00
Child* (summer)	£5.00
Child* (winter)	£4.20

* Age 6 - 17 yrs.

Extensive gift shop.

Award-winning guide book in English, French and German.

Comprehensive service for private and corporate entertainment. The Assembly Rooms, Guildhall, Victoria Art Gallery and Pump Room are all available for private hire, contact the Pump Room.

Free access to terrace. Restricted access to the Museum, special visits for disabled groups by appointment. People with special needs welcome, teaching sessions available.

Pump Room coffees, lunches and teas, no reservation needed. Music by Pump Room Trio or pianist.

Hourly. Private tours by appointment.

English, French, German, Italian, Japanese, Spanish, Dutch.

Teaching sessions available. Pre-booking necessary.

Civil Weddings in two private rooms with photographs around the Great Bath.

Rick Godley

Architects

Colen Campbell

d. 1729

Architect

An architect who took his inspiration from the works of Palladio and Inigo Jones. Look for an austere, plain style of exterior and monumental interiors – but with the occasional baroque flamboyance.

Visit Houghton Hall in Norfolk.

NO 1 ROYAL CRESCENT

BATH BA1 2LR

www.bath-preservation-trust.org.uk

Tel: 01225 428126   **Fax:** 01225 481850   **e-mail:** admin@bptrust.demon.co.uk

Owner: Bath Preservation Trust   **Contact:** Sue Duncan – Administrator

Number 1 was the first house to be built in the Royal Crescent. The house was given to the Bath Preservation Trust in 1968 and both the exterior and interior have been accurately restored. Visitors can see a grand town-house of the late 18th century with authentic furniture, paintings and carpets. In the basement there is a period kitchen and Museum shop.

Location: OS Ref. ST746 653. M4/J18. A46 to Bath. ¼ m NW of city centre.

Open: 10 Feb - 22 Oct: daily except Mons, 10.30am - 5pm. Closed Good Fri. Open BH Mons. 23 Oct - 28 Nov: daily except Mons, 10.30am - 4pm. Also open 4/5 & 11/12 Dec. Last admission 30 mins before closing. Evening tours and other times by arrangement.

Admission: Adult £4, Child (5-16yrs)/Student £3.50, Family £10. Groups: £3.

▣ ♿Unsuitable. 🚶 🅿The Royal Crescent & Bath centre. ▣

English Palladian Architects

Lord Burlington 1694-1753

William Kent 1685-1748

Colen Campbell d 1729

Giacomo Leoni c 1686-1746

Sir Robert Taylor 1714-1788

James Paine 1716-1789

John Carr of York 1723-1807

THE AMERICAN MUSEUM & GARDENS

CLAVERTON MANOR, BATH BA2 7BD

www.americanmuseum.org

Tel: 01225 460503   **Fax:** 01225 469160   **e-mail:** info@americanmuseum.org

Owner: The Trustees of the American Museum in Britain   **Contact:** R Hornshaw

Claverton Manor was built in 1820 by Jeffry Wyattville. In the late 1950s it became the home of the American Museum in Britain. Inside the Manor there are 18 period rooms which show the development of American decorative arts from the 1680s to the 1860s. In addition there are galleries devoted to Folk Art, Native American Art, and our large collection of quilts and other textiles. The extensive grounds contain a replica of part of the garden at Mount Vernon, George Washington's house in Virginia, and an

Arboretum of North American trees and shrubs. Light lunches and teas are available.

Location: OS Ref. ST784 640. 2m SE of Bath city centre.

Open: 20 Mar - 31 Oct: Tues - Sun (open BH Mon in Aug), 12 noon - 5pm. 20 Nov - 15 Dec: Tues - Sun, 1 -4 pm.

Admission: Adult £6.50, Child £4, Conc. £6. Groups (20-100): Adult £5.50, OAP £5.

▣ 🚾 ♿Partial. WC. ▣ 🚶By arrangement. 🅿 ▣ 🐕In grounds, on leads. ▣ Tel for details.

NTPL: Neil Campbell-Sharp

BARRINGTON COURT ✤

BARRINGTON, ILMINSTER, SOMERSET TA19 0NQ

www.nationaltrust.org.uk

Tel: 01460 241938 **e-mail:** barringtoncourt@nationaltrust.org.uk

Owner: The National Trust   **Contact:** Visitor Services Manager

An enchanting formal garden influenced by Gertrude Jekyll and laid out in a series of walled rooms, including the White Garden, the Rose and Iris Garden and the Lily Garden. The working Kitchen Garden has espaliered apple, pear and plum trees trained along high stone walls. The Tudor manor house was restored in the 1920s by the Lyle family. It is let to Stuart Interiors as showrooms with antique furniture for sale, thereby offering NT visitors a different kind of visit.

Location: OS Ref. ST395 181. In Barrington village, 5m NE of Ilminster, on B3168.

Open: 4 Mar - 28 Mar & Oct: Thur - Sun, 11am - 4.30pm. 1 Apr - 30 Sept: Thurs - Tues, 11am - 5.30pm. Open BH Mons. Restuarant (last orders 1hr before closing) & Shop as House & Garden. Coach groups by appointment only.

Admission: Adult £5.50, Child £2.50, Family (2+3) £13.50. Groups: £4.80.

🗓 ⚘ ♿Grounds. WC. Braille Guide. 🅿 ■ 💷Licensed. ♨Tel for details.

THE CHALICE WELL & GARDENS

CHILKWELL STREET, GLASTONBURY, SOMERSET BA6 8DD

www.chalicewell.org.uk

Tel: 01458 831154 **Fax:** 01458 835528 **e-mail:** info@chalicewell.org.uk

Owner: Chalice Well Trust   **Contact:** Michael Orchard

A jewel of a garden, nestling around one of Britain's oldest Holy Wells. Legend tells of the Well being visited by Joseph of Arimethea, bearing the Chalice of the Last Supper, and of King Arthur on his Grail Quest. Today, the beautifully landscaped grounds with the iron-rich waters are a haven of peace and tranquillity.

Location: OS Ref. ST507 384. On the A361 Glastonbury - Shepton Mallet road, at the foot of Glastonbury Tor.

Open: All year: 1 Apr - 31 Oct: 10am - 6pm; Nov, Feb & Mar: 11am - 5pm; Dec & Jan: 11am - 4pm.

Admission: Adult £2.60, Child £1.30.

ℹ️No smoking in gardens. 🗓 ♿ 𝒇By arrangement. 🅿Limited. At nearby Rural Life Museum. ■ 🐕Guide dogs only. ✱ ♨Tel for details.

BECKFORD'S TOWER & MUSEUM

Lansdown Road, Bath BA1 9BH

Tel: 01225 422212 **Fax:** 01225 481850 **e-mail:** beckford@bptrust.demon.co.uk

Owner: Bath Preservation Trust   **Contact:** The Administrator

Built in 1827 for eccentric William Beckford and recently restored by Bath Preservation Trust. The tower is a striking feature of the Bath skyline.

Location: OS Ref. ST735 676. Lansdown Road, 2m NNW of city centre.

Open: Easter weekend - end of October: Sats, Suns & BH Mons, 10.30am - 5pm.

Admission: Adult £2.50, Child/OAP £2, Family £6. BPT & NACF members: Free. Groups by arrangement – Tel: 01225 460705.

BREAN DOWN ✤

Brean, North Somerset

Tel: 01934 844518 www.nationaltrust.org.uk

Owner: The National Trust   **Contact:** Property Manager

Brean Down is one of the most dramatic landmarks of the Somerset coastline, extending 1¹⁄₂ m into the Bristol Channel. A Palmerston Fort built in 1865 and then re-armed in World War II, provides a unique insight into Brean's past.

Location: OS Ref. ST2959 Between Weston-super-Mare and Burnham-on-Sea about 8m from M5/J22. Rail: Highbridge 5m.

Open: All year.

Admission: Free.

ℹ️The cliffs are extremely steep. Please stay on the main paths and wear suitable footwear. 🗓 (Not NT.) ♿Partial. WC. ■(Not NT.) 𝒇Guided walks. 🅿 ■ 🐕On leads. ✱

THE BUILDING OF BATH MUSEUM

The Countess of Huntingdon's Chapel, The Vineyards, The Paragon, Bath BA1 5NA

Tel: 01225 333895 / 01225 445473 **e-mail:** amanda@bathmuseum.co.uk

Owner: Bath Preservation Trust   **Contact:** The Administrator

Discover the essence of life in Georgian Bath.

Location: OS Ref. ST751 655. 5 mins walk from city centre. Bath M4/J18.

Open: 10 Feb - 28 Nov: Tue - Sun and BH Mons, 10.30am - 5pm.

Admission: Adult £4, Child £1.50, Conc. £3. Groups: £2.50.

CLEEVE ABBEY ⌘

Washford, Nr Watchet, Somerset TA23 0PS

Tel: 01984 640377 **e-mail:** customers@english-heritage.org.uk

www.english-heritage.org.uk/visits

Owner: English Heritage   **Contact:** The Custodian

There are few monastic sites where you will see such a complete set of cloister buildings, including the refectory with its magnificent timber roof. Built in the 13th century, this Cistercian abbey was saved from destruction at the Dissolution by being turned into a house and then a farm.

Location: OS Ref. ST047 407. In Washford, ¹⁄₄ m S of A39.

Open: 1 Apr - 31 Oct: daily 10am - 6pm (5pm in Oct). 1 Nov - 31 Mar: daily 10am - 4pm (closed lunch 1 - 2pm). Closed 24 - 26 Dec & 1 Jan. Times subject to change April 2004.

Admission: Adult £3, Child £1.50, Conc. £2.30. 15% discount for groups (11+). Prices subject to change April 2004.

ℹ️WC. 🗓 ♿Partial. 🅿 🐕In grounds, on leads. ✱ ♨Tel for details.

CLEVEDON COURT ✤

Tickenham Road, Clevedon, North Somerset BS21 6QU

Tel: 01275 872257 www.nationaltrust.org.uk

Owner: The National Trust   **Contact:** The Administrator

Home of the Elton family since 1709, this 14th century manor house, once partly fortified, has a 12th century tower and 13th century hall. Collection of Nailsea glass and Eltonware. Beautiful terraced garden.

Location: OS Ref. ST423 716. 1¹⁄₂ m E of Clevedon, on B3130, signposted from M5/J20.

Open: 4 Apr - 30 Sept: Wed, Thur, Sun & BH Mons, 2 - 5pm.

Admission: Adult £5, Child £2.50. Admission by timed ticket in high season & BH weekends. Groups & coaches by arrangement.

♿Ground floor. 🅿Limited. ■ 🐕

COLERIDGE COTTAGE ✻
35 Lime Street, Nether Stowey, Bridgwater, Somerset TA5 1NQ
Tel: 01278 732662 **www.**nationaltrust.org.uk
Owner: The National Trust **Contact:** The Custodian
The home of Samuel Taylor Coleridge for three years from 1797, with mementoes of the poet on display. It was here that he wrote *The Rime of the Ancient Mariner*, part of *Christabel* and *Frost at Midnight*.
Location: OS Ref. ST191 399. At W end of Nether Stowey, on S side of A39, 8m W of Bridgwater.
Open: 1 Apr - 26 Sept: Thur - Sun, 2 - 5pm (open BH Mons).
Admission: Adult £3.20, Child £1.60, no reduction for groups, which must book.
ⓘNo WC. ⓖBraille guide. Ⓟ500yds (not NT). ⊠

COMBE SYDENHAM COUNTRY PARK ⌂
Monksilver, Taunton, Somerset TA4 4JG
Tel: 0800 7838572
Owner: Theed Estates **Contact:** John Burns
Built in 1580 on the site of a monastic settlement. Deer Park and woodland walks.
Location: OS Ref. ST075 366. Monksilver.
Open: Country Park: Easter - end Sept. House: All year.
Admission: Car park Free. House & Gardens by appointment, £5pp. Tel for details.

Christopher Simon Sykes

COTHAY MANOR
GREENHAM, WELLINGTON, SOMERSET TA21 0JR

Tel: 01823 672283 **Fax:** 01823 672345
Owner/Contact: Mr & Mrs Alastair Robb
It has been said that Cothay Manor is the finest example of a small classic, medieval manor house in England. The manor has remained virtually untouched since it was built in 1480. The gardens, laid out in the 1920s have been completely re-designed and replanted within the original framework of yew hedges. A white garden, scarlet and purple garden, herbaceous borders and bog garden are but a few of the delights to be found in this magical place.
Location: OS Ref. ST721 214. From M5 W J/27, take A38 dir Wellington. 3¹/₂ m left to Greenham. From N/J26 take A38 dir. Exeter. 3¹/₂ m right to Greenham (1¹/₂ m). On LH corner at bottom of hill turn right. Cothay 1m, always keeping left.
Open: May - Sept: Weds, Thurs, Suns & BHs, 2 - 6pm.
Admission: Garden: Adult £4, Child (under 12yrs) £2. House: Groups (20+): by arrangement throughout the year, £4.50.
ⓘNo photography in house. ⏢ ⓣ ⓖ ⓦ ⓕBy arrangement. Ⓟ ⊠ ❋

CROWCOMBE COURT
CROWCOMBE, TAUNTON, SOMERSET TA4 4AD

www.crowcombecourt.co.uk

Tel: 01984 618373 **Fax:** 01984 618222 **e-mail:** info@crowcombecourt.co.uk
Owner/Contact: Dr P J Smith
Handsome early Georgian squire's house, designed in 1734 by Nathaniel Ireson for Thomas Carew. Baroque façade set against sweeping parkland and wooded hills. Pevsner described the interiors as 'sumptuous'. The neo-Palladian great hall and richly decorated reception rooms are available for weddings and other functions.
Location: OS Ref. ST139 369. 1m NE of A358, 9m NW of Taunton.
Open: By arrangement for weddings, corporate hospitality and other functions. Tours for special interest groups by appointment.
Admission: Please contact for details.
ⓣ ⓖPartial. WC. ⓕBy arrangement. ⓅLimited for coaches. ⚐Guide dogs only. ♠

CROWE HALL
Widcombe Hill, Bath, Somerset BA2 6AR
Tel: 01225 310322
Owner/Contact: John Barratt Esq
Ten acres of romantic hillside gardens. Victorian grotto, classical Bath villa with good 18th century furniture and paintings.
Location: OS Ref. ST760 640. In Bath, 1m SE of city centre.
Open: Gardens only open 4 Apr, 9 May, 6 Jun, 11 Jul, 2 - 6pm. House and Gardens by appointment.
Admission: House & Gardens: Adult £5. Gardens only: Adult £3, Child £1.

DODINGTON HALL
Nr Nether Stowey, Bridgwater, Somerset TA5 1LF
Tel: 01278 741400
Owner: Lady Gass **Contact:** P Quinn (occupier)
Small Tudor manor house on the lower slopes of the Quantocks. Great Hall with oak roof. Semi-formal garden with roses and shrubs.
Location: OS Ref. ST172 405. ¹/₂ m from A39, 11m N of Bridgwater, 7m E of Williton.
Open: 5 - 15 Jun, 2 - 5pm.
Admission: Donations to Dodington Church.
ⓘNo inside photography. ⓖUnsuitable. ⓅLimited. No coach parking.

NTPL: Bill Batten

DUNSTER CASTLE

DUNSTER, NR MINEHEAD, SOMERSET TA24 6SL

www.nationaltrust.org.uk

Tel: 01643 821314 **Fax:** 01643 823000 **e-mail:** dunstercastle@nationaltrust.org.uk

Owner: The National Trust   **Contact:** The Property Manager

Dramatically sited on a wooded hill, a castle has existed here since at least Norman times. The 13th century gatehouse survives, but the present building was remodelled in 1868-72 by Antony Salvin for the Luttrell family, who lived here for 600 years. The fine oak staircase and plasterwork of the 17th century house he adapted can still be seen. There is a sheltered terrace to the south on which tender plants and shrubs grow, and beautiful parkland in which to walk. Dunster Castle is home to the National Collection of Strawberry Trees and Britain's oldest lemon tree.

Location: OS Ref. ST995 435. In Dunster, 3m SE of Minehead.

Open: Castle: 20 Mar - 23 Oct: daily except Thur & Fri (open Good Fri), 11am - 5pm. 24 Oct - 31 Oct: daily except Thur & Fri, 11am - 4pm. Garden & Park: 1 Jan - 19 Mar & 24 Oct - 31 Dec: daily (closed 25/26 Dec), 11am - 4pm. 20 Mar - 23 Oct: 10am - 5pm. Varied events programme, please telephone for full details.

Admission: Castle, Garden & Park: Adult £6.80, Child £3.40, Family (2+3) £16.80. Groups (15+): £5.80. Garden & Park only: Adult £3.70, Child £1.60, Family £9.

🖼 🎫 ♿Braille guide. 🎦 Out of hours by arrangement. 🅿 🖼

🐕In park, on leads. 📺 Tel for details (01985 843601).

DUNSTER WORKING WATERMILL ✤

Mill Lane, Dunster, Minehead, Somerset TA24 6SW

Tel: 01643 821759   www.nationaltrust.org.uk

Owner: The National Trust   **Contact:** The Tenant

Built on the site of a mill mentioned in the Domesday Survey of 1086, the present mill dates from the 18th century and was restored to working order in 1979. Note: the mill is a private business and all visitors, including NT members, are asked to pay the admission charge.

Location: OS Ref. SS991 434. On River Avill, beneath Castle Tor, approach via Mill Lane or Castle gardens on foot.

Open: 1 Apr - 30 Jun & 1 Sept - 31 Oct: Daily except Fri, 11am - 4.45pm. 1 Jul - 31 Aug: Daily, 11am - 4.45pm.

Admission: Adult £2.40, Child £1.40, OAP £2, Family £6.

🖼 ♿Ground floor. 🍴 🅿

ENGLISHCOMBE TITHE BARN

Rectory Farmhouse, Englishcombe, Bath BA2 9DU

Tel: 01225 425073

Owner/Contact: Mrs Jennie Walker

An early 14th century cruck-framed Tithe Barn built by Bath Abbey.

Location: OS172 Ref. ST716 628. Adjacent to Englishcombe Village Church. 1m SW of Bath.

Open: BHs, 2 - 6pm. Other times by appointment or please knock at house. Closed 1 Dec - 7 Jan.

Admission: Free.

FAIRFIELD

Stogursey, Bridgwater, Somerset TA5 1PU

Tel: 01722 327087   **Fax:** 01722 413229

Owner: Lady Gass   **Contact:** D W Barke FRICS

Elizabethan house of medieval origin, undergoing extensive repairs. Woodland garden. Views of Quantocks.

Location: OS Ref. ST187 430. 11m W of Bridgwater, 8m E of Williton. From A39 Bridgwater/Minehead turn North. House 1m W of Stogursey.

Open: 28 Apr - 30 June: Wed - Fri and BHs. Guided house tours at 2.30 & 3.30pm. Groups at other times by arrangement. Provisional dates. Please contact to confirm. Garden open for NGS & other charities on dates advertised in Spring.

Admission: £4 in aid of Stogursey Church.

ℹ️No inside photography. ♿ 🎦Obligatory. 🅿No coach parking.

🐕Guide dogs only.

FARLEIGH HUNGERFORD CASTLE ⌗

Farleigh Hungerford, Bath, Somerset BA3 6RS

Tel/Fax: 01225 754026   **e-mail:** customers@english-heritage.org.uk

www.english-heritage.org.uk/visits

Owner: English Heritage   **Contact:** The Custodian

Extensive ruins of 14th century castle with a splendid chapel containing wall paintings, stained glass and the fine tomb of Sir Thomas Hungerford, builder of the castle.

Location: OS173, ST801 577. In Farleigh Hungerford 3½ m W of Trowbridge on A366.

Open: 1 Apr - 31 Oct: daily 10am - 6pm (5pm in Oct). Nov - Mar: Wed - Sun, 10am - 4pm (closed for lunch 1 - 2 pm). Closed 24 - 26 Dec & 1 Jan. Times subject to change April 2004.

Admission: Adult £2.50, Child £1.30, Conc. £1.90. 15% discount for groups of 11+. Prices subject to change April 2004.

ℹ️WCs. 🖼 ♿Grounds. 🅿 🖼 🐕Guide dogs only. ❋ 📺Tel for details.

GATCOMBE COURT

Flax Bourton, Somerset BS48 3QT

Tel: 01275 393141   **Fax:** 01275 394274

Owner/Contact: Mrs Charles Clarke

A Somerset manor house, dating from early 13th century, which has evolved over the centuries since. It is on the site of a large Roman village, traces of which are apparent. Rose and herb garden.

Location: OS Ref. ST525 698. 5m W of Bristol, N of the A370, between the villages of Long Ashton and Flax Bourton.

Open: May - July: for groups of 15 - 40 people by appointment.

♿Unsuitable. 🎦By arrangement. 🍴 🅿 🖼 ❋

GAULDEN MANOR

Tolland, Lydeard St Lawrence, Nr Taunton, Somerset TA4 3PN

Tel: 01984 667213

Owner/Contact: James Le Gendre Starkie

Small historic manor of great charm. A real lived-in family home, guided tours by owner. Past seat of the Turberville family, immortalised by Thomas Hardy. Magnificent early plasterwork, fine furniture, many examples of embroidery by owner's wife. Interesting gardens include herb garden, old fashioned roses, bog garden and secret garden beyond monks' fish pond.

Location: OS Ref. ST111 314. 9m NW of Taunton off A358 and B3224.

Open: Garden: Jun - Aug. Thurs, Suns & BHs, 2 - 5pm. House & Garden: groups (15+): Jun, Jul & Aug: by written appointment at any time.

Admission: House & Garden: Adult £5.50, Child £1. Garden only: Adult £3.25, Child £1.

🖼 ♿Ground floor & grounds. 🎦Obligatory. 🅿 🖼 ❋

THE GEORGIAN HOUSE

7 Great George Street, Bristol, Somerset BS1 5RR

Tel: 0117 921 1362

Owner: City of Bristol Museums & Art Gallery   **Contact:** Karin Walton

Location: OS172 ST582 730. Bristol.

Open: 1 Apr - 31 Oct: Sat - Wed, 10am - 5pm.

Admission: Free.

GLASTONBURY ABBEY

Abbey Gatehouse, Magdalene Street, Glastonbury BA6 9EL

Tel/Fax: 01458 832267   **e-mail:** info@glastonburyabbey.com

Owner: Glastonbury Abbey Estate   **Contact:** F C Thyer - Deputy Custodian

Magnificent Abbey ruins set in 36 acres of glorious Somerset parkland, steeped in history and legend. Legendary burial place of King Arthur.

Location: OS Ref. ST499 388. 50 yds from the Market Cross, in the centre of Glastonbury. M5/J23, then A39.

Open: Daily (except Christmas Day), 9.30am - 6pm or dusk if earlier. Jun, Jul & Aug: opens 9am. Dec, Jan & Feb: opens 10am.

Admission: Adult £3.50, Child £1.50, Conc. £3. Groups (booked, 10+): Adult £3. Prices change 1 Sept 2004 to: Adult £4, Conc. £3.50. Groups (booked, 10+): Adult £3.50.

▣ ⬤ ⬤ ⬤ **P** ⬤ ⬤ ⬤ Tel for details.

GLASTONBURY TOR ⬤

Nr Glastonbury, Somerset

Tel: 01985 843600 / 01934 844518

Owner: The National Trust   **Contact:** The Regional Office

The dramatic and evocative Tor dominates the Somerset Levels and offers spectacular views over Somerset, Dorset and Wiltshire. An excavation has revealed the plans of two superimposed churches of St Michael, of which only the 15th-century tower remains.

Location: OS Ref. ST512 386. Signposted from Glastonbury, from where seasonal park-and-ride operates (not NT).

Open: All year.

Admission: Free.

P Park & ride from town centre Apr - Sept. Also free at Rural Life Museum. Tel 01458 831147.   ⬤ On leads only. ⬤

GLASTONBURY TRIBUNAL ⬤

Glastonbury High Street, Glastonbury, Somerset

Tel: 01458 832954   **e-mail:** glastonbury.tic@ukonline.co.uk

Owner: English Heritage   **Contact:** The TIC Manager

A well preserved medieval town house, reputedly once used as the courthouse of Glastonbury Abbey. Now houses Glastonbury Tourist Information Centre.

Location: OS182 Ref. ST499 390. In Glastonbury High Street.

Open: Apr - Sept: Sun - Thur 10am - 5pm (Fri & Sat to 5.30pm). Oct - Apr: Sun - Thur, 10am - 4pm (Fri & Sat, 4.30pm). Closed 25 - 26 Dec & 1 Jan. Times subject to change April 2004.

Admission: TIC Free. Display areas: Adult £2, Child £1.50. Prices subject to change April 2004.

⬤ Partial. **P** Charge. ⬤

THE WILLIAM HERSCHEL MUSEUM

19 New King Street, Bath BA1 2BL

Tel: 01225 311342   **Fax:** 01225 446865

Owner: The Herschel House Trust   **Contact:** The Curator

Georgian town-house. Home to astronomer William Herschel and site of discovery of planet Uranus in 1781. Georgian garden. Audio tour. Star Vault Astronomy Auditorium.

Location: OS Ref. ST750 648. Bath, Somerset.

Open: 10 Feb - 30 Nov: daily except Weds, 2 - 5pm, weekends 11am - 5pm.

Admission: Adult £3.50, Child £2, Family £7.50.

HESTERCOMBE ⬤ GARDENS

CHEDDON FITZPAINE, TAUNTON, SOMERSET TA2 8LG

www.hestercombegardens.com

Tel: 01823 413923 **Fax:** 01823 413747

Owner: Somerset County Council & Hestercombe Gardens Project

Contact: Mr P White

Lose yourself in 40 acres of walks, streams and temples, vivid colours, formal terraces, woodlands, lakes, cascades and views that take your breath away. This is Hestercombe: a unique combination of three period gardens. The Georgian landscape garden was created in the 1750s by Copelstone Warre Bampfylde, whose vision was complemented with the addition of a Victorian terrace and shrubbery and the stunning Edwardian gardens designed by Sir Edwin Lutyens and Gertrude Jekyll. All once abandoned, now being faithfully restored to their former glory. Each garden has its own quality – tranquility, wonder, inspiration – refreshing the visitor body and soul.

Location: OS Ref. ST241 287. 4m NE from Taunton, 1m NW of Cheddon Fitzpaine.

Open: All year: daily, 10am - 6pm (last admission 5pm). Groups & coach parties by arrangement.

Admission: Adult £5.20. Child (5-15yrs) £1.30, Child under 5 Free, OAP £4.90, Family £11.50. Guided tour (15+): £7.50.

▣ ⬤ ⬤ Partial. WC. ⬤ Licensed.

⬤ Licensed. ⬤ By arrangement.

P Limited for coaches. ⬤ On short leads. ⬤

HOLBURNE MUSEUM OF ART
Great Pulteney Street, Bath BA2 4DB

Tel: 01225 466669 **Fax:** 01225 333121

Owner: Trustees   **Contact:** Katie Jenkins

This jewel in Bath's crown houses the treasures collected by Sir William Holburne: superb English and continental silver, porcelain, majolica, glass and Renaissance bronzes, and paintings by Turner, Guardi and Stubbs.

Location: OS Ref. ST431 545. Via A4 or A431, follow brown signs.

Open: Mid Feb - mid Dec: Tue - Sat, 10am - 5pm, Sun, 2.30 - 5.30pm. Closed Mons except for group bookings by appointment.

Admission: Adult £4, Child £1.50, OAP £3.50, Students Free. Groups (10+): Adult £3, Child £1.

HOLNICOTE ESTATE 🍃
Selworthy, Minehead, Somerset TA24 8TJ

Tel: 01643 862452 **Fax:** 01643 863011 **e-mail:** holnicote@ntrust.org.uk

Owner: The National Trust   **Contact:** The Estate Office

The Holnicote Estate covers 5042ha (12,500 acres) of Exmoor National Park. The Estate also covers 4m of coastline between Porlock Bay and Minehead. There are over 100m of footpaths to enjoy through the fields, woods, moors and villages.

Location: OS Ref. SS920 469. Off A39 Minehead - Porlock, 3m W of Minehead. Station: Minehead 5m.

Open: All year.

Admission: Free.

🖻 🕭 ▣(Not NT.) ▮ ❋

KENTSFORD
Washford, Watchet, Somerset TA23 0JD

Tel: 01984 631307

Owner: Wyndham Estate   **Contact:** Mr R Dibble

Location: OS Ref. ST058 426.

Open: House open only by appointment with Mr R Dibble. Gardens: 2 Mar - 24 Aug: Tues & BHs.

Admission: House: £2, Gardens: Free.

🕭 Gardens only. ▣ Limited. ▮ In grounds, on leads. ❋

KING JOHN'S HUNTING LODGE 🍃
The Square, Axbridge, Somerset BS26 2AP

Tel: 01934 732012 **www.**nationaltrust.org.uk

Owner/Contact: The National Trust

An early Tudor merchant's house, extensively restored in 1971. Note: the property is run as a local history museum by Axbridge & District Museum Trust in co-operation with Sedgemoor District Council, County Museum's Service and Axbridge Archaeological & Local History Society.

Location: OS Ref. ST431 545. In the Square, on corner of High Street, off A371.

Open: 1 Apr - 30 Sept: Daily, 1 - 4pm.

Admission: Free. Donations welcome.

🕭 Ground floor. ▣ ▮ By arrangement.

LOWER SEVERALLS
Crewkerne, Somerset TA18 7NX

Tel: 01460 73234 **Fax:** 01460 76105 **e-mail:** mary@lowerseveralls.co.uk

Owner: Mrs Howard Pring   **Contact:** Mary Pring

2¹/₂ acre garden, developed over the last 25 years including herb garden, mixed borders and island beds with innovative features, ie a giant living dogwood basket and a wadi.

Location: OS Ref. ST457 112. 11/2 m NE of Crewkerne, between A30 & A356.

Open: 1 Mar - mid Oct: daily (except Thurs), 10am - 5pm (Suns, 2 - 5pm in May/Jun only).

Admission: Adult £3, Child (under 16yrs) Free.

LYTES CARY MANOR 🍃
Nr Charlton Mackrell, Somerset TA11 7HU

Tel: 01458 224471 (property) **e-mail:** lytescarymanor@nationaltrust.org.uk
www.nationaltrust.org.uk

Owner: The National Trust   **Contact:** The Property Manager

A charming manor house with a 14th century chapel and 15th century Great Hall, much added to in the 16th century and rescued from dereliction in the 20th century by Sir Walter Jenner. The interiors were refurnished in period style and are complemented by the attractive hedged garden and mixed borders. Due to essential roof repairs parts of the Manor may be scaffolded.

Location: OS Ref. ST534 265. 1m N of Ilchester bypass A303, signposted from roundabout at junction of A303. A37 take A372.

Open: 5 Apr - 31 Oct: Mon, Wed, Fri & Sun, 11am - 5pm. Closes dusk if earlier.

Admission: £5, Child £2. Garden only: Adult £3, Child £1.

🕭 Partial. Braille guide. 🎧 By arrangement.

▣ Free. Small coaches only by arrangement.

▮ On leads in car park and river walk only. 🎦 Tel for details.

MAUNSEL HOUSE
NORTH NEWTON, Nr BRIDGWATER, SOMERSET TA7 0BU

www.sirbenslade.co.uk

Tel: 01278 661076 **Fax:** 01278 661074 **e-mail:** bensladebt@aol.com

Owner: Sir Benjamin Slade   **Contact:** The Estate Office

This imposing 13th century manor house offers the ideal location for wedding receptions, corporate events, private and garden parties, filming and family celebrations. The ancestral seat of the Slade family and home of the 7th baronet Sir Benjamin Slade, the house can boast such visitors as Geoffrey Chaucer, who wrote part of the *Canterbury Tales* whilst staying there. The beautiful grounds and spacious rooms provide both privacy and a unique atmosphere for any special event. There are ten bedrooms (B&B basis) available for weekend parties and weddings.

Location: OS Ref. ST302 303. Bridgwater 4m, Bristol 20m, Taunton 7m, M5/J24, A38 to North Petherton. 2¹/₂ m SE of A38 at North Petherton via North Newton.

Open: Coaches and groups welcome by appointment. Caravan rally field available.

🍽 Functions. 🕭 Partial. ▮ In grounds, on leads. 🖾 ▲

MILTON LODGE GARDENS 🏛
Old Bristol Road, Wells, Somerset BA5 3AQ

Tel: 01749 672168

Owner/Contact: D Tudway Quilter Esq

"The great glory of the gardens of Milton Lodge is their position high up on the slopes of the Mendip Hills to the north of Wells ... with broad panoramas of Wells Cathedral and the Vale of Avalon", (Lanning Roper). Charming, mature, Grade II listed terraced garden dating from 1909. Replanned 1962 with mixed shrubs, herbaceous plants, old fashioned roses and ground cover; numerous climbers; old established yew hedges. Fine trees in garden and in 7-acre arboretum.

Location: OS Ref. ST549 470. ¹/₂ m N of Wells from A39. N up Old Bristol Road. Free car park first gate on left.

Open: Garden & Arboretum: Easter - end Oct: Tues, Weds, Suns & BHs, 2 - 5pm Parties & coaches by prior arrangement.

Admission: Adult £2.50, Child (under 14yrs) Free. Open certain Suns in aid of National Gardens Scheme.

🖻 🎴 🕭 Unsuitable. ▣ ▣ ▮

NT Photographic Library: Rupert Truman

MONTACUTE HOUSE ❧
MONTACUTE, SOMERSET TA15 6XP
www.nationaltrust.org.uk

Tel: 01935 823289 **Fax:** 01935 826921 **e-mail:** montacute@nationaltrust.org.uk

Owner: The National Trust **Contact:** The Property Manager

A glittering Elizabethan house, adorned with elegant chimneys, carved parapets and other Renaissance features, including contemporary plasterwork, chimney pieces and heraldic glass. The magnificent state rooms, including a long gallery which is the largest of its type in England, are full of fine 17th and 18th century furniture and Elizabethan and Jacobean portraits from the National Portrait Gallery.

Location: OS Ref. ST499 172. In Montacute village, 4m W of Yeovil, on S side of A3088, 3m E of A303.

Open: House: 19 Mar - 31 Oct: daily except Tue (open BH Mons), 11am - 5pm. Garden & Park only: 1 Jan - 18 Mar & 3 Nov - 25 Mar: daily except Mon & Tue, 11am - 4pm. 19 Mar - 31 Oct:: daily except Tue, 11am - 6pm.

Admission: House, Park & Garden: Adult £6.90, Child £3.40, Family £16. Groups (15+): Adult £5.80, Child £2.90. Garden & Park only (19 Mar - 31 Oct): Adult £3.70, Child £1.70. 3 Nov - 31 Mar 2005: Adult £2, Child £1. Group organisers please book in writing to House Manager with a SAE.

◻ 🏠 ♿Partial. Braille guide. WC.
🍴Licensed. Christmas lunches in Dec. (must book) 🅿 🐕In park, on leads. ◼ ❋

MUCHELNEY ABBEY ♯
Muchelney, Langport, Somerset TA10 0DQ

Tel: 01458 250664 **Fax:** 01458 253842 **e-mail:** customers@english-heritage.org.uk
www.english-heritage.org.uk/visits

Owner: English Heritage **Contact:** The Custodian

Well-preserved ruins of the cloisters, with windows carved in golden stone, and abbot's lodging of the Benedictine abbey, which survived by being used as a farmhouse after the Dissolution.

Location: OS193 Ref. ST428 248. In Muchelney 2m S of Langport.

Open: 1 Apr - 31 Oct: daily 10am - 6pm (5pm in Oct). Winter: closed. Times subject to change April 2004.

Admission: Adult £2.50, Child £1.30, Conc. £1.90. 15% discount for groups (11+). Prices subject to change April 2004.

ℹWCs. ◻ ♿Partial. 🅿 🐕 ▼Tel for details.

MUSEUM OF COSTUME ❧   *See page 239 for full page entry.*
& ASSEMBLY ROOMS

ORCHARD WYNDHAM
Williton, Taunton, Somerset TA4 4HH

Tel: 01984 632309 **Fax:** 01984 633526

Owner: Wyndham Estate **Contact:** Wyndham Estate Office

English manor house. Family home for 700 years encapsulating continuous building and alteration from the 14th to the 20th century.

Location: OS Ref. ST072 400. 1m from A39 at Williton.

Open: 30 July - 27 Aug: Thur & Fri, 2 - 5pm & Aug BH Mon, 11am - 5pm. Guided tours only. Last tour 4pm. Limited viewing space within the house. To avoid disappointment please advance book places on tour by telephone or fax. Access only suitable for cars.

Admission: Adult £5, Child (under 12) £1.

👤Obligatory & pre-booked. 🅿 Limited. No coach parking. 🐕In grounds, on leads.

PRIEST'S HOUSE ❧
Muchelney, Langport, Somerset TA10 0DQ

Tel: 01985 843600 (Regional Office) **www**.nationaltrust.org.uk

Owner: The National Trust **Contact:** The Administrator

A late medieval hall house with large gothic windows, originally the residence of priests serving the parish church across the road. Lived-in and recently repaired.

Location: OS Ref. ST429 250. 1m S of Langport.

Open: 21 Mar - 27 Sept: Sun & Mon, 1.30 - 5.30pm.

Admission: Adult £3, Child £1.50.

🐕

NTPL / David Noton

PRIOR PARK LANDSCAPE GARDEN ❧
RALPH ALLEN DRIVE, BATH BA2 5AH
www.nationaltrust.org.uk

Tel: 01225 833422 **Infoline:** 09001 335242
e-mail: priorpark@nationaltrust.org.uk

Owner: The National Trust **Contact:** Gardener-in-Charge

Beautiful and intimate 18th century landscape garden created by Bath entrepreneur Ralph Allen with advice from the poet Alexander Pope and 'Capability' Brown. Sweeping valley with magnificent views of the City of Bath, Palladian bridge and lakes. Restoration of the garden continues. New circuit walk into Bath Skyline (NT) Countryside adjacent to garden with further views to Bath. Newly planted 18th century shrubbery. All visitors must use public transport as there is no car park. For further details 01225 833422 or 24 hour information line 09001 335242 (60p per minute). Prior Park College, a co-educational school, operates from the mansion (not NT).

Location: OS Ref. ST760 632. Frequent bus service from City Centre. Badgerline 2 & 4.

Open: 1 Feb - 29 Nov: Wed - Mon, 11am - 5.30pm or dusk if earlier. 3 Dec - 31 Jan: Fri - Sun. 11am - dusk. Last adm. 1 hr before closing. Closed 25/26 Dec & 1 Jan.

Admission: Adult £4, Child £2.

♿Grounds. WC. Braille guide. ▣ 👤By arrangement. ◼ 🐕Nov - Feb. ❋
▼ Tel for details.

THE ROMAN BATHS & PUMP ROOM

See page 240 for full page entry.

STEMBRIDGE TOWER MILL

High Ham, Somerset TA10 9DJ

Tel: 01458 250818   **www**.nationaltrust.org.uk

Owner: The National Trust   **Contact:** The Administrator

The last thatched windmill in England, dating from 1822 and in use until 1910.

Location: OS Ref. ST432 305. 2m N of Langport, ¹/₂ m E of High Ham.

Open: 28 Mar - 27 Sept: Mon & Sun, 2 - 5pm.

Admission: Adult £2.30, Child £1.20. Arrangements may be made for coach/school groups with the tenant.

ⓘ No WC. **P** Limited. 🅱

STOKE-SUB-HAMDON PRIORY

North Street, Stoke-sub-Hamdon, Somerset TA4 6QP

Tel: 01985 843600 (Regional Office)   **www**.nationaltrust.org.uk

Owner/Contact: The National Trust

A complex of buildings, begun in the 14th century for the priests of the chantry of St Nicholas, which is now destroyed. The Great Hall is open to visitors.

Location: OS Ref. ST473 174. ¹/₂ m S of A303. 2m W of Montacute between Yeovil and Ilminster.

Open: 27 Mar - 31 Oct: daily, 10am - 6pm or dusk if earlier.

Admission: Free.

ⓘ No WC. **P** Limited. 🅱

TINTINHULL GARDEN

Farm Street, Tintinhull, Somerset BA22 9PZ

Tel: 01935 822545   **e-mail:** tintinhull@nationaltrust.org.uk   **www**.nationaltrust.org.uk

Owner: The National Trust   **Contact:** The Head Gardener

A delightful formal garden, created in the 20th century around a 17th century manor house. Small pools, varied borders and secluded lawns are neatly enclosed within walls and clipped hedges and there is also an attractive kitchen garden.

Location: OS Ref. ST503 198. 5m NW of Yeovil, ¹/₂m S of A303, on E outskirts of Tintinhull.

Open: 24 Mar - 30 Sept: Wed - Sun, 12 noon - 6pm (open BH Mon).

Admission: Adult £4.20, Child £2.10. No reduction for groups.

♿ Grounds. Braille guide. ⬛ ⓘBy arrangement. **P** Limited. 🅱

TREASURER'S HOUSE

Martock, Somerset TA12 6JL

Tel: 01935 825801   **www**.nationaltrust.org.uk

Owner/Contact: The National Trust

A small medieval house, recently refurbished by The Trust. The two-storey hall was completed in 1293 and the solar block is even earlier.

Location: OS Ref. ST462 191. 1m NW of A303 between Ilminster and Ilchester.

Open: 28 Mar - 28 Sept: Sun - Tue, 2 - 5pm. Only medieval hall, wall paintings and kitchen are shown.

Admission: Adult £2.70, Child £1.60. Groups by arrangement with tenant.

ⓘ No WC. **P** Limited for cars. None for coaches & trailer caravans.

TYNTESFIELD

Wraxall, North Somerset BS48 1NT

Tel: 0870 458 4500   **www**.nationaltrust.org.uk

Owner/Contact: The National Trust

A spectacular Victorian country house and estate. Situated on a ridge overlooking the beautiful Yeo Valley, Tyntesfield was inspired and remodelled by John Norton in c1864 for William Gibbs, a successful merchant. The mansion, an extraordinary Gothic Revival extravaganza, bristling with towers and turrets, survives with much of its original Victorian interior intact, an unrivalled collection of Victorian decorative arts, an insight into life below stairs and a sumptuously decorated private chapel. Its surrounding 200ha (500 acres) of land includes formal gardens and a wonderful walled kitchen garden. Tyntesfield was saved for the nation by the National Trust in June 2002 with funding from the National Heritage Memorial Fund, other heritage partners and a £3 million public appeal.

Location: OS Ref. SO506 716. Off B3130.

Open: Visits to Tyntesfield in 2004 are likely to be by pre-booked guided tour only, with a park and ride service in operation. For details please tel: 0870 458 4500.

♿ Ground floor only.

WELLS CATHEDRAL

Cathedral Green, Wells, Somerset BA5 2UE

Tel: 01749 674483   **Fax:** 01749 832210

Owner: The Chapter of Wells   **Contact:** Mr John Roberts

Fine medieval Cathedral. The West Front with its splendid array of statuary, the Quire with colourful embroideries and stained glass, Chapter House and 1392 astronomical clock should not be missed.

Location: OS Ref. ST552 458. In Wells, 20m S from both Bath & Bristol.

Open: Apr - Sept: 7am - 7pm; Oct - Mar: 7am - 6pm.

Admission: Suggested donation: Adult £4.50, Child/Student £1.50, OAP £3. Photo permit £2.

Cothay Manor, Somerset from the book *Historic Family Homes and Gardens from the Air*, see page 54.

BOWOOD HOUSE & GARDENS

CALNE

www.bowood.org

Owner:
The Marquis of
Lansdowne

▶ **CONTACT**

The Administrator
Bowood House and
Gardens
Calne
Wiltshire   SN11 0LZ

Tel: 01249 812102

Fax: 01249 821757

e-mail:
houseandgardens@
bowood.org

▶ **LOCATION**

OS Ref. ST974 700

From London M4/J17,
off the A4 in Derry Hill
village, midway
between Calne and
Chippenham.
Swindon 17m,
Bristol 26m,
Bath 16m.

Bus: to the gate,
1¹/₂ m through
park to House.

Rail: Chippenham
Station 5m.

Taxi: AA Taxis,
Chippenham 657777.

Bowood is the family home of the Marquis and Marchioness of Lansdowne. Begun c1720 for the Bridgeman family, the house was purchased by the 2nd Earl of Shelburne in 1754 and completed soon afterwards. Part of the house was demolished in 1955, leaving a perfectly proportioned Georgian home, over half of which is open to visitors. Robert Adam's magnificent Diocletian wing contains a splendid library, the laboratory where Joseph Priestley discovered oxygen gas in 1774, the orangery, now a picture gallery, the Chapel and a sculpture gallery in which some of the famous Lansdowne Marbles are displayed.

Among the family treasures shown in the numerous exhibition rooms are Georgian costumes, including Lord Byron's Albanian dress; Victoriana; Indiana (the 5th Marquess was Viceroy 1888-94); and superb collections of watercolours, miniatures and jewellery.

The House is set in one of the most beautiful parks in England. Over 2,000 acres of gardens and grounds were landscaped by 'Capability' Brown between 1762 and 1768, and are embellished with a Doric temple, a cascade, a pinetum and an arboretum. The Rhododendron Gardens are open for six weeks from late April to early June. All the walks have seats.

▶ **OPENING TIMES**

House & Garden
1 April - 31 October:
Daily, 11am - 6pm.
Last admission 5pm.

Rhododendron Walks
Off the A342 Chippenham
to Devizes road, midway
between Derry Hill and
Sandy Lane.

Open daily for 6 weeks
during the flowering
season, usually from late
April to early June,
11am - 6pm.
We recommend visitors
telephone or visit the
website to check the
progress of the
flowering season.

▶ **ADMISSION**

House & Garden
Adult £6.40
Child (2-4yrs).......... £3.25
Child (5-15yrs) £4.10
OAP £5.30
Groups (20+)
Adult £5.45
Child (2-4yrs).......... £3.05
Child (5-15yrs) £3.60
OAP £4.65

Rhododendron Walks
Adult £3.60
Child (0-15yrs) .... Free

Season Tickets available,
ask for details.

The charge for
Rhododendron Walks is
£2.60 if combined on same
day with a visit to Bowood
House & Gardens.

Receptions, film location, 2,000 acre park, 40 acre lake, 18-hole golf course and Country Club, open to all players holding a current handicap.

Visitors may alight at the House before parking. WCs.

Self-service snacks, teas etc.

The Restaurant (waitress-service, capacity 85). Parties that require lunch or tea should book in advance.

On request, groups can be given introductory talk, or for an extra charge, a guided tour. Tour time 1¹/₄ hrs. Guide sheets in French, German, Dutch, Spanish & Japanese.

1,000 cars, unlimited for coaches, 400 yds from house. Allow 2-3 hrs to visit house, gardens and grounds.

Welcome. Special guide books. Picnic areas. Adventure playground.

Sorry no dogs.

Map 2

CORSHAM COURT

CORSHAM

www.corsham-court.co.uk

Corsham Court is an Elizabethan house of 1582 and was bought by Paul Methuen in the mid-18th century, to house a collection of 16th and 17th century Italian and Flemish master paintings and statuary. In the middle of the 19th century, the house was enlarged to receive a second collection, purchased in Florence, principally of fashionable Italian masters and stone-inlaid furniture.

Paul Methuen (1723-95) was a great-grandson of Paul Methuen of Bradford-on-Avon and cousin of John Methuen, ambassador and negotiator of the Methuen Treaty of 1703 with Portugal which permitted export of British woollens to Portugal and allowed a preferential $33^{1}/3$ percent duty discount on Portuguese wines, bringing about a major change in British drinking habits.

The architects involved in the alterations to the house and park were Lancelot 'Capability' Brown in the 1760s, John Nash in 1800 and Thomas Bellamy in 1845-9. Brown set the style by retaining the Elizabethan Stables and Riding School, but rebuilding the Gateway, retaining the gabled Elizabethan stone front and doubling the gabled wings at either end and inside, by designing the East Wing as Stateroom Picture Galleries. Nash's work has now largely disappeared, but Bellamy's stands fast, notably in the Hall and Staircase.

The State Rooms, including the Music Room and Dining Room, provide the setting for the outstanding collection of over 150 paintings, statuary, bronzes and furniture. The collection includes work by such names as Chippendale, the Adam brothers, Van Dyck, Reni, Rosa, Rubens, Lippi, Reynolds, Romney and a pianoforte by Clementi.

GARDENS

'Capability' Brown planned to include a lake, avenues and specimen trees such as the Oriental Plane now with a 200-yard perimeter. The gardens, designed not only by Brown but also by Repton, contain a ha-ha, herbaceous borders, secluded gardens, lawns, a rose garden, a lily pool, a stone bath house and the Bradford Porch.

Owner:
J Methuen-
Campbell Esq

▶ **CONTACT**
Corsham Court
Corsham
Wiltshire SN13 0BZ

Tel/Fax: 01249 701610

▶ **LOCATION**
OS Ref. ST874 706

Corsham Court
is signposted
from the A4, approx.
4m W of Chippenham.
From Edinburgh, A1,
M62, M6, M5, M4,
8 hrs.
From London, M4,
$2^{1}/4$ hrs.
From Chester,
M6, M5, M4, 4 hrs.

Motorway: M4/J17 9m.

Rail: Chippenham
Station 6m.

Taxi: 01249 715959.

▶ **OPENING TIMES**
Summer

20 March - 30 September
Daily except Mons & Fris
but including BH Mons
2 - 5.30pm
Last admission 5pm.

Winter

1 October - 19 March
Weekends only
2 - 4.30pm
Last admission 4pm.

Closed December.

NB: Open throughout the year by appointment only for groups of 15+.

▶ **ADMISSION**
House & Garden
Adult £5.00
Child (5-15yrs)....... £2.50
OAP £4.50
Groups
(includes guided tour - 1 hr)
Adult £4.50

Garden only
Adult £2.00
Child (5-15yrs)....... £1.00
OAP £1.50

[i] Souvenir desk. No umbrellas, no photography.

[symbol] Visitors may alight at the entrance to the property, before parking in the allocated areas.

[symbol] Refreshments organised by prior arrangement for groups (15+).

[symbol] For up to 55. If requested the owner may meet the group. Tour time 1hr.

[P] 120 yards from the house. Coaches may park in Church Square. Coach parties must book in advance. No camper vans, no caravans.

[symbol] Available: rate negotiable. A guide will be provided.

[symbol] Must be kept on leads in the garden.

[symbol]

Map 2

Owner:
Marquess of Bath

▶ **CONTACT**

Estate Office
Longleat
Warminster
Wiltshire BA12 7NW

Tel: 01985 844400
Fax: 01985 844885
e-mail: enquiries@
longleat.co.uk

▶ **LOCATION**
OS Ref. ST809 430

Just off the A36
between Bath -
Salisbury (A362
Warminster - Frome).
2hrs from London
following M3, A303,
A36, A362 or
M4/J18 A46-A36.

Rail: Warminster Station
(5m) on the
Cardiff/Portsmouth line.
Westbury Station (12m)
on the Paddington/
Penzance line.
Taxi rank at Warminster
& Westbury Stations.

Air: Bristol 30m.

CONFERENCE/FUNCTION

ROOM	SIZE	MAX CAPACITY
Great Hall	8 x 13m	150
Banqueting Suite	2 x (7 x 10m)	50
Green Library	7 x 13m	80

LONGLEAT 🏛

WARMINSTER

www.longleat.co.uk

Set within 900 acres of 'Capability' Brown landscaped grounds, Longleat House is widely regarded as one of the best examples of high Elizabethan architecture in Britain and one of the most beautiful stately homes open to the public. Visited by Elizabeth I in 1574, Longleat House was built by Sir John Thynne from 1568 and is the current home of the 7th Marquess of Bath, Alexander Thynn. Many treasures are included within. The fine collection of paintings ranges from English portraits dating from the 16th century to hunting scenes by John Wootton c1736 (amongst his finest work) to Italian Old Masters.

Inspired by various Italian palace interiors, including the Ducal Palace in Venice, the ceilings are renowned for their ornate paintings and abundance of gilt with many made by the firm of John Dibblee Crace in the 1870s and 1880s. The furniture collection meanwhile includes English pieces from as early as the 16th century, 17th century chairs from the Coromandel coast of India,

fine French furniture of the 17th and 18th centuries and a collection of major Italian pieces very unusual for an English country house.

The Murals in the private apartments in the West Wing have been painted by the present Marquess and are a fascinating and unique addition to the House. Incorporating a mixture of oil paints and sawdust these private works of art offer a unique insight into Lord Bath's personality and beliefs. Mural Tours can be booked at the Front Desk of Longleat House on the date of a visit. They are subject to availability.

Apart from the ancestral home, Longleat has a wonderland of attractions to suit all ages. Discover some of the world's most magnificent animals including lions, tigers, rhinos and giraffes in the UK's original Safari Park; get lost in the 'World's Longest Hedge Maze'; voyage on the Safari Boats; journey on the Longleat Railway and much, much more!

🛍 ℹ️ Rooms in Longleat House can be hired for conferences, gala dinners and product launches. Extensive parkland for car launches, ride n' drives, company fun days, marquee based events, concerts, balloon festivals, equestrian events, caravan rallies & fishing. Film location.

🍴 Wessex Pavillion (300 capacity)

♿ ☕ 🍽 Cellar Café (capacity 80), licensed. Groups must book. From 3 course meals to cream teas, sandwiches & snacks. Traditional Wiltshire Fare. Not open all year.

🚶 Individuals & Groups (max 20; 15 for Murals). Booking essential.

🅿 Ample.

🏫 Welcome with 1 teacher free entry per 8 children. GNVQ talks and packs available on request. Booking essential. Education sheets.

🐕 In grounds, on leads.

🔔 Orangery. ❄ Tel for details.

▶ **OPENING TIMES**

House:
1 - 26 Mar: Weekends &
school holidays only;

Easter - Sept: Daily
10am - 5.30pm.

Oct - Dec (closed 25 Dec).
Guided tours on the hour
between 11am - 3pm.
Please telephone to
confirm tour times.

Safari Park:
27 Mar - 31 Oct: daily,
10am - 4pm (10am - 5pm
on weekends, BHs &
state school holidays).

Other attractions:
27 Mar - 31 Oct: daily,
11am - 5.30pm.

Note: last admission times may
be earlier in Mar, & Sept - Nov
due to shorter daylight hours.

▶ **ADMISSION**
House & Grounds
Adult £9.00
Child (3 -14yrs) £6.00
OAP £6.00
Longleat Passport
(see below)
Adult £16.00
Child (3 -14yrs) £13.00
OAP £13.00
Groups (12+)
Adult £12.00
Child (3 -14yrs) £9.75
OAP £9.75

**LONGLEAT PASSPORT -
includes all the following
attractions:**
Longleat House, Safari Park,
Safari Boats, World's Longest
Hedge Maze, King Arthur's
Mirror Maze, Pets Corner,
Adventure Castle (including
Blue Peter Maze (under 14yrs
only), Longleat Railway,
Motion Simulator, Butterfly
Garden, Postman Pat Village
(under 14yrs only), Grounds
& Gardens.

South West - England

NTPL / Nick Meers

Map 2

Owner:
The National Trust

▶ **CONTACT**

The Estate Office
Stourton
Nr Warminster
BA12 6QD

Tel: 01747 841152

Fax: 01747 842005

e-mail: stourhead@
nationaltrust.org.uk

▶ **LOCATION**

OS Ref. ST778 341

At Stourton off the
B3092, 3m NW of A303
(Mere), 8m S of A361
(Frome).

Rail: Gillingham 6¹/₂ m;
Bruton 7m.

Bus: South West
Coaches 80 Frome to
Stourhead on Sat;
First 58/0A.

STOURHEAD

STOURTON

www.nationaltrust.org.uk

An outstanding example of the English landscape style of garden. Designed by Henry Hoare II and laid out between 1741 and 1780. Classical temples, including the Pantheon and Temple of Apollo, are set around the central lake at the end of a series of vistas, which change as the visitor moves around the paths and through the magnificent mature woodland with its extensive collection of exotic trees. The house, begun in 1721 by Colen Campbell, contains furniture by the younger Chippendale and fine paintings. King Alfred's Tower, an intriguing red-brick folly built in 1772 by Henry Flitcroft, is almost 50m high and gives breathtaking views over the estate. Art Gallery in Spread Eagle Courtyard (not NT). What's new in 2004: Tree list. Introductory talks in house and garden.

NTPL

i Exhibition in Reception Buildings

Wheelchair accessible. Designated parking. Transfer available in main season to house & garden entrances. Powered mobility vehicles, recommended ground route map available. WCs. Braille guide.

Licensed.

Group tours, by arrangement.

P

Not in Tower or House. 1 Nov - 28 Feb: on short fixed leads in landscape garden.

❄

Tel for details.

▶ **OPENING TIMES**

Garden: All year, daily, 9am - 7pm or dusk if earlier.

House: 19 Mar - 31 Oct: Fri - Tue, 11am - 5pm. Last admission: Mar - Sept 4.30pm; Oct 4pm.

King Alfred's Tower: 19 Mar - 31 Oct: daily, 12 noon - 5pm.

Restaurant: All year, daily. Mar & Oct: 10am - 5pm; Apr - Sept: 10am - 5.30pm; Nov - Feb: 10.30am - 4pm.

Shop & Plant Centre: All year, daily. Mar & Oct: 10am - 5pm; Apr - Sept: 10am - 6pm; Nov - Feb: 11am - 4pm.

Closes dusk if earlier.

▶ **ADMISSION**

House & Garden:
Adult	£9.40
Child	£4.50
Family	£22.00
Groups (15+)	£8.90

House or Garden:
Adult	£5.40
Child	£3.00
Family	£13.40
Groups (15+)	£4.80

Garden only:
1 Nov - end Feb:
Adult	£4.10
Child	£2.00
Family	£9.90
Groups (15+)	£3.90

King Alfred's Tower:
Adult	£2.00
Child	£1.00
Family	£4.90
Groups (15+)	£1.80

NB. Groups must book.

Map 2

Owner:
The Earl of Pembroke

▶ **CONTACT**

The Estate Office
Wilton House
Wilton
Salisbury   SP2 0BJ

Tel: 01722 746720
Fax: 01722 744447
e-mail:
tourism@
wiltonhouse.com

▶ **LOCATION**

OS Ref. SU099 311

3m W of Salisbury
along the A3.

Rail: Salisbury
Station 3m.

Bus: Every 10 mins
from Salisbury,
Mon - Sat.

Taxi: Sarum Taxi
01722 334477.

CONFERENCE/FUNCTION

ROOM	SIZE	MAX CAPACITY
Double cube	60' x 30'	150
Exhibition Centre	50' x 40'	140
Film Theatre	34" x 20"	67

WILTON HOUSE 🏛

NR SALISBURY

www.wiltonhouse.com

Wilton House has been the ancestral home of the Earl of Pembroke and his family for 450 years. In 1544 Henry VIII gave the Abbey and lands of Wilton to Sir William Herbert who had married Anne Parr, sister of Katherine, sixth wife of King Henry.

The Clock Tower, in the centre of the east front, is reminiscent of this part of the Tudor building which survived a fire in 1647. Inigo Jones and John Webb were responsible for the rebuilding of the house in the Palladian style, whilst further alterations were made by James Wyatt from 1801.

The chief architectural features are the magnificent 17th century state apartments (including the famous Single and Double Cube rooms) and the 19th century cloisters.

The house contains one of the finest art collections in Europe, with over 230 original paintings on display, including works by Van Dyck, Rubens, Joshua Reynolds and Brueghel. Also on show are Greek and Italian statuary, a lock of Queen Elizabeth I's hair, Napoleon's despatch case, and Florence Nightingale's sash.

The Old Riding School houses a dynamic introductory film (narrated by Anna Massey), the reconstructed Tudor kitchen and the Estate's Victorian laundry. The house is set in magnificent landscaped parkland, bordered by the River Nadder which is the setting for the majestic Palladian Bridge. The 17th Earl of Pembroke was a keen gardener who created four new gardens since succeeding to the title in 1969 including the North Forecourt Garden, Old English Rose Garden, Water and Cloister Gardens.

🖻 ℹ Film location, fashion shows, product launches, equestrian events, garden parties, antiques fairs, concerts, vehicle rallies. No photography in house. French, German, Spanish, Italian, Japanese and Dutch information.

🍽 Exclusive banquets.

♿ Visitors may alight at the entrance. WCs.

🍷 Licensed.

🍴 Licensed. Self-service restaurant open 10.30am - 5pm. Groups must book. Hot lunches 12 noon - 2pm.

🚶 By arrangement.

🅿 200 cars and 12 coaches. Free coach parking. Group rates (min 15), meal vouchers, drivers' lounge.

📕 Teachers' handbook for National Curriculum. EFL students welcome. Free preparatory visit for group leaders.

🐕 Guide dogs only. ❄

▶ **OPENING TIMES**

Summer
2 Apr - 31 October
Daily: 10.30am - 5.30pm.

(House closed Mondays except BHs).

Last admission 4.30pm.

Winter
Closed, except for private parties by prior arrangement.

▶ **ADMISSION**

Summer
House, Grounds & Exhibition
Adult £9.75
Child (5 - 15yrs) £5.50
OAP/Student £8.00
Groups (15+)
Adult £7.00
Child £4.50
OAP £6.50

Membership
.... (from) £16.00

🎭 **SPECIAL EVENTS**

MAR 5 - 7
27th Annual Antiques Fair.

APR 16 - 18
Flower Show

JUL 17
Classical Firework Concert.

NTPL / David Norton

NT/Wessex region

AVEBURY MANOR & GARDEN, AVEBURY STONE CIRCLE ✳ ⊞
& ALEXANDER KEILLER MUSEUM
AVEBURY, Nr MARLBOROUGH, WILTSHIRE SN8 1RF

Tel: 01672 539250 **e-mail:** avebury@nationaltrust.org.uk

Owner: The National Trust   **Contact:** The Property Manager

Avebury Manor & Garden: A much-altered house of monastic origin, the present buildings date from the early 16th century, with notable Queen Anne alterations and Edwardian renovation by Col Jenner. The topiary and flower gardens contain medieval walls, ancient box and numerous 'rooms'. The Manor House is occupied and furnished by private tenants, who open a part of it to visitors. Owing to restricted space, guided tours will be in operation. Tours run every 40 mins from 2pm, last tour 4.40pm. Following periods of prolonged wet weather it may be necessary to close the house and garden.

Avebury Stone Circle (above left)**:** One of the most important Megalithic monuments in Europe, this 28 1/2 acre site with stone circles enclosed by a ditch and external bank, is approached by an avenue of stones.

Alexander Keiller Museum: The investigation of Avebury Stone Circle was largely the work of Alexander Keiller in the 1930s. He put together one of the most important prehistoric archaeological collections in Britain which can be seen at the Museum. The development of the Avebury landscape and the story of the people who discovered it is told, using interactive displays and CD ROMs, housed in the spectacular 17th century thatched barn.

Location: OS Ref. SU101 701 (Avebury Manor). OS Ref. SU102 699 (Stone Circle). OS Ref. SU100 699 (Alexander Keiller Museum). 6m W of Marlborough, 1m N of the A4 on A4361 & B4003.

Open: Avebury Manor: House: 4 Apr - 31 Oct: Sun - Tue & Good Fri, 2 - 4.40pm (last admission). Garden: 2 Apr - 31 Oct: Fri - Tue, 11am - 5.30pm, last admission 5pm or dusk if earlier. **Stone Circle:** all year, daily. **Alexander Keiller Museum & Barn Gallery Exhibition** (above right)**:** 1 Apr - 31 Oct: daily, 10am - 6pm; 1 Nov - 31 Mar: 10am - 4pm; close dusk if earlier. Closed 24/25 Dec.

Admission: Avebury Manor: House & Garden: Adult £3.80, Child £1.90. Groups (max 12): Adult £3.20, Child £1.60. Garden only: Adult £2.90, Child £1.40. Groups: Adult £2.45, Child £1.20. **Stone Circle: Free. Alexander Keiller Museum:** (including Barn Gallery): Adult £4.20, Child £2.10, Family (2+3) £10, Family (1+3) £7. Groups (15+): Adult £3.60, Child £1.80. Discount when arriving by public transport or cycle. EH members Free.

🎞 Alexander Keiller Museum, Granary. ♿ Avebury Manor: ground floor with assistance & grounds; Avebury: ground floor fully accessible. WCs. Braille guide.

🍴 Avebury, licensed. 🅿 £1 (pay & display). ▣

🐕 No dogs in house, guide dogs only in garden (Avebury Manor). On leads in Stone Circle.

✳ Stone Circle & Avebury Manor.

BOWOOD HOUSE & GARDENS 🏛   *See page 249 for full page entry.*

BRADFORD-ON-AVON TITHE BARN ⊞
Bradford-on-Avon, Wiltshire

Tel: 0117 975 0700

Owner: English Heritage   **Contact:** South West Regional Office

A magnificent medieval stone-built barn with a slate roof and wooden beamed interior.

Location: OS Ref. ST824 604. 1/4 m S of town centre, off B3109.

Open: Daily, 10.30am - 4pm. Closed 25 Dec. Times subject to change April 2004.

Admission: Free.

♿ 🅿 Charged. ▣ ✳

BROADLEAS GARDENS
Devizes, Wiltshire SN10 5JQ

Tel: 01380 722035

Owner: Broadleas Gardens Charitable Trust   **Contact:** Lady Anne Cowdray

10 acres full of interest, notably The Dell, where the sheltered site allows plantings of magnolias, camellias, rhododendrons and azaleas.

Location: OS Ref. SU001 601. Signposted SW from town centre at S end of housing estate, (coaches must use this entrance) or 1m S of Devizes on W side of A360.

Open: Apr - Oct: Sun, Weds & Thurs, 2 - 6pm or by arrangement for groups.

Admission: Adult £4, Child (under 12yrs) £1.50, Groups (10+) £3.50.

CORSHAM COURT 🏛   *See page 250 for full page entry.*

Website Information see front section

NT Photographic Library: George Wright

THE COURTS ✳
HOLT, TROWBRIDGE, WILTSHIRE BA14 6RR

Tel: 01225 782785 (opening hours)   **Tel:** 01225 782340 (other times)

Fax: 01225 782340

e-mail: courtsgarden@nationaltrust.org.uk

Owner: The National Trust   **Contact:** Head Gardener

One of Wiltshire's best-kept secrets, the English garden style at its best, full of charm and variety. There are many interesting plants and an imaginative use of colour surrounding water features, topiary and herbaceous borders. Complemented by an arboretum with natural planting of spring bulbs.

Location: OS Ref. ST861 618. 3m SW of Melksham, 3m N of Trowbridge, 2 1/2 m E of Bradford-on-Avon, on S side of B3107.

Open: 27 Mar - 17 Oct: daily except Weds, 11am - 5.30pm. Open out of season by appointment only.

Admission: Adult £4.50, Child £2.25, Family (2+2) £11.50. Groups Adult £4, Child £2 Guided tours £2 extra per person.

ℹ No WC. No picnics. 🎭 By appointment at an add. charge. 🅿 Limited. ▣ ✳
🐾 Tel for details.

GREAT CHALFIELD MANOR ✿
Nr Melksham, Wiltshire SN12 8NJ

Tel: 01225 782239   **Fax:** 01225 783379   **www.**nationaltrust.org.uk

Owner: The National Trust   **Contact:** The Tenant

A charming manor house enhanced by a moat and gatehouse and with beautiful oriel windows and a great hall. Completed in 1480, the manor and gardens were restored earlier last century (c1905 - 1911) by Major R Fuller, whose family live here and manage the property. The garden, designed by Alfred Parsons, to complement the Manor, has been replanted.

Location: OS Ref. ST860 633. 3m SW of Melksham off B3107 via Broughton Gifford Common, sign for Atworth. Rail: Bradford-on-Avon 3m.

Open: 30 Mar - 28 Oct: Tue - Thur, admission by guided tour only at 12.15, 2.15, 3, 3.45 & 4.30pm. The tours take 45 mins and numbers are limited to 25. Visitors arriving during a tour can visit the adjoining parish church and garden first. Note: Group visits are welcome on Fri & Sat (not BHs) by written arrangement with the tenant Mrs Robert Floyd. Organisers of coach parties should allow 2 hrs because of limit on numbers in the house.

Admission: Adult £4.40, Child £2.20, Family (2+2) £11. Groups £4, Child £2.

♿ Ground floor with assistance. Limited access to Garden. WC. 👤 Obligatory.
🅿 Limited. ✖

HAMPTWORTH LODGE 🏛
HAMPTWORTH, LANDFORD, SALISBURY, WILTSHIRE SP5 2EA

Tel: 01794 390215   **Fax:** 01794 390700

Owner/Contact: Mr N J M Anderson

Rebuilt Jacobean manor house standing in woodlands on the edge of the New Forest. Grade II* family house with period furniture including clocks. The Great Hall has an unusual roof construction. There is a collection of prentice pieces and the Moffatt collection of contemporary copies. Garden also open.

Location: OS Ref. SU227 195. 10m SE of Salisbury on road linking Downton on Salisbury/Bournemouth Road (A338) to Landford on A36, Salisbury - Southampton.

Open: 28 Mar - 30 Apr: 2.15 - 5pm except Suns. Coaches, by appointment only, 1 Apr - 30 Oct: except Suns.

Admission: £4, Child (under 11yrs) Free. Groups by arrangement.

♿ Ground floor & grounds. 👤 Obligatory.

THE KING'S HOUSE
Salisbury & South Wiltshire Museum
65 The Close, Salisbury, Wiltshire SP1 2EN

Tel: 01722 332151   **Fax:** 01722 325611   **www.**salisburymuseum.org.uk
e-mail: museum@salisburymuseum.org.uk

Owner: Occupied by Salisbury & South Wiltshire Museum Trust
                                                    Contact: P R Saunders

Location: OS Ref. SU141 295. In Salisbury Cathedral Close, W side, facing Cathedral.

Open: All year: Mon - Sat: 10am - 5pm. Suns in Jul & Aug: 2 - 5pm.

Admission: Adult £3.50, Child £1, Conc. £2.30, Groups £2.30.

📷 ♿ Ground floor only. ● ❋

NT Photographic Library

LACOCK ABBEY, FOX TALBOT MUSEUM & VILLAGE ✿
LACOCK, CHIPPENHAM, WILTSHIRE SN15 2LG

www.nationaltrust.org.uk

Tel/Fax: 01249 730227 (Abbey)   **Museum:** 01249 730459   **Fax:** 01249 730501

Owner: The National Trust   **Contact:** The Property Manager

Founded in 1232 and converted into a country house c1540, the fine medieval cloisters, sacristy, chapter house and monastic rooms of the abbey have survived largely intact. The handsome stable courtyard has half-timbered gables, a clockhouse, brewery and bakehouse. Victorian rose garden and a woodland garden boasting a fine display of spring flowers and magnificent trees. The Fox Talbot Museum commemorates William Fox Talbot, a previous resident of the Abbey and inventor of the modern photographic negative. The village has many limewashed half-timbered and stone houses, featured in the TV and film productions of *Pride & Prejudice*, *Moll Flanders*, *Emma* and the recent *Harry Potter* films.

Location: OS Ref. ST919 684. In the village of Lacock, 3m N of Melksham, 3m S of Chippenham just E of A350.

Open: Museum, Cloisters & Garden: 1 Mar - 31 Oct: daily, 11am - 5.30pm (closed Good Fri). Only Museum open winter weekends (closed 25 Dec - 2 Jan), 11am - 4pm. Abbey: 27 Mar - 31 Oct: daily, 1 - 5.30pm (closed Tues & Good Fri).

Admission: Abbey, Museum, Cloisters & Garden: Adult £7, Child £3.50, Family (2+2) £17.90. Groups: Adult £6.30, Child £3.20. Garden, Cloisters & Museum only: Adult £4.40, Child £2.20, Family £11.20. Groups: Adult £4, Child £2. Abbey, Cloisters & Garden only: Adult £5.60, Child £2.80, Family £14.30. Groups: Adult £5, Child £2.50. Museum (winter): Adult £3, Child £1.50, Family (2+2) £7.70. Groups: Adult £2.60, Child £1.30. Abbey guided tours £2 extra per person.

📷 ♿ Braille guides. ● 👤 By arrangement. 🅿 ■ ✖ ❋ ♿ Tel for details.

LARMER TREE GARDENS
RUSHMORE ESTATE, TOLLARD ROYAL, SALISBURY, WILTSHIRE SP5 5PT

www.larmertreegardens.co.uk

Tel: 01725 516228   **Fax:** 01725 516449   **e-mail:** larmer.tree@rushmore-estate.co.uk

Owner: Pitt-Rivers Trustees   **Contact:** Derek Lea

General Augustus Pitt Rivers created these extraordinary 11-acre pleasure grounds in 1880. They contain a unique collection of buildings including a Roman temple, open-air theatre, colonial style tea pavilion and Nepalese rooms. Beautifully laid out gardens with mature trees, laurel hedges, rides and stunning views of the Cranborne Chase. Concerts every Sunday throughout the summer. The gardens are well suited to weddings and corporate events.

Location: OS Ref. ST943 169. 2m S Tollard Royal.

Open: 1 Apr - 31 Oct: daily, 11am - 6pm except Sats & Jul.

Admission: Adult £3.75, Child £2.50 (under 5yrs Free), Conc./Groups £3, Family (2+4) £12.50.

📷 🍴 🍵 ● Licensed. 👤 By arrangement. 🅿 ■ By arrangement. ✖ ▲
♿ Tel for details.

LITTLE CLARENDON

Dinton, Salisbury, Wiltshire SP3 5DZ

Tel: 01985 843600 (Regional Office)   www.nationaltrust.org.uk

Owner: The National Trust   **Contact:** The Regional Office

A Tudor house, altered in the 17th century and with a 20th century Catholic chapel. The three principal rooms on the ground floor are open to visitors and furnished with vernacular oak furniture.

Location: OS Ref. SU015 316. ¼ m E of Dinton Church. 9m W of Salisbury.

Open: 2004 dates to be confirmed, please telephone 0870 458 4000 for details.

Admission: £2, no reductions. (2003 prices, subject to change for 2004.)

ℹ️No WC, no pushchairs or prams, no coaches. ♿Unsuitable.
🅿️At Dinton Post Office.

LONG HALL GARDENS

Stockton, Warminster, Wiltshire BA12 0SE

Tel: 01985 850424   **Owner/Contact:** N H Yeatman-Biggs Esq

4 acres of gardens. Long Hall Nursery is adjacent.

Location: OS Ref. ST982 381. Stockton 7m SE of Warminster, off A36, W of A303 Wylye interchange.

Open: The gardens will be closed during 2004 except to groups by appointment, Apr - Aug.

Admission: Please contact for details.

LONGLEAT 🏛

See page 251 for full page entry.

THE MERCHANT'S HOUSE

132 HIGH STREET, MARLBOROUGH, WILTSHIRE SN8 1HN

www.themerchantshouse.co.uk

Tel/Fax: 01672 511491   **e-mail:** manager@themerchantshouse.co.uk

Owner: Marlborough Town Council   **Contact:** Michael Gray

Situated in Marlborough's world-famous High Street, The Merchant's House is one of the finest middle-class houses in England. Its well-preserved Panelled Chamber was completed in 1656. Both the Dining Room and Great Staircase display recently uncovered 17th century wall paintings which have aroused much expert interest. Leased to the Merchant's House (Marlborough) Trust.

Location: OS Ref. SU188 691. N side of High Street, near Town Hall.

Open: Easter - end Sept: Fri - Sun, 11am - 4pm.

Admission: Adult £3, Child 50p. Booked groups (10-40): Adult £2.50, Child 50p.

ℹ️Photography only by arrangement. 📷 🎭By arrangement.
🅿️Outside house, also in Hillier's Yard. 🦮Guide dogs only. 📞Tel for details.

LYDIARD PARK

LYDIARD TREGOZE, SWINDON, WILTSHIRE SN5 3PA

www.swindon.gov.uk

Tel: 01793 770401   **Fax:** 01793 877909

Owner: Swindon Borough Council   **Contact:** The Keeper

Lydiard Park, ancestral home of the Bolingbrokes, is Swindon's treasure. Set in rolling lawns and woodland this beautifully restored Georgian mansion contains the family's furnishings and portraits, exceptional plasterwork, rare 17th century window and room devoted to 18th century society artist Lady Diana Spencer. Exceptional monuments such as the 'Golden Cavalier' in adjacent church.

Location: OS Ref. SU104 848. 4m W of Swindon, 1½ m N of M4/J16.

Open: House: Mon - Sat, 10am - 5pm, Sun, 2 - 5pm. Nov - Feb: early closing at 4pm. Grounds: all day, closing at dusk. Victorian Christmas decorations throughout December.

Admission: Adult £1.50, Child 75p. Groups by appointment.

ℹ️No photography in house. 📷 ♿ 📖Open all year, but groups must book.
🎭By arrangement. 🎧 🅿️ 🎁 🦮In grounds on leads. ✳️ 📞Tel for details.

MOMPESSON HOUSE 🌿

THE CLOSE, SALISBURY, WILTSHIRE SP1 2EL

www.nationaltrust.org.uk

Tel: 01722 335659   **Infoline:** 01722 420980   **Fax:** 01722 321559

e-mail: mompessonhouse@nationaltrust.org.uk

Owner: The National Trust   **Contact:** The Property Manager

An elegant and spacious 18th century house in the Cathedral Close. Featured in the award-winning film *Sense and Sensibility* and with magnificent plasterwork and a fine oak staircase. As well as pieces of good quality period furniture the house also contains the Turnbull collection of 18th century drinking glasses. Outside, the delightful walled garden has a pergola and traditional herbaceous borders.

Location: OS Ref. SU142 295. On N side of Choristers' Green in Cathedral Close, near High Street Gate.

Open: 9 Apr - 31 Oct: Sat - Wed, 11am - 5pm. Open Good Fri.

Admission: Adult £4, Child £2, Family (2+2) £9.85. Groups: £3.50. Garden only: 80p. Reduced rate when arriving by public transport.

📷 ♿Ground floor & grounds. Braille guide. WC. 📞 🎭By arrangement. 🎁 🦮

NT Photographic Library

NEWHOUSE 🏛

REDLYNCH, SALISBURY, WILTSHIRE SP5 2NX

Tel: 01725 510055 **Fax:** 01725 510284

Owner: George & June Jeffreys   **Contact:** Mrs Jeffreys

A brick, Jacobean 'Trinity' House, c1609, with two Georgian wings and a basically Georgian interior. Home of the Eyre family since 1633.

Location: OS184, SU218 214. 9m S of Salisbury between A36 & A338.

Open: 1 - 31 Mar; 1 - 8 Apr & 30 Aug: Mon - Fri, 2 - 5pm.

Admission: Adult £3.50, Child £2.50, Conc. £3.50. Groups (15+): Adult £3, Child £2.50, Conc. £3.

ℹ️No photography in house, except at weddings. 🅃 🄵By arrangement. 🅿Limited for coaches. 🐕Guide dogs only. ⬆

English Heritage Photo Library/ Skyscan Balloon photography

OLD SARUM ⌗

CASTLE ROAD, SALISBURY, WILTSHIRE SP1 3SD

www.english-heritage.org.uk/visits

Tel: 01722 335398 **Fax:** 01722 416037
e-mail: customers@english-heritage.org.uk

Owner: English Heritage   **Contact:** The Head Custodian

Built around 500BC by the Iron Age peoples, Old Sarum is the former site of the first cathedral and ancient city of Salisbury. A prehistoric hillfort in origin, Old Sarum was occupied by the Romans, the Saxons, and eventually the Normans who made it into one of their major strongholds, with a motte-and-bailey castle built at its centre. Old Sarum eventually grew into one of the most dramatic settlements in medieval England as castle, cathedral, bishop's palace and thriving township. When the new city we know as Salisbury was founded in the early 13th century the settlement faded away. With fine views of the surrounding countryside, Old Sarum is an excellent special events venue.

Location: OS184, SU138 327. 2m N of Salisbury off A345.

Open: Apr - 31 Oct: daily, 10am - 6pm (5pm in Oct). 1 Nov - 31 Mar: daily 10am - 4pm. Closed 24 - 26 Dec & 1 Jan. Times subject to change April 2004.

Admission: Adult £2.50, Child £1.30, Conc. £1.90. 15% discount for groups (11+). Prices subject to change April 2004.

ℹ️WCs. 📷 ♿Grounds. 🅿 🐕In grounds, on leads. ✳ ☎Tel for details.

NORRINGTON MANOR

Alvediston, Salisbury, Wiltshire SP5 5LL

Tel: 01722 780367 **Fax:** 01722 780667

Owner/Contact: T Sykes

Built in 1377 it has been altered and added to in every century since, with the exception of the 18th century. Only the hall and the 'undercroft' remain of the original. It is currently a family home and the Sykes are only the third family to own it.

Location: OS Ref. ST966 237. Signposted to N of Berwick St John and Alvediston road (half way between the two villages).

Open: By appointment in writing.

Admission: A donation to the local churches is asked for.

♿Unsuitable. 🄵By arrangement. 🅿Limited for cars, none for coaches. 🐕 ✳

Bowood, Wiltshire from the book *Historic Family Homes and Gardens from the Air*, see page 54.

Inigo Jones

1573-1652

Regarded by many as England's first true architect. A Londoner and son of a clothmaker, it is thought that he was largely self-taught. First known references to him are as a designer of costumes and décor for the masques at Court. In 1611 Jones was appointed Surveyor to Prince Henry of Wales and, having travelled through Europe and Italy, in 1615 he was appointed Surveyor-General. Look out for the use of true classical proportions in his building work.

Visit The Banqueting House, London to see what is generally regarded as his greatest work. The exterior façade uses two classical orders: the lower, Ionic and the upper, Composite. Visit also The Queen's House, Greenwich, London and Wilton House, Wiltshire.

Architects

© English Heritage Photo Library © Skyscan Balloon Photography

OLD WARDOUR CASTLE

Nr TISBURY, WILTSHIRE SP3 6RR

www.english-heritage.org.uk/visits

Tel/Fax: 01747 870487 **e-mail:** customers@english-heritage.org.uk

Owner: English Heritage   **Contact:** The Custodian

In a picture-book setting, the unusual hexagonal ruins of this 14th century castle stand on the edge of a beautiful lake, surrounded by landscaped grounds which include an elaborate rockwork grotto.

Location: OS184, ST939 263. Off A30 2m SW of Tisbury.

Open: 1 Apr - 31 Oct: daily, 10am - 6pm (5pm in Oct). 1 Nov - 31 Mar: Wed - Sun, 10am - 4pm. Closed for lunch 1 - 2pm. Closed 24 - 26 Dec & 1 Jan. Times subject to change April 2004.

Admission: Adult £2.60, Child £1.30, Conc. £2. 15% discount for groups (11+). Prices subject to change April 2004.

ⓘWCs. ⬜ ⬜Grounds. ⬜ Ⓟ ⬜In grounds, on leads. ✱ ⬜ Tel for details.

F A H Bloemendal

THE PETO GARDEN AT IFORD MANOR 🏛

BRADFORD-ON-AVON, WILTSHIRE BA15 2BA

www.ifordmanor.co.uk

Tel: 01225 863146 **Fax:** 01225 862364

Owner/Contact: Mrs E A J Cartwright-Hignett

This unique Grade I Italian-style garden is set on a romantic hillside beside the River Frome. Designed by the Edwardian architect Harold A Peto, who lived at Iford Manor from 1899 - 1933, the garden has terraces, a colonnade, cloister, casita, statuary, evergreen planting and magnificent rural views. Renowned for its tranquillity and peace, the Peto Garden won the 1998 HHA/Christie's Garden of the Year Award.

Location: OS Ref. ST800 589. 7m SE of Bath via A36, signposted Iford. ¹/₂ m SW of Bradford-on-Avon via Westwood on B3109.

Open: Apr & Oct: Suns only & Easter Mon, 2 - 5pm. May - Sept: Tue - Thur, Sats, Suns & BH Mons, 2 - 5pm. Coaches by appointment at other times. Children under 10yrs welcome weekdays only for safety reasons.

Admission: Adult £4, Conc. £3.50. Groups (10+) welcome outside normal opening hours, by appointment only, £4.50.

⬛Teas (May-Aug: Sats, Suns & BHs, 2.30 - 5pm). ⬜Partial. WCs. Ⓚ By arrangement. Ⓟ Limited for coaches. ⬜On leads, in grounds.

PHILIPPS HOUSE & DINTON PARK 🌿

Dinton, Salisbury, Wiltshire SP3 5HJ

Tel: 01985 843600 **www.**nationaltrust.org.uk

Owner: The National Trust   **Contact:** The Regional Office

A neo-Grecian house by Jeffry Wyatville, completed in 1820. Lovely walks in surrounding parkland.

Location: OS Ref. SU004 319. 9m W of Salisbury, N side of B3089, ¹/₂ m W of Little Clarendon. Car park off St Mary's Road next to church.

Open: 2004 dates to be confirmed, please telephone 0870 458 4000 for details.

Admission: House £3. Dinton Park Free. (2003 prices, subject to change for 2004.)

ⓘNo WC. ⬜House suitable, Park limited. Braille guide.

CHA

PYTHOUSE

TISBURY, WILTSHIRE SP3 6PB

www.cha.org.uk

Tel: 01747 870210 **Fax:** 01747 871786

Owner: Country Houses Association   **Contact:** The Administrators

Set under a well-wooded hill with panoramic views of the south Wiltshire countryside. Pythouse dates from 1725 and boasts an Ice-House and attractive 18th century orangery. The stone elevation was added in 1805 and two wings in 1891. Pythouse has been converted into apartments for active retired people.

Location: OS Ref. SJ909 285. 2¹/₂ m W of Tisbury, 4¹/₂ m N of Shaftesbury. Rail: Tisbury 2¹/₂ m.

Open: 1 May - 30 Sept: Wed & Thur, 2 - 5pm.

Admission: Adult £3, Child Free. Groups by arrangement.

Ⓣ ⬜ ⬜1 single & 1 double with bathroom, CHA members & Wolsey Lodge guests. ⬜

Hamptworth, Wiltshire from the book *Historic Family Homes and Gardens from the Air*, see page 54.

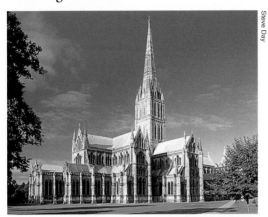

Steve Day

SALISBURY CATHEDRAL

33 THE CLOSE, SALISBURY SP1 2EJ

www.salisburycathedral.org.uk

Tel: 01722 555120 **Fax:** 01722 555116 **e-mail:** visitors@salcath.co.uk

Owner: The Dean & Chapter **Contact:** Visitor Services

Salisbury Cathedral is a building of world importance. Set within the elegant splendour of the Cathedral Close. It is probably the finest medieval building in Britain. Built in one phase from 1220 to 1258. Britain's tallest spire (123m/404ft) was added a generation later. Also, the best preserved Magna Carta, Europe's oldest working clock and a unique 13th century frieze of bible stories in the octagonal Chapter House. Boy and girl choristers sing daily services which follow a tradition of worship that goes back nearly 800 years. Join a tower tour climbing 332 steps to the base of the spire, and marvel at the medieval craftsmanship and the magnificent views.

Location: OS Ref. SU143 295. S of City. M3, A303, A30 from London or A36.

Open: Every Sunday 7.15am - 6.15pm. Mon - Sat, 1 Jan - 6 Jun, 29 Aug - 31 Dec: 7.15am - 6.15pm. 7 Jun - 28 Aug (excluding Sun): 7.15am - 7.15pm.

Admission: Donation: Adult £3.80, Child £2, Conc. £3.30, Family (2+2) £8.50.

◻ ⊤ ⅃ ▣ Licensed. ⅋ ⅌ By arrangement. 🄿 In city centre. ▣ ⤧ In grounds, on leads. ✳ ♒ Tel for details.

STONEHENGE DOWN ⚘

Amesbury, Nr Salisbury, Wiltshire SP4 7DE

Tel: 01985 843600 (Open Countryside, NT)

Tel: 01980 623108 (Monument Visitor Centre, EH)

Owner: The National Trust **Contact:** English Heritage Monument & Visitor Centre

The Trust own 850ha (2100 acres) of downland surrounding the famous monument, including some fine Bronze Age barrow groups and the Cursus, variously interpreted as an ancient racecourse or processional way. The monument itself is owned by English Heritage (see entry below).

Location: OS Ref. SU123 422. 2m W of Amesbury on junction of A303 and A344/ A360.

Open: Tel for details. NT land N of visitor centre: All year, but parts may be closed at the Summer Solstice (21 Jun) for up to 2 days.

Admission: Free.

◻ ⅃ Partial. ⤧ Not on archaeological walks, under close control at all times. ✳

STOURHEAD ⚘   *See page 252 for full page entry.*

STOURTON HOUSE FLOWER GARDEN

Stourton, Warminster, Wiltshire BA12 6QF

Tel: 01747 840417

Owner/Contact: Mrs E Bullivant

Four acres of peaceful, romantic garden. Rhododendrons, hydrangeas, daffodils and roses.

Location: OS Ref. ST780 340. A303, 2m NW of Mere next to Stourhead car park. Follow blue signs.

Open: Apr - end Nov: Weds, Thurs, Suns, and BH Mons, 11am - 6pm. Plants & dried flowers for sale during the winter on weekdays.

Admission: Adult £3, Child £50p. Group guided tours by appointment.

WILTON HOUSE 🏛   *See page 253 for full page entry.*

STONEHENGE ⊞

AMESBURY, WILTSHIRE SP4 7DE

www.english-heritage.org.uk/visits

Tel: 01980 624715 (Information Line) **Owner:** English Heritage

The mystical and awe-inspiring stone circle at Stonehenge is one of the most famous prehistoric monuments in the world, designated by UNESCO as a World Heritage Site. Stonehenge's orientation on the rising and setting sun has always been one of its most remarkable features. Whether this was simply because the builders came from a sun-worshipping culture, or because – as some scholars have believed – the circle and its banks were part of a huge astronomical calendar, remains a mystery. Visitors to Stonehenge can discover the history and legends which surround this unique stone circle, which began over 5,000 years ago, with a complimentary three part audio tour available in 9 languages (subject to availability).

Location: OS Ref. SU123 422. 2m W of Amesbury on junction of A303 and A344/A360.

Open: 16 Mar - 31 May: daily, 9.30am - 6pm, 1 June - 31 Aug: daily, 9am - 7pm, 1 Sept - 15 Oct: daily, 9.30am - 6pm. 16 Oct - 15 Mar: daily, 9.30am - 4pm. Closed 24 - 26 Dec & 1 Jan 2004. Last recommended adm. is ¹/₂ hr before advertised closing times and the site will be closed promptly 20mins after the advertised closing times. Times subject to change April 2004.

Admission: Adult £5, Child £2.50, Conc. £3.80. Family (2+3) £12. Groups (11+) 10% discount. Prices subject to change April 2004.

ⓘWCs. ◻ ⅃ ▣ ◻ ⅃ 🄿 ⤧ ✳ ♒ Tel for details.

eastern

Wimpole Hall, Cambridgeshire © NTPL

houghton hall

Houghton Hall lies 10 miles north-east of King's Lynn in Norfolk. As the guidebook tells, all over the house – in the pediment on the west front, on rainwater hoppers, in plaster, carved wood, and furniture – there appears the Saracen's head crest of the Walpoles. For even now this splendid Palladian mansion with its exquisite tapestries and swaggering State Rooms decorated with Kentian furnishings, oozes the personality of the man for whom it was built. This man, Sir Robert Walpole, 1st Earl of Orford (born in 1676) was one of England's most brilliant and flamboyant politicians of the 18th century. A man who held many of the great offices of State: Secretary of War, Paymaster General, First Lord of the Treasury and Chancellor of the Exchequer, and the man to become the first *de facto* British Prime Minister.

Houghton Hall, built on Walpole's Norfolk estate on the site of two earlier houses, provided that all important regional power-base from which to support his glittering parliamentary career. Begun in 1721, this great mansion, built by Colen Campbell and James Gibbs, was designed with the sole intention to impress – not for Walpole strict controlled Palladian elegance, he wanted something more – here is a house that mixes Italianate simplicity with rich dramatic baroque flourishes. The dome studded roof line makes no apology for its exuberance.

The first floor State Rooms are largely furnished as they would have been in Walpole's day – entered from a massive wooden staircase designed to lead up through the whole height of the building, a huge bronze *The Gladiator*, dominates the Staircase Hall. Wander through these rooms, and you cannot help but gasp at the lavish use of gilding, marble, tapestries and decorated plasterwork on the walls and ceilings. Houghton became the perfect backdrop for Walpole's family living, sporting life, and riotous political entertaining. Barely 30 years later his feckless grandson had to sell his famous collection of Old Masters, and had lost the great outside staircases in a wager.

The house and estate continued on an uneasy passage until the present Marquess' grandparents came to live at Houghton soon after the First World War. Only then did the 5th Marquess and his wife begin to breathe life back into the bones of the house and estate. Lady Cholmondeley, born Sybil Sassoon is perhaps the second most fascinating figure to have lived at Houghton. The daughter of Sir Edward Sassoon, and Aline de Rothschild, Lady Cholmondeley grew up to be the friend and confidante of numerous statesmen and artists. The Walled Garden was replanted in her memory in 1996 by the present Marquess and has become one of the highlights for visitors to the estate.

Today, under Lord Cholmondeley's direction, new projects abound – contemporary art works are to be found in the park and grounds – a mixing of the old with the new – and a way of keeping this old house vibrant and alive … Sir Robert would surely approve.

▶ **For further details about Houghton Hall see page 287.**

WOBURN ABBEY 🏛

WOBURN

www.woburnabbey.co.uk

Set in a beautiful 3,000 acre deer park, Woburn Abbey has been the home of the Dukes of Bedford for nearly 400 years, and is now occupied by the present Duke and Duchess and their family.

The Abbey houses one of the most important private art collections in the world, including paintings by Gainsborough, Reynolds, Van Dyck, Cuyp, and Canaletto, 21 of whose views hang in the Venetian Room.

The tour of the Abbey covers three floors, including the vaults, with 18th Century French and English furniture, silver and a wide range of porcelain on display. Amongst the highlights is the Sèvres dinner service presented to the 4th Duke by Louis XV of France.

The Deer Park is home to ten species of deer, including the Père David, descended from the Imperial Herd of China, which was saved from extinction at Woburn and is now the largest breeding herd of this species in the world. In 1985 the 14th Duke gave 22 Père David deer to the People's Republic of China and the herd is now well established in its natural environment and numbers several hundred.

Woburn Abbey is also noted for its excellent and unique 40 shop Antiques Centre (including 33 showcases), and has an enviable reputation for its in-house catering. Woburn Abbey specialises in banqueting, conferences, receptions and company days; and the Sculpture Gallery overlooking the Private Gardens provides a splendid setting for weddings and wedding receptions.

There are a number of events in the Park each year including the Woburn Garden Show, Craft Fair and the ever popular de Havilland Moth Club annual fly-in.

ℹ️ Suitable for fashion shows, product launches and company 'days out'. Use of parkland and garden. No photography in House.

🏠 Two shops.

🍴 Conferences, exhibitions, banqueting, luncheons, dinners in the Sculpture Gallery, Lantern & Long Harness rooms.

♿ Wheelchairs in the Abbey by prior arrangement (max. 8 per group).

☕ Group bookings in Sculpture Gallery. Flying Duchess Pavilion Coffee Shop.

🍽 Licensed.

🎧 £14, by arrangement, max 15. Tours in French, German & Dutch at an additional charge of £20 per guide. Audio tape tour available – £2pp. Lectures on the property, its contents, gardens and history can be arranged.

🅿 Ample. £2.

👶 Welcome. Special programme on request. Cost: £2.50pp (group rate).

🐕 In park on leads, and guide dogs in house.

🔔 Civil Wedding Licence. ❋

🎭 Tel for details.

Map 6

Owner:
The Duke and Duchess of Bedford &
The Trustees of Bedford Estates

▶ CONTACT

William Lash
Woburn Abbey
Woburn
Bedfordshire MK17 9WA

Tel: 01525 290666
Fax: 01525 290271

e-mail: enquiries@ woburnabbey.co.uk

▶ LOCATION
OS Ref. SP965 325

On A4012, midway between M1/J13, 3m, J14, 6m and the A5 (turn off at Hockliffe). London approx. 1hr by road (43m).

Rail: London Euston to Leighton Buzzard, Bletchley/Milton Keynes. Kings Cross Thameslink to Flitwick.

Air: Luton 14m. Heathrow 39m.

CONFERENCE/FUNCTION

ROOM	SIZE	MAX CAPACITY
Sculpture Gallery	130' x 25'	400 / 220 (sit-down)
Lantern Rm	24' x 21'	100

▶ OPENING TIMES
1 January - 13 March
Abbey: weekends only
11am - 4pm*
Deer Park:
Daily, 10.30am - 3.45pm

13 March - 31 October
Abbey:
Mon - Sat: 11am - 4pm*
Sun & BHs: 11am - 5pm
Deer Park:
Mon - Sat: 10am - 5pm
Sun & BHs: 10am - 5pm

Abbey: closed
1 Nov - end Dec

Antiques Centre:
All year, daily
(except 24 - 26,
31 Dec 2003 & 1 Jan,
24 - 26 Dec 2004).

*last entry time

▶ ADMISSION
Woburn Abbey
(Prices incl. Private Apts)
Adult £9.00
Child (5 - 15yrs) £4.50
OAP £8.00
Group rates & family tickets available.

**Grounds &
Deer Park only**
Car £2.00
Motorcycle............. £2.00
Coaches... £1 per person
Other £1.00

Reduced rates apply when Private Apartments are in use by the family.

BROMHAM MILL & GALLERY
Bridge End, Bromham, Bedfordshire MK43 8LP
Tel: 01234 824330
Owner: Bedfordshire County Council   **Contact:** Sally Wileman
Working water mill on River Ouse. Flour milling and changing contemporary art & craft exhibitions.
Location: OS Ref. TL010 506. Location beside the River Ouse bridge on N side of the former A428, 2^1/$_2$ m W of Bedford.
Open: Apr - Oct: Suns & BHs, 1 - 5pm. Other times for groups by arrangement.
Admission: Free. Group charges on application.

BUSHMEAD PRIORY ⌗
Colmworth, Bedford, Bedfordshire MK44 2LD
Tel: 01234 376614   **Regional Office:** 01223 582700
Owner: English Heritage   **Contact:** The Custodian
A rare survival of the medieval refectory of an Augustinian priory, with its original timber-framed roof almost intact and containing interesting wall paintings and stained glass.
Location: OS Ref. TL115 607. On unclassified road near Colmworth; off B660, 2m S of Bolnhurst. 5m W of St. Neots (A1).
Open: Jul - Aug weekends & BHs only: 10am - 6pm. Closed 1 - 2pm. Times subject to change April 2004.
Admission: Adult £2 Child £1, Conc. £1.50. Prices subject to change April 2004.
P ⊠ ,

MOOT HALL
Elstow Green, Church View, Elstow, Bedford
Tel: 01234 266889
Owner: Bedfordshire County Council
Timber framed market hall.
Location: OS Ref. TL048 475. 1m from Bedford, signposted from A6.
Open: Apr - Oct: Tue, Wed, Thur, Sat, Sun & BHs: 2 - 5pm.
Admission: Adult £1, Conc. 50p.

STOCKWOOD PERIOD GARDENS
Farley Hill, Luton, Bedfordshire
Tel: 01582 738714   **Fax:** 01582 546763   **e-mail:** museum.gallery@luton.gov.uk
Owner: Luton Borough Council   **Contact:** Keith Watts
Includes Knot, Medieval, Victorian and Italian gardens.
Location: OS Ref. TL085 200. 1^1/$_4$ m SW of Luton town centre by Farley Road B4546.
Open: Apr - Oct: Tue - Sun & BHs, 10am - 5pm. Nov - Mar: Sat - Sun, 10am - 4pm.
Admission: Free.

SWISS GARDEN
Old Warden Park, Bedfordshire
Tel: 01767 627666   **Fax:** 01767 627443   **e-mail:** swiss.garden@dial.pipex.co.uk
Operated By: Bedfordshire County Council
Laid out in the early 1800s and steeped in the indulgent romanticism of the time, Swiss Garden combines all the elements of high fashion: formal walks and vistas, classical proportions, tiny thatched buildings, woodland glades and, hidden away, a fairytale grotto with a brilliant glazed fernery, magnificent trees and a network of ponds and bridges.
Location: OS Ref. TL150 447. 1^1/$_2$ m W of Biggleswade A1 roundabout, signposted from A1 and A600.
Open: Apr - Oct: 10am - 5pm; Nov - Mar: 10am - 4pm. Closed Christmas week.
Admission: Adult £3, Child Free, Conc. £2. Special rates for groups, tours or private hire.
⌷ ⅃ ⊤ Catering. ▣ Refreshments adjacent. P ⊠ ▲ ✳

CECIL HIGGINS ART GALLERY
CASTLE LANE, BEDFORD MK40 3RP
www.cecilhigginsartgallery.org
Tel: 01234 211222   **Fax:** 01234 327149   **e-mail:** chag@bedford.gov.uk
Owner: Bedford Borough Council & Trustees of Gallery   **Contact:** The Gallery
A recreation of an 1880s home, with superb examples of 19th century decorative arts. Room settings include items from the Handley-Read collection and the famous Gothic bedroom containing works by William Burges. Adjoining gallery housing renowned collections of watercolours, prints and drawings (exhibitions changed regularly), ceramics, glass and lace. Situated in pleasant gardens near the river embankment.
Location: OS Ref. TL052 497. Centre of Bedford, just off The Embankment. E of High St.
Open: Tue - Sat, 11am - 5pm (last admission 4.45pm). Sun & BH Mons, 2 - 5pm. Closed Mons, Good Fri, 25/26 Dec & 1 Jan.
Admission: Adults £2.20, Conc. Free (includes visit to Bedford Museum). Free entry on Fri.
ⓘ Photography in house by arrangement. ⬚ ⊤ By arrangement. ⅃
▣ Self-service coffee bar. ⓘ By arrangement. ▣ ⬙ Guide dogs only. ✳
⬚ Tel for details.

HOUGHTON HOUSE ⌗
Ampthill, Bedford, Bedfordshire
Tel: 01223 582700 (Regional Office)
Owner: English Heritage   **Contact:** East of England Regional Office
Reputedly the inspiration for "*House Beautiful*" in Bunyan's "*Pilgrim's Progress*", the remains of this early 17th century mansion still convey elements which justify the description, including work attributed to Inigo Jones.
Location: OS Ref. TL039 394. 1m NE of Ampthill off A421, 8m S of Bedford.
Open: Any reasonable time.
Admission: Free.
P ⬙ ✳

WREST PARK GARDENS ⌗
SILSOE, LUTON, BEDFORDSHIRE MK45 4HS
www.english-heritage.org.uk/visits
Tel: 01525 860152
Owner: English Heritage   **Contact:** The Custodian
Over 90 acres of enchanting gardens originally laid out in the early 18th century, and inspired by the great gardens of Versailles and the Loire Valley in France. Marvel at the magnificent collection of stone and lead statuary, the Bath House and the vast Orangery, built by the Earl de Grey, and dream of days gone by. The gardens form a delightful backdrop to the house which is built in the style of an 18th century French château.
Location: OS153, TL093 356. ^{3}/$_4$ m E of Silsoe off A6, 10m S of Bedford.
Open: 1 Apr - 31 Oct: Weekends and BHs only, 10am - 6pm (5pm in Oct). Last admission 1hr before closing time. Times subject to change April 2004.
Admission: Adult £4, Child £2, Conc. £3. 15% discount for groups (11+). Family Ticket £9.50. Prices subject to change April 2004.
ⓘ WCs. ⬚ ⅃ ▣ P ⬚ Tel for details.

ANGLESEY ABBEY

LODE, CAMBRIDGE, CAMBRIDGESHIRE CB5 9EJ

www.nationaltrust.org.uk/angleseyabbey

Tel/Fax: 01223 810080   **e-mail:** angleseyabbey@nationaltrust.org.uk

Owner: The National Trust   **Contact:** The Property Manager

Dating from 1600, the house, built on the site of an Augustinian priory, contains the famous Fairhaven collection of paintings and furniture. Surrounded by an outstanding 100 acre garden and arboretum, with a wonderful display of hyacinths in spring and magnificent herbaceous borders and a dahlia garden in summer. A watermill in full working order is demonstrated on the first & third Saturday each month.

Location: OS Ref. TL533 622. 6m NE of Cambridge on B1102, signs from A14.

Open: Summer: House & Mill: 24 Mar - 7 Nov: Wed - Sun & BH Mons (closed Good Fri): 1 - 5pm. Garden, Shop, Plant Centre & Restaurant: 24 Mar - 7 Nov: Wed - Sun & BH Mons; 5 July - 29 Aug: daily (late opening Thurs to 8pm), 10.30am - 5.30pm. Winter: Winter Garden, Shop, Plant Centre & Restaurant: 10 Nov - 23 Dec & 29 Dec - 20 Mar 2005: Wed - Sun, 10.30am - 4pm; Mill: Sat & Sun, 11am - 3.30pm, last adm. 3pm. Groups must book, no groups on Sun & BHs.

Admission: House & garden: £6.60, Child £3.30. Groups: Adult £5.40, Child £2.70. Garden only: Adult £4.10, Child £2.05. Groups: Adult £3.35, Child £1.70. Winter (garden only): Adult £3.40, Child £1.70. Groups: Adult £2.90, Child £1.45.

☐ ☒ ☒ Partial. ☒ Licensed. ☒ ☒ ☒ ☒ ☒ Tel for details.

H Rice

CAMBRIDGE UNIVERSITY BOTANIC GARDEN

BATEMAN STREET, CAMBRIDGE CB2 1JF

www.botanic.cam.ac.uk

Tel: 01223 336265 **Fax:** 01223 336278 **e-mail:** enquiries@botanic.cam.ac.uk

Owner: University of Cambridge   **Contact:** Juliet Day

This 40 acre oasis of listed heritage landscape showcases over 8000 species, including alpines from every continent in the Rock Garden, nine national collections, the finest collection of trees in the Eastern Region, the historic Systematic Beds, the Dry Garden, the renowned Winter Garden and tropical forest in the Glasshouses.

Location: OS Ref. TL453 573. ³/₄m S of Cambridge city centre; entrance on Bateman Street off A1309 (Trumpington Rd). 10mins walk from railway station.

Open: 2 Jan - 24 Dec: daily, 10am - 6pm; closes 5pm in autumn & spring and 4pm in winter.

Admission: Adult £2.50, Child £2.

☐ Mar - Oct. ☒ ☒ ☒ By arrangement. ☒ Street/Pay & Display. ☒ ☒ Guide dogs only. ☒

OLIVER CROMWELL'S HOUSE

29 St Mary's Street, Ely, Cambridgeshire CB7 4HF

Tel: 01353 662062   **Fax:** 01353 668518   **e-mail:** tic@eastcambs.gov.uk

Owner: East Cambridgeshire District Council

The former home of the Lord Protector.

Location: OS Ref. TL538 803. N of Cambridge, ¼ m W of Ely Cathedral.

Open: 1 Nov - 31 Mar: Mon - Sat, 11am - 4pm; Suns, 11.15am - 4pm. 1 Apr -31 Oct: daily, 10am - 5.30pm.

Admission: Adult £3.75, Child £2.50, Conc. £3.25, Family £10.

DENNY ABBEY & THE FARMLAND MUSEUM ♯

Ely Road, Chittering, Waterbeach, Cambridgeshire CB5 9TQ

Tel: 01223 860489   www.english-heritage.org.uk/visits

Owner: English Heritage/Managed by the Farmland Museum Trust

                                                  Contact: The Custodian

What at first appears to be an attractive stone-built farmhouse is actually the remains of a 12th century Benedictine abbey which, at different times, also housed the Knights Templar and Franciscan nuns. Founded by the Countess of Pembroke.

Location: OS Ref. TL495 684. 6m N of Cambridge on the E side of the A10.

Open: 1 Apr - 31 Oct: daily, 12 noon - 5pm. Times subject to change April 2004.

Admission: Adult £3.60, Child £1.40, Conc. £2.60, Family £8.50. Prices subject to change April 2004.

☒ ☒

DOCWRA'S MANOR GARDEN ⬚

Shepreth, Royston, Hertfordshire SG8 6PS

Tel: 01763 261473 **Information:** 01763 260677

Owner: Mrs Faith Raven   **Contact:** Peter Rocket

Extensive garden around building dating from the 18th century.

Location: OS Ref. TL393 479. In Shepreth via A10 from Royston.

Open: All year: Weds & Fris, 10am - 4pm & 1st Sun in month from Apr - Oct: 2 - 5pm.

Admission: £3.

ELTON HALL
Nr PETERBOROUGH PE8 6SH

Tel: 01832 280468   **Fax:** 01832 280584   **e-mail:** office@eltonhall.com

Owner: Sir William Proby Bt   **Contact:** The Administrator

Elton Hall, the home of the Proby family for over 350 years is a fascinating mixture of styles. Every room contains treasures, magnificent furniture and fine paintings. The library is one of the finest in private hands and includes Henry VIII's prayer book. The beautiful gardens have been carefully restored, with the addition of a new gothic Orangery to celebrate the Millennium.

Location: OS Ref. TL091 930. Close to A1 in the village of Elton, off A605 Peterborough - Oundle road.

Open: 31 May (BH Mon). June: Weds. Jul & Aug: Wed, Thur & Sun and 30 Aug (BH Mon). 2 - 5pm. Private groups by arrangement Apr - Sept.

Admission: Hall & Gardens: £6. Gardens only: £3. Accompanied child under 16 free.
ⓘNo photography in house. 🅿️ Garden suitable. Obligatory. P
Guide dogs in gardens only. Tel for details.

ELY CATHEDRAL

The Chapter House, The College, Ely, Cambridgeshire CB7 4DL

Tel: 01353 667735 ext.261 **Fax:** 01353 665658

Contact: Marilyn Carpenter (Visits & Tours Manager)

A wonderful example of Romanesque architecture. Octagon and Lady Chapel are of special interest. Superb medieval domestic buildings surround the Cathedral. Stained Glass Museum. Brass rubbing. Octagon and West Tower tours peak season.

Location: OS Ref. TL541 803. Via A10, 15m N of Cambridge City centre.

Open: Summer: 7am - 7pm. Winter: Mon - Sat, 7.30am - 6pm, Suns and week after Christmas, 7.30am - 5pm. Sun services: 8.15am, 10.30am and 3.45pm. Weekday services: 7.40am, 8am, and 5.30pm (Thurs only also 12.30pm).

Admission: Adult £4.80, Child Free, Conc. £4.40. Discounts for groups of 15+. Separate rates for school visits.

ISLAND HALL
GODMANCHESTER, CAMBRIDGESHIRE PE29 2BA

Tel: 01480 459676   **e-mail:** cvp@cvpdesigns.com

Owner: Mr Christopher & Lady Linda Vane Percy   **Contact:** Mr C Vane Percy

An important mid 18th century mansion of great charm, owned and restored by an award-winning interior designer. This family home has lovely Georgian rooms, with fine period detail, and interesting possessions relating to the owners' ancestors since their first occupation of the house in 1800. A tranquil riverside setting with formal gardens and ornamental island forming part of the grounds in an area of Best Landscape. Octavia Hill wrote *"This is the loveliest, dearest old house, I never was in such a one before."*

Location: OS Ref. TL244 706. Centre of Godmanchester, Post Street next to free car park. 1m S of Huntingdon, 15m NW of Cambridge A14.

Open: Groups only, by arrangement: May - Jul & Sept.

Admission: (30+) Adult £4, (10-30 persons) Adult £4.50. Under 10 persons, min charge £45 per group (sorry but no children under 13).
Unsuitable. Home made teas.

KIMBOLTON CASTLE

Kimbolton, Huntingdon, Cambridgeshire PE28 0EA

Tel: 01480 860505 **Fax:** 01480 861763

www.kimbolton.cambs.sch.uk

Owner: Governors of Kimbolton School **Contact:** Mrs N Butler

A late Stuart house, an adaptation of a 13th century fortified manor house, with evidence of Tudor modifications. The seat of the Earls and Dukes of Manchester 1615 - 1950, now a school. Katharine of Aragon died in the Queen's Room - the setting for a scene in Shakespeare's Henry VIII. A minor example of the work of Vanbrugh and Hawksmoor; Gatehouse by Robert Adam; the Pellegrini mural paintings on the Staircase, in the Chapel and in the Boudoir are the best examples in England of this gifted Venetian decorator.

Location: OS Ref. TL101 676. 7m NW of St Neots on B645.

Open: 7 Mar & 7 Nov, 1 - 4pm.

Admission: Adult £3, Child £2, OAP £2.50. Groups by arrangement throughout the year, including evenings.

🅣 🅹Unsuitable. 🅿 🅘By arrangement. 🅿 🅿 🅷On leads in grounds. 🅰 ❄

THE MANOR, HEMINGFORD GREY

HUNTINGDON, CAMBRIDGESHIRE PE28 9BN

www.greenknowe.co.uk

Tel: 01480 463134 **Fax:** 01480 465026 **e-mail:** diana_boston@hotmail.com

Owner: Mrs D S Boston **Contact:** Diana Boston

Built about 1130 and reputedly the oldest continuously inhabited house in Britain. Made famous as 'Green Knowe' by the author Lucy Boston. Her patchwork collection is also shown. Four acre garden with topiary, old roses and herbaceous borders.

Location: OS Ref. TL290 706. Off A14, 3m SE of Huntingdon. 12m NW of Cambridge. Access is by a small gate on the riverside footpath.

Open: House: All year (except May), to individuals or groups by prior arrangement. May only: guided tours at 11am & 2pm (booking advisable). Garden: All year, daily, 11am - 5pm (4pm in winter).

Admission: Adult £4, Child £1.50, OAP £3.50. Garden only: Adult £2, Child Free.

🅘No photography in house. 🅾 🅗 🅿Locally, by arrangement. 🅘Obligatory. 🅿 🅿Disabled only. 🅷In garden, on leads. ❄

KING'S COLLEGE

KING'S PARADE, CAMBRIDGE CB2 1ST

www.kings.cam.ac.uk

Tel/Fax: 01223 331212 **e-mail:** derek.buxton@kings.cam.ac.uk

Owner: Provost and Fellows **Contact:** Mr D Buxton

Visitors are welcome, but remember that this is a working college. Please respect the privacy of those who work, live and study here. The Chapel is sometimes used for services, recordings, broadcasts, etc, and ideally visitors should check before arriving. Recorded message for services, concerts and visiting times: 01223 331155.

Location: OS Ref. TL447 584.

Open: Out of term: Mon - Sat, 9.30am - 4.30pm. Sun, 10am - 5pm. In term: Mon - Fri: 9.30am - 3.30pm. Sat: 9.30am - 3.15pm. Sun: 1.15 - 2.30pm, 5 - 5.30pm BST only.

Admission: Adult £4, Child (12-17yrs)/Student (ID required)/OAP £3. Child (under 12 & accompanied) Free (only as part of family unit).

🅘No photography inside Chapel. Conferences. 🅾 🅣By arrangement. 🅗 🅘By arrangement. 🅿None. 🅷Guide dogs only. ❄

PETERBOROUGH CATHEDRAL

Chapter Office, Minster Precincts, Peterborough PE1 1XS

Tel: 01733 343342 **Fax:** 01733 552465

e-mail: a.watson@peterborough-cathedral.org.uk

www.peterborough-cathedral.org.uk **Contact:** Andrew Watson

'An undiscovered gem.' With magnificent Norman architecture a unique 13th century nave ceiling, the awe-inspiring West Front and burial places of two Queens to make your visit an unforgettable experience. Exhibitions tell the Cathedral's story. Tours by appointment, of the cathedral, tower, Deanery Garden or Precincts. Freshly prepared meals and snacks at Beckets Restaurant (advance bookings possible). Cathedral gift shop and Tourist Information Centre in Precincts. Business meeting facilities.

Location: OS Ref. TL194 986. 4m E of A1, in City Centre.

Open: All year: Mon - Fri, 9am - 5.15pm. Sat, 9am - 5pm. Sun: services from 7.30am; visitors: 12 noon - 5pm.

Admission: No fixed charge – donations are requested.

🅘Visitors' Centre. 🅾 🅗 🅸 Mon - Sat. 🅘By arrangement. 🅿None. 🅿 🅷Guide dogs only. ❄

LONGTHORPE TOWER ⛫

Thorpe Rd, Longthorpe, Cambridgeshire PE1 1HA

Tel: 01733 268482 **www.**english-heritage.org.uk/visits

Owner: English Heritage **Contact:** The Custodian

The finest example of 14th century domestic wall paintings in northern Europe showing a variety of secular and sacred objects. The tower, with the Great Chamber that contains the paintings, is part of a fortified manor house. Special exhibitions are held on the upper floor.

Location: OS Ref. TL163 983. 2m W of Peterborough just off A47.

Open: 1 Apr - 31 Oct: weekends & BHs only: 12 noon - 5pm. Times subject to change April 2004.

Admission: Adult £1.70, Child 90p, Conc. £1.30. Prices subject to change April 2004.

🅾 🅿 🅷

RAMSEY ABBEY GATEHOUSE ⛨

Abbey School, Ramsey, Cambridgeshire PE17 1DH

Tel: 01480 301494 (Property Manager) **www.**nationaltrust.org.uk

Owner: The National Trust **Contact:** The Curator (in writing)

The remnants of a former Benedictine monastery, built on an island in the Fens. The late 15th century gatehouse is richly carved and contains an ornate oriel window.

Location: OS Ref. TL291 851. At SE edge of Ramsey at point where Chatteris Road leaves B1096, 10m SE of Peterborough.

Open: 29 Apr - 31 Oct: daily, 10am - 5pm, other times by written application to curator.

Admission: Free, donations welcome.

🅿Limited. 🅷Guide dogs only.

PECKOVER HOUSE & GARDEN ❧

NORTH BRINK, WISBECH, CAMBRIDGESHIRE PE13 1JR

www.nationaltrust.org.uk

Tel/Fax: 01945 583463   **e-mail:** peckover@nationaltrust.org.uk

Owner: The National Trust   **Contact:** The Property Manager

A town house, built c1722 and renowned for its very fine plaster and wood rococo decoration. The outstanding 2 acre Victorian garden includes an orangery, summer-houses, roses, herbaceous borders, fernery, croquet lawn and Reed Barn tearoom.

Location: OS Ref. TF458 097. On N bank of River Nene, in Wisbech B1441.

Open: House: 21 Mar - 31 Oct: Weds, Sats, Suns, Good Fri & BH Mons (also open Thurs May - Aug), 1.30 - 4.30pm. Garden: 21 Mar - 31 Oct: Sat - Thur, 12.30 - 5pm. Groups welcome when house open and at other times by appointment. Restaurant & Shop: Same days as House, 12.30 - 5pm.

Admission: Adult £4.25. Garden days: £2.75. Groups: £3.75.

🔲 ♿ Ⓣ ♿Partial. 🛒 🍴 🅿 Signposted. 🐕 🏠 ▲ 🔱Tel for details.

WIMPOLE HALL & HOME FARM ❧

ARRINGTON, ROYSTON, CAMBRIDGESHIRE SG8 0BW

www.nationaltrust.org.uk or www.wimpole.org

Tel: 01223 207257   **Fax:** 01223 207838   **e-mail:** wimpolehall@nationaltrust.org.uk

Owner: The National Trust   **Contact:** The Property Manager

Wimpole is a magnificent country house built in 18th century style with a colourful history of owners. The Hall is set in recently restored formal gardens including parterres and a rose garden. Home Farm is a working farm and is the largest rare breeds centre in East Anglia.

Location: OS154. TL336 510. 8m SW of Cambridge (A603), 6m N of Royston (A1198).

Open: Hall: 20 Mar - 31 Oct: daily except Mon & Fri (open Good Fri & BH Mon); Aug: Tue - Sun (open BH Mons); 7, 14, 21 & 28 Nov, Sun only; 1 - 5pm, BH Mon, 11am - 5pm, closes 4pm after 31 Oct. Garden: as Farm. Park: dawn - dusk. Farm: 20 Mar - 31 Oct: daily except Mon & Fri (open Good Fri & BH Mon); Jul & Aug: Tue - Sun & BH Mon; Nov - Mar 2005: Sat & Sun (open Feb half-term week); 20 Mar - 31 Oct: 10.30am - 5pm; 5 Nov - Mar 2005, 11am - 4pm.

Admission: Hall: Adult £6.60, Child £3.20. Joint ticket with Home Farm: Adult £9.80, Child £5.20, Family £25. Garden: £2.60. Group rates (not Suns or BH Mons). Farm: Adult £5.10, Child (3yrs & up) £3.20. Discount for NT members (not Suns or BH Mons).

🔲 ♿ Ⓣ ♿Partial. 🛒 🍴 Licensed. 🎨 By arrangement. 🅿 Limited for coaches. ▣ 🐕In park, on leads. ▲ 🔱Tel for details.

UNIVERSITY OF CAMBRIDGE

Christ's College
St Andrew's Street, Cambridge CB2 3BU
Tel: +44 1223 334900
Fax: +44 1223 334967
Email: admissions@christs.cam.ac.uk
Founder: Lady Margaret Beaufort
Founded: 1505

Churchill College
Storey's Way, Cambridge CB3 0DS
Tel: +44 1223 336000
Fax: +44 1223 336180
Email: admissions@chu.cam.ac.uk
Founded: 1960

Clare College
Trinity Lane, Cambridge CB2 1TL
Tel: +44 1223 333200
Fax: +44 1223 333219
Email: admissions@clare.cam.ac.uk
        enquiries@clare.cam.ac.uk
Founded: 1326

Clare Hall
Herschel Road, Cambridge CB3 9AL
Tel: +44 1223 332360
Fax: +44 1223 332333
Email: receptionist@clarehall.cam.ac.uk
Founded: 1965

Corpus Christi College
Trumpington Street, Cambridge CB2 1RH
Tel: +44 1223 338000
Fax: +44 1223 338061
Email: admissions@corpus.cam.ac.uk
Founded: 1352

Darwin College
Silver Street, Cambridge CB3 9EU
Tel: +44 1223 335660
Fax: +44 1223 335667
Email: deanery@dar.cam.ac.uk
Founded: 1964

Downing College
Regent Street, Cambridge CB2 1DQ
Tel: +44 1223 334800
Fax: +44 1223 467934
Email: admissions@dow.cam.ac.uk
        college-secretary@dow.cam.ac.uk
Founded: 1800

Emmanuel College
St Andrew's Street, Cambridge CB2 3AP
Tel: +44 1223 334200
Fax: +44 1223 334426
Email: admissions@emma.cam.ac.uk
Founded: 1584

Fitzwilliam College
Huntingdon Road, Cambridge CB3 0DG
Tel: +44 1223 332000
Fax: +44 1223 464162
Email: admissions@fitz.cam.ac.uk
Founded: 1966

Girton College
Huntingdon Road, Cambridge CB3 0JG
Tel: +44 1223 338999
Fax: +44 1223 338896
Email: admissions@girton.cam.ac.uk
Founded: 1869

Gonville & Caius College
Trinity Street, Cambridge CB2 1TA
Tel: +44 1223 332400
Fax: +44 1223 332456
Email: admissions@cai.cam.ac.uk
Founded: 1348

Homerton College
Hills Road, Cambridge CB2 2PH
Tel: +44 1223 507111
Fax: +44 1223 507120
Email: admissions@homerton.cam.ac.uk
Founded: 1976

Hughes Hall
Mortimer Road, Cambridge CB1 2EW
Tel: +44 1223 334898
Fax: +44 1223 311179
Email: admissions@hughes.cam.ac.uk
        enquiries@hughes.cam.ac.uk
Founded: 1885

Jesus College
Jesus Lane, Cambridge CB5 8BL
Tel: +44 1223 339339
Fax: +44 1223 324910
Email: undergraduate-admissions@jesus.cam.ac.uk
Founded: 1497

King's College
King's Parade, Cambridge CB2 1ST
Tel: +44 1223 331100
Fax: +44 1223 331315
Email: undergraduate.admissions@kings.cam.ac.uk
        graduate.admissions@kings.cam.ac.uk
Founded: 1441

Lucy Cavendish College
Lady Margaret Road, Cambridge CB3 0BU
Tel: +44 1223 332190
Fax: +44 1223 332178
Email: lcc-admission@lists.cam.ac.uk
Founded: 1965

Magdalene College
Magdalene Street, Cambridge CB3 0AG
Tel: +44 1223 332100
Fax: +44 1223 363637
Email: magd-admissions@lists.cam.ac.uk
Founded: 1428

New Hall
Huntingdon Road, Cambridge CB3 0DF
Tel: +44 1223 762100
Fax: +44 1223 352941
Email: admissions@newhall.cam.ac.uk
Founded: 1954

Newnham College
Sidgwick Avenue, Cambridge CB3 9DF
Tel: +44 1223 335700
Fax: +44 1223 359155/357898
Email: admissions@newn.cam.ac.uk
enquiries@newn.cam.ac.uk
Founded: 1871

Pembroke College
Trumpington Street, Cambridge CB2 1RF
Tel: +44 1223 338100
Fax: +44 1223 338163
Email: admissions@pem.cam.ac.uk
enquiries@pem.cam.ac.uk
Founded: 1347

Peterhouse
Trumpington Street, Cambridge CB2 1RD
Tel: +44 1223 338200
Fax: +44 1223 337578
Email: admissions@pet.cam.ac.uk
Founder: The Bishop of Ely
Founded: 1284

Queens' College
Silver Street, Cambridge CB3 9ET
Tel: +44 1223 335511
Fax: +44 1223 335522 (General)
Email: admissions@quns.cam.ac.uk
enquiries@quns.cam.ac.uk
Founder: Margaret of Anjou, Elizabeth Woodville
Founded: 1448

Robinson College
Grange Road, Cambridge CB3 9AN
Tel: +44 1223 339100
Fax: +44 1223 351794
Email: undergraduate-admissions
@robinson.cam.ac.uk
graduate-admissions@robinson.cam.ac.uk
Founded: 1979

St Catharine's College
Trumpington Street, Cambridge CB2 1RL
Tel: +44 1223 338300
Fax: +44 1223 338340
Email: undergraduate.admissions@caths.cam.ac.uk
Founded: 1473

St Edmund's College
Mount Pleasant, Cambridge CB3 0BN

Tel: +44 1223 336250
Fax: +44 1223 336111
Email: admissions@st-edmunds.cam.ac.uk
college.office@st-edmunds.cam.ac.uk
Founded: 1896

St John's College
St John's Street, Cambridge CB2 1TP
Tel: +44 1223 338600
Fax: +44 1223 337720
Email: admissions@joh.cam.ac.uk
Founded: 1511

Selwyn College
Grange Road, Cambridge CB3 9DQ
Tel: +44 1223 335846
Fax: +44 1223 335837
Email: admissions@sel.cam.ac.uk
Founded: 1882

Sidney Sussex College
Sidney Street, Cambridge CB2 3HU
Tel: +44 1223 338800
Fax: +44 1223 338884
Email: admissions@sid.cam.ac.uk
enquiries@sid.cam.ac.uk
Founded: 1596

Trinity College
Trinity Street, Cambridge CB2 1TQ
Tel: +44 1223 338400
Fax: +44 1223 338564
Email: admissions@trin.cam.ac.uk
college.office@trin.cam.ac.uk
Founded: 1546

Trinity Hall
Trinity Lane, Cambridge CB2 1TJ
Tel: +44 1223 332500
Fax: +44 1223 332537
Email: admissions@trinhall.cam.ac.uk
Founded: 1350

Wolfson College
Barton Road, Cambridge CB3 9BB
Tel: +44 1223 335900
Fax: +44 1223 335908 (Porter's Lodg)
Email: ug-admissions@wolfson.cam.ac.uk
pg-admissions@wolfson.cam.ac.uk
Founded: 1965

Visitors wishing to gain admittance to the Colleges (meaning the Courts, not to the staircases & students' rooms) are advised to contact the Tourist Office for further information. It should be noted that Halls normally close for lunch (12 - 2pm) and many are not open during the afternoon. Chapels may be closed during services. Libraries are not normally open, and Gardens do not usually include the Fellows' garden. Visitors, and especially guided groups, should always call on the Porters Lodge first.

For further details contact: Cambridge Tourism, The Old Library, Wheeler Street, Cambridge CB2 3QB.
Tel: +44 (0)1223 464132   Infoline: 0906 5862526   Fax: +44 (0)1223 457549

English Heritage Photographic Library

Map 6

AUDLEY END HOUSE & GDNS ⊞

SAFFRON WALDEN

www.english-heritage.org.uk/visits

Owner:
English Heritage

▶ **CONTACT**

The General Manager
Audley End House
Audley End
Saffron Walden
Essex CB11 4JF

Tel: 01799 522842
Fax: 01799 521276

**Venue Hire and
Hospitality:**
Tel: 01799 522842

▶ **LOCATION**

OS Ref. TL525 382

1m W of Saffron
Walden on B1383,
M11/J8 & 9 northbound
only & J10.

Rail: Audley End 1¼m.

Audley End was a palace in all but name. Built by Thomas Howard, Earl of Suffolk, to entertain King James I. The King may have had his suspicions, for he never stayed there; in 1618 Howard was imprisoned and fined for embezzlement.

Charles II bought the property in 1668 for £50,000, but within a generation the house was gradually demolished, and by the 1750s it was about the size you see today. There are still over 30 magnificent rooms to see, each with period furnishings.

The house and its gardens, including a 19th century parterre and rose garden, are surrounded by an enchanting 18th century landscaped park laid out by 'Capability' Brown.

Visitors can also visit the working organic walled garden and purchase produce from its shop. Extending to nearly 10 acres the garden includes a 170ft long, five-bay vine house, built in 1802.

English Heritage Photographic Library

▶ **OPENING TIMES***

House

1 April - 30 September
Wed - Sun and BHs
12 noon - 5pm.
Last admission 4pm.
1 - 26 October: Sat & Sun,
11am - 3pm.

Grounds

1 April - 30 September
Wed - Sun and BHs
11am - 6pm.
Last admission 5pm.
1 - 26 October: 11am - 5pm.
Last admission 4pm.

* Times subject to change
April 2004.

▶ **ADMISSION**

House & Grounds

Adult £8.00
Child (5 - 15yrs) £4.00
Child (under 5yrs ....Free
Conc. £6.00
Family (2+3).......... £20.00

Grounds only

Adult £4.00
Child (5 - 15yrs) £2.00
Child (under 5yrs ....Free
Concessions........... £3.00
Family (2+3).......... £10.00

Groups (11+)
15% discount.

* Prices subject to change
April 2004.

CONFERENCE/FUNCTION

ROOM	MAX CAPACITY
Grounds	Large scale events possible

🗗 🍽 Private and corporate hire.

ℹ Open air concerts and other events. WCs.

♿ Ground floor and grounds.

♿ Restaurant (max 50).

🚶 By arrangement for groups.

🅿 Coaches to book in advance, £5 per coach. Free entry for coach drivers and tour guides. One additional place for every extra 20 people.

▦ School visits free if booked in advance. Contact the Administrator or tel 01223 582700 for bookings.

🐕 On leads only. 🎭 Tel for details.

BOURNE MILL

Bourne Road, Colchester, Essex CO2 8RT

Tel: 01206 572422 **www**.nationaltrust.org.uk

Owner: The National Trust **Contact:** The Custodian
Originally a fishing lodge built in 1591. It was later converted into a mill with a 4 acre mill pond. Much of the machinery, including the waterwheel, is intact.
Location: OS Ref. TM006 238. 1m S of Colchester centre, in Bourne Road, off the Mersea Road B1025.
Open: 1 June - 31 August: Tues & Suns (& BH Mons), 2 - 5pm.
Admission: Adult £2, Child £1. No reduction for groups.
⌖ Guide dogs only.

CHELMSFORD CATHEDRAL

New Street, Chelmsford, Essex CM1 1AT

Tel: 01245 294480 **e-mail:** office@chelmsfordcathedral.org.uk

Contact: Mrs Bobby Harrington
15th century building became a Cathedral in 1914. Extended in 1920s, major refurbishment in 1980s and in 2000 with contemporary works of distinction and splendid new organs in 1994 and 1996.
Location: OS Ref. TL708 070. In Chelmsford.
Open: Daily: 8am - 5.30pm. Sun services: 8am, 9.30am, 11.15am and 6pm. Weekday services: 8.15am and 5.15pm daily. Holy Communion: Wed, 12.35pm & Thur, 10am. Tours by prior arrangement.
Admission: No charge but donation invited.

COGGESHALL GRANGE BARN

Grange Hill, Coggeshall, Colchester, Essex CO6 1RE

Tel: 01376 562226 **www**.nationaltrust.org.uk

Owner: The National Trust **Contact:** The Custodian
One of the oldest surviving timber-framed barns in Europe, dating from around 1240, and originally part of a Cistercian Monastery. It was restored in the 1980s by the Coggeshall Grange Barn Trust, Braintree District Council and Essex County Council. Features a small collection of farm carts and wagons.
Location: OS Ref. TL848 223. Signposted off A120 Coggeshall bypass. West side of the road southwards to Kelvedon.
Open: 4 Apr - 10 Oct: Tues, Thurs, Suns & BH Mons, 2 - 5pm.
Admission: Adult £1.70, Child 85p. Joint ticket with Paycocke's Adult £3.40, Child £1.70. ♿ **P** Coaches must book. ⌖ Guide dogs only.

COLCHESTER CASTLE MUSEUM

14 Ryegate Road, Colchester, Essex CO1 1YG

Tel: 01206 282939 **Fax:** 01206 282925

Owner: Colchester Borough Council **Contact:** Museum Resource Centre
The largest Norman Castle Keep in Europe with fine archaeological collections on show. Hands-on & interactive display brings history to life.
Location: OS Ref. TL999 253. In Colchester town centre, off A12.
Open: All year: Mon - Sat, 10am - 5pm, also Suns, 11am - 5pm.
Admission: Adult £4.25, Child/Conc. £2.80. Saver ticket: £11. Booked groups (20+): £3.75, Child £2.50. Prices may increase from 1 Apr 2004.

Henry VIII and his Happy Henchmen!

1509-1558

Many of the great Tudor mansions built at this time were erected by men who helped Henry VIII in the Dissolution of the Monasteries. Help dear Hal and you were sure to become wealthy! Most of these houses were built on the enclosed courtyard plan, with one or more courts, although the need for defence was not necessary. Entrance to the courts was through a large gatehouse, flanked by octagonal turrets.
Around the court stood the hall, chapel, offices, living and sleeping accommodation.

Visit Hengrave Hall, Suffolk and Layer Marney Tower, Essex. Other examples include Lacock Abbey, Wiltshire, Barrington Court, Somerset and The Vyne, Hampshire.

Great Houses of the Early Tudor Period

COPPED HALL

CROWN HILL, EPPING, ESSEX CM16 5HH

www.coppedhalltrust.org.uk

Tel: 020 7267 1679 **Fax:** 020 7482 0557

Owner: The Copped Hall Trust **Contact:** Alan Cox
Shell of 18th century Palladian mansion under restoration. Situated on ridge overlooking excellent landscaped park. Ancillary buildings including stables and small racquets court. Former elaborate gardens being rescued from abandonment. Large early 18th century walled garden – adjacent to site of 16th century mansion where *'A Midsummer Night's Dream'* was first performed. Ideal film location.
Location: OS Ref. TL433 016. 4m SW of Epping, N of M25.
Open: By appointment only for groups (20+). Special open days.
Admission: Gardens: £3. Part of Mansion: £2, Child under 15 Free.
♿ Partial. ⓕ Obligatory. **P** ▣ ⌖ In grounds on leads. ❋

CRESSING TEMPLE BARNS & GARDENS

Witham Road, Braintree, Essex CM7 8PD

Tel: 01376 584903 **Fax:** 01376 584864

Owner: Essex County Council **Contact:** Mark Sweeting
Built by the Knights Templar in the 13th century, Cressing Temple has the finest remaining pair of medieval barns in Europe. Also an Elizabethan Granary, thatched cart lodge and Tudor walled garden featuring knot gardens, flowery mead, nosegay garden and physic plant area. Full Summer Events Programme.
Location: OS Ref. TL798 187. Signposted off B1018 between Witham and Braintree.
Open: Mar - Oct: Suns; May - Sept: Wed - Fri, 10.30am - 4.30pm.
Admission: Adult £3.50, Conc. £2.50. Groups (booked, 15+): Adult £3, Conc. £2.
▣ ♿ ⓕ By arrangement. **P** ▣ ⌖ Tel for details.

FEERINGBURY MANOR

Coggeshall Road, Feering, Colchester, Essex CO5 9RB

Tel: 01376 561946

Owner/Contact: Mrs Giles Coode-Adams
Location: OS Ref. TL864 215. 1½ m N of A12 between Feering & Coggeshall.
Open: From 1st Thur in Apr to last Fri in Jul, Thur & Fri only, 8am - 4pm.
Admission: Adult £2.50, Child Free. In aid of National Gardens Scheme.

❋ **Plant Sales Index** see front section

Martin Sale

GARDENS OF EASTON LODGE 🏛

WARWICK HOUSE, EASTON LODGE, LITTLE EASTON, GT DUNMOW CM6 2BB

www.eastonlodge.co.uk

Tel/Fax: 01371 876979 **e-mail:** enquiries@eastonlodge.co.uk

Owner/Contact: Mr Brian Creasey

Beautiful gardens set in 23 acres. Horticultural associations from the 16th century to date. Visit the Italian gardens, currently undergoing restoration, designed by Harold Peto for 'Daisy' Countess of Warwick (Edward VII's mistress). In the dovecote, study the history of the house, garden and owners over 400 years. A peaceful and atmospheric haven! Millennium Project: Living yew and box sundial and Shakespeare border.

Location: OS Ref. TL593 240. 4m NW of Great Dunmow, off the B184 Dunmow to Thaxted road.

Open: Feb/Mar (snowdrops): daily. Easter - 31 Oct: Fri - Sun & BHs, 12 noon - 6pm or dusk if earlier. Groups at other times by appointment.

Admission: Adult £3.80, Child (3-12yrs) £1.50, Conc. £3.50. Group (20+): £3.50. Schools (20+) £1.50 per child, 1 teacher free per 10 children.

ℹ️Exhibition & Study Centre in Dovecote. 🏛 🚽 ♿Partial. WC. 🌭Picnics.
🎞By arrangement. 🅿Limited for coaches. 🏠 🐕In grounds on leads. ✳
📺Tel for details. €

HARWICH MARITIME & LIFEBOAT MUSEUMS

Harwich Green, Harwich, Essex

Tel/Fax: 01255 503429 **e-mail:** theharwichsociety@quista.net
www.harwich-society.com

Owner: The Harwich Society **Contact:** Mr Sheard

One housed in a disused lighthouse and the other in the nearby disused Victorian Lifeboat House, complete with full size lifeboat.

Location: OS Ref. TM263 325. On Harwich Green.

Open: 1 May - 31 Aug: daily, 10am - 1pm & 2 - 4.30pm. Groups by appointment at any time.

Admission: Adult 50p, Child Free (no unaccompanied children).

✳ €

HARWICH REDOUBT FORT

Main Road, Harwich, Essex

Tel/Fax: 01255 503429 **e-mail:** theharwichsociety@quista.net
www.harwich-society.com

Owner: The Harwich Society **Contact:** Mr Sheard

180ft diameter circular fort built in 1808 to defend the port against Napoleonic invasion. Being restored by Harwich Society and part is a museum. Eleven guns on battlements.

Location: OS Ref. TM262 322. Rear of 29 Main Road.

Open: 1 May - 31 Aug: daily, 10am - 4.30pm. Sept - Apr: Suns only, 10am - 4pm. Groups by appointment at any time.

Admission: Adult £1, Child Free (no unaccompanied children).

✳ €

CHA

GOSFIELD HALL

GOSFIELD, HALSTEAD, ESSEX CO9 1SF

www.cha.org.uk

Tel: 01787 472914 **Fax:** 01787 479551

Owner: Country Houses Association **Contact:** The Administrators

Built in 1545, Gosfield Hall is steeped in history. Elizabeth I really slept here and Lady Catherine Grey arrived from the Tower of London! The house looks out onto a large lake and is shaped around a Tudor courtyard. Gosfield Hall has been converted into apartments for active retired people.

Location: OS Ref. TL788 297. On the A1037 between Braintree and Sible Hedingham. 2¹/₂ m SW of Halstead.

Open: 1 May - 30 Sept: Wed & Thurs, 2 - 5pm. Groups by arrangement.

Admission: Adult £3, Child £1.50.

🚽 🌭 By arrangement. 🎞 🚫 🛏1 single & 1 double with bathroom, CHA members & Wolsey Lodge guests. 🔼

CHA

HEDINGHAM CASTLE 🏛

CASTLE HEDINGHAM, Nr HALSTEAD, ESSEX CO9 3DJ

www.hedinghamcastle.co.uk

Tel: 01787 460261 **Fax:** 01787 461473 **e-mail:** hedinghamcastle@aspects.net

Owner: The Hon Thomas Lindsay **Contact:** Mrs Diana Donoghue

Splendid Norman keep built in 1140 by the famous de Veres, Earls of Oxford. Visited by Kings Henry VII and VIII and Queen Elizabeth I and besieged by King John. Magnificent banqueting hall with minstrel's gallery and finest Norman arch in England. Beautiful grounds, peaceful woodland and lakeside walks. Beside medieval village with fine Norman church.

Location: OS Ref. TL787 358. On B1058, 1m off A1017 between Cambridge and Colchester.

Open: Apr - Oct: Thur, Fri & Sun, 11am - 4pm (4 - 16 Apr, 30 May - 3 Jun, 26 Jul - 26 Aug & 24 - 29 Oct: 10am - 5pm). Closed on Sats.

Admission: Adult £4, Child £3, Conc. £3.50, Family (2+3) £14. Groups (20+): £3.50.

📷 🚽 ♿Partial. 🌭 🎞By arrangement. 🅿 🏠 🐕In grounds, on leads. 🔔
📺Tel for details.

HYLANDS HOUSE

HYLANDS PARK, LONDON ROAD, CHELMSFORD CM2 8WQ

www.hylandshouse.gov.uk

Tel: 01245 496800 **Fax:** 01245 496804/606970

Owner: Chelmsford Borough Council   **Contact:** Ceri Lowen

This beautiful Grade II* listed villa, with its neo-classical exterior is surrounded by over 500 acres of parkland, including formal gardens. The house re-opened Easter 1999 after a period of restoration work. The Library, Drawing Room and Saloon have been restored to their early Victorian period. The Entrance Hall was restored to its Georgian origins in the 1995 restoration. It is possible to view the Victorian staircase, as yet unrestored. April 2003 saw the opening of the most recent phase of restoration, which includes the magnificent Victorian Banqueting Room and The Georgian Small Dining Room, as well as the original Cellar circa 1730. An Exhibition details the history of the house. A full programme of events throughout the year is available.

Location: OS Ref. TL681 054. 2m SW of Chelmsford. Signposted on A414 (formerly A1016) near Chelmsford.

Open: All year: Suns, Mons & BHs, 11am - 6pm, except Christmas Day.

Admission: Adult £3.20, Child (12-16 yrs) £2.20, (under 12yrs) Free, Conc. £2.20. Groups: £3.20pp or £75 (whichever greater).

ⓘ No photography in house. ⬚ 🏺 🍵 ⬚ 💺 Sun & Mon. 🎨 By arrangement. ℙ Limited for coaches. ◼ 🐕 In grounds. Guide dogs only in house. ⬛ ❄ 💺 Tel for details.

LAYER MARNEY TOWER ⬚

Nr COLCHESTER, ESSEX CO5 9US

www.layermarneytower.co.uk

Tel/Fax: 01206 330784   **e-mail:** info@layermarneytower.co.uk

Owner/Contact: Mr Nicholas Charrington

Built in the reign of Henry VIII, the tallest Tudor gatehouse in Great Britain. Lord Henry Marney clearly intended to rival Wolsey's building at Hampton Court, but he died before his masterpiece was finished. His son John died two years later, in 1525, and building work stopped. Layer Marney Tower has some of the finest terracotta work in the country, most probably executed by Flemish craftsmen trained by Italian masters. The terracotta is used on the battlements, windows, and most lavishly of all, on the tombs of Henry and John Marney. Visitors may climb the Tower, passing through the History Room, and enjoy the marvellous views of the Essex countryside. There are fine outbuildings, including the Long Gallery with its magnificent oak roof and the medieval barn which now houses some of the Home Farm's collection of Rare Breed farm animals. Function room available for receptions, etc.

Location: OS Ref. TL929 175. 7m SW of Colchester, signed off B1022.

Open: 1 Apr - 3 Oct: Sun - Fri, 12 noon - 5pm. Group visits/guided tours throughout the year by arrangement.

Admission: Adult £3.50, Child £2, Family £10. Groups (15+): Adult £3.25, Child £1.75. Guided tours (pre-booked) £4.75, min. charge £120. Schools by arrangement.

⬚ 🏺 🍵 ♿ Partial. WC. ⬚ ℙ 🎨 By arrangement. ◼ 🐕 In grounds, on leads. 🛏 1 dble, 2 single. ⬛ ❄ 💺 On BHs. Tel for details.

INGATESTONE HALL ⬚

HALL LANE, INGATESTONE, ESSEX CM4 9NR

Tel: 01277 353010 **Fax:** 01245 248979

Owner: The Lord Petre   **Contact:** The Administrator

16th century mansion, set in 11 acres of grounds (formal garden and wild walk), built by Sir William Petre, Secretary of State to four Tudor monarchs, which has remained in the hands of his family ever since. The two Priests' hiding places can be seen, as well as the furniture, portraits and family memorabilia accumulated over the centuries.

Location: OS Ref. TQ653 986. Off A12 between Brentwood & Chelmsford. Take Station Lane at London end of Ingatestone High Street, cross level-crossing and continue for ¹/₂ m to SE.

Open: 10 Apr - 26 Sept: Sats, Suns & BH Mons. 21 Jul - 3 Sept: Wed - Fri, 1 - 6pm.

Admission: Adult £4, Child £2 (under 5yrs Free), Conc. £3.50. 50p per head discount for groups (20+).

ⓘ No photography in house. ⬚ 🏺 ♿ Partial. ⬚ 🎨 By arrangement. ℙ ◼ 🐕 Guide dogs only. 💺 Tel for details.

MARKS HALL ARBORETUM & GARDEN

COGGESHALL, ESSEX CO6 1TG

www.markshall.org.uk

Tel: 01376 563796

Owner: The Thomas Philips Price Trust   **Contact:** Mrs G Nosworthy

Five individual gardens and a double long border, combining contemporary and traditional landscaping and planting, form the newly redesigned Walled Garden at Marks Hall. This unique garden is open on one side to a lake and on the opposite bank the Millennium Walk is designed to be at its best during the shortest days of the year. There is much to see in this Arboretum and Garden of over 100 acres on every day of the year.

Location: OS168 Ref. TQ840 252. Off B1024, 1¹/₂ m N of Coggeshall.

Open: Apr - Oct: Tues - Sun & BH Mons, 10.30am - 5pm. Winter weekends, 10.30am - dusk.

Admission: £3.80 per car.

♿ Transport for those with walking difficulties (must be booked in advance). ❄

MISTLEY TOWERS ⚑

Colchester, Essex

Tel: 01206 393884 / 01223 582700 (Regional Office)

Owner: English Heritage　　**Contact:** The Keykeeper (Mistley Quay Workshops)

The remains of one of only two churches designed by the great architect Robert Adam. Built in 1776. It was unusual in having towers at both the east and west ends.

Location: OS Ref. TM116 320. On B1352, 1¹/₂ m E of A137 at Lawford, 9m E of Colchester.

Open: Telephone for opening times.

Admission: Free.

🅰 Grounds only. 🐕 Restricted areas.

SIR ALFRED MUNNINGS ART MUSEUM

Castle House, Dedham, Essex　CO7 6AZ

Tel/Fax: 01206 322127　**www**.siralfredmunnings.co.uk

Owner: Castle House Trust　　**Contact:** Mrs C Woodage

The home, studios and grounds where Sir Alfred Munnings, KCVO, 1878 – 1959 (PRA 1944 – 1949) lived and painted for 40 years. Castle House, part Tudor part Georgian, restored and with original Munnings' furniture, exhibits over 200 Munnings' works representing his life's work and is augmented by private loans each season. Annual Special Exhibition.

Location: OS Ref. TM060 328. ³/₄m from Dedham centre. 8m from Colchester, 12m from Ipswich.

Open: Easter Sun - first Sun in Oct: Weds, Suns & BH Mons, 2 - 5pm. Additionally Thurs & Sats in Aug, 2 - 5pm.

Admission: Adult £4, Child £1, Conc. £3. Groups by arrangement.

ℹ No photography in house. 📷 🅰 Partial. 🅿 Limited for coaches.

🐕 In grounds, on leads.

PAYCOCKE'S 🌿

West Street, Coggeshall, Colchester, Essex　C06 1NS

Tel: 01376 561305　**www**.nationaltrust.org.uk

Owner: The National Trust　　**Contact:** The Tenant

A merchant's house, dating from about 1500, with unusually rich panelling and wood carving. A display of lace, for which Coggeshall was famous, is on show. Delightful cottage garden leading down to small river.

Location: OS Ref. TL848 225. Signposted off A120.

Open: 4 Apr - 10 Oct: Tues, Thurs, Suns & BH Mons, 2 - 5.30pm, last adm: 5pm.

Admission: Adult £2.30, Child £1.15. Groups (10+) by prior arrangement, no reduction for groups. Joint ticket with Coggeshall Grange Barn Adult £3.40, Child £1.70

🅰 Access to ground floor and garden. 🅿 NT's at the Coggeshall Grange Barn.

PRIOR'S HALL BARN ⚑

Widdington, Newport, Essex

Tel: 01233 582700 (Regional Office)

Owner: English Heritage　　**Contact:** East of England Regional Office

One of the finest surviving medieval barns in south-east England and representative of the group of aisled barns centred on north-west Essex.

Location: OS Ref. TL538 319. In Widdington, on unclassified road 2m SE of Newport, off B1383.

Open: 1 Apr - 30 Sept: Sats & Suns, 10am - 6pm. Times subject to change April 2004.

Admission: Free.

🅰 🐕

RHS GARDEN HYDE HALL

BUCKHATCH LANE, RETTENDON, CHELMSFORD, ESSEX　CM3 8ET

www.rhs.org.uk

Tel: 01245 400256　**Fax:** 01245 402100　**e-mail:** hydehall@rhs.org.uk

Owner: The Royal Horticultural Society　　**Contact:** Janet Uttley

Voted Small Visitor Attraction of the Year 2003, in the Regional Excellence Awards, RHS Hyde Hall is truly a garden of its time. Set on a hilltop amongst rolling hills of arable crops, the garden combines environmental and sustainable practices with the high standards of horticulture for which the RHS gardens are renowned. Highlights include the spectacular Dry Garden, colour themed Herbaceous Border, the Queen Mother's Garden, boldly planted Farmhouse Garden and ponds, Wildflower and Cornfield annual Meadows and, new for 2004, The Garden for Wildlife.

Location: OS Ref. TQ782 995. SE of Chelmsford, signposted from A130.

Open: Jan - Mar & Oct - Dec (except Christmas Day): 10am - dusk; Apr - Sept: 10am - 6pm. Last entry 1 hour before closing.

Admission: Adult £4.50, Child (6-16yrs) £1, Companion/Carer of disabled person Free. RHS member and one guest Free. Pre-booked Groups (10+): £3.50.

📷 ⚡ 🅰 🍴 Licensed. 🅿 🐕 Guide dogs only. ✳ ♿

SALING HALL GARDEN

Great Saling, Braintree, Essex　CM7 5DT

Tel: 01371 850 243　**Fax:** 01371 850 274

Owner/Contact: Hugh Johnson Esq

Twelve acres including a walled garden dated 1698. Water gardens and landscaped arboretum.

Location: OS Ref. TL700 258. 6m NW of Braintree, 2m N of A120.

Open: May, Jun & Jul: Weds, 2 - 5pm.

Admission: Adult £2.50, Child Free.

TILBURY FORT ⚑

No. 2 Office Block, The Fort, Tilbury, Essex　RM18 7NR

Tel: 01375 858489　**www**.english-heritage.org.uk

Owner: English Heritage　　**Contact:** The Custodian

The best and largest example of 17th century military engineering in England, commanding the Thames. The fort shows the development of fortifications over the following 200 years. Enlightening exhibitions, the powder magazine and the bunker-like 'casemates' demonstrate how the fort protected London from seaborne attack. Elizabeth I gave a speech near here on the eve of the Spanish Armada.

Location: OS Ref. TQ651 754. ¹/₂ m E of Tilbury off A126.

Open: 1 Apr - 31 Oct: daily, 10am - 6pm (5pm in Oct). 1 Nov - 31 Mar: Wed - Sun, 10am - 4pm. Closed 1 - 2pm in winter. Closed 24 - 26 Dec & 1 Jan. Times subject to change April 2004.

Admission: Adult £2.90, Child £1.50, Conc. £2.20, Family £7.30. Prices subject to change April 2004.

ℹ WCs. 📷 🅰 Grounds only. 📷 🅿 ✳ ♿ Tel for details.

WALTHAM ABBEY GATEHOUSE & BRIDGE ⚑

Waltham Abbey, Essex

Tel: 01992 702200 / 01223 582700 (Regional Office)

Owner: English Heritage　**Contact:** East of England Regional Office (01223 582700)

The late 14th century abbey gatehouse, part of the north range of the cloister and the medieval 'Harold's Bridge' of one of the great monastic foundations of the Middle Ages.

Location: OS Ref. TL381 008. In Waltham Abbey off A112. Just NE of the Abbey church.

Open: Any reasonable time.

Admission: Free.

🅰 Sensory trail guide. ✳

Jerry Harpur

Map 6

Owner:
The Marquess
of Salisbury

▶ **CONTACT**

The Curator
Hatfield House
Hatfield
Hertfordshire AL9 5NQ

Tel: 01707 287010

Fax: 01707 287033

e-mail:
curator@
hatfield-house.co.uk

▶ **LOCATION**

OS Ref. TL 237 084

21m N of London,
M25/J23 7m,
A1(M)/J4, 2m.

Bus: Local bus services
from St Albans and
Hertford.

Rail: From Kings Cross
every 30 mins.
Hatfield Station is
immediately opposite
entrance to Park.

Air: Luton (30 mins).
Stansted (45 mins).

HATFIELD HOUSE & GARDENS

HATFIELD

www.hatfield-house.co.uk

This celebrated Jacobean house, which stands in its own great park, was built between 1607 and 1611 by Robert Cecil, 1st Earl of Salisbury and Chief Minister to King James I. It has been the family home of the Cecils ever since.

The main designer was Robert Lyminge helped, it is thought, by the young Inigo Jones. The interior decoration was the work of English, Flemish and French craftsmen, notably Maximilian Colt.

The State Rooms are rich in world-famous paintings including The Rainbow Portrait of Queen Elizabeth I and The Ermine Portrait by Nicholas Hilliard. Other paintings include works by Hoefnagel, Mytens, John de Critz the Elder and Sir Joshua Reynolds. Fine furniture from the 16th, 17th and 18th centuries, rare tapestries and historic armour can be found in the State Rooms.

Within the delightful gardens stands the surviving wing of The Royal Palace of Hatfield (1485) where Elizabeth I spent much of her childhood and held her first Council of State in November 1558. Some of her possessions can be seen in the House.

GARDENS

John Tradescant the Elder, the celebrated plant hunter, was employed to plant and lay out the gardens after the completion of the house in 1611. During the 18th century, when landscape gardening became more fashionable, much of his work was neglected or swept away. The Dowager Marchioness of Salisbury (wife of the 6th Marquess) has for 30 years continued with the work of restoration and redevelopment, started in the mid 19th century, so that the 42 acres of gardens now include formal, knot, scented and wilderness areas which reflects their Jacobean origins.

▶ **OPENING TIMES**

Easter Sat - 30 September

House
Daily, 12 noon - 4pm.
Guided tours only on weekdays.

Park, West Gardens, Restaurant & Shop
Daily, 11am - 5.30pm.

East Gardens
Open only on Fridays (Connoisseurs' Day) – except during special events.

▶ **ADMISSION**

House, Park & Gardens
Adult £7.50
Child (5 - 15yrs) £4.00
Groups (20+)*
Adult £6.50
Park & Gardens
Adult £4.50
Child £3.50
Park only
Adult £2.00
Child (5 - 15yrs) £1.00
Connoisseurs' Day (Fri)
House, Park &
Gardens £10.50
Park & Gardens £6.50

Jerry Harpur

SPECIAL EVENTS

MAY 6 - 9
Living Crafts.

JUN 11 - 13
Flower Festival.

JUL 24
Battle Proms Concert.

AUG 6 - 8
Art in Clay.

SEPT 3 - 5
Country Homes, Gardens & Rare Breeds Show.

Please telephone for details of other events.

[i] No photography in house. National Collection of model soldiers, 5m of marked trails, children's play area.

[icon] Wedding receptions, functions. Elizabethan Banquets held in Old Palace throughout year: 01707 262055.

[icon] WCs. Parking next to house. Lift.

[icon] Seats 150. Pre-booked lunch and tea for groups 20+. Tel: 01707 262030.

[icon] Mon - Fri, no extra charge. Group tours available in French, German, Italian, Spanish or Japanese by prior arrangement. Garden tour for groups £15.

[P] Ample. Hardstanding for coaches.

[icon] 1:10 ratio. Teacher free. Guide provided. Resource books, play area & nature trails. Living History days: tel 01707 287042.

[icon] In park.

FUNCTION

ROOM	SIZE	MAX CAPACITY
The Old Palace	112' x 33'	280
Old Riding School	100' X 40'	180

Map 6

KNEBWORTH HOUSE

NR STEVENAGE

www.knebworthhouse.com

Owner: The Hon Henry Lytton Cobbold

▶ **CONTACT**

The Estate Office
Knebworth House
Knebworth
Hertfordshire SG3 6PY

Tel: 01438 812661
Fax: 01438 811908
e-mail: info@ knebworthhouse.com

▶ **LOCATION**

OS Ref. TL230 208

Direct access off the A1(M) J7 (Stevenage South A602).
28m N of London.
15m N of M25 J23.

Rail: Stevenage Station 2m (from Kings Cross).

Air: Luton Airport 15m Landing facilities.

Taxi: 01438 811122.

Home of the Lytton family since 1490, and still a lived-in family house. Transformed in early Victorian times by Edward Bulwer-Lytton, the author, poet, dramatist and statesman, into the unique high gothic fantasy house of today, complete with turrets, griffins and gargoyles.

Historically home to Constance Lytton, the Suffragette, and her father, Robert Lytton, the Viceroy of India who proclaimed Queen Victoria Empress of India at the Great Delhi Durbar of 1877. Visited by Queen Elizabeth I, Charles Dickens and Sir Winston Churchill.

The interior contains various styles including the magnificent Jacobean Banqueting Hall, a unique example of the 17th century change in fashion from traditional English to Italian Palladian. The high gothic State Drawing Room by John Crace contrasts with the Regency elegance of Mrs Bulwer-Lytton's bedroom and the 20th century designs of Sir Edwin Lutyens in the Entrance Hall, Dining Parlour and Library.

25 acres of beautiful gardens, simplified by Lutyens, including pollarded lime avenues, formal rose garden, maze, Gertrude Jekyll herb garden and newly designed Walled Garden. 250 acres of gracious parkland, with herds of red and sika deer, includes children's giant adventure playground and miniature railway. World famous for its huge open-air rock concerts, and used as a film location for *Batman*, *The Shooting Party*, *Wilde*, *Jane Eyre* and *The Canterville Ghost*, amongst others.

The Jacobean Banqueting Hall.

Suitable for fashion shows, air displays, archery, shooting, equestrian events, cricket pitch, garden parties, shows, rallies, filming, helicopter landing. No pushchairs, photography, smoking or drinking in House.

Indian Raj Evenings and Elizabethan Banquets with jousting. Full catering service.

Disabled parking. Ground floor accessible.

Licensed tearoom. Special rates for advance bookings, menus on request.

Unlimited parking. Group visits must be booked in advance with Estate Office.

Daily at 30 min intervals or at booked times including evenings. Tour time 1hr. Shorter tours by arrangement. Room Wardens on duty on busy weekends. Themed tours available.

National Curriculum based school activity days.

Guide dogs only in House. In Park, on leads.

Tel for details.

CONFERENCE/FUNCTION

ROOM	SIZE	MAX CAPACITY
Banqueting Hall	26' x 41'	80
Dining Parlour	21' x 38'	50
Library	32' x 21'	40
Manor Barn	70' x 25'	250
Lodge Barn	75' x 30'	150

▶ **OPENING TIMES**

Park, Gardens, Fort Knebworth Adventure Playground & Miniature Railway

3 - 18 Apr; 29 May - 6 Jun; 3 Jul - 31 Aug: daily.

27/28 Mar; 24 Apr - 23 May; 12 - 27 Jun; 4 - 26 Sept: weekends & BHs.

Park, Gardens & Playground

11am - 5.30pm.

House

12 noon - 5pm (last adm. 4.15pm)

Please telephone for details of pre-booked house tours for groups outside of normal opening times.

▶ **ADMISSION**

House, Gardens, Park, Playground & Railway

Adult £8.50
Child*/OAP............ £8.00
Family (2+2).......... £29.00
Groups (20+)
Adult £7.50
Child*/OAP............ £7.00
(subject to special events)

Gardens, Park, Playground & Railway

All persons £6.50
Family (2+2)......... £22.00
Groups (20+)
All persons £5.60
(subject to special events)

* 4 - 16yrs. Under 4s Free.

Season Tickets available.

ASHRIDGE

Ringshall, Berkhamsted, Hertfordshire HP4 1LT

Tel: 01442 851227 **Fax:** 01442 850000 **e-mail:** ashridge@nationaltrust.org.uk
Owner: The National Trust **Contact:** The Visitor Centre
The Ashridge Estate comprises over 1800ha of woodlands, commons and downland. At the northerly end of the Estate the Ivinghoe Hills are an outstanding area of chalk downland which supports a rich variety of plants and insects.
Location: OS Ref. SP970 131. Between Northchurch & Ringshall, just off B4506.
Open: Visitor Centre & Shop: 27 Mar - 12 Dec: Mon - Fri, 1 - 5pm. Weekends & BHs, 12 noon - 5pm. Monument: 27 Mar - 31 Oct: Sats & Suns, 12 noon - 5pm, Tearoom: 27 Mar - 12 Dec: Tues - Sun, 12 noon - 5pm. Please telephone for details of winter openings.
Admission: Monument: £1.20, Child 60p.
🛈Visitor Centre. 🗖 🕭Vehicles available. 🖰 🅿Limited for coaches. ⬛ 🐾In grounds, on leads. 🐾Tel for details

BENINGTON LORDSHIP GARDENS 🏛

Stevenage, Hertfordshire SG2 7BS

Tel: 01438 869668 **Fax:** 01438 869622 **e-mail:** rhbott@beningtonlordship.co.uk
www.beningtonlordship.co.uk
Owner: Mr C H A Bott **Contact:** Mr or Mrs C H A Bott
A hilltop garden which appeals to everyone with its intimate atmosphere, ruins, Queen Anne Manor, herbaceous borders, old roses, lakes and vegetable garden. For films, fashion shoots etc. the gardens and estate offer excellent facilities. Mediaeval barns, cottages and other unique countryside features.
Location: OS Ref. TL296 236. In village of Benington next to the church. 4m E of Stevenage.
Open: Gardens only: Easter & Spring/Summer BH weekends. Suns, 2 - 5pm. Mons, 12 noon - 5pm. Herbaceous Border week: 1st week in July, 2 - 5pm. By request all year, please telephone. Coaches must book. Snowdrops in Feb, tel for details end Jan.
Admission: Adult £3.50, Child Free.
🛈Air-strip. Suitable for filming & fashion shoots. 🕭Unsuitable. 🖰

BERKHAMSTED CASTLE 🏛

Berkhamsted, St Albans, Hertfordshire

Tel: 01223 582700 (Regional Office)
Owner: English Heritage **Contact:** East of England Regional Office
The extensive remains of a large 11th century motte and bailey castle which held a strategic position on the road to London.
Location: OS Ref. SP996 083. Adjacent to Berkhamsted rail station.
Open: All year: daily, 10am - 6pm; Winter: 10am - 4pm. Closed 24 - 26 Dec & 1 Jan. Times subject to change April 2004.
Admission: Free.
🐾 ❄

THE BRITISH SCHOOLS MUSEUM, HITCHIN

41 - 42 Queen Street, Hitchin, Hertfordshire SG4 9TS

Tel/Fax: 01462 420144 **e-mail:** brsch@britishschools.freeserve.co.uk
www.hitchinbritishschools.org.uk
Owner: Hitchin British Schools Trust **Contact:** Mrs Rosie Pinhorn
Unique complex of school buildings dating from 1837 to 1905. Incorporates 1837 Lancasterian Schoolroom, believed to be the only surviving example, a rare 1853 galleried classroom (both Grade II*), Girls and Infants School 1857 and two Edwardian classrooms. Related displays, small museum and Family Trail with activities.
Location: OS Ref. TL186 289. Hitchin town centre.
Open: Feb - Nov: Tue, 10am - 4pm. Apr - Oct: Sun, 2.30 - 5pm. Feb - Nov: School visits, Wed & Thur, 9.45am - 12.45pm.
Admission: Adult £2, Child £1. Education programme with teaching session £3 plus VAT per child.
🗖 🕭Partial. WC. 🖰 🚹Obligatory. 🅿 ⬛ 🐾Guide dogs only. ❄

CATHEDRAL & ABBEY CHURCH OF ST ALBAN

St Albans, Hertfordshire AL1 1BY

Tel: 01727 860780 **Fax:** 01727 850944 **Contact:** Deputy Administrator
Abbey church of Benedictine Monastery founded 793AD commemorating Britain's first martyr.
Location: OS Ref. TL145 071. Centre of St Albans.
Open: All year: 9am - 5.45pm. Tel for details of services, concerts and special events Mon - Sat, 11am - 4pm.
Admission: Free of charge.

CROMER WINDMILL

Ardeley, Stevenage, Hertfordshire SG2 7QA

Tel: 01279 843301
Owner: Hertfordshire Building Preservation Trust **Contact:** Cristina Harrison
17th century Post Windmill restored to working order.
Location: OS Ref. TL305 286. 4m NE of Stevenage on B1037. 1m SW of Cottered.
Open: Mid-May - mid-Sept: Sun, 2nd & 4th Sat & BHs, 2.30 - 5pm.
Admission: Adult £1.50, Child 25p. Groups (10+) by arrangement: Adult £1, Child 25p.

FORGE MUSEUM & VICTORIAN COTTAGE GARDEN

High Street, Much Hadham, Hertfordshire SG10 6BS

Tel/Fax: 01279 843301 **e-mail:** cristinaharrison@hotmail.com
Owner: The Hertfordshire Building Preservation Trust **Contact:** The Curator
The garden reflects plants that would have been grown in 19th century, also houses an unusual 19th century bee shelter.
Location: OS Ref. TL428 195. Village centre.
Open: Fri, Sat, Sun & BHs, 11am - 5pm (dusk in winter).
Admission: Adult £1, Child/Conc. 50p.

GORHAMBURY 🏛

St Albans, Hertfordshire AL3 6AH

Tel: 01727 854051 **Fax:** 01727 843675
Owner: The Earl Of Verulam **Contact:** The Administrator
Late 18th century house by Sir Robert Taylor. Family portraits from 15th - 20th centuries.
Location: OS Ref. TL114 078. 2m W of St Albans. Accessible via private drive from A4147 at St Albans.
Open: May - Sept: Thur, 2 - 5pm.
Admission: House & Gardens: Adult £6, Child £3, OAP £4. Guided tour only. Groups by arrangement: Thursdays £5, other days £6.

HATFIELD HOUSE & GARDENS See page 279 for full page entry.

HERTFORD MUSEUM

18 Bull Plain, Hertford

Tel: 01992 582686 **Fax:** 01992 552100
Owner: Hertford Museums Trust **Contact:** Helen Gurney
Local museum in 17th century house, altered by 18th century façade, with recreated Jacobean knot garden.
Location: OS Ref. TL326 126. Town centre.
Open: Tue - Sat, 10am - 5pm.
Admission: Free.

KNEBWORTH HOUSE 🏛 See page 280 for full page entry.

OLD GORHAMBURY HOUSE 🏛

St Albans, Hertfordshire

Tel: 01223 582700 (Regional Office)
Owner: English Heritage **Contact:** East of England Regional Office
The decorated remains of this Elizabethan mansion, particularly the porch of the Great Hall, illustrate the impact of the Renaissance on English architecture.
Location: OS Ref. TL110 077. On foot by permissive 2m path. By car, drive to Gorhambury Mansion and walk across the gardens.
Open: Access by car only on Thursday afternoons between 1 May & 30 Sept. Access on foot any reasonable time (except 1 June). Times subject to change April 2004.
Admission: Free.
🐾

THE WALTER ROTHSCHILD ZOOLOGICAL MUSEUM

Akeman Street, Tring, Hertfordshire HP23 6AP

Tel: 020 7942 6171 **Fax:** 020 7942 6150

Owner: The Natural History Museum **Contact:** General Organiser

The museum was opened to the public by Lord Rothschild in 1892. It houses his private natural history collection. More than 4,000 species of animal in a unique Victorian setting.

Location: OS Ref. SP924 111. S end of Akeman Street, ¹/₄ m S of High Street.

Open: Mon - Sat, 10am - 5pm, Suns, 2 - 5pm. Closed 24 - 26 Dec.

Admission: Free.

ST PAULS WALDEN BURY

Hitchin, Hertfordshire SG4 8BP

Tel/Fax: 01438 871218/871229 **e-mail:** boweslyon@aol.com

Owner: S Bowes Lyon **Contact:** S or C Bowes Lyon

Formal landscape garden, laid out in 1730. Avenues and allées lead to temples, statues, lake and ponds. Also more recent flower gardens. Grade I listed. Covers 60 acres. The childhood home of Queen Elizabeth, The Queen Mother.

Location: OS Ref. TL186 216. 30m N of London. 5m S of Hitchin on B651.

Open: Sundays: 18 Apr, 16 May: 2 - 7pm & 4 July, 2 - 6pm, followed by lakeside concert. Other times by appointment.

Admission: Adult £3, Child 50p. Private visits £6.

SCOTT'S GROTTO

Ware, Hertfordshire

Tel: 01920 464131

Owner: East Hertfordshire District Council **Contact:** J Watson

One of the finest grottos in England built in the 1760s by Quaker Poet John Scott.

Location: OS Ref. TL355 137. In Scotts Rd, S of the A119 Hertford Road.

Open: 1 Apr - 30 Sept: Sat & BH Mon, 2 - 4.30pm. Also by appointment.

Admission: Suggested donation of £1 for adults. Children Free. Please bring a torch.

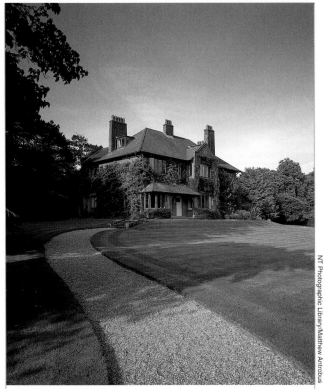

NT Photographic Library/Matthew Antrobus

Knot Garden

Formal beds edged often with box, planted in intricate geometric patterns, and infilled with herbs, flowers or sometimes stones. Extremely popular as a garden feature.
Visit Little Moreton Hall, Cheshire, Hatfield House & Gardens, Hertfordshire, Bourton House Garden, Gloucestershire, Sledmere House, Yorkshire, Broughton Castle, Oxfordshire and Wyken Hall Gardens in Suffolk.

Garden Jargon

SHAW'S CORNER ❧

AYOT ST LAWRENCE, WELWYN, HERTFORDSHIRE AL6 9BX

www.nationaltrust.org.uk/shawscorner

Tel/Fax: 01438 820307 **e-mail:** shawscorner@nationaltrust.org.uk

Owner: The National Trust **Contact:** The Custodian

The fascinating home of playwright George Bernard Shaw until his death in 1950. The modest Edwardian villa contains many literary and personal relics, and the interior is still set out as it was in Shaw's lifetime. The garden, with its richly planted borders and views over the Hertfordshire countryside, contains the revolving summerhouse where Shaw retreated to write.

NT Photographic Library/Matthew Antrobus

Ashridge, Hertfordshire.

Location: OS Ref. TL194 167. At SW end of village, 2m NE of Wheathampstead, approximately 2m N from B653. A1(M)/J4, M1/J10.

Open: 20 Mar - 31 Oct: Wed - Sun & BH Mons (open Good Fri), House: 1 - 5pm; Garden: 12 noon - 5.30pm. Last admission to House & Garden 4.30pm. No large hand luggage inside house. Groups by prior appointment only.

Admission: Adult £3.80, Child £1.90, Family £9.50. Discounts for groups (15+). ⓘWC. 🚻 ♿ Partial, ground floor. No WC. 🅿 ■ ⛟ Car park only. ⌚ Tel 01438 829221 for details.

HOLKHAM HALL 🏛

WELLS-NEXT-THE-SEA

www.holkham.co.uk

Map 6

Owner:
The Earl of Leicester

▶ **CONTACT**

The Marketing Manager
Holkham Estate Office
Wells-next-the-Sea
Norfolk NR23 1AB

Tel: 01328 713104
Fax: 01328 711707
e-mail: p.minchin@
holkham.co.uk

▶ **LOCATION**

OS Ref. TF885 428

From London 120m
Norwich 35m
King's Lynn 30m.

Rail: Norwich
Station 35m
King's Lynn
Station 30m.

Air: Norwich
Airport 32m.

Holkham Hall has been the home of the Coke family and the Earls of Leicester for almost 250 years. Built between 1734 and 1764 by Thomas Coke, 1st Earl of Leicester and based on a design by William Kent, this fine example of an 18th century Palladian style mansion reflects Thomas Coke's natural appreciation of classical art developed during his Grand Tour. The House is constructed of local yellow brick with a magnificent Entrance Hall of English alabaster.

The State Rooms occupy the first floor and contain Roman statuary, paintings by Rubens, Van Dyck, Claude, Gaspar Poussin and Gainsborough and original furniture.

On leaving the House, visitors pass Holkham Pottery and its adjacent shop, both under the supervision of the Countess of Leicester. Fine examples of local craftsmanship are for sale, including the Holkham Florist Ware.

Beyond are the 19th century stables now housing the Holkham Bygones Collection; some 4,000 items range from working steam engines, vintage cars and tractors to craft tools and kitchenware. A History of Farming Exhibition is adjacent to the Museum.

The House is set in a 3,000-acre park with a herd of 800 fallow deer. On the one-mile long lake, are many species of wildfowl. Two walks encircle either the lake or agricultural buildings.

Holkham Nursery Gardens occupy the 18th century walled Kitchen Garden and a large range of stock is on sale to the public.

i Grounds for shows, rallies and filming. Photography allowed. No smoking in the Hall.

In nursery gardens.

Visitors may alight at entrance, stairs in Hall. WC.

Licensed. Menus for pre-booked groups on request.

Audio tour £2, other times guided tours by arrangement.

P Unlimited for cars, 20+ coaches. Parking, admission, refreshments free to coach drivers, coach drivers' rest room.

Welcome. Areas of interest: Bygones Collection, History of Farming, two nature walks, deer park, lake and wildfowl.

No dogs in Hall, on leads in grounds.

❄ Deer Park open all year except Christmas Day.

▶ **OPENING TIMES**
Summer
Hall
3 Jun - 27 Sept, Thur - Mon (closed Tue & Wed), 1 - 5pm.

10 - 12 Apr; 1 - 3, 29 - 31 May & 28 - 30 Aug: 11.30am - 5pm.

Last admissions 4.30pm.

6 - 28 May: Hall audio tour on a "turn up and join in", daily (not Tue & Wed), 3pm. Latecomers will not be admitted and 40 people limit per tour.

The Bygones Museum
10 - 12 Apr; 1 - 3 May & 6 May - 27 Sept: daily except Tue & Wed, 12 noon - 5pm. Last adm. 4.30pm.

The Stables Café & Pottery Shop
10 - 12 Apr; 1 - 3 May & 6 May - 25 Oct: daily, except Wed, 10am - 5.30pm.

Acoustiguide hire: £2pp.

Boat trips on the lake:
Adult.........................£2.50
OAP/Child (5-16yrs).....£2.00

Winter: October - May
By appointment for private guided tours.

▶ **ADMISSION**
Summer
Hall
Adult.......................£6.50
Child (5-16yrs) £3.25

Bygones Museum
Adult £5.00
Child (5-16yrs) £2.50

Combined Ticket
Adult £10.00
Child (5-16yrs) £5.00

Family (Hall & Bygones)
2 adults + 2 children (5-16yrs)
...............................£25.00

Groups (20+).... 10% discount

Private guided tours by arrangement. Apply for rates.

Winter: Private guided tours by arrangement.

Visitors may walk in the Park without charge every day of the year, except Christmas Day.

HM Queen Elizabeth II

SANDRINGHAM

NORFOLK

www.sandringhamestate.co.uk

Sandringham House is the charming country retreat of Her Majesty The Queen, hidden in the heart of 60 acres of beautiful wooded gardens. Still maintained in the style of Edward and Alexandra, Prince and Princess of Wales (later King Edward VII and Queen Alexandra), all the main ground floor rooms used by The Royal Family, full of their treasured ornaments, portraits and furniture, are open to the public. Throughout 2004 an exhibition entitled 'Wildlife Art – The Duke of Edinburgh's Personal Collection' will be on display in the Ballroom.

More family possessions are displayed in the Museum housed in the old stable and coach houses including vehicles ranging in date from the first car owned by a British monarch, a 1900 Daimler, to a half-scale Aston Martin used by Princes William and Harry. A display tells the mysterious tale of the Sandringham Company who fought and died at Gallipolli in 1915, recently made into a TV film *'All the King's Men'*. Guided garden tours take place on Fridays and Saturdays and include the Walled Garden, unchanged since the days of Queen Alexandra and only accessible as part of a garden tour.

A free Land Train from within the entrance will carry passengers less able to walk through the grounds to the House and back.

Map 6

Owner:
H M The Queen

▶ CONTACT

The Public Enterprises
Manager
The Estate Office
Sandringham
Norfolk   PE35 6EN

Tel: 01553 612908
Fax: 01485 541571

▶ LOCATION
OS Ref. TF695 287

8m NE of King's Lynn
on B1440 off A148.

Rail: King's Lynn.

Air: Norwich.

▶ OPENING TIMES

**House, Museum &
Gardens**
10 Apr - 23 Jul &
1 Aug - 31 Oct.

▶ ADMISSION

**House, Museum
& Gardens**

Adult	£6.50
Child (5-15yrs)	£4.00
Conc.	£5.00
Family	£17.00

Museum & Garden

Adult	£4.50
Child (5-15yrs)	£2.50
Conc.	£3.50
Family	£11.50

Groups (20+)
10% discount for payment
one month in advance.

HM Queen Elizabeth II

CONFERENCE/FUNCTION

ROOM	MAX CAPACITY
Restaurant	200
Tearoom	60

BERNEY ARMS WINDMILL ⚘

c/o 8 Manor Road, Southtown, Gt Yarmouth NR31 0QA

Tel: 01493 700605   01223 582700 (Regional Office)

Owner: English Heritage   **Contact:** The Custodian
A wonderfully situated marsh mill, one of the best and largest remaining in Norfolk, with seven floors, making it a landmark for miles around. It was in use until 1951.

Location: OS Ref. TG465 051. 3^1/2 m NE of Reedham on N bank of River Yare, 5m from Gt. Yarmouth. Accessible by boat from Yarmouth or by footpath from Halvergate (3^1/2 m).

Open: 1 Apr - 31 Oct: daily, 9am - 5pm (closed 1 - 2pm). Subject to closure at times of essential maintenance. Please check with Regional Office. Times subject to change April 2004.

Admission: Adult £2, Child £1, Conc. £1.50. Prices subject to change April 2004.

BINHAM PRIORY ⚘

Binham-on-Wells, Norfolk

Tel: 01328 830434 / 01223 582700 (Regional Office)

Owner: English Heritage   **Contact:** East of England Regional Office
Extensive remains of a Benedictine priory, of which the original nave of the church is still in use as the parish church.

Location: OS Ref. TF982 399. ^{1}/4 m NW of village of Binham-on-Wells, on road off B1388.

Open: Any reasonable time.

Admission: Free.

BIRCHAM WINDMILL

Snettisham Road, Great Bircham, Norfolk PE31 6SJ

Tel: 01485 578393

Owner/Contact: Mr & Mrs S Chalmers
One of the last remaining complete windmills.

Location: OS Ref. TF760 326. ^{1}/2 m W of Bircham. N of the road to Snettisham.

Open: Easter - end Sept: Daily 10am - 5pm.

Admission: Adult £2.75, Child £1.50, Retired £2.50.

BURGH CASTLE ⚘

Breydon Water, Great Yarmouth, Norfolk

Tel: 01223 582700 (Regional Office)

Owner: English Heritage   **Contact:** East of England Regional Office
Impressive walls, with projecting bastions, of a Roman fort built in the late 3rd century as one of a chain to defend the coast against Saxon raiders.

Location: OS Ref. TG475 046. At far W end of Breydon Water, on unclassified road 3m W of Great Yarmouth. SW of the church.

Open: Any reasonable time.

Admission: Free.

CASTLE ACRE PRIORY ⚘

Stocks Green, Castle Acre, King's Lynn, Norfolk PE32 2XD

Tel: 01760 755394   www.english-heritage.org.uk/visits

Owner: English Heritage   **Contact:** The Custodian
Explore the romantic ruins of this 12th century Cluniac priory, set in the picturesque village of Castle Acre. The impressive Norman façade, splendid prior's lodgings and chapel, and delightful medieval herb garden should not be missed.

Location: OS Ref. TF814 148. ^{1}/4 m W of village of Castle Acre, 5m N of Swaffham.

Open: 1 Apr - 31 Oct: daily, 10am - 6pm (5pm in Oct). 1 Nov - 31 Mar: Wed - Sun, 10am - 4pm. Closed 24 - 26 Dec & 1 Jan. Times subject to change April 2004.

Admission: Adult £4, Child £2, Conc. £3, Family £9.30. Prices subject to change April 2004.
ⓘWC. Ground floor & grounds. P Tel for details.

CASTLE RISING CASTLE ⚘

Castle Rising, King's Lynn, Norfolk PE31 6AH

Tel: 01553 631330   **Fax:** 01553 631724

Owner: Greville Howard   **Contact:** The Custodian
Possibly the finest mid-12th century Keep left in England: it was built as a grand and elaborate palace. It was home to Queen Isabella, grandmother of the Black Prince. Still in surprisingly good condition, the Keep is surrounded by massive ramparts up to 120 feet high. Picnic area adjacent tearoom. Free audio tour.

Location: OS Ref. TF666 246. Located 4m NE of King's Lynn off A149.

Open: 1 Apr - 31 Oct: daily, 10am - 6pm, (5pm in Oct). 1 Nov - 31 Mar: Wed - Sun, 10am - 4pm. Closed 24 - 26 Dec & 1 Jan.

Admission: Adult £3.75, Child £2.10, Conc. £3. 15% discount for groups (11+). Prices include VAT.
ⓘPicnic area. Grounds. WC. P

NTPL / Nick Meers

BLICKLING HALL ✿

BLICKLING, NORWICH, NORFOLK NR11 6NF

www.nationaltrust.org.uk

Tel: 01263 738030   **Fax:** 01263 738035   **e-mail:** blickling@nationaltrust.org.uk

Owner: The National Trust   **Contact:** The Property Manager
Built in the early 17th century and one of England's great Jacobean houses. Blickling is famed for its spectacular long gallery, superb library and fine collections of furniture, pictures and tapestries.

Location: OS133 Ref. TG178 286. 1^1/2 m NW of Aylsham on B1354. Signposted off A140 Norwich (15m) to Cromer.

Open: House: 20 Mar - 31 Oct: Wed - Sun & BH Mons, 1 - 4.30pm (last admission, house closes at 5pm). Oct: 1 - 3.30pm (last admission, house closes at 4pm). Garden: Same days as house, also Tues in Aug, 10.15am - 5.15pm. 4 Nov - 19 Dec: Thur - Sun. 6 Jan - end Mar 2005: Thurs - Suns, 11am - 4pm. Park & Woods: daily, dawn - dusk.

Admission: Hall & Gardens: £7. Garden only: £4. Family & groups discounts. Groups must book.
Open as garden. Mostly suitable. Licensed. By arrangement. In park, on leads. Tel for details.

DRAGON HALL

115 - 123 King Street, Norwich, Norfolk NR1 1QE

Tel: 01603 663922 **e-mail:** dragon.hall@virgin.net

Owner: Norfolk & Norwich Heritage Trust Ltd **Contact:** Mr Neil Sigsworth

Magnificent medieval merchants' hall described as "one of the most exciting 15th century buildings in England". A wealth of outstanding features include living hall, screens passage, vaulted undercroft, superb timber-framed Great Hall, crown-post roof and intricately carved and painted dragon. Built by Robert Toppes, a wealthy and influential merchant. Dragon Hall is a unique legacy of medieval life, craftsmanship and trade.

Location: OS Ref. TG235 084. SE of Norwich city centre.

Open: Apr - Oct: Mon - Sat, 10am - 4pm. Nov - Mar: Mon - Fri, 10am - 4pm. Closed 23 Dec - 2 Jan & BHs.

Admission: Adult £2.50, Child £1, Conc. £2.

◻ ♿ House. ⓘ Obligatory. 🐕 Guide dogs only. ✳

FAIRHAVEN WOODLAND & WATER GARDEN

School Road, South Walsham NR13 6DZ

Tel/Fax: 01603 270449

Owner: The Fairhaven Garden Trust **Contact:** George Debbage, Manager

180 acre woodland & water garden with private broad in the beautiful Norfolk Broads.

Location: OS Ref. TG368 134. 9m NE of Norwich. Signed on A47 at junction with B1140.

Open: Daily (except 25 Dec), 10am - 5pm, also May - Aug: Wed & Thurs evenings until 9pm.

Admission: Adult £4, Child £1.50 (under 5yrs Free), OAP £3.50. Group reductions.

GRIME'S GRAVES ⌗

Lynford, Thetford, Norfolk IP26 5DE

Tel: 01842 810656

Owner: English Heritage **Contact:** The Custodian

These remarkable Neolithic flint mines, unique in England, comprise over 300 pits and shafts. The visitor can descend some 30 feet by ladder into one excavated shaft, and look along the radiating galleries, from where the flint used for making axes and knives was extracted.

Location: OS 144, TL818 898. 7m NW of Thetford off A134.

Open: 1 Apr - 31 Oct, daily, 10am - 6pm, (5pm in Oct). 1 Nov - 31 Mar: Wed - Sun, 10am - 4pm (closed 1 - 2pm) Closed 24 - 26 Dec & 1 Jan. Last visit to site 30 mins before close. NB: Visits to pit for children under 5yrs are at the discretion of the custodian. Times subject to change April 2004.

Admission: Adult £2.50, Child £1.50, Conc. £2, Family £5.80. Prices subject to change April 2004.

♿ Exhibition area only. 🅿 🐕 Restricted areas. ✳ 🖥 Tel for details.

HOLKHAM HALL 🏛

See page 283 for full page entry.

FELBRIGG HALL ❦

FELBRIGG, NORWICH, NORFOLK NR11 8PR

www.nationaltrust.org.uk

Tel: 01263 837444 **Fax:** 01263 837032 **e-mail:** felbrigg@nationaltrust.org.uk

Owner: The National Trust **Contact:** The Property Manager

One of the finest 17th century country houses in East Anglia. The hall contains its original 18th century furniture and one of the largest collections of Grand Tour paintings by a single artist. The library is outstanding. The Walled Garden has been restored and features a series of pottager gardens, a working dovecote and the National Collection of Colchicums. The Park, through which there are way-marked walks, is well known for its magnificent and aged trees. There are also walks to the church and lake and through the 500 acres of woods.

Location: OS133 Ref. TG193 394. Nr Felbrigg village, 2m SW of Cromer, entrance off B1436, signposted from A148 and A140.

Open: House: 20 Mar - 31 Oct: daily except Thur & Fri, 1 - 5pm. Gardens: As house, 11am - 5pm. Walled Garden: Also open Thur & Fri, 22 Jul - 3 Sep, 11am - 5pm.

Admission: House & Garden: Adult £6.30, Child £3, Family £15.50. Garden only: £2.60. Groups: (except BHs), £5.10. Groups please book with SAE to the Property Manager.

◻ 01263 837040. ✳ 🖥 01263 838237. ♿ Partial. ◼ Licensed. 🍴 Licensed. ⓘ By arrangement. 🅿 🐕 In grounds, on leads. 🖥 Tel 01263 837444 for details.

HOUGHTON HALL 🏛

HOUGHTON, KING'S LYNN, NORFOLK PE31 6UE

www.houghtonhall.com

Tel: 01485 528569 **Fax:** 01485 528167 **e-mail:** enquiries@houghtonhall.com

Owner: The Marquess of Cholmondeley **Contact:** Susan Cleaver

Houghton Hall is one of the finest examples of Palladian architecture in England. Built in the 18th century by Sir Robert Walpole, Britain's first prime minister. Original designs by James Gibbs & Colen Campbell, interior decoration by William Kent. The House has been restored to its former grandeur, containing many of its original furnishings. The spectacular 5-acre walled garden is divided into areas devoted to fruit and vegetables, elegant herbaceous borders, and a formal rose garden with over 150 varieties – full of colour throughout the summer. The unique Model Soldier Collection contains over 20,000 models arranged in various battle formations.

Location: OS Ref. TF792 287. 13m E of King's Lynn, 10m W of Fakenham 1¹/₂ m N of A148.

Open: Easter Sun - 30 Sept: Wed, Thur, Sun & BH Mons, 1 - 5.30pm. House: 2 - 5.30pm. Last admission 5pm.

Admission: Adult £6.50, Child (5-16) £3, Groups (20+): Adult £6, Child £2.50. Excluding house: Adult £4, Child £2, Groups (20+) Adult £3.50, Child £1.50.

ℹ️ 📷 🎁 ♿ 🍽 Licensed. 🍴 Licensed. 🎫 By arrangement. 🅿️ 🚌 ♿ On leads, in grounds.

HOVETON HALL GARDENS 🏛
Wroxham, Norwich, Norfolk NR12 8RJ

Tel: 01362 688109 **Fax:** 01362 688103 **e-mail:** info@hovetonhallgardens.co.uk

Owner: Mr & Mrs Andrew Buxton **Contact:** Mrs Buxton

15 acres of rhododendrons, azaleas, woodland and lakeside walks, walled herbaceous and vegetable gardens. Traditional tearooms and plant sales. The Hall (which is not open to the public) was built 1809 - 1812. Designs attributed to Humphry Repton.

Location: OS Ref. TG314 202. 8m N of Norwich. 1¹/₂ m NNE of Wroxham on A1151. Follow brown tourist signs.

Open: Easter Sun - mid-Sept: Weds, Fris, Suns & BH Mons, 11am - 5.30pm. Also open Thurs in May.

Admission: Adult £3.75, Child £1, Wheelchairs users £2. Family Season Ticket £20, Single Adult Season Ticket £9.50. Groups: £3.50 (if paid in advance).

Geoffrey Alan Jellicoe
1900-1996

An architect and landscape gardener heavily influenced by Italian gardens. Look for strong structural lines in his planting schemes and choice of plants.

Visit his public work at Runnymede, Surrey and the great private gardens of Sandringham, Norfolk, Hever Castle & Gardens, Kent, RHS Garden Wisley, Surrey and Mottisfont Abbey Garden, House & Estate, Hampshire and Kelmarsh Hall, Northamptonshire.

Architect, Landscape Architect & Writer

KIMBERLEY HALL
WYMONDHAM, NORFOLK NR18 0RT

www.kimberleyhall.co.uk

Tel/Fax: 01603 759447 **e-mail:** events@kimberleyhall.co.uk

Owner/Contact: R Buxton

Magnificent Queen Anne house built in 1712 by William Talman for Sir John Wodehouse, an ancestor of P G Wodehouse. Towers added after 1754 and wings connected to the main block by curved colonnades in 1835. Internal embellishments in 1770s include some very fine plasterwork by John Sanderson and a 'flying' spiral staircase beneath a coffered dome. The park, with its picturesque lake, ancient oak trees and walled gardens was laid out in 1762 by 'Capability' Brown.

Location: OS Ref. TG091 048. 10m SW of Norwich, 3m from A11.

Open: House & Park not open to the public. Grounds, certain rooms and extensive cellars available for corporate hospitality and weddings (licensed for Civil ceremonies) as well as product launches, film and fashion shoots.

Admission: Please telephone for details.

🍴 🏛

LETHERINGSETT WATERMILL
Riverside Road, Letheringsett, Holt, Norfolk NR25 7YD

Tel: 01263 713153 **e-mail:** watermill@ic24.net

Owner/Contact: M D Thurlow

Water-powered mill producing wholewheat flour from locally grown wheat. Built in 1802.

Location: OS Ref. TG062 387. Riverside Road, Letheringsett, Holt, Norfolk.

Open: Whitsun - Oct: Mon - Fri, 10am - 5pm, Sat 9am - 1pm. Working demonstration, Tue - Fri, 2 - 4.30pm. Viewing may take place at any other time. Oct - Whitsun: Mon - Fri, 9am - 4pm. Sat, 9am - 1pm. Working demonstration, Tue - Thur, 1.30 - 3.30pm. BH Suns & Mons, 2 - 5pm.

Admission: Adult £2.50, Child £1.50. When demonstrating: Adult £3.50, Child £2.50, OAP £3, Family (2+2) £10.

MANNINGTON GARDENS & COUNTRYSIDE
MANNINGTON HALL, NORWICH NR11 7BB

Tel: 01263 584175 **Fax:** 01263 761214

Owner: The Lord & Lady Walpole **Contact:** Lady Walpole

The gardens around this medieval moated manor house feature a wide variety of plants, trees and shrubs in many different settings. Throughout the gardens are thousands of roses especially classic varieties. The Heritage Rose and 20 century Rose Gardens have roses in areas with designs reflecting their date of origin from the 15th century to the present day.

Location: OS Ref. TG144 320. Signposted from Saxthorpe crossroads on the Norwich - Holt road B1149. 1¹/₂ m W of Wolterton Hall.

Open: Gardens: May - Sept: Suns 12 - 5pm. Jun - Aug: Wed - Fri, 11am - 5pm. Walks: daily from 9am. Medieval Hall open by appointment. Grounds & Park open all year.

Admission: Adult £3, Child (under 16yrs) Free, Conc. £2.50. Groups by arrangement.

⬚ ⬚ ⬚ ⬚ Grounds. WCs. ⬚Licensed. ⬚By arrangement. ⬚ ⬚
⬚In grounds on leads. Not in gardens. ⬚ Park. ⬚Tel for details.

NORWICH CASTLE MUSEUM & ART GALLERY
Norwich, Norfolk NR1 3JU

Tel: 01603 493625 **Fax:** 01603 493623 **e-mail:** museums@norfolk.gov.uk

Norman Castle Keep, housing displays of art, archaeology and natural history.

Location: OS Ref. TG233 085. City centre.

Open: All year: Mon - Fri, 10.30am - 4.30pm. Sat, 10am - 5pm. Sun, 1 - 5pm.

Admission: Single zone: Adult £2.90, Child £2.25, Conc. £2.55. Whole museum: Adult £4.95, Child (4-16yrs) £3.95, Conc. £4.50.

❄ **Open All Year Index** see front section

OXBURGH HALL & ESTATE ❧
OXBOROUGH, KING'S LYNN, NORFOLK PE33 9PS

www.nationaltrust.org.uk

Tel: 01366 328258 **Fax:** 01366 328066 **e-mail:** oxburghhall@nationaltrust.org.uk

Owner: The National Trust **Contact:** The Property Secretary

A moated manor house built in 1482 by the Bedingfeld family, who still live here. The rooms show the development from medieval austerity to Victorian comfort and include an outstanding display of embroidery done by Mary Queen of Scots. The attractive gardens include a French parterre, kitchen garden and orchard and woodland walks.

Location: OS143, TF742 012. At Oxborough, 7m SW of Swaffham on S side of Stoke Ferry road.

Open: House: 20 Mar - 7 Nov: Sat - Wed, 1 - 5pm; BH Mons, 11am - 5pm, last admission 4.30pm. Garden: 3 Jan - 14 Mar: Sat & Sun, 11am - 4pm; 20 Mar - 7 Nov: Sat - Wed & Aug: daily, 11am - 5.30pm. Shop & Restaurant: As garden 11am - 5pm; also 13 Nov - 19 Dec: weekends only, 11am - 4pm.

Admission: House & Garden: Adult £5.75, Child £2.90, Family £15. Garden & Estate only: Adult £2.90, Child £1.45. Booked Groups (15+): £4.65 (except BHs). Groups must book with SAE to the Property Secretary.

⬚ ⬚Licensed. ⬚Partial. ⬚By arrangement. ⬚ ⬚ ⬚ ⬚Send SAE for details.

RAVENINGHAM GARDENS 🏛

RAVENINGHAM, NORWICH, NORFOLK NR14 6NS

www.raveningham.com

Tel: 01508 548152 **Fax:** 01508 548958

e-mail: info@raveningham.com

Owner: Sir Nicholas Bacon Bt **Contact:** Mrs Janet Woodard

Superb herbaceous borders, 18th century walled kitchen garden, Victorian glass-house, herb garden, Edwardian rose garden, contemporary sculptures, 14th century church and much more. Also house guided tours.

Location: OS Ref. TM399 965. Between Norwich & Lowestoft off A146 then B1136/B1140.

Open: All BH Suns & Mons (including Easter); also 13/14 Jun: 2 - 5pm.

Admission: Garden only: Adult £2.50, Child (under 16yrs) Free, OAP £2. Garden & House tour: Adult £6, Child £2, OAP £5.50. Groups by prior arrangement.

🍴 Teas on Suns. 🎬 House tours by arrangement.

ROW 111 HOUSE, OLD MERCHANT'S HOUSE, 🏛 & GREYFRIARS' CLOISTERS

South Quay, Great Yarmouth, Norfolk NR30 2RQ

Tel: 01493 857900

Owner: English Heritage **Contact:** The Custodian

Two immaculately presented 17th century Row Houses, a type of building unique to Great Yarmouth. Row 111 House was almost destroyed by bombing in 1942/3 and contains items rescued from the rubble. Old Merchant's House boasts magnificent plaster-work ceilings and displays of local architectural fittings.

Location: OS134, TG525 072. In Great Yarmouth, make for South Quay, by riverside and dock, ½ m inland from beach. Follow signs to dock and south quay.

Open: 1 Apr - 31 Oct: daily, 10am - 5pm. Escorted tours of all 3 sites depart from Row 111 house at 10am, 12 noon, 2pm and 4pm. Times subject to change April 2004.

Admission: Adult £3. Child £1.50, Conc. £2. 15% discount for groups of 11+. Prices subject to change April 2004.

🎬 🎥

ST GEORGE'S GUILDHALL 🌿

27-29 King Street, King's Lynn, Norfolk PE30 1HA

Tel: 01553 765565 www.west-norfolk.gov.uk

Owner: The National Trust **Contact:** The Administrator

The largest surviving English medieval guildhall and now converted into an arts centre, but with many interesting surviving features.

Location: OS132, TF616 202. On W side of King Street close to the Tuesday Market Place.

Open: All year: Mon - Fri (closed Good Fri, BHs & 24 Dec - 1st Mon in Jan), 10am - 2pm. Times may vary in Jul & Aug. The Guildhall is not usually open on days when there are performances in the theatre, tel box office 01553 764864 for details.

Admission: Free.

🎬 🦽 Access to galleries. 🍴 🎭 Licensed. ✳

SANDRINGHAM

See page 284 for full page entry.

SHERINGHAM PARK 🌿

Upper Sheringham, Norfolk NR26 8TB

Tel: 01263 823778 **e-mail:** sheringhampark@nationaltrust.org.uk

www.nationaltrust.org.uk

Owner: The National Trust **Contact:** The Head Warden

One of Humphry Repton's most outstanding achievements, the landscape park contains fine mature woodlands, and the large woodland garden is particularly famous for its spectacular show of rhododendrons and azaleas (mid May - June). There are stunning views of the coast and countryside from the viewing towers and many delightful waymarked walks.

Location: OS133, TG135 420. 2m SW of Sheringham, access for cars off A148 Cromer - Holt road; 5m W of Cromer, 6m E of Holt.

Open: All year: daily, dawn - dusk.

Admission: Pay & Display: Cars £2.80 (NT members Free - display card in car). Coaches £8.40 (must book for May & Jun visits).

🦽 Partial. WC. 🍴 Easter - end Sept. 🅿 Limited for coaches. 🐕 In grounds, on leads. ✳

WALSINGHAM ABBEY GROUNDS & SHIREHALL MUSEUM 🏛

Little Walsingham, Norfolk NR22 6BP

Tel: 01328 820259 **Fax:** 01328 820098 **e-mail:** walsingham.estate@farmline.com

Owner: Walsingham Estate Company **Contact:** Estate Office

Set in the picturesque medieval village of Little Walsingham, a place of pilgrimage since the 11th century, the grounds contain the remains of the famous Augustinian Priory with attractive gardens and river walks. The Shirehall Museum includes a Georgian magistrates' court and displays on the history of Walsingham.

Location: OS Ref. TF934 367. B1105 N from Fakenham - 5m.

Open: 3 Apr - 31 Oct: daily, 10am - 4.30pm. Also daily during snowdrop season for snowdrop walks, 10am - 4pm. Abbey grounds: many other times, please ring for details.

Admission: Combined ticket: Adult £3, Conc. £1.50.

🎬 🎫 🦽 Partial. 🎬 By arrangement. 🔌 🐕 In grounds, on leads. ✳ 🎭 Tel for details.

WOLTERTON PARK 🏛

NORWICH, NORFOLK NR11 7BB

Tel: 01263 584175 **Fax:** 01263 761214

Owner: The Lord and Lady Walpole **Contact:** The Lady Walpole

18th century Hall. Historic park with lake.

Location: OS Ref. TG164 317. Situated near Erpingham village, signposted from Norwich - Cromer Rd A140.

Open: Park: daily from 9am. Hall: Fridays 30 Apr - 29 Oct: 2 - 5pm (last entry 4pm) & by appointment.

Admission: £2 car park fee only for walkers. Groups by application: from £4 groups, £5 individuals.

🎬 🦽 Partial. WC. 🎬 🅿 🔌 🐕 In park, on leads. 🔈 ✳ 🎭 Tel for details. €

Houghton Hall, Norfolk from the book *Historic Family Homes and Gardens from the Air*, see page 54.

THE ANCIENT HOUSE
Clare, Suffolk CO10 8NY

Tel: 01628 825920 or 825925 (bookings) **www**.landmarktrust.co.uk
Owner: Leased to the Landmark Trust by Clare PC **Contact:** The Landmark Trust
A 14th century house extended in the 15th and 17th centuries, decorated with high relief pargetting. Half of the building is managed by the Landmark Trust, which lets buildings for self-catering holidays. The other half of the house is run as a museum. Full details of The Ancient House and 178 other historic buildings available for holidays are featured in The Landmark Handbook (price £9.50 refundable against booking), from The Landmark Trust, Shottesbrooke, Maidenhead, Berkshire SL6 3SW.
Location: OS Ref. TL769 454. Village centre, on A1092 8m WNW of Sudbury.
Open: By appointment only and, 12 - 17 Jun 2004. Museum: Easter & May - Sept: Thur, Fri & Sun, 2 - 5pm, Sat & BHs 11.30am - 5pm.
Admission: Please contact the Landmark Trust for details.

BELCHAMP HALL
BELCHAMP WALTER, SUDBURY, SUFFOLK CO10 7AT
www.belchamphall.com

Tel: 01787 881961 **Fax:** 01787 466778
Owner/Contact: Mr C F V Raymond
Superb Queen Anne house on a site belonging to the Raymond family since 1611. Historic portraits and period furniture. Suitable for receptions and an ideal film location, often seen as 'Lady Jane's house' in 'Lovejoy'. Gardens including a cherry avenue, follies, a sunken garden, walled garden and lake. Medieval church with 15th century wall paintings.
Location: OS Ref. TL827 407. 5m SW of Sudbury, opposite Belchamp Walter Church.
Open: By appointment only: May - Sept: Tues, Thurs & BHs, 2.30 - 6pm.
Admission: Adult £5, Child £2. No reduction for groups.
ⓘNo photography in house. Conference facilities. Ⓣ Ⓓ By arrangement. ⒡Obligatory. Ⓟ Ⓗ Guide dogs only.

CHRISTCHURCH MANSION
Christchurch Park, Ipswich, Suffolk IP4 2BE

Tel: 01473 433554 **Fax:** 01473 433564 **Owner/Contact:** Ipswich Borough Council
A fine Tudor house set in beautiful parkland.
Location: OS Ref. TM165 450. Christchurch Park, near centre of Ipswich.
Open: All year: Tue - Sat, 10am - 5pm (dusk in winter). Suns, 2.30 - 4.30pm (dusk in winter). Also open BH Mons. Closed 24 - 26 Dec, 1/2 Jan & Good Fri.
Admission: Free.

EAST BERGHOLT PLACE GARDEN
East Bergholt, Suffolk CO7 6UP

Tel/Fax: 01206 299224
Owner: Mr & Mrs R L C Eley **Contact:** Sara Eley
Fifteen acres of garden and arboretum originally laid out at the beginning of the century by the present owner's great-grandfather. A wonderful collection of fine trees and shrubs, many of which are rarely seen growing in East Anglia and originate from the famous plant hunter George Forrest. Particularly beautiful in the spring when the rhododendrons, magnolias and camellias are in flower.
Location: OS Ref. TM084 343. 2m E of A12 on B1070, Manningtree Rd, on the edge of East Bergholt.
Open: Mar - Sept: daily, 10am - 5pm. Closed Easter Sun.
Admission: Adult £2.50, Child Free. (Proceeds to garden up-keep).
ⓘSpecialist Plant Centre in the Victorian walled garden. ⒡By arrangement. Ⓗ

EUSTON HALL 🏛
Estate Office, Euston, Thetford, Norfolk IP24 2QP

Tel: 01842 766366 **Fax:** 01842 766764 **e-mail:** lcampbell@euston-estate.co.uk
www.eustonhall.co.uk
Owner: The Duke of Grafton **Contact:** Mrs L Campbell
18th century house contains a famous collection of paintings including works by Stubbs, Van Dyck, Lely and Kneller. The Pleasure Grounds were were laid out by John Evelyn and William Kent. 17th century parish church in Wren style. River walk, watermill and picnic area.
Location: OS Ref. TL897 786. 12m N of Bury St Edmunds, on A1088. 2m E of A134.
Open: 17 Jun - 16 Sept: Thurs 2.30 - 5pm. Also Suns 27 Jun, 18 July & 5 Sept: 2.30 - 5pm.
Admission: Adult £4, Child £2, OAP £3. Groups (12+): £3pp.
Ⓐ Ⓑ Ⓒ Ⓓ

FLATFORD BRIDGE COTTAGE 🌿
Flatford, East Bergholt, Colchester, Essex CO7 6OL

Tel: 01206 298260 **Fax:** 01206 299193 **www**.nationaltrust.org.uk
Owner: The National Trust **Contact:** The Property Manager
Just upstream from Flatford Mill, the restored thatched cottage houses a display about John Constable, several of whose paintings depict this property. Facilities include a tea garden, shop, boat hire, an Information Centre and countryside walks.
Location: OS Ref. TM077 332. On N bank of Stour, 1m S of East Bergholt B1070.
Open: Mar & Apr: Wed - Sun, 11am - 5.30pm. May - end Sept: daily, 10am - 5.30pm. Oct: daily, 11am - 4.30pm. Nov & Dec: Wed - Sun, 11am - 3.30pm. Jan & Feb 2004: Sats & Suns only, 11am - 3.30pm. Closed Christmas & New Year.
Admission: Guided walks (when guide available) £2, accompanied child Free.
Ⓐ Ⓑ Tea garden & shop. WC. Ⓓ Ⓔ Ⓕ Charge applies. Ⓗ Guide dogs only.

© English Heritage Photo Library

FRAMLINGHAM CASTLE ⚜
FRAMLINGHAM, SUFFOLK IP8 9BT
www.english-heritage.org.uk/visits

Tel: 01728 724189
Owner: English Heritage **Contact:** The Custodian
A magnificent 12th century castle which, from the outside, looks almost the same as when it was built. From the continuous curtain wall linking 13 towers, there are excellent panoramic views of Framlingham and the charming reed-fringed mere. Throughout its colourful history the castle has been a fortress, an Elizabethan prison, a poor house and a school. The many alterations over the years have led to a pleasing mixture of historic styles.
Location: OS Ref. TM287 637. In Framlingham on B1116. NE of town centre.
Open: 1 Apr - 31 Oct: daily 10am - 6pm (5pm in Oct). 1 Nov - 31 Mar: daily 10am - 4pm. Closed 24 - 26 Dec & 1 Jan. Times subject to change April 2004.
Admission: Adult £3.90, Child £2, Conc. £2.90, Family £9.80. 15% discount for groups (11+). Prices subject to change April 2004.
Ⓐ Ⓑ Ground floor & grounds. WCs. Ⓓ Ⓟ Ⓕ Ⓖ Ⓗ Tel for details.

GAINSBOROUGH'S HOUSE

46 GAINSBOROUGH ST, SUDBURY, SUFFOLK CO10 2EU

www.gainsborough.org

Tel: 01787 372958 **Fax:** 01787 376991 **e-mail:** mail@gainsborough.org

Owner: Gainsborough's House Society **Contact:** Rosemary Woodward

Birthplace of Thomas Gainsborough RA (1727-88). Georgian-fronted town house, with attractive walled garden, displays more of the artist's work than any other gallery. The collection is shown together with 18th century furniture and memorabilia. Varied programme of contemporary exhibitions organised throughout the year includes: fine art, craft, photography, printmaking, sculpture and highlights the work of East Anglian artists.

Location: OS Ref. TL872 413. 46 Gainsborough Street, Sudbury town centre.

Open: All year: Mon - Sat, 10am - 5pm. BH Suns & Mons, 2 - 5pm. Closed: Suns, Good Fri and Christmas to New Year.

Admission: Adult £3.50, Child/Student £1.50, OAP £2.80, Family Ticket £8.

i No photography. ◻ & Ground floor. WCs. ▣ P None. ▣ ❋

HELMINGHAM HALL GARDENS ▥

STOWMARKET, SUFFOLK IP14 6EF

www.helmingham.com

Tel: 01473 890363 **Fax:** 01473 890776 **e-mail:** helminghamestate@aol.com

Owner: The Lord & Lady Tollemache **Contact:** Ms Jane Tresidder

The Tudor Hall surrounded by its wide moat is set in a 400 acre deer park. Two superb gardens, one surrounded by its own moat and walls extends to several acres and has wide herbaceous borders and an immaculate kitchen garden. The second enclosed within yew hedges, has a special rose garden with a herb and knot garden containing plants grown in England before 1750.

Location: OS Ref. TM190 578. B1077, 9m N of Ipswich, 5m S of Debenham.

Open: Gardens only: 2 May - 12 Sept: Suns, 2 - 6pm. Groups: by appointment only on Weds, 2 - 5pm. (We can also accept individual bookings on a Wed if a group is booked.)

Admission: Adult £4, Child (5-15yrs) £2. Groups (30+) £3.75.

◻ ▨ & Grounds. WCs. ▣ P ▦ In grounds, on leads.

HADLEIGH GUILDHALL
Hadleigh, Suffolk IP7 5DT

Tel: 01473 827752

Owner: Hadleigh Market Feoffment Charity **Contact:** Jane Haylock

Fine timber framed guildhall, one of the least known medieval buildings in Suffolk.

Location: OS Ref. TM025 425. S side of churchyard.

Open: Jun - end Sept: Building: Thurs & Suns; Garden: daily (except Sats), 2 - 5pm

Admission: Free. Donations welcome.

HAUGHLEY PARK ▥
Stowmarket, Suffolk IP14 3JY

Tel: 01359 240701 www.haughleyparkbarn.co.uk

Owner/Contact: Mr & Mrs Robert Williams

Mellow red brick manor house of 1620 set in gardens, park and woodland. Original five-gabled east front, north wing re-built in Georgian style, 1820. 6 acres of well tended gardens including walled kitchen garden. 17th century brick and timber barn restored as meeting rooms. Woodland walks with bluebells (special Sun opening), lily-of-the-valley (May), rhododendrons and azaleas.

Location: OS Ref. TM005 618. 4m W of Stowmarket signed off A14.

Open: Garden only: May - Sept: Tues & last Sun in Apr & 1st Sun in May, 2 - 5.30pm. House visits and groups by appointment (even outside normal times). Barn bookable for special lunches, teas, dinners, lectures etc. (capacity 120).

Admission: House: £2. Garden: £3. Child under 16 Free.

i Picnics allowed. ▨ Bluebell Sun. ▼ & ▣ Bluebell Sun. ▥ By arrangement. P ▦ On leads only. ▲ ❋

Somerleyton Hall, Suffolk from the book
Historic Family Homes and Gardens from the Air, see page 54.

▣ **Special Events Index** see front section

HENGRAVE HALL

BURY ST EDMUNDS, SUFFOLK IP28 6LZ

www.hengravehallcentre.org.uk

Tel: 01284 701561   **Fax:** 01284 702950   **e-mail:** info@hengravehallcentre.org.uk
Owner: Religious of the Assumption   **Contact:** Mr J H Crowe

Hengrave Hall is a unique Tudor house of stone and brick, built between 1525 and 1538 by Sir Thomas Kytson, Warden of the Mercers' Company. Former home to the Kytson and Gage families, it was visited by Elizabeth I on her Suffolk Progress in 1578. Set in 45 acres of cultivated grounds, the Hall is now run as a Conference and Retreat Centre by the Hengrave Community of Reconciliation. The Hall has many important and distinctive features, including beautiful stained glass and the magnificent Oriel Window and Frieze incorporating the Garter Arms and other Coats of Arms which were comprehensively restored in summer 2000. The ancient church with Saxon tower adjoins the Hall and continues to be used for daily prayer.

Location: OS Ref. TL824 686. 3½ m NW of Bury St Edmunds on the A1101.

Open: Please apply to the Warden (quoting ref. HHG) for conference facilities (day and residential); tours (by appointment); retreats; programme of events; schools' programme. Special group rates.

ⓘ Children's playground. 🄯 ♨ ♿ ✎ By arrangement. ▨ 🔲 ❉ ♿ Tel for details.

Maze

Garden Jargon

Often created from well clipped yew, or beech hedging – a man-made garden feature designed as narrow corridors that people can walk through. Paths often lead nowhere – and the maze becomes a puzzle to solve!

Visit Chatsworth House, Derbyshire, Chenies Manor House, Buckinghamshire, Greys Court, Oxfordshire, Longleat, Wiltshire, Glendurgan Garden, Cornwall, Somerleyton Hall & Gardens, Suffolk, Cawdor Castle and Scone Palace, Scotland.

NT Photographic Library: Rupert Truman

ICKWORTH HOUSE & PARK 🌿

THE ROTUNDA, HORRINGER, BURY ST EDMUNDS IP29 5QE

www.nationaltrust.org.uk/eastanglia

Tel: 01284 735270   **Fax:** 01284 735175   **e-mail:** ickworth@nationaltrust.org.uk
Owner: The National Trust   **Contact:** The Property Manager

One of the most unusual houses in East Anglia. The huge Rotunda of this 18th century Italianate house dominates the landscape. Inside are collections of Georgian silver, Regency furniture, Old Master paintings and family portraits.

Location: OS155 Ref. TL816 611. In Horringer, 3m SW of Bury St Edmunds on W side of A143.

Open: House: 19 Mar - 31 Oct: daily except Wed & Thur, 1 - 5pm, last admission 4.30pm (closes 4.30pm in Oct). Garden: 19 Mar - 31 Oct: daily; 10am - 5pm. 1 Nov - 22 Dec: Mon - Fri; 2 Jan - 22 Mar 2005, Daily, 10am - 4pm. Park: daily, 7am - 7pm. Note: Garden & Park closed 25 Dec.

Admission: Adult £6.40, Child £2.90. Family discounts. Park & Garden only (includes access to shop & restaurant): Adult £2.95, Child 85p. All Groups must pre-book: Adult £5.40, Child £2.40. No group discounts on Suns & BH Mons.

🄯 ♿ Partial. ▨ ⑪ Licensed. ✎ By arrangement. ▨ 🔲 In park, on leads. ♿ Tel for details.

KENTWELL HALL 🏛
LONG MELFORD, SUFFOLK CO10 9BA

www.kentwell.co.uk

Tel: 01787 310207 **Fax:** 01787 379318 **e-mail:** info@kentwell.co.uk

Owner: Patrick Phillips Esq **Contact:** Mrs J G Phillips

Heritage Building of the Year 2001. Atmospheric moated Tudor Hall with rare service building of c1500. Interior 'improved' by Thomas Hopper in 1820s. Still a lived-in family home. Famed for the long-time, long term, ongoing restoration works.

Re-Creations: Kentwell is renowned for its award-winning Re-Creations of Everyday Tudor Life. It has now added occasional Re-Creations of WW2 Life. Re-Creations take place on selected weekends. Telephone for dates.

Gardens: Over 30 years endeavour has resulted in Gardens which are a joy in all seasons. Moats predominate with massed spring bulbs, extensive wild flowers; ancient fruit blossom and clipped yews to large Herb Garden & Potager.

Corporate: Any sort of function including authentic Tudor Banquets.

Schools: Major education Programme based upon the Tudors.

Filming: Much used for medieval and Tudor periods for its wide range of perfectly equipped locations inside and out and access to Kentwell's 700 Tudors as extras.

Location: OS Ref. TL864 479. Off the A134. 4m N of Sudbury, 14m S of Bury St. Edmunds 1m NNW of Long Melford off A134.

Open: BHs, Sat - Mon (+Fri, Easter & Aug): 11am - 6pm. Feb half term & Suns - 4 Apr: for Lambing & Spring Bulbs only. Daily week before & week after Easter, otherwise Suns & summer half term only - 19 Jun: 12noon - 5pm; 20 Jun - 11 Jul Great Annual Re-Creation of Tudor Life (booked schools on weekdays, public on Sat, Sun & last Fri, 11am - 5pm). 14 Jul - early Sept: daily, 12noon - 5pm. Rest of Sept: Wed, Thur & Sun; Oct: Suns & half term only, 12 noon - 5pm.

Admission: House, Gardens & Farm: Adult £6.95, Child (5-15yrs) £4.45, OAP £5.95; Gardens & Farm only: Adult £4.90, Child (5-15yrs) £3.20, OAP £4.15; Special prices apply for all BH weekends and other Re-Creation & Special Event days.
ℹ️No photography in house. 🔲 🅃 ♿ 🍴Home-made food. 🅿 ⬛ ✖ ⬛
🐕 Tel for details.

LANDGUARD FORT ⚜
Felixstowe, Suffolk

Tel: 01394 277767 or 01473 218245

Owner: English Heritage **Contact:** The Custodian

Impressive 18th century fort with later additions built on a site originally fortified by Henry VIII and in use until after World War II. There is also a museum (not EH).

Location: OS Ref. TM284 318. 1m S of Felixstowe town centre - follow brown tourist signs to Landguard Point and Nature Reserve from A14.

Open: 6 Apr - 2 Nov: daily, 10am - 6pm (5pm from 1 Oct - 2 Nov). Times subject to change April 2004.

Admission: Adult £2.50, Child £1, Conc. £2. EH members Free. Prices subject to change April 2004.
🔲 🅿 ✖

NTPL / John Bethell

LAVENHAM: THE GUILDHALL OF CORPUS CHRISTI 🐛
THE MARKET PLACE, LAVENHAM, SUDBURY CO10 9QZ

www.nationaltrust.org.uk

Tel: 01787 247646 **e-mail:** lavenhamguildhall@nationaltrust.org.uk

Owner: The National Trust **Contact:** The Property Manager

This splendid 16th century timber-framed building dominates the Market Place of the picturesque town of Lavenham with its many historic houses and wonderful church. Inside are exhibitions on local history, farming and industry, as well as the story of the medieval woollen cloth trade. There is also a walled garden with dye plants.

Location: OS155, TL915 942. 6m NNE of Sudbury. Village centre. A1141 & B1071.

Open: 1 - 30 Mar: Sat & Sun, 11am - 4pm. 1 - 30 Apr: Wed - Sun, 11am - 5pm. 1 May - 31 Oct: daily, 11am - 5pm. 1 - 30 Nov: Sat & Sun, 11am - 4pm. Open BH Mon, closed Good Fri. Parts of the building may be closed occasionally for community use.

Admission: Adult £3.25, accompanied child Free. Groups: £2.75. School parties (by arrangement) 60p per child.
🔲 ♿ Shop & tearoom. ⬛

LEISTON ABBEY ⚜
Leiston, Suffolk

Tel: 01223 582700 (Regional Office)

Owner: English Heritage **Contact:** The East of England Regional Office

The remains of this abbey for Premonstratensian canons, including a restored chapel, are amongst the most extensive in Suffolk.

Location: OS Ref. TM445 642. 1m N of Leiston off B1069.

Open: Any reasonable time.

Admission: Free.
♿ 🅿 ✖ ✳

LITTLE HALL

Market Place, Lavenham, Sudbury, Suffolk CO10 9QZ

Tel: 01787 247179   **Fax:** 01787 248341

e-mail: info@suffolksociety.com **www.**suffolksociety.com

Owner: Suffolk Building Preservation Trust

Contact: Suffolk Preservation Society Trust

A beautifully presented 14th century hall house in the heart of historic Lavenham. A warm, friendly, furnished building with a lovely walled garden and courtyard. Its fascinating history mirrors the rise and fall of Lavenham's medieval woollen-cloth trade, the years of industrial decline and its eventual 20th century revival.

Location: OS Ref. TL915 942. 6m NNE of Sudbury. Bus: No.753 hourly from Sudbury & Bury St. Edmunds.

Open: Good Fri - 31 Oct: Sat, Sun, Wed & Thurs, 2 - 5.30pm. Last entry 5pm. Throughout Easter, May & Aug BH Mons: 11am - 5.30pm. Groups & school groups by arrangement throughout the year.

Admission: Adult £2, accompanied Child Free, OAP/Student £2. Groups (10+): Adult £1.50, Child 50p, OAP/Student £1.50, School parties 50p per child.

ⓘNo photography in house. 🅣 By arrangement. 🅿 Nearby for cars and coaches. ⊠

MANOR HOUSE MUSEUM

Honey Hill, Bury St Edmunds, Suffolk IP33 1RT

Tel: 01284 757076   **Fax:** 01284 747231   **e-mail:** manor.house@stedsbc.gov.uk

Owner: St Edmundsbury Borough Council   **Contact:** The Manager

A Georgian town house, built by the Earl of Bristol for his wife Elizabeth between 1736 and 1737.

Location: OS Ref. TL858 640. Bury town centre off A14. Just S of Abbey grounds.

Open: All year: Wed - Sun, 11am - 4pm.

Admission: Adult £2.50, Conc £2. Free to residents of the Borough.

MELFORD HALL 🐾

Long Melford, Sudbury, Suffolk CO10 9AA

Tel: 01787 880286   **e-mail:** melford@nationaltrust.org.uk

www.nationaltrust.org.uk

Owner: The National Trust   **Contact:** Visitor Services Co-ordinator

A turreted brick Tudor mansion, little changed since 1578 with the original panelled banqueting hall, an 18th century drawing room, a Regency library and Victorian bedrooms, showing fine furniture and Chinese porcelain. Small collection of Beatrix Potter memorabilia. The home of the Hyde-Parker family since 1786.

Location: OS Ref. TL867 462. In Long Melford off A134, 14m S of Bury St Edmunds, 3m N of Sudbury.

Open: 1 - 30 Apr: 1 - 31 Oct: Sat, Sun & BH Mon, 2 - 5.30pm. May - Sept: Wed - Sun & BH Mon, 2 - 5.30pm. Last admission 5pm.

Admission: Adult £4.50, Child (under 16) £2.25. Groups (15+): Adult £3.40. E-mail, phone or write with SAE to Visitor Services Coordinator.

ⓘNo photography in house. ♿Ramp at main door, stairlift to 1st floor. WC. 🅿 🐾In car park & park walk only, on leads.

ORFORD CASTLE ⊞

ORFORD, WOODBRIDGE, SUFFOLK IP12 2ND

www.english-heritage.org.uk/visits

Tel: 01394 450472

Owner: English Heritage   **Contact:** The Custodian

An enchanting royal castle built by Henry II for coastal defence in the 12th century. A magnificent keep survives almost intact with three immense towers offering beautiful views over Orford Ness and the surrounding countryside.

Location: OS169, TM419 499. In Orford on B1084, 20m NE of Ipswich.

Open: 1 Apr - 31 Oct: daily 10am - 6pm (5pm in Oct). 1 Nov - 31 Mar: Wed - Sun, 10am - 4pm. Closed 1 - 2pm. Closed 24 - 26 Dec & 1 Jan. Times subject to change April 2004.

Admission: Adult £3.60, Child £1.80, Conc. £2.70, Family £9. 15% discount for groups (11+). Prices subject to change April 2004.

🗀 🗀 🅿 ⊠ ❀ ♿ Tel for details.

Kentwell Hall, Suffolk from the book
Historic Family Homes and Gardens from the Air, see page 54.

ST EDMUNDSBURY CATHEDRAL

Angel Hill, Bury St Edmunds, Suffolk IP33 1LS

Tel: 01284 754933 **Fax:** 01284 768655 **e-mail:** cathedral@burycathedral.fsnet.co.uk
www.stedscathedral.co.uk

Owner: The Church of England   **Contact:** Sarah Friswell

Be among the first to see the magnificent Millennium Tower, which is to complete the last unfinished Anglican cathedral in England. Built over the past five years of English limestone, brick and lime mortar, the 150ft Lantern Tower, along with new chapels, cloisters and North Transept, will complete nearly fifty years of development in a style never likely to be repeated.

Location: OS Ref. TL857 642. Bury St Edmunds town centre.
Open: All year: daily 8.30am - 6pm, Jun - Aug: 8.30am - 7pm.
Admission: Donation invited.

🅿 🅺Partial. WC. 🌐 ℹ 🅼

SAXTEAD GREEN POST MILL ♯

Post Mill Bungalow, Saxtead Green, Woodbridge, Suffolk IP13 9QQ

Tel: 01728 685789 **www**.english-heritage.org.uk/visits

Owner: English Heritage   **Contact:** The Custodian

The finest example of a Suffolk Post Mill. Still in working order, you can climb the wooden stairs to the various floors, full of fascinating mill machinery. Ceased production in 1947.

Location: OS Ref. TM253 645. 2¹/₂ m NW of Framlingham on A1120.
Open: 1 Apr - 31 Oct: Mon - Sat, 10am - 6pm (5pm in Oct). Closed 1 - 2pm. Times subject to change April 2004.
Admission: Adult £2.30, Child £1.20, Conc. £1.70. Prices subject to change April 2004.

🅿 🅺

SHRUBLAND PARK GARDENS

Ipswich, Suffolk IP6 9QQ

Tel: 01473 830221 **Fax:** 01473 832202

Owner/Contact: Lord de Saumarez

One of the finest examples of an Italianate garden in England, designed by Sir Charles Barry.

Location: OS Ref. TM125 525. 6m N of Ipswich to the E of A14/A140.
Open: 4 Apr - 12 Sept: Suns & BH Mons, 2 - 5pm.
Admission: Adult £3, Child/OAP £2.

SOUTH ELMHAM HALL

ST CROSS, HARLESTON, NORFOLK IP20 0PZ

www.southelmham.co.uk   **www**.batemansbarn.co.uk

Tel: 01986 782526 **Fax:** 01986 782203 **e-mail:** enquiries@southelmham.co.uk

Owner/Contact: John Sanderson

A Grade I listed medieval manor house set inside moated enclosure. Originally built by the Bishop of Norwich around 1270. Much altered in the 16th century. Self guided trail through former deer park to South Elmham Minster, a ruined Norman chapel with Saxon origins.

Location: OS30 Ref. TM778 324. Between Harleston and Bungay from the A143 take the B1062.
Open: Minster, Walks (free) & Café: Easter - 31 Oct: Suns, Thurs, Fris & BH Mons. 1 Nov - Easter: Suns only, 10.30am - 5pm. Hall: Thurs, BH Mons. 1 May - 30 Sept: Guided tours only, 2pm.
Admission: House: Adult £6, Child £3. Groups (12 - 50): Adult £4, Child £2.50.

🅿 🕋 🅺WC. 🌐 ℹObligatory. 🅼 🅿 🅺In grounds, on leads. 🔺 ❄

SOMERLEYTON HALL & GARDENS 🏛

SOMERLEYTON, LOWESTOFT, SUFFOLK NR32 5QQ

www.somerleyton.co.uk

Tel: 01502 730224 office **Fax:** 01502 732143 **e-mail:** enquiries@somerleyton.co.uk

Owner: Hon Hugh Crossley   **Contact:** Edward Knowles

Splendid early Victorian mansion built in Anglo-Italian style by Sir Morton Peto, with lavish architectural features, magnificent carved stonework and fine state rooms. Paintings by Landseer, Wright of Derby and Stanfield, wood carvings by Willcox of Warwick and Grinling Gibbons. Somerleyton's 12-acre gardens are justly renowned with beautiful borders, specimen trees and the 1846 yew hedge maze which ranks amongst the finest in the country. Special features include glasshouses by Paxton, 300ft pergola, walled garden, Vulliamy tower clock, Victorian ornamentation. Film location for BBC drama *The Lost Prince* (2002).

Location: OS134 Ref. TM493 977. 5m NW of Lowestoft on B1074, 7m SW of Great Yarmouth off A143.
Open: 4 Apr - 31 Oct: Thurs, Suns, BH Mons. Jul & Aug: Tue - Thur, Suns & BH Mons. Gardens: 11am - 5.30pm. Hall: 1 - 5pm (last admission 4.30pm). Tearoom: 11am - 5pm.
Admission: Adult £6.20, Child £3.20, Conc. £5.80.

ℹNo photography in house. 🅿 ❄ 🕋Receptions/functions/conferences. 🅺 🌐 ℹBy arrangement. 🅿 🅼 🅺 🔺 ❄

The National Trust

SUTTON HOO ✤

TRANMER HOUSE, SUTTON HOO, WOODBRIDGE, SUFFOLK IP12 3DJ

www.nationaltrust.org.uk

Tel: 01394 389700 **Fax:** 01394 389702
e-mail: suttonhoo@nationaltrust.org.uk
Owner: The National Trust **Contact:** The Property Manager
The Anglo-Saxon royal burial site where the priceless Sutton Hoo treasure was discovered in a huge ship grave in 1939. The exhibition hall houses a full size reconstruction of the burial chamber from the ship grave and tells the story of the 'page one of English history'. The burial site (500m from visitor facilities) forms part of the 99ha estate given to the National Trust by the Annie Tranmer Charitable Trust in 1998. Excellent estate walks and modern bistro-style restaurant. Shop sells jewellery and ceramics based on Sutton Hoo artefacts.

Location: OS Ref. TM288 487. Off B1083 Woodbridge to Bawdsey road. Follow signs from A12. Train ¹/₂ m Melton. Bus: First 83 Ipswich - Bawdsey (passing Melton train station).
Open: Exhibition Hall, shop & restaurant: 20 Mar - 30 Sept: daily, 10am - 5pm. Oct: Wed - Sun, 10am - 5pm. 1 Nov - 31 Dec: Fri - Sun, 10am - 4pm. 1 Jan - 28 Feb 2005: Sat & Sun, 10am - 4pm.
Admission: Adult £4, Child £2. Groups: Adult £3.50, School groups £1.50. Discount entry fee for visitors arriving by cycle or on foot.
▢ T ⅙ ▣ Licensed. 🍴 Licensed. 🎨 By arrangement. P ▥
🐕 In grounds, on leads. 🎪 Programme of events, tel for details.

THE TIDE MILL

Woodbridge, Ipswich, Suffolk IP12 4SR
Tel: 01473 626618
Owner/Contact: Geoff Gostling
First recorded in 1170, now fully restored, machinery demonstrated at low tide. Ring for wheel turning times.
Location: OS Ref. TM275 487. By riverside ¹/₄ m SE of Woodbridge town centre. 1¹/₄ m off A12.
Open: Easter, then May - Sept: daily. Apr & Oct: Sats & Suns only, 11am - 5pm.
Admission: Adult £2, Child Free, Conc. £1.25.

WYKEN HALL GARDENS

STANTON, BURY ST EDMUNDS, SUFFOLK IP31 2DW

Tel: 01359 250287 **Fax:** 01359 253420
Owner: Sir Kenneth & Lady Carlisle **Contact:** Mrs Barbara Hurn
The Elizabethan manor house is surrounded by a romantic, plant-lover's garden with maze, knot and herb garden and rose garden featuring old roses. A walk through ancient woodlands leads to Wyken Vineyards, winner of EVA Wine of the Year. In the 16th century barn, the Vineyard Restaurant serves our wines along with a varied menu from fresh local produce. It is a 'Bib Gourmand' in the *Michelin Guide* and features also in *The Good Food Guide*.
Location: OS Ref. TL963 717. 9m NE of Bury St. Edmunds 1m E of A143. Follow brown tourist signs to Wyken Vineyards from Ixworth.
Open: 7 Jan - 24 Dec: daily, 10am - 6pm. Garden: 1 Apr - 1 Oct: daily except Sat, 2 - 6pm. Open for dinner from 7pm Fri & Sat.
Admission: Gardens: Adult £3, Child (under 12yrs) Free, Conc. £2.50. Groups by appointment.
▢ ⅙ Grounds. WC. 🍴 Licensed. 🐕 In grounds, on leads. ✳

eastmidlands

Rutland Water, Leicestershire. © David Osborn

299

tissingtonhall
derbyshire

> *"Tissington has been in the hands of my family for the past 500 years. If it is to remain as one of the prettiest and most attractive villages in the Peak District it must be allowed to evolve over the coming years in order to provide an income for the village and to retain its thriving community"*

Sir Richard FitzHerbert Bt

Tissington Hall and the pretty estate village that surrounds it, is to be found four miles north of Ashbourne off the A515 towards Buxton. It has been been the family home of the FitzHerberts for the past 500 years – and is today lived in by Sir Richard FitzHerbert, his wife Caroline and their two young children.

Approaching the village from the Ashbourne-Buxton road, the Hall is reached by driving through lovely large stone gates, and down a long meandering avenue of limes. Built in the early 17th century, the Hall is obviously the focal point of the village – a long, low mansion which has had many extensions over the years. The façade is plain with upright mullion windows and a projecting porch with the front door surmounted by the arms of the FitzHerberts, carved in stone. The West Front, re-faced in the 18th century, has a severe classical style with a projecting central bay and open arcading on the ground floor. Finally, in 1900, the major extension of the Library and Billiard Room wing was completed by the architect Arnold Mitchell for the 5th Baronet.

If the Hall is the focal point to life at Tissington, it is the cottages, houses, greens and pond scattered around it that create the real charm to the place. As one commentator put it *'no planner designed it; no bureaucrat decided how and where the houses were to be built. The village grew in that effortless and instinctive way that villages did before the Industrial Revolution began to change the face of England'.*

However, don't be deceived into thinking it is an easy task to maintain this idyll. On inheriting the Hall and estate from his uncle in 1989, Sir Richard spent a great deal of his early tenure carrying out essential repairs – re-roofing in 1991, re-wiring in 1992, and re-plumbing in 1998. The estate at Tissington consists of 2,400 acres comprising 13 farms, and 40 cottages. With the recent problems in the farming industry, there is a constant need to look at alternative ways of creating income. Many of the farms on the estate now provide Bed & Breakfast accommodation; one has a thriving pony-trekking operation. Within the village, Sir Richard has converted many redundant buildings into new business enterprises. Visit the Old Kitchen Garden, now a Plant Nursery; the Old Coach House is a Tearoom. The most wonderful organic meat can be bought from the White Peak Butchery housed in the Old Slaughterhouse, or visit the Craft Shop 'Acanthus' in the Old Joiner's Shop and candlemaker in the Old Forge. If you live locally you can even send your children to Tissington Pre-Prep & Kindergarten, founded by Lady FitzHerbert in 1995, and housed in the converted Old Stable Block – with an initial roll of 3 children, numbers have grown to over 90.

Since June 1998 the FitzHerberts have opened the Hall for 28 days each summer … walk through beautifully panelled and furnished rooms, and learn how to juggle the practicalities of living in such a house with a young energetic family. It sounds hard work … but fun. So why not enjoy this, and take the time also to buy something from the butcher, the baker and candlemaker!

▸ For further details about Tissington Hall see page 311.

Images courtesy of: © Heritage House Group Limited.

Gary Rogers Hamburg

Map 5

Owner: Trustees of the
Chatsworth Settlement.
Home of the Duke &
Duchess of Devonshire

▶ **CONTACT**

Mr John Oliver
Chatsworth
Bakewell
Derbyshire DE45 1PP

Tel: 01246 582204
01246 565300
Fax: 01246 583536

e-mail: visit@
chatsworth.org

▶ **LOCATION**

OS Ref. SK260 703

From London
3 hrs M1/J29,
signposted via
Chesterfield.

3m E of Bakewell,
off B6012,
10m W of Chesterfield.

Rail: Chesterfield
Station, 11m.

Bus: Chesterfield -
Baslow, 1½ m.

CHATSWORTH

BAKEWELL

www.chatsworth.org

The great Treasure House of Chatsworth was first built by Bess of Hardwick in 1552 and has been lived in by the Cavendish family, the Dukes of Devonshire, ever since. The House today owes its appearance to the 1st Duke who remodelled the building at the end of the 17th century, while the 6th Duke added a wing 130 years later. Visitors can see 26 rooms including the run of 5 virtually unaltered 17th century State Rooms and Chapel. There are painted ceilings by Verrio, Thornhill and Laguerre, furniture by William Kent and Boulle, tapestries from Mortlake and Brussels, a library of over 17,000 volumes, sculpture by Cibber and Canova, old master paintings by Rembrandt, Hals, Van Dyck, Tintoretto, Veronese, Landseer and Sargent; the collection of neo-classical sculpture, Oriental and European porcelain and the dazzling silver collection, including an early English silver chandelier. The present Duke has added to the collection.

The 2004 exhibition celebrates the centenary of the Duchess of Devonshire's sister, Nancy Mitford. Chatsworth was voted the nation's favourite stately home in 2003.

GARDEN

The 105 acre garden was created during three great eras in garden and landscape design. The 200 metre Cascade, the Willow Tree fountain and the Canal survive from the 1st Duke's formal garden. 'Capability' Brown landscaped the garden and park in the 1760s. The 6th Duke's gardener, Sir Joseph Paxton, built rockeries and designed a series of glasshouses. He also created the Emperor fountain, the tallest gravity-fed fountain in the world. More recent additions include the Rose, Cottage and Kitchen gardens, the Serpentine Hedge and the Maze.

🛍 ℹ Farmyard and Adventure Playground. Guide book translations and audio guides in French, German, Italian, Spanish and Japanese.

♿ No wheelchairs in house, but welcome in garden (3 electric, 7 standard available). WCs. Special leaflet.

🍽 New rooms available for conferences and private functions. Contact Head of Catering.

🍴 Restaurant (max 300); home-made food. Menus on request.

🚶 Private tours of house or Greenhouses and Behind the Scenes Days, by arrangement only (extra charges apply). Tape recorded tour may be hired at entrance. Groups please pre-book.

🅿 Cars 100 yds, Coaches 25 yds from house.

📷 Guided tours, packs, trails and school room. Free preliminary visit recommended.

❅

▶ **OPENING TIMES**

Summer
17 March - 19 December.
Daily: 11am - 4.30pm.
The Park is open free throughout the year.

▶ **ADMISSION**

House & Garden
Adult	£9.00
Child	£3.50
OAP/Student	£7.00
Family	£21.50

Pre-booked groups
Adult	£7.50
School (no tour)	£3.50
School (w/tour)	£4.50
OAP/Student	£6.00

Garden only
Adult	£5.50
Child	£2.50
OAP/Student	£4.00
Family	£13.50

House, Garden & Scots Suite
Adult	£10.50
Child	£4.00
OAP	£8.50
Family	£24.00

Groups
Adult	£9.00
OAP	£7.50

Farmyard & Adventure Playground
All	£4.00
Groups (5+)	£3.50
OAP/School	£3.00
Child under 3yrs	Free

Family ticket for all attractions £35.00

Rates differ during Christmas season (6 Nov - 19 Dec).

🛡 **SPECIAL EVENTS**
Tel for details.

CONFERENCE/FUNCTION

ROOM	MAX CAPACITY
Hartington Rm.	70
Coffee Rm.	24

HADDON HALL 🏛

BAKEWELL

www.haddonhall.co.uk

Map 5

Owner:
Lord Edward Manners

▶ CONTACT

Janet O'Sullivan
Estate Office
Haddon Hall
Bakewell
Derbyshire
DE45 1LA

Tel: 01629 812855
Fax: 01629 814379

e-mail: info@
haddonhall.co.uk

▶ LOCATION

OS Ref. SK234 663

From London 3 hrs
Sheffield 1/2 hr
Manchester 1 hr
Haddon is on the
E side of A6 1 1/2 m
S of Bakewell.
M1/J30.

Rail: Chesterfield
Station, 12m.

Bus: Chesterfield
Bakewell.

Haddon Hall sits on a rocky outcrop above the River Wye close to the market town of Bakewell, looking much as is would have done in Tudor times. There has been a dwelling here since the 11th century but the house we see today dates mainly from the late 14th century with major additions in the following 200 years and some alterations in the early 17th century including the creation of the Long Gallery.

William the Conqueror's illegitimate son Peverel, and his descendants, held Haddon for 100 years before it passed to the Vernon family. In the late 16th century the estate passed through marriage to the Manners family, in whose possession it has remained ever since.

When the Dukedom of Rutland was conferred on the Manners family in 1703 they moved to Belvoir Castle, and Haddon was left deserted for 200 years. This was Haddon's saving grace as the Hall thus escaped the major architectural changes of the 18th and 19th centuries ready for the great restoration at the beginning of the 20th century by the 9th Duke of Rutland. Henry VIII's elder brother Arthur, who was a frequent guest of the Vernons, would be quite familiar with the house as it stands today.

Haddon Hall is a popular location for film and television productions. Recent films include *Jane Eyre* and *Elizabeth*.

GARDENS

Magnificent terraced gardens with over 150 varieties of rose and clematis, many over 70 years old, provide colour and scent throughout the summer.

▶ OPENING TIMES

Summer
1 April - 30 September
Daily: 10.30am - 5pm
Last admission 4pm.

October: Thur - Sun
10.30am - 4.30pm
Last admission 3.30pm.

Winter
November - 31 March
Closed.

▶ ADMISSION

Summer

Adult	£7.25
Child (5 -15yrs)	£3.75
Conc	£6.25
Family (2+3)	£19.00

Groups (15+)

Adult	£6.25
Child (5 -15yrs)	£3.25
Conc	£5.25

🏠 ℹ️ Haddon Hall is ideal as a film location due to its authentic and genuine architecture requiring little alteration. Suitable locations are also available on the Estate.

♿ Unsuitable, steep approach, varying levels of house.

☕🍴 Self-service, licensed (max 75). Home-made food.

🚶 Special tours £30 extra for groups of 15, 7 days' notice.

🅿️ Ample, 450 yds from house. £1 per car.

🎭 Tours of the house bring alive Haddon Hall of old. Costume room also available, very popular!

🐕 Guide dogs only. 🎭 Tel for details.

PAVILION GARDENS

BUXTON, DERBYSHIRE

www.paviliongardens.org

Map 5

Owner: High Peak Borough Council

▶ CONTACT

Scott McCauley
Pavilion Gardens
St John's Road
Buxton
Derbyshire DE45 1PP

Tel: 01298 23114
Fax: 01298 27622

e-mail:
paviliongardens@
highpeak.gov.uk

▶ LOCATION

OS Ref. SK055 734

Situated on the A6 in the Peak District, within easy reach of Manchester, Sheffield and the East Midlands.

Rail: Buxton station
½ m.

PAVILION

With Grade II listed buildings dating from 1871 and 23 acres of beautiful Victorian landscaped gardens in the centre of Buxton on the River Wye, there are attractions to Suit all tastes and ages.

The Pavilion hosts a range of fairs and events such as Antique, Book and Toy fairs to Classic Car Auctions, Tea Dances and Farmers' Markets.

There are facilities for conferences, seminars and meetings with a capacity to cater for up to 400 people with a full meal menu.

Visitors can also use the Restaurant, Café and Coffee Lounge or browse in the Food and Gift Shop, which specialises in locally produced goods.

GARDENS

Over the last 125 years, various changes have been made to the Gardens (they hosted the only Open Tennis Championships in the UK outside Wimbledon). The Gardens, originally designed by the eminent landscape gardener Edward Milner, have recently been restored to their original Victorian splendour, following a £4.5 million Heritage Lottery grant.

The bandstand is used on most summer Sundays, with brass bands playing from 2 - 4pm, when deckchairs are available on the terrace promenade.

There is also a colourful and relaxing Conservatory, housing an extensive range of flowers and plants, and which adjoins the renowned, Frank Matcham designed, Buxton Opera House.

▶ OPENING TIMES

Every day except Christmas Day.

Opens: 10am.

▶ ADMISSION

Free entry into building.

Charges vary for different events and fairs.

ℹ️ Miniature train in gardens, crazy golf, adventure play areas.

Food & gift shops.

Wedding receptions, banquets, functions & conferences.

Partial.

Licensed.

P Charge applies

In gardens on leads. Guide dogs only in Pavilion.

 Tel for details.

BOLSOVER CASTLE ⌗

CASTLE STREET, BOLSOVER, DERBYSHIRE S44 6PR

www.english-heritage.org.uk/visits

Tel: 01246 822844

Owner: English Heritage   **Contact:** The Custodian

An enchanting and romantic spectacle, situated high on a wooded hilltop dominating the surrounding landscape. Built on the site of a Norman castle, this is largely an early 17th century mansion. Most delightful is the 'Little Castle', with intricate carvings, panelling and wall painting. See the restored interiors of the Little Castle and the Venus Fountain and statuary. There is also an impressive 17th century indoor Riding House built by the Duke of Newcastle. Enjoy the Visitor and Discovery Centre. Bolsover is now available for Civil weddings, receptions and corporate hospitality. Excitng new interpretation scheme includes Audio/Visual and scale model of Little Castle. Also contemporary Visitor Centre with information about Bolsover town's development. Picnickers are welcome.

Location: OS120, SK471 707. Signposted from M1/J29, 6m from Mansfield. In Bolsover 6m E of Chesterfield on A632.

Open: 1 Apr - 31 Oct: daily, 10am - 6pm (5pm in Oct). 1 Nov - 31 Mar: Thur - Mon, 10am - 4pm. Closed 24 - 26 Dec & 1 Jan. Times subject to change from April 2004.

Admission: Adult £6.20, Child £3.10, Conc. £4.60, Family £15.50. 15% discount for groups (11+). Prices subject to change from April 2004.

Grounds. WC. Airconditioned café. Free with admission. Tel for details.

CALKE ABBEY ❧

TICKNALL, DERBYSHIRE DE73 1LE

www.nationaltrust.org.uk

Tel: 01332 863822   **Fax:** 01332 865272   **e-mail:** calkeabbey@nationaltrust.org.uk

Owner: The National Trust   **Contact:** The Property Manager

The house that time forgot, this baroque mansion, built 1701 - 3 for Sir John Harpur is set in a landscaped park. Little restored, Calke is preserved by a programme of conservation as a graphic illustration of the English country house in decline; it contains the family's collection of natural history, a magnificent 18th century state bed and interiors that are virtually unchanged since the 1880s. Walled garden, pleasure grounds and orangery. Early 19th century Church. Historic parkland with Portland sheep and deer. Staunton Harold Church is nearby.

Location: OS128, SK356 239. 10m S of Derby, on A514 at Ticknall between Swadlincote and Melbourne.

Open: House, Garden & Church: 27 Mar - 31 Oct: Sat - Wed; House: 1 - 5.30pm (ticket office opens 11am); Garden & Church: 11am - 5.30pm. Park: most days until 9pm or dusk. Closed 14 Aug for concert. Shop & Restaurant: 27 Mar - 31 Oct: as house, 10.30am - 5.30pm (shop) & 10.30am - 5pm (restaurant). 6 - 28 Nov & Jan - Mar 2005: Sat & Sun, 11am - 4pm; also 29 Nov - 19 Dec: Sat - Wed, 11am - 4pm.

Admission: All sites: Adult £5.90, Child £2.90, Family £14.50. Garden only: Adult £3.40, Child £1.70, Family £8.50. Discount for pre-booked groups.

House. Braille guide. Wheelchairs. WCs. Licensed. By arrangement. In park, on leads only.

CARNFIELD HALL

SOUTH NORMANTON, Nr ALFRETON, DERBYSHIRE DE55 2BE

Tel: 01773 520084

Owner/Contact: J B Cartland

Unspoilt Elizabethan 'Mansion House'. Panelled rooms, two 17th century staircases, 18th century dining room, 1600 great parlour. Very atmospheric interior. Since 1502 seat of the Revell, Wilmot and now the Cartland families. 300 years of family possessions including needlework, costumes, and royal relics including Princess Charlotte's wedding stockings and a lock of Edward IV's hair. Old walled garden. Adjoining garden centre with restaurant in old stables.

Location: OS Ref. SK425 561. 1½ m W of M1/J28 on B6019. Alfreton Station 5 mins walk.

Open: By appointment. Guided tours (4+) by the owner.

Admission: £5. Evening visits £6.

No photography in Hall. Grounds. Obligatory. In grounds, on leads only.

CATTON HALL

CATTON, WALTON-ON-TRENT, SOUTH DERBYSHIRE DE12 8LN

www.catton-hall.com

Tel: 01283 716311 **Fax:** 01283 712876 **e-mail:** kneilson@catton-hall.com

Owner/Contact: Robin & Katie Neilson

Catton, built in 1745, has been in the hands of the same family since 1405 and is still lived in by the Neilsons as their private home. This gives the house, with its original collection of 17th and 18th century portraits, pictures and antique furniture, a unique, relaxed and friendly atmosphere. Catton is available for corporate entertaining throughout the year. With its spacious reception rooms and luxurious bedrooms, Catton is centrally located for business meetings/conferences, product launches, lunches and dinners, as well as for groups visiting Birmingham, the NEC, the Belfry, the Potteries and Dukeries. The acres of parkland alongside the River Trent are ideal for all types of corporate and public events, including motorised activities.

Location: OS Ref. SK206 154. 2m E of A38 at Alrewas between Lichfield & Burton-on-Trent (8m from each). Birmingham NEC 20m.

Open: By arrangement all year for corporate hospitality, shooting parties, wedding receptions, residential and non-residential tour groups. Guided tours: 5 Apr - 11 Oct: Mons only, 2pm.

Conference facilities. By arrangement. By arrangement for Groups. 3 x four posters, 5 twin, all en-suite. Tel for details.

CHATSWORTH *See page 304 for full page entry*

ELVASTON CASTLE COUNTRY PARK

Borrowash Road, Elvaston, Derbyshire DE72 3EP

Tel: 01332 571342 **Fax:** 01332 758751

Owner: Derbyshire County Council **Contact:** The Park Manager

200 acre park landscaped in 19th century by William Barron. Walled garden.

Location: OS Ref. SK407 330. 5m SE of Derby, 2m from A6 or A52.

Open: Please contact park for details.

Admission: Park and Gardens Free. Car park: Midweek 70p, weekends/BHs £1.30, Coaches £7.50.

Ground floor & grounds. WCs. By arrangement. In grounds, under close control.

© Henry Wilson

EYAM HALL

EYAM, HOPE VALLEY, DERBYSHIRE S32 5QW

www.eyamhall.com

Tel: 01433 631976 **Fax:** 01433 631603 **e-mail:** nicola@eyamhall.com

Owner: Mr R H V Wright **Contact:** Mrs N Wright

This small but charming manor house in the famous plague village of Eyam has been the home of the Wright family since 1671 and it retains the intimate atmosphere of a much-loved private home. Recent filming includes *Blue Peter*'s production about Eyam and the plague. Craft Centre in the historic farmyard with crafts people at work. Licensed for Civil wedding ceremonies with small in-house, or larger marquee receptions.

Location: OS119, SK216 765. Approx 10m from Sheffield, Chesterfield and Buxton. Eyam is off A623 between Stockport and Chesterfield. Eyam Hall is in the centre of the village, past the church.

Open: House & Garden: 30 Jun - 1 Sept : Wed, Thur, Sun & BH Mons, 11am - 4pm. Craft Centre: All year: Tue - Sun, 11am - 5pm.

Admission: Adult £4.75, Child £3.50, Conc. £4.25. Family (2+4) £15.50. Group rates available. Craft Centre: Free.

Craft Centre. Partial. Licensed. Obligatory. In grounds, on leads. Guide dogs only in house.

HADDON HALL *See page 305 for full page entry.*

HARDSTOFT HERB GARDEN

Hall View Cottage, Hardstoft, Chesterfield, Derbyshire S45 8AH

Tel: 01246 854268

Owner: Mr Stephen Raynor/L M Raynor **Contact:** Mr Stephen Raynor

Consists of four display gardens with information boards and well labelled plants.

Location: OS Ref. SK436 633. On B6039 between Holmewood & Tibshelf, 3m from J29 on M1.

Open: Gardens, Nursery & Tearoom: 15 Mar - 15 Sept: Wed - Sun, 10am - 5pm. Closed Mon & Tue except Easter and BHs when open throughout.

Admission: Adult £1.50, Child Free.

NT Photographic Library

NT Photographic Library: Gerry Sweethman

HARDWICK HALL, GARDENS, PARK & STAINSBY MILL

DOE LEA, CHESTERFIELD, DERBYSHIRE S44 5QJ

www.nationaltrust.org.uk

Tel: 01246 850430   **Fax:** 01246 854200   **Shop/Restaurant:** 01246 854088
e-mail: hardwickhall@nationaltrust.org.uk
Owner: The National Trust   **Contact:** The Property Manager
Hardwick Hall: A late 16th century 'prodigy house' designed by Robert Smythson for Bess of Hardwick. The house contains outstanding contemporary furniture, tapestries and needlework including pieces identified in an inventory of 1601; a needlework exhibition is on permanent display. Walled courtyards enclose fine gardens, orchards and a herb garden. The country park contains Whiteface Woodland sheep and Longhorn cattle.
Location: OS120, SK456 651. 7½ m NW of Mansfield, 9½ m SE of Chesterfield: approach from M1/J29 via A6175.
Open: Hall: 31 Mar - 31 Oct: Weds, Thurs, Sats, Suns, BH Mons & Good Fri: 12 noon - 4.30pm. Gardens: as Hall, Wed - Sun, 11am - 5.30pm. Parkland: daily. Shop: As Hall, 11am - 5pm. Restaurant: As Shop.

Admission: Hall & Garden: Adult £6.80, Child £3.40, Family £17.00. Garden only: Adult £3.70, Child £1.85, Family £9.25. Joint ticket for Hall (NT) and Old Hall (EH): Adult £9.20, Child £4.60, Family £23 (NT members Free). Pre-booking for groups essential, discount for groups of 15+. Timed tickets on busy days.
Hardwick Estate - Stainsby Mill is an 18th century water-powered corn mill in working order.
Location: OS120, SK455 653. From M1/J29 take A6175, signposted to Clay Cross then first left and left again to Stainsby Mill.
Open: 31 Mar - 30 Jun, 30 Aug - 31 Oc: Wed, Thur, Sat, Sun, BH Mons & Good Fri; 1 Jun - 29 Aug: Wed - Sun & BH Mons plus 26 Dec & 1 Jan 2005, 11am - 4.30pm.
Admission: Adult £2.30, Child £1.15, Family £5.75. No discounts for groups, suitable for school groups. Stainsby Mill and Hardwick Hall close 30 Jul 2004, for information send SAE to Property Manager at Hardwick Hall.

⬜ ♿ Garden, Hall: 3 display rooms only. 🍴 Licensed. 📷 🐕 In park, on leads.

Biagio Rebecca

1735-1808

A painter, who worked on painted panels and wall decoration for William Chambers and Robert Adam.

Look out for his work at Somerset House, London, Kedleston Hall, Derbyshire, and Harewood House, Yorkshire.

18th Century Stuccoist

English Heritage Photo Library

HARDWICK OLD HALL ⚏

DOE LEA, Nr CHESTERFIELD, DERBYSHIRE S44 5QJ

www.english-heritage.org.uk/visits

Tel: 01246 850431
Owner: National Trust, managed by English Heritage   **Contact:** The Custodian
This large ruined house, finished in 1591, still displays Bess of Hardwick's innovative planning and interesting decorative plasterwork. The views from the top floor over the country park and 'New' Hall are spectacular. Picknickers are welcome.
Location: OS120, SK463 638. 7½ m NW of Mansfield, 9½ m SE of Chesterfield, off A6175, from M1/J29.
Open: 1 Apr - 30 Sept: 11am - 6pm; 1 - 31 Oct: 11am - 5pm, Mon, Wed, Thur, Sat & Sun. Times subject to change from April 2004, please ring prior to visiting.
Admission: Adult £3, Child £1.50, Conc. £2.30, Family £7.50. 15% discount for groups (11+). Prices subject to change from April 2004.
ℹ️WC. ⬜ 🅿️Free with admission. 📷 🅿 🐕 On leads.

🛏️ **Accommodation Index** see front section

NT Photographic Library / Oliver Benn

KEDLESTON HALL ✤

DERBY DE22 5JH

www.nationaltrust.org.uk

Tel: 01332 842191 **Fax:** 01332 841972 **e-mail:** kedlestonhall@nationaltrust.org.uk

Owner: The National Trust **Contact:** The Property Manager

Experience the age of elegance in this neo-classical house built between 1759 and 1765 for the Curzon family and little altered since. Set in 800 acres of parkland with an 18th century pleasure ground, garden and woodland walks – a day at Kedleston is truly an experience to remember. The influence of the architect Robert Adam is everywhere, from the Park buildings to the decoration of the magnificent state rooms. Groups are welcome and an introductory talk can be arranged.

Location: OS Ref. SK312 403. 5m NW of Derby, signposted from roundabout where A38 crosses A52 Derby ring road.

Open: House: 20 Mar - 31 Oct: Sat - Wed (open Good Fri); Garden: as house: daily, 10am - 6pm. Park: 20 Mar - 31 Oct: daily; 10am - 6pm; 1 Nov - 31 Mar: daily, 10am - 4pm. Park: occasional day restrictions may apply in Dec & Jan 2005. Shop: 20 Mar - 31 Oct: Sat - Wed, 11.30am - 5.30pm; 1 Nov - 31 Mar: Sat & Sun, 12 noon - 4pm. Restaurant: 20 Mar - 31 Oct: Sat - Wed, 11am - 5pm; 1 Nov - 31 Mar: Sat & Sun, 12 noon - 4pm.

Admission: Adult £5.80, Child £2.80, Family £14.40. Garden & Park: Adult £2.60, Child £1.30, Family £6.50. Winter admission for Park only, £2.70.

⬜ ♿ Stairclimber & Batricar. 🍴 Licensed. 🐕 In park (but not Long Walk), on leads. 🔺 ♿ Tel for details.

MELBOURNE HALL & GARDENS 🏛

MELBOURNE, DERBYSHIRE DE73 1EN

Tel: 01332 862502 **Fax:** 01332 862263

Owner: Lord & Lady Ralph Kerr **Contact:** Mrs Gill Weston

This beautiful house of history, in its picturesque poolside setting, was once the home of Victorian Prime Minister William Lamb. The fine gardens, in the French formal style, contain Robert Bakewell's intricate wrought iron arbour and a fascinating yew tunnel. Upstairs rooms available to view by appointment.

Location: OS Ref. SK389 249. 8m S of Derby. From London, exit M1/J24.

Open: Hall: Aug only (not first 3 Mons) 2 - 5pm. Last admission 4.15pm. Gardens: 1 Apr - 30 Sept: Weds, Sats, Suns, BH Mons, 1.30 - 5.30pm.

Admission: Hall: Adult £3, Child £1.50, OAP £2.50. Gardens: Adult £3, Child/OAP £2. Hall & Gardens: Adult £5, Child £3, OAP £4.

ℹ Crafts. No photography in house. ⬜ ♿ Partial. 🐕 ✍ Obligatory.

🅿 Limited. No coach parking. 🦮 Guide dogs only.

PAVILION GARDENS *See page 306 for full page entry*

PEVERIL CASTLE ⌗

Market Place, Castleton, Hope Valley S33 8WQ

Tel: 01433 620613 **www.**english-heritage.org.uk/visits

Owner: English Heritage **Contact:** The Custodian

There are breathtaking views of the Peak District from this castle, perched high above the pretty village of Castleton. The great square tower of Henry II stands almost to its original height. Formerly known as Peak Castle. Walkway opens up new areas and views from the first floor of the Keep. Peveril Castle, mentioned in the Domesday Book of 1086, is one of the earliest Norman castles to be built in England. Picnickers are welcome.

Location: OS110, SK150 827. S side of Castleton, 15m W of Sheffield on A6187.

Open: 1 Apr - 31 Oct: daily, 10am - 6pm (5pm in Oct). 1 Nov - 31 Mar, Wed - Sun, 10am - 4pm. Closed 24 - 26 Dec & 1 Jan. Times subject to change from April 2004.

Admission: Adult £2.50, Child £1.30, Conc. £1.90. 15% discount for groups (11+). Prices subject to change from April 2004.

ℹ WC. ⬜ 🅿 🐕 🦮 ❄ ♿ Tel for details.

Patrick Lane

RENISHAW HALL
SHEFFIELD, DERBYSHIRE S31 3WB
www.sitwell.co.uk

Tel: 01246 432310   **Fax:** 01246 430760   **e-mail:** info@renishaw-hall.co.uk

Owner: Sir Reresby Sitwell Bt DL   **Contact:** The Administrator

Home of Sir Reresby and Lady Sitwell. Eight acres of Italian style formal gardens stand in 300 acres of mature parkland, encompassing statues, shaped yew hedges, herbaceous borders, a water garden and lakes. The Sitwell museum, art galleries (display of Fiori de Henriques sculptures and paintings by John Piper) are located in Georgian stables alongside craft workshops and Gallery café, furnished with contemporary art. Beautiful camellias and carpets of daffodils in April.

Location: OS Ref. SK435 786. On A6135 3m from M1/J30, equidistant from Sheffield and Chesterfield.

Open: 1 Apr - 26 Sept: Thurs - Sun & BH Mons, 10.30am - 4.30pm.

Admission: Garden only: Adult £3.60, Conc. £2.80. Museum & Galleries: Adult £3.60, Conc. £2.80. Garden, Museum & Galleries: Adult £6.50, Conc. £4.50. House: group tours (20+) by prior booking.

Conferences. By arrangement.
In grounds, on leads. Tel for details.

SUDBURY HALL
Ashbourne, Derbyshire DE6 5HT

Tel: 01283 585337   **Fax:** 01283 585139   **e-mail:** sudburyhall@nationaltrust.org.uk

Owner: The National Trust   **Contact:** The Property Manager

Late 17th century house with sumptuous interiors. The decoration includes wood carving by Grinling Gibbons, and painted murals and ceilings by Louis Laguerre.

Location: OS Ref. SK160 323. 6m E of Uttoxeter.

Open: 20 Mar - 31 Oct: Wed - Sun & BH Mons & Good Fri. Hall: 1 - 5pm. Grounds: 11am - 6pm. Tearoom: 12 noon - 5pm. Shop: 12.30 - 5pm.

Admission: Adult £4.80, Child £2, Family (2+3) £11.50. Groups (15+): Adult £4, Child £1.50.
Limited, braille guide. WC. Licensed. Car park only.

SUTTON SCARSDALE HALL
Chesterfield, Derbyshire

Tel: 01604 735400 (Regional Office)   www.english-heritage.org.uk/visits

Owner: English Heritage   **Contact:** The East Midlands Regional Office

The dramatic hilltop shell of a great early 18th century baroque mansion.

Location: OS Ref. SK441 690. Between Chesterfield & Bolsover, 1½ m S of Arkwright Town.

Open: Daily in summer: 10am - 6pm (5pm rest of year). Subject to change from April 2004.

Admission: Free.

WINGFIELD MANOR
Garner Lane, South Wingfield, Derbyshire DE5 7NH

Tel: 01773 832060

Owner: Mr S Critchlow (managed by English Heritage)   **Contact:** The Custodian

Huge, ruined, country mansion built in the mid-15th century. Mary Queen of Scots was imprisoned here in 1569, 1584 and 1585.

Location: OS Ref. SK374 548. S side of B5035, ½ m S of South Wingfield village. Access by 600yd drive (no vehicles). From M1 J28, W on A38, A615 (Matlock road) at Alfreton and turn onto B5035 after 1½ m.

Open: 1 Apr - 30 Sept: Wed - Sun, 10am - 6pm. 1 - 31 Oct: Wed - Sun, 10am - 5pm. 1 Nov - 31 Mar: 10am - 4pm. Closed 1 - 2pm in winter. Closed 24 - 26 Dec & 1 Jan. Times subject to change from April 2004. The Manor incorporates a working farm. Visitors are requested to respect the privacy of the owners, to keep to visitor routes and refrain from visiting outside official opening times.

Admission: Adult £3.20, Child £1.60, Conc. £2.40. Subject to change from April 2004.

Derbyshire Countryside Ltd

TISSINGTON HALL
ASHBOURNE, DERBYSHIRE DE6 1RA
www.tissington-hall.com

Tel: 01335 352200   **Fax:** 01335 352201   **e-mail:** tisshall@dircon.co.uk

Owner/Contact: Sir Richard FitzHerbert Bt

Home of the FitzHerbert family for over 500 years. The Hall stands in a superbly maintained estate village, and contains wonderful panelling and fine old masters. A 10 acre garden and arboretum. Schools very welcome. Award-winning Old Coach House Tearoom, open daily 11am - 5pm for lunch and tea.

Location: OS Ref. SK175 524. 4m N of Ashbourne off A515 towards Buxton.

Open: 12 - 16 Apr & 31 May - 4 Jun, daily. 20 Jul - 27 Aug, Tue - Fri, first tour 1.30pm - last tour 4pm. Groups and societies welcome by appointment throughout the year. Corporate days and events also available, contact: The Estate Office on 01335 352200.

Well-Dressings: 20 - 26 May. Six wells dressed in the village.

Admission: Hall & Gardens: Adult £5.50, Child (10-16yrs) £2.50, Conc. £4.50, Gardens only: Adult £2, Child £1.

No photography in house. Partial. WCs at tearooms.
Tearoom adjacent to Hall. Obligatory. Limited. Guide dogs only.
Tel for details.

BELVOIR CASTLE

GRANTHAM

www.belvoircastle.com

Belvoir Castle, home of the Duke and Duchess of Rutland, commands a magnificent view over the Vale of Belvoir. The name Belvoir, meaning beautiful view, dates back to Norman times, when Robert de Todeni, Standard Bearer to William the Conqueror, built the first castle on this superb site. Destruction caused by two Civil Wars and by a catastrophic fire in 1816 have breached the continuity of Belvoir's history. The present building owes much to the inspiration and taste of Elizabeth, 5th Duchess of Rutland and was built after the fire.

Inside the Castle are notable art treasures including works by Poussin, Holbein, Rubens, and Reynolds, Gobelin and Mortlake tapestries,

Chinese silks, furniture, fine porcelain and sculpture.

The Queen's Royal Lancers' Museum at Belvoir has a fascinating exhibition of the history of the Regiment, as well as a fine collection of weapons, uniforms and medals.

GARDENS

The Statue Gardens are built into the hillside below the castle and take their name from the collection of 17th century sculptures on view. The garden is planted so that there is nearly always something in flower. The Duchess' private Spring Gardens are available for viewing throughout the year by pre-booked groups of 15 persons or more. Details from the Castle Office.

Map 5

Owner:
Their Graces The Duke & Duchess of Rutland

▶ **CONTACT**

Mary McKinlay
Castle Opening Office
Belvoir Castle
Grantham
Leicestershire NG32 1PE

Tel: 01476 871002
Fax: 01476 871018
e-mail: info@ belvoircastle.com

▶ **LOCATION**

OS Ref. SK820 337

A1 from London 110m
York 100m
Grantham 7m.
A607 Grantham-Melton Mowbray.

Air: East Midlands International.

Rail: Grantham Stn 7m

Bus: Melton Mowbray - Vale of Belvoir via Castle Car Park.

Taxi: Grantham Taxis 01476 563944 / 563988.

CONFERENCE/FUNCTION

ROOM	SIZE	MAX CAPACITY
State Dining Room	52' x 31'	130
Regents Gallery	131' x 16'	220
Old Kitchen	45' x 22'	100

▶ **OPENING TIMES**

Summer
April - September:
Tues - Thurs, Sat & Sun,
(open BH Mon & Good Fri).

11am - 5pm.
Last entry 4pm.

Winter
March & October:
Sun only,
11am - 5pm.
Last entry 4pm.

Groups welcome by appointment.

Suitable for exhibitions, product launches, conferences, filming, photography welcomed (permit £2).

Banquets, private room available.

Ground floor and restaurant accessible. Please telephone for advice. WC.

Licensed restaurant. Groups catered for.

Tue - Thur, twice daily. Tour time: 1¼ hrs.

Ample. Coaches can take passengers to entrance by arrangement but should report to the main car park and ticket office on arrival.

Guided tours. Teacher's pack. Education room. Picnic area and adventure playground.

Guide dogs only.

Tel for details.

▶ **ADMISSION**

Adult	£8.00
Child (5-16yrs)	£5.00
OAP/Student	£7.00
Family (2+2)	£21.00
Groups (20-200)	
Adult	£7.00
Child (5-16yrs)	£4.00
OAP/Student	£6.00
School/Youth	£3.00

Spring Garden Tours (15+)

Adult	£6.00
OAP/Student	£5.00

Map 5

Owner:
Mr Frederick de Lisle

▶ CONTACT

Mrs F de Lisle
Quenby Hall
Hungarton
Nr Leicester LE7 9JF

Tel/Fax: 0116 2595224

e-mail: enquiries@
quenbyhall.co.uk

▶ LOCATION
OS Ref. SK702 065

7m E of Leicester,
20 mins from M1/J21A,
40 mins A1.

Air: East Midlands
International 25 mins.

Rail: Market
Harborough.

QUENBY HALL

HUNGARTON

www.quenbyhall.co.uk

Quenby Hall lies seven miles east of Leicester and is a perfect and unspoiled example of a Jacobean country house. It was built by George Ashby in 1627. Amidst ancient cedars and beeches, it commands magnificent views of the countryside, in the secluded setting of 1400 acres of gardens, parkland and farm.

Stilton cheese was invented by the housekeeper at Quenby Hall. It was sold by her daughter who lived at the popular staging inn at Stilton, on the Great North Road: hence its name.

It is the private home of the de Lisle family and has been extensively restored, making it exceptionally warm and comfortable whilst remaining true to its Jacobean style, with beautiful panelling, plaster and stonework and other architectural features. It is not open to the public and is available for exclusive hire as a film location and for conferences, weddings and special events. The Old Dairy, with its old beams, stone floor and more 'country' ambience, is also available for hire.

Full exclusive use of the rooms can be made by groups numbering up to 150. Dinners can be held for up to 80 in the house with dancing in the old Dairy, or up to 300 in a marquee on the back lawn. Four beautiful ensuite bedrooms, two with four posters, available by special arrangement.

▶ OPENING TIMES

Not open to the public. Available for exclusive hire as a film location and for conferences, weddings and special events.

▶ ADMISSION

Please contact property for details.

Banquets, private room available.

By arrangement.

Ample.

By arrangement.

Tel for details.

Map 5

STANFORD HALL

NR RUGBY

www.stanfordhall.co.uk

Stanford has been the home of the Cave family, ancestors of the present owner, since 1430. In the 1690s, Sir Roger Cave commissioned the Smiths of Warwick to pull down the old Manor House and build the present Hall, which is an excellent example of their work and of the William and Mary period.

As well as over 5000 books, the handsome Library contains many interesting manuscripts, the oldest dating from 1150. The splendid pink and gold Ballroom has a fine coved ceiling with four *trompe l'oeil* shell corners. Throughout the house are portraits of the family and examples of

furniture and objects which they collected over the centuries. There is also a collection of Royal Stuart portraits, previously belonging to the Cardinal Duke of York, the last of the male Royal Stuarts. An unusual collection of family costumes is displayed in the Old Dining Room, which also houses some early Tudor portraits and a fine Empire chandelier.

The Hall and Stables are set in an attractive Park on the banks of Shakespeare's Avon. There is a walled Rose Garden behind the Stables. An early ha-ha separates the North Lawn from the mile-long North Avenue.

Owner:
Nicholas Fothergill Esq

▶ CONTACT

Robert Thomas or
Sarah Maughan
Stanford Hall
Lutterworth
Leicestershire
LE17 6DH

Tel: 01788 860250
Fax: 01788 860870

e-mail: enquiries@
stanfordhall.co.uk

▶ LOCATION

OS Ref. SP587 793

M1/J18 6m,
M1/J19 (from/to
the N only) 2m,
M6 exit/access at
A14/M1(N)J 2m,
A14 2m.
Follow Historic
House signs.

Rail: Rugby Stn 7¹/₂ m.

Air: Birmingham
Airport 27m.

Taxi: Fone-A-Car.
01788 543333.

▶ OPENING TIMES

Summer
11 April - 26 September:
Sun & BH Mons,
1.30 - 5.30pm,
last admission 5pm.

NB. Grounds open
12 noon on BH Suns &
Mons and earlier on event
days.

House open any day or
evening for pre-booked
groups.

Winter
27 September - 26 March
2005: Closed to public.
Available during October
for corporate events.

▶ ADMISSION

House & Grounds
Adult	£5.00
Child (5-15yrs)	£2.00

Groups (20+)
Adult	£4.75
Child (5-15yrs)	£1.80

Grounds only
Adult	£3.00
Child (5-15yrs)	£1.00

Motorcycle Museum
Adult	£1.00
Child (5-15yrs)	£0.35

CONFERENCE/FUNCTION

ROOM	SIZE	MAX CAPACITY
Ballroom	39' x 26'	100
Old Dining Rm	30' x 20'	70
Crocodile Room	39' x 20'	60

Craft centre (most Suns). No photography in house. Corporate days, clay pigeon shoots, filming, photography, small conferences and fashion shows. Parkland, helicopter landing area, lecture room, Blüthner piano.

Lunches, dinners & wedding receptions (outside caterers).

Visitors may alight at the entrance. WC.

Teas, lunch & supper. Groups must book (70 max.)

Tour time: ³/₄ hr in groups of approx 25.

1,000 cars and 6 - 8 coaches. Free meals for coach drivers, coach parking on gravel in front of house.

£1.80 per child. Guide provided by prior arrangement, nature trail with guide book & map, motorcycle museum.

In Park, on leads.

Tel for details.

ASHBY-DE-LA-ZOUCH CASTLE ⌗
South Street, Ashby-de-la-Zouch, Leicestershire LE65 1BR
Tel: 01530 413343 **www.english-heritage.org.uk/visits**
Owner: English Heritage   **Contact:** The Custodian
The impressive ruins of this late medieval castle are dominated by a magnificent tower, over 80 feet high, which was split in two during the Civil War. Panoramic views. Explore the tunnel linking the kitchens to the Hastings Tower. Picnickers welcome.
Location: OS128, SK363 167. In Ashby de la Zouch, 12m S of Derby on A511. SE of town centre.
Open: 1 Apr - 31 Oct: daily, 10am - 6pm (5pm in Oct). 1 Nov - 31 Mar: Wed - Sun, 10am - 4pm. Closed 24 - 26 Dec & 1 Jan. Times subject to change April 2004.
Admission: Adult £3.20, Child £1.60, Conc. £2.40, Family £8. 15% discount for groups (11+). Prices subject to change April 2004.
ⓘWC. ▣ ♿Grounds. ⌖ Free with admission. 🅿 ▣ 🖼 On leads. ❄ ♒ Tel for details.

BELVOIR CASTLE 🏛
See page 312 for full page entry.

BRADGATE PARK & SWITHLAND WOOD COUNTRY PARK
Bradgate Park, Newtown Linford, Leics
Tel: 0116 2362713
Owner: Bradgate Park Trust   **Contact:** M H Harrison
Includes the ruins of the brick medieval home of the Grey family and childhood home of Lady Jane Grey. Also has a medieval deer park.
Location: OS Ref. SK534 102. 7m NW of Leicester, via Anstey & Newtown Linford. Country Park gates in Newtown Linford. 1¼ m walk to the ruins.
Open: All year during daylight hours.
Admission: No charge. Car parking charges.

DONINGTON-LE-HEATH MANOR HOUSE
Manor Road, Donington-le-Heath, Leicestershire LE67 2FW
Tel: 01530 831259 / 0116 2645810
Owner/Contact: Leicestershire County Council
Medieval manor c1280 with 16th-17th century alterations.
Location: OS Ref. SK421 126. ½ m SSW of Coalville. 4½ m W of M1/J22, by A511.
Open: Apr - Sept: daily, 11.30am - 5pm. Oct - Mar: 11.30am - 3pm. Dec - Feb: Sat & Sun, 11.30am - 3pm.
Admission: Free.

BOSWORTH BATTLEFIELD
VISITOR CENTRE & COUNTRY PARK, SUTTON CHENEY, MARKET BOSWORTH CV13 0AD

www.leics.gov.uk

Tel: 01455 290429 **Fax:** 01455 292841 **e-mail:** bosworth@leics.gov.uk
Owner: Leicestershire County Council   **Contact:** Ranger
Historic site of the Battle of Bosworth Field 1485, where King Richard III lost his crown and his life to the future Henry VII. Visitor Centre, film theatre, battle trail, picnic areas and car parks. Summer event programme: Medieval Spectacular 21/22 Aug 2004 (including battle re-enactment). Living history displays.
Location: OS Ref. SK404 001. Bounded by A5, A444, A447, B585. Clearly signposted from all these roads.
Open: 1 Apr - 31 Oct: daily, 11am - 5pm. Nov & Dec: Suns, 11am - 4pm. Mar: Sat & Sun, 11am - 5pm.
Admission: Adult £3, Child/Conc. £2, Family (2+3) £8.50. Groups (20+): Adult £2.30, Child/Conc. £1.70. (Opening times and charges subject to review.)
▣ ⌖ ♿Partial. ▣Licensed. 🅕By arrangement. 🅿 ▣ ❄ ♒ Tel for details.

EXTON PARK
OAKHAM, RUTLAND LE15 8AN

www.extonpark.co.uk

Tel: 01572 812208/812209 **Fax:** 01572 812473
e-mail: campden@extonpark.co.uk
Owner: Viscount Campden   **Contact:** Viscountess Campden
Early Victorian stone house, with large private Roman Catholic Chapel built by Buckler, set in a beautiful quintessential English garden and park with magnificent trees, lakes and garden ponds, together with two exquisite 18th century follies and ruins of Tudor mansion. Fascinating collection of 17th & 18th century portraits. Suitable for films, wedding receptions, product launches.
Location: Turn at Barnsdale cross roads off A606 Oakham to Stamford road, close to A1.
Open: Guided tours strictly by appointment only throughout the year.
Admission: Telephone for details.
⌖ 🅕By arrangement. 🅿Ample. ❖ ❄

James Wyatt
1746-1813

Although initially an architect who employed the Greek Revival style, in later career he became a well known Gothic Revivalist. Look for a style that uses gothic motifs applied in a decorative way – they do not form part of the structure of the building.

Visit Belvoir Castle, Leicestershire and Heaton Park, Lancashire.

Gothic Revival Architect

KIRBY MUXLOE CASTLE

Kirby Muxloe, Leicestershire LE9 9MD

Tel: 01162 386886 **www**.english-heritage.org.uk/visits

Owner: English Heritage **Contact:** East Midlands Regional Office (01604 735400)

Picturesque, moated, brick built castle begun in 1480 by William Lord Hastings. It was left unfinished after Hastings was executed in 1483. Picnickers welcome.

Location: OS140, SK524 046. 4m W of Leicester off B5380.

Open: 1 Apr - 31 Oct: weekends & BHs only, 12 noon - 5pm. Times subject to change April 2004.

Admission: Adult £2.20, Child £1.10, Conc. £1.70. Prices subject to change April 2004.

LYDDINGTON BEDE HOUSE

Blue Coat Lane, Lyddington, Uppingham, Rutland LE15 9LZ

Tel: 01572 822438 **www**.english-heritage.org.uk/visits

Owner: English Heritage **Contact:** The Custodian

Located in this picturesque 'Cotswold' village of honey coloured stone cottages and public houses lies the splendid former 'palace' of the powerful medieval Bishops of Lincoln. In 1600 the building was converted into an almshouse. Picnickers welcome.

Location: OS141, SP875 970. In Lyddington, 6m N of Corby, 1m E of A6003.

Open: 1 Apr - 31 Oct: daily, 10am - 6pm (5pm in Oct). Times subject to change April 2004.

Admission: Adult £3.20, Child £1.60, Conc. £2.40, Family £8. 15% group discount (11+). Prices subject to change April 2004.

Ground floor only. Free with admission. Tel for details.

OAKHAM CASTLE

Castle Lane (off Market Place), Oakham, Rutland LE15 6DF

Tel: 01572 758440 **www**.rutnet.co.uk/rcc/rutlandmuseums

Owner: Rutland County Council **Contact:** Rutland County Museum

Exceptionally fine Norman Great Hall of a late 12th century fortified manor house, with contemporary musician sculptures. Bailey earthworks and remains of earlier motte. The hall contains over 200 unique horseshoes forfeited by royalty and peers of the realm to the Lord of the Manor from Edward IV onwards.

Location: OS Ref. SK862 088. Near town centre, E of the church. Off Market Place, Oakham.

Open: All year: Mon - Sat, 10.30am - 1pm & 1.30 - 5pm; Sun, 2 - 4pm. Closed Good Fri & Christmas.

Admission: Free.

Great Hall. For disabled, on request.

QUENBY HALL

See page 313 for full page entry.

STANFORD HALL

See page 314 for full page entry.

STAUNTON HAROLD CHURCH

Staunton Harold Church, Ashby-de-la-Zouch, Leicestershire

Tel: 01332 863822 **Fax:** 01332 865272

One of the very few churches to be built during the Commonwealth, erected by Sir Robert Shirley, an ardent Royalist. The interior retains its original 17th century cushions and hangings and includes fine panelling and painted ceilings.

Location: OS Ref. SK379 208. 5m NE of Ashby-de-la-Zouch, W of B587.

Open: 1 Apr - 26 Sept: Wed - Sun & Good Fri, 1.30 - 4.30pm or sunset if earlier. Oct: Sats & Suns only, 1.30 - 4.30pm.

Admission: £1 donation.

Partial. At hall.

WARTNABY GARDENS

Melton Mowbray, Leicestershire LE14 3HY

Tel: 01664 822549 **Fax:** 01664 822231 **www**.wartnabygardenlabels.co.uk

Owner: Lord and Lady King

This garden has delightful little gardens within it, including a white garden, a sunken garden and a purple border of shrubs and roses, and there are good herbaceous borders, climbers and old-fashioned roses. A large pool has an adjacent bog garden with primulas, ferns, astilbes and several varieties of willow. There is an arboretum with a good collection of trees and shrub roses, and alongside the drive is a beech hedge in a Grecian pattern. Greenhouses, a fruit and vegetable garden with rose arches and cordon fruit.

Location: OS Ref. SK709 228. 4m NW of Melton Mowbray. From A606 turn W in Ab Kettleby for Wartnaby.

Open: Apr - Jul: Tue, 9.30am - 12.30pm. 25 Apr (Plants for sale) & 20 Jun (Plant Fair): 11am - 4pm. Groups by appointment at other times.

Admission: Adult £2.50, Child Free.

25 Apr & 20 June (Plant Fair) By arrangement. Limited for coaches. In grounds on leads. Tel for details.

Stanford Hall, Leicestershire from the book *Historic Family Homes and Gardens from the Air*, see page 54.

Map 6

Owner:
Burghley House
Preservation Trust Ltd

▶ CONTACT
The House Manager
Burghley House
Stamford
Lincolnshire PE9 3JY

Tel: 01780 752451
Fax: 01780 480125

e-mail: burghley@
burghley.co.uk

▶ LOCATION
OS Ref. TF048 062

Burghley House
is 1m SE of Stamford.
From London, A1 2hrs.

Visitors entrance
is on B1443.

Rail: London -
Peterborough 1hr
(GNER).
Stamford Station
1¹/₂ m, regular service
to Peterborough.

Taxi: Direct Line:
01780 481481.

CONFERENCE/FUNCTION

ROOM	SIZE	MAX CAPACITY
Great Hall	70' x 30'	150
Orangery	100' x 20'	120

BURGHLEY HOUSE 🏛
STAMFORD
www.burghley.co.uk

Burghley House, home of the Cecil family for over 400 years, was built as a country seat during the latter part of the 16th century by Sir William Cecil, later Lord Burghley, principal adviser and Lord Treasurer to Queen Elizabeth.

The House was completed in 1587 and there have been few alterations to the architecture since that date thus making Burghley one of the finest examples of late Elizabethan design in England. The interior was remodelled in the late 17th century by John, 5th Earl of Exeter who was a collector of fine art on a huge scale, establishing the immense collection of art treasures at Burghley. Burghley is truly a 'Treasure House', containing one of the largest private collections of Italian art, unique examples of Chinese and Japanese porcelain and superb items of 18th century furniture. The remodelling work of the 17th century means that examples of the work of

the principal artists and craftsmen of the period are to be found at Burghley: Antonio Verrio, Grinling Gibbons and Louis Laguerre all made major contributions to the beautiful interiors.

PARK AND GARDENS
The house is set in a 300-acre deer park landscaped by 'Capability' Brown. A lake was created by him and delightful avenues of mature trees feature largely in his design. The park is home to a large herd of Fallow deer, established in the 16th century. The Sculpture Garden contains many specimen trees and shrubs and is a display area for a number of dramatic art works by contemporary sculptors. The sculptures are varied in style, but their placement is designed to provoke thought and accentuate the beauty of the surroundings. The private gardens around the house are open in April for the display of spring bulbs. Please telephone for details.

▶ OPENING TIMES
Summer
27 March - 31 October
(closed 4 September)
Daily: 11am - 5pm
(last admission 4.30pm).

Specialist, VIP and Twilight Tours available. Please telephone for details. Access to the Private Apartments is available by appointment.

NB. The house is viewed by guided tour except on Sundays and BHs when there are guides in each room.

**Gift Shop &
Orangery Restaurant**
Daily, 11am - 5pm.

The South Garden
27 March - 30 April
Daily, 11am - 4pm.

The Sculpture Garden
Open all year. Admission charges apply on weekends in June - August and on event days.
Adults £3.00, Children 50p.

Park
All year. Admission is free except on event days.

▶ ADMISSION
Adult £7.80
Child (5 - 15yrs) £3.50
OAP £6.90
Family £19.50
Groups (20+)
Adult £6.60
School groups
(up to 14 yrs)........ £3.40

🛍 ℹ️ Suitable for a variety of events, large park, golf course, helicopter landing area, cricket pitch. No photography in house.

♿ Visitors may alight at entrance. WC. Chair lift to Orangery Restaurant, house tour has two staircases one with chairlift.

🍽 Restaurant/tearoom. Groups can book in advance.

👤 Obligatory, except Sundays.
Tour time: 1¹/₂ hrs at ¹/₂ hr intervals. Max. 25.

Ⓟ Ample. Free refreshments for coach drivers.

🏫 Welcome. Guide provided.

🐕 No dogs in house. In park on leads. 🛡 Tel for details.

Map 6

GRIMSTHORPE CASTLE, PARK & GARDENS

STAMFORD

www.grimsthorpe.co.uk

Owner:
Grimsthorpe and
Drummond Castle
Trust Ltd

▶ **CONTACT**

Ray Biggs
Grimsthorpe Estate
Office
Grimsthorpe
Bourne, Lincolnshire
PE10 0LY

Tel: 01778 591205
Fax: 01778 591259

e-mail: ray@
grimsthorpe.co.uk

▶ **LOCATION**

OS Ref. TF040 230

TF040 230. 4m NW of
Bourne on A151, 8m E
of Colsterworth
roundabout off A1.

Home of the Willoughby de Eresby family since 1516. Examples of 13th century architecture and building styles from the Tudor period. The dramatic 18th century North Front is Sir John Vanbrugh's last major work. State Rooms and picture galleries with magnificent contents including tapestries, furniture and paintings. Unusual collection of thrones, fabrics and objects from the old House of Lords, associated with the family's hereditary Office of Lord Great Chamberlain.

The Grounds and Gardens

3,000 acre landscaped park with lakes, ancient woods, woodland walk with all-weather footpath, adventure playground, red deer herd. Family cycle trail. Landrover tours with park ranger.

Unusual ornamental vegetable garden and orchard, created in the 1960s by the Countess of Ancaster and Peter Coates. Intricate parterres lined with box hedges. Herbaceous border with yew topiary framing views across to the lake. Woodland garden.

Groups can explore the park from the comfort of their coach by booking a one-hour, escorted Park Ranger tour, with opportunities to discover more about the site of the Cistercian Abbey, the ancient deer parks and extensive series of early tree-lined avenues.

Summer

1 Apr - 30 Sept: Suns,
Thurs & BH Mons.
Aug: Sun - Thur. Park &
Gardens: 11am - 6pm.
Castle: 1 - 4.30pm (last
admission).
Tearoom: 11am - 5.15pm
(last orders).
Groups: Apr - Sept:
anytime by arrangement.
Also evening candlelight
supper tours.

▶ **ADMISSION**

Park & Garden
   Adult £3.00
   Child £2.00
   Conc. £2.50
   Family (2+2) £8.00

Castle, Park & Garden
   Adult £7.00
   Child £3.50
   Conc. £6.00
   Family (2+2) £17.50

Special charges may be
made for special events.
Group rates on
application.

ℹ️ No photography in house.

🛍️ Conferences (up to 50), inc catering.

♿ Partial. WC.

🍽️ Licensed.

🚶 Obligatory except Suns.

🅿️ Ample.

🐕 In grounds, on leads.

🛡️ Tel for details.

AUBOURN HALL
Lincoln LN5 9DZ
Tel: 01522 788270 **Fax:** 01522 788199
Owner/Contact: Lady Nevile
Late 16th century house with important staircase and panelled rooms. Garden.
Location: OS Ref. SK928 628. 6m SW of Lincoln. 2m SE of A46.
Open: House not open on a regular basis in 2003. Garden: Occasional Suns for charity or by arrangement.
Admission: Please contact property for details.

AYSCOUGHFEE HALL MUSEUM & GARDENS
Churchgate, Spalding, Lincolnshire PE11 2RA
www.sholland.gov.uk
Tel: 01775 725468 **Fax:** 01775 762715 **e-mail:** museum@sholland.gov.uk
Owner: South Holland District Council **Contact:** Mr A Sandall
A late-Medieval wool merchant's house surrounded by five acres of walled gardens.
Location: OS Ref. TF240 230. E bank of the River Welland, 5 mins walk from Spalding town centre.
Open: Closed for renovation in 2004.

BURGHLEY HOUSE 🏛
See page 317 for full page entry

Francesco Zuccarelli
1702 –1788
An Italian painter, whose landscape paintings featuring small figures set in a classical background, was one of Polite Society's most sought after painters of the day. A founder member of the Royal Academy.

18th Century Painter

East Midlands - England

The NT Photographic Library / Nick Meers
The NT Photographic Library

BELTON HOUSE ❦
GRANTHAM, LINCOLNSHIRE NG32 2LS
www.nationaltrust.org.uk

Tel: 01476 566116 **Fax:** 01476 579071 **e-mail:** belton@nationaltrust.org.uk
Owner: The National Trust **Contact:** The Property Manager
Belton, considered by many to be the perfect English Country House, with stunning interiors, fine silver and furniture collections and the remnants of a collection of Old Masters. There are also huge garden scenes by Melchior d'Hondecoeter acquired by the last Earl. The 17th century saloon in the centre of the house is panelled and decorated with intricate limewood carvings of the Grinling Gibbons school. The virtually unaltered north-facing chapel has a baroque plaster ceiling by Edward Gouge. Built in 1685 - 88, Belton offers you a great day out whether you are looking for peace and tranquillity or lots to do. With magnificent formal gardens, Orangery, landscaped park with lakeside walk, woodland adventure playground and Bellmount Tower. Fine church with family monuments. Winners of "Excellence in Tourism" and Sandford Heritage Education awards 2002.
Location: OS Ref. SK929 395. 3m NE of Grantham on A607. Signed off the A1.
Open: House: 31 Mar - 31 Oct: Wed - Sun (open BH Mons & Good Fri), 12.30 - 5pm. Garden & Park: as house, 11am - 5.30pm (Aug: 10.30am - 5.30pm). Garden only: 6 Nov - 19 Dec: Sat & Sun, 12 noon - 4pm. Park only: on foot from Lion Lodge gates. Shop & Restaurant: 31 Mar - 31 Oct: 11am - 5.15pm. 6 Nov - 19 Dec: Sat & Sun, 12 noon - 4pm.
Admission: Adult £6.50, Child £3, Family £15. Discount for groups.
⬜ ♿ Partial. Please telephone for arrangements.
🍴 Licensed. P ■ ⬛

DODDINGTON HALL 🏛

LINCOLN LN6 4RU

www.doddingtonhall.free-online.co.uk

Tel: 01522 694308 **Fax:** 01522 685259

e-mail: estateoffice@doddingtonhall.com

Owner: A G Jarvis   **Contact:** The House Manager

Magnificent Smythson mansion which stands today as it was completed in 1600 with its contemporary walled gardens and gatehouse. The Hall is still very much the home of the Jarvis family and has an elegant Georgian interior with a fine collection of porcelain, furniture, paintings and textiles representing 400 years of unbroken family occupation. The beautiful gardens contain a superb layout of box-edged parterres, sumptuous borders that provide colour in all seasons, and a wild garden with a marvellous succession of spring bulbs and flowering shrubs set among mature trees. Sandford Award winning schools project, and a nature trail into the nearby countryside. HERO project member.

Location: OS Ref. SK900 710. 5m W of Lincoln on the B1190, signposted off the A46 Lincoln bypass.

Open: Gardens only: 15 Feb - 26 Sept: Suns, 2 - 6pm. House & Gardens: 2 May - 26 Sept: Weds & Suns, 2 - 6pm.

Admission: House & Garden: Adult £5.20, Child £2.60, Family (2 adults & 2 - 4 children of 2 - 14yrs/1 OAP) £14.50. Gardens only: Adult £3.60, Child £1.80. Groups (20 - 100) on open days: Adult £4.70. Special groups (20+) at other times by appointment only £6.70.

ℹ️ No photography in Hall. No stilettos. ⬜ 🔼 Occasional. 🎧 ♿ Gardens. WC. 🍽 Licensed. 🚶 By arrangement. 🏠 🅿 🚌 Guide dogs only. 🏠 In Little House, not Hall. 📞 Tel for details. €

GAINSBOROUGH OLD HALL ⌗

Parnell Street, Gainsborough, Lincolnshire DN21 2NB

Tel: 01427 612669   www.english-heritage.org.uk/visits

Owner: English Heritage   **Contact:** The Custodian

A large medieval house with a magnificent Great Hall and suites of rooms. A collection of historic furniture and a re-created medieval kitchen are on display.

Location: OS121, SK815 895. In centre of Gainsborough, opposite library.

Open: Easter Sun - 31 Oct: Mon - Sat, 10am - 5pm. Suns, 2 - 5.30pm. 1 Nov - Easter Sat: Mon - Sat, 10am - 5pm (closed Good Fri, Suns Nov - Mar, 24 - 26 Dec & 1 Jan). Prices subject to change April 2004.

Admission: Adult £2.50, Child £1, Conc. £1.50. Prices subject to change April 2004.

ℹ️ WC. ♿ 🍽 🚌

GRIMSTHORPE CASTLE, 🏛   *See page 318 for full page entry*
PARK & GARDENS

See page 318 for full page entry

GUNBY HALL 🦌

Gunby, Spilsby, Lincolnshire PE23 5SS

Tel: 01909 486411 **Fax:** 01909 486377 **www.**nationaltrust.org.uk

Owner: The National Trust   **Contact:** Regional Office

A red brick house with stone dressings, built in 1700 and extended in 1870s. Within the house, there is good early 18th century wainscoting and a fine oak staircase, also English furniture and portraits by Reynolds. Also of interest is the contemporary stable block, a walled kitchen and flower garden, sweeping lawns and borders and an exhibition of Field Marshal Sir Archibald Montgomery-Massingberd's memorabilia. Gunby was reputedly Tennyson's 'haunt of ancient peace'.

Location: OS122, TF466 672. 2¹/₂ m NW of Burgh Le Marsh, 7m W of Skegness. On S side of A158 (access off roundabout).

Open: Ground floor of house & garden: 31 Mar - 30 Sept: Weds, 2 - 6pm. Last admission 5.30pm. Closed BHs. Garden also open Thurs, 2 - 6pm. House & garden also open Tues, Thurs & Fris by written appointment to J D Wrisdale at above address.

Admission: House & Garden: Adult £4, Child £2, Family £10. Garden only: Adult £2.80, Child £1.40, Family £7. No reduction for groups. Access roads unsuitable for coaches which must park in layby at gates ¹/₂ m from Hall.

♿ Grounds. 🚌 In grounds, on leads.

HARLAXTON MANOR

Harlaxton, Grantham, Lincolnshire NG32 1AG

Tel: 01476 403000 **Fax:** 01476 403030

Owner: University of Evansville   **Contact:** Mrs A Clark

Neo-Elizabethan house. Grandiose and imposing exterior by Anthony Salvin. Internally an architectural tour de force with various styles and an unparalleled Cedar Staircase.

Location: OS Ref. SK895 323. 3m W of Grantham (2m from A1) A607. SE of the village.

Open: House: Sun 6 Jun & Sun 22 Aug: 11am - 5pm. House open at other times for group tours by appointment only.

Admission: House open days: Adult £5, Child (under 12yrs) £2, OAP £4.

HECKINGTON WINDMILL

Heckington, Sleaford, Lincolnshire

Tel: 01529 461919   **Contact:** Derek James

Britain's last surviving eight sail windmill.

Location: OS Ref. TF145 436. W side of B1394, S side of Heckington village.

Open: Contact property for details.

Admission: Ground floor & Shop: Free. Mill: Adult £1.50, Child 75p. (2003 prices.)

LEADENHAM HOUSE

Leadenham House, Lincolnshire LN5 0PU

Tel: 01400 273256   **Fax:** 01400 272237

Owner: Mr P Reeve   **Contact:** Mr and Mrs P Reeve

Late eighteenth century house in park setting.

Location: OS Ref. SK949 518. Entrance on A17 Leadenham bypass (between Newark and Sleaford).

Open: 19 - 23 Apr; 10 - 14 May; 1 - 4, 7 - 12 & 16 - 18 June; 5 - 7 July & Spring & Aug BHs: 2 - 5pm.

Admission: £3.50. Groups by prior arrangement only.

ℹ️ No photography. ♿ 🚌

LINCOLN CASTLE

Castle Hill, Lincoln LN1 3AA

Tel: 01522 511068   **e-mail:** lincoln_castle@lincolnshire.gov.uk

Contact: The Manager

Built by William the Conqueror in 1068. Informative exhibition of the 1215 Magna Carta.

Location: OS Ref. SK975 718. Opposite west front of Lincoln Cathedral.

Open: BST: Sats, 9.30am - 5.30pm, Suns, 11am - 5.30pm. GMT: Mon - Sat: 9.30am - 4pm, Suns, 11am - 4pm. Closed Christmas Day, Boxing Day & New Year's Day. Opening times are subject to change.

Admission: Adult £3.50, Child £2, Family (2+3) £9. Prices are subject to change.

LINCOLN CATHEDRAL

Lincoln LN2 1PZ

Tel: 01522 544544   **e-mail:** visitors@lincolncathedral.com

www.lincolncathedral.com   **Contact:** Communications Office

Lincoln Cathedral is one of the finest medieval buildings in Europe, of outstanding historical interest and architectural merit. Dominating the skyline for many miles, visitors are urged not to miss St Hugh's shrine, the tomb of Katherine Swynford and to seek out the notorious Lincoln Imp!

Location: OS Ref. SK978 718. At the centre of Uphill, Lincoln.

Open: All year: Summer, 7.15am - 8pm. Winter, 7.15am - 6pm. Sun closing 6pm in Summer & 5pm in Winter. Roof tours available. Pre-booked groups welcome.

Admission: £4, Child up to 14yrs Free, Conc. £3. Optional guided tours & photography Free. No charge on Sun or for services.

⬜ 🍽 🎧 ♿ 🚶 🅿 🚌 ✳ 📞 Tel for details.

LINCOLN MEDIEVAL BISHOPS' PALACE ⌗

Minster Yard, Lincoln LN2 1PU

Tel: 01522 527468   www.english-heritage.org.uk/visits

Owner: English Heritage   **Contact:** The Custodian

Sitting alongside the South door and 'Bishops Eye' window of the Cathedral is the entrance to the Precincts & remains of the Medieval Bishops' Palace. Seat of the most powerful Bishops in England when the Magna Carta was returned to Lincoln in 1215. See a virtual tour of the Palace and explore the grounds and see the award winning Contemporary Garden and Vineyard (most northerly exposed vineyard in Europe).

Location: OS121 Ref. SK981 717. S side of Lincoln Cathedral, in Lincoln.

Open: 1 Apr - 31 Oct: daily, 10am - 6pm (5pm in Oct). 1 Nov - 31 Mar: weekends only, 10am - 4pm. Closed 24 - 26 Dec & 1 Jan. Open daily for Lincoln Christmas Market. Times subject to change April 2004.

Admission: Adult £3.20, Child £1.60, Conc. £2.40, Family £8. 15% discount for groups (11+). Prices subject to change April 2004.

⬜ 🔼 🅿 🚌 ✳ 📞 Tel for details.

NTPL / Nick Meers

MARSTON HALL
Marston, Grantham NG32 2HQ

Tel/Fax: 01400 250225 **e-mail:** thorold@fsworld.co.uk

Owner/Contact: J R Thorold

The ancient home of the Thorold family. The building contains Norman, Plantaganet, Tudor and Georgian elements through to the modern day.

Location: OS Ref. SK893 437. 5m N of Grantham and about 1m E of A1.

Open: 28/29 Feb; 1, 13 - 15 Mar; 8 - 13 Apr; 1 - 3, 29 - 31 May; 30 Aug; 18 - 20 Sep; 2 - 4, 16 - 18 Oct: 1 - 6pm.

Admission: Adult £3.50, Child £1.50. Groups must book.

ℹ️No photography.

SIBSEY TRADER WINDMILL ♯
Sibsey, Boston, Lincolnshire

Tel: 01205 750036 **www**.english-heritage.org.uk/visits

Owner: English Heritage   **Contact:** The East Midlands Regional Office

An impressive old mill built in 1877, with its machinery and six sails still intact. Flour milled on the spot can be bought here.

Location: OS Ref. TF345 511. ^{1}/2 m W of village of Sibsey, off A16, 5m N of Boston.

Open: Mill can be seen in action during the year, please telephone for details. Opening times subject to change Apr 2004, please ring prior to visiting.

Admission: Adult £2, Child £1, Conc. £1.50. Prices subject to change April 2004.

ℹ️WC. ♿ 🖼 🅿 ✖

TATTERSHALL CASTLE ✄
TATTERSHALL, LINCOLN, LINCOLNSHIRE LN4 4LR

www.nationaltrust.org.uk

Tel: 01526 342543 **e-mail:** tattershallcastle@nationaltrust.org.uk

Owner: The National Trust   **Contact:** The Property Manager

A vast fortified tower built c1440 for Ralph Cromwell, Lord Treasurer of England. The Castle is an important example of an early brick building, with a tower containing state apartments, rescued from dereliction and restored by Lord Curzon 1911-14. Four great chambers, with ancillary rooms, contain late gothic fireplaces and brick vaulting. There are tapestries and information displays in turret rooms.

Location: OS122 Ref. TF209 575. On S side of A153, 15m NE of Sleaford, 10m SW of Horncastle.

Open: 6 - 28 Mar: Sat & Sun, 12 noon - 4pm. 3 Apr - 29 Sept: Sat - Wed, 11am - 5.30pm; 2 - 31 Oct: Sat - Wed, 11am - 4pm. 6 Nov - 12 Dec: Sat & Sun, 12 noon - 4pm.

Admission: Adult £3.50, Child £1.80, Family £8.80. Group discounts.

♿Ground floor. WC. 🅿Free. ✖Car park only. ▲

NTPL / Andrew Butler

WOOLSTHORPE MANOR ✄
23 NEWTON WAY, WOOLSTHORPE-BY-COLSTERWORTH, GRANTHAM NG33 5NR

www.nationaltrust.org.uk

Tel/Fax: 01476 860338 **e-mail:** woolsthorpemanor@nationaltrust.org.uk

Owner: The National Trust   **Contact:** The Property Manager

This small 17th century farmhouse was the birthplace and family home of Sir Isaac Newton. Some of his major work was formulated here, during the Plague years (1665 - 67); an early edition of the Principia is on display. The orchard has a descendant of the famous apple tree. Science Discovery Centre and exhibition of Sir Isaac Newton's work.

Location: OS130 Ref. SK924 244. 7m S of Grantham, 1/2 m NW of Colsterworth, 1m W of A1.

Open: House & Science Discovery Centre: 6 - 28 Mar: Sat & Sun, 1 - 5pm; 1 Apr - 30 Sept: Wed - Sun (open BH Mons & Good Fri), 1 - 5pm (Jul & Aug: 1 - 6pm). 2 - 31 Oct: Sat & Sun, 1 - 5pm.

Admission: Adult £4, Child £2, Family £10, no reduction for groups which must book in advance.

♿Ground floor. 🅿Limited. ✖Car park only.

Sir Christopher Wren
1632-1723

Architects

Born in Wiltshire, Sir Christopher Wren is today as much a phenomenon as he was in his own lifetime. **Visit London, and you will see St Paul's Cathedral still dominating the City of London skyline. Walk down a street within the City and marvel at one of the 51 churches he designed and built – St James's, Piccadilly and St Clement Danes being the only two outside the City boundaries. Visit the Royal Palaces of Kensington, Hampton Court and the master's hand is at work. All this, even before you start talking about his rebuilding of London after the Great Fire in 1666! Look for buildings based on classical themes that, although inspired by the French and Italian architecture, are always designed to suit the classical proportions of their site.**

The Stable Block

ALTHORP

NORTHAMPTON

www.althorp.com

The history of Althorp is the history of a family. The Spencers have lived and died here for nearly five centuries and twenty generations.

Since the death of Diana, Princess of Wales, Althorp has become known across the world, but before that tragic event, connoisseurs had heard of this most classic of English stately homes on account of the magnificence of its contents and the beauty of its setting.

Next to the mansion at Althorp lies the honey-coloured stable block, a truly breathtaking building which at one time accommodated up to 100 horses and 40 grooms. The stables are now the setting for the Exhibition celebrating the life of Diana, Princess of Wales and honouring her memory after her death. The freshness and modernity of the facilities are a unique tribute to a woman who captivated the world in her all-too-brief existence.

All visitors are invited to view the House, Exhibition and Grounds as well as the Island in the Round Oval where Diana, Princess of Wales is laid to rest.

Map 5

Owner:
The Earl Spencer

▶ **CONTACT**

Visitor Manager
Althorp
Northampton NN7 4HQ

Tel: 01604 770107
Fax: 01604 770042

Book online
www.althorp.com

e-mail:
mail@althorp.com

▶ **LOCATION**
OS Ref. SP682 652

From the M1/J16, 7m
J18, 10m.
Situated on A428
Northampton - Rugby.
London on average 85
mins away.

Rail: 5m from
Northampton station.
14m from Rugby
station.

The Picture Gallery

▶ **OPENING TIMES**

Summer

1 July - 30 September
(closed 31 August)
Daily, 10am - 5pm.

Last admission 4pm.

**Pre-booking
recommended.**

Winter
Closed.

▶ **ADMISSION**

House & Garden

Adult	£11.50
Child* (5-17yrs)	£5.50
OAP	£9.50
Family (2+3)	£28.50

£1 discount on all tickets
for advanced internet
bookings.

Groups (by arrangement
only, tel 01604 772110):

Adult	£10.00
Child* (5-17yrs)	£5.00
OAP	£10.00

* under 5yrs Free.

Carers accompanying
visitors with disabilities are
admitted free.

There is a supplement to
view the upstairs rooms
of the House of £2.50pp.

Numbers are limited each
day. Advance booking is
recommended.

Information leaflet issued to all ticket holders who book in advance. No indoor photography with still or video cameras.

Café.

Limited for coaches.

Visitor Centre & ground floor of house accessible. WCs.

Guide dogs only.

Map 6

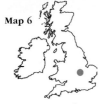

BOUGHTON HOUSE 🏛

KETTERING

www.boughtonhouse.org.uk

Boughton House is the Northamptonshire home of the Duke of Buccleuch and Queensberry KT, and his Montagu ancestors since 1528. A 500 year old Tudor monastic building gradually enlarged around seven courtyards until the French style addition of 1695, which has lead to Boughton House being described as 'England's Versailles'.

The house contains an outstanding collection of 17th and 18th century French and English furniture, tapestries, 16th century carpets, porcelain, painted ceilings and notable works by El Greco, Murillo, Caracci and 40 Van Dyck sketches. There is an incomparable Armoury and Ceremonial Coach.

Beautiful parkland with historic avenues, lakes, picnic area, gift shop, adventure woodland play area, plant centre and tearoom. Boughton House is administered by The Living Landscape Trust, which was created by the present Duke of Buccleuch to show the relationship between the historic Boughton House and its surrounding, traditional, working estate.

For information on the group visits programme, educational services and our new Insight Programme, please contact The Living Landscape Trust. Our newly developed Internet website gives information on Boughton House and The Living Landscape Trust, including a 'virtual' tour, together with full details of our schools' educational facilities (Sandford Award winner 1988, 1993, 1998 and 2003).

In 2003, the Boughton State Bed returned on long term loan from the Victoria & Albert Museum, following over 6000 hours of restoration. It is now on show, as originally intended, in the State Apartments designed for the visit of William III in 1695.

Owner:
His Grace The Duke of Buccleuch & Queensberry KT

▶ **CONTACT**
Charles Lister
The Living Landscape Trust
Boughton House
Kettering
Northamptonshire
NN14 1BJ

Tel: 01536 515731
Fax: 01536 417255

e-mail:
llt@boughtonhouse.org.uk

▶ **LOCATION**
OS Ref. SP900 815

3m N of Kettering on A43 - junction from A14.

Signposted through Geddington.

CONFERENCE/FUNCTION

ROOM	MAX CAPACITY
Lecture	100
Seminar Rm	25
Conference facilities available in stable block adjacent to House	

🏛 ✳ ℹ Parkland available for film location and other events. Stable block contains 100 seats and lecture theatre. No inside photography. No unaccompanied children. Browse our website for a 'virtual' tour of the house

♿ Access and facilities, no charge for wheelchair visitors. WCs.

☕ Tearoom seats 80, groups must book. Licensed.

🚶 By arrangement.

🅿

🏫 Heritage Education Trust Sandford Award winner 1988, 1993, 1998 & 2003. School groups free, teachers' pack.

🐕 No dogs in house and garden, welcome in Park on leads.

✳ By arrangement.

▶ **OPENING TIMES**

Summer

House
1 August - 1 September
Daily, 2 - 4.30pm.

Grounds
1 May - 1 September
Daily: (except Fris, May - July)1 - 5pm.

Opening of the Woodland Adventure Play Area is subject to weather conditions for reasons of health and safety. Children must be supervised at all times by parents.

Winter

Daily by appointment throughout the year for educational groups - contact for details.

▶ **ADMISSION**

Summer
House & Grounds
Adult £6.00
Child/Conc. £5.00

Grounds
Adult £1.50
Child/Conc. £1.00

Wheelchair visitors free. HHA Friends are admitted Free in August.

Winter
Group rates available – contact for further details.

Map 6

Owner:
E Brudenell Esq

▶ **CONTACT**

The House Keeper
Deene Park
Corby
Northamptonshire
NN17 3EW

Tel: 01780 450278
or 01780 450223

Fax: 01780 450282

e-mail: admin@
deenepark.com

▶ **LOCATION**
OS Ref. SP950 929

6m NE of
Corby off A43.
From London via
M1/J15 then A43.
or via A1, A14,
A43 - 2 hrs.

From Birmingham
via M6, A14, A43, 90
mins.

Rail: Kettering
Station
20 mins.

CONFERENCE/FUNCTION

ROOM	MAX CAPACITY
Great Hall	150
Tapestry Rm	75
East Room	18

DEENE PARK 🏛

CORBY

www.deenepark.com

A most interesting house, occupied and developed by the Brudenell family since 1514, from a mediaeval manor around a courtyard into a Tudor and Georgian mansion. Visitors see many rooms of different periods, providing an impressive yet intimate ambience of the family home of many generations. The most flamboyant member of the family to date was the 7th Earl of Cardigan, who led the charge of the Light Brigade at Balaklava and of whom there are many historic relics and pictures on view.

Mr Edmund Brudenell, the current owner, has taken considerable care in restoring the house after the Second World War. The gardens have also been improved during the last thirty years or so, with long, mixed borders of shrubs, old-fashioned roses and flowers, together with a parterre designed by David Hicks and long walks under fine old trees by the water. The car park beside the main lake is a good place for visitors to picnic.

🏛ℹ️ Suitable for indoor and outdoor events, filming, specialist lectures on house, its contents, gardens and history. No photography in house.

🍽 Including buffets, lunches and dinners.

♿ Partial. Visitors may alight at the entrance, access to ground floor and garden. WC.

☕ Special rates for groups, bookings can be made in advance, menus on request.

🍴 By arrangement.

🚶 Tours inclusive of admittance, tour time 90 mins. Owner will meet groups if requested.

🅿 Unlimited for cars, space for 3 coaches 10 yards from house.

🐕 In car park only.

🛏 Residential conference facilities by arrangement.

❄

 Tel for details.

▶ **OPENING TIMES**
Summer

Open Suns & Mons of
Easter - August BH
weekends.
Also, June - August
Suns, 2 - 5pm

Open at all other times
by arrangement, including
pre-booked parties.

Winter

Gardens only
Suns 8 & 15 Feb:
11am - 4pm for
snowdrops.
Refreshments available
in the Old Kitchen.

Otherwise House and
Gardens closed to casual
visitors. Open at all other
times by arrangement for
groups.

▶ **ADMISSION**
Public Open Days

House & Gardens
Adult £6.00
Child (10-14yrs)........ £2.50
Conc. £5.50
Gardens only
Adult £3.50
Child (10-14yrs)........ £1.50

Groups (20+)
by arrangement:
Weekdays £5.00
(Min £100)
Weekends & BHs .. £5.50
(Min £110)

* Child up to 10yrs free with
an accompanying adult.

Winter
Groups visits only by prior
arrangement.

Map 5

ROCKINGHAM CASTLE

LEICESTERSHIRE

www.rockinghamcastle.com

Rockingham Castle stands on the edge of an escarpment with dramatic views over five counties and the Welland Valley below. Built by William the Conqueror, the Castle was a royal residence for 450 years. In the 16th century Henry VIII granted it to Edward Watson, and for 450 years it has remained a family home. The predominantly Tudor building, within Norman walls, has architecture, furniture and works of art from practically every century including, unusually, a remarkable collection of 20th century pictures. Charles Dickens was a regular visitor to the Castle and based *Chesney Wolds* in *Bleak House* on Rockingham.

Surrounding the Castle are some 12 acres of gardens largely following the foot print of the medieval castle. The vast 400 year old "Elephant Hedge" dissects the formal 17th century terraced gardens. The circular yew hedge stands on the site of the motte and bailey and provides shelter for the rose garden. Below the Castle is the beautiful 19th century "Wild Garden" replanted with advice from Kew Gardens during the early 1960s. Included in the gardens are many specimen trees and shrubs including the remarkable Handkerchief Tree.

Owner:
James Saunders Watson

▶ CONTACT

Andrew Norman
Operations Manager
Rockingham Castle
Market Harborough
Leicestershire
LE16 8TH

Tel: 01536 770240

e-mail: a.norman@
rockinghamcastle.com

▶ LOCATION
OS Ref. SP867 913.

1m N of Corby on A6003.
9m E of Market
Harborough. 14m SW of
Stamford on A427.

▶ OPENING TIMES

Apr, May & Sept: Suns &
BH Mons, 1 - 5pm.

Jun - Aug: Tue, Sun &
BH Mon, 1 - 5pm.

Grounds: 12 noon - 5pm.

Last entrance: 4.30pm.

▶ ADMISSION
House & Grounds

Adult	£7.00
Child (5 - 16yrs)	£4.00
OAP	£6.00

Groups (20+)	
Adult	£6.00
Child	£4.00

i	No photography in Castle.	In grounds, on leads.
Licensed.	Partial. WC.	
By arrangement.	P	Tel for details.

ALTHORP *See page 322 for full page entry.*

AYNHOE PARK

AYNHO, BANBURY, OXFORDSHIRE OX17 3BQ

www.cha.org.uk

Tel: 01869 810636 **Fax:** 01869 811054 **e-mail:** aynhoepark@cha.org.uk

Owner: Country Houses Association **Contact:** The Administrator

Former home of the Cartwright family until 1960. The house was burned by the royalist troops in the Civil War, then rebuilt in rectangular form. Various alterations were made by Thomas Archer and later additions by Sir John Soane. Aynhoe Park has been converted into apartments for active retired people.

Location: OS Ref. SP513 331. M40/J10 then 3m W of B4100. Stations: Banbury 6m, Bicester 8m.

Open: May - Sept: Wed & Thur, 2 - 4.30pm.

Admission: Adult £3, Child/Conc. £1.50. Groups by arrangement.

2 twins with bathroom, CHA members & Wolsey Lodge guests.

BOUGHTON HOUSE *See page 323 for full page entry.*

CANONS ASHBY

CANONS ASHBY, DAVENTRY, NORTHAMPTONSHIRE NN11 3SD

www.nationaltrust.org.uk

Tel: 01327 861900 **Fax:** 01327 861909 **e-mail:** canonsashby@nationaltrust.org.uk

Owner: The National Trust **Contact:** The Property Manager

Home of the Dryden family since the 16th century, this Elizabethan manor house was built c1550, added to in the 1590s, and altered in the 1630s and c1710; largely unaltered since. Within the house, Elizabethan wall paintings and outstanding Jacobean plasterwork are of particular interest. A formal garden includes terraces, walls and gate piers of 1710. There is also a medieval priory church and a 70 acre park.

Location: OS Ref. SP577 506. Access from M40/J11, or M1/J16. Signposted from A5 2m S of Weedon crossroads. Then 7m to SW.

Open: 22 Mar - 3 Nov: Sat - Wed. House, Park & Church: 1 - 5.30pm (Oct: 12 noon - 4.30pm). Gardens: 11am - 5.30pm (Oct: 11am - 4.30pm). Shop & Tearoom: 12 noon - 5pm (Oct: 11am - 4.30pm). Gardens, Shop, Tearoom, Park & Church: 6 Nov - 19 Dec: Sat & Sun, 11am - 3pm.

Admission: Adult £5.60, Child £2.80, Family £14. Garden only: £2. Discount for booked groups, contact Property Manager.

Some steps. WC. In Home Paddock, on leads.

COTON MANOR GARDEN

GUILSBOROUGH, NORTHAMPTONSHIRE NN6 8RQ

www.cotonmanor.co.uk

Tel: 01604 740219 **Fax:** 01604 740838

e-mail: pasleytyler@cotonmanor.fsnet.co.uk

Owner: Ian & Susie Pasley-Tyler **Contact:** Sarah Ball

Traditional English garden laid out on different levels surrounding a 17th century stone manor house. Many herbaceous borders, with extensive range of plants, old yew and holly hedges, rose garden, water garden and fine lawns set in 10 acres. Also wild flower meadow and bluebell wood.

Location: OS Ref. SP675 716. 9m NW of Northampton, between A5199 (formerly A50) and A428.

Open: 1 Apr - 30 Sept: Tue - Sat & BH weekends; also Suns Apr - May: 12 noon - 5.30pm.

Admission: Adult £4, Child £2, Conc. £3.50. Groups: £3.50.

Grounds. WC. By arrangement.

COTTESBROOKE HALL & GDNS 🏛

COTTESBROOKE, NORTHAMPTONSHIRE NN6 8PF

www.cottesbrookehall.co.uk

Tel: 01604 505808 **Fax:** 01604 505619 **e-mail:** hall@cottesbrooke.co.uk

Owner: Mr & Mrs A R Macdonald-Buchanan   **Contact:** The Administrator
Architecturally magnificent house built in the reign of Queen Anne. The identity of the original architect remains a mystery but the house has stayed essentially the same since that time. Renowned picture collection, particularly of sporting and equestrian subjects. Fine English and Continental furniture and porcelain. House reputed to be the pattern for Jane Austen's *Mansfield Park*. Winner of the *HHA/Christie's Garden of the Year* award (2000). Celebrated gardens of great variety including herbaceous borders, water and wild gardens, fine old cedars and specimen trees. Magnolia, cherry and acer collections and several fine vistas across the Park. Notable planting of containers. A number of distinguished landscape designers have been involved including Rober Weir Schultz, the late Sir Geoffrey Jellicoe and the late Dame Sylvia Crowe.

Location: OS Ref. SP711 739. 10m N of Northampton near Creaton on A5199 (formerly A50). Signed from J1 on A14.

Open: House & Gardens: 3 May - end Sept. May & Jun: Wed & Thur, 2 - 5pm. Jul, Aug & Sept: Thur, 2 - 5pm. Open BH Mons (May - Sept), 2 - 5pm.

Admission: House & Gardens: Adult £6. Gardens only: Adult £4, Child half price. RHS members Free access to gardens. Private groups welcome by prior arrangement.

ℹ️No photography in house. Filming & outside events. ✷Unusual plants.
🍴Banqueting facilities, corporate hospitality & catering for functions.
♿Gardens. WC. ☐ ☐Obligatory. P ✗

Deene Park, Northamptonshire from the book *Historic Family Homes and Gardens from the Air*, see page 54.

DEENE PARK 🏛   *See page 324 for full page entry.*

EDGCOTE HOUSE

Edgcote, Banbury, Oxfordshire OX17 1AG
Owner/Contact: Christopher Courage
Early Georgian house with good rococo plasterwork.
Location: OS Ref. SP505 480. 6m NE of Banbury off A361.
Open: By written appointment only.

ELEANOR CROSS ⚜

Geddington, Kettering, Northamptonshire
Tel: 01604 735400 (Regional Office) www.english-heritage.org.uk/visits
Owner: English Heritage   **Contact:** The East Midlands Regional Office
One of a series of famous crosses, of elegant sculpted design, erected by Edward I to mark the resting places of the body of his wife, Eleanor, when brought for burial from Harby in Nottinghamshire to Westminster Abbey in 1290. Picnickers are welcome.
Location: OS Ref. SP896 830. In Geddington, off A43 between Kettering and Corby.
Open: Any reasonable time. Opening times subject to change April 2004, please ring prior to visiting.
☐ ☐ Free with admission. ✗ ✷

HADDONSTONE SHOW GARDEN

The Forge House, East Haddon, Northampton NN6 8DB
Tel: 01604 770711 **Fax:** 01604 770027
e-mail: info@haddonstone.co.uk www.haddonstone.co.uk
Owner: Haddonstone Ltd   **Contact:** Marketing Director
See Haddonstone's classic garden ornaments in the beautiful setting of the walled manor gardens – including urns, troughs, fountains, statuary, bird baths, sundials and balustrading. The garden is on different levels with shrub roses, conifers, clematis and climbers. The Jubilee garden features a pavilion, temple and Gothic grotto. An Orangery was opened in 2002.
Location: OS Ref. SP667 682. 7m NW of Northampton off A428. Signposted.
Open: Mon - Fri, 9am - 5.30pm. Closed weekends, BHs & Christmas period.
Admission: Free. Groups by appointment only. Not suitable for coach groups.
☐ ♿ ☐By arrangement. PLimited. ✗Guide dogs only. ✷

HOLDENBY HOUSE GARDENS & FALCONRY CENTRE 🏛

HOLDENBY, NORTHAMPTONSHIRE NN6 8DJ

www.holdenby.com

Tel: 01604 770074 **Fax:** 01604 770962 **e-mail:** enquiries@holdenby.com

Owner: James Lowther Esq **Contact:** The Administrator

Just across the fields from Althorp stands Holdenby, a house whose regal history is now complemented by an equally regal collection of birds of prey. Built by Sir Christopher Hatton as the largest house in England in order to entertain Elizabeth I, Holdenby subsequently became the palace and then the prison of Charles I. Now over the beautiful gardens, restored with the help of Rosemary Verey and Rupert Golby, soar magnificent birds of prey. The Falconry Centre, recently upgraded, boasts over 50 birds, embracing many species of falcons, hawks, buzzards, kite, owls and eagles, including the only naturally reared male Black Eagle on display anywhere.

Visitors can watch our trained falconers fly these beautiful creatures or even fly some themselves by appointment.

Location: OS Ref. SP693 681. M1/J15a. 7m NW of Northampton off A428 and A5199.

Open: Garden & Falconry Centre: Apr - end Sept: Suns, 1 - 5pm; BH Suns & Mons, 11am - 6pm. Jul & Aug: daily except Sat, 1 - 5pm. House: 12 Apr, 3 & 31 May & 30 Aug; for groups by appt. BHs special events: see special events index and/or website.

Admission: Garden & Falconry: Adult £4.50 Child (3-15yrs) £3, OAP £4, Family £12. BH & special events: Adult £5/£6, Child £4, OAP £4/£5, Family £16/£18.

ⓘ Children's play area. ◻ ⛔ ⊤ ♿ Partial. WC.
🍽 Home-made teas. Groups must book. 🐕 By arrangement. 🅿
🏛 Sandford Award-winner. 🐾 In grounds, on leads. ▲ ▨

KELMARSH HALL 🏛

KELMARSH, NORTHAMPTONSHIRE NN6 9LT

www.kelmarsh.com

Tel: 01604 686543 **Fax:** 01604 686437 **e-mail:** administrator@kelmarsh.com

Owner: The Kelmarsh Trust **Contact:** Administrator

Built in 1732 to a James Gibbs design, Kelmarsh Hall is surrounded by its working estate, grazed parkland and beautiful gardens. In 1928 Ronald and Nancy Tree rented the Palladian house from the Lancaster family and decorated the rooms in the manner that has become known as the English country house look. In the 1950s she returned to Kelmarsh as Nancy Lancaster and continued to develop her style both in the house and in the gardens. Additional schemes and designs by Geoffrey Jellicoe and Norah Lindsay have created a remarkable garden. Gifted to the Kelmarsh Trust by the Lancaster family the house, gardens and estate are now available for study, group and general visits.

Location: OS Ref. SP736 795. 500 metres N of A14 - A508 junction. Rail & Bus: Market Harborough.

Open: House & Garden: 11 Apr - 5 Sept: Suns & BH Mons & Thurs in Jul & Aug, 2.30 - 5pm. Garden: 11 Apr - 30 Sept: Tue - Thur, 2.30 - 5pm.

Admission: House & Garden: Adult £4.50, Child (5-16yrs) £2.50, Conc. £4. Access to house by guided tour only. Garden only: Adult £3.50, Child (5-16yrs) £2, Child under 5yrs Free, Conc £3.

ⓘ No photography in house. ⛔ ⊤ Conferences & functions ♿ Partial. WC.
🍽 Licensed. 🐕 Obligatory. 🅿 🏛 🐾 In grounds, on leads. ▲
▨ Art workshops throughout year.

English Heritage Photo Library

KIRBY HALL

DEENE, CORBY, NORTHAMPTONSHIRE NN17 5EN

www.english-heritage.org.uk/visits

Tel: 01536 203230

Owner: English Heritage   **Contact:** The Custodian

The peaceful ruins of a large, stone-built Elizabethan mansion, begun in 1570 with 17th century alterations. The richly carved decoration is exceptional, full of amazing Renaissance detail. There are fine gardens with topiary, home to peacocks. Jane Austen's *Mansfield Park* was filmed at Kirby Hall in 1998. Newly restored Elizabethan decorative schemes in the Great Hall, Billiard Room, Library & Best Bedchamber. Located in beautiful countryside close to both Rockingham Castle & Deene Park. Picnickers are welcome.

Location: OS Ref. SP926 927. On unclassified road off A43, Corby to Stamford road, 4m NE of Corby. 2m W of Deene Park.

Open: 1 Apr - 31 Oct: daily 10am - 6pm (5pm in Oct). 1 Nov - 31 Mar: Sats & Suns, 10am - 4pm. Closed 24 - 26 Dec & 1 Jan. Opening times subject to change April 2004, please ring prior to visiting. Times subject to change April 2004.

Admission: Adult £3.50, Child £1.80, Conc. £2.60, Family £8.80. 15% discount for groups (11+). Prices subject to change April 2004.

ⓘ WC. ▣ ⓹ Grounds, gardens & ground floor only. ⓝ Free with admission. Ⓟ ▣ ⓕ Restricted areas. ✳ ⓥ Tel for details.

✳ Open All Year Index see front section

LAMPORT HALL & GARDENS 🏛

LAMPORT, NORTHAMPTONSHIRE NN6 9HD

www.lamporthall.co.uk

Tel: 01604 686272 **Fax:** 01604 686224 **e-mail:** admin@lamporthall.co.uk

Owner: Lamport Hall Trust   **Contact:** Executive Director

Home of the Isham family from 1560 to 1976. The 17th and 18th century façade is by John Webb and the Smiths of Warwick. The Hall contains an outstanding collection of furniture, china and paintings including portraits by Van Dyck, Kneller and Lely. The Library contains books dating back to the 16th century and the Cabinet Room houses rare Venetian cabinets. The first floor includes a replicated 17th century bedchamber and a photographic record of Sir Gyles Isham, a Hollywood actor, who initiated the restoration. The gardens owe much to the 10th Baronet who, in the mid 19th century, created the famous rockery.

Location: OS Ref. SP759 745. Entrance on A508. 8m N of Northampton, 3m S of A14 J2. Bus: Limited Stagecoach from Northampton and Leicester.

Open: Easter - 3 Oct: Suns & BH Mons, 2.15 - 5pm. 16/17 Oct: 2.15 - 5pm. Group visits: Aug: Mon - Sat, 2.30pm for one tour. Group visits on other days by arrangement.

Admission: Adult £5, Child £2, OAP. £4.50. Groups (max 60): £5. Min £150.

ⓘ No photography in house. ▣ ⓣ Conferences & functions ⓹ Partial. WC. ◉ Licensed. Ⓚ Obligatory other than Fair Days. Ⓟ Limited for coaches. ▣ ⓕ In grounds, on leads. ▲ ✳ ⓥ

LYVEDEN NEW BIELD ⅍

Nr Oundle, Peterborough PE8 5AT
Tel: 01832 205358 **e-mail:** lyvedennewbield@nationaltrust.org.uk
www.nationaltrust.org.uk
Owner: The National Trust   **Contact:** The Property Manager
An incomplete Elizabethan garden house and moated garden. Begun in 1595 by
Sir Thomas Tresham to symbolise his Catholic faith, Lyveden remains virtually
unaltered since work stopped when Tresham died in 1605. Fascinating Elizabethan
architectural detail; remains of one of the oldest garden layouts; set amongst beautiful
open countryside.
Location: OS141, SP983 853. 4m SW of Oundle via A427, 3m E of Brigstock, off
Harley Way. Access by foot along a $^1/_2$ m farm track.
Open: House, Elizabethan water garden & visitor information room: 31 Mar - 31 Oct:
Wed - Sun (open BH Mons & Good Fri), 10.30am - 5pm (Aug: daily); 6 Nov - 27 Mar
2005: Sat & Sun, 10.30am - 4pm. Groups by arrangement with Property Manager.
Admission: Adult £2.50, Child £1.20, Family £6.20.
🅿 Limited. 🐕 On leads. ✳

NORTHAMPTON CATHEDRAL

Catholic Cathedral House, Primrose Hill, Northampton NN2 6AG
Tel: 01604 714556   **Contact:** Father Ivor Parrish
Partly 19th century Pugin.
Location: OS Ref. SP753 617. $^3/_4$ m N of town centre on A508.
Open: Apply at house: Sun Mass: 7pm (Sat) 8.30am, 10.30am 5.15pm. Weekday Mass
9.30am and 7pm.
Admission: Visits welcomed by appointment.

THE PREBENDAL MANOR HOUSE

Nassington, Peterborough PE8 6QG
Tel: 01780 782575 **e-mail:** info@prebendal-manor.co.uk
www.prebendal-manor.co.uk
Owner/Contact: Mrs J Baile
Grade I listed, dating from the early 13th century, it retains many fine original
medieval features and included in the visit are the 15th century dovecote, tithe barn
museum and medieval fish ponds. Encompassing 6 acres are the largest 14th century
re-created medieval gardens in Europe.
Location: OS Ref. TL063 962. 6m N of Oundle, 9m W of Peterborough, 7m S of
Stamford.
Open: Easter Monday - end Sept: Sun & Wed, also BH Mons, 1 - 5.30pm. Closed
Christmas.
Admission: Adult £4.50, Child £2. Groups (20 - 50) outside normal opening times by
arrangement: Adult £4, Child £1.
ⓘNo photography. 🍴 ♿ Partial. 🍴 Home-made teas. 🅿 Limited. 🎦 🔲 Free.
🐕 Guide dogs only.

ROCKINGHAM CASTLE 🏛   *See page 325 for full page entry.*

RUSHTON TRIANGULAR LODGE ⌘

Rushton, Kettering, Northamptonshire NN14 1RP
Tel: 01536 710761 **www**.english-heritage.org.uk
Owner: English Heritage   **Contact:** The Custodian
This extraordinary building, completed in 1597, symbolises the Holy Trinity. It has
three sides, 33 ft wide, three floors, trefoil windows and three triangular gables on
each side. Picnickers are welcome.
Location: OS141, SP830 831. 1m W of Rushton, on unclassified road 3m from
Desborough on A6.
Open: 1 Apr - 31 Oct: daily, 10am - 6pm (5pm in Oct) Opening times subject to
change April 2004, please ring prior to visiting. Times subject to change April 2004.
Admission: Adult £2, Child £1, Conc. £1.50. Prices subject to change April 2004.
📷 🔲 Free with admission. 🅿 🐕 Restricted areas.

SOUTHWICK HALL 🏛

Nr Oundle, Peterborough PE8 5BL
Tel: 01832 274064
Owner: Christopher Capron Esq   **Contact:** G & C Bucknill
A family home since 1300, retaining medieval building dating from 1300, with Tudor
rebuilding and 18th century additions. Exhibitions: Victorian and Edwardian Life,
collections of agricultural and carpentry tools and local archaeological finds.
Location: OS152, TL022 921. 3m N of Oundle, 4m E of Bulwick.
Open: BH Suns & Mons: 11/12 Apr, 2/3 & 30/31 May, 29/30 Aug: 2 - 5pm. Last
admission 4.30pm. Groups at other times by arrangement.
Admission: House & Grounds: Adult £4, Child £2.
♿ Partial. WC. ☕ 🎦 By arrangement. 🅿 🐕 In grounds on leads.

STOKE PARK PAVILIONS

Stoke Bruerne, Towcester, Northamptonshire NN12 7RZ
Tel: 01604 862172
Owner: A S Chancellor Esq   **Contact:** Mrs C Cook
The two Pavilions, dated c1630 and attributed to Inigo Jones, formed part of the first
Palladian country house built in England by Sir Francis Crane. The central block, to
which the Pavilions were linked by quadrant colonnades, was destroyed by fire in
1886. The grounds include extensive gardens and overlook the former park, now
farmland.
Location: OS Ref. SP740 488. 7m S of Northampton.
Open: Aug: daily, 3 - 6pm. Other times by appointment only.
Admission: Adult £3, Child £1.
♿ Grounds. 🅿 Limited. 🐕 In grounds, on leads. ✳

Rockingham Castle, Northamptonshire from the book *Historic Family Homes and Gardens from the Air*, see page 54.

SULGRAVE MANOR
MANOR ROAD, SULGRAVE, BANBURY, OXON OX17 2SD
www.sulgravemanor.org.uk

Tel: 01295 760205 **Fax:** 01295 768056 **e-mail:** sulgrave-manor@talk21.com

A delightful 16th century Manor House that was the home of George Washington's ancestors. Today it presents a typical wealthy man's home and gardens of Elizabethan times. Restored with scholarly care and attention to detail that makes a visit both a pleasure and an education. New gardens being created by the Herb Society, now based at Sulgrave. New Courtyard development with fine visitor/education facilities.

Location: OS152, SP561 457. Off Banbury - Northampton road (B4525) 5m from M40/J11. 15m from M1/J15A.

Open: 1 Apr - 30 Oct: 2 - 5pm. Closed Mon & Fri except BHs & event days. Last admission 1 hour before closing. Open for booked groups on any day or evening throughout the year (except Jan). Access to house may be restricted during private wedding ceremonies. Closed 30 May, 8 Aug.

Admission: Adult £5, Child (5-16) £2.50. Garden only: £2.50. Groups: Adult £4.50, Child £2.25. Special Events: All visitors on non-event days are taken round the Manor House on regularly organized guided tours.

[i]No photography in house. Partial. Obligatory. In grounds, on leads. Various. Send for details.

Elizabethan Great Houses
1558-1603

An era when the owner designed his own house, and employed an army of craftsmen in the building trades: carpenters, glaziers, plasterworkers, and masons, who were generally managed by a master mason or surveyor. Two of the great master surveyors of this period are John Thorpe and Robert Smythson.

This was the era of building big, and building bold. Although Queen Elizabeth was responsible for comparatively little building work for herself, her courtiers vied with each other to provide the most comfortable and magnificent accommodation for her and her Court on its annual summer progress around its kingdom.

Look out for the E-plan great house, i.e. two wings extended on each side of the house whilst, in the centre, the short arm of the E was provided by the projecting porch. The house was completely symmetrical, with the hall, solar and reception-rooms at one side of the porch, and screens passage and offices at the other. Look also for the H-plan, i.e. where the side wings of the house extended as far back as forward.

Visit Longleat in Wiltshire, Wollaton Hall in Nottinghamshire, Hardwick Hall in Derbyshire, Montacute House in Somerset, Burghley House in Lincolnshire and Kirby Hall in Northamptonshire. For small country houses of this period visit Coughton Court in Warwickshire, Little Moreton Hall in Cheshire and Chavenage in Gloucestershire.

WAKEFIELD LODGE
Potterspury, Northamptonshire NN12 7QX
Tel: 01327 811218
Owner/Contact: Mrs J Richmond-Watson
Georgian Hunting Lodge with deer park.
Location: OS Ref. SP739 425. 4m S of Towcester on A5. Take signs to farm shop for advice on tour times.
Open: House: 22 Apr - 4 June: Mon - Fri (closed BHs), 12 noon - 4pm. Appointments by phone or take signs to Farm Shop for advice on tour times.
Admission: £5.
[i]No photography. Unsuitable. Obligatory. Guide dogs only.

Plant Sales Index see front section

BREWHOUSE YARD
THE MUSEUM OF NOTTINGHAM LIFE
Castle Boulevard, Nottingham NG7 1FB
Tel: 0115 9153600 **Fax:** 0115 9153601 **e-mail:** bhyoffice@ncmg.demon.co.uk
Owner/Contact: Ann Inskuer
Set in a group of 18th century cottages, the museum presents a realistic glimpse of life in Nottingham over the past 200 years.
Location: OS Ref. SK570 393. 500yds SW of City Centre.
Open: Daily, 10am - 4.30pm.
Admission: Weekdays: Free. Weekends & BHs: Adult £1.50, Conc. 80p, Family £3.80.
✳

CARLTON HALL
Carlton-on-Trent, Nottinghamshire NG23 6LP
Tel: 01636 821421 **Fax:** 01636 821554
Owner/Contact: Lt Col & Mrs Vere-Laurie
Mid 18th century house by Joseph Pocklington of Newark. Stables attributed to Carr of York. Family home occupied by the same family since 1832.
Location: OS Ref. SK799 640. 7m N of Newark off A1. Opposite the church.
Open: 1 Apr - 30 Sept: Weds only, 2 - 5pm. Other dates and times by appointment.
Admission: Hall and Garden £4.
📧Conferences. ♿Unsuitable. 🐕In grounds, on leads. Guide dogs in house. ✳

CLUMBER PARK 🌿
Clumber Park, Worksop, Nottinghamshire S80 3AZ
Tel: 01909 476592 **Fax:** 01909 500721 **www**.nationaltrust.org.uk
Owner: The National Trust   **Contact:** Property Manager
Historic parkland with peaceful woods, open heath and rolling farmland around a serpentine lake.
Location: OS120 Ref SK626 746. 4^1/$_2$ m SE of Worksop, 6^1/$_2$ m SW of Retford, just off A1/A57 via A614. 11m from M1/J30.
Open: Park: All year except 10 Jul & 21 Aug & 25/26 Dec. Walled Kitchen Garden: 28 Mar - 30 Oct: Mon - Fri & BH Mons, 10am - 5.30pm, Sats & Suns, 10am - 6pm. Chapel: 28 Mar - 30 Oct: Mon - Fri, 10.30am - 5.30pm, Sat & Sun 10am - 6pm. 31 Oct - 11 Jan 2005: daily, 10am - 4pm. Closed 12 Jan - end Mar for conservation cleaning.
Admission: Pedestrians, Cyclists & Coaches: Free, NT Members Free, Cars & Motorbikes £3.80, Minibuses & caravans £5. Walled Kitchen Garden £1.
🅿 ♿Partial. Wheelchairs available. 🍴 🅿 🛏 🐕In grounds on leads. ✳

GREEN'S MILL
Windmill Lane, Sneinton, Nottingham NG2 4QB
Tel: 0115 9156878 **www**.greensmill.org.uk
Owner/Contact: Graham Armitage
This fully operational windmill was once owned and operated by George Green, mathematician and physicist. Includes interactive science centre.
Location: OS Ref. SK585 398. ^{1}/$_2$ m due E of City Centre, between A612 and B686.
Open: Wed - Sun & BH Mons, 10am - 4pm.
Admission: Free.

HODSOCK PRIORY GARDEN
Blyth, Nr Worksop, Nottinghamshire S81 0TY
Tel: 01909 591204 **Fax:** 01909 591578
Owner: Sir Andrew & Lady Buchanan   **Contact:** Lady Buchanan
Sensational snowdrops, winter flowering plants and shrubs, woodland walk.
Location: OS Ref. SK612 853. W of B6045 Worksop/Blyth road, 1m SW of Blyth, less than 2m from A1.
Open: 31 Jan - 7 Mar: daily, 10am - 4pm. Please telephone for details.
Admission: Adult £3.50, accompanied Child (6-16yrs) 50p.

HOLME PIERREPONT HALL 🏛
HOLME PIERREPONT, Nr NOTTINGHAM NG12 2LD
www.holmepierreponthall.com
Tel: 0115 933 2371
Owner: Mr & Mrs Robin Brackenbury   **Contact:** Robert Brackenbury
This charming late medieval manor house is set in 30 acres of Park and Gardens with regional furniture and family portraits. The Ball Room, Drawing Room and Long Gallery are available to hire for functions on an exclusive basis. Filming welcome.
Location: OS Ref. SK628 392. 5m ESE of central Nottingham. Follow signs to the National Water Sports Centre and continue for 1^1/$_2$ m.
Open: Easter, Spring & Summer BH Suns & Mons. Jun: Thurs, Jul: Weds & Thurs. Aug: Tue - Thurs, 2 - 5.30pm. Corporate/private and wedding venue. Functions at other times by arrangement.
Admission: Adult £4, Child £1.50. Gardens only £2.
ℹNo photography or video recording in house when open to the public.
♿Partial. 📧Business & charity functions, wedding receptions.
🐕In grounds on leads. 🔔 ⚭Tel for details.

NEWARK TOWN HALL
Market Place, Newark, Nottinghamshire NG24 1DU
Tel: 01636 680333 **Fax:** 01636 680350
Owner: Newark Town Council   **Contact:** The Curator
A fine Georgian Grade I listed Town Hall containing a museum of the town's treasures. Disabled access – lift and WC.
Location: OS Ref. SK570 395. Close to A46 and A1.
Open: All year: Mon - Fri, 11am - 4pm. Sats, 12 noon - 4pm. Closed BHs.
Admission: Free.

NEWSTEAD ABBEY
Newstead Abbey Park, Nottinghamshire NG15 8NA
Tel: 01623 455900 **Fax:** 01623 455904 **www**.newsteadabbey.org.uk
                                              Contact: The Manager
Historic home of the poet, Lord Byron, set in grounds of over 300 acres. Mementoes of Byron and period rooms from medieval to Victorian times.
Location: OS Ref. SK540 639. 12m N of Nottingham 1m W of the A60 Mansfield Rd.
Open: House: 1 Apr - 30 Sept: 12 noon - 5pm, last adm. 4pm. Grounds: All year: 9am - dusk except for the last Friday in November and 25 Dec.
Admission: House & Grounds: Adult £5, Conc. £2.50, Family (2+4) £12. Grounds only: Adult £2.50, Family £7 (Oct - Mar: Adult £2, Conc. £1.50).

East Midlands - England

NOTTINGHAM CASTLE
Nottingham NG1 6EL

Tel: 0115 9153700 **Fax:** 0115 9153653 **e-mail:** castle@ncmg.demon.co.uk
17th century ducal mansion, home to a museum and art gallery. Lively and often interactive galleries display paintings, glass, silver and Wedgwood.
Location: OS Ref. SK569 395. Just SW of the city centre on hilltop.
Open: Daily, 10am - 5pm (4pm during winter). Closed 24 - 26 Dec & 1 Jan.
Admission: Weekdays Free. Weekends: Adult £2, Child/Conc. £1, Family £5.
⁂

PAPPLEWICK HALL
Papplewick, Nottinghamshire NG15 8FE

Tel: 0115 963 3491 **Fax:** 0115 964 2767
Owner/Contact: Dr R Godwin-Austen
A beautiful stone built classical house set in a park with woodland garden laid out in the 18th century. The house is notable for its very fine plasterwork and elegant staircase. Grade I listed.
Location: OS Ref. SK548 518. Halfway between Nottingham & Mansfield, 3m E of M1/J27. A608 & A611 towards Hucknall. Then A6011 to Papplewick and B683 N for ½ m.
Open: By appointment and 1st, 3rd & 5th Wed in each month, 2 -5pm.
Admission: Adult £5. Groups (10+): £4.
ⁱNo photography. ℐObligatory. ℙLimited for coaches. ℍIn grounds on leads. ⁂

RUFFORD ABBEY ⌗
Ollerton, Nottinghamshire NG22 9DF

Tel: 01623 822944 **www**.english-heritage.org.uk/visits
Owner: English Heritage **Contact:** Nottinghamshire County Council
The remains of a 17th century country house; displaying the ruins of a 12th century Cistercian Abbey. It is set in what is now Rufford Country Park. Picnickers welcome.
Location: OS120, SK645 646. 2m S of Ollerton off A614.
Open: 1 Apr - 31 Oct: Daily, 10am - 5pm. 1 Nov - 31 Mar: daily, 10am - 4pm. (Closed 24 - 26 Dec & 1 Jan). (Opening times subject to change April 2004, please ring prior to visit.)
Admission: Free - parking charge applies.
ⁱWC. ⌂ ♿ ℙ ℍ ⁂

UPTON HALL 🏛
Upton, Newark, Nottinghamshire NG23 5TE

Tel: 01636 813795 **Fax:** 01636 812258 **www**.bhi.co.uk
Owner: British Horological Institute **Contact:** The Museum Manager
A fine country house dating from the 16th century, but extensively altered in the 19th century, set within its own grounds. Since 1972, it has been the headquarters of the British Horological Institute and its fascinating museum containing a large historic collection of public and domestic clocks and watches.
Location: OS Ref. SK735 544. A612 between Newark and Southwell.
Open: Apr - Oct: Sats & BH Mons, 11am - 5pm, Suns, 2 - 5pm. (Closed Nov - Mar.)
Admission: Adult £3.50, Child £2, (under 10yrs free), OAP £3. Members free.
ℐBy arrangement. ℙ

WINKBURN HALL
Winkburn, Newark, Nottinghamshire NG22 8PQ

Tel: 01636 636465 **Fax:** 01636 636717
Owner/Contact: Richard Craven-Smith-Milnes Esq
A fine William and Mary house.
Location: OS Ref. SK711 584. 8m W of Newark 1m N of A617.
Open: Throughout the year by appointment only.
Admission: £5.

WOLLATON HALL & PARK
Wollaton, Nottingham NG8 2AE

Tel: 0115 915 3900 **e-mail:** wollatonhall@ncmg.demon.co.uk
Contact: The Manager
Flamboyant 16th century Robert Smythson Building set in 500 acre deer park, home to Natural History Museum, Steam Beam Engine House and Contemporary Art Gallery.
Location: OS Ref. SK532 392. Wollaton Park, Nottingham. 3m W of city centre.
Open: Hall: Summer, 11am - 5pm; Winter, 11am - 4pm. Park: All year, 9am - dusk.
Admission: Weekdays Free. Weekends & BHs: Joint ticket for all museums: Adult £2, Child £1. Grounds £2/car (free for disabled badge holders). Yard Gallery Free.
⁂

THRUMPTON HALL 🏛
THRUMPTON, NOTTINGHAM NG11 0AX

www.thrumptonhall.co.uk

Tel: 01159 830333 **Fax:** 01159 831309
Owner: Miranda Seymour **Contact:** The Hon Mrs R Seymour
Fine Jacobean house, built in 1607 incorporating an earlier manor house. Priest's hiding hole, magnificent carved Charles II staircase, carved and panelled saloon. Other fine rooms containing beautiful 17th and 18th century furniture and many fine portraits. Large lawns separated from landscaped park by ha-ha and by lake in front of the house. The house is still lived in as a home and Mrs Seymour will show parties around when possible. Dining room with capacity for 52 with silver service or buffet. Free access and meal for coach drivers.
Location: OS Ref. SK508 312. 7m S of Nottingham, 3m E M1/J24, 1m from A453.
Open: By appointment throughout the year. Groups of (20+) 10.30am - 7.30pm.
Admission: Adult £5.50, Child Free.
⌂ ℐWedding receptions. ♿Ground floor & grounds. WC. ℍ ℍIn grounds on leads. ⁂

Do You Know Your Dates?

Norman and Early English Gothic 1066-1275

Decorated Gothic 1275-1375

Perpendicular Gothic 1375-1509

Tudor 1509-1603

Stuart 1603-1660

Restoration Stuart & Queen Anne 1660-1714

Early Georgian 1714-1760

Late Georgian 1760-1800

Regency and Early Victorian 1800-1850

Victorian 1850-1901

Architectural Periods

westmidlands

Broadway Tower, Worcestershire. © David Osborn

uptonhouse
warwickshire

Upton is also rare, in that its story really revolves around the life of one man, William Samuel, 2nd Viscount Bearsted and his wife Lady Dorothy. Upton estate was purchased by the Viscount, on the death of his father in 1927. Marcus Samuel, 1st Viscount Bearsted was the founder of Shell Transport and Trading Company (known today as Royal Dutch Shell, one of the largest companies in the world). The family fortune was founded on trading with the Far East, and from the building of a huge tanker fleet capable of passing through the Suez Canal, carrying oil in one direction and, after steam-cleaning, other goods in the opposite. Having developed an extensive lighting oil business, William's father was in a perfect position to exploit the market for oil, when this first began to replace coal in ships, and to produce petroleum for cars. By the end of the century Marcus Samuel's operation was so extensive that an observer who counted 54 ships in Yokohama harbour noted that 45 of them belonged to, or were on charter to Shell.

Although the 2nd Viscount Bearsted inherited his father's country retreat near Maidstone in Kent, he preferred instead to sell this and acquire the Upton estate which joined an existing Warwickshire estate he already owned.

Between 1927-1929 Lord Bearsted employed the architect Percy Morley Horder to remodel the 17th century house. Horder raised the one-storey wings on the garden front of the house to the height of the main block and he regularised and the lengthened the entrance front. He also created the 100ft Long Gallery to display Lord Bearsted's collection of English soft-paste porcelain and some of his Old Master paintings.

The gardens at Upton are spectacular in all seasons and use all the surprises created by the natural steeply undulating fall of the land. The gardens' long wide terraces, the bog garden, the rock garden, the kitchen garden ... the list goes on, are primarily the result of the partnership between Lady Bearsted and the garden designer and plantswoman Kitty Lloyd-Jones.

Upton remained Lord Bearsted's country residence until his death in 1948. Like his father he was a highly successful businessman. He became the Chairman of Shell, the owner of the bankers M Samuel (now part of Lloyd's TSB) and Samuel Estates. However it is at Upton that you see the private man – the compulsive collector and the philanthropist. A man passionate about 18th century soft-paste porcelain from the French and English factories, a lover of paintings ranging from Hieronymus Bosch and Bruegel through El Greco and Guardi to Hogarth, and Stubbs.

A visit to Upton House is to an idyllic world – something Lord Bearsted and his wife felt, after the horrors of the First and Second World Wars, should be preserved for all to enjoy. In 1948 they gifted the estate to the National Trust ... it remains today as complete and well loved as the day it first opened its doors to the public ... make time to visit it.

▸ **For further details about Upton House see page 363.**

NT Photographic Library

Map 5

Owner:
The National Trust

▶ CONTACT

The Property
Manager
Berrington Hall
Nr Leominster
Herefordshire
HR6 0DW

Tel: 01568 615721
Fax: 01568 613263

Restaurant:
01568 610134

Shop:
01568 610529

Costume Curator:
01568 613720

e-mail: berrington
@nationaltrust.org.uk

▶ LOCATION
OS137 SP510 637

3m N of Leominster,
7m S of Ludlow on
W side of A49.

Rail: Leominster 4m.

BERRINGTON HALL 🌳

NR LEOMINSTER

www.nationaltrust.org.uk/berrington

Berrington Hall is the creation of Thomas Harley, the 3rd Earl of Oxford's remarkable son, who made a fortune from supplying pay and clothing to the British Army in America and became Lord Mayor of London in 1767 at the age of thirty-seven. The architect was the fashionable Henry Holland. The house is beautifully set above the wide valley of a tributary of the River Lugg, with views west and south to the Black Mountains and Brecon Beacons. This was the site advised by 'Capability' Brown who created the lake with its artificial island. The rather plain neo-classical exterior with a central portico

gives no clue to the lavishness of the interior. Plaster ceilings decorated in muted pastel colours adorn the principal rooms. Holland's masterpiece is the staircase hall rising to a central dome. The rooms are set off with a collection of French furniture, including pieces which belonged to the Comte de Flahault, natural son of Talleyrand, and Napoleon's step-daughter Hortense.

In the dining room, vast panoramic paintings of battles at sea, three of them by Thomas Luny, are a tribute to the distinguished Admiral Rodney.

NT Photographic Library

▶ OPENING TIMES
House
6 Mar - 4 Apr: Sats & Suns
5 Apr - 30 Sept:
Daily except Thur & Fri
(open Good Fri).

Sats & Suns,
12 noon - 4.30pm
(opens 1pm in Oct);
Mon - Wed, 1 - 4.30pm.

Garden
6 Mar - 4 Apr:
12 noon - 5pm
Sat & Sun only.

5 April - 31 Oct:
Daily except Thurs & Fri
12 noon - 5pm
(closes 4.30pm in Oct).

1 Nov - 14 Dec:
Sat & Sun only.
12 noon - 4.30pm

Park Walk
1 Jul - 31 Oct:
Daily except Thur & Fri,
1 Nov - 14 Dec Sat & Sun
12 noon - 5pm.

Shop
6 Mar - 4 Apr: as house
5 Apr - 31 Oct:
12 noon - 5pm
1 Nov - 14 Dec:
12 noon - 4.30pm
Sat & Sun only.

Restaurant
6 Mar - 4 Apr Sat & Sun
only: 12 noon - 5pm.

5 Apr - 14 Dec: as shop.

Last admission to House, Shop and Restaurant 30 minutes before stated closing time.

▶ ADMISSION
Adult £4.80
Child (5-12yrs) £2.40
Family (2+3).......... £12.00
Groups (15-25)*
Adult £4.20
Child £2.10

Garden Ticket £3.40

Groups must pre-book. Two groups can visit at a time.

Joint Ticket for Berrington & Croft Castle £6.00

No photography in the house. Groups by arrangement only.

Single seater batricar; pre-booking essential. Audio tours for the visually impaired.

Licensed restaurant: open as house: 12 noon - 5pm (4.30pm in Oct & Nov).

By arrangement only. Tour time: 1 hr.

Ample for cars. Parking for coaches limited; instructions given when booking is made.

Children's quizzes. Play area in walled garden.

Guide dogs only.   Tel for details.

Owner:
Mr J Hervey-Bathurst

▶ **CONTACT**

Simon Foster
Portcullis Office
Eastnor Castle
Nr Ledbury
Herefordshire HR8 1RL

Tel: 01531 633160
Fax: 01531 631776
e-mail: enquiries@
eastnorcastle.com

▶ **LOCATION**

OS Ref. SO735 368

2m SE of Ledbury on
the A438 Tewkesbury
road. Alternatively
M50/J2 & from Ledbury
take the A449/A438.

Tewkesbury 20 mins,
Malvern 20 mins, Gloucester
25 mins, Hereford 25 mins,
Worcester 30 mins,
Cheltenham 30 mins,
B'ham 1 hr, London 2¼ hrs.

Taxi: Richard James
07836 777196.

EASTNOR CASTLE 🏛

LEDBURY

www.eastnorcastle.com

Encircled by the Malvern Hills and surrounded by a famous arboretum and lake, this fairytale castle looks as dramatic inside as it does outside.

The atmosphere Everyone is struck by it. The vitality of a young family brings the past to life and the sense of warmth and optimism is tangible. Eastnor, however grand, is a home.

'Sleeping' for the past fifty years, the Castle has undergone a triumphant renaissance – 'looking better than it probably ever has', Country Life 1993.

Hidden away in attics and cellars since 1939, many of the castle's treasures are now displayed for the first time – early Italian Fine Art, 17th century Venetian furniture and Flemish tapestries, mediaeval armour and paintings by Van Dyck, Romney, Wootton and Watts, photographs by Julia Margaret Cameron. Drawing Room by Pugin.

'The princely and imposing pile' as it was described in 1812 when it was being built to pitch the owner into the aristocracy, remains the home of his descendants. The Castle contains letters diaries, clothes and furnishings belonging to friends and relations who include: Horace Walpole, Elizabeth Barrett Browning, Tennyson, Watts, Julia Margaret Cameron and Virginia Woolf.

Encircled by the Malvern Hills, the medieval beauty of the estate remains unchanged.

GARDENS

Castellated terraces descend to a 21 acre lake with a restored lakeside walk. The arboretum holds a famous collection of mature specimen trees. There are spectacular views of the Malvern hills across a 300 acre deer park, once part of a mediaeval chase and now designated a Site of Special Scientific Interest.

ℹ Tree trail, maze, assault course, off-road driving, clay-pigeon shooting, quad bikes, archery and falconry. Survival training, team building activity days. Product launches, fashion shows, concert, charity events, craft fairs, television and feature films. No photography in Castle.

🍴 Wedding receptions. Catering for booked events.

♿ Partially suitable. Visitors may alight at the castle. Priority parking.

☕ By arrangement.

🅿 Ample 10 - 200 yds from castle. Coaches phone in advance to arrange parking & catering. Free meal for drivers.

📖 Welcome. Guides available if required. Children's fun worksheets.

🐕 On leads in grounds.

🛏 Luxury accommodation within castle for small groups (min. 10 guests). 1 single room, 11 double. Ensuite available.

🔔

▶ **OPENING TIMES**

Summer
11 April - 3 October:
Suns & BH Mons.
July - August: Sun - Fri
11am - 5pm.
(Last admission 4.30pm).

▶ **ADMISSION**

Summer
Castle & Grounds

Adult	£6.50
Child (5-15yrs)	£4.00
OAP	£6.00
Family (2+2)	£17.00

Groups (20+)
(with guide)

Adult	£8.50

Groups (20+)
(without guide)

Adult	£5.50

Grounds only

Adult	£4.50
Child (5-15yrs)	£3.00
OAP	£4.00

🎭 **SPECIAL EVENTS**

APRIL 11/12
Easter Treasure Hunt

MAY 2/3
Spring Crafts Festival

MAY 30/31
Steam & Woodland Fair

AUG 29/30
Medieval Treasure Hunt

OCT 2/3
Festival of Fine Food & Drink

CONFERENCE/FUNCTION

ROOM	SIZE	MAX CAPACITY
Great Hall	16 x 8m	150
Dining Rm	11 x 7m	80
Gothic Rm	11 x 7m	80
Octagon Rm	9 x 9m	50

ABBEY DORE COURT GARDEN

Abbey Dore, Herefordshire HR2 0AD

Tel/Fax: 01981 240419

Owner/Contact: Mrs C L Ward

6 acres of new and established garden with a wild river walk leading to a meadow planted with a variety of interesting trees.

Location: OS Ref. SO387 309. 3 m W of A465 midway Hereford - Abergavenny.

Open: Apr - Sept: Sat, Sun, Tue, Thur & BHs, 11am - 5.30pm. Other times by appointment.

Admission: Adult £3, Child 50p.

BERRINGTON HALL ※   *See page 340 for full page entry.*

BERNITHAN COURT

Llangarron, Nr Ross on Wye, Herefordshire HR9 6NG

Tel: 020 7962 8361   **e-mail:** michael.richardson@dwp.gsi.gov.uk

Owner: Bernithan Court Farm Partnership   **Contact:** M J Richardson
William and Mary house with walled gardens. Set in rolling countryside with spectacular views to Welsh mountains. Surrounded by farmland. A perfect setting for weddings and receptions.

Location: OS Ref. SO542 215. 4m from Ross on Wye off A40 Ross - Monmouth road.

Open: By arrangement only for Civil weddings and receptions.

⬤ P ⬤

BROCKHAMPTON ESTATE ※

Bringsty, Worcestershire WR6 5UH

Tel: 01885 488099/482077   **www.**nationaltrust.org.uk/brockhampton

Owner: The National Trust   **Contact:** The Property Manager
Wood and parkland estate with waymarked walks. inc. Lower Brockhampton, a 14th century moated manor house with timber framed gatehouse.

Location: OS Ref. SO682 546. 2m E of Bromyard on A44.

Open: Lower Brockhampton: 3 Mar - 31 Oct: Wed - Sun & BHs, 12 noon - 5pm (Mar & Oct: 4pm). Woodland walks: All year: daily during daylight hours.

Admission: Lower Brockhampton: Adult £3.50, Child £1.75, Family £8.50. Estate Car Park: £2.

⬤ Partial. ⬤ ⬤ Dogs in woodland walks, on leads. ❉

CROFT CASTLE ※

Leominster, Herefordshire HR6 9PW

Tel: 01568 780246   **e-mail:** croft@nationaltrust.org.uk   **www.**nationaltrust.org.uk

Owner: The National Trust   **Contact:** The House Manager
Home of the Croft family since Domesday. Walls and corner towers date from 14th and 15th centuries, interior mainly 18th century.

Location: OS Ref. SO455 655. 5m NW of Leominster, 9m SW of Ludlow, approach from B4362.

Open: House: 6 - 28 Mar & 2 - 31 Oct: Sat & Sun; Apr - Sept: Wed - Sun & BH Mons, 1 - 5pm. Garden: 6 - 28 Mar & 2 - 31 Oct: Sat, Sun & BH Mons, 11.30am - 5pm; Apr - Sept: Wed - Fri, 12 noon - 5pm. Park: All year. Tea Room: 6 - 28 Mar & 2 - 31 Oct: Sat & Sun; Apr - Sept: Wed - Sun & BH Mons, 11am - 5pm.

Admission: House & Garden: Adult £4.40, Child £2.20, Family £11, Group (15+) £4. Garden only: Adult £3.10, Child £1.50.

⬤ ⬤ ⬤

EASTNOR CASTLE ⬚   *See page 341 for full page entry.*

English Heritage Photo Library

GOODRICH CASTLE ⬚

ROSS-ON-WYE, HEREFORDSHIRE HR9 6HY

www.english-heritage.org.uk/visits

Tel: 01600 890538

Owner: English Heritage   **Contact:** The Custodian
This magnificent red sandstone castle is remarkably complete with a 12th century keep and extensive remains from 13th & 14th centuries. From the battlements there are fine views over the Wye Valley to Symonds Yat. Marvel at the maze of small rooms and the 'murder holes'.

Location: OS Ref. SO579 199. 5m S of Ross-on-Wye, off A40.

Open: Contact site for details and special event dates. Closed 24 - 26 Dec & 1 Jan.

Admission: Contact site for details. Family ticket available. 15% discount for groups (11+).

ℹ WC. ⬚ ⬚ P ⬚ ❉ ⬚ Tel for details.

Hergest Croft Gardens, Herefordshire from the book
Historic Family Homes and Gardens from the Air, see page 54.

HELLENS 🏛

MUCH MARCLE, LEDBURY, HEREFORDSHIRE HR8 2LY

Tel: 01531 660504

Owner: Pennington-Mellor-Munthe Charity Trust   **Contact:** The Administrator

Built as a monastery and then a stone fortress in 1292 by Mortimer, Earl of March, with Tudor, Jacobean and Stuart additions and lived in ever since by descendants of the original builder. Visited by the Black Prince, Bloody Mary and the 'family ghost'. Family paintings, relics and heirlooms from the Civil War and possessions of the Audleys, Walwyns and Whartons as well as Anne Boleyn. Also beautiful 17th century woodwork carved by the 'King's Carpenter', John Abel. All those historical

stories incorporated into guided tours, revealing the loves and lives of those who lived and died here. Goods and chattels virtually unchanged.

Location: OS Ref. SO661 332. Off A449 at Much Marcle. Ledbury 4m, Ross-on-Wye 4m.

Open: Easter Sat - 3 October: Wed, Sat, Sun & BH Mon. Guided tours only at 2pm, 3pm & 4pm. Other times by arrangement with the Administrator throughout the year.

Admission: Adult £5, Child £2.50, OAP £4, Family ticket £10.

ℹ️No photography inside house. 🍴 ♿Partial. 📷Obligatory. 🎥 🅿️
🐕In grounds, on leads. 💷 Tel for details.

HEREFORD CATHEDRAL

MAPPA MUNDI AND CHAINED LIBRARY EXHIBITION.

Hereford HR1 2NG   www: herfordcathedral.co.uk

Tel: 01432 374202   **Fax:** 01432 374220   **e-mail:** visits@herefordcathedral.co.uk

Contact: Mrs C Quinto - The Visits Manager

Location: OS Ref. SO510 398. Hereford city centre on A49.

Open: 7.30am - 5pm. Sun services: 8am, 10am, 11.30am & 3.30pm. Weekday services: 8am and 5.30pm. Mappa Mundi: May - Sept: Mon - Sat, 10am - 4.15pm, Suns 11am - 3.15pm.   Oct - Apr: Mon - Sat (closed Sun), 11am - 3.15pm.

Admission: Admission only for Mappa Mundi and Chained Library Exhibition: Adult £4.50, OAP/Student/Unemployed £3.50, Child under 5yrs Free. Family ticket (2+3) £10. (2003 details, please telephone to confirm prices)

🏠 🍴 ♿ 🍴 🎥 📷 🐕 ✱ 💷Tel for details.

HERGEST COURT

c/o Hergest Estate Office, Kington HR5 3EG

Tel: 01544 230160   **Fax:** 01544 232031   **e-mail:** gardens@hergest.co.uk

Owner/Contact: W L Banks

The ancient home of the Vaughans of Hergest, dating from the 13th century.

Location: OS Ref. SO283 554. 1m W of Kington on unclassified road to Brilley.

Open: Strictly by appointment only through Estate Office.

Admission: Adult £4, Child £1.50. Groups: Adult £3.50, Child £1.

♿Unsuitable. 🅿️Limited. 🐕Guide dogs only. ✱

HERGEST CROFT GARDENS 🏛

KINGTON, HEREFORDSHIRE HR5 3EG

www.hergest.co.uk

Tel: 01544 230160   **Fax:** 01544 232031   **e-mail:** gardens@hergest.co.uk

Owner: W L Banks   **Contact:** Melanie Lloyd

From spring bulbs to autumn colour, this is a garden for all seasons. An old-fashioned kitchen garden has spring and summer borders and roses. Over 59 Champion trees and shrubs grow in one of the finest collections in the British Isles. Holds National Collection of birches, maples and zelkovas. Park Wood is a hidden valley with rhododendrons up to 30 ft tall.

Location: OS Ref. SO281 565. On W side of Kington. $^1/_2$ m off A44, left at Rhayader end of bypass. Turn right and gardens are $^1/_4$ m on left. Signposted from bypass.

Open: 3 Apr - 31 Oct: 12.30 - 5.30pm, May & June: 12 noon - 6pm. Season tickets and groups by arrangement throughout the year. Winter by appointment.

Admission: Adult £4.50, Child (under 16yrs) Free. Pre-booked groups (20+) £4pp. Pre-booked guided groups (20+) £6pp. Season ticket £15.

ℹ️Gift sales.♿Limited. 🌱Rare plants. 🍴 🐕In grounds, on leads. ✱
💷 Tel for details.

✱ Plant Sales Index see front section

LANGSTONE COURT

Llangarron, Ross on Wye, Herefordshire HR9 6NR

Tel: 01989 770254

Owner/Contact: R M C Jones Esq

Mostly late 17th century house with older parts. Interesting staircases, panelling and ceilings.

Location: OS Ref. SO534 221. Ross on Wye 5m, Llangarron 1m.

Open: 20 May - 31 Aug: Wed & Thur, 11am - 2.30pm, also spring & summer BHs.

Admission: Free.

LONGTOWN CASTLE ⚏

Abbey Dore, Herefordshire

Tel: 0121 625 6820 (Regional Office)

Owner: English Heritage   **Contact:** The West Midlands Regional Office

An unusual cylindrical keep built c1200 with walls 15ft thick. There are magnificent views of the nearby Black Mountains.

Location: OS Ref. SO321 291. 4m WSW of Abbey Dore.

Open: Any reasonable time.

Admission: Free.

MOCCAS COURT 🏠

Moccas, Herefordshire HR2 9LH

Tel: 01981 500019   **Fax:** 01981 500095   **e-mail:** mimi@moccas.freeserve.co.uk

Owner: Trustees of the Baunton Trust   **Contact:** Ben & Mimi Chester-Master

18th century Adam interiors, 'Capability' Brown park.

Location: OS Ref. SO359 434. 1m N of B4352, 3¹/₂ m SE of Bredwardine.

Open: Apr - Sept: Thurs, 2 - 6pm. Last admission 5.15pm.

Admission: £4.

OLD SUFTON

Mordiford, Hereford HR1 4EJ

Tel: 01432 870268/850328   **Fax:** 01432 850381   **e-mail:** jameshereford@aol.com

Owner: Trustees of Sufton Heritage Trust   **Contact:** Mr & Mrs J N Hereford

A 16th century manor house which was altered and remodelled in the 18th and 19th centuries and again in this century. The original home of the Hereford family (see Sufton Court) who have held the manor since the 12th century.

Location: OS Ref. SO575 384. Mordiford, off B4224 Mordiford - Dormington road.

Open: By written appointment to Sufton Court or by fax.

Admission: Adult £3, Child 50p.

♿Partial. 🎥Obligatory. 🅿 ▣Small school groups. No special facilities. 🐾 ✳

ROTHERWAS CHAPEL ⚏

Hereford

Tel: 0121 625 6820 (Regional Office)

Owner: English Heritage   **Contact:** The West Midlands Regional Office

This Roman Catholic chapel, dating from the 14th and 16th centuries, is testament to the past grandeur of the Bodenham family and features an interesting mid-Victorian side chapel and High Altar.

Location: OS Ref. SO537 383. 1¹/₂ m SE of Hereford 500yds N of B4399.

Open: Any reasonable time. Keykeeper at nearby filling station.

Admission: Free.

♿ 🅿 🐾 ✳

SUFTON COURT 🏠

Mordiford, Hereford HR1 4LU

Tel: 01432 870268/850328   **Fax:** 01432 850381   **e-mail:** jameshereford@aol.com

Owner: J N Hereford   **Contact:** Mr & Mrs J N Hereford

Sufton Court is a small Palladian mansion house. Built in 1788 by James Wyatt for James Hereford. The park was laid out by Humphrey Repton whose 'red book' still survives. The house stands above the rivers Wye and Lugg giving impressive views towards the mountains of Wales.

Location: OS Ref. SO574 379. Mordiford, off B4224 on Mordiford to Dormington road.

Open: 18 - 31 May & 17 - 30 Aug: 2 - 5pm. Guided tours: 2, 3 and 4pm.

Admission: Adult £4, Child 50p.

♿ 🎥Obligatory. 🅿Only small coaches. ▣Small school groups. No special facilities. 🐾In grounds, on leads.

THE WEIR 🌿

Swainshill, Hereford

Tel: 01981 590509   **www**.nationaltrust.org.uk

Owner: The National Trust   **Contact:** Gardener-in-Charge

Delightful riverside garden particularly spectacular in early spring, with fine view over the River Wye and Black Mountains.

Location: OS Ref. SO435 421. 5m W of Hereford on S side of A438.

Open: 17 Jan - 1 Feb: Sat & Sun only, 11am - 4pm. 4 - 29 Feb: Wed - Sun, 11am - 5pm. Mar: daily, 11am - 6pm. 1 Apr - 30 Sept: Wed - Sun, 11am - 6pm. Oct: Wed - Sun only, 11am - 5pm.

Admission: Adult £3.50, Child £1.75, Family £8.

♿Unsuitable. 🅿Unsuitable for coaches. 🐾

Eastnor Castle, Herefordshire from the book *Historic Family Homes and Gardens from the Air*, see page 54.

OAKLEY HALL

MARKET DRAYTON

Map 5

Owner:
Mr & Mrs F Fisher

▶ **CONTACT**

Mrs Ann E Fisher
Oakley Hall
Market Drayton
Shropshire TF9 4AG

Tel: 01630 653472
Fax: 01630 653282

Wedding Enquiries:
Mrs D Hastie
Tel: 01244 572021

▶ **LOCATION**
OS Ref. SJ701 367

From London 3hrs:
M1, M6/J14, then A5013
to Eccleshall, turn right
at T-junction, 200 yards,
then left onto B5026.
Mucklestone is 1³/₄ m
from Loggerheads on
B5026. 3m NE of
Market Drayton
N of the A53,
1¹/₂ m W of
Mucklestone,
off B5145.

Oakley Hall is situated in magnificent countryside on the boundary of Shropshire and Staffordshire. The present Hall is a fine example of a Queen Anne mansion house and was built on the site of an older dwelling mentioned in the Domesday Survey of 1085. Oakley Hall was the home of the Chetwode family until it was finally sold in 1919.

GARDENS

Set in 100 acres of rolling parkland, the Hall commands superb views over the surrounding countryside and the gardens include wild areas in addition to the more formal parts.

Oakley Hall is a privately owned family house and since it is not open to the general public it provides a perfect location for exclusive private or corporate functions. The main hall can accommodate 120 people comfortably and has excellent acoustics for concerts. The secluded location and unspoilt landscape make Oakley an ideal setting for filming and photography.

The surrounding countryside is rich in historical associations. St Mary's Church at Mucklestone, in which parish the Hall stands, was erected in the 13th century and it was from the tower of this Church that Queen Margaret of Anjou observed the Battle of Blore Heath in 1459. This was a brilliant victory for the Yorkist faction in the Wars of the Roses and the blacksmith at Mucklestone was reputed to have shod the Queen's horse back to front in order to disguise her escape.

▶ **OPENING TIMES**

All Year
Not open to the public. The house is available all year round for private or corporate events.

▶ **ADMISSION**

Please telephone for details.

ℹ️ Concerts, conferences (see left for rooms available). Slide projector, word processor, fax and secretarial assistance are all available by prior arrangement, fashion shows, product launches, seminars, clay pigeon shooting, garden parties and filming. Grand piano, hard tennis court, croquet lawn, horse riding. No stiletto heels.

🍸 Wedding receptions, buffets, lunches and dinners can be arranged for large or small groups, using high quality local caterers.

♿ Visitors may alight at the entrance to the Hall, before parking in allocated areas. WCs.

🚶 By prior arrangement groups will be met and entertained by members of the Fisher family.

🅿️ 100 cars, 100/200 yds from the Hall.

 3 double with baths.

CONFERENCE/FUNCTION

ROOM	SIZE	MAX CAPACITY
Hall	50' x 30'	100
Dining Rm	40' x 27'	60
Ballroom	40' x 27'	60

Map 5

Owner:
The Weston Park
Foundation

▶ **CONTACT**

Kate Thomas
Weston Park
Weston-under-Lizard
Nr Shifnal
Shropshire TF11 8LE

Tel: 01952 852100
Fax: 01952 850430
e-mail: enquiries@
weston-park.com

▶ **LOCATION**

OS Ref. SJ808 107

Birmingham 40 mins.
Manchester 1 hr.
Motorway access
M6/J12 or M54/J3.
House situated on A5 at
Weston-under-Lizard.

Rail: Nearest Railway
Stations: Wolverhampton,
Stafford or Telford.

Air: Birmingham,
West Midlands,
Manchester.

WESTON PARK 🏛

NR SHIFNAL

www.weston-park.com

Weston Park is a magnificent Stately Home and Parkland situated on the Staffordshire/Shropshire border. The former home of the Earls of Bradford, the Park is now held in trust for the nation by The Weston Park Foundation.

Built in 1671 by Lady Elizabeth Wilbraham, this warm and welcoming house boasts a superb collection of paintings, including work by Van Dyck, Gainsborough and Stubbs, furniture and *objets d'art*, providing continued interest and enjoyment for all of its visitors.

Step outside to enjoy the 1,000 acres of glorious Parkland, take one of a variety of woodland and wildlife walks, all landscaped by the legendary 'Capability' Brown in the 18th Century. Then browse through the Gift Shop before relaxing in The Stables Restaurant and Bar.

With the exciting Woodland Adventure Playground, Animal Centre and Deer Park, as well as the Miniature Railway, there is so much for children to do.

Weston Park has a long-standing reputation for staging outstanding events. The exciting and varied programme of entertainment includes Music Festivals, Opera Evenings, Model Air Shows and Game Fairs.

▶ **OPENING TIMES**

Easter week:
10 - 16 April

17 April - 27 June:
weekends & BHs.

3 July - 31 August:
Daily (closed 3, 31 July &
19 - 25 August).

1 - 5 September.

House: 1 - 5pm
Last admission 4.30pm.

Park: 11am - 7pm
Last admission 5pm.

NB. Visitors are advised to telephone first to check this information.

▶ **ADMISSION**

Park & Gardens
Adult £3.00
Child (3 - 14yrs) £2.00
OAP £2.50
Family (2+3 or 1+4)...........
(inc House)...........£10.00

House
Adult £2.50
Child (3 - 14yrs) £1.50
OAP £2.00

CONFERENCE/FUNCTION

ROOM	SIZE	MAX CAPACITY
Dining Rm	52' x 23'	120
Orangery	51' x 20'	120
Music Rm	50' x 20'	80
The Old Stables	58' x 20'	60
Conference Room	40' x 7'6"	60

ℹ House available on an exclusive use basis. Conferences, product launches, outdoor concerts and events, filming location. Helipad and airstrip. Sporting activities organised for private groups eg. clay pigeon shooting, archery, hovercrafts, rally driving. Interior photography by prior arrangement only.

🛍 Gift Shop.

🍴 Full event organisation service. Residential parties, special dinners, wedding receptions. Dine and stay arrangements in the house on selected dates.

♿ House and part of the grounds. WCs.

🍽🍴 The Stables Bar and Restaurant provide meals and snacks. Licensed.

🅿 Ample 100 yds away. Private booked groups may park vehicles at front door.

🎒 Award-winning educational programme available during all academic terms. Private themed visits aligned with both National Curriculum and QCA targets.

🐕 In grounds, on leads.

🛏 Weston Park offers 28 delightful bedrooms with bathrooms, 22 doubles, 2 twins, 4 singles.

🔔

🎫 Tel for details.

ACTON BURNELL CASTLE ⊞
Acton Burnell, Shrewsbury, Shropshire
Tel: 0121 625 6820 (Regional Office)
Owner: English Heritage   **Contact:** The West Midlands Regional Office
The warm red sandstone shell of a fortified 13th century manor house.
Location: OS Ref. SJ534 019. In Acton Burnell, on unclassified road 8m S of Shrewsbury.
Open: Any reasonable time.
Admission: Free.

♿ 📷 ✻

ADCOTE SCHOOL
Little Ness, Shrewsbury, Shropshire SY4 2JY
Tel: 01939 260202   **Fax:** 01939 261300
www.adcoteschool.co.uk
Owner: Adcote School Educational Trust Ltd   **Contact:** The Bursar
Adcote is a Grade I listed building designed by Norman Shaw, and built to a Tudor design in 1879. Its features include a Great Hall, Minstrels' Gallery, William De Morgan tiled fireplaces and stained glass windows. Landscaped gardens include many fine trees.
Location: OS Ref. SJ418 294. 7m NW of Shrewsbury. 2m NE of A5.
Open: By appointment only.
Admission: Free, but the Governors reserve the right to make a charge.

🔺 ✻

NT Photographic Library

NTPL - James Mortimer

ATTINGHAM PARK ⚘
SHREWSBURY, SHROPSHIRE SY4 4TP

Infoline: 01743 708123   **Tel:** 01743 708162   **Fax:** 01743 708175
Owner: The National Trust   **Contact:** The Property Manager
Late 18th century house, sitting in 500 acres of wonderful parkland. Built for the 1st Lord Berwick, the Georgian house contains some beautiful Italian furniture and a large silver collection. Lord Berwick, and subsequently his two elder sons, had a passion for art and music and this is seen in the Picture Gallery with fine paintings and a Samuel Green organ, which is often played for visitors' enjoyment during the season. Woodland walks along the River Tern and through the Deer Park take in picturesque views of the Wrekin and Shropshire Hills. Costumed guided tours of the House are on offer every day the house is open. Events planned for 2004 include Easter Egg Trail,

1940s Day, Spring Plant Fair, Food Fayre, In Service and Apple Weekend.
Location: OS127, SJ837 083. 4m SE of Shrewsbury on N side of B4380 in Atcham village.
Open: 19 Mar - 31 Oct: daily (closed Wed & Thur), 12 noon - 5pm, last admission to house 4pm.
Admission: House & Grounds: Adult £5.50, Child £2.75, Family £13.75. Grounds only: Adult £2.70, Child £1.35. Booked groups (15+): Adult £4.50, Child £2.25.
ℹ No photography in house. 📷 ♿ 💿 Licensed. 𝑓 By arrangement. 🅿 📷
🐾 In grounds on leads. ✻ 📺 Tel for details.

BENTHALL HALL ⚘
Benthall, Nr Broseley, Shropshire TF12 5RX
Tel: 01952 882159
Owner: The National Trust   **Contact:** Mr E Benthall or Custodian
A 16th century stone house with mullioned windows and moulded brick chimneys.
Location: OS Ref. SJ658 025. 1m NW of Broseley (B4375), 4m NE of Much Wenlock, 1m SW of Ironbridge.
Open: 6 Apr - 30 June: Tues & Weds & BH Suns & Mons, 2 - 5.30pm. 3 Jul - 26 Sept: Tues, Weds & Suns, 2 - 5.30pm. Garden: 1 - 5.30pm.
Admission: Adult: £4, Child: £2. Garden: £2.50, Child £1.25.
🔺 Partial. Ground floor. WC. 𝑓 By arrangement. 🅿 Limited.

English Heritage Photo Library

BOSCOBEL HOUSE & THE ROYAL OAK ⚌

BREWOOD, BISHOP'S WOOD, SHROPSHIRE ST19 9AR

Tel: 01902 850244

Owner: English Heritage   **Contact:** The Custodian

This 17th century hunting lodge was destined to play a part in Charles II's escape from the Roundheads. A descendant of the Royal Oak, which sheltered the fugitive King from Cromwell's troops after the Battle of Worcester in 1651, still stands in the fields near Boscobel House. The timber-framed house where the King slept in a tiny 'sacred hole' has been fully restored and furnished in Victorian period and there are panelled rooms and secret hiding places. There is an exhibition in the house as well as the farmyard and smithy.

Location: OS127, SJ837 083. On unclassified road between A41 & A5. 8m NW of Wolverhampton.

Open: Contact site for details and special events dates.

Admission: Contact site for details. Family ticket available.

⬜ ♿Grounds. WC. 🍴 👤Obligatory. ⊠ ✳ 🛡 Tel for details.

BUILDWAS ABBEY ⚌

Iron Bridge, Telford, Shropshire TF8 7BW

Tel: 01952 433274

Owner: English Heritage   **Contact:** The Custodian

Extensive remains of a Cistercian abbey built in 1135, set beside the River Severn against a backdrop of wooded grounds. The remains include the church which is almost complete except for the roof.

Location: OS Ref. SJ642 044. On S bank of River Severn on A4169, 2m W of Ironbridge.

Open: Contact site for details. Closed Oct - Mar.

Admission: Contact site for details and special events dates.

⬜ ♿ 🅿

CLUN CASTLE ⚌

Clun, Ludlow, Shropshire

Tel: 0121 625 6820 (Regional Office)

Owner: English Heritage   **Contact:** The West Midlands Regional Office

Remains of a four-storey keep and other buildings of this border castle are set in outstanding countryside. Built in the 11th century.

Location: OS Ref. SO299 809. In Clun, off A488, 18m W of Ludlow. 9m W of Craven Arms.

Open: Any reasonable time.

Admission: Free.

⊠ ✳

COLEHAM PUMPING STATION

Longden Coleham, Shrewsbury, Shropshire SY3 7DN

Tel: 01743 361196   **Fax:** 01743 358411

e-mail: museums@shrewsbury.gov.uk   **www.**shrewsburymuseums.com

Owner: Shrewsbury & Atcham Borough Council   **Contact:** Mary White

Two Renshaw beam engines of 1901 are being restored to steam by members of Shrewsbury Steam Trust. One is now 'in steam' during the summer.

Location: OS Ref. SJ497 122. Shrewsbury town centre, near the River Severn.

Open: Apr - July & Sept: 4th Sun in each month, 10am - 4pm. Plus occasional other days. Details: 01743 361196.

Admission: Adult £1, Child 50p, Student £1.

♿Partial. 👤By arrangement. 🅿 No parking. ▮ 🦮 Guide dogs only.

COMBERMERE ABBEY

Whitchurch, Shropshire SY13 4AJ

Tel: 01948 662880   **Fax:** 01948 871604

e-mail: estate@combermereabbey.co.uk   **www.**combermereabbey.co.uk

Owner: Mrs S Callander Beckett   **Contact:** Mrs Jill Parker

Combermere Abbey, originally a Cistercian Monastery, and remodelled as a Gothic house in 1820 sits in a magnificent 1000 acre private parkland setting. Host to many remarkable historical personalities, the splendid 17th century Library and elegant Porter's Hall are licensed for weddings, receptions and corporate events. Excellent accommodation is available on the Estate.

Location: OS Ref. SJ590 440. 5m E of Whitchurch, off A530.

Open: By arrangement for groups.

Admission: Groups: £7 per person inclusive of refreshments.

ⓘNo photography. 📶 ♿Unsuitable. 👥By arrangement. 👤By arrangement. 🅿 Limited. 🔲 ⛺ ✳

DAVENPORT HOUSE

WORFIELD, Nr BRIDGNORTH, SHROPSHIRE WV15 5LE

www.davenporthouse.co.uk

Tel: 01746 716221 / 716345   **Fax:** 01746 716021

e-mail: murphy@davenporthouse.co.uk

Owner/Contact: Roger Murphy

A Grade I listed country house of 1726 by the architect Francis Smith of Warwick. The house sits within an extensive estate and is a popular regional venue for wedding receptions, Civil marriage ceremonies and corporate and social group entertainment.

Location: OS Ref. SO756 955. Worfield village, drive entrance by war memorial.

Open: Available for weddings and other functions throughout the year.

Admission: Please telephone for details.

📶 ♿ 🍴Licensed. 🅿 ⊠ ⛺ ✳

Michael Caldwell

DUDMASTON ✤
QUATT, BRIDGNORTH, SHROPSHIRE WV15 6QN

Tel: 01746 780866 **Fax:** 01746 780744 **e-mail:** dudmaston@nationaltrust.org.uk

Owner: The National Trust   **Contact:** The House & Visitor Services Manager

Late 17th century manor house. Contains furniture and china, Dutch flower paintings, watercolours, botanical art and modern pictures and sculpture, family and natural history. 9 acres of lakeside gardens and Dingle walk. Two estate walks 5½ m and 3½m starting from Hampton Loade car park.

Location: OS Ref. SO748 888. 4m SE of Bridgnorth on A442.

Open: 4 Apr - 29 Sept: Hall: Tues, Weds, Suns & BH Mons, 2 - 5.30pm. Last admission to house 5pm. Mons booked groups by arrangement. Garden: Mon - Wed & Suns, 12 noon - 6pm. Tearoom: 11.30am - 5.30pm.

Admission: House & Garden: Adult £4.50, Child £2.20, Family £10.50. Groups £3.50. Garden only: Adult £3.20, Child £1.40, free tours Mon afternoons.

ⓘ Countryside walks. ⬜ ♿ ▣ ⬛ In parkland and estate, on leads, not garden.

HAUGHMOND ABBEY ⌗
Upton Magna, Uffington, Shrewsbury, Shropshire SY4 4RW

Tel: 01743 709661

Owner: English Heritage   **Contact:** The Custodian

Extensive remains of a 12th century Augustinian abbey, including the Chapter House which retains its late medieval timber ceiling, and including some fine medieval sculpture.

Location: OS Ref. SJ542 152. 3m NE of Shrewsbury off B5062.

Open: Contact site for details. Closed Oct - Mar.

Admission: Contact site for details and special events dates.

⬜ ♿ ▣ ⬛ ☎ Tel for details.

HAWKSTONE HALL & GARDENS
Marchamley, Shrewsbury SY4 5LG

Tel: 01630 685242 **Fax:** 01630 685565

Owner: The Redemptorists   **Contact:** Guest Mistress

Grade I Georgian mansion and restored gardens set in spacious parkland.

Location: OS Ref. SJ581 299. Entrance 1m N of Hodnet on A442.

Open: Please contact for details.

Admission: Adult £4, Child £1.

HODNET HALL GARDENS 🏛
HODNET, MARKET DRAYTON, SHROPSHIRE TF9 3NN

Tel: 01630 685786 **Fax:** 01630 685853

Owner: Mr and the Hon Mrs A Heber-Percy   **Contact:** Mrs M Revie

There have been gardens at Hodnet since the 11th century when the Heber-Percy family constructed their first house in the parkland. Their serious development began in 1921 by the late Brigadier Heber-Percy. Today, the 60+ acres are renowned as amongst the finest in the country. Forest trees provide a wonderful backdrop for formal gardens planted to give delight during every season, and for woodland walks amongst flowering shrubs. There is a daisy chain of ornamental pools and lakes.

Tearooms serve light lunches and afternoon teas and adjacent is a gift shop.. The walled kitchen garden sells plants and produce in their season.

Location: OS Ref. SJ613 286. 12m NE of Shrewsbury on A53; M6/J15, M54/J3.

Open: 1 Apr - 30 Sept: Tue - Sun & BH Mons; Oct: Sun only, 12 noon - 5pm.

Admission: Adult £3.75, Child £1.75, OAP £3.25. Reduced rates for groups.

⬜ Gift Shop. ▣ Kitchen garden plants & produce. ☎ For groups. ⬛ ▣

⬛ Educational package linked to Key stages I & 2 of National Curriculum.

⬛ On leads.

West Midlands - England

IRON BRIDGE ⚏

Ironbridge, Shropshire

Tel: 0121 625 6820 (Regional Office)

Owner: English Heritage   **Contact:** The West Midlands Regional Office

The world's first iron bridge and Britain's best known industrial monument. Cast in Coalbrookdale by local ironmaster, Abraham Darby, it was erected across the River Severn in 1779. Iron Bridge is a World Heritage Site. Visit the recently refurbished Toll House on the Bridge, with interpretation displays.

Location: OS Ref. SJ672 034. In Ironbridge, adjacent to A4169.

Open: Any reasonable time.

Admission: Free crossing.

⊠ ✳

LANGLEY CHAPEL ⚏

Acton Burnell, Shrewsbury, Shropshire

Tel: 0121 625 6820 (Regional Office)

Owner: English Heritage   **Contact:** The West Midlands Regional Office

A delightful medieval chapel, standing alone in a field, with a complete set of early 17th century wooden fittings and furniture.

Location: OS Ref. SJ538 001. 1½ m S of Acton Burnell, on unclassified road 4m E of the A49, 9½ m S of Shrewsbury.

Open: Any reasonable time during the day. Key at farmhouse. Closed 24- 26 Dec & 1 Jan.

Admission: Free.

⊠ ✳

LILLESHALL ABBEY ⚏

Oakengates, Shropshire

Tel: 0121 625 6820 (Regional Office)

Owner: English Heritage   **Contact:** The West Midlands Regional Office

Extensive ruins of an abbey of Augustinian canons including remains of the 12th and 13th century church and the cloister buildings. Surrounded by green lawns and ancient yew trees.

Location: OS Ref. SJ738 142. On unclassified road off the A518, 4m N of Oakengates.

Open: Any reasonable time.

Admission: Free.

⊠ ✳

LONGNER HALL 🏠

Uffington, Shrewsbury, Shropshire SY4 4TG

Tel: 01743 709215

Owner: Mr R L Burton   **Contact:** Mrs R L Burton

Designed by John Nash in 1803, Longner Hall is a Tudor Gothic style house set in a park landscaped by Humphry Repton. The home of one family for over 700 years. Longner's principal rooms are adorned with plaster fan vaulting and stained glass.

Location: OS Ref. SJ529 110. 4m SE of Shrewsbury on Uffington road, ¼ m off B4380, Atcham.

Open: Apr - Oct: Tues & BH Mons, 2 - 5pm. Tours at 2pm & 3.30pm. Groups at any time by arrangement.

Admission: Adult £5, Child/OAP £3.

ⓘNo photography in house. ♿ Partial. ☛ By arrangement for groups. ⓕObligatory. ⓟLimited for coaches. ⬛By arrangement. ⬚ Guide dogs only. ✳

LUDLOW CASTLE

CASTLE SQUARE, LUDLOW, SHROPSHIRE SY8 1AY

www.ludlowcastle.com

Tel: 01584 873355

Owner: The Earl of Powis & The Trustees of the Powis Estate

Contact: Helen J Duce

900 year old castle of the Marches, dates from 1086 and extended over the centuries to a fortified Royal Palace. Seat of government for the Council for Wales and the Marches. Privately owned by the Earls of Powis since 1811. A magnificent ruin set in the heart of medieval Ludlow.

Location: OS Ref. SO509 745. Shrewsbury 28m, Hereford 26m. A49 centre of Ludlow.

Open: Jan: weekends only, 10am - 4pm, Feb - Mar & Oct - Dec: 10am - 4pm. Apr - Jul & Sept: 10am - 5pm. Aug: 10am - 7pm. Last adm. 30mins before closing. Closed 25 Dec.

Admission: Adult £3.50, Child £1.50, Conc. £3, Family £9.50. 10% reduction for groups (10+).

⌖ ♿Partial. ⓕBy arrangement. ⌂ ⓟNone. ⬛ ⊠ ✳ ⬚

MAWLEY HALL

CLEOBURY MORTIMER, DY14 8PN

www.mawley.com

Tel: 01299 270869 **Fax:** 01299 270022 **e-mail:** administration@mawley.com

Owner: R Galliers-Pratt Esq   **Contact:** Mrs R Sharp

Built in 1730 and attributed to Francis Smith of Warwick, Mawley is set in 18th century landscaped parkland with extensive gardens and walks down to the River Rea. Magnificent plasterwork and a fine collection of English and Continental furniture and porcelain.

Location: OS137, SO688 753. 1m N of Cleobury Mortimer on the A4117 and 7m W of Bewdley.

Open: 19 Apr - 22 Jul: Mons & Thurs, 3 - 5pm and throughout the year by appointment.

Admission: Adult £5, Child/OAP £3.

ⓘLunches, dinners & functions in association with Sean Hill of the Michelin starred restaurant, The Merchant House, in Ludlow.

🍽 ⓕBy arrangement. ⓟ ⬛ ⬚In grounds, on leads. ✳

MORETON CORBET CASTLE ⊞

Moreton Corbet, Shrewsbury, Shropshire
Tel: 0121 625 6820 (Regional Office)
Owner: English Heritage **Contact:** The West Midlands Regional Office
A ruined medieval castle with the substantial remains of a splendid Elizabethan mansion, captured in 1644 from Charles I's supporters by Parliamentary forces.
Location: OS Ref. SJ562 232. In Moreton Corbet off B5063, 7m NE of Shrewsbury.
Open: Any reasonable time.
Admission: Free.

MORVILLE HALL ⚘

Bridgnorth, Shropshire WV16 5NB
Tel: 01746 780838
Owner: The National Trust **Contact:** Dr & Mrs C Douglas
An Elizabethan house of mellow stone, converted in the 18th century and set in attractive gardens.
Location: OS Ref. SO668 940. Morville, on A458 3m W of Bridgnorth.
Open: By written appointment only with the tenants.

OAKLEY HALL

See page 345 for full page entry.

PREEN MANOR GARDENS

Church Preen, Church Stretton, Shropshire SY6 7LQ
Tel: 01694 771207
Owner/Contact: Mrs P Trevor-Jones
Six acre garden on site of Cluniac monastery, with walled, terraced, wild, water, kitchen and chess gardens. 12th century monastic church.
Location: OS Ref. SO544 981. 10m SSE of Shrewsbury. 7m NE of Church Stretton, 6m SW of Much Wenlock.
Open: 2 May: 2 - 5pm; 10 & 24 Jun, 15 & 29 Jul: 2 - 6pm; 3 Oct: 2 - 5pm.
Admission: Adult £3.50, Child 50p.

SHIPTON HALL 🏛

Much Wenlock, Shropshire TF13 6JZ
Tel: 01746 785225 **Fax:** 01746 785125
Owner: Mr J N R Bishop **Contact:** Mrs M J Bishop
Built around 1587 by Richard Lutwyche who gave the house to his daughter Elizabeth on her marriage to Thomas Mytton. Shipton remained in the Mytton family for the next 300 years. The house has been described as 'an exquisite specimen of Elizabethan architecture set in a quaint old fashioned garden, the whole forming a picture which as regards both form and colour, satisfies the artistic sense of even the most fastidious'. The Georgian additions by Thomas F Pritchard include some elegant rococo interior decorations. There is some noteworthy Tudor and Jacobean panelling. Family home. In addition to the house visitors are welcome to explore the gardens, the dovecote and the parish church which dates back to Saxon times.
Location: OS Ref. SO563 918. 7m SW of Much Wenlock on B4378. 10m W of Bridgnorth.
Open: Easter - end Sept: Thurs, 2.30 - 5.30pm. Also Suns and Mons of BH, 2.30 - 5.30pm. Groups of 20+ at any time of day or year by prior arrangement.
Admission: Adult £4, Child £2. Discount of 10% for groups (20+).
♿Unsuitable. ◼By arrangement for groups (20+). ⚑Obligatory. ⌨Guide dogs only.

SHREWSBURY CASTLE & THE SHROPSHIRE REGIMENTAL MUSEUM

Castle Street, Shrewsbury SY1 2AT
Tel: 01743 358516 **Fax:** 01743 358411 **e-mail:** museums@shrewsbury.gov.uk
www.shrewsburymuseums.com
Owner: Shrewsbury & Atcham Borough Council **Contact:** Louise Cliffe
Norman Castle with 18th century work by Thomas Telford. Free admission to attractive floral grounds. The main hall houses The Shropshire Regimental Museum and displays on the history of the castle. Open-air theatre, music and events throughout the summer.
Location: OS Ref. SJ495 128. Town centre, adjacent BR and bus stations.
Open: Main building & Museum: Late May BH - end Sept: Tue - Sat, 10am - 5pm; Sun & Mon, 10am - 4pm. Winter: Please call for details. Grounds: Mon - Sat, 10am - 5pm & Suns as above.
Admission: Museum: Adult £2, OAP £1, Shrewsbury residents, under 18s, Students & members of the regiments Free. Grounds: Free.
ⓘNo photography. ◻ ♿ 🅿None. ◼ ⌨Guide dogs only. ▲ ⌨Tel for details.

SHREWSBURY MUSEUM & ART GALLERY

Barker Street, Shrewsbury, Shropshire SY1 1QH
Tel: 01743 361196 **Fax:** 01743 358411
e-mail: museums@shrewsbury.gov.uk **www.**shrewsburymuseums.com
Owner: Shrewsbury and Atcham Borough Council **Contact:** Mary White
Impressive timber-framed building and attached 17th century brick mansion with archaeology and natural history, geology, social history and special exhibitions, including contemporary art.
Location: OS Ref. SJ490 126. Barker Street.
Open: Late May BH - end Sept: Tue - Sat, 10am - 5pm; Sun & Mon, 10am - 4pm. Rest of year: Tue - Sat, 10am - 4pm. Closed 21 Dec - 5 Jan.
Admission: Free.
ⓘNo photography. ◻ ♿Ground floor only. 🅿Adjacent public. ◼ ⌨Guide dogs only. ✳

STOKESAY CASTLE ⊞

Nr CRAVEN ARMS, SHROPSHIRE SY7 9AH

Tel: 01588 672544
Owner: English Heritage **Contact:** The Custodian
This perfectly preserved example of a 13th century fortified manor house gives us a glimpse of the life and ambitions of a rich medieval merchant. Lawrence of Ludlow built this country house to impress the landed gentry. Lawrence built a magnificent Great Hall where servants and guests gathered on feast days, but the family's private quarters were in the bright, comfortable solar on the first floor. From the outside the castle forms a picturesque grouping of castle, parish church and timber-framed Jacobean gatehouse set in the rolling Shropshire countryside.
Location: OS Ref. SO436 817. 7m NW of Ludlow off A49. 1m S of Craven Arms off A49.
Open: Contact site for details and special event dates.
Admission: Contact site for details. Family ticket available. 15% discount for groups (11+). Closed 24 - 26 Dec & 1 Jan.
◻ ♿Great Hall & gardens. WC. ⍰ ◻ 🅿 ✳ ⌨Tel for details.

West Midlands - England

WENLOCK GUILDHALL

Much Wenlock, Shropshire TF13 6AE

Tel: 01952 727509

Owner/Contact: Much Wenlock Town Council

16th century half-timbered building has an open-arcade market area.

Location: OS Ref. SJ624 000. In centre of Much Wenlock, next to the church.

Open: 1 Apr - 31 Oct: Mon - Sat, 10.30am - 1pm & 2 - 4pm. Suns: 2 - 4pm.

Admission: Adult 50p, Child Free.

WENLOCK PRIORY ⌗

Much Wenlock, Shropshire TF13 6HS

Tel: 01952 727466

Owner: English Heritage   **Contact:** The Custodian

A prosperous, powerful priory at its peak in the Middle Ages. A great deal of the structure still survives in the form of high, romantic ruined walls and it is the resting place of St Milburga the first Abbess. A monastery was first founded at Wenlock in the 7th century, and little more is known of the site until the time of the Norman Conquest when it became a Cluniac monastery. These majestic ruins of the priory church are set in green lawns and topiary, and there are substantial remains of the early 13th century church and Norman Chapter House.

Location: OS Ref. SJ625 001. In Much Wenlock.

Open: Contact site for details and special events. Closed 24 - 26 Dec & 1 Jan.

Admission: Contact site for details. Family ticket available.

ⓘWC. 🔲 🔲 **P** 🖀 ☀ 🔰Tel for details.

WESTON PARK 🏛   *See page 346 for full page entry.*

WOLLERTON OLD HALL GARDEN

Wollerton, Market Drayton, Shropshire TF9 3NA

Tel: 01630 685760 **Fax:** 01630 685583

Owner: Mr & Mrs J D Jenkins   **Contact:** Mrs Di Oakes

Three acre plantsman's garden created around a 16th century house (not open).

Location: OS Ref. SJ623 296. 14m NE of Shrewsbury off A53 between Hodnet and Market Drayton.

Open: Easter Good Fri - end Aug: Fris, Suns & BHs (Suns only in Sept), 12 noon - 5pm. Groups (25+) by appointment at other times.

Admission: Adult £4, Child £1.

WROXETER ROMAN CITY ⌗

Wroxeter, Shrewsbury, Shropshire SY5 6PH

Tel: 01743 761330

Owner: English Heritage   **Contact:** The Custodian

The part-excavated centre of the fourth largest city in Roman Britain, originally home to some 6,000 men and several hundred houses. Impressive remains of the 2nd century municipal baths. There is a site museum in which many finds are displayed, including those from recent work by Birmingham Field Archaeological Unit.

Location: OS Ref. SJ568 088. At Wroxeter, 5m E of Shrewsbury, on B4380.

Open: Contact site for details and special events. Closed 24 - 26 Dec & 1 Jan.

Admission: Contact site for details. Family ticket available.

ⓘWC. 🔲 🔲 🔲 **P** 🖀 ☀ 🔰Tel for details.

Weston Park, Shropshire from the book *Historic Family Homes and Gardens from the Air*, see page 54.

THE ANCIENT HIGH HOUSE

Greengate Streetm Stafford ST16 2JA

Tel: 01785 619131 **Fax:** 01785 619132 **e-mail:** ahh@staffordbc.gov.uk
www.staffordbc.gov.uk

Owner: Stafford Borough Council   **Contact:** Mark Hartwell

Over four hundred years of history are waiting to be discovered within the walls of Stafford's Ancient High House - England's largest timber-framed town house and one of the finest Tudor buildings in the country. Now fully restored, the superb period room settings reflect its fascinating story.

Location: OS Ref. SJ922 232. Town centre.

Open: All year: Tues - Sat, 10am - 4pm.

Admission: Free. Check for events, charges may apply.

🖥 🚫Unsuitable. 🛈By arrangement. 🖼School tours by arrangement. 🐕 Guide dogs only. ✳ 💺 Tel for details.

CHILLINGTON HALL 🏛

CODSALL WOOD, WOLVERHAMPTON, STAFFORDSHIRE WV8 1RE

www.chillingtonhall.co.uk

Tel: 01902 850236   **Fax:** 01902 850768
e-mail: mrsplod@chillingtonhall.co.uk
Owner/Contact: Mr & Mrs J W Giffard

Home of the Giffards since 1178. Built during 18th century by Francis Smith of Warwick and John Soane. Park designed by 'Capability' Brown. Smith's Staircase, Soane's Saloon, the legend of Giffard's Cross and the Pool (a lake of 70 acres) are splendid examples of the days of the Georgian landowner.

Location: OS Ref. SJ864 067. 2m S of Brewood off A449. 4m NW of M54/J2.

Open: Easter Sun; Suns prior to both May BHs; Jul: Thur & Sun; Aug: Wed - Fri & Sun, 2 - 5pm.

Admission: Adult £4, Child £2. Grounds only: half price.

🚫 Partial. 🛈 Obligatory. 🅿 🐕In grounds, on leads. €

BIDDULPH GRANGE GARDEN 🌿

GRANGE ROAD, BIDDULPH, STOKE-ON-TRENT ST8 7SD

Tel: 01782 517999 **Fax:** 01782 510624

Owner: The National Trust   **Contact:** The Garden Office

A rare and exciting survival of a High Victorian garden, restored by the National Trust. The garden is divided into a series of themed gardens within a garden, with a Chinese temple, Egyptian court, pinetum, dahlia walk, glen and many other settings. Difficult uneven levels, unsuitable for wheelchairs.

Location: OS Ref. SJ891 592. E of A527, 3¹/₂ m SE of Congleton, 8m N of Stoke-on-Trent.

Open: 27 Mar - 31 Oct: Wed - Fri, 12 noon - 5.30pm. Sats, Suns & BH Mons, 11am - 5.30pm or dusk. 1 Nov - 19 Dec: Sats & Suns, 11am - 3pm.

Admission: Adult £4.80, Child £2.40, Family (2+2) £12. Booked guided tours: £6.60. Groups (15+): £4. Nov & Dec: Adult £2, Child £1, Family £5. Voucher to visit Little Moreton Hall at a reduced fee when purchasing Adult ticket.

🖥 🚫Unsuitable for wheelchairs and people with mobility problems. 💻 🐕In car park, on leads.

THE DOROTHY CLIVE GARDEN

WILLOUGHBRIDGE, MARKET DRAYTON, SHROPSHIRE TF9 4EU

www.dorothyclivegarden.co.uk

Tel: 01630 647237 **Fax:** 01630 647902

Owner: Willoughbridge Garden Trust   **Contact:** Mrs M Grime

The Dorothy Clive Garden accommodates a wide range of choice and unusual plants providing year round interest. Features include a quarry with spectacular waterfall, flower borders, a scree and water garden. Tearoom serving home-baked hot and cold snacks throughout the day.

Location: OS Ref. SJ753 400. A51, 2m S of Woore, 3m from Bridgemere.

Open: 14 Mar - 31 Oct: daily, 10am - 5.30pm.

Admission: Adult £3.80, Child (11-16yrs) £1, (under 16yrs Free), OAP £3.30. Groups (20+) £3.30.

🚫 💻 🅿 🐕In grounds on leads.

CASTERNE HALL 🏛

Ilam Nr Ashbourne, Derbyshire DE6 2BA

Tel: 01335 310489 **e-mail:** info@casterne.co.uk **www.**casterne.co.uk

Owner/Contact: Charles & Susannah Hurt

Manor house in fine location.

Location: OS Ref. SK123 523. Take first turning on left N of Ilam and continue past 'No through Road' sign.

Open: 1 Apr - 7 May: weekdays only (except 9 & 12 Apr), plus May Day & Aug BH weekends, 10am - 1pm & 2 - 5pm. Please telephone in advance.

Admission: £4.

🚫 Partial. 🛈 Obligatory. 🖼 💺 🔺 €

DUNWOOD HALL

Longsdon, Nr Leek, Stoke-on-Trent, Staffordshire ST9 9AR

Tel: 01538 372978 **e-mail:** info@dunwoodhall.co.uk

www.dunwoodhall.co.uk

Owner: Dr R V Kemp/C Lovatt **Contact:** Camilla Lovatt

A fine example of Gothic Revival architecture built in 1871 as the country residence of a Victorian gentleman, who was Mayor of Burslem (a Potteries' town), and his family. The Hall features wrought iron and carved stone work and an impressive three-storey, galleried hall over an extensive Minton encaustic tiled floor.

Location: OS Ref. SJ947 544. On the A53 between Stoke-on-Trent and Leek, 3 miles West of Leek. Regular bus service on A53.

Open: Groups (15 - 50), by arrangement only.

Admission: Please telephone for details.

⊗ T & Partial. ⊞ ⊠ Obligatory. P Limited for cars, none for coaches. ⊠ Guide dogs only. ⊠ 3 doubles.

FORD GREEN HALL

Ford Green Road, Smallthorne, Stoke-on-Trent ST6 1NG

Tel: 01782 233195 **Fax:** 01782 233194

e-mail: ford.green.hall@stoke.gov.uk **www.**stoke.gov.uk/fordgreenhall

Owner: Stoke-on-Trent City Council **Contact:** Angela Graham

A 17th century house, home to the Ford family for two centuries. The hall has been designated a museum with an outstanding collection of original and reproduction period furniture, ceramics and textiles. There is a Tudor-style garden. The museum has an award-winning education service and regular events. Children's parties available.

Location: OS Ref. SJ887 508. NE of Stoke-on-Trent on B505, signposted from A500.

Open: All year: (closed 25 Dec - 1 Jan), Sun - Thurs, 1 - 5pm.

Admission: Charge applies. Special group packages & packages with other visitor attractions (must book, min 10).

⊡ ⊗ & Partial. WC. ⊞ P ⊞ ⊠ In grounds, on leads. ⊠ ⊞ ⊞ Tel for details.

IZAAK WALTON'S COTTAGE

Worston Lane, Shallowford, Nr Stafford ST15 0PA

Tel/Fax: 01785 760278 (Apr - Oct) 01785 619619 (Nov - Mar)

e-mail: ahh@staffordbc.gov.uk **www.**staffordbc.gov.uk.heritage

Owner: Stafford Borough Council **Contact:** Gillian Bould

Stafford's rural heritage is embodied in Izaak Walton's Cottage, the charming 17th century home of the celebrated author of *The Compleat Angler*. Izaak Walton's Cottage gives a fascinating insight into the history of angling and the life of a writer whose work remains 'a unique celebration of the English countryside.'

Location: OS Ref. SJ876 293. M6/J14, A5013 towards Eccleshall, signposted on A5013.

Open: Apr - Oct: Wed - Sun & BHs, 1 - 5pm. Closed Nov - Mar.

Admission: Free. Check for events, charges may apply.

⊡ & Partial. WCs. ⊞ P Limited for cars. ⊠ Guide dogs only. ⊠

ERASMUS DARWIN HOUSE ⌂

BEACON STREET, LICHFIELD, STAFFORDSHIRE WA13 7AD

www.erasmusdarwin.org

Tel: 01543 306260 **e-mail:** erasmus.d@virgin.net

Owner: The Erasmus Darwin Foundation **Contact:** Judith Franklin

Grandfather of Charles Darwin and a founder member of the Lunar Society, Erasmus Darwin (1731-1802) was a leading doctor, scientist, inventor and poet. This elegant Georgian house was his home and contains an exhibition of his life, theories, and inventions. There is also an 18th century herb garden.

Location: OS Ref. SK115 098. Situated at the W end of Lichfield Cathedral Close.

Open: Please telephone for details.

Admission: Adult £3, Child/Conc. £2.50. Groups (10-50) Adult £2.50, Child/Conc. £2.

⊡ ⊗ T & ⊠ By arrangement. ⊡ P Disabled only. ⊞ ⊠ Guide dogs only. ⊞

Shugborough, Staffordshire.

NT Photographic Library / Nick Meers

Website Information see front section

NT Photographic Library / Andreas Von Einsiedel

NT Photographic Library / Nick Meers

MOSELEY OLD HALL ✣
FORDHOUSES, WOLVERHAMPTON WV10 7HY

Tel: 01902 782808

Owner: The National Trust   **Contact:** The Property Manager

An Elizabethan timber-framed house encased in brick in 1870; with original interiors. Charles II hid here after the Battle of Worcester. The bed in which he slept is on view as well as the hiding place he used. An exhibition retells the story of the King's dramatic escape from Cromwell's troops, and there are optional, free guided tours. The garden has been reconstructed in 17th century style with formal box parterre, only 17th century plants are grown. The property is a Sandford Education Award Winner.

Location: OS Ref. SJ932 044. 4m N of Wolverhampton between A449 and A460.

Open: 20 Mar - 31 Oct: Sats, Suns, Weds, BH Mons & following Tues. 7 Nov - 19 Dec: Suns (guided tour only). Times: Mar - end Oct: 1 - 5pm (garden & tearoom from 12 noon). BH Mons: 11am - 5pm (whole property). Nov & Dec: 1 - 4pm (garden & tearoom from 12 noon). Sun 7 Mar: pre-season preview: Ground floor of house, garden, tearoom & shop: 1 - 4pm (garden & tearoom from 12 noon). Pre-booked groups at other times.

Admission: Adult £4.60, Child £2.30, Family £11.50.

⬚ ♿ Ground floor & grounds. WC. ☕ Tearoom in 18th century barn.
🐕 Guide dogs only.

SAMUEL JOHNSON BIRTHPLACE MUSEUM
Breadmarket Street, Lichfield, Staffordshire WS13 6LG

Tel: 01543 264972   **Fax:** 01543 414779

Owner: Lichfield City Council   **Contact:** Annette French

The house where his father had a bookshop is now a museum with many of Johnson's personal belongings.

Location: OS Ref. SK115 094. Breadmarket Street, Lichfield.

Open: 1 Apr - 30 Sept: daily: 10.30am - 4.30pm. 1 Oct - 31 Mar: daily, 12 noon- 4.30pm.

Admission: Free. Check for events, charges may apply.

Josiah Wedgwood
18th Century Potter & Designer of Decorative Ware
1730-1795

Potter and Designer

Wedgwood established a hugely successful pottery company which still exists today and is known for its high quality chinaware. Wedgwood introduced new designs and processes for the production of pottery, and became famous for innovations such as 'Jasper Ware' – much of which was made into medallions and plaques to go over chimney-pieces and on mural decorations. Look for his decorative collaborations with the architects and decorators, Robert Adam and James Wyatt.

SANDON HALL
SANDON, STAFFORDSHIRE ST18 0BZ

www.sandonhall.co.uk

Tel/Fax: 01889 508004   **e-mail:** info@sandonhall.co.uk

Owner: The Earl of Harrowby   **Contact:** Michael Bosson

Ancestral seat of the Earls of Harrowby, conveniently located in the heart of Staffordshire. The imposing neo-Jacobean house was rebuilt by William Burn in 1854. Set amidst 400 acres of glorious parkland, Sandon, for all its grandeur and elegance, is first and foremost a home. The family museum which opened in 1994 has received considerable acclaim, and incorporates several of the State Rooms. The 50 acre landscaped gardens feature magnificent trees and are especially beautiful in May and autumn.

Location: OS Ref. SJ957 287. 5m NE of Stafford on the A51, between Stone and Lichfield, easy access from M6/J14.

Open: All year: for events, functions and for pre-booked visits to the museum and gardens. Evening tours by special arrangement. Closed 22 Dec - 4 Jan.

Admission: Museum: Adult £4, Child £3, OAP £3.50. Gardens: Adult £1.50, Child £1, OAP £1. NB. Max group size 22 or 45 if combined Museum and Gardens.

⛲ ♿ Grounds. ☕ By arrangement. 👥 Obligatory. 🅿 Limited for coaches.
🐕 In grounds, on leads. ▲ ✳ ☎ Tel for details.

SHUGBOROUGH 🌺
STAFFORD

www.staffordshire.gov.uk/shugborough

Tel: 01889 881388 **Fax:** 01889 881323
e-mail:shugborough.promotions@staffordshire.gov.uk

Owner: The National Trust   **Contact:** Sales and Marketing Office

Shugborough is the magnificent 900-acre ancestral home of the 5th Earl of Lichfield. The 18th century mansion house contains a fine collection of ceramics, silver, paintings and French furniture. Part of the house is still lived in by the Earl and his family. Visitors can enjoy the splendid 18-acre Grade I Historic Garden with its Riverside Walk and terraces. A unique collection of neo-classical monuments by James Stuart can be found in the parkland which also includes walks and trails. The working laundry, kitchens and brewhouse have all been restored and are staffed by costumed guides. Shugborough Park Farm is a Georgian working farm which features an agricultural museum, restored working corn mill and is also a rare breeds

centre. In the farmhouse kitchen visitors can see bread baked in brick ovens and in the dairy, cheese and butter being made. Throughout the year themed tours are in operation for the coach market and there is an award-winning educational programme for schools. Shugborough is an ideal venue for weddings, conferences, corporate activity days and product launches.

Location: OS Ref. SJ992 225. 10mins from M6/J13 on A513 Stafford/Lichfield Road. Rail: Stafford 6m. Taxi: Anthony's 01785 252255

Opening Times: Please call 01889 881388 for full details.

Admission: Please call 01889 881388 for full details.

⬜ℹ️No photography in house. 🚻 ♿WCs. Stairclimber to house. Batricars available. 🍷Licensed. 🐕 ⬜ 🅿 ⬜ 🐾In grounds, on leads.⬜✳️📺Tel for details.

STAFFORD CASTLE & VISITOR CENTRE
Newport Road, Stafford ST16 1DJ

Tel/Fax: 01785 257698 **e-mail:** castlebc@btconnect.com

Owner: Stafford Borough Council   **Contact:** Mark Hartwell

Stafford Castle has dominated the Stafford landscape for over 900 years of turbulent history. William the Conqueror first built Stafford Castle as a fortress to subdue the local populace. The visitor centre – built in the style of a Norman guardhouse – features an audio-visual area that brings its turbulent past to life.

Location: OS Ref. SJ904 220. On N side of A518, 1¹⁄₂ m WSW of town centre.

Open: Apr - Oct: Tue - Sun, 10am - 5pm (open BHs). Nov - Mar: Sat & Sun, 10am - 4pm.

Admission: Free (admission charges may apply for events).

🐕By arrangement. ✳️

WALL ROMAN SITE (Letocetum) ⚏ 🌺
Watling Street, Nr Lichfield, Staffordshire WS14 0AW

Tel: 01543 480768

Owner: English Heritage   **Contact:** The Custodian

The remains of a staging post alongside Watling Street. Foundations of an Inn and a Bath House can be seen and there is a display of finds in the site museum.

Location: OS139, SK099 067. Off A5 at Wall, nr Lichfield.

Open: Contact site for details & Special Events.

Admission: Contact site for details.

ℹ️WC. ⬜ ⬜ 🅿 🐾 📺 Tel for details.

🖼️ **Accommodation Index** see front section

WHITMORE HALL 🏛️
WHITMORE, NEWCASTLE-UNDER-LYME ST5 5HW

Tel: 01782 680478 **Fax:** 01782 680906

Owner: Mr Guy Cavenagh-Mainwaring   **Contact:** Mr Michael Cavenagh-Thornhill

Whitmore Hall is a Grade I listed building, designated as a house of outstanding architectural and historical interest, and is a fine example of a small Carolinian manor house, although parts of the hall date back to a much earlier period. The hall has beautifully proportioned light rooms, curving staircase and landing. There are some good family portraits to be seen with a continuous line, from 1624 to the present day. It has been the family seat, for over 900 years, of the Cavenagh-Mainwarings who are direct descendants of the original Norman owners. The interior of the hall has recently been refurbished and is in fine condition. The grounds include a beautiful home park with a lime avenue leading to the house, as well as landscaped gardens encompassing an early Victorian summer house. One of the outstanding features of Whitmore is the extremely rare example of a late Elizabethan stable block, the ground floor is part cobbled and has nine oak-carved stalls.

Location: OS Ref. SJ811 413. On A53 Newcastle - Market Drayton Road, 3m from M6/J15.

Open: 1 May - 31 Aug: Tues, Weds, 2 - 5pm (last tour 4.30pm). Groups (15+) by arrangement only outside normal opening days (between 1 Apr - 31 Aug). Groups (15+) may be booked in other months of the year, if convenient to the owner.

Admission: Adult £3, Child 50p.

♿ Ground floor & grounds.

🍷Afternoon teas for booked groups (15+), May - Aug. 🅿 ✳️

Map 5

Owner:
The Viscount Daventry

▶ **CONTACT**

Miss Brenda Newell
Arbury Hall
Nuneaton
Warwickshire
CV10 7PT

Tel: 024 7638 2804
Fax: 024 7664 1147
e-mail: brenda.newell@
arburyhall.net

▶ **LOCATION**
OS Ref. SP335 893

London, M1, M6/J3
(A444 to Nuneaton),
2m SW of Nuneaton.
1m W of A444.

Chester A51, A34, M6
(from J14 to J3),
2¹/₂ hrs.
Nuneaton 10 mins.

London 2 hrs,
Birmingham ¹/₂ hr,
Coventry 20 mins.

Bus: Nuneaton 3m.

Rail: Nuneaton
Station 3m.

Air: Birmingham
International 17m.

CONFERENCE/FUNCTION

ROOM	SIZE	MAX CAPACITY
Dining Room	35' x 28'	120
Saloon	35' x 30'	70
Long Gallery	48' x 11'	40
Stables Tearooms	31' x 18'	80

ARBURY HALL 🏛

NUNEATON

Arbury Hall has been the seat of the Newdegate family for over 400 years and is the ancestral home of Viscount Daventry. This Tudor/Elizabethan House was gothicised by Sir Roger Newdegate in the 18th century and is regarded as the 'Gothic Gem' of the Midlands. The Hall contains a fine collection of both oriental and Chelsea porcelain, portraits by Lely, Reynolds, Devis and Romney and furniture by Chippendale and Hepplewhite. The principal rooms, with their soaring fan vaulted ceilings and plunging pendants and filigree tracery, stand as a most breathtaking and complete example of early Gothic Revival architecture and provide a unique and

fascinating venue for corporate entertaining, product launches, receptions, fashion shoots and activity days. Exclusive use of this historic Hall, its gardens and parkland is offered to clients. The Hall stands in the middle of beautiful parkland with landscaped gardens of rolling lawns, lakes and winding wooded walks. Spring flowers are profuse and in June rhododendrons, azaleas and giant wisteria provide a beautiful environment for the visitor.

George Eliot, the novelist, was born on the estate and Arbury Hall and Sir Roger Newdegate were immortalised in her book *'Scenes of Clerical Life'*.

🎁 ℹ️ Corporate hospitality, film location, small conferences, product launches and promotions, marquee functions, clay pigeon shooting, archery and other sporting activities, grand piano in Saloon, helicopter landing site. No cameras or video recorders indoors,.

🍽 Exclusive lunches and dinners for corporate parties in dining room, max. 50, buffets 120.

♿ Visitors may alight at the Hall's main entrance. Parking in allocated areas. Ramp access to main hall.

☕ By arrangement for groups.

🚶 Obligatory. Tour time: 1hr.

🅿 200 cars and 3 coaches 250 yards from house. Follow tourist signs. Approach map available for coach drivers.

🎒 Welcome, must book. School room available.

🐕 In gardens on leads. Guide dogs only in house.

❄️ 🛡 Tel for details.

▶ **OPENING TIMES**
All Year

Open all year on Tues, Weds & Thurs only, for corporate events.

Pre-booked visits to the Hall and Gardens for groups of 25+ on Tues, Weds & Thurs (until 4pm) from Easter to the end of September.

Hall & Gardens open 2 - 5pm on BH weekends only (Suns & Mons) Easter - September.

▶ **ADMISSION**
Summer

Hall & Gardens
Adult £6.50
Child (up to 14 yrs.).. £4.00
Family (2+2) £16.00

Gardens Only
Adult £4.50
Child (up to 14 yrs.).... £3.00

Groups (25+)
Adult £5.50

Special rates for pre-booked groups of 25+.

Map 5

BADDESLEY CLINTON ❧

KNOWLE

www.nationaltrust.org.uk

Enjoy a day at Baddesley Clinton, the medieval moated manor house with hidden secrets! One of the most enchanting properties owned by the National Trust, Baddesley Clinton has seen little change since 1633 when Henry Ferrers 'the Antiquary' died. He was Squire at Baddesley for almost seventy years and remodelled the house over a long period of time, introducing much of the panelling and chimney pieces. Henry was proud of his ancestry and began the tradition at Baddesley of armorial glass, which has continued until the present day. Henry let the house in the 1590s when it became a refuge for Jesuit priests, and hiding places, called 'priest holes', created for their concealment, survive from this era. Pictures painted by Rebecca, wife of Marmion Edward Ferrers, remain to show how the romantic character of Baddesley was enjoyed in the late 19th century when the family also re-created a sumptuously furnished Chapel.

The garden, which surrounds the house, incorporates many features including stewponds: a small lake (the 'Great Pool'); a walled garden with thatched summer house and a lakeside walk with nature trail and wildflower meadow. Make a day of it! Revised opening times and substantial discounts on joint ticket prices make a combined visit to Baddesley Clinton and Packwood House even more attractive, especially since both properties are only two miles apart.

Owner:
The National Trust

▶ CONTACT

Rising Lane, Baddesley Clinton, Knowle, Solihull B93 0DQ

Tel: 01564 783294
Fax: 01564 782706

e-mail:
baddesleyclinton@
nationaltrust.org.uk

▶ LOCATION
OS Ref. SP199 715

³/₄m W of A4141 Warwick/Birmingham road at Chadwick End.

▶ OPENING TIMES

House
3 Mar - 7 Nov:
Wed - Sun, Good Friday & BH Mons.

Mar, Apr, Oct & Nov:
1.30 - 5pm;

May - end Sept:
1.30 - 5.30pm.

Grounds
3 Mar - 12 Dec:
Wed - Sun, Good Friday & BH Mons.

Mar, Apr, Oct & 3 - 7 Nov:
12 noon - 5pm;

May - end Sept:
12 noon - 5.30pm;

10 Nov - 12 Dec:
12 noon - 4.30pm.

▶ ADMISSION

Adult	£6.20
Child	£3.10
Family	£15.50

Grounds only

Adult	£3.10
Child	£1.55
Groups per person	£5.00
Guided tours (out of hours)	£10.00

Combined Ticket with Packwood House

Adult	£9.00
Child	£4.50
Family	£22.50

Gardens only

Adult	£4.50
Child	£2.25
Groups	£7.20

 ❀ ⊤ ♿ Partial. WC. Licensed. ⚑ By arrangement. ▣ ⌁ Guide dogs only. ⛨ Tel for details.

Map 5

COUGHTON COURT 🏛

ALCESTER

www.coughtoncourt.co.uk

Owner:
Mrs C Throckmorton

▶ **CONTACT**

Sales Office
Coughton Court
Alcester
Warwickshire   B49 5JA

Tel: 01789 400777
Fax: 01789 765544

Visitor Information:
01789 762435

e-mail: sales@
throckmortons.co.uk

▶ **LOCATION**

OS Ref. SP080 604

Located on A435,
2m N of Alcester,
8m NW of
Stratford-on-Avon.
18m from Birmingham
City Centre.

Rail: Birmingham
International.

Air: Birmingham
International.

Coughton Court has been the home of the Thockmortons since the 15th century and the family still live here today. The magnificent Tudor gatehouse was built around 1530 with the north and south wings completed 10 or 20 years later. The gables and the first storey of these wings are of typical mid-16th century half-timbered work.

Of particular interest to visitors is the Thockmorton family history from Tudor times to the present generation. On view are family portraits through the centuries with other family memorabilia and recent photographs. Also furniture, tapestries and porcelain.

A long-standing Roman Catholic theme runs through the family history as the Thockmortons have maintained their Catholic religion until the present day. The house has a strong connection with the Gunpowder Plot and also suffered damage during the Civil War. Exhibitions on the Gunpowder Plot as well as Children's Clothes (included in price).

GARDENS

The house stands in 25 acres of gardens and grounds along with two churches (both open to visitors) and a lake. A formal garden was constructed in 1992 with designs based on an Elizabethan knot garden in the courtyard. A new 1½ acre garden was opened in 1996 and is now one of Britain's finest walled gardens. Visitors can also enjoy a specially created walk beside the River Arrow and a new bog garden opened in 1997.

ⓘ Receptions, special dinners, filming, buffets, business meetings, fairs and company activity days. The excellent acoustics of the Saloon make it ideal for concerts, especially chamber music. Marquees can be erected on the large lawn area, grand piano. No photography or stiletto heels in house.

🅰 ❄

🍽 Buffet or sit-down meals can be provided by arrangement, in the Dining Room and Saloon. In-house catering can be arranged for other events. Civil marriages & wedding receptions welcome.

♿ Ground floor of house, gardens & restaurant. WC.

🍽🍴 Licensed restaurant, 11am - 5.30pm. Capacity 100 inside and 60 outside.

👤 By arrangement. Ask for group organisers brochure.

🅿 Unlimited for cars plus 4 coaches. 75p charge.

📕 Teacher's pack available.

🐕 Car park only.

🔔   🛡 Tel for details.

CONFERENCE/FUNCTION

ROOM	SIZE	MAX CAPACITY
Dining Rm	45' x 27'	60
Saloon	60' x 36'	100

The Saloon, which has particularly good acoustics, is often used for music recording.

▶ **OPENING TIMES**

House

March & October:
Sat & Sun only;

April - June & September:
Wed - Sun, BH Mons & Tues (12/13 Apr, 3/4 & 31 May & 1 Jun).
Closed Good Fri (9 Apr) & 26 Jun;

July & August:
Tue - Sun, BH Mons & Tues (30/31 Aug);
11.30am - 5pm.

House may close early some Sats, check on the visitor information line:
01789 762435.

Gardens, Restaurant, Shop & Plant Centre:
Dates as house,
11am - 5.30pm.

Walled Garden
Dates as house,
11.30am - 4.45pm.

▶ **ADMISSION**

House & Gardens

Adult £8.25
Child* (5-15yrs)........ £4.15
Family (2+2).......... £23.90
Family (2+3).......... £27.65
Booked Groups (15+)
   per person £7.00

Gardens only

Adult £5.50
Child* (5-15yrs)........ £2.75
Family (2+2).......... £16.00
Family (2+3).......... £18.50
Groups (15+)
   per person £4.10

*under 5yrs Free.

PACKWOOD HOUSE 🌿

LAPWORTH

www.nationaltrust.org.uk

Map 5

Owner:
The National Trust

▶ **CONTACT**

Packwood House
Lapworth
Solihull B94 6AT

Tel: 01564 783294
Fax: 01564 782706

e-mail:
packwoodhouse@
nationaltrust.org.uk

▶ **LOCATION**
OS Ref. SP174 722

2m E of Hockley Heath
(on A3400), 11m SE of
central Birmingham.

Packwood lies in the pleasantly wooded Forest of Arden and was, for many years, the home of the Fetherstons, who allowed Cromwell's General, Henry Ireton, to stay overnight before the Battle of Edgehill in 1642. There is also a tradition that Charles II was given refreshment at Packwood after his defeat at Worcester in 1651. Many of Packwood's interiors were designed in the 1920s and 30s in idealised Elizabethan or Jacobean styles for Graham Baron Ash. They offer a wonderful insight into the taste, rich decoration and way of life of a wealthy connoisseur in the period between the wars. Packwood still retains the intimate atmosphere of a real home, with lavishly furnished rooms containing French and Flemish tapestries and fine 17th & 18th century furniture. The oak panelled bedrooms with their sumptuous four-poster beds give you a glimpse of what it was like to stay the night as Baron Ash's

guest. Queen Mary, another regal guest who took refreshment here, visited in August 1927. Look out for several reminders of that historic visit throughout the house.

The house is surrounded by its own delightful, tranquil grounds. A large flower garden complete with long terraced herbaceous borders, enclosed by red brick walls with a gazebo in each corner, is a blend of the traditional country house garden and the Carolean Garden of the Fetherstons. The famous 17th century Yew Garden is traditionally said to represent 'The Sermon on the Mount' and is a highly unusual and attractive feature. Make a day of it! Revised opening times and substantial discounts on joint ticket prices make a combined visit to Packwood House and Baddesley Clinton even more attractive, especially since both properties are only two miles apart.

▶ **OPENING TIMES**

House
3 March - 7 November:
Wed - Sun, Good Friday
& BH Mons:
12 noon - 4.30pm.

Garden
3 March - 7 November:
Wed - Sun, Good Friday
& BH Mons;

March , April, October &
November:
11am - 4.30pm;

May - end September:
11am - 5.30pm.

Park & Woodland Walks
All year: daily.

▶ **ADMISSION**

Adult	£5.60
Child	£2.80
Family	£14.00

Garden only

Adult	£2.80
Child	£1.40
Groups	£4.50pp

Guided tours
out of hours | £9.00

Combined Ticket with Baddesley Clinton

Adult	£9.00
Child	£4.50
Family	£22.50

Gardens only

Adult	£4.50
Child	£2.25
Groups	£7.20pp

Partial. By arrangement.
Guide dogs only. Parkland only. Tel for details.

Map 5

RAGLEY HALL

ALCESTER

www.ragleyhall.com

Ragley Hall, the family home of the Marquess and Marchioness of Hertford, was designed by Robert Hooke, the inventive genius, in 1680 and is one of the earliest and loveliest of England's great Palladian Houses. The perfect symmetry of the architecture of Ragley remains unchanged save for the spectacular portico by Wyatt added in 1780.

The majestic Great Hall, soaring two storeys high, is adorned with some of England's finest and most exquisite baroque plasterwork by James Gibbs, dated 1750.

Ragley houses a superb collection of 18th century and earlier paintings, china, and furniture and wonderful ceilings decorated with Grisaille panels and insets by Angelica Kauffman.

A most striking feature of Ragley is the breathtaking mural "The Temptation" by Graham Rust in the south staircase hall, that was painted between 1969 and 1983.

Ragley is a working estate with more than 6000 acres of land. The house is set in 400 acres of picturesque parkland landscaped by Lancelot "Capability" Brown and 27 acres of fascinating gardens including the enchanting rose garden, richly planted borders and mature woodland.

Near to the Hall the working stables, designed by James Gibbs in 1751, house a collection of carriages dating back to 1760 and equestrian equipment.

For children there is an exciting woodland adventure playground, 3D maze and an extensive lakeside play and picnic area, and for walkers the delightful woodland walk.

Owner:
The Marquess of Hertford

▶ **CONTACT**

Bryan McDonald
General Manager
Ragley Hall
Alcester
Warwickshire B49 5NJ

Tel: 01789 762090
Fax: 01789 764791

e-mail:
bryanmcdonald@
ragleyhall.com

▶ **LOCATION**

OS Ref. SP073 555

Off A46/A435 1m SW of Alcester. From London 100m, M40 via Oxford and Stratford-on-Avon.

Rail: Evesham Station 9m.

Air: Birmingham International 20m.

Taxi: 007 Taxi 01789 414007

CONFERENCE/FUNCTION

ROOM	SIZE	MAX CAPACITY
Great Hall	70' x 40'	150
Red Saloon	30' x 40'	40
Hertford	45' x 22'	60
Seymour	25' x 23'	30

i Product launches, dinners and activity days, film and photographic location, park, lake and picnic area, marquee. No photography or camcorders in the house.

🛍

🍽 Wedding ceremonies and receptions, private and corporate entertainment, conferences and seminars.

♿ Visitors may alight at entrance. Parking in allocated areas. WCs. Lifts. Tearoom on ground floor. Electric scooter for visiting the gardens may be available. Please enquire.

☕ Tearoom in the Park and licensed Terrace tearoom. Groups please book.

🍴 Licensed.

🚶 By arrangement.

P Coach drivers admitted free and receive info pack and voucher. Please advise of group visits.

📋 Welcome. Teachers' packs and work modules on request. Adventure Wood and Woodland Walk.

🐕 In grounds, on leads. 🔔

🛡 Please visit website or telephone for details.

▶ **OPENING TIMES**

Summer:
3 April - 26 September

House
Thur - Sun & BH Mons
12 noon - 5.30pm (last admission 4.30pm).

Garden, Park & Adventure Playground
Thur - Sun & BH Mons, also daily in school holidays:
3 - 18 Apr, 29 May - 6 Jun, 17 Jul - 5 Sept.
10am - 6pm (last admission 4.30pm).

Winter:
October - March

Open by special arrangement with the General Manager.

▶ **ADMISSION**

House, Garden, Park & Adventure Playground incl.

Adult £7.50
Child (5-16yrs)....... £4.50
Conc. £6.50
Family (2+4) £25.00

Garden, Park & Adventure Playground only

Adult £6.00
Child (5-16yrs)....... £4.50
Conc. £5.50
Family (2+4) £22.00

Concessionary admission for groups, please enquire.

Season tickets available for families and individuals, please enquire.

THE SHAKESPEARE HOUSES

STRATFORD-UPON-AVON

www.shakespeare.org.uk

Map 5

Owner:
The Shakespeare Birthplace Trust

▶ **CONTACT**

The Shakespeare Birthplace Trust
Henley Street
Stratford-upon-Avon
CV37 6QW

Tel: 01789 204016
(General enquiries)
Tel: 01789 201806/201836
(Group Visits)
01789 201808
(Special/Evening Visits).
Fax: 01789 263138

e-mail: info@shakespeare.org.uk
groups@shakespeare.org.uk

▶ **LOCATION**

OS Refs:
Birthplace - SP201 552
New Place - SP201 548
Hall's Croft - SP200 546
Hathaway's - SP185 547
Arden's - SP166 582

Rail: Direct service from London (Paddington)

2 hrs from London
45 mins from Birmingham by car.

4m from M40/J15 and well signed from all approaches.

These five Shakespeare Houses, all authentic and directly linked to William Shakespeare and his family, offer a great insight into the world of the famous writer, his life and his work. Experience and enjoy the architectural character, period furniture, special collections, attractive gardens, grounds and walks, and craft displays.

In Town: Shakespeare's Birthplace: The half-timbered house, where William Shakespeare was born in 1564, continued as the family home until the 19th century and has welcomed visitors for well over 250 years. The house offers a fascinating insight into life as it was when Shakespeare was a child. Includes Shakespeare Exhibition – an introduction to his life, work and times, and a beautiful traditional English garden.

Nash's House and New Place: Once owned by Thomas Nash, who married Shakespeare's granddaughter Elizabeth. In addition to exceptional furnishings of Shakespeare's time, the house also contains displays on the history of Stratford. Outside lies the site of Shakespeare's final Stratford home – discover why it was demolished. Stroll in the Elizabethan-style knot garden and rest awhile in Shakespeare's Great Garden.

Hall's Croft: Named after Dr John Hall who married Shakespeare's daughter Susanna. This impressive 16th century house, with Jacobean additions, includes outstanding furniture and paintings. See the exhibition of medicine in Shakespeare's time with references to remedies and potions mentioned in the plays. The large peaceful garden is home to an ancient mulberry tree and a herbal bed.

Out of Town: Anne Hathaway's Cottage: This world famous, picturesque thatched cottage, childhood home of Shakespeare's wife, continued to be owned by Anne Hathaway's descendants until the late 19th century. It still contains the Hathaway bed. Outside lies a beautiful cottage garden and a tree and sculpture garden including a maze. There are many pleasant walks leading from the cottage.

Mary Arden's House and The Shakespeare Countryside Museum: Great for a family day out, the site includes the home of Shakespeare's mother before she married John Shakespeare. The site today, with its many farm buildings, activities and rare breeds of farm animals, brings to life for visitors and families the work and traditions of the countryside around Stratford-upon-Avon from Shakespeare's time to the early 20th century. The grounds also feature rare livestock and a falconry with displays throughout the day.

© Shakespeare Houses

ℹ City Sightseeing guided bus tour service connecting the town houses with Anne Hathaway's Cottage and Mary Arden's House, does not include admission to houses. No photography inside houses.

🛍 Shops at Shakespeare's Birthplace, Hall's Croft, Anne Hathaway's Cottage and Mary Arden's House.

🍽 Available, details upon request.

♿ WCs. Naturally difficult levels but much for disabled to enjoy at Mary Arden's House, ground floor & gardens accessible. Virtual reality tour at Shakespeare's Birthplace & Anne Hathaway's Cottage.

🍴 Available on site or close by.

🚶 By special arrangement.

🅿 The Trust provides a free coach terminal for delivery and pick-up of groups, maximum stay 30 mins at Shakespeare's Birthplace. Parking at Anne Hathaway's Cottage and Mary Arden's House.

👤 Available for all houses. For information 01789 201804.

🐕 Guide dogs only. ❄

▶ **OPENING TIMES**

Mid Season:
Apr - May & Sept - Oct.

Birthplace & Mary Arden's House
Mon - Sat: 10am - 5pm.
Suns: 10.30am - 5pm.

Hall's Croft & Nash's House & New Place
Daily: 11am - 5pm.

Anne Hathaway's
Mon - Sat: 9.30am - 5pm.
Suns: 10am - 5pm.

Summer Season:
Jun - Aug.

Birthplace & Anne Hathaway's
Mon - Sat: 9am - 5pm.
Suns: 9.30am - 5pm.

Mary Arden's House, Hall's Croft & Nash's House & New Place
Mon - Sat: 9.30am - 5pm.
Suns: 10am - 5pm.

Winter Season:
Nov - Mar.

Birthplace & Anne Hathaway's & Mary Arden's House
Mon - Sat: 10am - 4pm.
Suns: 10.30am - 4pm.
(Anne Hathaway's 10am - 4pm)

Hall's Croft & Nash's House
Daily: 11am - 4pm.

Closed 23 - 26 Dec.
All times are for admission to last entry.

▶ **ADMISSION**

Multiple house tickets for all five houses and the three in-town houses and single house tickets are available. Please telephone 01789 204016 for further information or visit www.shakespeare.org.uk

© NT Severn/R Charlton

UPTON HOUSE

BANBURY

www.nationaltrust.org.uk

Upton House stands less than a mile to the south of the battlefield of Edgehill and there has been a house on this site since the Middle Ages. The present house was built at the end of the 17th century and remodelled 1927 - 29 for the 2nd Viscount Bearsted.

He was a great collector of paintings, china and many other valuable works of art, and adapted the building to display them. The paintings include works by El Greco, Bruegel, Bosch, Memling, Guardi, Hogarth and Stubbs. The rooms provide an admirable setting for the china collection which includes Chelsea figures and superb examples of beautifully decorated Sèvres porcelain. The set of 17th century Brussels tapestries depict the Holy Roman Emperor Maximilian I's boar and stag hunts.

Artists and Shell Exhibition of Paintings and Posters commissioned by Shell for use in its publicity 1921 - 1949, while the 2nd Viscount Bearsted was chairman of the company, founded by his father.

GARDEN

The outstanding garden is of interest throughout the season with terraces descending into a deep valley from the main lawn. There are herbaceous borders, the national collection of asters, over an acre of kitchen garden, a water garden laid out in the 1930s and pools stocked with ornamental fish.

An 80-seat licensed restaurant in the grounds serves full lunches and afternoon teas. It is available for hire throughout the year for dinners and functions by arrangement.

Map 5

Owner:
The National Trust

▶ **CONTACT**

The Property Manager
Upton House
Banbury
Oxfordshire OX15 6HT

Tel: 01295 670266
Fax: 01295 671144

e-mail: uptonhouse
@nationaltrust.org.uk

▶ **LOCATION**
OS Ref. SP371 461

On A422, 7m NW of Banbury. 12m SE of Stratford-upon-Avon

Rail: Banbury Station, 7m.

▶ **OPENING TIMES**

Spring
Restaurant, Shop & Exhibition:
6 - 28 March, Sat & Sun,
12 noon - 4pm.

Summer
3 April - 31 October
House: Sat - Wed including BH Mons & Good Fri: 1 - 5pm (last admission to house 4.30pm). (shop open until 5.30pm).

Garden & Restaurant:
Sat, Sun & BHs: 11am - 5pm.
Mon - Wed: 12 noon - 5pm.

Winter
Garden, Restaurant & Shop:
6 Nov - 19 Dec, Sat & Sun,
12 noon - 4pm.

▶ **ADMISSION**

House & Garden
Adult £6.50
Child £3.50
Family £16.00
Groups (15+) £5.20
Garden only
Adult £3.50
Child £2.00
Groups (15+) £2.80
6 - 28 Mar &
6 Nov - 19 Dec
Adult £2.00
Child 1.00

⬛ **SPECIAL EVENTS**
ALL YEAR
Art tours, conservation demonstrations, concerts and other events, please send SAE or telephone.

© NT Severn/R Charlton

ℹ️ Parent & baby room. No indoor photography.

♿ Wheelchair available. Access to ground floor. WC. Motorised buggy to/from reception/lower garden on request.

🍴 Licensed. Self-service.

🚶 Tour time 1½ - 2hrs. Groups (15+) must pre-book. Evening tours by written appointment (no reduction).

🅿️ 350 yds from House.　🐕 In car park, on leads.

WARWICK CASTLE

WARWICK

www.warwick-castle.co.uk

From the moment you walk through the gates of Warwick Castle, beneath the murder holes used to repel invaders in the past, you can sense that this is no ordinary day out. Nowhere else in Britain gives you the chance to be involved in the grim preparations for a mediaeval battle, before walking through the elegance of an aristocratic Victorian party. This is not history behind glass, this is history you live for yourself.

Join a mediaeval household in our Kingmaker attraction, watching them prepare for the final battle of the Earl of Warwick. Enter the eerie Ghost Tower, where it is said that the unquiet spirit of Sir Fulke Greville, murdered most foully by a manservant, still roams.

Descend into the gloomy depths of the Dungeon and Torture Chamber, then step forward in time and marvel at the grandeur of the Great Hall and State Rooms. In our newest attraction, the Mill and Engine House, you can discover how the Earl generated electricity in 1900.

Witness the perfect manners and hidden indiscretions of Daisy, Countess of Warwick and her friends at the Royal Weekend Party 1898 or stroll through the 60 acres of grounds and gardens, landscaped by 'Capability' Brown, which surround the Castle today.

There are special events to enjoy throughout the year, with a unique opportunity to witness mediaeval life at the Mediaeval Festival.

Warwick Castle really is one of the best days out in history.

Map 5

▶ CONTACT

Sales Office
Warwick Castle
Warwick CV34 4QU

Tel: 0870 442 2000

Fax: 01926 401692

e-mail:
customer.information@
warwick-castle.com

▶ LOCATION

OS Ref. SP284 648

2m from M40/J15.
Birmingham 35 mins
Leeds 2 hrs 5 mins
London, 1 hr 30 mins
Vehicle entrance from
A429 ¹/₂ m SW of town
centre.

Rail: Intercity from
London Euston to
Coventry. Direct
service from
Marylebone &
Paddington to Warwick.

CONFERENCE/FUNCTION

ROOM	SIZE	MAX CAPACITY
Great Hall	61' x 34'	130
State Dining Room	40' x 25'	32
Undercroft	46' x 26'	120
Coach House	44' x 19'	80
Marquees		3000

ℹ️ Corporate events, receptions, Kingmaker's Feasts and Highwayman's Supper. Guide books available in English, French, German, Japanese and Spanish.

🛍️ Three shops.

♿ Parking spaces in Stables Car Park, free admission for registered blind and visitors in wheelchairs.

🍴 Available, ranging from cream teas to three-course hot meals. During the summer there is an open air barbecue and refreshment pavilion in the grounds (weather permitting).

🚶 For groups (must be pre-booked). Guides in every room.

🅿️ A charge is made for car parking. Free coach parking, free admission and refreshment voucher for coach driver.

🏰 Ideal location, being a superb example of military architecture dating back to the Norman Conquest and with elegant interiors up to Victorian times. Group rates apply. To qualify for group rates, groups must book in advance. Education packs available.

🐕 Registered assistance dogs only.

❄️ 🎭 Tel for details.

▶ OPENING TIMES

Every day except 25 Dec
10am - 6pm
(closes 5pm during
October - March).

▶ ADMISSION

8 Sept - 28 Feb 2004 (excl. 15 Feb - 2 Mar, 18 Oct - 2 Nov, 29 Nov - 7 Dec, w/ends & BHs)

Adult	£11.25
Child	£6.95
Student	£8.50
OAP	£8.00
Family (2+2)	£32.00

*Groups (20+)

Adult	£8.95
Child	£5.90
Student	£7.75
OAP	£7.20

6 May - 18 July (excl. w/ends & BHs) & 15 Feb - 2 Mar, 18 Oct - 2 Nov & 29 Nov - 7 Dec. (2003 prices)

Adult	£12.50
Child	£7.50
Student	£9.40
OAP	£9.00
Family (2+2)	£34.00

*Groups (20+)

Adult	£9.95
Child	£6.20
Student	£8.25
OAP	£7.95

3 May - 13 July w/ends, 19 July - 7 Sept & BHs, inc Easter. (2003 prices)

Adult	£13.50
Child	£8.00
Student	£10.00
OAP	£9.75
Family(2+2)	£36.00

*Groups (20+) as above.

*Group rates apply to pre-booked groups.

Admission prices are subject to change without prior notice.

ARBURY HALL 🏛   *See page 357 for full page entry.*

BADDESLEY CLINTON 🌿   *See page 358 for full page entry.*

NT Photographic Library

NT Severn SWT / D Sellman

CHARLECOTE PARK 🌿

WARWICK CV35 9ER

www.nationaltrust.org.uk

Tel: 01789 470277   **Fax:** 01789 470544   **e-mail:** charlecotepark@nationaltrust.org.uk

Owner: The National Trust   **Contact:** Sal Ransome

Owned by the Lucy family since 1247, Sir Thomas Lucy built the house in 1558. Now, much altered, it is shown as it would have been a century ago, complete with Victorian kitchen, brewhouse and family carriages in the coach house and two bedrooms, a dressing room and the main staircase. A video of Victorian life can be viewed. The formal gardens and informal parkland lie to the north and west of the house. Jacob Sheep were brought to Charlecote in 1756 by Sir Thomas Lucy. It is reputed that William Shakespeare was apprehended for poaching c1583 and Sir Thomas Lucy is said to be the basis of Justice Shallow in Shakespeare's *'Merry Wives of Windsor'*.

Location: OS151, SP263 564. 1m W of Wellesbourne, 5m E of Stratford-upon-Avon.

Open: Please telephone or see our website for opening times and dates and details of special events.

Admission: NT Members and those joining at Charlecote Park: Free. Adult £6.40, Child (5-16yrs) £3.20, Family £16. Grounds only: Adult £3, Child £1.50.

⬛ℹ️Children's play area. 🍴 ♿ 📷 🍴Licensed. ✗For booked groups. 🅿️Limited for coaches. ⬛By arrangement. 🐕On leads, in car park. 🛏Tel for details.

Arbury Hall, Warwickshire from the book *Historic Family Homes and Gardens from the Air*, see page 54.

COUGHTON COURT 🏛️   *See page 359 for full page entry.*

FARNBOROUGH HALL ❦
BANBURY, OXFORDSHIRE OX17 1DU

www.nationaltrust.org.uk

Tel: 01295 690002

Owner: The National Trust   **Contact:** Mrs A Beddall

A classical mid-18th century stone house, home of the Holbech family for 300 years; notable plasterwork, the entrance hall, staircase and 2 principal rooms are shown; the grounds contain charming late 17th century temples, a ²/₃ mile terrace walk and an obelisk.

Location: OS151, SP430 490. 6m N of Banbury, ¹/₂ m W of A423.

Open: House, Garden & Terrace Walk: 1 Apr - 30 Sept: Weds & Sats, also 2/3 May, 2 - 6pm. Terrace Walk only: (by prior telephone appointment only), 2 - 6pm. Closed Good Fri. Last admission to house 5.30pm.

Admission: House, Garden & Terrace Walk: Adult £3.80, Child £1.90, Family £9.50. Garden & Terrace Walk: £1.90. Visits may be possible outside normal opening hours, please telephone.

♿ House & grounds, but steep terrace walk.   🐕 In grounds, on leads.

THE HILLER GARDEN
Dunnington Heath Farm, Alcester, Warwickshire B49 5PD

Tel: 01789 491342   **Fax:** 01789 490439

Owner: A H Hiller & Son Ltd   **Contact:** Mr Jeff Soulsby

2 acre garden of unusual herbaceous plants and over 200 rose varieties.

Location: OS Ref. SP066 539. 1¹/₂ m S of Ragley Hall on B4088 (formerly A435).

Open: All year: daily 10am - 5pm.

Admission: Free.

Bath Houses

– popular in the 17th and 18th centuries, inspired by Greek and Roman designs and, as the name suggests, they were the noble gentlemen's equivalent of today's swimming pool.

Visit Packwood House, Warwickshire and Rousham House, Oxfordshire.

Garden Jargon

HONINGTON HALL 🏛️
SHIPSTON-ON-STOUR, WARWICKSHIRE CV36 5AA

Tel: 01608 661434   **Fax:** 01608 663717

Owner/Contact: Benjamin Wiggin Esq

This fine Caroline manor house was built in the early 1680s for Henry Parker in mellow brickwork, stone quoins and window dressings. Modified in 1751 when an octagonal saloon was inserted. The interior was also lavishly restored around this time and contains exceptional mid-Georgian plasterwork. Set in 15 acres of grounds.

Location: OS Ref. SP261 427. 10m S of Stratford-upon-Avon. 1¹/₂ m N of Shipston-on-Stour. Take A3400 towards Stratford, then signed right to Honington.

Open: Jun - Aug: Weds only. BH Mon, 2.30 - 5pm. Groups at other times by appointment.

Admission: Adult £4, Child £2.

♿ Unsuitable.   📷 Obligatory.   🐕

English Heritage Photo Library

KENILWORTH CASTLE ⚜️
KENILWORTH, WARWICKSHIRE CV8 1NE

Tel: 01926 852078

Owner: English Heritage   **Contact:** The Custodian

Kenilworth is the largest castle ruin in England, the former stronghold of great Lords and Kings. Its massive walls of warm red stone tower over the peaceful Warwickshire landscape. The Earl of Leicester entertained Queen Elizabeth I with 'Princely Pleasures' during her 19 day visit. He built a new wing for the Queen to lodge in and organised all manner of lavish and costly festivities. The Great Hall, where Gloriana dined with her courtiers, still stands and John of Gaunt's Hall is second only in width and grandeur to Westminster Hall. Climb to the top of the tower beside the hall and you will be rewarded by fine views over the rolling wooded countryside. Exhibition, interactive castle model and café in Leicester's Barn. Recreated Tudor garden and atmospheric audio tour.

Location: OS140, SP278 723. In Kenilworth, off A452, W end of town.

Open: Contact site for details and special event dates. (Closed 24 - 26 Dec & 1 Jan.)

Admission: Contact site for details. Family ticket available. 15% discount for groups (11+)

ℹ️ WC. 📷 ♿ 🔲 🎧 🅿️ 🐕 ✳️ ♿ Tel for details.

LORD LEYCESTER HOSPITAL

HIGH STREET, WARWICK CV34 4BH

Tel/Fax: 01926 491422

Owner: The Governors   **Contact:** The Master

This magnificent range of 14th century half-timbered buildings was adapted into almshouses by Robert Dudley, Earl of Leycester, in 1571. The Hospital still provides homes for ex-servicemen and their wives. The Guildhall, Great Hall, Chapel, Brethren's Kitchen and galleried Courtyard are still in everyday use. The Queen's Own Hussars regimental museum is here. The historic Master's Garden, featured in BBC TV's *Gardener's World*, has been restored.

Location: OS Ref. 280 648. 1m N of M40/J15 on the A429 in town centre.

Open: All year: Tue - Sun & BHs (except Good Fri & 25 Dec), 10am - 5pm (4pm in winter). Garden: Apr - Sept: 10am - 4.30pm.

Admission: Adult £3.40, Child £2.40, Conc. £2.90. 5% discount for adult groups (20+).

⬛❄❆⏹️♿Partial. ⬛ 🏠 📷By arrangement. 🅿Limited. ⬛ 🔲Guide dogs only. ❄

RYTON ORGANIC GARDENS

COVENTRY, WARWICKSHIRE CV8 3LG

www.hdra.org.uk

Tel: 024 7630 3517   **Fax:** 024 7663 9229   **e-mail:** enquiry@hdra.org.uk

Owner: HDRA - The Organic Organisation   **Contact:** Angela Bull

The UKs national centre for organic gardening now has major new tourist attraction – Vegetable Kingdom, a £2 million fully interactive visitor centre, telling the story of Britain's vegetables. Plus ten acres of stunning gardens and displays, award winning organic restaurant and extensive shop. Regularly seen on TV.

Location: OS Ref. SP400 745. 5m SE of Coventry off A45 on the road to Wolston.

Open: Daily (closed Christmas week): 9am - 5pm.

Admission: Adult £3.95 (no concessions), accompanied Child £1.50. Groups (14+) £3.50, Child £1.

⬛ ❄ ⏹️ ♿ 🔲Licensed. 🍴Licensed. 📷By arrangement. 🅿 ⬛ 🐕Dog shelter available.. ❄ 🔲Tel for details.

MIDDLETON HALL

Middleton, Tamworth, Staffordshire B78 2AE

Tel: 01827 283095   **Fax:** 01827 285717   **e-mail:** middletonhall@btconnect.com

Owner: Middleton Hall Trust   **Contact:** Carol Sullivan

Hall (1285 - 1824). Former home of Hugh Willoughby (Tudor explorer), Francis Willughby and John Ray (17th century naturalists).

Location: OS Ref. SP193 982. A4091, S of Tamworth.

Open: 6 Apr - 28 Sept: Suns, 2 - 5pm, BH Mons, 11am - 5pm.

Admission: £2.50, OAP £1.50. BHs & Special Events: Adult £4, Child 50p, OAP £3.

PACKWOOD HOUSE 🌿   *See page 360 for full page entry.*

RAGLEY HALL 🏛   *See page 361 for full page entry.*

THE SHAKESPEARE HOUSES   *See page 362 for full page entry.*

UPTON HOUSE 🌿   *See page 363 for full page entry.*

WARWICK CASTLE   *See page 364 for full page entry.*

STONELEIGH ABBEY

KENILWORTH

www.stoneleighabbey.org

Tel: 01926 858535   **Fax:** 01926 850724   **e-mail:** enquire@stoneleighabbey.org

Owner: Stoneleigh Abbey Ltd   **Contact:** Enquiry Office

Stoneleigh Abbey was founded in 1154 and features seven magnificent 18th century Baroque state rooms and chapel, a medieval Gatehouse, the Gothic Revival style Regency Stables and riverside gardens. Stoneleigh Abbey has been restored with funding from the Heritage Lottery Fund, English Heritage and the European Regional Development Fund.

Location: OS Ref. SP318 712. Off A46/B4115, 2m W of Kenilworth. From London 100m, M40 to Warwick.

Open: Good Fri - end October, West Wing & Stables: Tue - Thur, Sun & BHs: Guided tours at 11am, 1pm & 3pm. Grounds: 10am - 5pm.

Admission: Tours: Adult (inc. 1 child) £5, additional child £2.50, OAP £3.50. Grounds only: £2pp. Discounts for Groups 20+.

ℹ️Available for public & commercial hire. ⬛ ♿House only. WCs. ⬛ 📷Obligatory. 🅿 ⬛ 🐕In grounds, on leads. ⬛ 🔲Tel for details.

❄ **Open All Year Index** see front section

CJB Photography

HAGLEY HALL 🏛

HAGLEY

www.hagleyhall.com

Hagley Hall is set in a 350-acre landscaped park yet is only 25 minutes from Birmingham city centre, the NEC and ICC and close to the motorway network of M5, M6, M40 and M42. The house is available throughout the year on an exclusive basis for conferences, product launches, presentations, lunches, dinners, country sporting days, team building activities, themed evenings, murder mysteries, concerts, filming and wedding receptions. The elegant Palladian house, completed in 1760, contains some of the finest examples of Italian plasterwork. Hagley's rich rococo decoration is a remarkable tribute to the artistic achievement of great 18th century amateurs and is the much loved home of the 11th Viscount Cobham.

Map 5

Owner:
Viscount Cobham

▸ CONTACT

Miss Lucy Carpenter
Hagley Hall
Hagley
Worcestershire DY9 9LG

Tel: 01562 882408
Fax: 01562 882632

e-mail: enquiries@
hagleyhall.info

▸ LOCATION

OS Ref. SO920 807

Easily accessible from
all areas of the country.
¼ m S of A456 at
Hagley.

Close to the M42, M40,
M6 and only 5m from
M5/J3/J4.

Birmingham City
Centre 12m.

Rail: Railway Station
and the NEC 25 mins.

Air: Birmingham
International Airport
25 mins.

CONFERENCE/FUNCTION

ROOM	SIZE	MAX CAPACITY
Gallery	85' x 17'	120
Crimson Rm	23' x 31'	40
The Saloon	34' x 27'	70
Westcote	31' x 20'	60

▸ OPENING TIMES

House
5 - 30 January,
1 - 27 February,
12 - 16 April:
daily except Saturdays.

31 May - 4 June, and
30 August - 3 September,
2 - 5pm. Guided tours.

Afternoon tea available
during house opening.

Please telephone prior
to visit to ensure the
house is open.

▸ ADMISSION

House

Adult	£4.00
Child (under 14 yrs)	£1.50
Conc.	£2.50
Student	£2.50

ℹ️ Available on an exclusive basis for conferences, presentations, lunches, dinners, product launches, themed evenings, murder mysteries, concerts, wedding receptions. Extensive parkland for country sporting days, team-building activities, off-road driving and filming.

♿ Visitors may alight at the entrance. No WC.

☕ Teas available during opening times.

🚶 Obligatory. Please book parties in advance, guided tour of house time: 1hr. Colour guidebook.

🅿️ Unlimited for coaches and cars.

By arrangement.

Guide dogs only.

ASTON HALL

TRINITY ROAD, BIRMINGHAM, WEST MIDLANDS B6 6JD

www.bmag.org.uk

Tel: 0121 327 0062 **Fax:** 0121 327 7162

Owner: Birmingham City Council   **Contact:** Curator/Manager

A large Jacobean mansion built 1618 - 1635 from plans by John Thorpe. The Hall is brick-built with a fairytale skyline of gables and turrets. The interior has period rooms from the 17th, 18th and 19th centuries and a splendid long gallery measuring 136ft. A large kitchen and servants' rooms are also on display.

Location: OS139, SP080 899. 3m NE of Birmingham, 1/4 m from A38(M).

Open: 9 Apr - 31 Oct: Tue - Sun & BH Mons, 11.30am - 4pm.

Admission: Free.

⬛ ♿Ground floor & grounds. ⬛ 👤By arrangement, all year (charge made). 🅿 🐕Guide dogs only.

THE BIRMINGHAM BOTANICAL GARDENS AND GLASSHOUSES

WESTBOURNE ROAD, EDGBASTON, BIRMINGHAM B15 3TR

www.birminghambotanicalgardens.org.uk

Tel: 0121 454 1860 **Fax:** 0121 454 7835

e-mail: admin@birminghambotanicalgardens.org.uk

Owner: Birmingham Botanical & Horticultural Society   **Contact:** Mrs L Keen

Tropical, Mediterranean and Arid Glasshouses contain a wide range of exotic and economic flora. 15 acres of beautiful gardens with the finest collection of plants in the Midlands. Home of the National Bonsai Collection. Children's adventure playground, aviaries, gallery and sculpture trail.

Location: OS Ref. SP048 855. 2m W of city centre. Follow signs to Edgbaston then brown tourist signs.

Open: Daily: 9am - Dusk (7pm latest except pre-booked groups). Suns opening time 10am. Closed Christmas Day.

Admission: Adult £5.70 (£6 on summer Suns & BHs), Conc. £3.30, Family £16 (£17 on summer Suns & BHs). Groups (10+): Adult £4.70, Conc. £3.

⬛ ♿ 🍴Licensed. 🅿 🐕Guide dogs only. ⬛ ❄ 🎥Tel for details.

BLAKESLEY HALL

BLAKESLEY ROAD, YARDLEY, BIRMINGHAM B25 8RN

www.bmag.org.uk

Tel: 0121 464 2193

Owner: Birmingham City Council   **Contact:** Curator/Manager

Blakesley Hall is a late 16th century farmhouse. Following a major development scheme funded by Birmingham City Council and the Heritage Lottery Fund, the site reopened in 2002, with new displays and facilities. The house contains period furniture and displays of excavated finds and social customs of the time. An upstairs chamber contains extensive remains of Elizabethan wall paintings.

Location: OS139, SP130 862. 6m E of Birmingham city centre off A4040 from A45.

Open: 9 Apr - 31 Oct: Tue - Sun & BH Mons, 11.30am - 4pm.

Admission: Free.

⬛ ♿Ground floor. ⬛ 👤All year, by arrangement. 🅿

CASTLE BROMWICH HALL GARDENS

CHESTER ROAD, CASTLE BROMWICH, BIRMINGHAM B36 9BT

www.cbhgt.colebridge.net

Tel/Fax: 0121 749 4100   **e-mail:** admin@cbhgt.colebridge.net

Owner: Castle Bromwich Hall Gardens Trust   **Contact:** Visitor Services Manager

A unique example of 17th and 18th century formal garden design within a 10 acre walled area, comprising historic plants, vegetables, herbs and fruit, with a 19th century holly maze. Classical patterned parterres can be seen at the end of the holly walk, together with restored green house and summer house.

Location: OS Ref. SP142 898. Off B4114, 4m E of Birmingham city centre, 1m from M6/J5 (exit northbound only). Southbound M6/J6 and follow A38 & A452.

Open: Apr - end Oct: Tue - Thur, 1.30 - 4.30pm. Sats, Suns & BHs 2 - 6pm. Closed Mons & Fris including Good Fri.

Admission: Adult £3.50, Child £1.50, OAP £2.50.

🖸 ⓘ 🔌 💻 🎦Daily. 🅿Limited for coaches. ▦ 🐾In grounds, on leads. ♿Tel for details.

MUSEUM OF THE JEWELLERY QUARTER

75 - 79 VYSE STREET, HOCKLEY, BIRMINGHAM B18 6HA

www.bmag.org.uk

Tel: 0121 554 3598   **Fax:** 0121 554 9700

Owner: Birmingham City Council   **Contact:** The Curator

Built around the preserved workshops and offices of Smith and Pepper, a Birmingham jewellery firm. This lively working Museum offers a fascinating insight into the city's historic jewellery trade. Enjoy a tour of the factory with one of our knowledgeable guides and see demonstrations of the machinery. You can also explore the displays which tell the story of the Quarter and the jeweller's craft, practiced in this distinctive part of Birmingham for over 200 years.

Location: OS Ref. SP060 880. ³/₄ m NW of city centre, just within A4540 (ring road).

Open: 9 Apr - 31 Oct: Tue - Sun & BH Mons, 11.30am - 4pm.

Admission: Free.

ⓘTemporary exhibitions. 🖸 🔌 💻 🎦 🅿On street parking only. ▦ 🐾Guide dogs only. ✱ ♿Tel for details.

COVENTRY CATHEDRAL

1 Hill Top, Coventry CV1 5AB

Tel: 024 7652 1200   **Fax:** 024 7652 1220

e-mail: information@coventrycathedral.org   **www.**coventrycathedral.org.uk

Owner: Dean & Canons of Coventry Cathedral   **Contact:** The Visits Secretary

The remains of the medieval Cathedral, bombed in 1940, stand beside the new Cathedral by Basil Spence, consecrated in 1962. Modern works of art include a huge tapestry by Graham Sutherland, a stained glass window by John Piper and a bronze sculpture by Epstein. 'Reconciliation' statue by Josefina de Vasconcellos.

Location: OS Ref. SP336 790. City centre.

Open: Cathedral: All year: 9am - 6pm. Visitors Centre & Video show: opening times vary.

Admission: Cathedral: £3 donation. Groups must book in advance.

ⓘPhoto permit required. 🖸 🔌Partial.WC. 💻 🍴 🎦By arrangement. 🅿None. ▦ 🐾Guide dogs only. ✱

HAGLEY HALL 🏛

See page 368 for full page entry.

HALESOWEN ABBEY ⌗

Halesowen, Birmingham, West Midlands

Tel: 0121 625 6820 (Regional Office)

Owner: English Heritage   **Contact:** The West Midlands Regional Office

Remains of an abbey founded by King John in the 13th century, now incorporated into a 19th century farm. Parts of the church and the monks' infirmary can still be made out.

Location: OS Ref. SO975 828. Off A456 Kidderminster road, ¹/₂ m W of M5/J3, 6m W of Birmingham city centre.

Open: By appointment only. Contact Regional Office for details.

Admission: Free.

SELLY MANOR

MAPLE ROAD, BOURNVILLE, WEST MIDLANDS B30 2AE

www.bvt.org.uk/sellymanor

Tel/Fax: 0121 472 0199   **e-mail:** sellymanor@bvt.org.uk

Owner: Bournville Village Trust   **Contact:** Gillian Ellis

A beautiful half-timbered manor house in the heart of the famous Bournville village. The house has been lived in since the 14th century and was rescued from demolition by George Cadbury. It houses furniture dating back several centuries and is surrounded by a delightful typical Tudor garden.

Location: OS Ref. SP045 814. N side of Sycamore Road, just E of Linden Road (A4040). 4m SSW of City Centre.

Open: All year: Tue - Fri, 10am - 5pm. Apr - Sept: Sats, Suns & BHs, 2 - 5pm. Closed Mons.

Admission: Adult £2, Child 50p, Conc. £1.50, Family £4.50.

🖸 🔌Partial. WC. 🎦By arrangement. 🅿Limited. ▦ 🐾In grounds, on leads. ⛰ ✱

SOHO HOUSE

SOHO AVENUE, HANDSWORTH, BIRMINGHAM B18 5LB

www.bmag.org.uk

Tel: 0121 554 9122 **Fax:** 0121 554 5929

Owner: Birmingham City Council **Contact:** Curator/Manager

Soho House was the elegant home of the industrial pioneer Matthew Boulton between 1766 and 1809. The house contains period rooms and displays on Boulton's businesses, family and associates and the architectural development of the site.

Location: OS Ref. SP054 893. S side of Soho Avenue, just SW of Soho Hill/Soho Road (A41). 2m NW of city centre. Follow signs for Handsworth then brown tourist signs.

Open: 9 Apr - 31 Oct: Tue - Sun & BH Mons, 11.30am - 4pm.

Admission: Free.

ⓘMeeting room. 🔲 ♿ 🎧 ⚡All year, by arrangement. 🅿 Limited for cars. ▉ 🐕 Guide dogs only.

National Trust Photographic Library

WIGHTWICK MANOR 🌿

WIGHTWICK BANK, WOLVERHAMPTON, WEST MIDLANDS WV6 8EE

Tel: 01902 761400 **Fax:** 01902 764663

Owner: The National Trust **Contact:** The Property Manager

Begun in 1887, the house is a notable example of the influence of William Morris, with many original Morris wallpapers and fabrics. Also of interest are pre-Raphaelite pictures, Kempe glass and De Morgan ware. The 17 acre Victorian/Edwardian garden designed by Thomas Mawson has formal beds, pergola, yew hedges, topiary and terraces, woodland and two pools.

Location: OS Ref. SO869 985. 3m W of Wolverhampton, up Wightwick Bank (A454), beside the Mermaid Inn.

Open: 1 Mar - 24 Dec: Thurs & Sats, 1.30 - 5pm (last entry 4.30pm). Admission by timed ticket. Guided groups through ground floor, freeflow upstairs (min. tour time approx. 1 hr). Also open BH Sats, Suns & Mons, 1.30 - 5pm (last entry 4.30pm) - ground floor only, no guided tours. booked groups Weds & Thurs. Garden: Weds, Thurs & Sats, 11am - 6pm; BH Suns & Mons, 11am - 6pm.

Admission: Adult £6, Child £3. Garden only: £3, Child Free.

🔲 ♿ Ground floor & grounds. 🎧 🅿 400 yds. 🐕 In grounds, on leads.

Orders of Classical Architecture

There are five Orders of classic architecture, the first three being Greek, the other two Roman.

Doric Ionic Corinthian

Doric

The most massive and probably the oldest of the orders. The Greek doric had no base, the Romans added one. Shafts are fluted, numbers vary, but there are usually around twenty. The height of the column is between four-and-and-a-quarter and eight diameters. The entablature is around a quarter of the height of the order. Decoration is copied from timber construction, the cornice projects strongly, the frieze is divided into metopes and triglyphs, the architrave is usually plain.

Tuscan

Confined mainly to the north of Italy, it was employed by the Romans but replaced by the doric. Very plain, the columns are not fluted, and in height it is usually around seven diameters.

Ionic

Later than the doric, the ionic order has a distinctive capital, with two volutes, and an echinus based on a water lily shape. The Greek capital was straight sided, the volutes on the Roman capital angled outwards. The columns, on attic bases, usually have about twenty four flutes, and are between eight and nine diameters in height. The entablature is usually about one-fifth of the whole. The cornice projects and often has dentil ornamentation, the frieze can be decorated, the architrave is usually divided into three fascias.

Corinthian

Invented by the Greeks, but not widely used, it was developed by the Romans. The capital has acanthus leaf decoration, which legend bases on a hanging basket. The columns are usually ten diameters in height. The entablature is heavily decorated, with a particularly deep cornice, usually supported on modillions.

Composite

Developed by the Romans, the composite is a mixture of the ionic and corinthian orders. Usually ten-and-a-half diameters in height, the order was richly ornate and was mainly used on triumphal arches.

Architectural Styles

BROADWAY TOWER
BROADWAY, WORCESTERSHIRE WR12 7LB

Tel: 01386 852390 **Fax:** 01386 858038 **e-mail:** broadwaytower1@aol.com
Owner: Broadway Tower Country Park Ltd **Contact:** Annette Gorton

Broadway Tower is a unique historic building on top of the Cotswold ridge, having been built by the 6th Earl of Coventry in the late 1790s. Its architecture, the fascinating views as well as its exhibitions on famous owners and occupants (including William Morris) make the Tower a "must" for all visitors to the Cotswolds. The Tower is surrounded by 35 acres of parkland, picnic/ BBQ facilities. A complete family day out.

Location: OS Ref. SP115 362. ^{1}/$_2$ m SW of the A44 Evesham to Oxford Rd. 1^1/$_2$ m E of Broadway.

Open: 1 Apr – 31 Oct: daily, 10.30am - 5pm. Nov - Mar: Sats & Suns (weather permitting), 11am - 3pm.

Admission: Adult £3, Child £1.50, Conc. £2.50. Group rate on request.

⬚ ⊤ Wedding receptions. ♿ WC. Ⓟ ▣ ⑪ Licensed. ▣
🐕 In grounds, on leads. ❄

CROOME PARK
SEVERN STOKE, WORCESTERSHIRE WR8 9JS

www.nationaltrust.org.uk

Tel: 01905 371006 **Fax:** 01905 371090 **e-mail:** croomepark@nationaltrust.org.uk
Owner: The National Trust **Contact:** The Property Manager

Croome was 'Capability' Brown's first complete landscape, making his reputation and establishing a new parkland aesthetic which became universally adopted over the next fifty years. The elegant park buildings and other structures are mostly by Robert Adam and James Wyatt. The Trust acquired most of the park in 1996 with substantial grant aid from the Heritage Lottery Fund. The Trust has embarked on a ten year restoration plan, including dredging the water features, clearance and replanting of the gardens and parkland. Royal & SunAlliance is making a major financial contribution towards the cost of this restoration.

Location: OS150, SO878 448. 8m S of Worcester and E of A38 and M5, 6m W of Pershore and B4084.

Open: Park & Church: 5 Mar - 31 Oct, Wed - Sun, 10am - 5.30pm; 3 Nov - 19 Dec: Wed - Sun, 10am - 4pm. Open BH Mons. Last admission 30 min before park closes. Church open in association with the Churches Conservation Trust

Admission: Adult £3.50, Child £1.70, Family £8.50.

♿ Partial. Ⓟ 🐕 ▣ Tel for details.

THE GREYFRIARS ❧
Worcester WR1 2LZ
Tel: 01905 23571 **e-mail:** greyfriars@nationaltrust.org.uk www.nationaltrust.org.uk
Owner: The National Trust **Contact:** The Custodian

Built about 1480 next to a Franciscan friary in the centre of medieval Worcester, this timber-framed house has 17th and late 18th century additions. It was rescued from demolition at the time of the Second World War and was carefully restored. The panelled rooms have noteworthy textiles and interesting furniture. An archway leads through to a delightful walled garden.

Location: OS150, SO852 546. Friar Street, in centre of Worcester.

Open: 3 Mar - 18 Dec: Wed - Sat, 1 - 5pm. 4 Jul - 29 Aug: Sun only, 1 - 5pm.

Admission: Adult £3.20, Child £1.60, Family £8.

HANBURY HALL ❧
DROITWICH, WORCESTERSHIRE WR9 7EA

www.nationaltrust.org.uk

Tel: 01527 821214 **Fax:** 01527 821251 **e-mail:** hanburyhall@nationaltrust.org.uk
Owner: The National Trust **Contact:** The Property Manager

In its beautiful setting of Worcestershire parkland, this delightful William and Mary style country house retains its lived in and friendly atmosphere. With its superb staircase murals by Thornhill, and the unique Watney collection of fine porcelain, Hanbury Hall also boasts tranquil 18th century formal gardens including a playable bowling green and a stunning Orangery and working mushroom house.

Location: OS150, SO943 637. 4^1/$_2$ m E of Droitwich, 4m SE M5/J5.

Open: 1 Mar - 31 Oct: Sat - Wed, 11am - 5pm (House 1 - 5pm). Guided tours: Sat & Sun, 11am - 1pm.

Admission: House & Garden: Adult £5.40, Child £2.70, Family £13. Gardens only: Adult £3.50, Child £1.80, Family £8.50.

⬚ 🏛 ⊤ ♿ Partial. WC. ▣ 🎦 For pre-booked groups. Ⓟ 🐕 Guide dogs only.
▣ ▣ Tel for details.

Queen Anne Houses to Visit

As well as the great palaces of Blenheim and Castle Howard, you can visit the smaller Queen Anne houses of Uppark and Petworth in Sussex, Hanbury Hall in Worcestershire, Fawley Court in Oxfordshire, and Chatsworth in Derbyshire.

HARTLEBURY CASTLE
HARTLEBURY, NR KIDDERMINSTER DY11 7XZ

Tel: 01299 250416 **Fax:** 01299 251890 **e-mail:** museum@worcestershire.gov.uk
Owner: The Church Commissioners   **Contact:** The County Museum
Hartlebury Castle has been home to the Bishops of Worcester for over a thousand years. The three principal State Rooms – the medieval Great Hall, the Saloon and the unique Hurd Library – contain period furniture, fine plasterwork and episcopal portraits. In the former servants' quarters in the Castle's North Wing, the County Museum brings to life the past inhabitants of the county, from Roman times to the twentieth century. A wide range of temporary exhibitions and events are held each year, and detailed listings are available from the Museum.
Location: OS Ref. SO389 710. N side of B4193, 2m E of Stourport, 4m S of Kidderminster.
Open: 1 Feb - 30 Sept. County Museum: Mon - Thur, 10am - 5pm. Fris & Suns, 2 - 5pm. Closed Good Fri and Sats. Staterooms: Tue - Thur, 10am - 5pm.
Admission: Combined ticket (Museum & State Rooms): Adult £3, Child/OAP £1.50. Family (2+3) £8.
🖾 🚻 Ground floor & grounds. WC. 🖾 🎔 By arrangement for groups. 🅿 🖾 🐕 Guide dogs only. 🖾 Tel for details.

HARVINGTON HALL 🏛
HARVINGTON, KIDDERMINSTER, WORCESTERSHIRE DY104LR

www.harvingtonhall.com

Tel: 01562 777846   **Fax:** 01562 777190
e-mail: thehall@harvington.fsbusiness.co.uk
Owner: Roman Catholic Archdiocese of Birmingham   **Contact:** The Hall Manager
Harvington Hall is a moated, medieval and Elizabethan manor house. Many of the rooms still have their original Elizabethan wall paintings and the Hall contains the finest series of priest hides in the country. A full programme of events throughout the year including outdoor plays, craft fairs, living history weekends and a pilgrimage is available.

Location: OS Ref. SO877 745. On minor road, ½ m NE of A450/A448 crossroads at Mustow Green. 3m SE of Kidderminster.
Open: Mar & Oct: Sats & Suns; Apr - Sept: Wed - Sun & BH Mons (closed Good Fri), 11.30am - 5pm. Open throughout the year for pre-booked groups and schools. Occasionally the Hall may be closed for a private function.
Admission: Adult £4.20, Child £3, OAP £3.50, Family £12.50. Garden: £1.
🖾 🚻 🚻 Partial. 🍴 Licensed. 🅿 Limited for coaches. 🖾 🐕 Guide dogs only. 🖾 🖾 Tel for details.

HAWFORD DOVECOTE ✻

Hawford, Worcestershire

Tel: 01743 708100 (Regional Office) www.nationaltrust.org.uk

Owner: The National Trust   **Contact:** Regional Office

A 16th century half-timbered dovecote.

Location: OS Ref. SO846 607. 3m N of Worcester, ¹/₂ m E of A449.

Open: 1 Apr - 31 Oct: daily 9am - 6pm or sunset if earlier. Closed Good Fri, other times by prior appointment with the Regional Office.

Admission: £1.

LEIGH COURT BARN ⌗

Worcester

Tel: 0121 625 6820 - Regional Office

Owner: English Heritage   **Contact:** The West Midlands Regional Office

Magnificent 14th century timber-framed barn built for the monks of Pershore Abbey. It is the largest of its kind in Britain.

Location: OS Ref. SO784 534. 5m W of Worcester on unclassified road off A4103.

Open: 1 Apr - 30 Sept: Thur - Sun & BH Mons, 10am - 6pm. Times subject to change April 2004.

Admission: Free.

✻

LITTLE MALVERN COURT ⌂

Nr Malvern, Worcestershire WR14 4JN

Tel: 01684 892988   **Fax:** 01684 893057

Owner: Trustees of the late T M Berington   **Contact:** Mrs T M Berington

Prior's Hall, associated rooms and cells, c1480, of former Benedictine Monastery. Formerly attached to, and forming part of the Little Malvern Priory Church which may also be visited. It has an oak-framed roof, 5-bay double-collared roof, with two tiers of cusped windbraces. Library. Collections of religious vestments, embroideries and paintings. Gardens: 10 acres of former monastic grounds with spring bulbs, blossom, old fashioned roses and shrubs. Access to Hall only by flight of steps.

Location: OS Ref. SO769 403. 3m S of Great Malvern on Upton-on-Severn Rd (A4104).

Open: 14 Apr - 15 Jul: Weds & Thurs, 2.15 - 5pm. Last admission 4.30pm.

Admission: House & Garden: Adult £5, Child £2.50, Garden only: Adult £4, Child £1.50. Groups must book, max 35.

♿ Garden (partial). 🅵 ✻

MADRESFIELD COURT

Madresfield, Malvern WR13 5AU

Tel: 01684 573614   **Fax:** 01684 569197   **e-mail:** madresfield@clara.co.uk

Owner: The Trustees of Madresfield Estate   **Contact:** Mr Peter Hughes

Elizabethan and Victorian house with medieval origins. Fine contents. Extensive gardens and arboretum.

Location: OS Ref. SO809 474. 6m SW of Worcester. 1¹/₂ m SE of A449. 2m NE of Malvern.

Open: Guided tours: 14 Apr - 29 Jul: Wed & Thur, also Sats 24 Apr, 22 May, 12 Jun & 17 Jul: 10.45am & 2.30pm. Numbers are restricted and prior booking, by telephone to The Estate Office (01684 573614), is strongly recommended to avoid disappointment.

Admission: £6.

🅵 Obligatory. ✻

SPETCHLEY PARK GARDENS ⌂

SPETCHLEY PARK, WORCESTER WR5 1RS

www.spetchleygardens.co.uk

Tel: 01905 345213/345224   **Fax:** 01453 511915   **e-mail:** hb@spetchleygardens.co.uk

Owner: Spetchley Gardens Charitable Trust   **Contact:** Mr R J Berkeley

This lovely 30 acre private garden contains a large collection of trees, shrubs and plants, many rare or unusual. A garden full of secrets, every corner reveals some new vista, some treasure of the plant world. The exuberant planting and the peaceful walks make this an oasis of beauty, peace and quiet. Deer Park close by.

Location: OS Ref. SO895 540. 2m E of Worcester on A44. Leave M5/J6 or J7.

Open: 1 Apr - 30 Sept: Tue - Fri & BH Mons, 11am - 6pm (last admission at 4pm each open day). Suns, 2 - 6pm (last admission at 4pm each open day). Closed all Sats and all other Mons.

Admission: Adult £4, Child £2. Groups: Adult £3.80, Child £1.90.

♿ 🏪 🅿 🔲 ✻

THE TUDOR HOUSE

16 Church Street, Upton-on-Severn, Worcestershire WR8 0HT

Tel: 01684 592447/592754

Owner: Mrs Lavender Beard   **Contact:** Mrs Wilkinson

Upton past and present, exhibits of local history.

Location: OS Ref. SO852 406. Centre of Upton-on-Severn, 7m SE of Malvern by B4211.

Open: Apr - Oct: daily, 2 - 5pm (Suns until 4pm). Winter Suns only, 2 - 4pm.

Admission: Adult £1, Conc. 50p, Family £2.

WICHENFORD DOVECOTE ✻

Wichenford, Worcestershire

Tel: 01743 708100 (Regional Office)   www.nationaltrust.org.uk

Owner: The National Trust   **Contact:** Regional Office

A 17th century half-timbered black and white dovecote.

Location: OS Ref. SO788 598. 5¹/₂ m NW of Worcester, N of B4204.

Open: Apr - 31 Oct: daily, 9am - 6pm or sunset if earlier. Closed Good Fri, other times by appointment with Regional Office.

Admission: £1.

✻ Open All Year Index see front section

English Heritage Photo Library

WITLEY COURT ⊞

GREAT WITLEY, WORCESTER WR6 6JT

Tel: 01299 896636

Owner: English Heritage

Contact: The Custodian

The spectacular ruins of a once great house. An earlier Jacobean manor house, converted in the 19th century into an Italianate mansion, with porticoes by John Nash. The adjoining church, by James Gibbs, has a remarkable 18th century baroque interior. The gardens, William Nesfield's 'Monster Work' were equally elaborate and contained immense fountains, which survive today. The largest is the Perseus and Andromeda Fountain which has been restored and now fires daily throughout the summer, contact the site for details and timings. The landscaped grounds, parterres, fountains and woodlands have recently been restored to their former glory. The historic parkland contains the Jerwood Sculpture Park, eventually consisting of 40 modern British sculptures. An atmospheric audio tour leads visitors through the Court.

Location: OS150, SO769 649. 10m NW of Worcester off A443.

Open: Contact site for details and special event dates. Closed 24 - 26 Dec & 1 Jan.

Admission: Contact site for details, Family ticket available. 15% discount for groups of 11+.

ⓘVisitor welcome point. ⬛ ♿Grounds. WC. ⬛ 🍴 ⬛ 🅿 ❊ ⬛Tel for details.

Croome Park, Worcestershire.

National Trust Photographic Library / David Norton

yorkshire
& the humber

Whitby Abbey, Yorkshire. © David Osborn

burtonagneshall
yorkshire

Few great country houses stand today as beautifully maintained and unchanged in appearance as the day they were built ... but Burton Agnes Hall must fall into this category. On the edge of the Yorkshire Wolds and only six miles south west of the boisterous and bustling seaside town of Bridlington, it stands as a perfect peaceful gem of early 17th Century late Elizabethan building design. Built between 1601 - 1610 for Sir Henry Griffith, by Robert Smythson (architect of Longleat, Wollaton Hall, and Hardwick), Burton Agnes is unique in that a plan for the house still exists in the RIBA collection. Here too, lives the same family who have owned the property since Roger de Stuteville first built a manor house on the site in 1173.

Burton Agnes is approached through a charming red-brick band stone turreted gatehouse, built for decorative display rather than defence. From here you will see for the first time the south front of the hall – its symmetry retained by putting the entrance door at the side of one of the projecting bays. Wander around to the east side of the hall, and you can see how the front of the house was built higher than the rear in order to accommodate the Long Gallery on the top floor. The Palladian windows at each end of the Gallery were 18th century additions, and the top floor Gallery itself was fully restored in 1974.

This is a house full of the most wonderful treasures; heavily panelled Jacobean rooms with intricate decorative plasterwork ceilings sit easily with other softly painted interiors remodelled in the 18th century. All the rooms are brimming with family portraits and fine furniture. But what adds such freshness and life to this house are the Impressionist and Modern Art collection acquired by the late Marcus Wickham-Boynton that fill the house. Marcus Wickham-Boynton took over Burton Agnes Hall in 1942 and lived here until his death in 1989. He started his collections of English and French paintings of the 18th, 19th and 20th centuries in 1937 with the encouragement of two collector friends: Lord Ivor Spencer Churchill and the Right Hon Harcourt 'Crinks' Johnstone. You will find works by Boudin, Courbet, Gauguin, Manet, Pissarro and Sickert ... the list goes on. But what makes the house feel so dynamic is that Susan Cunliffe-Lister and her son, Simon (heir to the estate) are still adding to this collection. In the Gallery you can enjoy works by some of today's most innovative craftsmen – furniture by John Makepeace, vibrantly coloured tapestries and embroideries by designers such as Kaffe Fassett and Janet Haigh. It all creates a feeling of great optimism.

Since coming to live at the Hall in 1990, Susan Cunliffe-Lister has also spent a huge amount of time on the restoration of the Walled Garden – it now contains a maze, potager, jungle garden, colour gardens: it incorporates giant games' boards and, importantly, a children's corner!

Burton Agnes is open from April - October, daily. So don't just head for the seaside if you are in this part of the country, make sure to give time to visit this very unspoilt and charming place.

▶ For further details about Burton Agnes Hall see page 393.

Map 8

BRAMHAM PARK

WETHERBY

www.bramhampark.co.uk

Owner:
George Lane Fox

▶ CONTACT

The Estate Office
Bramham Park
Wetherby
West Yorkshire
LS23 6ND

Tel: 01937 846000
Fax: 01937 846007
e-mail: enquiries@
bramhampark.co.uk

▶ LOCATION
OS Ref. SE410 416

A1/M1 1m,
Wetherby 5m,
Leeds 7m,
Harrogate 12m,
York 14m.

Rail: Leeds or York.

Bus: 770; Bus stop
$^1/_2$ m.

Air: Leeds/Bradford
15m.

Bramham Park is the stunning family home of the Lane Fox family, who are direct descendants of Robert Benson, the founder of Bramham over 300 years ago. The gardens extend to some 66 acres and, with the Pleasure Grounds, extend to over 100 acres.

The focus at Bramham has always been the landscape (the house was merely built as a 'villa' from which to admire it). Inspiration for the design of the Garden at Bramham was French and formal, but the manner in which it was adapted to the national landscape is relaxed and entirely English. It is completely original and few other parks of this period survive; none on

the scale and complexity of Bramham. It is a rare and outstanding example of the formal style of the late 17th century and early 18th century.

Bramham is a garden of walks and vistas, architectural features and reflecting water. A broad vista stretches away at an angle from the house and a number of other allées have focal points – temples and vistas. This creates an experience of anticipation when walking around the grounds.

The house, gardens and surrounding parkland make an ideal venue for events, private dinners, corporate entertaining, product launches and filming.

▶ OPENING TIMES
House
For groups of 10+ by appointment only (separate fee).

Gardens
1 April - 30 September: daily, 11.30am - 4.30pm. Closed 7 - 14 June & 16 August - 4 September.

▶ ADMISSION
Gardens only

Adult	£4.00
Child (under 16yrs)	£2.00
Child (under 5yrs)	Free
OAP	£2.00

 Grounds. WC.
Guide dogs only.

CONFERENCE/FUNCTION

ROOM	SIZE	MAX CAPACITY
Gallery	80' x 20'	110
Hall	30' x 30'	50
North Room	27' x 48'	100
East Room	20' x 18'	14
Old Kitchen	22' x 23'	50

▶ SPECIAL EVENTS
JUN 10 - 13
Bramham International 3-Day Event.

AUG 27 - 30
Leeds Festival.

© English Heritage Photo Library / John Critchley

Map 8

BRODSWORTH HALL & GARDENS

NR DONCASTER

Owner:
English Heritage

▶ **CONTACT**

The Custodian
Brodsworth Hall
Brodsworth
Nr Doncaster
Yorkshire DN5 7XJ

Tel: 01302 722598

Fax: 01302 337165

▶ **LOCATION**
OS Ref. SE507 071

In Brodsworth, 5m NW
of Doncaster off A635.
Use A1(M)/J37.

Rail: Doncaster.

Brodsworth Hall is a rare example of a Victorian country house that has survived largely unaltered. Designed and built in the 1860s it remains an extraordinary time capsule. The now faded grandeur of the reception rooms speaks of an opulent past whilst the cluttered servants' wing, with its great kitchen from the age of Mrs Beeton, recalls a vanished way of life. Careful conservation has preserved the patina of time to produce an interior that is both fascinating and evocative. The Hall is set within beautiful Victorian gardens rich in features which are a delight in any season and are currently being restored to their original design.

New for 2004: *'Maids and Mistresses' - the rôle of women in the country house revealed.*

© English Heritage Photo Library / John Critchley

▶ **OPENING TIMES***

Summer

April - October
Tue - Sun, & BHs.

House: 1 - 6pm
(last admission 1 hour
before closing).

Gardens: 12 noon - 6pm
Mon, 11am - 4pm (summer
only).

Winter

**Gardens, Shop &
Tearoom only**
November - March
Sats & Suns: 11am - 4pm.

* Times subject to change
April 2004.

▶ **ADMISSION***

Summer

House

Adult	£6.00
Child (5-15yrs)	£3.00
Child (under 5yrs)	Free
Conc.	£4.50

Groups (11+) 15% discount

Free admission for tour
leaders and coach drivers.

Gardens

Adult	£3.50
Child (5-15yrs)	£1.80
Child (under 5yrs)	Free
Conc.	£2.60

Winter Gardens

Adult	£2.00
Child	£1.00
Conc.	£1.50

* Prices subject to change
April 2004.

Exhibitions about the family and their love of yachting, the servants and the gardens.

Most of house is accessible. WCs.

Seating for 70.

Groups must book. Booked coach parties: 10am - 1pm.

220 cars and 3 coaches. Free.

Education Centre. Free if booked in advance.

No dogs in gardens.

Tel for details.

CASTLE HOWARD

YORK

www.castlehoward.co.uk

Map 8

Owner:
The Hon Simon Howard

▶ CONTACT

Visitor Services
Castle Howard
York, North Yorks,
YO60 7DA

Tel: 01653 648333
Fax: 01653 648529

e-mail:
house@
castlehoward.co.uk

▶ LOCATION
OS Ref. SE716 701

Approaching from S, A64
to Malton, on entering
Malton, take Castle
Howard road via
Coneysthorpe village.
Or from A64 following
signs to Castle Howard
via the Carrmire Gate
9' wide by 10' high.

York 15m (20 mins), A64.
From London: M1/J32,
M18 to A1(M) to A64,
York/Scarborough Road,
3½ hrs.

Train: London Kings
Cross to York 1hr. 50
mins. York to Malton
Station 30 mins.

Bus: Service and tour
buses from York Station.

CONFERENCE/FUNCTION

ROOM	SIZE	MAX CAPACITY
Long Gallery	197' x 24'	280
Grecian Hall	40' x 40'	160

In a dramatic setting between two lakes with
extensive gardens and impressive fountains, this
18th century Palace was designed by Sir John
Vanbrugh in 1699. Undoubtedly the finest
private residence in Yorkshire it was built for
Charles Howard, 3rd Earl of Carlisle, whose
descendants still live here.

With its painted and gilded dome reaching 80ft into
the Yorkshire sky, this impressive house has
collections of antique furniture, porcelain and
sculpture, while its fabulous collection of
paintings is dominated by the famous Holbein
portraits of Henry VIII and the Duke of Norfolk.

GARDENS

Designed on a heroic scale covering 1,000 acres.
The gardens include memorable sights like the
Temple of the Four Winds and the Mausoleum, the
New River Bridge and the recently restored
waterworks of the South Lake, Cascade, Waterfall
and Prince of Wales Fountain. The walled garden
has collections of old and modern roses.

Ray Wood, acknowledged by the Royal Botanic
Collection, Kew, as a "rare botanical jewel"
has a unique collection of rare trees, shrubs,
rhododendrons, magnolias and azaleas.

🏠 ✳ ℹ️ Suitable for concerts, craft fairs, fashion
shows, clay pigeon shooting, equestrian events, garden
parties, filming, product launches. Helicopter landing.
Firework displays.

🍸 Booked private parties and receptions, min. 25.

♿ Transport equipped for wheelchairs. Wheelchair lift in
house to main floor. WCs.

☕ Two cafeterias.

🚶 Guides posted throughout house. Private tours and
lectures by arrangement covering house, history, contents
and garden.

🅿️ 400 cars, 20 coaches.

📚 1:10 teacher/pupil ratio required. Special interest: 18th
century architecture, art, history, wildlife, horticulture.

❄️

▶ OPENING TIMES
Summer
14 February - 31 October
Daily, 10am - 4pm
(last admission).

Grounds, Rose Gardens,
Plant Centre and Stable
Courtyard Complex
open 10am.

Winter
November - mid February

Grounds open most days
November, December and
January - telephone
for confirmation.

Access to Pretty Wood
Pyramid is available from
1 July to 31 August.
For more information
please contact Castle
Howard Estate Office
on 01653 648444.

▶ ADMISSION
Summer

House & Garden
Adult	£9.50
Child (4-16yrs)	£6.50
Senior	£8.50

Groups (12+)
Adult	£8.00
Child (4-16yrs)	£5.50
OAP	£7.50

Garden only
Adult	£6.50
Child*	£4.50
Senior	£6.00

Winter
Garden only.

Map 8

FAIRFAX HOUSE

YORK

www.fairfaxhouse.co.uk

Owner:
York Civic Trust

▶ **CONTACT**

Mr Peter Brown
Fairfax House
Castlegate
York YO1 9RN

Tel: 01904 655543
Fax: 01904 652262

e-mail: peterbrown@
fairfaxhouse.co.uk

▶ **LOCATION**

OS Ref. SE605 515

In centre of York
between Castle
Museum and
Jorvik Centre.

London 4 hrs by car,
2 hrs by train.

Rail: York Station,
10 mins walk.

Taxi: Station Taxis
01904 623332.

Fairfax House was acquired and fully restored by the York Civic Trust in 1983/84. The house, described as a classic architectural masterpiece of its age and certainly one of the finest townhouses in England, was saved from near collapse after considerable abuse and misuse this century, having been converted into a cinema and dance hall.

The richly decorated interior with its plasterwork, wood and wrought-iron, is now the home for a unique collection of Georgian furniture, clocks, paintings and porcelain.

The Noel Terry Collection, gift of a former treasurer of the York Civic Trust, has been described by Christie's as one of the finest private collections formed this century. It enhances and complements the house and helps to create that special 'lived-in' feeling, providing the basis for a series of set-piece period exhibitions which bring the house to life in a very tangible way.

▶ **OPENING TIMES**

Summer
14 February - 6 January

Mon - Thur: 11am - 5pm.
Fridays: Guided tours only at 11am and 2pm.
Saturdays: 11am - 5pm.
Sundays: 1.30 - 5pm.

Last admission 4.30pm.

Winter
Closed
7 January - 13 February,
24 - 26 & 31 December
and 1 January.

▶ **ADMISSION**

Adult......................£4.50
Child......... Free with full
paying adult.
Conc. £3.75
Groups*
Adult.....................£4.00
Child.....................£1.00
Conc. £3.25

* Min payment 15 persons.

◆ **SPECIAL EVENTS**

MAR 1 - MAY 30
Gilray & Gout - an 18th century view of men behaving badly.

JUNE 7 - AUG 31
The Glory of Glass 1700-1850.

SEPT 8 - JAN 6
Tales from the Teatable 1700-1850. The English obsession with tea explained.

DEC 3 - JAN 6
The Keeping of Christmas.

ℹ️ Suitable for filming. No photography in house. Liveried footmen, musical & dancing performances can be arranged.

🛍️

🍽️ Max. 28 seated. Groups up to 50: buffet can be provided.

♿ Visitors may alight at entrance prior to parking. No WCs except for functions.

🧑 A guided tour can be arranged at a cost of £5. Evening and daytime guided tours, telephone for details. Available in French and German. Tour time: 1½ hrs.

🅿️ 300 cars, 50 yds from house. Coach park is ½ m away, parties are dropped off; drivers please telephone for details showing the nearest coach park and approach to the house.

❄️

Mike Williams

Map 8

Owner:
The National Trust

▶ **CONTACT**

The National Trust
Fountains Abbey
and Studley Royal
Ripon
North Yorkshire
HG4 3DY

Tel: 01765 608888
Fax: 01765 601002
e-mail:
fountainsenquiries@
nationaltrust.org.uk

▶ **LOCATION**
OS Ref. SE275 700

Abbey entrance;
4m W of Ripon off
B6265.
8m W of A1.

Rail: Harrogate 12m.

Bus: Regular
season service
tel: 0870 608 2608
for details.

FOUNTAINS ABBEY 🌿
& STUDLEY ROYAL

RIPON

One of the most remarkable sites in Europe, sheltered in a secluded valley, Fountains Abbey and Studley Royal, a World Heritage Site, encompasses the spectacular remains of a 12th century Cistercian abbey with one of the finest surviving monastic watermills in Britain, an Elizabethan mansion, and one of the best surviving examples of a Georgian green water garden. Elegant ornamental lakes, avenues, temples and cascades provide a succession of unforgettable eye-catching vistas in an atmosphere of peace and tranquillity. St Mary's Church, built by William Burges in the 19th century, provides a dramatic focal point to the medieval deer park with over 500 deer.

Small museum near to the Abbey. Exhibitions in Fountains Hall, Swanley Grange and the Mill.

▶ **OPENING TIMES**

April - September
Daily: 10am - 6pm.

October - March
Daily: 10am - 4pm.

Closes early on
special event days.

Closed 24/25 December,
and Fri Nov - Jan.

▶ **ADMISSION**

Adult	£5.50
Child* (5-16yrs)	£3.00
Family	£15.00

Groups (15+)
Adult	£4.50
Child* (5-16yrs)	£2.20

Group discount
applicable only with
prior booking.

Group visits and disabled
visitors, please telephone
in advance, 01765 643197.

* NT, EH Members &
Under 5s Free.

The Abbey is maintained
by English Heritage.
St Mary's Church is owned
by English Heritage and
managed by the
National Trust.

ℹ Events held throughout the year. Exhibitions. Seminar facilities. Outdoor concerts, meetings, activity days, walks.

▣ Two shops.

Ⴒ Dinners and dances.

♿ Free Batricars & wheelchairs, please book, tel. 01765 643185. 3-wheel Batricars not permitted due to terrain. Tours for visually impaired, please book. WC.

▦ Groups please book, discounted rates. Licensed.

⊓ Licensed.

🏃 Free, but seasonal. Groups (please book on 01765 643197), please use Visitor Centre entrance.

P Drivers must book groups.

🐕 In grounds, on leads.

🔔 Fountains Hall, an Elizabethan Mansion is an ideal setting for weddings. For details or a Wedding pack tel: 01765 643196/643197.

✳

⬡ Tel for details.

Harewood House

HAREWOOD HOUSE

LEEDS

www.harewood.org

Map 8

Owner:
The Earl of Harewood

▶ **CONTACT**

Harewood House Trust
Moor House
Harewood Estate
Harewood
Leeds
West Yorkshire
LS17 9LQ

Tel: 0113 2181010
Fax: 0113 2181002
e-mail: business@
harewood.org

▶ **LOCATION**

OS Ref. SE311 446

A1 N or S to Wetherby.

A659 via Collingham, Harewood is on A61 between Harrogate and Leeds. Easily reached from A1, M1, M62 and M18. Half an hour from York,

15 mins from centre of Leeds or Harrogate.

Rail: Leeds Station 7m.

Bus: No. 36 from Leeds or Harrogate.

CONFERENCE/FUNCTION

ROOM	SIZE	MAX CAPACITY
State Dining Rm.		32
Gallery		96
Courtyard Suite		120
Courtyard Marquee	20' x 24'	400

Harewood House is the magnificent Yorkshire home of the Queen's cousin, the Earl of Harewood. Harewood is now consistently the most visited historic house in Yorkshire, has been The Yorkshire Tourist Board's Visitor Attraction of the Year in 1995 and 2002 and recently was awarded Silver in the same category for England.

The house is renowned for its stunning architecture and exquisite Adam interiors, and contains a rich collection of Chippendale furniture, fine porcelain and outstanding art collections.

A highlight of 2004 will be 'Maids & Mistresses' – an exhibition celebrating the rôle of women and highlighting their achievements and contributions to running these great households since the 17th century. HRH Princess Mary, the Princess Royal (Lord Harewood's mother), lived at Harewood for 35 years and much of her fascinating memorabilia is part of the exhibition.

Following the success of the restored Old Kitchen, the Servants' Hall, Housekeeper's Room, and corridors of 'Below Stairs' Harewood, will open for the first time ever in 2004 with fascinating tales to tell. Through hands-on discovery (including peeking in drawers and cupboards) visitors will find out how the servants lived, what they wore and their rôles.

Harewood's stunning gardens enfold lakeside and woodland walks, a Rock Garden, Walled Garden and the restored Parterre Terrace. The Lakeside Bird Garden contains around 100 species of threatened and exotic birds as well as popular favourites, penguins and flamingos.

Throughout the season Harewood plays host to many special events, including concerts, craft festivals and car rallies, while the Terrace Gallery features a changing programme of contemporary exhibitions.

Harewood House

🏠 ✳ ℹ️ Marquees can be accommodated, concerts and product launches. No photography in the house.

🍴 Ideal for corporate entertaining including drinks receptions, buffets and wedding receptions. Specific rooms available for corporate entertaining plus Courtyard Suite for conferences/ product launches.

♿ Visitors may alight at entrance. Parking in allocated areas. Most facilities accessible. Wheelchair available at House and Bird Garden. WC. Special concessions apply to disabled groups. Some steep inclines.

☕ Licensed. 🍴 Licensed.

🅿 Cars 400 yds from house. 50+ coaches 500 yds from house. Drivers to verify in advance.

🚶 🎧 By arrangement. Audio tour of house available. Lectures by arrangement. Daily free talks.

🎓 Sandford Award for Education.

🐕 Dogs on leads in grounds, guide dogs only in house.

💒 Civil Wedding Licence.

▶ **OPENING TIMES**

House
17 March - 31 October:
Daily.

Garden & Grounds
11 February - 31 October:
Daily;
November - 12 December:
Sats & Suns only,
10am - 6pm.

Please call for opening times of specific areas.

▶ **ADMISSION**

All attractions*

Adult	£10.00
Child/Student	£5.50
OAP	£8.25
Family (2+3)	£30.50

Bird Garden, Grounds, Terrace Gallery & Below Stairs*

Adult	£7.25
Child/Student	£4.50
OAP	£6.25
Family (2+3)	£23.00

Groups (15+):
please telephone for details.

* Prices are for Mon - Sat. Prices on Suns and BH Mons are slightly higher.

🎭 **SPECIAL EVENTS**

MAY 1 - 3
Noddy & Friends!

JUN 15
Classic Car Rally.

Please telephone for details of other events.

NEWBY HALL & GARDENS

RIPON

www.newbyhall.com

Map 8

Owner:
Mr Richard Compton

▶ CONTACT

The Opening
Administrator
Newby Hall
Ripon
North Yorkshire
HG4 5AE

Tel: 01423 322583
Information Hotline:
0845 450 4068

Fax: 01423 324452

e-mail:
info@newbyhall.com

▶ LOCATION

OS Ref. SE348 675

Midway between
London and Edinburgh,
4m W of A1, towards
Ripon. S of Skelton 2m
NW of (A1)
Boroughbridge.
4m SE of Ripon.

Taxi: Ripon Taxi Rank
01765 601283.

Bus: On Ripon - York
route.

CONFERENCE/FUNCTION

ROOM	SIZE	MAX CAPACITY
Grantham Room	90' x 20'	200

The home of Richard and Lucinda Compton, Newby Hall was built in the 1690s by Sir Christopher Wren's number two, John Etty. In the 1760s William Weddell, an ancestor of the Comptons, acquired a magnificent collection of Ancient Roman sculpture and Gobelins tapestries. He commissioned Robert Adam to alter the interior of the house and Thomas Chippendale to make furniture. The result is a perfect example of the Georgian 'Age of Elegance'.

GARDENS

25 acres of glorious award-winning gardens contain rare and beautiful shrubs and plants, including the National Collection of the Genus Cornus. Newby's famous double herbaceous borders, flanked by great bastions of yew hedges, sweep down to the River Ure. Formal gardens such as the Autumn and Rose Gardens – each with splashing fountains – a Victorian rock garden, the tranquillity of Sylvia's Garden, pergolas and even a tropical garden, make Newby a 'Garden for all Seasons'. The gardens incorporate an exciting children's adventure garden and miniature railway. There is also an unusual exhibition of contemporary sculptures, set in ornamental woodland.

▶ OPENING TIMES

Summer

House
1 April - 26 September

April, May, June &
September:
Tues - Sun & BH Mons;
July - August: Daily
12 noon - 5pm.
Last admission 4.30pm.

Garden
Dates as House,
11am - 5.30pm.
Last admission 5pm.

Winter
October - end March
Closed.

▶ ADMISSION

House & Garden
Adult £7.80
Child/Disabled £5.30
OAP £6.80
Group (15+)
Adult/OAP £6.50
Child/Disabled £4.80

Garden only
Adult £6.30
Child/Disabled £4.80
OAP £5.30
Group (15+)
Adult £5.30
Child (4-16yrs) £4.30

Suitable for filming and for special events, craft and country fairs, vehicle rallies etc, promotions and lectures. No indoor photography. Allow a full day for viewing house and gardens.

Wedding receptions & special functions.

5 wheelchairs available. Access to ground floor of house and key areas in gardens. WC.

Garden restaurant, teas, hot and cold meals. Booked groups in Grantham Room. Menus/rates on request.

Ample. Hard standing for coaches.

Welcome. Rates on request. Grantham Room for use as wet weather base subject to availability. Woodland discovery walk, adventure gardens and train rides on 10¼" gauge railway.

Guide dogs only.

Map 8

RIPLEY CASTLE 🏛

HARROGATE

www.ripleycastle.co.uk

Ripley Castle has been the home of the Ingilby family for twenty-six generations and Sir Thomas and Lady Ingilby together with their five children continue the tradition. The guided tours are amusing and informative, following the lives and loves of one family for over 670 years and how they have been affected by events in English history. The Old Tower dates from 1555 and houses splendid armour, books, panelling and a Priest's Secret Hiding Place, together with fine paintings, china, furnishings and chandeliers collected by the family over the centuries. The extensive Victorian Walled Gardens have been transformed and are a colourful delight through every season. In the Spring you can appreciate 150,000 flowering bulbs which create a blaze of colour through the woodland walks, and also the National Hyacinth Collection whose scent is breathtaking. The restored Hot Houses have an extensive tropical plant collection, and in the Kitchen Gardens you can see an extensive collection of rare vegetables from the Henry Doubleday Research Association.

Ripley village on the Castle's doorstep is a model estate village with individual charming shops, an art gallery, delicatessen and Farmyard Museum.

Owner:
Sir Thomas Ingilby Bt

▶ CONTACT

Tours: Wendy McNae
Meetings/Dinners:
Chloe Drummond
Ripley Castle
Ripley
Harrogate
North Yorkshire
HG3 3AY

Tel: 01423 770152
Fax: 01423 771745
e-mail: enquiries@
ripleycastle.co.uk

▶ LOCATION

OS Ref. SE283 605

W edge of village. Just off A61, 3$^{1}/_{2}$ m N of Harrogate, 8m S of Ripon. M1 18m S, M62 20m S.

Rail: London -
Leeds/York 2hrs.
Leeds/York - Harrogate
30mins.

Taxi: Blueline taxis
Harrogate
(01423) 503037.

CONFERENCE/FUNCTION

ROOM	SIZE	MAX CAPACITY
Morning Rm	27' x 22'	80
Large Drawing Rm	30' x 22'	80
Library	31' x 19'	70
Tower Rm	33' x 21'	70
Map Rm	19' x 14'	20
Dining Rm	23' x 19'	20

No photography inside Castle unless by prior written consent. Parkland for outdoor activities & concerts. Murder mystery weekends.

VIP lunches & dinners (max. 66): unlimited in marquees. Full catering service, wedding receptions, banquets and medieval banquets.

5/7 rooms accessible. Gardens accessible (not Tropical Collection). WCs. Parking 50 yds.

The Castle Tearooms (seats 54) in Castle courtyard. Licensed. Pub lunches or dinner at hotel (100 yds). Groups must book.

Obligatory. Tour time 75 mins.

290 cars - 300 yds from Castle entrance. Coach park 50 yds. Free.

Welcome by arrangement, between 10.30am - 7.30pm.

Guide dogs only.

Boar's Head Hotel (RAC***) 100 yds. Owned and managed by the estate.

Civil Wedding Licence.

Open all year.

▶ OPENING TIMES

Summer
Castle & Gardens
January - June,
September - December:
Tues, Thurs, Sats & Suns:
10.30am - 3pm.

July - August:
Daily: 10.30am - 3pm.

Gardens
Daily, 10am - 5pm.

Winter
December - May &
September - December:
Tues, Thurs, Sats & Suns.

10.30am - last guided tour 3pm.

▶ ADMISSION

All Year
Castle & Gardens
Adult £6.00
Child (5-16yrs) £3.50
OAP £5.00
Groups (15+)
Adult £5.00
Child (5-16yrs) £3.00

Gardens only
Adult £3.50
Child (5-16yrs) £2.00
OAP £3.00
Groups (15+)
Adult £3.00

🛡 SPECIAL EVENTS

JUN 10 - 13
Grand Summer Sale.

OCT 8 - 9
Fashion Sale.

SKIPTON CASTLE

SKIPTON

www.skiptoncastle.co.uk

Map 8

Judith Parker
Skipton Castle
Skipton
North Yorkshire
BD23 1AQ

Tel: 01756 792442

Fax: 01756 796100

e-mail: info@
skiptoncastle.co.uk

▶ **LOCATION**
OS Ref. SD992 520

In the centre of
Skipton, at the N end
of High Street.

Skipton is 20m W of
Harrogate on the A59
and 26m NW
of Leeds on A65.

Rail: Regular services
from Leeds & Bradford.

Guardian of the gateway to the Yorkshire Dales for over 900 years, this unique fortress is one of the most complete and well-preserved medieval castles in England. Standing on a 40-metre high crag, fully-roofed Skipton Castle was founded around 1090 by Robert de Romille, one of William the Conqueror's Barons, as a fortress in the dangerous northern reaches of the kingdom.

Owned by King Edward I and Edward II, from 1310 it became the stronghold of the Clifford Lords withstanding successive raids by marauding Scots. During the Civil War it was the last Royalist bastion in the North, yielding only after a three-year siege in 1645. 'Slighted' under the orders of Cromwell, the castle was skilfully restored by the redoubtable Lady Anne Clifford and today visitors can climb from the depths of the Dungeon to the top of the Watch Tower, and explore the Banqueting Hall, the Kitchens, the Bedchamber and even the Privy!

Every period has left its mark, from the Norman entrance and the Medieval towers, to the beautiful Tudor courtyard with the great yew tree planted by Lady Anne in 1659. Here visitors can see the coat of arms of John Clifford, the infamous 'Bloody' Clifford of Shakespeare's *Henry VI*, who fought and died in the Wars of the Roses whereupon the castle was possessed by Richard III. Throughout the turbulent centuries of English history, the Clifford Lords fought at Bannockburn, at Agincourt and in the Wars of the Roses. The most famous of them all was George Clifford, 3rd Earl of Cumberland, Champion to Elizabeth I, Admiral against the Spanish Armada and conqueror of Puerto Rico in 1598.

In the castle grounds visitors can see the Tudor wing built as a royal wedding present for Lady Eleanor Brandon, niece of Henry VIII, the beautiful Shell Room decorated in the 1620s with shells and Jamaican coral and the ancient medieval chapel of St John the Evangelist. The Chapel Terrace, with its delightful picnic area, has fine views over the woods and Skipton's lively market town.

▶ **OPENING TIMES**

All Year
(closed 25 December)

Mon - Sat: 10am - 6pm
Suns: 12 noon - 6pm
(October - February 4pm)

▶ **ADMISSION**

Adult £5.00
Child (0 - 4yrs)........ Free
Child (5-17yrs)....... £2.50
OAP £4.40
Student (with ID) .. £4.40
Family (2+3) £13.90
Groups (15+)
Adult £4.00
Child (0-17yrs)....... £2.50

Includes illustrated tour sheet in a choice of eight languages, plus free badge for children.

Groups welcome: Guides available for booked groups at no extra charge.

Unsuitable.

Tearoom. Indoor and outdoor picnic areas.

By arrangement.

Large public coach and car park off nearby High Street. Coach drivers' rest room at Castle.

Welcome. Guides available. Teachers free.

In grounds on leads.

Tel for details.

ALDBOROUGH ROMAN SITE ⌗

High Street, Aldborough, Boroughbridge, North Yorkshire YO51 9EP

Tel: 01423 322768

Owner: English Heritage   **Contact:** The Custodian

Site of the principal town of Britain's largest Roman tribe. Discover original Roman mosaics still in situ. A small museum displays finds from the site.

Location: OS Ref. SE405 661. Close to Boroughbridge off A1.

Open: Please ring for details.

Admission: Adult £2, Child £1, Conc. £1.50. 15% discount for groups (11+). Prices subject to change April 2004.

ⓘ WC. ⬚ ▦ ⛟

ARCHAEOLOGICAL RESOURCE CENTRE

St Saviour's Church, St Saviourgate, York YO1 8NN

Tel: 01904 543403   **Fax:** 01904 627097

e-mail: jorvik@yorkarchaeology.co.uk   **www.vikingjorvik.com**

Owner: York Archaeological Trust   **Contact:** Reservations Team

Housed in the restored medieval church of St Saviour, the ARC offers a glimpse behind the scenes of a leading archaeological unit. Visitors take part in hands-on activities with real finds, investigating a section of a layer from an archaeological dig and even examining Viking-Age artefacts.

Location: OS Ref. SE606 519. Central York, close to the Shambles.

Open: School holidays: Mon - Sat, 11am - 3pm. Term time: Mon - Fri, 10am - 3.30pm. Closed last two weeks of Dec & first week of Jan. For details of opening times on the day of your visit please phone 01904 543403.

Admission: £4.50, Conc. £4. Pre-booked groups (15+) £4 (valid until 31 Mar 2004).

⬚ ⛾ ⛓ Partial. 🛈 Obligatory. 🅿 None. ▦ ⛟ Guide dogs only.

ASKE HALL 🏛

Richmond, North Yorkshire DL10 5HJ

Tel: 01748 822000   **Fax:** 01748 826611

e-mail: mhairi.mercer@aske.co.uk   **www.aske.co.uk**

Owner: The Marquess of Zetland   **Contact:** Mhairi Mercer

Aske Hall lies in Capability Brown landscaped parkland and has been the family seat of the Dundas family since 1763. This Georgian treasure house boasts exquisite 18th century furniture, paintings and porcelain, including works by Robert Adam, Chippendale, Gainsborough, Raeburn and Meissen.

Location: OS Ref. NZ179 035. 2m SW of A1 at Scotch Corner, 1m from the A66, on the Gilling West road (B6274).

Open: Public Access days as per the website – dates shown. Group tours by appointment only. Mon - Fri, 10am - 3pm.

Admission: House & grounds: Adult £7, Child £5. Groups (10 - 30).

🛈 By arrangement. 🅿 Limited ⛟ In grounds on leads.

BAGSHAW MUSEUM

Wilton Park, Batley, West Yorkshire WF17 0AS

Tel: 01924 326155   **Fax:** 01924 326164

Owner: Kirklees Cultural Services   **Contact:** Melanie Brook

A Victorian Gothic mansion set in Wilton Park.

Location: OS Ref. SE235 257. From M62/J27 follow A62 to Huddersfield. At Birstall, follow tourist signs.

Open: Mon - Fri, 11am - 5pm. Sat & Sun, 12 noon - 5pm. Pre-booked groups and school parties welcome.

Admission: Free.

BENINGBROUGH HALL & GARDENS ✤

BENINGBROUGH, NORTH YORKSHIRE YO30 1DD

Tel: 01904 470666   **Fax:** 01904 470002

e-mail: beningbrough@nationaltrust.org.uk

Owner: The National Trust   **Contact:** The Visitor Services Manager

Imposing 18th century house with over 100 portraits from the National Portrait Gallery. Walled garden, children's playground, Victorian laundry. Herbaceous borders and parkland.

Location: OS Ref. SE516 586. 8m NW of York, 3m W of Shipton, 2m SE of Linton-on-Ouse, follow signposted route.

Open: 27 Mar - 31 Oct: Sat - Wed & Good Fri, also Fri in Jul & Aug. House: 12 noon - 5pm. Last admission 4.30pm. Grounds: 11am - 5.30pm.

Admission: House & Garden: Adult £6, Child £3, Family £14. Garden: Adult £5, Child £2.50, Family £11.50.

⬚ ⛾ ⛓ Partial. WC. ⛾ 🅿 Reduced rates for groups (15+), not Suns or BHs. ▦ ⛟ ⌂

BOLTON ABBEY

SKIPTON, NORTH YORKSHIRE BD23 6EX

www.boltonabbey.com

Tel: 01756 718009   **Fax:** 01756 710535   **e-mail:** tourism@boltonabbey.com

Owner: Trustees of the Chatsworth Settlement   **Contact:** Visitor Manager

Wordsworth, Turner and Landseer were inspired by this romantic and varied landscape. The Estate, centred around Bolton Priory (founded 1154), is the Yorkshire home of the Duke and Duchess of Devonshire and provides 80 miles of footpaths to enjoy some of the most spectacular landscape in England.

Location: OS Ref. SE074 542. On B6160, N from the junction with A59 Skipton - Harrogate road, 23m from Leeds.

Open: All year.

Admission: £4 per car, £2.50 for disabled (car park charge only).

⬚ ⛾ ⛓ ▦ Licensed. ⛾ Licensed. 🛈 By arrangement. 🅿 ▦ ⛟ In grounds, on leads.   🍴 Devonshire Arms Country House Hotel & Devonshire Fell Hotel nearby. ✱

BOLTON CASTLE

LEYBURN, NORTH YORKSHIRE DL8 4ET

www.boltoncastle.co.uk

Tel: 01969 623981 **Fax:** 01969 623332 **e-mail:** harry@boltoncastle.co.uk

Owner/Contact: Lord Bolton

A fine medieval castle that overlooks beautiful Wensleydale. Bolton Castle celebrated its 600th anniversary in 1999. Set your imagination free as you wander round this fascinating castle, which once held Mary Queen of Scots prisoner for 6 months and succumbed to a bitter Civil War siege. Don't miss the beautiful medieval garden and vineyard.

Location: OS Ref. SE034 918. Approx 6m W of Leyburn. 1m NW of Redmire.

Open: All year: daily, 10am - 5pm or dusk. Please telephone to confirm times from 14 Dec - 14 Feb.

Admission: Adult £5, Child/OAP. £3.50, Family £12.

🎥 ⓉWedding receptions. ⓀPartial. 🖭 🅿 💻 🐾In grounds, on leads. ⬆ ❋

BRAMHAM PARK 🏛

See page 382 for full page entry.

BROCKFIELD HALL 🏛
Warthill, York YO19 5XJ

Tel: 01904 489362

Owner/Contact: Mr & Mrs Simon Wood

A fine late Georgian house designed by Peter Atkinson, whose father had been assistant to John Carr of York, for Benjamin Agar Esq. Begun in 1804, its outstanding feature is an oval entrance hall with a fine cantilevered stone staircase curving past an impressive Venetian window. It is the family home of Mr and Mrs Simon Wood. Mrs Wood is the daughter of the late Lord and of Lady Martin Fitzalan Howard. He was the brother of the 17th Duke of Norfolk and son of the late Baroness Beaumont of Carlton Towers, Selby. There are some interesting portraits of her old Roman Catholic family, the Stapletons, and some good English furniture.

Location: OS Ref. SE664 550. 5m E of York off A166 or A64.

Open: 31 July and Aug: daily except Mons (open Aug BH Mon), 1 - 4pm. Other times by appointment.

Admission: Adult £4, Child £1.

Ⓚ Partial. ⓉObligatory. 🅿 💻 Guide dogs only.

BRODSWORTH HALL ♯
& GARDENS

See page 383 for full page entry.

BRONTË PARSONAGE MUSEUM
Church St, Haworth, Keighley, West Yorkshire BD22 8DR

Tel: 01535 642323   **Fax:** 01535 647131   **e-mail:** bronte@bronte.org.uk
www.bronte.info

Owner: The Brontë Society   **Contact:** The Administrator

Georgian parsonage, former home of the Brontë family, now a museum with rooms furnished as in the sisters' day and displays of their personal treasures as seen on BBC1's "In search of the Brontës".

Location: OS Ref. SE029 373. 8m W of Bradford, 3m S of Keighley.

Open: Apr - Sept: 10am - 5pm, Oct - Mar: 11am - 4.30pm. Daily except 24 - 27 Dec & 2 Jan - 2 Feb 2003.

Admission: Adult £4.80, Child £1.50 (5-16 inclusive), Conc. £3.50, Family £10.50. Discounts for booked groups.

Castle Howard, North Yorkshire from the book *Historic Family Homes and Gardens from the Air*, see page 54.

BROUGHTON HALL

SKIPTON, NORTH YORKSHIRE BD23 3AE

www.broughtonhall.co.uk www.ruralsolutions.co.uk

Tel: 01756 799608   **Fax:** 01756 700357

e-mail: tempest@broughtonhall.co.uk   **e-mail:** info@ruralsolutions.co.uk

Owner: The Tempest Family   **Contact:** The Estate Office

Stephen Tempest built Broughton Hall in 1597 and it was extended in the 18th and 19th centuries into the handsome and graceful form we see today. It is the private home of the Tempest family and is a Grade I listed building, the rooms containing fine Gillow furniture and interesting family portraits. Groups may visit for tours by prior arrangement. A 3,000 acre parkland setting and Italianate gardens which include a stunning conservatory, make Broughton Hall a desirable location for film makers and for corporate and promotional events, the owners being very experienced in successfully meeting the needs of such clients.

Nearby Estate buildings have been skilfully converted into the Broughton Hall Business Park. Here forty companies employ over five hundred people in quality offices in unspoilt historic buildings and peaceful surroundings, thanks to the innovative approach of Rural Solutions, the rural regeneration specialists (01756 799955) who conceived and completed the project.

Location: OS Ref. SD943 507. On A59, 3m W of Skipton midway between the Yorkshire and Lancashire centres. Good air and rail links.

Open: Year round tours for groups by arrangement.

Admission: £5.

By arrangement. **P**

BURTON AGNES HALL

DRIFFIELD, EAST YORKSHIRE YO25 0ND

www.burton-agnes.com

Tel: 01262 490324 **Fax:** 01262 490513

Owner: Burton Agnes Hall Preservation Trust Ltd   **Contact:** Mrs Susan Cunliffe-Lister

A lovely Elizabethan Hall containing treasures collected by the family over four centuries from the original carving and plasterwork to modern and Impressionist paintings. The Hall is surrounded by lawns and topiary yew. The old walled garden contains a maze, potager, jungle garden, campanula collection and colour gardens incorporating giant game boards. Children's corner.

Location: OS Ref. TA103 633. Off A614 between Driffield and Bridlington.

Open: 1 Apr - 31 Oct: daily, 11am - 5pm.

Admission: House & Gardens: Adult £5.20, Child £2.60, OAP £4.70. Gardens only: Adult £2.60, Child £1.20, OAP £2.35. 10% reduction for groups of 30+.

Ground floor & grounds. Café. Ice-cream parlour.
In grounds, on leads.

BURTON AGNES MANOR HOUSE

Burton Agnes, Bridlington, East Yorkshire

Tel: 01904 601901

Owner: English Heritage   **Contact:** The Yorkshire Regional Office

A rare example of a Norman house, altered and encased in brick in the 17th & 18th centuries.

Location: OS Ref. TA103 633. Off A614 between Driffield and Bridlington.

Open: 1 Apr - 31 Oct: daily, 11am - 5pm. Times subject to change April 2004.

Admission: Free.

Antonio Zucchi

1726-1795

Italian painter, doing much of the paintings on the decorative panelwork on Adam interiors.

Look at his work in Syon Park, Kenwood House, Osterley Park in London, and Harewood House, Yorkshire.

Kenneth Berry Studios & Associates

BURTON CONSTABLE HALL 🏠

SKIRLAUGH, EAST YORKSHIRE HU11 4LN

www.burtonconstable.com

Tel: 01964 562400   **Fax:** 01964 563229   **e-mail:** enquiries@burtonconstable.com

Owner: Burton Constable Foundation   **Contact:** Mrs Helen Dewson

One of the most fascinating country houses to survive with its historic collections, Burton Constable is a large Elizabethan mansion set in a 300 acre park with nearly 30 rooms open. The interiors of faded splendour are filled with fine furniture, paintings and sculpture, a library of 5,000 books and a remarkable 18th century 'cabinet of curiosities'. Occupied by the Constable family for over 400 years, the house still maintains the atmosphere of a home. Pleasure grounds with a delightful orangery ornamented with coade stone, a stable block and park landscaped by 'Capability' Brown in the 1770s.

Location: OS Ref. TA193 369. 14m E of Beverley via A165 Bridlington Road, follow Historic House signs. 7m NE of Hull via B1238 to Sproatley then follow Historic House signs.

Open: Hall, Grounds & Tearoom: 3 Apr - 31 Oct: Sat - Thur. Grounds & Tearoom: 12.30 - 5pm. Hall: 1 - 5pm. Last admission 4pm.

Admission: Hall & Grounds: Adult £5, Child £2, OAP £4.50, Family £11. Grounds only: Adult £1, Child 50p. Groups (20-80): £4. Connoisseur Study Visits: prices on application.

ℹ️No photography in house. 📷 ♿Suitable. WCs. ☕ 🐕By arrangement. 🅿️ 🛏️ 🦽In grounds on leads. ♨️

BYLAND ABBEY ⌗

Coxwold, Helmsley, North Yorkshire YO61 4BD

Tel: 01347 868614

Owner: English Heritage   **Contact:** The Custodian

Byland was once one of the three largest Cistercian monasteries in the North and inspired the design for the Rose Window in York Minster.

Location: OS Ref. SE549 789. 2m S of A170 between Thirsk and Helmsley, NE of Coxwold village.

Open: Please ring for details.

Admission: Adult £2, Child £1, Conc. £1.50 (valid to 31.3.04). 15% discount for groups (11+). Prices subject to change April 2004.

ℹ️WC. ♿ 🅿️Limited. 🦽 🛏️On leads. ♨️Tel for details.

CANNON HALL MUSEUM, PARK & GARDENS

Cawthorne, Barnsley, South Yorkshire S75 4AT

Tel: 01226 790270   **Fax:** 01226 792117   **e-mail:** cannonhall@barnsley.gov.uk

www.barnsley.gov.uk

Owner: Barnsley Metropolitan Borough Council   **Contact:** The Museum Manager

Set in 70 acres of historic parkland and gardens, Cannon Hall was for 200 years the home of the Spencer-Stanhope family with alterations in the 1760s by John Carr. The Hall now contains collections of fine furniture, old master paintings, stunning glassware and colourful pottery, much of which is displayed in period settings. Plus 'Charge', the Regimental museum of the 13th/18th Royal Hussars (QMO). Events and education programme and an ideal setting for conferences and Civil wedding ceremonies. Victorian tea room and gift shop.

Location: OS Ref. SE272 084. 6m NW of Barnsley of A635. M1/J38.

Open: Nov, Dec & Mar: Sun, 12 noon - 4pm; closed Jan & Feb. Apr - Oct: Wed - Fri, 10.30am - 5pm; Sat & Sun, 12 noon - 5pm. Last admission 4.15pm for 5pm. Open all year for weddings, school visits and corporate hospitality.

Admission: Free except for some events. Charge for car parking.

📷 🍴 ♿Partial. WC. ☕Weekends. 🅿️ 🦽 🛏️In grounds, on leads. 🔔 ❄️ ♨️Tel for details.

CASTLE HOWARD 🏠   *See page 384 for full page entry.*

CAWTHORNE VICTORIA JUBILEE MUSEUM

Taylor Hill, Cawthorne, Barnsley, South Yorkshire S75 4HQ

Tel: 01226 790545/790246

Owner: Cawthorne Village   **Contact:** Mrs Mary Herbert

A quaint and eccentric collection in a half-timbered building. Museum has a ramp and toilet for disabled visitors. School visits welcome.

Location: OS Ref. SE285 080. 4m W of Barnsley, just off the A635.

Open: Palm Sun - end Oct: Sats, Suns & BH Mons, 2 - 5pm. Groups by appointment throughout the year.

Admission: Adult 50p, Child 20p.

CLIFFE CASTLE

Keighley, West Yorkshire BD20 6LH

Tel: 01535 618231

Owner: City of Bradford Metropolitan District Council   **Contact:** Alison Armstrong

Victorian manufacturer's house of 1878 with tall tower and garden. Now a museum.

Location: OS Ref. SE057 422. ³/₄ m NW of Keighley off the A629.

Open: Please telephone for details.

Admission: Free.

CLIFFORD'S TOWER ⌗

Tower Street, York YO1 9SA

Tel: 01904 646940

Owner: English Heritage   **Contact:** The Custodian

A 13th century tower on one of two mottes thrown up by William the Conqueror to hold York. There are panoramic views of the city from the top of the tower.

Location: OS Ref. SE 605 515. York city centre.

Open: 1 Apr - 30 Sept: daily, 10am - 6pm; 1 - 31 Oct: daily, 10am - 5pm. 1 Nov - 31 Mar: daily, 10am - 4pm. Closed 24-26 Dec & 1 Jan. 14 - 22 Feb 2004: 10am - 5pm. Times subject to change April 2004.

Admission: Adult £2.50, Child £1.30, Conc. £1.90. Family ticket £6.30 (valid to 31.3.04). 15% discount available for groups (11+). Prices subject to change April 2004.

📷 ♿Unsuitable. 🅿️ 🦽 🛏️In grounds, on leads. ❄️

Skyscan/William Cross

CLIFTON PARK MUSEUM
Clifton Lane, Rotherham, South Yorkshire S65 2AA
Tel: 01709 823635
Owner: Rotherham Metropolitan Borough Council.   **Contact:** Steven Blackbourn
Furnished period rooms and one of the best collections of Rockingham porcelain in the country in an 18th century house set within a delightful park.
Location: OS Ref. SK435 926.
Open: Due to major refurbishment the Museum will be closed from 24 Dec 2002 and will reopen autumn 2004. For details of reopening contact 01709 823635.
Admission: Free.

CONISBROUGH CASTLE ⚓
Conisbrough, South Yorkshire
Tel: 01709 863329
Owner: English Heritage   **Contact:** The Administrator
The oldest circular keep in England and one of the finest medieval buildings, inspiration for Sir Walter Scott's *Ivanhoe.*
Location: OS Ref. SK515 989. 4¹/₂ m SW of Doncaster.
Open: For opening times and confirmed prices please contact 01709 863329.
Admission: Adults £3.75, Child £2, Conc. £2.50, Family £9.50. Prices subject to change April 2004.
🏠 ♿ 🅿

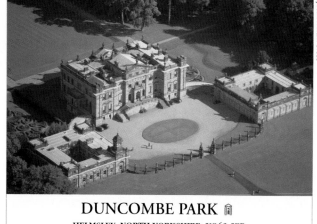

DUNCOMBE PARK 🏛
HELMSLEY, NORTH YORKSHIRE YO62 5EB

www.duncombepark.com

Tel: 01439 770213 **Fax:** 01439 771114
e-mail: liz@duncombepark.com
Owner/Contact: Lord & Lady Feversham
Lord and Lady Feversham's restored family home in the North York Moors National Park. Built on a virgin plateau overlooking Norman Castle and river valley, it is surrounded by 35 acres of beautiful 18th century landscaped gardens and 400 acres of parkland with national nature reserve and veteran trees.
Location: OS Ref. SE604 830. Entrance just off Helmsley Market Square, signed off A170 Thirsk - Scarborough road.
Open: 13 Apr - 24 Oct: Sun - Thur.
Admission: House & Gardens: Adult £6.50, Child (10 - 16yrs) £3, Conc. £5, Family (2+2) £13.50 Groups (15+): £4.75. Gardens & Parkland: Adult £3.50, Child (10-16yrs) £1.75, Conc £3. Parkland: Adult £2, Child (10-16yrs) £1. Season ticket (2+2) £25.
ℹ️ Country walks, nature reserve, orienteering, conferences. 🏠 🎁
🍽 Banqueting facilities. ♿Partial. 🍷Licensed. 🚻Obligatory. 🅿 🎦
🐕 In park on leads. ♨ ♨ Tel for details.

CONSTABLE BURTON HALL GARDENS 🏛
LEYBURN, NORTH YORKSHIRE DL8 5LJ

www.constableburtongardens.co.uk

Tel: 01677 450428 **Fax:** 01677 450622
Owner/Contact: M C A Wyvill Esq
A delightful terraced woodland garden of lilies, ferns, hardy shrubs, roses and wild flowers, attached to a beautiful Palladian house designed by John Carr (not open). Garden trails, rockery with an interesting collection of alpines. Stream garden with large architectural plants and reflection ponds. Impressive spring display of daffodils and tulips.
Location: OS Ref. SE164 913. 3m E of Leyburn off the A684.
Open: Garden only: 21 Mar - 10 Oct: daily, 9am - 6pm.
Admission: Adult £2.50, Child (under 16yrs) 50p, OAP £2.
🎁 ♿Partial. 🚻Group tours by arrangement. 🅿Limited for coaches.
🐕In grounds, on leads. ♨

EASBY ABBEY ⚓
Nr Richmond, North Yorkshire
Tel: 01748 822493
Owner: English Heritage   **Contact:** Head Custodian, Richmond Castle
Substantial remains of the medieval abbey buildings stand by the River Swale, a short walk from Richmond Castle.
Location: OS Ref. NZ185 003. 1m SE of Richmond off B6271.
Open: Apr - Sept: 10am - 6pm. Oct: 10am - 5pm. Nov - Mar: Wed - Sun, 11am - 4pm. (Closed 24 - 26 Dec & 1 Jan.) Times subject to change April 2004.
Admission: Free.
🅿 🐕 ✳

🍸 **Corporate Hospitality** see front section

EAST RIDDLESDEN HALL

BRADFORD ROAD, KEIGHLEY, WEST YORKSHIRE BD20 5EL

www.nationaltrust.org.uk

Tel: 01535 607075 **Fax:** 01535 691462 **e-mail:** eastriddlesden@ntrust.org.uk

Owner: The National Trust   **Contact:** Property Manager

Homely 17th century merchant's house with beautiful embroideries and textiles, Yorkshire carved oak furniture and fine ceilings. Delightful garden with lavender and herbs. Also wild garden with old varieties of apple trees. Magnificent oak framed barn. Handling collection, children's play area. Costumed tours July and August. Events.

Location: OS Ref. SE079 421. 1m NE of Keighley on S side of B6265 in Riddlesden. 50yds from Leeds/Liverpool Canal. Bus: Frequent services from Skipton, Bradford and Leeds. Railway station at Keighley 2m.

Open: 30 Mar - 2 Nov: daily except Mons, Thurs & Fris (open Good Fri, BH Mons & Mons in Jul & Aug), 12 noon - 5pm, Sats, 1 - 5pm.

Admission: Adult £3.80, Child £1.90, Family £9.50. Booked groups (15+): Adult £3.20, Child £1.60.

Partial. By arrangement. Limited for coaches, please book. In grounds, on leads. Tel for details.

EPWORTH OLD RECTORY

1 Rectory Street, Epworth, Doncaster, South Yorkshire DN9 1HX

Tel: 01427 872268 **e-mail:** curator@epwortholdrectory.org.uk

Owner: World Methodist Council   **Contact:** A Milson (Curator)

1709 Queen Anne period house, John and Charles Wesley's boyhood home. Portraits, period furniture, Methodist memorabilia. Garden, picnic facilities, cinematic presentation.

Location: OS Ref. SE785 036. Epworth lies on A161, 3m S M180/J2. 10m N of Gainsborough. When in Epworth follow the Wesley Trail information boards.

Open: 1 Mar - 31 Oct. Mar, Apr & Oct: Mon - Sat, 10am - 12 noon & 2 - 4pm, Suns, 2 - 4pm. May - Sept: Mon - Sat, 10am - 4.30pm, Suns, 2 - 4.30pm.

Admission: Adult £3, Child £1, OAP £2.50, Student £2, Family £7.

Ground floor & grounds. By arrangement. Obligatory. Limited. Guide dogs only.

FAIRFAX HOUSE   *See page 385 for full page entry.*

FOUNTAINS ABBEY & STUDLEY ROYAL   *See page 386 for entry.*

THE GEORGIAN THEATRE ROYAL & THEATRE MUSEUM

Victoria Road, Richmond, North Yorkshire DL10 4DW

Tel: 01748 823710 **Box Office:** 01748 823021/ 01748 825252

Owner: Georgian Theatre Royal Trust   **Contact:** Jayne Duncan

A unique example of Georgian theatre with the majority of its original features intact. Built in 1788 by actor/manager, Samuel Butler. Closed since January for major restoration work.

Location: OS Ref. NZ174 013. 4m from the A1 (Scotch Corner) on the A6108.

Open: All year: Mon - Sat, 10am - 5pm. Guided tours: 10 & 11am, 12 noon, 1, 1.30, 2.30, 3.30 & 4.30pm.

Admission: Suggested donation £2.50. Child Free.

HANDS ON HISTORY

Market Place, Hull, East Yorkshire HU1 1EP

Tel: 01482 613902 **Fax:** 01482 613710

Owner: Hull City Council   **Contact:** S R Green

Housed in the Old Grammar School this history resource centre offers hands on activities for the public and schools alike.

Location: OS Ref. TA099 285. 50 yds SW of the Church at centre of the Old Town.

Open: School holidays and weekends open to the public. Please phone for details.

Admission: Free.

HAREWOOD HOUSE   *See page 387 for full page entry.*

HELMSLEY CASTLE

Helmsley, North Yorkshire YO22 5AB

Tel: 01439 770442

Owner: English Heritage   **Contact:** The Custodian

Explore the changing military needs of this castle with its 12th century keep, Tudor mansion and spectacular earthworks cut from solid rock.

Location: OS Ref. SE611 836. In Helmsley town.

Open: 1 Apr - 30 Sept: daily, 10am - 6pm. 1 - 31 Oct, daily, 10am - 5pm. 1 Nov - 31 Mar: Wed - Sun, 11am - 4pm (closed 1 - 2pm). (Closed 24 - 26 Dec & 1 Jan.) Times subject to change April 2004.

Admission: Adult £2.60, Child £1.30, Conc £2, Family £6.50 (valid to 31.3.04). 15% discount for groups (11+). Prices subject to change April 2004.

WC. Tel for details.

HELMSLEY WALLED GARDEN

Cleveland Way, Helmsley, North Yorkshire YO62 5AH

Tel/Fax: 01439 771427

Owner: Helmsley Walled Garden Ltd   **Contact:** Paul Radcliffe/Lindsay Tait

A 5 acre walled garden under restoration. Orchid house restored. Plant sales area and café conservatory.

Location: OS Ref. SE611 836. 25m N of York, 15m from Thirsk. In Helmsley follow signs to Cleveland Way.

Open: 1 Apr - 31 Oct: daily, 10.30am - 5pm. Nov - Mar: Sats/Suns, 12 noon - 4pm.

Admission: Adult £3, Child Free, Conc. £2.

HOVINGHAM HALL

YORK, NORTH YORKSHIRE YO62 4LU

www.hovingham.co.uk

Tel: 01653 628771 **Fax:** 01653 628668 **e-mail:** office@hovingham.co.uk

Owner: William Worsley   **Contact:** Mrs Lamprey

Palladian house built c1760 by Thomas Worsley to his own design. Unique entry by huge riding school. This family home has extensive gardens with magnificent yew hedges and is in beautiful parkland setting. The private cricket ground in front of the house is reported to be the oldest in England.

Location: OS Ref. SE666 756. 18m N of York on Malton/Helmsley Road (B1257).

Open: 7 Jun - 10 Jul: daily except Suns, 1.45 - 4.30pm (last entry 4pm).

Admission: Adult £5.50, Child £3. Gardens only: £3.

No photography in house. Partial. By arrangement. Limited. Guide dogs only.

JERVAULX ABBEY
Ripon, North Yorkshire HG4 4PH
Tel: 01677 460226
Owner/Contact: Mr I S Burdon
Extensive ruins of a former Cistercian abbey.
Location: OS Ref. SE169 858. Beside the A6108 Ripon - Leyburn road, 5m SE of Leyburn and 5m NW of Masham.
Open: Daily during daylight hours. Tearoom: Mar - 1 Nov (all home baking).
Admission: Adult £2, Child £1.50 in honesty box at Abbey entrance.

KIPLIN HALL
KIPLIN, Nr SCORTON, RICHMOND, NORTH YORKSHIRE DL10 6AT
www.kiplinhall.co.uk www.herriotdaysout.com
Tel/Fax: 01748 818178 **e-mail:** info@kiplinhall.co.uk
Owner: Kiplin Hall Trustees   **Contact:** The Administrator
A Grade I Listed Jacobean house built in 1620 by George Calvert, 1st Lord Baltimore, founder of the State of Maryland, USA, containing paintings and furniture collected by four families over four centuries. Continuing major restoration has brought the Hall back to life as a comfortable Victorian family home.
Location: OS Ref. SE274 976. Signposted from Scorton - Northallerton road (B6271).
Open: Easter weekend; May & Sept: Sun & Tue; Jun, Jul & Aug: Sun - Wed, 2 - 5pm. Open at other times of the year by appointment with the Administrator.
Admission: Adult £4, Child £2 Conc. £3. Groups (15-50) by arrangement.
⬚ ⬚Partial. ⬚ ⬚By arrangement. ⬚Limited. ⬚
⬚In grounds, on leads. Guide dogs only in house. ⬚ ⬚Tel for details.

KIRKHAM PRIORY
Kirkham, Whitwell-on-the-Hill, North Yorkshire YO60 7JS
Tel: 01653 618768
Owner: English Heritage   **Contact:** The Custodian
Set in peaceful valley, discover the ruins of an elaborate gatehouse and washroom. Find out also why Churchill visited during the Second World War.
Location: OS Ref. SE735 657. 5m SW of Malton on minor road off A64.
Open: 1 Apr - 30 Sept: daily, 10am - 6pm. 1 - 31 Oct: daily, 10am - 5pm. Times subject to change April 2004.
Admission: Adult £2, Child £1, Conc. £1.50 (valid to 31.3.04). 15% discount for groups (11+). Prices subject to change April 2004.
⬚WC. ⬚ ⬚ ⬚Limited. ⬚ ⬚On leads.

KNARESBOROUGH CASTLE & MUSEUM
Knaresborough, North Yorkshire HG5 8AS
Tel: 01423 556188 **Fax:** 01423 556130
Owner: Duchy of Lancaster   **Contact:** Miss Janine Taylor
Ruins of 14th century castle standing high above the town. Local history museum housed in Tudor Courthouse. Gallery devoted to the Civil War.
Location: OS Ref. SE349 569. 5m E of Harrogate, off A59.
Open: Easter BH - 30 Sept: daily, 10.30am - 5pm.
Admission: Adult £2.50, Child £1.25, OAP £1.50, Family £6.50, Groups (10+) £2.

LEDSTON HALL
Hall Lane, Ledston, Castleford, West Yorkshire WF10 2BB
Tel: 01423 523423 **Fax:** 01423 521373 **e-mail:** james.hare@carterjonas.co.uk
Owner/Contact: James Hare
17th century mansion with some earlier work.
Location: OS Ref. SE437 289. 2m N of Castleford, off A656.
Open: Exterior only: May - Aug, Mon - Fri, 9am - 4pm. Other days by appointment.
Admission: Free.

THE LINDLEY MURRAY SUMMERHOUSE
The Mount School, Dalton Terrace, York YO24 4DD
Tel: 01904 667506 www.mount.n-yorks.sch.uk
Owner/Contact: The Mount School
Location: OS Ref. SE593 510. Dalton Terrace, York.
Open: By prior arrangement: Mon - Fri, 9am - 4.30pm all the year (apart from BHs).
Admission: Free.
⬚ ⬚ ⬚Guide dogs only. ⬚

LING BEECHES GARDEN
Ling Lane, Scarcroft, Leeds, West Yorkshire LS14 3HX
Tel: 0113 2892450
Owner/Contact: Mrs A Rakusen
A 2 acre woodland garden designed by the owner.
Location: OS Ref. SE354 413. Off A58 midway between Leeds & Wetherby. At Scarcroft turn into Ling Lane, signed to Wike on brow of hill.
Open: By appointment, please telephone for details.
Admission: Adult £2.50, Child Free.

LONGLEY OLD HALL
Longley, Huddersfield, West Yorkshire HD5 8LB
Tel: 01484 430852 **e-mail:** gallagher@longleyoldhall.co.uk
www.longleyoldhall.co.uk
Owner: Christine & Robin Gallagher   **Contact:** Christine Gallagher
This timber framed Grade II* manor house dates from the 14th century. It was owned by the Ramsden family, the former Lords of the Manors of Almondbury and Huddersfield, for over 400 years.
Location: OS Ref. SE154 150. 1¹/₂ m SE of Huddersfield towards Castle Hill, via Dog Kennel Bank.
Open: Easter, early May, Spring & Summer BH weekends and 27 - 30 Dec for guided tours. Available at other times by appointment. Candlelit evenings – contact for details. Group viewings (10 - 25) of Tudor decorations by candlelight throughout Nov & Dec.
Admission: £6 for open days - please telephone for other times.
⬚ ⬚Unsuitable. ⬚Obligatory. ⬚Limited for coaches. ⬚ ⬚

MARKENFIELD HALL
Nr Ripon, North Yorkshire HG4 3AD
Tel: 01765 603411 / 692303 **Fax:** 01765 607195 www.markenfield.com
Owner: Lady Deirdre Curteis   **Contact:** The Administrator
Fine example of a moated English Manor House (14th and 15th century).
Location: OS Ref. SE294 672. Access from W side of A61, 1¹/₂m S of Safeways roundabout, Ripon.
Open: 2 - 15 May & 13 - 26 Jun: daily, 2 - 5pm. Groups all year round by appointment.
Admission: Adult £3, Child (under 16)/OAP £2. Booked groups (min charge £60).
⬚ ⬚

MIDDLEHAM CASTLE
Middleham, Leyburn, North Yorkshire DL8 4RJ
Tel: 01969 623899
Owner: English Heritage   **Contact:** The Custodian
The childhood home and favourite castle of King Richard III. Climb the massive keep, one of the largest in England, and enjoy magnificent views.
Location: OS Ref. SE128 875. At Middleham, 2m S of Leyburn on A6108.
Open: 1 Apr - 30 Sept: daily, 10am - 6pm. 1 - 31 Oct, daily, 10am - 5pm. 1 Nov - 31 Mar: Wed - Sun, 11am - 4pm (closed 1 - 2pm). Closed 24 - 26 Dec & 1 Jan. Times subject to change April 2004.
Admission: Adult £3, Child £1.50, Conc. £2.30 (valid to 31.3.04). 15% discount for groups (11+). Prices subject to change April 2004.
⬚Exhibition. WCs. ⬚ ⬚Grounds. ⬚ ⬚ ⬚In grounds, on leads. ⬚
⬚Tel for details.

English Heritage Photo Library

MOUNT GRACE PRIORY

STADDLEBRIDGE, NORTHALLERTON, NORTH YORKSHIRE DL6 3JG

Tel: 01609 883494

Owner: National Trust   **Managed by:** English Heritage   **Contact:** The Custodian

Set amid woodland below the North York Moors and Cleveland Way National Trail, the site's history spans several centuries. The 14th century ruins are the best preserved of any Carthusian monastery in Britain. Experience the simple and austere life of a monk in the reconstructed cell and herb garden. The 17th century manor house, built on the ruins of the monastery guest house, and which now forms the entrance to the site, is a rare building of the Commonwealth period. The gardens were also re-modelled in the 20th century to enhance the mansion, and are a haven for the famous 'Priory Stoats'.

Location: OS Ref. SE449 985. 12m N of Thirsk, 7m NE of Northallerton on A19.

Open: 1 Apr - 30 Sept: daily, 10am - 6pm. 1 - 31 Oct: daily, 10am - 5pm. 1 Nov - 31 Mar: Wed - Sun, 11am - 4pm (closed 1 - 2pm). Closed 24 - 26 Dec & 1 Jan. Times subject to change April 2004.

Admission: Adult £3.20, Child £1.60, Conc. £2.40, Family £8 (valid to 31.3.04). 15% discount for groups (11+). Prices subject to change April 2004.

⒤WCs. ⬚ ♿Ground floor & grounds. ℙ ▣ ❋ ⬚Tel for details.

NEWBURGH PRIORY

COXWOLD, NORTH YORKSHIRE YO61 4AS

Tel: 01347 868435

Owner/Contact: Sir George Wombwell Bt

Originally 1145 with major alterations in 1568 and 1720, it has been the home of the Earls of Fauconberg and of the Wombwell family since 1538. Tomb of Oliver Cromwell (3rd daughter Mary married Viscount Fauconberg) is in the house. Extensive grounds contain a water garden, walled garden, topiary yews and woodland walks.

Location: OS Ref. SE541 764. 4m E of A19, 18m N of York, 1/2 m E of Coxwold.

Open: Easter Sun & Mon; Spring BH Sun & Mon. 4 Apr - 30 Jun: Wed & Sun only. House: 2.30 - 4.45pm. Garden: 2 - 6pm. Tours every 1/2 hour, take approximately 50mins. Booked groups by arrangement.

Admission: Gardens only: £2.50, Child Free. House & Grounds: £5. Child £1.50. Special tours of Private Apartment in addition to the above: 4 Apr - 2 May: Wed & Sun only: £6pp.

⒤No photography in house. ♿Partial. ▣ ⒤Obligatory. ℙLimited for coaches. ❧In grounds, on leads. ⬚

THE MUSEUM OF SOUTH YORKSHIRE LIFE

Cusworth Hall & Park, Cusworth Lane, Doncaster, South Yorkshire DN5 7TU

Tel: 01302 782342

Owner: Doncaster Metropolitan Borough Council **Contact:** Mr F Carpenter, Curator

A magnificent Grade I country house set in a landscaped parkland and built in 1740, with a chapel and other rooms designed by James Paine, the house is now the home of a museum showing the changing home, work and social conditions of the region over the last 250 years. Regular events and activities.

Location: OS Ref. SE547 039. A1(M)/J37, then A635 and right into Cusworth Lane.

Open: Some parts of the building will be closed due to extensive renovation during 2004. Please telephone for more information.

NATIONAL CENTRE FOR EARLY MUSIC

St Margaret's Church, Walmgate, York YO1 9TL

Tel: 01904 632220   **Fax:** 01904 612631   **e-mail:** info@ncem.co.uk

www.ncem.co.uk

Owner: York Early Music Foundation   **Contact:** Mrs G Baldwin

The National Centre for Early Music is based in the medieval church of St Margaret's York. The church boasts a 12th century Romanesque doorway and a 17th century brick tower of considerable note. The Centre hosts concerts, music education activities, conferences, recordings and events.

Location: OS Ref. SE609 515. Inside Walmgate Bar, within the city walls, on the E side of the city.

Open: Mon - Fri, 10am - 4pm. Also by appointment. Access is necessarily restricted when events are taking place.

Admission: Free, donations welcome.

♿ ⒤By arrangement. ℙLimited. No coaches. ❧Guide dogs only. ▣ ❋ ⬚Tel for details.

NEWBY HALL & GARDENS 🏛 See page 388 for full page entry.

NORMANBY HALL

Scunthorpe, North Lincolnshire DN15 9HU

Tel: 01724 720588   **Fax:** 01724 721248   **e-mail:** normanby.hall@northlincs.gov.uk

www.northlincs.gov.uk/normanby

Managed by: North Lincolnshire Council   **Contact:** Park Manager

Set in 300 acres of Park, the restored working Victorian Walled Garden has something to impress at every turn. Victorian varieties of fruit, vegetables and flowers are grown using traditional and organic methods of cultivation. Glasshouses display a wonderful collection of exotic plants and ferns. Visitors may tour the Regency Mansion, discovering re-creations of Regency, Victorian and Edwardian interiors.

Location: OS Ref. SE886 166. 4m N of Scunthorpe off B1430. Follow signs for M181 & Humber Bridge. Tours by arrangement.

Open: Hall & Farming Museum: 31 Mar - 28 Sept: 1 - 5pm. Park & Adventure Playground: daily, 9am - dusk. Walled Garden: daily, 10.30am - 5pm (4pm in winter). Last admission at all venues 1/2 hour before closing.

Admission: Adult £4, Child £2, Conc. £3.60. Season ticket £12.

⒤Fishing available. ⬚ ❋ ⬚Wedding receptions. ♿Ground floor & grounds. WC. ▣ ⒤By arrangement. ℙ ▣ ❧In grounds, on leads. ⬚ ❋ ⬚Tel for details.

Special Events Index see front section

NORTON CONYERS
NR RIPON, NORTH YORKSHIRE HG4 5EQ

Tel/Fax: 01765 640333 **e-mail:** norton.conyers@ripon.org

Owner: Sir James and Lady Graham **Contact:** Lady Graham

Visited by Charlotte Brontë in 1839, Norton Conyers is an original of 'Thornfield Hall' in *Jane Eyre*, and a family legend was an inspiration for the mad Mrs Rochester. Building is late medieval with Stuart and Georgian additions. Friendly atmosphere, resulting from 380 years of occupation by the Grahams. Family pictures, furniture, costumes and ceramics on display. 18th century walled garden near house, with Orangery and herbaceous borders. Small plants sales area specialising in unusual hardy plants. Pick your own fruit in season.

Location: OS Ref. SF319 763. 4m N of Ripon. $3^1/2$m from the A1.

Open: House & Garden: Easter Sun & Mon. BH Suns & Mons. Suns: 25 Apr - 29 Aug. Daily: 28 June - 3 July. House: 2 - 5pm. Garden: 12 - 5pm. Last admissions 4:40pm. Garden also open Thurs throughout the year 10 - 4pm (please check beforehand). Also some Sundays for charity; telephone for details.

Admission: House: Adult £4, Child (10-16yrs)/Conc. £3. Reduced rate for two or more children. Garden: Free (donations welcome), but charges are made at charity openings. Groups: by arrangement.

No interior photography. No stilettos in house. Partial. WC.
Only on Sunday Charity Days, please tel for dates. By arrangement. P
In grounds, on leads, guide dogs only in house. Tel for details.

NOSTELL PRIORY
Doncaster Road, Wakefield, West Yorkshire WF4 1QE

Tel: 01924 863892 **Fax:** 01924 865282 **www.**nationaltrust.org.uk

Owner: The National Trust **Contact:** Visitor Services Manager

Nostell Priory, one of Yorkshire's finest jewels, is an 18th century architectural masterpiece by James Paine.

Location: OS Ref. SE403 175. 6m SE of Wakefield, off A638.

Open: House: 27 Mar - 31 Oct: daily except Mon/Tues, 1 - 5pm & 6 Nov - 9 Dec: Sat & Sun, 12 noon - 4pm (open BH Mons). Grounds, Shop, Stables & Tearoom: 6 - 21 Mar: Sat & Sun 11am - 4.30pm & 27 Mar - 31 Oct: Wed - Sun. 11am - 5.30pm & 6 Nov - 9 Dec, Sat & Sun, 11am - 4.30pm.

Admission: House & Grounds: Adult £5, Child £2.50, Family (2+4) £12.50. Grounds only: Adult £2.50, Child £1.20.

Baby facilities. Partial. WC. By arrangement. P
In grounds, on leads. Send SAE for details.

NUNNINGTON HALL
Nunnington, North Yorkshire YO62 5UY

Tel: 01439 748283 **Fax:** 01439 748284

Owner: The National Trust **Contact:** The Property Manager

17th century manor house with magnificent oak-panelled hall, nursery, haunted room, and attics, with their fascinating Carlisle collection of miniature rooms fully furnished to reflect different periods.

Location: OS Ref. SE670 795. In Ryedale, $4^1/2$ m SE of Helmsley, $1^1/2$ m N of B1257.

Open: 20 Mar - 31 Oct. Apr & Oct: daily except Mon & Tues (open BH Mons). 1.30 - 4.30pm. May & Sept: daily except Mon & Tues (open BH Mons). 1.30 - 5pm. June - Aug: daily except Mon (open BH Mons). 1.30 - 5pm.

Admission: House & Garden: Adult £5, Child (5 - 16yrs) £2.50. Garden: Adult £2.50 Child Free. Family (2+3) £12.50. Groups: Adult £4.50 (groups of 15; enquiries to Linzi)

Ground floor and grounds.WC. Guide dogs only. Tel for details.

ORMESBY HALL
Ladgate Lane, Ormesby, Middlesbrough TS7 9AS

Tel: 01642 324188 **Fax:** 01642 300937 **e-mail:** ormesbyhall@nationaltrust.org.uk

Owner: The National Trust **Contact:** The House Manager

A mid 18th century house with opulent decoration inside, including fine plasterwork by contemporary craftsmen. A Jacobean doorway with a carved family crest survives from the earlier house on the site. The stable block, attributed to Carr of York, is a particularly fine mid 18th century building with an attractive courtyard leased to the Mounted Police; also an attractive garden with holly walk.

Location: OS Ref. NZ530 167. 3m SE of Middlesbrough.

Open: 30 Mar- 31 Oct: Tue, Wed, Thur & Sun (open Good Fri & BH Mons), 1.30 - 4.30pm. Tearoom: open 12.30pm for light lunches.

Admission: House, garden & model railways: Adult £3.90, Child £1.90, Family £9.50. Garden & railways: Adult £2.70, Child £1.20.

Ground floor & grounds. WC.

PARCEVALL HALL GARDENS
Skyreholme, Skipton, North Yorkshire BD23 6DE

Tel: 01756 720311 **Fax:** 01756 720441 **Contact:** Phillip Nelson (Head Gardener)

Owner: Walsingham College (Yorkshire Properties) Ltd.

Location: OS Ref. SE068 613. E side of Upper Wharfedale, $1^1/2$ m NE of Appletreewick. 12m NNW of Ilkley by B6160 and via Burnsall.

Open: 1 Apr - 31 Oct: 10am - 6pm.

Admission: £3.50, Child 50p.

PICKERING CASTLE
Pickering, North Yorkshire YO18 7AX

Tel: 01751 474989

Owner: English Heritage **Contact:** The Custodian

A splendid motte and bailey castle built by William the Conqueror, it was later used as a royal ranch. Discover more of its fascinating history in the chapel exhibition.

Location: OS Ref. SE800 845. In Pickering, 15m SW of Scarborough.

Open: 1 Apr - 30 Sept: daily, 10am - 6pm. 1 - 31 Oct: daily, 10am - 5pm. 1 Nov - 31 Mar: Wed - Sun, 11am - 4pm (closed 1 - 2pm). Closed 24 - 26 Dec & 1 Jan. Times subject to change April 2004.

Admission: Adult £2.60, Child £1.30, Conc. £2, Family £6.50. 15% discount for groups (11+). Prices subject to change April 2004.

WCs. Partial. P Limited. In grounds, on leads.

PLUMPTON ROCKS
Plumpton, Knaresborough, North Yorkshire HG5 8NA

Tel: 01423 863950 **www.**plumptonrocks.co.uk

Owner: Edward de Plumpton Hunter **Contact:** Robert de Plumpton Hunter

Grade II* listed garden extending to over 30 acres including an idyllic lake, dramatic millstone grit rock formation, romantic woodland walks winding through bluebells and rhododendrons. Declared by English Heritage to be of outstanding interest. Painted by Turner. Described by Queen Mary as 'Heaven on earth'.

Location: OS Ref. SE355 535. Midway between Harrogate and Wetherby on the A661, 1m SE of A661 junction with the Harrogate southern bypass.

Open: Mar - Oct: Sat, Sun & BHs, 11am - 6pm.

Admission: Adult £2, Child/OAP £1.

Unsuitable. By arrangement. P Limited for coaches. In grounds, on leads.

RHS GARDEN HARLOW CARR

CRAG LANE, HARROGATE, NORTH YORKSHIRE HG3 1QB

www.rhs.org.uk

Tel: 01423 565418 **Fax:** 01423 530663 **e-mail:** admin-harlowcarr@rhs.org.uk

Owner/Contact: Royal Horticultural Society

Beautiful 58 acre garden with new BBC 'Gardens through Time' to mark the RHS Bicentenary in 2004, flower and vegetable trials, ornamental grasses, woodland and streamside... to name a few. Courses on gardening and horticulture, family events, playground, Gardening Museum, Plant Centre and Gift Shop, Café bar, free parking – one of Yorkshire's most relaxing locations.

Location: OS Ref. SE285 543. 1¹/₂m W from town centre on B6162.

Open: Daily: 9.30am - 6pm or dusk if earlier. Last entry 1 hour before closing.

Admission: Adult £5, Child (6-16yrs) £1, Child (under 6yrs) Free, OAP £4.50. Groups (10+): £4. Groups must book in advance.

ⓘPicnic area. ⬚ ⬚ ⬚Partial. WC. ⬚Licensed. ⬚Licensed. ⬚By arrangement. ⬚ ⬚ ⬚Guide dogs only. ⬚ ⬚

© English Heritage Photo Library

RICHMOND CASTLE ⌗

TOWER ST, RICHMOND, NORTH YORKSHIRE DL10 4QW

Tel: 01748 822493

Owner: English Heritage   **Contact:** The Custodian

Set amid woodland below the North York Moors and built shortly after 1066, this is the best preserved castle of such scale and age in Britain. The magnificent Keep, with breathtaking views of the River Swale, is reputed to be the place where the legendary King Arthur sleeps. An exhibition and contemporary garden reflect the castle's military history from the 11th to 20th centuries.

Location: OS Ref. NZ174 006. In Richmond.

Open: 1 Apr - 30 Sept: daily, 10am - 6pm. 1 - 31 Oct: daily, 10am - 5pm. 1 Nov - 31 Mar: Wed - Sun, 11am - 4pm. Closed 24- 26 Dec & 1 Jan. Times subject to change April 2004.

Admission: Adult £3, Child £1.50, Conc. £2.30 (valid to 31.3.04). 15% discount for groups (11+). Prices subject to change April 2004.

ⓘNew interactive exhibition. WCs. ⬚ ⬚Partial. ⬚ ⬚In grounds, on leads. ⬚ ⬚Tel for details.

English Heritage Photo Library

RIEVAULX ABBEY ⌗

RIEVAULX, Nr HELMSLEY, NORTH YORKSHIRE YO62 5LB

Tel: 01439 798228

Owner: English Heritage   **Contact:** The Custodian

In a deeply wooded valley by the River Rye you can see some of the most spectacular monastic ruins in England, dating from the 12th century. The church has the earliest large Cistercian nave in Britain. A fascinating exhibition shows how successfully the Cistercians at Rievaulx ran their many businesses and explains the part played by Abbot Aelred, who ruled for twenty years. New museum, exhibition and interactive display.

Location: OS Ref. SE577 849. 2¹/₄ m W of Helmsley on minor road off B1257.

Open: 1 Apr - 30 Sept: daily, 10am - 6pm. 1 - 31 Oct: daily, 10am - 5pm. 1 Nov - 31 Mar: Wed - Sun, 11am - 4pm. Closed 24- 26 Dec & 1 Jan. Times subject to change April 2004.

Admission: Adult £3.80, Child £1.90, Conc. £2.90 (valid to 31.3.04). 15% discount for groups (11+). Prices subject to change April 2004.

ⓘWCs. ⬚ ⬚Partial. ⬚ ⬚ ⬚ ⬚On leads. ⬚ ⬚Tel for details.

RIEVAULX TERRACE & TEMPLES 🌿
Rievaulx, Helmsley, North Yorkshire YO62 5LJ
Tel: 01439 748283 **Fax:** 01439 748284
Owner: The National Trust   **Contact:** The Property Manager
A ¹/₂ m long grass-covered terrace and adjoining woodlands with vistas over Rievaulx Abbey and Rye valley. There are two mid-18th century temples. Note: no access to property Nov - end Mar.
Location: OS Ref. SE579 848. 2¹/₂ m NW of Helmsley on B1257. E of the Abbey.
Open: 20 Mar - 31 Oct: daily, 10.30am - 6pm (5pm Oct & Nov). Last admission 1hr before closing. Ionic Temple closed 1 - 2pm. Events: for details contact Property Secretary at Nunnington Hall, tel. 01439 748283.
Admission: Adult £3.80, Child (5 - 16yrs) £2, Family (2+3) £9.60. Groups (15+): £3.20 (enquiries to Linzi).
📷 ♿Grounds. Batricar available. 🐕In grounds, on leads. 🌐Tel for details.

RIPLEY CASTLE 🏛
See page 389 for full page entry.

RIPON CATHEDRAL
Ripon, North Yorkshire HG4 1QR
Tel: 01765 604108 (information on tours etc.)   **Contact:** Canon Keith Punshon
One of the oldest crypts in Europe (672). Marvellous choir stalls and misericords (500 years old). Almost every type of architecture. Treasury.
Location: OS Ref. SE314 711. 5m W signposted off A1, 12m N of Harrogate.
Open: All year: 8am - 6pm.
Admission: Donations: £3 pp. Pre-booked guided tours available.

ROCHE ABBEY 🏛
Maltby, Rotherham, South Yorkshire S66 8NW
Tel: 01709 812739
Owner: English Heritage   **Contact:** The Custodian
Set in a beautiful, secluded valley landscaped by 'Capability' Brown in the 18th century, the early Gothic transepts of this 'miniature Fountains Abbey' still survive to their original height.
Location: OS Ref. SK544 898. 1m S of Maltby off A634.
Open: 1 Apr - 30 Sept: daily, 10am - 6pm. 1 - 31 Oct: daily, 10am - 5pm. Times subject to change April 2004.
Admission: Adult £2, Child £1, Conc. £1.50 (valid to 31.3.04). 15% discount for groups (11+). Prices subject to change April 2004.
ℹ️WCs. 📷♿Partial. 🅿Limited. 🔲 🐕In grounds, on leads. 🌐Tel for details.

RYEDALE FOLK MUSEUM
Hutton le Hole, York, North Yorkshire YO62 6UA
Tel: 01751 417367 **e-mail:** info@ryedalefolkmuseum.co.uk
Owner: The Crosland Foundation   **Contact:** Mick Krupa
13 historic buildings showing the lives of ordinary folk from earliest times to the present day.
Location: OS Ref. SE705 902. Follow signs from Hutton le Hole. 3m N of Kirkbymoorside.
Open: 7 Mar - 7 Nov: 10am - 5.30pm, last admission 4.30pm.
Admission: Adult £3.50, Child £2, Conc. £3, Family (2+2) £9.

ST WILLIAM'S COLLEGE
5 College Street, York YO1 7JF
Tel: 01904 557233 **Fax:** 01904 557234
Owner: The Dean and Chapter of York   **Contact:** Sandie Clarke
15th century medieval home of Minster Chantry Priests. Three large medieval halls.
Location: OS Ref. SE605 522. College Street, York. Adjoining E end of York Minster.
Open: 10am - 5pm.
Admission: Adult £1, Child 50p. For further details please telephone.

🪴 **Plant Sales Index** see front section

THE WALLED GARDEN
AT SCAMPSTON
SCAMPSTON HALL, MALTON, NORTH YORKSHIRE YO17 8NG

www.scampston.co.uk

Tel: 01944 758224 / 758123 **Fax:** 01944 758700 **e-mail:** info@scampston.co.uk
Owner: Sir Charles Legard Bt   **Contact:** Lady Legard
An exciting new garden opens at Scampston in 2004. Designed by Piet Oudolf, winner of Gold and 'Best in Show' at Chelsea 2000, the contemporary layout in the 4¹/₂ acre walled garden uses perennial meadow planting to splendid effect and will be an inspiration to every gardener.
Location: OS Ref. SE865 755. 4m E of Malton, off A64.
Open: House: 18 Jun - 25 Jul: Wed - Sun, 1.30 - 5pm. (Last admission 4pm.) Walled Garden: 30 May - 17 Oct: Wed - Sun & BH Mons, 10am - 5pm.
Admission: Garden: Adult £4, Conc £3.50, Child £2. House £5 extra. Groups by arrangement.
🍴 🚻 ♿Partial. 🍴 📷Obligatory for house. 🔲 🅿Limited for coaches. 🐕 Guide dogs only.

English Heritage Photo Library

SCARBOROUGH CASTLE 🏛
CASTLE ROAD, SCARBOROUGH, NORTH YORKSHIRE YO11 1HY

Tel: 01723 372451
Owner: English Heritage   **Contact:** The Custodian
This 12th Century castle conceals over 2,500 years of turbulent history, and played a key role in national events up to the 20th century. Famous visitors include the Viking warlord, Harald Hardrada, and King Richard III. Indeed, it is alleged that Richard enjoyed the views so much that he still returns today to walk the battlements.
Location: OS Ref. TA050 893. Castle Road, E of town centre.
Open: 1 Apr - 30 Sept: daily, 10am - 6pm. 1 - 31 Oct: daily, 10am - 5pm. 1 Nov - 31 Mar: Wed - Sun, 11am - 4pm. Closed 24 - 26 Dec & 1 Jan. Times subject to change April 2004.
Admission: Adult £3, Child £1.50, Conc. £2.30, Family £7.50 (valid to 31.3.04). 15% discount for groups (11+). Prices subject to change April 2004.
ℹ️WCs. 📷♿Partial. 🔲 📷Inclusive. 🅿🔲 🐕In grounds, on leads. ✴️ 🌐Tel for details.

SEWERBY HALL & GARDENS

Church Lane, Sewerby, Bridlington, East Yorkshire YO15 1EA

Tel: 01262 673769　**Fax:** 01262 673090　**e-mail:** sewerby.hall@eastriding.gov.uk
www.bridlington.net/sewerby

Owner: East Riding of Yorkshire Council　　**Contact:** Customer Service Officer

Sewerby Hall and Gardens, set in 50 acres of parkland, dates back to 1715. The Georgian house contains: 19th century orangery; history/archaeology displays; art galleries and an Amy Johnson Room. The Grounds include: walled gardens, woodland, children's zoo and play area, golf and putting.

Location: OS Ref. TA203 690. 2m N of Bridlington in Sewerby village.

Open: Please telephone for details.

Admission: Please telephone for admission prices.

⬚ Craft units. 🚻 🚻 ♿ 📷 Licensed. 🅿 🚻
🐕 In grounds, on leads. Guide dogs in hall. ⬛ 🚻 Tel for details.

SION HILL HALL 🏛

KIRBY WISKE, THIRSK, NORTH YORKSHIRE YO7 4EU

www.sionhillhall.co.uk

Tel: 01845 587206　**Fax:** 01845 587486　**e-mail:** sionhill.hall@virgin.net

Owner: H W Mawer Trust　　**Contact:** R M Mallaby

Designed in 1912 by the renowned York architect Walter H Brierley, 'the Lutyens of the North', receiving an award from the Royal Institute of British Architects as being of 'outstanding architectural merit'. Sion Hill contains the H W Mawer collection of fine furniture, porcelain, paintings and clocks in superb settings.

Location: OS Ref. SE373 844. 6m S of Northallerton off A167, signposted. 4m W of Thirsk, 6m E of A1 via A61.

Open: Jun - Sept: Weds only, 1 - 5pm, last entry 4pm. Also Easter Sun and all BH Mons. Guided tours during public opening times/Connoisseur tours at any time May - Oct by arrangement.

Admission: House: Adult £4.50, Child 12 - 16yrs, £2, Child under 12yrs £1, Conc. £4. Guided tours during public opening times: £5.75ea. Connoisseur Tours: £8.50. Grounds: £1.50.

♿Partial. WC. 📷 🎟 🅿

SHANDY HALL

COXWOLD, NORTH YORKSHIRE YO61 4AD

www.shandy-hall.org.uk

Tel/Fax: 01347 868465

Owner: The Laurence Sterne Trust　　**Contact:** Mr P Wildgust

Here in 1760-1767 the witty and eccentric parson Laurence Sterne wrote *Tristram Shandy* and *A Sentimental Journey*. Shandy Hall was built as a timber-framed open-hall in the 15th century and added to by Sterne in the 18th. It houses the world's foremost collection of editions of Sterne's work, and is surrounded by a walled garden full of old-fashioned roses and cottage garden plants. Also an acre of wild garden in the adjoining old quarry. It is a lived-in house where you are sure of a personal welcome. May - Sept: exhibitions.

Location: OS Ref. SE531 773. W end of Coxwold village, 4m E of A19 between Easingwold and Thirsk. 20m N of York.

Open: 1 May - 30 Sept: Weds, 2 - 4.30pm. Suns, 2.30 - 4.30pm. Garden: 1 May - 30 Sept: Sun - Fri, 11am - 4.30pm. Other times by appointment.

Admission: Hall & Garden: Adult £4.50, Child £1.50. Garden only: Adult £2.50, Child £1.

ℹ️No photography in house. ⬚ 🚻 ♿Partial. 📷 In nearby village. 🎟 Obligatory.
🅿 🐕

SKIPTON CASTLE 　　　　*See page 390 for full page entry.*

William Kent

1685-1748

A Yorkshireman, Kent started his career as a painter studying in Italy. Here he met Lord Burlington, who encouraged him to study architecture. On his return to England, through Burlington's patronage, Kent won important commissions during the 1730s and 1740s, becoming known as the great Palladian architect in England. Look for an architectural style that is monumental, plain and severe. You will see this in his treatment both of the exterior and interiors of his buildings.

Visit Houghton Hall and Holkham Hall in Norfolk and Chiswick House in London. William Kent's role as an 18th century landscape designer should not be understated – inspired not only by the classical buildings of Palladio, he drew inspiration from the Arcadian paintings of Claude Lorraine and Poussin. Kent took these painted scenes and literally transplanted them into creating a landscape scene. Visit Rousham, Oxfordshire.

Architect, Painter & Landscape Designer

SHIBDEN HALL

Lister's Road, Halifax, West Yorkshire HX3 6XG

Tel: 01422 352246　**Fax:** 01422 348440　**www.**calderdale.gov.uk

Owner: Calderdale MBC　　**Contact:** Valerie Stansfield

A half-timbered manor house, the home of Anne Lister set in a landscaped park. Oak furniture, carriages and an array of objects make Shibden an intriguing place to visit.

Location: OS Ref. SE106 257. 1½ m E of Halifax off A58.

Open: 1 Mar - 30 Nov: Mon - Sat, 10am - 5pm. Suns, 12 noon - 5pm. Last admission 4.15pm. Dec - Feb: Mon - Sat, 10am - 4pm. Suns, 12 noon - 4pm. Last admission 3.30pm.

Admission: Adult £3.50, Child/Conc. £2.50, Family £10. Prices subject to change Apr 2004.

⬚ ♿ Ground floor & grounds. 📷 🅿 🚻 🐕Guide dogs only. 🚻

SLEDMERE HOUSE 🏛

SLEDMERE, DRIFFIELD, EAST YORKSHIRE YO25 3XG

Tel: 01377 236637 **Fax:** 01377 236560

Owner: Sir Tatton Sykes Bt   **Contact:** Mrs Anne Hines

Sledmere House is the home of Sir Tatton Sykes, 8th Baronet. There has been a manor house at Sledmere since medieval times. The present house was designed and built by Sir Christopher Sykes, 2nd Baronet, a diary date states "June 17th, 1751 laid the first stone of the new house at Sledmere." Sir Christopher employed a fellow Yorkshireman, Joseph Rose, the most famous English plasterer of his day, to execute the decoration of Sledmere. Rose's magnificent work at Sledmere was unique in his career. A great feature at Sledmere is the 'Capability' Brown parkland and the beautiful 18th century walled rose gardens. Also worthy of note is the recently laid out knot-garden, all accessible by wheelchair.

Location: OS Ref. SE931 648. Off the A166 between York & Bridlington. ¹/₂ hr drive from York, Bridlington & Scarborough.

Open: 9 - 12 Apr & 2 May - 19 Sept: closed Mons & Sats except BHs: 11.30am - 4.30pm. Famous pipe organ played Weds, Fris & Suns.

Admission: House & Gardens: Adult £5, Child £2, OAP £4.50. Gardens & Park: Adult £3, Child £1.

ℹ️No photography in house. 🅿️ 🚻 🇹 ♿ 🍴Licensed. 🎦By arrangement. 🅿️ 🔲 🐕In grounds on leads. Guide dogs in house. ⬆️

STOCKELD PARK

WETHERBY, NORTH YORKSHIRE LS22 4AW

Tel: 01937 586101 **Fax:** 01937 580084

Owner: Mr and Mrs P G F Grant   **Contact:** Mrs L A Saunders

Stockeld is a beautifully proportioned Palladian villa designed by James Paine in 1763, featuring a magnificent cantilevered staircase in the central oval hall. Stockeld is still very much a family home, with a fine collection of 18th and 19th century furniture and paintings. The house is surrounded by lovely gardens of lawns, large herbaceous and shrub borders, fringed by woodland, and set in 100 acres of fine parkland in the midst of an extensive farming estate. A beautiful and interesting house which is a popular location and venue for filming and photography. Perfect parkland setting for exclusive outdoor activites.

Location: OS Ref. SE376 497. York 12m, Harrogate 5m, Leeds 12m.

Open: Privately booked events only. Please contact the Estate Office: 01937 586101.

Admission: Prices on application.

♿House only. 🔲

SPOFFORTH CASTLE ⌗

Harrogate, North Yorkshire

Tel: 01904 601901

Owner: English Heritage   **Contact:** The Yorkshire Regional Office

This manor house has some fascinating features including an undercroft built into the rock. It was once owned by the Percy family.

Location: OS Ref. SE360 511. 3¹/₂ m SE of Harrogate on minor road off A661 at Spofforth.

Open: 1 Apr - 30 Sept: daily, 10am - 6pm. 1 Oct - 31 Mar: daily, 10am - 4pm. Times subject to change April 2004.

Admission: Free.

🐕 ❄️

STUDLEY ROYAL: ST MARY'S CHURCH ⌗

Ripon, North Yorkshire

Tel: 01765 608888

Owner: English Heritage   **Contact:** The Custodian

A magnificent Victorian church, designed by William Burges in the 1870s, with a highly decorated interior. Coloured marble, stained glass, gilded and painted figures and a splendid organ.

Location: OS Ref. SE278 703. 2¹/₂ m W of Ripon off B6265, in grounds of Studley Royal estate.

Open: 1 Apr - 30 Sept: daily, 1 - 5pm. Times subject to change April 2004.

Admission: Free.

ℹ️WCs. 🔲 🔲 🅿️

Newby Hall, North Yorkshire from the book *Historic Family Homes and Gardens from the Air*, see page 54.

SUTTON PARK 🏛

SUTTON-ON-THE-FOREST, NORTH YORKSHIRE YO61 1DP

www.statelyhome.co.uk

Tel: 01347 810249/811239 **Fax:** 01347 811251 **e-mail:** suttonpark@fsbdial.co.uk

Owner: Sir Reginald & Lady Sheffield   **Contact:** Administrator

The Yorkshire home of Sir Reginald and Lady Sheffield. Charming example of early Georgian architecture. Magnificent plasterwork by Cortese. Rich collection of 18th century furniture, paintings, porcelain, needlework, beadwork. All put together with great style to make a most inviting house. Award winning gardens attract enthusiasts from home and abroad.

Location: OS Ref. SE583 646. 8m N of York on B1363 York - Helmsley Road.

Open: House: 4 Apr - end Sept: Wed & Sun; Good Fri - Easter Mon, 18 - 21 Apr & BH Mons, 1.30 - 5pm. Gardens: 4 Apr - end Sept: 11am - 5pm. Tearoom: Wed - Sun, 12 noon - 5pm. Private groups any other day or evening by appointment. House open Oct - Mar for private groups only.

Admission: House & Garden: Adult £5.50, Child £3, Conc. £4.50. Coaches £5. Gardens only: Adult £3, Child 50p, Conc. £2. Private Groups (15+): £6. Caravans: £6 per unit per night. Electric hookup: £7.50/night. (2003 prices.)

ⓘNo photography. ⓉHosted lunches & dinners. ♿Partial. ●Home-baked fayre. 🄵Obligatory. 🅿Limited for coaches. ✖ 🛏3 double with ensuite bathrooms. ⓋTel for details.

TREASURER'S HOUSE 🌿

MINSTER YARD, YORK, NORTH YORKSHIRE YO1 7JL

Tel: 01904 624247 **Fax:** 01904 647372 **e-mail:** yorkth@nationaltrust.org.uk

Owner: The National Trust   **Contact:** The Property Manager

Named after the Treasurer of York Minster and built over a Roman road, the house is not all that it seems! Nestled behind the Minster, the size and splendour and contents of the house are a constant surprise to visitors – as are the famous ghost stories. Free trails for children and free access to the National Trust tearoom.

Location: OS Ref. SE604 523. The N side of York Minster. Entrance on Chapter House St.

Open: 27 Mar - 31 Oct: daily except Fri, 11am - 4.30pm. Last adm. 4.30pm.

Admission: Adult £4.50, Child £2.20, Family £11. Booked groups (15+): Adult £3.50, Child £1.70.

Ⓣ ♿Partial. WC. ●Licensed. 🄵Licensed. 🅿None. 🔲 🛏In grounds, on leads. 🔺

THORNTON ABBEY & GATEHOUSE ♯

Scunthorpe, North Lincolnshire

Tel: 01904 601901

Owner: English Heritage   **Contact:** The Yorkshire Regional Office

The 14th century Gatehouse to the Abbey is recognised as one of the grandest in England, and the remains of a beautiful octagonal chapter house are also notably fine.

Location: OS Ref. TA115 190. 18m NE of Scunthorpe on minor road N of A160.

Open: Grounds: daily, 10am - 6pm. Gatehouse: 1 Apr - 30 Sept: 1st & 3rd Sun of the month, 12 noon - 6pm; 1 Oct - 31 Mar: 3rd Sun of the month, 12 noon - 4pm. Times subject to change April 2004.

Admission: Free.

♿🅿🛏❄

THORP PERROW ARBORETUM & WOODLAND GARDEN & FALCONRY CENTRE

Bedale, North Yorkshire DL8 2PR

Tel/Fax: 01677 425323

e-mail: louise@thorpperrow.freeserve.co.uk **www**.thorpperrow.com

Owner: Sir John Ropner Bt   **Contact:** Louise McNeill

85 acres of woodland walks. One of the largest collections of trees and shrubs in the north of England, including a 16th century spring wood and 19th century pinetum, and holds four National Collections - Ash, Lime, Walnut and Laburnum. The Falcons of Thorp Perrow is a captive breeding and conservation centre. Three flying demonstrations daily throughout the season.

Location: OS Ref. SE258 851. Bedale - Ripon road, S of Bedale, 4m from Leeming Bar on A1.

Open: All year: dawn - dusk. Telephone for winter opening times.

Admission: Arboretum & Falcons: Adult £5.75, Child £2.95, OAP £4.40, Family (2+2) £16, (2+4) £21. Groups (20+): Adult £5.20, OAP £4.

ⓘPicnic area. Children's playground. 🔲 🄵♿Partial. WCs. ●Licensed. 🄵By arrangement. 🅿Limited for coaches. 🔲 🛏In grounds, on leads. ❄ ⓋTel for details.

WAKEFIELD CATHEDRAL

Northgate, Wakefield, West Yorkshire WF1 1HG

Tel: 01924 373923 **Fax:** 01924 215054 **www**.wakefield-cathedral.org.uk

Owner: Church of England   **Contact:** Mr F Arnold, Head Verger

Built on the site of a previous Saxon church, this 14th century Parish Church became a cathedral in 1888.

Location: OS Ref. SE333 208. Wakefield city centre. M1/ J39-41, M62/J29W, J30 E.

Open: Mon - Sat: 8am - 5pm. Suns: between services only. For service details contact Cathedral.

Admission: Free, but donations welcome.

❄

WASSAND HALL

Seaton, Hull, East Yorkshire HU11 5RJ

Tel: 01964 534488 **Fax:** 01964 533334

Owner/Contact: R E O Russell - Resident Trustee

Fine Regency house 1815 by Thomas Cundy the Elder. Beautifully restored walled gardens, woodland walks parks and vistas. House contains fine collection of 18/19th century paintings, English and Continental silver, furniture and porcelain.

Location: OS Ref. TA174 460. On the B1244 Seaton - Hornsea road. Approximately 2m from Hornsea.

Open: 28 - 31 May; 10 - 14 & 24 - 29 June; 16 - 17 July; 6, 8/9, 12 - 15 & 27 - 30 Aug.

Admission: Please contact property for details.

♿ ● 🄵By arrangement. 🅿Ample for cars, limited for coaches. 🛏In grounds, on leads.

WENTWORTH CASTLE GARDENS

Lowe Lane, Stainborough, Barnsley, South Yorkshire S75 3ET

Tel: 01226 731269

Owner: Barnsley MBC   **Contact:** Chris Margrave

300 years old, these gardens are the only Grade I listed gardens in South Yorkshire, 28 listed buildings and monuments and the National Collections of rhododendrons, magnolias and williamsii camellias. Conservatory 3rd in the BBC2 series 'Restoration'.

Location: OS Ref. SE320 034. 5km W of Barnsley, M1/J36 via Birdwell & Rockley Lane then Lowe Lane.

Open: Mid April - end June, mainly by guided tours. Please telephone 01226 731269 for a recorded message.

Admission: £2.50, Conc. £2. (2003 prices, subject to change.)

© English Heritage Photo Library
John Whitaker

WHITBY ABBEY ⌗
WHITBY, NORTH YORKSHIRE YO22 4JT

Tel: 01947 603568

Owner: English Heritage   **Contact:** The Custodian

A new visitor centre has been created within the 17th century banqueting hall exploring the 1500 year old story of the Abbey and town with displays of archaeological artefacts and state-of-the-art technology. An ancient holy place, once a burial place of kings and an inspiration for saints. A religious community was first established at Whitby in 657 by Abbess Hilda and was the home of Caedmon, the first English poet. The remains we can see today are of a Benedictine church built in the 13th and 14th centuries, and include a magnificent three-tiered choir and north transept. It is perched high above the picturesque harbour town of Whitby.

Location: OS Ref. NZ904 115. On cliff top E of Whitby.

Open: 1 Apr - 30 Sept: daily 10am - 6pm. 1 - 31 Oct: daily, 10am - 5pm. 1 Nov - 31 Mar: Wed - Sun, 11am - 4pm. Closed 24 - 26 Dec & 1 Jan. Times subject to change April 2004.

Admission: Adult £3.80, Child £1.90, Conc. £2.90, Family £9 (valid to 31.3.04). 15% discounts for groups (11+). Prices subject to change April 2004.

ⓘWCs. 🔲 ♿Ground floor. 🅿 Charged. ▣ 🐕In grounds, on leads. ❄ 🛏Tel for details.

YORK GATE GARDEN
BACK CHURCH LANE, ADEL, LEEDS, WEST YORKSHIRE LS16 8DW

www.perennial.org.uk

Tel: 0113 2678240

Owner: Perennial   **Contact:** The Garden Co-ordinator

Inspirational one acre garden renowned for its outstanding design and exquisite detail. A series of smaller gardens, separated by hedges and stone walls, are linked by a succession of delightful vistas. One of many highlights is the famous herb garden with topiary.

Location: OS Ref. 275 403. $2^{1}/4$m SE of Bramhope. $^{1}/2$m E of A660.

Open: Apr - Sept: Thur, Sun & BH Mons, 2 - 5pm.

Admission: Adult £3, Child Free.

ⓘCoach parties must book. ♿Partial. ☕Tea & Biscuits: June - Sept & BH w/ends. 🅵By arrangement. 🅿Limited. 🐕Guide dogs only. €

WILBERFORCE HOUSE
25 High Street, Hull, East Yorkshire HU1 1NQ

Tel: 01482 613902 **Fax:** 01482 613710

Owner: Hull City Council   **Contact:** S R Green

Birthplace of William Wilberforce – slavery abolitionist. Displays include costume gallery, the history of slavery, clocks and the Hull Silver Collection.

Location: OS Ref. TA102 286. High Street, Hull.

Open: Mon - Sat, 10am - 5pm. Suns, 1.30 - 4.30pm. Closed Good Fri & Christmas Day.

Admission: Free.

THE WORKHOUSE MUSEUM OF POOR LAW
Allhallowgate, Ripon, North Yorkshire HG1 4LE

Tel: 01765 690799   **Contact:** The Curator

"Vacancies for Vagrants: bath, 2 nights' bed and board; payment - stone breaking & wood chopping".

Location: OS Ref. SE312 712 Close to Market Square.

Open: 1 Apr - 26 Oct: daily, 1pm - 4pm. During school holidays & July & August open 11am - 4pm. (2003 details, please telephone for current details.)

Admission: Adult £1.50, Child (6 - 16yrs) 50p, Child under 6yrs Free, Conc/Student £1.25. (2003 details, please telephone for current details.)

WORTLEY HALL
Wortley, Sheffield, South Yorkshire S35 7DB

Tel: 0114 2882100 **Fax:** 0114 2830695

Owner: Labour, Co-operative & Trade Union Movement   **Contact:** Marc Mallender

15 acres of formal Italianate gardens surrounded by 11 acres of informal pleasure grounds.

Location: OS Ref. SK313 995. 10kms S of Barnsley in Wortley on A629.

Open: Gardens: All year. 6 Jun & 29 Aug: Specialist Plant Sales.

Admission: Free. Groups must book for gardeners' tour, £1.60.

YORK MINSTER
Deangate, York YO1 7HH

Tel: 01904 557216 **Fax:** 01904 557218 **e-mail:** visitors@yorkminster.org

Owner: Dean and Chapter of York   **Contact:** Stephen Hemming

Large gothic church housing the largest collection of medieval stained glass in England.

Location: OS Ref. SE603 522. Centre of York.

Open: Summer: 7am - 6.30pm. Winter: 7am - 6pm.

Admission: Adult £4.50, Child (under 16yrs) Free, Conc. £3. Tour companies: Unbooked: Adult £4, Conc. £2.50, Booked: £3.50, Conc. £2.

Accommodation Index see front section

Yorkshire & The Humber - England

northwest

Cumbria. © David Osborn

leightonhall
lancashire

> *"My ancestors have lived at Leighton for over four centuries, and each generation has cherished it and in one way or another left its mark. Because we love this place so much, my wife and I and all the family are keen that others should share our enjoyment of it both now and in the future ... and be able to absorb the unique atmosphere of this old house and its incomparable setting."*
>
> Richard Gillow Reynolds

If there was a competition for a country house in Britain with the loveliest setting – Leighton Hall near Carnforth in Lancashire would surely be in the top ten favourites.

Leighton Hall is situated in a huge bowl of parkland, a pretty white limestone neo-gothic house, with its turreted and battlemented roofline, behind which the Lakeland fells rise as a huge protective canopy surrounding the scene. Few houses could be more beautifully situated; its impact is all the greater because the house is approached downward through the park with the house nestling well below you.

The present owner, Mr Richard Reynolds, is descended from Adam d'Avranches who built a fortified manor on this site in 1246. Since then there have been 26 owners, with more than one bringing to the estate their fair share of political intrigue and catastrophes, including Sir George Middleton, loyal Cavalier and High Sheriff of Lancashire, and Albert Hodgson who was jailed after the Jacobite rebellion in 1715. It was following the 1715 Jacobite uprising that d'Avranches' original manor was sacked and burned by government troops, and Leighton was to be rebuilt in 1760 in the Adam style by George Towneley.

The gothic façade and interiors we see today were superimposed onto Adam's building in 1822, by Richard Gillow, grandson of the famous Lancastrian furniture makers, Gillow & Sons, whose name became the byword for Victorian and Edwardian quality of furniture design and finish. Guided tours around the house must be pre-booked, but they are well worth it ... and Mr and Mrs Reynolds will often take you around the house themselves. Wander with them, through these comfortable, cosy and lived-in rooms with unique pieces of Gillow furniture and you will find that the interiors of the house are only gently gothicised – all except for the magnificent stoned flagged Entrance Hall which is a wonderful excitable statement to the early gothic revival.

If you only have time to visit the gardens and parkland, there is plenty to do and see. Depending on the amount of time you have, there is a Woodland Walk which is especially lovely in the spring. The main garden has a huge herbaceous border, and there is a Walled Garden within which are a Herb Garden, and ornamental Vegetable Garden with caterpillar maze.

Leighton offers something for everyone... school programmes, corporate event facilities, and if you are planning a wedding you might just have found your fairytale venue ... or perhaps you should just make a visit to it to enjoy one of the many special events held here every year. Whatever it is, Leighton Hall offers a wonderful day out.

▶ For further details about Leighton Hall see page 431.

Map 5

ADLINGTON HALL

MACCLESFIELD

www.adlingtonhall.com

Adlington Hall, the home of the Leghs of Adlington from 1315 to the present day, was built on the site of a Hunting Lodge which stood in the Forest of Macclesfield in 1040. Two oaks, part of the original building, remain with their roots in the ground and support the east end of the Great Hall, which was built between 1480 and 1505.

The Hall is a manor house, quadrangular in shape, and was once surrounded by a moat. Two sides of the Courtyard and the east wing were built in the typical 'Black and White' Cheshire style in 1581. The south front and west wing (containing the Drawing Room and Dining Room) were added between 1749 and 1757 and are built of red brick with a handsome stone portico with four Ionic columns on octagonal pedestals. Between the trees in the Great Hall stands an organ built by 'Father' Bernard Smith (c1670-80). Handel subsequently played on this instrument and, now fully restored, it is the largest 17th century organ in the country.

GARDENS

The gardens were landscaped in the style of 'Capability' Brown in the middle of the 18th century. Visitors may walk round the 'wilderness' area; among the follies to be seen are 'Temple to Diana', a 'Shell Cottage', Chinese bridge and T'ing house. There is a fine yew walk and a lime avenue planted in 1688. An old fashioned rose garden and yew maze have recently been planted. In this continually evolving garden, the 'Father Tiber' water garden was created in 2002 and the Penstemon garden in 2003.

Owner:
Mrs C J C Legh

▶ CONTACT

Corporate Enquiries:
Tessa Quayle
The Estate Office
Adlington Hall
Macclesfield
Cheshire SK10 4LF

Tel: 01625 829206
Fax: 01625 828756

e-mail: enquiries@
adlingtonhall.com

Hall Tours:
The Guide
Tel: 01625 820875

▶ LOCATION

OS Ref. SJ905 804

5m N of
Macclesfield, A523,
13m S of Manchester.
London 178m.

Rail: Macclesfield
& Wilmslow
stations 5m.

Air: Manchester
Airport 8m.

▶ OPENING TIMES

June - August
Wed only, 2 - 5pm.

Also by prior arrangement for groups weekdays throughout the year. Please contact for details.

▶ ADMISSION

Hall & Gardens

Adult	£5.00
Child	£2.00
Student	£2.00
Groups of 20+	£4.00

 Suitable for corporate events, product launches, business meetings, conferences, concerts, fashion shows, garden parties, rallies, clay-pigeon shooting, filming and weddings.

The Great Hall and Dining Room are available for corporate entertaining. Catering can be arranged.

Visitors may alight at entrance to Hall. WCs.

Tearoom.

By arrangement.

For 100 cars and 4 coaches, 100 yds from Hall.

Schools welcome. Guide can be provided.

No dogs.

Tel for details.

CONFERENCE/FUNCTION

ROOM	SIZE	MAX CAPACITY
Great Hall	11 x 8m	80
Dining Rm	10.75 x 7m	80
Courtyard	27 x 17m	300

Map 5

CAPESTHORNE HALL 🏛

MACCLESFIELD

www.capesthorne.com

Capesthorne Hall, set in 100 acres of picturesque Cheshire parkland, has been touched by nearly 1,000 years of English history - Roman legions passed across it, titled Norman families hunted on it and, during the Civil War, a Royalist ancestress helped Charles II to escape after the Battle of Worcester. The Jacobean-style Hall has a fascinating collection of fine art, marble sculptures, furniture and tapestries. Originally designed by the Smiths of Warwick it was built between 1719 and 1732. It was altered by Blore in 1837 and partially rebuilt by Salvin in 1861 following a disastrous fire.

The present Squire is William Bromley-Davenport, Lord Lieutenant of Cheshire, whose ancestors have owned the estate since Domesday times when they were appointed custodians of the Royal Forest of Macclesfield.

In the grounds near the family Chapel the 18th century Italian Milanese Gates open onto the herbaceous borders and maples which line the beautiful lakeside gardens. But amid the natural spectacle and woodland walks, Capesthorne still offers glimpses of its man-made past... the remains of the Ice House, the Old Boat House and the curious Swallow Hole.

Facilities at the Hall can be hired for corporate occasions and family celebrations including Civil wedding ceremonies.

Owner:
Mr & Mrs
Bromley-Davenport

▶ **CONTACT**
Gwyneth Jones,
Hall Manager
Capesthorne Hall
Siddington
Macclesfield
Cheshire SK11 9JY

Tel: 01625 861221
Fax: 01625 861619
e-mail: info@
capesthorne.com

▶ **LOCATION**
OS Ref. SJ840 727

5m W of Macclesfield.
30 mins S of
Manchester on A34.
Near M6, M63 and M62.

Air: Manchester
International 20 mins.

Rail: Macclesfield 5m
(2 hrs from London).

Taxi: 01625 533464.

▶ **OPENING TIMES**

Summer
April - October
Weds, Suns & BHs.

Hall
1.30 - 4pm.
Last admission 3.30pm.

Gardens & Chapel
12 noon - 5pm.

Groups welcome by
appointment.

Caravan Park also open
Easter - end October.

Corporate enquiries:
March - December.

▶ **ADMISSION**

Sundays & BHs only
Hall, Gardens & Chapel
Adult £6.50
Child (5-18yrs) £3.00
OAP £5.50
Family £15.00

Gardens & Chapel only
Adult £4.00
Child (5-18yrs) £2.00
OAP £3.00

Transfers from Gardens
& Chapel to Hall
Adult/OAP £3.50
Child (5-18yrs) £1.50

Wednesdays only Hall,
Chapel & Gardens
Car
(up to 4 pass.) £10.00
Additional person . £2.50
Minibus
(up to 12 pass) £25.00
Coach
(up to 50 pass) ... £50.00

Caravan Park
Up to 2 people £12.00 pn
Over 2 people. £14.00 pn

CONFERENCE/FUNCTION

ROOM	SIZE	MAX CAPACITY
Theatre	45' x 19'	150
Garden Room	52' x 20'	80
Saloon	40' x 25'	80
Queen Anne Room	34' x 25'	80

ℹ️ Available for corporate functions, meetings, product launches, promotions, exhibitions, presentations, seminars, activity days, Civil weddings and receptions, family celebrations, still photography, fishing, clay shooting, car rallies, garden parties, barbecues, concerts, antique, craft, country and game fairs. No photography in Hall.

🍽 Catering can be provided for groups (full menus on request). Function rooms available for wedding receptions, corporate hospitality, meetings and other special events.

The Butler's Pantry' serves tea, coffee and ices.

♿ Compacted paths, ramps. WCs.

👥 For up to 50. Tours are by staff members or Hall Manager. Tour time 1 hr.

🅿 100 cars/20 coaches on hard-standing and unlimited in park, 50 yds from house.

🐕 Guide dogs in Hall. Under control in Park.

💍 Civil Wedding Licence. 🎭 Tel for details.

The National Trust Photographic Library

TATTON PARK

KNUTSFORD

www.tattonpark.org.uk

Tatton is one of the most splendid historic estates in Europe. The 1000 acres of parkland are home to herds of red and fallow deer and provide the setting for a Georgian Mansion, over 50 acres of Gardens, Tudor Old Hall and a working Farm. These attractions, plus private functions and a superb events programme attract over 700,000 visits each year.

Archaeologists have found evidence of occupation at Tatton since 8000 BC with the discovery of flints in the park. There is also proof of people living here in the Iron Age, Roman times, Anglo-Saxon and medieval periods.

The neo-classical Mansion by Wyatt is the jewel in Tatton's crown and was built in stages from 1780 - 1813. The Egerton family collection of Gillow furniture, Baccarat glass, porcelain and paintings by Italian and Dutch masters is found in the splendid setting of the magnificent staterooms. In stark contrast, the Victorian kitchens and cellars provide fascinating insight into life as it would have been 'downstairs'. Guided tours are available for a small extra charge at 12 noon and 12.15pm.

The Gardens extend over 50 acres and feature rare species of plants, shrubs and trees, and in fact are considered to be one of the most important gardens within the National Trust. Features include: a conservatory by Wyatt, Fernery by Paxton, Italian terraced garden and recently restored Japanese garden. The rare collection of plants including rhododendrons, tree ferns, bamboo and pines are the result of 200 years of collecting by the Egerton family.

The Home Farm has traditional breeds of animals including rare sheep and cattle, pigs and horses plus estate workshops. The Tudor Old Hall shows visitors how life would have been at Tatton Park over centuries past for the estate workers. Tours start in the smoky 16th century Great Hall lit by flickering candles and end in the 1950s home of an estate employee.

Map 5

Owner:
The National Trust

▶ **CONTACT**

Conferences, exhibitions, weddings etc.
Sheila Hetherington
01625 534406

Party Visits
01625 534428

Tatton Park
Knutsford
Cheshire WA16 6QN

Tel: 01625 534400
info: 01625 534435
Fax: 01625 534403

▶ **LOCATION**

OS Ref. SJ745 815

From M56/J7 follow signs. From M6/J19, signed on A56 & A50.

Rail: Knutsford or Altrincham Station, then taxi.

Air: Manchester Airport 6m.

OPENING TIMES

Summer
27 March - 3 October

Park: Daily, 10am - 7pm.
Gardens: Tue - Sun, 10.30am - 6pm.

Mansion:
Tue - Sun, 1 - 5pm.
(12 noon & 12.15pm guided tours by timed ticket, limited numbers)

Tudor Old Hall: Guided tours: Sats & Suns, hourly, 12 noon - 4pm.

Farm: 12 noon- 5pm.

Restaurant: Tue - Sun, 10.30am - 5pm.

Gift, Garden & Housekeeper's Store:
Tue - Sun, 11am - 5pm.

Winter
4 October - 25 March.

Park: Tue - Sun, 11am - 5pm.

Gardens: Tue - Sun, 11am - 4pm.

Farm: Sat & Sun, 11am - 4pm

Last admissions 1 hour before closing.

(Oct half-term & Dec special opening of Mansion, Farm & Old Hall)

ADMISSION

Any two attractions

	Single	Group*
Adult	£4.60	£3.80
Child**	£2.60	£2.10
Family	£12.80	

Mansion, Gardens, Tudor Old Hall, Farm

	Single	Group*
Adult	£3.00	£2.40
Child**	£2.00	£1.60
Family	£8.00	

(50% reduction for NT members to Tudor Old Hall & Farm.)

Parking
Per car £3.90
Coaches .... Free

*Min. 12   ** Aged 4 - 15yrs.

Tours available outside normal openings phone for details.

CONFERENCE/FUNCTION

Room	Size	Max Capacity
Tenants' Hall	125' x 45'	330 - 400
Foyer	23' x 20'	50 - 100
Tenants' Hall Event Wing – total of 8,000 sq.ft. available		
Lord Egerton's Apartment	20' x 16'	16 - 40
	24' x 18'	19 - 40
Stable Block	31' x 20'	80

Conferences, trade exhibitions, presentations, product launches, concerts and fashion shows. Special family days. Spotlights, stages, dance floor, PA system. The Tenants' Hall seats up to 400 for presentations.

Telephone for details. Dinners, dances, weddings.

Upstairs in Mansion, Tudor Old Hall & areas of farm not accessible. Wheelchairs & electric vehicles available. WCs.

Self-service. Tuck shop.

By arrangement.

200-300 yds away. Meal vouchers for coach drivers.

Award-winning educational programmes, please book. Environmental days, Orienteering, adventure playground.

In grounds, on leads.

Civil Wedding Licence.

Tel for details.

ADLINGTON HALL  *See page 412 for full page entry.*

ARLEY HALL & GARDENS

ARLEY, NR NORTHWICH, CHESHIRE CW9 6NA

www.arleyhallandgardens.com

Tel: 01565 777353   **Fax:** 01565 777465
e-mail: enquiries@arleyhallandgardens.com
Owner: Viscount Ashbrook   **Contact:** Estate Secretary
Recently voted one of the top 50 gardens in Europe, these Grade II listed gardens have been created by generations of the same family. The Woodland Grove, created by the present owner, overlooks the Chapel. The Hall, a delightful family home, is a popular wedding and corporate venue and is open to the public on Tuesdays and Sundays only. Family Chapel, Gift Shop, Plant Nursery and Restaurant. Arley offers a peaceful day out.

Location: OS Ref. SJ675 809. 5 miles WNW Knutsford.
Open: 11 April – 26 Sept & Oct weekends. Hall: Tues & Sun. Gardens, grounds & Chapel: Tues - Sun & BHs, 11am - 5am. Gardens open 3 April.
Admission: Gardens, grounds & Chapel: Adult £4.50, Child (5-15) £2, OAP £3.90, Family £11.25. Season ticket £20. Hall & Gardens: £7, Child (5-15) £3, OAP £5.90, Family £17.75. Group discounts available.

ℹ️ Photography in garden only. 🔲 Ⓣ ♿ Partial. ⬛ 🍴 ✗ By arrangement. 🅿️ 🖼
🐕 In grounds on leads. ⬛ ♿ Tel for details.

BEESTON CASTLE ⊞
Beeston, Tarporley, Cheshire CW6 9TX
Tel: 01829 260464
Owner: English Heritage   **Contact:** The Custodian
Standing majestically on sheer, rocky crags which fall sharply away from the castle walls, Beeston has stunning views across 8 counties. (Access by steep paths.) Exhibition on the site's 4,000 year history.
Location: OS Ref. SJ537 593. 11m SE of Chester on minor road off A49, or A41. 2m SW of Tarporley.
Open: 1 Apr - 30 Sept: 10am - 6pm. 1 - 31 Oct: daily, 10am - 5pm. 1 Nov - 31 Mar: daily, 10am - 4pm. Closed 24 & 25 Dec. Times subject to change April 2004.
Admission: Adult £3.20, Child £1.60, Conc. £2.40, Family £8. 15% discount for groups (11+). Prices subject to change April 2004.
ℹ️ Exhibition. WCs. 🔲 ♿ Unsuitable. 🅿️ 🐕 In grounds on leads. ✳️
♿ Tel for details.

CAPESTHORNE HALL    *See page 413 for full page entry.*

CHESTER ROMAN AMPHITHEATRE ⊞
Vicars Lane, Chester, Cheshire
Tel: 0161 242 1400
Owner: English Heritage   **Contact:** The North West Regional Office
The largest Roman amphitheatre in Britain, partially excavated. Used for entertainment and military training by the 20th Legion, based at the fortress of Deva.
Location: OS Ref. SJ404 660. On Vicars Lane beyond Newgate, Chester.
Open: Any reasonable time.
Admission: Free.
🐕 On leads. ✳️

North West - England

CHOLMONDELEY CASTLE GARDEN 🏚

MALPAS, CHESHIRE SY14 8AH

Tel: 01829 720383   **Fax:** 01829 720877

Owner: The Marchioness of Cholmondeley   **Contact:** The Secretary

Extensive ornamental gardens dominated by romantic Gothic Castle built in 1801 of local sandstone. Visitors can enjoy the beautiful Temple Water Garden, Rose Garden and many mixed borders. Lakeside picnic area, children's play areas, rare breeds of farm animals, including llamas, children's corner with rabbits, chickens and free flying aviary birds. Private chapel in the park.

Location: OS Ref. SJ540 515. Off A41 Chester/Whitchurch Rd. & A49 Whitchurch/

Tarporley Road. 7m N of Whitchurch.

Open: 4 Apr - 26 Sept: Weds, Thurs, Suns & BHs (open Good Fri), 11.30am - 5pm. May be open Suns in Oct for Autumn tints, please confirm with the Secretary. Groups (25+): other days by prior arrangement at reduced rates.

The castle is not open to the public except by prior arrangement to organised groups.

Admission: Adult £3.50, Child £1.50, no concessions.

🖸 🖼 🎨 🅣 🚾 Limited. WCs. ♿ 🐕 In grounds on leads only. ❋

DORFOLD HALL 🏚

ACTON, Nr NANTWICH, CHESHIRE CW5 8LD

Tel: 01270 625245   **Fax:** 01270 628723

Owner/Contact: Richard Roundell

Jacobean country house built in 1616 for Ralph Wilbraham. Family home of Mr & Mrs Richard Roundell. Beautiful plaster ceilings and oak panelling. Attractive woodland gardens and summer herbaceous borders.

Location: OS Ref. SJ634 525. 1m W of Nantwich on the A534 Nantwich - Wrexham road.

Open: Apr - Oct: Tues only and BH Mons, 2 - 5pm.

Admission: Adult £5, Child £3.

🖾 Obligatory. 🅿 Limited. Narrow gates with low arch prevent coaches.
🐕 In grounds on leads.

Patrick Lane

DUNHAM MASSEY 🌿

ALTRINCHAM, CHESHIRE WA14 1SJ

www.nationaltrust.org.uk

Tel: 0161 941 1025 **Fax:** 0161 929 7508

e-mail: dunhammassey@nationaltrust.org.uk

Owner: The National Trust   **Contact:** Property Manager

Originally an early Georgian house, Dunham Massey has sumptuous interiors with collections of walnut furniture, paintings and magnificent Huguenot silver. The richly planted garden contains waterside plantings, late flowering azaleas, an Orangery and Elizabethan mount. The surrounding deer park escaped the attentions of 18th century landscape gardeners and contains some notable specimen trees.

Location: OS Ref. SJ735 874. 3m SW of Altrincham off A56. M6/J19. M56/J7. Station Altrincham (BR & Metro) 3m.

Open: House: 27 Mar - 3 Nov: Sat - Wed, 12 noon - 5pm (11am - 5pm Good Fri, BH Sun & Mon; late Oct & Nov: 12 noon - 4pm). Garden: 27 Mar - 3 Nov: daily, 11am - 5.30pm (4.30pm in late Oct & Nov). Last admission normally ½ hr before closing. Mill: as House. Park open daily, all year.

Admission: House & Garden: Adult £6, Child £3, Family £15 (2+3 max). House or Garden: Adult £4, Child £2. Car entry: £3.50 per car. Coach/minibus entry: £10 (free to booked groups). Motorcycle £1. Groups tel for details.

ℹ️ No photography in house. 🖸 🖼 🚾 ♿ Partial. WC. Batricars. 🍽 Licensed.
🖾 Optional. No extra charge. 🅿 ♿ 🐕 In grounds, on leads. ❋

GAWSWORTH HALL
MACCLESFIELD, CHESHIRE SK11 9RN

www.gawsworthhall.com

Tel: 01260 223456 **Fax:** 01260 223469 **e-mail:** enquiries@gawsworthhall.com

Owner: Mr and Mrs T Richards **Contact:** Mr T Richards

Fully lived-in Tudor half-timbered manor house with Tilting Ground. Former home of Mary Fitton, Maid of Honour at the Court of Queen Elizabeth I, and the supposed 'Dark Lady' of Shakespeare's sonnets. Pictures, sculpture and furniture. Open air theatre with covered grandstand - June, July and August, please telephone for details. Situated halfway between Macclesfield and Congleton in an idyllic setting close to the lovely medieval church.

Location: OS Ref. SJ892 697. 3m S of Macclesfield on the A536 Congleton to Macclesfield road.

Open: Easter - 29 Sept: Sun - Wed (open daily 20 Jun - 31 Aug), 2 - 5pm. Also Special Events and BH weekends.

Admission: Adult £5, Child £2.50. Groups (20+): £4.

◻ ▣ ▣ ▣ Guide dogs in garden only. ▣ ▣ Tel for details.

LITTLE MORETON HALL ❧
CONGLETON, CHESHIRE CW12 4SDN

www.nationaltrust.org.uk

Tel: 01260 272018 **Fax:** 01260 292802

e-mail: littlemoretonhall@nationaltrust.org.uk

Owner: The National Trust **Contact:** The Property Manager

Begun in 1450 and completed 160 years later, Little Moreton Hall is regarded as the finest example of a timber-framed moated manor house in the country. The drunkenly reeling South Front topped by its Elizabethan Long Gallery opens onto a cobbled courtyard and the main body of the Hall. The Chapel, Great Hall, wall paintings and Knot Garden are of particular interest.

Location: OS Ref. SJ833 589. 4m SW of Congleton on E side of A34.

Open: 20 Mar - 31 Oct: Wed - Sun (open BH Mons & Good Fri), 11.30am - 5pm. 6 Nov - 19 Dec: Sat & Sun, 11.30am - 4pm or dusk.

Admission: Adult £5, Child £2.50, Family £12. Groups: £4.25 (must book).

◻ ▣ ▣ Braille guide, wheelchair. WCs. ▣ ▣ ▣ Car park only.

HARE HILL ❧

Over Alderley, Macclesfield, Cheshire SK10 4QB

Tel: 0161 928 0075 (Regional Office) 01625 584412 (Countryside Office)

www.nationaltrust.org.uk

Owner: The National Trust **Contact:** The Head Gardener

A woodland garden surrounding a walled garden with pergola, rhododendrons hollies and hostas. Parkland.

Location: OS Ref. SJ875 765. Between Alderley Edge and Macclesfield (B5087). Turn off N onto Prestbury Road, continue for ³/₄ m.

Open: 1 Apr - 30 Oct: Weds, Thurs, Sats & Suns, 10am - 5pm. Also 10 - 30 May: daily, 10am - 5pm.

Admission: Adult £2.70, Child £1.25. Car park fee £1.50 (refundable on entry to garden). Groups by written appointment c/o Garden Lodge at address above.

▣ Gravel paths - strong companion advisable. ▣ On leads in park.

HOLMSTON HALL BARN

Little Budworth, Tarporley, Cheshire CW6 9AY

Tel/Fax: 01829 760366

Owner/Contact: Mr Richard & Dr Yvonne Hopkins

15th century barn. Newly restored.

Location: OS Ref. SJ607 626. Off A49. 2m from Eaton village.

Open: All year by appointment only.

Admission: Free.

✳

© NTPL/ Nick Meers

LYME PARK ❧
DISLEY, STOCKPORT, CHESHIRE SK12 2NX

www.nationaltrust.org.uk

Tel: 01663 762023 **Fax:** 01663 765035 **e-mail:** lymepark@nationaltrust.org.uk

Owner: The National Trust **Contact:** The Property Manager

Legh family home for 600 years. Part of the original Elizabethan house survives with 18th and 19th century additions by Giacomo Leoni and Lewis Wyatt. Four centuries of period interiors – Mortlake tapestries, Grinling Gibbons carvings, unique collection of English clocks. Historic gardens with conservatory by Wyatt, a lake and a 'Dutch' garden. A 1,400 acre medieval deer park, home to red and fallow deer. Exterior featured as 'Pemberley' in BBC's *Pride and Prejudice*.

Location: OS Ref. SJ966 843. Off the A6 at Disley. 6¹/₂ m SE of Stockport.

Open: House: 29 Mar - 30 Oct: Fri - Tue, 1 - 5pm (last adm 4.30pm) (BH Mons & Good Fri, 11am - 5pm). Park: 1 Apr - 31 Oct: daily, 8am - 8.30pm; Nov - Mar: 8am - 6pm. Gardens: 29 Mar - 30 Oct: Fri - Tue, 11am - 5pm. Shop: 30 Mar - 30 Oct: daily, 11am - 5pm. 6 Nov - 27 Mar: Sats & Suns, 12 noon - 4pm. 27/28 Dec: 12 noon - 4pm. Coffee Shop: 29 Mar - 31 Oct: daily 10.30am - 5pm; 6 Nov - 22 Mar: Sat & Sun, 11am - 4pm. Restaurant: 29 Mar - 30 Oct, 11am- 5pm.

Admission: House & Garden: £5.80, House only: £4.20, Garden only: £2.70, Park only: car £3.80 (refundable on purchase of adult house & garden ticket), motorbike £2, coach/minibus £6. Booked coach groups Park admission Free. NT members Free.

ℹ No photography in house. ◻ ▣ Partial. WC. ▣ ▣ Licensed. ▣ By arrangement. ▣ ▣ ▣ In park, close control. Guide dogs only in house & garden. ✳

MACCLESFIELD SILK MUSEUMS
THE HERITAGE CENTRE, ROE STREET, MACCLESFIELD SK11 6UT

www.silk-macclesfield.org

Tel: 01625 613210/01625 612045 **Fax:** 01625 617880
e-mail: silkmuseum@tiscali.co.uk

Owner: Macclesfield Museums Trust **Contact:** Richard de Peyer

Three museums devoted to the silk industry in this historic town. The Silk Museum, housed in former Georgian Sunday School, tells the development of the industry through audio visual programmes, models, textiles and costume. Café. Silk Shop. Displays in the new extension opened in former Macclesfield School of Art look at properties of silk, design education, Macclesfield's other textile industries, social history and machinery. Temporary exhibition gallery. Guides at Paradise Mill give demonstrations on the last surviving silk handlooms.

Location: OS Ref. SJ917 733. Centre of Macclesfield.

Open: All year (except 25/26 Dec & 1 Jan). Groups at any time by prior booking.

Admission: All Museums: Adult £5.95, Child/Conc. £4.95, Family £18. Heritage Museum: Adult £3.20, Child/Conc. £2.20, Family £9. Industry Museum: Adult £3.75, Child/Conc. £2.75, Family £10.80.

🖥 🇹 🦽Partial. 🍴Licensed. 🍴Licensed. 🎫By arrangement. 🎧 ▪
🐕Guide dogs only. ❄

NTPL/ John Blake

NETHER ALDERLEY MILL ❧
CONGLETON RD, NETHER ALDERLEY, MACCLESFIELD SK10 4TW

www.nationaltrust.org.uk

Tel: 01625 584412 **e-mail:** netheralderleymill@national trust.org.uk

Owner: The National Trust **Contact:** Property Manager

Watermill dating from the 15th century, with working machinery. The mill has overshot tandem wheels and is powered by water from the adjacent lake. After lying derelict for 30 years, the Victorian machinery was restored in the 1960s and regular flour grinding demonstrations take place. Further restoration is planned.

Location: OS Ref. SJ844 763. 1¹/₂ m S of Alderley Edge, on E side of A34. Bus: Arriva North Midlands 130 Manchester - Macclesfield (Passing BR Alderley Edge). Station: Alderley Edge 2m.

Open: Apr - Oct: Wed, Thur, Fri & BH Mons, 1 - 5pm.

Admission: Adult £2.70, Child £1.10. Groups by prior arrangement (max. 20).

🎫By arrangement. 🅿Limited. Coaches must book. ▪ By arrangement. 🐕

NESS BOTANIC GARDENS
Ness, Neston, Cheshire CH64 4AY
Tel: 01513 530123 **Fax:** 01513 531004
Owner: University of Liverpool **Contact:** Dr E J Sharples
Location: OS Ref. SJ302 760 (village centre). Off A540. 10m NW of Chester. 1¹/₂ m S of Neston.
Open: 1 Mar - 31 Oct: 9.30am - 5pm. Nov - Feb: 9.30am - 4pm.
Admission: Charge for Adults & Conc. Accompanied child (under 18yrs) Free. 10% discount for groups. Please telephone for details.

Parterre

Garden Jargon

– Larger than a knot garden, normally planted in large formal geometric beds in front of the house. Popular in the 16th century, they were swept away by 'Capability' Brown, and became popular again with the Victorians and Edwardians.

Visit Manderston and Mellerstain in the Scottish Borders, Holkham Hall and Oxburgh Hall, Norfolk, Tatton Park, Cheshire, and Waddesdon Manor, Buckinghamshire, and Moseley Old Hall, Staffordshire.

NORTON PRIORY MUSEUM & GARDENS
TUDOR ROAD, MANOR PARK, RUNCORN WA7 1SX

www.nortonpriory.org

Tel: 01928 569895 **e-mail:** info@nortonpriory.org
Owner/Contact: The Norton Priory Museum Trust

Discover the 800 year old priory range, excavated priory remains, museum gallery, the St Christopher statue – one of the great treasures of medieval Europe – exciting sculpture trail and award winning Walled Garden. Set in 38 acres of tranquil, woodland gardens, Norton Priory also has a coffee shop, retail area and temporary exhibitions gallery.

Location: OS Ref. SJ545 835. 3m from M56/J11. 2m E of Runcorn.

Open: All year: daily, from 12 noon. Telephone for details.

Admission: Adult £4.25, Child/Conc. £2.95. Family £10, Groups £2.50.

🖥 🇹 🦽Wheelchairs, braille guide, audio tapes & WC. ▪ 🎫By arrangement. 🅿 ▪ 🐕In grounds, on leads. ❄ 🍴Tel for details.

PEOVER HALL 🏛
OVER PEOVER, KNUTSFORD WA16 9HN

Tel: 01565 632358

Owner: Randle Brooks   **Contact:** I Shepherd

An Elizabethan house dating from 1585. Fine Carolean stables. Mainwaring Chapel, 18th century landscaped park. Large garden with topiary work, also walled and herb gardens.

Location: OS Ref. SJ772 734. 4m S of Knutsford off A50 at Whipping Stocks Inn.

Open: Apr - Oct: House, Stables & Gardens: Mons except BHs, 2 - 5pm. Tours of the House at 2.30 & 3.30pm. Stables & Gardens only: Thurs, 2 - 5pm.

Admission: House, Stables & Gardens: Adult £4.50, Child £3. Stables & Gardens only: Adult £3, Child £2.

📷 Mondays only. 🎟 Obligatory. 🅿

RODE HALL 🏛
CHURCH LANE, SCHOLAR GREEN, CHESHIRE ST7 3QP

Tel: 01270 873237   **Fax:** 01270 882962   **e-mail:** rodehall@scholargreen.fsnet.co.uk

Owner/Contact: Sir Richard Baker Wilbraham Bt

The Wilbraham family have lived at Rode since 1669; the present house was constructed in two stages, the earlier two storey wing and stable block around 1705 and the main building was completed in 1752. Later alterations by Lewis Wyatt and Darcy Braddell were undertaken in 1812 and 1927 respectively. The house stands in a Repton landscape and the extensive gardens include a woodland garden, with a terraced rock garden and grotto, which has many species of rhododendrons, azaleas, hellebores and climbing roses following snowdrops and daffodils in the early spring. The formal rose garden was designed by W Nesfield in 1860 and there is a large walled kitchen garden which is at its best from the middle of June. The icehouse in the park has recently been restored.

Location: OS Ref. SJ819 573. 5m SW of Congleton between the A34 and A50. Kidsgrove railway station 2m NW of Kidsgrove.

Open: 1 Apr - 30 Sept: Weds & BHs (closed Good Fri) and by appointment. Garden only: Tues & Thurs, 2 - 5pm. Snowdrop Walk: 7 - 22 Feb: 12 noon - 4pm. NGS: 9 May.

Admission: House, Garden & Kitchen Garden: Adult £5, OAP £3.50. Garden & Kitchen Garden: Adult £3, OAP £2. Snowdrop Walk: £3.

🏛 📷 Home-made teas. 🐕 On leads.

QUARRY BANK MILL 🌿
& STYAL ESTATE
STYAL, WILMSLOW SK9 4LA

www.quarrybankmill.org.uk

Tel: 01625 527468   **Fax:** 01625 539267

e-mail: quarrybankmill@nationaltrust.org.uk

Owner: The National Trust   **Contact:** Nikky Braithwaite

Unique Georgian Cotton Mill with working machinery, daily demonstrations and fascinating living history. See the steam engines and mighty watermill in action. Experience the grim conditions in the Apprentice House. Enjoy the beautiful 300 acre Styal Estate.

Location: OS Ref. SJ835 830. 1¹/₂m N of Wilmslow off B5166. 2¹/₂ m from M56/J5. Styal Shuttle Bus, Airport 2¹/₂m.

Open: Mill: Apr - Sept: daily, 10.30am - 5.30pm, last adm. 4pm. Oct - Mar: daily except Mons, 10.30am - 5pm, last adm. 3.30pm. Apprentice House & Garden: Tue - Fri, 2 - 4.30pm, Sats, Suns: 11am - 4.30pm. Booked Groups (20+) at child rate.

Admission: Adult £7.30, Child/Conc. £4.50, Family £15 (2+3). Mill only: Adult £5.20, Child/Conc. £3.50. Booked Groups (20+) at child rate.

📷 📺 ♿ Partial. 📷 🍴 Licensed. 🎟 By arrangement. 🅿 📷 🐕 In grounds on leads. ▲ ❄ 📷 Tel for details.

TABLEY HOUSE
Knutsford, Cheshire WA16 0HB

Tel: 01565 750151   **Fax:** 01565 653230

e-mail: inquiries@tableyhouse.co.uk   **www**.tableyhouse.co.uk

Owner: The University of Manchester   **Contact:** The Assistant Administrator

The finest Palladian mansion in the North West of England, Grade I, by John Carr of York completed 1767 for the Leicester family who lived at Tabley for over 700 years. The first collection of English paintings ever made, furniture and fascinating memorabilia, can be seen in the State Rooms. Private chapel 1678 re-erected due to salt brine pumping.

Location: OS Ref. SJ725 777. M6/J19, A556 S on to A5033. 2m W of Knutsford.

Open: Apr - end Oct inclusive: Thurs, Fris, Sats, Suns & BHs, 2 - 5pm.

Admission: Adult £4. Child/Student £1.50. Groups by arrangement.

📷 ♿ 📷 🅿 ▲ Civil Wedding Licence plus Civil Naming Ceremonies & Re-affirmation of Vows. 📷 Tel for details.

TATTON PARK 🦌   *See page 414 for full page entry.*

WOODHEY CHAPEL
Faddiley, Nr Nantwich, Cheshire CW5 8JH

Tel: 01270 524215

Owner: The Trustees of Woodhey Chapel   **Contact:** Mr Robinson, The Curator

Small private chapel that has been recently restored.

Location: OS Ref. SJ573 528. Proceeding W from Nantwich on A534, turn left 1m W of the Faddiley - Brindley villages onto narrow lane, keep ahead at next turn, at road end obtain key from farmhouse.

Open: Apr - Oct: Sats & BHs, 2 - 5pm, or apply for key at Woodhey Hall.

Admission: £1.

❄ **Open All Year Index** see front section

ABBOT HALL ART GALLERY

KENDAL

www.abbothall.org.uk

Abbot Hall is a jewel of a building in a beautiful setting on the banks of the River Kent, surrounded by a park and overlooked by the ruins of Kendal Castle. This is one of Britain's finest small art galleries and a wonderful place in which to see and enjoy changing exhibitions in the elegantly proportioned rooms of a Grade I Listed Georgian building. The collection includes works by Romney, Ruskin, Turner and Freud. The adjacent Museum of Lakeland Life is a popular family attraction with a Victorian street scene, farmhouse rooms, Arthur Ransome room and displays of Arts and Crafts Movement furniture and fabrics.

Map 7

Owner:
Lakeland Arts Trust

▶ **CONTACT**

Abbot Hall Art Gallery
Kendal
Cumbria   LA9 5AL

Tel: 01539 722464

Fax: 01539 722494

e-mail: info@
abbothall.org.uk

▶ **LOCATION**
OS Ref. SD516 922

10 mins from M6/J36.
Follow brown museum
signs to South Kendal.

Rail: Oxenholme.

Air: Manchester.

▶ **OPENING TIMES**

20 January - 23 December
Mon - Sat
10.30am - 5pm
(4pm, Jan - Mar, Nov/Dec.)

Closed Sun.

▶ **ADMISSION**

Exhibition incl. free entry
to collection £4.75
Collection only £3.75

All ages welcome.

i No photography. No mobile phones.

Bookshop.

Chairlifts in split level galleries. WCs.

Licensed.   By arrangement.

P Ample. Free.

Guide dogs only.

Lakeland Arts Trust/Jonathan Lynch

Map 7

Owner:
Lakeland Arts Trust

▶ **CONTACT**

Alice Pearson
Blackwell
The Arts & Crafts House
Bowness on
Windermere
Cumbria   LA23 3JR

Tel: 01539 446139

Fax: 01539 488486

e-mail: info@
blackwell.org.uk

▶ **LOCATION**

OS Ref. SD400 945

1¹/₂ m S of Bowness
just off the A5074 on
the B5360.

Rail: Windermere.

Air: Manchester.

BLACKWELL - THE ARTS & CRAFTS HOUSE

BOWNESS ON WINDERMERE

www.blackwell.org.uk

Blackwell is a superb house situated in the Lake District. Completed in 1900, it sits in an elevated position overlooking Lake Windermere. Blackwell is the most important, and the largest, surviving early example of work by the architect Mackay Hugh Baillie Scott. Changing exhibitions of the highest quality applied arts and crafts can be seen in the setting of the Arts and Crafts Movement architecture itself.

In this treasure trove of 1890s Arts and Crafts design are fine examples of the decorative arts, drawn from natural forms. Lakeland birds and local wild flowers, trees and berries can be seen in the many original stained glass windows, pristine oak panelling and plasterwork. These rooms were designed for relaxation and everywhere you turn you will find inglenooks and places to sit and enjoy the views and garden terraces.

Lakeland Arts Trust/Jonathan Lynch

▶ **OPENING TIMES**

9 February - 23 December
Daily, 10.30am - 5pm,
(4pm, Feb/Mar, Nov/Dec.).

▶ **ADMISSION**

Adult.....................£4.75

All ages welcome.

 No photography. No mobile phones. Ground floor & part of 1st floor. WCs. Licensed. By arrangement. Limited for cars and coaches. Guide dogs only.

Map 7

DALEMAIN 🏛

PENRITH

www.dalemain.com

Owner:
Robert Hasell-McCosh Esq

▸ CONTACT

Marta Bakinowska
Administrator
Dalemain Estate Office
Dalemain
Penrith
Cumbria
CA11 0HB

Tel: 017684 86450

Fax: 017684 86223

e-mail:
admin@dalemain.com

▸ LOCATION

OS Ref. NY477 269

On A592 1m S of A66.
4m SW of Penrith.
From London, M1,
M6/J40: 5 hrs.

From Edinburgh,
A73, M74,
M6/J40: 2¹/₂ hrs.

Rail: Penrith 4m.

Taxi: Lakeland Taxis:
Penrith 01768 865722.

Dalemain is a fine mixture of mediaeval, Tudor and early Georgian architecture. The imposing Georgian façade strikes the visitor immediately but in the cobbled courtyard the atmosphere of the north country Tudor manor is secure. The present owner's family have lived at Dalemain since 1679 and have collected china, furniture and family portraits. Visitors can see the grand Drawing Rooms with 18th century Chinese wallpaper and fine oak panelling, also the Nursery and Housekeeper's Room. The Norman pele tower contains the regimental collection of the Westmorland and Cumberland Yeomanry. The house is full of the paraphernalia of a well established family house which is still very much lived in by the family.

The 16th century Great Barn holds a collection of agricultural bygones and a Fell Pony Museum.

Do not miss Mrs Mouse's house on the back stairs or the Nursery with toys from all ages. Something of interest for all the family. Location for ITV's production of *Jane Eyre*.

GARDENS

Delightful and fascinating 5 acre plantsman's gardens set against the picturesque splendour of the Lakeland Fells and Parkland. Richly planted herbaceous borders. Rose Walk with over 100 old-fashioned roses and ancient apple trees of named varieties. Magnificent Abies Cephalonica and Tulip Tree. Tudor Knot Garden. Wild Garden with profusion of flowering shrubs and wild flowers and in early summer the breathtaking display of blue Himalayan Poppies. Glorious woodland walk high above Dacre Beck. The gardens have been featured on *BBC Gardeners' World* and in *Country Life* and *English Garden*.

Val Corbett

▸ OPENING TIMES

Summer
28 March - 21 October
Sunday - Thursday

House:
11am - 4pm
(September & October:
11am - 3pm, last
admission 2pm).

Gardens, restaurant and tearoom, gift shop, plant sales & museums:
10.30am - 5pm
(September & October:
10.30am - 4pm).

NB. Groups (10+)
please book.

Winter
Gardens, restaurant and tearoom open for delicious homemade food, please call for opening times.

▸ ADMISSION

House & Garden
Adult £5.50
Child (6-16yrs) £3.50
Family £14.50

Gardens only
Adult £3.50
Child (6-16yrs) .... Free
Groups (10+)
Adult £4.50
Child (6-16yrs) £3.50

All prices include VAT.

🎭 SPECIAL EVENTS

JUL 17/18
Dalemain Craft Fair.

AUG 22
Cumbria Classic Car Show.

SEP 12
Plant Fair.

Please telephone for further details.

Fashion shows, archery, clay pigeon shooting, garden parties, rallies, filming, caravan rallies, antique fairs and children's camps. Business meetings and conferences. Grand piano available. Deer Park. Lectures on the house, gardens and history by arrangement (max 50). No photography in house. Moorings available on Ullswater.

Corporate events: telephone for details.

Visitors may drive into the Courtyard and alight near the gift shop. Electric scooter for visiting the gardens. Admission free for visitors in wheelchairs. WCs.

Licensed (in Mediaeval Hall). Seats 50. Groups must book for lunches/high teas. Free admission.

1 hr tours. German and French translations in every room. Garden tour for groups extra.

50 yds from house. Free.

Welcome. Guides can be arranged. Interest includes Military, Country Life, Agricultural and Fell Pony collections, also country walk past Dacre Castle to St Andrew's Church, Dacre where there is a fine Laurence Whistler window.

Guide dogs in house only. Strictly no dogs in garden but allowed in grounds.

CONFERENCE/FUNCTION

ROOM	MAX CAPACITY
Dining Room	40
Old Hall	50

Map 7

Owner: C H Bagot

▶ **CONTACT**

Peter Milner
Levens Hall
Kendal
Cumbria LA8 0PD

Tel: 01539 560321

Fax: 01539 560669

e-mail: email@
levenshall.fsnet.co.uk

▶ **LOCATION**

OS Ref. SD495 851

5m S of Kendal on the
A6. Exit M6/J36.

Rail: Oxenholme 5m.

Air: Manchester.

LEVENS HALL 🏛

KENDAL

www.levenshall.co.uk

Levens Hall is an Elizabethan mansion built around a 13th century pele tower. The much loved home of the Bagot family, visitors comment on the warm and friendly atmosphere. Fine panelling and plasterwork, period furniture, Cordova leather wall coverings, paintings by Rubens, Lely and Cuyp, the earliest English patchwork and Wellingtoniana combine with other beautiful objects to form a fascinating collection.

The world famous Topiary Gardens were laid out by Monsieur Beaumont from 1694 and his design has remained largely unchanged to this day. Over ninety individual pieces of topiary, some over nine metres high, massive beech hedges and colourful seasonal bedding provide a magnificent visual impact. *"One of the world's great gardens"* – *Sunday Times*. Also featured on BBC Gardeners' World Top Ten Gardens.

On Sundays and Bank Holidays 'Bertha', a full size Showman's Engine, is in steam. Delicious home-made lunches and teas are available, together with the award-winning Levens beer 'Morocco Ale', in the Bellingham Buttery.

▶ **OPENING TIMES**

Summer
4 April - mid October
Sun - Thur
(closed Fris & Sats).

House: 12 noon - 5pm
Last admission 4.30pm.

Group tours of Hall to
start between 10 - 10.30am
by prior arrangement.

Gardens, Plant Centre, Gift
Shop & Tearoom:
10am - 5pm.

Winter
Closed.

▶ **ADMISSION**

House & Gardens
Adult £7.50
Child £3.70
Groups (20+)
Adult...................... £6.00
School £3.50
Family (2+3).......... £21.00

Gardens
Adult £5.80
Child £2.60
Groups (20+)
Adult...................... £5.00
School £2.40
Family (2+3) £16.00

Evening Tours
House & Garden for
groups (20+) by prior
arrangement only
(Mon - Thur) £8.50

Gardens only
guided tour by the Head
Gardener or his Assistant
for groups (20+) by prior
arrangement only..... £6.50

Morning Tours
House tours starting
between 10 - 10.30am
for pre-arranged groups
(20+/min charge £140)
..................................£7.00

No admission charge for gift
shop, tearoom and plant
centre.

 No indoor photography. Partial. WC. Wheelchair loan - gardens only suitable.

 Licensed.  By arrangement. Schools welcome. **P** Guide dogs only.

Map 7

MUNCASTER CASTLE 🏛

GARDENS & OWL CENTRE, RAVENGLASS

www.muncaster.co.uk

Owner: Mrs Phyllida
Gordon-Duff-
Pennington

▶ CONTACT

Peter Frost-Pennington
Muncaster Castle
Ravenglass
Cumbria   CA18 1RQ

Tel: 01229 717614
Fax: 01229 717010

e-mail: info@
muncaster.co.uk

▶ LOCATION

OS Ref. SD103 965

On the A595 1m S of
Ravenglass, 19m S of
Whitehaven.

From London 6 hrs,
Chester 2¹/₂ hrs,
Edinburgh 3¹/₂ hrs,
M6/J36, A590,
A595 (from S). M6/J40,
A66, A595 (from E).
Carlisle, A595 (from N).

Rail: Ravenglass
(on Barrow-in-Furness-
Carlisle Line) 1¹/₂ m.

Air: Manchester 2¹/₂ hrs.

CONFERENCE/FUNCTION

ROOM	MAX CAPACITY
Drawing Rm	120
Dining Rm	50
Family Dining Rm	60
Great Hall	110
Old Laundry	120
Library	40

Visitor Attraction of the year (up to 100,000 visitors) Excellence in England Awards 2003.

Muncaster Castle has been owned by the Pennington family since 1208. It has grown from the original pele tower built on Roman foundations to the impressive structure visible today. Outstanding features are the Great Hall and Salvin's Octagonal Library and the Drawing Room with its barrel ceiling.

The haunted castle contains many treasures including beautiful furniture, exquisite needlework panels, tapestries and oriental rugs. The family silver is very fine and is accompanied in the Dining Room by the Ongley Service, the most ornamental set of porcelain ever created by the Derby factory, Florentine 16th century bronzes and an alabaster lady by Giambologna can be seen. The family are actively involved in entertaining their many visitors.

The woodland gardens cover 77 acres and command spectacular views of the Lakeland Fells, with many delightful walks including a 3 hour Wild Walk allowing visitors into areas not previously accessible. From mid-March to June the rhododendrons, azaleas, camellias and magnolias are at their best.

The Owl Centre boasts a fine collection of owls from all over the world. 'Meet the Birds' occurs daily at 2.30pm (14 Mar - 7 Nov), when a talk is given on the work of the centre. Weather permitting, the birds fly free.

Imagine being a meadow vole - just two and a half inches tall - living in meadowland, where dangers lurk at every turn. It's no picnic. Great for kids of all ages! Then revert to size and wander into the real wildflower meadow with glorious views of the Castle.

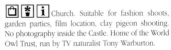 Church. Suitable for fashion shoots, garden parties, film location, clay pigeon shooting. No photography inside the castle. Home of the World Owl Trust, run by TV naturalist Tony Warburton.

Wedding receptions. For catering and functions in the Castle Tel: 01229 717614.

By prior arrangement visitors alight near Castle. Wheelchairs for loan. WCs. Special audio tour tapes for the partially sighted/those with learning difficulties. Allocated parking.

Creeping Kate's Kitchen (licensed) (max 80) – full menu. Groups can book: 01229 717614 to qualify for discounts.

Individual audio tour (40mins) included in price. Private tours with a personal guide (family member possible) can be arranged at additional fee. Lectures by arrangement.

P 500 cars 800 yds from House; coaches may park closer.

Guides available. Historical subjects, horticulture, conservation, owl tours.

In grounds, on leads.

'Georgie' star of the 3rd Millenium Muncaster stamp may be seen in the World Owl Centre.

▶ OPENING TIMES

Castle
14 March - 7 November
Daily (closed Sat),
12 noon - 5pm.

Gardens & Owl Centre
All year: Daily:
10.30am - 6pm or dusk
if earlier.

'Meet the Birds'
14 March - 7 November
Daily at 2.30pm.

Watch the wild herons feeding during the 'Heron Happy Hour'.
Daily at 4.30pm.

Winter
Castle closed. Open by appointment for groups.

▶ ADMISSION

Castle, Gardens, Owl Centre & MeadowVole Maze
Adult £8.50
Child (5-15yrs) £5.50
Under 5yrs .... Free
Family (2+2) £23.00
Groups
Adult £7.00
Child (5-15yrs) £4.00

Gardens, Owl Centre & MeadowVole Maze
Adult £6.00
Child (5-15yrs) £4.00
Under 5yrs .... Free
Family (2+2) £18.00
Groups
Adult £5.50
Child (5-15yrs) £3.00

ABBOT HALL ART GALLERY   *See page 420 for full page entry.*

ACORN BANK GDN & WATERMILL �

TEMPLE SOWERBY, PENRITH, CUMBRIA CA10 1SP

www.nationaltrust.org.uk

Tel: 01768 361893   **e-mail:** acornbank@nationaltrust.org.uk

Owner: The National Trust   **Contact:** The Custodian

A one hectare garden protected by fine oaks under which grow a vast display of daffodils. Inside the walls there are orchards containing a variety of fruit trees surrounded by mixed borders with shrubs, herbaceous plants and roses, while the impressive herb garden has the largest collection of culinary and medicinal plants in the north. A circular woodland walk runs beside the Crowdundle Beck to Acorn Bank Watermill, which although under restoration, is open to visitors. The house is not open to the public.

Location: Gate: OS Ref. NY612 281. Just N of Temple Sowerby, 6m E of Penrith on A66.

Open: 27 Mar - 31 Oct: daily except Tue, 10am - 5pm. Last admission 4.30pm. Tearoom: 6 - 26 Mar, 11am - 4pm.

Admission: Adult £2.75, Child £1.80, Family £6.80. Pre-arranged groups £2.
◻ ♿ Grounds only. WCs. ⛓

BEATRIX POTTER GALLERY ✲

MAIN STREET, HAWKSHEAD, CUMBRIA LA22 0NS

www.nationaltrust.org.uk

Tel: 01539 436355   **Fax:** 01539 436187

e-mail: beatrixpottergallery@nationaltrust.org.uk

Owner: The National Trust   **Contact:** Ticket Office / House Steward

An annually changing exhibition of original sketches and watercolours painted by Beatrix Potter for her children's stories. One of many historic buildings in this picturesque village, the gallery was once the office of Beatrix Potter's husband, William Heelis, and the interior remains substantially unaltered since his day. The gallery is ideally matched with a visit to Beatrix Potter's house, Hill Top, two miles away, where she wrote and illustrated many of her children's stories.

Location: OS Ref. SD352 982. 5m SSW of Ambleside. In the Square.

Open: 3 Apr - 31 Oct: Sat - Wed (closed Thur & Fri except Good Fri) 10.30am - 4.30pm. Last admission 4pm. Admission is by timed ticket (incl. NT members).

Admission: Adult £3, Child £1.50, Family £7.50. No reduction for groups. Discount for Hill Top ticket holders (not groups). Group booking essential.
ⓘ No photography inside. ◻ ▪ ⛓ Guide dogs only.

BLACKWELL -   *See page 421 for full page entry.*
THE ARTS & CRAFTS HOUSE

BROUGH CASTLE ⌗
Brough, Cumbria
Tel: 0191 269 1227/8
Owner: English Heritage   **Contact:** The North East Regional Office
This ancient site dates back to Roman times. The 12th century keep replaced an earlier stronghold destroyed by the Scots in 1174.
Location: OS Ref. NY791 141. 8m SE of Appleby S of A66. South part of the village.
Open: Any reasonable time.
Admission: Free.
⛓ On leads. 🅿 ✳

BROUGHAM CASTLE ⌗
Penrith, Cumbria CA10 2AA
Tel: 01768 862488
Owner: English Heritage   **Contact:** The Custodian
These impressive ruins on the banks of the River Eamont include an early 13th century keep and later buildings. You can climb to the top of the keep and survey the domain of its eccentric one-time owner Lady Anne Clifford. Exhibition about the Roman fort, medieval castle and Lady Anne Clifford.
Location: OS Ref. NY537 290. 1¹/₂ m SE of Penrith, between A66 & B6262.
Open: 1 Apr - 30 Sept: daily, 10am - 6pm. 1 - 31 Oct: daily, 10am - 5pm. Times subject to change April 2004.
Admission: Adult £2.50, Child £1.50, Conc. £2. 15% discount for groups (11+). Prices subject to change April 2004.
ⓘ WCs. ◻ ♿ Grounds. 🅿 Limited. ▪ ⛓ In grounds, on leads. ⛓ Tel for details.

© English Heritage Photo Library

CARLISLE CASTLE ⌗

CARLISLE, CUMBRIA CA3 8UR

Tel: 01228 591922

Owner: English Heritage   **Contact:** The Custodian

This impressive medieval castle, where Mary Queen of Scots was once imprisoned, has a long and tortuous history of warfare and family feuds. A portcullis hangs menacingly over the gatehouse passage, there is a maze of passages and chambers, endless staircases to lofty towers and you can walk the high ramparts for stunning views. There is also a medieval manor house in miniature: a suite of medieval rooms furnished as they might have been when used by the castle's former constable. The castle includes the King's Own Royal Border Regimental Museum.

Location: OS Ref. NY397 563. In Carlisle town, at N end of city centre.

Open: 1 Apr - 30 Sept: daily, 9.30am - 6pm. 1 - 31 Oct: daily, 10am - 5pm. 1 Nov - 31 Mar: daily, 10am - 4pm. Closed 24 - 26 Dec & 1 Jan. Times subject to change April 2004.

Admission: Adult £3.50, Child £1.80, Conc £2.70. 15% discount for groups (11+). Prices subject to change April 2004.
◻ ♿ Partial, wheelchairs available. 𝕂 By arrangement.
🅿 Disabled parking only. ▪ ⛓ Dogs on leads. ✳ ⛓ Tel for details.

CARLISLE CATHEDRAL
Carlisle, Cumbria CA3 8TZ
Tel: 01228 548151 **Fax:** 01228 547049 **Contact:** Ms C Baines
Fine sandstone Cathedral, founded in 1122. Medieval stained glass.
Location: OS Ref. NY399 559. Carlisle city centre, 2m from M6/J43.
Open: Mon - Sat: 7.45am - 6.15pm, Suns, 7.45 - 5pm. Closes 4pm between Christmas Day & New Year. Sun services: 8am, 10.30am & 3pm. Weekday services: 8am, 5.30pm & a 12.30 service on Weds, Fris and Saints' Days.
Admission: Donation.

CONISHEAD PRIORY & MANJUSHRI BUDDHIST TEMPLE
ULVERSTON, CUMBRIA LA12 9QQ

www.manjushri.org.uk

Tel: 01229 584029 **Fax:** 01229 580080
e-mail: info@manjushri.org.uk
Owner: Manjushri Mahayana Buddhist Centre **Contact:** Mr D Coote
A Georgian gothic mansion on site of a medieval Augustinian Priory. Special features include decorative ceilings, a vaulted great hall with fine stained glass and a 177 feet long cloister corridor. This historic treasure has been rescued from collapse by the resident community and is still under careful restoration. 'A very important Gothic revival country house... it has few peers in the North West...', English Heritage. There is also a unique Buddhist Temple in the former Kitchen garden.
Location: OS Ref. SD300 750. 2m S of Ulverston on Bardsea Coast Rd A5087.
Open: Easter - Oct: Sat, Sun & BHs, 2 - 5pm. Closed 22 May - 6 Jun & 24 Jul - 23 Aug. Opening times sometimes vary, please telephone to confirm.
Admission: Free. House Tours and audio visual: Adult £2.50, Child/Conc: £1.50.
🖼 ❄ ♿Partial. WC. ☕ ℱBy arrangement. 🅿 ⬛
🐕Guide dogs only in House, In grounds, on leads. ⬛ ❄

DALEMAIN 🏛 *See page 422 for full page entry.*

Website Information see front section

DOVE COTTAGE & THE WORDSWORTH MUSEUM
GRASMERE, CUMBRIA LA22 9SH

www.wordsworth.org.uk

Tel: 01539 435544 **Fax:** 01539 435748
e-mail: enquiries@wordsworth.org.uk
Owner: The Wordsworth Trust **Contact:** Bookings Officer
Situated in the heart of the English Lake District, Dove Cottage is the beautifully preserved Grasmere home of England's finest poet William Wordsworth. Visitors are offered fascinating guided tours of his world-famous home. The award-winning Museum displays priceless Wordsworth manuscripts and memorabilia. Onsite tearooms and book and gift shop.
Location: OS Ref. NY342 070. Immediately S of Grasmere village on A591. Main car/coach park next to Dove Cottage Tea Rooms and Restaurant.
Open: All year: daily, 9.30am - 5pm. Closed 5 Jan - 1 Feb & 24 - 26 Dec.
Admission: Adult £5.80, Child £2.60, OAP £4.90, Family Tickets available. Pre-arranged groups (10-60): Adult £4.70. Reciprocal discount ticket with Rydal Mount and Wordsworth House.
ℹ️No photography. 🖼 ♿Partial. WC. ☕ 🍽 ℱObligatory. 🅿Limited. ⬛
🐕Guide dogs only. ❄ ♿ Tel for details.

FELL FOOT PARK 🌿
Newby Bridge, Cumbria LA12 8NN
Tel: 01539 531273 **Fax:** 01539 539926 **e-mail:** fellfootpark@nationaltrust.org.uk
Owner: The National Trust **Contact:** Visitor Services Manager
Come and explore this lakeshore Victorian park on the edge of Windermere. A great place for the family, with boat hire, tearoom, play area, family activity sheets and wildlife room showing birds and bats who live around the park. Fantastic views of the Lakeland fells. Wonderful colour in spring.
Location: OS Ref. SD381 869. S end of Lake Windermere on E shore, entrance from A592. Near Aquarium of the Lakes and Haverthwaite Steam Railway.
Open: Daily, 9am - dusk.
Admission: Car park: 2hrs £2.50, 4hrs £4.50, all day £6. Coaches by arrangement.
🖼 ♿Partial. ☕ 🅿Charge. 🐕On leads. ❄ ♿ Tel for details.

FURNESS ABBEY ⧉
Barrow-in-Furness, Cumbria LH13 0TJ
Tel: 01229 823420
Owner: English Heritage **Contact:** The Custodian
Hidden in a peaceful green valley are the beautiful red sandstone remains of the wealthy abbey founded in 1123 by Stephen, later King of England. This abbey first belonged to the Order of Savigny and later to the Cistercians. There is a museum and exhibition.
Location: OS Ref. SD218 717. 1¹/₂ m NE of Barrow-in-Furness.
Open: 1 Apr - 30 Sept: daily, 10am - 6pm. 1 - 31 Oct:, daily, 10am - 5pm. 1 Nov - 31 Mar: Wed - Sun, 10am - 4pm. Closed 1 - 2pm in winter. Closed 24 - 26 Dec & 1 Jan. Times subject to change April 2004.
Admission: Adult £3, Child £1.50, Conc. £2.30. 15% discount for groups (11+). Prices subject to change April 2004.
ℹ️WC. 🖼 ♿Grounds. 🎧Inclusive. 🅿 ⬛ 🐕In grounds, on leads. ❄
♿ Tel for details.

HARDKNOTT ROMAN FORT ⧉
Ravenglass, Cumbria
Tel: 0161 242 1400
Owner: English Heritage **Contact:** The North West Regional Office
This fort, built between AD120 and 138, controlled the road from Ravenglass to Ambleside.
Location: OS Ref. NY219 015. At the head of Eskdale. 9m NE of Ravenglass, at W end of Hardknott Pass.
Open: Any reasonable time. Access may be hazardous in winter.
Admission: Free.
🅿 🐕On leads. ❄

HERON CORN MILL & MUSEUM OF PAPERMAKING

c/o Henry Cooke, Waterhouse Mills, Beetham, Milnthorpe LA7 7AR

Tel: 015395 65027 **Fax:** 015395 65033 **e-mail:** nt.stobbs@virgin.net

Owner: Heron Corn Mill Beetham Trust **Contact:** Mr Neil Stobbs

Location: OS Ref. SD497 800. At Beetham. 1m S of Milnthorpe on the A6.

Open: Easter: 1 Apr - 30 Sept: Tue - Sun & BH Mon, 11am - 5pm.

Admission: Adult £2, Child £1, OAP £1.50, Family (2+2) £5, Coach parties/groups 10% discount if pre-booked.

HOLEHIRD GARDENS

Patterdale Road, Windermere, Cumbria LA23 1NP

Tel: 01539 446008

Owner: Lakeland Horticultural Society **Contact:** The Hon Secretary

Over 10 acres of hillside gardens overlooking Windermere, including a walled garden and national collections of Astilbe, Hydrangea and Polystichum ferns. Organised and maintained entirely by volunteers.

Location: OS Ref. NY410 008. On A592, 3/4 m N of junction with A591. 1/2 m N of Windermere. 1m from Townend.

Open: All year: dawn to dusk.

Admission: Free. Donation appreciated (at least £2 suggested).

NT Photographic Library: Stephen Robson

HILL TOP

NEAR SAWREY, AMBLESIDE, CUMBRIA LA22 0LF

www.nationaltrust.org.uk

Tel: 01539 436269 **Fax:** 01539 436118 **e-mail:** hilltop@nationaltrust.org.uk

Owner: The National Trust **Contact:** Ticket Office/Property Assistant

Beatrix Potter wrote many of her famous children's stories in this little 17th century house, which contains her furniture and china. There is a traditional cottage garden attached. A selection of the original illustrations may be seen at the Beatrix Potter Gallery. Shop specialises in Beatrix Potter items.

Location: OS Ref. SD370 955. 2m S of Hawkshead, in hamlet of Near Sawrey, behind the Tower Bank Arms.

Open: 3 Apr - 31 Oct: Sat - Wed & Good Fri, 10.30am - 4.30pm. Garden & Shop: Sat - Wed, 10.30am - 5pm, Thur & Fri, 11am - 4pm. Last admission 4pm. Admission by timed ticket. Group booking essential.

Admission: Adult £4.50, Child £2, Family £11. No reduction for groups. Discount for Beatrix Potter Gallery ticket holders (not groups). Shop & Garden: Free on Thur & Fri.

No photography in house. Partial. None for coaches. Guide dogs only. Tel for details.

HOLKER HALL & GARDENS

CARK-IN-CARTMEL, GRANGE-OVER-SANDS, CUMBRIA LA11 7PL

www.holker-hall.co.uk

Tel: 01539 558328 **Fax:** 01539 558378 **e-mail:** publicopening@holker.co.uk

Owner: Lord Cavendish of Furness **Contact:** Elizabeth Ward

Holker Hall, home of Lord and Lady Cavendish, shows the confidence, spaciousness and prosperity of Victorian style on its grandest scale. The New Wing was designed by architects Paley and Austin and built by the 7th Duke of Devonshire during 1871-4. Despite this grand scale, Holker is very much a family home with visitors able to wander freely throughout the New Wing. Varying in period and style, Louis XV pieces happily mix with the Victorian, including an early copy of the famous triple portrait of Charles I by Van Dyck. The award-winning gardens include formal and woodland areas covering 25 acres. Designated 'amongst the best in the world in terms of design and content' by the *Good Gardens Guide*. This inspiring garden includes a lime stone cascade, fountain, the Sunken Garden, the Elliptical and Summer Gardens and many rare plants and shrubs. Newly created Labyrinth designed by Lady Cavendish and international designer Jim Buchanen.

Location: OS Ref. SD359 773. Close to Morecambe Bay, 5m W of Grange-over-Sands by B5277. From Kendal, A6, A590, B5277, B5278: 16m. Motorway: M6/J36.

Open: 28 Mar - 31 Oct: Sun - Fri, 10am - 6pm (closed Sat). Last admission 4.30pm. All other facilities open daily from 1 Mar 2004.

Admission: House & Garden: Adult £8.75, Child £5, Family £25.75. Groups (20-100): Adult £5, Child £3.50, OAP £4.50. Under 6yrs Free.

No photography in house. Visitors alight at entrance. WCs. Licensed. By arrangement. 150 yds from Hall. In grounds, on leads.

HUTTON-IN-THE-FOREST 🏠

PENRITH, CUMBRIA CA11 9TH

www.hutton-in-the-forest.co.uk

Tel: 01768 484449 **Fax:** 01768 484571 **e-mail:** hutton-in-the-forest@talk21.com

Owner: Lord Inglewood   **Contact:** Edward Thompson

The home of Lord Inglewood's family since 1605. Built around a medieval pele tower with 17th, 18th and 19th century additions. Fine collections of furniture, paintings, ceramics and tapestries. Outstanding grounds with terraces, topiary, walled garden, dovecote and woodland walk through magnificent specimen trees.

Location: OS Ref. NY460 358. 6m NW of Penrith & 2 ¹/₂ m from M6/J41 on B5305.

Open: 9 - 18 Apr & 2 May - 3 Oct: Thur, Fri, Suns & BHs. 12.30 - 4pm (last entry). Tearoom: As house: 11am - 4.30pm. Gardens & Grounds: Easter - Oct, daily except Sats, 11am - 5pm.

Admission: House, Gardens & Grounds: Adult £4.50, Child £2.50, Family £12. Gardens & Grounds: Adult £2.50, Child Free. (2003 prices.)

ℹ️ Picnic area. 🎁 Gift stall. 🍽 By arrangement. ♿ Partial. 🅿

🚫 Obligatory (except Jul/Aug & BHs). 🅿 🔲 🐕 On leads. ❋ 🛏 Tel for details.

LANERCOST PRIORY ⚜

Brampton, Cumbria CA8 2HQ

Tel: 01697 73030

Owner: English Heritage   **Contact:** The Custodian

This Augustinian priory was founded c1166. The nave of the church, which is intact and in use as the local parish church, contrasts with the ruined chancel, transepts and priory buildings. Free audio tour.

Location: OS Ref. NY556 637. 2m NE of Brampton. 1m N of Naworth Castle.

Open: 1 Apr - 30 Sept: daily, 10am - 6pm. 1 - 31 Oct: daily, 10am - 5pm. Times subject to change April 2004.

Admission: Adult £2.50, Child £1.50, Conc. £2. Groups (11+): 15% discount. Prices subject to change April 2004.

🔲 ♿ Ground floor. 🔄 Inclusive. 🅿 Limited. 🔲 🐕 🛏 Tel for details.

LEVENS HALL 🏠   *See page 423 for full page entry.*

MIREHOUSE 🏠

KESWICK, CUMBRIA CA12 4QE

www.mirehouse.com

Tel: 017687 72287 **Fax:** 017687 75356 **e-mail:** info@mirehouse.com

Owner: James Fryer-Spedding   **Contact:** Clare Spedding

Mirehouse is a remarkably literary house, linked with Tennyson, Wordsworth, Thomas Carlyle and Francis Bacon. Our visitors also like the classical music, poetry walk, varied gardens, walks by Bassenthwaite Lake (home to the English ospreys) and the natural adventure playgrounds. *The Lake District with its hand on its heart* – Simon Jenkins in *The Times*.

Location: OS Ref. NY235 284. Beside A591, 3¹/₂ m N of Keswick. Good bus service.

Open: 1 Apr - 31 Oct: Gardens & Tearoom: daily, 10am - 5.30pm. House: Suns & Weds (also Fris in Aug), 2 - 5pm (4.30pm last entry). At other times for groups by appointment.

Admission: House & Garden: Adult £4.60, Child £2.30, Family £13.80. Gardens only: Adult £2.20, Child £1.10. 10% discount for groups (20+), booked in advance.

ℹ️ No photography in house. ♿ 🔲 🚫 By arrangement. 🅿 Limited. 🔲

🐕 Dogs on leads only. ❋ Booked groups only.

MUNCASTER CASTLE 🏛 *See page 424 for full page entry.*

PENRITH CASTLE ⌗
Penrith, Cumbria
Tel: 0161 242 1400
Owner: English Heritage   **Contact:** The North West Regional Office
This 14th century castle, set in a park on the edge of the town, was built to defend Penrith against repeated attacks by Scottish raiders.
Location: OS Ref. NY513 299. Opposite Penrith railway station. W of the town centre. Fully visible from the street.
Open: Park opening hours.
Admission: Free.
ⓘ WC 🐕 On leads.

SIZERGH CASTLE & GARDEN 🌿
Nr KENDAL, CUMBRIA LA8 8AE
www.nationaltrust.org.uk
Tel: 01539 560070   **Fax:** 01539 560951   **e-mail:** sizergh@nationaltrust.org.uk
Owner: The National Trust   **Contact:** Property Administrator
The Strickland family has lived here for more than 750 years. The impressive 14th century tower was extended in Tudor times, with some of the finest Elizabethan carved overmantels in the country. Contents include good English and French furniture and family portraits. A visit culminates in the important and impressive Inlaid Chamber. The castle is surrounded by gardens of beauty and interest, including the Trust's largest limestone rock garden; good autumn colour. Large estate; walks leaflet available in shop.
Location: OS Ref. SD498 878. 3½ m S of Kendal, NW of the A590/A591 interchange.
Open: Castle: 1 Apr - 31 Oct: Sun - Thur & BHs except Good Fri, 1.30 - 5.30pm. Garden: As house: 12.30 - 5.30pm. Last admission 5pm. Shop: as garden, also open Nov & Dec.
Admission: Adult £5.50, Child £2.70, Family £13.70. Garden only: Adult £3, Child £1.50. Groups (15+): £4.50 by arrangement (not on BHs).
🗎 🍴 ♿ Partial. ☕ Ⓟ Limited for coaches. 🐕 📺 Tel for details.

RYDAL MOUNT & GARDENS
RYDAL, CUMBRIA LA22 9LU
www.rydalmount.co.uk
Tel: 01539 433002 **Fax:** 01539 431738 **e-mail:** rydalmount@aol.com
Owner: Rydal Mount Trustees   **Contact:** Peter & Marian Elkington
Nestling in the beautiful fells between Lake Windermere and Rydal Water, lies the 'most beloved home' of William Wordsworth from 1813 - 1850. *Experience* the splendid historic home of Wordsworth's descendants; *Enjoy* the beautiful terraced gardens landscaped by the poet; *Feel* the peaceful relaxed 'romantic' atmosphere; *The freedom* of wandering through this 'spot of more perfect and enjoyable beauty' as wrote Dr Thomas Arnold.
Location: OS Ref. NY364 063. 1½ m N of Ambleside on A591 Grasmere Road.
Open: Mar - Oct: daily, 9.30am - 5pm. Nov - Feb: daily except Tues, 10am - 4pm.
Admission: Adult £4.50, Child £1.50, Student £3.25, OAP £3.50, Family £10. Pre-arranged groups £3. Garden only: £2. Free parking. Reciprocal discount ticket with Dove Cottage & Wordsworth House.
ⓘ No inside photography. 🗎 ♿ Partial. ✗ By arrangement. Ⓟ Limited. ▪
🐕 In grounds, on leads. Guide dogs only in house. ✳

STEAM YACHT GONDOLA 🌿
NT GONDOLA BOOKINGS OFFICE, THE HOLLENS, GRASMERE LA22 9QZ
www.nationaltrust.org.uk
Tel: 015394 41288 **Fax:** 015394 35353   **e-mail:** gondola@nationaltrust.org.uk
Owner: The National Trust   **Contact:** The Manager
The Steam Yacht Gondola, first launched in 1859 and now completely renovated by the Trust, provides a steam-powered passenger service, carrying 86 passengers in opulently upholstered saloons. A superb way to see Coniston's scenery.
Location: OS Ref. SD305 975. Coniston (½ m to Coniston Pier).
Open: Sails from Coniston Pier daily, 1 Apr - 31 Oct. The Trust reserves the right to cancel sailings in the event of high winds. Piers at Coniston and Brantwood (not NT). Groups from Coniston Pier only.
Admission: Ticket prices & timetable on application and published locally. Family ticket available. No reduction for NT members as Gondola is an enterprise and not held solely for preservation. Groups & private charters by prior arrangement.
ⓘ WC at Coniston Pier. ♿ Unsuitable. Ⓟ Free at Coniston.
🐕 Dogs on leads, outside saloons.

STAGSHAW GARDEN 🌿
Ambleside, Cumbria LA22 0HE
Tel /Fax: 015394 46027 **e-mail:** stagshaw@nationaltrust.org.uk
Owner: The National Trust
This woodland garden contains a fine collection of azaleas and rhododendrons, planted to give good blends of colour under thinned oaks on the hillside; also magnolias, camellias and embothriums. Adjacent to the woods are Skelghyll Woods which offer delightful walks and access to the fells beyond.
Location: OS Ref. NY380 029. ½ m S of Ambleside on A591. Ferry Waterhead ½ m.
Open: 1 Apr - 30 Jun: daily. Colours best Apr - Jun, Jul - end Oct: by appointment through the property office at St Catherines, Patterdale Road, Windermere LA23 1NH.
Admission: £2, by honesty box.
♿ Unsuitable. Ⓟ Limited. 🐕

STOTT PARK BOBBIN MILL ⌗

Low Stott Park, Nr Newby Bridge, Cumbria LA12 8AX

Tel: 01539 531087

Owner: English Heritage   **Contact:** The Custodian

When this working mill was built in 1835 it was typical of the many mills in the Lake District which grew up to supply the spinning and weaving industry in Lancashire but have since disappeared. A remarkable opportunity to see a demonstration of the machinery and techniques of the Industrial Revolution. Steam days: Tues - Thurs.

Location: OS Ref. SD373 883. Near Newby Bridge on A590.

Open: 1 Apr - 30 Sept: daily, 10am - 6pm. 1 - 31 Oct: daily, 10am - 5pm. Last admission 1hr before closing. Times subject to change April 2004.

Admission: Adult £3.50, Child £1.80, Conc. £2.70, Family £8.50. Groups: discount for groups (11+). Prices subject to change April 2004.

🔲 ♿Ground floor. WC. ⓕFree. 🅿 ▣ ✖

HELENA THOMPSON MUSEUM

Park End Road, Workington, Cumbria CA14 4DE

Tel: 01900 326255   **e-mail:** heritage.arts@allerdale.gov.uk

Owner: Allerdale Borough Council   **Contact:** Heritage & Arts Unit

The museum is housed in a fine listed mid-Georgian building. Displays include pottery, silver, glass, furniture and dress collection.

Location: OS Ref. NY007 286. Corner of A66, Ramsey Brow & Park End Road.

Open: All year: daily, 10.30am - 4pm.

Admission: Free.

Education Index see front section

TOWNEND ✿

TROUTBECK, WINDERMERE, CUMBRIA LA23 1LB

www.nationaltrust.org.uk

Tel: 01539 432628   **e-mail:** townend@nationaltrust.org.uk

Owner: The National Trust   **Contact:** The Administrator

An exceptional relic of Lake District life during past centuries. Originally a 'statesman' (wealthy yeoman) farmer's house, built about 1626. Townend contains carved woodwork, books, papers, furniture and fascinating implements of the past which were accumulated by the Browne family who lived here from 1626 until 1943. Regular 'Living History' programme - Meet George Browne c1900.

Location: OS Ref. NY407 020. 3m SE of Ambleside at S end of Troutbeck village. 1m from Holehird, 3m N of Windermere.

Open: 1 Apr - 31 Oct: Tue - Fri, Suns & BH Mons, 1 - 5pm or dusk if earlier. Last entry 4.30pm.

Admission: Adult £3.20, Child £1.50, Family £8. No reduction for groups which must be pre-booked.

♿Unsuitable for wheelchairs.   ✖ ▣ Tel for details.

Levens Hall, Cumbria from the book *Historic Family Homes and Gardens from the Air*, see page 54.

WORDSWORTH HOUSE ✿

MAIN STREET, COCKERMOUTH, CUMBRIA CA13 9RX

www.wordsworthhouse.org.uk

Tel/Fax: 01900 824805   **e-mail:** wordsworthhouse@ntrust.org.uk

Owner: The National Trust   **Contact:** The Custodian

This Georgian town house was the birthplace of William Wordsworth. Imaginatively presented as the home of the Wordsworth family in the 1770s, the house offers a lively and participative visit with costumed living history. The garden, with terraced walk overlooking the River Derwent, has been restored to its 18th century appearance.

Location: OS Ref. NY118 307. Main Street, Cockermouth.

Open: Following refurbishment the house re-opens in Jun - 5 Nov: Mon - Sat, 11am - 4.30pm. Last entry 4pm. Shop: 29 Mar - 24 Dec. Telephone for details.

Admission: Adult £4.50, Child £2.50. Pre-booked groups (15+): Adult £3.50, Child £1.50.

ⓘNo photography. 🔲 ♿Partial. WCs. ⓕBy arrangement only. ▣ 🐕Guide dogs only.

English Life Publication Ltd

LEIGHTON HALL

CARNFORTH

www.leightonhall.co.uk

Leighton Hall is one of the most beautifully sited houses in the British Isles, situated in a bowl of parkland, with the whole panorama of the Lakeland Fells rising behind. The Hall's neo-gothic façade was superimposed on an 18th century house, which, in turn, had been built on the ruins of the original medieval house. The present owner is descended from Adam d'Avranches who built the first house in 1246.

The whole house is lived in today by the Reynolds family and emphasis is put on making visitors feel welcome in a family home.

Mr Reynolds is also descended from the founder of Gillow and Company of Lancaster. Connoisseurs of furniture will be particularly interested in the many 18th century Gillow pieces, some of which are unique. Fine pictures, clocks, silver and *objets d'art* are also on display.

Leighton Hall is home to a varied collection of Birds of Prey. These birds are flown daily during opening hours, weather permitting.

GARDENS

The main garden has a continuous herbaceous border with rose covered walls, while the Walled Garden contains flowering shrubs, a herb garden, and an ornamental vegetable garden with a caterpillar maze. Beyond is the Woodland Walk where wild flowers abound from early Spring.

Owner:
Richard Gillow
Reynolds Esq

▶ CONTACT

Mrs C S Reynolds
Leighton Hall
Carnforth
Lancashire LA5 9ST

Tel: 01524 734474
Fax: 01524 720357

e-mail: info@
leightonhall.co.uk

▶ LOCATION

OS Ref. SD494 744

9m N of Lancaster,
10m S of Kendal,
3m N of Carnforth.
1½ m W of A6.
3m from M6/A6/J35,
signed from J35A.

Rail: Carnforth
Station 3m.

Bus: The Carnforth
Connect (line 1) bus
from Carnforth Railway
Station stops at the
gates of Leighton Hall
(info 01524 734311)

Air: Manchester
Airport 65m.

Taxi: Carnforth Radio
Taxis, Carnforth 732763.

CONFERENCE/FUNCTION

ROOM	SIZE	MAX CAPACITY
Music Room	24' x 21'6"	80
Dining Rm		30
Other		80

🏛 ❄ ℹ Product launches, seminars, filming, garden parties, conferences, rallies, overland driving, archery and clay pigeon shooting. No photography in house. Gifts & unusual plants for sale.

🍽 Buffets, lunches, dinners and wedding receptions.

♿ Partial. WC. Visitors may alight at the entrance to Hall.

☕ 🍴 Booking essential for group catering, menus on request.

🚶 Obligatory. By prior arrangement owner may meet groups,. The 45 minute tour includes information on the property, its gardens and history. House and flying display tour time: 2 hrs. .

🅿 Ample for cars and coaches.

🏫 School programme: all year round. Choice of Countryside Classroom, Victorian Leighton or Local History. Sandford Award for Heritage Education winner in 1983 & 1989.

🐾 In Park, on leads.

❄ For booked groups & functions.

🔔 An unusual, but spectacular venue, Leighton Hall is a fairytale choice.

🛡 Visit website for details.

▶ OPENING TIMES

Summer

1 May - 30 September
Daily except Mons & Sats
2 - 5pm. Open BH Mons.

August only:
12.30 - 5pm.

NB. Booked groups (25+) at any time by arrangement.

Winter

1 October - 30 April
Open to booked
groups (25+).

▶ ADMISSION

Summer
House, Garden & Birds
  Adult £5.00
  Child (5-12yrs)....... £3.50
  Student/OAP £4.50
Groups (25+)
  Adult £4.00
  Child (5-12yrs)....... £3.00
  Family (2+3) £15.00
  School................... £3.00

Child under 5yrs, Free

Grounds only
(after 4.30pm)
  Per person £1.50

Winter

As above but groups by appointment only.

Pre-booked candlelit tours Nov - Jan.

Note: The owners reserve the right to close or restrict access to the house and grounds for special events, or at any other time without prior notice.

ASTLEY HALL MUSEUM & ART GALLERY
ASTLEY PARK, CHORLEY PR7 1NP

www.astleyhall.co.uk

Tel: 01257 515555 **Fax:** 01257 515556 **e-mail:** astleyhall@lineone.net

Owner/Contact: Chorley Borough Council

Timber-framed Tudor house, with spectacular 17th century additions. Interiors include sumptuous plaster ceilings, fine 17th century oak furniture and tapestries, plus displays of fine and decorative art. Set in parkland.

Location: OS Ref. SD574 183. Off Hallgate, Astley Village, between A581 and B5252. Close to M61/J8 and M6/J28.

Open: Apr - end Oct: Tue - Sun, 12 noon - 5pm. Plus BH Mons. Nov - Mar: Sat & Sun, 12 noon - 4pm (last admission ¹/₂hr before closing time). Closed Christmas & New Year.

Admission: Rates to be confirmed. Please telephone for details.

ⓘNo photography. 🖭 🕇 🛇Partial. Braille guide. 🖤 ⓕBy arrangement. 🖭 🖭 🅿 🖼Guide dogs only. 🔺 ❋

BLACKBURN CATHEDRAL
Cathedral Close, Blackburn, Lancashire BB1 5AA

Tel: 01254 51491 **Fax:** 01254 689666 **Contact:** Mrs Alison Feeney

On an historic Saxon site in town centre. The 1826 Parish Church dedicated as the Cathedral in 1977 with new extensions to give a spacious and light interior.

Location: OS Ref. SD684 280. 9m E of M6/J31, via A59 and A677. City centre.

Open: Daily, 9am - 5pm. Sun services: at 8am, 9am, 10.30am and 4pm. Catering: Tues - Fri, 10am - 2.30pm or Sat by arrangement.

Admission: Free. Donations invited.

BROWSHOLME HALL 🖼
Clitheroe, Lancashire BB7 3DE

Tel: 01254 826719 **e-mail:** rrp@browsholme.co.uk **www.**browsholme.co.uk

Owner/Contact: Robert Parker

Ancestral home of the Parker Family, built in 1507 with a major collection of oak furniture and portraits, arms and armour, stained glass and many unusual antiquities from the Civil War to a fragment of a Zeppelin.

Location: OS Ref. SD683 452. 5m NW of Clitheroe off B6243.

Open: 23 May with Garden and Craft Fair. 28 - 31 May, 22 - 30 June, 24 - 31 July and 21 - 31 Aug : Daily except Mons (but open BH Mons), 2 - 4pm. Groups welcome by appointment.

Admission: Adult £4, Child £1.

GAWTHORPE HALL 🌿
Padiham, Nr Burnley, Lancashire BB12 8UA

Tel: 01282 770353 **Fax:** 01282 770178 **e-mail:** gawthorpe@nationaltrust.org.uk

Owner: The National Trust **Contact:** Property Office

The house was built in 1600-05, and restored by Sir Charles Barry in the 1850s. Barry's designs have been re-created in the principal rooms. Gawthorpe was the home of the Shuttleworth family, and the Rachel Kay-Shuttleworth textile collections are on display in the house, private study by arrangement. Collection of portraits on loan from the National Portrait Gallery.

Location: OS Ref. SD806 340. M65/J8. On E outskirts of Padiham, ³/₄ m to house on N of A671. Signed to Clitheroe, then signed from 2nd set of traffic lights.

Open: Hall & Tearoom: 1 Apr - 2 Nov: daily except Mons & Fris, open Good Fri & BH Mons, 1 - 5pm. Last adm. 4.30pm. Garden: All year: daily, 10am - 6pm.

Admission: Hall: Adult £3, Family £8 (prices may change). Garden: Free. Groups must book.

🛇Please ring in advance. 🖤 🖼In grounds on leads. ❋

HALL I'TH'WOOD
off Green Way, off Crompton Way, Bolton BL1 8UA

Tel: 01204 332370

Owner: Bolton Metropolitan Borough Council **Contact:** Liz Shaw

Late medieval manor house with 17/18th century furniture, paintings and decorative art.

Location: OS Ref. SD724 116. 2m NNE of central Bolton. ¹/₄ m N of A58 ring road between A666 and A676 crossroads.

Open: 31 Mar - 31 Oct: Wed - Sun, 11am - 5pm. 1 Nov - 27 Mar: Sat & Sun, 11am - 5pm.

Admission: Adult £2, Child/Conc. £1.

HOGHTON TOWER 🖼
HOGHTON, PRESTON, LANCASHIRE PR5 0SH

Tel: 01254 852986 **Fax:** 01254 852109

Owner: Sir Bernard de Hoghton Bt **Contact:** Office

Hoghton Tower, home of 14th Baronet, is one of the most dramatic looking houses in northern England. Three houses have occupied the hill site since 1100 with the present house re-built by Thomas Hoghton between 1560 - 1565. Rich and varied historical events including the Knighting of the Loin 'Sirloin' by James I in 1617.

Location: OS Ref. SD622 264. M65/J3. Midway between Preston & Blackburn on A675.

Open: Jul, Aug & Sept: Mon - Thur, 11am - 4pm. Suns, 1 - 5pm. BH Suns & Mons excluding Christmas & New Year. Group visits by appointment all year.

Admission: Gardens & House tours: Adult £5, Child/Conc. £4, Family £16. Gardens, Shop & Tearoom only: £2. Children under 5yrs Free. Private tours by arrangement (25+) £6, OAP £5.

🖭 🕇Conferences, wedding receptions. 🛇Unsuitable. 🖤 ⓕObligatory. 🅿 🖭 ❋

LEIGHTON HALL 🖼

See page 431 for full page entry.

MANCHESTER CATHEDRAL
Manchester M3 1SX

Tel: 0161 833 2220 **Fax:** 0161 839 6218

In addition to regular worship and daily offices, there are frequent professional concerts, day schools, organ recitals, guided tours and brass-rubbing. The cathedral contains a wealth of beautiful carvings and has the widest medieval nave in Britain. Visitor Centre and restaurant.

Location: OS Ref. SJ838 988. Manchester.

Open: Daily. Visitor Centre: daily, 9am - 4pm (10am - 4pm on Mons).

Admission: Donations welcome.

ⓘVisitor Centre. ❋

MARTHOLME
Great Harwood, Blackburn, Lancashire BB6 7UJ

Owner: Mr & Mrs T H Codling **Contact:** Miss P M Codling

Part of medieval manor house with 17th century additions and Elizabethan gatehouse.

Location: OS Ref. SD753 338. 2m NE of Great Harwood off A680 to Whalley.

Open: Groups (8+) by written appointment only.

Admission: £4.50.

RUFFORD OLD HALL ✤

RUFFORD, Nr ORMSKIRK, LANCASHIRE L40 1SG

www.nationaltrust.org.uk

Tel: 01704 821254 **Fax:** 01704 823823 **e-mail:** ruffordhall@nationaltrust.org.uk

Owner: The National Trust   **Contact:** The Property Manager

There is a legend that William Shakespeare performed here for the owner Sir Thomas Hesketh in the Great Hall of this, one of the finest 16th century buildings in Lancashire. The playwright would have delighted in the magnificent hall with its intricately carved movable wooden screen. Built in 1530, it established the Hesketh family seat for the next 250 years. In the Carolean Wing, altered in 1821, there are fine collections of 16th and 17th century oak furniture, arms, armour and tapestries. An audio tour is available to guide visitors around the house. The attractive garden includes sculpture and topiary.

Location: OS Ref. SD463 160. 7m N of Ormskirk, in village of Rufford on E side of A59.

Open: House: 3 Apr - 27 Oct: Sat - Wed, 1 - 5pm. Garden: as house, 11am - 5.30pm. Shop & Tearoom: as house, 11am - 5pm. Open BHs & Good Fri.

Admission: House & Garden: Adult £4.50, Child £2, Family £11. Garden only: Adult £2.50, Child £1. Booked groups (15+): Adult £2.75, Child £1 (no groups on Suns & BH Mons). Group joint ticket for Rufford Old Hall/Martin Mere Wildfowl Trust £5.

ⓘ No photography in house. 🅿️ 🆃 ♿ Partial. 🅱 Licensed. 🅵 By arrangement. 🎧 🅿 Limited for coaches. 🐕 🐾 In grounds, on leads. ⬆ 🆃 Tel for details.

SAMLESBURY HALL

Preston New Road, Samlesbury, Preston PR5 0UP

Tel: 01254 812010 **Fax:** 01254 812174

Owner: Samlesbury Hall Trust   **Contact:** S Jones - Director

Built in 1325, the hall is an attractive black and white timbered manor house set in extensive grounds. Weddings & events welcome. Antiques & crafts all year.

Location: OS Ref. SD623 305. N side of A677, 4m WNW of Blackburn.

Open: All year: daily except Sats: 11am - 4.30pm.

Admission: Adult £3, Child £1.25.

SMITHILLS HALL HISTORIC HOUSE

Smithills Dean Road, Bolton BL1 7NP

Tel: 01204 332377 **e-mail:** office@smithills.org

Owner: Smithills Hall & Park Trust   **Contact:** Mrs Margaret Koppens

14th century manor house with Tudor panelling. Stuart furniture. Stained glass.

Location: OS Ref. SD699 119. 2m NW of central Bolton, ½ m N of A58 ringroad.

Open: Apr - Sept: Tue - Sat, 11am - 5pm; Sun, 2 - 5pm. Oct - Mar: Tues & Sat, 1 - 5pm, Sun, 2 - 5pm. Closed Mon except BH Mons.

Admission: Adult £3, Conc. £1.75, Family (2+3) £7.75.

TOWNELEY HALL ART GALLERY & MUSEUMS

Burnley BB11 3RQ

Tel: 01282 424213 **Fax:** 01282 436138 **www.**towneleyhall.org.uk

Owner: Burnley Borough Council   **Contact:** Miss Susan Bourne

House dates from the 14th century with 17th and 19th century modifications. Collections include oak furniture, 18th and 19th century paintings. There is a Museum of Local Crafts and Industries and a Natural History Centre with an aquarium in the grounds.

Location: OS Ref. SD854 309. ½ m SE of Burnley on E side of Todmorden Road (A671).

Open: All year: Mon - Thur, 10am - 5pm. Sat & Sun, 12 noon - 5pm. Closed Fris. Closed Christmas - New Year.

Admission: Free. Guided tours: Tues, Weds & Thurs afternoons or as booked for groups.

🅿️ ♿ WC. 🅵 ❋ 🆃 Tel for details.

TURTON TOWER

Chapeltown Road, Turton BL7 0HG

Tel: 01204 852203 **Fax:** 01204 853759 **e-mail:** turtontower@mus.lancscc.gov.uk

Owner: Lancashire County Council   **Contact:** Martin Robinson-Dowland

Country house based on a medieval tower, extended in the 16th, 17th and 19th centuries.

Location: OS Ref. SD733 153. On B6391, 4m N of Bolton.

Open: Feb & Nov: Suns, 1 - 4pm. Mar - Sept: Mon - Thur, 11am - 5pm; Sat & Sun, 1 - 5pm. Apr: Sat - Wed, 1 - 5pm. Mar & Oct: Mon - Wed, 1 - 5pm. Sats & Suns 1 - 4pm.

Admission: Adult £3, Child Free, OAP £1.50. Season ticket available.

WARTON OLD RECTORY ⌗

Warton, Carnforth, Lancashire

Tel: 0161 242 1400

Owner: English Heritage   **Contact:** The North West Regional Office

A rare medieval stone house with remains of the hall, chambers and domestic offices.

Location: OS Ref. SD499 723. At Warton, 1m N of Carnforth on minor road off A6.

Open: Any reasonable time.

Admission: Free.

🐾 On leads. ❋

Special Events Index see front section

Leighton Hall, Lancashire from the book *Historic Family Homes and Gardens from the Air*, see page 54.

BLUECOAT ARTS CENTRE
School Lane, Liverpool L1 3BX
Tel: 0151 709 5297 **Fax:** 0151 707 0048

Owner: Bluecoat Arts Centre Ltd   **Contact:** Building Manager
Built in 1717, the Bluecoat is of outstanding historical and architectural interest, with Grade I listed building status, and is a popular tourist attraction in the heart of Liverpool.
Location: OS Ref. SJ346 902. ¼ m S of Lime Street station.
Open: Mon - Sat, 9.30am - 6pm (unless there is an evening performance, outside hire or exhibition opening). Gallery closed Suns & Mons.
Admission: Free admission to Building and Gallery, with varying prices for the Performing Arts events.

CROXTETH HALL & COUNTRY PARK
Liverpool, Merseyside L12 0HB
Tel: 0151 228 5311 **Fax:** 0151 228 2817

Owner: Liverpool City Council   **Contact:** Mrs Irene Vickers
Ancestral home of the Molyneux family. 500 acres country park. Special events and attractions most weekends.
Location: OS Ref. SJ408 943. 5m NE of Liverpool city centre.
Open: Parkland: daily throughout the year. Hall, Farm & Garden: daily, 10.30am - 5pm during main season. Telephone for exact dates.
Admission: Parkland: Free. Hall, Farm & Garden: prices on application.

LIVERPOOL CATHEDRAL
ST JAMES' MOUNT, LIVERPOOL, MERSEYSIDE L1 7AZ
www.liverpoolcathedral.org.uk

Tel: 0151 709 6271 **Fax:** 0151 702 7292 **e-mail:** info@liverpoolcathedral.org.uk
Owner: The Dean and Chapter   **Contact:** Lew Eccleshall (Visitor Manager)
Sir Giles Gilbert Scott's greatest creation. Built last century from local sandstone with superb glass, stonework and major works of art, it is the largest Anglican cathedral in Europe and has a fine musical tradition, a tower offering panoramic views, and an award-winning refectory. There is a unique collection of church embroidery, and SPCK shop with a full range of souvenirs, cards and religious books.
Location: OS Ref. SJ354 893. Central Liverpool, ½ m S of Lime Street Station.
Open: Daily, 8am - 6pm. Sun services: 8am, 10.30am, 3pm, 4pm. Weekdays: 8am & 5.30pm (Fri only: 12.05pm). Sats: 8am & 3pm.
Admission: Donation. Lift to Tower & Embroidery Exhibition: £2.50, Conc. £1.50.
◻ Ⳁ ⳇGround floor. WC. ▣ ⅲ By arrangement. ⅌Limited for cars. None for coaches. ▣ ⅲ Guide dogs only. ✱

LIVERPOOL METROPOLITAN CATHEDRAL OF CHRIST THE KING
Liverpool, Merseyside L3 5TQ
Tel: 0151 709 9222 **Fax:** 0151 708 7274 **e-mail:** met.cathedral@boltblue.com
www.liverpoolmetrocathedral.org.uk
Owner: Roman Catholic Archdiocese of Liverpool   **Contact:** Rt Rev P Cookson
Modern circular cathedral with spectacular glass by John Piper and numerous modern works of art. Extensive earlier crypt by Lutyens. Grade II* listed.
Location: OS Ref. SJ356 903. Central Liverpool, ½ m E of Lime Street Station.
Open: 8am - 6pm (closes 5pm Suns in Winter). Sun services: 8.30am, 10am, 11am, 3pm & 7pm. Weekday services: 8am, 12.15pm, 5.15pm & 5.45pm. Sats, 9am & 6.30pm. Gift shop: Mon - Sat, 10am - 5pm; Sun, 11am - 4pm. Restaurant: Mon - Fri, 10am - 7pm; Sat, 10am - 5pm; Sun, 11am - 4pm.
Admission: Donation.
◻ ⳇExcept crypt. WCs. ⅲ By arrangement. ⅌Ample for cars. ▣ ⅲ Guide dogs only. ✱

MEOLS HALL 🏛
Churchtown, Southport, Merseyside PR9 7LZ
Tel: 01704 228326 **Fax:** 01704 507185 **e-mail:** events@meolshall.com
www.meolshall.com
Owner: Robert Hesketh Esq   **Contact:** Pamela Whelan
17th century house with subsequent additions. Interesting collection of pictures and furniture. Tithe Barn available for wedding ceremonies and receptions all year.
Location: OS Ref. SD365 184. 3m NE of Southport town centre in Churchtown. SE of A565.
Open: 14 Aug - 14 Sept: daily, 2 - 5pm.
Admission: Adult £3, Child £1. Groups only (25+) £8.50 (inclusive of afternoon tea).
Ⳁ Wedding receptions now available in the Tithe Barn. ⳇ ⅌ ▲ ⅲ

PORT SUNLIGHT VILLAGE & HERITAGE CENTRE
95 Greendale Road, Port Sunlight CH62 4XE
Tel: 0151 6446466 **Fax:** 0151 6458973   **Contact:** The Centre
Port Sunlight is a picturesque 19th century garden village on the Wirral.
Location: OS Ref. SJ340 845. Follow signs from M53/J4 or 5 or follow signs on A41.
Open: All year, 10am - 4pm in summer; 11am - 4pm in winter.
Admission: Adult £1, Child 60p, Conc. 80p. Group rates on application.

SPEKE HALL GARDEN & ESTATE 🌿
The Walk, Liverpool L24 1XD
Tel: 0151 427 7231 **Fax:** 0151 427 9860 **Info Line:** 08457 585702
www.spekehall.org.uk www.nationaltrust.org.uk
Owner: The National Trust   **Contact:** The Property Manager
One of the most famous half-timbered houses in the country.
Location: OS Ref. SJ419 825. North bank of the Mersey, 6m SE of city centre. Follow signs for Liverpool John Lennon airport.
Open: House: 20 Mar - 31 Oct: Daily except Mons & Tues (open BH Mons), 1 - 5.30pm; 6 Nov - 5 Dec: Sats & Suns only, 1 - 4.30pm. Grounds: Daily, 11am - 5.30pm. Home Farm: dates as House, 11am - 5.30pm. Check for winter opening, additional opening Jul & Aug.
Admission: Adult £6, Child £3.50, Family £17. Grounds only: Adult £3, Child £1.50, Family £9.

northeast

Bamburgh Castle, Northumberland © David Osborn

wallington
northumberland

439

Wallington is to be found near the village of Cambo in Northumberland, 20 miles north-west of Newcastle-upon-Tyne and only 20 miles from Hadrian's Wall. This huge 13,000 acre estate, with its house and contents, was given by Sir Charles Philips Trevelyan to the National Trust in 1941.

Many country houses are hidden from view by high walls, long drives or screens of trees. The visitor must wait, anticipate and then gasp at a house's exterior aspect – this is not the case with Wallington, which comes immediately into sight as one climbs the hill after crossing James Paine's Palladian bridge. The exterior of Wallington is plain, solid and dignified, built of local sandstone – only the four griffins' heads sitting on the front lawn seem to grin at you. Begun in 1688 by Sir William Blackett, a successful Newcastle businessman, the house is designed around a courtyard plan. In the 18th century, Sir William's grandson, Sir Walter Calverley Blackett, made further improvements to both the house and grounds. He laid out the garden and the park, and for the house commissioned Daniel Garrett, a member of Lord Burlington's circle, to create a new suite of state rooms on the south front. The Francini brothers were employed to decorate the rooms with rococo plasterwork. Their work creates the exuberant yet delicate feel to the interiors.

Wallington passed to the Trevelyan family on Sir Walter's death in 1771. When Sir Walter Trevelyan inherited the estate in 1846, he and his wife Pauline, Lady Trevelyan, made Wallington a meeting place for writers, scientists, and particularly painters and sculptors of the Pre-Raphaelite circle. The central courtyard, roofed over in 1853-54, is decorated with murals on Northumbrian history by William Bell Scott. The mural entitled *'The Northumbrian shows the world what can be done with Iron & Coal'*, is renowned for its depiction of an image from the Industrial Revolution. The stone columns were painted with flowers by Pauline, Lady Trevelyan and Ruskin. Later generations of the family used the Hall as a central sitting room.

The Trevelyans are a family of distinguished intellectuals, politicans, historicans and civil servants. Sir Charles Trevelyan, who gave Wallington to the National Trust, was a leading Socialist, and Labour MP. As early as 1929 he opened parts of the house to the public – gifting Wallington to the Trust gave him immense satisfaction that everyone could enjoy this beautiful place.

The garden and grounds are worth a visit just for themselves. The Walled Garden, half a mile from the house, has a Victorian peach house, a terrace lined with 18th century statues, and an Edwardian conservatory. There are a number of helpful leaflets describing walks on the estate.

The House is re-opening in 2004 after a year of extensive works – the sparkling interiors are the perfect backdrop to consider for a corporate function, or even as a wedding venue – a peaceful tranquil world which you should take time to enjoy.

▸ For further details about Wallington see page 452.

RABY CASTLE 🏛

NR BARNARD CASTLE

www.rabycastle.com

Map 8

Owner:
The Lord Barnard

▶ **CONTACT**

Clare Simpson/
Catherine Turnbull
Raby Castle
Staindrop
Darlington
Co. Durham DL2 3AH

Tel: 01833 660202
Fax: 01833 660169

e-mail: admin@
rabycastle.com

▶ **LOCATION**
OS Ref. NZ129 218

On A688, 1m N of
Staindrop. 8m NE of
Barnard Castle, 12m
WNW of Darlington.

Rail: Darlington
Station, 12m.

Air: Teesside Airport,
20m.

The magnificent Raby Castle, in the beautiful North Pennines, has been home to Lord Barnard's family since 1626 when it was purchased by his ancestor, Sir Henry Vane the Elder, the eminent statesman and politician. The Castle was built mainly in the 14th century by the Nevill family on the site of an earlier manor house. The Nevills continued to live at Raby until 1569 when, after the failure of the Rising of the North, the Castle and its land were forfeited to the Crown.

The impressive Entrance Hall (below) was created into its present dramatic form by John Carr for the 2nd Earl of Darlington, to celebrate the coming of age of his heir in 1787. The roof was raised to enable carriages to pass through the Hall and the result is a stunning interior in the Gothic Revival

style. Raby's treasures include an important collection of Meissen porcelain, fine furniture and artworks, including paintings by Munnings, De Hooch, Reynolds, Van Dyck, Batoni, Teniers, Amigoni, Vernet and De Vos.

There is a 200-acre Deer Park with two lakes and a beautiful walled garden with formal lawns, ancient yew hedges and an ornamental pond. The 18th century stable block contains a horse-drawn carriage collection including the State Coach last used by the family for the Coronation of Edward VII in 1902.

Part of the Stables has been converted into a gift shop and tearooms, where the former stalls have been incorporated to create an atmospheric setting. A Woodland Adventure Playground is close to the picnic area.

Summer

Castle
Easter & BHs
Sat - Wed, 1- 5pm.

May & September:
Weds & Suns only, 1 - 5pm.

June, July & August:
Daily except Sats, 1 - 5pm.

Guided tours by
arrangement Easter -
end September:
Mon - Fri, mornings only.

Park & Gardens
On Castle open days:
11am - 5.30pm.

Winter
October - Easter: Closed.

▶ **ADMISSION**

Castle, Park & Gardens
Adult £7.00
Child (5-15yrs) £3.00
OAP/Student £6.00
Family (2+3) £16.00
Groups (12+)
Adult £6.00
Child (5-15yrs). £3.00
OAP/Student £5.50

*Please book in advance for group visits.

Guided Tour (20+, must book)
(incl. tea/coffee) £8.50

Park & Gardens
Adult £4.00
Child (5-15yrs) £2.50
OAP/Student £3.50
Groups (12+)
Adult £3.50
Child (5-15yrs). £2.50
OAP/Student £3.00

Park & Gardens
Season ticket
Adult £10.00
Child (5-15yrs) £5.00
OAP/Student £7.50

 i Film locations, product launches, corporate events, fairs & concerts. Raby Estates venison & game sold in tearooms. Soft fruit when in season. Lectures on Castle, its contents, gardens & history. No photography or video filming is permitted inside. Colour illustrated guidebook and slides are on sale.

 Partial. WC. Licensed.

By arrangement (20+). Tour time: 1½ hrs. **P**

By arrangement (20+). Primary & junior £3; Secondary £3.50, 1 adult free per 20 pupils. Tours: Easter - Sept: weekday am.

Guide dogs welcome, others on leads in park only.

Tel for details or see website.

AUCKLAND CASTLE 🏛

BISHOP AUCKLAND, CO. DURHAM DL14 7NR

www.auckland-castle.co.uk

Tel: 01388 601627 **Fax:** 01388 609323 **e-mail:** auckland.castle@zetnet.co.uk

Owner: Church Commissioners   **Contact:** The Manager

Principal country residence of the Bishops of Durham since Norman times and now the official residence of the present day Bishops. The Chapel, reputedly one of the largest private chapel in Europe, was originally the 12th century banquet hall. Chapel and State Rooms including the Throne Room, Long Dining Room and King Charles Dining Room are open to the public. Access to the adjacent Bishop's Park with its 18th century Deer House.

Location: OS Ref. NZ214 303. Bishop Auckland, N end of town centre.

Open: Easter Mon - 30 Sept: Suns & Mons (plus Weds in August) , 2 - 5pm. Last admission 4.30pm. The managment reserves the right to close the castle to visitors.

Admission: Adult £4, Child/Conc. £3. Child (up to 12yrs) Free. Special openings for groups (25+).

ℹ️Exhibitions. No indoor photography. 📷📺Wedding receptions, functions. ♿ Wheelchair access to chapel, ground floor. WC. Stairwalker available for upstairs staterooms by prior arrangement. 🅿️ 🍴 🐕Guide dogs only.

AUCKLAND CASTLE DEER HOUSE ⚏

Bishop Auckland, Durham

Tel: 0191 2691200

Owner: English Heritage   **Contact:** The Regional Office

A charming building erected in 1760 in the Park of the Bishops of Durham so that the deer could shelter and find food.

Location: OS Ref. NZ216 305. In Bishop Auckland Park, just N of town centre on A689. About 500 yds N of the castle.

Open: Park opening times – see Auckland Castle.

Admission: Free.

🐕On leads.

BARNARD CASTLE ⚏

Barnard Castle, Castle House, Durham DL12 9AT

Tel: 01833 638212

Owner: English Heritage   **Contact:** The Custodian

The substantial remains of this large castle stand on a rugged escarpment overlooking the River Tees. Parts of the 14th century Great Hall and the cylindrical 12th century tower, built by the Baliol family can still be seen. Sensory garden.

Location: OS92, NZ049 165. In Barnard Castle.

Open: 1 Apr - 30 Sept: daily, 10am - 6pm. 1 - 31 Oct: daily, 10am - 5pm. 1 Nov - 31 Mar: Wed - Sun, 10am - 4pm. Closed 24 - 26 Dec & 1 Jan. Closed 1 - 2pm. Times subject to change April 2004.

Admission: Adult £2.60, Child £1.30, Conc. £2. 15% discount for groups (11+). Prices subject to change April 2004.

ℹ️WCs in town. 📷♿Grounds. 🍴Inclusive. 🐕In grounds, on leads. ❋ 📺Tel for details.

BINCHESTER ROMAN FORT

Bishop Auckland, Co. Durham

Tel: 01388 663089 / 0191 3834212 (outside opening hours)

Owner: Durham County Council   **Contact:** Fiona Macdonald

Once the largest Roman fort in Co Durham, the heart of the site has been excavated.

Location: OS92 Ref. NZ210 312. 1½ m N of Bishop Auckland, signposted from A690 Durham - Crook and from A688 Spennymoor - Bishop Auckland roads.

Open: Under review. Please contact for details.

Admission: Please contact for details.

THE BOWES MUSEUM

BARNARD CASTLE, CO. DURHAM DL12 8NP

www.bowesmuseum.org.uk

Tel: 01833 690606 **Fax:** 01833 637163 **e-mail:** info@bowesmuseum.org.uk

Owner: The Bowes Museum Ltd

This world class visitor attraction houses a designated collection of European fine and decorative art, together with displays of archaeology and local history. A busy programme brings new exhibitions and events including concerts, craft markets, family fun days and theatre.

Location: OS Ref. NZ055 164. ¼ m E of Market Place in Barnard Castle, just off A66.

Open: All year: Daily, 11am - 5pm. Closed 25/26 Dec & 1 Jan.

Admission: Adult £6, Conc £5, Under 16s & disabled carers Free. Groups (20+): Adult £5, Conc. £4.

📷📺♿ Licensed. 🍴By arrangement. 🅿️🐕In grounds. ❋ 📺Tel for details.

CROOK HALL & GARDENS
Sidegate, Durham DH1 5SZ
Tel: 0191 3848028
Owner: Keith & Maggie Bell   **Contact:** Mrs Maggie Bell
Medieval manor house set in rural landscape on the edge of Durham city.
Location: OS Ref. NZ274 432. 1/2 m N of city centre.
Open: Easter weekend, BHs, Suns in May & Sept; Jun, Jul & Aug: daily except Sats, 1 - 5pm.
Admission: Adult £4, Conc. £3.50, Family £12.

DERWENTCOTE STEEL FURNACE ⌗
Newcastle, Durham
Tel: 0191 2691200
Owner: English Heritage   **Contact:** The Custodian
Built in the 18th century it is the earliest and most complete authentic steel making furnace to have survived.
Location: OS Ref. NZ131 566. 10m SW of Newcastle N of the A694 between Rowland's Gill and Hamsterley.
Open: 1 Apr - 30 Sept: Suns, 1 - 5pm. Times subject to change April 2004.
Admission: Free.
🅿 🐕 On leads in restricted areas.

DURHAM CASTLE
Palace Green, Durham DH1 3RW
Tel: 0191 3343800 **Fax:** 0191 3343801   **Contact:** Mrs Julie Marshall
Durham Castle, founded in the 1070s, with the Cathedral is a World Heritage Site.
Location: OS Ref. NZ274 424. City centre, adjacent to cathedral.
Open: Mar - Sept: 10am - 12 noon & 2 - 4.30pm. Oct - Mar: 2 - 4pm.
Admission: Adult £3.50, Child £2.50, OAP £3, Family £8. Guide book £3.

DURHAM CATHEDRAL
Durham DH1 3EH
Tel: 0191 3864266 **Fax:** 0191 3864267 **e-mail:** enquiries@durhamcathedral.co.uk
                                                Contact: Miss A Heywood
A World Heritage Site. Norman architecture. Burial place of St Cuthbert and the Venerable Bede.
Location: OS Ref. NZ274 422. Durham city centre.
Open: Summer: 31 May - 5 Sept: 9.30am - 8pm. Open only for worship and private prayer: All year: Mon - Sat, 7.30am - 9.30am and Suns, 7.45am - 12.30pm. The Cathedral is closed to visitors during evening recitals and concerts. Visitors welcome Mon - Sat, 9.30 - 5pm, Suns 12.30 - 3.30pm.
Admission: Cathedral: Request a donation of min. £4. Tower: Adult £2.50, Child (under 16) £1.50, Family £7. Monk's Dormitory: Adult £1, Child 30p, Family £2.10. AV: Adult £1.10, Child 30p, Family £2.

EGGLESTONE ABBEY ⌗
Durham
Tel: 0191 2691200
Owner: English Heritage   **Contact:** The Regional Office
Picturesque remains of a 12th century abbey, located in a bend of the River Tees. Substantial parts of the church and abbey buildings remain.
Location: OS Ref. NZ062 151. 1 1/2 m SE of Barnard Castle on minor road off B6277.
Open: Any reasonable time.
Admission: Free.
♿ 🅿 🐕 On leads.

ESCOMB CHURCH
Escomb, Bishop Auckland DL14 7ST
Tel: 01388 458358
Owner: Church of England   **Contact:** Mrs E Kitching (01388 662265)
Saxon church dating from the 7th century built of stone from Binchester Roman Fort.
Location: OS Ref. NZ189 302. 3m W of Bishop Auckland.
Open: Summer: 9am - 8pm. Winter: 9am - 4pm. Key available from 22 Saxon Green, Escomb.
Admission: Free.

FINCHALE PRIORY ⌗
Finchdale Priory, Brasside, Newton Hall DH1 5SH
Tel: 0191 3863828
Owner: English Heritage   **Contact:** The Custodian
These beautiful 13th century priory remains are located beside the curving River Wear.
Location: OS Ref. NZ297 471. 4 1/2 m NE of Durham.
Open: 1 Apr - 30 Sept: daily, 10am - 6pm. Times subject to change April 2004.
Admission: Adult £2, Child £1, Conc. £1.50. 15% discount for groups (11+). Prices subject to change April 2004.
ℹ WC. 🚻 ♿ (Not managed by EH.) 🅿 On S side of river. 🐕 On leads.

PIERCEBRIDGE ROMAN FORT
Piercebridge, Co. Durham
Tel: 01325 460532
Owner: Darlington Borough Council   **Contact:** Heritage Manager
Visible Roman remains include the east gate and defences, courtyard building and Roman road. Also remains of a bridge over the Tees.
Location: OS Ref. NZ211 157. Through narrow stile and short walk down lane opposite car park off A67 NE of the village. Bridge via signposted footpath from George Hotel car park.
Open: At all times.
Admission: Free.

RABY CASTLE 🏰   *See page 442 for full page entry.*

ROKEBY PARK 🏛
Nr Barnard Castle, Co Durham DL12 9RZ
Tel: 01833 637334
Owner: Trustees of Mortham Estate   **Contact:** Mrs P I Yeats (Curator)
Rokeby, a fine example of a 18th century Palladian-style country house.
Location: OS Ref. NZ082 142. Between A66 & Barnard Castle.
Open: May BH Mon then each Mon & Tue from Spring BH until the first Tue in Sept: 2 - 5pm (last admission 4.30pm). Groups (25+) on other days by appointment.
Admission: Please telephone for details.

THE WEARDALE MUSEUM & HIGH HOUSE CHAPEL
Ireshopeburn, Co. Durham DL13 1EY
Tel: 01388 517433   **Contact:** D T Heatherington
Small folk museum and historic chapel. Includes 1870 Weardale cottage room, John Wesley room and local history displays.
Location: OS Ref. NZ872 385. Adjacent to 18th century Methodist Chapel.
Open: Easter & May - Sept: Wed - Sun & BH, 2 - 5pm. Aug: daily, 2 - 5pm.
Admission: Adult £1.50, Child 50p.

Map 10

ALNWICK CASTLE

ALNWICK

www.alnwickcastle.com   www.alnwickgarden.com

Set in magnificent 'Capability' Brown landscape, Alnwick Castle is the home of the Duke of Northumberland. Owned by his family, the Percies, since 1309, the Castle was a major stronghold during the Scottish wars.

Restorations by the First and Fourth Dukes have transformed this massive fortress into a comfortable family home. The Italian Renaissance-style State Rooms are filled with fine furniture, porcelain and paintings by Canaletto, Van Dyck and Titian.

Within the grounds are the recently refurbished museums of the Northumberland Fusiliers,

Northumberland Archaeology and the Percy Tenantry Volunteers 1798 - 1814. Quizzes and a location for the *Harry Potter* film make it a magical place for the whole family.

Events include: birds of prey demonstrations, live music, open-air theatre and Wellington's Redcoat camp.

The Castle's splendid Guest Hall is available for entertaining, concerts, wedding receptions and dinner dances. (Not open to the public.)

For details of events visit the website or telephone 01665 510777.

Owner:
His Grace the Duke of Northumberland

▶ **CONTACT**
Alnwick Castle Estate Office Alnwick Northumberland NE66 1NQ

Tel: 01665 510777
Info: 01665 511100
Group bookings: 01665 511367
Fax: 01665 510876
e-mail: enquiries@ alnwickcastle.com

▶ **LOCATION**
OS Ref. NU187 135

In Alnwick 1½ m W of A1. From London 6hrs, Edinburgh 2hrs, Chester 4hrs, Newcastle 40mins North Sea ferry terminal 30mins.

Bus: From bus station in Alnwick.
Rail: Alnmouth Station 5m. Kings Cross, London 3½hrs
Air: Newcastle 40mins.

CONFERENCE/FUNCTION

ROOM	SIZE	MAX CAPACITY
The Guest Hall	100' x 30'	300

ⓘ Conference facilities. Fashion shows, fairs, filming, parkland for hire. No photography inside the castle. No unaccompanied children.

🛍

🍽 Wedding receptions.
♿ Unsuitable.
☕ Coffee, light lunches and teas.
🅿 200 cars and 6 coaches.
📖 Guidebook and worksheet, special rates for children and teachers.
🐕 Guide dogs only.
❄ Garden only.
🛡 Tel for details.

▶ **OPENING TIMES**
Castle
1 April - 29 October Daily, 11am - 5pm, last admission 4.15pm.

Private functions by arrangement.

The Alnwick Garden
Daily except 25 Dec: opens 10am - (closing time varies during the year tel: 01665 511350 for details).

▶ **ADMISSION**
Castle
Adult £7.50
Child* (under 16yrs) ... Free
Conc. £7.00

Pre-booked Groups (14+)
Adult £6.50
Child £1.20
Conc. £6.00

The Alnwick Garden
Adult £4.00
Conc. £3.50
Child..................... Free

Discounts available for joint tickets with The Alnwick Garden.

* max. 3 per adult

HHA friends free access to Castle only.

Jarrold Colour Publications

Map 10

BAMBURGH CASTLE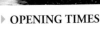

BAMBURGH

www.bamburghcastle.com

Owner:
Trustees Lord Armstrong
dec'd.

▶ **CONTACT**

The Administrator
Bamburgh Castle
Bamburgh
Northumberland
NE69 7DF

Tel: 01668 214515

Fax: 01668 214060

e-mail: bamburghcastle
@aol.com

▶ **LOCATION**

OS Ref. NU184 351

42m N of
Newcastle-upon-Tyne.
20m S of Berwick upon
Tweed. 6m E of Belford
by B1342 from
A1 at Belford.

Bus: Bus service
200 yards.

Rail: Berwick-upon-
Tweed 20m.

Taxi: J Swanston
01289 306124.

Air: Newcastle-upon-
Tyne 45m.

Bamburgh Castle is the home of the Armstrong family. The earliest reference to Bamburgh shows the craggy citadel to have been a royal centre by AD 547. Recent archaeological excavation has revealed that the site has been occupied since prehistoric times.

The Norman Keep has been the stronghold for nearly nine centuries, but the remainder has twice been extensively restored, initially by Lord Crewe in the 1750s and subsequently by the 2nd Lord Armstrong at the beginning of the 20th century. This Castle was the first to succumb to artillery fire – that of Edward IV.

The public rooms contain many exhibits, including the loan collections of armour from HM Tower of London, the John George Joicey Museum, Newcastle-upon-Tyne and other private sources, which complement the castle's armour. Porcelain, china, jade, furniture from many periods, oils, water-colours and a host of interesting items are all contained within one of the most important buildings of Britain's national heritage.

VIEWS

The views from the ramparts are unsurpassed and take in Holy Island, the Farne Islands, one of Northumberland's finest beaches and, landwards, the Cheviot Hills.

▶ **OPENING TIMES**

13 March - 31 October
Daily, 11am - 5pm.
Last entry 4.30pm.

Tours by arrangement
at any time.

▶ **ADMISSION**

Summer

Adult	£5.00
Child (6 - 15yrs)	£2.00
OAP	£4.00
Groups *	
Adult	£3.50
Child (6 - 15yrs)	£1.50
OAP	£2.50

* Min payment £50

Winter
Group rates only quoted.

ℹ️ Filming. No photography in house.

📷 Limited access. WC.

☕ Tearooms for light refreshments. Groups can book.

🚶 By arrangement at any time, min charge out of hours £50.

🅿️ 100 cars, coaches park on tarmac drive at entrance.

Welcome. Guide provided if requested, educational pack.

🐕 Guide dogs only.

Map 10

CHILLINGHAM CASTLE 🏛

NR ALNWICK

www.chillingham-castle.com

This remarkable castle, the home of Sir Humphry Wakefield Bt, with its alarming dungeons has, as now and since the 1200s, been continuously owned by the family of the Earls Grey and their relations. You will see active restoration of complex masonry, metalwork and ornamental plaster as the great halls and state rooms are gradually brought back to life with antique furniture, tapestries, arms and armour as of old and even a torture chamber.

At first a 12th century stronghold, Chillingham became a fully fortified castle in the 14th century. Wrapped in the nation's history it occupied a strategic position as a fortress during Northumberland's bloody border feuds, often besieged and at many times enjoying the patronage of royal visitors. In Tudor days there were additions but the underlying medieval character has always been retained. The 18th and 19th centuries saw decorative refinements and extravagances including the lake, garden and grounds laid out by Sir Jeffrey Wyatville, fresh from his triumphs at Windsor Castle.

GARDENS

With romantic grounds, the castle commands breathtaking views of the surrounding countryside. As you walk to the lake you will see, according to the season, drifts of snowdrops, daffodils or bluebells and an astonishing display of rhododendrons. This emphasises the restrained formality of the Elizabethan topiary garden, with its intricately clipped hedges of box and yew. Lawns, the formal gardens and woodland walks are all fully open to the public.

Owner:

Sir Humphry Wakefield Bt

▶ CONTACT

Administrator
Chillingham Castle
Northumberland
NE66 5NJ

Tel: 01668 215359
Fax: 01668 215463

e-mail: enquiries@
chillingham-castle.com

▶ LOCATION

OS Ref. NU062 258

45m N of Newcastle
between A697 & A1.
2m S of B6348
at Chatton.
6m SE of Wooler.

Rail: Alnmouth
or Berwick.

▶ OPENING TIMES

Summer

Easter
1 May - 30 September
Daily except Sat,
Castle, 1 - 5pm,
Grounds & Tearoom,
12 noon - 5pm

Winter

October - April: Groups
any time by appointment.
All function activities
available.

▶ ADMISSION

Summer

Adult	£6.00
Child (under 16yrs)	£2.50
Child (under 5yrs)	£0.50
OAP	£5.50

Groups (10+)	
Per person	£5.30
Tour	£25.00

CONFERENCE/FUNCTION

ROOM	MAX CAPACITY
King James I Room	
Great Hall	100
Minstrels' Hall	60
2 x Drawing Room	
Museum	
Tea Room	35
Lower Gallery	
Upper Gallery	

Corporate entertainment, lunches, drinks, dinners, wedding ceremonies and receptions.

Partial.

Booked meals for up to 100 people.

By arrangement.

Avoid Lilburn route, coach parties welcome by prior arrangement. Limited for coaches.

Apartments.

Civil Wedding Licence.

North East - England

ALNWICK CASTLE

See page 445 for full page entry.

AYDON CASTLE

Corbridge, Northumberland NE45 5PJ

Tel: 01434 632450

Owner: English Heritage   **Contact:** The Custodian

One of the finest fortified manor houses in England, dating from the late 13th century. Its survival, intact, can be attributed to its conversion to a farmhouse in the 17th century.

Location: OS Ref. NZ002 663. 2m NE of Corbridge, on minor road off B6321 or A68.

Open: 1 Apr - 30 Sept: daily, 10am - 6pm. 1- 31 Oct: daily, 10am - 5pm. Times subject to change April 2004.

Admission: Adult £2.50, Child £1.30, Conc. £1.90. 15% discount for groups (11+). Prices subject to change April 2004.

⒤WC. ▢ ♿Ground floor & grounds. **P** Limited. ▣ ⛖In grounds, on leads. ☏Tel for details.

BAMBURGH CASTLE

See page 446 for full page entry.

BELSAY HALL, CASTLE & GARDENS

See right for half page entry.

BERWICK BARRACKS

The Parade, Berwick-upon-Tweed, Northumberland TD15 1DF

Tel: 01289 304493

Owner: English Heritage   **Contact:** The Custodian

Among the earliest purpose built barracks, these have changed very little since 1717. They house an exhibition 'By Beat of Drum', which recreates scenes such as the barrack room from the life of the British infantryman, the Museum of the King's Own Scottish Borderers and the Borough Museum with fine art, local history exhibition and other collections. Guided tours available.

Location: OS Ref. NT994 535. On the Parade, off Church Street, Berwick town centre.

Open: 1 Apr - 30 Sept: daily, 10am - 6pm. 1 - 31 Oct: daily, 10am - 5pm. 1 Nov - 31 Mar: Wed - Sun, 10am - 4pm. Closed 24 - 26 Dec and 1 Jan. Times subject to change April 2004.

Admission: Adult £3, Child £1.50, Conc. £2.30. 15% discount for groups (11+). Prices subject to change April 2004.

▢ **P** In town. ▣ ⛖In grounds, on leads. ❋ ☏Tel for details.

BERWICK RAMPARTS

Berwick-upon-Tweed, Northumberland

Tel: 0191 269 1200

Owner: English Heritage   **Contact:** The Regional Office

A remarkably complete system of town fortifications consisting of gateways, ramparts and projecting bastions built in the 16th century.

Location: OS Ref. NT994 535. Surrounding Berwick town centre on N bank of River Tweed.

Open: Any reasonable time.

Admission: Free.

❋

BRINKBURN PRIORY

Long Framlington, Morpeth, Northumberland NE65 8AF

Tel: 01665 570628

Owner: English Heritage   **Contact:** The Custodian

This late 12th century church is a fine example of early gothic architecture, almost perfectly preserved, and is set in a lovely spot beside the River Coquet.

Location: OS Ref. NZ116 984. 4¹/₂ m SE of Rothbury off B6344 5m W of A1.

Open: 1 Apr - 30 Sept: daily, 10am - 6pm. 1 - 31 Oct, daily, 10am - 5pm. Closed 24 - 26 Dec and 1 Jan. Times subject to change April 2004.

Admission: Adult £2, Child £1, Conc. £1.50. 15% discount for groups (11+). Prices subject to change April 2004.

▢ **P** ▣ ⛖On leads. ❋ ☏Tel for details.

CAPHEATON HALL

Newcastle-upon-Tyne NE19 2AB

Tel/Fax: 01830 530253

Owner/Contact: J Browne-Swinburne

Built for Sir John Swinburne in 1668 by Robert Trollope, an architect of great and original talent.

Location: OS Ref. NZ038 805. 17m NW of Newcastle off A696.

Open: By written appointment only.

❋

© English Heritage Photo Library

BELSAY HALL, CASTLE & GARDENS

BELSAY, Nr PONTELAND, NORTHUMBERLAND NE20 0DX

www.english-heritage.org.uk/visits

Tel: 01661 881636   **Fax:** 01661 881043

Owner: English Heritage   **Contact:** The Custodian

Belsay is one of the most remarkable estates in Northumberland's border country. The buildings, set amidst 30 acres of magnificent landscaped gardens, have been occupied by the same family for nearly 600 years. The gardens, created largely in the 19th century, are a fascinating mix of the formal and the informal with terraced gardens, a rhododendron garden, magnolia garden, mature woodland and even a winter garden. The buildings comprise a 14th century castle, a manor house and Belsay Hall, an internationally famous mansion designed by Sir Charles Monck in the 19th century in the style of classical buildings he had encountered during a tour of Greece.

© English Heritage Photo Library

Location: OS87, NZ088 785. In Belsay 14m (22.4 km) NW of Newcastle on SW of A696. 7m NW of Ponteland. Nearest airport and station is Newcastle.

Open: 1 Apr - 30 Sept: daily, 10am - 6pm. 1 - 31 Oct: daily, 10am - 5pm. 1 Nov - 31 Mar: daily, 10am - 4pm. Closed 24 - 26 Dec and 1 Jan. Times subject to change April 2004.

Admission: Adult £4.50, Child £2.30, Conc. £3.40, Family £11.30. 15% discount for groups (11+). Prices subject to change April 2004.

▢ ⒤ ♿Partial. WC. ⬛During summer & weekends Apr - Oct. **P** ▣ ⛖In grounds, on leads. ☏Tel for details.

CHERRYBURN – THOMAS BEWICK BIRTHPLACE

Station Bank, Mickley, Stocksfield, Northumberland NE43 7DD

Tel: 01661 843276 **www.**nationaltrust.org.uk

Owner: The National Trust **Contact:** The Administrator

Birthplace of Northumbria's greatest artist, wood engraver and naturalist, Thomas Bewick, b1753. The Museum explores his famous works. Farmyard animals, picnic area, garden.

Location: OS Ref. NZ075 627. 11m W of Newcastle on A695 (400yds signed from Mickley Square). 1½ m W of Prudhoe.

Open: 1 Apr - 31 Oct: daily except Tues & Weds, 1 - 5.30pm. Last admission 5pm.

Admission: Adult £3.20, Child (under 5yrs) Free. Tel for group rate.

⬜ ♿ Some steps. WC. ☕ Morning coffee for booked groups. ▦ Tel for details.

© English Heritage Photo Library

© Skyscan Balloon Photography

CHESTERS ROMAN FORT & MUSEUM

CHOLLERFORD, Nr HEXHAM, NORTHUMBERLAND NE46 4EP

Tel: 01434 681379

Owner: English Heritage **Contact:** The Custodian

The best preserved example of a Roman cavalry fort in Britain, including remains of the bath house on the banks of the River North Tyne. The museum houses a fascinating collection of Roman sculpture and inscriptions.

Location: OS87, NY913 701. 1½ m from Chollerford on B6318.

Open: 1 Apr - 30 Sept: daily, 9.30am - 6pm. 1 - 31 Oct: daily, 10am - 5pm. 1 Nov - 31 Mar: daily, 10am - 4pm. Closed 24 - 26 Dec and 1 Jan. Times subject to change April 2004.

Admission: Adult £3.10, Child £1.60, Conc. £2.30. 15% discount for groups (11+). Prices subject to change April 2004.

⬜ ♿ Grounds. WC. ☕ Summer only. 🅿 ▣ 🐕In grounds, on leads. ✳
▦ Tel for details.

CHILLINGHAM CASTLE 🏚

See page 447 for full page entry.

CHIPCHASE CASTLE 🏚

Wark, Hexham, Northumberland NE48 3NT

Tel: 01434 230203 **Fax:** 01434 230740

Owner/Contact: Mrs P J Torday

The castle overlooks the River North Tyne and is set in formal and informal gardens. One walled garden is used as a nursery specialising in unusual perennial plants.

Location: OS Ref. NY882 758. 10m NW of Hexham via A6079 to Chollerton. 2m SE of Wark.

Open: Castle: 1 - 28 Jun: daily 2 - 5pm. Tours by arrangement at other times. Castle Gardens & Nursery: Easter - 31 Jul, Thur - Sun & BH Mons, 10am - 5pm.

Admission: Castle £5, Garden £3, concessions available. Nursery Free.

♿ Unsuitable. 🅵 Obligatory. ▣

CORBRIDGE ROMAN SITE 🏛

Corbridge, Northumberland NE45 5NT

Tel: 01434 632349

Owner: English Heritage **Contact:** The Custodian

A fascinating series of excavated remains, including foundations of granaries with a grain ventilation system. From artefacts found, which can be seen in the site museum, we know a large settlement developed around this supply depot.

Location: OS Ref. NY983 649. ½ m NW of Corbridge on minor road, signposted for Corbridge Roman Site.

Open: 1 Apr - 30 Sept: daily, 10am - 6pm. 1 - 31 Oct: daily, 10am - 5pm. 1 Nov - 31 Mar: Wed - Sun, 10am - 4pm. Closed 1 - 2pm during winter & 24 - 26 Dec and 1 Jan. Times subject to change April 2004.

Admission: Adult £3.10, Child £1.60, Conc. £2.30. 15% discount for groups (11+). Prices subject to change April 2004.

⬜ ♿Partial. 🅾 Inclusive. 🅿 Limited for coaches. ▣ 🐕In grounds, on leads. ✳
▦ Tel for details.

CRAGSIDE 🏚

Rothbury, Morpeth, Northumberland NE65 7PX

Tel: 01669 620150 **Fax:** 01669 620066 **www.**nationaltrust.org.uk

Owner: The National Trust **Contact:** Property Manager

Revolutionary home of Lord Armstrong, Victorian inventor and landscape genius, Cragside sits on a rocky crag high above the Debdon Burn. Crammed with ingenious gadgets, it was the first house in the world lit electrically. Armstrong constructed 5 lakes, one of Europe's largest rock gardens and planted over 7 million trees and shrubs. Today, this magnificent estate can be explored on foot and by car and provides one of the last shelters for the endangered red squirrel. Children will love the tall trees, tumbling streams, adventure play area and labyrinth.

Location: OS Ref. NU073 022. ½ m NE of Rothbury on B6341.

Open: House: 30 Mar - 31 Oct: daily except Mons (open BH Mons), 1 - 5.30pm (28 Sept - 31 Oct closes 4.30pm), last admission 1hr prior to closing time. Estate & Gardens: as house, 10.30am - 7pm, last admission 5pm.

Admission: House, Estate & Gardens: Adult £8, Child (5-17yrs) £4, Family (2+3) £20. Groups (15+) £6.50. Estate & Gardens: Adult £5.50, Child (5-17yrs) £2.50, Family (2+3) £13.50. Groups (15+) £4.50.

⬜ ♿Partial. ▣ 🍴 🅿 ▣ 🏠 🐕In grounds, on leads. ▦ Tel for details.

DUNSTANBURGH CASTLE 🏛 🏚

c/o Grieves Garage, Embleton, Northumberland NE66 3TT

Tel: 01665 576231

Owner: The National Trust **Guardian:** English Heritage **Contact:** The Custodian

An easy, but bracing, coastal walk leads to the eerie skeleton of this wonderful 14th century castle sited on a basalt crag, rearing up more than 100 feet from the waves crashing on the rocks below. The surviving ruins include the large gatehouse, which later became the keep, and curtain walls.

Location: OS75, NU258 220. 8m NE of Alnwick.

Open: 1 Apr - 30 Sept: daily, 10am - 6pm. 1 - 31 Oct, daily, 10am - 5pm. 1 Nov - 31 Mar: Wed - Sun, 10am - 4pm. Closed 24 - 26 Dec and 1 Jan. Times subject to change April 2004.

Admission: Adult £2.20, Child £1.10, Conc. £1.70. 15% discount for groups (11+). Prices subject to change April 2004.

🅿None. ▣ 🐕In grounds, on leads. ✳

EDLINGHAM CASTLE 🏛

Edlingham, Alnwick, Northumberland

Tel: 0191 269 1200

Owner: English Heritage **Contact:** The Regional Office

Set beside a splendid railway viaduct this complex ruin has defensive features spanning the 13th and 15th centuries.

Location: OS Ref. NU115 092. At E end of Edlingham village, on minor road off B6341 6m SW of Alnwick.

Open: Any reasonable time.

Admission: Free.

🐕In grounds, on leads. ✳

ETAL CASTLE 🏛

Cornhill-on-Tweed, Northumberland

Tel: 01890 820332

Owner: English Heritage **Contact:** The Custodian

A 14th century castle located in the picturesque village of Etal. Award-winning exhibition about the castle, Border warfare and the Battle of Flodden.

Location: OS75, NT925 394. In Etal village, 10m SW of Berwick.

Open: 1 Apr - 30 Sept: daily, 10am - 6pm. 1 - 31 Oct: daily, 10am - 5pm. Times subject to change April 2004.

Admission: Adult £3, Child £1.50, Conc. £2.30, Family £7. 15% discount for groups (11+). Prices subject to change April 2004.

ℹ WC in village. ⬜ ♿Partial. WC. 🅾 Inclusive. 🅿 Limited. ▣
🐕In grounds, on leads. ▦ Tel for details.

HERTERTON HOUSE GARDENS

Hartington, Cambo, Morpeth, Northumberland NE61 4BN

Tel: 01670 774278

Owner/Contact: C J "Frank" Lawley

One acre of formal garden in stone walls around a 16th century farmhouse, including a small topiary garden, physic garden, flower garden, fancy garden and gazebo.

Location: OS Ref. NZ022 881. 2m N of Cambo, just off B6342, Signposted (brown).

Open: 1 Apr - 30 Sept: Mons, Weds, Fri - Sun, 1.30 - 5.30pm.

Admission: Adult £2.50, Child (5-15yrs) £1. Groups by arrangement.

⚫ ♿Unsuitable. 📷By arrangement. 🅿 Limited for coaches.
🎥 Guided tours for adult students only. ✖

English Heritage Photo Library

HOUSESTEADS ROMAN FORT ⊞ 🌿

NR HAYDON BRIDGE, NORTHUMBERLAND NE47 6NN

Tel: 01434 344363

Owner: The National Trust **Guardian:** English Heritage **Contact:** The Custodian

Perched high on a ridge overlooking open moorland, this is the best known part of the Wall. The fort covers five acres and there are remains of many buildings, such as granaries, barrack blocks and gateways. A small exhibition displays altars, inscriptions and models.

Location: OS Ref. NY790 687. 2m NE of Bardon Mill.

Open: 1 Apr - 30 Sept: daily, 10am - 6pm. 1 - 31 Oct: daily, 10am - 5pm. 1 Nov - 31 Mar: daily, 10am - 4pm. Closed 24 - 26 Dec and 1 Jan. Times subject to change April 2004.

Admission: Adult £3.10, Child £1.60, Conc. £2.30, Family £7.80. 15% discount for groups (11+). Prices subject to change April 2004.

📷 🅿Charge. ⚫ 🎥In grounds, on leads. ✱

HOWICK HALL GARDENS

Howick, Alnwick, Northumberland NE66 3LB

Tel: 01665 577285 **e-mail:** estateoffice@howickuk.com

Owner: Howick Trustees Ltd **Contact:** Mrs D Spark

Romantically landscaped grounds surrounding the house in a little valley, with rare rhododendrons and flowering shrubs and trees.

Location: OS Ref. NU249 175. 6m NE of Alnwick. 1m E of B1339.

Open: Apr - Oct: daily 1 - 6pm.

Admission: Adult £3, Child (under 16) Free, OAP £2. Season tickets available.

♿Grounds partial. WC. ⚫ 🅿Limited. 🎥Guide dogs only.

KIRKLEY HALL GARDENS

Ponteland, Northumberland NE20 0AQ

Tel: 01670 841200 **Fax:** 01661 860047 **Contact:** Steve Nicholson

Over 9 acres of beautiful gardens incorporating a Victorian walled garden, woodland walks, sunken garden and wildlife areas and ponds.

Location: OS Ref. NZ150 772. 10m from the centre of Newcastle upon Tyne. 2 ½ m N of Ponteland on byroad to Morpeth.

Open: All year: daily, 10am - 4pm.

Admission: Free.

THE LADY WATERFORD HALL & MURALS

Ford, Berwick-upon-Tweed TD15 2QA

Tel: 01890 820503 **Fax:** 01890 820384

Owner: Ford & Etal Estates **Contact:** The Caretaker

Commissioned in 1860 the walls of this beautiful building are decorated with beautiful murals depicting Bible stories.

Location: OS Ref. NT945 374. On the B6354, 9m from Berwick-upon-Tweed, midway between Newcastle-upon-Tyne and Edinburgh, close to the A697.

Open: 13 Mar - 31 Oct: daily, 10.30am - 12.30pm & 1.30 - 5.30pm. By arrangement with the caretaker during winter months. Note: the Hall may be closed on occasion for private functions. Please telephone prior to travelling.

Admission: Adult £1.75, Child 75p, Child (under 12yrs) Free, Conc. £1.25. Groups by arrangement.

LINDISFARNE CASTLE 🌿

Holy Island, Berwick-upon-Tweed, Northumberland TD15 2SH

Tel: 01289 389244 **www.**nationaltrust.org.uk

Owner: The National Trust **Contact:** The Administrator

Built in 1550 to protect Holy Island harbour from attack, the castle was restored and converted into a private house for Edward Hudson by Sir Edwin Lutyens in 1903.

Location: OS Ref. NU136 417. On Holy Island, ¾ m E of village, 6m E of A1 across causeway. Usable at low tide.

Open: 14 Feb - 22 Feb, 20 Mar - 31 Oct: daily except Mon (but open BHs incl. Scottish BHs), 10.30am - 3pm or 12 noon - 4.30pm, depending on tides. Visitors are advised to check tide times before visiting.

Admission: £5, Family £12.50. Out of hours Group tours (15+) by arrangement £6pp.

📷NT Shop (in Main St.) 🎥In grounds, on leads.

© English Heritage Photo Library

LINDISFARNE PRIORY ⊞

HOLY ISLAND, BERWICK-UPON-TWEED TD15 2RX

Tel: 01289 389200

Owner: English Heritage **Contact:** The Custodian

The site of one of the most important early centres of Christianity in Anglo-Saxon England. St Cuthbert converted pagan Northumbria, and miracles occurring at his shrine established this 11th century priory as a major pilgrimage centre. The evocative ruins, with the decorated 'rainbow' arch curving dramatically across the nave of the church, are still the destination of pilgrims today. The story of Lindisfarne is told in an exhibition which gives an impression of life for the monks, including a reconstruction of a monk's cell.

Location: OS Ref. NU126 418. On Holy Island, check tide times.

Open: 1 Apr - 30 Sept: daily, 10am - 6pm. 1 - 31 Oct: daily, 10am - 5pm. 1 Nov - 31 Mar: daily, 10am - 4pm. Closed 24 - 26 Dec and 1 Jan. Times subject to change April 2004.

Admission: Adult £3, Child £1.50, Conc. £2.30. 15% discount for groups (11+). Prices subject to change April 2004.

📷 ♿Partial. Disabled parking. 🅿Charge. ⚫ 🎥Restricted. ✱ 🎥Tel for details.

NORHAM CASTLE ⛫
Norham, Northumberland

Tel: 01289 382329

Owner: English Heritage   **Contact:** The Custodian

Set on a promontory in a curve of the River Tweed, this was one of the strongest of the Border castles, built c1160.

Location: OS75, NT907 476. 6m SW of Berwick.

Open: 1 Apr - 30 Sept: daily, 10am - 6pm. Times subject to change April 2004.

Admission: Adult £2, Child £1, Conc. £1.50. 15% discount for groups (11+). Prices subject to change April 2004.

⊡ ⬧ Partial. ⌂ ⬛ ⬚ On leads. ☎ Tel for details.

PRESTON TOWER ⌂
Chathill, Northumberland NE67 5DH

Tel: 01665 589227

Owner/Contact: Major T Baker Cresswell

The Tower was built by Sir Robert Harbottle in 1392 and is one of the few survivors of 78 pele towers listed in 1415. The tunnel vaulted rooms remain unaltered and provide a realistic picture of the grim way of life under the constant threat of "Border Reivers". Two rooms are furnished in contemporary style and there are displays of historic and local information. Visitors are welcome to walk in the grounds which contain a number of interesting trees and shrubs. A woodland walk to the natural spring from which water is now pumped up to the Tower for the house and cottages.

Location: OS Ref. NU185 253. Follow Historic Property signs on A1 7m N of Alnwick.

Open: All year: daily, 9am - 6pm.

Admission: Adult £1.50, Child 50p, Conc. £1. Groups £1.

⬧ Grounds. ⬚ ✳

PRUDHOE CASTLE ⛫
Prudhoe, Northumberland NE42 6NA

Tel: 01661 833459

Owner: English Heritage   **Contact:** The Custodian

Set on a wooded hillside overlooking the River Tyne are the extensive remains of this 12th century castle including a gatehouse, curtain wall and keep. Small exhibition and video presentation.

Location: OS88 Ref. NZ092 634. In Prudhoe, on minor road N from A695.

Open: 1 Apr - 30 Sept: daily, 10am - 6pm. 1 - 31 Oct: daily, 10am - 5pm. Times subject to change April 2004.

Admission: Adult £2, Child £1, Conc. £1.50. 15% discount for groups (11+). Prices subject to change April 2004.

ⓘWC. ⊡ ⬧ Partial. ⬛ Ⓟ Limited. ⬛ ⬚ In grounds, on leads. ☎ Tel for details.

SEATON DELAVAL HALL ⌂
SEATON SLUICE, WHITLEY BAY, NORTHUMBERLAND NE26 4QR

Tel: 0191 237 1493 / 0191 237 0786   **e-mail:** lordhastings@onetel.net.uk

Owner: Lord Hastings   **Contact:** Mrs Mills

The home of Lord and Lady Hastings, half a mile from Seaton Sluice, is the last and most sensational mansion designed by Sir John Vanbrugh, builder of Blenheim Palace and Castle Howard. It was erected 1718 - 1728 and comprises a high turreted block flanked by arcaded wings which form a vast forecourt. The centre block was gutted by fire in 1822, but was partially restored in 1862 and again in 1959 - 1962 and 1999 - 2000. The remarkable staircases are a visual delight, and the two surviving rooms are filled with family pictures and photographs and royal seals spanning three centuries as well as various archives. This building is used frequently for concerts and charitable functions. The East Wing contains immense stables in ashlar stone of breathtaking proportions. Nearby are the Coach House with farm and passenger vehicles, fully documented, and the restored ice house with explanatory sketch and description. There are beautiful gardens with herbaceous borders, rose garden, rhododendrons, azaleas, laburnum walk, statues, and a spectacular parterre by internationally famous Jim Russell, also a unique Norman Church.

Location: OS Ref. NZ322 766. 1/2m from Seaton Sluice on A190, 3m from Whitley Bay.

Open: May & Aug BH Mons; Jun - 30 Sept: Weds & Suns, 2 - 6pm.

Admission: Adult £4, Child £1, OAP £3, Student £2. Groups (20+): Adult £3, Child/Student £1.

⊡ ⬧ Partial. WC. ⬛ Ⓟ Free. ⬛ ⬚ In grounds, on leads.

NT Photographic Library/Andrea Jones

WALLINGTON ✹

CAMBO, MORPETH, NORTHUMBERLAND NE61 4AR

www.nationaltrust.org.uk

Tel: 01670 773600 **Fax** 01670 774420 **e-mail:** wallington@nationaltrust.org.uk

Owner: The National Trust   **Contact:** The Estate Office

After extensive conservation work, the house will open again in Easter 2004. Dating from 1688, the much-loved home of the Trevelyan family contains magnificent rococco plasterwork, fine ceramics and a collection of doll's houses. The Pre-Raphaelite Central Hall depicts floral wall paintings and a series of scenes of Northumbrian history by William Bell Scott.

There are extensive walks through a variety of lawns, shrubberies, lakes and woodland to the exuberant walled garden, which remain open throughout the year.

Location: OS Ref. NZ030 843. Near Cambo, 6m NW of Belsay (A696).

Open: House & Restaurant: 1 Apr - 31 Oct: daily except Tue, 1 - 5.30pm (close 4.30pm from 6 Sep). Last admissions 1 hr (House)/30 min (Restaurant) prior to closing times. Walled garden: 1 Apr - 30 Sept: daily, 10am - 7pm. Oct: daily, 10am - 6pm. 1 Nov - 31 Mar: daily, 10am - 4pm. Shop: 5 Jan - 15 Feb: Wed - Sun, 10.30am - 4.30pm; 16 Feb - 5 Sep: daily (closed Tue during 16 Feb - 30 May), 10.30am - 5.30pm; 6 Sep - 31 Oct: daily except Tue, 10.30am - 4.30pm; 1 Nov -21 Dec: Wed - Sun, 10.30am - 4.30pm. Restaurant as shop. Farm shop: 1 Apr - 24 Dec: daily, 10.30am - 5pm; 28 Dec - 31 Mar (outside turnstile): 10.30am - 4pm. Grounds: daily in daylight hours.

Admission: Adult £7, Child £3.50, Family £17.50, Group £6.50pp. Walled garden & grounds only: Adult £5, Child £2.50, Family £12.50, Group £4.50.

⬚ ⛲ ⊤ ⬚Partial. ◨ ⓕBy arrangement. Ⓟ ▣ ⬚In grounds on leads. ▲ ✳ ⬚ Tel for details.

English Heritage Photo Library

WARKWORTH CASTLE ⌗

WARKWORTH, MORPETH, NORTHUMBERLAND NE66 0UJ

Tel: 01665 711423

Owner: English Heritage   **Contact:** The Custodian

The great towering keep of this 15th century castle, once the home of the mighty Percy family, dominates the town and River Coquet. Warkworth is one of the most outstanding examples of an aristocratic fortified residence. Upstream by boat from the castle lies Warkworth Hermitage, cutting into the rock of the river cliff (separate charge applies).

Location: OS Ref. NU247 057. 7m S of Alnwick on A1068.

Open: 1 Apr - 30 Sept: daily, 10am - 6pm. 1 - 31 Oct: daily, 10am - 5pm. 1 Nov - 31 Mar: daily, 10am - 4pm (closed 1 - 2pm). Closed 24 - 26 Dec and 1 Jan. Times subject to change April 2004.

Admission: Adult £3, Child £1.50, Conc. £2.30. 15% discount for groups (11+). Prices subject to change April 2004.

ⒾWC. ⬚ ⬚Grounds. ⬚Inclusive. Ⓟ ▣ ⬚ On leads. ✳ ⬚ Tel for details.

WARKWORTH HERMITAGE ⌗

Warkworth, Northumberland

Tel: 01665 711423

Owner: English Heritage   **Contact:** The Custodian

Upstream by boat from the castle this curious hermitage cuts into the rock of the river cliff.

Location: OS Ref. NU247 057. 7¹/2 m SE of Alnwick on A1068.

Open: 1 Apr - 30 Sept: Weds, Suns & BHs, 11am - 5pm. Times subject to change April 2004.

Admission: Adult £2, Child £1, Conc. £1.50. Prices subject to change April 2004.

⬚ ⬚Grounds. ⬚Inclusive. Ⓟ ▣ ⬚On leads. ✳ ⬚Tel for details.

Special Events Index see front section

ARBEIA ROMAN FORT
Baring Street, South Shields, Tyne & Wear NE33 2BB
Tel: 0191 456 1369 **Fax:** 0191 427 6862
Owner: South Tyneside Metropolitan Borough Council   **Contact:** The Curator
Managed by: Tyne & Wear Museums
More than 1,500 years on, the remains at Arbeia represent the most extensively excavated example of a military supply base anywhere in the Roman Empire. Museum includes weapons, jewellery and tombstones.
Location: OS Ref. NZ365 679. Near town centre and Metro Station.
Open: Easter - Sept: Mon - Sat: 10am - 5.30pm, Suns, 1 - 5pm. Open BH Mons. Oct - Easter: Mon - Sat, 10am - 4pm. Closed 25/26 Dec, 1 Jan & Good Friday.
Admission: Free, except for Time Quest Gallery: Adult £1.50, Child/Conc. 80p.

BEDE'S WORLD MUSEUM
Church Bank, Jarrow, Tyne & Wear NE32 3DY
Tel: 0191 489 2106 **Fax:** 0191 428 2361
Managed by: Jarrow 700AD Ltd   **Contact:** Visitor Services
A museum telling the story of the Venerable Bede and Anglo-Saxon Northumbria.
Location: OS Ref. NZ339 652. Just off A19, S end of Tyne Tunnel. 300yds N of St Paul's.
Open: Apr - Oct: Mon - Sat, 10am - 5.30pm, Suns, 12 noon - 5.30pm. Nov - Mar: Mon - Sat, 10am - 4.30pm, Suns, 12 noon - 4.30pm. Also open BH Mons but closed Good Fri.
Admission: Adult £4.50, Conc. £3, Family £10. Groups by arrangement.

BESSIE SURTEES HOUSE ⚎
41 - 44 Sandhill, Newcastle, Tyne & Wear
Tel: 0191 269 1200
Owner: English Heritage   **Contact:** The Custodian
Two 16th and 17th century merchants' houses stand on the quayside near the Tyne Bridge. One is a rare example of Jacobean domestic architecture. 3 rooms open.
Location: OS Ref. NZ252 639. 41- 44 Sandhill, Newcastle. Riverside. City centre.
Open: Weekdays only: 10am - 4pm. Closed BHs, 24 - 26 Dec and 1 Jan. Times subject to change April 2004.
Admission: Free.
ℹ️ WC. ⬚ ▣ ✖

GIBSIDE ✿
Nr Rowlands Gill, Burnopfield, Newcastle-upon-Tyne NE16 6BG
Tel: 01207 541820 **e-mail:** gibside@nationaltrust.org.uk **www**.nationaltrust.org.uk
Owner: The National Trust   **Contact:** The Property Manager
Gibside is one of the finest 18th century designed landscapes in the north of England. The Chapel was built to James Paine's design soon after 1760. Outstanding example of Georgian architecture approached along a terrace with an oak avenue. Walk along the River Derwent through woodland.
Location: OS Ref. NZ172 583. 6m SW of Gateshead, 20m NW of Durham. Entrance on B6314 between Burnopfield and Rowlands Gill.
Open: Grounds: 23 Mar - 3 Nov: daily except Mons (open BH Mons), 10am - 6pm. Last admission 4.30pm. 4 Nov - 31 Mar: 10am - 4pm. Last admission 1 hour before closing. Chapel 23 Mar - 3 Nov: as grounds, otherwise by arrangement.
Admission: Chapel and Grounds: Adult £3.50, Child £2, Family (2+4) £10, Family (1+3) £7. Booked groups £3. NT members free.
♿ Partial. ▣ ℹ️ By arrangement. 🅿 Limited for coaches. 🐕 On leads, in grounds. ✱ ☎ Tel for details.

NEWCASTLE CASTLE KEEP
Castle Keep, Castle Garth, Newcastle-upon-Tyne NE1 1RQ
Tel: 0191 232 7938
Owner: Newcastle City Council   **Contact:** Paul MacDonald
The Keep originally dominated the castle bailey. The 'new' castle was founded in 1080.
Location: OS Ref. NZ251 638. City centre between St Nicholas church and the High Level bridge.
Open: All year: daily, 9.30am - 5.30pm (4.30pm winter).
Admission: Adult £1.50, Child/Conc. 50p.

ST PAUL'S MONASTERY ⚎
Jarrow, Tyne & Wear
Tel: 0191 489 7052
Owner: English Heritage   **Contact:** The Regional Office – 0191 269 1200
The home of the Venerable Bede in the 7th and 8th centuries, partly surviving as the chancel of the parish church. It has become one of the best understood Anglo-Saxon monastic sites.
Location: OS Ref. NZ339 652. In Jarrow, on minor road N of A185. 300yds S of Bede's World.
Open: Any reasonable time.
Admission: Free.
⬚ ♿ ▣ 🅿

SOUTER LIGHTHOUSE ✿
Coast Road, Whitburn, Sunderland, Tyne & Wear SR6 7NH
Tel: 0191 529 3161 **Fax:** 0191 529 0902 **e-mail:** souter@nationaltrust.org.uk
www.nationaltrust.org.uk
Owner: The National Trust   **Contact:** The Property Manager
Dramatic red and white lighthouse tower on rugged coast. Built in 1871, the first to be powered by alternating electric current.
Location: OS Ref. NZ408 641. 2¹/₂m S of South Shields on A183. 5m N of Sunderland.
Open: 14 - 29 Feb & 27 Mar - 31 Oct: daily except Fri (open Good Fri), 11am - 5pm. Last admission 4.30pm.
Admission: Adult £3, Child £1.50, Family £7.50. Booked Groups: £2.50. NT members Free: membership available from shop.
⬚ ❂ ☵ ♿ Partial. WCs. ▣ 🍴 ℹ️ By arrangement. 🅿 ▣ 🐕 In grounds, on leads.

TYNEMOUTH PRIORY & CASTLE ⚎
North Pier, Tynemouth, Tyne & Wear NE30 4BZ
Tel: 0191 257 1090
Owner: English Heritage   **Contact:** The Custodian
The castle walls and gatehouse enclose the substantial remains of a Benedictine priory founded c1090 on a Saxon monastic site. Their strategic importance has made the castle and priory the target for attack for many centuries. In World War I, coastal batteries in the castle defended the mouth of the Tyne.
Location: OS Ref. NZ374 695. In Tynemouth.
Open: 1 Apr - 30 Sept: daily, 10am - 6pm. 1 - 31 Oct: daily, 10am - 5pm. 1 Nov - 31 Mar: Wed - Sun, 10am - 4pm (closed 1 - 2 pm). Closed 24 - 26 Dec & 1 Jan. Times subject to change April 2004.
Admission: Adult £2.50, Child £1.30, Conc. £1.90, Family £5.80. 15% discount for groups (11+). Prices subject to change April 2004.
⬚ ♿ Grounds. ℹ️ By arrangement. 🐕 In grounds, on leads. ✱ ☎ Tel for details.

WASHINGTON OLD HALL ✿
The Avenue, Washington Village, District 4, Washington, Tyne & Wear NE38 7LE
Tel: 0191 416 6879 **Fax:** 0191 419 2065 **www**.nationaltrust.org.uk
Owner: The National Trust   **Contact:** The Property Manager
Jacobean manor house incorporating portions of 12th century house of the Washington family. Small Jacobean knot garden.
Location: OS Ref. NZ312 566. In Washington on E side of The Avenue. 5m W of Sunderland (2m from A1), S of Tyne Tunnel, follow signs for Washington District 4 and then village.
Open: 28 Mar - 31 Oct: Sun - Wed. Closed Thur - Sat (open Good Fri), 11am - 5pm. Last admission 4.30pm.
Admission: Adult £3.50, Child £2. Booked groups (15+): £3. Membership available from reception.
⬚ ☵ Conferences. ♿ Ground floor and grounds. ▣ ℹ️ By arrangement. 🅿 Limited. 🐕 In grounds, on leads. 🅰

Website Information see front section

Allée

Just as it sounds, a French word, meaning a straight walk or straight avenue.

Visit Melbourne Hall & Gardens in Derbyshire.

Garden Jargon

Torosay Castle, Isle of Mull from the book *Historic Family Homes and Gardens from the Air*, see page 54.

SCOTLAND

scotland

Glencoe, Highlands. © David Osborn

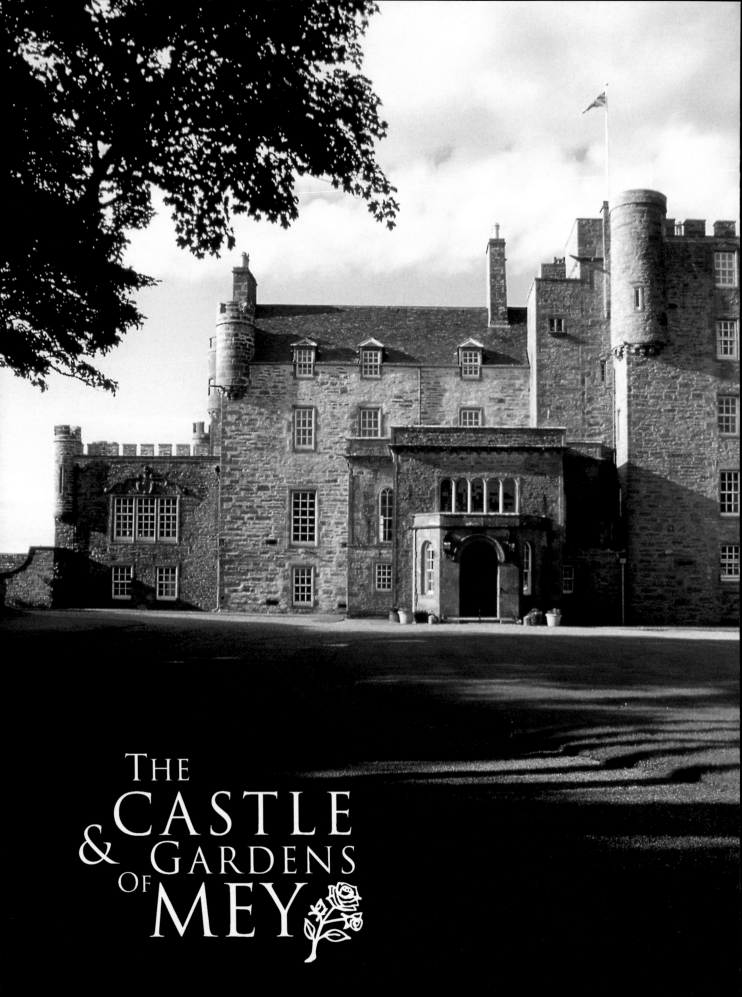

THE CASTLE & GARDENS OF MEY

We're proud today,
For the beloved Queen Mother comes here to stay,
Not alone a Royal smile passing this way –
But coming to rest in her Castle of Mey.

So there shall be
A hundred thousand welcomes o'er land and sea,
The greeting of the Celts, its ancient heraldry,
For a Queen who has served right loyally.

Lest any dare,
To say this land is bleak or bare –
Pray have a care, yea have a care,
For the eyes of a Queen have rested there –
And behold the land is forever fair.

"Caithness Makes Her Curtsey" – read by the Provost of Wick, Miss Bessie Leith, after the Queen Mother had received the Freedom of Wick in 1956.

Huge painters' skies, the sea stretching out before you and, on a fine day, … islands in the Pentland Firth that bewitch you into thinking that they are nothing more than mere stepping stones inviting you to the Orkney Islands beyond. These are the views of The Castle and Gardens of Mey in the county of Caithness in the Highlands; mainland Britain's most northerly castle, and the former home of Her Majesty Queen Elizabeth, The Queen Mother.

It was in the summer of 1952, while staying with Commander and Lady Doris Vyner, that Her Majesty first saw the Castle looking very run down and badly in need of repair. The Queen Mother and Lady Doris opened the front door to be greeted by a pair of shoes left on the stairs in the hall. They were green with mould. Her Majesty then and there determined to save Barrogill Castle (as it was then called) and restore it to its former glory. The Queen Mother was clearly taken by the peace and tranquillity of the place and she succeeded in buying it. So began a story of nearly 50 years, of many happy holidays at the only home Her Majesty ever actually owned.

The Castle of Mey is not large. It is thought to have been built between 1566 and 1572 after George, 4th Earl Caithness, acquired the Barony of Mey from the Bishop of Caithness. The Castle's 'Z-plan' shape, tower, and corbelled turrets and numerous gun slits are typical of the late 16th century design. The Castle remained in the ownership of the Sinclairs of Mey until the 15th Earl of Caithness died without issue in 1889. He bequeathed the Castle and its estates to his great friend PG Heathcote. It was later bought from Mr Heathcote's widow by Captain Imbert-Terry, from whom The Queen Mother bought the Castle and estate in 1952. She was delighted in 1996 to appoint the 20th Earl of Caithness as one of the Trustees of the Queen Elizabeth Castle of Mey Trust – so re-establishing the Sinclair's family's historical link with the Castle.

Whilst the exterior of the Castle of Mey is plain and castellated, the interiors are deceptively comfortable and intimate. Although the Queen Mother consulted a London firm about decoration and curtains, much of the furniture you see was acquired in Thurso either in *Miss Miller Calder's* shop or in the *Ship's Wheel*. Sadly, these shops are no longer in existence. The wonderfully ornate clam shell jardinière, which is the centrepiece of the Front Hall and always filled with flowers, is one such local purchase. Many of the paintings are also by local artists, bought in Thurso and Wick and at exhibitions held by the Society of Caithness Artists. All the rooms contain reminders of The Queen Mother's royal status, but set in a wonderfully elegant yet informal atmosphere. The fabulous tapestry of her Royal Coat of Arms sits as easily here as the simple rush chair next to the walking-stick stand.

Visiting the Castle of Mey is to visit a private and happy world – a world which revolved around local events, the community, the estate, the champion Aberdeen Angus herd and North Country Cheviot sheep, Canisbay Church, the garden, picnics, beachcombing and reading – it is an enchanting world to visit.

▶ For further details about the Castle of Mey see page 505.

'The Pink Boy' - Sir Joshua Reynolds

Map 10

Owner: His Grace the
Duke of Buccleuch &
Queensberry KT

▶ **CONTACT**

Buccleuch Heritage
Trust
Bowhill House &
Country Park
Bowhill
Selkirk TD7 5ET

Tel/Fax: 01750 22204

e-mail:
bht@buccleuch.com

▶ **LOCATION**
OS Ref. NT426 278

3m W of Selkirk off
A708 Moffat Road,
A68 from Newcastle,
A7 from Carlisle
or Edinburgh.

Bus: 3m Selkirk.

Taxi: 01750 20354.

BOWHILL HOUSE & 🏛
COUNTRY PARK

SELKIRK

Scottish Borders home of the Duke and Duchess of Buccleuch, dating mainly from 1812 and christened 'Sweet Bowhill' by Sir Walter Scott in his *Lay of the Last Minstrel*.

Many of the works of art were collected by earlier Montagus, Douglases and Scotts or given by Charles II to his natural son James, Duke of Monmouth and Buccleuch. Paintings include Canaletto's *Whitehall*, works by Guardi, Claude, Ruysdael, Gainsborough, Raeburn, Reynolds, Van Dyck and Wilkie. Superb French furniture, Meissen and Sèvres porcelain, silver and tapestries.

Historical relics include Monmouth's saddle and execution shirt, Sir Walter Scott's plaid and some proof editions, Queen Victoria's letters and gifts to successive Duchesses of Buccleuch, her Mistresses of the Robes.

There is also a completely restored Victorian Kitchen, 19th century horse-drawn fire engine, 'Bowhill Theatre', a lively centre for the performing arts and where, prior to touring the house, visitors can see 'The Quest for Bowhill', a 20 minute audio-visual presentation by Dr Colin Thompson. James Hogg Exhibition.

Conference centre, arts courses, literary lunches, education service, visitor centre. Shop, tearoom, adventure playground, woodland walks, nature trails, picnic areas. Garden and landscape designed by John Gilpin.

'Winter' - Sir Joshua Reynolds

🛍 ✻ ℹ Fashion shows, air displays, archery, clay pigeon shooting, equestrian events, charity garden parties, shows, rallies, filming, lecture theatre. House is open by appointment outside public hours to groups led by officials of a recognised museum, gallery or educational establishment. No photography inside house.

🍵 Inside caterers normally used but outside caterers considered.

♿ Visitors may alight at entrance. WC. Wheelchair visitors free.

🍴 Groups can book in advance (special rates), menus on request.

🚶 For groups. Tour time 1¼ hrs.

🅿 60 cars and 6 coaches within 50yds of house.

📖 Welcome. Projects in Bowhill House and Victorian kitchen, Education Officers (service provided free of charge), schoolroom, ranger-led nature walks, adventure playground. Heritage Education Trust Sandford Award winner '93 and '98.

🐕 On leads. ✱

▶ **OPENING TIMES**

House
June: Thurs & Suns,
1 - 4pm;
July: Daily, 1 - 5pm;
August: please telephone
for details.

Outwith stated times to
educational groups by
appointment.

Country Park
Easter - end August.
Times vary, please
telephone for details.

▶ **ADMISSION**
Summer

House & Country Park
Adult £6.00
Child (5-16yrs) £2.00
OAP £4.50

Country Park only
All ages £2.00
Child (under 5yrs) &
Wheelchair
visitors .... Free

Family tickets and group
tickets available.

CONFERENCE/FUNCTION

ROOM	MAX CAPACITY
Bowhill Little Theatre	72

Skyscan Photo Library

Map 10

Owner: His Grace the
Duke of Roxburghe

▶ CONTACT

Judy Potts
Sales & Events
Organiser
Roxburghe Estates
Office
Kelso
Roxburghshire
Scotland TD5 7SF

Tel: 01573 223333

Fax: 01573 226056

e-mail:
jpotts@floorscastle.com

▶ LOCATION
OS Ref. NT711 347

From South A68, A698.

From North A68,
A697/9
In Kelso follow signs.

Bus: Kelso Bus Station
1m.

Rail: Berwick 20m.

FLOORS CASTLE 🏛

KELSO

www.floorscastle.com

Floors Castle, home of the Duke and Duchess of Roxburghe, is situated in the heart of the Scottish Border Country. It is reputedly the largest inhabited castle in Scotland. Designed by William Adam, who was both masterbuilder and architect, for the first Duke of Roxburghe, building started in 1721.

It was the present Duke's great-great-grand-father James, the 6th Duke, who embellished the plain Adam features of the building. In about 1849 Playfair, letting his imagination and talent run riot, transformed the castle, creating a multitude of spires and domes.

The apartments now display the outstanding collection of French 17th and 18th century furniture, magnificent tapestries, Chinese and European porcelain and many other fine works of art. Many of the treasures in the castle today were collected by Duchess May, American wife of the 8th Duke.

The castle has been seen on cinema screens worldwide in the film *Greystoke*, as the home of Tarzan, the Earl of Greystoke.

GARDENS
The extensive parkland and gardens overlooking the River Tweed provide a variety of wooded walks. The garden centre and walled gardens contain splendid herbaceous borders and in the outer walled garden a parterre to commemorate the Millennium can be seen. An excellent children's playground and picnic area are very close to the castle.

ℹ️ Gala dinners, conferences, product launches, 4 x 4 driving, incentive groups, highland games and other promotional events. Extensive park, helicopter pad, fishing, clay pigeon and pheasant shooting. No photography inside the castle.

🛍 ♿ 🍷

♿ Visitors may alight at the entrance. WC.

🍽 Self-service, licensed, seats 125 opens 10am.

🚶 By arrangement. Tour time 1¼ hrs.

🅿️ Unlimited for cars, 100 yds away, coach park 50 yds. Coaches can be driven to the entrance, waiting area close to restaurant exit. Lunch or tea for coach drivers.

👤 Welcome, guide provided. Playground facilities.

🐕 On leads, in grounds.

▶ OPENING TIMES
Summer
3 April - 31 October:
Daily: 10am - 4.30pm.

Last admission 4pm.

Winter
November - March
Closed to the general public, available for events.

▶ ADMISSION
Summer
Adult	£5.75
Child* (5 - 15yrs)	£3.25
OAP/Student	£4.75
Family	£15.00

Groups (20+)
Adult	£4.50
Child* (5 - 15yrs)	£2.00
OAP/Student	£4.00

*Under 5yrs Free.

🎭 SPECIAL EVENTS
APR 11
Easter Eggstravaganza.

MAY 22/23
Floors Castle Horse Trials.

JULY 3/4
Gardeners' Festival –
Herbaceous Perennials.

JULY 22
As You Like It (Shakespeare Open Air Theatre).

AUG 29
Massed Pipe Bands Family Day.

CONFERENCE/FUNCTION
ROOM	SIZE	MAX CAPACITY
Dining Rm	18m x 7m	150
Ballroom	21m x 8m	150

Map 10

Owner:
The Lord Palmer

► **CONTACT**

The Lord or Lady
Palmer
Manderston
Duns
Berwickshire
Scotland   TD11 3PP

Tel: 01361 883450
Secretary: 01361 882636
Fax: 01361 882010
e-mail: palmer@
manderston.co.uk

► **LOCATION**

OS Ref. NT810 544

From Edinburgh
47m, 1hr.
1¹/₂ m E of Duns on
A6105.
Bus: 400 yds.
Rail: Berwick
Station 12m.
Taxi: Chirnside 818216.
Airport: Edinburgh or
Newcastle both
60m or 80 mins.

CONFERENCE/FUNCTION

ROOM	SIZE	MAX CAPACITY
Dining Rm	22' x 35'	100
Ballroom	34' x 21'	150
Hall	22' x 38'	130
Drawing Rm	35' x 21'	150

MANDERSTON 🏛

DUNS

www.manderston.co.uk

Manderston, together with its magnificent stables, stunning marble dairy and 56 acres of immaculate gardens, forms an ensemble which must be unique in Britain today.

The house was completely rebuilt between 1903 and 1905, with no expense spared.

Visitors are able to see not only the sumptuous State rooms and bedrooms, decorated in the Adam manner, but also all the original domestic offices, in a truly 'upstairs downstairs' atmosphere. Manderston boasts a unique and recently restored silver staircase.

There is a special museum with a nostalgic display of valuable tins made by Huntly and Palmer from 1868 to the present day. Winner of the AA/NPI Bronze Award UK 1994.

GARDENS

Outside, the magnificence continues and the combination of formal gardens and picturesque landscapes is a major attraction unique amongst Scottish houses.

The stables, still in use, have been described by *Horse and Hound* as 'probably the finest in all the wide world'.

Manderston has often been used as a film location, most recently it was the star of Channel 4's *'The Edwardian Country House'*.

🖼️ ℹ️ Corporate & incentives venue. Ideal retreat: business groups, think-tank weekends. Fashion shows, air displays, archery, clay pigeon shooting, equestrian events, garden parties, shows, rallies, filming, product launches and marathons. Two airstrips for light aircraft, approx 5m, grand piano, billiard table, fox-hunting, pheasant shoots, sea angling, salmon fishing, stabling, cricket pitch, tennis court, lake. Nearby: 18-hole golf course, indoor swimming pool, squash court. No photography in house.

🍽️ Available. Buffets, lunches and dinners. Wedding receptions.

♿ Special parking available outside the House.

☕ Tearoom (open as house) with waitress service. Can be booked in advance, menus on request.

🚶 Included. Available in French. Guides in rooms. If requested, the owner may meet groups. Tour time 1¹/₄ hrs.

🅿️ 400 cars 125yds from house, 30 coaches 5yds from house. Appreciated if group fees are paid by one person.

🎒 Welcome. Guide can be provided. Biscuit Tin Museum of particular interest.

🐕 Grounds only, on leads.

🛏️ 6 twin, 4 double.

❄️

► **OPENING TIMES**

Summer

Mid-May - end September
Thurs & Suns
2 - 5pm. Gardens open
until dusk.

BH Mons, late May
& late August, 2 - 5pm.
Gardens open until dusk.

Groups welcome all year
by appointment.

Winter

September - May
Group visits welcome
by appointment.

► **ADMISSION**

House & Grounds

Adult £6.50
Child £3.00
Groups (20+ on open days)
Per person £5.00

Grounds only

Including Stables &
Marble Dairy
Adult £3.50
Child £1.50

On days when the house is closed to the public, groups viewing by appointment will have personally conducted tours. The Gift Shop will be open. On these occasions reduced party rates (except for school children) will not apply. Group visits (20+) other than open days are £6.50 (minimum £130). Edwardian teas on open days only.

AYTON CASTLE

AYTON, EYEMOUTH, BERWICKSHIRE TD14 5RD

Tel: 018907 81212 **Fax:** 018907 81550

Owner: D I Liddell-Grainger of Ayton **Contact:** The Curator

Built in 1846 by the Mitchell-Innes family and designed by the architect James Gillespie Graham. Over the last ten years it has been fully restored and is now a family home. It is a unique restoration project and the quality of the original and restored workmanship is outstanding. The castle stands on an escarpment surrounded by mature woodlands containing many interesting trees and has been a film-making venue due to this magnificent setting.

Location: OS Ref. NT920 610. 7m N of Berwick-on-Tweed on Route A1.

Open: 19 May - 15 Sept: Weds and Suns, 2 - 5 pm or by appointment.

Admission: Adult £3, Child (under 15yrs) Free.

Partial. Obligatory. In grounds, on leads.

ABBOTSFORD

Melrose, Roxburghshire TD6 9BQ

Tel: 01896 752043 **Fax:** 01896 752916 **e-mail:** abbotsford@melrose.bordernet.co.uk

Sir Walter Scott purchased the Cartley Hall farmhouse on the banks of the Tweed in 1812. Scott had the old house demolished in 1822 and replaced it with the main block of Abbotsford as it is today.

Location: OS Ref. NT508 343. 35m S of Edinburgh. Melrose 3m, Galashiels 2m. On B6360.

Open: 17 Mar - 31 Oct: Mon - Sat. 9.30am - 5pm. Suns in Jun - Sept: 9.30am - 5pm; Suns in Mar - May & Oct: 2 - 5pm. Other dates by arrangement. (2003 times, please contact property for current times)

Admission: Adult £4.20, Child £2.10. Groups: Adult £3.40 Child £1.70. (2003 prices)

BOWHILL HOUSE & COUNTRY PARK

See page 462 for full page entry.

DAWYCK BOTANIC GARDEN

Stobo, Peeblesshire EH45 9JU

Tel: 01721 760254 **Fax:** 01721 760214 **e-mail:** dawyck@rbge.co.uk

Contact: The Curator

Renowned historic arboretum. Amongst mature specimen trees – some over 40 metres tall – are a variety of flowering trees, shrubs and herbaceous plants. Explore the world's first Cryptogamic Sanctuary and Reserve for 'non-flowering' plants.

Location: OS Ref. NT168 352. 8m SW of Peebles on B712.

Open: 14 Feb - 14 Nov: Daily, 10am - 6pm (Feb & Nov closes 4pm; Mar & Oct closes 5pm). Last admission 30 mins before closing.

Admission: Adult £3.50, Child £1, Conc. £3, Family £8. Group discounts & membership programme available.

DRYBURGH ABBEY

St Boswells, Melrose

Tel: 01835 822381

Owner: Historic Scotland **Contact:** The Steward

Remarkably complete ruins of Dryburgh Abbey.

Location: OS Ref. NT591 317. 5m SE of Melrose off B6356. 1½ m N of St Boswells.

Open: 1 Apr - 30 Sept: daily, 9.30am - 6.30pm. Last ticket 6pm. 1 Oct - 31 Mar: Mon - Sat, 9.30am - 4.30pm, Suns, 2 - 4.30pm, last ticket 4pm.

Admission: Adult £3, Child £1, Conc. £2.30.

€

DUNS CASTLE

DUNS, BERWICKSHIRE TD11 3NW

www.dunscastle.co.uk

Tel: 01361 883211 **Fax:** 01361 882015 **e-mail:** aline_hay@lineone.net

Owner: Alexander Hay of Duns **Contact:** Mrs Aline Hay

This historical 1320 pele tower has been home to the Hay family since 1696, and the current owners Alexander and Aline Hay offer it as a welcoming venue for individuals, groups and corporate guests to enjoy. They have renovated it to produce high standards of comfort while retaining all the character of its rich period interiors. Wonderful lakeside and parkland setting.

Location: OS Ref. NT777 544. 10m off A4. Rail: Berwick station 16m. Airports: Newcastle & Edinburgh, 1 hr.

Open: Available all year by reservation for individuals, groups and companies for day visits or residential stays, on an exclusive use basis. Not open to the general public.

Admission: Rates for private and corporate visits, wedding receptions, filming on application.

4 x 4-poster, 4 x double, 3 x twin (all with bathrooms), 1 single plus 6 cottages in grounds.

FERNIEHIRST CASTLE
JEDBURGH, ROXBURGHSHIRE TD8 6NX

Tel: 01835 862201 **Fax:** 01835 863992
Owner: The Ferniehirst Trust
Contact: Mrs J Fraser

Ferniehirst Castle – Scotland's Frontier Fortress. Ancestral home of the Kerr family. Restored (1984/1987) by the 12th Marquess of Lothian. Unrivalled 16th century Border architecture. Grand Apartment and Turret Library. A 16th century Chamber Oratory. The Kerr Chamber – Museum of Family History. A special tribute to Jedburgh's Protector to Mary Queen of Scots – Sir Thomas Kerr. Riverside walk by Jed Water. Archery Field opposite the Chapel where sheep of Viking origin still graze as they did four centuries ago.

Location: OS Ref. NT653 181. 2m S of Jedburgh on the A68.

Open: Jul: Tue - Sun (closed Mons), 11am - 4pm.

Admission: Adult £3, Child £1.50. Groups (max. 50) by prior arrangement (01835 862201).

🔲 ♿Suitable. WCs.
🚶Guided tours only, groups by arrangement.
🅿 Ample for cars and coaches.
🐕In grounds, on leads.

FLOORS CASTLE 🏛

See page 463 for full page entry.

HALLIWELL'S HOUSE MUSEUM
Halliwell's Close, Market Place, High Street, Selkirk
Tel: 01750 20096 **Fax:** 01750 23282
Owner: Scottish Borders Council   **Contact:** Shona Sinclair
Re-creation of buildings, formerly used as a house and ironmonger's shop.
Location: OS Ref. NT472 286. In Selkirk town centre.
Open: Apr - Sept: Mon - Sat, 10am - 5pm (July & Aug 10am - 5.30pm), Suns, 10am - 12 noon.Oct: Mon - Sat, 10am - 4pm.
Admission: Free.

HARMONY GARDEN 🌺
St Mary's Road, Melrose TD6 9LJ
Tel: 01721 722502 **Fax:** 01721 724700
Owner: The National Trust for Scotland   **Contact:** Head Gardener
A tranquil garden offering herbaceous and mixed borders, lawns, vegetable and fruit areas. Fine views of Melrose Abbey and the Eildon Hills. Garden set around 19th century house (not open to visitors).
Location: OS Ref. NT549 342. In Melrose, opposite the Abbey.
Open: Good Fri - Easter Mon and 1 Jun - 30 Sept: Mon - Sat, 10am - 5pm, Sun 1 - 5pm.
Admission: Adult £2, Conc. £1 (honesty box).

HERMITAGE CASTLE 🏛
Liddesdale, Newcastleton
Tel: 01387 376222
Owner: In the care of Historic Scotland   **Contact:** The Steward
Eerie fortress at the heart of the bloodiest events in the history of the Borders. Mary Queen of Scots made her famous ride here to visit her future husband.
Location: OS Ref. NY497 961. In Liddesdale 5¹/₂ m NE of Newcastleton, B6399.
Open: 1 Apr - 30 Sept: daily, 9.30am - 6.30pm, last ticket 6pm.
Admission: Adult £2.20, Child 75p, Conc. £1.60.
€

THE HIRSEL GARDENS, COUNTRY PARK 🏛
& HOMESTEAD MUSEUM
Coldstream, Berwickshire TD12 4LP
Tel/Fax: 01573 224144   **e-mail:** rogerdodd@btconnect.com
www.hirselcountrypark.co.uk
Owner: Lord Home of the Hirsel   **Contact:** Roger G Dodd
Wonderful spring flowers and rhododendrons. Homestead museum and crafts centre. The Cottage Tearoom. Displays of estate life and adaptation to modern farming.
Location: OS Ref. NT838 393. Immediately W of Coldstream off A697.
Open: All year during daylight hours.
Admission: £2 per car, coaches by appointment.
🔲 🍴 ♿WCs. 🅿 Limited for coaches. 🐕In grounds, on leads. ❄

Accommodation Index see front section

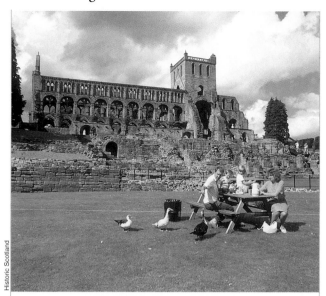

Historic Scotland

JEDBURGH ABBEY

4/5 ABBEY BRIDGEND, JEDBURGH TD8 6JQ

Tel: 01835 863925

Owner: In the care of Historic Scotland   **Contact:** The Steward

Founded by David I c1138 for Augustinian Canons. The church is mostly in the Romanesque and early Gothic styles and is remarkably complete. The award-winning visitor centre contains the priceless 12th century 'Jedburgh Comb' and other artefacts found during archaeological excavations.

Location: OS Ref. NT650 205. In Jedburgh on the A68.

Open: Apr - Sept: daily, 9.30am - 6.30pm. Oct - Mar: Mon - Sat, 9.30am - 4.30pm, Suns, 2 - 4.30pm. Last ticket 30 mins before closing. 10% discount for groups (10+).

Admission: Adult £3.50, Child £1.20, Conc. £2.60.

i Picnic area. 🗓 & Partial. WC. P ■ Free when booked. 🐕 Guide dogs only. ❋ €

MELLERSTAIN HOUSE 🏛

MELLERSTAIN, GORDON, BERWICKSHIRE TD3 6LG

www.mellerstain.com

Tel: 01573 410225   **Fax:** 01573 410636   **e-mail:** enquiries@mellerstain.com

Owner: The Earl of Haddington   **Contact:** Rosemary Evans

One of Scotland's great Georgian houses and a unique example of the work of the Adam family; the two wings built in 1725 by William Adam, the large central block by his son, Robert 1770-78. Rooms contain fine plasterwork, colourful ceilings and marble fireplaces. The library is considered to be Robert Adam's finest creation. Many fine paintings and period furniture.

Location: OS Ref. NT648 392. From Edinburgh A68 to Earlston, turn left 5m, signed.

Open: Easter weekend (4 days), 1 May - 30 Sept: daily except Tue & Sat. Oct: Sat & Sun only, 12.30 - 5pm. Groups at other times by appointment. Last admission 4pm. Tearoom, shop & gardens: daily, except Tue & Sat, 11.30am - 5.30pm.

Admission: Adult £5.50, child with adult free. Groups (20+) £5. Grounds only: £3.

i No photography or video cameras. 🗓 🍴 🅃 & Partial. ■ Licensed. 🍽 Licensed. 🎟 By arrangement. P

🐕 In grounds, on leads. Guide dogs only in house. 🛏 Tel for details.

MANDERSTON 🏛   *See page 464 for full page entry.*

MELROSE ABBEY 🏛

MELROSE, ROXBURGHSHIRE TD6 9LG

Tel: 01896 822562

Owner: Historic Scotland   **Contact:** The Steward

The Abbey was founded about 1136 by David I as a Cistercian Abbey and at one time was probably the richest in Scotland. Richard II's English army largely destroyed it in 1385 but it was rebuilt and the surviving remains are mostly 14th century. Burial place of Robert the Bruce's heart. Local history displays.

Location: OS Ref. NT549 342. In the centre of Melrose off the A68 or A7.

Open: Apr - Sept: daily, 9.30am - 6.30pm. Oct - Mar: Mon - Sat, 9.30am - 4.30pm, Suns, 2 - 4.30pm. Last ticket 30 mins before closing.

Admission: Adult £3.50, Child £1.20, Conc. £2.60. 10% discount for groups (10+).

i Picnic area. 🗓 & Tape for visitors with learning difficulties. 🎧 P ■ Pre-booked visits free. 🐕 Guide dogs only. ❋ €

MERTOUN GARDENS 🏛

St Boswells, Melrose, Roxburghshire TD6 0EA

Tel: 01835 823236 **Fax:** 01835 822474

Owner: His Grace the Duke of Sutherland **Contact:** Angela Dodds/Susan Murdoch

26 acres of beautiful grounds. Walled garden and well-preserved circular dovecote.

Location: OS Ref. NT617 318. Entrance off B6404 2m NE of St Boswells.

Open: Apr - Sept: weekends & Public Holiday Mons only, 2 - 6pm. Last admission 5.30pm.

Admission: Adult £2, Child 50p, OAP £1.50. Groups by arrangement: 10% reduction.

🅵 By arrangement. 🅿 ✖

OLD GALA HOUSE

Scot Crescent, Galashiels TD1 3J

Tel: 01750 20096 **Fax:** 01750 23282

Owner: Scottish Borders Council

Dating from 1583, the former house of the Lairds of Gala. Particularly memorable is the painted ceiling dated 1635.

Location: OS Ref. NT492 357. S of town centre, signed from A7.

Open: Apr - Sept: Tue - Sat, 10am - 4pm. Jun - Aug: Mon - Sat, 10am - 4pm, Suns, 2 - 4pm. Oct: Tue - Sat, 1 - 4pm.

Admission: Free.

MONTEVIOT HOUSE
JEDBURGH, ROXBURGHSHIRE TD8 6UQ

Tel: 01835 830380 (mornings only) / 01835 830704 **Fax:** 01835 830288

Owner: The Earl of Ancram **Contact:** The Administrator

The river garden planted with herbaceous shrub borders, has a beautiful view of the River Teviot. A semi-enclosed rose garden with a collection of hybrid teas, floribunda and shrub roses. The pinetum is full of unusual trees and nearby a water garden of islands is linked by bridges.

Location: OS Ref. NT648 247. 3m N of Jedburgh. S side of B6400 (to Nisbet). 1m E of A68.

Open: House: First two weeks in Jul: 1 - 5pm. Garden: Apr - Oct: daily, 12 noon - 5pm. Coach parties by prior arrangement.

Admission: House or Garden only: Adult £2.50. House & Garden: Adult £4.50. Under 16yrs Free.

♿ 🅰Partial. Parking & WCs. 🅵By arrangement. 🅿

PAXTON HOUSE, GALLERY & COUNTRY PARK 🏛
BERWICK-UPON-TWEED TD15 1SZ

www.paxtonhouse.com

Tel: 01289 386291 **Fax:** 01289 386660 **e-mail:** info@paxtonhouse.com

Owner: The Paxton Trust **Contact:** The Director

Award-winning country house and country park built from 1758-62 to the design of John and James Adam for Patrick Home, Laird of Wedderburn. The house boasts the pre-eminent collection of Chippendale furniture in Scotland and a fine collection of regency furniture by William Trotter of Edinburgh. The largest picture gallery in a Scottish country house built by Robert Reid in 1814 houses over 70 paintings from the National Galleries of Scotland, recently re-hung in November 2002. The estate has woodland trails, riverside walks, gardens, parkland, red squirrel hide, Highland cattle and croquet. There is a shop, stables tearoom, a function suite and an ever-changing exhibition programme.

Location: OS Ref. NT931 520. 3m off the A1 Berwick-upon-Tweed bypass on B6461.

Open: 1 Apr - 31 Oct: House: 11am - 5pm. Last house tour 4.15pm. Grounds: 10am - sunset. Open to groups/schools all year by appointment.

Admission: Adult £6, Child £3. Groups (pre-arranged, 12+). Adult £5, Child £2.50. Grounds only: Adult £3, Child £1.50.

ℹ️No photography. 📷 🎦 📺Conferences, weddings. 🅰Partial. 🍴 🍽Licensed. 🅵Obligatory. 🅿 📷 ✖In grounds, on leads. ♿ 🐾Tel for details.

SMAILHOLM TOWER
Smailholm, Kelso
Tel: 01573 460365
Owner: In the care of Historic Scotland **Contact:** The Steward
Set on a high rocky knoll this well preserved 16th century tower houses an exhibition of tapestries and costume dolls depicting characters from Sir Walter Scott's Minstrelsy of the Scottish Borders.
Location: OS Ref. NT638 347. Nr Smailholm Village, 6m W of Kelso on B6937.
Open: 1 Apr - 30 Sept: daily, 9.30am - 6.30pm. Last tickets ½ hour before closing.
Admission: Adult £2.20, Child 75p, Conc. £1.60.

€

TRAQUAIR
INNERLEITHEN, PEEBLESSHIRE EH44 6PW

www.traquair.co.uk

Tel: 01896 830323 **Fax:** 01896 830639 **e-mail:** enquiries@traquair.co.uk

Contact: Ms C Maxwell Stuart

Traquair, situated amidst beautiful scenery and close by the River Tweed, is the oldest inhabited house in Scotland - visited by twenty-seven kings. Originally a Royal hunting lodge, it was owned by the Scottish Crown until 1478 when it passed to a branch of the Royal Stuart family whose descendants still live in the house today. Nearly ten centuries of Scottish political and domestic life can be traced from the collection of treasures in the house. It is particularly rich in associations with the Catholic Church in Scotland, Mary Queen of Scots and the Jacobite Risings. There is an 18th century working brewery in one of the wings of the house where the famous Traquair House Ales are produced. Maze, Craft Workshops, Children's Adventure Playground. 1745 cottage restaurant, gift shop, brewshop and museum.

Location: OS Ref. NY330 354. On B709 near junction with A72. Edinburgh 1hr,

Glasgow 1½ hrs, Carlisle 1½ hrs, Newcastle 1½ hrs.

Open: 3 Apr - 31 Oct: daily. House: 3 Apr - 31 May: 12 noon - 5pm; Jun - Aug: 10.30am - 5.30pm (last admission 5pm); Oct: 11am - 4pm. Guided tours outside normal opening times by arrangement (see below).

Admission: House & Grounds: Adult £5.75, Child (under 15yrs) £3.20, OAP £5.30, Family (2+3) £16.75. Grounds only: Adult £2.50, Child (under 15yrs) £1.25. Groups (20+): Adult £5.25, Child £2.50, OAP £5.10. Guided tours (must be booked in advance): £6.25pp (20+); Personal guided tours by Catherine Maxwell Stuart, 21st Lady of Traquair, £10pp; Reception in the High Drawing Room or Dining Room with Traquair or Sherry £4pp, with canapés £5pp, Coffee & shortbread £3.50pp.

No photography in house. Licensed, self-service.
Outside opening hours. Coaches please book. In grounds on leads.
3 en-suites. B&B.

Floors Castle, Kelso, Scotland from the book
Historic Family Homes and Gardens from the Air, see page 54.

Website Information *see front section*

South West Scotland, Dumfries & Galloway, Ayrshire and the Isle of Arran

Christine Ottewill

BLAIRQUHAN CASTLE

MAYBOLE

www.blairquhan.co.uk

Blairquhan is the home of James Hunter Blair, the great-great-grandson of Sir David Hunter Blair, 3rd Baronet for whom it was designed by William Burn and built in 1821-24.

All the Regency furniture bought for the house remains, and the house has not been altered except discreetly to bring it up-to-date. There are ten double bedrooms including four four-poster beds, with en-suite bathrooms, five singles, and many public rooms which can be used for conferences and every sort of occasion.

The Castle is approached by a 3 mile private drive along the River Girvan and is situated in one of the most charming parts of south west Scotland. There is a well-known collection of pictures. It is particularly suitable for conferences because the house is entirely at your disposal.

A five minute walk from the Castle are the walled gardens, laid out around the 1800s and recently replanned and replanted.

Blairquhan is only 50 miles from Glasgow. It is within about half an hour's drive of the world-famous golf courses of Prestwick, Troon and Turnberry, the last two of which are venues for the British Open Golf Championships.

Christine Ottewill

Map 9

Owner:
James Hunter Blair

▶ **CONTACT**

James Hunter Blair
Blairquhan Castle
Maybole
Ayrshire   KA19 7LZ

Tel: 01655 770239
Fax: 01655 770278
e-mail: enquiries@
blairquhan.co.uk

▶ **LOCATION**

OS Ref. NS366 055

From London M6 to Carlisle, A75 to Crocketford, A712 to A713 nr New Galloway, B741 to Straiton, B7045 to Ayr. Turn left ¼ m beyond village. 6m SE of Maybole off B7045.

Rail: Maybole 7m.

Air: Prestwick Airport, 15m. Direct flights to London, Dublin, Paris, Frankfurt, Brussels & Oslo. Executive Travel: contact 01655 882666.

CONFERENCE/FUNCTION

ROOM	SIZE	MAX CAPACITY
Drawing Rms	1200 sq ft	100
Dining Rm	750 sq ft	100
Library	400 sq ft	25
Saloon	600 sq ft	100
Meeting Rm	255 sq ft	50

Tree trail, fashion shows, shooting, equestrian events, garden parties, shows, rallies, filming, grand piano, snooker, fishing. Slide projector, overhead projector, screen, and secretarial assistance for meetings. No photography in castle.

Wedding receptions.

Two main floors suitable. WC.

Teas, lunches, buffets and dinners. Groups can book in advance, special rates for groups.

By arrangement. Also available in French.

Unlimited.

Guide and schoolroom provided, cost negotiable.

10 doubles (4x4-posters) with bathrooms en-suite, 5 singles. The Dower House at Milton has 10 doubles, 1 single, 6 bathrooms. 7 holiday cottages on the Estate.

In grounds on leads.

▶ **OPENING TIMES**

Summer
24 July - 22 August
Daily (except Mons)
1.30 - 4.15pm
(last admission).

Open at all other times by appointment.

Winter
Open by appointment.

▶ **ADMISSION**

House & Garden

Adult	£5.00
Child (6-16yrs)	£3.00
Conc	£4.00

Groups*
Negotiable

* Minimum payment £20.

▶ **SPECIAL EVENTS**

EVENTS EVERY WEEKEND INCLUDING:
Model aeroplane flying
Battle re-enactments
Kite-flying
Highland Dancing
Music

His Grace the Duke of Buccleuch & Queensberry KT

South West Scotland, Dumfries & Galloway, Ayrshire and the Isle of Arran

DRUMLANRIG CASTLE

THORNHILL

www.buccleuch.com

Map 10

Owner: His Grace the Duke of Buccleuch & Queensberry KT

▶ **CONTACT**

Claire Oram
Drumlanrig Castle
Thornhill
Dumfriesshire
DG3 4AQ

Tel: 01848 330248
Fax: 01848 331682

Countryside Service:
01848 331555

e-mail: bre@
drumlanrigcastle.org.uk

▶ **LOCATION**
OS Ref. NX851 992

18m N of Dumfries,
3m NW of Thornhill
off A76.
16m from M74 at
Elvanfoot.
Approx. 1½ hrs
by road from
Edinburgh, Glasgow
and Carlisle.

Drumlanrig Castle, Gardens and Country Park, the home of the Duke of Buccleuch and Queensberry KT was built between 1679 and 1691 by William Douglas, 1st Duke of Queensberry. Drumlanrig is rightly recognised as one of the first and most important buildings in the grand manner in Scottish domestic architecture. James Smith, who made the conversion from a 15th century castle, made a comparable transformation at Dalkeith a decade later.

The Castle, of local pink sandstone, offers superb views across Nithsdale. It houses a renowned art collection, including work by Holbein and Rembrandt, as well as cabinets made for Louis XIV's Versailles, relics of Bonnie Prince Charlie and a 300 year old silver chandelier.

The story of Sir James Douglas, killed in Spain while carrying out the last wish of Robert Bruce, pervades the Castle in the emblem of a winged heart. Douglas family historical exhibition. Working forge. The gardens, now being restored to the plan of 1738, add to the overall effect. The fascination of Drumlanrig as a centre of art, beauty and history is complemented by its role in the Queensberry Estate, a model of dynamic and enlightened land management.

No photography inside the castle.

Suitable. WC. Please enquire about facilities before visit.

Licensed.

Snacks, lunches and teas during opening hours.

P Adjacent to the castle.

Children's quiz and worksheets. Ranger-led activities, including woodlands and forestry. Adventure playground. School groups welcome throughout the year by arrangement.

In grounds on leads.

▶ **OPENING TIMES**
Summer

Castle
9 - 12 April;
1 May - 22 August:
Mon - Sat: 11am - 4pm.
Suns: 12 noon - 4pm.

Country Park, Gardens & Adventure Woodland
9 April - 30 September:
daily, 11am - 5pm.

Winter
By appointment only.

▶ **ADMISSION***

Castle and Country Park
Adult £6.00
Child £2.00
OAP/Student £4.00
Family (2+4) £14.00
Disabled in
wheelchairs............ Free
Pre-booked groups (20+)
Adult £4.00
Child £2.00
Outside normal
opening times........... £8.00

Country Park only
Adult £3.00
Child £2.00
Family (2+4) £8.00

* Half price entry
on Tuesdays.

CONFERENCE/FUNCTION

ROOM	SIZE	MAX CAPACITY
Visitors' Centre	6m x 13m	50

ARDWELL GARDENS
Ardwell, Nr Stranraer, Dumfries and Galloway DG9 9LY

Tel: 01776 860227

Owner: Mr Francis Brewis   **Contact:** Mrs Terry Brewis
The gardens include a formal garden, wild garden and woodland.
Location: OS Ref. NX102 455. A716 10m S of Stranraer.
Open: 1 Apr - 30 Sept: daily, 10am - 5pm.
Admission: Adult £2, Child/Conc. £1.

AUCHINLECK HOUSE
Ochilltree, Ayrshire

Tel: 01628 825920 or 825925   **Fax:** 01628 825417
e-mail: bookings@landmarktrust.co.uk   **www**.landmarktrust.co.uk
Owner/Contact: The Landmark Trust
One of the finest examples of an 18th century Scottish country house, the importance of which is further enhanced by its association with James Boswell, author of *The Life of Samuel Johnson*. The house has been restored by the Landmark Trust and is let for holidays for up to 13 people. Full details of staying at Auchinleck House and 178 other historic buildings are featured in the Landmark Trust Handbook.
Location: OS Ref. NS507 230. Ochilltree, Ayrshire.
Open: Parts of the house will be open to the public Easter - Oct: Wed afternoons. Grounds: dawn - dusk in the Spring & Summer season.
Admission: By appointment only. Tickets £3 from 01628 825920.
⊞In grounds, on leads. ⊞Up to 13 people, self-catering.

BACHELORS' CLUB ♛
Sandgate Street, Tarbolton KA5 5RB

Tel: 01292 541940

Owner: The National Trust for Scotland   **Contact:** The Manager
17th century thatched house in which poet Robert Burns and friends formed a debating society in 1780.
Location: OS Ref. NS430 270. In Tarbolton, B744, 7^1/2 m NE of Ayr, off B743.
Open: 1 Apr - 30 Sep: Fri - Tue, 1 - 5pm. Morning visits for pre-booked groups.
Admission: Adult £2.50, Conc. £1.90, Family £7. Groups: Adult £2, Child/School £1.

BARGANY GARDENS
Girvan, Ayrshire KA26 9QL

Tel: 01465 871249   **Fax:** 01465 871282
Owner/Contact: Mr John Dalrymple Hamilton
Lily pond, rock garden and a fine collection of hard and softwood trees.
Location: OS Ref. NX851 992. 18m N of Dumfries, 3m NW of Thornhill off A76. 16m from M74 at Elvanfoot.
Open: Weekends & Mons in May only, 12 noon - 5pm.
Admission: £2 per head, Child Free. Buses by arrangement.

BLAIRQUHAN CASTLE ⌂   *See page 470 for full page entry.*

BRODICK CASTLE, COUNTRY PARK & GOATFELL ♛
Isle of Arran KA27 8HY   **Tel:** 01770 302202   **Fax:** 01770 302312

Owner: The National Trust for Scotland
Castle built on the site of a Viking fortress with interesting contents.
Location: OS Ref. NX684 509. Off A711/A755, in Kirkcudbright, at 12 High St.
Open: Castle: 1 Apr - 31 Oct: daily 11am - 4.30pm (closes 3.30pm in Oct). Reception Centre, restaurant, shop & walled garden: same dates but open at 10am. Reception Centre also open 1 Nov - 21 Dec: Fri - Sun 10am - 3.30pm. Country Park: All year: daily, 9.30am - sunset.
Admission: Adult £7, Conc. £5.25. Groups: Adult £5.60, Child/School £1, Family £19. Garden & Country Park only: 1 Apr - 31 Oct: Adult £3.50, Conc. £2.60, Family £9.50. Groups: Adult £2.80, Child/School £1; 1 Nov - 31 Mar: Free. Car parking £2.

BROUGHTON HOUSE & GARDEN ♛
High Street, Kirkcudbright DG6 4JX

Tel/Fax: 01557 330437

Owner: The National Trust for Scotland
18th century house which was the home and studio from 1901 - 1933 of the artist E A Hornel, one of the 'Glasgow Boys'.
Location: OS Ref. NX684 509. Off A711 / A755, in Kirkcudbright, at 12 High St.
Open: Garden: 1 Feb - 31 Mar & 1 - 31 Oct: Mon - Fri, 11am - 4pm; 1 Apr - 30 Sep: Mon - Sat, 11am - 5pm, Sun 1 - 5pm (but closed mid - Oct 2004 - 1 Feb 2005). Some restrictions may apply at certain times: please check with property.
Admission: Adult £2, Conc. £1 (honesty box).

BURNS' COTTAGE
Alloway, Ayrshire KA7 4PY

Tel: 01292 441215   **Fax:** 01292 441750   **Contact:** J Manson
Thatched cottage, birthplace of Robert Burns in 1759, with adjacent museum.
Location: OS Ref. NS335 190. 2m SW of Ayr. Two separate sites, 600yds apart.
Open: Apr - Sept: daily, 9.30am - 5.30pm. Oct - Mar: daily 10am - 5pm. Closed 25/26 Dec & 1 Jan.
Admission: Adult £3, Child/OAP £1.50, Family £9.

CAERLAVEROCK CASTLE ⌂
GLENCAPLE, DUMFRIES DG1 4RU

Tel: 01387 770244

Owner: In the care of Historic Scotland   **Contact:** Alec Little
One of the finest castles in Scotland on a triangular site surrounded by moats. Its most remarkable features are the twin-towered gatehouse and the Renaissance Nithsdale lodging. The site of two famous sieges. Children's park, replica siege engines and nature trail to site of earlier castle.
Location: OS84 NY025 656. 8m S of Dumfries on the B725.
Open: Apr - Sept: daily, 9.30am - 6.30pm. Oct - Mar: Mon - Sat, 9.30am - 4.30pm, Suns, 2 - 4.30pm. Last ticket sold 30 mins before closing.
Admission: Adult £4, Child £1, Conc. £3. 10% discount for groups (10+).
⊡ ⌖Partial. WCs. ⏸Limited for coaches. ⬛Free if pre-booked.
⊞In grounds, on leads. ⊛ €

CARDONESS CASTLE ⌂
Gatehouse of Fleet

Tel: 01557 814427

Owner: In the care of Historic Scotland   **Contact:** The Steward
Well preserved ruin of a four storey tower house of 15th century standing on a rocky platform above the Water of Fleet. Ancient home of the McCullochs. Very fine fireplaces.
Location: OS Ref. NX591 553. 1m SW of Gatehouse of Fleet, beside the A75.
Open: 1 Apr - 30 Sept: daily, 9.30am - 6.30pm. Last ticket 6pm. 1 Oct - 31 Mar: Sats, 9.30am - 4.30pm, Suns, 2 - 4.30pm. Last ticket 4pm.
Admission: Adult £2.50, Child 75p, Conc. £1.90.
€

THOMAS CARLYLE'S BIRTHPLACE ♛
Ecclefechan, Dumfriesshire DG11 3DG

Tel: 01576 300666

Owner: The National Trust for Scotland   **Contact:** The Manager
House of Thomas Carlyle, brilliant essayist, historian, social reformer, visionary and literary giant.
Location: OS Ref. NY193 745. Off M74, 6m SE of Lockerbie. In Ecclefechan village.
Open: 1 May - 30 Sep: Thur - Mon, 1 - 5pm.
Admission: Adult £2.50, Conc. £1.90, Family £7. Groups: Adult £2, Child/School £1.

CASTLE KENNEDY GARDENS
Stair Estates, Rephad, Stranraer, Dumfries and Galloway DG9 8BX
Tel: 01776 702024 **Fax:** 01776 706248
Owner: The Earl & Countess of Stair   **Contact:** The Earl of Stair
75 acres of gardens, originally laid out in 1730, includes rhododendrons, pinetum, walled garden and circular lily pond.
Location: OS Ref. NX109 610. 3m E of Stranraer on A75.
Open: Apr - Sept: daily, 10am - 5pm.
Admission: Adult £4, Child £1, OAP £3.

CRAIGDARROCH HOUSE
Moniaive, Dumfriesshire DG3 4JB
Tel: 01848 200202
Owner/Contact: Mr Alexander Sykes
Location: OS Ref. NX741 909. S side of B729, 2m W of Moniaive, 19m WNW of Dumfries.
Open: Jul: daily, 2 - 4pm. Please note: no WCs.
Admission: £2.

CRAIGIEBURN GARDEN
Craigieburn House, Nr Moffat, Dumfriesshire DG10 9LF
Tel: 01683 221250
Owner/Contact: Janet Wheatcroft
A plantsman's garden with a huge range of rare and unusual plants surrounded by natural woodland.
Location: OS Ref. NT117 053. NW side of A708 to Yarrow & Selkirk, 2¹/₂ m E of Moffat.
Open: May - Sept: Sats & Suns (open for charity).
Admission: Adult £2, Child Free.

CROSSRAGUEL ABBEY
Maybole, Strathclyde
Tel: 01655 883113
Owner: In the care of Historic Scotland   **Contact:** The Steward
Founded in the early 13th century by the Earl of Carrick. Remarkably complete remains include church, cloister, chapter house and much of the domestic premises.
Location: OS Ref. NS275 083. 2m S of Maybole on the A77.
Open: 1 Apr - 30 Sept: daily, 9.30am - 6.30m. Last ticket 6pm.
Admission: Adult £2.20, Child 75p, Conc. £1.60.
€

CULZEAN CASTLE & COUNTRY PARK
Maybole KA19 8LE
Tel: 01655 884455 **Fax:** 01655 884503
Owner: The National Trust for Scotland
Romantic 18th century Robert Adam clifftop mansion with adjacent Country Park.
Location: OS Ref. NS240 100. 12m SW of Ayr, on A719, 4m W of Maybole.
Open: Castle: 1 Apr - 31 Oct: daily, 10.30am - 5pm; 1 Nov - 21 Dec: Sun, 11am - 4pm. Visitor Centre: 1 Apr - 31 Oct: daily, 9am - 5pm; 1 Nov - 31 Mar: Sat/Sun, 11am - 4pm. Other visitor facilities: 1 Apr - 31 Oct: daily, 10.30am - 5.30pm. Country Park: All year: daily, 9.30am - sunset.
Admission: Combined Ticket: Adult £9, Conc. £6.50, Family £23. Groups: Adult £7, Country Park only, 1 Apr - 31 Oct: Adult £5, Conc. £3.75, Family £13.50. Groups: Adult £4, Child/School £1. 1 Nov - 31 Mar: Free. Car parking £2.

DALGARVEN MILL MUSEUM
Dalgarven, Dalry Road, Nr Kilwinning, Ayrshire KA13 6PL
Tel/Fax: 01294 552448 **e-mail:** admin@dalgarvenmill.org.uk
Owner: Dalgarven Mill Trust   **Contact:** The Administrator
Museum of Ayrshire Country Life and Costume.
Location: OS Ref. NS295 460. On A737 2m from Kilwinning.
Open: All year: Summer: Easter - end Oct: Tue - Sat, 10am - 5pm. Suns, 11am - 5pm. Winter: Tue - Sat, 10am - 4pm. Suns, 11am - 5pm. Closed Mons.
Admission: Charges.

DEAN CASTLE COUNTRY PARK
Dean Road, Kilmarnock, East Ayrshire KA3 1XB
Tel: 01563 522702 **Fax:** 01563 572552
Owner: East Ayrshire Council   **Contact:** Andrew Scott-Martin
Set in 200 acres of Country Park. Visits to castle by guided tour only.
Location: OS Ref. NS437 395. Off A77. 1¹/₄ m NNE of town centre.
Open: Country Park & Visitor Centre: All year. Castle: Easter - end Oct: daily, 12 noon - 5pm (last tour 4.15pm). Oct - Easter: weekends only, 12 noon - 4pm (last tour 3.15pm).
Admission: Free (group charge on application). Conducted tours.

DRUMLANRIG CASTLE 🏛
See page 471 for full page entry.

DUNDRENNAN ABBEY
Kirkcudbright
Tel: 01557 500262
Owner: Historic Scotland   **Contact:** The Steward
Mary Queen of Scots spent her last night on Scottish soil in this 12th century Cistercian Abbey founded by David I. The Abbey stands in a small and secluded valley.
Location: OS Ref. NX749 4750. 6¹/₂ m SE of Kirkcudbright on the A711.
Open: 1 Apr - 30 Sept: daily, 9.30am - 6.30pm. Last ticket 6pm. 1 Oct - 31 Mar: Sats, 9.30am - 4.30pm, Suns, 2 - 4.30pm.
Admission: Adult £2, Child 75p, Conc. £1.50.
€

GILNOCKIE TOWER
Hollows, Canonbie, Dumfriesshire
Tel: 01387 371876 **e-mail:** tedarmclan@aol.com
Owner/Contact: Edward Armstrong
16th century tower house, occupied by the Clan Armstrong Centre.
Location: OS Ref. NY383 787. 2m N of Canonbie on minor road E of A7 just N of Hollows.
Open: Summer months by guided tour at 2.30pm sharp (1 tour daily). Winter months open by appointment. Tours to be booked in advance by telephone.
Admission: Adult £3, Child (under 14yrs) £1.50.

GLENLUCE ABBEY
Glenluce
Tel: 01581 300541
Owner/Contact: In the care of Historic Scotland
A Cistercian Abbey founded in 1190. Remains include a 16th century Chapter House.
Location: OS Ref. NX185 587. 2m NW of Glenluce village off the A75.
Open: 1 Apr - 30 Sept: daily 9.30am - 6.30pm. Last ticket 6pm. 1 Oct - 31 Mar: Sats, 9.30am - 4.30pm, Suns, 2 - 4.30pm. Last ticket 4pm.
Admission: Adult £2, Child 75p, Conc. £1.50.
€

GLENWHAN GARDENS
Dunragit, Stranraer, Wigtownshire DG9 8PH
Tel/Fax: 01581 400222   **Contact:** Tessa Knott
Beautiful 12 acre garden overlooking Luce Bay and the Mull of Galloway. Licensed tearoom, groups catered for.
Location: OS Ref. NX150 580. N side of A75, 6m E of Stranraer.
Open: 1 Apr - 30 Sept: daily, 10am - 5pm or by appointment at other times.
Admission: Adult £3.50, Child £1, Conc. £3.

KELBURN CASTLE & COUNTRY CENTRE

FAIRLIE, BY LARGS, AYRSHIRE KA29 0BE

www.kelburncountrycentre.com

For Country Park and Castle tours:- Earl of Glasgow
Tel: 01475 568685　　**Fax:** 01475 568121　　**e-mail:** admin@kelburncountrycentre.com
For functions in the Castle:- Countess of Glasgow
Tel: 01475 568204　　**e-mail:** isabelglasgow@aol.com
Owner/Contact: The Earl of Glasgow
Kelburn is the home of the Earls of Glasgow and has been in the Boyle family for over 800 years. It is notable for its waterfalls, historic family gardens, romantic glen and unique trees, including two of the hundred most important in Scotland, and its outstanding views over the Firth of Clyde.
The Country Centre includes exhibitions, craft shop, licensed café, riding school, pottery workshop, stockade, adventure course, pet's corner and Scotland's most

unusual attraction – The Secret Forest. The Castle is open for guided tours in July and August and available for weddings, conferences, dinner parties and other functions all the year round.
Location: OS Ref NS210 580. A78 to Largs, 2m S of Largs.
Open: Country Centre: Easter - October: daily. Castle: July & Aug. Open by arrangement for groups at other times of the year.
Admission: Castle: Adult: £1.75, plus entrance fee to Country Centre: Adult £5, Conc. £3.50, Groups (10+): Adult: £3.50, Conc. £2.50, Family (2+3) £15.
⬛ 🔻 ♿ Partial. 🐕 🍴 Licensed.
✗ July & August. By arrangement at other times of the year. 🅿 ⬛
🐕 In grounds on leads. ✳

LOGAN BOTANIC GARDEN
Port Logan, Stranraer, Wigtownshire DG9 9ND
Tel: 01776 860231　**Fax:** 01776 860333　**e-mail:** logan@rbge.org.uk
Owner: Royal Botanic Garden Edinburgh　　　**Contact:** The Curator
Scotland's most exotic garden. Take a trip to the south west of Scotland and experience the southern hemisphere!
Location: OS Ref. NX097 430. 14m S of Stranraer on B7065, off A716.
Open: 1 Mar - 31 Oct: daily, 10am - 5pm (Apr - Sept: closes 6pm).
Admission: Adult £3.50, Child £1, Conc. £3, Family £8. Group discount and membership programme available.

MACLELLAN'S CASTLE
Kirkcudbright
Tel: 01557 331856
Owner: In the care of Historic Scotland　　　**Contact:** The Steward
Castellated mansion, built in 1577 using stone from an adjoining ruined monastery by the then Provost. Elaborately planned with fine architectural details, it has been a ruin since 1752.
Location: OS Ref. NX683 511. Centre of Kirkcudbright on the A711.
Open: 1 Apr - 30 Sept: daily, 9.30am - 6.30pm. Last ticket 6pm.
Admission: Adult £2.20, Child 75p, Conc. £1.60.
€

NEW ABBEY CORN MILL
New Abbey Village
Tel: 01387 850260
Owner: Historic Scotland　　　**Contact:** The Custodian
This carefully renovated 18th century water-powered oatmeal mill is in full working order and regular demonstrations are given for visitors in the summer.
Location: OS Ref. NX962 663. 8m S of Dumfries on the A710. Close to Sweetheart Abbey.
Open: 1 Apr - 30 Sept: daily, 9.30am - 6.30pm. Last ticket 6pm. 1 Oct - 31 Mar: Mon - Wed & Sat, 9.30am - 4.30pm, Thurs, 9.30am - 12 noon, Fris closed, Suns, 2 - 4.30pm. Last ticket 4pm.
Admission: Adult £3, Child £1, Conc. £2.30. Joint entry ticket with Sweetheart Abbey: Adult £3.50, Child £1.20, Conc. £2.50.
€

Harold Peto
1854-1933
An Edwardian architect who loved the formal gardens of Italy. Look for wide terraces, colonnades, statuary, and evergreen planting schemes.
Visit Peto's own garden at Iford Manor, Wiltshire.

Architect & Gardener

RAMMERSCALES
Lockerbie, Dumfriesshire DG11 1LD
Tel: 01387 810229　**Fax:** 01387 810940
Owner/Contact: Mr M A Bell Macdonald
Georgian house.
Location: OS Ref. NY080 780. W side of B7020, 3m S of Lochmoben.
Open: Last week in Jul, 1st three weeks in Aug: daily (excluding Sats), 2 - 5pm.
Admission: Adult £5, Conc. £2.50.

SORN CASTLE

Ayrshire KA5 6HR

Tel: 01290 551555

Owner/Contact: Mrs R G McIntyre

Dating from the 14th century, the Castle stands on a cliff overlooking the River Ayr, surrounded by wooded grounds. It has been enlarged throughout the centuries, most recently in 1908. Sorn contains many fine Scottish paintings and artifacts.

Location: OS Ref. NS555 265. 4m E of Mauchline on B743.

Open: 17 Jul - 14 Aug: daily, 2 - 4pm and by appointment.

Admission: Adult £4.

SOUTER JOHNNIE'S COTTAGE

Main Road, Kirkoswald KA19 8HY

Tel: 01655 760603

Owner: The National Trust for Scotland

Home of John Davidson, original 'Souter' (cobbler) of Robert Burns' famous narrative poem *Tam O' Shanter*.

Location: OS Ref. NS240 070. On A77, in Kirkoswald village, 4m SW of Maybole.

Open: 1 Apr - 30 Sep: Fri - Tue, 11.30am - 5pm.

Admission: Adult £2.50, Conc. £1.90, Family £7. Groups: Adult £2, Child/School £1.

STRANRAER CASTLE

Stranraer, Galloway

Tel: 01776 705088   **Fax:** 01776 705835

Owner: Dumfries & Galloway Council   **Contact:** John Pickin

Also referred to as the Castle of St John. A much altered 16th century L-plan tower house, now a museum.

Location: OS Ref. NX061 608. In Stranraer, towards centre, 1/4 m short of the harbour.

Open: Easter - mid-Sept: Mon - Sat, 10am - 1pm & 2 - 5pm.

Admission: Free.

SWEETHEART ABBEY

New Abbey Village

Tel: 01387 850397

Owner: In the care of Historic Scotland   **Contact:** The Steward

Cistercian abbey founded in 1273 by Devorgilla, in memory of her husband John Balliol. A principal feature is the well-preserved precinct wall enclosing 30 acres.

Location: OS Ref. NX965 663. In New Abbey Village, on A710 8m S of Dumfries.

Open: 1 Apr - 30 Sept: daily, 9.30am - 6.30pm. Last ticket 6pm. 1 Oct - 31 Mar: Mon - Wed & Sat, 9.30am - 4.30pm, Thurs, 9.30am - 12 noon, Fris closed, Suns, 2 - 4.30pm. Last ticket 4pm.

Admission: Adult £2, Child 75p, Conc. £1.50. Joint entry ticket with New Abbey Corn Mill: Adult £3.50, Child £1.20, Conc. £2.50.

€

THREAVE CASTLE

Castle Douglas

Tel: 07711 223101

Owner: The National Trust for Scotland   **Contact:** Historic Scotland

Built by Archibald the Grim in the late 14th century, early stronghold of the Black Douglases. Around its base is an artillery fortification built before 1455 when the castle was besieged by James II. Ring the bell and the custodian will come to ferry you over. Long walk to property. Owned by The National Trust for Scotland but under the guardianship of Historic Scotland.

Location: OS Ref. NX739 623. 2m W of Castle Douglas on the A75.

Open: 1 Apr - 30 Sept: daily, 9.30am - 6.30pm. Last ticket 6pm.

Admission: Adult £2.50, Child 75p, Conc. £1.90. Charges include ferry trip.

€

THREAVE GARDEN & ESTATE

Castle Douglas DG7 1RX

Tel: 01556 502575   **Fax:** 01556 502683

Owner: The National Trust for Scotland

The garden has a wide range of features and a good collection of plants. There are peat and woodland garden plants and a colourful rock garden. A garden for all seasons.

Location: OS Ref. NX752 605. Off A75, 1m SW of Castle Douglas.

Open: Estate & garden, All year:, daily, 9.30am - sunset. Walled garden & glasshouses: All year: daily 9.30am - 5pm. Visitor Centre, Countryside Centre & exhibition: 1 Feb - 31 Mar & 1 Nov - 23 Dec: daily, 10am - 4pm; 1 Apr - 31 Oct: daily 9.30am - 5.30pm. House: 1 Mar - 31 Oct: Wed - Fri & Sun, 11am - 4 pm (guided tours only, admission by timed ticket).

Admission: House & garden: Adult £9, Conc. £6.50, Family £23. Groups: Adult £7, Child/School £1. Garden only: Adult £5, Conc. £3.75, Family £13.50. Groups: Adult £4, Child/School £1.

WHITHORN PRIORY

Whithorn

Tel: 01988 500508

Owner: In the care of Historic Scotland   **Contact:** The Project Manager

The site of the first Christian church in Scotland. Founded as 'Candida Casa' by St Ninian in the early 5th century it later became the cathedral church of Galloway.

Location: OS Ref. NX445 403. At Whithorn on the A746. 18m S of Newton Stewart.

Open: Please telephone for details.

Admission: Joint ticket gives entry to Priory, Priory Museum and archaeological dig.

Caerlaverock, Dumfrieshire.

Historic Scotland

Map 10

DALMENY HOUSE

SOUTH QUEENSFERRY

www.dalmeny.co.uk

Dalmeny House rejoices in one of the most beautiful and unspoilt settings in Great Britain, yet it is only seven miles from Scotland's capital, Edinburgh, fifteen minutes from Edinburgh airport and less than an hour's drive from Glasgow. It is an eminently suitable venue for group visits, business functions, meetings and special events, including product launches. Outdoor activities, such as off-road driving, can be arranged.

Dalmeny House, the family home of the Earls of Rosebery for over 300 years, boasts superb collections of porcelain and tapestries, fine paintings by Gainsborough, Raeburn, Reynolds and Lawrence, together with the exquisite Mentmore Rothschild collection of 18th century French furniture. There is also the Napoleonic collection, assembled by the 5th Earl of Rosebery, Prime Minister, historian and owner of three Derby winners.

The Hall, Library and Dining Room will lend a memorable sense of occasion to corporate receptions, luncheons and dinners. A wide range of entertainment can also be provided, from a clarsach player to a floodlit pipe band Beating the Retreat.

Owner:
The Earl of Rosebery

▶ CONTACT

The Administrator
Dalmeny House
South Queensferry
Edinburgh
EH30 9TQ

Tel: 0131 331 1888
Fax: 0131 331 1788

e-mail: events@
dalmeny.co.uk

▶ LOCATION
OS Ref. NT167 779

From Edinburgh A90,
B924, 7m N, A90 ½ m.

On south shore
of Firth of Forth.

Bus: From St Andrew
Square to Chapel Gate
1m from House.

Rail: Dalmeny
station 3m.

Taxi: Queensferry Fare
Radio Cabs
0131 331 1041.

▶ OPENING TIMES
Summer
July and August
Sun - Tue, 2 - 5.30pm.
Last admission 4.30pm.

Winter
Open at other times by
appointment only.

▶ ADMISSION
Summer

Adult	£5.00
Child (10-16yrs)	£3.00
OAP	£4.00
Student	£4.00
Groups (20+)	£4.00

ℹ️ Fashion shows, product launches, archery, clay pigeon shooting, shows, filming, background photography, small meetings and special events. Lectures on House, contents and family history. Helicopter landing area. House is centre of a 4½ m shore walk from Forth Rail Bridge to small foot passenger ferry at Cramond (ferry 9am - 1pm, 2 - 7pm in summer, 2 - 4pm winter, closed Fri). No fires, picnics or photography.

🍽️ Conferences and functions, buffets, lunches, dinners.

♿ Partially suitable. Visitors may alight at entrance. WC.

☕ Teas, groups can book in advance.

🚶 Obligatory. Special interest tours can be arranged outside normal opening hours.

🅿️ 60 cars, 3 coaches. Parking for functions in front of house.

Map 10

Owner:
Hopetoun House
Preservation Trust

▶ **CONTACT**

Mhairi MacDougall
Hopetoun House
South Queensferry
Edinburgh
West Lothian
EH30 9SL

Tel: 0131 331 2451
Fax: 0131 319 1885

e-mail: marketing@
hopetounhouse.com

▶ **LOCATION**
OS Ref. NT089 790

2¹/₂ m W of Forth Road
Bridge.

12m W of Edinburgh
(25 mins. drive).

34m E of Glasgow
(50 mins. drive).

HOPETOUN HOUSE 🏛
Edinburgh

www.hopetounhouse.com

Hopetoun House is a unique gem of Europe's architectural heritage and undoubtedly 'Scotland's Finest Stately Home'. Situated on the shores of the Firth of Forth, it is one of the most splendid examples of the work of Scottish architects Sir William Bruce and William Adam. The interior of the house, with opulent gilding and classical motifs, reflects the aristocratic grandeur of the early 18th century, whilst its magnificent parkland has fine views across the Forth to the hills of Fife. The house is approached from the Royal Drive, used only by members of the Royal Family, notably King George IV in 1822 and Her Majesty Queen Elizabeth II in 1988.

Hopetoun is really two houses in one, the oldest part of the house was designed by Sir William Bruce and built between 1699 and

1707. It shows some of the finest examples in Scotland of carving, wainscotting and ceiling painting. In 1721 William Adam started enlarging the house by adding the magnificent façade, colonnades and grand State apartments which were the focus for social life and entertainment in the 18th century.

The house is set in 100 acres of rolling parkland including fine woodland walks, the red deer park, the spring garden with a profusion of wild flowers, and numerous picturesque picnic spots.

Hopetoun has been home of the Earls of Hopetoun, later created Marquesses of Linlithgow, since it was built in 1699 and in 1974 a charitable trust was created to preserve the house with its historic contents and surrounding landscape for the benefit of the public for all time.

▶ **OPENING TIMES**
Summer
9 April - 26 September:
Daily, 10am - 5.30pm.
Last admission 4.30pm.

Winter
By appointment only
for groups of 15+.

▶ **ADMISSION**
House & Grounds
Adult £6.50
Child (5-16yrs)* £3.50
Conc/Student £5.50
Family (2+2) £18.00
Additional Child £2.00
Groups £5.50ppß

School Visits
Child £4.50
Teachers .... Free

*Under 5yrs Free.

Winter prices on request.

Admission to Adam Stables
Tearoom Free.

📷 ℹ️ Private functions, special events, antiques fairs, concerts, Scottish gala evenings, conferences, wedding ceremonies and receptions, grand piano, helicopter landing. No smoking or flash photography in house.

🍸 Receptions, gala dinners.

♿ Licensed.

🍽 Licensed. Groups (up to 250) can book in advance, menus on request tel: 0131 331 4305.

🚶 By arrangement.

🅿 Close to the house for cars and coaches. Book if possible, allow 1-2hrs for visit (min).

👥 Special tours of house and/or grounds for different age/ interest groups.

🐕 No dogs in house, on leads in grounds.
❄

CONFERENCE/FUNCTION

ROOM	SIZE	MAX CAPACITY
Ballroom	92' x 35'	300
Tapestry Rm	37' x 24'	100
Red Drawing Rm	44' x 24'	100
State Dining Rm	39' x 23'	20
Stables	92' x 22'	200

PALACE OF HOLYROODHOUSE
& THE QUEEN'S GALLERY
EDINBURGH
www.royal.gov.uk

Map 10

Owner:
Official Residence of
Her Majesty The Queen

▶ **CONTACT**
Ticket Sales &
Information Office
Official Residences of
The Queen
London SW1A 1AA

Tel: 0131 556 5100
Fax: 020 7930 9625
e-mail: information@
royalcollection.org.uk

▶ **LOCATION**
OS Ref. NT269 739

Central Edinburgh,
end of Royal Mile.

The Palace of Holyroodhouse, the official residence in Scotland of Her Majesty The Queen, stands at the end of Edinburgh's Royal Mile against the spectacular backdrop of Arthur's Seat. This fine baroque palace is closely associated with Scotland's rich history. Today the Royal Apartments are used by The Queen for State ceremonies and official entertaining. They are finely decorated with magnificent works of art from the Royal Collection.

The Palace is perhaps best known as the home of Mary, Queen of Scots, and was the setting for many dramatic episodes in her short and turbulent reign. Mary, Queen of Scots' chambers are housed in the Palace's west corner tower and are approached up a small winding staircase. These intimate apartments were home to Mary following her return from France in 1561.

The Queen's Gallery, Palace of Holyroodhouse
opened in November 2002 as part of Her Majesty The Queen's Golden Jubilee celebrations. The new Gallery provides purpose-built facilities and state-of-the-art environmental controls, which enable exhibitions of the most delicate works from the Royal Collection to be shown.

King of the World: The Padshahnama, an Imperial Mughal Manuscript (until 3 May 2004.)

The jewel-like manuscript known as the *Padshahnama*, or *Chronicle of the King of the World*, is among the greatest treasures of the Royal Collection and ranks as one of the finest examples of Mughal art. It forms an official record of the first ten years of the reign of Shah-Jahan, fifth Mughal emperor and builder of the Taj Mahal.

Enchanting the Eye: Dutch Paintings of the Golden Age (15 May - 7 November 2004.)

The Royal Collection contains one of the world's finest groups of Dutch 17th-century paintings. Among the most enduringly popular images in Western art, these pictures have for centuries been admired for their masterful compositions, close observation of detail, subtle light effects and meticulous finish. The 51 outstanding examples selected for the exhibition include works by Rembrandt, Vermeer, Cuyp and de Hooch.

▶ **OPENING TIMES**
Palace of Holyroodhouse
April - October:
Daily (closed 9 April),
9.30am - 6pm,
last admission 5.15pm.

November - March:
Daily (closed 25/26
December),
9.30am - 4.30pm,
last admission 3.45pm.

Closed during Royal visits.
Opening times are subject
to change at short notice.
Please check before
planning a visit.

The Queen's Gallery
Open daily, except 9 April,
4 - 13 May, 8 - 18 November
& 25/26 December, opening
times as Palace.

Each exhibition is priced
separately. Entry by timed
ticket.

▶ **ADMISSION**
(Price incl. Audio tours)
Adult £8.00
Child (under 17yrs).... £4.00
Child (under 5yrs) ...... Free
OAP/Student £6.50
Family (2+3) £20.00

Groups (15+) discounts
available.

Note: A combined Palace &
Gallery ticket is available.

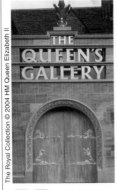

📷 ♿ Please book in advance. 🎧 Palace. 🅿 ▪ 🐕 Guide dogs only. ❄

AMISFIELD MAINS

Nr Haddington, East Lothian EH41 3SA

Tel: 01875 870201 **Fax:** 01875 870620

Owner: Wemyss and March Estates Management Co Ltd **Contact:** M Andrews

Georgian farmhouse with gothic barn and cottage.

Location: OS Ref. NT526 755. Between Haddington and East Linton on A1 Edinburgh-Dunbar Road.

Open: Exterior only: By appointment, Wemyss and March Estates Office, Longniddry, East Lothian EH32 0PY.

Admission: Please contact for details.

ARNISTON HOUSE

GOREBRIDGE, MIDLOTHIAN EH23 4RY

www.arniston-house.co.uk

Tel/Fax: 01875 830515 **e-mail:** henrietta.d.bekker2@btinternet.com

Owner: Mrs A Dundas-Bekker **Contact:** Miss H Dundas-Bekker

Magnificent William Adam mansion started in 1726. Fine plasterwork, Scottish portraiture, period furniture and other fascinating contents. Beautiful country setting beloved by Sir Walter Scott.

Location: OS Ref. NT326 595. Off B6372, 1m from A7, Temple direction.

Open: Apr, May & Jun: Tue & Wed; 1 Jul - 12 Sept: Mon - Fri & Sun, guided tours at 2pm & 3.30pm. Pre-arranged groups (10-50) accepted throughout the rest of the year.

Admission: Adult £5, Child £2, Conc. £4.

No inside photography. WC. Obligatory. In grounds, on leads.

BEANSTON

Nr Haddington, East Lothian EH41 3SB

Tel: 01875 870201 **Fax:** 01875 870620

Owner: Wemyss and March Estates Management Co Ltd **Contact:** M Andrews

Georgian farmhouse with Georgian orangery.

Location: OS Ref. NT546 763. Between Haddington and East Linton on A1 Edinburgh-Dunbar Road.

Open: Exterior only: By appointment, Wemyss and March Estates Office, Longniddry, East Lothian EH32 0PY.

Admission: Please contact for details.

BLACKNESS CASTLE

Blackness

Tel: 01506 834807

Owner: In the care of Historic Scotland **Contact:** The Steward

One of Scotland's most important strongholds. Built in the 14th century and massively strengthened in the 16th century as an artillery fortress, it has been a Royal castle and a prison armaments depot and film location for *Hamlet*. It was restored by the Office of Works in the 1920s. It stands on a promontory in the Firth of Forth.

Location: OS Ref. NT055 803. 4m NE of Linlithgow on the Firth of Forth, off the A904.

Open: 1 Apr - 30 Sept: daily, 9.30am - 6.30pm, last ticket 6pm. 1 Oct - 31 Mar: Mon - Sat, 9.30am - 4.30pm, last ticket 4pm. Closed Thur pm, Fri & Sun in winter.

Admission: Adult £2.50, Child 75p, Conc. £1.90.

€

CRAIGMILLAR CASTLE

Edinburgh

Tel: 0131 661 4445

Owner: In the care of Historic Scotland **Contact:** The Steward

Mary Queen of Scots fled to Craigmillar after the murder of Rizzio. This handsome structure with courtyard and gardens covers an area of one and a quarter acres. Built around an L-plan tower house of the early 15th century including a range of private rooms linked to the hall of the old tower.

Location: OS Ref. NT285 710. 2½ m SE of Edinburgh off the A68.

Open: 1 Apr - 30 Sept: daily, 9.30am - 6.30pm, last ticket 6pm. 1 Oct - 31 Mar: Mon - Sat, 9.30am - 4.30pm, Suns, 2 - 4.30pm, last ticket 4pm. Closed Thur pm & Fri in winter.

Admission: Adult £2.50, Child 75p, Conc. £1.90.

€

CRICHTON CASTLE

Pathhead

Tel: 01875 320017

Owner: In the care of Historic Scotland **Contact:** The Steward

A large and sophisticated castle with a spectacular façade of faceted stonework in an Italian style added by the Earl of Bothwell between 1581 and 1591 following a visit to Italy. Mary Queen of Scots attended a wedding here.

Location: OS Ref. NT380 612. 2½ m SSW of Pathhead off the A68.

Open: 1 Apr - 30 Sept: daily, 9.30am - 6.30pm, last ticket 6pm.

Admission: Adult £2.20, Child 75p, Conc. £1.60.

€

DALMENY HOUSE

See page 476 for full page entry.

DIRLETON CASTLE & GARDEN

DIRLETON, EAST LOTHIAN EH39 5ER

Tel: 01620 850330

Owner: In the care of Historic Scotland **Contact:** The Steward

The oldest part of this romantic castle dates from the 13th century, when it was built by the De Vaux family. The renowned gardens, first laid out in the 16th century, now include a magnificent Arts and Crafts herbaceous border (the longest in the world) and a re-created Victorian Garden. In the picturesque village of Dirleton.

Location: OS Ref. NT516 839. In Dirleton, 2m W of North Berwick on the A198.

Open: Apr - Sept: daily, 9.30am - 6.30pm. Oct - Mar: Mon - Sat, 9.30am - 4.30pm, Suns, 2 - 4.30pm. Last ticket 30 mins before closing.

Admission: Adult £3, Child £1, Conc. £2.30. 10% discount for groups (10+).

Partially. Free if booked. Guide dogs only. €

DUNGLASS COLLEGIATE CHURCH 🏛

Cockburnspath

Tel: 0131 668 8800

Owner: In the care of Historic Scotland

Founded in 1450 for a college of canons by Sir Alexander Hume. A handsome cross-shaped building with vaulted nave, choir and transepts.

Location: OS67 NT766 718. 1m NW of Cockburnspath. SW of A1.

Open: All year.

Admission: Free.

Historic Scotland.

EDINBURGH CASTLE 🏛

CASTLEHILL, EDINBURGH EH1 2NG

Tel: 0131 225 9846   **Fax:** 0131 220 4733

Owner: Historic Scotland   **Contact:** Barbara Smith

Scotland's most famous castle, dominating the capital's skyline and giving stunning views of the city and countryside. Home to the Scottish crown jewels, the Stone of Destiny and Mons Meg. Other highlights include St Margaret's Chapel, the Great Hall and the Scottish National War Memorial.

Location: OS Ref. NT252 736. At the top of the Royal Mile in Edinburgh.

Open: Apr - Sept: daily, 9.30am - 6pm. Oct - Mar: daily, 9.30am - 5pm. Last ticket 45 mins before closing.

Admission: Adult £9.50, Child £2, Conc. £7. Pre-booked school visits available free, except May - Aug.

🖼 📅 Private evening hire. ♿ Partial. WCs. Courtesy vehicle. 🍴 Licensed. 🛍 🎁 🎧 In 6 languages. 🅿 Ample (except Jun-Oct). ▨ 🐕 Guide dogs. ✳ €

THE GEORGIAN HOUSE ♛

7 Charlotte Square, Edinburgh EH2 4DR

Tel: 0131 226 3318

Owner: The National Trust for Scotland

A splendid example of the neo-classical 'palace front'. Three floors are delightfully furnished as they would have been around 1796. There is an array of china and silver, pictures and furniture, gadgets and utensils.

Location: OS Ref. NT045 608. Off B7008, 2^1/$_2$ m S of A71. 2m N of A70. 20m SW of Edinburgh.

Open: House & Shop: 1 - 31 Mar and 1 Nov - 24 Dec: daily 11am - 3pm; 1 Apr - 31 Oct: daily, 10am - 5pm.

Admission: Adult £5, Conc. £3.75, Family £13.50. Groups: Adult £4, Child/School £1.

GLADSTONE'S LAND ♛

477b Lawnmarket, Royal Mile, Edinburgh EH1 2NT

Tel: 0131 226 5856   **Fax:** 0131 226 4851

Owner: The National Trust for Scotland

Gladstone's Land was the home of a prosperous Edinburgh merchant in the 17th century. It is decorated and furnished with great authenticity to give visitors an impression of life in Edinburgh's Old Town some 300 years ago.

Location: OS Ref. NT255 736. In Edinburgh's Royal Mile, near the castle.

Open: 1 Apr - 31 Oct: Mon - Sat, 10am - 5pm, Sun, 2 - 5pm.

Admission: Adult £3.50, Conc. £2.60, Family £9.50. Groups: Adult £2.80, Child/School £1.

GOSFORD HOUSE 🏛

LONGNIDDRY, EAST LOTHIAN EH32 0PX

Tel: 01875 870201   **Owner/Contact:** The Earl of Wemyss

Though the core of the house is Robert Adam, the family home is in the South Wing built by William Young in 1890. This contains the celebrated Marble Hall and a fine collection of paintings and works of art. The house is set in extensive policies with an 18th century Pleasure Garden and Ponds. Greylag geese and swans abound.

Location: OS Ref. NT453 786. Off A198 2m NE of Longniddry.

Open: 17 June then 18 June - 8 Aug (inclusive): Fri - Sun, 2 - 5pm.

Admission: Adult £5, Child £1.

🅿 🐕 In grounds, on leads.

GREYWALLS 🏛

MUIRFIELD, GULLANE, EAST LOTHIAN EH31 2EG

www.greywalls.co.uk

Tel: 01620 842144   **Fax:** 01620 842241   **e-mail:** hotel@greywalls.co.uk

Owner: Giles Weaver   **Contact:** Mrs Sue Prime

Stunning Edwardian Country House Hotel only 30 minutes from the centre of Edinburgh. Close to wonderful golf courses and beaches. Designed by Sir Edwin Lutyens with secluded walled gardens attributed to Gertrude Jekyll. Greywalls offers the delights of an award-winning menu and an excellent wine list in this charming and relaxed environment (non residents welcome).

Location: OS Ref. NT490 835. Off A198, 5m W of North Berwick, 30 mins from Edinburgh.

Open: Apr - Oct.

📅 🍴 ♿

HAILES CASTLE

East Linton

Tel: 0131 668 8800

Owner: In the care of Historic Scotland

Beautifully-sited ruin incorporating a fortified manor of the 13th century. It was extended in the 14th and 15th centuries. There are two vaulted pit prisons.

Location: OS Ref. NT575 758. 1½ m SW of East Linton. 4m E of Haddington. S of A1.

Open: All year.

Admission: Free.

HARELAW FARMHOUSE

Nr Longniddry, East Lothian EH32 0PH

Tel: 01875 870201 **Fax:** 01875 870620

Owner: Wemyss and March Estates Management Co Ltd   **Contact:** M Andrew

Early 19th century 2-storey farmhouse built as an integral part of the steading. Dovecote over entrance arch.

Location: OS Ref. NT450 766. Between Longniddry and Drem on B1377.

Open: Exteriors only: By appointment, Wemyss and March Estates Office, Longniddry, East Lothian EH32 0PY.

Admission: Please contact for details.

HOPETOUN HOUSE ⌂

See page 477 for full page entry.

HOUSE OF THE BINNS ⚘

Linlithgow, West Lothian EH49 7NA

Tel: 01506 834255

Owner: The National Trust for Scotland

17th century house, home of the Dalyells, one of Scotland's great families, since 1612. Here in 1681, General Tam Dalyell raised the Royal Scots Greys Regiment, named after the colour of their uniforms.

Location: OS Ref. NT051 786. Off A904, 15m W of Edinburgh. 3m E of Linlithgow.

Open: House: 1 Jun - 30 Sep: daily except Fri, 2 - 5pm. Parkland: 1 Apr - 31 Oct: daily, 10am - 7pm; 1 Nov - 31 Mar: daily, 10am - 4pm.

Admission: House & Parkland: Adult £5, Conc. £3.75, Family £13.50. Groups: Adult £4, Child/School £1. Group visits must be booked. Members of the Royal Scots Dragoon Guards admitted Free.

INVERESK LODGE GARDEN ⚘

24 Inveresk Village, Musselburgh, East Lothian EH21 7TE

Tel: 01721 722502 **Fax:** 01721 724700

Owner: The National Trust for Scotland

Small garden in grounds of 17th century house, with large selection of plants. House closed.

Location: OS Ref. NT348 718. A6124, S of Musselburgh, 6m E of Edinburgh.

Open: All year: daily, 10am - 6pm or dusk if earlier. House not open.

Admission: Adult £2, Conc. £1 (honesty box).

Ha-Ha

A man-made boundary formed of a deep ditch at the edge of the garden to prevent livestock coming into the garden and creating an uninterrupted view merging garden with park. Apparently got its name 'ha-ha' from the surprise it caused unsuspecting visitors!

Garden Jargon

Baroque Architects

Nicholas Hawksmoor 1661-1736

Sir John Vanburgh 1664-1726

Thomas Archer 1668-1743

Baroque Architects

LENNOXLOVE HOUSE ⌂

HADDINGTON, EAST LOTHIAN EH41 4NZ

www.lennoxlove.com

Tel: 01620 823720 **Fax:** 01620 825112 **e-mail:** enquiries@lennoxlove.com

Owner: Lennoxlove House Ltd   **Contact:** Events Manager

Lennoxlove was acquired by the 14th Duke of Hamilton in 1947. It is set in 460 acres of mixed woodland and is home to much of the famous Hamilton Palace collection of works of art. In the medieval keep are many 16th century artefacts, including Mary, Queen of Scots' silver casket which once contained the incriminating letters that helped to send her to her death, a sapphire ring given to Lord John Hamilton and a death mask said to be hers. In the 17th and 18th century parts of the house are highly important works of art including pictures, furniture and porcelain collected by the Douglas, Hamilton and Stewart families for over 500 years.

Location: OS Ref. NT515 721. 18m E of Edinburgh, 1m S of Haddington.

Open: Easter - end Oct: Wed, Thur & Sun, 2 - 4.30pm. Guided tours.

Admission: Adult £4.25, Child £2.25. Group charges on application.

ⓘ No photography in house. Ⓣ Corporate/Private functions. ♿ ▣ Ⓕ Obligatory. ▣ Ⓟ ⌂ Grounds only.

LIBERTON HOUSE

73 Liberton Drive, Edinburgh EH16 6NP

Tel: 0131 467 7777 **Fax:** 0131 467 7774 **e-mail:** mail@ngra.co.uk

Owner/Contact: Nicholas Groves-Raines

Built around 1600 for the Littles of Liberton, this harled L-plan house has been carefully restored by the current architect owner using original detailing and extensive restoration of the principal structure. Public access restricted to the Great Hall and Old Kitchen. The restored garden layout suggests the original and there is a late 17th century lectern doocot by the entrance drive.

Location: OS Ref. NT267 694. 73 Liberton Drive, Edinburgh.

Open: 1 Mar - 31 Oct: 10am - 4.30pm, by prior appointment only.

Admission: Free.

♿ Unsuitable. Ⓟ Limited. ⌂

LINLITHGOW PALACE 🏛

LINLITHGOW, WEST LOTHIAN EH49 7AL

Tel: 01506 842896

Owner: Historic Scotland   **Contact:** The Steward

The magnificent remains of a great royal palace set in its own park and beside Linlithgow Loch. A favoured residence of the Stewart monarchs, James V and his daughter Mary Queen of Scots were born here. Bonnie Prince Charlie stayed here during his bid to regain the British crown.

Location: OS Ref. NT003 774. In the centre of Linlithgow off the M9.

Open: Apr - Sept: daily, 9.30am - 6.30pm. Oct - Mar: Mon - Sat, 9.30am - 4.30pm, Suns, 2 - 4.30pm. Last ticket 30 mins before closing.

Admission: Adult £3, Child £1, Conc. £2.30. 10% discount for groups (10+).
ℹ Picnic area. 🍽 Private evening hire. ♿ Partial. 🎫 Free if booked.
🅿 Cars only. 🐕 In grounds, off leads. ✹ €

NEWLISTON 🏠

Kirkliston, West Lothian EH29 9EB

Tel: 0131 333 3231

Owner/Contact: Mrs Caroline Maclachlan

Late Robert Adam house. Costumes on display. 18th century designed landscape, rhododendrons, azaleas and water features. On Sundays tea is in the Edinburgh Cookery School in the William Adam Coach House. Also on Sundays there is a ride-on steam model railway from 2 - 5pm.

Location: OS Ref. NT110 735. 8m W of Edinburgh, 3m S of Forth Road Bridge, off B800.

Open: 1 May - 4 Jun: Wed - Sun, 2 - 6pm. Also by appointment.

Admission: Adult £2, Conc. £1.
♿ Grounds. 🍽 🐕 In grounds, on leads. ✹

PALACE OF HOLYROOD HOUSE & THE QUEEN'S GALLERY

See page 478 for full page entry.

PRESTON MILL 🏛

East Linton, East Lothian EH40 3DS

Tel: 01620 860426

Owner: The National Trust for Scotland   **Contact:** Property Manager

For centuries there has been a mill on this site and the present one operated commercially until 1957.

Location: OS Ref. NT590 770. Off the A1, in East Linton, 23m E of Edinburgh.

Open: 1 Apr - 30 Sep: Thur - Mon, 12 noon - 5pm (Sun 1 - 5pm).

Admission: Adult £3.50, Conc. £2.60, Family £9.50. Groups: Adult £2.80, Child/School £1. Group visits must book.

RED ROW

Aberlady, East Lothian

Tel: 01875 870201   **Fax:** 01875 870620

Owner: Wemyss & March Estates Management Co Ltd   **Contact:** M Andrews
Terraced Cottages.

Location: OS Ref. NT464 798. Main Street, Aberlady, East Lothian.

Open: Exterior only. By appointment, Wemyss & March Estates Office, Longniddry, East Lothian EH32 0PY.

Admission: Please contact for details.

ROYAL BOTANIC GARDEN EDINBURGH

20A Inverleith Row, Edinburgh EH3 5LR

Tel: 0131 552 7171   **Fax:** 0131 248 2901   **e-mail:** info@rbge.org.uk

Contact: Press Office

Scotland's premier garden. Discover the wonders of the plant kingdom in over 70 acres of beautifully landscaped grounds.

Location: OS Ref. NT249 751. Off A902, 1m N of city centre.

Open: Daily (except 25 Dec & 1 Jan): open 10am, closing: Nov - Feb 4pm; Mar & Oct 6pm; Apr - Sept 7pm.

Admission: Free, with an admission charge on the Glasshouses.

ST MARY'S EPISCOPAL CATHEDRAL

Palmerston Place, Edinburgh EH12 5AW

Tel: 0131 225 6293   **Fax:** 0131 225 3181   **e-mail:** office@thecathedral.org.uk

Contact: Cathedral Secretary

Neo-gothic grandeur in the classical new town. Designed by G Gilbert Scott.

Location: OS Ref. NT241 735. 1/2 m W of west end of Princes Street.

Open: Mon - Fri, 7.30am - 6pm; Sat & Sun, 7.30am - 5pm. Sun services: 8am, 10.30am and 3.30pm. Services: Weekday, 7.30am, 1.05pm & 5.30pm; Sat, 7.30am, Sun, 11.30am.

Admission: Free.

SCOTTISH NATIONAL PORTRAIT GALLERY

1 Queen Street, Edinburgh EH2 1JD

Tel: 0131 624 6200

Unique visual history of Scotland.

Location: OS Ref. NT256 742. At E end of Queen Street, 300yds N of Princes Street.

Open: All year to permanent collection: daily, 10am - 5pm (Thurs closes 7pm). Closed 25 & 26 Dec.

Admission: Free

TANTALLON CASTLE 🏛

BY NORTH BERWICK, EAST LOTHIAN EH39 5PN

Tel: 01620 892727

Owner: In the care of Historic Scotland   **Contact:** The Steward

Set on the edge of the cliffs, looking out to the Bass Rock, this formidable castle was a stronghold of the powerful Douglas family. The castle has earthwork defences and a massive 80-foot high 14th century curtain wall. Interpretive displays include a replica gun.

Location: OS Ref. NT595 850. 3m E of North Berwick off the A198.

Open: Apr - Sept: daily, 9.30am - 6.30pm. Oct - Mar: Mon - Sat, 9.30am - 6.30pm (but closed Thur pm & all day Fri), Suns, 2 - 4.30pm.

Admission: Adult £3, Child £1, Conc. £2.30. 10% discount for groups (10+).
ℹ Picnic area. 🍽 ♿ Partial. 🅿 🍽 Booked school visits free.
🐕 In grounds, on leads. ✹ €

BURRELL COLLECTION

Pollok Country Park, 2060 Pollokshaws Road, Glasgow G43 1AT

Tel: 0141 287 2550   **Fax:** 0141 287 2597

Owner: Glasgow Museums

An internationally renowned, outstanding collection of art.

Location: OS Ref. NS555 622. Glasgow 15 min drive.

Open: All year: Mon - Thur & Sats, 10am - 5pm. Fri & Sun, 11am - 5pm. Closed Christmas Day, Boxing Day & 1 & 2 Jan.

Admission: Free. Small charge may apply for temporary exhibitions.

COLZIUM HOUSE & WALLED GARDEN

Colzium-Lennox Estate, off Stirling Road, Kilsyth G65 0RZ

Tel/Fax: 01236 828156

Owner: North Lanarkshire Council   **Contact:** Charlie Whyte

A walled garden with an extensive collection of conifers, rare shrubs and trees. Kilsyth Heritage Museum, curling pond, picnic tables, woodland walks.

Location: OS Ref. NS722 786. Off A803 Banknock to Kirkintilloch Road. 1/2 m E of Kilsyth.

Open: House available for weddings, conferences, etc. Walled garden: Apr - Sept: daily, 12 noon - 7pm; Oct - Mar: Sats & Suns, 12 noon - 4pm.

Admission: Free.

COREHOUSE

Lanark ML11 9TQ

Tel: 01555 663126 or 0131 667 1514

Owner: The Trustees of the late Lt Col A J E Cranstoun MC   **Contact:** Estate Office

Designed by Sir Edward Blore and built in the 1820s, Corehouse is a pioneering example of the Tudor Architectural Revival in Scotland.

Location: OS Ref. NS882 416. On S bank of the Clyde above the village of Kirkfieldbank.

Open: 9 May - 2 Jun & 12 - 19 Sep: Sat - Wed. Guided tours: weekdays: 1 & 2pm, weekends: 1.30 & 2.30pm. Closed Thur & Fri.

Admission: Adult £5, Child (under 14yrs)/OAP £2.

Obligatory.

CRAIGNETHAN CASTLE

Lanark, Strathclyde

Tel: 01555 860364

Owner: Historic Scotland   **Contact:** The Steward

In a picturesque setting overlooking the River Nethan and defended by a wide and deep ditch with an unusual caponier, a stone vaulted artillery chamber, unique in Britain.

Location: OS Ref. NS815 463. 5 1/2 m WNW of Lanark off the A72. 1/2 m footpath to W.

Open: 1 Apr - 30 Sept: daily, 9.30am - 6.30pm.

Admission: Adult £2.50, Child 75p, Conc. £1.90.

€

Colzium Walled Garden.

Patrick Lane

GLASGOW CATHEDRAL

Glasgow

Tel: 0141 552 6891

Owner: Historic Scotland   **Contact:** The Steward

The only Scottish mainland medieval cathedral to have survived the Reformation complete. Built over the tomb of St Kentigern. Notable features in this splendid building are the elaborately vaulted crypt, the stone screen of the early 15th century and the unfinished Blackadder Aisle.

Location: OS Ref. NS603 656. E end of city centre. In central Glasgow.

Admission: Free.

GREENBANK GARDEN

Clarkston, Glasgow G76 8RB

Tel: 0141 639 3281

Owner: The National Trust for Scotland

Several small gardens including a parterre layout illustrating different aspects of gardening.

Location: OS Ref. NS563 566. Flenders Road, off Mearns Road, Clarkston. Off M77 and A726, 6m S of Glasgow city centre.

Open: Garden: All year: daily, 9.30am - sunset. Shop & tearoom: 3 Jan - 31 Mar: Sat/Sun, 2 - 4pm; 1 Apr - 31 Oct: daily, 11am - 5pm. House: 1 Apr - 31 Oct: Sun 2 - 4pm.

Admission: Adult £3.50, Conc. £2.60, Family £9.50. Groups: Adult £2.80, Child/School £1.

HOLMWOOD HOUSE

61 Netherlee Road, Cathcart, Glasgow G1 1EJ

Tel: 0141 637 2129

Owner: The National Trust for Scotland

Villa described as Alexander 'Greek' Thomson's finest domestic design, built in 1857-8.

Location: OS Ref. NS580 593. Netherlee Road, off Clarkston road (off A77 and B767).

Open: 1 Apr - 31 Oct: daily, 12 noon - 5pm. Morning visits available for pre-booked groups.

Admission: Adult £3.50, Conc. £2.60, Family £9.50. Groups: Adult £2.80, Child/School £1.

HUTCHESONS' HALL

158 Ingram Street, Glasgow G1 1EJ

Tel: 0141 552 8391   **Fax:** 0141 552 7031

Owner: The National Trust for Scotland

Described as one of Glasgow city centre's most elegant buildings, the Hall by David Hamilton, replaced the earlier 1641 hospice founded by George and Thomas Hutcheson.

Location: OS Ref NS594 652. Glasgow city centre, near SE corner of George Square.

Open: Gallery, shop & function hall: 20 Jan - 24 Dec: Mon - Sat, 10am - 5pm. Hall on view subject to functions in progress.

Admission: Function hall & A/V programme: Adult £2, Conc. £1.

DAVID LIVINGSTONE CENTRE

165 Station Road, Blantyre, Glasgow G72 9BT

Tel: 01698 823140

Owner: The National Trust for Scotland

Scotland's most famous explorer and missionary was born here in 1813 and today the Centre commemorates his life and work. Livingstone's childhood home - consisting of just one room - remains much as it would have done in his day.

Location: OS Ref NS690 575. In Blantyre town centre, at N end of Station Road.

Open: 1 Apr - 24 Dec: Mon - Sat, 10am - 5pm, Sun 12.30 - 5pm.

Admission: Adult £3.50, Conc. £2.60, Family £9.50. Groups: Adult £2.80, Child/School £1.

MOTHERWELL HERITAGE CENTRE

High Road, Motherwell ML1 3HU

Tel: 01698 251000

Owner: North Lanarkshire Council   **Contact:** The Manager

Multimedia exhibition and other displays of local history. STB 4-Star attraction.

Location: OS Ref. NS750 570. In High Road, 200 yds N of A723 (Hamilton Road).

Open: Wed - Sat, 10am - 5pm. Suns, 12 noon - 5pm. (closed 25/26 Dec & 1/2 Jan). Closed Mons & Tues.

Admission: Free.

NEW LANARK WORLD HERITAGE SITE

NEW LANARK MILLS, LANARK, S. LANARKSHIRE ML11 9DB

www.newlanark.org

Tel: 01555 661345 **Fax:** 01555 665738 **e-mail:** visit@newlanark.org

Owner: New Lanark Conservation Trust   **Contact:** Richard Evans

Surrounded by native woodlands and close to the famous Falls of Clyde, this cotton mill village was founded in 1785 and became famous as the site of Robert Owen's radical reforms. Now beautifully restored as both a living community and attraction, the fascinating history of the village is interpreted in an award-winning Visitor Centre. Accommodation is available in the New Lanark Mill Hotel and Waterhouses, a stunning conversion from an original 18th century mill. New Lanark is now a World Heritage Site.

Location: OS Ref. NS880 426. 1m S of Lanark.

Open: All year: daily, 11am - 5pm (closed 25 Dec & 1 Jan).

Admission: Visitor Centre: Adult £5.95, Child/Conc. £3.95. Groups: 1 free/10 booked.

i Conference facilities. 🗐 🔲 Partial. WC. Visitor Centre wheelchair friendly. ⬛ 🔍 By arrangement. P 5 min walk. ⬛ 🔍 In grounds, on leads. ⬛ ⬛

NEWARK CASTLE

Port Glasgow, Strathclyde

Tel: 01475 741858

Owner: In the care of Historic Scotland   **Contact:** The Steward

The oldest part of the castle is a tower built soon after 1478 with a detached gatehouse, by George Maxwell. The main part was added in 1597 - 99 in a most elegant style. Enlarged in the 16th century by his descendent, the wicked Patrick Maxwell who murdered two of his neighbours.

Location: OS Ref. NS329 744. In Port Glasgow on the A8.

Open: 1 Apr - 30 Sept: daily, 9.30am - 6.30pm. Last ticket 6pm.

Admission: Adult £2.50, Child 75p, Conc. £1.90.

€

POLLOK HOUSE

Pollok Country Park, Pollokshaws Road, Glasgow G43 1AT

Tel: 0141 616 6410

Owner: The National Trust for Scotland

Three earlier castles here were replaced by the present house (c1740). The house contains an internationally famed collection of paintings as well as porcelain and furnishings appropriate to an Edwardian house.

Location: OS Ref. NS550 616. In Pollok Country Park, off M77/J1, follow signs for Burrell Collection.

Open: House, shop & restaurant: All year: daily 10am - 5pm (closed 25/26 Dec & 1/2 Jan).

Admission: 1 Apr - 31 Oct: Adult £5, Conc. £3.75, Family £13.50. Groups: Adult £4, Child/School £1. 1 Nov - 31 Mar, admission free. Gardens, Country Park & Burrell Collection open all year: daily. Admission free.

ST MARY'S EPISCOPAL CATHEDRAL

300 Great Western Road, Glasgow G4 9JB

Tel: 0141 339 6691 **Fax:** 0141 334 5669   **Contact:** Very Rev Griff Dines

Newly restored, fine Gothic Revival church by Sir George Gilbert Scott, with outstanding contemporary murals by Gwyneth Leech. Regular concerts and exhibitions.

Location: OS Ref. NS578 669. ¼ m after the Dumbarton A82 exit from M8 motorway.

Open: Daily, 9.30am - 10.30am, 4 - 5pm and at other service times. Please telephone for details of services.

SUMMERLEE HERITAGE PARK

Heritage Way, Coatbridge, North Lanarkshire ML5 1QD

Tel: 01236 431261

Owner: North Lanarkshire Council   **Contact:** The Manager

STB 4-star attraction. 22 acres of industrial heritage including Scotland's only remaining electric tramway; a re-created addit mine and mine workers' cottages.

Location: OS Ref. NS729 655. 600yds NW of Coatbridge town centre.

Open: All year. Summer, 10am - 5pm. Winter: 10am - 4pm (closed 25/26 Dec & 1/2 Jan).

Admission: Free. Tram ride: Adult 80p, Child 45p.

THE TENEMENT HOUSE ♥

145 Buccleuch Street, Glasgow G3 6QN

Tel: 0141 333 0183

Owner: The National Trust for Scotland

A typical Victorian tenement flat of 1892, and time capsule of the first half of the 20th century.

Location: OS Ref. NS583 662. Garnethill (three streets N of Sauchiehall Street, near Charing Cross), Glasgow.

Open: 1 Mar - 31 Oct: daily, 1 - 5pm; weekday morning visits available for pre-booked educational and other groups.

Admission: Adult £3.50, Conc. £2.60, Family £9.50. Groups: Adult £2.80, Child/School £1.

THE TOWER OF HALLBAR

Braidwood Road, Braidwood, Lanarkshire

Tel: 0845 090 0194 **Fax:** 0845 090 0174 **e-mail:** enquiries@vivat.org.uk
www.vivat.org.uk

Owner: The Vivat Trust   **Contact:** Miss Lisa Simm

A 16th century defensive tower and Bothy set in ancient orchards and meadowland. Converted into self-catering holiday accommodation by The Vivat Trust and furnished and decorated in keeping with its history. Hallbar sleeps up to seven people, including facilities for a disabled person and their carer.

Location: OS Ref. NS842 471. S side of B7056 between Crossford Bridge & Braidwood.

Open: All year: Sats, 2 - 3pm, or by appointment. Also four open days a year.

Admission: Free.

🔲 Partial. 🔍 By arrangement. P Limited. 🔍 In grounds, on leads. ⬛ 3 single, 1 twin & 1 double. ⬛

WEAVER'S COTTAGE ♥

Shuttle Street, Kilbarchan, Renfrew PA10 2JG

Tel: 01505 705588

Owner: The National Trust for Scotland

Typical cottage of an 18th century handloom weaver contains looms, weaving equipment and domestic utensils.

Location: OS Ref. NS402 633. Off A740 (off M8) and A737, at The Cross, Kilbarchan, (nr Johnstone, Paisley) 12m SW of Glasgow.

Open: 1 Apr - 30 Sep: Fri - Tue, 1 - 5pm; morning visits available for pre-booked groups.

Admission: Adult £3.50, Conc. £2.60, Family £9.50. Groups: Adult £2.80, Child/School £1.

Map 10

Owner: Blair
Charitable Trust

▶ CONTACT

Administration Office
Blair Castle
Blair Atholl
Pitlochry
Perthshire PH18 5TL

Tel: 01796 481207
Fax: 01796 481487
e-mail: office@
blair-castle.co.uk

▶ LOCATION
OS Ref. NN880 660

From Edinburgh 80m,
M90 to Perth, A9,
follow signs for Blair
Castle, 1½ hrs.
Trunk Road A9 2m.

Bus: Bus stop 1m
in Blair Atholl.

Train: 1m, Blair Atholl
Euston-Inverness line.

Taxi: Elizabeth Yule,
01796 472290.

FUNCTION

ROOM	SIZE	MAX CAPACITY
Ballroom	88' x 36'	400
Ballroom Dining	36' x 25'	200
Exhibition Hall	55' x 27'	90

BLAIR CASTLE 🏛

BLAIR ATHOLL, BY PITLOCHRY

www.blair-castle.co.uk

Perthshire's 5 star historic home. Blair Castle has been the ancient home and fortress of the Earls and Dukes of Atholl for over 725 years. Its central location makes it easily accessible from all major Scottish centres in less than two hours.

The castle has known the splendour of Royal visitations, submitted to occupation by opposing forces on no less than four occasions, suffered siege and changed its architectural appearance to suit the taste of successive generations.

Today 30 rooms of infinite variety display beautiful furniture, fine collections of paintings, arms, armour, china, costumes, lace and embroidery, Jacobite relics and other unique treasures giving a stirring picture of Scottish life from the 16th to 20th centuries.

The Duke of Atholl has the unique distinction of having the only remaining private army in Europe - The Atholl Highlanders.

GARDENS
Blair Castle is set in extensive grounds. Near the car and coach parks, there is a picnic area, a deer park and a unique two acre plantation of large trees known as 'Diana's Grove.' It has been said that *"it is unlikely that any other two acres in the world contain such a number of different conifers of such heights and of such small age."* A restored 18th century garden re-opened to visitors in 1996.

ℹ️ Fashion shows, equestrian events, shows, rallies, filming, highland and charity balls, piping championships, grand piano, helicopter pad, cannon firing by Atholl Highlanders, resident piper, needlework displays. No smoking.

🍷 Buffets, dinners, wedding receptions and banquets.

♿ May alight at entrance. WC & wheelchair facilities.

🍴 Non-smoking. Seats up to 125. Private group lunches for up to 35 can be arranged in the Garry Room.

🎧 Audio visual presentation.

🚶 In English, German and French at no extra cost. Tour time 1½ hrs (max).

🅿️ 200 cars, 20 coaches. Coach drivers/couriers free, plus free meal and shop voucher, information pack.

🖼 Nature walks, deer park, ranger service & pony trekking, children's play area.

🐕 Grounds only. ❄️

🛡 Event programme available on application.

▶ OPENING TIMES
Summer
1 April - 29 October
Daily, 9.30am - 4.30pm
(last admission). Other
times by special
arrangement.

Winter
Groups by arrangement,
plus limited public
opening – enquire for
details.

▶ ADMISSION
House & Grounds

Adult	£6.70
Child (5-16yrs)	£4.20
OAP	£5.70
Student	£5.40
Family	£17.00
Disabled	£2.00

Groups* (12+)
(Please book)

Adult	£5.40
Child(5-16yrs)	£4.00
Primary School	£3.00
OAP	£4.90
Student	£4.40
Disabled	£2.00

Grounds only
(with access to restaurant,
gift shop & WC)

Adult	£2.00
Child (5-16yrs)	£1.00
Family	£5.00
Disabled	Free
Scooter Hire	£3.00

Groups* (12+)
(Please book)

Adult	£2.00
Child(5-16yrs)	£1.00
Disabled	Free

* Group rates only apply if tickets
bought by the Driver, Courier,
group leader at one time.

GLAMIS CASTLE

BY FORFAR

www.glamis-castle.co.uk

Glamis Castle is the family home of the Earls of Strathmore and Kinghorne and has been a royal residence since 1372. It was the childhood home of Her Majesty Queen Elizabeth The Queen Mother, the birthplace of Her Royal Highness The Princess Margaret and the legendary setting of Shakespeare's play Macbeth. Although the castle is open to visitors it remains a family home lived in and loved by the Strathmore family.

The castle, a five-storey 'L' shaped tower block, was originally a royal hunting lodge. It was remodelled in the 17th century and is built of pink sandstone. It contains the Great Hall, with its magnificent plasterwork ceiling dated 1621, a beautiful family Chapel constructed inside the Castle in 1688, an 18th century billiard room housing what is left of the extensive library once at Glamis, a 19th century dining room containing family portraits and the Royal Apartments which have been used by Her Majesty Queen Elizabeth The Queen Mother.

The castle stands in an extensive park, landscaped towards the end of the 18th century, and contains the beautiful Italian Garden and the Pinetum which reflect the peace and serenity of the castle and grounds.

Map 10

Owner: The Earl of Strathmore & Kinghorne

▶ CONTACT
Mr David Adams
Castle Administrator
Estates Office
Glamis
by Forfar
Angus   DD8 1RJ

Tel: 01307 840393
Fax: 01307 840733

e-mail: admin@
glamis-castle.co.uk

▶ LOCATION
OS Ref. NO386 480

From Edinburgh M90,
A94, 81m.
From Forfar A94, 6m.
From Glasgow 93m.
Motorway: M90.

Rail: Dundee
Station 12m.

Air: Dundee
Airport 12m.

Taxi: K Cabs
01575 573744.

▶ OPENING TIMES
27 March - 31 October
Daily, 10am - 6pm.

Last admission 4.30pm.

Groups welcome. Out of hours visits can also be arranged.

Winter
By arrangement.

▶ ADMISSION
Summer
Castle & Grounds
Adult £6.80
Child* (5-16yrs)........ £3.70
OAP/Student £5.50
Family £19.00
Groups (20+)
Adult £5.80
Child* (5-16yrs)....... £3.20
OAP/Student £5.00

**Grounds only
ticket available.**

CONFERENCE/FUNCTION

ROOM	SIZE	MAX CAPACITY
Dining Rm	84 sq.m	90
Restaurant	140 sq.m	100
16th century Kitchens		50

ℹ️ Fashion shoots, archery, equestrian events, shows, rallies, filming, product launches, highland games, new shopping development, grand piano. No photography in the castle.

🛍️ Shopping complex. ✳️

🍽️ The State Rooms are available for grand dinners, lunches and wedding receptions.

♿ Disabled visitors may alight at entrance. Those in wheelchairs will be unable to tour the castle but may visit the two exhibitions. WC.

☕🍴 Morning coffees, light lunches, afternoon teas. Self-service, licensed restaurant.

🚶 All visits are guided, tour time 50 - 60 mins. Tours leave every 10 - 15 mins. Tours in French, German, Italian and Spanish by appointment at no additional cost. Three exhibitions.

🅿️ 500 cars and 20 coaches 200 yds from castle. Coach drivers and couriers admitted free. Beware narrow gates; they are wide enough to take buses (10ft wide).

📚 One teacher free for every 10 children. Nature trail, family exhibition rooms, dolls' house, play park. Glamis Heritage Education Centre in Glamis village. Education pack. Winner of Sandford Award in 1997. Children's Quest.

 🐕 In grounds, on leads. ✳️ 🎭 Tel for details. €

Perthshire, Angus & Dundee and The Kingdom of Fife

Map 10

SCONE PALACE & GROUNDS 🏛

PERTH

www.scone-palace.co.uk

Owner: The Earl of Mansfield

▸ CONTACT

The Administrator
Scone Palace
Perth   PH2 6BD

Tel: 01738 552300
Fax: 01738 552588

e-mail: visits@
scone-palace.co.uk

▸ LOCATION

OS Ref. NO114 266

From Edinburgh
Forth Bridge M90,
A93 1hr.

Bus: Regular buses
from Perth.

Rail: Perth Station 3m.

Motorway: M90 from
Edinburgh.

Taxi: 01738 636777.

Scone Palace is the home of the Earl and Countess of Mansfield and is built on the site of the former Bishop's Palace. 1500 years ago it was the capital of the Pictish kingdom and the centre of the ancient Celtic church. In the intervening years, it has been the seat of the parliaments and crowning place of kings, including Macbeth, Robert the Bruce and Charles II. The State Rooms house a superb collection of *objets d'art*, including items of Marie Antoinette, bought by the 2nd Earl of Mansfield. Notable works of art are also on display, including paintings by Sir David Wilkie, Sir Joshua Reynolds, and Johann Zoffany. The Library boasts one of Scotland's finest collections of porcelain, including Sèvres, Ludwigsburg and Meissen, whilst the unique 'Vernis Martin' *papier mâché* may be viewed in the Long Gallery.

Gardens

The grounds of the Palace house magnificent collections of shrubs, with woodland walks through the pinetum containing David Douglas' original fir and the unique Murray Star Maze. There are Highland cattle and peacocks to admire and an adventure play area for children. The 100 acres of mature Policy Parks, flanked by the River Tay, are available for a variety of events, including corporate and private entertaining.

▸ OPENING TIMES

Summer
1 April - 31 October
Daily: 9.30am - 6pm.

Last admission 4.45pm.

Evening tours by appointment.

Winter
By appointment.

Grounds only: Fri,
11am - 4pm.

▸ ADMISSION

Summer
Palace & Grounds

Adult	£6.75
Child (under 16yrs)	£3.80
OAP/Student	£5.70
Family	£20.00

Groups (20+)

Adult	£5.50
Child (5-16yrs)	£3.40
OAP/Student	£4.75

Grounds only

Adult	£3.40
Child (5-16yrs)	£2.00
OAP/Student	£2.80

Under 5s Free
Private Tour £35
supplement.

Winter
On application.

▸ SPECIAL EVENTS

APR - SEPT
Perth Races (01738 551597).

JUL
Game Fair.

FEB & NOV
Antiques Fair.

Please telephone for further information.

CONFERENCE/FUNCTION

ROOM	SIZE	MAX CAPACITY
Long Gallery	140' x 20'	200
Queen Victoria's Rm	20' x 20'	20
Drawing Rm	48' x 25'	80

Receptions, fashion shows, war games, archery, clay pigeon shooting, equestrian events, garden parties, shows, rallies, filming, shooting, fishing, floodlit tattoos, product launches, highland games, parkland, cricket pitch, helicopter landing, croquet, racecourse, polo field, firework displays, adventure playground. No photography in state rooms. Gift shop & food shop.

Grand dinners in state rooms, buffets, receptions, wedding receptions, cocktail parties.

All state rooms on one level, wheelchair access to restaurants. Stairlift in gift shop.

Licensed. Teas, lunches & dinners, can be booked, menus upon request, special rates for groups.

By arrangement. Guides in rooms, tour time 45 mins. French and German guides available by appointment.

Welcome.

300 cars and 15 coaches, groups please book, couriers and coach drivers free meal and admittance.

In grounds on leads.

❄ €

ABERDOUR CASTLE

Aberdour, Fife

Tel: 01383 860519

Owner: In the care of Historic Scotland   **Contact:** The Steward

A 14th century castle built by the Douglas family. The gallery on the first floor gives an idea of how it was furnished at the time. The castle has a 14th century tower extended in the 16th and 17th centuries, a delightful walled garden and a circular dovecote.

Location: OS Ref. NT193 854. In Aberdour 5m E of the Forth Bridge on the A921.

Open: 1 Apr - 30 Sept: daily, 9.30am - 6.30pm, last ticket 6pm. 1 Oct - 31 Mar: Mon - Sat, 9.30am - 4.30pm, Suns, 2 - 4.30pm, last ticket 4pm. Closed Thur pm & Fris in winter.

Admission: Adult £2.50, Child 75p, Conc. £1.90.

€

ANGUS FOLK MUSEUM

Kirkwynd, Glamis, Forfar, Angus DD8 1RT

Tel: 01307 840288   **Fax:** 01307 840233

Owner: The National Trust for Scotland   **Contact:** The Manager

Where will you find cruisie lamps, pirn winders, cloutie rugs, bannock spades and a thrawcrook? All these items, and more, are to be found in the Angus Folk Museum.

Location: OS Ref. NO385 467. Off A94, in Glamis, 5m SW of Forfar.

Open: 1 Apr - 30 Jun & 1 - 30 Sep: Fri - Tue, 12 noon - 5pm; 1 Jul - 31 Aug: daily 12 noon - 5pm.

Admission: Adult £3.50, Conc. £2.60, Family £9.50. Groups: Adult £2.80, Child/School £1.

ARBROATH ABBEY

Arbroath, Tayside

Tel: 01241 878756

Owner: In the care of Historic Scotland   **Contact:** The Steward

The substantial ruins of a Tironensian monastery, notably the gate house range and the abbot's house. Arbroath Abbey holds a very special place in Scottish history. Scotland's nobles swore their independence from England in the famous 'Declaration of Arbroath' in 1320. New visitor centre.

Location: OS Ref. NO644 414. In Arbroath town centre on the A92.

Open: 1 Apr - 30 Sept: daily 9.30am - 6.30pm, last ticket 6pm. 1 Oct - 31 Mar: Mon - Sat, 9.30am - 4.30 pm, Suns, 2 - 4.30pm, last ticket 4pm.

Admission: Adult £3.30, Child £1, Conc. £2.50.

€

BALCARRES

Colinsburgh, Fife KY9 1HL

Tel: 01333 340206

Owner: Balcarres Trust   **Contact:** The Earl of Crawford

16th century tower house with 19th century additions by Burn and Bryce. Woodland and terraced gardens

Location: OS Ref. NO475 044. 1/2 m N of Colinsburgh.

Open: Woodland & Gardens: 2 - 18 Feb & 1 Apr - 14 Jun, 2 - 5pm. House not open except by written appointment and 12 - 28 Apr, excluding Sun.

Admission: Adult £5. Garden only: £3.

By arrangement.

BALGONIE CASTLE

Markinch, Fife KY7 6HQ

Tel: 01592 750119   **Fax:** 01592 753103

Owner/Contact: The Laird of Balgonie

14th century tower, additions to the building up to 1702. Still lived in by the family. 14th century chapel for weddings.

Location: OS Ref. NO313 006. 1/2 m S of A911 Glenrothes - Leven road at Milton of Balgonie on to B921.

Open: All year: daily, 10am - 5pm.

Admission: Adult £3, Child £1.50, OAP £2.

BALHOUSIE CASTLE (BLACK WATCH MUSEUM)

Hay Street, North Inch Park, Perth PH1 5HR

Tel: 0131 310 8530

Owner: MOD   **Contact:** Major Proctor

Regimental museum housed in the castle.

Location: OS Ref. NO115 244. 1/2 m N of town centre, E of A9 road to Dunkeld.

Open: May - Sept: Mon - Sat, 10am - 4.30pm. Oct - Apr: Mon - Fri, 10am - 3.30pm. Closed 23 Dec - 5 Jan & last Sat in Jun.

Admission: Free.

J M BARRIE'S BIRTHPLACE

9 Brechin Road, Kirriemuir, Angus DD8 4BX

Tel: 01575 572646

Owner: The National Trust for Scotland

The creator of the eternal magic of *Peter Pan*, J M Barrie, was born here in 1860.

Location: OS Ref. NO388 542. On A926/B957, in Kirriemuir, 6m NW of Forfar.

Open: 1 Apr - 30 Jun & 1 - 30 Sep: Fri - Tue, 1 - 5pm; 1 Jul - 31 Aug: daily, 1 - 5pm.

Admission: Adult £5, Conc. £3.75, Family £13.50. Groups: Adult £4, Child/School £1. Includes admission to Camera Obscura.

BARRY WATER MILL

Barry, Carnoustie, Angus DD7 7RJ

Tel: 01241 856761

Owner: The National Trust for Scotland

19th century meal mill. Waymarked walks. Picnic area.

Location: OS Ref. NO533 349. N of village between A92 & A930, 2m W of Carnoustie.

Open: 1 Apr - 30 Sep: Fri - Tue, 12 noon - 5pm.

Admission: Adult £3.50, Conc. £2.60, Family £9.50. Groups: Adult £2.80, Child/School £1.

BLAIR CASTLE

See page 485 for full page entry.

BOLFRACKS GARDEN

Aberfeldy, Perthshire PH15 2EX

Tel: 01887 820344   **Fax:** 01887 829522   **e-mail:** info@bolfracks.fsnet.co.uk www.bolfracks.com

Owner/Contact: Mr R A Price

A garden of approximately 4 acres with splendid views over the River Tay to the hills beyond. A walled garden contains a wide collection of trees, shrubs and perennials. Also a burn garden with rhododendrons, azaleas, meconopsis, primulas etc. with peat wall arrangements. Lots of bulbs and good autumn colour.

Location: OS Ref. NN822 481. 2m W of Aberfeldy on A827 towards Kenmore.

Open: 1 Apr - 31 Oct: daily, 10am - 6pm.

Admission: Adult £3, Child (under 16 yrs) Free.

Not ideal. Self catering cottages with fishing.

BRANKLYN GARDEN

Dundee Road, Perth PH2 7BB

Tel: 01738 625535

Owner: The National Trust for Scotland

Small garden with an impressive collection of rare and unusual plants.

Location: OS Ref. NO125 225. On A85 at 116 Dundee Road, Perth.

Open: 1 - 30 Apr & 1 Jul - 30 Sep: Fri - Tue 10am - 5pm; 1 May - 30 Jun: daily 10am - 5pm.

Admission: Adult £3.50, Conc. £2.60, Family £9.50. Groups: Adult £2.80, Child/School £1.

BRECHIN CASTLE

Brechin, Angus DD9 6SG

Tel: 01356 624566   **e-mail:** fay@dalhousieestates.co.uk www.dalhousieestates.co.uk

Owner: Dalhousie Estates   **Contact:** Fay Clark

Dating from 1711 the Castle contains many family pictures and artefacts. Beautiful gardens.

Location: OS Ref. NO593 602. Off A90 on A935.

Open: 10 Jul - 8 Aug: guided tours only.

Admission: Adult £5.

No photography. Unsuitable. Obligatory.

CAMBO GARDENS

Cambo Estate, Kingsbarns, St Andrews, Fife KY16 8QD

Tel: 01333 450054   **Fax:** 01333 450987   **e-mail:** cambo@camboestate.com www.camboestate.com

Owner: Mr & Mrs T P N Erskine   **Contact:** Catherine Erskine

Victorian walled garden with burn, willow, waterfall and rose-clad bridges. Naturalistic plantings of rare and interesting herbaceous perennials, spectacular bulbs, including acres of woodland walks leading to sea carpeted in snowdrops, roses, September borders, woodland garden with colchicum meadow. "All seasons plantsman's paradise."

Location: OS Ref. NO603 114. 3m N of Crail. 7m SE of St Andrews on A917.

Open: All year: daily except Christmas and New Year, 10am - dusk.

Admission: Adult £3, Child Free.

Conferences. Mail order snowdrops in the green. Limited for coaches. In grounds, on leads. 2 doubles & self-catering apartments/cottages.

CASTLE CAMPBELL 🏰 🏛
Dollar Glen, Central District
Tel: 01259 742408
Owner: The National Trust for Scotland   **Contact:** Historic Scotland
Known as 'Castle Gloom' this spectacularly sited 15th century fortress was the lowland stronghold of the Campbells. Stunning views from the parapet walk.
Location: OS Ref. NS961 993. At head of Dollar Glen, 10m E of Stirling on the A91.
Open: 1 Apr - 30 Sept: daily, 9.30am - 6.30pm, last ticket 6pm. 1 Oct - 31 Mar: Mon - Sat, 9.30am - 4.30pm (closed Thurs pm & Fris all day) Suns, 2 - 4.30pm, last ticket 4pm.
Admission: Adult £3, Child £1, Conc. £2.30.

€

CHARLETON HOUSE
Colinsburgh, Leven, Fife KY9 1HG
Tel: 01333 340249   **Fax:** 01333 340583
Location: OS Ref. NO464 036. Off A917. 1m NW of Colinsburgh. 3m NW of Elie.
Open: Sept: 12 noon - 3pm. Admission every ½ hr with guided tours only.
Admission: £8.
🚶 Obligatory.

CORTACHY ESTATE
Cortachy, Kirriemuir, Angus DD8 4LX
Tel: 01575 540222   **Fax:** 01575 540400
e-mail: walks@airlieestates.com   **www**.airlieestates.com
Owner: Trustees of Airlie Estates   **Contact:** Estate Office
Countryside walks including access through woodlands to Airlie Monument on Tulloch Hill with spectacular views of the Angus Glens and Vale of Strathmore. Footpaths are waymarked and colour coded.
Location: OS Ref. N0394 596. Off the B955 Glens Road from Kirriemuir.
Open: Woodland Walk: all year. Gardens: 9 - 12 Apr; 3 & 17 May - 6 Jun; 2 & 30 Aug: 10am - 4pm, last admission 3.30pm. Castle not open.
Admission: Please contact for details.
♿ Not suitable. 🅿 Limited. 🐕 ❄

CULROSS PALACE 🏰
Culross, Fife KY12 8JH   **Tel:** 01383 880359   **Fax:** 01383 882675
Owner: The National Trust for Scotland   **Contact:** Property Manager
Relive the domestic life of the 16th and 17th centuries at this Royal Burgh fringed by the River Forth. Enjoy too the Palace, dating from 1597 and the medieval garden.
Location: OS Ref. NS985 860. Off A985. 12m W of Forth Road Bridge and 4m E of Kincardine Bridge, Fife.
Open: Palace, Study, Town House, shop & tearoom: Good Fri- - Easter Mon, Jun & Sep: daily, 12 noon - 5pm; 1 Jul - 31 Aug: daily, 11am - 5pm.
Admission: Adult £5, Conc. £3.75, Family £13.50. Groups: Adult £4, Child/School £1.

DUNFERMLINE ABBEY & PALACE 🏛
Dunfermline, Fife
Tel: 01383 739026
Owner: In the care of Historic Scotland   **Contact:** The Steward
The remains of the Benedictine abbey founded by Queen Margaret in the 11th century. The foundations of her church are under the 12th century Romanesque-style nave. Robert the Bruce was buried in the choir. Substantial parts of the Abbey buildings remain, including the vast refectory.
Location: OS Ref. NY090 873. In Dunfermline off the M90.
Open: 1 Apr - 30 Sept: daily, 9.30am - 6.30pm, last ticket 6pm. 1 Oct - 31 Mar: Mon - Sat, 9.30am - 4.30pm, Suns, 2 - 4.30pm, last ticket 4pm. Closed Thur pm and Fris in winter.
Admission: Adult £2.50, Child 75p, Conc. £1.90.

€

DUNNINALD 🏛
Montrose, Angus DD10 9TD
Tel: 01674 674842   **Fax:** 01674 674860   **Owner/Contact:** J Stansfeld
This house, the third Dunninald built on the estate, was designed by James Gillespie Graham in the gothic Revival style, and was completed for Peter Arkley in 1824. It has a superb walled garden and is set in a planned landscape dating from 1740. It is a family home.
Location: OS Ref. NO705 543 2m S of Montrose, between A92 and the sea.
Open: 1 Jul - 1 Aug: Tue - Sun, 1 - 5pm. Garden: from 12 noon.
Admission: Adult £5, Child £2.50, Conc. £3.50. Garden only: £2.
ℹ No photography in house. 📷 ♿ Unsuitable. 🐕 🚶 Obligatory. 🅿 ■
🐕 In grounds, on leads. €

DRUMMOND CASTLE GARDENS 🏛
MUTHILL, CRIEFF, PERTHSHIRE PH5 2AA
www.drummondcastlegardens.co.uk

Tel: 01764 681257   **Fax:** 01764 681550 Weekends: 01764 681433
e-mail: the gardens@drummondcastle.sol.co.uk
Owner: Grimsthorpe & Drummond Castle Trust   **Contact:** Pat Keith
Scotland's most important formal gardens, among the finest in Europe. A mile of beech-lined avenue leads to a formidable ridge top tower house. Enter through the woven iron yett to the terraces and suddenly revealed is a magnificent Italianate parterre, celebrating the saltire and family heraldry, surrounding the famous multiplex sundial by John Milne, master mason to Charles I. First laid out in the early 17th century by John Drummond, the 2nd Earl of Perth and renewed in the early 1950s by Phyllis Astor, Countess of Ancaster.
Location: OS Ref. NN844 181. 2m S of Crieff off the A822.
Open: Easter weekend, then 1 May - 31 Oct: 1 - 6pm, last entry 5pm.
Admission: Adult £3.50, Child £1.50, OAP £2.50. 10% discount for groups (20+). Prices subject to change.

📷 ♿ Partial. Viewing platform. WC. 🚶 By arrangement. 🅿 🐕 🛏 Tel for details.

EDZELL CASTLE AND GARDEN

Edzell, Angus

Tel: 01356 648631

Owner: In the care of Historic Scotland　　　　　　**Contact:** The Steward

The beautiful walled garden at Edzell is one of Scotland's unique sights, created by Sir David Lindsay in 1604. The 'Pleasance' is a delightful formal garden with walls decorated with sculptured stone panels, flower boxes and niches for nesting birds. The fine tower house, now ruined, dates from the last years of the 15th century. Mary Queen of Scots held a council meeting in the castle in 1562 on her way north as her army marched against the Gordons.

Location: OS Ref. NO585 691. At Edzell, 6m N of Brechin on B966. 1m W of village.

Open: 1 Apr - 30 Sept: daily, 9.30am - 6.30pm, last ticket 6pm. 1 Oct - 31 Mar: Mon - Sat, 9.30am - 4.30pm, Suns, 2 - 4.30pm, last ticket 4pm. Closed Thur pm and Fris in winter.

Admission: Adult £3, Child £1, Conc. £2.30.

€

ELCHO CASTLE

Perth

Tel: 01738 639998

Owner: In the care of Historic Scotland

This handsome and complete fortified mansion of 16th century date has four projecting towers. The original wrought-iron grilles to protect the windows are still in place.

Location: OS Ref. NO164 211. On the Tay, 3m SE of Perth.

Open: 1 Apr - 30 Sept: daily, 9.30am - 6.30pm, last ticket 6pm.

Admission: Adult £2.20, Child 75p, Conc. £1.60.

€

FALKLAND PALACE

Falkland KY15 7BU

Tel: 01337 857397

Owner: The National Trust for Scotland

Built between 1502 and 1541, the Palace is a good example of Renaissance architecture. Surrounded by gardens, laid out in the 1950s.

Location: OS Ref. NO253 075. A912, 11m N of Kirkcaldy.

Open: 1 Mar - 31 Oct: Mon - Sat, 10am - 6pm, Sun, 1 - 5pm. Shop also open: 1 Nov - 24 Dec: daily, 10am - 4pm; 3 Jan - 28/29 Feb, hours vary: please contact property for details.

Admission: Palace & Grounds: Adult £7, Conc. £5.25, Family £19. Groups: Adult £5.60, Child/School £1. Member of Scots Guard's Association Free.

GLAMIS CASTLE

See page 486 for full page entry.

Stobhall, Perthshire from the book *Historic Family Homes and Gardens from the Air*, see page 54.

GLENEAGLES

Auchterarder, Perthshire PH3 1PJ

Tel: 01764 682388

Owner: Gleneagles 1996 Trust　　　　　　**Contact:** J Martin Haldane of Gleneagles

Gleneagles has been the home of the Haldane family since the 12th century. The 18th century pavilion is open to the public by written appointment.

Location: OS Ref. NS931 088. ³/₄ m S of A9 on A823. 2¹/₂ m S of Auchterarder.

Open: By written appointment only.

✳

HILL OF TARVIT MANSIONHOUSE

Cupar, Fife KY15 5PB

Tel/Fax: 01334 653127

Owner: The National Trust for Scotland　　　　　　**Contact:** The Manager

House rebuilt in 1906 by Sir Robert Lorimer, the renowned Scottish architect, for a Dundee industrialist, Mr F B Sharp.

Location: OS Ref. NO379 118. Off A916, 2¹/₂ m S of Cupar, Fife.

Open: 1 Apr - 30 Sep: daily, 1 - 5pm; 1 - 31 Oct: Sat/Sun 1 - 5pm. Tearoom, same dates, but opens at 12 noon. Garden & grounds, All year: daily, 9.30am - sunset.

Admission: Adult £5, Conc. £3.75, Family £13.50. Groups: Adult £4, Child/School £1. Garden and grounds only, £2.

HOUSE OF DUN

Montrose, Angus DD10 9LQ

Tel: 01674 810264　　**Fax:** 01674 810722

Owner: The National Trust for Scotland　　　　　　**Contact:** The Manager

Georgian house, overlooking the Montrose Basin, was designed by William Adam and built in 1730 for David Erskine, Lord Dun.

Location: OS Ref. NO670 599. 3m W Montrose on A935.

Open: House & shop: 1 Apr - 30 Jun & 1 - 30 Sep: Fri - Tue, 12 noon - 5pm; 1 Jul - 31 Aug: daily, 12 noon - 5pm. Garden & grounds, All year: daily 9.30am - sunset.

Admission: Adult £7, Conc. £5.25, Family £19. Groups: Adult £5.60, Child/School £1. Garden and grounds only, £1 (honesty box).

HUNTINGTOWER CASTLE

Perth

Tel: 01738 627231

Owner: In the care of Historic Scotland　　　　　　**Contact:** The Steward

The splendid painted ceilings are especially noteworthy in this castle, once owned by the Ruthven family. Scene of a famous leap between two towers by a daughter of the house who was nearly caught in her lover's room. The two towers are still complete, one of 15th - 16th century date, the other of 16th century origin. Now linked by a 17th century range.

Location: OS Ref. NO084 252. 3m NW of Perth off the A85.

Open: 1 Apr - 30 Sept: daily, 9.30am - 6.30pm, last ticket 6pm. 1 Oct - 31 Mar: Mon - Sat, 9.30am - 4.30pm, Suns, 2 - 4.30pm, last ticket 4pm. Closed Thur pm & Fris in winter.

Admission: Adult £2.50, Child 75p, Conc. £1.90.

€

INCHCOLM ABBEY

Inchcolm, Fife

Tel: 01383 823332

Owner: In the care of Historic Scotland　　　　　　**Contact:** The Steward

Known as the 'Iona of the East'. This is the best preserved group of monastic buildings in Scotland, founded in 1123. Includes a 13th century octagonal chapter house.

Location: OS Ref. NT190 826. On Inchcolm in the Firth of Forth. Reached by ferry from South Queensferry (30 mins). Tel. 0131 331 4857 for times/charges.

Open: 1 Apr - 30 Sept: daily, 9.30am - 6.30pm, last ticket 6pm.

Admission: Adult £3, Child £1, Conc. £2.30. Additional charge for ferries.

€

KELLIE CASTLE & GARDEN

Pittenweem, Fife KY10 2RF

Tel: 01333 720271　　**Fax:** 01333 720326

Owner: The National Trust for Scotland　　　　　　**Contact:** The Property Manager

Fine example of domestic architecture in Lowland Scotland dates from the 14th century and was sympathetically restored by the Lorimer family in the late 19th century.

Location: OS Ref. NO519 051. On B9171, 3m NW of Pittenweem, Fife.

Open: Castle: Good Fri - Easter Mon & 1 Jun - 30 Sep: daily, 1 - 5pm. Tearoom, same dates, but opens at 12 noon. Garden & grounds: All year: daily, 9.30am - sunset.

Admission: Adult £5, Conc. £3.75, Family £13.50. Groups: Adult £4, Child/School £1. Garden, grounds & parking: £2.

KILLIECRANKIE 🏱
Pitlochry, Perth & Kinross PH16 5LG
Tel: 01796 473233
Owner: The National Trust for Scotland   **Contact:** The Administrator
The first shots in the Jacobite cause were fired in 1689 at the Battle of Killiecrankie about one mile from the Trust's property.
Location: OS Ref. NN915 620. B8079 (old A9), 3m N of Pitlochry.
Open: Site: All year: daily. Visitor Centre, shop & snack-bar: 1 Apr - 30 Jun & 1 Sep - 31 Oct: daily, 10am - 5.30pm; 1 Jul - 31 Aug, daily, 9.30am - 6pm.
Admission: Car parking £2.

LOCH LEVEN CASTLE 🏛
Loch Leven, Kinross
Tel: 0388 040483
Owner: In the care of Historic Scotland   **Contact:** The Steward
Mary Queen of Scots endured nearly a year of imprisonment in this 14th century tower before her dramatic escape in May 1568. During the First War of Independence it was held by the English, stormed by Wallace and visited by Bruce.
Location: OS Ref. NO138 018. On island in Loch Leven reached by ferry from Kinross off the M90.
Open: 1 Apr - 30 Sept: daily, 9.30am - 6.30pm, last ticket 6pm.
Admission: Adult £3.50, Child £1.20, Conc. £2.50. Prices include ferry trip.
€

MEGGINCH CASTLE GARDENS
Errol, Perthshire PH2 7SW
Tel: 01821 642222 **Fax:** 01821 642708
Owner: Captain Drummond of Megginch and Lady Strange
15th century castle, 1,000 year old yews, flowered parterre, double walled kitchen garden, topiary, astrological garden, pagoda dovecote in courtyard. Part used as a location for the film *Rob Roy.*
Location: OS Ref. NO241 245. 8m E of Perth on A90.
Open: Apr - Oct: Weds. Aug: daily, 2.30 - 6pm. (2002 details.)
Admission: Adult £4, Child £1.
🅣 🅑 Partial. 𝕀 By arrangement. 🅟 Limited for coaches. 🖼 In grounds, on leads.

MEIGLE SCULPTURED STONE MUSEUM 🏛
Meigle
Tel: 01828 640612
Owner: In the care of Historic Scotland
A remarkable collection of 25 sculptured monuments of the Celtic Christian period. This is one of the finest collections of Dark Age sculpture in Western Europe.
Location: OS Ref. NO287 446. In Meigle on the A94.
Open: 1 Apr - 30 Sept: daily, 9.30am - 6.30pm, last ticket 6pm.
Admission: Adult £2.20, Child 75p, Conc. £1.60.
€

MONZIE CASTLE 🏠
Crieff, Perthshire PH7 4HD
Tel: 01764 653110
Owner/Contact: Mrs C M M Crichton
Built in 1791. Destroyed by fire in 1908 and rebuilt and furnished by Sir Robert Lorimer.
Location: OS Ref. NN873 244. 2m NE of Crieff.
Open: 15 May - 13 Jun: daily, 2 - 5pm. By appointment at other times.
Admission: Adult £3, Child £1. Group rates available, contact property for details.
❊

PITTENCRIEFF HOUSE MUSEUM
Dunfermline, Fife
Tel: 01383 313838/722935
Owner: Fife Council   **Contact:** Museum Co-ordinator
A temporary exhibition programme.
Location: OS Ref. NN087 873. In Dunfermline, S of A994 in Pittencrieff Park. 5mins walk W from Abbey.
Open: 1 Apr - 30 Sept: 11am - 5pm; 1 Oct - 31 Mar: 11am - 4pm.
Admission: Free.

Website Information see front section

ST ANDREWS CASTLE 🏛
THE SCORES, ST ANDREWS, KY16 9AR
Tel: 01334 477196
Owner: Historic Scotland   **Contact:** David Eaton
This was the castle of the Bishops of St Andrews and has a fascinating mine and counter-mine, rare examples of medieval siege techniques. There is also a bottle dungeon hollowed out of solid rock. Cardinal Beaton was murdered here and John Knox was sent to the galleys when the ensuing siege was lifted.
Location: OS Ref. NO513 169. In St Andrews on the A91.
Open: Apr - Sept: daily, 9.30am - 6.30pm. Oct - Mar: Daily, 9.30am - 4.30pm. Last ticket 30 mins before closing.
Admission: Adult £3, Child £1, Conc. £2.30. 10% discount for groups (10+). Free pre-booked school visits. Joint ticket with St Andrews Cathedral: Adult £4, Child £1.25, Conc. £3.
ℹ️Visitor centre. ⬜ 🅣Private evening hire. 🅑Partial. WCs. 𝕀 By arrangement. 🅟On street. ⬛ Free if booked. 🖼 Guide dogs. ❊ €

ST ANDREWS CATHEDRAL 🏛
St Andrews, Fife
Tel: 01334 472563
Owner: Historic Scotland   **Contact:** The Administrator
The remains still give a vivid impression of the scale of what was once the largest cathedral in Scotland along with the associated domestic ranges of the priory.
Location: OS Ref. NO514 167. In St Andrews.
Open: 1 Apr - 30 Sept: daily, 9.30am - 6.30pm, last ticket 6pm. 1 Oct - 31 Mar: Mon - Sat, 9.30am - 4.30pm, Suns, 2 - 4.30pm, last ticket 4pm.
Admission: Adult £2.50, Child 75p, Conc. £1.90. Joint entry ticket with St Andrews Castle: Adult £4, Child £1.25, Conc. £3.
€

SCONE PALACE & GROUNDS 🏠   *See page 487 for full page entry.*

STOBHALL 🏠
Stobhall, Cargill, Perthshire PH2 6DR
Tel: 01821 640332
Owner: Viscount Strathallan
Dramatic shrub gardens surround this unusual and charming cluster of historic buildings in a magnificent situation overlooking the River Tay. 14th century chapel with a unique painted ceiling (1642).
Location: OS Ref. NO132 343. 8m N of Perth on A93.
Open: No general opening in 2004 due to major works. Those with special interest may visit by prior appointment.

STRATHTYRUM HOUSE & GARDENS
St Andrews, Fife
Tel: 01334 473600
Owner: The Strathtyrum Trust   **Contact:** Elizabeth Smith
Location: OS Ref: NO490 172. Entrance from the St Andrews/Guardbridge Road which is signposted when open.
Open: 3 -7, 10 - 12 May, 31 May - 4 Jun, 5 - 9 Jul, 2 - 6 Aug & 30 Aug - 3 Sept: 2 - 4.30pm.
Admission: Adult £5, Child £2.50.
🅟 Free. 🖼 Guide dogs only.

Historic Scotland.

ARGYLL'S LODGING
STIRLING

Map 10

Owner: Historic Scotland

▶ CONTACT

Neil Young
Argyll's Lodging
Castle Wynd
Stirling FK8 1EJ

Tel: 01786 431319

Fax: 01786 448194

▶ LOCATION
OS Ref. NS793 938

At the top and on E side of Castle Wynd in Stirling. One way route from town centre from Albert Street.

Rail: Stirling.

Air: Edinburgh or Glasgow.

This attractive townhouse, sitting at the foot of Stirling Castle, is decorated as it would have been during the 9th Earl of Argyll's occupation around 1680. Before coming into Historic Scotland's care the building was a youth hostel, but restoration revealed hidden secrets from the Lodging's past. Perhaps the best of these was a section of 17th century *trompe l'oeil* panelling in the dining room, created by painter David McBeath.

Visitors to Argyll's Lodging might wonder at the highly decorated walls and rich materials and colours used but the restoration relied on a household inventory of 1680 found among the then Duchess's papers. But no matter how rich the decoration, it cannot match the colourful lives of Argyll Lodging's inhabitants.

The 9th Earl, Archibald Campbell, was sentenced to death for treason and imprisoned in Edinburgh Castle. However he escaped when his stepdaughter smuggled him out dressed as her page. Archibald escaped to Holland, but his stepdaughter was arrested and placed in public stocks – a major humiliation. He didn't cheat death a second time, however. Joining plots over the succession following Charles II's death, he was captured and beheaded in 1685.

An earlier inhabitant of Argyll's Lodging, Sir William Alexander, was tutor to James VI's son, Prince Henry and in 1621 he attempted to colonise Nova Scotia in Canada. Great wealth eluded him all his life, however, and he died a bankrupt in 1640, leading to the town council taking over the lodging and selling it to the Earl of Argyll in the 1660s.

▶ OPENING TIMES

April - September:
Daily: 9.30am - 6pm.

October - March:
Daily: 9.30am - 5pm.

▶ ADMISSION

Adult £3.30
Child* £1.20
Conc.......................£2.50

*up to 16 years

FUNCTION

ROOM	SIZE	MAX CAPACITY
Laigh Hall	11 x 6m	60 for receptions
High Dining Room	11 x 6m	26 for dinner
Both rooms: 120 for receptions		

Interpretation scheme includes computer animations; joint ticket with Stirling Castle available.

Evening receptions/dinners.

Partial. No wheelchair access to upper floor.

Ample parking for coaches and cars on Stirling Castle Esplanade.

Free pre-booked school visits scheme.

Guide dogs only. ❄

INVERARAY CASTLE 🏛

INVERARAY

www.inveraray-castle.com

The Duke of Argyll's family have lived in Inveraray since the early 15th century. The present Castle was built between 1745 and 1790.

The ancient Royal Burgh of Inveraray lies about 60 miles north west of Glasgow by Loch Fyne in an area of spectacular natural beauty combining the ruggedness of highland scenery with the sheltered tidal loch 90 miles from the open sea.

The Castle is the home of the Duke and Duchess of Argyll. Its fairytale exterior belies the grandeur of its gracious interior. The building was designed by Roger Morris and decorated by Robert Mylne, the clerk of works being William Adam, father of Robert and John, who did much of the laying out of the present Royal Burgh, an unrivalled example of an early planned town.

Visitors may see the famous Armoury Hall containing some 1300 pieces, French tapestries made especially for the Castle, fine examples of Scottish, English and French furniture together with a wealth of other works of art including china, silver and family artifacts, all of which form a unique collection spanning the generations which are identified by a magnificent genealogical display in the Clan Room.

Owner:
Duke of Argyll

▶ CONTACT
The Factor
Dept HHD
Argyll Estates Office
Cherry Park
Inveraray
Argyll PA32 8XE

Tel: 01499 302203
Fax: 01499 302421

e-mail: enquiries@
inveraray-castle.com

▶ LOCATION
OS Ref. NN100 090

From Edinburgh
2½ - 3hrs via Glasgow.

Just NE of Inveraray
on A83. W shore
of Loch Fyne.

Bus: Bus route
stopping point within
½ m.

Map 9

▶ OPENING TIMES

Summer

3 April - 31 October

April, May & October:
Mon - Thur & Sats:
10am - 1pm & 2 - 5.45pm
Fridays: Closed
Suns: 1 - 5.45pm.
Last admissions
12.30 & 5pm.

June, July, August &
September:
Daily: 10am - 5.45pm
(including Friday)
Suns: 1 - 5.45pm.
Last admission 5pm.

Winter
Closed.

▶ ADMISSION
House only
Adult £5.90
Child (under 16yrs) .. £3.90
OAP/Student £4.90
Family (2+2) £16.00

Groups of
(20+) .... 20% discount

🚫📷 ℹ No photography. Guide books in French, Italian, Japanese and German translations.

♿ Visitors may alight at the entrance. 2 wheelchair ramps to castle. All main public rooms suitable but two long flights of stairs to the smaller rooms upstairs. WCs.

🍴 Seats up to 50. Licensed. Menus available on request. Groups book in advance. Tel: 01499 302112.

👥 Available for up to 100 people at no additional cost. Groups please book. Tour time: 1 hr.

🅿 100 cars. Separate coach park close to Castle

🎒 £1.50 per child. A guide can be provided. Areas of interest include a nature walk.

🐕 In grounds, on leads. Guide dogs only inside Castle.

West Highlands & Islands, Loch Lomond, Stirling and Trossachs

ACHAMORE GARDENS
Isle of Gigha, Argyll PA41 7AD
Tel: 01583 505254
Owner: Isle of Gigha Heritage Trust   **Contact:** Nic Macaulay-Smith
Gardens only open. Sub-tropical gardens created by Sir James Horlick who bought Gigha in 1944.
Location: OS Ref. NR650 500. Off the Mull of Kintyre. Ferry from Tayinloan.
Open: Dawn until dusk every day.
Admission: Adult £2, Child £1.

ALLOA TOWER
Alloa Park, Alloa, Clackmannanshire FK10 1PP
Tel: 01259 211701
Owner: The National Trust for Scotland   **Contact:** The Manager
Restored and furnished 14th century Tower House with an unusual 18th century interior. The ancestral home of the Erskines, Earls of Mar.
Location: OS Ref. NS886 925. On A907, in Alloa.
Open: 1 Apr - 31 Oct: Daily 1 - 5pm. Weekday morning visits for pre-booked groups.
Admission: Adult £3.50, Conc. £2.60, Family £9.50. Groups: Adult £2.80, Child/School £1. 25% discount to Clackmannanshire residents.

ANGUS'S GARDEN
Barguillean, Taynuilt, Argyll, West Highlands PA35 1HY
Tel: 01866 822335   **Fax:** 01866 822048   **Contact:** Sean Honeyman
Memorial garden of peace, tranquillity and reconciliation.
Location: OS Ref. NM978 289. 4m SW on Glen Lonan road from A85.
Open: All year: daily, 9am - 5pm.
Admission: Adult £2, Child Free.

ARDENCRAIG GARDENS
Ardencraig, Rothesay, Isle of Bute, West Highlands PA20 9BP
Tel: 01700 505339   **Fax:** 01700 502492
Owner: Argyll and Bute Council   **Contact:** Allan Macdonald
Walled garden, greenhouses, aviaries.
Location: OS Ref. NS105 645. 2m from Rothesay.
Open: May - Sept: Mon - Fri, 10am - 4.30pm, Sats & Suns, 1 - 4.30pm.

ARDKINGLAS ESTATE
CAIRNDOW, ARGYLL PA26 8BH
www.ardkinglas.com

Tel: 01499 600261   **Fax:** 01499 600241   **e-mail:** ardkinglas@btinternet.com
Contact: The Estate Manager
Ardkinglas House, a superb neo-baronial house near the head of Loch Fyne was built by Sir Robert Lorimer in 1907 and has retained many original features. Although not open to the public, the house is available for weddings, corporate days or as a film location. The Woodland Gardens, which are open to the public, are part of a designed landscape and are of outstanding horticultural and scenic significance and include many champion trees.
Location: OS Ref. NN179 106. Head of Loch Fyne, just off the A83 at Cairndow, 10m W of Arrochar. About 1hr from Glasgow.
Open: Woodland Garden & woodland trails: All year, dawn - dusk.
Admission: Garden admission charge for adults.
⬛ Tree shop. 🐾 🍴 🔲 Partial. 🎦 🍴 𝒊 By arrangement. 🅿 Limited.
🐕 In grounds, on leads. ✻ €

ARDUAINE GARDEN
Arduaine, By Oban, Argyll PA34 4XQ
Tel/Fax: 01852 200366
Owner: The National Trust for Scotland
A haven of tranquillity nestling on the west coast, Arduaine Garden is best in the late spring and early summer.
Location: OS Ref. NM798 105. On A816, 20m S of Oban and 17m N of Lochgilphead.
Open: All year: daily, 9.30am - sunset.
Admission: Adult £3.50, Conc. £2.60, Family £9.50. Groups: Adult £2.80, Child/School £1.

ARGYLL'S LODGING   *See page 493 for full page entry.*

BALLOCH CASTLE COUNTRY PARK
Balloch, Dunbartonshire G83 8LX
Tel: 01389 722230   **Fax:** 01389 720922
                        Contact: Loch Lomond & The Trossachs National Park
A 200 acre country park on the banks of Loch Lomond.
Location: OS Ref. NS390 830. SE shore of Loch Lomond, off A82 for Balloch or A811 for Stirling.
Open: Visitor Centre: Easter - Oct: variable hours, please phone for details. Country Park: All year: dawn - dusk.
Admission: Free for both Visitor Centre and Country Park.

BANNOCKBURN HERITAGE CENTRE
Glasgow Road, Stirling FK7 0LJ
Tel: 01786 812664   **Fax:** 01786 810892
Owner: The National Trust for Scotland
In 1314 from this battlefield the Scots 'sent them homeward to think again', when Edward II's English army was soundly defeated by King Robert the Bruce.
Location: OS Ref. NS810 910. Off M80 & M9/J9, 2m S of Stirling.
Open: Site: All year:, daily. Heritage Centre, Shop & Café: 1 Feb - 31 Mar & 1 Nov - 24 Dec: daily 10.30am - 4pm; 1 Apr - 31 Oct: daily, 10am - 5.30pm (last audio-visual show half-an-hour before closing).
Admission: Adult £3.50, Conc. £2.60, Family £9.50. Groups: Adult £2.80, Child/School £1. Car parking £2.

BENMORE BOTANIC GARDEN
Dunoon, Argyll PA23 8QU
Tel: 01369 706261   **Fax:** 01369 706369   **Contact:** The Curator
A botanical paradise. Enter the magnificent avenue of giant redwoods and follow trails through the Formal Garden and hillside woodlands with its spectacular outlook over the Holy Loch and the Eachaig Valley.
Location: OS Ref. NS150 850. 7m N of Dunoon on A815.
Open: 1 Mar - 31 Oct: daily, 10am - 6pm. Closes 5pm in Mar & Oct.
Admission: Adult £3.50, Child £1, Conc. £3, Family £8. Group discounts available.

BONAWE IRON FURNACE
Taynuilt, Argyll
Tel: 01866 822432
Owner: In the care of Historic Scotland   **Contact:** The Steward
Founded in 1753 by Cumbrian iron masters this is the most complete remaining charcoal fuelled ironworks in Britain. Displays show how iron was once made here.
Location: OS Ref. NN005 310. By the village of Taynuilt off the A85.
Open: 1 Apr - 30 Sept: daily, 9.30am - 6.30pm, last ticket 6pm.
Admission: Adult £3, Child £1, Conc. £2.30.
€

CASTLE STALKER
Portnacroish, Appin, Argyll PA38 4BA
Tel: 01883 622768   **Fax:** 01883 626238   www.castlestalker.com
Owner: Mrs M Allward   **Contact:** Messrs R & A Allward
Early 15th century tower house and ancient seat of the Stewarts of Appin. Picturesquely set on a rocky islet approx 400 yds off the mainland on the shore of Loch Linnhe. Reputed to have been used by James IV as a hunting lodge. Garrisoned by Government troops during the 1745 rising. Restored from a ruin by the late Lt Col Stewart Allward following acquisition in 1965 and now retained by his family.
Location: OS Ref. NM930 480. Approx. 20m N of Oban on the A828. On islet ¼ m offshore.
Open: 7 - 11 & 14 - 18 Jun; 23 - 27, 30 & 31 Aug; 1 - 3 & 6 - 10 Sept. Telephone for appointments. Times variable depending on tides and weather.
Admission: Adult £6, Child £3.
𝒊 Not suitable for coach parties. 🔲 Unsuitable.

West Highlands & Islands, Loch Lomond, Stirling and Trossachs

DOUNE CASTLE

Doune

Tel: 01786 841742

Owner: Earl of Moray (leased to Historic Scotland) **Contact:** The Steward

A formidable 14th century courtyard castle, built for the Regent Albany. The striking keep-gatehouse combines domestic quarters including the splendid Lord's Hall with its carved oak screen, musicians' gallery and double fireplace.

Location: OS Ref. NN720 020. In Doune, 8m S of Callendar on the A84.

Open: 1 Apr - 30 Sept: daily, 9.30am - 6.30pm. 1 Oct - 31 Mar: Mon - Wed, Sat & Sun, 9.30am - 4.30pm, last admission ½ hr before closing.

Admission: Adult £3, Child £1, Conc. £2.30.

€

DUART CASTLE

ISLE OF MULL, ARGYLL PA64 6AP

www.duartcastle.com

Tel: 01680 812309 or 01577 830311   **e-mail:** duartguide@isle-of-mull.demon.co.uk

Owner/Contact: Sir Lachlan Maclean Bt

Duart is a fortress, one of a line of castles stretching from Dunollie in the east to Mingary in the north, all guarding the Sound of Mull. The earliest part of the Castle was built in the 12th century, the keep was added in 1360 by the 5th Chief Lachlan Lubanach and the most recent alterations were completed in 1673. The Macleans were staunchly loyal to the Stuarts. After the rising of 1745 they lost Duart and their lands were forfeited. Sir Fitzroy Maclean, 25th Chief, restored the Castle in 1910. Duart remains the family home of the Chief of the Clan Maclean.

Location: OS Ref. NM750 350. Off A849 on the east point of the Isle of Mull.

Open: 1 - 30 Apr: Sun - Thurs, 11am - 4pm. 1 May - 10 Oct: daily, 10.30am - 5.30pm.

Admission: Adult £4.50, Child £2.25, Conc. £4, Family £11.25.

Unsuitable. By arrangement. In grounds, on leads.

Sir John Vanbrugh

1664-1726

Baroque Architect

Born into a wealthy family, Vanbrugh initially had a career in the army, and then after travelling extensively in his mid-thirties, he turned to architecture as a career. Don't just look for large designs, look for huge, flamboyant, monumental statements of design which are best seen from a distance to appreciate the sheer swagger of their style – huge drums and cupola dominate the exteriors of his facades.

Visit Blenheim Palace, Oxfordshire, Castle Howard, Yorkshire, Seaton Delaval Hall, Northumberland.

Baroque Architect

DUMBARTON CASTLE

Dumbarton, Strathclyde

Tel: 01389 732167

Owner: Historic Scotland **Contact:** The Steward

Location: OS Ref. NS401 744. 600yds S of A84 at E end of Dumbarton.

Open: 1 Apr - 30 Sept: daily, 9.30am - 6.30pm, last ticket 6pm. 1 Oct - 31 Mar: Mon - Wed & Sats, 9.30am - 4.30pm, Thurs, 9.30am - 12 noon, Fris closed, Suns, 2 - 4.30pm, last ticket 4pm.

Admission: Adult £2.50, Child 75p, Conc £1.90.

€

DUNBLANE CATHEDRAL

Dunblane

Tel: 01786 823388

Owner: Historic Scotland **Contact:** The Steward

One of Scotland's noblest medieval churches. The lower part of the tower is Romanesque but the larger part of the building is of the 13th century. It was restored in 1889 - 93 by Sir Rowand Anderson.

Location: OS Ref. NN782 015. In Dunblane.

Open: All year: Suns, from 1.30pm.

Admission: Free.

Crown Copyright

DUNSTAFFNAGE CASTLE 🏛
BY OBAN, ARGYLL PA37 1PZ

Tel: 01631 562465

Owner: In the care of Historic Scotland   **Contact:** The Steward

A very fine 13th century castle built on a rock with a great curtain wall. The castle's colourful history stretches across the Wars of Independence to the 1745 rising. The castle was briefly the prison of Flora Macdonald. Marvellous views from the top of the curtain wall. Close by are the remains of a chapel with beautiful architectural detail.

Location: OS49 NM882 344. 3¹/₂ m NE of Oban off A85.

Open: Apr - Sept: daily, 9.30am - 6.30pm, last ticket ¹/₂ hr before closing. Oct - Mar: daily, 9.30am - 4.30pm (closed Thurs & Fri).

Admission: Adult £2.50, Child 75p, Conc. £1.90. 10% discount for groups (10+).
🖱 🖐Partial. 🎬 By arrangement. 🅿 ▣ Free pre-booked school visits. 🐕 In grounds, on leads. ✳ €

THE HILL HOUSE ♥
Upper Colquhoun Street, Helensburgh G84 9AJ

Tel: 01436 673900   **Fax:** 01436 674685

Owner: The National Trust for Scotland

Charles Rennie Mackintosh set this 20th century masterpiece high on a hillside overlooking the Firth of Clyde. Mackintosh also designed furniture, fittings and decorative schemes to complement the house, and suggested a layout for the garden which has been renovated by the Trust.

Location: OS Ref. NS300 820. Off B832, between A82 & A814, 23m NW of Glasgow.

Open: 1 Apr - 31 Oct: daily, 1.30 - 5.30pm. Morning visits available for pre-booked groups.

Admission: Adult £7, Conc. £5.25, Family £19 (no group rates).

INCHMAHOME PRIORY 🏛
Port of Menteith

Tel: 01877 385294

Owner: In the care of Historic Scotland   **Contact:** The Steward

A beautifully situated Augustinian priory on an island in the Lake of Menteith founded in 1238 with much of the building surviving. The five year old Mary Queen of Scots was sent here for safety in 1547.

Location: OS Ref. NN574 005. On an island in Lake of Menteith. Reached by ferry from Port of Menteith, 4m E of Aberfoyle off A81.

Open: 1 Apr - 30 Sept: daily, 9.30am - 6.30pm, last ticket 6pm.

Admission: Adult £3.50, Child £1.20, Conc. £2.50. Charge includes ferry trip.
€

INVERARAY CASTLE 🏛
See page 494 for full page entry.

INVERARAY JAIL
Church Square, Inveraray, Argyll PA32 8TX

Tel: 01499 302381   **Fax:** 01499 302195   **e-mail:** inverarayjail@btclick.com
www.inverarayjail.co.uk

Owner: Visitor Centres Ltd   **Contact:** J Linley

A living 19th century prison! Uniformed prisoners and warders, life-like figures, imaginative exhibitions, sounds, smells and trials in progress, bring the 1820 courtroom and former county prison back to life. See the 'In Prison Today' exhibition.

Location: OS Ref. NN100 090. Church Square, Inveraray, Argyll.

Open: Apr - Oct: 9.30am - 6pm, last adm. 5pm. Nov - Mar: 10am - 5pm, last adm. 4pm.

Admission: Adult £5.75, Child £2.80, OAP £3.75, Family £15.70. Groups (10+): Adult £3.95, OAP £2.60.
🖱 🖐Partial (FOC). ▣ 🖐 ✳

IONA ABBEY & NUNNERY 🏛
Iona, West Highlands

Tel/Fax: 01681 700512   **e-mail:** hs.ionaabbey@scotland.gov.uk
www.historic-scotland.gov.uk

Owner: In the care of Historic Scotland   **Contact:** Chris Calvert

One of Scotland's most historic and venerated sites, Iona Abbey is a celebrated Christian centre and the burial place for many Scottish kings. The abbey and nunnery grounds house one of the most comprehensive collections of Christian carved stones in Scotland, dating from 600AD to the 1600s. Includes the Columbia Centre, Fionnphort exhibition and giftshop.

Location: OS Ref. NM270 240. Ferry service from Fionnphort, Mull.

Open: All year:, daily.

Admission: Adult £3.30, Child (under 16) £1.20, Conc. £2.50. Columba Centre, exhibition & giftshop: Free.
🖱 ✳ €

KILCHURN CASTLE 🏛
Loch Awe, Dalmally, Argyll

Tel: 01786 431323

Owner: In the care of Historic Scotland   **Contact:** The Steward

A square tower, built by Sir Colin Campbell of Glenorchy c1550, it was much enlarged in 1693 to give the building, now a ruin, its present picturesque outline. Spectacular views of Loch Awe.

Location: OS Ref. NN133 276. At the NE end of Loch Awe, 2¹/₂ m W of Dalmally.

Open: Ferry service operates in the summer. Tel: 01838 200440 for times & prices.

Admission: Please telephone for details.

ROTHESAY CASTLE 🏛
Rothesay, Isle of Bute

Tel: 01700 502691

Owner: In the care of Historic Scotland   **Contact:** The Steward

A favourite residence of the Stuart Kings, this is a wonderful example of a 13th century circular castle of enclosure with 16th century forework containing the Great Hall. Attacked by Vikings in its earlier days.

Location: OS Ref. NS088 646. In Rothesay, Isle of Bute. Ferry from Wemyss Bay on the A78.

Open: 1 Apr - 30 Sept: daily, 9.30am - 6.30pm, last ticket 6pm. 1 Oct - 31 Mar: Mon - Wed & Sats, 9.30am - 4.30pm, Thurs 9.30am - 12 noon, Fris closed, Suns, 2 - 4.30pm, last ticket 4pm.

Admission: Adult £2.50, Child 75p, Conc. £1.90.
€

ST BLANE'S CHURCH 🏛
Kingarth, Isle of Bute

Tel: 0131 668 8800

Owner: In the care of Historic Scotland

This 12th century Romanesque chapel stands on the site of a 12th century Celtic monastery.

Location: OS Ref. NS090 570. At the S end of the Isle of Bute.

Open: All year: daily.

Admission: Free.
€

Accommodation Index see front section

Historic Scotland

STIRLING CASTLE

CASTLE WYND, STIRLING FK8 1EJ

Tel: 01786 450000   **Fax:** 01786 464678

Owner: Historic Scotland   **Contact:** Neil Young

Stirling Castle has played a key role in Scottish history, dominating the North–South and East–West routes through Scotland. The battles of Stirling Bridge and Bannockburn were fought in its shadow and Mary Queen of Scots lived here as a child. Renaissance architecture, restored Great Hall and tapestry weaving.

Location: OS Ref. NS790 941. At the top of Castle Wynd in Stirling.

Open: Apr - Sept: 9.30am - 6pm. Oct - Mar: 9.30am - 5pm, last ticket 45 mins before closing.

Admission: Adult £8, Child £2, Conc. £6. 10% discount for groups (10+). Free booked school visits, except May - August.

ℹ️Picnic area. Joint ticket with Argyll's Lodging. 📷 🅃Private hire. ♿Partial. WC. 🍽️Licensed. 🎫 🅿 ◼ 🐕Guide dogs. ❋ €

TOROSAY CASTLE & GARDENS 🏛️

CRAIGNURE, ISLE OF MULL PA65 6AY

www.torosay.com

Tel: 01680 812421   **Fax:** 01680 812470   **e-mail:** torosay@aol.com

Owner/Contact: Mr Chris James

Torosay Castle and Gardens set on the beautiful Island of Mull, was completed in 1858 by the eminent architect David Bryce in the Scottish baronial style, and is surrounded by 12 acres of spectacular gardens which offer a dramatic contrast between formal terraces, impressive statue walk and informal woodland, also rhododendron collection, alpine, walled, water and oriental gardens. The house offers family history, portraits, scrapbooks and antiques in an informal and relaxed atmosphere.

Location: OS Ref. NM730 350. 1¹/₂ m SE of Craignure by A849.

Open: House: 1 Apr - 31 Oct: daily, 10.30am - 5pm. Gardens: All year: daily, 9am - 7pm or daylight hours in winter.

Admission: Adult £5, Child £1.75, Conc. £4, Family £12.

📷 🎫 🅃 ♿Grounds. WC. 🍽️ 🅿 🏠Holiday cottages. ❋ € 🅥Tel for details.

Inveraray Castle, Argyll from the book *Historic Family Homes and Gardens from the Air*, see page 54.

ALTYRE ESTATE

Altyre Estate, Forres, Moray IV36 2SH

Tel: 01463 715585 **Fax:** 01463 715601 **e-mail:** acampbell@bidwells.co.uk

Contact: Managing Agent

Altyre Estate comprises architecturally interesting buildings including Italianate farm buildings, standing stones and access to areas of natural and ornithological interest. Altyre Estate may interest scientific groups, students, and the general public.

Location: OS Ref. NJ028 552. Details given on appointment.

Open: Visitors are welcome by appointment on the first working day of Apr, May Jun, Jul & Aug.

Admission: Free.

ARBUTHNOTT HOUSE

Arbuthnott, Laurencekirk AB30 1PA

Tel: 01561 361226 **e-mail:** keith@arbuthnott.co.uk **www**.arbuthnott.co.uk

Owner: The Viscount of Arbuthnott   **Contact:** The Master of Arbuthnott

Arbuthnott family home for 800 years with formal 17th century walled garden on unusually steep south facing slope. Well maintained grass terraces, herbaceous borders, shrubs and greenhouses.

Location: OS Ref. NO796 751. Off B967 between A90 and A92, 25m S of Aberdeen.

Open: House: 2/3 May; 1/2, 8/9, 15/16 & 22/23 Aug and by prior arrangement. Guided tours: 2 - 5pm. Garden: All year: 9am - 5pm.

Admission: House: £4. Garden: £2.

♿ Ground floor. Ⓓ Obligatory. 🗿 ❌ ✳

BALFLUIG CASTLE

Alford, Aberdeenshire AB33 8EJ

Tel: 020 7624 3200

Owner/Contact: Mark Tennant of Balfluig

Small 16th century tower house in farmland, restored in 1967.

Location: OS Ref. NJ586 151. Alford, Aberdeenshire.

Open: Please write to M I Tennant Esq, 30 Abbey Gardens, London NW8 9AT. Occasionally let by the week for holidays. Scottish Tourist Board ***.

♿ Unsuitable. ❌ 🗼1 single, 4 double. ✳

BALMORAL CASTLE (GROUNDS & EXHIBITIONS)

Balmoral, Ballater, Aberdeenshire AB35 5TB

Tel: 013397 42534 **Fax:** 013397 42034

Owner: Her Majesty The Queen   **Contact:** Garry Marsden

Holiday home of The Royal Family, bought by Prince Albert in 1852. Grounds, gardens and exhibition of paintings and works of art in the Ballroom. Exhibitions, commemorative china and a display of native wildlife in their natural habitat in the Carriage Hall. Display of carriages and Upper Deeside Art Society exhibition on view in the Stables.

Location: OS Ref. NO256 951. Off A93 between Ballater and Braemar. 50m W of Aberdeen.

Open: 1 Apr - 29 Jul: daily, 10am - 5pm (last recommended admission 4pm).

Admission: Adult £5, Child (5-16yrs) £1, OAP £4.

BALVENIE CASTLE ⛩

Dufftown

Tel: 01340 820121

Owner: In the care of Historic Scotland   **Contact:** The Steward

Picturesque ruins of 13th century moated stronghold originally owned by the Comyns. Visited by Edward I in 1304 and by Mary Queen of Scots in 1562. Occupied by Cumberland in 1746.

Location: OS Ref. NJ326 408. At Dufftown on A941.

Open: 1 Apr - 30 Sept: daily, 9.30am - 6.30pm, last ticket 6pm.

Admission: Adult £1.80, Child 50p, Conc. £1.30.

€

BRODIE CASTLE ⛩

Forres, Moray IV36 0TE

Tel: 01309 641371 **Fax:** 01309 641600

Owner: The National Trust for Scotland

This imposing Castle stands in rich Morayshire parkland. The lime harled building is a typical 'Z' plan tower house with ornate corbelled battlements and bartizans, with 17th & 19th century additions.

Location: OS Ref. NH980 577. Off A96 41/2 m W of Forres and 24m E of Inverness.

Open: 1 - 30 Apr & 1 Jul - 31 Aug: daily, 12 noon - 4pm; 1 May - 30 Jun & 1 - 30 Sep: Sun - Thur, 12 noon - 4pm. Grounds, All year: daily 9.30am - sunset.

Admission: Castle, garden & grounds: Adult £5, Conc. £3.75, Family £13.50. Groups: Adult £4, Child/School £1. Garden & grounds only: £1 (honesty box).

CAIRNESS HOUSE

Lonmay, Fraserburgh, Aberdeenshire AB43 8XP

Tel: 01346 582078 **Fax:** 01346 582314 **e-mail:** cairnesshouse@hotmail.com

Owner: Mr Julio Soriano y Ruiz   **Contact:** Mr K H Khairallah

Scotland's most extraordinary neo-classical house: James Playfair's architectural masterpiece built in 1790s. Largely neglected and forgotten for 60 years. Magnificent and unique semi-circular service wing, icehouse, and earliest Egyptian room in Britain. Elaborate plasterwork and finest private collection of Regency furniture and paintings in Buchan. House and grounds undergoing restoration.

Location: OS Ref. NK038 609. Off A952, 4m SE of Fraserburgh, 1/4 m W of B9033 about 2m S of St Comb's.

Open: All year by written appointment only.

Admission: Adult £6, OAP/Student £5.

ⓘNo photography. No smoking. ⒹObligatory. 🗿 Limited. ❌ ✳

CASTLE FRASER & GARDEN ⛩

Sauchen, Inverurie AB51 7LD

Tel: 01330 833463

Owner: The National Trust for Scotland   **Contact:** The Manager

Begun in 1575 by the 6th Laird, Michael Fraser, the two low wings contribute to the scale and magnificence of the towers rising above them, combining to make this the largest and most elaborate of the Scottish castles built on the 'Z' plan.

Location: OS Ref. NJ723 125. Off A944, 4m N of Dunecht & 16m W of Aberdeen.

Open: 1 Apr - 30 Jun & 1 - 30 Sep: Fri - Tue, 12 noon - 5.30 pm; 1 Jul - 31 Aug: daily 11am - 5.30pm.

Admission: Castle & Garden: Adult £7, Conc. £5.25, Family £19. Groups: Adult £5.60, Child/School £1. Car parking, £2.

Drum Castle, Grampian Highlands.

CORGARFF CASTLE

Strathdon

Tel: 013398 83635

Owner: In the care of Historic Scotland   **Contact:** The Steward

A 16th century tower house converted into a barracks for Hanoverian troops in 1748.

Location: OS Ref. NJ255 086. 8m W of Strathdon on A939. 14m NW of Ballater.

Open: 1 Apr - 30 Sept: daily, 9.30am - 6.30pm. 1 Oct - 31 Mar: Sats, 9.30am - 4.30pm. Suns, 2 - 4.30pm, last admission 1/2 hr before closing.

Admission: Adult £3, Child £1, Conc. £2.30.

€

CRAIG CASTLE

Rhynie, Huntly, Aberdeenshire AB54 4LP

Tel: 01464 861705 **Fax:** 01464 861702

Owner: Mr A J Barlas   **Contact:** The Property Manager

The Castle is built round a courtyard and consists of a 16th century L-shaped Keep, a Georgian house (architect John Adam) and a 19th century addition (architect Archibald Simpson of Aberdeen). The Castle was a Gordon stronghold for 300 years. It has a very fine collection of coats-of-arms.

Location: OS Ref. NJ472 259. 3m W of Rhynie and Lumsden on B9002.

Open: May - Sept: Wed and every 2nd weekend in each month, 2 - 5pm.

Admission: Adult £5, Child £1.

⊤ ⓖ Unsuitable. ⓕ By arrangement. ⓟ Limited for coaches. ⓖ Guide dogs only.

CRAIGSTON CASTLE

Turriff, Aberdeenshire AB53 5PX

Tel: 01888 551228/551640

Owner: William Pratesi Urquhart   **Contact:** Mrs Fiona Morrison

Built in 1607 to John Tutor of Cromarty's individualistic plan. An arch and ornate sculptured balcony joins two towers, to accommodate the Laird's private apartments. The largely unchanged interior, still lived in by the Urquhart family, includes remarkable series of carved oak panels on doors and shutters, early 16th century.

Location: OS Ref. NJ762 550. On B9105, 4 1/2 m NE of Turriff.

Open: 1 - 9 May, 26 Jun - 4 Jul & 24 Jul - 8 Aug: daily, 11am - 3pm. Groups throughout the year by appointment.

Admission: Adult £5, Child £1, Conc. £3.75. Groups: Adult £4, Child/School £1.

ⓖ Unsuitable. ⓕ Obligatory. ⓟ ⓖ In grounds on leads. ✲

CRATHES CASTLE & GARDEN ♛

Banchory AB31 3QJ

Tel: 01330 844525 **Fax:** 01330 844797

Owner: The National Trust for Scotland

The building of the castle began in 1553 and took 40 years to complete. Just over 300 years later, Sir James and Lady Burnett began developing the walled garden and created not just one but eight superb gardens

Location: OS Ref. NO733 969: On A93, 3m E of Banchory and 15m W of Aberdeen.

Open: Castle & Visitor Centre: 1 Apr - 30 Sep: daily 10am - 5.30pm; 1 - 31 Oct: daily 10am - 4.30pm. Restaurant & shop: 18 Jan - 31 Mar & 1 Nov - 21 Dec: Wed - Sun, 10am - 4pm; 1 Apr - 30 Sep: daily 10am - 5.30pm; 1 - 31 Oct: daily 10am - 4.30pm. To help you enjoy your visit and for safety reasons, admission to the castle is by timed ticket (limited numbers: entry may be delayed). Garden and grounds, All year: daily 9am - sunset.

Admission: Castle & Garden: Adult £9, Conc. £6.50. Groups: Adult £7, Child/School £1, Family £23. Car parking £2. Castle/walled garden/grounds only: Adult £7, Conc. £5.25.

CRUICKSHANK BOTANIC GARDEN

St Machar Drive, Aberdeen AB24 3UU

Tel: 01224 272704 **Fax:** 01224 272703

Owner: University of Aberdeen   **Contact:** R B Rutherford

Extensive collection of shrubs, herbaceous and alpine plants and trees. Rock and water gardens.

Location: OS Ref. NJ938 084. In old Aberdeen. Entrance in the Chanonry.

Open: All year: Mon - Fri, 9am - 4.30pm. May - Sept: Sats & Suns, 2 - 5pm.

Admission: Free.

DALLAS DHU DISTILLERY

Forres

Tel: 01309 676548

Owner: In the care of Historic Scotland   **Contact:** The Steward

A completely preserved time capsule of the distiller's craft. Wander at will through this fine old Victorian distillery then enjoy a dram. Visitor centre, shop and audio-visual theatre.

Location: OS Ref. NJ035 566. 1m S of Forres off the A940.

Open: 1 Apr - 30 Sept: daily, 9.30am - 6.30pm, last ticket 6pm. 1 Oct - 31 Mar: Mon - Sat, 9.30am - 4.30pm, Suns, 2 - 4.30pm, last ticket 4pm. Closed Thurs pm and Fris in winter.

Admission: Adult £3.50, Child £1, Conc. £2.60.

€

DELGATIE CASTLE

TURRIFF, ABERDEENSHIRE AB53 5TD

www.delgatiecastle.com

Tel/Fax: 01888 563479 **e-mail:** jjohnson@delgatie-castle.freeserve.co.uk

Owner: Delgatie Castle Trust   **Contact:** Mrs Joan Johnson

Dating from 1030 the Castle is steeped in Scottish history yet still has the atmosphere of a lived in home. It has some of the finest painted ceilings, Mary Queen of Scots' bed-chamber and armour, Victorian clothes, fine furniture and paintings are displayed. Widest turnpike stair of its kind in Scotland. Clan Hay Centre.

Location: OS Ref. NJ754 506. Off A947 Aberdeen to Banff Road.

Open: Apr - Oct: 10am - 5pm (Tue & Wed open till 8pm). Also 11 Nov - 18 Mar 2004: Tue - Thur, 10am - 4pm (excluding Christmas & New Year week).

Admission: Adult £4, Conc. £3. Groups (10+): £3.

ⓘ No photography. ⊤ ⓖ Ground floor. WC. ⓖ Home-baking. ⓕ By arrangement. ⓟ ⓖ ⓖ ⓖ 6 x houses for self catering. ✲

DRUM CASTLE & GARDEN ♛

Drumoak, by Banchory AB31 3EY

Tel: 01330 811204

Owner: The National Trust for Scotland   **Contact:** The Property Manager

Owned for 653 years by one family, the Irvines. The combination over the years of a 13th century square tower, a very fine Jacobean mansion house and the additions of the Victorian lairds make Drum Castle unique among Scottish castles.

Location: OS Ref. NJ796 004. Off A93, 3m W of Peterculter and 10m W of Aberdeen.

Open: 1 Apr - 31 May: daily, 12.30 - 5.30pm; 1 Jun - 31 Aug: daily 10am - 5.30pm. Grounds: All year: daily, 9.30am - sunset.

Admission: Castle & Garden: Adult £7, Conc. £5.25, Family £19. Groups: Adult £5.60, Child/School £1. Garden & grounds only: Adult £2.50, Conc. £1.90, Family £7. Groups: Adult £2, Child/School £1.

DRUMMUIR CASTLE

Drummuir, by Keith, Banffshire AB55 5JE

Tel: 01542 810332 **Fax:** 01542 810302

Owner: The Gordon-Duff Family   **Contact:** Joy James

Castellated Victorian Gothic-style castle built in 1847 by Admiral Duff. 60ft high lantern tower with fine plasterwork. Family portraits, interesting artefacts and other paintings. Organic walled garden and plant sales.

Location: OS Ref. NJ372 442. Midway between Keith (5m) and Dufftown, off the B9014.

Open: 21/22 & 28/29 Aug and 4 - 24 Sept: Tours 2pm - 5pm.

Admission: Adult £2, Child £1.50. Pre-arranged groups: Adult £2, Child £1.50.

ⓣ ⓖ ⓕ Obligatory. ⓟ ⓖ In grounds on leads.

DUFF HOUSE

Banff, AB45 3SX

Tel: 01261 818181 **Fax:** 01261 818900   **Contact:** The Chamberlain

One of the most imposing and palatial houses in Scotland, with a strong classical façade and a grand staircase leading to the main entrance.

Location: OS Ref. NJ691 634. Banff. 47m NW of Aberdeen on A947.

Open: Contact property for details.

Admission: Adult £4.50, Conc. £3.50, Family £10. Groups (10+): £3.50. Free admission to shop, tearoom, grounds & woodland walks. (2003 prices.)

DUNNOTTAR CASTLE

Dunnottar Castle Lodge, Stonehaven, Kincardineshire AB39 2TL
Tel: 01569 762173   **e-mail:** info@dunechtestates.co.uk
www.dunechtestates.co.uk   **Contact:** P McKenzie
Spectacular ruined cliff top fortress, home to the Earls Marischals of Scotland. The Crown Jewels of Scotland were hidden at this site, then smuggled away during the dark days of Cromwell's occupation.
Location: OS Ref. NO881 839. Just off A92. 1^1/$_2$ m SE of Stonehaven.
Open: Easter weekend - 28 Oct: Mon - Sat, 9am - 6pm. Suns, 2 - 5pm. 29 Oct - Easter Sat: Fri - Mon, 9.30am - dusk. Closed Tue - Thur. Last admission: 30 mins before closing.
Admission: Adult £3.50, Child £1.

ELGIN CATHEDRAL

Elgin
Tel: 01343 547171
Owner: Historic Scotland   **Contact:** The Steward
When entire this was perhaps the most beautiful of Scottish cathedrals, known as the Lantern of the North. 13th century, much modified after almost being destroyed in 1390 by Alexander Stewart, the infamous 'Wolf of Badenoch'. The octagonal chapterhouse is the finest in Scotland. You can see the Bishop's home at Spynie Palace, 2m north of the town.
Location: OS Ref. NJ223 630. In Elgin on the A96.
Open: 1 Apr - 30 Sept: daily, 9.30am - 6.30pm, last ticket 6pm. 1 Oct - 31 Mar: Mon - Sat, 9.30am - 4.30pm, Suns, 2 - 4.30pm, last ticket 4pm. Closed Thurs pm & Fris in winter.
Admission: Adult £3, Child £1, Conc. £2.30. Joint entry ticket with Spynie Palace: Adult £3.50, Child £1.20, Conc. £2.60.
€

FYVIE CASTLE

Turriff, Aberdeenshire AB53 8JS
Tel: 01651 891266   **Fax:** 01651 891107
Owner: The National Trust for Scotland   **Contact:** The Property Manager
The five towers of the castle bear witness to the five families who have owned it. Fyvie Castle has a fine wheel stair and a collection of arms and armour and paintings, including works by Batoni, Raeburn, Romney, Gainsborough, Opie and Hoppner.
Location: OS Ref. NJ763 393. Off A947, 8m SE of Turriff, and 25m N of Aberdeen.
Open: 1 Apr - 30 Jun & 1 - 30 Sep: Fri - Tue, 12 noon - 5pm; 1 Jul - 31 Aug: daily, 11am - 5pm. Grounds: All year: daily, 9.30am - sunset.
Admission: Adult £7, Conc. £5.25, Family £19. Groups: Adult £5.60, Child/School £1. Car parking £2.

HADDO HOUSE

Tarves, Ellon, Aberdeenshire AB41 0ER
Tel: 01651 851440   **Fax:** 01651 851888
Owner: The National Trust for Scotland
Designed by William Adam in 1731 for William, 2nd Earl of Aberdeen. Much of the splendid interior is 'Adam Revival' carried out about 1880 for John, 7th Earl and 1st Marquess of Aberdeen and his Countess, Ishbel.
Location: OS Ref. NJ868 348. Off B999, 4m N of Pitmedden, 10m NW of Ellon.
Open: House & Garden: Jun: Fri - Mon, 11am - 4.30pm; 1 Jul - 31 Aug: daily 11am - 4.30pm. Guided tours only, departing at set times. All admissions (incl members) from Stables Shop. Shop & tearoom, Good Fri - Easter Mon: daily, 11am - 5pm; 1 May - 30 Jun & 1 Sep - 31 Oct: Fri - Mon, 11am - 5pm; 1 Jul - 31 Aug: daily, 11am - 5pm. Aberdeenshire Council Country Park: All year: daily, 9.30am - sunset.
Admission: Adult £7, Conc. £5.25, Family £19. Groups: Adult £5.60, Child/School £1.

HUNTLY CASTLE

Huntly
Tel: 01466 793191
Owner: In the care of Historic Scotland   **Contact:** The Steward
Known also as Strathbogie Castle, this glorious ruin stands in a beautiful setting on the banks of the River Deveron. Famed for its fine heraldic sculpture and inscribed stone friezes.
Location: OS Ref. NJ532 407. In Huntly on the A96. N side of the town.
Open: 1 Apr - 30 Sept: daily, 9.30am - 6.30pm, last ticket 6pm. 1 Oct - 31 Mar: Mon - Sat, 9.30am - 4.30pm, Suns, 2 - 4.30pm, last ticket 4pm. Closed Thur pm & Fris in winter.
Admission: Adult £3.30, Child £1, Conc £2.50.
€

Open All Year Index see front section

KILDRUMMY CASTLE

Alford, Aberdeenshire
Tel: 01975 571331
Owner: In the care of Historic Scotland   **Contact:** The Steward
Though ruined, the best example in Scotland of a 13th century castle with a curtain wall, four round towers, hall and chapel of that date. The seat of the Earls of Mar, it was dismantled after the first Jacobite rising in 1715.
Location: OS Ref. NJ455 164. 10m W of Alford on the A97. 16m SSW of Huntley.
Open: 1 Apr - 30 Sept: daily, 9.30am - 6.30pm, last ticket 6pm.
Admission: Adult £2.20, Child 75p, Conc. £1.60.
€

KILDRUMMY CASTLE GARDEN

Kildrummy, Aberdeenshire
Tel: 01975 571203 / 571277   **Contact:** Alastair J Laing
Ancient quarry, shrub and alpine gardens renowned for their interest and variety. Water gardens below ruined castle.
Location: OS Ref. NJ455 164. On A97 off A944 10m SW of Alford. 16m SSW of Huntly.
Open: Apr - Oct: daily, 10am - 5pm.
Admission: Adult £2.50, Child Free.

LEITH HALL & GARDEN

Huntly, Aberdeenshire AB54 4NQ
Tel: 01464 831216   **Fax:** 01464 831594
Owner: The National Trust for Scotland   **Contact:** The Property Manager
This mansion house is built around a courtyard and was the home of the Leith family for almost 400 years. With an enviable family record of military service over the centuries, the house contains a unique collection of military memorabilia displayed in an exhibition 'For Crown and Country'.
Location: OS Ref. NJ541 298. B9002, 1m W of Kennethmont, 7m S of Huntley.
Open: House & tearoom, Good Fri - Easter Mon: daily, 12 noon - 5pm; 1 May - 30 Sep: Fri - Tue, 12 noon - 5pm. Garden & grounds: All year: daily 9.30am - sunset.
Admission: Adult £7, Conc. £5.25, Family £19. Groups: Adult £5.60, Child/School £1. Garden and grounds only, Adult £2.50, Conc. £1.90, Family £7. Groups: Adult £2, Child/School £1.

LICKLEYHEAD CASTLE

Auchleven, Insch, Aberdeenshire AB52 6PN
Tel: 01464 821359
Owner: The Leslie family   **Contact:** Zoë Lemon
A beautifully restored Laird's Castle, Lickleyhead was built by the Leslies c1450 and extensively renovated in 1629 by John Forbes of Leslie, whose initials are carved above the entrance. It is an almost unspoilt example of the transformation from 'Chateau-fort' to 'Chateau-maison' and boasts many interesting architectural features.
Location: OS Ref. NJ628 237. Auchleven is 2m S of Insch on B992. Twin pillars of castle entrance on left at foot of village.
Open: 1 May - 4 Sept: Sats, 12 noon - 3pm; 8 - 15 May: daily, 12 noon - 3pm.
Admission: Free.
Unsuitable. Limited. No coaches. In grounds, on leads.

PITMEDDEN GARDEN

Ellon, Aberdeenshire AB41 0PD
Tel: 01651 842352   **Fax:** 01651 843188
Owner: The National Trust for Scotland   **Contact:** The Property Manager
The centrepiece of this property is the Great Garden which was originally laid out in 1675 by Sir Alexander Seton, 1st Baronet of Pitmedden.
Location: OS Ref. NJ885 280. On A920 1m W of Pitmedden village & 14m N of Aberdeen.
Open: 1 May - 30 Sep: daily, 10am - 5.30pm. Grounds: All year: daily.
Admission: Adult £5, Conc. £3.75, Family £13.50. Groups: Adult £4, Child/School £1.

PLUSCARDEN ABBEY

Nr Elgin, Moray IV30 8UA
Tel: 01343 890257   **Fax:** 01343 890258
e-mail: monks@pluscardenabbey.org   **Contact:** Father Giles
Valliscaulian, founded 1230.
Location: OS Ref. NJ142 576. On minor road 6m SW of Elgin. Follow B9010 for first mile.
Open: All year: 4.45am - 8.30pm. Shop open 8.30am - 5pm.
Admission: Free.

PROVOST SKENE'S HOUSE

Guestrow, off Broad Street, Aberdeen AB10 1AS
Tel: 01224 641086   **Fax:** 01224 632133
Owner: Aberdeen City Council   **Contact:** Christine Rew
Built in the 16th century, Provost Skene's House is one of Aberdeen's few remaining examples of early burgh architecture. Splendid room settings include a suite of Georgian rooms, an Edwardian nursery, magnificent 17th century plaster ceilings and wood panelling.
Location: OS Ref. NJ943 064. Aberdeen city centre, off Broad Street.
Open: Contact property for details.
Admission: Free.

ST MACHAR'S CATHEDRAL TRANSEPTS

Old Aberdeen

Tel: 0131 668 8800

Owner: In the care of Historic Scotland

The nave and towers of the Cathedral remain in use as a church, and the ruined transepts are in care. In the south transept is the fine altar tomb of Bishop Dunbar (1514 - 32).

Location: OS Ref. NJ939 088. In old Aberdeen. 1/2 m N of King's College.

Admission: Free.

SPYNIE PALACE

Elgin

Tel: 01343 546358

Owner: In the care of Historic Scotland   **Contact:** The Steward

Spynie Palace was the residence of the Bishops of Moray from the 14th century to 1686. The site is dominated by the massive tower built by Bishop David Stewart (1461-77) and affords spectacular views across Spynie Loch.

Location: OS Ref. NJ231 659. 2m N of Elgin off the A941.

Open: 1 Apr - 30 Sept: daily, 9.30am - 6.30pm. 1 Oct - 31 Mar: Sats, 9.30am - 4.30pm, Suns, 2 - 4.30pm. Last ticket 30 mins before closing.

Admission: Adult £2.20, Child 75p, Conc. £1.60. Joint entry ticket with Elgin Cathedral: Adult £3.50, Child £1.20, Conc. £2.60.

€

TOLQUHON CASTLE

Aberdeenshire

Tel: 01651 851286

Owner: In the care of Historic Scotland   **Contact:** The Steward

Tolquhon was built for the Forbes family. The early 15th century tower was enlarged between 1584 and 1589 with a large mansion around the courtyard. Noted for its highly ornamented gatehouse and pleasance.

Location: OS Ref. NJ874 286. 15m N of Aberdeen on the A920. 6m N of Ellon.

Open: 1 Apr - 30 Sept: daily, 9.30am - 6.30pm. 1 Oct - 31 Mar: Sats, 9.30am - 4.30pm, Suns, 2 - 4.30pm. Last ticket 30 mins before closing.

Admission: Adult £2.20, Child 75p, Conc. £1.60.

€

DAVID WELCH WINTER GARDENS – DUTHIE PARK

Polmuir Road, Aberdeen, Grampian Highlands AB11 7TH

Tel: 01224 585310 **Fax:** 01224 210532 **e-mail:** wintergardens@aberdeen.nct.uk

www.aberdeencity.gov.uk

Owner: Aberdeen City Council   **Contact:** Alan Findlay

One of Europe's largest indoor gardens with many rare and exotic plants on show from all around the world.

Location: OS Ref. NJ97 044. Just N of River Dee, 1m S of city centre.

Open: All year: daily from 9.30pm.

Admission: Free.

❋

Elgin Cathedral, Grampian Highlands.

Historic Scotland

Map 12

Owner: The Dowager Countess Cawdor

▶ **CONTACT**

The Secretary
Cawdor Castle
Nairn
Scotland IV12 5RD

Tel: 01667 404401

Fax: 01667 404674

e-mail: info@
cawdorcastle.com

▶ **LOCATION**

OS Ref. NH850 500

From Edinburgh
A9, 3¹/₂ hrs,
Inverness 20 mins,
Nairn 10 mins.
Main road: A9, 14m.

Rail: Nairn
Station 5m.

Bus: Inverness to Nairn
bus route 200 yds.

Taxi: Cawdor Taxis
01667 404315.

Air: Inverness
Airport 5m.

CONFERENCE/FUNCTION

ROOM	MAX CAPACITY
Cawdor Hall	40

CAWDOR CASTLE

NAIRN

www.cawdorcastle.com

This splendid romantic castle dating from the late 14th century was built as a private fortress by the Thanes of Cawdor, and remains the home of the Cawdor family to this day. The ancient medieval tower was built around the legendary holly tree.

Although the house has evolved over 600 years, later additions mainly of the 17th century were all built in the Scottish vernacular style with slated roofs over walls and crow-stepped gables of mellow local stone. This style gives Cawdor a strong sense of unity, and the massive, severe exterior belies an intimate interior that gives the place a surprisingly personal, friendly atmosphere.

Good furniture, fine portraits and pictures, interesting objects and outstanding tapestries are arranged to please the family rather than to echo fashion or impress. Memories of Shakespeare's *Macbeth* give Cawdor an elusive, evocative quality that delights visitors.

GARDENS

The flower garden also has a family feel to it, where plants are chosen out of affection rather than affectation. This is a lovely spot between spring and late summer. The walled garden has been restored with a holly maze, paradise garden, knot garden and thistle garden. The wild garden beside its stream leads into beautiful trails through a spectacular mature mixed woodland, through which paths are helpfully marked and colour-coded.

ℹ️ 9 hole golf course, putting green, golf clubs for hire, Conferences, whisky tasting, musical entertainments, specialised garden visits. No photography, video taping or tripods inside.

📷 Gift, book and wool shops.

🍷 Lunches, sherry or champagne receptions.

♿ Visitors may alight at the entrance. WC. Only ground floor accessible.

☕ Licensed buttery, May-Oct, groups should book.

🅿️ 250 cars and 25 coaches. Two weeks' notice for group catering, coach drivers/couriers free.

🎒 £3.00 per child. Room notes, quiz and answer sheet can be provided.

🐕 Guide dogs only.

▶ **OPENING TIMES**

Summer

1 May - 10 October
Daily: 10am - 5.30pm.

Last admission 5pm.

Winter

11 October - 30 April
Closed.

▶ **ADMISSION**

Summer
House & Garden

Adult	£6.50
Child (5-15yrs)	£3.70
OAP/Student	£5.50
Family (2+5)	£19.20

Groups (20+)

Adult	£5.70
Child (5-15yrs)	£3.00
OAP/Student	£5.50

Garden only

Per person	£3.50

SPECIAL EVENTS

JUN 5/6
Special Gardens Weekend:
Guided tours of gardens.

Map 11

DUNVEGAN CASTLE

ISLE OF SKYE

www.dunvegancastle.com

Owner: John Macleod of Macleod

▶ **CONTACT**

The Administrator
Dunvegan Castle
Isle of Skye
Scotland IV55 8WF

Tel: 01470 521206
Fax: 01470 521205
Seal Tel: 01470 521500

e-mail: info@
dunvegancastle.com

▶ **LOCATION**

OS Ref. NG250 480

1m N of village. NW
corner of Skye.

From Inverness A82 to
Invermoriston, A887 to
Kyle of Lochalsh 82m.
From Fort William A82
to Invergarry, A87 to
Kyle of Lochalsh 76m.

Kyle of Lochalsh to
Dunvegan 45m via
Skye Bridge (toll).

Ferry: To the Isle of
Skye, 'roll-on, roll-off',
30 minute crossing.

Rail: Inverness to
Kyle of Lochalsh 3 - 4
trains per day - 45m.

Bus: Portree 25m,
Kyle of Lochalsh 45m.

Dunvegan is unique. It is the only Great House in the Western Isles of Scotland to have retained its family and its roof. It is the oldest home in the whole of Scotland continuously inhabited by the same family – the Chiefs of the Clan Macleod. A Castle placed on a rock by the sea - the curtain wall is dated before 1200 AD – its superb location recalls the Norse Empire of the Vikings, the ancestors of the Chiefs.

Dunvegan's continuing importance as a custodian of the Clan spirit is epitomised by the famous Fairy Flag, whose origins are shrouded in mystery but whose ability to protect both Chief and Clan is unquestioned. To enter Dunvegan is to arrive at a place whose history combines with legend to make a living reality.

GARDENS

The gardens and grounds extend over some ten acres of woodland walks, peaceful formal lawns and a water garden dominated by two spectacular natural waterfalls. The temperate climate aids in producing a fine show of rhododendrons and azaleas, the chief glory of the garden in spring. One is always aware of the proximity of the sea and many garden walks finish at the Castle Jetty, from where traditional boats make regular trips to view the delightful Seal Colony.

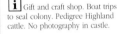

ℹ️ Gift and craft shop. Boat trips to seal colony. Pedigree Highland cattle. No photography in castle.

♿ Visitors may alight at entrance. WC.

🍴 Licensed restaurant, (cap. 70) special rates for groups, menus upon request. Tel: 01470 521310. Open late peak season for evening meals.

🚶 By appointment in English or Gaelic at no extra charge. If requested owner may meet groups, tour time 45mins.

🅿️ 120 cars and 10 coaches. Do not attempt to take passengers to Castle Jetty (long walk). If possible please book. Seal boat trip dependent upon weather.

🏫 Welcome by arrangement. Guide available on request.

🐕 In grounds only, on lead.

🛏️ 4 self-catering units, 3 of which sleep 6 and 1 of which sleeps 7.

Summer
22 March - 31 October
Daily: 10am - 5.30pm.
Last admission 5pm.

Winter
November - March
Daily: 11am - 4pm.
Last admission 3.30pm.

Closed Christmas Day,
Boxing Day, New Year's
Day and 2 January.

▶ **ADMISSION**

(2003 prices)

Summer
Castle & Gardens
  Adult £6.00
  Child* (5 -15yrs) £3.50
  OAP/Student £5.50

Groups (10+) £5.50

Gardens only
  Adult £4.00
  Child* (5 -15yrs) £2.50

Seal Boats
  Adult £4.00
  Child* (5 -15yrs) £2.50

*Child under 5yrs Free.

Winter
11am - 4pm.
No boat trips.

BALLINDALLOCH CASTLE 🏰 📷
Grantown-on-Spey, Banffshire AB37 9AX

Tel: 01807 500206　**Fax:** 01807 500210　**e-mail:** enquiries@ballindallochcastle.co.uk
www.ballindallochcastle.co.uk

Owner: Mr & Mrs Russell　　　　　　　　**Contact:** Mrs Clare Russell

Ballindalloch is a much loved family home and one of the few castles lived in continuously by its original owners, the Macpherson-Grants, since 1546. Filled with family memorabilia and a magnificent collection of 17th century Spanish paintings. The Estate is home to the oldest herd of Aberdeen Angus cattle and the Castle grounds have beautiful rock and rose gardens and river walks to savour.

Location: OS Ref. NJ178 366. 14m NE of Grantown-on-Spey on A95, 22m S of Elgin on A95.

Open: Good Fri - 30 Sept: 10.30am - 5.30pm, closed Sats. Coaches all year by appt.

Admission: Castle & Grounds: Adult £6, Child (6-16yrs) £2.50, Conc. £5, Family (2+3) £12, Season ticket £12. Grounds only: Adult £2, Child (6-16yrs) £1, Season ticket £5. Groups: (20+) Adult £4, Child £2.

📷 ♿Ground floor & grounds. WC. 🍴 P 📷 Audio-visual.
🐕In grounds, on leads in dog walking area.

CASTLE OF MEY
THURSO, CAITHNESS KW14 8XH
www.castleofmey.org.uk

Tel: 01847 851473　**Fax:** 01847 851475

Owner: The Queen Elizabeth Castle of Mey Trust　　**Contact:** James Murray

The home of The Queen Mother in Caithness and the only property in Britain that she owned. She bought the Castle in 1952, saved it from becoming a ruin and developed the gardens. It became her ideal holiday home because of the beautiful surroundings and the privacy she was always given.

Location: OS Ref. ND290 739. On A836 between Thurso and John O'Groats, just outside the village of Mey. 12m Thurso station, 18m Wick airport.

Open: 18 May - 29 Jul & 11 Aug - 30 Sept: Tue - Sat, 11am - 4.30pm, Sun, 2 - 5pm.

Admission: Adult £7, Child (12-16yrs) £3, (under 11yrs) Free, Conc. £6, Family £18. Booked groups (30+): £6.

ℹNo photography in the Castle. 📷 🍴 ♿Partial. 📷By arrangement. P
🐕In grounds, on leads.

CASTLE LEOD
Strathpeffer IV14 9AA

Tel/Fax: 01997 421264　**e-mail:** cromartie@castle-leod.freeserve.co.uk

Owner/Contact: The Earl of Cromartie

15th century tower house of rose-pink stone complete with turrets. Lived in by the Mackenzie family, chiefs of the clan, for 500 years and still very much a home where the family ensure a personal welcome. Magnificent setting below Ben Wyvis and amongst some of the finest trees in Scotland.

Location: OS Ref. NH485 593. 1km E of Strathpeffer on the A834 Strathpeffer to Dingwall road.

Open: 6 - 9 & 20 - 23 May; 3 - 6 & 24 - 27 Jun; 18 - 22 Aug; 2 - 5 Sept: 2 - 5.30pm (last admission 4.45pm).

Admission: Adult £5, Child £2, OAP/Student £4.

ℹNo coaches. 🍴 ♿Grounds only. WC. 📷By arrangement, all year.
P No coach parking. 🐕Guide dogs only. 🕐Tel for details.

CAWDOR CASTLE 🏰　　　　　　*See page 503 for full page entry.*

CULLODEN ⚜
Culloden Moor, Inverness IV1 2ED

Tel: 01463 790607　**Fax:** 01463 794294

Owner: The National Trust for Scotland

Culloden, the bleak moor which in 1746 saw the hopes of the young Prince Charles Edward Stuart crushed, and the end of the Jacobite Rising, the 'Forty-Five'.

Location: OS Ref. NH745 450. On B9006, 5m E of Inverness.

Open: Site: All year: daily. Visitor Centre, restaurant & shop, 1 - 28/29 Feb & 1 Nov - 31 Dec: daily 11am - 4pm (closed 25/26 Dec); 1 - 31 Mar: daily, 10am - 4pm; 1 Apr - 30 Jun & 1 Sep - 31 Oct: daily, 9am - 6pm; 1 Jul - 31 Aug: daily, 9am - 7pm.

Admission: Visitor Centre & Old Leanach Cottage: Adult £5, Conc. £3.75, Family £13.50. Groups: Adult £4, Child/School £1.

THE DOUNE OF ROTHIEMURCHUS 🏰
By Aviemore PH22 1QH

Tel: 01479 812345　**www.**rothiemurchus.net

Owner: J P Grant of Rothiemurchus　　**Contact:** Rothiemurchus Visitor Centre

The family home of the Grants of Rothiemurchus was nearly lost as a ruin and has been under an ambitious repair programme since 1975. This exciting project may be visited on selected Mondays throughout the season. Book with the Visitor Centre for a longer 2hr 'Highland Lady' tour which explores the haunts of Elizabeth Grant of Rothiemurchus, born 1797, author of *Memoirs of a Highland Lady*, who vividly described the Doune and its surroundings from the memories of her childhood.

Location: OS Ref. NH900 100. 2m S of Aviemore on E bank of Spey river.

Open: House: selected Mons. Grounds: May - Aug: Mon, 10am - 12.30pm & 2 - 4.30pm, also 1st Mon in the month during winter.

Admission: House only £1. Tour (booking essential, min 4) £5.

ℹVisitor Centre. 📷 📷Obligatory. P Limited. 🐕In grounds, on leads.

DUNROBIN CASTLE 🏰
GOLSPIE, SUTHERLAND KW10 6SF
www.highlandescape.com

Tel: 01408 633177　**Fax:** 01408 634081　**e-mail:** info@dunrobincastle.net

Owner: The Sutherland Trust　　　　　**Contact:** Keith Jones, Curator

Dates from the 13th century with additions in the 17th, 18th and 19th centuries. Wonderful furniture, paintings, library, ceremonial robes and memorabilia. Victorian museum in grounds with a fascinating collection including Pictish stones. Set in fine woodlands overlooking the sea. Magnificent formal gardens, one of few remaining French/Scottish formal parterres. Falconry display.

Location: OS Ref. NC850 010. 50m N of Inverness on A9. 1m NE of Golspie.

Open: 1 Apr - 15 Oct. 1 Apr - 31 May & 1 - 15 Oct: Mon - Sat, 10.30am - 4.30pm. Suns, 12 noon - 4.30pm. 1 Jun - 30 Sept: Mon - Sat, 10.30am - 5.30pm. Suns, 12 noon - 5.30pm (Jul & Aug: Suns, opens at 10.30am).

Admission: Adult £6.60, Child £4.60, Conc. £5.70, Family (2+2) £18. Booked groups: Adult £5.50, Child/Conc. £4.50.

📷 🍴 ♿Unsuitable for wheelchairs. 🍴 🍴 📷By arrangement. P 🐕

DUNVEGAN CASTLE

See page 504 for full page entry.

EILEAN DONAN CASTLE

Dornie, Kyle of Lochalsh, Wester IV40 8DX
Tel: 01599 555202 **Fax:** 01599 555262 **e-mail:** info@donan.f9.co.uk
www.eileandonancastle.com   **Contact:** Rod Stenson – Castle Keeper
Location: OS Ref. NG880 260. On A87 8m E of Skye Bridge.
Open: Mar & Nov: 10am - 3.30pm. Apr - Oct: 10am - 5.30pm.
Admission: Adult £4.50, Conc. £3.40.

GLENFINNAN MONUMENT

Inverness-shire PH37 4LT
Tel/Fax: 01397 722250
Owner: The National Trust for Scotland
The monument, situated on the scenic road to the Isles, is set amid superb Highland scenery at the head of Loch Shiel. It was erected in 1815 in tribute to the clansmen who fought and died in the Jacobite cause.
Location: OS Ref. NM906 805. On A830, 18m W of Fort William, Lochaber.
Open: Site: All year: daily. Visitor Centre, shop & snack-bar: 1 Apr - 30 Jun & 1 Sep - 31 Oct: daily 10am - 5pm; 1 Jul - 31 Aug: daily, 9.30am - 5.30pm.
Admission: Adult £2, Conc. £1 (honesty box).

HUGH MILLER'S COTTAGE

Cromarty IV11 8XA
Tel: 01381 600245
Owner: The National Trust for Scotland
Furnished thatched cottage of c1698, birthplace of eminent geologist and writer Hugh Miller. Exhibition and video.
Location: OS Ref. NH790 680. Via Kessock Bridge & A832, in Cromarty, 22m NE of Inverness.
Open: Good Fri - 30 Sep: daily, 12 noon - 5pm; 1 - 31 Oct: Sun - Wed, 12 noon - 5pm.
Admission: Adult £2.50, Conc. £1.90, Family £7. Groups: Adult £2, Child/School £1.

INVEREWE GARDEN

Poolewe, Ross & Cromarty IV22 2LQ
Tel: 01445 781200 **Fax:** 01445 781497
Owner: The National Trust for Scotland
In a spectacular lochside setting among pinewoods, Osgood Mackenzie's Victorian dreams have produced a glorious 50 acre mecca for garden lovers.
Location: OS Ref. NG860 820. On A832, by Poolewe, 6m NE of Gairloch, Highland.
Open: Garden: 1 Apr - 31 Oct: daily, 9.30am - 9pm; 1 Nov - 31 Mar: daily, 9.30am - 4pm (or sunset if earlier). Visitor Centre & shop, 1 Apr - 30 Sep: daily 9.30am - 5pm; 1 - 31 Oct: daily 9.30am - 4pm. Restaurant, same dates, but opens at 10am. Extended hours during 50th anniversary events in 2003, especially in May: contact property for details.
Admission: Adult £7, Conc. £5.25, Family £19. Groups: Adult £5.60 (pre-booked £5.25 in 2003), Child/School £1.

FORT GEORGE

ARDERSIER BY INVERNESS IV1 2TD

Owner: In the care of Historic Scotland   **Contact:** Brian Ford
Tel: 01667 460232 **Fax:** 01667 462698
Built following the Battle of Culloden to subdue the Highlands, Fort George never saw a shot fired in anger. One of the most outstanding artillery fortifications in Europe with reconstructed barrack room displays. The Queen's Own Highlanders' Museum.
Location: OS Ref. NH762 567. 11m NE of Inverness off the A96 by Ardersier.
Open: Apr - Sept: daily, 9.30am - 6.30pm. Oct - Mar: Mon - Sat, 9.30am - 4.30pm; Suns, 2 - 4.30pm. Last ticket sold 45 mins before closing.
Admission: Adult £6, Child £1.50, Conc. £4.50. 10% discount for groups (10+).
ⓘPicnic tables. ☐ ☎Private evening hire. ♿Wheelchairs available. WCs.
▣In summer. Ⓟ ◼Free if pre-booked. 🐕In grounds, on leads. ✳ €

URQUHART CASTLE

DRUMNADROCHIT, LOCH NESS

Tel: 01456 450551
Owner: In the care of Historic Scotland   **Contact:** Euan Fraser
The remains of one of the largest castles in Scotland dominate a rocky promontory on Loch Ness. Most of the existing buildings date from the 16th century. New visitor centre with original artefacts, audio-visual presentation, shop and café.
Location: OS Ref. NH531 286. On Loch Ness, 1^1/2m S of Drumnadrochit on A82.
Open: 1 Apr - 30 Sept: daily, 9.30am - 6.30pm, last ticket 5.45pm. 1 Oct - 31 Mar: daily, 9.30am - 4.30pm, last ticket 3.45pm.
Admission: Adult £6, Child £1.20, Conc. £4.50.
☐ ◨Partial. WCs. ▣ Ⓟ ☐ ◼Free if pre-booked. 🐕Guide dogs only. ✳ €

John Webb

1611-1674

An Architect, who worked for 24 years for Inigo Jones, and only really acknowledged for his own successes after Jones's death in 1652.

Visit Lamport Hall, Northamptonshire, Belvoir Castle, Leicestershire (later rebuilt) and the portico of The Vyne, Hampshire.

Architect

BALFOUR CASTLE

Shapinsay, Orkney Islands KW17 2DY

Tel: 01856 711282   **Fax:** 01856 711283

Owner/Contact: Mrs Lidderdale

Built in 1848.

Location: OS Ref. HY475 164 on Shapinsay Island, 3½ m NNE of Kirkwall.

Open: 9, 12, 16, 19, 23, 26 & 30 May; Jun - 3 Oct: Sun, 2.15 - 5.30pm.

Admission: Adult £17, Child £8.50, including boat fare, guided tour, gardens & afternoon tea.

BISHOP'S & EARL'S PALACES

Kirkwall, Orkney

Tel: 01856 875461

Owner: In the care of Historic Scotland   **Contact:** The Steward

The Bishop's Palace is a 12th century hall-house with a round tower built by Bishop Reid in 1541-48. The adjacent Earl's Palace built in 1607 has been described as the most mature and accomplished piece of Renaissance architecture left in Scotland.

Location: Bishop's Palace: OS Ref. HY447 108. Earl's Palace: OS Ref. HY448 108. In Kirkwall on A960.

Open: 1 Apr - 30 Sept: daily, 9.30am - 6.30pm, last ticket 6pm.

Admission: Adult £2.20, Child 75p, Conc. £1.60. Joint entry ticket available for all the Orkney monuments: Adult £11, Child £3.50, Conc. £8.

€

BLACK HOUSE

Arnol, Isle of Lewis

Tel: 01851 710395

Owner: In the care of Historic Scotland   **Contact:** The Steward

A traditional Lewis thatched house, fully furnished, complete with attached barn, byre and stockyard. A peat fire burns in the open hearth. New visitor centre open and restored 1920s croft house.

Location: OS Ref. NB320 500. In Arnol village, 11m NW of Stornoway on A858.

Open: 1 Apr - 30 Sept: Mon - Sat, 9.30am - 6.30pm, last ticket 6pm. 1 Oct - 31 Mar: Mon - Thur & Sat, 9.30am - 4.30pm, last ticket 4pm.

Admission: Adult £3, Child £1, Conc. £2.30.

€

BROCH OF GURNESS

Aikerness, Orkney

Tel: 01831 579478

Owner: In the care of Historic Scotland   **Contact:** The Steward

Protected by three lines of ditch and rampart, the base of the broch is surrounded by a warren of Iron Age buildings.

Location: OS Ref. HY383 268. At Aikerness, about 14m NW of Kirkwall on A966.

Open: 1 Apr - 30 Sept: daily, 9.30am - 6.30pm, last ticket 6pm.

Admission: Adult £3, Child £1, Conc. £2.30. Joint entry ticket available for all Orkney monuments: Adult £11, Child £3.50, Conc. £8.

€

CARRICK HOUSE

Carrick, Eday, Orkney KW17 2AB

Tel: 01857 622260

Owner: Mr & Mrs Joy   **Contact:** Mrs Rosemary Joy

17th century house of 3 storeys, built by John Stewart, Lord Kinclaven Earl of Carrick younger brother of Patrick, 2nd Earl of Orkney in 1633.

Location: OS Ref. NT227 773. N of island of Eday on minor roads W of B9063 just W of the shore of Calf Sound. Regular ferry service.

Open: Jun - Sept: occasional Suns by appointment only.

Admission: Adult £2.50, Child £1.

🎫Obligatory.

JARLSHOF PREHISTORIC & NORSE SETTLEMENT

Shetland

Tel: 01950 460112

Owner: In the care of Historic Scotland   **Contact:** The Steward

Over 3 acres of remains spanning 3,000 years from the Stone Age. Oval-shaped Bronze Age houses, Iron Age broch and wheel houses. Viking Long Houses, medieval farmstead and 16th century laird's house.

Location: OS Ref. HY401 096. At Sumburgh Head, 22m S of Lerwick on the A970.

Open: 1 Apr - 30 Sept: daily, 9.30am - 6.30pm. Last adm. ½ hr before closing.

Admission: Adult £3.30, Child £1, Conc. £2.50.

€

MAES HOWE

Orkney

Tel: 01856 761606

Owner: In the care of Historic Scotland   **Contact:** The Steward

This world-famous tomb was built in Neolithic times, before 2700 BC. The large mound covers a stone-built passage and a burial chamber with cells in the walls. Runic inscriptions tell of how it was plundered of its treasures by Vikings.

Location: OS Ref. NY318 128. 9m W of Kirkwall on the A965.

Open: 1 Apr - 30 Sept: daily, 9.30am - 6.30pm. 1 Oct - 31 Mar: daily, 9.30am - 5pm except Thurs pm, Fris and Suns am.

Admission: Adult £3, Child £1, Conc. £2.30. Joint entry ticket available for all Orkney monuments: Adult £12, Child £3.50, Conc. £9. Admission, shop and refreshments at nearby Tormiston Mill.

€

RING OF BRODGAR STONE CIRCLE & HENGE

Stromness, Orkney

Tel: 0131 668 8800

Owner/Contact: In the care of Historic Scotland

A magnificent circle of upright stones with an enclosing ditch spanned by causeways. Of late Neolithic date.

Location: OS Ref. HY294 134. 5m NE of Stromness.

Open: Any reasonable time.

Admission: Free.

Historic Scotland

SKARA BRAE & SKAILL HOUSE

SANDWICK, ORKNEY

Tel: 01856 841815

Owner: Historic Scotland/Major M R S Macrae   **Contact:** Anne Marwick

Skara Brae is one of the best preserved groups of Stone Age houses in Western Europe. Built before the Pyramids, the houses contain stone furniture, hearths and drains. New visitor centre and replica house with joint admission with Skaill House – 17th century home of the Laird who excavated Skara Brae.

Location: OS6 HY231 188. 19m NW of Kirkwall on the B9056.

Open: Apr - Sept: daily, 9.30am - 6.30pm. Oct - Mar: Mon - Sat, 9.30am - 4.30pm, Suns, 2 - 4.30pm.

Admission: Apr - Sept: Adult £5, Child £1.30, Conc. £3.75. Oct - Mar: Adult £4, Child £1.20, Conc. £3. 10% discount for groups (10+). Joint ticket with other Orkney sites available.

ℹ️Visitor centre. 📷 ♿Partial. WCs. 🍴Licensed. 🅿️ 🏫 Free school visits when booked. 🦮Guide dogs only. ❄️ €

TANKERNESS HOUSE

Broad Street, Kirkwall, Orkney

Tel: 01856 873191   **Fax:** 01856 871560

Owner: Orkney Islands Council   **Contact:** Bryce S Wilson

A fine vernacular 16th century town house contains The Orkney Museum.

Location: OS Ref. HY446 109. In Kirkwall opposite W end of cathedral.

Open: Oct - Apr: Mon - Sat, 10.30am - 12.30pm & 1.30 - 5pm. May - Sept: Mon - Sat, 10.30am - 5pm, Suns, 2 - 5pm. Gardens always open.

Admission: Free.

WALES

wales

River Ogwen waterfall, Conwy. © David Osborn

caernarfoncastle
wales

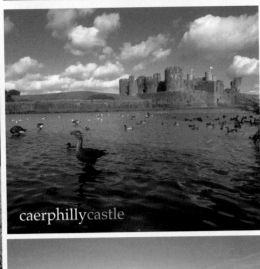

caerphilly castle

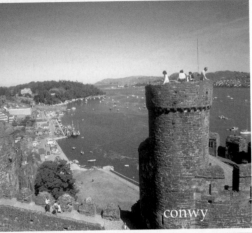

caerphilly castle

conwy

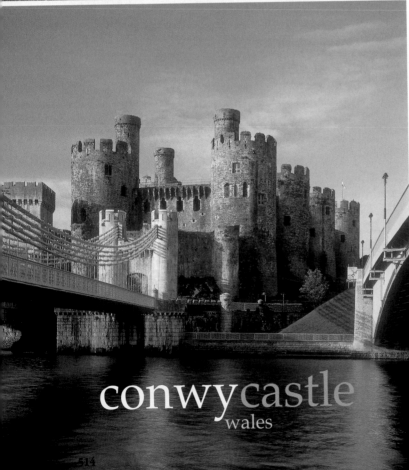

conwy castle
wales

Caernarfon Castle

Caernarfon Castle must be one of the best known images in North Wales, begun in 1283 and still not completely finished when building work stopped in about 1330. It is one of the most striking buildings the Middle Ages has left to us. Small wonder that it has caught the imagination of scores of writers and painters, as a stronghold brimming with image and symbolism.

Caernarfon was built to be the capital of a new dominion and the palace of a new dynasty of princes. Its future status as a seat of government and royal palace was finally secured on 25th April 1284 by the birth of a prince within the Castle precincts. It was not, however, until 1301 that Edward of Caernarfon was formally created Prince of Wales and endowed with the rule and revenues of all the Crown's Welsh lands. Interrupted by a Welsh revolt of 1294, and successfully suppressed by Edward I, building work continued until 1330. The structure we see today is much as it was in 1330.

Conwy Castle

Anyone looking at the grey gritty exterior of Conwy Castle, set against the backdrop of the Snowdonian hills, cannot fail to be impressed and humbled by the unity and compactness of so great a mass of building, with its eight almost identical towers and soaring curtain walls.

Conwy is one of the richest symbols of the medieval age – constructed by the English Monarch, Edward I between 1283 and 1287, it was one of the key fortresses in his 'iron-ring' of castles to contain the Welsh. Conceived and created in just four years, Conwy Castle remains one of the outstanding achievements of medieval architecture, its great strategist strength coming from the massive rock upon which it stands.

The views from the battlements are breathtaking – the surrounding mountains and sea wrap around you like a protective blanket. It is from here you can best see Conwy's other great glory – the $^3/_4$ of a mile long town walls, guarded by no less than 21 towers and three double-towered gateways.

Caerphilly Castle

Caerphilly has been called a 'sleeping giant' of a castle. Surrounded today by shops, offices and houses, it effortlessly dominates the town. Sprawling over a huge area (30 acres in all) it is the biggest castle in Wales and, along with Windsor and Dover, one of the largest in Britain.

Caerphilly's size, is perhaps all the more remarkable in that it was not raised for an English king, but for a leading Anglo-Norman Lord, Gilbert de Clare, Earl of Gloucester and Hertford, and Marcher Lord of Glamorgan. Built at breakneck speed between 1268-1271, de Clare used the Castle to exert his territorial control over the minor Welsh kingdoms of upland Glamorgan. The fortress impressed onlookers right from the start, and remains the supreme example of the concentric 'walls within walls' system of defence. The castle building shape, coupled with the moat and three artificial lakes would have made it almost impregnable.

▸ For further details about Caernarfon Castle see page 517, for Conwy Castle see page 518 and for Caerphilly Castle see page 524.

caerphillycastle
wales

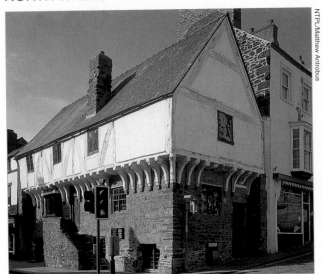

NTPL/Matthew Antrobus

ABERCONWY HOUSE ✣

CASTLE STREET, CONWY LL32 8AY

Tel: 01492 592246   **Fax:** 01492 585153

Owner: The National Trust

Dating from the 14th century, this is the only medieval merchant's house in Conwy to have survived the turbulent history of this walled town for nearly six centuries. Furnished rooms and an audio-visual presentation show daily life from different periods in its history.

Location: OS Ref. SH781 777. At junction of Castle Street and High Street.

Open: 27 Mar - 31 Oct: daily except Tues, 11am - 5pm. Last adm. 30 mins before close. Shop: All year: Mon - Sat, 9.30am - 5.30pm; Sun, 11am - 5.30pm.

Admission: Adult £2.40, Child £1.20, Family (2+2) £6. Pre-booked groups (15+) Adult £2, Child £1. National Trust members Free.

🛈No indoor photography. 🅾All year. 🅕By arrangement. 🎧 🅿In town car parks only. ▦ ♿Guide dogs only.

CADW: Welsh Historic Monuments. Crown copyright

BEAUMARIS CASTLE ✤

BEAUMARIS, ANGLESEY LL58 8AP

www.cadw.wales.gov.uk

Tel: 01248 810361

Owner: In the care of Cadw   **Contact:** The Custodian

The most technically perfect medieval castle in Britain, standing midway between Caernarfon and Conwy, commanding the old ferry crossing to Anglesey. A World Heritage Listed Site.

Location: OS Ref. SH608 762. 5m NE of Menai Bridge (A5) by A545. 7m from Bangor.

Open: Daily, phone site for details. Closed 24 - 26 Dec & 1 Jan.

Admission: Adult £3, Child/Conc. £2.50, Family £8.50 (subject to review Mar 2004).

🅾 ♿ 🅕 🅿 ♿Guide dogs only. ✺

BODELWYDDAN CASTLE

BODELWYDDAN, DENBIGHSHIRE LL18 5YA

www.bodelwyddan-castle.co.uk

Tel: 01745 584060   **Fax:** 01745 584563   **e-mail:** enquiries@bodelwyddan-castle.co.uk

Owner: Bodelwyddan Castle Trust   **Contact:** Kevin Mason

Set within 200 acres of historical parkland, Bodelwyddan Castle is the Welsh home of the National Portrait Gallery, displaying works from its 19th century collection. Complementary collection of sculpture and furniture in a period setting. New interactive displays show how portraits were made and used in the Victorian era. Free audio tour. Victorian games gallery. Temporary exhibitions and events. Terrace tearoom and shop. An ideal wedding venue.

Location: OS Ref. SH999 749. Follow signs off A55 expressway. 2m W of St Asaph, opposite Marble Church.

Open: Easter - end Sept: daily: 10.30am - 5pm (4pm in Winter). Oct - Mar: daily except Mon & Fri. (Times subject to change, please telephone for details.)

Admission: Adult £4.50, Child (5-16yrs) £2 (under 5yrs Free), Conc. £4, Family (2+2) £12. Discounts for schools, groups & disabled. Season ticket available.

🅾 🅃 ♿Partial. WCs. ▣ 🅕By arrangement. 🎧 Free. 🅿 ▦ ♿Guide dogs only. ✺ ⛰ ◪ Tel for details.

BODNANT GARDEN ❀

TAL-Y-CAFN, COLWYN BAY LL28 5RE

www.bodnantgarden.co.uk

Tel: 01492 650460 **Fax:** 01492 650448 **e-mail:** office@bodnantgarden.co.uk

Owner: The National Trust

Bodnant Garden is one of the finest gardens in the country not only for its magnificent collections of rhododendrons, camellias and magnolias but also for its idyllic setting above the River Conwy with extensive views of the Snowdonia range. Visit in early Spring and be rewarded by the sight of masses of golden daffodils and other spring bulbs, as well as the beautiful blooms of the magnolias, camellias and flowering cherries. The spectacular rhododendrons and azaleas will delight from mid-April until late May, whilst the famous original Laburnum Arch is an overwhelming mass of yellow bloom from mid-May to mid-June. The herbaceous borders, roses, hydrangeas, clematis and water lilies flower from the middle of June until September. This 32-ha garden has many interesting features including the Lily Terrace, pergola, Canal Terrace, Pin Mill and the Dell Garden.

Location: OS Ref. SH801 723. 8 miles S of Llandudno and Colwyn Bay, off A470. Signposted from A55, exit at Junction 19.

Open: 13 Mar - 31 Oct: daily, 10am - 5pm.

Admission: Adult £5.50, Child £2.75. Groups (20+) £5. Refreshment Pavilion: daily from 11am (Entrance fee does not have to be paid for the Pavilion). RHS & NT members Free.

⬚ ✦ ♿ Partial. WCs. ☕ P ▨ Guide dogs only.

CADW: Welsh Historic Monuments. Crown copyright

CAERNARFON CASTLE ✚

CASTLE DITCH, CAERNARFON LL55 2AY

www.cadw.wales.gov.uk

Tel: 01286 677617

Owner: In the care of Cadw   **Contact:** The Custodian

The most famous, and perhaps the most impressive castle in Wales. Taking nearly 50 years to build, it proved the costliest of Edward I's castles. A World Heritage Listed Site.

Location: OS Ref. SH477 626. In Caernarfon, just W of town centre.

Open: Daily, please phone site for details. Closed 24 - 26 Dec & 1 Jan.

Admission: Adult £4.50, Child/Conc. £3.50, Family £12.50 (subject to review Mar 2004).

⬚ P ▨ Guide dogs only. ✳

BODRHYDDAN 🏛

Rhuddlan, Clwyd LL18 5SB

Tel: 01745 590414 **Fax:** 01745 590155 **e-mail:** bodrhyddan@hotmail.com

www: bodrhyddan.co.uk

Owner/Contact: Colonel The Lord Langford OBE DL

The home of Lord Langford and his family, Bodrhyddan is basically a 17th century house with 19th century additions by the famous architect, William Eden Nesfield, although traces of an earlier building exist. The house has been in the hands of the same family since it was built over 500 years ago. There are notable pieces of armour, pictures, period furniture, a 3,000 year old mummy, a formal parterre, a woodland garden and attractive picnic areas. Bodrhyddan is a Grade I listing, making it one of few in Wales to remain in private hands.

Location: OS Ref. SJ045 788. On the A5151 midway between Dyserth and Rhuddlan, 4m SE of Rhyl.

Open: Jun - Sept inclusive: Tues & Thurs, 2 - 5.30pm.

Admission: House & Gardens: Adult £4, Child £2. Gardens only: Adult £2, Child £1.

Partial. ☕ 📷Obligatory. P

BRYN BRAS CASTLE

Llanrug, Caernarfon, Gwynedd LL55 4RE

Tel/Fax: 01286 870210 **e-mail:** holidays@brynbrascastle.co.uk

www.brynbrascastle.co.uk

Owner: Mr & Mrs N E Gray-Parry   **Contact:** Marita Gray-Parry

Built in the Neo-Romanesque style in 1830, on an earlier structure and probably designed by Thomas Hopper. Elegantly romantic family home with fine stained-glass, panelling, interesting ceilings and richly carved furniture. The castle stands in the beautiful Snowdonian range and the extensive gardens include herbaceous borders, walled knot garden, woodland walks, stream and pools, 1/4 m mountain walk with superb views of Snowdon, Anglesey and the sea. Picnic area.

Location: OS Ref. SH543 625. 1/2 m off A4086 at Llanrug, 41/2 m E of Caernarfon.

Open: Only for groups by appointment.

Admission: By arrangement. No young children please.

☕ ✖ ▨ Self-catering apartments for twos within castle. ✳

NT Photographic Library / Matthew Antrobus

CHIRK CASTLE ❀

CHIRK LL14 5AF

Tel: 01691 777701 **Fax:** 01691 774706 **e-mail:** chirkcastle@nationaltrust.org.uk

Owner: The National Trust

700 year old Chirk Castle, a magnificent marcher fortress, commands fine views over the surrounding countryside. Rectangular with a massive drum tower at each corner, the castle has beautiful formal gardens with clipped yews, roses and a variety of flowering shrubs. Voted best National Trust garden in 1999. The dramatic dungeon is a reminder of the castle's turbulent history, whilst later occupants have left elegant state rooms, furniture, tapestries and portraits. The castle was sold for five thousand pounds to Sir Thomas Myddelton in 1595, and his descendants continue to live in part of the castle today.

Location: OS Ref. SJ275 388. 8m S of Wrexham off A483, 2m from Chirk village.

Open: Castle & Shop: 20 Mar - 31 Oct, Wed - Sun & BH Mons, 12 noon - 5pm (Oct closes 4pm). Garden: as Castle, 11am - 6pm (Oct closes 5pm). Tearoom: as Castle, 11am - 5pm (Oct closes 4pm).

Admission: Adult £6, Child £3, Family £15. Pre-booked groups (15+): Adult £4.80, Child £2.40. Garden only: Adults £3.80, Child £1.90, Family £9. Groups: Adult £3, Child £1.50.

ℹ️No indoor photography. ⬚ ♿ ☕Licensed. 📷By arrangement. P ▨ ▨Guide dogs only.

COCHWILLAN OLD HALL

Talybont, Bangor, Gwynedd LL57 3AZ

Tel: 01248 355853

Owner: R C H Douglas Pennant   **Contact:** Miss M D Monteith

A fine example of medieval architecture with the present house dating from about 1450. It was probably built by William Gryffydd who fought for Henry VII at Bosworth. Once owned in the 17th century by John Williams who became Archbishop of York. The house was restored from a barn in 1971.

Location: OS Ref. SH606 695. 3¹/₂ m SE of Bangor. 1m SE of Talybont off A55.

Open: By appointment.

Admission: Please telephone for details.

✳

DENBIGH CASTLE ✚

Denbigh, Clwyd

Tel: 01745 813385   **www**.cadw.wales.gov.uk

Owner: In the care of Cadw   **Contact:** The Custodian

Crowning the summit of a prominent outcrop dominating the Vale of Clwyd, the principal feature of this spectacular site is the great gatehouse dating back to the 11th century. Some of the walls can still be walked by visitors.

Location: OS Ref. SJ052 658. Denbigh via A525, A543 or B5382.

Open: Daily – winter open site. Phone site for details.

Admission: Castle: Adult £2.50, Child/Conc. £2, Family £7 (subject to review Mar 2004).

⬜ 🅿 ♿ Guide dogs only. ✳

DOLWYDDELAN CASTLE ✚

Blaenau Ffestiniog, Gwynedd

Tel: 01690 750366   **www**.cadw.wales.gov.uk

Owner: In the care of Cadw   **Contact:** The Custodian

Standing proudly on a ridge, this stern building remains remarkably intact and visitors cannot fail to be impressed with the great solitary square tower, built by Llewelyn the Great in the early 13th century.

Location: OS Ref. SH722 522. A470(T) Blaenau Ffestiniog to Betws-y-Coed, 1m W of Dolwyddelan.

Open: Daily, phone site for details. Closed 24 - 26 Dec & 1 Jan.

Admission: Adult £2, Child/Conc. £1.50, Family £5.50 (subject to review Mar 2004).

🅿 ♿ Guide dogs only. ✳

Cadw: Welsh Historic Monuments. Crown Copyright

CONWY CASTLE ✚

CONWY LL32 8AY

www.cadw.wales.gov.uk

Tel: 01492 592358

Owner: In the care of Cadw   **Contact:** The Custodian

Taken together the castle and town walls are the most impressive of the fortresses built by Edward I, and remain the finest and most impressive in Britain. A World Heritage Listed Site.

Location: OS Ref. SH783 774. Conwy by A55 or B5106.

Open: Daily, phone site for details. Closed 24 - 26 Dec & 1 Jan.

Admission: Adult £3.50, Child/OAP £3, Family £10 (subject to review Mar 2004). Joint ticket for entry to Conwy Castle and Plas Mawr available.

⬜ 🎬 By arrangement. 🅿 ♿ Guide dogs only. ✳

ERDDIG 🌼

Nr WREXHAM LL13 0YT

Tel: 01978 355314   **Fax:** 01978 313333   **Info Line:** 01978 315151

Owner: The National Trust

One of the most fascinating houses in Britain, not least because of the unusually close relationship that existed between the family of the house and their servants. The beautiful and evocative range of outbuildings includes kitchen, laundry, bakehouse, stables, sawmill, smithy and joiner's shop, while the stunning state rooms display most of their original 18th & 19th century furniture and furnishings, including some exquisite Chinese wallpaper. The large walled garden has been restored to its 18th century formal design with Victorian parterre and yew walk, and also contains the National Ivy Collection. There is an extensive park with woodland walks.

Location: OS Ref. SJ326 482. 2m S of Wrexham.

Open: House: 20 Mar - 31 Oct: Sat - Wed, 12 noon - 5pm (Oct closes 4pm). Garden: 20 Mar - 30 Jun & Sept: Sat - Wed, 11am - 6pm; Jul - Aug: Sat - Wed, 10am - 6pm; Oct: Sat - Wed, 11am - 5pm; 7 Nov - 21 Dec: Fri, Sat & Sun, 11am - 4pm. Shop, restaurant & grounds: 6 Nov - 21 Dec: as Garden.

Admission: All-inclusive ticket: Adult £7, Child £3.50, Family (2+3) £17.50. Pre-booked group (15+) £5.50, Child £2.80. NT members Free.

⬜ 🎫 ♿ Partial. WCs. 🍴 Licensed. 🎥 AV presentation. 🅿 ⬛ ♿ Guide dogs only.

CRICCIETH CASTLE ✚

Castle Street, Criccieth, Gwynedd LL52 0DP

Tel: 01766 522227   **www**.cadw.wales.gov.uk

Owner: In the care of Cadw   **Contact:** The Custodian

Overlooking Cardigan Bay, Criccieth Castle is the most striking of the fortresses built by the native Welsh Princes. Its inner defences are dominated by a powerful twin-towered gatehouse.

Location: OS Ref. SH500 378. A497 to Criccieth from Porthmadog or Pwllheli.

Open: Daily – winter open site. Phone site for details.

Admission: Adult £2.50, Child/Conc. £2, Family £7 (subject to review Mar 2004).

⬜ 🅿 ♿ Guide dogs only. ✳

FFERM

Pontblyddyn, Mold, Flintshire

Tel/Fax: 01352 770217

Owner/Contact: Dr M Jones-Mortimer

17th century farmhouse. Viewing is limited to 7 persons at any one time. Prior booking is recommended. No toilets or refreshments.

Location: OS Ref. SJ279 603. Access from A541 in Pontblyddyn, 3½ m SE of Mold.

Open: 2nd Wed in every month, 2 - 5pm. Pre-booking is recommended.

Admission: £4.

HARLECH CASTLE ✤

HARLECH LL46 2YH

www.cadw.wales.gov.uk

Tel: 01766 780552

Owner: In the care of Cadw   **Contact:** The Custodian

Set on a towering rock above Tremadog Bay, this seemingly impregnable fortress is the most dramatically sited of all the castles of Edward I. A World Heritage Listed Site.

Location: OS Ref. SH581 312. Harlech, Gwynedd on A496 coast road.

Open: Daily, phone site for details. Closed 24 - 26 Dec & 1 Jan.

Admission: Adult £3.50, Child/OAP £2.50, Family £8.50 (subject to review Mar 2004).

Guide dogs only.

CADW: Welsh Historic Monuments. Crown copyright

GWYDIR CASTLE

LLANRWST, GWYNEDD LL26 0PN

www.gwydircastle.co.uk

Tel/Fax: 01492 641687   **e-mail:** info@gwydircastle.co.uk

Owner/Contact: Mr & Mrs Welford

Gwydir Castle is situated in the beautiful Conwy Valley and is set within a Grade I listed, 10 acre garden. Built by the illustrious Wynn family c1500, Gwydir is a fine example of a Tudor courtyard house, incorporating re-used medieval material from the dissolved Abbey of Maenan. Further additions date from c1600 and c1826. The important 1640s panelled Dining Room has now been reinstated, following its repatriation from the New York Metropolitan Museum.

Location: OS Ref. SH795 610. ½ m W of Llanrwst on B5106.

Open: 1 Mar - 31 Oct: daily, 10am - 5pm. Limited openings at other times. Occasional weddings on Sats.

Admission: Adult £3.50, Child £1.50. Group discount 10%.

Partial. By arrangement. By arrangement. 2 doubles.

HARTSHEATH

Pontblyddyn, Mold, Flintshire

Tel/Fax: 01352 770217

Owner/Contact: Dr M Jones-Mortimer

18th and 19th century house set in parkland. Viewing is limited to 7 persons at any one time. Prior booking is recommended. No toilets or refreshments.

Location: OS Ref. SJ287 602. Access from A5104, 3½ m SE of Mold between Pontblyddyn and Penyffordd.

Open: 1st, 3rd & 5th Wed in every month, 2 - 5pm.

Admission: £4.

ISCOYD PARK

Nr Whitchurch, Shropshire SY13 3AT

Owner/Contact: Mr P C Godsal

18th century Grade II* listed redbrick house in park.

Location: OS Ref. SJ504 421. 2m W of Whitchurch on A525.

Open: By written appointment only.

GYRN CASTLE

Llanasa, Holywell, Flintshire CH8 9BG

Tel/Fax: 01745 853500

Owner/Contact: Sir Geoffrey Bates BT

Dating, in part, from 1700, castellated 1820. Large picture gallery, panelled entrance hall. Pleasant woodland walks and fantastic views to the River Mersey and the Lake District.

Location: OS Ref. SJ111 815. 26m W of Chester, off A55, 4½ m SE of Prestatyn.

Open: All year by appointment.

Admission: £4. Discount for groups. (2003 price.)

Grounds. By arrangement. Obligatory. Limited for coaches. On leads.

PENRHYN CASTLE 🌺
BANGOR LL57 4HN

Tel: 01248 353084   **Infoline:** 01248 371337   **Fax:** 01248 371281

Owner: The National Trust

This dramatic neo-Norman fantasy castle sits between Snowdonia and the Menai Strait. Built by Thomas Hopper between 1820 and 1845 for the wealthy Pennant family, who made their fortune from Jamaican sugar and Welsh slate. The castle is crammed with fascinating things such as a 1-ton slate bed made for Queen Victoria.

Location: OS Ref. SH602 720. 1m E of Bangor, at Llandygai (J11, A55).

Open: 27 Mar - 31 Oct: daily except Tues. Castle: 27 Mar - 30 Jun & Sept - 31 Oct: 12 noon - 5pm; Jul - Aug: 11am - 5pm. Grounds: 27 Mar - 30 Jun & Sept - 31 Oct: 11am - 5pm; Jul - Aug: 10am - 5pm.

Admission: Adult £7, Child £3.50, Family (2+2) £17.50. Pre-booked groups (15+) £5.50. Garden & Stableblock Exhibitions only: Adult £5, Child £2.50. Audio tour: £1 (including NT members). NT members Free.

▢ ☯ Licensed. ⏸ ▢ ☒ Guide dogs only. ▣

PLAS BRONDANW GARDENS 🏛
Plas Brondanw, Llanfrothen, Gwynedd LL48 6SW

Tel: 07880 766741/ 01743 241181

Owner: Trustees of the Second Portmeirion Foundation

Italianate gardens with topiary.

Location: OS Ref. SH618 423. 3m N of Penrhyndeudraeth off A4085, on Croesor Road.

Open: All year: daily 9am - 5pm. Coaches accepted, please book.

Admission: Adult £3, Subsequent adult £2pp, Child Free.

PLAS NEWYDD 🌺
LLANFAIRPWLL, ANGLESEY LL61 6DQ

Tel: 01248 714795   **Infoline:** 01248 715272   **Fax:** 01248 713673

Owner: The National Trust

Set amidst breathtaking beautiful scenery and with spectacular views of Snowdonia. Fine spring garden and Australasian arboretum with an understorey of shrubs and wildflowers. Summer terrace, and, later, massed hydrangeas and Autumn colour. A woodland walk gives access to a marine walk on the Menai Strait. Rhododendron garden open April - early June only. Elegant 18th century house by James Wyatt, famous for its association with Rex Whistler whose largest painting is here. Military museum contains relics of 1st Marquess of Anglesey and Battle of Waterloo. A historic cruise, a boat trip on the Menai Strait operates from the property weather and tides permitting (additional charge). 5 seater buggy to rhododendron garden and woodland walk.

Location: OS Ref. SH521 696. 2m S of Llanfairpwll and A5.

Open: 27 Mar - 3 Nov: Sat - Wed (open Good Fri). House: 12 noon - 5pm. Garden: 11am - 5.30pm. Last admission 4.30pm.

Admission: House & Garden: Adult £5, Child £2.50 (under 5s Free), Family (2+3) £12. Groups (15+) £4.50. Garden only: Adult £3, Child £1.50. NT members Free.

ℹ No indoor photography. ▢ ♿ Partial. WCs. Minibus from car park to house. ☯ Licensed. ⏸ 🅵 By arrangement. Ⓟ ▣ ☒ Guide dogs only. ▣ Tel for details.

PLAS MAWR ✤
HIGH STREET, CONWY LL32 8EF

www.cadw.wales.gov.uk

Tel: 01492 580167

Owner: In the care of Cadw   **Contact:** The Custodian

The best preserved Elizabethan town house in Britain, the house reflects the status of its builder Robert Wynn. A fascinating and unique place allowing visitors to sample the lives of the Tudor gentry and their servants, Plas Mawr is famous for the quality and quantity of its decorative plasterwork.

Location: OS Ref. SH781 776. Conwy by A55 or B5106 or A547.

Open: Tue - Sun & BH Mons, phone site for details. Last admission ½ hour before closing. Closed Nov - Mar.

Admission: Adult £4.50, Child/OAP £3.50, Family £12.50 (subject to review Mar 2004). Joint ticket for Plas Mawr and Conwy Castle available.

▢ Ⓟ Limited. ▢ ☒ Guide dogs only.

PLAS YN RHIW 🌺
RHIW, PWLLHELI LL53 8AB

Tel/Fax: 01758 780219

Owner: The National Trust

A small manor house, with garden and woodlands, overlooking the west shore of Porth Neigwl (Hell's Mouth Bay) on the Llyn Peninsula. The house is part medieval, with Tudor and Georgian additions, and the ornamental gardens have flowering trees and shrubs, divided by box hedges and grass paths, rising behind to the snowdrop wood.

Location: OS Ref. SH237 282. 16m SW of Pwllheli, 3m S of the B4413 to Aberdaron. No access for coaches.

Open: 27 Mar - 31 Oct: 12 noon - 5pm (last entry 4.30pm). Closed Tues & Wed 27 Mar - 31 May & Tues 2 Jun - 1 Oct. Open weekends only 2 - 24 Oct and daily 25 - 31 Oct.

Admission: Adult £3.40, Child £1.70, Family (2+3) £8. Groups: £2.70. Gardens only: Adult £2, Child £1, Family (2+3) £5. Garden & snowdrop wood (Jan & Feb only): £2.50. NT members free.

▢ ♿ Partial. WCs. 🅵 By arrangement. Ⓟ Limited. ☒ Guide dogs only.

PORTMEIRION

Portmeirion, Gwynedd LL48 6ET

Tel: 01766 770000 **Fax:** 01766 771331 **e-mail:** info@portmeirion-village.com
Owner: The Portmeirion Foundation   **Contact:** Mr R Llywelyn
Built by Clough Williams-Ellis as an 'unashamedly romantic' village resort.
Location: OS Ref. SH590 371. Off A487 at Minffordd between Penrhyndeudraeth and Porthmadog.
Open: All year (except Christmas Day): daily, 9.30am - 5.30pm.
Admission: Adult £5.70, Child £2.80, OAP £4.60, Family (2+2) £13.80.

NTPL/Andrew Butler

POWIS CASTLE & GARDEN ❧

Nr WELSHPOOL SY21 8RF

Tel: 01938 551929 **Infoline:** 01938 551944 **Fax:** 01938 554336
e-mail: powiscastle@nationaltrust.org.uk
Owner: The National Trust   **Contact:** Visitor Services Manager
The world-famous garden, overhung with enormous clipped yew trees, shelters rare and tender plants in colourful herbaceous borders. Laid out under the influence of Italian and French styles, the garden retains its original lead statues and, an orangery on the terraces. Perched on a rock above the garden terraces, the medieval castle contains one of the finest collections of paintings and furniture in Wales.
Location: OS Ref. SJ216 064. 1m W of Welshpool, car access on A483.
Open: Castle & Museum: 21 Mar - 31 Oct: daily except Tues & Weds, 1 - 4pm (1 Apr - 30 Sep: 1 - 5pm). Garden: as Castle, 11am - 6pm. Shop & restaurant: as Castle, 11am - 5.30pm. Christmas shop & restaurant: 5 Nov - 12 Dec: Fri - Sun only, 11am - 4pm.
Admission: Castle & Garden: Adult £8.40, Child £4.20, Family £21. Groups: (15+ booked): £7.40. Garden only: Adult £5.80, Child £2.90, Family £14.40. Groups (15+ booked): £4.80. No groups rates on Suns or BHs. NT members & under 5s Free.
ⓘNo indoor photography. ◻ ⛩ ♿Partial. ▣Licensed. 🚻By arrangement.
▣Limited for coaches. ♿Guide dogs only.

RHUDDLAN CASTLE ✚

Castle Gate, Castle Street, Rhuddlan LL18 5AD

Tel: 01745 590777 **www.**cadw.wales.gov.uk
Owner: In the care of Cadw   **Contact:** The Custodian
Guarding the ancient ford of the River Clwyd, Rhuddlan was the strongest of Edward I's castles in North-East Wales. Linked to the sea by an astonishing deep water channel nearly 3 miles long, it still proclaims the innovative genius of its architect.
Location: OS Ref. SJ025 779. SW end of Rhuddlan via A525 or A547.
Open: Apr - Sept: daily, 10am - 5pm. Winter: closed.
Admission: Adult £2, Child/OAP £1.50, Family £5.50. (Subject to review Mar 2004.)
◻ ▣ ♿Guide dogs only.

RUG CHAPEL & LLANGAR CHURCH ✚

c/o Coronation Cottage, Rug, Corwen LL21 9BT

Tel: 01490 412025 **www.**cadw.wales.gov.uk
Owner: In the care of Cadw   **Contact:** The Custodian
Prettily set in a wooded landscape, Rug Chapel's exterior gives little hint of the wonders within. Nearby the attractive medieval Llangar Church still retains its charming early Georgian furnishings.
Location: Rug Chapel: OS Ref. SJ065 439. Off A494, 1M N of Corwen. Llangar Church: OS Ref. SJ064 423. Off B4401, 1m S of Corwen (obtain key at Rug).
Open: Rug Chapel: Apr - end Sept: 10am - 5pm. Closed Mon & Tues except BHs. Llangar Church: access arranged through the Custodian at Rug Chapel. Both sites closed in winter (subject to review Mar 2004).
Admission: Adult £2.50, Child/Conc. £2, Family £7. (Subject to review Mar 2004.)
▣ ♿Guide dogs only.

ST ASAPH CATHEDRAL

St Asaph, Denbighshire LL17 0RL

Tel: 01745 583429   **Contact:** Chapter Office
Britain's smallest ancient cathedral founded in 560AD by Kentigern, a religious community enclosed in a 'llan', hence Llanelwy.
Location: OS Ref. SJ039 743. In St Asaph, S of A55.
Open: Summer: 8am - 6.30pm. Winter: 8am - dusk. Sun services: 8am, 11am, 3.30pm.

TOWER

Nercwys, Mold, Flintshire CH7 4EW

Tel: 01352 700220 **e-mail:** enquiries@towerwales.co.uk **www:** towerwales.co.uk
Owner/Contact: Charles Wynne-Eyton
This Grade I listed building is steeped in Welsh history and bears witness to the continuous warfare of the time. A fascinating place to visit or for overnight stays.
Location: OS Ref. SJ240 620. 1m S of Mold.
Open: 3 - 25 & 31 May & 30 Aug: 1.30 - 4pm. Groups welcome at other times by appointment.
Admission: Adult £3, Child £2.
🚻

TREBERFYDD

Bwlch, Powys LD3 7PX

Tel: 01874 730205 **e-mail:** david.raikes@btinternet.com
www: treberfydd.net
Owner: David Raikes   **Contact:** David Garnons-Williams
Treberfydd is a Victorian country house, built in the Gothic style in 1847 - 50. The house was designed by J L Pearson, and the garden and grounds by W A Nesfield.
Location: From A40 in Bwlch take road to Llangors, after ¼m turn left, follow lane for 2m until white gates and Treberfydd sign.
Open: Aug: Guided tours of the House & Grounds, ring or e-mail to secure a place on a tour.
Admission: Adult £3, Child (under 8yrs) Free.
♿Partial. 🚻Obligatory. ▣Limited. None for coaches. ♿On leads, in grounds.

The National Trust Wales Photographic Library/ Pierino

TŶ MAWR WYBRNANT ❧

PENMACHNO, BETWS-Y-COED, CONWY LL25 0HJ

Tel: 01690 760213

Owner: The National Trust

Situated in the beautiful and secluded Wybrnant Valley, Tŷ Mawr was the birthplace of Bishop William Morgan, first translator of the entire Bible into Welsh. The house has been restored to its probable 16th-17th century appearance and houses a display of Welsh Bibles. A footpath leads from the house through woodland and the surrounding fields, which are traditionally managed.

Location: OS Ref. SH770 524. From A5 3m S of Betws-y-Coed, take B4406 to Penmachno. House is 2¹/₂ m NW of Penmachno by forest road.

Open: 1 Apr - 31 Oct: Thur - Sun, 12 noon - 5pm; Oct: 12 noon - 4pm.

Admission: Adult £2.40, Child £1.20, Family £6. Booked groups (15+): Adult £2, Child £1. NT members Free.

⯊ Ground floor. 🅿 🐕 Guide dogs only.

The National Trust Wales Photographic Library/ Pierino

TY'N Y COED UCHAF ❧

PENMACHNO, BETWS-Y-COED, CONWY LL24 0PS

www.nationaltrust.org.uk

Tel: 01690 760229

Owner: The National Trust   **Contact:** The Custodian

A small farm which provides an unique record of the traditional way of life in a Welsh speaking community. The house is approached by an interesting walk (³/₄ mile) along the river Machno through unspoilt meadows, therefore waterproof shoes are advisable.

Location: OS Ref. SH802 521. Follow signs for Penmachno, off the A5, 2m E of Betws y Coed.

Open: 1 Apr - 31 Oct: Thur, Fri & Sun, 12 noon - 5pm; Oct: 12 noon - 4pm.

Admission: Adult £2.40, Child £1.20, Family £6. Booked groups (15+): Adult £2, Child £1. NT members Free.

⯊ Unsuitable. 𝑓 By arrangement. 🅿 Limited, no coaches. ⬛ 🐕 Guide dogs only.

VALLE CRUCIS ABBEY ✪

Llangollen, Clwyd

Tel: 01978 860326   **www**.cadw.wales.gov.uk

Owner: In the care of Cadw   **Contact:** The Custodian

Set in a beautiful valley location, Valle Crucis Abbey is the best preserved medieval monastery in North Wales, enhanced by the only surviving monastic fish pond in Wales.

Location: OS Ref. SJ205 442. B5103 from A5, 2m NW of Llangollen, or A542 from Ruthin.

Open: Open daily - phone site for details. Winter: open site.

Admission: Adult £2, Child/Conc. £1.50. Family £5.50. (Subject to review Mar 2004.)

⬜ 🅿 🐕 Guide dogs only. ✳

WERN ISAF

Penmaen Park, Llanfairfechan LL33 0RN

Tel: 01248 680437

Owner/Contact: Mrs P J Phillips

This Arts and Crafts house was built in 1900 by the architect H L North as his family home and it contains much of the original furniture and William Morris fabrics. It is situated in a woodland garden and is at its best in the Spring. It has extensive views over the Menai Straits and Conwy Bay. One of the most exceptional houses of its date and style in Wales.

Location: OS Ref. SH685 75. Off A55 midway between Bangor and Conwy.

Open: 8 Mar - 6 Apr: daily except Thur, 1 - 4pm. Please telephone for details.

Admission: £1

WWW **Website Information** see front section

ABERCAMLAIS
Brecon, Powys LD3 8EY

Tel: 01874 636206 **Fax:** 01874 636964 **e-mail:** susan.ballance@virgin.net
www.abercamlais.co.uk

Owner/Contact: Mrs S Ballance

Splendid Grade II* mansion dating from middle ages, altered extensively in early 18th century with 19th century additions, in extensive grounds beside the river Usk. Still in same family ownership and occupation since medieval times. Exceptional octagonal pigeon house, formerly a privy.

Location: OS Ref. SN965 290. 5m W of Brecon on A40.

Open: Apr - Oct: by appointment.

Admission: Adult £5, Child Free.

ℹ️No photography in house. ♿ 🚻Obligatory. 🅿️ ▨

ABERDULAIS FALLS ※
Aberdulais, Vale of Neath SA10 8EU

Tel: 01639 636674 **Fax:** 01639 645069

Owner: The National Trust **Contact:** The Property Warden

For over 300 years this famous waterfall has provided the energy to drive the wheels of industry, from the first manufacture of copper in 1584 to present day remains of the tinplate works. It has also been visited by famous artists such as J M W Turner in 1796. The site today houses a unique hydro-electrical scheme which has been developed to harness the waters of the Dulais river.

Location: OS Ref. SS772 995. On A4109, 3m NE of Neath. 4m from M4/J43, then A465.

Open: 5 - 28 Mar: Fri - Sun, 11am - 4pm. 29 Mar - 31 Oct: Mon - Fri, 10am - 5pm; Sats/Suns & BHs, 11am - 6pm. 5 Nov - 19 Dec: Fri - Sun, 11am - 4pm; 20/21 Dec: 11am - 4pm.

Admission: Adult £3.20, Child £1.60, Family £8. Groups (15+): Adult £2.40, Child £1.20. Children must be accompanied by an adult.

📷 🍴Light refreshments (summer only). 🅿️Limited. ▨

BLAENAVON IRONWORKS ♣
Nr Brecon Beacons National Park, Blaenavon, Gwent

Tel: 01495 792615 **Winter Bookings:** 01633 648082 **www.**cadw.wales.gov.uk

Owner: In the care of Cadw **Contact:** The Custodian

The famous ironworks at Blaenavon were a milestone in the history of the Industrial Revolution. Visitors can view much of the ongoing conservation work as well as 'Stack Square' - a rare survival of housing built for pioneer ironworkers. Part of a World Heritage Site.

Location: OS Ref. SO248 092. Via A4043 follow signs to Big Pit Mining Museum and Blaenavon Ironworks. Abergavenny 8m. Pontypool 8m. From car park, cross road, then path to entrance gate.

Open: End Mar - end Oct: 9.30am - 4.30pm. For opening times outside this period call the above number or 029 2050 0200.

Admission: Adult £2, Child/Conc. £1.50, Family £5.50. (Subject to review March 2004.)

📷 ♿Partial. 🚻By arrangement. 🅿️ ▨Guide dogs only.

CAE HIR GARDENS
Cae Hir, Cribyn, Lampeter, Cardiganshire SA48 7NG

Tel: 01570 470839 **Owner/Contact:** Mr W Akkermans

This transformed 19th century smallholding offers a succession of pleasant surprises and shows a quite different approach to gardening.

Location: OS Ref. SN521 520. NW on A482 from Lampeter, after 5m turn S on B4337. Cae Hir is 2m on left.

Open: Daily, excluding Mons (open BH Mons), 1 - 6pm.

Admission: Adult £2.50, Child 50p, OAP £2. Groups: (20+) £2.

CAERLEON ROMAN BATHS & AMPHITHEATRE ♣
High Street, Caerleon NP6 1AE

Tel: 01633 422518 **www.**cadw.wales.gov.uk

Owner: In the care of Cadw **Contact:** The Custodian

Caerleon is the most varied and fascinating Roman site in Britain – incorporating fortress and baths, well-preserved amphitheatre and a row of barrack blocks, the only examples currently visible in Europe.

Location: OS Ref. ST340 905. 4m ENE of Newport by B4596 to Caerleon, M4/J25 (westbound), M4/J26 (eastbound).

Open: Daily, phone site for details. Closed 24 - 26 Dec & 1 Jan.

Admission: Adult £2.50, Child/Conc. £2, Family £7. (Subject to review March 2004.)

📷 🅿️ ▨Guide dogs only. ✳️

ABERGLASNEY GARDENS
LLANGATHEN, CARMARTHENSHIRE SA32 8QH

www.aberglasney.org

Tel/Fax: 01558 668998 **e-mail:** info@aberglasney.org.uk

Owner: Aberglasney Restoration Trust **Contact:** Booking Department

Aberglasney is one of the most remarkable restoration projects of recent years. When acquired in 1995 the Mansion and grounds were so derelict they were considered by most to be beyond restoration. It was not until the undergrowth was cleared and extensive archaeological surveys undertaken, that the importance of this historical garden was realised. The parapet walkway, dating from 1600, is the only example that survives in the United Kingdom. The nine acre garden is already planted with many rare and unusual plants, giving interest throughout the year. Aberglasney is destined to become one of the most fascinating gardens in the country.

Location: OS Ref. SN581 221. 4m W of Llandeilo. Follow signs from A40.

Open: All year: daily (except Christmas Day). Summer: 10am - 6pm, last entry 5pm. Winter: 10.30am - 4pm.

Admission: Adult £5.50, Child £2.50, OAP £4.50. Booked groups (10+): Adult £5, Child £2, OAP £4.

📷 🚻 ♿ 🍴Licensed. 🍽️Licensed. 🚻Daily: 11.30am & 2.30pm. 🅿️Limited for coaches. ▨ ▨Guide dogs only. 📷 ✳️

CADW: Welsh Historic Monuments. Crown Copyright

CAERPHILLY CASTLE ✠

CAERPHILLY CF8 1JL

www.cadw.wales.gov.uk

Tel: 029 2088 3143

Owner: In the care of Cadw   **Contact:** The Custodian

Often threatened, never taken, this vastly impressive castle is much the biggest in Wales. 'Red Gilbert' de Clare, Anglo-Norman Lord of Glamorgan, flooded a valley to create the 30 acre lake, setting his fortress on 3 artificial islands. Famous for its leaning tower, its fortifications are scarcely rivalled in Europe.

Location: OS Ref. ST156 871. Centre of Caerphilly, A468 from Newport, A470, A469 from Cardiff.

Open: Daily, phone site for details. Closed 24 - 26 Dec & 1 Jan.

Admission: Adult £3, Child/Conc. £2.50, Family £8.50. (Subject to review March 2004.)

▢ ▢ **P** Limited. ▦ Guide dogs only. ▲ ✳

CALDICOT CASTLE & COUNTRY PARK

Church Road, Caldicot, Monmouthshire NP26 4HU

Tel: 01291 420241   **Fax:** 01291 435094

e-mail: caldicotcastle@monmouthshire.gov.uk   **www.**caldicotcastle.co.uk

Owner: Monmouthshire County Council   **Contact:** Castle Development Officer

Caldicot's magnificent castle is set in fifty acres of beautiful parkland. Founded by the Normans, developed in royal hands in the Middle Ages and restored as a Victorian home. Discover the Castle's past with an audio tour. Visitors can relax in tranquil gardens, explore medieval towers, discover children's activities and play giant chess.

Location: OS Ref. ST487 887. From M4 take J23a and B4245 to Caldicot. From M48 take J2 and follow A48 & B4245. Castle signposted from B4245.

Open: Mar - Oct: Daily, 11am - 5pm. Open in winter to pre-booked groups.

Admission: Adult £3, Child/Conc £1.50. Groups (10 - 100): Adult £2, Child/Conc£ £1.

▢ ▣ **T** ⅃ Partial. WCs **T** By arrangement. ▢ **P** ▦ In Castle, on leads.
▣ Free for formal educational visits. ▲ ▣ Tel for details.

CARDIFF CASTLE

Castle Street, Cardiff CF10 3RB

Tel: 029 2087 8100   **Fax:** 029 2023 1417

Owner: City and County of Cardiff   **Contact:** Booking Office

2000 years of history, including Roman Walls, Norman Keep and Victorian interiors.

Location: OS Ref. ST181 765. Cardiff city centre, signposted from M4.

Open: 1 Mar - 30 Oct: daily, 9.30am - 6pm, last entry 5pm. Nov - Feb: daily, 9.30am - 5pm, last entry 4pm. Closed 25/26 Dec & 1 Jan.

Admission: Adult £6, Child/OAP £3.70.

🎭 **Special Events Index** see front section

CAREW CASTLE & TIDAL MILL

Tenby, Pembrokeshire SA70 8SL

Tel/Fax: 01646 651782   **e-mail:** enquiries@carewcastle.com   **www.**carewcastle.com

Owner: Pembrokeshire Coast National Park   **Contact:** Mr G M Candler

A magnificent Norman castle which later became an Elizabethan country house. Royal links with Henry Tudor and the setting for the Great Tournament of 1507. The Mill is one of only four restored tidal mills in Britain. Introductory slide programme, automatic 'talking points' and special exhibition on 'The Story of Milling'.

Location: OS Ref. SN046 037. ¹/₂ m N of A477, 5m E of Pembroke.

Open: 1 Apr - end Oct: daily, 10am - 5pm.

Admission: Adult £2.80, Child/OAP £1.90, Family £7.50 (prices under review).

▢ ⅃ Partial. WC. **T** By arrangement. **P** ▣ ▦ In grounds on leads. ▣ Tel for details.

CARMARTHEN CASTLE

Carmarthen, South Wales

Tel: 0126 7224923   **e-mail:** clgriffiths@carmarthenshire.gov.uk

Owner/Contact: The Conservation Department, Carmarthenshire County Council

The fortress, originally founded by Henry I in 1109, witnessed several fierce battles, notably in the 15th century when the Welsh hero Owain Glyndwr burnt the town and took the castle from the English.

Location: OS Ref. SN413 200. In the town centre.

Open: Throughout the year.

Admission: Free (guided tours while archaeologists continue to work at the site).

CARREG CENNEN CASTLE ✠

Tir-y-Castell Farm, Llandeilo

Tel: 01558 822291   **www.**cadw.wales.gov.uk

Owner: In the care of Cadw   **Contact:** The Custodian

Spectacularly crowning a remote crag 300 feet above the River Cennen, the castle is unmatched as a wildly romantic fortress sought out by artists and visitors alike. The climb from Rare Breeds Farm is rewarded by breathtaking views and the chance to explore intriguing caves beneath.

Location: OS Ref. SN668 190. Minor roads from A483(T) to Trapp village. 5m SE of A40 at Llandeilo.

Open: Early Apr - late Oct: 9.30am - 7.30pm. Late Oct - late Mar: 9.30am - dusk. Closed 24 - 26 Dec & 1 Jan.

Admission: Adult £3, Child/Conc. £2.50, Family £8.50. (Subject to review March 2004.)

▢ ▣ ▢ **P** ▦ Guide dogs only. ✳

CADW: Welsh Historic Monuments. Crown Copyright

CASTELL COCH ✠

TONGWYNLAIS, CARDIFF CF4 7JS

www.cadw.wales.gov.uk

Tel: 029 2081 0101

Owner: In the care of Cadw   **Contact:** The Custodian

A fairytale castle in the woods, Castell Coch embodies a glorious Victorian dream of the Middle Ages. Designed by William Burges as a country retreat for the 3rd Lord Bute, every room and furnishing is brilliantly eccentric, including paintings of Aesop's fables on the drawing room walls.

Location: OS Ref. ST131 826. M4/J32, A470 then signposted. 5m NW of Cardiff city centre.

Open: Daily, phone site for details. Closed 24 - 26 Dec, 1 Jan.

Admission: Adult £3, Child/Conc. £2.50, Family £8.50. (Subject to review March 2004.)

▢ ⅃ ▣ ▢ **P** ▦ Guide dogs only. ▲ ✳

CHEPSTOW CASTLE ♣
Chepstow, Gwent

Tel: 01291 624065   **www.**cadw.wales.gov.uk

Owner: In the care of Cadw   **Contact:** The Custodian

This mighty fortress has guarded the route from England to South Wales for more than nine centuries. So powerful was this castle that it continued in use until 1690, being finally adapted for cannon and musket after an epic Civil War siege. This huge, complex, grandiosely sited castle deserves a lengthy visit.

Location: OS Ref. ST533 941. Chepstow via A466, B4235 or A48. 1¹/₂ m N of M4/J22.

Open: Daily, phone site for details. Closed 24 - 26 Dec & 1 Jan.

Admission: Adult £3, Child/OAP £2,50, Family £8.50. (Subject to review March 2004.)

🖻 ⑤ Partial. 🅿 ☒ Guide dogs only. ✽

CILGERRAN CASTLE ♣ ☒
Cardigan, Dyfed

Tel: 01239 615007   **www.**cadw.wales.gov.uk

Owner: In the care of Cadw   **Contact:** The Custodian

Perched high up on a rugged spur above the River Teifi, Cilgerran Castle is one of the most spectacularly sited fortresses in Wales. It dates from the 11th - 13th centuries.

Location: OS Ref. SN195 431. Main roads to Cilgerran from A478 and A484. 3¹/₂ m SSE of Cardigan.

Open: Daily, phone site for details. Closed 24 - 26 Dec & 1 Jan.

Admission: Adult £2.50, Child/OAP £2, Family £7. (Subject to review March 2004.)

🖻 🅿 ☒ Guide dogs only. ✽

CLYNE GARDENS
Mill Lane, Blackpill, Swansea SA3 5BD

Tel: 01792 401737

Owner: City and County of Swansea   **Contact:** Steve Hopkins

50 acre spring garden, large rhododendron collection, 4 national collections, extensive bog garden, native woodland.

Location: OS Ref. SS614 906. S side of Mill Lane, 500yds W of A4067 Mumbles Road, 3m SW of Swansea.

Open: All year: daily.

Admission: Free.

COLBY WOODLAND GARDEN ☒
Amroth, Narbeth, Pembrokeshire SA67 8PP

Tel: 01834 811885   **Fax:** 01834 831766

Owner: The National Trust   **Contact:** The Centre Manager

An attractive woodland garden. Walks through secluded valleys along open woodland pathways.

Location: OS Ref. SN155 080. ¹/₂ m inland from Amroth beside Carmarthen Bay. Signs from A477.

Open: 1 Apr - 31 Oct: daily. Woodland Garden: 10am - 5pm; Walled Garden: 11am - 5pm; Shop/Gallery & Tea room: as Garden. Open evenings by arrangement.

Admission: Adult £3.40, Child £1.70, Family £7.50. Groups: Adult £2.70, Child £1.30.

ⓘ Gallery events. 🖻 ☞

CRESSELLY
Kilgetty, Pembrokeshire SA68 0SP

Fax: 01646 687045   **e-mail:** aha@cresselly.org.uk   **www.**cresselly.org.uk

Owner/Contact: H D R Harrison-Allen Esq MFH

Home of the Allen family for 250 years. The house is of 1770 with matching wings of 1869 and contains good plasterwork and fittings of both periods. The Allens are of particular interest for their close association with the Wedgwood family of Etruria and a long tradition of foxhunting. Grade II listed holiday cottage nearby on river.

Location: OS Ref. SN065 065. W of the A4075.

Open: 3 - 28 May & 2 - 11 Jun: Mon - Fri, 10am - 1pm. Guided tours only, on the hour. Coaches and other times by arrangement.

Admission: Adult £4, no children under 12.

⑤ Ground floor only. ⓘ Obligatory. 🅿 Coaches by arrangement. ☒ ☒ (Holiday cottage).

CYFARTHFA CASTLE MUSEUM
Brecon Road, Merthyr Tydfil, Mid Glamorgan CF47 8RE

Tel/Fax: 01685 723112   **e-mail:** museum@cyfarthfapark.freeserve.co.uk

Owner: Merthyr Tydfil County Borough Council   **Contact:** Scott Reid

Castle originates from 1824/1825, now a museum and school.

Location: OS Ref. SO041 074. NE side of A470 to Brecon, ¹/₂ m NW of town centre.

Open: 1 Apr - 30 Sept: Mon - Sun, 10am - 5.30pm. Winter: Tue - Fri (closed Mon), 10am - 4pm, Sat & Sun, 12 noon - 4pm.

Admission: Free.

DINEFWR ☒
Llandeilo SA19 6RT

Tel: 01558 825912   **Fax:** 01558 822036   **e-mail:** gdroff@nationaltrust.org.uk

Owner: The National Trust   **Contact:** The House Manager

Historic site with particular connections to the medieval Princes of Wales.

Location: OS Ref. SN625 225. On outskirts of Llandeilo.

Open: 1 Apr - 31 Oct: daily except Tue & Wed, 11am - 5pm.

Admission: House & Park: Adult £3.50, Child £1.70, Family £8.50. Groups (15+): £2.88. Park only: Adult £2.50, Child £1.20, Family £6. Groups: £2.

⑤ ☞ ⓘ By arrangement. 🅿 Limited for coaches. ☒ ☒ In grounds on leads. ✽

THE DINGLE
Dingle Lane, Crundale, Haverfordwest, Pembrokeshire SA62 4DJ

Tel: 01437 764370   **Fax:** 01437 768844

Owner/Contact: Andrew Barton

18th century country gentleman's home, surrounded by gardens. Gardens only open.

Location: OS Ref. SM973 175. 2m NE of Haverfordwest 600yds SE of B4329.

Open: 10am - 6pm.

Admission: Gardens: Adult £2, Child under 16 Free. Nursery & tearooms Free.

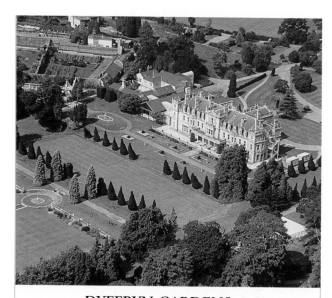

DYFFRYN GARDENS 🏛
ST NICHOLAS, NR CARDIFF CF5 6SU

www.dyffryngardens.org.uk

Tel: 029 2059 3328   **Fax:** 029 2059 1966

Owner: The Vale of Glamorgan Council   **Contact:** Ms G Donovan

Dyffryn Gardens is a delightful Edwardian garden set in the heart of the Vale of Glamorgan and currently being restored with the aid of a Heritage Lottery Grant. Many themed Garden Rooms, an Italianate design, floral bedding displays, herbaceous borders and a well stocked arboretum.

Location: OS Ref. ST095 723. 3m NW of Barry, J33/M4. 1¹/₂ m S of St Nicholas on A48.

Open: Visitor Centre: Apr - Oct.

Admission: Adult £3.50. Please telephone for details of concessions and tours.

🖻 ⚑ ⑤ Partial. ☞ ⓘ 🅿 ☒ ⬆ ✽ ⬚ Tel for details.

Skyscan

FONMON CASTLE 🏛
RHOOSE, BARRY, SOUTH GLAMORGAN CF62 3ZN

Tel: 01446 710206 **Fax:** 01446 711687 **e-mail:** sophie@fonmoncastle.fsnet.co.uk

Owner: Sir Brooke Boothby Bt   **Contact:** Sophie Katzi

Occupied as a home since the 13th century, this medieval castle has the most stunning Georgian interiors and is surrounded by extensive gardens. Available for weddings, concerts, corporate entertainment and multi-activity days.

Location: OS Ref. ST047 681. 15m W of Cardiff, 1m W of Cardiff airport.

Open: 1 Apr - 30 Sept: Tues & Weds, 2 - 5pm (last tour 4pm). Other times by appointment. Groups: by appointment.

Admission: Adult £5, Child Free.

ℹ️ Conferences. 🅣 By arrangement (up to 120). ♿ Partial. WC. 🅿
🐕 Guide dogs only. 🔼 ✳

Alex Ramsay

THE JUDGE'S LODGING
BROAD STREET, PRESTEIGNE, POWYS LD8 2AD

www.judgeslodging.org.uk

Tel: 01544 260650 **Fax:** 01544 260652 **e-mail:** info@judgeslodging.org.uk

Owner: Powys County Council   **Contact:** Gabrielle Rivers

Explore the fascinating world of the Victorian judges, their servants and felonious guests at this award-winning, totally hands-on historic house. From the stunning restored judge's apartments to the gas lit servants' quarters below. Follow an 'eavesdropping' audio tour featuring actor Robert Hardy. Damp cells, vast courtroom and local history rooms included.

Location: OS Ref. SO314 644. In town centre, off A44 and A4113. Easy reach from Herefordshire and mid-Wales.

Open: 1 Mar - 31 Oct: daily, 10am - 6pm. 1 Nov - 22 Dec: Wed - Sun, 10am - 4pm. Bookings by arrangement accepted all year.

Admission: Adult £4.50, Child £3.50, Conc. £3.95. Groups (10-80): Adult £3.95, Child/Conc. £3.50, Family £13.50.

📷 🅣 ♿ Partial (access via lift). 🅕 By arrangement. 🎧 🅿 In town. ▪
🐕 Guide dogs only. ✳

KIDWELLY CASTLE ♣
Kidwelly, West Glamorgan SA17 5BG

Tel: 01554 890104 **www.**cadw.wales.gov.uk

Owner: In the care of Cadw   **Contact:** The Custodian

A chronicle in stone of medieval fortress technology this strong and splendid castle developed during more than three centuries of Anglo-Welsh warfare. The half-moon shape stems from the original 12th century stockaded fortress, defended by the River Gwendraeth on one side and a deep crescent-shaped ditch on the other.

Location: OS Ref. SN409 070. Kidwelly via A484. Kidwelly Rail Station 1m.

Open: Daily, phone site for details. Closed 24 - 26 Dec & 1 Jan.

Admission: Adult £2.50, Child/OAP £2, Family £7. (Subject to review March 2004.)
📷 ♿ 🅕 By arrangement. 🎧 🅿 🐕 Guide dogs only. ✳

KYMIN 🍂
Kymin, Monmouth NP5 3SE

Tel/Fax: 01600 719241 **www.**nationaltrust.org.uk

Owner: The National Trust   **Contact:** The Custodian

Once visited by Nelson and set in 4ha (9acres) of woods and pleasure grounds, this property encompasses a small two-storey circular Georgian banqueting house and naval temple.

Location: OS Ref. SO528 125. 1m E of Monmouth between A466 and A4136.

Open: House: 4 Apr - 25 Oct: daily except Sun & Mon, 11am - 4pm. Temple & Grounds: All year, daily, 11am - 4pm.

Admission: House: Adult £2, Child £1, Family £5. Groups (15+): £1.60. Grounds: Free.
♿ Partial. 🅿 Limited, no coaches. 🐕 Guide dogs only.

LAMPHEY BISHOP'S PALACE ♣
Lamphey, Dyfed

Tel: 01646 672224 **www.**cadw.wales.gov.uk

Owner: In the care of Cadw   **Contact:** The Custodian

Lamphey marks the place of the spectacular Bishop's Palace but it reached its height of greatness under Bishop Henry de Gower who raised the new Great Hall. Today the ruins of this comfortable retreat reflect the power enjoyed by the medieval bishops.

Location: OS Ref. SN018 009. A4139 from Pembroke or Tenby. N of village (A4139).

Open: Daily, 10am - 5pm. Closed 24 - 26 Dec & 1 Jan.

Admission: Adult £2.50, Child/Conc. £2, Family £7. (Subject to review March 2004.)
📷 🎧 🅿 🐕 Guide dogs only. ✳

LAUGHARNE CASTLE ♣
King Street, Laugharne SA33 4SA

Tel: 01994 427906 **www.**cadw.wales.gov.uk

Owner: In the care of Cadw   **Contact:** The Custodian

Picturesque Laugharne Castle stands on a low ridge overlooking the wide Taf estuary, one of a string of fortresses controlling the ancient route along the South Wales coast.

Location: OS Ref. SN303 107. 4m S of A48 at St Clears via A4066.

Open: Apr - Sept: daily, 10am - 5pm. Winter: closed.

Admission: Adult £2.50, Child/Conc. £2, Family £7. (Subject to review March 2004.)
📷 🅿 🐕 Guide dogs only.

LLANCAIACH FAWR MANOR
Nelson, Treharris CF46 6ER

Tel: 01443 412248 **Fax:** 01443 412688

Owner: Caerphilly County Borough Council   **Contact:** The Administrator

Tudor fortified manor dating from 1530 with Stuart additions. Costumed guides.

Location: OS Ref. ST114 967. S side of B4254, 1m N of A472 at Nelson, in the county borough of Caerphilly.

Open: All year: weekdays, 10am - 5pm. weekends, 10am - 6pm. Last admission 1½ hours before closing. Nov - Feb: closed Mons. Closed Christmas week.

Admission: Adult £4.95, Child/Conc. £3.50, Family £13.95.

South Wales

NTPL/ Paul Kay

LLANERCHAERON ✻

ABERAERON, CEREDIGION SA48 8DG

Tel: 01545 570200 **Infoline:** 01558 825147 **Fax:** 01545 571759

Owner: The National Trust   **Contact:** The Property Manager

A small 18th century Welsh gentry estate which survived virtually unaltered into the 20th century. The house was designed and built by John Nash in 1794-96. Llanerchaeron was a self sufficient estate – evident in the dairy, laundry, brewery and salting house of the service courtyard as well as the home farm buildings from the stables to the threshing barn. Llanerchaeron today is a working organic farm and the two restored walled gardens also produce home grown fruit and herbs. There are extensive walks around the estate and pleasure grounds.

Location: OS Ref. SN480 602. 2¹/₂m E of Aberaeron off A482.

Open: 31 Mar - 31 Oct: Wed - Sun (open BH Mons). House: 11.30am - 4.30pm. Last entry to house 4pm. Home Farm & Garden: 11am - 5pm. Parkland: All year, daylight hours.

Admission: House & Garden: Adult £5, Child £2.50, Family £12. Groups (15+): Adult £4, Child £2. Home Farm & Garden: Adult £4, Child £2. Discounted entry when walking, cycling or arriving at the property by public transport. Bike or foot: Adult £4.20, Child £2.10. NT members Free.

LLANVIHANGEL COURT 🏛

Nr Abergavenny, Monmouthshire NP7 8DH

Tel: 01873 890217   **Fax:** 01873 890380   www.llanvihangel-court.co.uk

Owner/Contact: Julia Johnson

A Grade I Tudor Manor. The home in the 17th century of the Arnolds who built the imposing terraces and stone steps leading up to the house. The interior has a fine hall, unusual yew staircase and many 17th century moulded plaster ceilings. Delightful grounds. Includes 17th century features, notably Grade I stables.

Location: OS Ref. SO433 139. 4m N of Abergavenny on A465.

Open: 30 April - 4 May, 28 May - 1 June & 16 - 30 Aug: 2.30 - 5.30pm. Last tour 5pm.

Admission: Adult £4, Child/Conc. £2.50.

ℹ️No inside photography. ♿Partial. 🅿Limited.

MUSEUM OF WELSH LIFE

St Fagans, Cardiff CF5 6XB

Tel: 029 2057 3500   **Fax:** 029 2057 3490

St Fagans Castle, a 16th century building built within the walls of a 13th century castle.

Location: OS Ref. ST118 772. 4m W of city centre, 1¹/₂ m N of A48, 2m S of M4/J33. Entrance drive is off A4232 (southbound only).

Open: All year: daily, 10am - 5pm. Closed 24 - 26 Dec.

Admission: Free.

OXWICH CASTLE ♣

c/o Oxwich Castle Farm, Oxwich SA3 1NG

Tel: 01792 390359   www.cadw.wales.gov.uk

Owner: In the care of Cadw   **Contact:** The Custodian

Beautifully sited in the lovely Gower peninsula, Oxwich Castle is a striking testament to the pride and ambitions of the Mansel dynasty of Welsh gentry.

Location: OS159 Ref. SS497 864. A4118, 11m SW of Swansea, in Oxwich village.

Open: Apr - Sept: daily, 10am - 5pm. Winter: closed.

Admission: Adult £2, Child/OAP £1.50, Family £5.50. (Subject to review March 2004.)

🅿 Guide dogs only.

MIDDLETON, THE NATIONAL BOTANIC GARDEN OF WALES

CARMARTHENSHIRE SA32 8HG

Tel: 01558 668768   **Fax:** 01558 668933   **e-mail:** info@gardenofwales.org.uk

Owner: The National Botanic Garden of Wales   **Contact:** Ben Thomas

Set in the glorious parkland of the former Regency estate of Middleton Hall, this remarkable 21st century botanic garden is just 7 miles from the market town of Carmarthen. The spectacular Great Glasshouse embodies the achievements of contemporary architecture and science, whilst the recently restored Double Walled Garden represents horticultural methods of a bygone age combined with an entirely modern approach to planting. A 220m herbaceous Broadwalk, with a small rill running down its length, forming the spine of the garden and leading to the exciting willow play area. Enjoy a trip on the land train around the lakes and wander in the Shop amongst

the unique branded merchandise followed by a meal in the Seasons Restaurant.

Location: OS159 Ref. SN518 175. ¹/₄ m from the A48 midway between Crosshands and Carmarthen. Clearly signposted from A48 and Carmarthen. Train & Bus in Carmarthen (7m).

Open: Mar - Sept: 10am - 6pm. Oct - Mar: 10am - 4.30pm. Closed Christmas Day.

Admission: Adult £6.95, Child £3.50, OAP/Student £5, Family (2+4) £17.50. Groups (10+): Adult £5.75, Child £2.50, OAP/Student £4.

♿ Free disability scooter hire, booking advisable. Licensed. Licensed. By arrangement. 🅿 Guide dogs only.

South Wales

PEMBROKE CASTLE
PEMBROKE SA71 4LA

www.pembrokecastle.co.uk

Tel: 01646 681510 **Fax:** 01646 622260 **e-mail:** pembroke.castle@talk21.com

Owner: Trustees of Pembroke Castle **Contact:** Mrs A Williams

Pembroke Castle is situated within minutes of beaches and the breathtaking scenery of the Pembrokeshire Coastal National Park. This early Norman fortress, birthplace of the first Tudor King, houses many fascinating displays and exhibitions. Enjoy a picnic in the beautifully kept grounds, or on the roof of St. Anne's Bastion and take in the views along the estuary. Events every weekend in July and August.

Location: OS Ref. SM983 016. W end of the main street in Pembroke.

Open: All year. 1 Apr - Sept: daily, 9.30am - 6pm. Mar & Oct: daily, 10am - 5pm. Nov - Feb: daily, 10am - 4pm. Closed 24 - 26 Dec & 1 Jan. Brass rubbing centre open Summer months & all year by arrangement.

Admission: Adult £3, Child/Conc. £2. Groups (20+): Adult £2.60, OAP/Student £1.70.
⬜ 🅰 ▣ Summer only. 🅘 By arrangement. ▣ 🅗 In grounds on leads. ✳
🅥 Tel for details.

PICTON CASTLE 🏛
HAVERFORDWEST, PEMBROKESHIRE SA62 4AS

www.pictoncastle.co.uk

Tel/Fax: 01437 751326 **e-mail:** pct@pictoncastle.freeserve.co.uk

Owner: The Picton Castle Trust **Contact:** Mr D Pryse Lloyd

Built in the 13th century by Sir John Wogan, his direct descendants still use the Castle as their family home. The medieval castle was modernised in the 1750s, above the undercroft and extended around 1790 with fine Georgian interiors. The 40 acres of woodland and walled gardens are part of The Royal Horticultural Society access scheme for beautiful gardens. There is a unique collection of rhododendrons and azaleas, mature trees, unusual shrubs, wild flowers, fern walk, fernery, maze, restored dewpond, a herb collection labelled with medicinal remedies and a children's nature trail. The Picton Gallery is used for nationally acclaimed exhibitions. Events include spring and autumn plant sales.

Location: OS Ref. SN011 135. 4m E of Haverfordwest, just off A40.

Open: 1 Apr - 30 Sept: daily except Mon (open BH Mons), 10.30am - 5pm. Entrance to Castle by guided tours only, between 12 noon - 4pm. Oct: Gardens only, daily, 10.30am - dusk.

Admission: Castle, Garden & Gallery: Adult £4.95, Child £1.95, OAP £4.75. Garden & Gallery: Adult £3.95, Child £1.95, OAP £3.75. Groups (20+): reduced prices by prior arrangement.

🅘 No indoor photography. ⬜ 🅣 🖵 🅣 ⑪ Licensed. 🅘 Obligatory. ▣
🅗 In grounds, on leads. 🅰 🅥 Tel for details.

RAGLAN CASTLE ✤
Raglan NP5 2BT

Tel: 01291 690228 www.cadw.wales.gov.uk

Owner: In the care of Cadw **Contact:** The Custodian

Undoubtedly the finest late medieval fortress-palace in Britain, it was begun in the 1430s by Sir William ap Thomas who built the mighty 'Yellow Tower'. His son William Lord Herbert added a palatial mansion defended by a gatehouse and many towered walls. The high quality is still obvious today.

Location: OS Ref. SO415 084. Raglan, NE of Raglan village off A40 (eastbound) and signposted.

Open: Daily, phone site for details. Closed 24 - 26 Dec & 1 Jan.

Admission: Adult £2.50, Child/Conc. £2, Family £7. (Subject to review March 2004.)
⬜ ▣ 🅗 Guide dogs only. ✳

ST DAVIDS BISHOP'S PALACE ♣
St Davids, SA62 6PE

Tel: 01437 720517 www.cadw.wales.gov.uk

Owner: In the care of Cadw **Contact:** The Custodian

The city of St Davids boasts not only one of Britain's finest cathedrals but also the most impressive medieval palace in Wales. Built in the elaborate 'decorated' style of gothic architecture, the palace is lavishly encrusted with fine carving.

Location: OS Ref. SM750 254. A487 to St Davids, minor road past the Cathedral.

Open: Daily, phone site for details. Closed 24 - 26 Dec & 1 Jan.

Admission: Adult £2.50, Child/Conc. £2, Family £7 (Subject to review March 2004.)
⬜ 🅰 Partial. ▣ 🅗 Guide dogs only. ✳

ST DAVIDS CATHEDRAL
St Davids, Dyfed SA62 6QW

Tel: 01437 720691 **Fax:** 01437 721885 **Contact:** Mr R G Tarr

Over eight centuries old. Many unique and 'odd' features.

Location: OS Ref. SM751 254. 5-10mins walk from car/coach parks: signs for pedestrians.

Open: Daily: 7.30am - 6.30pm. Suns: 12.30 - 5.30pm, may be closed for services in progress. Sun services: 8am, 9.30am, 11.15am & 6pm. Weekday services: 8am & 6pm. Weds extra service: 10am.

Admission: Donations. Guided tours (Adult £3, Child £1.20) must be booked.

STRATA FLORIDA ABBEY ✤
Ystrad Meurig, Pontrhydfendigaid SY25 6BT

Tel: 01974 831261 www.cadw.wales.gov.uk

Owner: In the care of Cadw **Contact:** The Custodian

Remotely set in the green, kite-haunted Teifi Valley with the lonely Cambrian mountains as a backdrop, the ruined abbey has a wonderful doorway with Celtic spiral motifs and preserves a wealth of beautiful medieval tiles.

Location: OS Ref. SN746 658. Minor road from Pontrhydfendigaid 14m SE of Aberystwyth by the B4340.

Open: End Mar - end Sept: daily. Phone site for details. Winter: open site.

Admission: Adult £2, Child/Conc. £1.50, Family £5.50. (Subject to review March 2004.)
⬜ 🅰 ▣ 🅗 Guide dogs only. ✳

TINTERN ABBEY ✤
Tintern NP6 6SE

Tel: 01291 689251 www.cadw.wales.gov.uk

Owner: In the care of Cadw **Contact:** The Custodian

Tintern is the best preserved abbey in Wales and ranks among Britain's most beautiful historic sites. Elaborately decorated in 'gothic' architecture style this church stands almost complete to roof level. Turner sketched and painted here, while Wordsworth drew inspiration from the surroundings.

Location: OS Ref. SO533 000. Tintern via A466, from M4/J23. Chepstow 6m.

Open: Daily, phone site for details. Closed 24 - 26 Dec & 1 Jan. Opening/admission details subject to review Mar 2004.

Admission: Adult £2.50, Child/Conc. £2, Family £7. (Subject to review March 2004.)
⬜ 🅰 ⬜ ▣ 🅗 Guide dogs only. ✳

TREBINSHWN
Nr Brecon, Powys LD3 7PX

Tel: 01874 730653 **Fax:** 01874 730843

Owner/Contact: R Watson

16th century mid-sized manor house. Extensively rebuilt 1780. Fine courtyard and walled garden.

Location: OS Ref. SO136 242. 1¹/2m NW of Bwlch.

Open: Easter - 31 Aug: Mon - Tue, 10am - 4.30pm.

Admission: £1.
▣

TREDEGAR HOUSE & PARK 🏛

NEWPORT, SOUTH WALES NP1 9YW

Tel: 01633 815880 **Fax:** 01633 815895 **e-mail:** tredegar.house@newport.gov.uk
Owner: Newport County Borough Council **Contact:** The Manager
South Wales' finest country house, ancestral home of the Morgan family. Parts of a medieval house remain, but Tredegar owes its reputation to lavish rebuilding in the 17th century. Visitors have a lively and entertaining tour through 30 rooms, including glittering State Rooms and 'below stairs'. Set in 90 acres of parkland with formal gardens. Winner of Best Public Park and Garden in Great Britain 1997. Craft workshops.
Location: OS Ref. ST290 852. M4/J28 signposted. From London 2½hrs, from Cardiff 20 mins. 2m SW of Newport town centre.
Open: Easter - Sept: Wed - Sun & BHs, 11.30am - 4pm. Evening tours & groups by appointment. Oct - Mar: Groups only by appointment. For visits between 31 July & 7 Aug please telephone 01633 815880 for change to published tour information.
Admission: Adult £5.25, Child Free (when accompanied by paying adult), Conc. £3.85. Special discounts for Newport residents. (2003 prices.)
ℹ️ Conferences. No photography in house. 📷 🆃 ♿ Partial. WC. 🍴
🎥 Obligatory. 🅿 ■ 🐕 In grounds, on leads. ▲ 🖥 Tel for details.

TREOWEN 🏛

Wonastow, Nr Monmouth NP25 4DL
Tel/Fax: 01600 712031 **e-mail:** john.wheelock@virgin.net **www.**treowen.co.uk
Owner: R A & J P Wheelock **Contact:** John Wheelock
Early 17th century mansion built to double pile plan with magnificent well-stair to four storeys.
Location: OS Ref. SO461 111. 3m WSW of Monmouth.
Open: May, Jun Aug & Sept: Fri. Also Sat & Sun: 8/9 & 15/16 May; 11/12, 18/19 & 25/26 Sept. HHA Friends Free on Fri only.
Admission: £5 (£3 if appointment made). Groups by appointment only.
🆃 ■ Entire house let, self-catering. Sleeps 24+. ▲

TRETOWER COURT & CASTLE ♣

Tretower, Crickhowell NP8 2RF
Tel: 01874 730279 **www.**cadw.wales.gov.uk
Owner: In the care of Cadw **Contact:** The Custodian
A fine fortress and an outstanding medieval manor house, Tretower Court and Castle range around a galleried courtyard, now further enhanced by a beautiful recreated medieval garden.
Location: OS Ref. SO187 212. Signposted in Tretower Village, off A479, 3m NW of Crickhowell.
Open: Mar - Oct: daily, phone site for details. Winter: closed.
Admission: Adult £2.50, Child/Conc. £2, Family £7. (Subject to review March 2004.)
📷 🖨 🅿 🐕 Guide dogs only.

TUDOR MERCHANT'S HOUSE 🌿

QUAY HILL, TENBY SA70 7BX
Tel/Fax: 01834 842279
Owner: The National Trust **Contact:** The Custodian
A late 15th century town house, characteristic of the building tradition of south west Wales.
Location: OS Ref. SN135 004. Tenby. W of alley from NE corner of town centre square.
Open: 1 Apr - 31 Oct: daily, 10am - 5pm (closes 3pm in Oct).
Admission: Adult £2, Child £1, Family £5. Groups: Adult £1.60, Child 80p.
ℹ️ No indoor photography. 🅿 No parking. ■ 🐕 Guide dogs only.

TYTHEGSTON COURT

Tythegston, Bridgend CF32 0NE
e-mail: cknight@tythegston.com **www.**tythegston.com
Owner/Contact: C Knight
Location: OS Ref. SS857 789. 2m E of Porthcawl on Glamorgan coast.
Open: By written appointment (no telephone calls please).
Admission: Adult £10, Child £2.50, Conc. £5.
🆃 ♿ Partial. 🎥 Obligatory. 🅿 Limited. No coaches. 🐕 Guide dogs only.

USK CASTLE

Usk, Monmouthshire NP5 1SD
Tel: 01291 672563 **e-mail:** info@uskcastle.co.uk **www.**uskcastle.com
Owner/Contact: J H L Humphreys
Romantic, ruined castle overlooking the picturesque town of Usk. Inner and outer baileys, towers and earthwork defences. Surrounded by enchanting gardens (open under NGS) incorporating The Castle House, the former medieval gatehouse.
Location: OS Ref. SO376 011. Up narrow lane off Monmouth road in Usk, opposite fire station.
Open: Castle ruins: daily, 11am - 5pm. Groups by appointment. Gardens: private visits welcome & groups by arrangement. House: Jun & BHs: 2 - 5pm (except 26/27 Jun), small groups & guided tours only.
Admission: Castle ruins: Adult £2, Child Free. Gardens: Adult £2. House: Adult £5, Child £2.
🆃 ♿ Partial. 🎥 By arrangement. ■ 🅿 No coaches. 🐕 In grounds, on leads. ✳️

WEOBLEY CASTLE ♣

Weobley Castle Farm, Llanrhidian SA3 1HB
Tel: 01792 390012 **www.**cadw.wales.gov.uk
Owner: In the care of Cadw **Contact:** The Custodian
Perched above the wild northern coast of the beautiful Gower peninsula, Weobley Castle was the home of the Knightly de Bere family. Its rooms include a fine hall and private chamber as well as numerous 'garderobes' or toilets and an early Tudor porch block.
Location: OS Ref. SN477 928. B4271 or B4295 to Llanrhidian Village, then minor road for 1½ m.
Open: Daily, phone site for details. Closed 24 - 26 Dec & 1 Jan.
Admission: Adult £2, Child/Conc. £1.50, Family £5.50. (Subject to review March 2004.)
📷 🅿 🐕 Guide dogs only. ✳️

WHITE CASTLE ♣

Llantillio Crossenny, Gwent
Tel: 01600 780380 **www.**cadw.wales.gov.uk
Owner: In the care of Cadw **Contact:** The Custodian
With its high walls and round towers reflected in the still waters of its moat, White Castle is the ideal medieval fortress. It was rebuilt in the mid-13th century by the future King Edward I to counter a threat from Prince Llywelyn the Last.
Location: OS Ref. SO380 167. By minor road 2m NW from B4233 at A7 Llantilio Crossenny. 8m ENE of Abergavenny.
Open: Apr - Sept: phone site for details. Winter: Open site.
Admission: Adult £2, Conc. £1.50, Family £5.50. (Subject to review March 2004.)
📷 🅿 🐕 Guide dogs only. ✳️

Giacomo Leoni

c1686 – 1746

A Venetian, who came to England to prepare the illustrations for the English translation of the works of Palladio. Look for strong classical lines, and strict adherence to the rules of Palladio i.e. the use of harmonic proportions, Roman planning, and symmetry of design.

Visit Clandon Park in Surrey and Lyme Park in Cheshire.

Architect & Illustrator

Audley's Castle, a 15th century tower house on the Castle Ward Estate. © NTPL / Matthew Antrobus

NORTHERN

IRELAND

northern ireland

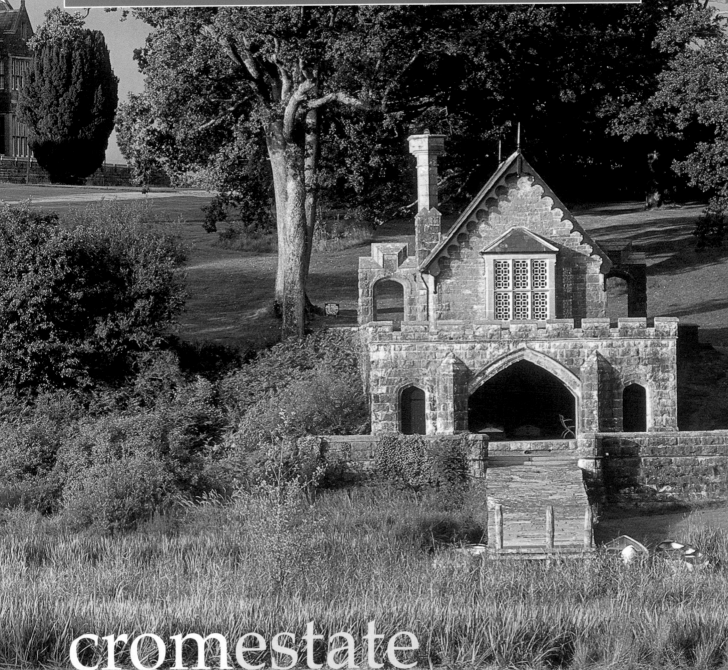

cromestate
co fermanagh

Crom Estate, acquired by the National Trust in 1987, is one of Northern Ireland's best kept secrets – a place of remoteness, peace and quiet, and great beauty. Set within the winding waters of Upper Lough Erne, Crom is a hidden gem on Fermanagh's waterways. Its varied habitats host a wealth of wildlife, making it a magical world to visit on foot or by boat.

Within Crom's 2,000 acres there are ancient woodlands, tranquil islands and historic ruins. Plants such as wood anemone, dog violet, wood sedge and the rare bird's nest orchid occur. Birds include blackcaps, jays and garden warblers, while butterflies such as the purple hairstreak and silver-washed fritillary may be seen in late summer. Fallow deer, badgers, red squirrels and the elusive pine marten also make Crom their home.

There are few other places within the British Isles where the transition from open water through swamp, fen, wet grassland and carr to mature broadleaf woodland is as well developed and occurs on such a large scale. Herons, great crested grebe, sedge warblers and the shy water rail can be found in the dense reed swamp, and with luck an otter might be spotted hunting along the shores.

Much of Crom's appeal is owed to William Sawry Gilpin. Gilpin's 1830s design for Crom's landscape is regarded as the best example of his picturesque style in the British Isles – a style of *"lots of sky, lots of water, lots of (dense) plantations, lots of grassland"*. This created a landscape where the parkland seems to disappear effortlessly into the surrounding Lough, and then re-emerges at some distant view.

The focal point of the estate was Crom Castle. The Scottish Planter, Michael Balfour, built the original castle in 1610 during the Ulster Plantation. It withstood two sieges by the Jacobites in 1689, but succumbed to accidental fire in 1764. It was replaced by a second castle, built in 1834-6 for Colonel John Crichton, to a design by the architect Edward Blore near to the site of the original castle. The Castle is not open to the public.

It is easy to visualise the estate of 200 years ago – a small world of its own, complete with church and school, remote and isolated yet vibrant and part of the wider Lough Erne area. Today, The National Trust ensures the estate is used and enjoyed all year by a mixed community of permanent residents, holiday cottage guests, tenant farmers and the donor family. Crom Castle, however, remains privately owned and is **not** open to the public. To stay in one of the seven 4* holiday cottages contact the Booking Office on tel: +44 (0) 870 4584422. You can even arrange conferences and weddings here. Visit Crom once, and you will surely want to return.

▸ For further details about Crom Estate see page 539.

ANTRIM CASTLE GARDENS
Randalstown Road, Antrim BT41 4LH

Tel: 028 9442 8000 **Fax:** 028 9446 0360 **e-mail:** clotworthyarts@antrim.gov.uk
Owner: Antrim Borough Council **Contact:** Philip Magennis
Situated adjacent to Antrim Town, the Sixmilewater River and Lough Neagh's shore, these recently restored, 17th century Anglo-Dutch water gardens are maintained in a manner authentic to the period. The gardens comprise of ornamental canals, round pond, ancient motte and a parterre garden planted with 17th century plants - many with culinary or medicinal uses. An interpretative display introducing the history of the gardens and the process of their restoration, along with a scale model of former Antrim Castle is located in the reception of Clotworthy Arts Centre.
Location: Outside Antrim town centre off A26 on A6.
Open: All year: Mon - Fri, 9.30am - 9.30pm (dusk if earlier). Sats, 10am - 5pm. Jul & Aug: also open Suns, 2 - 5pm.
Admission: Free. Charge for guided group tours (by arrangement only).

ARDRESS HOUSE & FARMYARD
64 Ardress Road, Portadown, Co Armagh BT62 1SQ

Tel/Fax: 028 3885 1236 **e-mail:** ardress@ntrust.org.uk **www**.ntni.org.uk

Owner: The National Trust **Contact:** The Custodian
A 17th century farmhouse with elegant 18th century additions by owner-architect George Ensor. Includes a display of antique farming implements in the farmyard.
Location: On B28, 5m from Moy, 5m from Portadown, 3m from M1/J13.
Open: 13 Mar - Sept: Sat, Sun & BH/PHs, 2 - 6pm.
Admission: House tour: Adult £3, Child £1.50, Family £7.50. Groups £2.50 (outside normal hours £4.50).
Ground floor. WC. Obligatory. On leads.

THE ARGORY
Moy, Dungannon, Co Tyrone BT71 6NA

Tel: 028 8778 4753 **Fax:** 028 8778 9598

e-mail: argory@ntrust.org.uk **www**.ntni.org.uk
Owner: The National Trust **Contact:** The Property Manager
The Argory is a handsome 19th century Victorian house furnished as it was in 1900, providing an excellent illustration of Victorian/Edwardian interior taste and interests.
Location: On Derrycaw road, 4m from Moy, 3m from M1/J13 or J14 (coaches J13).
Open: House: 13 Mar - May; Sat, Sun & BH/PHs (incl. 9 - 18 Apr); Jun - Aug: daily, 1 - 6pm; Sept: weekends, 1 - 6pm; 2 - 10 Oct: Sat & Sun, 1 - 5pm. Grounds: Oct - Apr: daily, 10am - 4pm; May - Sept: daily, 10am - 8pm (2 - 8pm on Event Days).
Admission: House tour: Adult £4.30, Child £2.30, Family £10.80. Groups: Adult £3.90 (outside normal hours £4.70). Grounds only (car park charge): £2.30 (refunded on purchase of house ticket).
Ground floor. WC. Obligatory. On leads.

BALLYWALTER PARK
Nr Newtownards, Co Down BT22 2PP

Tel: 028 4275 8264 **Fax:** 028 4275 8818

e-mail: enquiries@dunleath-estates.co.uk **www**.ballywalterpark.com
Owner: Lord Dunleath **Contact:** The Secretary, The Estate Office
Victorian mansion, situated in 40 acres of landscaped grounds, built in the mid-19th century by Charles Lanyon, with Edwardian additions by W J Fennell. Currently undergoing major restoration works. Self-catered (4 star) listed gatelodge overlooking beach available for holiday lets (sleeps four).
Location: 1km S of Ballywalter village.
Open: By appointment, please telephone the Estate Office.
Admission: House or Gardens: Adult £5. House and gardens: Adult £8. Groups (max 50): Adult £5.
No photography indoors. Pick-your-own, Jun - Aug. By prior arrangement. Obligatory. Self-catering.

BARONS COURT
Newtownstewart, Omagh, Co Tyrone BT78 4EZ

Tel: 028 8166 1683 **Fax:** 028 8166 2059 **Contact:** The Agent
The home of the Duke and Duchess of Abercorn, Barons Court was built between 1779 and 1782, and subsequently extensively remodelled by John Soane (1791), William and Richard Morrison (1819-1841), Sir Albert Richardson (1947-49) and David Hicks (1975-76).
Location: 5km SW of Newtownstewart.
Open: By appointment only.
Admission: Adult £4.50. Groups max. 50.
Partial. WCs. By arrangement.

CASTLE COOLE
Enniskillen, Co Fermanagh BT74 6JY

Tel: 028 6632 2690 **Fax:** 028 6632 5665 **e-mail:** castlecoole@ntrust.org.uk
www.ntni.org.uk
Owner: The National Trust **Contact:** The Property Manager
One of the finest neo-classical houses in Ireland, built by James Wyatt in the late 18th century, and sited in a rolling landscape park right on the edge of Enniskillen.
Location: On A4, 1m from Enniskillen on A4, Belfast - Enniskillen road.
Open: House: 13 Mar - May & Sept: Sat, Sun & BH/PHs (incl. 9 - 18 Apr); Jun: daily except Tue; Jul - Aug: daily, 12 noon - 6pm; 2 - 10 Oct: Sat & Sun, 1 - 5pm. Last tour 1hr before closing. Grounds: Oct - Mar: daily, 10am - 4pm; Apr - Sept: daily, 10am - 8pm.
Admission: House tour: Adult £4, Child £2, Family £10. Groups: £3 (outside normal hours £4).
Partial. WC. In grounds, on leads.

CASTLE WARD
STRANGFORD, DOWNPATRICK, Co DOWN BT30 7LS

www.ntni.org.uk

Tel: 028 4488 1204 **Fax:** 028 4488 1729 **e-mail:** castleward@ntrust.org.uk
Owner: The National Trust **Contact:** The Property Manager
Castle Ward is a beautiful 750 acre walled estate in a stunning location overlooking Strangford Lough. The mid-Georgian mansion is one of the architectural curios of its time, built inside and out in two distinct architectural styles. Due to a difference of opinion between its 18th century owners, Bernard and Anne Ward, the house features Classical styling on one side and Gothic on the other. The picturesque estate also includes a Victorian laundry and children's playroom, water-driven cornmill demonstrations, a disused leadmine and sawmill, which provide a fascinating insight into how the house and estate worked. Paths and horse trails wind their way throughout the estate. Also formal gardens, the Old Castle Ward tower house from 1610, the Temple Water (a man-made lake) and the Strangford Lough Wildlife Centre. Stableyard includes tearoom and a large Trust shop.
Location: On A25, 7m from Downpatrick and 1 1/2 m from Strangford.
Open: House & Wildlife Centre: 13 Mar - Apr: weekends & BH/PHs (open daily during 9 -18 Apr); May - Aug: daily (closed Tues in May), 1 - 6pm. Grounds: Oct - Apr: daily, 10am - 4pm; May - Sept: daily, 10am - 8pm.
Admission: Grounds, Wildlife Centre & House Tour: Adult £5, Child £2.30, Family £10.80. Group: £4 (outside normal hours £5). Grounds & Wildlife Centre only: Adult £3.50, Child £1.50, Family £8, Group £2.50.
Ground floor & grounds. WC. Obligatory. In grounds, on leads. Caravan park, holiday cottages, basecamp.

CROM ESTATE
Newtownbutler, Co Fermanagh BT92 8AP

Tel/Fax: 028 6773 8118 (Visitor Centre) 028 6773 8174 (Estate)
e-mail: crom@ntrust.org.uk **www**.ntni.org.uk
Owner: The National Trust **Contact:** The Visitor Facilities Manager
Crom is one of Ireland's most important nature conservation areas. It is set in 770 hectares of romantic and tranquil islands, woodland and ruins on the shores of Upper Lough Erne. Things to look out for include the spotted flycatcher, curlew, purple hairstreak butterfly, pine marten and fallow deer. Lots of well-maintained nature trails take in the Old Castle, boathouse and summer house. Wildlife exhibition, information point and tearoom for light snacks in visitor centre. Further facilities include jetty for boats, boat hire, award-winning holiday cottages, coarse angling, pike fishing, overnight woodland hide, lecture and conference facilities. The 19th century castle within the estate is private.
Location: 3m from A34, well signposted from Newtownbutler. Jetty at Visitor Centre.
Open: Grounds: 13 Mar - Jun: daily, 10am - 6pm; Jul & Aug: daily, 10am - 8pm; Sept: daily, 10am - 6pm; Oct: Sats & Suns, 12 noon - 6pm. All Suns: 12 noon - 6pm. Visitor Centre: 13 Mar - 25 Apr: Weekends, BHs and public holidays, 10am - 6pm; May - Sept: daily 10am - 6pm. 2 - 10 Oct: Sats & Suns, 1 - 5pm.
Admission: Grounds & Visitor Centre: Car or Boat £4.50. Minibus £12.50, Coach £16.
7 x 4-star holiday cottages & play-area.

DERRYMORE HOUSE ❧

Bessbrook, Newry, Co Armagh BT35 7EF

Tel: 028 3083 8361 **www**.ntni.org.uk

Owner: The National Trust

An elegant late 18th century thatched cottage, built by Isaac Corry, who represented Newry in the Irish House of Commons. Park laid out in the style of 'Capability' Brown.

Location: On A25, 2m from Newry on road to Camlough.

Open: House: May - Aug: Thur - Sat, 2pm - 5.30pm. Grounds: Oct - Apr: daily, 10am - 4pm; May - Sept: daily, 10am - 8pm.

Admission: House tour: Adult £2.50, Child £1.20, Family £5. Groups: £1.50 (outside normal hours £3).

P ⛔ On leads.

FLORENCE COURT ❧

Enniskillen, Co Fermanagh BT92 1DB

Tel: 028 6634 8249 **Fax:** 028 6634 8873 **e-mail:** florencecourt@ntrust.org.uk **www**.ntni.org.uk

Owner: The National Trust   **Contact:** The Property Manager

Florence Court is a fine mid-18th century house and estate set against the stunning backdrop of the Cuilcagh Mountains. House tour includes service quarters popular with all ages. Beautiful walled garden and lots of walks in grounds.

Location: 8m SW of Enniskillen via A4 then A32 to Swanlinbar.

Open: House: 13 Mar - May: Sat, Sun & BH/PHs (incl. 9 - 18 Apr); Jun: daily, (Mon - Fri from 1pm); Jul & Aug: daily; Sept: Sat & Sun: 12 noon - 6pm; Oct: Sat & Sun, 1 - 5pm. Grounds: Oct - Mar: daily, 10am - 4pm. Apr - Sept: daily, 10am - 8pm.

Admission: House tour: Adult £4, Child £2, Family £10. Groups: £3 (outside normal hours £4). Grounds only: Car £2.50 (refundable on purchase of house tour).

⬛ ⊤ ♿ Ground floor. WC. ⬛ 🎟 Obligatory. **P** ⛔ In grounds, on leads. ⬛ Holiday cottage. ▲

GRAY'S PRINTING PRESS ❧

49 Main Street, Strabane, Co Tyrone BT82 8AU

Tel: 028 7188 0055 **www**.ntni.org.uk

Owner: The National Trust   **Contact:** The Administrator

Historic printworks, featuring 18th century printing press and 19th century hand-printing machines. Tour includes audio-visual presentation.

Location: In the centre of Strabane.

Open: Apr - May: Sat only, 2 - 5pm; Jun - Sep: Tue - Sat, 2 - 5pm (Jul & Aug from 11am).

Admission: Press Tour: Adult £2.70, Child £1.60, Family £6. Group £2.20 (outside normal hours £3.50).

🎟 🔂

HEZLETT HOUSE ❧

107 Sea Road, Castlerock, Coleraine, Co Londonderry BT51 4TW

Tel/Fax: 028 7084 8567 **e-mail:** downhillcastle@ntrust.org.uk **www**.ntni.org.uk

Owner: The National Trust   **Contact:** The Custodian

Charming 17th century thatched house with 19th century furnishings. One of only a few pre-18th century Irish buildings still surviving.

Location: 5m W of Coleraine on Coleraine - Downhill coast road, A2.

Open: 13 Mar - May: Sat, Sun & BH/PHs (incl. 9 - 18 Apr); Jun - Aug: daily except Tue (unless BH/PH Tue); Sept: Sat & Sun: 1 - 6pm; 2 - 10 Oct: Sat & Sun, 1 - 5pm.

Admission: Adult £3.60, Child £2.10, Family £8.30. Groups £3.10 (outside normal hours £4.50).

♿ Ground floor. 🎟 Obligatory. **P** ⛔ In grounds, on leads.

KILLYLEAGH CASTLE

Killyleagh, Downpatrick, Co Down BT30 9QA

Tel/Fax: 028 4482 8261 **e-mail:** polly@killyleaghcastle.fsnet.co.uk **www**.killyleaghcastle.com

Owner/Contact: Mrs G Rowan-Hamilton

Oldest occupied castle in Ireland. Self-catering towers available to sleep 4-15. Swimming pool and tennis court available. Access to garden.

Location: At the end of the High Street.

Open: By arrangement. Groups (30-50): by appointment.

Admission: Adult £3.50, Child £2. Groups: Adult £2.50, Child £1.50.

ℹ️ No photography in house. ⊤ Wedding receptions. ♿ Unsuitable. 🎟 Obligatory. **P** 🅿️ ▲ ❋

MOUNT STEWART ❧

NEWTOWNARDS, Co DOWN BT22 2AD

www.ntni.org.uk

Tel: 028 4278 8387 **Fax:** 028 4278 8569

e-mail: mountstewart@nationaltrust.org.uk

Owner: The National Trust   **Contact:** The Property Manager

Home of the Londonderry family since the early 18th century, Mount Stewart was Lord Castlereagh's house and played host to many prominent political figures. The magnificent gardens planted in the 1920s have made Mount Stewart famous and earned it a World Heritage Site nomination. They feature a series of formal outdoor 'rooms', vibrant parterres, and formal and informal vistas, some with Strangford Lough views. Many rare and unusual plants thrive in the mild climate of the Ards, including eucalyptus, beschorneria, mimosa, and cordyline. The garden is also home to national collections of phormium and libertia. The house includes the famous painting 'Hambletonian', as well as the full set of chairs used at Congress of Vienna. The Temple of the Winds, a 1785 banqueting hall, is in the grounds. New café-bistro restaurant, gift shop and exhibition areas.

Location: On A20, 5m from Newtownards on the Portaferry road.

Open: House: 13 Mar - Apr & Oct: Sats, Suns & BH/PHs, 12 noon - 6pm. May - Jun: Mon & Wed - Fri, 1 - 6pm, Sats & Suns, 12 noon - 6pm; Jul - Sept: daily except Tue in Sept. Formal Gardens: Mar: Sats, Suns & BH/PHs, 10am - 4pm; Apr - Oct: daily, 10am - 6pm (closes 8pm during May - Sept). Lakeside Gardens: daily; Nov - Mar, 10am - 4pm; Apr & Oct: 10am - 6pm; May - Sept: 10am - 8pm. Temple of the Winds: Apr - Oct: Sats & Suns, 2 - 5pm.

Admission: House tour, Gardens & Temple: Adult £5.20, Child £2.50, Family £10.80. Group: £4.50, Outside normal hours £6. Gardens only: Adult £4.20, Child £2.20, Family £9.30, Group: £3.90.

⬛ ⊤ ♿ 🍴 🎟 Obligatory. **P** ⛔ In grounds, on leads. ▲

MUSSENDEN TEMPLE ❧

Castlerock, Co. Londonderry

Tel/Fax: 028 7084 8728 **e-mail:** downhillcastle@ntrust.org.uk **www**.ntni.org.uk

Owner: The National Trust

Set on a stunning and wild headland with fabulous views over Ireland's north coast is the landscaped estate of Downhill.

Location: 1m W of Castlerock.

Open: Temple: 13 Mar - May: Sat, Sun & BH/PHs (incl. 9 - 18 Apr); Jun - Aug: daily, (Jul & Aug closes 7.30pm); Sept: Sat & Sun: 11am - 6pm; Oct: Sat & Sun, 11am - 5pm. Grounds: All year, dawn - dusk.

Admission: Car park charge at Lion's Gate during Temple opening: Car £3.60, Minibus £7.30, Motorbike £2.20.

⊤ **P** ⛔ On leads. ▲

PATTERSON'S SPADE MILL ✂

Templepatrick, Co Antrim BT39 0AP

Tel/Fax: 028 9443 3619   **www.**ntni.org.uk

Owner: The National Trust
Founded in 1919, this is the last surviving water-driven spade mill in Ireland. The original equipment is working for visitors to see, complete with hammers, a turbine and a press.
Location: On A6 (between Sandyknowes roundabout and Templepatrick roundabout), M2/J4. 1st left at Templepatrick roundabout after exiting motorway.
Open: Mar: Sun only (open 17 Mar); Apr - May: Sat, Sun & BH/PHs (incl. 9 - 18 Apr); Jun - Aug: daily except Tue; Sept & 2 - 10 Oct: Sat & Sun: 2 - 6pm.
Admission: Mill Tour: Adult £3.60, Child £2.10, Family £8.80. Groups £2.50 (outside normal hours £4.50).
⬛ 🚹 Ⓟ 🐾 On leads.

ROWALLANE GARDEN ✂

Saintfield, Ballynahinch, Co Down BT24 7LH

Tel: 028 9751 0131   **Fax:** 028 9751 1242

e-mail: rowallane@ntrust.org.uk   **www.**ntni.org.uk

Owner: The National Trust   **Contact:** Head Gardener
Rowallane is a natural landscape of some 21 hectares, planted with an outstanding collection of trees, shrubs and other plants from many parts of the world, creating a beautiful display of form and colour throughout the year. The garden was established in the 1860s by the Rev John Moore, and carried on by his plant-collecting nephew in the early 1900s. Planting and collecting continue today. In spring the garden features a magnificent display of rhododendrons, azaleas, bulbs, flowering trees and shrubs. Summer brings hypericum, viburnum, shrub roses and fuschias in the walled garden; primulas and heathers in the rock garden and wild flower meadows rich with orchids. The scarlet and gold foliage of autumn gives way to winter, when Rowallane's plentiful supplies of fruit and berries attracts an array of interesting birds.
Location: On A7, 1m from Saintfield on road to Downpatrick.
Open: Daily. Oct - Apr: 10am - 4pm (closed 25/26 Dec & 1 Jan). May - Sept: 10am - 8pm.
Admission: Adult £3.50, Child £1.50, Family £8. Groups £2.80.
⬛ Grounds. WC. ▣ Apr - Aug. 🐾 In grounds, on leads. ✳

SEAFORDE GARDENS 🏛

Seaforde, Co Down BT30 8PG

Tel: 028 44811 225   **Fax:** 028 44811 370   **e-mail:** plants@seafordegardens.com
www.seafordegardens.com

Owner/Contact: Patrick Forde
18th century walled garden and adjoining pleasure grounds, containing many rare and beautiful trees and shrubs; many of them tender. There are huge rhododendrons and the National Collection of Eucryphias. The oldest maze in Ireland is in the centre of the walled garden, which can be viewed from the Mogul Tower. The tropical butterfly house contains hundreds of beautiful highly coloured butterflies; also a collection of parrots, insects and reptiles. The nursery garden contains many interesting plants for sale.
Location: 20m S of Belfast on the main road to Newcastle.
Open: Easter - end Sept: Mon - Sat, 10am - 5pm; Suns, 1 - 6pm. Gardens only: Oct - Mar: Mon - Fri, 10am - 5pm.
Admission: Butterfly House or Gardens: Adult £2.80, Child £1.70. Groups (10+): Adult £2.20. Child £1.40. Butterfly House & Gardens: Adult £5, Child £2.80. Groups: Adult £4, Child £2.50, Family (2+2) £14.
◻ 🚹 🔽 🍴 🍴 🚻By arrangement. Ⓟ ◼ 🐾 ✳ €

SPRINGHILL ✂

20 Springhill Road, Moneymore, Co Londonderry BT45 7NQ

Tel/Fax: 028 8674 8210   **e-mail:** springhill@ntrust.org.uk   **www.**ntni.org.uk

Owner: The National Trust   **Contact:** The Property Manager
A charming and atmospheric 17th century 'plantation' house, said by many to be one of the prettiest houses in Ulster. It was home to ten generations of the Conyngham family, originally from Ayr. 50 minutes drive from Belfast or Londonderry, 35 minutes from Coleraine. House tour takes in exceptional library, gun room, nursery, and includes the story of resident ghost. Colourful costume collection, with some Irish 17th century pieces. Beautiful walks in walled gardens and way-marked paths in estate. Excellent tearoom, small shop and children's play area.
Location: 1m from Moneymore on B18 to Coagh, 5m from Cookstown.
Open: 13 Mar - Jun: Sat, Sun & BH/PHs (incl. 9 - 18 Apr); Jul & Aug: daily; Sept: Sat & Sun: 12 noon - 6pm; 2 - 10 Oct: Sat & Sun, 12 noon - 5pm.
Admission: House & Costume Collection Tour: Adult £3.90, Child £2.10, Family £8.50. Group £3.50 (outside normal hours £4.70).
◻ 🔽 ⬛ Partial. WC. ▣ 🚹 Ⓟ 🐾 In grounds, on leads. ▲

WELLBROOK BEETLING MILL ✂

20 Wellbrook Road, Corkhill, Co. Tyrone BT80 9RY

Tel: 028 8674 8210/8675 1735   **e-mail:** wellbrook@ntrust.org.uk   **www.**ntni.org.uk

Owner: The National Trust   **Contact:** The Custodian
Wellbrook is an 18th century water-powered beetling mill with the only working beetling engines on show in Northern Ireland. New exhibition on the history of linen and its importance to Ireland.
Location: 4m from Cookstown, following signs from A505 Cookstown - Omagh road.
Open: 13 Mar - Jun: Sat, Sun & BH/PHs (incl. 9 - 18 Apr); Jul & Aug: daily; Sept: Sat & Sun: 1 - 6pm; 2 - 10 Oct: Sat & Sun, 1 - 5pm.
Admission: Mill Tour: Adult £2.80, Child £1.60, Family £6. Group: £2.20 (outside normal hours £3.50).
◻ Ⓟ

Republic of Ireland

The Cobbe Collection at Hatchlands (see feature on pages 90-93) can also, in part, be seen at Newbridge House, Donabate, Co. Dublin.

THE COBBE COLLECTION AT NEWBRIDGE HOUSE

Newbridge House is a Palladian villa in a landscaped park. It was designed by James Gibbs (1747-50) for Charles Cobbe, Archbishop of Dublin. Gibbs' first proposal was for a palatial building the size of Leinster House or Houghton Hall, but the Archbishop settled for a villa that is Gibbs' only executed work in Ireland. The building of the house was overseen by the Irish architect/engineer, George Semple. Thomas Cobbe the (Archbishop's son) considerably enlarged the house in the 1760s, but without disturbing the integrity of Gibbs' design. He incorporated a large picture gallery/drawing room which survives, untouched for nearly 200 years, as one of the most magnificent C18th interiors in Ireland.

The house transferred to Fingal County Council in 1985 under arrangements in which the Cobbe family remain in residence and keep the original pictures and furniture *in-situ*. The offices and yards have been sensitively restored as a model farm. The park offers splendid walks and the walled garden is open by special arrangement.
Open: 1 April - 30 Sept: Tue - Sat, 10am - 5pm (closed 1 - 2pm), Sun & BH, 2 - 6pm. 1 Oct - 1 April: Sat, Sun & BH, 2 - 5pm. Closed 25 Dec & St Stephen's Day.
Admission: Park: Free. House: Adult €6.20, Child €3.70, Conc. €5.20, Family €17. Farm: Adult €3, Child €2, Conc. €5.20, Family (2+2) €8, (2+3/4) €10.50. Group rates available on request.
ⓘNo photography. No smoking. ◻ ⬛ Partial. ▣ 🍴Light meals. 🚹Obligatory. Ⓟ ✳

Information contact: Brigid Dunn, Administrator
Tel: +353 1 843 6534 Fax: +353 1 843 6535
Newbridge House, Donabate, Co Dublin

Opening Arrangements at Properties grant-aided by English Heritage

ENGLISH HERITAGE

ENGLISH HERITAGE

23 Savile Row, London W1S 2ET

I am very pleased to introduce this year's list of opening arrangements at properties grant-aided by English Heritage. Over half the properties are open free, but we give details of admission charges where appropriate. There is also a brief description of each property, where it is located, and information on access for people with disabilities and parking.

The extent of public access varies from one property to another. The building's size, nature and function are all taken into account. Some buildings, such as town halls, museums or railway stations, are of course open regularly. For other properties, especially those which are family homes or work places, access may need to be arranged in a way which also recognises the vulnerability of the building or the needs of those who live or work in it. Usually this will mean opening by appointment or on an agreed number of days each year. This is made clear by each entry.

Some properties are open by written appointment only. In most cases you should still be able to make initial contact by telephone, but you will be asked to confirm your visit in writing. This is to confirm the seriousness of the visitor's interest as you would for example with a hotel booking. It also provides a form of identification, enabling owners to feel more secure about inviting strangers into their house.

It has always been a condition of grant-aid from English Heritage that the public should have a right to see the buildings to whose repair they have contributed. We therefore welcome feedback from visitors on the quality of their visit to grant-aided properties. In particular, please let us know if you are unable to gain access to any of the buildings on the list on the days or at the times specified, or if you have difficulty in making an appointment to visit and do not receive a satisfactory explanation from the owner. Please contact English Heritage Customer Services at PO Box 569, Swindon SN2 2YP (telephone: 0870 3331181; e-mail: customers@english-heritage.org.uk).

Information about public access is also included on our website (www.english-heritage.org.uk). The website is regularly updated to include new properties, any subsequent changes which have been notified to us or any corrections. We suggest that you consult our website for up to date information before visiting. If long journeys or special requirements are involved, we recommend that you telephone the properties in advance, even if no appointment is required.

Finally, may I use this introduction to thank all those owners with whom we work. Their support for the access arrangements has been hugely encouraging. That the public can enjoy a visit to a grant-aided property is not only good in itself, it demonstrates that the historic environment is in a very real sense a common wealth, part of the richness and diversity that makes the English landscape – both urban and rural – so special. It also illustrates how important the private owner is in maintaining that quality and distinctiveness.

I hope you will enjoy the sites and properties you find in this list – from the famous to the many lesser-known treasures. They are all worth a visit – I hope we have helped you to find, and enjoy, them.

Neil Cossons.

Sir Neil Cossons
Chairman

Opening arrangements at properties grant-aided by English Heritage ⌗

BERKSHIRE

Welford Park

Welford, Newbury, Berkshire RG20 8HU

Red brick country house c1652 and remodelled in 1702, when a third storey was added and the front façade was decorated with Ionic columns. Other alterations were made in the Victorian period.

Grant Recipient/Owner: Mr J H L Puxley

Access contact: Mr J H L Puxley

Tel: 01488 608203 **Fax:** 01488 608853

Open: Mon 24 May, Mon 31 May & 5 - 30 June: 11am - 5pm. Interior of house (4 principal rooms) by arrangement only.

P Spaces: 40. 80 more spaces within ¼ mile walk.

Yes. No WC for the disabled. Guide Dogs: Yes

£ **House: Adult:** £5 **Child:** £3.50 **Other:** £3.50 Free entry to garden & grounds, except on occasional charity days.

BUCKINGHAMSHIRE

Abbey Farmhouse

Church Street, Great Missenden, Bucks HP16 0AZ

Thought to have been the gatehouse to Missenden Abbey. The major part was built in the early 15th century and was converted to a farmhouse probably in the mid 16th century with further 19th century alterations.

Grant Recipient/Owner/Access contact:

Mr N F Pearce

Tel: 01494 862767

Open: By arrangement (written appointments preferred). A few days notice will usually be sufficient.

P Spaces: 2

Wheelchair access to ground floor only. No WC for the disabled. Guide Dogs: Yes

£ No

Claydon House

Middle Claydon, nr. Buckingham, Bucks MK18 2EY

18th century house with fine rococo decoration. A series of great rooms have wood carvings in Chinese and gothic styles, and tall windows overlook parkland and a lake. In continuous occupation by the Verney family for over 380 years, the house has mementoes of their relation Florence Nightingale who was a regular visitor.

www.nationaltrust.org.uk

Grant Recipient/Owner: The National Trust

Access contact: The Custodian

Tel: 01296 730349 **Fax:** 01296 738511

E-mail: claydon@nationaltrust.org.uk

Open: House: 27 Mar - 25 October, daily except Thurs & Fri 1 - 5pm; 26 - 31 Oct 1 - 4pm. Open BH Mons but closed Good Fri. Grounds: as house 1 - 5pm.

P Additional parking in parkland. Spaces: 30

Wheelchair access to ground floor with assistance and all of garden. WC for the disabled. Guide Dogs: Yes

£ **Adult:** £4.70, £1 (garden only) **Child:** £2.30

Family: £11.70, £3.60 (groups 15+ Sats & Mons - Weds)

Cliveden Mansion & Clock Tower

Cliveden, Taplow, Maidenhead, Bucks SL6 0JA

Built by Charles Barry in 1851, once lived in by Lady Astor, now let as an hotel. Series of gardens, each with its own character, featuring roses, topiary, water gardens, a formal parterre, informal vistas, woodland and riverside walks.

www.nationaltrust.org.uk

Grant Recipient/Owner: The National Trust

Access contact: Property Manager

Tel: 01628 605069 **Fax:** 01628 669461

E-mail: cliveden@nationaltrust.org.uk

Open: House (main ground floor rooms) and Octagon Temple: 1 Apr - 31 Oct, Thurs & Sun 3 - 6pm. Estate & garden: 10 Mar - 31 Dec, daily 11am - 6pm (closes at 4pm from 1 Nov).

P Woodlands car park: open all year, daily 11am - 5.30pm (closes at 4pm Nov - Mar). Spaces: 300. Overflow car park with 1000 spaces available.

Wheelchair access to house (some steps in house) and much of garden. WC for the disabled. Guide Dogs: Yes

£ **House: Adult:** £1, **Child:** 50p.

Grounds: Adult: £6, **Child:** £3, **Family:** £15 (family), £7.50 (family: woodlands car park)

Woodlands Car Park: Adult: £3, **Child:** £1.50

Hughenden Manor Disraeli Monument

High Wycombe, Bucks HP14 4LA

The home of Prime Minster Benjamin Disraeli from 1848-1881. Hughenden has a red brick 'gothic' exterior. Much of his furniture, books and paintings remain. The garden has been recreated in the spirit of his wife, Mary Anne, with colourful designs. Park and woodland walks.

www.nationaltrust.org.uk

Grant Recipient/Owner: The National Trust

Access contact: Property Manager

Tel: 01494 755573 **Fax:** 01494 474284

E-mail: hughenden@nationaltrust.org.uk

Open: House: 6 - 28 Mar, Sat & Sun 1 - 5pm; 31 Mar - 31 Oct, Wed - Sun (open Good Fri & BH Mons), 1 - 5pm. Gardens: as house 12 noon - 5pm. Park and woodlands all year. Note: long and steep walk to house entrance if arriving by public transport.

P Spaces: 100

Wheelchair access to ground floor of house, terrace, stable yard restaurant and shop. WC for the disabled. Guide Dogs: Yes

£ **House: Adult:** £4.70 **Child:** £2.30 **Family:** £12.

Garden: Adult: £1.70 **Child:** 80p. Parks & woods free.

Princes Risborough Market House

Market Square, Princes Risborough, Bucks HA27 0AS

17th/18th century brick building, with slate roof, built on wooden stilts. Originally used to store grain, straw and hay. The market was held under the store room. Now used as an information centre and display area to promote heritage, conservation and environmental projects in the area. New use developed by the Risborough Countryside Group, a local voluntary community organisation.

Grant Recipient/Owner: Princes Risborough Town Council

Access contact: Mr D J Phillips

Tel: 01844 275912 **Fax:** 01844 342991

E-mail: prtowncouncil@tisgali.co.uk

Open: Occasional weekdays and weekends all year for visitors to the information centre: this is a volunteer operation and details will be publicised locally. Otherwise access can be arranged by contacting Frances Gomme on 01844 274865.

P Short term parking in High St public car park, within 100 yds (next to parish church). Spaces: 10

No. £ No

Stowe House

Buckingham, Bucks MK18 5EH

Mansion built 1680 and greatly altered and enlarged in the 18th century, surrounded by important 18th century gardens. House and gardens variously worked on by Vanbrugh, Gibbs, Kent and Leoni. Many of the greatest alterations carried out for Viscount Cobham, one of Marlborough's Generals, between 1715 and 1749. Gardens cover 325 acres and contain 6 lakes and 32 garden temples. Kent designed the Elysian Fields in the 1730s, one of the first experiments in 'natural' landscaping, and 'Capability' Brown worked here for 10 years as head gardener and was married in the church in the grounds in 1744. The House is now occupied by the Preservation Trust's tenant, Stowe School. The Gardens are owned by the National Trust.

www.stowe.co.uk

Grant Recipient/Owner: The Stowe House Preservation Trust

Access contact: Lucy Beckett / Bill Kemp

Tel: 01280 818280 / 818282 **Fax:** 01280 818186

E-mail: sses@stowe.co.uk

Open: 24 - 25 Jan, 7 - 8 Feb, 14 - 15 Feb, 13 - 14 Mar open Sat & Sun for guided tour only at 2pm. 27 Mar - 25 Apr open Wed - Sun 12 - 5pm (last adm 4pm) with guided tour at 2pm. 30 May - 6 June open Wed - Sun for guided tour only at 2pm. 7 July - 28 Aug open Wed - Sun (and BH Mon) 12 - 5pm (last adm 4pm) with guided tour at 2pm. 2 Sept - 17 Oct open Wed - Sun for guided tours only at 2pm. 20 - 21 Nov, 11 - 19 Dec open Sat & Sun for guided tours only at 2pm. Group visits by arrangement all year. Times may vary, please phone prior to your visit.

P Spaces: 30

Stowe House is accessed via a flight of stone steps: a wheelchair lift can be made available by arrangement. The State Rooms are on one level. WC for the disabled. Guide Dogs: Yes

£ **Adult:** £2 **Child:** £1 Guided tours (excluding group bookings): **Adult:** £3 **Child:** £1.50

Stowe Landscape Gardens

Buckingham, Bucks MK18 5EH

Extensive and complex pleasure grounds and park around a country mansion. Begun late 17th century but substantially developed in the 18th and 19th centuries by, among others, Charles Bridgeman, Sir John Vanbrugh, James Gibbs, William Kent and Lancelot 'Capability' Brown (Brown was originally head gardener here before leaving to set up his landscape practice). The park and gardens contain over 30 buildings, many of great architectural importance. Stowe was supremely influential on the English landscape garden during the 18th century.

www.nationaltrust.org.uk

Grant Recipient/Owner: The National Trust

Access contact: Property Manager

Tel: 01280 822850 **Fax:** 01280 822437

E-mail: stowegarden@nationaltrust.org.uk

Open: 28 Feb - 31 Oct: daily, except Mon &Tues, 10am - 5.30pm (last adm 4pm); 1 Nov - 28 Feb 2005: Sat & Sun, 10am - 4pm (last adm 3pm).

P Spaces: 100

Yes. WC for the disabled. Guide Dogs: Yes

£ **Adult:** £5 **Child:** £2.50 **Family:** £12.50

West Wycombe Park (West Portico)

West Wycombe, Bucks HP14 3AJ

House built early 18th century, extensively remodelled between 1750 and 1780 by Sir Francis Dashwood (creator of the Hell-Fire Club). Porticoes were added to the east and west fronts by Nicholas Revett (his work is relatively rare), and on the south, linking the wings, John Donovell added a two storey colonnade. Although the latter is based on Renaissance prototypes, it too is a rare feature. Frescoes were painted on the ceiling of the west Portico by one of the Borgnis.

www.nationaltrust.org.uk

Grant Recipient/Owner: The National Trust

Access contact: Property Manager

Tel: 01494 513569

Open: Grounds only: 1 Apr - 31 May, daily 2 - 6pm except Fri and Sat (open BHs). House & Grounds: 1 June - 31 Aug, daily 2 - 6pm except Fri & Sat. Weekdays: entry by guided tour every 20 minutes (approx). Last adm 5.15pm.

P Spaces: 30

Wheelchair access to ground floor only. No WC for the disabled. Guide Dogs: Yes

£ **House & Grounds: Adult:** £5.20 **Child:** £2.60

Grounds: Adult: £2.70 **Child:** £1.30 **Family:** £13

Widmere Farm Chapel

Widmere, nr. Marlow, Bucks SL7 3DF

Chapel attached to farmhouse, early 13th century with traces of 14th century windows and later alterations, grade II*. 11th or 12th century crypt and medieval roof.

Grant Recipient/Owner: Mr G J White

Access contact: Mr G J White

Tel: 01628 484204

Open: Access by arrangement.

P Parking on site. Spaces: 6 No £ No

CAMBRIDGESHIRE

The Almonry

High Street, Ely, Cambs CB7 4JU

The Almonry (now a restaurant) is part of a long range of buildings which back onto the High Street on the north side of the Cathedral. Originally built by Alan of Walsingham soon after he became Sacrist in 1322, but mainly rebuilt in the 19th century.

www.cathedral.ely.anglican.org

Grant Recipient/Owner: The Dean & Chapter of Ely

Access contact: The Events Manager

Tel: 01353 667735 **Fax:** 01353 665658

E-mail: events.co ordinator@cathedral.ely. anglican.org

Open: Mon - Sat 10am - 5pm, Sun 11am - 5pm

P Town centre car parks. Parking for disabled in Cathedral car park by arrangement.

Wheelchair access to ground floor only. WC for the disabled. Guide Dogs: Yes

£ No

Anglesey Abbey Gardens

Quy Road, Lode, Cambridge CB5 9EJ

98 acres of formal and landscape gardens surrounding a 17th century house on the site of a 12th century priory. Contains over 100 pieces of sculpture and a working 18th century water mill.

www.nationaltrust.org.uk

Grant Recipient/Owner: The National Trust
Access contact: Property Manager
Tel: 01223 810080 **Fax:** 01223 810088
E-mail: angleseyabbey@nationaltrust.org.uk
Open: Garden, shop, plant centre and restaurant: 31 Dec 2003 - 21 Mar, Wed - Sun 10.30am - 4pm; 24 Mar - 7 Nov, Wed - Sun 10.30am - 5.30pm; July and Aug, daily 10.30am - 5.30pm (Thurs 8pm); 10 Nov - 23 Dec, Wed - Sun 10.30am - 4pm. Closed Good Fri, open BH Mons. House and mill are also open to the public, please contact the National Trust for details.
Ⓟ Spaces: 10
♿ Grounds largely accessible for wheelchairs; level entrance to shop and restaurant; access to ground floor of House and lower floor of Mill only. WC for the disabled. Guide Dogs: Yes
£ **Adult:** £4.10 (garden only), £3.40 (winter) **Child:** £2.05 (garden only), £1.70 (winter)

The Black Hostelry

The College, Ely, Cambs CB7 4DL

Built c1291-2 of Carr stone rubble with Barnack, or similar, stone dressings, upper storey is timber-framed and plastered on the south and east sides with stone on the west side. Has early 13th century undercroft with ribbed vaults, 13-14th century King Post roof, and 15th century red brick chimney and doorway. Constructed to accommodate visiting monks from other Benedictine monasteries.

www.cathedral.ely.anglican.org

Grant Recipient/Owner: The Dean & Chapter of Ely
Access contact: The Events Manager
Tel: 01353 667735 **Fax:** 01353 665658
E-mail: events.coordinator@cathedral.ely.anglican.org
Open: By written arrangement with the Events Manager, The Chapter House, The College, Ely, Cambs CB7 4DL.
Ⓟ Town centre car parks. Parking for disabled in Cathedral car park by arrangement.
♿ Wheelchair access to rear entrance hall only. Disabled WC in Cathedral. Guide Dogs: Yes
£ No

Buckden Towers

High Street, Buckden, Cambs PE19 5TA

Victorian house set in 15 acres of gardens and grounds, which include a grade I listed gatehouse built in 1480, and a late 15th century Great Tower. The grounds include an Elizabethan Knot Garden. Famous occupants include St Hugh of Lincoln (12th century) and Katherine of Aragon (1533-4).

www.claretcentre.fsnet.co.uk

Grant Recipient/Owner: The Claretian Missionaries
Access contact: Mrs Jill Davies
Tel: 01480 810344 **Fax:** 01480 811918
E-mail: claret_centre@claret.org.uk
Open: By arrangement. Tea shop open on Sat & Sun afternoons in summer. Grounds open throughout the year. New visitor centre expected to open Autumn 2004 with guided tours at weekends (to be confirmed).
Ⓟ Spaces: 50
♿ Yes. WC for the disabled. Guide Dogs: Yes
£ No

The Chapter House

The College, Ely, Cambridgeshire CB7 4DL

Originally part of the chapel of the Infirmary, now the remains of this house the Deanery and the Chapter Office. Contains part of the arch, ribbed vaulting and arcade of the 12th century chancel.

www.cathedral.ely.anglican.org

Grant Recipient/Owner: The Dean & Chapter of Ely
Access contact: The Events Manager
Tel: 01353 667735 **Fax:** 01353 665658
E-mail: events.coordinator@cathedral.ely.anglican.org
Open: By written arrangement with the Events Manager, The Chapter House, The College, Ely, Cambs CB7 4DL.
Ⓟ Town centre car parks. Parking for disabled in Cathedral car park by arrangement.
♿ Wheelchair access to ground floor only. WC for disabled in Cathedral. Guide Dogs: Yes
£ No

Elton Hall

Elton, nr. Peterborough, Cambs PE8 6SH

Grade I historic building and country house. Late 15th century gatehouse and chapel built by Sapcote family. Main entrance façade built by Sir Thomas Proby in the 17th century and remodelled by Henry Ashton for 3rd Earl of Carysfort in the 19th century. South Garden façade built between 1789 and 1812 in Gothic style.

Grant Recipient/Owner/Access contact:
Sir William Proby Bt
Tel: 01832 280468 **Fax:** 01832 280584
E-mail: whp@eltonhall.com
Open: 31 May; Weds in June; Weds, Thurs & Suns in July & Aug, plus Aug BH Mon 2 - 5pm. Private groups by arrangement on weekdays Apr - Oct.
Ⓟ Parking 300m from the Hall. Spaces: 500
♿ Wheelchair and guide dog access to garden only. WC for the disabled. Guide Dogs: Yes
£ **Adult:** £6 (house), £3 (garden)
Child: Free if accompanied

Madingley Post Mill

Mill Farm, Madingley Road, Coton, Cambs CB3 7PH

Historic post mill with machinery intact.

Grant Recipient/Owner/Access contact:
Mr Matthew Mortlock
Tel: 01954 211047 **Fax:** 01954 210752
E-mail: mattcb37ph@aol.com
Open: Weekdays & Sats 11am - 4pm by prior telephone arrangement.
Ⓟ At American Cemetery (next door). Spaces: 5
♿ Wheelchair access around base of Windmill only. No WC for the disabled. Guide Dogs: Yes
£ No

The Manor

Hemingford Grey, Huntingdon, Cambs PE28 9BN

Built c1130 and one of the oldest continuously inhabited houses in Britain. Made famous as Green Knowe by the author Lucy Boston. Her patchwork collection is also shown. Four acre garden with topiary, old roses and herbaceous borders.

www.greenknowe.co.uk

Grant Recipient/Owner: Mrs Diana Boston
Access contact: Mrs Diana Boston
Tel: 01480 463134 **Fax:** 01480 465026
E-mail: diana_boston@hotmail.com
Open: House: all year (except May) to individuals or groups by arrangement. May: guided tours at 11am and 2pm (booking advisable). Garden: all year, daily 11am - 5pm (4pm in winter).
Ⓟ For disabled only adjacent to property. Spaces: 2
♿ Wheelchair access to garden and dining room only. No WC for the disabled. Guide Dogs: Yes
£ **Adult:** £4, £2 (garden only) **Child:** £1.50, 50p (garden only) **Other:** £3.50, £2 (garden only)

Minster Precincts

Peterborough Cathedral, Peterborough, Cambs PE1 1XS

The Minster Precincts incorporate many remains from the medieval monastery of which the Cathedral church was a part. These include the richly decorated 13th century arcades of the former infirmary, the originally 13th century Little Prior's Gate and the 15th century Table Hall.

www.peterborough-cathedral.org.uk

Grant Recipient/Owner: The Dean & Chapter of Peterborough Cathedral
Access contact: The Dean & Chapter of Peterborough Cathedral
Tel: 01733 343342 **Fax:** 01733 552465
E-mail: a.watson@peterborough-cathedral.org.uk
Open: All year, exterior only.
Ⓟ City centre car parks.
♿ Disabled toilet in Cathedral restaurant and Tourist Information Centre. Guide Dogs: Yes
£ No

The Old Palace

Sue Ryder Care, Palace Green, Ely, Cambs CB7 4EW

Grade I listed building formerly a bishops palace opposite cathedral, with an Elizabethan promenading gallery, bishops chapel and monks' room. 2 acre garden contains the oldest plane tree in Europe. Used as a neurological centre for the physically disabled.

Grant Recipient/Owner: The Sue Ryder Care
Access contact: Mrs Mavis Garner
Tel: 01353 667686 **Fax:** 01353 669425
E-mail: suerely@dialstart.net
Open: By arrangement for access to the Long Gallery and Chapel. Gardens: open during the Open Gardens Scheme May - June. Other events held all year, contact Mrs Garner for details.
Ⓟ Nearest car park: St Mary's Street & Barton Road.
♿ Wheelchair access to garden and Long Gallery. WC for the disabled. Guide Dogs: Yes
£ No charge made on garden open days: adult £1, child 50p

Prior Crauden's Chapel

The College, Ely, Cambs CB7 4DL

Private chapel built by Prior Crauden in 1524-5 of Barnack stone ashlar with clunch carved interior, over a 13th century vaulted undercroft. Has windows in the "Decorated" style, octagonal entrance and tower with spiral staircase, richly carved interior and a 14th century mosaic tile floor.

www.cathedral.ely.anglican.org

Grant Recipient/Owner: The Dean & Chapter of Ely Cathedral
Access contact: The Events Manager
Tel: 01353 667735 **Fax:** 01353 665658
E-mail: events.coordinator@cathedral.ely.anglican.org
Open: By written arrangement with the Events Manager, The Chapter House, The College, Ely, Cambs CB7 4DL.
Ⓟ Town centre car parks. Parking for disabled in Cathedral car park by arrangement.
♿ Wheelchair access to the undercroft only. WC for disabled in Cathedral. Guide Dogs: Yes
£ No

Queen's Hall

The Gallery, Ely, Cambs CB7 4DL

Built by Prior Crauden c1330 of Carr stone rubble with Barnack, or similar, stone dressings and much brick patching. Has original undercroft with ribbed vaulting, 14th century pointed arched windows with curvilinear tracery and corbels carved in the shape of crouching figures. Reputedly constructed for entertaining Queen Philippa, wife of Edward III.

Grant Recipient/Owner: The Dean & Chapter of Ely Cathedral
Access contact: The Assistant Bursar
Tel: 01353 660700 **Fax:** 01353 662187
E-mail: nigelc@kings-ely.cambs.sch.uk
Open: By written arrangement with the Assistant Bursar, the King's School, Ely, Cambs CB7 4DN.
Ⓟ Town centre car parks. Parking for disabled in Cathedral car park by arrangement. Spaces: 5
♿ Wheelchair access to ground floor only. Disabled WC in Cathedral. Guide Dogs: Yes
£ No

Sir John Jacob's Almshouse Chapel

Church Street, Gamlingay, Cambs SG19 3JH

Built 1745 of Flemish bond red brick with plain tiled roof, in keeping with adjoining terrace of 10 almshouses constructed 80 years before. Now used as parish council offices.

Grant Recipient/Owner: The Trustees of Sir John Jacob's Almshouses
Access contact: Mrs D Royal
Tel: 01767 650310 **Fax:** 01767 650310
E-mail: gamlingaypc@lineone.net
Open: The office is generally open on Mons, Weds & Fris 9.15am - 3.15pm.
Ⓟ On-street parking.
♿ WC for the disabled. Guide Dogs: Yes £ No

Stoker's Cottage at Stretham Old Engine

Ely, Cambs

Four-roomed bungalow constructed in 1840 as a Toll Keeper's Cottage. Subsequently used to house the stoker of Stretham Old Engine, which it adjoins.

Grant Recipient/Owner: The Trustees of the Stretham Engine Preservation Trust
Access contact: Mr E Langford
Tel: 01353 649210
Open: Second Sun in each month and BHs from Good Fri to Aug, 1.30 - 5pm. Otherwise by arrangement.
Ⓟ Limited parking in lay-by in front of Old Engine.
♿ Guide Dogs: Yes
£ Old Engine Complex & Displays: **Adult:** £2
Child: £1 **Other:** £1.50

Sulehay House

32 Old Market, Wisbech, Cambs PE13 1NF

Grade II* town house, built 1723, with fine original staircase.

Grant Recipient/Owner: Cambridgeshire Historic

Buildings Preservation Trust
Access contact: Mr Arne Maynard
Tel: 020 7689 8100 **Fax:** 020 7689 8101
Open: By arrangement.
P Free public space at the Old Market. Spaces: 1
♿ Guide Dogs: Yes

Thomas à Becket Chapel

**(Becket's Restaurant & Gift Shop),
The Song School, Minster Precincts, Peterborough,
Cambs PE1 1XX**
The Chapel was originally built by Abbot Benedict, c1180, along with the Norman Arch giving access to the Cathedral precincts from Cathedral Square. Now houses a restaurant and shop alongside the Tourist Information Office.
www.peterborough-cathedral.org.uk
Grant Recipient/Owner/Access contact:
The Dean & Chapter of Peterborough Cathedral
Tel: 01733 343342 **Fax:** 01733 552465
E-mail: bk@peterborough-cathedral.org.uk
Open: All year, Mon - Sat 9.30am - 5pm, Restaurant 9.30am - 4pm.
P City centre car parks.
♿ Yes. WC for the disabled. Guide Dogs: No £ No

Thorpe Hall Hospice

**Sue Ryder Care, Longthorpe, Peterborough,
Cambs PE3 6LW**
Built in the 1650s by Peter Mills for Oliver St John, Oliver Cromwell's Lord Chief Justice. Ground floor retains many original features.
Grant Recipient/Owner: Sue Ryder Care
Access contact: Mr Bruce Wringe
Tel: 01733 330060 **Fax:** 01733 269078
E-mail: thorpe@sueryderthorpe.fsnet.co.uk
Open: Access to the Hall by arrangement. Gardens: open all year.
P Spaces: 30 ♿ Yes. WC for the disabled. Guide Dogs: Yes
£ Donations welcome

The Verger's House & The Old Sacristy

High Street, Ely, Cambs CB7 4JU
The Old Sacristy is part of a long range of buildings which back onto the High Street on the north side. Originally built by Alan of Walsingham soon after he became sacrist in 1322, but mainly rebuilt in the 19th century.
www.cathedral.ely.anglican.org
Grant Recipient/Owner: The Dean & Chapter of Ely
Access contact: The Events Manager
Tel: 01353 667735 **Fax:** 01353 665658
E-mail: events.coordinator@
cathedral.ely.anglican.org
Open: By written arrangement with the Events Manager, The Chapter House, The College, Ely, Cambs CB7 4DL.
P Town centre car parks. Parking for disabled in Cathedral car park by arrangement.
♿ Wheelchair access to ground floor only. Disabled WC in Cathedral. Guide Dogs: Yes
£ No

Walsingham House

The College, Ely, Cambs CB7 4DL
Originally a 14th century Hall built by the Sacrist, Alan of Walsingham, adjoining the monastic infirmary. Famed for its "painted chamber", a first floor decorated hall used for entertaining guests of the monastery. Now houses the Cathedral choristers.
Grant Recipient/Owner: The Dean & Chapter of Ely Cathedral
Access contact: The Assistant Bursar
Tel: 01353 660700 **Fax:** 01353 622187
E-mail: nigelc@kings-ely.cambs.sch.uk
Open: By written arrangement with the Assistant Bursar, King's School, Ely, Cambs CB7 4DN.
P Town centre car parks. Parking for disabled in Cathedral car park by arrangement. Spaces: 5
♿ Wheelchair access to ground floor only. Disabled WC in Cathedral. Guide Dogs: Yes
£ No

Wimpole Estate

Arrington, Royston, Cambs SG8 0BW
18th century house set in extensive wooded park. Interior features work by Gibbs, Flitcroft and Soane. The park was landscaped by Bridgeman, Brown and Repton featuring a grand folly, Chinese bridge and lake. Walled garden restored to a working vegetable garden - best seen from June to Aug.
www.nationaltrust.org.uk
Grant Recipient/Owner: The National Trust
Access contact: Property Manager
Tel: 01223 207257 **Fax:** 01223 207838
E-mail: wimpolehall@nationaltrust.org.uk
Open: Hall: 20 Mar - 31 July & 1 Sept - 31 Oct, daily except Mon & Fri (but open Good Fri & BH Mons), 1 - 5pm (BH Mons 11am - 5pm, closes 4pm after 28 Oct); Aug, daily except Mon (but open BH Mon); 10, 17 & 24 Nov, Sun only. Garden: 2 Mar - 1 Apr & 20 Apr - 19 Dec, daily except Mon & Fri (but open Good Fri & BH Mons); Aug, daily except Mon (but open BH Mons); 27 Dec - 4 Jan 2005, daily 11am - 4pm; 8 Jan - 28 Feb 2005, daily except Mon & Fri 11am - 4pm.
P Spaces: 500
♿ Wheelchair access to garden (gravel paths) and restaurant. Disabled visitors may be set down near Hall. Telephone in advance for details. WC for the disabled. Guide Dogs: Yes
£ Adult: £6.60, £2.60 (garden only)
Child: £3.20 Other: £9.80 (joint ticket with Wimpole Home Farm, adult), £5.20 (joint ticket, child), £25 (family)

CHESHIRE

Bache House Farm

Chester Road, Hurleston, Nantwich, Cheshire CW5 6BO
A timber-framed house with slate roof dating from 17th century with an 18th century extension. The house is a four square house with two gables at the rear. The interior shows timbers in the house walls and an oak staircase.
Grant Recipient/Owner: P R Posnett
Access contact: R J Posnett
Tel: 01829 260251
Open: By arrangement at all reasonable times.
P Spaces: 10 ♿ No £ No

Belmont Hall

Great Budworth, Northwich, Cheshire CW9 6HN
Country house, built 1755, initial design by James Gibbs, with fine plasterwork interiors. Set in parkland. Now a private day school with family apartments in the East Wing. Also accessible is surrounding farmland, woods and medieval moat.
Grant Recipient/Owner: The Trustees of Belmont Hall
Access contact: Mr R C Leigh
Tel: 01606 891235 **Fax:** 01606 892349
Open: Guided tours during the school holidays and on weekends by arrangement. with the Estate Manager, Belmont Hall, Great Budworth, Northwich, Cheshire CW9 6HN (tel:01606 891235). Please note: the property and adjacent area are also open by way of a Countryside Stewardship Access Educational Agreement for school as well as adult parties.
P Unlimited free parking on site. ♿ Guide Dogs: Yes
£ Adult: £5

Bramall Hall

Bramhall Park, Stockport, Cheshire SK7 3NX
Black and white timber-framed manor house dating back to the 14th century, with subsequently several renovations (many during the Victorian period). Contains 14th century wallpaintings, an Elizabethan plaster ceiling and Victorian kitchen and servants quarters.
www.stockport.gov.uk/tourism/bramall
Grant Recipient/Owner: Stockport Metropolitan Borough Council
Access contact: Ms Caroline Egan
Tel: 0161 485 3708 **Fax:** 0161 486 6959
E-mail: bramall.hall@stockport.gov.uk
Open: Good Fri - end Sept: Mon - Sat 1 - 5pm. Suns and BHs 11am - 5pm. Oct - 1 Jan: Tues - Sat 1 - 4pm. Sun & BHs 11am 4pm. 2 Jan - Easter: weekends only 1 - 4pm.
P Pay parking. Spaces: 60
♿ Wheelchair access to ground floor only. WC for the disabled. Guide Dogs: Yes
£ Adult: £3.95 Child: £2.50 Conc: £2.50

Capesthorne Hall

Macclesfield, Cheshire SK11 9JY
Jacobean style hall with a collection of fine art, sculpture, furniture, tapestry and antiques from Europe, America and the Far East. The Hall dates from 1719 when it was originally designed by the Smith's of Warwick. Altered in 1837 by Blore and rebuilt by Salvin in 1861 following a disastrous fire.
www.capesthorne.com
Grant Recipient/Owner: Mr William Arthur Bromley-Davenport
Access contact: Mrs Gwyneth Jones
Tel: 01625 861221 **Fax:** 01625 861619
E-mail: info@capesthorne.com
Open: Apr - Oct: Sun, Wed and BHs. Gardens and Chapel 12 noon - 5.00pm, Hall from 1.30 - 4pm (last adm 3.30pm). Groups on other days by arrangement.
P Spaces: 2000
♿ Wheelchair access to ground floor and butler's pantry. WC for the disabled. Guide Dogs: Yes
£ Adult: £6.50 (Suns & BHs), £4 (garden & chapel) Child: £3 (5-18 yrs), £2 (garden & chapel only) Senior: £5.50 , £3 (garden & chapel), £15 (family). Wed only: £10 (Car: 4 people) £25 (minibus) £50 (coach)

Chester Town Hall

Northgate Street, Chester, Cheshire CH1 2HS
Victorian town hall situated in centre of city, home to the Chester Tapestry, portraits of the Grosvenor family, and World War I memorial dedicated to Chester citizens. There is also a memorial to the Polish air force. One of many stained glass windows shows the Common Seal of the city.
www.chestercc.gov.uk
Grant Recipient/Owner: Chester City Council
Access contact: Ms Rebecca Pinfold
Tel: 01244 402320 **Fax:** 01244 341965
E-mail: b.pinfold@chestercc.gov.uk
Open: Mon - Fri, 8.30am - 7pm. Sat by arrangement.
P In Princess Street (pay & display).
♿ Yes. WC for the disabled. Guide Dogs: Yes
£ No

Dixon's Almshouses

1-6 The Pit, Little Heath Lane, Christleton, Chester, Cheshire CH3 7AN
Originally six almshouses, built in 1868 by J. Oldrid Scott in Tudor style in memory of James Dixon of Littleton. A good, early example of Victorian timber framing. Order of Malta Homes carried out a major refurbishment in 1998 which won a council award for design.
Grant Recipient/Owner: Order of Malta Homes Trust
Access contact: Order of Malta Homes Trust
Open: Property can be viewed from the outside with access to the interior by arrangement with the Reverend Peter Lee (tel: 01244 335663).
P On-street parking. ♿ No £ No

Highfields

Audlem, nr. Crewe, Cheshire CW3 0DT
Small half-timbered manor house dating back to c1600.
Grant Recipient/Owner: Mr J B Baker
Access contact: Mrs Susan Baker
Tel: 01630 655479
Open: Guided tour of hall, drawing room, dining room, parlour, bedrooms and gardens by written arrangement.
P Spaces: 20
♿ Wheelchair access to ground floor only, disabled WC with assistance (down 2 steps). Guide Dogs: Yes
£ Adult: £4 Child: £2

Lightshaw Hall Farm

Lightshaw Lane, Golborne, Warrington, Cheshire WA3 3UJ
16th century timber-framed farmhouse largely rebuilt in the 18th and 19th centuries. Historical evidence suggests there was an estate and probably a house on the site by the end of the 13th century if not before. The west range is supposed to represent the solar apartments of an early post-medieval house. External walls were replaced by bricks in the 18th and 19th centuries. Timber trusses and main roof timbers survive.
Grant Recipient/Owner/Access contact: Mrs J Hewitt
Tel: 01942 717429
Open: All year by telephone arrangement.
P Spaces: 20
♿ Wheelchair access to ground floor only. Video and photographs available for those unable to climb stairs. No WC for the disabled. Guide Dogs: Yes
£ No

Lyme Park

Disley, Stockport, Cheshire SK12 2NX
Home to the Legh family for 600 years, Lyme Park comprises a 1400 acre medieval deer park, a 17 acre Victorian garden and a Tudor hall which was transformed into an Italianate palace in the 18th century. Location for 'Pemberley' in the BBC TV's production of *Pride and Prejudice*.
www.nationaltrust.org.uk
Grant Recipient/Owner: Stockport Metropolitan Borough Council
Access contact: Mr Philip Burt
Tel: 01663 762023 **Fax:** 01663 765035
E-mail: lymepark@nationaltrust.org.uk
Open: Hall: 29 Mar - 30 Oct, daily except Wed and Thurs 1 - 5pm. Garden: 29 Mar - 30 Oct, Fri - Tues 11am - 5pm, Wed & Thurs 1 - 5pm; Nov - 15 Dec, weekends 12 - 3pm. Park: Apr - Oct, daily 8am - 8.30pm; Nov - Mar, daily 8am - 6pm.
P Spaces: 1500
♿ Wheelchair access to garden, first floor of house, parts of park, shop and restaurant. WC for the disabled. Guide Dogs: Yes
£ **Adult:** £5.80 **Child:** £2.90 NT members free

Quarry Bank Mill

Styal, Cheshire SK9 4LA
Georgian cotton mill, now a museum and the only water powered cotton mill in the world. Working demonstrations of cotton processing, a giant iron water wheel and two mill engines steaming daily. Restored Apprentice House once housed child workers.
www.quarrybankmill.org.uk
Grant Recipient/Owner: The National Trust
Access contact: Ms Josselin Hill
Tel: 01625 527468 **Fax:** 01625 539267
E-mail: quarrybankmill@nationaltrust.org.uk
Open: Mill: Apr - Sept, daily 10.30am - 5.30pm (last adm 4pm); Oct - Mar (closed Mons) 10.30am - 5pm (last adm 3.30pm). Apprentice House and Garden: Easter and daily during Aug as Mill, weekends all year as Mill and Tues - Fri all year 2pm - Mill closing time.
P Spaces: 350
♿ Wheelchair access to ground and lower ground floors only. WC for the disabled. Guide Dogs: Yes
£ Mill: **Adult:** £5.20 **Child:** £3.50 **Family:** £15 Mill & Apprentice House: **Adult:** £7.30 **Child:** £4.50 **Family:** £18

Rode Hall

Church Lane, Scholar Green, Cheshire ST7 3QP
Country house built early - mid 18th century, with later alterations. Set in a parkland designed by Repton. Home to the Wilbraham family since 1669.
Grant Recipient/Owner/Access contact:
Sir Richard Baker Wilbraham Bt
Tel: 01270 873237 **Fax:** 01270 882962
E-mail: rodehall@scholargreen.fsnet.co.uk
Open: Hall & Gardens: 1 Apr - 30 Sept, Wed & BHs (closed Good Fri) 2 - 5pm; Gardens only: Tues and Thurs 2 - 5pm. Snowdrop Walks: 7 - 22 Feb 12 - 4pm.
P Parking for disabled available adjacent to entrance by arrangement. Spaces: 200
♿ Wheelchair access with assistance to ground floor. No WC for the disabled. Guide Dogs: Yes
£ **Adult:** £5 (house & garden), £3 (garden) **Child:** £3.50 over 12s (house & garden), £2 (garden) **Other:** £3.50 (house & garden, seniors), £2 (garden)

St Chad's Church Tower

Wybunbury, Nantwich, Cheshire CW5 7LS
Grade II* listed 15th or 16th century church tower, rest of Church demolished in 1977. 96ft high and containing six restored bells, spiral staircase, charity boards, monuments and affords panoramic views over the South Cheshire plain.
www.wybunburytower.org.uk
Grant Recipient/Owner: Wybunbury Tower Preservation Society
Access contact: Mrs D Lockhart
Tel: 01270 841481 **Fax:** 01270 842659
Open: Sat 29 May 'Fig Pie Wakes' (local race and festival) 2 - 5pm. Heritage Open Days 11am - 4pm. At other times by arrangement. with Mrs D Lockhart (tel:01270 841481) or Mr John Colbert (tel:01270 841158).
P Spaces: 20
♿ Wheelchair access to ground floor only. No WC for the disabled. Guide Dogs: Yes
£ **Adult:** £1 **Child:** 50p

CLEVELAND

Former Holy Trinity Church

Yarn Lane, Stockton-on-Tees, Cleveland
Built 1837-8 by John & Benjamin Green, chancel enlarged 1906. Wide 4-bay nave, 2-bay chancel. Spire removed in 1957, interior gutted by fire in 1991.
Grant Recipient/Owner: Stockton-on-Tees Borough Council
Access contact: Miss Fiona Short
Tel: 01642 395 798 **Fax:** 01642 391282
E-mail: fiona.short@stockton.gov.uk
Open: Exterior only at all times.
P On-street parking. ♿ No £ No

Marske Hall

Marske by the Sea, Redcar and Cleveland TS11 6AA
Country house built by Sir William Pennyman in 1625. 2 storeys with 3-storey projecting towers in a 9-bay range forming a symmetrical front approx. 115ft long. Altered in the late 19th and 20th centuries. Varied uses during 20th century include as quarters for the Royal Flying Corps in WWI, Army quarters in WWII, school 1948-58 and since 1963 a Cheshire Foundation nursing home.
Grant Recipient/Owner: Teesside Cheshire Homes
Access contact: Mrs Sue O'Brien
Tel: 01642 482672 **Fax:** 01642 759973
E-mail: marske@ney.leonard-cheshire.org.uk
Open: Hall by arrangement only. Grounds open to public at all fund raising events such as the Summer Fete.
P Spaces: 20
♿ Yes. WC for the disabled. Guide Dogs: Yes £ No

CO DURHAM

Barnard Castle Market Cross

Barnard Castle, Co. Durham, DL12 8EL
Two-storey building dating from 1747 with a colonnaded ground floor and enclosed upper storey. Two slate roofs crowned by a bell tower and gilded weather vane with two bullet holes from 1804. Formerly used as Town Hall, butter market, lock-up, Court room and fire station.
Grant Recipient/Owner: Teesdale District Council
Access contact: Mr James Usher
Tel: 01833 696209 **Fax:** 01833 637269
E-mail: j.usher@teesdale.gov.uk
Open: Colonnaded area (ground floor) is open to the public at all times. The first floor is only accessible through organised tours with keys available from Teesdale House, Galgate, Barnard Castle, Co. Durham DL12 8EL (tel: 01833 696209) by special arrangement.
P On-street parking. ♿ No £ No

Christ Church

(Hartlepool Art Gallery & Tourist Information Centre)
Church Square, Hartlepool, Co. Durham TS24 7EQ
Built as the parish church for the new town of West Hartlepool in 1854 to a design by E.B. Lamb, Christ Church closed as a church in 1971 due to population movement in the town centre. Converted in the 1990s into a new art gallery, café and tourist information centre complete with a new staircase giving tower access to a viewing platform.
Grant Recipient/Owner: Hartlepool Borough Council
Access contact: The Museums Officer Hartlepool Borough Council
Tel: 01429 523443 **Fax:** 01429 523477
E-mail: arts-museums@hartlepool.gov.uk
Open: Open Tues - Sat 10am - 5pm; Sun 2 - 5pm; BH Mon 2 - 5pm. Closed on Mons and Christmas Day, Boxing Day and New Year's Day.
P Public parking 200 metres. Parking for disabled adjacent. Spaces: 200
♿ Wheelchair access to all areas except Tower. WC for the disabled. Guide Dogs: Yes
£ (Tower) **Adult:** 50p **Child:** 30p. Art Gallery free

Croxdale Hall

Durham, County Durham DH6 5JP
18th century re-casing of an earlier Tudor building, containing comfortably furnished mid-Georgian rooms with Rococo ceilings. There is also a private chapel in the north elevation, walled gardens, a quarter-of-a-mile long terrace, an orangery and lakes which date from the mid-18th century.
Grant Recipient/Owner: Captain G M Salvin

Access contact: Mr W H T Salvin
Tel: 01833 690100 **Fax:** 01833 637004
E-mail: whtsalvin@aol.com
Open: By arrangement on Tues & Weds from the first Tues in May to the second Wed in July, 11am - 1pm.
P Spaces: 20 ♿ Yes. WC for disabled. Guide Dogs: No
£ £5

Durham Castle

Palace Green, Durham, Co. Durham DH1 3RW
Dating from 1072, the Castle was the seat of the Prince Bishops until 1832. Together with the Cathedral, the Castle is a World Heritage site. It now houses University College, the Foundation College of Durham University, and is a conference, banqueting and holiday centre in vacations.
www.durhamcastle.com
Grant Recipient/Owner: University of Durham
Access contact: The Bursar
Tel: 0191 33 43800 **Fax:** 0191 33 43801
E-mail: e.a.gibson@dur.ac.uk
Open: Easter - end of Sept: guided tours daily from 10am - 4pm; 1 Oct - Easter Mon: Wed, Sat & Sun (afternoons only). Tours may not take place when the Castle is being used for functions.
P Parking in city car parks.
♿ Wheelchair access to courtyard only. No WC for disabled. Guide Dogs: Yes
£ **Adult:** £3.50 **Child:** £2.50
Group (10+): £3 **Family:** £8 (family)

Former Stockton & Darlington Railway Booking Office

48 Bridge Road, Stockton-on-Tees, Co. Durham TS18 3AX
Original booking office of the Stockton and Darlington Railway. Cottage of plain brick with slate roof facing railway line. A bronze tablet on the gable ends "Martin 1825 the Stockton and Darlington Company booked first passenger, thus marking an epoch in the history of mankind". The first rail of the Railway was laid outside the building. Now used as an administration office and accommodation for single homeless men.
Grant Recipient/Owner: Stockton Church's Mission to the Single Homeless
Access contact: Ms Margaret McCarthy
Tel: 01642 800322 **Fax:** 01642 800322
Open: Mon - Fri, 9am - 3pm.
P Opposite side of road. Spaces: 50
♿ Wheelchair access to exterior of site. No WC for the disabled. Guide Dogs: Yes
£ No

Hamsteels Hall

Hamsteels Lane, Quebec, Co. Durham DH7 9RS
Early 18th century farmhouse with 19th century alterations. Panelled window shutters; ground-floor room with full early 18th century panelling; similar panelling and cupboards in first-floor room. Good quality dogleg stair with turned balusters.
Grant Recipient/Owner: Mr G F Whitfield
Access contact: Mrs June Whitfield
Tel: 01207 520 388 **Fax:** 01207 520 388
E-mail: june@hamsteelshall.co.uk
Open: By arrangement.
P Spaces: 8
♿ Wheelchair access to Dining Room and Front Parlour only. No WC for the disabled. Guide Dogs: No
£ No

Kepier Farm Hospital

Kepier Lane, Durham, Co. Durham DH1
Ruins of Kepier Hospital which was the wealthiest of the county's medieval hospitals. Re-founded c1180 after the original hospital was destroyed in 1144. As well as caring for the sick and elderly it provided accommodation for pilgrims to the shrine of St Cuthbert. At the Reformation the hospital was dissolved and a new house, with a fashionable renaissance loggia, was built after 1588. The loggia survives within the medieval hospital enclosure.
Grant Recipient/Owner: Mrs R A Watson
Access contact: Mrs R A Watson
Tel: 0191 3842761
Open: Weekends by arrangement.
P No ♿ No £ No

Low Butterby Farmhouse

Croxdale & Hett, Co. Durham DH6 5JN
Stone built farmhouse constructed on medieval site incorporating elements of 17th, 18th and 19th century

phases of development.

Grant Recipient/Owner: The Trustees of Captain GM Salvin's 1983 Settlement

Access contact: Mr W H T Salvin

Tel: 01833 690100 **Fax:** 01833 637004

E-mail: whtsalvin@aol.com

Open: By written or telephone arrangement with Mr W H T Salvin, The Estate Office, Egglestone Abbey, Barnard Castle, Co. Durham DL12 9TN.

Ⓟ Spaces: 2

♿ Limited wheelchair access with assistance (some changes in floor level). No WC for the disabled. No Guide Dogs.

£ No

The Priest's House

Croxdale Hall, Croxdale, Co. Durham DH6 5JP

18th century stone built cottage with 19th century extension adjacent to and ancillary to the Old Church and Croxdale Hall.

Grant Recipient/Owner: The Trustees of the Low Butterby Settlement

Access contact: Mr W H T Salvin

Tel: 01833 690100 **Fax:** 01833 637004

E-mail: whtsalvin@aol.com

Open: By written or telephone arrangement with Mr W H T Salvin, The Estate Office, Egglestone Abbey, Barnard Castle, Co. Durham DL12 9TN.

Ⓟ Spaces: 2

♿ Wheelchair access to ground floor only. No WC for the disabled. Guide Dogs: Yes

£ No

Raby Castle

PO Box 50, Staindrop, Darlington, Co Durham DL2 3AY

Medieval castle, built in the 14th century. Once the seat of the Nevills, it has been home to Lord Barnard's family since 1626. Contains a collection of art, fine furniture and highly decorated interiors. Also has a deer park, gardens, carriage collection and woodland adventure playground.

www.rabycastle.com

Grant Recipient/Owner: Lord Barnard TD

Access contact: Miss Catherine Turnbull

Tel: 01833 660888/660202 **Fax:** 01833 660169

E-mail: admin@rabycastle.com

Open: Easter & BH weekends, Sat - Wed; May and Sept, Wed & Sun only; June, July & Aug, daily except Sat. Castle open 1 - 5pm. Garden, park and tea room 11am - 5.30pm. Guided tours including tea/coffee and reception (groups 20+) £8.50. Educational visits (groups 20+) £3 per pupil (primary & junior), £3.50 (secondary school). Both are available weekday mornings from Easter to end of Sept by arrangement. Group rates (12+) available preferably by advance booking: Castle, park & gardens £6 (adult), £3 (child), £5.50 (over 60/students); park & gardens £3.50 (adult), £2.50 (child), £3 (over 60/student).

Ⓟ Spaces: 500

♿ Limited wheelchair access to lower floor with assistance (3 steps to entrance and some internal steps to be negotiated). 3 wheelchairs available. WC for the disabled. Guide Dogs: Yes

£ **Adult:** £7 (castle, park & gardens), £4 (park & gardens) **Child:** Age 5-15 £3 (castle, park & gardens), £2.50 (park & gardens) **Other:** £6 (castle, park & gardens), £3.50 (park & gardens), £16 (family), £10, £5 & £7.50 (season ticket park & gardens)

Rectory Farm Barn

Hall Walks, Easington, Peterlee, Co. Durham SR8 3BS

Barn, possibly 13th century with extensive alterations. May originally have been an oratory connected with Seaton Holme. Limestone rubble construction; first floor contains medieval windows. Purchased by Groundwork in 1997 and recently renovated. Listed Grade II*.

Grant Recipient/Owner: Groundwork East Durham

Access contact: Mr Peter Richards

Tel: 0191 5273333 **Fax:** 0191 5273665

E-mail: peter.richards@groundwork.org.uk

Open: Access to the exterior at all reasonable times.

Ⓟ Available. ♿ Yes. WC for disabled. Guide Dogs: Yes

£ No

Rokeby Hall

Barnard Castle, Co Durham DL12 9RZ

Early 18th century Palladian country house with fine needlework pictures.

Grant Recipient/Owner: Executors of R A Morritt

Access contact: Mr W H T Salvin

Tel: 01833 690100 **Fax:** 01833 637004

E-mail: whtsalvin@aol.com

Open: May BH Mon and Spring BH Mon & Tues, then Mon & Tues until the second Tues in Sept, 2 - 5pm (last adm 4.30pm).

Ⓟ Spaces: 15

♿ Wheelchair access to ground floor only. No WC for the disabled. No Guide Dogs.

£ **Adult:** £5

CORNWALL

Caerhays Castle & Garden

Gorran, St Austell, Cornwall PL26 6LY

Built by John Nash in 1808. Set in 60 acres of informal woodland gardens created by J C Williams, who sponsored plant hunting expeditions to China at the turn of the 19th century.

www.caerhays.co.uk

Grant Recipient/Owner: The Trustees of Charles Williams (Caerhays Estate)

Access contact: Mrs Janette Coombe

Tel: 01872 501144/501312 **Fax:** 01872 501870

E-mail: estateoffice@caerhays.co.uk

Open: House: 15 Mar - 31 May (incl. BHs), Mon - Fri 1 - 4pm. Conducted tours every 45 mins. Gardens: 16 Feb - 31 May, daily 10am to 5.30pm (last entry 4.30pm).

Ⓟ Spaces: 500

♿ Limited wheelchair access to gardens (area around castle). Access to ground floor of castle with assistance, please telephone 01872 501144 or 01872 501312 in advance to check. No WC for the disabled. Guide Dogs: Yes

£ **Adult:** £9.50 (garden & house), £5.50 (house tour only), £5.50 (gardens) **Child:** £3.50 (garden & house), £2.50 (house tour only), £2.50 (gardens) Under 5s free **Other:** £5 (groups 15+, house tour), £6.50 (groups, garden tour), £4 (groups, garden without tour)

Cotehele

St Dominick, Saltash, Cornwall PL12 6TA

Cotehele, situated on the west bank of the River Tamar, was built mainly between 1485-1627. Home of the Edgcumbe family for centuries. Its granite and slatestone walls contain intimate chambers adorned with tapestries, original furniture and armour.

www.nationaltrust.org.uk

Grant Recipient/Owner: The National Trust

Access contact: Property Manager

Tel: 01579 351346 **Fax:** 01579 351222

E-mail: cotehele@nationaltrust.org.uk

Open: House and restaurant: 15 Mar - 31 Oct, daily except Fri (but open Good Fri) 11am - 5pm; Oct and Nov 11am - 4.30pm. Mill: 20 Mar - 30 June and 1 Sept - 31 Oct, daily except Fri (but open Good Fri) July and Aug, daily; Mar, June and Sept: 1 - 5.30pm, July and Aug: 1- 6pm, Oct: 1 - 4.30pm. Garden: all year round daily 10.30am until dusk. Tea room on quay: 20 Mar - 31 Oct, daily 11am - 5pm; Nov and Dec Christmas opening telephone 01579 351346.

Ⓟ Spaces: 100. Parking space available for pre-booked coaches.

♿ Wheelchair access to house (hall, kitchen and Edgcumbe Room only), garden, area around house, restaurant and shop. Ramps available. Woodland walks: some paths accessible. WC for the disabled. Guide Dogs: Yes

£ **Adult:** £7 (house, garden & mill) £4 (garden & mill) **Child:** £3.50 (house, garden & mill), £2 (garden & mill) **Other:** £17.50 (family: house, garden & mill), £10 (family: garden & mill), £6 (pre-booked groups)

Cullacott Farmhouse

Werrington, Launceston, Cornwall PL15 8NH

Grade I listed medieval hall house, built in the 1480s as a long house, and extended 1579. Contains wall paintings of fictive tapestry, Tudor arms, St James of Compostella and remains of representation of St George and the Dragon. Extensively restored 1995-7 but still retains many original features. Now used as holiday accommodation.

www.cullacottholidays.co.uk

Grant Recipient/Owner/Access contact:
Mr & Mrs J Cole

Tel: 01566 772631

E-mail: marycole@cullacottholidays.co.uk

Open: By arrangement.

Ⓟ Spaces: 20

♿ Wheelchair access to Great Hall, through passage and disabled toilet. Guide Dogs: Yes

£ **Adult:** £2 **Child:** Free

Godolphin House

Godolphin Cross, Helston, Cornwall, TR13 9RE

Tudor-Stuart mansion of granite round a courtyard. For many generations seat of the Godolphin family who were courtiers from the 16th to the 18th century, the 1st Earl (who was born here) rose to be Queen Anne's Lord Treasurer. Has late Elizabethan stables with wagon collection and a large medieval and other gardens.

www.godolphinhouse.com

Grant Recipient/Owner: Mrs S E Schofield

Access contact: Mrs Joanne Schofield

Tel: 01736 763194 **Fax:** 01736 763194

E-mail: godo@euphony.net

Open: Easter Mon - end Sept. Call for dates and times. Groups all year by arrangement.

Ⓟ Spaces: 100. Parking for 3 coaches.

♿ Wheelchair access to all of the house except one room, but no access to the stables and gardens may be difficult. WC for the disabled. Guide Dogs: Yes

£ **Adult:** £6 (house and gardens) **Child:** £1.50 (5-15 yrs) **Gardens:** £2

Mount Edgcumbe House & Country Park

Cremyll, Torpoint, Cornwall PL10 1HZ

Grade II former home of the Earls of Mount Edgcumbe in Grade I registered landscape park of 850 acres. Includes 52 listed buildings and 16 acres of formal gardens. 16th - 18th centuries. Spectacular setting above River Tamar and Plymouth Sound. Landscape noted by Horace Walpole and Alexander Pope in 18th century. Used as starting point for D-Day landings by American troops in 1944.

Grant Recipient/Owner: Mount Edgcumbe Country Park Joint Committee

Access contact: The Manager

Tel: 01752 822236 **Fax:** 01752 822199

Open: Country Park (with listed structures): all year from dawn to dusk. Mount Edgcumbe House and Earls Garden: 1 Apr - 29 Sept, Thurs - Sun & BHs 11am - 4.30pm.

Ⓟ Spaces: 120

♿ Wheelchair access to flat areas of garden and most of house. WC for the disabled. Guide Dogs: Yes

£ **Adult:** £4.50 (house only) **Child:** £2.25 **Other:** £3.50 (concessions & groups)

Porth-en-Alls Lodge

Prussia Cove, St Hilary, Cornwall TR20 9BA

Originally a chauffeur's lodge, built c1910-1914 and designed by Philip Tilden. The Lodge is built into the cliff and sits in close proximity to the main house. The chauffeur's lodge is one of a number of historic houses on the Porth-en-Alls Estate.

Grant Recipient/Owner: Trustees of Porth-en-Alls Estate

Access contact: Mr P Tunstall-Behrens

Tel: 01736 762 014 **Fax:** 01736 762 014

E-mail: penapc@dial.pipex.com

Open: Available as self-catering holiday lets all year. Members of the public may view the property by arrangement, but only if it is unoccupied at the time.

Ⓟ Public car park approx. ¹/₂ mile from the Lodge, off the A394 (near Rosudgeon village). Spaces: 50

♿ Wheelchair access to the lodge is difficult. No WC for the disabled. Guide Dogs: Yes

£ No

Tresco Abbey Gardens

Tresco Estate, Isles of Scilly, Cornwall TR24 0QQ

25 acre garden with plants mainly from the Mediterranean region. Plant groups include protea, aloe from South Africa, succulents from Canary Isles and palms from Mexico. All grown outside all year round. Unique, frost-free climate.

www.tresco.co.uk

Grant Recipient/Owner: Tresco Estate

Access contact: Mr Michael Nelhams

Tel: 01720 424105 **Fax:** 01720 422868

E-mail: mikenelhams@tresco.co.uk

Open: Daily 10am - 4pm.

Ⓟ No

♿ Wheelchair access to all garden areas but some gravel slopes which may be difficult. WC for the disabled. Guide Dogs: Yes

£ **Adult:** £8.50 **Child:** Free (under 14) **Other:** £12.50 (weekly ticket)

Trevelver Farmhouse

St Minver, Wadebridge, Cornwall PL27 6RJ
Remains of manor house now farmhouse. Dining room with 17th century painted panelling, a painted frieze and an over-mantel painted picture.
Grant Recipient/Owner/Access contact: Mr Wills
Tel: 01208 863415 **Fax:** 01208 869024
Open: By arrangement at any reasonable time. Access to dining room only.
P Spaces: 4 &No £No

CUMBRIA

13-26 Lowther Village

Penrith, Cumbria CA10 2HG
Dwelling houses in a model village built 1766-73 by Robert Adam as estate houses for Sir James Lowther, part of a model village which was never completed.
Grant Recipient/Owner/Access contact:
Lowther & District Housing Association Ltd
Tel: 01931 712577 **Fax:** 01931 712679
E-mail: jn.ldha@talk21.com
Open: Access to exterior at all times.
P Available. &No £No

Brantwood

Coniston, Cumbria LA21 8AD
Brantwood, situated on Coniston Water, was the former home of Victorian writer and artist, John Ruskin, from 1872 to 1900. Displays a collection of paintings by Ruskin and his circle, his furniture, books and personal items. Video, bookshop, craft gallery and restaurant on site. Gardens include the Harbour Walk and Professor's Garden where Ruskin experimented with native flowers and fruit.
www.brantwood.org.uk
Grant Recipient/Owner: Brantwood Education Trust Ltd
Access contact: Mr Howard Hull
Tel: 015394 41396 **Fax:** 015394 41263
E-mail: enquiries@brantwood.org.uk
Open: All year: mid Mar - mid Nov, daily 11am - 5.30pm; mid Nov - mid Mar, Wed - Sun 11am - 4.30pm (closed Christmas Day & Boxing Day).
P Spaces: 50
& Wheelchair access to house, toilets and restaurant only. WC for the disabled. Guide Dogs: Yes
£ Adult: £5.50 Child: £1 Other: £4 (student)

Coop House

Netherby, nr. Carlisle, Cumbria CA6 5PX
Stands on the bank of the River Esk where 'coops' or traps were set to catch salmon. This summerhouse was built c1765 by Dr Robert Graham as an ornament in the landscape around Netherby Hall and as a place to enjoy the river. By 1980 it was completely derelict.
www.landmarktrust.co.uk
Grant Recipient/Owner: The Landmark Trust
Access contact: Mrs Victoria O'Keeffe
Tel: 01628 825920 **Fax:** 01628 825417
E-mail: vokeeffe@landmarktrust.co.uk
Open: The Landmark Trust is an independent charity, which rescues small buildings of historic or architectural importance from decay or unsympathetic improvement. Landmark's aim is to promote the enjoyment of these historic buildings by making them available to stay in for holidays. Coop House can be rented by anyone, at all times of the year, for periods ranging from a weekend to three weeks. Bookings can be made by telephoning the Booking Office on 01628 825925. As the building is in full-time use for holiday accommodation, it is not normally open to the public. However the public can view the building by arrangement. by telephoning the access contact (Victoria O'Keeffe on 01628 825920) to make an appointment. Potential visitors will be asked to write to confirm the details
P No &No. Guide Dogs: Yes £No

Crown & Nisi Prius Court

The Courts, English Street, Carlisle, Cumbria CA3 8NA
Former Crown Court in Carlisle situated at southern entrance to the city. One of a pair of sandstone towers built in the early 19th century as replicas of the medieval bastion. The towers were built to house the civil and criminal courts, used until the 1980s.
Grant Recipient/Owner: Cumbria Crown Court
Access contact: Mr Mike Telfer
Tel: 01228 606116
Open: Guided Tours July and Aug, Mon - Fri 1pm &

2.30pm (excl. Aug BH Mon).
P Town centre car parks.
& Wheelchair access to Grand Jury Room, Court No.2 and Public Area Crown Court Room. WC for the disabled. Guide Dogs: Yes
£ Adult: £3 Child: £2 (age 5-15) Other: £2.50

Dean Tait's Lane Arch

Carlisle, Cumbria CA3 8TZ
16th century stone arch across the Dean Tait Lane pedestrian footpath and adjoining the Prior Slee Gatehouse.
Grant Recipient/Owner: The Chapter of Carlisle Cathedral
Access contact: Mr T I S Burns
Tel: 01228 548151 **Fax:** 01228 547049
E-mail: office@carlislecathedral.org.uk
Open: Exterior visible at all times - the arch spans a public footpath.
P No &Yes. No WC for the disabled. Guide Dogs: Yes
£No

Dixon's Chimney

Shaddongate, Carlisle, Cumbria CA2 5TZ
270ft chimney, formerly part of Shaddongate Mill. Built in 1836 by Peter Dixon. At its original height of 306ft the chimney was the tallest cotton mill chimney to have been constructed. Structural problems meant that the decorative stone capping had to be removed in the 1950s.
Grant Recipient/Owner: Carlisle City Council
Access contact: Mr Peter Messenger
Tel: 01228 871195 **Fax:** 01228 817199
E-mail: PeterMe@carlisle-city.gov.uk
Open: Chimney can be viewed from Shaddongate and Junction Street.
P No &No £No

Drawdykes Castle

Brampton Old Road, Carlisle, Cumbria CA6 4QE
Pele tower, probably 14th century, converted to house 1676 by William Thackery and John Aglionby. Original tower with Classical Revival facade. Grade II* listed.
Grant Recipient/Owner/Access contact:
Mr J M Milbourn
Tel: 01228 525 804
Open: By prior arrangement.
P No &No £No

Kirkby Hall Wallpaintings

Kirkby-in-Furness, Cumbria LA17 7UX
Chapel in west wing, accessible only from trap door in dairy passage. Wallpaintings in red ochre and black consisting of panels with stylised trees, animals and birds with texts above of the Lord's Prayer, Creed, Ten Commandments and Galations 5, 16-21 from the Great Bible of 1541.
Grant Recipient/Owner: Holker Estates Company Ltd
Access contact: Mr D P R Knight
Tel: 015395 58313 **Fax:** 015395 58966
E-mail: estateoffice@holker.co.uk
Open: By written arrangement with the Holker Estate Office, Cark-in-Cartmel, Grange-over-Sands, Cumbria LA11 7PH (tel:015395 58313).
P Spaces: 3 &No £No

Levens Hall

Kendal, Cumbria LA8 0PD
Elizabethan house built around a 13th century pele tower, containing fine furniture, panelling, plasterwork and an art collection. The gardens, which include much topiary, were laid out in the late 17th century by Monsieur Beaumont for Colonel James Graham and are of national importance.
www.levenshall.co.uk
Grant Recipient/Owner: Mr C H Bagot
Access contact: Mr P E Milner / Mrs J Smedley
Tel: 01539 560321 **Fax:** 01539 560669
E-mail: email@levenshall.fsnet.co.uk
Open: House: 4 Apr - mid Oct, Sun - Thurs 12 noon - 5pm (last adm 4.30). Garden: as house 10am - 5pm. Admission prices are under review at time of publication, please check with Mr Milner at the Estate Office for current information.
P Spaces: 80
& House unsuitable for wheelchair users due to stairs and narrow doorways but all other facilities (topiary garden, plant centre, gift shop, and tea room) are accessible. WC for the disabled. Guide Dogs: Yes
£ Adult: £7 (house & garden), £5.50 (garden only)
Child: £3.50 (house & garden), £2.50 (garden only)

Muncaster Castle

Ravenglass, Cumbria CA18 1RQ
Large house incorporating medieval fortified tower, remodelled by Anthony Salvin for the 4th Lord Muncaster in 1862-66. Ancestral home of the Pennington family for 800 years containing a panelled Hall and octagonal library. Headquarters of the World Owl Trust. Woodland garden, Lakeland setting. World-famous rhododendrons, camelias and magnolias with a terrace walk along the edge of the Esk valley.
www.muncaster.co.uk
Grant Recipient/Owner: Mrs P R Gordon-Duff-Pennington
Access contact: Mrs Iona Frost-Pennington
Tel: 01229 717614 **Fax:** 01229 717010
E-mail: info@muncaster.co.uk
Open: Castle: 14 Mar - 7 Nov and half-term week in Feb, daily (except closed Sat) 12 noon - 5pm. Gardens, Owl Centre and Maze open all year 10.30am - 6.30pm (or dusk if earlier). Refreshments available.
P Spaces: 150
& Wheelchair access to ground floor of Castle only but other attractions and facilities accessible. The hilly nature of the site can create access difficulties so please ask for further information on arrival. WC for the disabled. Guide Dogs: Yes
£ Adult: £8.50 (Castle, Gardens, Owls & Maze), £6 (Gardens, Owls & Maze)
Child: £5.50 (Castle, Gardens, Owls & Maze), £4 (Gardens, Owls & Maze). Under 5s free
Other: £23 (family: Castle, Gardens, Owls & Maze), £18 (family: Gardens, Owls & Maze)

Orthwaite Hall Barn

Uldale, Wigton, Cumbria CA7 1HL
Grade II* listed agricultural barn. Former house adjoining later Hall, probably late 16th or early 17th century, now used for storage and housing animals.
Grant Recipient/Owner: Mrs S Hope
Access contact: Mr Jonathan Hope
Tel: 016973 71344
Open: By prior telephone arrangement.
P Spaces: 3 &No. Guide Dogs: Yes
£No

Prior Slee Gatehouse

Carlisle Cathedral, Carlisle, Cumbria CA3 8TZ
Dated 1528, the Gatehouse would have replaced an earlier one. It has a large chamber over the gate, with two Tudor fireplaces. Graffiti carved in the stonework is believed to include merchants' marks. One of two integral lodges survives on the north-east side of the building. Now used as residential accommodation.
Grant Recipient/Owner: The Chapter of Carlisle Cathedral
Access contact: Mr T I S Burns
Tel: 01228 548151 **Fax:** 01228 547049
E-mail: office@carlislecathedral.org.uk
Open: By arrangement with Mr T I S Burns, The Chapter of Carlisle Cathedral, 7 The Abbey, Carlisle, Cumbria CA3 8TZ.
P Parking in nearby City centre car parks. 2 disabled parking spaces in Cathedral grounds.
& WC for the disabled. Guide Dogs: Yes £ No

Prior's Tower

The Abbey, Carlisle, Cumbria CA3 8TZ
This Grade I listed three storey pele tower type building was constructed c1500. It formed part of the Prior's Lodgings and until relatively recently was part of the Deanery. Of special interest is the magnificent ceiling of 45 hand-painted panels dating from c1510 and associated with Prior Senhouse.
Grant Recipient/Owner: The Chapter of Carlisle Cathedral
Access contact: Mr T I S Burns
Tel: 01228 548151 **Fax:** 01228 547049
E-mail: office@carlislecathedral.org.uk
Open: By arrangement with Mr T I S Burns, The Chapter of Carlisle Cathedral, 7 The Abbey, Carlisle, Cumbria CA3 8TZ.
P Nearby City centre car parks. 2 disabled parking spaces in Cathedral grounds.
& WC for the disabled. Guide Dogs: Yes
£No

Sizergh Castle

nr. Kendal, Cumbria LA8 8AE
Sizergh Castle has been the home of the Strickland family for over 760 years. Its core is the 14th century pele tower, later extended and containing some fine

Elizabethan carved wooden chimney-pieces and inlaid chamber. The Castle is surrounded by gardens, including a rock garden.
www.nationaltrust.org.uk
Grant Recipient/Owner: The National Trust
Access contact: Property Manager
Tel: 015395 60070 **Fax:** 015395 61621
E-mail: ntrust@sizerghcastle.fsnet.co.uk
Open: Castle: 1 Apr - 31 Oct, daily except Fri and Sat 1.30 - 5.30pm. Garden: 1 Apr - 31 Oct, daily except Fri and Sat 12.30 - 5.30pm. Closed Good Fri.
Ⓟ Parking for disabled visitors available near the house. Spaces: 250
♿ Wheelchair access to Castle Lower Hall and garden gravel paths only. WC for the disabled. Guide Dogs: Yes
£ **Adult:** £5.50, £3 (garden only)
Child: £2.70, £1.50 (garden only)
Other: £13.70 (family), £4.50 per person (pre-booked parties, minimum 15 persons, not BHs)

Smardale Gill Viaduct

Kirkby Stephen, Cumbria
Rail overbridge, built 1860-1 by Sir Thomas Bouch for the South Lancashire and Durham Union Railway. 550ft long with 14 arches spanning Scandal Beck at Smardale Gill, a National Nature Reserve. A well-preserved example of a large road bridge on this line.
Grant Recipient/Owner: The Trustees of the Northern Viaduct Trust
Access contact: Mr Michael Sewell
Tel: 01768 371456
Open: All year, access by footpaths from Newbiggin-on-Lune or Smardale. Path along former railway.
Ⓟ Parking at Smardale. Spaces: 8
♿ Wheelchair access from Smardale only. No WC for the disabled. Guide Dogs: Yes
£ No

St Anne's Hospital

Boroughgate, Appleby, Cumbria
17th century almshouses. There are 13 dwellings and a chapel set round a cobbled courtyard. Founded by Lady Anne Clifford in 1653.
Grant Recipient/Owner: The Trustees of St Anne's Hospital
Access contact: Lord Hothfield
Tel: 017683 51487 **Fax:** 017683 53259
E-mail: lulieant@aol.com
Open: All year, daily 9am - 5pm.
Ⓟ On-street parking. Spaces: 50
♿ Guide Dogs: Yes £ No

Wray Castle

Low Wray, Ambleside, Cumbria
A large Gothic mock castle and arboretum. Built in the 1840s over looking the western shore of Lake Windermere.
www.nationaltrust.org.uk
Grant Recipient/Owner: The National Trust
Access contact: Property Manager
Tel: 015394 47997 **Fax:** 015394 47997
Open: Castle (entrance hall only): July and Aug, weekdays 2 - 4 pm by arrangement. Gardens and grounds all year. Telephone the Property Manager for further details.
Ⓟ Spaces: 20 ♿ No £ No

DERBYSHIRE

Assembly Rooms

The Crescent, Buxton, Derbyshire SK17 6BH
The Crescent was designed by John Carr of York and built by the Fifth Duke of Devonshire between 1780-89. It provided hotels, lodgings and a suite of elaborately decorated Assembly Rooms. The front elevation of three storeys is dominated by Doric pilasters over a continuous rusticated ground floor arcade.
Grant Recipient/Owner: Derbyshire County Council
Access contact: Mr Allan Morrison
Tel: 01629 580000 **Fax:** 01629 585143
E-mail: allan.morrison@derbyshire.gov.uk
Open: Exterior accessible from public highway. No interior access until refurbishment works completed, other than special agreement.
Ⓟ On-street parking available. ♿ No £ No

Barlborough Hall

Barlborough, Chesterfield, Derbyshire S43 4TL
Built by Sir Francis Rhodes in the 1580s, the Hall is

square in plan and stands on a high basement with a small internal courtyard to provide light. Contains Great Chamber, now a chapel, bearing a date of 1584 on the overmantel whilst the porch is dated 1583. Now a private school.
Grant Recipient/Owner: The Governors of Barlborough Hall School
Access contact: Mr C F A Bogie
Tel: 01246 435138 **Fax:** 01246 435090
Open: By arrangement only 29 Mar - 17 Apr, 31 May - 5 June, 7 July - 3 Sept and most weekends all year. External visits (without guide) any evening after 6pm or weekend.
Ⓟ Spaces: 50 ♿ No. Guide Dogs: Yes
£ No

Bennerley Viaduct

Erewash Valley, Ilkeston, Derbyshire
Disused railway viaduct over the Erewash vally, c1878-9, and approximately 500 yards long with 15 piers. It is one of two remaining wrought iron lattice-girder bridges in the British Isles.
Grant Recipient/Owner: Railway Paths Ltd
Access contact: Mr Simon Ballantine
Tel: 01548 550 331 **Fax:** 01548 550 331
E-mail: simonb@sustrans.org.uk
Open: There is access to the viaduct by a public footpath running underneath it, but the deck itself is inaccessible.
Ⓟ No ♿ No £ No

Buxton Opera House

Water Street, Buxton, Derbyshire SK17 6XN
The Buxton Opera House was designed by Frank Matcham and opened in 1903. Its Baroque guilded plasterwork and painted ceiling panels by De Jong were restored in Spring 2001 following extensive research into the original colour scheme.
www.buxton-opera.co.uk
Grant Recipient/Owner: High Peak Borough Council
Access contact: Mr Steve Sloan
Tel: 01298 72050 **Fax:** 01298 27563
E-mail: genmanager@buxtonopera.co.uk
Open: The theatre is open all year round for performances (mostly evenings), exact schedule varies. Theatre tours are offered most Sat mornings. Box Office and Foyer open Mon - Sat 10am - 6pm (or 8pm) and some Suns.
Ⓟ Limited on-street parking.
♿ Wheelchair access to stalls only. WC for the disabled. Guide Dogs: Yes
£ **Adult:** £2 **Child:** Free

Calke Abbey

Ticknall, Derbyshire DE73 1LE
Baroque mansion, built 1701-3 for Sir John Harpur and set in a landscaped park. Little restored, Calke is preserved by a programme of conservation as a graphic illustration of the English house in decline. It contains the natural history collection of the Harpur Crewe family, an 18th century state bed and interiors that are essentially unchanged since the 1880s.
www.nationaltrust.org.uk
Grant Recipient/Owner: The National Trust
Access contact: Property Manager
Tel: 01332 863822 **Fax:** 01332 865272
E-mail: calkeabbey@nationaltrust.org.uk
Open: House, garden and Church: 27 Mar - 31 Oct: daily except Thurs and Fri. House: 1 - 5.30pm (ticket office opens at 11am). Garden and Church: 11am - 5.30pm. Park: most days until 9pm or dusk if earlier. Timed ticket system is in operation. All visitors (including NT members) require a ticket from the ticket office.
Ⓟ Spaces: 75
♿ Wheelchair access to ground floor of house, stables, shop and restaurant. Garden and park partly accessible. WC for the disabled. Guide Dogs: Yes
£ **Adult:** £5.90 **Child:** £2.90 **Other:** £14.50 (family), £3.40 (garden only)

Catton Hall

Catton, Walton-on-Trent, Derbyshire DE12 8LN
Country house built c1741 by Smith of Warwick for Christopher Horton. Property owned by the same family since 1405. Contains an interesting collection of 17th and 18th century pictures, including Royal and Family portraits; also Byron and Napoleon memorabilia. Gardens, which run down to the River Trent, include a family chapel.
www.catton-hall.com

Grant Recipient/Owner: Mr R Neilson
Access contact: Mrs C Neilson
Tel: 01283 716311 **Fax:** 01283 712876
E-mail: kneilson@catton-hall.com
Open: 5 Apr - 11 Oct, tours of the house, chapel and gardens every Mon at 2pm. Group tours (12 or more) at any time by arrangement.
Ⓟ Unlimited parking.
♿ Wheelchair access by separate entrance to all rooms. No WC for the disabled. Guide Dogs: Yes
£ **Adult:** £4 **Conc:** £3

Cromford Mill

Mill Lane, Cromford, nr. Matlock, Derbyshire DE4 3RQ
Grade I listed mill complex established by Sir Richard Arkwright in 1771. The world's first successful water powered cotton spinning mill situated in the Derwent Valley Mills World Heritage Site. Currently being conserved by the Arkwright Society, an educational charity. The Mill is home to four shops and a restaurant.
www.cromfordmill.co.uk
Grant Recipient/Owner: The Arkwright Society
Access contact: Mr Jon Charlton
Tel: 01629 823256 **Fax:** 01629 824297
E-mail: info@arkwright.net
Open: Daily 9am - 5pm, closed on Christmas Day. Free entry to main site, charges for guided tours.
Ⓟ Spaces: 100
♿ Wheelchair access to shops, lavatories and restaurant.WC for the disabled. Guide Dogs: Yes
£ **Adult:** £2 **Child:** £1.50 **Other:** £1.50

Hardwick Hall

Doe Lea, Chesterfield, Derbyshire S44 5QJ
A late 16th century 'prodigy house' designed by Robert Smythson for Bess of Hardwick. Contains an outstanding collection of 16th century furniture, tapestries and needlework. Walled courtyards enclose gardens, orchards and herb garden.
www.nationaltrust.org.uk
Grant Recipient/Owner: The National Trust
Access contact: Property Manager
Tel: 01246 850430 **Fax:** 01246 854200
E-mail: hardwickhall@nationaltrust.org.uk
Open: 31 Mar - 31 Oct: daily except Mon, Tues and Fri (but open BH Mons and Good Fri), 12.30 - 4.30pm. Garden: Wed - Sun, 11am - 5.30pm. Parkland: daily, 8am - 6pm.
Ⓟ Spaces: 200
♿ WC for the disabled. Guide Dogs: Yes
£ **Adult:** £6.80 **Child:** £3.40 **Other:** £17 (family), £3.70 (garden only), £9.20 (joint ticket with Hardwick Old Hall, EH property)

Kedleston Hall

Derby, Derbyshire DE22 5JH
A classical Palladian mansion built 1759-65 for the Curzon family and little altered since. Robert Adam interior with state rooms retaining their collection of paintings and original furniture. The Eastern museum houses a range of objects collected by Lord Curzon when Viceroy of India (1899-1905). Set in 800 acres of parkland and 18th century pleasure ground, garden and woodland walks.
www.nationaltrust.org.uk
Grant Recipient/Owner: The National Trust
Access contact: Property Manager
Tel: 01332 842191 **Fax:** 01332 841972
E-mail: kedlestonhall@nationaltrust.org.uk
Open: House: 20 Mar - 31 Oct: daily except Thurs and Fri, 12 noon - 4.30pm. Garden: as house, 10am - 6pm. Park: All year (occasional day restrictions may apply in Dec and Jan 2005): 20 Mar - 31 Oct, 10am - 6pm; 1 Nov - Mar 2005, 10am - 4pm.
Ⓟ Winter admission for park only, parking charge of £2.70. Spaces: 60
♿ Wheelchair access to ground floor of house via stairclimber, garden, restaurant and shop. WC for the disabled. Guide Dogs: Yes
£ **Adult:** £5.80 **Child:** £2.80 **Family:** £14.40 . **Park & garden only:** £2.60

Masson Mills

(Sir Richard Arkwright's), Derby Road, Matlock Bath, Derbyshire DE4 3PY
Sir Richard Arkwright's 1783 showpiece Masson Mills are the finest surviving example of one of Arkwright's cotton mills. The "Masson Mill pattern" of design was an important influence in nascent British and American mill development. Museum with historic

working textile machinery. Part of the Derwent Valley Mills World Heritage Site.
www.massonmills.co.uk
Grant Recipient/Owner: Mara Securities Ltd
Access contact: The Co-ordinator
Tel: 01629 581001 **Fax:** 01629 581001
Open: All year except Christmas Day & Easter Day: Mon - Fri 10am - 4pm, Sat 11am - 5pm & Sun 11am - 4pm.
P Spaces: 200
♿ Wheelchair access to most areas. WC for the disabled. Guide Dogs: No
£ **Adult:** £2.50 **Child:** £1.50 **Other:** £2

St Ann's Hotel

The Crescent, Buxton, Derbyshire SK17 6BH
The Crescent was designed by John Carr of York and built by the Fifth Duke of Devonshire between 1780-89. It provided hotels, lodgings and a suite of elaborately decorated Assembly Rooms. The front elevation of three storeys is dominated by Doric pilasters over a continuous rusticated ground floor arcade.
Grant Recipient/Owner: High Peak Borough Council
Access contact: Mr Richard Tuffrey
Tel: 01457 851653 **Fax:** 01457 860290
E-mail: richard.tuffrey@highpeak.gov.uk
Open: Exterior accessible from public highway. No interior access until refurbishment works completed.
P On-street parking available. ♿ No £ No

Sudbury Hall

Sudbury, Ashbourne, Derbyshire DE6 5HT
17th century house with rich interior decoration including wood carvings by Laguerre. The Great Staircase (c1676) with white-painted balustrade with luxuriantly carved foliage by Edward Pierce, is one of the finest staircases of its date in an English house. 19th century service wing houses the National Trust Museum of Childhood.
www.nationaltrust.org.uk
Grant Recipient/Owner: The National Trust
Access contact: Property Manager
Tel: 01283 585305 **Fax:** 01283 585139
E-mail: sudburyhall@nationaltrust.org.uk
Open: Hall: 20 Mar - 31 Oct: Wed - Sun (but open BH Mons & Good Fri) 1 - 5pm. Museum: 20 Mar - 31 Oct: as Hall 1 - 5pm; 4 - 12 Dec: Sats & Suns only 11am - 4pm. Grounds: as House to 31 Oct 11am - 6pm.
P Car park is a short distance from the Hall; six-seater volunteer driven buggy available. Spaces: 100
♿ Wheelchair access to lake, tea room and shop. Ground floor access to museum. Access to Hall difficult – please contact the Property Manager in advance. WC for the disabled. Guide Dogs: Yes
£ **Adult:** £4.80 (house), £4.80 (museum), £8 (house & museum) **Child:** £2 (house), £3.20 (museum), £4 (house & museum) **Family:** £11.50 (house), £12 (museum), £19 (house & museum)

Tissington Hall

Tissington, Ashbourne, Derbyshire DE6 1RA
Grade II* listed Jacobean manor house altered in the 18th century and extended in the 20th. Contains fine furniture, pictures and interesting early 17th century panelling. Home of the FitzHerbert family for over 500 years.
www.tissington-hall.com
Grant Recipient/Owner: Sir Richard FitzHerbert Bt
Access contact: Sir Richard FitzHerbert Bt
Tel: 01335 352200 **Fax:** 01335 352201
E-mail: tisshall@dircon.co.uk
Open: 12 - 16 Apr, 31 May - 4 June and 20 July - 27 Aug Tues - Fri.
P Spaces: 100
♿ Wheelchair access to gardens and various rooms. Guide Dogs: by arrangement. WC for the disabled. Guide Dogs: Yes
£ **Adult:** £5.50 (house & garden), £2 (garden) **Child:** (10-16yrs): £2.50 (house & garden), £1 (garden) **Other:** £4.50 (house & garden), £2 (garden)

DEVON

21 The Mint

Exeter, Devon EX4 3BL
The refectory range of St Nicholas Priory, converted into a substantial town house in the Elizabethan period and later into tenements. Features include medieval arch-braced roof, traces of the Norman priory and later Elizabethan panelling. Recently restored, now dwellings and meeting room.

Grant Recipient/Owner: Exeter Historic Buildings Trust
Access contact: Katharine Chant
Tel: 01392 436000 / 496653 **Fax:** 01392 496653
E-mail: the-chants@tiscali.co.uk
Open: Every Mon all year, 10am - 12 noon (except BHs). Also Easter Sat (10 Apr), May Day BH (3 May), Spring BH (29 - 31 May), first Sat in July (3 July) and first Sat in Aug for Exeter Living History Weekend (7 Aug) 11am - 4pm. Heritage Open Days (10 - 13 Sept) 11am - 4pm. Pre-booked groups at any time all year.
P No
♿ Wheelchair access to ground floor and courtyard garden only. No WC for the disabled. Guide Dogs: Yes
£ No, but meeting room available for hire

Ayshford Chapel

Ayshford, Burlescombe, Devon
Grade I listed private medieval chapel with a simple medieval screen. Distinctive stained glass of 1848 and 17th century monuments to the Ashford family.
www.friendsoffriendlesschurches.org.uk
Grant Recipient/Owner: Friends of Friendless Churches
Access contact: Mr & Mrs Kelland
Tel: 01884 820271
Open: At any reasonable time. Keyholder lives in nearby bungalow.
P On-street parking. Spaces: 2
♿ Wheelchair access possible with assistance: access to church through field and up one step. No WC for the disabled. Guide Dogs: Yes
£ No

Broomham Farm

King's Nympton, Devon EX37 9TS
Late medieval Grade II* listed Devon long-house of stone and cob construction with thatched roof. Contains a smoking room. Currently undergoing renovation.
Grant Recipient/Owner: Mr Clements
Access contact: Miss J Clements
Tel: 01769 572322
Open: By prior telephone arrangement.
P Spaces: 3 ♿ No £ No

Coldharbour Mill

Uffculme, Devon EX15 3EE
Woollen mill, earliest reference 1707, rebuilt as a grist mill after a flood. Now a working textile mill museum with demonstrations of textile machinery. Exhibition gallery, picnic area, café, waterside walks and shop.
www.coldharbourmill.org.uk
Grant Recipient/Owner: The Coldharbour Mill Trust
Access contact: Mr Ashley Smart
Tel: 01884 840960 **Fax:** 01884 840858
E-mail: info@coldharbourmill.org.uk
Open: Provisional dates: Jan & Feb, Mon - Fri 10.30am - 5pm; Mar - Dec, daily 10.30am - 5pm. However under review at time of publication: please contact the Mill for current information (tel:01884 840960).
P Spaces: 100
♿ Wheelchair access to all areas except café. WC for the disabled. Guide Dogs: Yes
£ **Adult:** £5.50 **Child:** £2.50 **Family:** £15 Admission charges under review at time of publication: please contact the Mill for details

Colleton Manor Chapel

Chulmleigh, Devon EX18 7JS
Small chapel over gatehouse, possibly one mentioned in licence of 1381. Stone walls, slate roof, west wall recently rebuilt in stone and cob. Plain interior with Edwardian matchboard panelling and exposed timbers. Still used as a chapel.
Grant Recipient/Owner/Access contact: Mr and Mrs Phillips
Tel: 01769 580240
Open: By prior telephone arrangement with Mr & Mrs Phillips at Colleton Manor.
P Spaces: 3 ♿ No
£ Voluntary donation requested towards chapel maintenance

Cookworthy Museum of Rural Life in South Devon

The Old Grammar School, 108 Fore Street, Kingsbridge, Devon TQ7 1AW
17th century schoolroom with 19th century annex in Tudor style. Original entrance arch. Now a local museum with Victorian kitchen, Victorian pharmacy and walled garden.

www.devonmuseums.net
Grant Recipient/Owner: William Cookworthy Museum Society
Access contact: Miss Margaret Lorenz
Tel: 01548 853235
E-mail: wcookworthy@talk21.com
Open: 31 Mar - 31 Oct: Mon - Sat 10.30am - 5pm (Oct 10am - 4pm). Booked groups all year (contact Mr Clifford Peach at the Cookworthy Museum). Local History Resource Centre open all year.
P Public car park on Fore Street, 100 metres from Museum. Spaces: 100
♿ Wheelchair access with assistance to Victorian kitchen, photographic display, Farm Gallery, walled garden and shop and Local Heritage Resource Centre. WC for the disabled. Guide Dogs: Yes
£ **Adult:** £2 **Child:** 90p **Seniors:** £1.50 **Family:** £5

Dartington Hall

Dartington, Totnes, Devon TQ9 6EL
Medieval mansion and courtyard built 1388-1399 by John Holland, Earl of Huntingdon and later Duke of Exeter, half brother to Richard II. Set in a landscaped garden and surrounded by a 1200 acre estate. The Champernowne family owned Dartington for 400 years before selling the estate to Leonard and Dorothy Elmhirst who founded the Dartington Hall Trust.
www.dartington.u-net.com
Grant Recipient/Owner: The Dartington Hall Trust
Access contact: Mrs K Hockings
Tel: 01803 847002 **Fax:** 01803 847007
E-mail: trust@dartingtonhall.org.uk
Open: All year for courses, events and activities. The Hall, courtyard and gardens are accessible for external viewing all year. Access to the interior by arrangement. Coach parties by arrangement only.
P Spaces: 250
♿ Wheelchair access to Great Hall, courtyard and top garden paths. WC for the disabled. Guide Dogs: Yes
£ Some activities have an entry fee

The Devon & Exeter Institution Library & Reading Rooms

7 Cathedral Close, Exeter, Devon EX1 1EZ
Building housing the Library and Reading Rooms of the Devon and Exeter Institution since 1813 but was formerly the town house of the Courtenay family and one time home of the Parliamentary General, Sir William Waller. Part of the Tudor house remains at the rear and also the gatehouse range which fronts The Close. In the early 19th century the two lofty libraries were built on the site of the old hall and kitchen.
Grant Recipient/Owner: The Devon & Exeter Institution Library & Reading Rooms
Access contact: Mrs M M Rowe
Tel: 01392 274727 **Fax:** 01392 274727
Open: Mon - Fri 9am - 5pm. Closed for a week at Easter & Christmas. Guide available if requested in advance.
P No ♿ Yes. WC for the disabled. Guide Dogs: Yes
£ No

Dunkeswell Abbey

nr. Honiton, Devon EX14 4RP
Ruins of Cistercian abbey.
Grant Recipient/Owner: Dunkeswell Abbey Preservation Fund
Access contact: Reverend N J Wall
Tel: 01404 891243
Open: Open at all times.
P Roadside parking.
♿ Yes. No WC for the disabled. Guide Dogs: Yes £ No

Exeter Custom House

The Quay, Exeter, Devon EX1 1NN
Located on the historic quayside, the Custom House was constructed in 1680-1 and is the earliest purpose-built customs house in Britain. Contains many original fittings and 3 exceptionally ornamental plaster ceilings by John Abbot of Frithelstock (amongst the finest such work of this date in the south west).
www.exeter.gov.uk/visiting/attractions
Grant Recipient/Owner: Exeter City Council
Access contact: Mrs Alison Flack
Tel: 01392 265203 **Fax:** 01392 265695
E-mail: guidedtours@exeter.gov.uk
Open: Tours: May - Sept, Thurs and Sat at 2pm (lasts 30 minutes).
P Cathedral and Quay car park (75 metres). 5 disabled public spaces in front of Custom House. Spaces: 400
♿ Wheelchair access to ground floor stair area only. WC for disabled in car park. Guide Dogs: Yes
£ No

Finch Foundry

Sticklepath, Okehampton, Devon EX20 2NW
19th century water-powered forge, which produced agricultural and mining hand tools. Still in working order with regular demonstrations. The foundry has three water-wheels driving the huge tilt hammer and grindstone.
www.nationaltrust.org.uk
Grant Recipient/Owner: The National Trust
Access contact: Property Manager
Tel: 01837 840046
Open: 29 Mar - 2 Nov, daily except Tues 11am - 5.30pm (last entry 5pm).
P Access to car park is narrow and unsuitable for coaches and wide vehicles. Spaces: 50
♿ Wheelchair access to museum and workshop is difficult, Foundry can be viewed through shop window. No WC for the disabled. Guide Dogs: Yes
£ **Adult:** £3.30 **Child:** £1.60 (5-16 yrs), Free (under 5s)

Higher Thornham

Romansleigh, South Molton, Devon EX36 4JS
16th century through passage house, remodelled in the 17th century. Built of stone and cob, with a thatched roof. Beamed ceilings on ground floor and one moulded door frame. Recently renovated using traditional materials.
Grant Recipient/Owner/Access contact:
Mr S W Chudley
Open: By written arrangement 1 May - end of Sept: Mon or Fri 2 - 4.30pm. Dogs not allowed and children must be accompanied by an adult. No Photography. Guide dog access to ground floor only.
P Spaces: 2
♿ No. Guide Dogs: Yes
£ **Adult:** £4 **Child:** £1.50

Kilworthy Farm Cow Houses & Granary

Tavistock Hamlets, Devon PL9 7QY
Kilworthy Farm was part of the Duke of Bedford's Devon estates. The farm buildings dated 1851 consist of three parallel ranges of cowhouses situated over an undercroft of granite construction. A two storey granary adjoins the cowhouses to the east and a stableyard of single storey buildings lies separately to the west. An unusually large and complete example of a planned farmyard covering all functions of the farm for dairy and arable. The cowhouses with underground dung pit are of exceptional interest.
Grant Recipient/Owner: Mesdames Coren, Dennis & Edworthy
Access contact: Mrs Sandra Vallance
Tel: 01822 614477 **Fax:** 01822 614477
Open: 25 July - 20 Aug, daily except Sun and excluding Thurs in Aug. Open both May & Aug BH weekends. At other times by arrangement with Mr & Mrs A Vallance 10am - 5pm.
P Please ensure access for farm traffic is not obstructed. Spaces: 4
♿ Wheelchair access to the ground floor of the granary and the lengthwise walkways of the cowhouses. The undercroft is cobbled and the central passages are passable but rough. Guide dogs are welcome but as a working farm care is requested. No WC for the disabled.
£ **Adult:** £2 **Child:** £1 (under 10)

Lawrence Castle Haldon Belvedere

Higher Ashton, nr. Dunchideock,
Exeter, Devon EX6 7QY
Grade II* listed building built in 1788 as the centrepiece to a 11,600 acre estate. Stands 800ft above sea level overlooking the cathedral city of Exeter, the Exe estuary and the surrounding countryside. Contains a spiral staircase and miniature ballroom.
www.haldonbelvedere.co.uk
Grant Recipient/Owner:
Devon Historic Buildings Trust
Access contact: Mr Ian Turner
Tel: 01392 833668 **Fax:** 01392 833668
E-mail: turner@haldonbelvedere.co.uk
Open: Mar - Oct: Suns and BHs 2 - 5pm. At other times by arrangement. Further public access under review at time of publication, please check the English Heritage website or with the access contact for current information.
P For disabled adjacent to building. Spaces: 15
♿ Wheelchair access to ground floor only. No WC for the disabled. Guide Dogs: Yes
£ **Adult:** £1.75 **Child:** Free
Other: Pre 01/03/04 £1.50 (adult), 75p (child)

Lynton Town Hall

Lee Road, Lynton, Devon EX35 6HT
Grade II* listed Town Hall. Cornerstone laid 1898, opened by the donor Sir George Newnes, 15 Aug 1900. Neo-Tudor design with Art Nouveau details: a very striking building. Now functions as Town Hall and community facility.
Grant Recipient/Owner: Lynton & Lynmouth Town Council
Access contact: Mr Dwyer
Tel: 01598 752384 **Fax:** 01598 752677
E-mail: ltc@northdevon.gov.uk
Open: Mon - Fri 9.30am - 11am. Other times by arrangement.
P No
♿ Wheelchair access to ground floor only. No WC for the disabled. Guide Dogs: Yes
£ No

Old Quay Head

The Quay, Ilfracombe, Devon EX34 9EQ
Grade II* listed quay originally constructed early in the 16th century by William Bourchier, Lord Fitzwarren. The Quay was paved with stone in the 18th century and extended further in the 19th. This extension is marked by a commemorative stone plaque at its southern end. The Quay separates the inner harbour basin from the outer harbour.
Grant Recipient/Owner: North Devon District Council
Access contact: Mr Paul Hollis
Tel: 01271 388418 **Fax:** 01271 372196
E-mail: paul_hollis@northdevon.gov.uk
Open: All year.
P Charges apply from Mar - Oct. Disabled places available. Spaces: 144
♿ WC for disabled immediately adjacent to the Old Quay Head. Guide Dogs: Yes
£ No

Saltram House

Plympton, Plymouth, Devon PL7 1UH
A remarkable survival of a George II mansion, complete with its original contents and set in a landscaped park. Robert Adam worked here on two occasions to create the state rooms and produced what are claimed to be the finest such rooms in Devon. These rooms show his development as a designer, from using the conventional Rococo, to the low-relief kind of Neo-Classical detail that became his hallmark and with which he broke new ground in interior design.
www.nationaltrust.org.uk
Grant Recipient/Owner: The National Trust
Access contact: Property Manager
Tel: 01752 333500 **Fax:** 01752 336474
E-mail: saltram@nationaltrust.org.uk
Open: House: 27 Mar - 31 Oct, daily except Fri (but open Good Fri), 27 Mar - 30 Sept, 12 - 4.30pm, 1 - 31 Oct, 11.30am - 3.30pm Garden: daily all year except Fri (but open Good Fri) 27 Mar - 31 Oct, 11am - 5pm and 1 Nov - 31 Mar 2005, 11am - 4pm .
P 500 metres from house, 30 marked spaces on tarmac, remainder on grass. Spaces: 250
♿ Wheelchair access to first floor via lift (66cm wide by 86.5cm deep), restaurant, tea room, ticket offices over cobbles. Wheelchairs available at house. WC for the disabled. Guide Dogs: Yes
£ **Adult:** £6.60 (house & garden), £3.30 (garden only) **Child:** £3.20 (house & garden), £1.60 (garden only). Under 5s Free
Other: £16.30 (family). £5.80 (Groups 15+)

Smeaton's Tower

The Hoe, Plymouth, Devon PL1 2NZ
Re-sited upper part of the former Eddystone Lighthouse. Built 1759 by John Smeaton, erected here on new base in 1882. Circular tapered tower of painted granite with octagonal lantern. When this lighthouse was first constructed it was considered to be an important technical achievement.
Grant Recipient/Owner: Plymouth City Museum & Art Gallery
Access contact: Mr Andrew Gater
Tel: 01752 304386 **Fax:** 01752 256361
E-mail: andrew.gater@plymouth.gov.uk
Open: Easter - end Oct, daily 10am - 4pm; beginning Nov - Easter, Tues - Sat 10am - 3pm.
P On-street parking. Spaces: 40 ♿ No
£ **Adult:** £2 **Child:** £1

South Molton Town Hall and Pannier Market

South Molton, Devon EX36 3AB
Guild Hall, dating from 1743 and Grade I listed.

Incorporates Court Room, Old Assembly Room and Mayors Parlour with Museum on ground floor. Adjacent to Pannier Market and New Assembly Room.
Grant Recipient/Owner: South Molton Town Council
Access contact: Mr Malcolm Gingell
Tel: 01769 572501 **Fax:** 01769 574008
E-mail: smtc@northdevon.gov.uk
Open: Museum open May - Oct, Mon - Thurs and Sat. All other rooms used for meetings, functions etc as and when required. Constable Room rented by Devon County Council.
P In Pannier Market except Thurs and Sats.
♿ All areas except Court Room, Mayors Parlour & Old Assembly Room. WC for the disabled. Guide Dogs: Yes
£ No

Ugbrooke Park

Chudleigh, Devon TQ13 0AD
House and chapel built c1200 and redesigned by Robert Adam in the 1760s for the 4th Lord Clifford. Chapel and library wing in Adam's characteristic castle style. Set in 'Capability' Brown landscaped park with lakes and 18th century Orangery. Home of the Lords Clifford of Chudleigh for 400 years.
Grant Recipient/Owner: Clifford Estate Company Ltd
Access contact: Lord Clifford
Tel: 01626 852179 **Fax:** 01626 853322
Open: 18 July - 9 Sept: Tues, Wed, Thurs, Sun and Aug BH Mon 1.00 - 5.30pm. Group tours and private functions by arrangement.
P Spaces: 200
♿ Yes. WC for the disabled. Guide Dogs: Yes
£ **Adult:** £5.50 (house & garden), £3 (garden)
Child: £3 (house & garden), £2 (garden)
Other: £5 (senior citizens, house & garden)

DORSET

Blandford Forum Town Hall & Corn Exchange

Market Place, Blandford Forum, Dorset DT1 7PY
The Town Hall built by the Bastard Brothers and completed in 1734, has a Portland stone facade. On the ground floor is a loggia with 3 semi-circular arches enclosed by iron gates. The former magistrates room and the mid 20th century Council Chamber sit at 1st floor level. Attached to the rear of the building is the Corn Exchange, built in 1858, with interesting elliptical roof-trusses.
Grant Recipient/Owner: Blandford Forum Town Council
Access contact: The Town Clerk
Tel: 01258 454500 **Fax:** 01258 454432
E-mail: admin@blandford-tc.co.uk
Open: All year for markets, civic functions and other events. At other times by prior telephone arrangement with The Town Clerk, Mon - Fri 9.30am - 12.30pm.
P On-street meter parking, except on market days on Thurs and Sats. Other parking in the town. Spaces: 20
♿ Wheelchair access to ground floor only. WC for the disabled. Guide Dogs: Yes
£ No

The Chantry

128 South Street, Bridport, Dorset DT6 3PA
14th or 15th century two-storey stone rubble house, originally situated on a promontory of the River Brit. At one time known as the "Prior's House", more probably the house of a chantry priest. Interesting internal details including fragments of 17th century domestic wall paintings.
www.vivat.org.uk
Grant Recipient/Owner: The Vivat Trust Ltd
Access contact: Mrs F Lloyd
Tel: 0845 090 2212 **Fax:** 0845 090 0174
E-mail: enquiries@vivat.org.uk
Open: Heritage Open Days in Sept 10am - 5pm. At other times by arrangement with The Vivat Trust (tel: 020 7930 2212, fax: 020 7930 2295)
P Additional on-street parking. Spaces: 1
♿ Wheelchair access with difficulty through back entrance to kitchen and sitting room on ground floor. No WC for the disabled. Guide Dogs: Yes
£ No

Highcliffe Castle

Rothesay Drive, Highcliffe-on-Sea,
Christchurch, Dorset BH23 4LE
Cliff-top mansion built in the 1830s by Charles Stuart. Constructed in the romantic, picturesque style, much of its stonework is medieval coming from France. Exterior

has been restored, interior houses changing exhibitions and the 16th century stained glass Jesse window. Gift shop and tea rooms on site with 14 acre cliff-top park. www.highcliffecastle.co.uk

Grant Recipient/Owner: Christchurch Borough Council

Access contact: Mr Mike Allen

Tel: 01425 278807 **Fax:** 01425 280423

E-mail: m.allen@christchurch.gov.uk

Open: 1 Apr - 31 Oct: daily 11am - 5pm. 1 Nov - 23 Dec: daily 11am - 4pm. Also some weekends in Mar for Special Events. Tea Rooms open all year 10am - late afternoon; grounds all year from 7am.

P Charged parking in Council car park Apr - Sept (free Oct - Mar) with additional parking in Highcliffe Village (1 mile from Castle). Spaces: 120

♿ Currently no wheelchair access to the building but there are toilet facilities for the disabled at the site. Guide Dogs: Yes

£ Adult: £1.50 **Child:** Free **Other:** HHA/Season Ticket holders free

EAST RIDING OF YORKSHIRE

Church of Our Lady & St Everilda

Everingham, East Riding of Yorkshire YO42 4JA

Roman Catholic parish church for Everingham, built between 1836 and 1839 to the designs of Agostino Giorgiola. Interior has columned walls and a barrelled ceiling with a semi-dome above the high altar. Also of note are the altar, font and statues and the 1839 organ by William Allen.

Grant Recipient/Owner: The Herries Charitable Trust

Access contact: Mr N J M Turton

Tel: 01759 304105 **Fax:** 01759 304105

E-mail: nturton@btconnect.com

Open: Key available during reasonable hours by telephoning 01430 861443 or 01759 302226.

P Spaces: 12

♿ No. Guide Dogs: Yes

£ No

Constable Mausoleum

Halsham, nr. Kingston-upon-Hull, East Riding of Yorkshire

The Constable Mausoleum was commissioned by Edward Constable in 1792, built by Atkinson and York and completed in 1802 at a cost of £3,300. It comprises a central domed rotunda of stone, internally lined with black marble and surrounded by heraldic shields. The external raised and railed podium is part of a vaulted ceiling to the crypt below, in which various generation of the Constable family are interned.

Grant Recipient/Owner/Access contact: Mr John Chichester-Constable

Tel: 01964 562316 **Fax:** 01964 563283

E-mail: bchall@dircon.co.uk

Open: By written arrangement with Mr John Chichester-Constable, South Wing - Estate Office, Burton Constable Hall, nr Kingston-upon-Hull, East Riding of Yorkshire HU11 4LN.

P On street parking. Spaces: 1 **♿** No **£** No

Maister House

160 High Street, Kingston-upon-Hull, East Riding of Yorkshire HU1 1NL

Rebuilt in 1743 during Hull's heyday as an affluent trading centre, this house is a typical but rare survivor of a contemporary merchant's residence. The restrained exterior belies the spectacular plasterwork staircase inside. The house is now let as offices. www.nationaltrust.org.uk

Grant Recipient/Owner: The National Trust

Access contact: Property Manager

Tel: 01482 324114 **Fax:** 01482 227003

Open: Daily except Sat & Sun (closed Good Fri and all BHs) 10am - 4pm. Access is to entrance hall and staircase only. Unsuitable for groups. No WC.

P No **♿** No. Guide Dogs: Yes

£ Donations welcome

Old Lighthouse

Flamborough, nr. Bridlington, East Riding of Yorkshire

Grade II* light tower, built in 1674. 24 metres high, designed for a coal and brushwood fire to have been burnt on top although it is uncertain whether it was ever lit. The octagonal tower has four floors, several windows and a fireplace so it was possibly built to be lived in.

Grant Recipient/Owner: East Riding of Yorkshire Council

Access contact: Miss Helen Kerr

Tel: 01482 395208

Open: Access to interior by arrangement. with Helen Kerr, Countryside Officer (tel:01482 395208).

P Public parking at Flamborough headland, 1/4 mile

♿ No **£** No

Stamford Bridge Viaduct

Stamford Bridge, East Riding of Yorkshire

Built 1847 for the York & North Midland Railway Company, East Riding lines. Mainly red brick with 10 unadorned round brick arches. The railway line was closed in the mid 1960s and is now repaired as part of a circular pedestrian walkway around the village.

Grant Recipient/Owner: East Riding of Yorkshire Council

Access contact: Mr Darren Stevens

Tel: 01482 391678 **Fax:** 01482 391660

E-mail: darren.stevens@eastriding.gov.uk

Open: The site is permanently open as a footpath.

P Informal parking for approximately 20 cars near sports hall.

♿ No. Guide Dogs: Yes **£** No

ESSEX

150 High Street

Kelvedon, nr. Colchester, Essex CO5 9JD

A timber framed building with 14th/15th century origins. It may have once been an Inn but is now a private dwelling. The house has a front range comprising former hall and crosswing with a long addition with several unique features – a rare assemblage for structures in Essex.

Grant Recipient/Owner: Mr J Loy

Access contact: Mr & Mrs J Loy

Tel: 01376 570200 **Fax:** 01376 570200

E-mail: jorolo@fish.co.uk

Open: By prior telephone arrangement.

P On-street parking (restricted 10-11am).

♿ Wheelchair access with assistance to ground floor of front and rear range. No WC for the disabled. Guide Dogs: Yes

£ Adult: £1.50 (donation to charity requested)

The Great Dunmow Maltings

Mill Lane, Great Dunmow, Essex CM6 1BD

Grade II* maltings complex (listed as Boyes Croft Maltings, White Street), early 16th century and later, timber-framed and plastered, part weatherboarding and brick. Now fully restored, the building houses the Great Dunmow Museum Society on the ground floor with displays of local history. The first floor is available for community use.

Grant Recipient/Owner: Great Dunmow Maltings Preservation Trust

Access contact: Mr David A Westcott

Tel: 01371 873958 **Fax:** 01371 873958

E-mail: david.westcott2@btinternet.com

Open: Open all year: Sat, Sun & BHs 11am - 4pm. In addition, from Easter - end Oct: Tues 11am - 4pm. Groups at any reasonable time by arrangement. Closed over Christmas/New Year holiday week.

P Public car park nearby (pay and display, free on Suns and BHs). Spaces: 100

♿ Yes. WC for the disabled. Guide Dogs: Yes

£ Adult: £1 **Child:** 50p **Senior:** 50p

Harwich Redoubt Fort

behind 29 Main Road, Harwich, Essex CO12 3LT

180ft diameter circular fort commanding the harbour entrance built in 1808 to defend the port against a Napoleonic invasion. Surrounded by a dry moat, there are 11 guns on the battlements. 18 casements which originally sheltered 300 troops in siege conditions now house a series of small museums. www.harwich-society.com

Grant Recipient/Owner: The Harwich Society

Access contact: Mr A Rutter

Tel: 01255 503429 **Fax:** 01255 503429

E-mail: theharwichsociety@quista.net

Open: 1 May - 31 Aug: daily 10am - 4.30pm. Rest of year: Suns only 10am - 4pm.

P No

♿ No. Guide Dogs: Yes

£ Adult: £1 **Child:** Accompanied children free

Hylands House

Hylands Park, London Road, Widford, Chelmsford, Essex CM2 8WQ

Grade II* listed building, surrounded by 600 acres of landscaped parkland, partly designed by Humphry Repton. Built c1730, the original house was a red brick Queen Anne style mansion, subsequent owners set about enlarging the property, which produced a neo-classical style house. Internal inspection of the house reveals its Georgian and Victorian features. www.hylandshouse.org.uk

Grant Recipient/Owner: Chelmsford Borough Council

Access contact: Mrs Linda Palmer

Tel: 01245 496800 **Fax:** 01245 496804

E-mail: linda.palmer@chelmsford.gov.uk

Open: Suns and BHs (except Christmas Day) all year and Mons between Apr - end Sept, 11am - 6pm. Mons between Oct - end Mar, 11am - 4pm. Tea Room: Suns all year & Mons between Apr - end Sept, 11am - 4.30pm; Mons between Oct - end Mar 11am - 4.30pm. Group visits by arrangement with Mrs Ceri Lowen, Assistant Hylands House Manager, Leisure Services, Chelmsford Borough Council, Civic Centre, Duke Street, Chelmsford, Essex CM1 1JE (tel:012450496800). Events programme.

P 4 disabled parking spaces, coaches by arrangement. Spaces: 84

♿ Yes. WC for the disabled. Guide Dogs: Yes

£ Adult: £3.20 **Child:** Free (under 12) **Other:** £2.20

John Webb's Windmill

Fishmarket Street, Thaxted, Essex CM6 2PG

Brick tower mill built in 1804 consisting of five floors. Has been fully restored as a working mill. On two floors there is a museum of rural and domestic bygones. There is also a small picture gallery of early photographs of the mill and the surrounding countryside.

Grant Recipient/Owner: Thaxted Parish Council

Access contact: Mr L A Farren

Tel: 01371 830285 **Fax:** 01371 830285

Open: May - Sept, Sat - Sun and BHs, 2pm - 6pm. Groups during weekdays by special arrangement. For further information please contact Mr L A Farren, Borough Hill, Bolford Street, Thaxted, Essex CM6 2PY (tel: 01371 830285).

P Public parking in Thaxted. Spaces: 80

♿ Wheelchair access to ground floor only. Disabled toilet in public car park (Margaret Street). Guide Dogs: Yes

£ Adult: £1 **Child:** Free

Maldon Moot Hall

High Street, Maldon, Essex CM9 4RL

15th century listed building which once housed a police station and still has the exercise yard, a brick built spiral staircase with brick handrail, courtroom and council chamber. Access to the roof gives good views of the Blackwater estuary and surrounding district.

Grant Recipient/Owner: Maldon Town Council

Access contact: The Town Clerk

Tel: 01621 857373 **Fax:** 01621 850793

E-mail: maldontowncouncil@u.genie.co.uk

Open: By prior telephone arrangement with the Town Clerk of Maldon Town Council (tel:01621 857373). Otherwise open Mar - end of Oct Sat afternoons for visits at 2 & 3.30pm. (This may be extended).

P No

♿ Wheelchair access to ground floor only. No WC for the disabled. Guide Dogs: Yes

£ Adult: £1 **Child:** 50p **Senior:** 50p

Monks Barn

Netteswellbury Farm (Harlow Study Centre), Harlow, Essex CM18 6BW

A medieval tithe barn built around 1440, now housing Harlow Study Centre. Schoolchildren and visitors can learn how the new town was designed and plans for the future. Many original features are visible.

Grant Recipient/Owner: Harlow District Council

Access contact: Ms Sandra Farrington

Tel: 01279 446745 **Fax:** 01279 421945

E-mail: sandra.farrington@harlow.gov.uk

Open: Opening by arrangement.

P Spaces: 16

♿ Full wheelchair access but cobbled flooring may prove uncomfortable. WC for disabled. Guide Dogs: Yes

£ No

Old Friends Meeting House

High Street, Stebbing, Essex CM6 3SG
The Stebbing Meeting House is the earliest Quaker meeting House in Essex. Built c1674 it is a particularly fine and complete example of an early Quaker meeting house and its historical importance is recognised by its Grade II* listing.
Grant Recipient/Owner: The Trustees of the Old Friends Meeting House
Access contact: Mr J B Newbrook
Tel: 01371 856464
E-mail: jnewbrook@aol.com
Open: By prior telephone or written arrangement with Mr J B Newbrook, 7 Oakfield, Stebbing, Essex CM6 3SX (tel: 01371 856464).
P Spaces: 10
Yes. WC for the disabled. Guide Dogs: Yes
£ No

St Mary

Mundon, Essex
Listed Grade I church, now redundant and owned by the Friends of Friendless Churches since 1975. Two-tier timber-framed weatherboarded tower of the 16th century and roughly contemporary north porch. The nave is partly 14th century and retains a complete set of 18th century box pews. The chancel is also Georgian but with simple 19th century fittings. Naïve Baroque trompe l'oeil painting of murals on the east wall.
www.friendsoffriendlesschurches.org.uk
Grant Recipient/Owner: Friends of Friendless Churches
Access contact: Mr Matthew Saunders
Tel: 020 7236 3934   **Fax:** 020 7329 3677
E-mail: office@ancientmonumentssociety.org.uk
Open: At all reasonable times.
P No
Wheelchair access possible with assistance: access to church along rough track and up one step. Also interior poorly lit. No WC for the disabled. Guide Dogs: Yes
£ No

Stansted Windmill

Millside, Stansted Mountfitchet, Essex CM24 8BL
Brick tower mill, built 1787 and a scheduled ancient monument. Ceased working in 1910 but most of the original machinery remains in situ. Given in trust to the village by Lord Blyth in 1935.
Grant Recipient/Owner: Stansted Mountfitchet Council
Access contact: Mrs D P Honour
Tel: 01279 647213   **Fax:** 01279 813160
Open: Apr - Oct: first Sun of each month 2 - 6pm; plus BH Suns and Mons. Parties at any reasonable time of the year by arrangement. with Mrs D P Honour, 59 Blythwood Gardens, Stansted, Essex CM24 8HH (tel:01279 647213). For school groups contact Mrs Minshull (01279 812230). Children must be accompanied. Small souvenir shop.
P No No
£ Adult: 50p Child: 25p
Other: £25 (group guided tours up to approx. 30)

Valentines Mansion

Emerson Road, Ilford, Essex IG1 4XA
Valentines Mansion is a late 17th century house, largely Georgian in appearance with Regency additions. Of particular interest is the unusual curved early 19th century porte cochere. The exterior was extensively repaired and restored in 2000.
Grant Recipient/Owner: London Borough of Redbridge
Access contact: Mr Nigel Burch
Tel: 020 8708 3619   **Fax:** 020 8708 3178
E-mail: nigel.burch@redbridge.gov.uk
Open: 10 May for annual May Fair and for London Open House weekend in Sept. At other times by arrangement. with Nigel Burch, Chief Leisure Officer, London Borough of Redbridge, Lynton House, 255/259 High Road, Ilford, Essex IG1 1NY (tel:020 8708 3619).
P No
Wheelchair access to ground floor only. No WC for the disabled. Guide Dogs: Yes
£ No

GLOUCESTERSHIRE

Acton Court

Latteridge Road, Iron Acton,
South Gloucestershire BS37 9TJ
Seat of the Poyntzes, an influential courtier family who

occupied the house until 1680 when it was converted into a farm house. A Tudor range, constructed in 1535 to accommodate King Henry VIII and Queen Anne Boleyn survives along with part of the North range. The rooms are unfurnished but contain important traces of original decoration.
Grant Recipient/Owner: Rosehill Corporation
Access contact: Ms Lisa Kopper
Tel: 01454 228224   **Fax:** 01454 227256
E-mail: actonct@dircon.co.uk
Open: Guided tours and events 16 June - 23 Aug. Closed Mons except Aug BH. Pre-booking essential. Ring information line for details 01454 228224.
P Spaces: 40
Wheelchair access to ground floor only. WC for the disabled. Guide Dogs: Yes
£ Adult: £5   Child: £3.50   Other: £3.50 (senior citizens & disabled), £100 (exclusive group tours maximum 25). Special events priced separately

Chastleton House

Chastleton, Moreton-in-Marsh, Glos GL56 0SU
Jacobean house filled with a mixture of rare and everyday objects, furniture and textiles collected since 1612. Continually occupied for 400 years by the same family. Emphasis here lies on conservation rather than restoration.
www.nationaltrust.org.uk
Grant Recipient/Owner: The National Trust
Access contact: The Custodian
Tel: 01608 674355   **Fax:** 01608 674355
E-mail: chastleton@nationaltrust.org.uk
Open: 31 Mar - 2 Oct: Wed - Sat, 1 - 5pm (last adm 4pm); 6 - 30 Oct: Wed - Sat, 1 - 4pm (last adm 3pm). Booking is essential at all times (tel:01494 755585 between 9.30am - 4pm, Mon - Fri, for advance booking). Groups by written arrangement with the Custodian.
P Spaces: 50
Wheelchair access to ground floor with assistance and parts of garden only. WC for the disabled. Guide Dogs: Yes
£ Adult: £5.80   Child: £2.90   Other: £14.50 (family), Private View £7.50 (£2.50 NT members)

Chavenage

Tetbury, Gloucestershire GL8 8XP
Elizabethan Manor House (c1576), contains tapestry rooms, furniture and relics from the Cromwellian Period. Has been the home of only two families since the time of Elizabeth I. Used as a location for television and film productions.
www.chavenage.com
Grant Recipient/Owner: Trustees of the Chavenage Settlement
Access contact: Miss Caroline Lowsley-Williams
Tel: 01666 502329   **Fax:** 01453 836778
E-mail: info@chavenage.com
Open: May - Sept: Thurs, Sun & BHs 2 - 5pm; plus Easter Sun and Mon. Groups at other times by arrangement.
P Spaces: 40
Wheelchair access to ground floor only. WC for the disabled. Guide Dogs: Yes
£ Adult: £5   Child: £2.50

Court Farm Dovecote

Quenington, Cirencester, Gloucestershire GL7 5BN
Reputed to be dovecote mentioned in 1338, belonging to the Knights Hospitallers, but possibly 17th century. Small round structure of rubble stone with conical stone slate roof with retractable lantern "lid". Contains 600 dove holes stacked at an angle one above another inside wall, above rat rail around which moves revolving ladder on central wooden pin.
Grant Recipient/Owner/Access contact: Mrs B Gollins
Tel: 01285 750371   **Fax:** 01285 750322
Open: By arrangement with Mrs B Gollins.
P Spaces: 5
Yes. No WC for the disabled. Guide Dogs: Yes
£ No

East Banqueting House

Calf Lane, Chipping Campden, Gloucestershire
The East Banqueting House stands opposite the West Banqueting House across a broad terrace that ran in front of Sir Baptist Hick's mansion, which was deliberately destroyed by the Royalists in 1645 only 30 years after it had been built. It is elaborately decorated with spiral chimney stacks, finials and ebullient strapwork parapets. Steep staircases.
www.landmarktrust.co.uk

Grant Recipient/Owner: The Landmark Trust
Access contact: Mrs Victoria O'Keeffe
Tel: 01628 825920   **Fax:** 01628 825417
E-mail: vokeeffe@landmarktrust.co.uk
Open: The Landmark Trust is an independent charity, which rescues small buildings of historic or architectural importance from decay or unsympathetic improvement. Landmark's aim is to promote the enjoyment of these historic buildings by making them available to stay in for holidays. East Banqueting House can be rented by anyone, at all times of the year, for periods ranging from a weekend to three weeks. Bookings can be made by telephoning the Booking Office on 01628 825925. The public can also view the building on eight Open Days all year (dates to be set) or by arrangement.; telephone the access contact Victoria O'Keeffe on 01628 825920 to make an appointment. Potential visitors will be asked to write to confirm the details of their visit.
P Parking available in town only.   No £ No

Ebley Mill

Westward Road, Stroud, Gloucestershire GL5 4UB
19th century riverside textile mill, now restored and converted into offices occupied by Stroud District Council. Has Gothic-style clock tower and block designed by George Bodley.
www.stroud.gov.uk
Grant Recipient/Owner: Stroud District Council
Access contact: Mr D Marshall
Tel: 01453 754646   **Fax:** 01453 754942
E-mail: information@stroud.gov.uk
Open: Mon - Thurs 8.45am - 5pm; Fris 8.45am - 4.30pm. Closed BHs. Tours by arrangement.
P Spaces: 30 Yes. WC for the disabled. Guide Dogs: Yes
£ No

Elmore Court Entrance Gates

Elmore, Gloucestershire GL2 3NT
Early 18th century carriage and pedestrian gateway, with 19th century flanking walls. By William Edney, blacksmith of Bristol for Sir John Guise at Rendcomb. Gateway was removed from Rendcomb and re-erected here in early 19th century.
Grant Recipient/Owner: Trustees of the Elmore Court Estate
Access contact: Trustees of the Elmore Court Estate
Tel: 01452 720293
Open: Visible at all times from public highway.
P Off-road parking on forecourt in front of Gates. Spaces: 5
Yes. No WC for the disabled. Guide Dogs: Yes £ No

Frampton Manor Barn

(The Wool Barn, Manor Farm), The Green, Frampton-on-Severn, Gloucestershire GL2 7EP
Grade I listed timber framed barn built c1560. Re-used worked stones in ashlar plinth wall were found during repair works.
www.framptoncourtestate.uk.com
Grant Recipient/Owner/Access contact:
Mr P R H Clifford
Tel: 01452 740698   **Fax:** 01452 740698
E-mail: clifford.fce@farming.co.uk
Open: During normal office hours (8.30am - 4.30pm Mon - Fri). Other times by arrangement (tel:01452 740698).
P Spaces: 30
Yes. WC for the disabled. Guide Dogs: Yes
£ Adult: £1 Child/Conc: Free (special rates for schools)

The Malt House

High Street, Chipping Campden, Gloucestershire GL55 6AH
18th century malt house converted to a dwelling in 1905. Now part of an hotel and used as a conference room.
Grant Recipient/Owner: Seymour House Hotel Ltd
Access contact: The Director
Tel: 01386 840429   **Fax:** 01386 840369
E-mail: enquiry@seymourhousehotel.com
Open: Open to the public at all times except when in use for functions.
P Spaces: 30 Guide Dogs: Yes £ No

Newark Park

Ozleworth, Wotton-under-Edge, Glos GL12 7PZ
Tudor hunting lodge built c1550 for one of Henry VIII's courtiers, Sir Nicholas Poyntz (who married into the

equally wealthy Berkeley family), reputedly with stone from the destroyed Kingswood Abbey. Enlarged in early 17th century and then remodelled into a castellated country house by James Wyatt in the late 18th century. Retains many original features and is located on the edge of a 40ft cliff with outstanding views of the surrounding countryside.
www.nationaltrust.org.uk
Grant Recipient/Owner: The National Trust
Access contact: Property Manager
Tel: 01985 842644 **Fax:** 01985 842644
E-mail: michael@newark98.freeserve.co.uk
Open: 31 Jan - 15 Feb Sat & Sun, 11am - 5pm; 1 Apr - 27 May Wed and Thurs, 11am - 5pm; 2 June - 31 Oct Wed, Thurs, Sat & Sun 11am - 5pm. Open BH Mons.
P Spaces: 10
& No. Guide Dogs: Yes
£ Adult: £4.50 Child: £2.20 Family: £11

St Mary Magdalene Chapel

Hillfield Gardens, London Road, Gloucestershire
Chancel of former church serving the inmates of St Mary Magdalene Hospital, originally a leper hospital, then later almshouses. Medieval graffiti visible on exterior, perhaps mementos of visiting pilgrims. Interior contains south and west doorways rebuilt after the church was demolished in 1861 and tomb of 13th century lady, removed from St Kyneburgh's Chapel near the South Gate in 1550.
Grant Recipient/Owner: Gloucester Historic Buildings Trust Ltd
Access contact: Mr Malcolm J Watkins
Tel: 01452 396620 **Fax:** 01452 396622
E-mail: culture@gloucester.gov.uk
Open: Building currently closed on safety grounds; works to enable re-opening planned for 2004. For further information please contact Mr Malcolm J Watkins, Strategic Cultural Manager, Gloucester City Council, Herbert Warehouse, The Docks, Gloucestershire GL1 2EQ (tel:01452 396620). When open, access will be by arrangement and as part of the Heritage Open Days weekend. Exterior accessible at all times in public park.
P No
& Wheelchair access to exterior and to interior with assistance (entrance steps to be negotiated). No WC for the disabled. Guide Dogs: Yes
£ No

Stancombe Park Temple

Dursley, Gloucestershire GL11 6AU
One in a series of buildings built in the folly gardens at Stancombe Park, in the form of a Greek temple.
www.thetemple.info
Grant Recipient/Owner: Mr N D Barlow
Access contact: Mrs G T Barlow
Tel: 01453 542815
E-mail: nicb@nicbarlow.com
Open: All year by prior telephone arrangement.
P Spaces: 50
& No. Guide Dogs: Yes
£ Adult: £3 (charity donation for visits to garden)
Other: No charge is made for anyone specifically wishing to see the temple only

Stanley Mill

Kings Stanley, Stonehouse, Gloucestershire GL10 3HQ
Built 1813, with large addition c1825, of Flemish bond red brick with ashlar dressings and Welsh slate roof. Early example of fireproof construction (which survived a major fire in 1884).
Grant Recipient/Owner: Stanley Mills Ltd
Access contact: Mr Mark Griffiths
Tel: 01453 824444
Open: By written arrangement as the Mill is used by various manufacturing companies.
P By arrangement. **&** No **£** No

West Banqueting House

Chipping Campden, Gloucestershire
The West Banqueting House stands opposite the East Banqueting House across a broad terrace. It is elaborately decorated with spiral chimney stacks, finials and strapwork parapets.
Grant Recipient/Owner: The Landmark Trust
Access contact: Mrs Victoria O'Keeffe
Tel: 01628 825920 **Fax:** 01628 825417
E-mail: vokeeffe@landmarktrust.co.uk
Open: The Landmark Trust is an independent charity, which rescues small buildings of historic or

architectural importance from decay or unsympathetic improvement. Landmark's aim is to promote the enjoyment of these historic buildings by making them available to stay in for holidays. West Banqueting House can be rented by anyone, at all times of the year, for periods ranging from a weekend to three weeks. Bookings can be made by telephoning the Booking Office on 01628 825925. The public can also view the building on eight Open Days all year (dates to be set) or by arrangement.; telephone the access contact Victoria O'Keeffe on 01628 825920 to make an appointment. Potential visitors will be asked to write to confirm the details of their visit.
P In town only. **&** No **£** No

Wick Court

Overton Lane, Arlingham, Gloucestershire GL2 7JJ
Medieval, 16th and 17th century Grade II* listed manor house with a range of farm buildings enclosed by a moat. The house is now a Farms for City Children centre.
www.farmsforcitychildren.co.uk
Grant Recipient/Owner: Farms for City Children
Access contact: Ms Heather Tarplee
Tel: 01452 741023 **Fax:** 01452 741366
E-mail: wickcourt@yahoo.co.uk
Open: 5 - 23 Jan; 29 May - 6 June; 23 July - 2 Sept. At other times by arrangement with Heather Tarplee, Farm School Manager (tel:01452 741023).
P Spaces: 20
& Wheelchair access to ground floor of manor house only. WC for the disabled. Guide Dogs: Yes
£ Adult: £2.50 (guided tour).

GREATER MANCHESTER

1830 Warehouse

The Museum of Science & Industry in Manchester, Liverpool Road, Castlefield, Manchester, Greater Manchester M3 4FP
Former railway warehouse, c1830, originally part of the Liverpool Road Railway Station (the oldest surviving passenger railway station in the world) which was the terminus of the Liverpool and Manchester Railway built by George Stephenson and his son Robert. Now part of The Museum of Science and Industry in Manchester.
www.msim.org.uk
Grant Recipient/Owner: The Museum of Science & Industry in Manchester
Access contact: Miss Val Smith
Tel: 0161 832 2244 **Fax:** 0161 833 1471
E-mail: marketing@msim.org.uk
Open: Daily (except 24/25/26 Dec) 10am - 5pm.
P Spaces: 50
& Yes. WC for the disabled. Guide Dogs: Yes
£ No. Free entry to all to main museum building. Charge for special exhibitions.

Albion Warehouse

Penny Meadow, Ashton-under-Lyne, Greater Manchester OL6 6HG
School, now warehouse. Built 1861-2 by Paull and Ayliffe in Italianate style.
Grant Recipient/Owner: G A Armstrong Ltd
Access contact: Mr David Armstrong
Tel: 0161 339 5353 **Fax:** 0161 339 5353
E-mail: enquiries@gaarmstrong.co.uk
Open: Mon - Sat 9am - 5pm. Closed Suns, BHs, Christmas Day and New Year's Day.
P Spaces: 10
& No. Guide Dogs: Yes **£** No

Dam House

Astley Hall Drive, Astley, Tyldesley, Greater Manchester M29 7TX
17th century house with extensive additions in the 19th century. Formerly a hospital, now a community facility. Retains many original and Regency features.
www.damhouse.org
Grant Recipient/Owner: Morts Astley Heritage Trust
Access contact: Mrs Helen Bolton
Tel: 01942 876417 **Fax:** 01942 876417
Open: Daily 9am - 5pm.
P Parking at rear. Spaces: 50
& Yes. WC for the disabled. Guide Dogs: Yes **£** No

Hall i' th' Wood Museum

Green Way, Bolton, Greater Manchester BL1 8UA

Grade I listed manor house, early 16th century, where Samuel Crompton invented and built his spinning mule in 1779. Part of the Hall is timber-framed and shows the development of a house in the 16th and 17th centuries. Now a museum.
www.boltonmuseums.org.uk
Grant Recipient/Owner: Bolton Metropolitan Borough Council
Access contact: Miss Elizabeth Shaw
Tel: 01204 332370 **Fax:** 01204 332215
Open: Provisional: Easter to end of Oct: Wed - Sun 11am - 5pm. Dates to be confirmed at time of publication, please contact the museum for information.
P Spaces: 8 **&** No **£** Adult: £2 Child: £1

Heaton Park Temple

Prestwich, Greater Manchester M25 2SW
Grade II* listed ornamental temple. Probably late 18th century, by James Wyatt. Situated on a hill in Heaton Park near Heaton Hall. The form is a simple, small rotunda of Tuscan columns with domed roof and lantern. It is said that Sir Thomas Egerton may have used the structure as an observatory.
www.manchester.gov.uk/leisure/parks/heaton.htm
Grant Recipient/Owner: Manchester City Council
Access contact: Mr Edward Flanagan
Tel: 0161 773 1085 **Fax:** 0161 798 0107
E-mail: e.flanagan@notes.manchester.gov
Open: The temple can be viewed externally 365 days a year. Access to the interior by arrangement. or when local artist is in residence (usually during summer months). Internal access also available in the winter through the park warden's team: please phone for details.
P Spaces: 500
& External viewing only possible: pathway to the temple on a steep incline. WC for the disabled. Guide Dogs: Yes
£ No

Kirkless Hall Farm

Farm Lane, New Springs, Wigan, Greater Manchester, WN2 1JP
Timber framed house enclosed in brick and divided into two houses. One of the two houses has been grant-aided. Timber frame partly repaired.
Grant Recipient/Owner/Access contact:
Mr Colin Hesketh
Tel: 01942 253014
Open: Access to the repaired timber-framed wall and exterior at all reasonable times. Access to the rooms in poor condition and non-public areas of the building by arrangement.
P Spaces: 2 **&** No. Guide Dogs: Yes **£** No

Manchester Law Library

14 Kennedy Street, Manchester M2 4BY
Built in Venetian Gothic style in 1885 to a design by Manchester architect, Thomas Hartas. Has stained glass windows by Evans of Birmingham.
www.manchester-law-library.co.uk
Grant Recipient/Owner: The Manchester Incorporated Law Library Society
Access contact: Mrs Jane Riley
Tel: 0161 236 6312 **Fax:** 0161 236 6119
E-mail: librarian@manchester-law-library.co.uk
Open: By prior telephone or written arrangement.
P No **&** No. Guide Dogs: Yes
£ No

Old Grammar School

Boarshaw Road, Middleton, Greater Manchester M24 6BR
Endowed by Elizabeth I in 1572, completed in 1584 with house added 1830s. Restored in 1998. Grade II* listed building with fine original oak beams and items of historical and local interest. An important early example of a building type for which there was little architectural precedent.
Grant Recipient/Owner: The Old Grammar School Trust
Access contact: Revd Canon N J Feist
Tel: 0161 643 2693 **Fax:** 0161 643 2693
E-mail: nickjfeist@ntlworld.com
Open: All year except Christmas/New Year period: Tues, Wed & Thurs 2 - 4pm. Parties by arrangement on 0161 643 7442 or 0161 643 2693. Regular

Opening arrangements at properties grant-aided by English Heritage

programme of events and use by community groups.

P Spaces: 9

& Yes. WC for the disabled. Guide Dogs: Yes

£ £1 (donation per person requested.

Ordsall Hall

Ordsall Lane, Salford, Greater Manchester M5 3AN

Ordsall Hall is a Grade I listed early 16th century timber-framed house, extended in brick and incorporating the remains of the original 14th century house. Once an important manor house and home to the wealthy and influential Radclyffe family.

www.ordsallhall.org.uk

Grant Recipient/Owner: Salford City Council

Access contact: The Director of Technical Services

Tel: 0161 793 3770

Open: Mon - Fri, 10am - 4pm; Sun, 1 - 4pm. Closed on Sats, Christmas Day and New Year's Day. For further information contact the Director of Technical Services at Salford City Council (tel: 0161 793 3770) or Ordsall Hall (tel: 0161 872 0251, fax: 0161 872 4951).

P Free parking in grounds. Spaces: 40

& Wheelchair access to ground floor only. WC for the disabled. Guide Dogs: Yes

£ No

Portico Library

57 Mosley Street, Manchester,

Greater Manchester M2 3HY

19th century subscription library with Reading Room and Gallery, situated in Manchester city centre. 25,000 volumes, mainly 19th century. Particularly valuable for Victorian studies. Gallery shows mainly art exhibitions of new and established artists' work - local, national and international. Occasionally literary/local history exhibitions also shown.

www.theportico.org.uk

Grant Recipient/Owner: The Trustees of the Portico Library

Access contact: Emma Marigliano

Tel: 0161 236 6785 **Fax:** 0161 236 6803

E-mail: librarian@theportico.org.uk

Open: Mon - Fri & 3rd Sun of each month: 9.30am - 4.30pm. Closed over Christmas period (usually 22 Dec - 2 Jan) & BHs.

P No **&** No. Guide Dogs: Yes **£** No

Tonge Hall

Middleton, Manchester, M24 2JT

Grade II* listed timber-framed hall c1580s with 18th and 19th century alterations. The Hall is a good example of 16th century carpentry and has a distinctive display of quatrefoil panels to front and left elevations.

Grant Recipient/Owner: Mr Norman Wolstonecroft

Access contact: Mr Norman Wolstonecroft

Tel: 01224 867893 or 0161 6431258

Open: By arrangement.

P Parking for disabled at front door. Spaces: 100

& Wheelchair access to ground floor only. No WC for the disabled. Guide Dogs: Yes

£ No

Victoria Baths

Hathersage Road, Manchester M13 0FE

Swimming pool complex built 1906, with 2 pools, Turkish and Russian Bath suite, Aerotone and extensive stained glass and tilework.

www.victoriabaths.org.uk

Grant Recipient/Owner: The Manchester Victoria Baths Trust

Access contact: Ms Gill Wright

Tel: 0161 224 2020 **Fax:** 0161 224 0707

E-mail: victoriabaths@aol.com

Open: At time of publication opening times still to be finalised. provisionally Mar - Oct, the first Sun in each month 12 - 3pm, and additional opening days including Heritage Open Days in Sept, but please ring to confirm. At other times by arrangement. with Ms Gill Wright of the Manchester Victoria Baths Trust, Studio 20, Imex Business Park, Hamilton Road, Longsight, Manchester M13 0PD (tel: 0161 224 2020).

P On-street parking during the week. Use of large adjacent car park at weekends by arrangement. Spaces: 5

& Wheelchair access to ground floor with assistance. No WC for the disabled. Guide Dogs: Yes

---

£ Admission charges may be introduced in 2004, please ring to confirm

HAMPSHIRE

Avington Park

Winchester, Hampshire SO21 1DB

Palladian mansion dating back to the 11th century, enlarged in 1670 by the addition of two wings and a classical Portico surmounted by three statues. Visited by Charles II and George IV. Has highly decorated State rooms and a Georgian church in the grounds.

www.avingtonpark.co.uk

Grant Recipient/Owner/Access contact:

Mrs Sarah Bullen

Tel: 01962 779260 **Fax:** 01962 779864

E-mail: sarah@avingtonpark.co.uk

Open: May - Sept: Suns and BHs (and every Mon in Aug) 2.50 - 5.30pm. At other times by arrangement.

P Spaces: 150

& Wheelchair access to ground floor only. Church with assistance (one step to interior). WC for the disabled. Guide Dogs: Yes

£ Adult: £3.75 Child: £1.75

Breamore Home Farm Tithe Barn

Breamore, nr. Fordingbridge, Hampshire SP6 2DD

Late 16th century tithe barn with dwarf walls supporting a timber-frame and external cladding under a tiled roof with massive timber aisle posts, double doors in the centre of each side and an area of threshing boards.

Grant Recipient/Owner: Breamore Ancient Buildings Conservation Trust

Access contact: Mr Michael Hulse

Tel: 01725 512858 **Fax:** 01725 512858

Open: Weekdays by arrangement. with Mr Michael Hulse of Breamore House.

P Spaces: 10 **&** Yes. No WC for the disabled. Guide Dogs: Yes

£ No

Calshot

Activities Main Hanger, Games Hanger & FFF Hanger, Calshot, Fawley, Hampshire SO45 1BR

Part of the most outstanding group of early aircraft structures of this type in Britain and the largest hanger built for use by fixed-wing aircraft during World War I. Now an activities centre.

Grant Recipient/Owner: Hampshire County Council

Access contact: Mr Peter Davies

Tel: 01962 841841 **Fax:** 01962 841326

E-mail: arccpd@pbrs.hants.gov.uk

Open: Daily except Christmas Day, Boxing Day and New Year's Day.

P Ample free on-site.

& Yes. WC for the disabled. Guide Dogs: Yes **£** No

The Deanery

The Close, Winchester, Hampshire SO23 9LS

Earliest remains are late 12th or early 13th century, fragments visible in a stairwell cupboard of the Prior's Hall. The hall itself is probably 13th century in origin. Until 1539 the Prior's House, now home of the Dean of Winchester.

www.winchester-cathedral.org.uk

Grant Recipient/Owner: The Chapter of Winchester

Access contact: Ms Kathryn Vere

Tel: 01962 857225 **Fax:** 01962 857201

E-mail: cathedral.office@winchester-cathedral.org.uk

Open: By written arrangement with the Cathedral Office, 1 The Close, Winchester, Hampshire SO23 9LS. Heritage Open Days in Sept, 2 - 4pm.

P No **&** No

£ Adult: £2.50 Child: £1 Booked groups: £2pp.

Highclere Castle & Park

Highclere, Newbury, Hampshire RG20 9RN

Early Victorian mansion rebuilt by Sir Charles Barry in 1842, surrounded by 'Capability' Brown parkland with numerous listed follies. Family home of the 8th Earl and Countess of Carnarvon.

www.highclerecastle.co.uk

Grant Recipient/Owner: Executors of the 7th Earl of Carnarvon & Lord Carnarvon

Access contact: Mr Alec Tompson

Tel: 01223 351421 **Fax:** 01223 324554

E-mail: agent@hwdean.co.uk

Open: Easter Sun & Mon (11 - 12 Apr); May BHs (2

- 3 May & 30 - 31 May); Aug BH (30 Aug); 6 July - 5 Sept, daily 11am- 5pm (closed Sats and Mons). Access enquiries may be made direct to the Castle (01635 253210).

P Unlimited parking.

& Wheelchair access to ground floor only. WC for the disabled. Guide Dogs: Yes

£ Adult: £7 Child: £3.50 Senior: £5.50

Manor Farmhouse

Hambledon, Hampshire PO7 4RW

12th century stone built house with later medieval wing. 17th and 18th century re-fronting of part and minor renovation.

Grant Recipient/Owner/Access contact: Mr Stuart Mason

Tel: 023 92632433

Open: By arrangement only.

P Spaces: 2 **&** Yes. No WC for the disabled. Guide Dogs: Yes

£ No

St Michael's Abbey

Farnborough, Hampshire GU14 7NQ

Grade I listed church and Imperial Mausoleum crypt of Napoleon III and his family. Abbey Church also built for the Empress Eugenie so the monks could act as custodians of the tombs. Now a Benedictine priory, raised to Abbey status in 1903.

www.farnboroughabbey.org

Grant Recipient/Owner: Empress Eugenie Memorial Trust

Access contact: Fr Magnus Wilson

Tel: 01252 546105 **Fax:** 01252 372822

E-mail: prior@farnboroughabbey.org

Open: Sats and Public Holidays at 3.30pm. Contact Fr Magnus Wilson, Bursar, or Fr D C Brogan, Prior, for further information.

P No **&** No **£** No

Whitchurch Silk Mill

28 Winchester Street, Whitchurch, Hampshire RG28 7AL

Grade II* watermill built c1800 and has been in continuous use as a silk weaving mill since the 1820s. Now a working museum, the winding, warping and weaving machinery installed between 1890 and 1927 produces traditional silks for theatrical costume, historic houses, fashion and artworks.

www.whitchurchsilkmill.org.uk

Grant Recipient/Owner: Hampshire Buildings Preservation Trust

Access contact: General Manager

Tel: 01256 892065 **Fax:** 01256 893882

E-mail: silkmill@btinternet.com

Open: Mill and shop: Tues - Sun 10.30am - 5pm (last adm 4.15pm). Mill and shop closed Mons (except BHs) and between Christmas and New Year.

P Free parking next to Mill, 2 disabled spaces next to shop and in adjacent car park. Spaces: 20

& Partial. WC for the disabled. Guide Dogs: Yes

£ Adult: £3.50 Child: £1.75 Other: £3

Family: £8.75

HEREFORDSHIRE

Chandos Manor

Rushall, Ledbury, Herefordshire HR8 2PA

Farmhouse, probably late 16th century with 18th century extensions. Timber-frame, partly rendered.

Grant Recipient/Owner: Mr Richard White

Access contact: Mr Richard White

Tel: 01531 660208

Open: Easter - Sept: Suns by arrangement.

P Spaces: 12

& No. Guide Dogs: Yes

£ Donations to charity requested

Chapel Farm

Wigmore, nr. Leominster, Herefordshire HR6 9UQ

Timber-framed farmhouse c1400 of rectangular plan, originally a hall-house with first floor inserted in the 16th century. Contains an open roof with foliate carved windbraces, ornate post-heads and late Elizabethan wall painting. Associated with the Lollards around 1400.

Grant Recipient/Owner/Access contact: Mr M Pollitt

Open: By written arrangement Mons (except BHs) May - Sept 2 - 4.30pm. Maximum 2 persons per visit. No children under 16 and no animals.

P Spaces: 1 **&** No **£** No

Eastnor Castle

nr. Ledbury, Herefordshire HR8 1RL
Norman-style castellated mansion set in the western slopes of the Malvern Hills. Constructed 1812 - 1820 and designed by Sir Robert Smirke, the castle has 15 state and other rooms fully-furnished and open to visitors. The decoration includes tapestries, paintings, armour and a drawing room by Augustus Pugin.
www.eastnorcastle.com
Grant Recipient/Owner: Mr J Hervey-Bathurst
Access contact: Mr S Foster
Tel: 01531 633160 **Fax:** 01531 631776
E-mail: enquiries@eastnorcastle.com
Open: Easter - end Sept: Suns & BH Mons, plus every day in July & Aug except Sat, 11am - 5pm.
P Spaces: 150
Wheelchair access to grounds and ground floor with assistance (always available). WC for the disabled. Guide Dogs: Yes
£ **Adult:** £6.50 **Child:** £4 **Senior:** £6

Hergest Court

Kington, Herefordshire HR5 3EG
House dates back to 1267 and was the ancestral home of the Clanvowe and Vaughan families. It is an unusual example of a fortified manor in the Welsh Mardes. It has literary associations with Sir John Clanvowe and Lewis Glyn Cothi.
Grant Recipient/Owner/Access contact: Mr W L Banks
Tel: 01544 230160 **Fax:** 01544 232031
E-mail: gardens@hergest.co.uk
Open: By arrangement with the Hergest Estate Office, Kington, Herefordshire HR5 3EG. Bookings by phone or fax with five days' notice.
P Spaces: 5
Wheelchair access to ground floor only. No WC for the disabled. Guide Dogs: Yes
£ **Adult:** £4 **Child:** Free **Groups:** £3.50

Lower Brockhampton

Brockhampton-by-Bromyard, Herefordshire WR6 5UH
A late 14th century moated manor house with a detached half-timbered 15th century gatehouse. Also, the ruins of a 12th century chapel. Woodland walks.
www.nationaltrust.org.uk
Grant Recipient/Owner: The National Trust
Access contact: Property Manager
Tel: 01885 488099 **Fax:** 01885 482151
E-mail: brockhampton@nationaltrust.org.uk
Open: House: 3 Mar - 30 Sept, Wed - Sun (open BH Mons) 12 - 5pm; 1 Oct - 31 Oct, Wed - Sun 12 noon - 4pm.
P Parking for disabled near house. Spaces: 60
Wheelchair access to ground floor of house, chapel and estate. No WC for the disabled. Guide Dogs: Yes
£ **Adult:** £3.50 **Child:** £1.75 **Family:** £8.50 Car Park: £2. Estate free to pedestrians

The Painted Room

Town Council Offices, Church Street,
Ledbury, Herefordshire HR8 1DH
The wall paintings, discovered here in 1989, are a unique example of domestic wall painting dating from the Tudor period. They are clearly the work of a commoner, created to imitate the rich tapestries or hangings that would have been found in the homes of the gentry.
Grant Recipient/Owner: Ledbury Town Council
Access contact: Mrs J McQuaid
Tel: 01531 632306 **Fax:** 01531 631193
E-mail: ledburytowncouncil@ledbury.org.uk
Open: Easter - end Sept: guided tours Mon - Fri, 11.00am - 1pm & 2 - 4pm; Sun, 2 - 5pm (from end of May - end Sept). Rest of year: Mon, Tues, Wed and Fri, 10am - 2pm, if member of staff available. Tours may be arranged out of these hours at a cost of £1 per adult (minimum 10 persons). Children's parties are free.
P Town centre car parks nearby.
No WC for the disabled. Guide Dogs: Yes
£ No charge when open normally (£1 for adults on out of hours tours) but donations welcome

HERTFORDSHIRE

Berkhamsted Town Hall

196 High Street, Berkhamsted, Hertfordshire HP4 3AP
Berkhamsted Town Hall and Market House, built in 1859, also housed the Mechanics' Institute. It has a gothic façade and retains much of the original stonework. There are three rooms: the Great Hall, Clock Room, Sessions Hall. In the Great Hall many of the original features have been preserved, including the fireplace and barrel vaulted ceiling.
Grant Recipient/Owner: Berkhamsted Town Hall Trust
Access contact: Ms Janet Few
Tel: 01442 862288
E-mail: janet_few@lineone.net
Open: Mon - Fri 10am - 1pm. At other times the Town Hall is let for functions. Additional opening by arrangement with the Town Hall Manager (tel:01442 862288).
P Parking in nearby public car parks.
Yes. WC for the disabled. Guide Dogs: Yes £ No

Bishop Seth Ward's Almshouses

Market Hill, High Street, Buntingford, Herts SG9 9AB
Almshouses c1684 (possibly by Robert Hooke) for Seth Ward, Bishop of Exeter and Salisbury, mathematician and astronomer and friend of Wren.
Grant Recipient/Owner: Bishop Seth Ward 's Almshouse Trust
Access contact: Mr R C Woods
Tel: 01763 271974 **Fax:** 01763 271974
Open: The exterior and gardens by arrangement. with Mr R C Woods, Chairman of the Trustees, Bishop Seth Ward's Almshouse Trust, 58 Hare Street Road, Buntingford, Hertfordshire SG9 9HN.
P No No £ No

Bridgewater Monument

Aldbury, Hertfordshire HP4 1LT
The monument was erected in 1832 to commemorate the Duke of Bridgewater. It is the focal point of Ashridge Estate which runs across the borders of Hertfordshire and Bucks along the main ridge of the Chilterns.
www.nationaltrust.org.uk
Grant Recipient/Owner: The National Trust
Access contact: Property Manager
Tel: 01442 851227 **Fax:** 01442 850000
E-mail: ashridge@nationaltrust.org.uk
Open: Estate: open all year. Visitor Centre: 27 Mar - 12 Dec, daily Mon - Fri 1 - 5pm; Sat, Sun, BH Mons & Good Fri 12 noon - 5pm. Monument: 27 Mar - Oct, Sat, Sun and BH Mons 12 noon - 5pm; Mon - Fri by arrangement., weather permitting.
P Spaces: 100
Wheelchair access to monument area, monument drive and visitor centre. WC for the disabled. Guide Dogs: Yes
£ **Adult:** £1.20 **Child:** 60p

Cromer Windmill

Ardeley, Stevenage, Hertfordshire SG2 7QA
Grade II* postmill dated 1674, last surviving postmill in Hertfordshire. Restored to working order (but not actually working). Houses displays about Hertfordshire's lost windmills, television and video display on the history of Cromer Mill and audio sound effects of a working mill.
www.hertsmuseums.org.uk
Grant Recipient/Owner: Hertfordshire Building Preservation Trust
Access contact: Ms Cristina Harrison
Tel: 01279 843301/07944 928552   **Fax:** 01279 841295
E-mail: cristinaharrison@hotmail.com
Open: Open Sat before National Mill Day, ie. second Sun in May. Thereafter Suns and BHs, and second and fourth Sats, until Heritage Open Days, 2.30 - 5pm. 30 minute video available for schools and other groups. Guided tours. Special parties by arrangement with Ms Cristina Harrison, The Forge Museum, High Street, Much Hadham, Hertfordshire SG10 6BS (tel:01279 843301 or 07944 928552). Refreshments available.
P Spaces: 20
Wheelchair access to ground floor only but video of upper floors showing all the time. No WC for the disabled. Guide Dogs: Yes
£ **Adult:** £1.50 **Child:** 25p

Ducklake House Wallpainting

Springhead, Ashwell, Baldock, Hertfordshire SG7 5LL
16th century wall painting, located on the ground floor, containing classical grotesques holding cartouches.
Grant Recipient/Owner: Mr P W H Saxton
Access contact: Mr P W H Saxton
Open: By written arrangement to view the wall painting only.
P Spaces: 1 No £ No

Knebworth House

Knebworth, nr. Stevenage, Hertfordshire SG3 6PY
Originally a Tudor manor house, rebuilt in gothic style in 1843. Contains rooms in various styles, which include a Jacobean banqueting hall. Set in 250 acres of parkland with 25 acres of formal gardens. Home of the Lytton family since 1490.
www.knebworthhouse.com
Grant Recipient/Owner: Knebworth House Education & Preservation Trust
Access contact: Mrs Christine Smith
Tel: 01438 812661 **Fax:** 01438 811908
E-mail: info@knebworthhouse.com
Open: 3 - 18 Apr, 29 May - 6 June, 3 July - 31 Aug: daily. 27 - 28 Mar, 24 Apr - 23 May, 12 - 27 June, 4 - 26 Sept: weekends & BHs only. Gardens, Park and Playground: 11am - 5.30pm. House: 12 noon - 5pm (last adm 4.15pm). Groups (20+) between 3 Apr - 26 Sept by arrangement.
P 50-75 parking spaces on gravel, unlimited space on grass.
Wheelchair access to ground floor of House only. Gravel paths around gardens and House but level route from car park to House entrance. WC for the disabled. Guide Dogs: Yes
£ **Adult:** £8.50 (£7.50 group) **Child:** £8 **Senior:** £8 (£7 group)

The Old Clockhouse

Cappell Lane, Stanstead Abbots, Hertfordshire SG12 8BU
Grammar school, now private residence, c1636 also used for Sun services in 17th century.
Grant Recipient/Owner/Access contact: Mr Michael Hannon
Tel: 01920 871495
Open: Access to exterior at all times; Bell Tower can only be viewed from High Street.
P Public car park in Stansted Abbots High Street.
No £ No

Redbournbury Mill

Redbournbury Lane, Redbourn Road,
St Albans, Hertfordshire AL3 6RS
18th century watermill in full working order after 10 year restoration programme following 1987 fire. Supplementary power from Crossley oil engine.
www.redbournmill.co.uk
Grant Recipient/Owner: Mr J T James
Access contact: Mrs A L James
Tel: 01582 792874 **Fax:** 01582 792874
E-mail: redbrymill@aol.com
Open: 21 Mar - 3 Oct: Suns 2.30 - 5pm, plus Easter, late May and Aug BHs. National Mills Weekend, Heritage Open Days and New Year's Day open all day. Special events all year. Private parties by arrangement. Refreshments available. Milling demonstrations. Organic flour and bread for sale.
P Spaces: 30
Wheelchair access to ground floor only. No WC for the disabled. Guide Dogs: No
£ **Adult:** £1.50 **Child:** 80p **Other:** 80p

Torilla

11 Wilkins Green Lane, Nast Hyde,
Hatfield, Hertfordshire AL10 9RT
'Torilla' (house at Nast Hyde) was built by F R S Yorke in 1935 in the international style and features a flat roof, 2 balconies and a large double height living room. Constructed of concrete with large steel framed windows. F R S Yorke was a key figure in the evolution of modern architecture in Britain.
Grant Recipient/Owner/Access contact: Mr Alan Charlton
Tel: 01707 259582
Open: By arrangement (written or telephone) 11am - 5pm on Sun 16 May and Sun 15 Aug. At other times by prior written arrangement.
P Spaces: 5
Wheelchair access to ground floor only. No WC for the disabled. Guide Dogs: Yes
£ No

Woodhall Park

Watton-at-Stone, Hertfordshire SG14 3NF
Country house, now school. Designed and built by Thomas Leverton in 1785 in neo-Classical style. Normally associated with London houses, this is one of

his few country houses. Highly decorated interiors which include the Print Room with walls covered in engraved paper, reproductions of paintings with frames, ribbons, chains, busts, candelabra and piers with vases.

Grant Recipient/Owner/Access contact: The Trustees of R M Abel Smith 1991 Settlement

Tel: 01920 830286 **Fax:** 01920 830162

E-mail: woodhallest@dial.pipex.com

Open: At all reasonable times, preferably school holidays, by arrangement. with the Trustees.

Ⓟ Parking limited to 10 spaces during school terms. Spaces: 30

Ⓗ Wheelchair access to ground floor only. No WC for the disabled. Guide Dogs: Yes

£ No

KENT

The Archbishops' Palace

Mill Street, Maidstone, Kent ME15 6YE

14th century Palace built by the Archbishops of Canterbury. Much altered and extended over the centuries, the interior contains 16th century panelling and fine wood or stone fireplaces. Now used as Kent County Council's Register Office.

Grant Recipient/Owner: Maidstone Borough Council

Access contact: Ms Annette Masters

Tel: 01622 752891

Open: Open all year for weddings and at other times by arrangement. with the Registrar.

Ⓟ Public parking in town centre car parks (pay and display). Spaces: 100

Ⓗ No. Guide Dogs: Yes £ No

Chiddingstone Castle

Chiddingstone, nr. Edenbridge, Kent TN8 7AD

Tudor mansion subsequently twice remodelled by the Streatfeilds whose seat it was. William Atkinson "Master of the picturesque" is responsible for the romantic design, c1805, of the building as it is today. Rescued from dereliction by Denys Bower in the 20th century, now managed by a charitable trust.

www.chiddingstone-castle.org.uk

Grant Recipient/Owner: Trustees of the Denys Eyre Bower Bequest

Access contact: Miss M R Eldridge MBE

Tel: 01892 870347

Open: Apr and May: Easter and Spring BHs only. June - Sept: Thurs, Sun and BHs. Weekdays: 2pm - 5.30pm. Sun and BHs: 11.30am - 5.30pm (last admittance 5pm). Groups (minimum 20), including school groups, all year by arrangement. No mobile phones.

Ⓟ Disabled parking available at entrance. Spaces: 50

Ⓗ Wheelchair access to ground floor (includes everything except the Egyptian collection) and tea room. WC for the disabled. Guide Dogs: Yes

£ **Adult:** £5 **Child:** £3 (5-15, under 5 free but must be accompanied by an adult)

Church House

72 High Street, Edenbridge, Kent TN8 5AR

Late 14th century timber-framed farmhouse, Tudor additions include fireplace and 18th century brick frontage. Now houses the Eden Valley Museum which illustrates economic and social changes during the 14th to 20th centuries.

www.evmt.org.uk

Grant Recipient/Owner: Edenbridge Town Council

Access contact: Mrs Jane Higgs

Tel: 01732 868102 **Fax:** 01732 867866

E-mail: curator@evmt.org.uk

Open: Oct - Mar: Tues and Wed 2 - 4.30pm; Thurs and Sat 10am - 4.30pm. Apr - Sept: Tues, Wed, Sun 2 - 4.30pm; Thurs & Sat 10am - 4.30 pm. Private/educational groups by arrangement.

Ⓟ Free parking in town centre car park, 200 yards from House. Spaces: 150

Ⓗ Wheelchair access grnd floor only (visual computer link to upstairs). WC for the disabled. Guide Dogs: Yes

£ **Adult:** £2 **Child:** 75p **Other:** 75p (disabled)

Cobham Hall and Dairy

Cobham, Kent DA12 3BL

Gothic-style dairy in grounds of Cobham Hall, built by James Wyatt c1790.

Grant Recipient/Owner: Cobham Hall Heritage Trust

Access contact: Mr N G Powell

Tel: 01474 823371 **Fax:** 01474 825904

E-mail: cobhamhall@aol.com

Open: Easter - July / Aug: Hall open Wed and Sun 2 - 5pm (last tour 4.30pm). Please telephone to confirm opening times. At other times (and coach parties) by arrangement. Self-guided tour of Gardens and Parkland (historical/conservation tour by arrangement.)

Ⓟ Spaces: 100

Ⓗ Wheelchair access to ground floor, manual assistance required for first floor access. WC for the disabled. Guide Dogs: Yes

£ **Adult:** £4.50 **Conc:** £3.50

Crabble Corn Mill

Lower Road, River, nr. Dover, Kent CT17 0UY

Georgian watermill with millpond, cottages and gardens. Guided and non-guided tours and demonstrations of milling techniques. Flour produced and sold on site. Cafeteria and art gallery. Available for group tours, functions and events.

Grant Recipient/Owner: Crabble Corn Mill Trust

Access contact: Mr Alan Davis

Tel: 01304 823292 **Fax:** 01304 823292

E-mail: miller@ccmt.org.uk

Open: Feb - Apr: Suns 11am - 5pm. Apr - Sept: Daily 11am - 5pm. Open to group visits all year round by arrangement. (contact Alan Davis, Tony Staveley, Anne Collins or Anthony Reid, tel: 01304 823292).

Ⓟ In recreation ground opposite site. Spaces: 32

Ⓗ Wheelchair access to ground and first floor, art gallery, cafeteria and milling floor. No WC for the disabled. Guide Dogs: Yes

£ **Adult:** £2.50 **Child:** £2 (age 5-15)

Conc: £2 **Family:** £6

Dover Town Hall

Biggin Street, Dover, Kent CT16 1DL

The Town Hall incorporates the remains of a medieval hospital, 14th century chapel tower, 19th century prison, town hall and assembly rooms. The Maison Dieu Hall of c1325 was originally part of a hospital founded by Hubert de Burgh in the early 13th century. The Town Hall designed by Victorian Gothic architect William Burges was built in 1881 on the site of the hospital.

www.dover.gov.uk/townhall/home.htm

Grant Recipient/Owner: Dover District Council

Access contact: Dover Town Hall

Tel: 01304 201 200

Open: Normally open during the week for functions & other bookings. Guided tours to be organised on two Suns per month June - Sept and one Sun per month Oct - May. To ensure access please telephone in advance.

Ⓟ Parking at the rear of the building.

Ⓗ Yes. WC for the disabled. Guide Dogs: Yes £ No

Gad's Hill Place

Higham, Rochester, Kent ME3 7PA

Former home of Charles Dickens, who lived here from 1856, until his death in 1870 whilst writing The Mystery of Edwin Drood. Built c1780 with Dickensian additions, it is now an Independent School and stands in 11 acres of playing fields and gardens.

Grant Recipient/Owner: Gad's Hill School

Access contact: Mrs Sheena Fitzgerald

Tel: 01474 822366 **Fax:** 01474 822977

E-mail: info@gadshill.org

Open: Sun 11 Apr; 2 May; 4 July; 1 Aug; 29 Aug; 3 Oct 2 - 5pm. Dickens Festival: 5 - 6 June and 4 - 5 Dec 11am - 4.30pm. Guided tours at other times by arrangement. Refreshments available.

Ⓟ Spaces: 40

Ⓗ Access for certain types of wheelchair only, please check with the Place for details. WC for the disabled. Guide Dogs: Yes

£ **Adult:** £5 **Child:** £2.50

Herne Windmill

Mill Lane, Herne Bay, Kent CT6 7DR

Kentish smock mill built 1789, worked by wind until 1952 and then by electricity until 1980. Bought by Kent County Council in 1985, which carried out some restoration. Now managed by Friends of Herne Mill on behalf of the County Council. Much of the original machinery is in place, some is run for demonstration and the sails used when the wind conditions permit.

www.kentwindmills.co.uk

Grant Recipient/Owner: Kent County Council

Access contact: Mr Ken Cole

Tel: 01227 361326

Open: Easter - end Sept: Sun and BHs, plus Thurs in Aug, 2 - 5pm. National Mills Weekend, Sat & Sun, 2 - 5pm. For further information contact Ken Cole, Secretary, Friends of Herne Mill (tel:01227 361326) or

---

Bill Martin (tel:01227 374539).

Ⓟ Six parking spaces in Mill grounds. Free on-street parking (Windmill Road). Spaces: 6

Ⓗ Wheelchair and guide dog access to ground floor of Mill and meeting room.WC for the disabled. Guide Dogs: Yes

£ **Adult:** £1 **Child:** 25p (accompanied by adult)

Ightham Mote

Ivy Hatch, Sevenoaks, Kent TN15 0NT

Moated manor house covering 650 years of history from medieval times to 1960s. Extended visitor route now includes the newly refurbished north-west quarter with Tudor Chapel, Billiards Room and Drawing Room. Interpretation displays and special exhibition featuring conservation in action.

www.nationaltrust.org.uk

Grant Recipient/Owner: The National Trust

Access contact: Property Manager

Tel: 01732 810378 **Fax:** 01732 811029

E-mail: ighthammote@nationaltrust.org.uk

Open: 28 Mar - 7 Nov, daily except Tues & Sat. House: 10.30am - 5.30pm; Garden 10am - 5.30pm. Estate open all year Dawn - Dusk.

Ⓟ Spaces: 420

Ⓗ Wheelchair access to ground floor with help and part of the exterior only. WC for the disabled. Guide Dogs: Yes

£ **Adult:** £6.50. **Child:** £3.50 **Other:** £16.50 (family), £5.50 (groups), no reduction on Sun or BHs

Penshurst Place Park

Tonbridge, Kent TN11 8DG

Open parkland, formerly a medieval deer park, circa 80 hectares. Scattered mature trees, lake with a small island and Lime Avenue originally planted in 1730s.

www.penshurstplace.com

Grant Recipient/Owner: Lord De L'Isle

Access contact: Mr Ian R Scott

Tel: 01892 870307 **Fax:** 01892 870866

E-mail: ianscott@penshurstplace.com

Open: Footpaths through parkland open 365 days a year.

Ⓟ Parking available. Spaces: 50

Ⓗ No. Guide Dogs: Yes £ No

Sissinghurst Tower

Sissinghurst, Cranbrook, Kent TN17 2AB

Red-brick prospect tower and walls - surviving part of an Elizabethan mansion. Surrounded by a world-famous garden. The study where Vita Sackville-West worked and Long Library are open to the public.

www.nationaltrust.org.uk

Grant Recipient/Owner: The National Trust

Access contact: Property Manager

Tel: 01580 710700 **Fax:** 01580 710702

E-mail: sissinghurst@nationaltrust.org.uk

Open: 20 Mar - 31 Oct, daily except Wed and Thurs 11am - 6.30pm. Sat, Sun & BHs 10am - 6.30pm. Last adm 1 hour before closing.

Ⓟ Spaces: 610

Ⓗ Wheelchair access to garden but some narrow paths and steps. For further detailed information contact the Property Manager (01580 710700). WC for the disabled. Guide Dogs: Yes

£ **Adult:** £7 **Child:** £3.50 **Other:** £17.50 (family)

Somerhill

Tonbridge, Kent TN11 0NJ

Grade I Jacobean mansion with Victorian addition set in 150 acres of parkland. Now used as a school, but original ceilings, panelling and stables have been retained.

Grant Recipient/Owner: Somerhill Charitable Trust Ltd

Access contact: Diane M Huntingford

Tel: 01732 352124 **Fax:** 01732 363381

Open: By written or telephone arrangement with Diane Huntingford, Administrator, plus the Sun of Heritage Open Days weekend.

Ⓟ Spaces: 170

Ⓗ Wheelchair access to ground floor only. No WC for the disabled. Guide Dogs: Yes

£ No

LANCASHIRE

Gawthorpe Hall

Padiham, nr. Burnley, Lancashire BB12 8UA

An Elizabethan property in the heart of industrial Lancashire. Restored and refurbished in the mid 19th

century by Sir Charles Barry. There are many notable paintings on display loaned to the National Trust by the National Portrait Gallery, and a collection of needlework, assembled by the last family member to live there, Rachel Kay-Shuttleworth.
www.nationaltrust.org.uk
Grant Recipient/Owner: The National Trust
Access contact: Property Manager
Tel: 01282 771004 **Fax:** 01282 770178
E-mail: gawthorpehall@nationaltrust.org.uk
Open: Hall: 1 Apr - 2 Nov, daily except Mon & Fri (but open Good Fri & BH Mons) 1 - 5pm. Garden: all year 10am - 6pm.
P Spaces: 50
♿ Wheelchair access to garden only. WC for the disabled. Guide Dogs: Yes
£ **Adult:** £3 **Child:** Free when accompanied by an adult **Other:** £1.50 (concessions), garden free

Grand Theatre

33 Church Street, Blackpool, Lancashire FY1 1HT
Grade II* 1200-seat theatre designed by Frank Matcham, 1894. Major restoration completed, Jan 2002.
www.blackpoolgrand.co.uk
Grant Recipient/Owner: Blackpool Grand Theatre Trust Ltd
Access contact: Mr David Fletcher
Tel: 01253 290111 **Fax:** 01253 751767
E-mail: info@blackpoolgrand.co.uk
Open: Daily. Tours take place on a semi-regular basis. Shows in the auditorium once or twice a day. Contact David Fletcher for more information.
P In West Street car park (2 min walk). Spaces: 200
♿ Wheelchair access to stalls and bar. WC for the disabled. Guide Dogs: Yes
£ **Adult:** £4 (guided tour). Charges made for performances

Harris Museum & Art Gallery

Market Square, Preston, Lancashire PR1 2PP
The Harris is a Grade I listed Greek Revival style building which opened in 1893, designed by James Hibbert. Collections of paintings, sculpture, textiles, costume, glass and ceramics and a permanent local history gallery, 'The Story of Preston'. Temporary exhibitions.
www.visitpreston.com/harris
Grant Recipient/Owner: Preston City Council
Access contact: Ms Alexandra Walker
Tel: 01772 258248 **Fax:** 01772 886764
E-mail: harris.museum@preston.gov.uk
Open: All year Mon - Sat 10am - 5pm, Suns 11am - 4pm. Closed on BHs.
P Public parking in Bus Station car park. Parking for disabled by museum entrance. Spaces: 1000
♿ Wheelchair access to all areas except Egyptian Balcony. WC for the disabled. Guide Dogs: Yes
£ No

Hoghton Tower

Hoghton, Preston, Lancashire PR5 0SH
16th century fortified manor house, ancestral home of the de Hoghton family since William the Conqueror. Associated with many kings and queens (the Banqueting Hall is where James I knighted the Loin of Beef 'Sirloin') and William Shakespeare. Various staterooms open to the public, as well as a Tudor horse-drawn well, dungeons and underground passages.
www.hoghtontower.co.uk
Grant Recipient/Owner:
Hoghton Tower Preservation Trust
Access contact: Mr John Graver
Tel: 01254 852986 **Fax:** 01254 852109
E-mail: mail@hoghtontower.co.uk
Open: July - Sept: Mon - Thurs, 11am - 4pm (Suns 1 - 5pm). Guided tours: BH Suns/Mons (excl. Christmas & New Year); private tours all year by arrangement.
P Spaces: 250
♿ Wheelchair access to Gardens, Banqueting Hall and Kings Hall. WC for the disabled. Guide Dogs: Yes
£ **Adult:** £5 **Conc:** £4 **Family:** £12

India Mill Chimney

Bolton Road, Darwen, Blackburn, Lancashire BB3 1AE
Chimney, 1867, built as part of cotton spinning mill. Brick with ashlar base. Square section, 300 feet high, in the style of an Italian campanile. Rests on foundation stone said to have been the largest single block quarried since Cleopatra's Needle. Listed Grade II*.
Grant Recipient/Owner/Access contact: Brookhouse Managed Properties Ltd
Open: Chimney visible from public highway (no interior access).
P On-street parking.
♿ Yes. No WC for the disabled. Guide Dogs: Yes £ No

Judges Lodgings

Church Street, Lancaster, Lancashire LA1 1YS
The home of Thomas Covell, Keeper of the Castle at the time of the Lancashire witch trials in 1612. For two centuries a Judges' Lodgings, now a museum with Regency period rooms, Gillow furniture, portraits by Wright of Derby, Romney and Lawrence. Museum of Childhood with historic doll collection.
Grant Recipient/Owner: Lancashire County Council
Access contact: Stephen Sartin
Tel: 01524 32808 **Fax:** 01524 846315
E-mail: judges.lodgings@mus.lancscc.gov.uk
Open: Good Fri - 30 June: Mon - Fri 1 - 4pm, Sat - Sun 12noon - 4pm. 1 July - 30 Sept: Mon - Fri 10am - 4pm, Sat - Sun 12noon - 4pm. Oct: Mon - Fri 1pm - 4pm, Sat - Sun 12noon - 4pm. Open BH weekends.
P Large car park nearby.
♿ Wheelchair access to ground floor only via side entrance. Please telephone in advance. No WC for the disabled. Guide Dogs: Yes
£ **Adult:** £2 **Child:** Free (accompanied by adult) **Conc:** £1

Leighton Hall

Carnforth, Lancashire LA5 9ST
Country House, 1765, probably by Richard Gillow, with earlier remains. Gothic south-east front early 19th century, possibly by Thomas Harrison. Tower at west end of the façade 1870 by Paley and Austin. Ancestral home of the Gillow family with fine furniture, paintings and objets d'art.
www.leightonhall.co.uk
Grant Recipient/Owner: Mr Richard Reynolds
Access contact: Mr & Mrs Richard Reynolds
Tel: 01524 734474 **Fax:** 01524 720357
E-mail: leightonhall@yahoo.co.uk
Open: 1 May - end of Sept: daily (except Sats and non-BH Mons), 2 - 5pm (12.30 - 5pm in Aug). Groups all year by arrangement. The owner reserves the right to close or restrict access to the Hall and grounds for special events (dates to be confirmed). Refreshments available.
P Spaces: 100
♿ Wheelchair access to ground floor, shop and tea rooms. WC for the disabled. Guide Dogs: Yes
£ **Adult:** £5 **Child:** £3.50 (age 5-12) **Conc:** £4.50 **Family:** £15

Rufford Old Hall

Rufford, nr. Ormskirk, Lancashire L40 1SG
Fine 16th century building with intricately carved movable wooden screen and hammerbeam roof. Owned by the Hesketh family for 400 years, the house contains collections of 16th and 17th century oak furniture, arms, armour and tapestries.
www.nationaltrust.org.uk
Grant Recipient/Owner: The National Trust
Access contact: Property Manager
Tel: 01704 821254 **Fax:** 01704 821254
E-mail: ruffordoldhall@nationaltrust.org.uk
Open: House: 3 Apr - 27 Oct, daily except Thurs & Fri 1 - 5pm. Garden: as house 11am - 5.30pm. Shop & Restaurant: 11am - 5pm. Open BH Mons and Good Fri. Winter opening: please telephone for details.
P Spaces: 130
♿ Wheelchair access to ground floor, restaurant, shop and garden. WC for the disabled. Guide Dogs: Yes
£ **Adult:** £4.50 **Child:** £2 **Family:** £11 **Garden only:** £2.50 **Booked Groups:** £2.75 (adult) £1 (child).

Samlesbury Hall

Preston New Road, Samlesbury, Preston, Lancs PR5 0UP
Built in 1325, the hall is an attractive black and white timbered manor house set in extensive grounds. Independently owned and administered since 1925 by The Samlesbury Hall Trust whose primary aim is to maintain and preserve the property for the enjoyment and pleasure of the public. Currently open to the public as an antiques/craft centre.
www.samlesburyhall.co.uk
Grant Recipient/Owner: Samlesbury Hall Trust
Access contact: Ms Sharon Jones
Tel: 01254 812010/01254 812229
Fax: 01254 812174
E-mail: samlesburyhall@btconnect.com
Open: Daily except Sats, 11am - 4.30pm. Open BHs. For Christmas closing times please contact the Hall (tel:01254 812010 or 01254 812229).
P Additional parking for 100 cars in overflow car park. Spaces: 70
♿ Wheelchair access to ground floors of historical part of Hall. WC for the disabled. Guide Dogs: Yes
£ **Adult:** £3 **Child:** £1.25 (age 4-16)

Smithills Hall

Smithills Dean Road, Bolton, Lancashire BL1 7NP
Grade I listed Hall, some parts of which date back to the medieval period. The early East Wing contains collection of mainly 17th century oak furniture. The largely Victorian West Wing has been recently conserved and includes Victorian period rooms, a shop, toilets and refreshments. Also a Grade II listed garden.
www.smithills.org
Grant Recipient/Owner: Bolton Metropolitan Borough Council
Access contact: Mr Ian Greenhalgh
Tel: 01204 332377 **Fax:** 01204 332377
E-mail: smithills_hall@hotmail.com
Open: Easter - end Sept: Tues - Sat 11am - 5pm, plus Suns 2 - 5pm. Oct - Easter: Winter opening, please telephone for further details (tel:01204 332377). Groups at other times of the year by arrangement with Administration, Smithills Hall and Park Trust, Smithills Hall, Smithills Dean Road, Bolton, Lancs BL1 7NP.
P Spaces: 40
♿ Wheelchair access to ground floor only. WC for the disabled. Guide Dogs: Yes
£ **Adult:** £3 **Child:** £1.75 **Other:** £1.75

Stonyhurst College

Stonyhurst, Clitheroe, Lancashire BB7 9PZ
16th century manor house, now home to a Catholic independent co-education boarding and day school. Contains dormitories, library, chapels, school-rooms and historical apartments.
www.stonyhurst.ac.uk
Grant Recipient/Owner: Stonyhurst College
Access contact: Miss Frances Ahearne
Tel: 01254 826345 **Fax:** 01254 826732
E-mail: domestic-bursar@stonyhurst.ac.uk
Open: House: 19 July - 30 Aug daily (except Fri), plus Aug BH Mon, 1 - 5pm; Gardens: 1 July - 30 Aug daily (except Fri), plus Aug BH Mon, 1 - 5pm. Coach parties by arrangement.
P Spaces: 200
♿ Limited wheelchair access but assistance is available by arrangement. WC for the disabled. Guide Dogs: Yes
£ **Adult:** £5 **Conc:** £4

Todmorden Unitarian Church

Honey Hole Road, Todmorden, Lancashire OL14 6LE
Grade I church with a large wooded burial ground and ornamental gardens designed by John Gibson, 1865-69. Victorian Gothic style with tall tower and spire. Detached smaller burial ground nearby and listed lodge in churchyard. Lavish interior with highly decorated fittings and furnishings. One of the most elaborate Nonconformist churches of the High Gothic Revival.
www.hct.org.uk
Grant Recipient/Owner: Historic Chapels Trust
Access contact: Mr Rob Goldthorpe
Tel: 01706 815648
E-mail: rob.goldthorpe@btinternet.com
Open: At all reasonable times by application to the keyholder, Mr Rob Goldthorpe, 14 Honey Hole Close, Todmorden, Lancashire OL14 6LH or by calling at the caretaker's house, Todmorden Lodge, at the entrance to the churchyard. Additional keyholders: Tristan Molloy (01706 813498); John Crabbe (01706 812446).
P Spaces: 10 ♿ Yes. WC for the disabled. Guide Dogs: Yes
£ No

Towneley Hall Art Gallery & Museum

Todmorden Road, Burnley, Lancashire BB11 3RQ
Former home of the Towneley family on outskirts of Burnley, Towneley Hall has been the town's art gallery and museum since 1903. The earliest part of the building dates from c1450. There is a 16th century chapel and Long Gallery, Baroque entrance hall and two reception rooms by Jeffrey Wyatville c1820.
www.towneleyhall.org.uk
Grant Recipient/Owner: Burnley Borough Council
Access contact: Ms Jackie Simm

Tel: 01282 424213 **Fax:** 01282 436138
E-mail: towneleyhall@burnley.gov.uk
Open: Mon - Thurs 10am - 5pm. Closed Fri. Sat & Sun 12 - 5pm. Open BHs but closed Christmas & New Year.
Ⓟ Free parking for cars and coaches.
⧗ Wheelchair access to 80% of the Hall, lifts available to all floors. Long Gallery can be viewed via a 'virtual tour'. WC for the disabled. Guide Dogs: Yes
£ Donations welcome

LEICESTERSHIRE

Rearsby Packhorse Bridge

Rearsby, Leicestershire LE7 4YE
Low narrow medieval bridge, perhaps 16th century, comprising 7 arches of random granite masonry and brick coping. On the upstream side there are 4 cutwaters, 3 of granite and 1 of brick. The bridge has recently been restored.
Grant Recipient/Owner: Leicestershire County Council
Access contact: Mr P Steer
Tel: 0116 265 7151 **Fax:** 0116 265 7135
E-mail: psteer@leics.gov.uk
Open: In use as a public highway.
Ⓟ Street parking.
⧗ Yes. No WC for the disabled. Guide Dogs: Yes £ No

Stanford Hall

Lutterworth, Leicestershire LE17 6DH
William and Mary house, built by the Smiths of Warwick (begun 1697), for Sir Roger Cave, ancestor of present owner whose family home it is. Visitors see every room on the ground floor (except modern kitchen), the "flying staircase" and two bedrooms. Contents include collection of Royal Stuart paintings.
Grant Recipient/Owner: Lady Braye
Access contact: Mr Robert Thomas
Tel: 01788 860250 **Fax:** 01788 860870
E-mail: enquiries@stanfordhall.co.uk
Open: 11 Apr - 26 Sept: Sun & BH Mon's, 1.30pm - 5.30pm (last adm 5pm). On BH Sun's & Mon's Grounds open at 12noon and earlier on Event Days. Open day or evening during the Season for booked groups of 20+.
Ⓟ Disabled parking adjacent to the house. Spaces: 1500
⧗ Wheelchair access to the Park, the Gardens, the Motorcycle Museum, the 1898 Flying Machine and the ground floor of the Hall if entrance steps can be negotiated. WC for the disabled. Guide Dogs: Yes
£ **Adult:** £5 (house and grounds), £3 (grounds only), £1 (museum) **Child:** £2 (house & grounds), £1 (grounds only), 35p (museum) **Other:** £4.75 (groups 20+, adult), £1.80 (group 20+, child)

Tomb of Andrew Lord Rollo

St Margaret's Church, Canning Place, Leicester
Grade II* listed tomb of 1765. Each face has a large rectangular plaque with ornate carved pilaster panels. The west front has a long inscription on the slate plaque recording the life and exploits of Andrew Lord Rollo, who died in 1765. The remaining three fronts each have a shallow carved relief of Lord Rollo's arms and military trophies.
Grant Recipient/Owner: The Abbey Parish PCC
Access contact: Mr Jack Adams
Tel: 0116 2897432
Open: The churchyard is open at all times.
Ⓟ Spaces: 3
⧗ Yes. No WC for disabled. Guide Dogs: Yes £ No

LINCOLNSHIRE

12 Minster Yard

Lincoln, Lincolnshire LN2 1PJ
House of early 14th, late 17th and 19th centuries.
Grant Recipient/Owner:
Dean & Chapter of Lincoln Cathedral
Access contact: Mrs Carol Heidschuster
Tel: 01522 527637 **Fax:** 01522 575 688
E-mail: worksmanager@lincolncathedral.com
Open: By written arrangement with the Works Manager, Lincoln Cathedral, 28 Eastgate, Lincoln LN2 4AA.
Ⓟ No ⧗ No. Guide Dogs: Yes £ No

13/13a Minster Yard

Lincoln, Lincolnshire LN2 1PW
Houses, mid-18th century, with late 18th and 19th century alterations.
Grant Recipient/Owner:
Dean & Chapter of Lincoln Cathedral
Access contact: Mrs Carol Heidschuster
Tel: 01522 527637 **Fax:** 01522 575 688
E-mail: worksmanager@lincolncathedral.com
Open: By written arrangement with the Works Manager, Lincoln Cathedral, 28 Eastgate, Lincoln LN2 4AA.
Ⓟ No ⧗ No. Guide Dogs: Yes £ No

17 Minster Yard

Lincoln, Lincolnshire LN2 1PX
13th and 14th century building with 15th century additions. Sacked in 1644 and restored 1671-94 and 1704-32 with internal alterations, c1813, by William Fowler. Further additions to the building were made in the late 19th century.
Grant Recipient/Owner: Dean & Chapter of Lincoln Cathedral
Access contact: Mrs Carol Heidschuster
Tel: 01522 527637 **Fax:** 01522 575 688
E-mail: worksmanager@lincolncathedral.com
Open: By written arrangement with the Works Manager, Lincoln Cathedral, 28 Eastgate, Lincoln LN2 4AA.
Ⓟ No ⧗ No. Guide Dogs: Yes £ No

18/18a Minster Yard

Lincoln, Lincolnshire LN2 1PX
13th and 14th century building with 17th century additions. Remodelled and extended in 1827 and re-fronted 1873 by J L Pearson.
Grant Recipient/Owner:
Dean & Chapter of Lincoln Cathedral
Access contact: Mrs Carol Heidschuster
Tel: 01522 527637 **Fax:** 01522 575 688
E-mail: worksmanager@lincolncathedral.com
Open: By written arrangement with the Works Manager, Lincoln Cathedral, 28 Eastgate, Lincoln LN2 4AA.
Ⓟ No ⧗ No. Guide Dogs: Yes £ No

3/3a Pottergate

Lincoln, Lincolnshire LN2 1PH
17th century house, now 2 houses, incorporating medieval walling. Remodelled in early 18th century with late 18th and 19th century alterations.
Grant Recipient/Owner: Dean & Chapter of Lincoln Cathedral
Access contact: Mrs Carol Heidschuster
Tel: 01522 527637 **Fax:** 01522 575688
E-mail: worksmanager@lincoln.cathedral.com
Open: By written arrangement with the Works Manager, Lincoln Cathedral, 28 Eastgate, Lincoln LN2 4AA.
Ⓟ Public parking in local authority car parks.
⧗ No £ No

3/3a Vicars Court

Lincoln, Lincolnshire LN2 1PT
Former priests' vicars lodgings, now 2 houses. Begun late 13th century by Bishop Sutton and completed c1309. Altered 15th century, re-roofed and altered late 16th, 17th, 18th and 19th centuries.
Grant Recipient/Owner: Dean & Chapter of Lincoln Cathedral
Access contact: Mrs Carol Heidschuster
Tel: 01522 527637 **Fax:** 01522 575688
E-mail: worksmanager@lincolncathedral.com
Open: By written arrangement with the Works Manager, Lincoln Cathedral, 28 Eastgate, Lincoln LN2 4AA.
Ⓟ No ⧗ No. Guide Dogs: Yes £ No

4 Pottergate

Lincoln, Lincolnshire LN2 1PH
14th and 15th century house, with mid-17th century additions. Altered c1760 and in the 19th century.
Grant Recipient/Owner: Dean & Chapter of Lincoln Cathedral
Access contact: Mrs Carol Heidschuster
Tel: 01522 527637 **Fax:** 01522 575688
E-mail: worksmanager@lincolncathedral.com

Open: By written arrangement with the Works Manager, Lincoln Cathedral, 28 Eastgate, Lincoln LN2 4AA.
Ⓟ No ⧗ No. Guide Dogs: Yes £ No

Arabella Aufrere Temple

Brocklesby Park, Grimsby, Lincolnshire DN41 8PN
Garden Temple of ashlar and red brick with coupled doric columns on either side of a central arch leading to a rear chamber. Built c1787 and attributed to James Wyatt. Inscription above inner door: "Dedicated by veneration and affection to the memory of Arabella Aufrere."
Grant Recipient/Owner: The Earl of Yarborough
Access contact: Mr H A Rayment
Tel: 01469 560214 **Fax:** 01469 561346
E-mail: office@brocklesby-estate.co.uk
Open: 1 Apr - 31 Aug: viewable from permissive paths through Mausoleum Woods at all reasonable times.
Ⓟ Free parking in village or walks car park, ¼ mile from site. Spaces: 10
⧗ No £ No

Brocklesby Mausoleum

Brocklesby Park, Grimsby, Lincolnshire DN41 8PN
Family Mausoleum designed by James Wyatt and built between 1787 and 1794 by Charles Anderson Pelham, who subsequently became Lord Yarborough, as a memorial to his wife Sophia who died at the age of 33. The classical design is based on the Temples of Vesta at Rome and Tivoli.
Grant Recipient/Owner: The Earl of Yarborough
Access contact: Mr H A Rayment
Tel: 01469 560214 **Fax:** 01469 561346
E-mail: office@brocklesby-estate.co.uk
Open: Exterior: 1 Apr - 31 Aug: viewable from permissive paths through Mausoleum Woods at all reasonable times. Interior (excluding private crypt) by arrangement with the Estate Office. Admission charge for interior.
Ⓟ Free parking in village or walks car park, ¼ mile from site. Spaces: 10
⧗ No. Guide Dogs: Yes
£ **Adult:** £2

Burghley House

Stamford, Lincolnshire PE9 3JY
Large country house built by William Cecil, Lord High Treasurer of England, between 1555 and 1587, and still lived in by descendants of his family. Eighteen State Rooms, many decorated by Antonio Verrio in the 17th century, housing a collection of artworks including 17th century Italian paintings, Japanese ceramics, European porcelain and wood carvings by Grinling Gibbons and his followers. There are also four State Beds, English and continental furniture, and tapestries and textiles. 'Capability' Brown parkland.
www.burghley.co.uk
Grant Recipient/Owner: Burghley House Preservation Trust Ltd
Access contact: Mr Philip Gompertz
Tel: 01780 752451 **Fax:** 01780 480125
E-mail: burghley@burghley.co.uk
Open: 27 Mar - 31 Oct: daily (except 4 Sept) 11am - 4.30pm. By guided tour only apart from Sun afternoons when there are guides in each room.
Ⓟ Parking for disabled available close to visitors' entrance. Spaces: 500
⧗ Yes. Please telephone the Property Manager for information on wheelchair access. WC for the disabled. Guide Dogs: Yes
£ **Adult:** £7.80 **Child:** £3.50 **Other:** £6.90 (senior citizens & students), £6.60 (per person for groups 20+), £3.40 (school groups up to 15 years of age), £19 (Family)

Harding House

48-54 Steep Hill, Lincoln, Lincolnshire LN2
Grade II listed house of the 16th century, remodelled in the 18th and restored in the 20th. Built of coursed rubble and brick with a pantile roof. The building is divided up into several studios predominately used for a variety of craft uses.
Grant Recipient/Owner: Lincoln City Council
Access contact: Mr Mark Wheater
Tel: 01522 873464 **Fax:** 01522 560049
E-mail: mark.wheater@lincoln.gov.uk
Open: During normal shop opening hours.
Ⓟ No ⧗ No. Guide Dogs: Yes £ No

Harlaxton Manor

Harlaxton, Grantham, Lincolnshire NG32 1AG

Grade I listed county house 1832-1844. Elizabethan, Revival style. Now a university. The owner, Gregory Gregory, acted largely as his own architect, in collaboration with Anthony Salvin 1832-1838. The interior decoration, c1837-1854, incorporates important plasterwork probably by Bernasconi.
www.ueharlax.ac.uk

Grant Recipient/Owner: University of Evansville-Harlaxton College

Access contact: Mr Ian Welsh

Tel: 01476 403000 **Fax:** 01476 403030

E-mail: iwelsh@ueharlax.ac.uk

Open: 6 June and 22 Aug 11am - 5pm open house. Guided tours (for approx. 20 plus) at other times by arrangement.

Ⓟ Spaces: 150 Ⓖ Yes. WC for disabled. Guide Dogs: Yes

£ **Adult:** £5 **Child:** £2 **Conc:** £4 (concessions), £4.80 (guided tours, including refreshments)

Heggy's Cottage

Hall Road, Haconby, nr. Bourne, Lincolnshire PE10 0UY

Built c1500 of mud and stud construction, a good example of early conversion to two storeys. Restored to its original state in 1995.

Grant Recipient/Owner: J E Atkinson & Son

Access contact: Mrs J F Atkinson

Tel: 01778 570790

Open: By written arrangement with Mrs J F Atkinson, Haconby Hall, nr. Bourne, Lincolnshire PE10 0UY.

Ⓟ Spaces: 1 Ⓖ No £ No

Jews Court

(the Society for Lincolnshire History & Archaeology), 2/3 Steep Hill, Lincoln, Lincolnshire LN2 1LS

Grade I two storey stone building, c12th century, with cellar and attic. Traditionally the medieval synagogue. Now used by the Society for Lincolnshire History & Archaeology and for worship.
www.lincolnshirepast.org.uk

Grant Recipient/Owner: Jews' Court Trust

Access contact: Ms Pearl Wheatley

Tel: 01522 521337 **Fax:** 01522 521337

Open: Daily except Suns, 10am - 4pm. Also closed over the Christmas period.

Ⓟ Ample public parking within 300 yards.

Ⓖ No. Guide Dogs: Yes £ No

Kyme Tower

Manor Farm, South Kyme, Lincoln, Lincolnshire LN4 4JN

23.5m high tower with one storey and a stair turret. Remainder of a fortified medieval manor house, built on the site of an Auginian priory, itself built on an Anglo-Saxon religious establishment. There are also visible earthworks of the former moat and fishponds on the site.

Grant Recipient/Owner: The Crown Estate Commissioners

Access contact: Mr W B Lamyman

Tel: 01526 860603

Open: By prior telephone arrangement with Mr W B Lamyman of Manor Farm (tel: 01526 860603). At least one week's notice required.

Ⓟ Spaces: 3 Ⓖ No £ No

Lincoln Castle

Castle Hill, Lincoln, Lincolnshire LN1 3AA

Lincoln Castle was begun by William the Conqueror in 1068. For 900 years the castle has been used as a court and prison. Many original features still stand and the wall walks provide magnificent views of the cathedral, city and surrounding countryside.
www.lincolnshire.gov.uk/lincolncastle

Grant Recipient/Owner: Lincolnshire County Council

Access contact: Mr Peter Allen

Tel: 01522 511068 **Fax:** 01522 512150

E-mail: allenp@lincolnshire.gov.uk

Open: Mon - Sat: 9.30am - 5.30pm. Sun 11am - 5.30pm. Winter closing at 4pm. Also closed 24 - 26 Dec, 31 Dec and 1 Jan.

Ⓟ Paid parking available in the Castle / Cathedral area.
Ⓖ Wheelchair access to grounds, Magna Carta exhibition, audio visual presentation and café. WC for the disabled. Guide Dogs: Yes

£ **Adult:** £2.50 **Child:** £1 (under 5s free) **Conc:** £1.50 **Family:** £6.50

Tattershall Castle

Tattershall, Lincoln, Lincolnshire LN4 4LR

A vast fortified and moated red-brick tower, built c1440 for Ralph Cromwell, Treasurer of England. The building was rescued from becoming derelict by Lord Curzon 1911-14 and contains four great chambers with enormous Gothic fireplaces, tapestries and brick vaulting. Gatehouse with museum room.
www.nationaltrust.org.uk

Grant Recipient/Owner: The National Trust

Access contact: The Custodian

Tel: 01526 342543 **Fax:** 01526 342543

E-mail: tattershallcastle@nationaltrust.org.uk

Open: 6 Mar - 28 Mar and 6 Nov - 12 Dec: Sat & Sun 12 noon - 4pm; 3 Apr - 31 Oct: Sat - Wed 11am - 5.30pm (11am - 4pm in Oct). Ground floor of Castle may occasionally be closed for functions or events.

Ⓟ Spaces: 40

Ⓖ Wheelchair access to ground floor via ramp. Photograph album of inaccessible parts of Castle. WC for the disabled. Guide Dogs: Yes

£ **Adult:** £3.50 **Child:** £1.80 **Other:** £8.80 (family)

Uffington Manor Gatepiers

Main Street, Uffington, nr. Stamford, Lincs PE9 4SN

Pair of Grade II* listed gatepiers, possibly by John Lumley c1700, surmounted by urns with wrought iron entrance gates with a coat of arms over of later 19th century date.

Grant Recipient/Owner/Access contact:
Mr David Pike

Tel: 01780 751944 **Fax:** 01780 489218

Open: Can be viewed from public roadway, otherwise by written arrangement.

Ⓟ Spaces: 2 Ⓖ No. Guide Dogs: Yes £ No

Westgate House

Westgate, Louth, Lincolnshire LN11 9YQ

Georgian town house in brick and stone, with 1775 additions and early Regency remodelling c1799 on Westgate façade. Interior contains fine plasterwork, mahogany doors, marble fireplaces and many original details. Used as a school 1937-1980s but now in course of restoration as a residence by the present owners, after dereliction.

Grant Recipient/Owner: Professor P Byrne

Access contact: Professor & Mrs P Byrne

Tel: 01507 354215

Open: Ground floor only: Easter Mon - 30 Sept, Wed, Sat & BH Mons 11.30am - 4.30pm. At other times by written arrangement.

Ⓟ Public parking in town centre (5 mins walk).
Ⓖ No. Guide Dogs: Yes

£ **Adult:** £2.50 **Child:** Free (when accompanied by an adult) **Other:** £2.50

LONDON

Bruce Castle Museum

(Haringey Libraries Archives & Museum Service), Lordship Lane, London N17 8NU

Once a 16th century manor house, Bruce Castle has been modified over the 17th, 18th and 19th centuries. Past owners include Sir Rowland Hill, the postal reformer, who ran a school here. Now a museum, set in parkland, it houses displays about the building, local history & art, and an archive.
www.haringey.gov.uk

Grant Recipient/Owner: London Borough of Haringey

Access contact: Ms Deborah Hedgecock

Tel: 020 8808 8772 **Fax:** 020 8808 4118

E-mail: museum.services@haringey.gov.uk

Open: Museum: Wed - Sun 1 - 5pm & all BH Mons. Closed Good Fri, 25/26 Dec & 1 Jan. Groups at other times by arrangement. Archive: Wed - Thurs 1 - 4.45pm, Fri 9.15am - 12noon & 1 - 4.45pm, Sat 1 - 4.45pm. Visitors to archive are advised to book.

Ⓟ Spaces: 15

Ⓖ Yes. WC for the disabled. Guide Dogs: Yes £ No

Charlton House Gateway

Charlton Road, London SE7 8RE

Located on the front lawn of Charlton House, the arch (previously known as the Gateway) marks the original front boundary to the House. The House is a Grade I listed Jacobean mansion, built 1607 - 1612 by Sir Adam Newton with later additions.
www.greenwich.gov.uk

Grant Recipient/Owner: London Borough of Greenwich

Access contact: Mrs Sue Brown

Tel: 020 8921 8337 **Fax:** 020 8921 8322

E-mail: sue.brown@greenwich.gov.uk

Open: All year: Mon - Fri 9am - 10pm, Sat 10am - 5pm. Closed on Suns.

Ⓟ Spaces: 25

Ⓖ Yes. WC for the disabled. Guide Dogs: Yes £ No

Clissold House

Stoke Newington Church Street, London N16

House built c1770 for Jonathan Hoare, a Quaker banker. Located in middle of Clissold Park, a late 18th Century park, developed in 1880s into a public park.

Grant Recipient/Owner: London Borough of Hackney

Access contact: Ms Carole Stewart

Tel: 020 8356 7476 **Fax:** 020 8356 7575

E-mail: carole.stewart@hackney.gov.uk

Open: Cafe is open throughout the year.

Ⓟ On street parking. Ⓖ No £ No

College of Arms

Queen Victoria Street, London EC4V 4BT

Built in 1670s/1680s to the design of Francis Sandford and Morris Emmett to house the Heralds' offices, on the site of their earlier building, Derby Place, which was destroyed in the Great Fire of 1666. The principal room is Earl Marshal's Court, which is two floors high with gallery, panelling and throne. New record room added 1842 and portico and terrace in 1867.
www.college-of-arms.gov.uk

Grant Recipient/Owner: College of Arms

Access contact: The Bursar

Tel: 020 7248 2762 **Fax:** 020 7248 6448

E-mail: enquiries@college-of-arms.gov.uk

Open: Earl Marshal's Court only: all year (except Public Holidays and State and Special Occasions), Mon - Fri 10am - 4pm. Group visits (up to 10) by arrangement. with the Bursar. Group tours of Record Room (up to 20) also by arrangement.

Ⓟ No Ⓖ No. Guide Dogs: Yes £ No

Countess of Derby's Almshouses

Church Hill, Harefield, London UB9 6DU

16th century range, established in 1636 for poor women of good character in the Parish of Harefield, known as the Countess of Derby Almshouses. Four stacks of paired or tripled diagonal brick chimney stacks. Originally housed six residents in 'one up one down' 'apartments' each with their own front door and staircase, hence the windows at first floor level. Converted to accommodate four on the ground floor only in the 1950s and undergoing conversion again in 2003/4 into two self-contained flats. Listed Grade II*.
www.harefieldcharities.co.uk

Grant Recipient/Owner: Harefield Parochial Charities

Access contact: Mrs Joyce Willis

Tel: 01895 822657 **Fax:** 01895 823644

E-mail: hpc@harefieldcharities.co.uk

Open: Acces to exterior from main road, Church Hill, Harefield.

Ⓟ On-street parking. Ⓖ No £ No

Dissenters' Chapel

Kensal Green Cemetery, Harrow Road, London W10 4RA

Grade II* building within Grade II* cemetery. Cemetery dates from 1832 and is London's oldest. The Chapel was designed in Greek Revival style by John Griffith in 1834. Now used by the Friends of Kensal Green Cemetery as a headquarters, exhibition space and art gallery and as a centre for their guided walks, lectures and special events.
www.hct.org.uk or www.kensalgreen.co.uk

Grant Recipient/Owner: Historic Chapels Trust

Access contact: Mr Henry Vivian-Neal

Tel: 020 8960 1030

E-mail: hvn@cix.co.uk

Open: Cemetery: daily; Dissenters' Chapel: Sun and at other times by arrangement. Guided tours of chapels and cemetery for modest charge, also tours of the Catacombs 1st and 3rd Sun in every month.

Ⓟ In adjacent streets, parking for disabled in cemetery.
Ⓖ Yes. WC for the disabled. Guide Dogs: Yes

£ £4 (donation requested for guided tours only)

Dr Johnson's House

17 Gough Square, London EC4A 3DE

Fine 18th century town house in the heart of the City of London. Here Dr Johnson compiled his dictionary

(published 1755). Original staircase and woodwork throughout and collection of prints, paintings and Johnson memorabilia.
www.drjohnsonshouse.org
Grant Recipient/Owner: Dr Johnson's House Trust
Access contact: Chair of Dr Johnson's House Trust
Tel: 020 7353 3745 **Fax:** 020 7353 3745
E-mail: curator@drjohnsonshouse.org
Open: Mon - Sat: May - Sept 11am - 5.30pm, Oct - Apr 11am - 5pm. Closed Suns and BHs.
Ⓟ On-street metered. Ⓖ No. WC for the disabled. Guide Dogs: Yes
£ **Adult:** £4 **Child:** £1 **Conc:** £3

Dulwich College

College Road, Dulwich, London SE21 7LD
Dulwich College was founded in 1619; the main buildings date from 1866-70 by the younger Charles Barry and are listed Grade II*. Three blocks lined by arcades in ornate Northern Italian Renaissance style. Close to Dulwich Village.
www.dulwich.org.uk
Grant Recipient/Owner: Dulwich College
Access contact: Ms Julia Field
Tel: 020 8693 3737 **Fax:** 020 8693 6319
E-mail: skinneraw@dulwich.org.uk
Open: Exterior visible from South Circular. Interior by arrangement with the Bursar.
Ⓟ 200 parking spaces in school holidays. Spaces: 50
Ⓖ Wheelchair access with help (a few steps at entrance). WC for the disabled. Guide Dogs: Yes
£ **Tour and archives:** £4, £6

Fulham Palace Stableyard Wall

Bishop's Avenue, London SW6
Home to the Bishops of London for over a thousand years to 1973. The two storey medieval west court is red brick with terracotta roof tiles. The mainly three storey Georgian east court is brown and yellow brick with parapets and slate roofs. Set in historic grounds near the river.
Grant Recipient/Owner: London Borough of Hammersmith & Fulham
Access contact: Ms Stella Washington
Tel: 020 8753 4960
E-mail: stella.washington@lbhf.gov.uk
Open: Palace grounds are open daily all year during daylight hours, admission free. Museum of Fulham Palace: Mar - Oct, Wed - Sun 2 - 5pm; Nov - Feb, Thurs - Sun 1 - 4pm. Display of principal rooms & gardens every 2nd & 4th Sun. Restoration works due to begin Aug 2004 will affect access to the Museum and Palace: please check for current information.
Ⓟ On-street meter parking. Spaces: 50
Ⓖ Prior notice required for wheelchair users wishing to visit ground floor to enable the ramp to be installed. Gardens accessible. WC for the disabled. Guide Dogs: Yes. £ No

Garrick's Temple

Hampton Court Rd, Richmond-upon-Thames, London TW12 2EN
The actor-manager David Garrick built the Temple in 1756 to celebrate the genius of William Shakespeare. The Temple was restored between 1997-1999 and now houses an exhibition of Garrick's acting career and life at Hampton, while the grounds have been landscaped to echo their original 18th century layout.
www.hampton-online.co.uk
Grant Recipient/Owner: London Borough of Richmond-upon-Thames
Access contact: Sara Bird/Mark De Novellis
Tel: 020 8831 6000 **Fax:** 020 8744 0501
E-mail: m.denovellis@richmond.gov.uk
Open: Temple: Suns, Apr - Sept 2 - 5pm. Also pre-arranged visits for small groups all year. Lawn: open all year 7.30am - dusk.
Ⓟ On Molesey Hurst, access via Ferry, running all day in summer.
Ⓖ Wheelchair access to lawn gardens only. No WC for the disabled. Guide Dogs: Yes £ No

Gunnersbury Park Temple

Gunnersbury Park, Popes Lane, Acton, London W3 8LQ
Grade II* listed temple. Built before 1760. Red brick with stone Doric portico. Situated in Gunnersbury Park, the estate of Princess Amelia in the 18th century. The 185 acre park became a public park in 1926.
Grant Recipient/Owner: London Borough of Hounslow
Access contact: The Curator

Tel: 020 8992 1612 **Fax:** 020 8752 0686
E-mail: gp-museum@cip.org.uk
Open: Park open daily 8am - dusk. The interior open for London Open House and at other times by arrangement. The Temple is used for events throughout the year and is available for hire.
Ⓟ Spaces: 120
Ⓖ Wheelchair access to exterior only. Two WCs for disabled within the park, but not close to Temple. Guide Dogs: Yes £ No

Hackney Empire

291 Mare Street, London E8 1EJ
Hackney Empire, designed and built by Frank Matcham in 1901, is one of the finest surviving variety theatres in Britain. Currently undergoing restoration and renovation and due to reopen in early 2004, providing modern facilities and access for all.
www.hackneyempire.co.uk
Grant Recipient/Owner: Hackney Empire Ltd
Access contact: Mr S Thomsett
Tel: 020 8510 4500 **Fax:** 020 8510 4530
E-mail: info@hackneyempire.co.uk
Open: Scheduled to open early 2004 after refurbishment.
Ⓟ On-street parking. Ⓖ Yes. WC for the disabled. Guide Dogs: Yes
£ No, but charges are made for performances. Free tours planned after re-opening

Highpoint

North Hill, Highgate, London N6 4BA
Two blocks of flats built in 1935 & 1938 by Lubetkin and Tecton. Constructed of reinforced concrete with decorative features.
Grant Recipient/Owner: Mantra Ltd
Access contact: Mr Stephen Ellman
Tel: 020 7554 5800 **Fax:** 020 7554 5801
E-mail: smc@grossfine.com
Open: By arrangement with Mr Stephen Ellman of Gross Fine, 14/16 Stephenson Way, London NW1 2HD.
Ⓟ No Ⓖ No. Guide Dogs: Yes £ No

The House Mill

Three Mill Lane, Bromley-by-Bow, London E3 3DU
Industrial water mill, originally built 1776 as part of a distillery. Four floors with remains of un-restored machinery, four water wheels and gearing. Originally had 12 pairs of millstones and has unique survival of Fairbairn-style "silent millstone machinery".
Grant Recipient/Owner: River Lea Tidal Mill Trust
Access contact: Ms Patricia Wilkinson
Tel: 020 8539 6726 **Fax:** 020 8539 2317
E-mail: pwilkinson@whippx.demon.co.uk
Open: Sun of National Mills Week, Heritage Open Days & the first Sun of each month Apr - Dec: 11am - 4pm. Other Suns May - Oct: 2 - 4pm. Groups by arrangement. with Ms Patricia Wilkinson, 1B Forest Drive East, Leytonstone, London E11 1JX. For further information tel. 020 8539 6726.
Ⓟ Nearby. Ⓖ Yes. WC for the disabled. Guide Dogs: Yes
£ **Adult:** £3 **Child:** Free **Other:** £1.50

Kew Bridge Steam Museum

Kew Bridge Pumping Station, Green Dragon Lane, Brentford, London TW8 0EN
19th century Victorian waterworks with original steam pumping engines which are operated every weekend. "Water for Life" gallery exploring 2000 years of London's water.
www.kbsm.org
Grant Recipient/Owner/Access contact: Kew Bridge Engines Trust & Water Supply Museum Ltd
Tel: 020 8568 4757 **Fax:** 020 8569 9978
E-mail: info@kbsm.org
Open: Daily 11am - 5pm. Closed Good Fri & 20 Dec 2003 - 2 Jan 2004. Prices may be increased for 2004, contact the Museum for up-to-date information.
Ⓟ Spaces: 45 Ⓖ Wheelchair access to 80% of museum. Two wheelchairs available. WC for the disabled. Guide Dogs: Yes
£ **Adult:** £4.60 **Child:** £2.50 **Other:** £3.70

Orleans House Gallery

Riverside, Twickenham, London TW1 3DJ
Orleans House Gallery comprises the Octagon Room with its fine Baroque interior, and the surviving wing/stable block of the 18th century Orleans House, the rest having been demolished in 1926. Overlooking

---

the Thames and residing in preserved natural woodland, the Gallery presents a programme of temporary exhibitions, organises educational projects/activities and is responsible for the Richmond Borough Art Collection.
www.richmond.gov.uk/orleanshouse
Grant Recipient/Owner: London Borough of Richmond-upon-Thames
Access contact: Mr Mark De Novellis
Tel: 020 8831 6000 **Fax:** 020 8744 0501
E-mail: m.denovellis@richmond.gov.uk
Open: All year, Tues - Sat 1 - 5.30pm; Suns 2 - 5.30pm. Oct - Mar, closes 4.30pm. Grounds open daily from 9am - dusk. For BH & Christmas opening hours please call in advance.
Ⓟ Spaces: 60
Ⓖ Wheelchair access to ground floor only. WC for the disabled. Guide Dogs: Yes £ No

Pitzhanger Manor House and Gallery

Walpole Park, Mattock Lane, London W5 5EQ
Pitzhanger Manor House is set in Walpole Park, Ealing and was owned and rebuilt by architect and surveyor Sir John Soane (1753-1837). Much of the house has been restored to its early 19th century style and a Victorian wing houses a collection of Martinware Pottery (1877-1923). Pitzhanger Manor Gallery opened in 1996 in a 1940s extension and exhibitions of professional contemporary art in all media are shown in both the House and Gallery.
www.ealing.gov.uk/pmgallery&house
Grant Recipient/Owner: London Borough of Ealing
Access contact: Pitzhanger Manor House and Gallery
Tel: 020 8567 1227 **Fax:** 020 8567 0596
E-mail: pmgallery&house@ealing.gov.uk
Open: Tues - Fri, 1 - 5pm, Sat 11am - 5pm. Summer Sun openings (ring for details). Closed BHs, Christmas and Easter.
Ⓟ For orange badge holders. Parking meters. Spaces: 2
Ⓖ Access for certain types of wheelchair with help (domestic lift & some steps). Please phone for further information. WC for the disabled. Guide Dogs: Yes
£ No

Prendergast School Murals

Hilly Fields, Adelaide Avenue, London SE4 1LE
Painted in the school hall in the 1930s by students of the Royal College of Art, the murals depict classical tales and incorporate local features.
Grant Recipient/Owner: Governors of Prendergast School
Access contact: Miss E Pienaar
Tel: 020 8690 3710 **Fax:** 020 8690 3155
E-mail: ericapienaar@yahoo.com
Open: By written arrangement in school hours in term-time.
Ⓟ No Ⓖ Yes. No WC for the disabled. Guide Dogs: Yes
£ No

Priory Church of the Order of St John

St John's Square, Clerkenwell, London EC1M
Remains of the Priory Church of the Knights Hospitallers' London headquarters, including choir and 12th century crypt. Museum in adjacent St John's Gate presents information on the Order of St John and conducts guided tours.
www.sja.org.uk/history
Grant Recipient/Owner: The Order of St John of Jerusalem
Access contact: Ms Pamela Willis
Tel: 020 7324 4071 **Fax:** 020 7336 0587
E-mail: museum@nhq.sja.org.uk.
Open: Guided tours: Tues, Fri & Sat 11am & 2.30pm. Other days & times by arrangement with the Museum.
Ⓟ Metered parking available in St John's Square.
Ⓖ Wheelchair access to Church with help, but not crypt. WC for disabled at St John's Gate. Guide Dogs: Yes
£ Donations requested for guided tours

The Queen's Chapel of the Savoy

Savoy Hill, Strand, London WC2R 0DA
Originally part of a hospital founded in 1512 by Henry VII. Rebuilt by Robert Smirke after a fire in 1864, from which time the ceiling covered with heraldic emblems dates. Recently restored.
Grant Recipient/Owner: Duchy of Lancaster
Access contact: Mr Phillip Chancellor
Tel: 020 7836 7221 **Fax:** 020 7379 8088
Open: All year except Aug & Sept: Tues - Fri 10.30am - 3.30pm; Sun for Morning Service only. Closed week

after Christmas Day and the week after Easter Day.
P Parking on meters in adjoining streets. Spaces: 2
♿ Wheelchair access to chapel via portable ramps.
No WC for the disabled. Guide Dogs: Yes **£** No

Rainham Hall

The Broadway, Rainham, Havering, London RM13 9YN
Georgian house built in 1729 to a symmetrical plan and with fine wrought iron gates, carved porch and interior panelling plasterwork.
www.nationaltrust.org.uk
Grant Recipient/Owner: The National Trust
Access contact: Property Manager
Tel: 01708 555 360
Open: Apr - end Oct: Wed & BH Mons 2 - 6pm. Sats by written arrangement with the tenant of the Hall.
P On-street pay-and-display parking nearby.
♿ Wheelchair access to ground floor only. Guide dogs by arrangement. WC for the disabled. Guide Dogs: Yes
£ Adult: £2.10 **Child:** £1 **Other:** No group reductions

Richmond Weir & Lock

Riverside, Richmond-upon-Thames, London
The lock and weir are important examples in the history of hydraulic engineering. Constructed in 1894 to control river levels between Richmond & Teddington at half-tide level, the weir was engineered to ensure that the river remained navigable at all times. Operated and maintained by the Port of London Authority since its establishment in 1909, the machinery was designed and built by Ransomes & Rapier.
www.portoflondon.co.uk
Grant Recipient/Owner: Port of London Authority
Access contact: Mr James Trimmer
Tel: 020 7743 7900 **Fax:** 020 7743 7998
E-mail: james.trimmer@pola.co.uk
Open: Open at all times for passage by river except for 3 weeks in Nov/Dec for maintenance undertaken by the Port of London Authority. The footbridge over the lock is currently open at all times, but this is under review due to sustained vandalism. Other works/facilities open as part of London Open House weekend.
P On-street parking. Please note this area is liable to flooding at high spring tides. Spaces: 50
♿ No **£** No

The Round Chapel (Clapton Park United Reformed Church)

1d Glenarm Road, London E5 0LY
Grade II* listed United Reformed Church, c1871. Horseshoe-shaped plan with roof and gallery supported by iron pillars. Detailed columns form a continuous iron arcade at roof level with latticework effects. Contemporary pulpit with double flight of stairs, organ and organ case.
Grant Recipient/Owner: Hackney Historic Buildings Trust
Access contact: Dr Ann Robey
Tel: 020 8525 0706 **Fax:** 020 8533 9517
E-mail: roundchapel@pop3.poptel.org.uk
Open: Many public/community events take place in the Round Chapel which the public can attend. Also available to hire for private events, otherwise access by arrangement.
P Spaces: 3
♿ Wheelchair access to ground floor only. WC for the disabled. Guide Dogs: Yes
£ No

Royal Geographical Society (with the Institute of British Geographers)

Lowther Lodge, 1 Kensington Gore, London SW7 2AR
Built by Norman Shaw, c1874-5, as a private house with a 2-acre garden for the Lowthers, the Lodge was one of the earliest and most influential works in the Queen Anne style. Bought by the RGS in 1912 and extended by them in 1930 to provide a lecture theatre. 'Unlocking the Archives' project, supported by the Heritage Lottery Fund, is underway. It will provide improved access, education facilities & increased conservation storage facilities for the Society's extensive heritage collections.
www.rgs.org
Grant Recipient/Owner: Royal Geographical Society
Access contact: Ms Denise Prior
Tel: 020 7591 3090 **Fax:** 020 7591 3091
E-mail: d.prior@rgs.org
Open: Weekdays (except BHs) 9.30am - 5.30pm. Closed 25 Dec - 1 Jan. Picture library 10am - 5pm by arrangement only. The remaining Collections (maps,

library, archives & artifacts) will reopen as a combined resource in June 2004. Contact Denise Prior for current information. Charges made for use of collections.
P On-street parking.
♿ Wheelchair access difficult above ground floor level. Contact House Manager for details. WC for the disabled. Guide Dogs: Yes
£ No

The Royal Institution of Great Britain

21 Albemarle Street, London W1S 4BS
Houses the Michael Faraday Museum and a 200 year old lecture theatre. Regular public lectures on scientific themes.
www.rigb.org
Grant Recipient/Owner: Royal Institution of Great Britain
Access contact: Mr Alan Winter
Tel: 020 7409 2992 **Fax:** 020 7629 3569
E-mail: alanw@ri.ac.uk
Open: Mon - Fri 9am - 5pm. Public lectures/events on various days of the week, usually starting at 6.30 or 7.30pm. Lecture lists published on RI website (www.rigb.org).
P No ♿ Yes. WC for the disabled. Guide Dogs: Yes
£ Adult: £1 (museum), £8.00 (lecture)**Child:** 50p (museum), £5 (lecture) **Other:** Schools free

St Alban (now the Landmark Arts Centre)

Ferry Road, Teddington, London TW11 9NN
Grade II* former church, c1889, in French-Gothic style by architect William Niven. A number of intended architectural features were never in the end built, due to insufficient funds (hence the incomplete flying buttresses for example). Redundant as a church in 1977. Following renovation now used as an Arts Centre with a variety of arts events, classes and private events.
www.landmarkartscentre.org
Grant Recipient/Owner: London Diocesan Fund
Access contact: Mr Graham Watson
Tel: 020 8614 8036 **Fax:** 020 8614 8080
Open: Mon - Fri 10am - 5pm (shorter hours at w/e when public events are held), visitors advised to contact Lorna Henderson at the Landmark Arts Centre (tel:020 8977 7558, fax: 020 8977 4830, email: landmarkinfo@aol.com) to check. Other times by arrangement with Lorna Henderson, subject to staff availability.
P Additional on-street parking nearby. Spaces: 4
♿ Yes. WC for the disabled. Guide Dogs: Yes
£ No. Admission charges for some public events

St Ethelburga's Centre for Reconciliation and Peace

78 Bishopgate, London EC2N 4AG
Church of St Ethelburga the Virgin built in the late 14th and early 15th centuries. Devastated by a terrorist bomb in Apr 1993 and re-opened in Nov 2002, after restoration, for use as a Centre for Reconciliation and Peace.
www.stethelburgas.org
Grant Recipient/Owner: St Ethelburga's Centre for Reconciliation & Peace
Access contact: Mr Ronald Smith
Tel: 020 7496 1610 **Fax:** 020 7638 1440
E-mail: enquiries@stethelburgas.org
Open: Wed 11am - 3pm & first Fri in every month 12 noon - 2.30pm. Groups may visit at other times by arrangement. Details of services, public lectures and other events available from the website or by telephone.
P No ♿ Yes. WC for the disabled. Guide Dogs: Yes
£ No

St Matthias Old Church

113 Poplar High Street, Poplar, London E14 0AE
Built by in 1650-54 by the East India Company, St Matthias Old Church is the oldest building in Docklands. Declared redundant in 1977, the building became derelict. In 1990 the building was restored and is now used as a community arts/cultural centre.
Grant Recipient/Owner: London Diocesan Fund
Access contact: Mrs Kathleen Haley
Tel: 020 7987 0459 **Fax:** 020 7531 9973
Open: Mons: 11am - 1pm.
P Car park for limited number of cars. ♿ Yes. WC for the disabled. Guide Dogs: Yes **£** No.

St Pancras Chambers

Euston Road, London NW1 2QR
Grade I listed Gothic-style building fronting St Pancras Station. Built as the Midland Grand Hotel 1868 - 1876 to designs by Sir George Gilbert Scott. Key features are its impressive grand gothic façade and sweeping 'fairytale' staircase.
www.lcrproperties.co.uk
Grant Recipient/Owner: British Railways Board/London & Continental Stations & Property Ltd
Access contact: Miss Laura Peck
Tel: 020 7304 3927 **Fax:** 020 7304 3901
E-mail: lpeck@lcsp.co.uk
Open: The front entrance & former ground floor coffee lounge are generally open each weekday 11.30am - 3.30pm without charge (except during filming & events). Tours Sat & Sun 11am & 1.30pm last approx. 1 hour (max 25 on a first come first serve basis). Tours are conducted by experienced guides who have a unique understanding of the building & its history. Please note that tours involve climbing several flights of stairs and that there are no working lifts or other facilities for disabled visitors. For further information on tours please telephone 020 7304 3921.
P No ♿ No **£** Adult: £7.50 (private tour), £5.00 (public tour)
Child: Free (must be accompanied by a paying adult)

Victoria Embankment Gardens

Whitehall Court, Westminster, London SW1
Part of Victoria Embankment Gardens which run along the side of the Embankment from Westminster to Temple tube. The gardens are formal and have a wide range of monuments. The Whitehall section has been restored to the original design and retains many original trees and specimens of note.
Grant Recipient/Owner: Westminster City Council
Access contact: Mr Colin Buttery
Tel: 020 7641 2693 **Fax:** 020 7641 2959
E-mail: cbuttery@westminster.gov.uk
Open: Daily 7.30am - dusk all year. **P** Limited on-street parking at meters. ♿ Yes. WC for the disabled. Guide Dogs: Yes **£** No

Walpole's House

St Mary's College, Strawberry Hill, Waldegrave Road, Twickenham, London TW1 4SX
Bought by Horace Walpole in 1749 and over the next half century converted into his own vision of a 'gothic' fantasy with 14 rooms open to the public containing chimneypieces based on medieval tombs & a collection of 16th century painted glass roundels. Reputedly the first substantial building of the Gothic Revival.
Grant Recipient/Owner: St Mary's, Strawberry Hill
Access contact: Head of Catering and Conference Services
Tel: 020 8240 4044 **Fax:** 020 8255 4255
E-mail: gallaghs@smuc.ac.uk
Open: 2 May - 26 Sept, Sun only 2 - 3.30pm. Guided group tours (10+) by arrangement on any day except Sat.
P Spaces: 60
♿ Wheelchair access to ground floor & grounds with difficulty, doorways are small. WC for the disabled. Guide Dogs: Yes
£ Adult: £5 **Other:** £4.25.

Wapping Hydraulic Power Pumping Station

Wapping Wall, London E1W 3ST
Wapping Hydraulic Power Station was built by the London Hydraulic Power Company in 1890. One of the 5 London Stations of its kind, it used Thames water to provide power throughout the central London area. The showcase building of the LHPC, used as a model for power stations in Argentina, Australia, New York & Europe, it now houses an art gallery & restaurant.
Grant Recipient/Owner/Access contact: Women's Playhouse Trust
Tel: 020 7680 2080 **Fax:** 020 7680 2081
E-mail: info@wapping-wpt.com
Open: Mon - Fri: 12 noon - Midnight. Sat 10am - Midnight, Sun 10am - 6pm. Open all year except Christmas & New Year BHs.
P Spaces: 30 ♿ Yes. WC for the disabled. Guide Dogs: Yes **£** No

Whitechapel Art Gallery

Whitechapel High Street, London E1 7QX
Grade II* listed Arts and Crafts building constructed in the late 1890s by C H Townsend. Occupied by the

Whitechapel Art Gallery, which was founded in 1901 by the Revd Canon Barnett 'to bring great art to the people of the East End'.
www.whitechapel.org
Grant Recipient/Owner: Trustees of the Whitechapel Art Gallery
Access contact: Annette Graham / Demitra Procopiou
Tel: 020 7522 7888/7865 **Fax:** 020 7377 1685
E-mail: info@whitechapel.org
Open: All year: Tues - Sun 11am - 6pm, Thurs 11am - 9pm. Various exhibitions (5 - 6 per year).
[P] Paid parking in Spreadeagle Yard off Whitechapel High Street.
[♿] Yes. WC for the disabled. Guide Dogs: Yes
[£] No. But one exhibition per year will have entrance fee

MERSEYSIDE

Bluecoat Arts Centre

School Lane, Liverpool, Merseyside L1 3BX
Grade I listed Queen Anne building dated 1717 housing contemporary art gallery, performance space, artists' studios, café bar, crafts centre, shops and garden courtyard. Originally a charity school and the oldest building in Liverpool city centre. Reputedly the oldest arts centre in the country.
www.bluecoatartscentre.com
Grant Recipient/Owner: Bluecoat Arts Centre Ltd
Access contact: Anne Jones
Tel: 0151 709 5297 **Fax:** 0151 707 0048
E-mail: admin@bluecoatartscentre.com.uk
Open: All year (except Sun & BHs) Mon - Sat 9am - 5.30pm. Art Gallery open Tues - Sat 10.30am - 5.00pm except during exhibition changeovers. Performances of music, dance, poetry and other events take place in the evening.
[P] NCP car parks in Paradise St and Hanover St. Disabled parking spaces in College Lane close to buildings rear entrance.
[♿] Wheelchair access to ground floor only inc. cafe, gallery, crafts centre & some shops. Building will undergo access improvements in 2005. WC for the disabled. Guide Dogs: Yes
[£] No, but charges for performances (concessions available)

Broughton Hall Conservatory

Convent of Mercy, Yew Tree Lane, West Derby, Liverpool, Merseyside L12 9HH
Victorian conservatory of rectangular shape with an entrance porch at one end and an access bay to main building, at the other. The cast iron structure is mounted on a stone plinth. The elevations are divided into a series of panels with decorated cast iron circular columns. From the capitols spring semi-circular arches. These form the bases of the frieze moulding which runs round the periphery of the building. The flooring is of quarry tiles.
Grant Recipient/Owner: The Institute of Our Lady of Mercy
Access contact: The Sister Superior
Tel: 0151 228 9232 **Fax:** 0151 259 0677
Open: By written arrangement only, Mon - Sat 10am - 4pm. No access on Suns or BHs.
[P] Spaces: 4 [♿] Yes. WC for the disabled. Guide Dogs: Yes [£] No

Ince Blundell Hall & Garden Temple

Hightown, Liverpool, Merseyside L38 6JN
New Hall built c1720-50 with 19th century additions. Brick with stone dressings in nine bays with central Corinthian pilasters and demi-columns. Domed Pantheon added 1802. Rococo stucco ceiling in Drawing Room c1750 and Dining Room decoration by Crace. Garden Temple c1780 by William Everard of Liverpool with Tuscan columns and antique reliefs.
Grant Recipient/Owner/Access contact: Auginian Nursing Sisters of the Mercy of Jesus
Tel: 0151 929 2596 **Fax:** 0151 929 2188
Open: By telephone or written arrangement.
[P] Spaces: 10 [♿] No [£] No

Liverpool Collegiate Apartments

Shaw Street, Liverpool, Merseyside L6 1NR
Grade II* former school built 1843 of red sandstone in Tudor Gothic style, gutted by fire, now converted into residential block.
Grant Recipient/Owner: Urban Splash Ltd
Access contact: Mr Bill Maynard
Tel: 0161 839 2999 **Fax:** 0161 839 8999
E-mail: billmaynard@urbansplash.co.uk
Open: Exterior only, visible from Shaw Street.
[P] No [♿] Yes. No WC for the disabled. Guide Dogs: No
[£] No

Meols Hall

Churchtown, Southport, Merseyside PR9 7LZ
17th century house with 18th & 19th century alterations. Substantially rebuilt in 1960-94 by amateur architect Roger Hesketh, using materials from other houses demolished after the Second World War. For its mix of old and new Meols Hall has been acclaimed as one of the most convincing country houses created since the war.
www.meolshall.com
Grant Recipient/Owner/Access contact: Mr Robert Hesketh
Tel: 01704 228326 **Fax:** 01704 507185
E-mail: events@meolshall.com
Open: 1 - 3 May (as part of the Southport Spring Garden Festival), 14 Aug - 14 Sept daily 2 - 5pm.
[P] Spaces: 200
[♿] Yes. WC for the disabled. Guide Dogs: Yes
[£] **Adult:** £4 **Child:** £1 **Other:** Concession for Garden Festival visitors only in May

Sefton Park

Liverpool, Merseyside L18 3JD
108 hectare public park, designed in 1867, the first to introduce French influence to the design of parks through the designer Edouard André who had worked on the design of major Parisian parks. Sefton Park is Grade II* registered and contains several listed statues and other features. The Grade II* listed Palm House, 1896 by Mackenzie and Moncur, is an octagonal iron frame structure which appears as 3 domed roofs, one above the other.
www.palmhouse.org.uk
Grant Recipient/Owner: Liverpool City Council
Access contact: Ms Elizabeth-Anne Williams
Tel: 0151 726 9304 **Fax:** 0151 726 2419
E-mail: info@palmhouse.org.uk
Open: Park open at all times. Palm House: Jan - 31 Mar: Mon - Sun 10.30am - 4pm, may close on Tues and Thurs for events; 1 Apr - 31 Dec: Mon - Sat 10.30am - 5pm, Sun 10.30am - 4pm, may close on Tues & Thurs & from 4pm for events. The Trust reserves the right to shut the Palm House on other occasions and will endeavour to give as much notice as possible on the website and information line (tel:0151 726 2415).
[P] On-street parking available on edge of park.
[♿] Yes. No WC for the disabled. Guide Dogs: Yes [£] No

Speke Hall

The Walk, Liverpool, Merseyside L24 1XD
One of the most important timber framed manor houses in the country, dating from 1530. The interior spans many periods: the Great Hall and priest holes evoke Tudor times, the Oak Parlour and smaller rooms, some with William Morris wallpapers, show the Victorian desire for privacy and comfort. There is some Jacobean plasterwork and intricately carved furniture. Restored garden and woodland walks.
www.nationaltrust.org.uk
Grant Recipient/Owner: The National Trust
Access contact: Property Manager
Tel: 0151 427 7231 **Fax:** 0151 427 9860
E-mail: spekehall@nationaltrust.org.uk
Open: House: 20 Mar - end Oct, Wed - Sun (open BHs); Nov and Dec, Sat & Sun only. Times: Mar - mid Oct 1 - 5.30pm; mid Oct - Dec 1 - 4.30pm. Woodland and garden: open daily throughout the year, closed 24 - 26 and 31 Dec, 1 Jan. Times: Mar - mid Oct 11am - 5.30pm; mid Oct - mid Mar 2004 11am - dusk.
[P] 500 yards from property. Courtesy shuttle service available. Spaces: 400
[♿] Wheelchair access to ground floor of house. WC for the disabled. Guide Dogs: Yes
[£] **Adult:** £6, £3 (grounds only) **Child:** £3.50, £1.50 (grounds only) **Other:** £17 (family), £9 grounds only)

NORFOLK

The Deanery

56 The Close, Norwich, Norfolk NR1 4EG
13th century with later additions, originally the Prior's lodgings. It remains the residence of the Dean of Norwich. The interior is closed to the public.
www.cathedral.org.uk
Grant Recipient/Owner: The Chapter of Norwich Cathedral
Access contact: Mr Tim Cawkwell
Tel: 01603 218300 **Fax:** 01603 766032
E-mail: steward@cathedral.org.uk
Open: Exterior visible from The Close which is open to visitors during daylight hours throughout the year.
[P] No [♿] Yes. No WC for the disabled. Guide Dogs: No
[£] No

Felbrigg Hall

Felbrigg, Norwich, Norfolk NR11 8PR
17th century house containing its original 18th century furniture and paintings. The walled garden has been restored and features a working dovecote, small orchard and the national collection of Colchicum. The park is renowned for its fine and aged trees.
www.nationaltrust.org.uk
Grant Recipient/Owner: The National Trust
Access contact: Property Manager
Tel: 01263 837444 **Fax:** 01263 837032
E-mail: felbrigg@nationaltrust.org.uk
Open: House: 20 Mar - 31 Oct: daily except Thurs & Fri, 1 - 5pm. Garden: 20 Mar - 31 Oct: daily except Thurs & Fri, 11am - 5pm (22 July - 3 Sept: daily 11am - 5pm) Estate walks: daily, dawn to dusk.
[P] Visitors with disabilities may be set down at Visitor Reception by arrangement. Spaces: 200
[♿] Wheelchair access to ground floor, photograph album of first floor. Garden, shop & bookshop (ramp), tearoom & restaurant accessible. WC for the disabled. Guide Dogs: Yes
[£] **Adult:** £6.30 **Child:** £3 **Other:** £15.50 (family), £2.60 (gardens only)

Hales Hall Barn

Loddon, Norfolk NR14 6QW
Late 15th century brick and thatch barn 180ft long, built by James Hobart, Henry VII's Attorney General. Queen post roof, and crown post roof to living accommodation, and richly patterned brickwork. The Barn and similar sized gatehouse, ranged around defended courtyards, are all that remains of the house that once stood on this site. Large garden with topiary and yew hedges, and national collections of citrus, grapes and figs.
www.haleshall.com
Grant Recipient/Owner/Access contact: Mr & Mrs Terence Read
Tel: 01508 548507 **Fax:** 01508 548040
E-mail: judy@haleshall.com
Open: All year, Tues - Sat 10am - 5pm (or dusk if earlier); plus Easter - Oct, Sun pms & BH Mons 11am - 4pm. Closed 25 Dec - 5 Jan & Good Fri. Garden with yew & box topiary included in charge. Parties & guided tours by arrangement with owners. Barn and garden may be used for wedding receptions, particularly Sat afternoon: telephone to ensure access.
[P] Spaces: 40
[♿] Yes. WC for the disabled. Guide Dogs: Yes
[£] **Adult:** £2 (including guide) **Child:** Free
Other: £1.50, £3 (guided tours by arrangement)

King's Lynn Custom House

Purfleet Quay, King's Lynn, Norfolk PE30 1HP
Built 1683 as a merchants exchange, became official Custom House in 1703. Building purchased by the Crown in 1717 for £800 and was used by HM Customs until 1989. The Borough Council of King's Lynn and West Norfolk obtained a lease of the building in 1995 and restored it.
Grant Recipient/Owner: King's Lynn & West Norfolk Council
Access contact: Mrs Karen Cooke
Tel: 01553 763044 **Fax:** 01553 819441
E-mail: kings-lynn.tic@west-norfolk.gov.uk
Open: Daily 10.3am - 4pm. Opening times likely to be longer during summer, check with contact for current information
[P] Public car parks. Pay & display spaces within 10 min. walk.
[♿] Wheelchair access to ground floor only. No WC for the disabled. Guide Dogs: Yes [£] No

Old Buckenham Cornmill

Green Lane, Old Buckenham, Norfolk NR17
Mill with the largest diameter tower in England, which had five sets of stones when it was working. Once owned by the Colmans of Norwich and Prince Duleep Singh. Built by John Burlingham in 1818.
www.norfolkwindmills.co.uk
Grant Recipient/Owner: Norfolk Windmills Trust

Access contact: Mrs A L Rix
Tel: 01603 222708 **Fax:** 01603 224413
E-mail: amanda.rix@norfolk.gov.uk
Open: Apr - Sept: second Sun of each month 2 - 5pm. Groups at other times by arrangement. with Mrs A L Rix, Conservation Officer, Building Conservation Section, Dept of Planning & Transportation, Norfolk County Council, County Hall, Martineau Lane, Norwich, Norfolk NR1 2SG.
P Spaces: 6 No £ Adult: 70p Child: 30p

Old Hall

Norwich Road, South Burlingham, Norfolk NR13 4EY
Small Elizabethan manor house with a painted stucco fireplace, painted stucco mermaids and scrollwork on the front porch, and a long gallery of hunting scenes in grisaille, c1600.
Grant Recipient/Owner/Access contact:
Mr P Scupham
Tel: 01493 750804 **Fax:** 01493 750804
E-mail: goodman@dircon.co.uk
Open: By prior telephone arrangement with Mr P Scupham or Ms M Steward. No access for guide dogs to the Long Gallery.
P Spaces: 8 Wheelchair access to ground floor and garden, painted gallery inaccessible. No WC for the disabled. Guide Dogs: Yes
£ No

Oxburgh Hall

Oxborough, King's Lynn, Norfolk PE33 9PS
Moated manor house with Tudor gatehouse, built in 1482 by the Bedingfeld family who still live there. The rooms show the development from medieval austerity to Victorian comfort, and include a display of embroidery by Mary, Queen of Scots and Bess of Hardwick. Gardens include a French Parterre and woodland walks, as well as a Catholic chapel.
www.nationaltrust.org.uk
Grant Recipient/Owner: The National Trust
Access contact: Property Manager
Tel: 01366 328258 **Fax:** 01366 328066
E-mail: oxburghhall@nationaltrust.org.uk
Open: House: 20 Mar - 7 Nov: daily except Thurs/Fri, 1 - 5pm, BHs 11am - 5pm (last adm 4.30pm). Garden: 28 Feb - 14 Mar: Sat/Sun 11am - 4pm; 20 Mar - 7 Nov: daily except Thurs/Fri 11am - 5.30pm; Aug: daily; 13 Nov - 27 Feb 2005: Sat/Sun 11am - 4pm.
P Spaces: 100
Wheelchair access to 4 ground floor rooms (shallow ramp), difficult stairs to upper floors. Garden largely accessible, restaurant and shop accessible. WC for the disabled. Guide Dogs: Yes
£ Adult: £5.75 Child: £2.90 Other: £15.00 (family), £2.90 (garden & estate only)

Ruined Church of St Mary the Virgin

Houghton-on-the-Hill, Norfolk PE37 8DP
Ancient church at least 900 years old. Many original features remain including double splay windows, keyhole chancel, Roman brick arch, 12th century North door and early wall paintings. All areas open.
Grant Recipient/Owner: Norfolk County Council
Access contact: Mr & Mrs R Davey
Tel: 01760 440470
Open: All year at any reasonable time.
P Spaces: 40
Yes. No WC for the disabled. Guide Dogs: Yes £ No

Ruined Church of St Peter

Wiggenhall St Peter with Wigge, Norfolk
Former parish church, largely 15th century, now ruined. South aisle was demolished in 1840.
Grant Recipient/Owner: Wiggenhall St Peter PCC
Access contact: Ms Caroline Davison
Tel: 01603 222706 **Fax:** 01603 224413
E-mail: caroline.davison.pt@norfolk.gov.uk
Open: At all times.
P Spaces: 2 No £ No

Shotesham Park Dairy Farm Barn

Newton Flotman, Norfolk NR15 1XA
Built c1500 with later additions, part weather-boarded and part-rendered 5-bay timber framed barn with double queen post thatched roof.
Grant Recipient/Owner: Norfolk Historic Buildings Trust/ Mr Christopher Bailey
Access contact: Mr John Nott
Tel: 01508 470113
Open: All year by arrangement. with either Mr John Nott or Mr Christopher Bailey (tel: 01508 499285).
P The Barn is in a busy farmyard but parking can

usually be found (apart from at harvest time) for at least two cars by arrangement. Spaces: 2
Partial. Wheelchair access with assistance, rough surface outside Barn. WC for the disabled. Guide Dogs: Yes £ No

St Andrew's Hall

St Andrew's Plain, Norwich, Norfolk NR3 1AU
Remains of medieval friary, including the nave (St Andrew's Hall), choir (Blackfriars Hall), crypt, cloisters, private chapel (Beckets) and chapter house. Hammerbeam roof in nave, medieval bosses in choir and a 13th century 7-light East Window. A civic hall in use since 1540.
www.norwich.gov.uk
Grant Recipient/Owner: Norwich City Council
Access contact: Mr Russell Wilson
Tel: 01603 628477 **Fax:** 01603 762182
E-mail: TheHalls@norwich.gov.uk
Open: Mon - Sat 9am - 4pm. Subject to events.
P Multi-storey car park in city centre. Blue Badge on site, Orange Badge if space is available.
Partial. Wheelchair access to ground floor only. WC for the disabled. Guide Dogs: Yes £ No

St Benet's Level Mill

Ludham, Norfolk
Typical example of a Broadland drainage mill with tapering red brick tower, white boat shaped cap, sails and fantail. Built in 18th century and altered over the years, it became redundant in the 1940s. Ground and first floors accessible. Information boards on site.
Grant Recipient/Owner: Crown Estates Commissioners
Access contact: Mr D L Ritchie
Tel: 01692 678232 **Fax:** 01692 678055
E-mail: d.l.ritchie@farming.me.au
Open: Second Sun in May & first Sun in Aug. Other times by arrangement. with Mr D L Ritchie at Hall Fm, Ludham, Gt Yarmouth, Norfolk NR29 5NU or Mrs Jenny Scaff, Carter Jonas, 6-8 Hills Road, Cambridge CB2 1NH (tel:01223 346628).
P No
No. Guide dog access possible to ground floor only.
£ No

St Clement, Colegate

Norwich, Norfolk NR3 1BQ
15th century church, now a pastoral care and counselling centre. Has a slender tower decorated with lozenges of flushwork (patterns made from flint and stone).
Grant Recipient/Owner: Norwich Historic Churches Trust
Access contact: Reverend Jack Burton
Tel: 01603 622747
Open: Daily 10am-4pm (sometimes longer). Occasionally closed when steward on leave.
P In city centre car parks. Partial. Wheelchair access to Nave at street level. No WC for the disabled. Guide Dogs: Yes £ No

St Lawrence

The Street, South Walsham, Norfolk NR13 6DQ
Medieval church destroyed by fire and rebuilt in 1832 as a parish church and used for worship until c1890. Formerly redundant but now re-licensed for worship. Now houses St Lawrence Centre for Training and the Arts, open to the public and used for exhibitions, classes and concerts. Access to Sacristans Garden.
Grant Recipient/Owner: South Walsham Parochial Church Council
Access contact: Mrs Caroline Linsdell
Tel: 01603 270522
Open: Daily 9am - 6pm or dusk in winter.
P Spaces: 8
Yes. WC for the disabled. Guide Dogs: Yes £ No

St Martin at Oak

Norwich, Norfolk
15th century former church, now redundant.
Grant Recipient/Owner: Norwich Historic Churches Trust
Access contact: Mrs J Jones
Tel: 07867 801995 **Fax:** 01603 722008
E-mail: hall.farm@btinternet.com
Open: By arrangement. Use of building under review at time of publication. Please contact Mrs J Jones of Norwich Historic Churches Trust for current information.
P In city centre car parks. No £ No

St Martin at Palace

Norwich, Norfolk NR3 1RW
Medieval former church, now housing the Norfolk Association for the Care and Resettlement of Offenders (NACRO). Has a fine 16th century tomb for Lady Elizabeth Calthorpe.
Grant Recipient/Owner: Norwich Historic Churches Trust
Access contact: Mr Richard Hawthorn
Tel: 01603 763555
E-mail: director.norfolkacro@btinternet.com
Open: By prior written arrangement.
P In city centre car parks.
No. WC for the disabled. Guide Dogs: Yes
£ No

St Mary's Abbey

West Dereham, Norfolk
The present six bay house is the remains of the service block of Sir Thomas Dereham's Renaissance style mansion, built after 1689 incorporating the surviving parts of a Premonstratensian Abbey founded in 1188 by Hubert Walter. Had become a ruin and was only recently restored, with the building re-roofed, re-fenestrated and a first floor and stair tower added. The house is now a private residence.
Grant Recipient/Owner: Mr G Shropshire
Access contact: Mrs Ann King
Tel: 01353 727200 **Fax:** 01353 727325
Open: By prior arrangement with Mrs Ann King, G's Marketing Ltd, Barway, Ely, Cambridgeshire CB7 5TZ (tel: 01353 727200, Mon-Fri only). Up to one month's notice may be required.
P Spaces: 20 Yes. WC for the disabled available on request, although they are not specifically designed for such use. Guide Dogs: Yes £ No

St Mary

Fordham, Norfolk
Medieval aisleless church in rural landscape, now redundant. Listed Grade II*.
Grant Recipient/Owner: Fordham St Mary Preservation Trust
Access contact: Mr Chris Clare
Tel: 01223 513026
Open: Key may be available from farm opposite church or by arrangement.
P Available. No. Guide Dogs: Yes £ No

St Peter & St Paul

Tunstall, Norfolk
Chancel and ruined nave and tower of medieval church.
Grant Recipient/Owner: Tunstall (Norfolk) Church Preservation Trust
Access contact: The Secretary
Tel: 01493 700279
Open: Normally all year. If locked, it is due to severe weather. Key available at the Manor House in Tunstall.
P Spaces: 6 Yes. Wheelchair access across uneven path. No WC for the disabled. Guide Dogs: Yes £ No

Thornage Hall Dovecote

Thornage, Holt, Norfolk NR25 7QH
Square dovecote, dated 1728, built of red brick in English bond with hipped roof in red black and black glazed pantiles terminating in square wooden glover. Contains 20 tiers of holes on all four sides and on brick spokes projecting from each corner toward the centre.
Grant Recipient/Owner: Norfolk Dovecote Trust/ Camphill Communities East Anglia
Access contact: Ms A Gimelli
Tel: 01263 860305
Open: For village fete in July, & first Sun in Sept, 2 - 5pm. Other times by written arrangement with Ms A Gimelli at the Hall.
P Spaces: 50 No. Guide Dogs: Yes £ No

Thurne Dyke Drainage Mill

Thurne Staithe, Thurne, Norfolk
Broadland drainage mill c1820 with classic 'hained' appearance and turbine pump. Originally 2 storey tapering circular whitewashed brick tower, raised to 3 storeys in mid 19th century, with timber weatherboarded boat shaped cap, sails and fan.
www.norfolkwindmills.co.uk
Grant Recipient/Owner: Norfolk Windmills Trust
Access contact: Ms A Yardy
Tel: 01603 222705 **Fax:** 01603 224413
Open: Exterior can be viewed at all times. Interior open Apr - Oct, 1st and 3rd Sun afternoon in each month,

however opening arrangements for 2004 to be confirmed at time of publication, please check with the Norfolk Windmills Trust.
P Parking at parish staithe, approx. 100 yds. Pub also allows parking for visitors. Spaces: 4 ♿ No £ No

Waxham Great Barn

Sea Palling, Norfolk NR1 2DH
Grade I listed barn, 1570s-80s, with later additions. Flint with ashlar dressings and thatched roof. Much of its fabric is reused material from dissolved monasteries.
Grant Recipient/Owner: Norfolk County Council
Access contact: Ms Caroline Davison
Tel: 01603 222706 **Fax:** 01603 224413
E-mail: caroline.davison.pt@norfolk.gov.uk
Open: Provisional: Easter (3 Apr 2004) - end Sept. Times to be finalised. Check with the access contact for current information.
P Free. Spaces: 100 ♿ Wheelchair access with help (gravel path from car park to Barn). WC for the disabled. Guide Dogs: Yes
£ **Adult:** £2.50 **Child:** Free

NORTH YORKSHIRE

Aiskew Water Cornmill

Bedale, North Yorkshire DL8 1AW
Grade II* watermill, late 18th and early 19th century. Sold in 1918 in a major dispersal of estate properties. Roof & main structure restored. Restoration of interior with original wooden machinery is planned.
Grant Recipient/Owner: David Clark
Access contact: Jared and Duncan Clark
Tel: 01677 422125 **Fax:** 01677 425205
E-mail: oakwood.ent@btinternet.com
Open: Access to the exterior at all reasonable times.
P Spaces: 40 ♿ Yes. No WC for the disabled. Guide Dogs: Yes. £ No

Beningbrough Hall

Shipton-by-Beningbrough, North Yorkshire YO30 1DD
Country house, c1716, contains an impressive baroque interior. A very high standard of craftsmanship is displayed throughout, most of the original work surviving with extremely fine woodcarving and other ornate decoration, and an unusual central corridor running the full length of the house. Over 100 pictures on loan from the National Portrait Gallery are on display. There is a fully equipped Victorian laundry and walled garden.
www.nationaltrust.org.uk
Grant Recipient/Owner: The National Trust
Access contact: Property Manager
Tel: 01904 470666 **Fax:** 01904 470002
E-mail: beningbrough@nationaltrust.org.uk
Open: House: 27 Mar - 30 Jun, daily except Thurs & Fri 12 noon - 5pm; 1 Jul - 31 Aug daily except Thurs 12 noon - 5pm; 1 Sept - 31 Oct daily except Thurs & Fri 12 noon - 5pm. Grounds & shop: as house 11am - 5.30pm. Restaurant: as house 11am - 5pm.
P Spaces: 250 ♿ Partial. Wheelchair access (ramped) to ground floor only. WC for the disabled. Guide Dogs: Yes
£ **Adult:** £6.00 (house), £5.00 (garden & exhibition)
Child: £3 (house), £2.50 (garden & exhibition)
Other: £14.00 (family, house), £12.50 (family, garden & exhibition). Discount for cyclists

Castle Howard

York, North Yorkshire YO60 7DA
Large stately home dating from the beginning of the 18th century and designed by Sir John Vanbrugh. Situated in 10,000 acres of landscaped grounds, which includes numerous monuments.
www.castlehoward.co.uk
Grant Recipient/Owner: The Hon. Simon Howard
Access contact: Mr D N Peake
Tel: 01653 648444 **Fax:** 01653 648529
E-mail: estatemanager@castlehoward.co.uk
Open: 14 Feb - 31 Oct: daily 11am - 4.45pm (Grounds only from 10am); Nov - mid-Mar: grounds open most days but please telephone for confirmation in Nov, Dec and Jan.
P Spaces: 300 ♿ Wheelchair access to all but chapel & first floor of exhibition wing. WC for the disabled. Guide Dogs: Yes
£ **Adult:** £9.50 **Child:** £6.50 **Other:** £8.50

Cawood Castle

nr. Selby, North Yorkshire
This decorated gatehouse, and wing to one side, is all that remains of the castle, once a stronghold of the Archbishops of York. Visitors have included Thomas Wolsey, Henry III, Edward I, and Henry VIII. In the 18th century it was used as a courtroom eventually ending up in domestic use. Extremely steep spiral staircase.
www.landmarktrust.co.uk
Grant Recipient/Owner: The Landmark Trust
Access contact: Mrs Victoria O'Keeffe
Tel: 01628 825920 **Fax:** 01628 825417
E-mail: vokeeffe@landmarktrust.co.uk
Open: The Landmark Trust is an independent charity, which rescues small buildings of historic or architectural importance from decay or unsympathetic improvement. Landmark's aim is to promote the enjoyment of these historic buildings by making them available to stay in for holidays. Cawood Castle can be rented by anyone, at all times of the year, for periods ranging from a weekend to three weeks. Bookings can be made by telephoning the Booking Office on 01628 825925. As the building is in full-time use for holiday accommodation, it is not normally open to the public. However the public can view the building by arrangement. by telephoning the access contact to make an appointment. Potential visitors will be asked to write to confirm the details of their visit.
P Spaces: 1 ♿ No £ No

Duncombe Park

Helmsley, York, North Yorkshire YO62 5EB
Recently restored family home of Lord and Lady Feversham. Originally built in 1713 and then rebuilt after a fire in 1879 largely to the original design. Early 18th century gardens.
www.duncombepark.com
Grant Recipient/Owner: Lord Feversham
Access contact: Duncombe Park Estate Office
Tel: 01439 770213 **Fax:** 01439 771114
E-mail: liz@duncombepark.com
Open: 12 Apr - 24 Oct, Sun - Thurs: House & Garden 12 noon - 5.30pm (tours hourly 12.30pm - 3.30pm, last adm to gardens and parkland 4.30pm). Parkland Centre Tearoom, shop & parkland walks 11am - 5.30pm (last orders in tearoom 5.15pm). Special Events all year. Duncombe Park reserve the right to alter opening arrangements without prior notice - please telephone to check. Closed 9/10, & 14 June 2004.
P Spaces: 200 ♿ Wheelchair access to ground & first floor only. WC for the disabled. Guide Dogs: Yes
£ **Adult:** £6.50 (house & gardens), £3.50 (gardens & parkland), £2.00 (parkland) **Child:** £3 (10-16, house & garden), £2.00 (10-16, gardens & parkland), £1 (10-16, parkland) **Other:** £5.00 (concessions, house & garden), £13.50 (family, house & garden), £4.75 (groups, house & garden), £25.00 (family season ticket)

Fountains Hall

Studley Royal, Ripon, North Yorkshire HG4 3DY
Elizabethan mansion, built between 1589 and 1604 for Stephen Proctor. Two rooms; the Stone Hall and the Arkell Room, both unfurnished, are open to the public. The conservation of a third room, the Great Chamber, has recently been completed. This upper room features an ornate chimney piece depicting the Biblical story of the Judgement of Solomon. The mansion is situated within a World Heritage Site which also includes the ruins of a 12th century Cistercian Abbey, monastic water mill and Georgian water garden.
www.fountainsabbey.org.uk
Grant Recipient/Owner: The National Trust
Access contact: Property Manager
Tel: 01765 608888 **Fax:** 01765 601002
E-mail: fountainsenquiries@nationaltrust.org.uk
Open: As part of the Fountain's Abbey and Studley Royal Estate. Jan - Mar, 10am - 4pm; Apr - Sept, 10am - 6pm; Oct - Dec, 10am - 4pm. Estate closed 24/25 Dec and Fris in Jan, Nov and Dec.
P Spaces: 500 ♿ Yes. WC for the disabled. Guide Dogs: Yes
£ **Adult:** £5.50 **Child:** £3 **Other:** £15 (family)

Giggleswick School Chapel

Giggleswick, Settle, North Yorkshire BD24 0DE
Built 1897-1901 by T G Jackson for Walter Morrison as a gift to the school to commemorate the Diamond Jubilee of Queen Victoria. Constructed of Gothic banded rockfaced millstone grit sandstone and limestone, with lead hipped roof to nave and copper covered terracotta dome to chancel. Contains Italian sgrafitto work throughout.
www.giggleswick.org.uk/school_life/chapel_main.htm
Grant Recipient/Owner: The Governors of Giggleswick School
Access contact: The Bursar and Clerk to the Governors
Tel: 01729 893000/893012 **Fax:** 01729 893150
E-mail: bursar@giggleswick.org.uk
Open: Mon - Fri 9 am - 5pm, closed BHs. Other times by arrangement. Visitors must report to reception to obtain the key to the Chapel.
P Spaces: 25 ♿ Wheelchair access to ground floor only. Disabled WC in main school premises. Guide Dogs: Yes
£ No

Hackfall

Grewelthorpe, North Yorkshire
Developed as a wild gothic woodland landscape in the 18th century, remains of a number of man-made features can still be seen. The woodland is known to have existed since at least 1600 and the ground flora is characteristic of ancient woodland. Beech, oak, ash and wild cherry can also be seen together with spindle, an unusual tree found in chalk and limestone. The site is very steep and paths can sometimes be narrow and difficult to negotiate.
www.woodland-trust.org.uk
Grant Recipient/Owner: The Woodland Trust
Access contact: Ms Karen Fisher
Tel: 01476 581146 **Fax:** 01476 590808
E-mail: karenfisher@woodland-trust.org.uk
Open: The site is open to the public at all times. For further information contact Karen Fisher (tel:01476 581146).
P Parking on opposite side of road. Spaces: 6 ♿ No
£ No

Jervaulx Abbey

Ripon, North Yorkshire HG4 4PH
Ruins of Cistercian Abbey moved to this site in 1156, built of sandstone ashlar in Early English style. Remains of nave, transepts and choir, with a cloister on the south side of the nave, flanked by a chapter house to the east and a kitchen and dorter to the south.
Grant Recipient/Owner/Access contact: Mr Ian Burdon
Tel: 01677 460391/01677 460226
E-mail: ba123@btopenworld.com
Open: At any reasonable time throughout the year.
P Spaces: 55 ♿ lWheelchair access to church, infirmary, frater and cloisters. Uneven terrain and steps on other parts of site. WC for the disabled. Guide Dogs: Yes
£ **Adult:** £2.00 (honesty box) **Child:** £1.50 (honesty box)

Kiplin Hall

Scorton, Richmond, North Yorkshire DL10 6AT
Grade I listed Jacobean house with 19th century additions. Built in 1620 by George Calvert, 1st Lord Baltimore, founder of the State of Maryland, USA, the Hall contains fine paintings and furniture collected by four families over four centuries. Recent major restoration work has brought the Hall back to life as a comfortable Victorian family home.
www.kiplinhall.co.uk
Grant Recipient/Owner: Kiplin Hall Trust
Access contact: Ms Dawn Webster
Tel: 01748 818178 **Fax:** 01748 818178
E-mail: info@kiplinhall.co.uk
Open: Easter weekend: daily, 2 - 5pm. May and Sept: Sun and Tues, 2 - 5pm; June - Aug: Sun - Wed, 2 - 5pm; BH Mons, 2 - 5pm. Special events, contact the Hall for further details.
P Free parking a short walk along drive to Hall, overflow into coach area. Disabled parking adjacent to Hall, 12 spaces.
♿ lWheelchair access to ground floor and tea room only. No WC for the disabled. Guide Dogs: Yes
£ **Adult:** £4.00 **Child:** £2 **Other:** £3

Lindley Murray Summerhouse

The Mount School, Dalton Terrace, York, N Yorkshire YO24 4DD
Grade II* listed summerhouse built c1774, formerly situated in the grounds of Holgate House, York. Octagonal timber structure on raised stepped circular base with lead ogee roof and decorated with Doric

columns. Restored in 1997.
Grant Recipient/Owner: The Mount School
Access contact: Ms Anne Bolton
Tel: 01904 667506 **Fax:** 01904 667524
E-mail: abolton@mount.n-yorks.sch.uk
Open: By arrangement Mon-Fri all year (except BHs) 9am - 4.30pm.
Ⓟ Spaces: 3 ♿ Yes. WC for the disabled. Guide Dogs: Yes
£ No, but donations welcome

Markenfield Hall

Ripon, North Yorkshire HG4 3AD
Fortified moated manor house, built 1310-1323 for John de Markenfield, with further additions and alterations in the 16th, 18th and 19th centuries. Restored 1981-4.
www.markenfield.com
Grant Recipient/Owner: Lady Deirdre Curteis
Access contact: Mrs C M Wardroper
Tel: 01845 597226 / 01765 603411 **Fax:** 01845 597023
E-mail: wardroper@aol.com
Open: 2 - 15 May & 13 - 26 June 2 - 5pm. Groups by arrangement. at any time.
Ⓟ Spaces: 25
♿ Wheelchair access to ground floor only. No WC for the disabled. Guide Dogs: Yes £ **Adult:** £3 **Child:** £2
Other: £2 (senior citizens), £60 (minimum charge groups out of opening times)

Norton Conyers

nr. Ripon, North Yorkshire HG4 5EQ
Medieval house with Stuart and Georgian additions. 18th century walled garden nearby. Family pictures, furniture and costumes. Visited by Charlotte Brontë in 1839; a family legend of a mad woman confined in an attic room contributed towards the mad Mrs Rochester in 'Jane Eyre' and the house was a model for 'Thornfield Hall'.
Grant Recipient/Owner/Access contact: Sir James Graham Bt
Tel: 01765 640333 **Fax:** 01765 640333
E-mail: norton.conyers@ripon.org
Open: House & Garden: Easter Sun and Mon, BH Suns and Mons, and Suns 25 Apr - 29 Aug; 28 June - 3 July daily. House: 2 - 5pm (last adm 4.40pm). Garden: 12.00 noon - 5pm. Garden also open on Thurs throughout the year 10am - 4pm but please check beforehand. Groups by arrangement.
Ⓟ Free car park approx. 50m from the house; disabled parking available near front door by arrangement. Spaces: 60
♿ Wheelchair access to ground floor of house only. Some gravelled paths in garden may be difficult. WC for the disabled. Guide Dogs: Yes
£ **Adult:** £4 **Child:** £3 (10-16 yrs, reduced rate for two or more children) **Other:** £3 (senior citizens). Admission to garden only is free but donations are welcome; a charge is made when the garden is open for charity.

Ormesby Hall

Church Lane, Ormesby, Middlesbrough, North Yorkshire TS7 9AS
A mid-18th century Palladian mansion, notable for its fine plasterwork and carved wood decoration. The Victorian laundry and kitchen with scullery and game larder are interesting. 18th century stable block, attributed to Carr of York, is leased to the Cleveland Mounted Police. Large model railway and garden with holly walk.
www.nationaltrust.org.uk
Grant Recipient/Owner: The National Trust
Access contact: Property Manager
Tel: 01642 324188 **Fax:** 01642 300937
E-mail: ormesbyhall@nationaltrust.org.uk
Open: Hall: 30 Mar - 2 Nov, daily except Mon, Fri & Sat (open Good Fri & BH Mons) 1.30 - 5pm (last adm 4.30pm). Shop & tea room: as Hall 12.30 - 5pm.
Ⓟ 100 metres from House. Spaces: 100
♿ Wheelchair access to ground floor of Hall (shallow step at entrance), shop, tearoom & garden. No WC for the disabled. Guide Dogs: Yes
£ **Adult:** £3.90, £2.70 (garden, railway & exhibition) **Child:** £1.90, £1.20 (garden, railway & exhibition) **Family:** £9.50

Ribblehead Viaduct

Ribblehead, North Yorkshire
Railway viaduct, 1870-74, rockfaced stone and brick. 104 feet high at highest point. Largest and most impressive of the viaducts of the Settle - Carlisle line of the Midland Railway.
Grant Recipient/Owner: British Rail
Access contact: Mr David Wiggins
Tel: 0161 228 8584 **Fax:** 0161 228 8711
E-mail: david.wiggins@networkrail.co.uk
Open: Viewing from ground level only. Strictly no access from Network Rail property.
Ⓟ On-street parking in Cave. ♿ No £ No

St Margaret's Church

(National Centre for Early Music), Walmgate, York, North Yorkshire YO1 9TL
14th century church with highly decorated 12th century Romanesque doorway (removed from chapel of the ruined hospital of St Nicholas, probably during 1684-5 rebuilding of church (orange-red brick tower of same date) occasioned by Civil War damage). Now houses the National Centre for Early Music and used for concerts, music educational activities, conferences, recordings and events.
www.ncem.co.uk
Grant Recipient/Owner: York Early Music Foundation
Access contact: Mrs G Baldwin
Tel: 01904 632220 **Fax:** 01904 612631
E-mail: info@ncem.co.uk
Open: All year, Mon - Fri 10am - 4pm. Also by arrangement. Access is necessarily restricted when events are taking place.
Ⓟ 2 disabled parking places. Spaces: 9
♿ Yes. WC for the disabled. Guide Dogs: Yes £ No

St Paulinus

Brough Park, Richmond, North Yorkshire DL10 7PJ
Catholic neo-Gothic chapel designed by Bonomi with priest's accommodation and school room in undercroft.
Grant Recipient/Owner/Access contact: Mr Greville Worthington
Tel: 01748 812127
E-mail: grev@saintpaulinus.co.uk
Open: By prior arrangement.
Ⓟ Spaces: 2
♿ No. Guide Dogs: Yes £ No

St Saviour's Church

(Archaeological Resource Centre), St Saviourgate, York, North Yorkshire YO1 8NN
Church on site by late 11th century, present building dates from the 15th and extensively remodelled in 1845. Now houses the Archaeological Resource Centre, which contains an archaeological collection excavated by the York Archaeological Trust and promotes access to archaeological material through hands-on displays.
www.yorkarchaeology.co.uk
Grant Recipient/Owner: York Archaeological Trust
Access contact: Miss Christine McDonnell
Tel: 01904 654324 / 619264 **Fax:** 01904 663024
E-mail: cmcdonnell@yorkarchaeology.co.uk
Open: School terms: Mon - Sat 10am - 3.30pm. School holidays: Mon - Sat 11am - 3.30pm. Groups by arrangement. in school term. 24-hr infoline (01904 643211); advance bookings (01904 543403). Visitors who simply want to view the building may look round free of charge, otherwise admission charged for entrance to Archaeological Resource Centre. Sensory garden on architectural theme.
Ⓟ Disabled on-street parking at entrance; public car parks nearby.
♿ Full wheelchair access for exhibition areas, but no access to offices on mezzanine floor. WC for the disabled. Guide Dogs: Yes
£ **Adult:** £4.50 (ARC) **Child:** £4 **Other:** £15 (family). Carers/enablers free when helping disabled person

St William's College

5 College Street, York, North Yorkshire YO1 7JF
St William's College is one of the most important timber framed buildings in York and is named after St William, Archbishop of York in 1154. Founded in 1461 as a home for the Chantry Priests of the Minster until the Reformation, it was also used to house a printing press and mint for King Charles I in 1642 as well as being the home of the Earls of Carlisle in 1719 (builders of Castle Howard). Now used as York Minster's Conference & Banqueting Centre.

www.yorkminster.org
Grant Recipient/Owner: The Trustees of St William's College
Access contact: Mr A S Clarke
Tel: 01904 557233 **Fax:** 01904 557234
E-mail: info@yorkminster.org
Open: Daily 9am - 5pm, subject to functions - please check with Mr A S Clarke. Closed: Good Fri, Christmas Day, Boxing Day.
Ⓟ Public car parks in York City centre. ♿ No
£ **Adult:** £1 **Child:** 50p

Scampston Hall

Scampston, Malton, North Yorkshire, YO17 8NG
Late 17th century country house, extensively remodelled in 1801 by Thomas Leverton. Contains Regency interiors and an art collection. Set in a parkland designed by 'Capability' Brown with 10 acres of lakes and a Palladian bridge.
www.scampston.co.uk
Grant Recipient/Owner/Access contact:
Sir Charles Legard Bt
Tel: 01944 758224 **Fax:** 01944 758700
E-mail: legard@scampton.co.uk
Open: 18 June - 25 July (closed Mons and Tues) 1.30 - 5.00pm.
Ⓟ Spaces: 50
♿ Wheelchair access to ground floor only. WC for the disabled. Guide Dogs: Yes
£ **Adult:** £5 (house, garden & park)

Thompson Mausoleum

Little Ouseburn Churchyard, Little Ouseburn, N Yorkshire YO26 9TS
18th century Mausoleum in magnesian limestone. It is a rotunda encircled by 13 Tuscan columns, above which a frieze and cornice support a plain drum and ribbed domed roof. Listed Grade II*. Built for the use of the Thompson family of Kirby Hall.
Grant Recipient/Owner: Little Ouseburn Mausoleum Ltd
Access contact: Mr H Hibbs
Tel: 01423 330414
E-mail: helier@clara.net
Open: Always available to view from the outside, interior visible through a replica of the original wrought iron gate. Access to interior by arrangement and upon completion of repairs (scheduled to complete 2004). Contact Mr Hibbs, Friends of Ouseburn Mausoleum Ltd, Hilltop Cottage, Little Ouseburn, North Yorks YO26 9TD (tel: 01423 330414) for current information.
Ⓟ Spaces: 4
♿ Wheelchair access with assistance (gravel path and grass). No WC for the disabled. Guide Dogs: Yes
£ No

NORTHAMPTONSHIRE

Hall Farmhouse

Hall Yard, Kings Cliffe, Peterborough, Northamptonshire PE8 6XQ
Former medieval open hall. Music room, c1795, with coved and ornamented ceiling. Home of William Law 1740-61.
Grant Recipient/Owner/Access contact:
Mr J A R Grove
Tel: 01780 470748
Open: By prior arrangement.
Ⓟ Spaces: 3
♿ No. Guide Dogs: Yes £ No

Laxton Hall

Corby, Northamptonshire NN17 3AU
Stone built 18th century manor house, enlarged and modified in 19th century and set in 60 acres of parkland. Stable block by Repton. Formerly a boys' school, now a residential home for elderly Poles.
Grant Recipient/Owner: Polish Benevolent Housing Association Ltd
Access contact: Mr B R Baumgart
Tel: 020 7359 8863 **Fax:** 020 7226 7677
E-mail: pbf.pmk@ukonlinke.co.uk
Open: By written arrangement with Mr B R Baumgart, PBF Housing Association, 2 Devonia Road, London N1 8JJ, access will be arranged through the manager of the Residential Home.
Ⓟ Spaces: 10
♿ Wheelchair access to ground floor only. WC for the disabled. Guide Dogs: Yes £ No

The Manor House

Hardwick, Wellingborough, Northamptonshire NN9 5AL

Manor house dating back to the 12th century. The exterior of the building has been restored including a fine example of a Collyweston roof. Now part of a modern working farm.
Grant Recipient/Owner/Access contact: Mr Siddons
Tel: 01933 678785 **Fax:** 01933 678166
E-mail: siddons@siddons.fsbusiness.co.uk
Open: By prior arrangement with Mr Siddons (please allow at least 48 hours notice).
P Spaces: 4 No No

NORTHUMBERLAND

27/28 Market Place

Hexham, Northumberland NE46 3PB

Grade II* listed 4 storey house built 1749. Ground floor is a shop and the upper floors have been converted into flats. Imposing rear elevation to Back Row.
Grant Recipient/Owner: Two Castles Housing Association
Access contact: Ms Julie Cuthbert
Tel: 0191 261 4774 **Fax:** 0191 2619629
E-mail: julie.cuthbert@twocastles.org.uk
Open: Exterior only.
P No No No

Belford Hall

Belford, Northumberland NE70 7EY

Country house, 1754-56 by James Paine, wings and rear entrance added 1818 by John Dobson. The property stood derelict for 40 years until it was restored by the North East Civic Trust and the Monument Trust between 1984-87.
Grant Recipient/Owner: North East Civic Trust
Access contact: Ms Sheila Fairbairn
Tel: 01668 213794
Open: Interior: any day 9am - 5pm, subject to prior arrangement with Ms Fairbairn or Mrs Harrison (tel:01668 213810), but excluding Christmas & Easter. Exterior: any day 9am - 5pm (3pm in winter months), but excluding Christmas & Easter. No WC
P Spaces: 8 Wheelchair access to ground floor with assistance (three steps to main entrance). No WC for the disabled. Guide Dogs: Yes
No

Cragside

Rothbury, Morpeth, Northumberland NE65 7PX

High Victorian mansion by Norman Shaw, with original furniture and fittings including William Morris's stained glass and earliest wallpapers. Built for the inventor-industrialist and armaments manufacturer, Lord Armstrong, who installed the world's first hydro-electric lighting. The mansion is set in a 1,000-acre wooded estate, with rock garden, formal garden, man-made lakes and hydro-electric machinery.
www.nationaltrust.org.uk
Grant Recipient/Owner: The National Trust
Access contact: Mr John O'Brien
Tel: 01669 620333 x101 **Fax:** 01669 620066
E-mail: cragside@nationaltrust.org.uk
Open: House: Tues - Sun (& BH Mons) 30 Mar - 26 Sept 1 - 5.30pm (last adm 4.30pm); 28 Sept - 31 Oct 1 - 4.30pm (last adm 3.30pm). Estate & formal gardens: Tues - Sun (& BH Mons) 30 Mar - 31 Oct 10.30am - 7pm (last adm 5pm). Wed - Sun 3 Nov - 19 Dec 11am - 4pm.
P Spaces: 400
Wheelchair access to ground floor of house and one landing area on first floor. WC for the disabled. Guide Dogs: Yes
Adult: £8 (house & garden), £5.50 (estate only) Child: £4 (house & garden), £2.50 (estate only) Other: £20 (family, house & garden), £13.50 (family, estate), £6.50 (booked groups 15 +, house & garden), £4.50 (booked groups15 +, estate)

Felton Park Greenhouse

Felton, Northumberland NE65 9HN

Grade II* listed curvilinear cast-iron hothouse, with hollow/heated wall attached, designed by J C Loudon c1830. Greenhouse supports 2 large camelias imported from China at time of construction.
Grant Recipient/Owner/Access contact: Major B D S Burton
Tel: 01670 787319 **Fax:** 01670 787319
Open: All year, 2pm - 5.30pm or by arrangement.

P Spaces: 15 Wheelchair access exterior only. No WC for the disabled. Guide Dogs: Yes No

High Meadows Cottage Barn

Whitshields, Bardon Mill, Northumberland NE47 7BN

18th century stone walled, cruck roofed heather thatched barn with flagged floor. Perhaps a unique survival of a once-common vernacular building type, remaining virtually unaltered.
Grant Recipient/Owner: Mr D W Collinson
Access contact: Dr M Crick
Tel: 0777 1996 838
Open: By prior telephone arrangement.
P Spaces: 4
Wheelchair access possible with assistance: across grass track and cobbled yard. No WC for the disabled. Guide Dogs: Yes No

High Staward Farm

Langley-on-Tyne, Hexham, Northumberland NE47 5NS

Georgian farmhouse standing inside a walled garden surrounded by the farm steading. Has a ging gang, threshing machine, pig stys with stone troughs and a blacksmiths' shop. Most of the house and buildings are of dressed stone and the house has flagged floors, ceiling hooks, cheeseboard and rail, large pantry and servants' staircase. Still a working hill farm.
Grant Recipient/Owner/Access contact: Mr R J Coulson
Tel: 01434 683619
Open: By prior arrangement.
P Spaces: 2
No. Guide Dogs: Yes No

Lady's Well

Holystone, Harbbottle, Northumberland

The Lady's Holy Well is considered to be of Roman origin and is located on a halting place along the Roman road. The main feature of the well today is a rectangular stone tank which is fed by a natural spring.
www.nationaltrust.org.uk
Grant Recipient/Owner: The National Trust
Access contact: Mr John O'Brien
Tel: 01669 620333 ext. 101 **Fax:** 01669 620066
Open: Open at all times.
P No No. Guide Dogs: Yes No

Lambley Viaduct

Lambley, Tynedale, Northumberland

17 arch stone viaduct, 100ft high and 1650ft long, spanning the South Tyne river. Originally carried single track, now a footpath.
www.npht.com
Grant Recipient/Owner: British Rail Property Board/North Pennines Heritage Trust
Access contact: Mr David Flush
Tel: 01434 382045 **Fax:** 01434 382294
E-mail: np.ht@virgin.net
Open: At all times as part of the South Tyne Trail between Featherstone Park and Alston.
P Spaces: 30
Yes. No WC for the disabled. Guide Dogs: Yes
No

Lindisfarne Castle

Holy Island, Berwick-upon-Tweed, Northumberland TD15 2SH

Built in 1550 to protect Holy Island harbour from attack, the castle was converted into a private house for Edward Hudson by Sir Edwin Luytens in 1903. Small walled garden was designed by Gertrude Jekyll. 19th century lime kilns in field by the castle.
www.nationaltrust.org.uk
Grant Recipient/Owner: The National Trust
Access contact: Property Manager
Tel: 01289 389244 **Fax:** 01289 389349
Open: Castle: 14 Feb - 22 Feb daily except Mon; 20 Mar - 31 Oct daily except Mon (open Scottish & English BH Mons). Open for 4½ hours either 10.30am - 3pm or 12 noon - 4.30pm, depending on the tide. Garden: 14 Feb - 31 Oct daily 12 noon - 5pm.
P Local authority car park 1 mile from site.
No. Guide Dogs: Yes
Adult: £5 Child: £2.50 Other: £12.50 (family), NT members free, £6 (groups 10+ out-of-hours by arrangement.)

Little Harle Tower

Kirkwhelpington, Newcastle-upon-Tyne, Northumberland NE19 2PD

Medieval tower with 17th century range and a Victorian wing which contains a recently restored

1740s drawing room. It has been one family's home since 1830 though part is now let.
Grant Recipient/Owner: Mr J P P Anderson
Access contact: Mr Simon Rowarth
Tel: 01434 609000 **Fax:** 01434 606900
E-mail: simon.rowarth@youngscs.com
Open: By prior arrangement (at least two weeks notice required) with Mr Simon Rowarth of Youngs, 3 Wentworth Place, Hexham, Northumberland NE46 1XB.
P Spaces: 6
Wheelchair access to ground floor only. No WC for the disabled. Guide Dogs: Yes Donations to the church requested.

Mitford Hall Camellia House

Morpeth, Northumberland NE61 3PZ

East wing and conservatory of country house built c1820 by John Dobson, detached from main house by demolition of north-east wing in the 20th century. The conservatory houses a superb specimen of a red flowering camellia dating to c1826.
Grant Recipient/Owner: Shepherd Offshore plc
Access contact: Mr B Shepherd
Tel: 01670 512637 **Fax:** 0191 2639872
Open: By prior written arrangement during the summer.
P Spaces: 3
Wheelchair access by arrangement. Ordinary WC on site may be accessible for some disabled persons, contact Hall for further information. Guide Dogs: Yes
No

Netherwitton Hall

Morpeth, Northumberland NE61 4NW

Grade I listed mansion house built c1685 by Robert Trollope for Sir Nicholas Thornton. Access to main ground floor rooms and external elevations. Built as a family home and remains the current family home.
Grant Recipient/Owner/Access contact: Mr J H T Trevelyan
Tel: 01670 772 249 **Fax:** 01670 772 510
Open: 3 May - 9 June, Mon - Fri 11am - 2pm by compulsory tour. Groups by arrangement.
P Spaces: 20
No. Guide Dogs: Yes
Adult: £3 Child: £1

Pottergate Tower

Pottergate, Alnwick, Northumberland

Built as part of the town's defences, Pottergate Tower was one of the many gates providing access into Alwick. Rebuilt in 1768 to a design by Mr Henry Bell with a crown spire (removed in 1812). Above the archway is a St Michael and Dragon (the symbol of the Town), a blank roundel (formerly with a clock) and a memorial tablet: 'This tower was rebuilt at the expense of the Borough of Alnwick and the new foundation laid April 28 AD. 1768.' The Tower is approximately 50 feet in height and has a spiral stone staircase leading on an inner room. Listed Grade II*.
Grant Recipient/Owner: The Freemen of Alnwick
Access contact: Mr Dennis Nixon
Tel: 01665 603517 **Fax:** 01665 603517
Email: Opening Arrangements: To the exterior at all times; to the interior by prior arrangement.
P No
Guide dogs and wheelchair access to the exterior only. No guide dogs.
No

St Cuthbert's Chapel

Farne islands, Northumberland

St Cuthbert's Chapel was completed in 1370. By the early 19th century it was in a ruinous condition. Restored in 1840 by Archdeacon Thorp it includes some fine 17th century woodwork from Durham Cathedral and a memorial to Grace Darling. Remains of an original window.
www.nationaltrust.org.uk
Grant Recipient/Owner: The National Trust
Access contact: Mr John Walton (Property Manager)
Tel: 01665 720651 **Fax:** 01665 720651
E-mail: john.walton@nationaltrust.org.uk
Open: 1 - 30 Apr & 1 Aug - 30 Sept: daily 10.30am - 6pm. 1 May - 31 July (breeding season) daily Staple Island 10.30am - 1.30pm, Inner Farne 1.30 - 5pm.
P Public parking in Seahouses (nearest mainland village).
Inner Farne is accessible for wheelchairs (tel Property Manager in advance). Staple Island not

accessible. Disabled WC on Inner Farne. Guide dogs on boat but not on islands.

£Adult: £4.80 (breeding season), £3.80 (outside breeding season) **Child:** £2.40 (breeding season), £1.90 (outside breeding season) **Other:** £2.20 (booked school parties, breeding season, per island), £1.90 (outside breeding season, per island). Admission fees do not include boatmen's charges.

St Michael's Pant

Alnwick, Northumberland

St Michael's Pant (drinking fountain) was built in 1765 by Matthew Mills, designed by Mr Bell. St Michael and Dragon (the symbol of the Town) on top of an octagonal drum, gargoyle for the water spout with large square trough which measures approximately ten square metres. Listed Grade II*.
Grant Recipient/Owner: The Freemen of Alnwick
Access contact: Mr D Nixon
Tel: 01665 603517 **Fax:** 01665 603517
Open: To the exterior at all times.
PNo.
Wheelchair Access. No WC for the disabled. Guide Dogs: Yes
£ No

Swinburne Castle

Hexham, Northumberland NE48 4DQ

Kitchen range 1600-1650, incorporating earlier fabric and with later alterations, stands at right angles to the footprint of the now demolished (1966) mid 18th century house which stood on the site of the medieval castle. East (laundry) wing 1770, restored in 2000. Orangery early 19th century.
Grant Recipient/Owner: Trustees of R W Murphy
Access contact: Major R P Murphy
Tel: 01434 681610
Open: 1 - 3, 5 - 8, 12 - 16, 19 - 23 and 26 - 30 Apr; 3 - 6 and 31 May; 30 Aug: 12 noon - 4.30pm.
PSpaces: 6
Wheelchair access to East Wing ground floor only. No WC for the disabled. Guide Dogs: No **£**No

The Tower

Elsdon, Northumberland NE19 1AA

14th century Tower House, residence of the Rector until 1961 and originally used as a refuge from the Border Reivers. Fine example of a medieval tower house and listed Grade I.
Grant Recipient/Owner/Access contact:
Dr J F Wollaston
Fax: 01830 520904
Open: By previously arranged guided tour, weekends only, 1 Apr - 30 Oct.
PSpaces: 30
No. Guide Dogs: Yes
£Adult: £5

Vindolanda Roman Fort

Bardon Mill, Hexham, Northumberland, NE47 7NJ

Roman Fort and civilian settlement in central sector of Hadrian's Wall with active excavation and education programmes. The site is owned and administered by the Vindolanda Charitable Trust and has an on-site museum, with full visitor services, reconstructed Roman buildings and gardens.
www.vindolanda.com
Grant Recipient/Owner: Vindolanda Trust
Access contact: Mrs Patricia Birley
Tel: 01434 344277 **Fax:** 01434 344060
E-mail: info@vindolanda.com
Open: 14 Feb - 14 Nov. Feb - Mar & Oct - Nov: daily 10am - 5pm. Apr - Sept: daily 10am - 6pm. Winter 2004 to be decided.
PCoach parking available on-site. Spaces: 60
Wheelchair access to parts of the site and all of the museums, gardens & open air museum. WC for the disabled. Guide Dogs: Yes
£Adult: £4.10 (10% reduction for EH members)
Child: £2.90 (10% reduction for EH members)
Other: £3.50 (10% reduction for EH members)

Wallington Hall & Clock Tower

Cambo, Morpeth, Northumberland NE61 4AR

Dating from 1688, the house was home to many generations of the Blackett and Trevelyan family. Contains Rococo plasterwork, fine ceramics, paintings and a doll's house collection. Pre-Raphaelite central

hall with scenes from Northumbrian history. Hall, Clock Tower and stable buildings set among lawns, lakes and woodland with walled garden.
www.nationaltrust.org.uk
Grant Recipient/Owner: The National Trust
Access contact: Property Manager
Tel: 01670 773600 **Fax:** 01670 774420
E-mail: wallington@nationaltrust.org.uk
Open: House: daily except Tues; 1 Apr - 5 Sept 1pm - 5.30pm; 6 Sept - 31 Oct 1pm - 4.30pm. Walled garden: daily; 1 Apr - 30 Sept 10am - 7pm; 1 Oct - 31 Oct 10am - 6pm; 1 Nov - 31 Mar 10am - 4pm. Grounds: daily in daylight hours.
PSpaces: 500
Lift to first floor for visitors with mobility problems. WC for the disabled. Guide Dogs: Yes
£ Adult: £7 (house & gardens), £5 (gardens)
Child: £3.50 (house & gardens), £2.50 (gardens)
Other: £17.50 (family, house & gardens), £12.50 (family, gardens only), £6.50 (groups 15+ house & gardens), £4.50 (groups 15+ gardens only)

NOTTINGHAMSHIRE

Kiln Warehouse

Mather Road, Newark, Nottinghamshire NG24 1FB

Grade II* former warehouse. Early example of the use of massed concrete construction. Interior completely destroyed by fire in the early 1990s, the exterior walls have been restored and warehouse converted into offices.
Grant Recipient/Owner: British Waterways Midlands & South West
Access contact: Mrs Karen Tivey
Tel: 0115 950 7577 **Fax:** 0115 950 7688
E-mail: karen@fhp.co.uk
Open: The exterior walls for which the property is notable can be viewed without arrangement. Access to the internal courtyard is by arrangement with Elizabeth Blackhurst of Fisher Hargreaves Proctor, Chartered Surveyors, 10 Oxford Street, Nottingham NG1 5BG (tel: 0115 950 7577).
PParking is available on adjacent land.
Yes. WC for the disabled. Guide Dogs: Yes **£**No

Newdigate House

Castle Gate, Nottingham, Nottinghamshire NG1 6AF

House, c1675, built for Thomas Newdigate. Stucco with ashlar dressings, hipped slate roof, sash windows, panelled rooms and Adam-style plasterwork. Crested wrought-iron railings, central gateway and overthrow, probably by Francis Foulgham, to the exterior. Marshal Tallard was held prisoner here after the battle of Blenheim. The ground floor is now a restaurant.
Grant Recipient/Owner: Nottingham and Nottinghamshire United Sevices Club
Access contact: Mr Ashley Walters
Tel: 0115 8475587 **Fax:** 0115 8475584
E-mail: enquiries@worldservicerestaurant.com
Open: Daily 11am - 6pm, preferably by arrangement.
PNo Help may be required for wheelchair access, please check with Mr Walters. No WC for the disabled. Guide Dogs: Yes
£No

Upton Hall (the British Horological Institute)

Upton, Newark, Nottinghamshire NG23 5TE

Grade II* listed house in Greek revival style, 1832, incorporating the earlier 17th century house. Large addition and interior remodelled in 1895. During the Second World War the house was a school for partially-sighted children. Now houses the British Horological Institute watch and clock museum featuring clocks from the 17th - 20th centuries.
www.bhi.co.uk/tour/start.htm
Grant Recipient/Owner/Access contact:
British Horological Institute
Tel: 01636 813795 **Fax:** 01636 812258
E-mail: clocks@bhi.co.uk
Open: Museum 28 Mar - 31 Oct: Sat 11am - 5pm, Sun 2pm - 5pm and BHs 11am - 5pm. Groups and guided tours by arrangement.
PCoach parking available. Spaces: 50 Wheelchair access to ground floor only. No WC for the disabled. Guide Dogs: Yes
£Adult: £3.50 **Child:** £2 (under 10s free)
Other: £3 (seniors), £10 (family)

OXFORDSHIRE

Aston Martin Heritage Trust

Drayton St Leonard, Wallingford, Oxon OX10 7BG

15th century tithe barn, 6 bays. Constructed of elm with hipped roof. Listed Grade II*.
Grant Recipient/Owner: Aston Martin Owners Club
Access contact: Ms Christine Sharrock
Tel: 01491 837736 **Fax:** 01491 825454
E-mail: amht@email.com
Open: Wed afternoons, 2 - 4pm. At other times by arrangement.
PSpaces: 30
Wheelchair access to ground floor only. WC for the disabled. Guide Dogs: Yes **£**No

Blenheim Palace & Park

Woodstock, Oxfordshire OX20 1PX

Ancestral home of the Dukes of Marlborough & birthplace of Winston Churchill. Built 1705-22 for John Churchill, the 1st Duke, in recognition of his victory at the Battle of Blenheim (1704). Designed by Sir John Vanbrugh, the house has in its many state rooms a collection of paintings, furniture, bronzes & the Marlborough Victories tapestries. 5-room Churchill Exhibition includes his birth room. 'Capability' Brown park & gardens.
www.blenheimpalace.com
Grant Recipient/Owner: Duke of Marlborough
Access contact: Mr J Blades
Tel: 01993 811325/811091 **Fax:** 01993 813527
E-mail: administrator@blenheimpalace.com
Open: Palace: 14 Feb - 12 Dec, daily 10.30am - 5.30pm (last adm 4.45pm), Nov & Dec closed Mon & Tues. Park: daily (except Christmas Day) 9am - 6pm (last adm 4.45pm). High Lodge may be visited by prior written arrangement with the Estate Office. Admission charges seasonal: off-peak 14 Feb - 28 May & 13 Sept - 12 Dec; peak: 29 May - 12 Sept & Easter.
PSpaces: 10000
Yes. WC for the disabled. Guide Dogs: Yes
£Adult: £11 off peak, £12.50 peak
Child: £5.50 off peak, £7 peak
Other: £8.50 off peak, £10 peak (senior citizens)

Broughton Castle

Banbury, Oxfordshire OX15 5EB

Originally built c1300, the castle stands on an island site surrounded by a 3 acre moat. Greatly enlarged in 1550 and decorated with plaster ceilings, panelling and fireplaces. Ancestral home of the Lords Saye and Sele since 1450.
www.broughtoncastle.demon.co.uk
Grant Recipient/Owner/Access contact: Lord Saye and Sele
Tel: 01295 262624 **Fax:** 01295 276070
Open: 1 May - 15 Sept: Wed and Sun, plus Thurs in July and Aug and BH Suns and BHs Mons (including Easter) 2 - 5pm. Groups at any time throughout the year by arrangement.
PSpaces: 150
Wheelchair access to ground floor only. WC for the disabled. Guide Dogs: Yes
£Adult: £5.50 **Child:** £2.50 (age 5-15)
Other: £4.50 (seniors/students)

Clattercote Priory Farm

Claydon, Banbury, Oxfordshire OX17 1QB

Founded c1150, the Priory is now a family house - part farmhouse, part tenanted. A rare example of a Gilbertine Priory with cellars and 'chapel', probably medieval.
Grant Recipient/Owner/Access contact:- Mr Adrian Taylor
Tel: 01295 690476 **Fax:** 01295 690476
E-mail: clattercote1@aol.com
Open: By prior written arrangement.
PSpaces: 4
No. Guide Dogs: Yes
£Adult: £5 (to cancer charity)

Cornbury Park

Charlbury, Oxford, Oxfordshire OX7 3EH

400 acre deer park adjacent to Wychwood forest containing newly restored/replanted beech avenues, ancient English oak trees and several ancient monuments.
www.cornburypark.co.uk
Grant Recipient/Owner: The Lord Rotherwick
Access contact: Helen Spearman & Richard Watkins
Tel: 01608 811276 **Fax:** 01608 811252

E-mail: estate@cpark.co.uk

Open: 1 Mar - 31 Oct: Tues and Thurs 10am - 4pm. Please note that a permit is required for access to the Park; permit must be applied for in advance. Organised educational access walks for groups by arrangement.
Ⓟ Spaces: 20 ♿ No £ No

Culham Manor Dovecote

The Green, Culham, Oxfordshire OX14 4LZ

Dovecote constructed from brick and stone, with a datestone above the door of 1685. Reputed to be the second largest dovecote in England, being formed of two large cells each with an entry lantern for dove access. In total it has over 3,000 nesting boxes.

Grant Recipient/Owner/Access contact: Mr James Wilson MacDonald

Tel: 01235 527009 **Fax:** 01865 744520

E-mail: wil.mac@virgin.net

Open: By prior arrangement at any time.
Ⓟ Spaces 20 ♿ No. Guide dogs: Yes. £ No

Farnborough Hall

Farnborough, Banbury, Oxfordshire OX17 1DU

Mid-18th century honey-coloured stone built home of the Holbech family for over 300 years, contains impressive plasterwork. Set in grounds with 18th century temples, a terrace walk and an obelisk.

www.nationaltrust.org.uk

Grant Recipient/Owner: The National Trust

Access contact: Mr & Mrs G Holbech

Tel: 01295 690002

E-mail: farnboroughhall@nationaltrust.org.uk

Open: House and grounds: Apr - end Sept, Weds and Sats 2 - 6pm; also 2 & 3 May 2 - 6pm. Terrace walk: Apr - end Sept, same days as house by arrangement.
Ⓟ Spaces: 10
♿ Wheelchair access to ground floor & garden. Terrace walk may be difficult(very steep). No WC for the disabled. Guide Dogs: Yes
£ **Adult:** £3.80, £1.90 (terrace walk only)
Child: £1.90 **Other:** £9.50 (family)

Freeman Mausoleum

St Mary's Churchyard, Fawley, Henley-on-Thames, Oxon RG9 6HZ

Built in 1752 for the Freeman family who owned the Fawley Estate. Design by John Freeman based on the mausoleum of Cecilia Metella on the Appian Way in Rome, which he visited while on his Grand Tour. It contains 30 coffin slots with 12 being filled by the Freemans before they sold the Estate in 1850.

Grant Recipient/Owner: St Mary's Parochial Church Council

Access contact: Mr R A Sykes

Tel: 01491 573778 **Fax:** 01491 411406

Open: Mausoleum permanently open. For further information please contact Mr R A Sykes (tel:01491 573778).
Ⓟ On-street parking adjacent to church. Spaces: 10
♿ Yes. No WC for the disabled. Guide Dogs: Yes
£ No

The Old Rectory Dovecote

Mill Street, Kidlington, Oxford, Oxfordshire OX5 2EE

Large round medieval dovecote.

Grant Recipient/Owner/Access contact: Ms Felicity Duncan

Tel: 01865 513816

Open: Daily, 10am - 5.30pm.
Ⓟ No ♿ No. Guide Dogs: Yes £ No

Shotover Park

Wheatley, Oxfordshire OX33 1QS

Early 18th century garden follies. The Gothic Temple (designer unknown) lies east of the house at the end of a long canal vista. Has a battlemented gable with a central pinnacle and a rose-window, below which is an open loggia of three pointed arches. The other Temple west of the house, designed by William Kent, is of a domed octagonal construction.

Grant Recipient/Owner/Access contact: Sir John Miller

Tel: 01865 872450 or 874095

Open: Access to Temples at all reasonable times (lie close to public rights of way). Parking for a few cars at the Gothic Temple, otherwise other arrangements can be made in advance with Sir John Miller or Mrs Price on 01865 874095.
Ⓟ Spaces: 50
♿ Wheelchair access to the Gothic Temple with assistance. WC for the disabled. Guide Dogs: Yes
£ No

Swalcliffe Tithe Barn

Shipston Road, Swalcliffe, Banbury, Oxfordshire OX15 5DR

15th century barn built for the Rectorial Manor of Swalcliffe by New College, who owned the Manor. Constructed between 1400 and 1409, much of the medieval timber half-cruck roof remains intact. It is now a museum.

www.oxfordshire-collections.org.uk

Grant Recipient/Owner: Oxfordshire Historic Building Trust Ltd

Access contact: Mr Martyn Brown

Tel: 01993 814114 **Fax:** 01993 813239

E-mail: martyn.brown@oxfordshire.gov.uk

Open: Easter - end of Sept: Sun and BHs, 2 - 5pm. At other times by arrangement. (contact Jeff Demmar tel:01295 788278).
Ⓟ Spaces: 10 ♿ Yes. WC for the disabled. Guide Dogs: Yes £ No

SHROPSHIRE

2/3 Milk Street

Shrewsbury, Shropshire SY1 1SZ

Timber-framed two and a half storey building dating from the 15th century with later alterations and additions. Medieval shop front to rear. Still a shop.

Grant Recipient/Owner: Mr M J Cockle

Access contact: Mr H Carter

Tel: 01743 236789 **Fax:** 01743 242140

E-mail: htc@pooks.co.uk

Open: Ground floor shop 6 days a week all year. Mon - Sat 9.30am - 5.30pm. Upper floor flats can be visited only by arrangement with Mr H Carter, Pooks, 26 Claremont Hill, Shrewsbury, Shropshire SY1 1RE.
Ⓟ No ♿ Wheelchair access to ground floor only. No WC for the disabled. Guide Dogs: Yes £ No

Attingham Park

Atcham, Shrewsbury, Shropshire SY4 4TP

Built 1785 by George Steuart for the 1st Lord Berwick, with a picture gallery by John Nash. Contains Regency interiors, Italian neo-classical furniture and Grand Tour paintings. Park landscaped by Repton in 1797.

www.nationaltrust.org.uk

Grant Recipient/Owner: The National Trust

Access contact: The Property Manager

Tel: 01743 708162 **Fax:** 01743 708175

E-mail: attingham@nationaltrust.org.uk

Open: House: 19 Mar - 31 Oct, daily except Wed and Thurs 12 - 5pm (last adm 4.30pm). Park: all year except Christmas Day, Mar - end Oct 10am - 8pm, Nov - Feb 10am - 5pm.
Ⓟ Spaces: 150 ♿ Yes. WC for the disabled. Guide Dogs: Yes
£ **Adult:** £5.20, £2.60 (park & grounds) **Child:** £2.60 **Family:** £13 **Booked Parties:** £4.50 (15+)

Benthall Hall

Broseley, Shropshire TF12 5RX

16th century stone house situated on a plateau above the gorge of the River Severn, with mullioned and transomed windows, carved oak staircase, decorated plaster ceilings and oak panelling. Also has a restored plantsman's garden, old kitchen garden and a Restoration church.

www.nationaltrust.org.uk

Grant Recipient/Owner: The National Trust

Access contact: The Custodian

Tel: 01952 882159

E-mail: benthall@nationaltrust.org.uk

Open: 6 Apr - 30 June: Tues and Wed 2 - 5.30pm. 3 July - 26 Sept: Tues, Wed and Sun 2 - 5.30pm. Also open BH Suns and Mons. Groups by arrangement with the custodian.
Ⓟ Spaces: 50
♿ Wheelchair access to ground floor of Hall & part of garden. No WC for the disabled. Guide Dogs: Yes
£ **Adult:** £4 **Child:** £2 **Other:** £2.50 (garden only)

Blodwell Summerhouse

Blodwell Hall, Llanyblodwell, Oswestry, Shropshire SY10 8LT

Square red brick summerhouse with ashlar dressings and slate roof, built 1718, at end of terrace in a restored formal garden.

Grant Recipient/Owner: Trustees of the Bradford Estate

Access contact: Mr R J Taylor

Tel: 07977 239955

Broseley Pipeworks

King Street, Broseley, Shropshire TF8 7AW

19th century clay pipe factory comprising a three storey factory range, bottle kiln, workers cottage and school room. Contents include pipe-making machinery and collection of smoking pipes. Main rooms contain the original equipment installed in the 1880s and used until the site was abandoned at the end of the 1950s.

www.ironbridge.org.uk

Grant Recipient/Owner: Ironbridge Gorge Museum Trust

Access contact: Mr Glen Lawes

Tel: 01952 433 522 **Fax:** 01952 432 204

E-mail: info@ironbridge.org.uk

Open: Apr to end of Oct 1 - 5pm.
Ⓟ Spaces: 10. Overflow at adjacent site for 20.
♿ Wheelchair access to ground floor and yard. WC for the disabled. Guide Dogs: Yes
£ **Adult:** £2.90 **Other:** £2.15 (senior citizens)

Dudmaston

Quatt, Bridgnorth, Shropshire WV15 6QN

Queen Anne mansion of red brick with stone dressings, situated in parkland overlooking the Severn. Contains furniture, Dutch flower paintings, contemporary paintings and sculpture. Gardens, wooded valley and estate walks starting from Hampton Loade.

www.nationaltrust.org.uk

Grant Recipient/Owner: The National Trust

Access contact: The Administrator

Tel: 01746 780866 **Fax:** 01746 780744

E-mail: dudmaston@nationaltrust.org.uk

Open: 4 Apr - 29 Sept: House: Tues, Wed and Sun 2 - 5.30pm; Garden: Mon, Tues, Wed & Sun 12 noon - 6pm; Shop: open same days as house 1 - 5.30pm; Tea Room: open same days as garden 11.30am - 5.30pm.
Ⓟ Spaces: 150
♿ Wheelchair access to main and inner halls, Library, oak room, No 1 and Derby galleries, old kitchen, garden and grounds (some estate walks), shop and tea room. WC for the disabled. Guide Dogs: Yes
£ **Adult:** £4.50 **Child:** £2.20
Other: £10.50 (family), £3.20 (garden only), £3.50 (booked groups of 15+)

Hospital of the Holy and Undivided Trinity

Hospital Lane, Clun, Shropshire SY7 8LE

Founded in 1607 by Henry Howard, Earl of Northampton and built in 1618 with alterations of 1857. Dwellings and other rooms arranged around a square courtyard. A well preserved example of a courtyard-plan almshouses.

Grant Recipient/Owner: The Trustees of Trinity Hospital

Access contact: Mrs J S Woodroffe

Tel: 01588 672303

Open: Gardens and chapel open each day apart from Christmas Day. Further public access under review at time of publication, please check the English Heritage website or with the access contact for current information.
Ⓟ Spaces: 70
♿ Yes. No WC for the disabled. Guide Dogs: Yes
£ No

John Rose Building

High Street, Coalport, Telford, Shropshire TF8 7HT

A range of china painting workshops, centre part dating from late 18th century, outer wings rebuilt early 20th century. Restored and converted to a Youth Hostel, with café, Coalport China Museum, craft workshops and shop. Main entrance is paved with mosaic celebrating the amalgamation of Coalport, Swansea and Nantgarw brands. Coalbrookdale cast iron windows of large dimension line both major elevations.

www.ironbridge.org.uk

Grant Recipient/Owner: Ironbridge Gorge Museum Trust

Access contact: Mr Glen Lawes

Tel: 01952 433 522 **Fax:** 01952 432 204

E-mail: info@ironbridge.org.uk

Open: Open all year except Jan. Café: 10am - 5pm daily. Workshops: 11am - 5pm Mon - Fri.

P Museum car park. Spaces: 65

⬆ Youth Hostel: wheelchair access to ground and first floor (stair lift) with disabled WC & shower facilities. China Museum: majority accessible, visiting guide available on arrival. WC for the disabled. Guide Dogs: Yes £No

Langley Gatehouse

Acton Burnell, Shropshire SY5 7PE

This gatehouse has two quite different faces: one is of plain dressed stone; the other, which once looked inwards to long demolished Langley Hall, is timber-framed. It was probably used for the Steward or important guests. It was rescued from a point of near collapse and shows repair work of an exemplary quality.

www.landmarktrust.co.uk

Grant Recipient/Owner: The Landmark Trust

Access contact: Mrs Victoria O'Keeffe

Tel: 01628 825920 **Fax:** 01628 825417

E-mail: vokeeffe@landmarktrust.co.uk

Open: The Landmark Trust is an independent charity, which rescues small buildings of historic or architectural importance from decay or unsympathetic improvement. Landmark's aim is to promote the enjoyment of these historic buildings by making them available to stay in for holidays. Langley Gatehouse can be rented by anyone, at all times of the year, for periods ranging from a weekend to three weeks. Bookings can be made by telephoning the Booking Office on 01628 825925. As the building is in full-time use for holiday accommodation, it is not normally open to the public. However the public can view the building by arrangement. by telephoning the access contact to make an appointment. Potential visitors will be asked to write to confirm the details of their visit.

P Spaces: 2 ⬆No. Guide Dogs: Yes £No

Lord Hill Column

Abbey Foregate, Shrewsbury, Shropshire SY2 6LU

Giant fluted Greek Doric column surmounted by a statue of Lord Hill (1772-1842). Erected 1814 to 1816 and designed by Edward Haycock of Shrewsbury and Thomas Harrison of Chester, the monument stands 132 feet, 6 inches high and was built by public subscription to honour Lord Hill's achievements during the Napoleonic Wars as a Lieutenant-General under Wellington.

Grant Recipient/Owner: Shropshire County Council

Access contact: Mr Peter Hepper

Tel: 01743 252896 **Fax:** 01743 252862

Open: The monument can be viewed from the exterior at all times, access to the interior by prior booking of escorted ascent on open days (3 per annum in June, July and a Heritage Open Day in Sept). Access at other times by arrangement.

P Free parking (150 metres). Spaces: 100

⬆No £No

Loton Hall

Alberbury, Shropshire SY5 9AJ

Country house, c1670, but extensively altered and enlarged in the early 18th and 19th centuries. Set in parkland which includes the ruins of the early 13th century Alberbury Castle. Home of the Leighton family since the 14th century.

Grant Recipient/Owner: Sir Michael Leighton

Access contact: Mr Mark Williams

Tel: 01691 655334 **Fax:** 01691 657798

Open: House: 5 Jan - 8 Apr, Mons and Thurs by guided tour only at 10am or 12 noon. Garden and castle also can be viewed at the same times.

P Spaces: 30

⬆No. Guide Dogs: Yes

£Adult: £5 Child: Free Senior: £3

The Lyth

Ellesmere, Shropshire SY12 0HR

Grade II* listed small country house, c1820, with minor later additions. Cast-iron verandah with trellised supports, one of the earliest and largest examples in the country. Birthplace of E & D Jebb, founders of Save the Children.

Grant Recipient/Owner/Access contact: Mr L R Jebb

Tel: 01691 622339 **Fax:** 01691 624134

Open: To the exterior on the following Suns: 11 Apr, 30 May, 19 Sept, 10 Oct, 2 - 6pm. Other times by arrangement with Mr Jebb.

P Spaces: 40

⬆Yes. No WC for the disabled. Guide Dogs: Yes

£Adult: £2 Child: £1 (charity donation for visits to garden)

Newport Guildhall

High Street, Newport, Shropshire TF10 7TX

15th century timber framed Guildhall now used as town council offices and registered as a venue for Civil Weddings.

www.newportsaloptowncouncil.co.uk

Grant Recipient/Owner: Newport Town Council

Access contact: Miss Dee Halliday

Tel: 01952 814338 **Fax:** 01952 825353

E-mail: townclerk@newportsaloptowncouncil.co.uk

Open: Mon - Fri, 9am - 1pm (closed BHs). 3 other Special Open Days in July & Aug planned, contact Town Council for details.

P Spaces: 5 ⬆Wheelchair access via chair lift to first floor. No WC for the disabled. Guide Dogs: Yes £No

The Old Mansion

St Mary's Street, Shrewsbury, Shropshire SY1 1UQ

Early 17th century house with original staircase. The building was renovated in 1997 and now provides 4 bedroom suites for the Prince Rupert Hotel.

Grant Recipient/Owner/Access contact:: Mr A Humphreys

Tel: 01291 672 563**Open:** By arrangement with the Prince Rupert Hotel (tel: 01743 499955).

P Public car park in town centre. ⬆No £No

Old Market Hall

The Square, Shrewsbury, Shropshire SY1 1HJ

Old market hall and court house, dated 1596 and listed Grade I. Recently repaired and refurbished to accommodate a Film and Digital Media Centre, including auditorium and café/bar.

www.musichall.co.uk

Grant Recipient/Owner: Shrewsbury & Atcham Borough Council

Access contact: Miss Lezley Picton

Tel: 01743 281287 **Fax:** 01743 281283

E-mail: lezley@musichall.co.uk

Open: Daily 10am - 11pm. Auditorium closed to public when film being screened. Current screening times: Mon - Sat evening films, Tues and Sat matinees starting at 2.30pm.

P No

⬆Yes. WC for the disabled. Guide Dogs: Yes

£No. Charges for performances only (Adult £4.50, Child £3)

Pradoe

West Felton, Oswestry, Shropshire SY11 4ER

Georgian country house set in park and garden designed by John Webb. Grade II* listed house contains furniture dating from 1803 - 1812 during initial occupation by the Kenyon family. Attached service ranges, walled kitchen garden and outbuildings including dairy, malthouse and carpenter's shop, contain original early 19th century features, recently restored.

Grant Recipient/Owner/Access contact: Colonel John F Kenyon

Tel: 01691 610218 **Fax:** 01691 610913

Open: Apr - Sept, dates to be confirmed. Please check with the house or the English Heritage website for current information.

P Spaces: 50 ⬆Wheelchair access to gardens only. No WC for the disabled. Guide Dogs: Yes

£Please contact access contact for details.

Weston Park

Weston-under-Lizard, Shifnal, Shropshire TF11 8LE

Stately home, built 1671, designed by Lady Wilbraham. Houses collection of paintings by Van Dyck, Gainsborough, Lely and Stubbs, and is surrounded by 1000 acres of 'Capability' Brown parkland and formal gardens. Formerly home to the Earls of Bradford, now held in trust for the nation by The Weston Park Foundation.

www.weston-park.com

Grant Recipient/Owner: Weston Park Foundation

Access contact: Mr Colin Sweeney

Tel: 01952 852100 **Fax:** 01952 850430

E-mail: enquiries@weston-park.com

Open: Easter 10 Apr, then every weekend and BH in Apr, May and June; July & Aug: daily (excluding 1, 2, 31 July and 19 - 25 Aug); 4 - 5 Sept. House 1 - 5pm (last adm 4.30pm). Park and Gardens 11am - 7pm (last adm 5pm).

P Spaces: 300 ⬆Wheelchair access to all areas except open parkland and some formal gardens. WC for the disabled. Guide Dogs: Yes

£Adult: £2.50 (house), £3 (park) Child: £1.50 (house), £2 (park) Other: £2 (house), £2.50 (park), £10 (family)

Yeaton Peverey Hall

Yeaton Peverey, Shrewsbury, Shropshire SY4 3AT

Mock Jacobean country house, 1890-2 by Aston Webb. Previously a school, now reinstated as a family home. Principal rooms on the ground floor open to visitors.

Grant Recipient/Owner/Access contact: Mr Martin Ebelis

Tel: 01743 851185 **Fax:** 01743 851186

E-mail: mae@earlstone.co.uk

Open: By arrangement all year. Opening arrangements under review at time of publication, please check with Mr Ebelis or English Heritage website for current information.

P Parking adjacent to the property for disabled. Spaces: 6

⬆Yes. WC for the disabled. Guide Dogs: No

£Adult: £5 Child: £2

SOMERSET

29 Queen Square

Bristol BS1 4ND

Early Georgian town house, 1709-11, listed Grade II*. Brick with limestone dressings. One of the few surviving original houses in Queen Square which was laid out in 1699 and has claim to be the largest square in England.

Grant Recipient/Owner: The Queen Square Partnership

Access contact: Reception

Tel: 0117 975 0700 **Fax:** 0117 975 0701

E-mail: southwest@english-heritage.org.uk

Open: Mon - Fri 9am - 5pm, except BHs.

P Paid parking in Queen Square and The Grove behind 29 Queen Square.

⬆Partial. Wheelchair access to ground and first floors. WC for the disabled. Guide Dogs: Yes £No

Bath Assembly Rooms

Bennett Street, Bath, Somerset BA1 2QH

Built in 1771 by John Wood the Younger, now owned by the National Trust and administered by Bath & North East Somerset District Council. Each room has a complete set of original chandeliers. Museum of Costume is on the lower ground floor.

www.museumofcostume.co.uk

Grant Recipient/Owner: Bath City Council/National Trust

Access contact: Ms Rosemary Harden

Tel: 01225 477752 **Fax:** 01225 444793

E-mail: rosemary_harden@bathnes.gov.uk

Open: Daily 10am - 5pm when not in use for pre-booked functions. Telephone in advance (01225 477789) to check availability. There are no pre-booked functions during the day during Aug. Closed Christmas Day and Boxing Day.

P On street car parking (pay and display).

⬆Yes. WC for the disabled. Guide Dogs: Yes

£No, but charge for Museum of Costume

British Empire and Commonwealth Museum

Clock Tower Yard, Temple Meads, Bristol BS1 6QH

Museum housed in world's earliest surviving railway terminus, which was completed in 1840 and was originally part of the Great Western Railway designed by I K Brunel. Over 220ft long with timber and iron roof spans of 72ft, this Grade I listed building has been nominated as a World Heritage Site. Contains the Passenger shed and the adjoining former Engine and Carriage shed.

www.empiremuseum.co.uk

Grant Recipient/Owner: Empire Museum Ltd

Access contact: Mr Stephen Barber

Tel: 0117 925 4980 **Fax:** 0117 925 4983

E-mail: stephen.barber@empiremuseum.co.uk

Open: Daily 10am - 5pm, except 25 & 26 Dec. Access to exterior is unrestricted.

P Parking in Station car park. Spaces: 25

⬆Yes. WC for the disabled. Guide Dogs: Yes

£Adult: £5.95 Child: £3.95 Other: £4.95 (subject to change)

Clevedon Pier

The Beach, Clevedon, Somerset BS21 7QU

Pier with attached toll house built c1860s to serve steamers bound for South Wales. Wrought and cast iron structure and shelters consisting of eight 100ft arched spans leading to a landing stage. The exceptionally slender spans are constructed from riveted broad-gauge railway track as designed by W H

Barlow for the Great Western Railway. Scottish baronial style toll house contains shop and art gallery. Pier restored in 1999 after partial collapse 30 years earlier and is one of only two Grade I listed piers. This pier is of outstanding importance for its delicate engineering and the relationship of pier to landward buildings, which creates an exceptionally picturesque ensemble.

Grant Recipient/Owner: The Clevedon Pier and Heritage Trust

Access contact: Miss Mikhael Munday

Tel: 01275 878846   **Fax:** 01275 790077

E-mail: clevedonpier@zoom.co.uk

Open: All year except Christmas Day: Mon - Wed 10am - 5pm, Thurs - Sun 9am - 5pm

P On seafront.   No wheelchair access to art gallery. No WC for the disabled. Guide Dogs: Yes

£ Adult: £1   Child: 50p   Other: 75p (senior citizens)

Englishcombe Tithe Barn

Rectory Farmhouse, Englishcombe, Bath, Somerset BA2 9DU

Early 14th century cruck framed tithe barn. Recently restored with new crucks, masonry and straw lining to the roof, and filigree windows unblocked. There are masons and other markings on the walls. Now used as a venue, principally for Civil weddings and wedding receptions.

www.barnhire.com

Grant Recipient/Owner/Access contact: Mrs Jennie Walker

Tel: 01225 425073   **E-mail:** jennie@barnhire.com

Open: BHs 2 - 6pm; all other times by arrangement with Mrs Walker. Closed 1-19 Jan 2004.

P Spaces: 34

Yes. WC for the disabled. Guide Dogs: Yes   **£** No

Fairfield, Stogursey

nr. Bridgwater, Somerset TA5 1PU

Elizabethan manor house, medieval in origin and listed Grade II*. Built by an ancestor of the present owner. Undergoing extensive repairs. Set in woodland garden with views of the Quantocks.

Grant Recipient/Owner: Lady Gass

Access contact: Mr D W Barke

Tel: 01722 327087 or 01278 732251

Fax: 01722 413229

Open: Provisional: House: 28 Apr - 30 June: Wed, Thurs, Fri & BHs by guided tour at 2.30pm & 3.30pm. Groups at other times by arrangement. (Dates to be confirmed. Please contact the agent or check the English Heritage website for current information). Garden: open for NGS and other charities on dates advertised in Spring. No inside photography.

P No parking for coaches. Spaces: 30

Yes. WC for the disabled. Guide Dogs: Yes

£ Adult: £4   Child: £1

Other: Admission charges in aid of Stogursey Church

Forde Abbey

Chard, Somerset TA20 4LU

Cistercian monastery founded in 1140 and dissolved in 1539 when the church was demolished. The monks quarters were converted in 1640 into an Italian style "palazzo" by Sir Edmund Prideaux. Interior has plaster ceilings and Mortlake tapestries.

www.fordeabbey.co.uk

Grant Recipient/Owner: Trustees of the Roper Settlement

Access contact: Mrs Clay

Tel: 01460 220231

E-mail: forde.abbey@virgin.net

Open: Gardens: daily 10am - 4.30pm. House: Apr - Oct; Tues - Fri, Sun & BHs 12 noon - 4pm.

P Spaces: 500   Wheelchair access to ground floor and garden. WC for the disabled. Guide Dogs: Yes

£ Adult: £7.00   Child: Free

Gants Mill

Gants Mill Lane, Bruton, Somerset BA10 0DB

Working watermill with deeds dating back to owner John le Gaunt in 1290. The documents were saved for posterity by the model for "Tom Jones's" Sophia Weston. Corn grinding demonstrations, historical displays. Designer watergarden with sculptures, ponds, streams, rose pergolas. Collections of iris, delphiniums, penstemons, day lilies and dahlias. Riverside walk.

www.gantsmill.co.uk

Grant Recipient/Owner: Mr Brian Shingler

Access contact: Brian & Alison Shingler

Tel: 01749 812393 **E-mail:** shingler@gantsmill.co.uk

Open: 15 May - end Sept, Suns, Thurs & BHs 2 - 5pm. Groups by arrangement. Refreshments available.

P Spaces: 40

Wheelchair access to gardens only. No WC for the disabled. Guide Dogs: Yes

£ Adult: £4   Child: £1   Other: Group reductions by arrangement

Goldney Hall Hercules Statue

Lower Clifton Hill, Bristol BS8 1BH

Grade II* listed lead statue of Hercules. Erected 1758. Part of a notable and well-preserved mid 18th century garden layout. Located approximately 100 metres south of Goldney Hall.

Grant Recipient/Owner: University of Bristol

Access contact: Dr Paul O'Prey

Tel: 0117 903 4873/0117 954 4792

Fax: 0117 9034877

E-mail: goldney@bristol.ac.uk

Open: Hall: 25 Apr 2 - 6pm; charity open days: 23 May & 1 Aug 2 - 5.30pm. Group tours at other times by arrangement. Events throughout the year. Available for hire during the summer vacation.

P On site parking during University vacations. Spaces: 22

Wheelchair access to the statue and grounds. No WC for the disabled. Guide Dogs: Yes

£ Adult: £2.50   Child: £1.50 (under 5s free) Other: £1. (open days)

Great House Farm

Theale, Wedmore, Somerset BS28 4SJ

17th century farmhouse with Welsh slate roof, oak doors and some original diamond paned windows. Inside is a carved well staircase with two murals on the walls. There are four servants' rooms at the top, three of which are dark and occupied by Lesser Horseshoe bats.

Grant Recipient/Owner/Access contact: Mr A R Millard

Tel: 01934 713133

Open: Apr-Aug: Tues & Thurs 2 - 6pm by telephone arrangement.

P Spaces: 6

No. Guide Dogs: Yes

£ Adult: £2   Child: Free   Other: £1 (senior citizens)

Gurney Manor

Cannington, Somerset TA5 2MW

Late medieval house built around a courtyard. Used as a tenant farm before converted into flats in the 1940s, now restored to its original undivided state.

www.landmarktrust.co.uk

Grant Recipient/Owner: The Landmark Trust

Access contact: Mrs Victoria O'Keeffe

Tel: 01628 825920   **Fax:** 01628 825417

E-mail: vokeeffe@landmarktrust.co.uk

Open: The Landmark Trust is an independent charity, which rescues small buildings of historic or architectural importance from decay or unsympathetic improvement. Landmark's aim is to promote the enjoyment of these historic buildings by making them available to stay in for holidays. Gurney Manor can be rented by anyone, at all times of the year, for periods ranging from a weekend to three weeks. Bookings can be made by telephoning the Booking Office on 01628 825925. As the building is in full-time use for holiday accommodation, it is not normally open to the public. However the public can view the building by arrangement, by telephoning the access contact (Victoria O'Keeffe on 01628 825920) to make an appointment. Potential visitors will be asked to write to confirm the details of their visit.

P Spaces: 3   No. Guide Dogs: Yes   **£** No

Hall Farm High Barn

Stogumber, Taunton, Somerset TA4 3TQ

17th century Grade II* listed building with seven bays of red local sandstone rubble with jointed cruck roof. South wall supported by four buttresses but there are none on the North wall. There are blocked windows on the South wall and two stub walls extend north. Lines of joist holes were provided for internal flooring and the two main entrances were to the north and south.

Grant Recipient/Owner/Access contact: C M & R Hayes

Tel: 01984 656321

Open: By prior arrangement with C M & R Hayes at Hall Farm.

P Spaces: 4

Yes. No WC for the disabled. Guide Dogs: Yes

£ No

Hestercombe

Cheddon Fitzpaine, Taunton, Somerset TA2 8LG

Formal gardens, featuring terraces, rills and an orangery, designed by Sir Edwin Lutyens and Gertrude Jekyll. The newly restored Landscape Garden was designed by Bampfylde in 1750 and comprises 40 acre pleasure grounds with classical temples and a Great Cascade.

www.hestercombegardens.com

Grant Recipient/Owner: Somerset County Council

Access contact: Mr Philip White

Tel: 01823 413923   **Fax:** 01823 413747

E-mail: info@hestercombegardens.com

Open: Daily, including Christmas Day, 10am - 5pm (last adm).

P Spaces: 100

Limited wheelchair access to Gardens. Full access to toilets and tea room. WC for the disabled. Guide Dogs: Yes

£ Adult: £5.20   Child: £1.20 (age 5-15)   Other: £4.90 (senior citizens), £4.20 (groups 20+)

Lancin Farmhouse

Wambrook, Chard, Somerset TA20 3EG

14th century farmhouse with old oak beams, fireplaces with the original smoking thatch, flagstone floors and breadoven.

Grant Recipient/Owner: Mr S J Smith

Access contact: Mrs R A Smith

Tel: 01460 62290

Open: 5 May; 25 May; 10 June; 24 June; 1 July; 22 July; 19 Aug; 25 Aug; 2 Sept; 22 Sept. At other times Tues, Wed or Thurs 10am - 5pm by arrangement.

P Spaces: 5   No   **£** Adult: £2.

The Old Manse

4 Bath Road, Beckington, Somerset BA11 6SW

Late 16th/early 17th century gabled stone built dwelling with mullioned windows with transoms to front elevation and stone tiled roof. Contains 2 large Plantagenet/Tudor fireplaces, 16th century oak staircase, strapwork ceilings and transitional rococo fireplaces. Gallery of attic rooms reveal an unusual roof structure.

www.old-manse.co.uk

Grant Recipient/Owner/Access contact: Mr M J Evans

Tel: 01373 831401   **Fax:** 01373 831401

E-mail: jennie@old-manse.co.uk

Open: By prior arrangement.

P On-street parking.   No. Guide Dogs: Yes   **£** No

Orchard Wyndham

Williton, Somerset TA4 4HH

Manor house, originally medieval but with many subsequent alterations and additions. Family home of the Wyndhams and their ancestors, the Orchards and Sydenhams, for 700 years.

Grant Recipient/Owner: The Wyndham Estate

Access contact: Dr K S H Wyndham

Tel: 01984 632309   **Fax:** 01984 633526

E-mail: wyndhamest@talk21.com

Open: 30 July - 27 Aug: Thurs and Fri 2 - 5pm, BH Mon 11am - 5pm, by guided tour (groups max 8 persons, last tour 4pm). Other times by arrangement. (min 2 weeks notice requested).

P Spaces: 25

Wheelchair access to ground floor and gardens only. No WC for the disabled. Guide Dogs: Yes

£ Adult: £5   Child: £1 (under 12)

Prior Park College Chapel, Mansion & Old Gymnasium

Ralph Allen Drive, Bath, Somerset BA2 5AH

Built for Ralph Allen in the mid-18th century as an early and successful demonstration of the quality of Bath stone. The Chapel and Old Gymnasium are part of the mid-19th century additions to adapt the property as a Catholic seminary for Bishop Baines. Now a boarding and day school.

www.priorpark.co.uk

Grant Recipient/Owner: Governors of Prior Park College

Access contact: C J Freeman

Tel: 01225 837491   **Fax:** 01225 835753

E-mail: bursar@priorpark.co.uk

Open: Chapel: Suns all year for public worship, & 13 June 2 - 5pm, or by arrangement. Mansion: certain Suns Mar - July 11.30am - 6pm, please tel or e-mail for details, & 13 June 2 - 5pm; Limited number of group tours in July and Aug by arrangement. Old

Gymnasium: 5 July - 15 Aug, Mon - Fri 10am - 4pm but please telephone in advance.
🅿Spaces: 50 ♿Wheelchair access to ground floor of Mansion via wooden ramp and to Chapel. No access to upper floors of Mansion or Old Gymnasium. WC for the disabled. Guide Dogs: Yes
♿Adult: £3 Child: £3 Other: £3

Rowes Leadworks

('Wildscreen at Bristol' and Firehouse restaurant), Harbourside, Bristol BS1 5DB
A former leadworks built in the 19th century. One of a few surviving structures associated with the industrial character of this area with a goods station and nearby warehouses. Now transformed into a restaurant/bar, The Firehouse Rotisseries. Attached to this is a modern canopied, large open structure, the entrance to 'Wildscreen at Bristol' which features imagery and interactive exhibits of the natural world. It includes an IMAX cinema and living botanical house.
www.at-bristol.org.uk
Grant Recipient/Owner: Bristol City Council
Access contact: Mr John Durant
Tel: 0117 9092000 **Fax:** 0117 9157202
E-mail: john.durant@at-bristol.org.uk
Open: All venues: daily 10am - 6pm. Possible late openings for Aug (please ring for confirmation). Public squares and spaces around the leadworks open all year round.
🅿Pay parking operated by Bristol City Council. Spaces: 500
♿WC for the disabled. Guide Dogs: Yes
£No, but charges for access to 'Wildscreen at Bristol' and the IMAX theatre

Rowlands Mill

Rowlands, Ilminster, Somerset TA19 9LE
Grade II* stone and brick 3-storey millhouse and machinery, c1620, with a mill pond, mill race, overshooting wheel and waterfall. The millhouse is now a holiday let but the machinery has separate access and is in working condition.
Grant Recipient/Owner/Access contact:
Mr P G H Speke
Tel: 01460 52623 **Fax:** 01460 52623
Open: Millhouse Fris and machinery Mon - Fri 10am - 4pm by written arrangement (at least 1 week's notice required). Heritage Open Days machinery only unless a Fri, then whole building.
🅿Spaces: 7
♿Wheelchair access to ground floor only. No WC for the disabled. Guide Dogs: Yes
£Adult: £3 Child: Free

Royal West of England Academy

Queen's Road, Clifton, Bristol BS8 1PX
Bristol's first Art Gallery, founded in 1844 and Grade II* listed. A fine interior housing five naturally lit art galleries, a new commercial gallery and a permanent fine art collection. Open to the public throughout the year.
www.rwa.org.uk
Grant Recipient/Owner: Royal West of England Academy
Access contact: Miss Clare Wood
Tel: 0117 9735129 **Fax:** 0117 9237874
E-mail: info@rwa.org.uk
Open: Mon - Sat 10am - 5.30pm, Sun 2pm - 5pm. BHs 11am - 4pm. Closed 25 Dec - 1 Jan & Easter Day.
🅿5 spaces for Disabled Badge Holders only.
♿Wheelchair access to New Gallery on ground floor and Main Galleries accessible by lift. Downstairs gallery not accessible. No WC for the disabled. Guide Dogs: Yes
£Adult: £2.50 Child: Free (under 16) Conc: £1.25

St George's Bristol

Great George Street, Bristol, Somerset BS1 5RR
Grade II* listed Georgian former church, c1821-3, by Robert Smirke in Greek Revival style, now 550 seater concert hall. A Waterloo church, built as a chapel-of-ease to Cathedral of St Augine, and converted to a concert hall in 1987. The crypt now houses a café and art gallery.
www.stgeorgesbristol.co.uk
Grant Recipient/Owner: St George's Bristol
Access contact: Mrs Catherine Freda
Tel: 0117 929 4929 **Fax:** 0117 927 6537
E-mail: c.freda@stgeorgesbristol.co.uk
Open: For seasonal concert programmes - mainly evenings, some lunchtimes and Sun afternoons,

contact Box Office on 0117 9230359 for brochure. Free access to crypt and art gallery from 1 hour before concerts. Tours can be arranged if dates comply with events schedule.
🅿Disabled parking & evenings only. Pay & display around building and 2 NCPs within 5 mins walk. Spaces: 3
♿Wheelchair access via Charlotte Street. The auditorium stalls, crypt/café/gallery and Box Office are accessible but preferable if you ring in advance as entry is not straightforward. WC for the disabled. Guide Dogs: Yes
£No, but tickets required for concerts

Temple of Harmony

Halswell Park, Goathurst, Bridgwater, Somerset TA5 2DH
18th century folly, a copy of the Temple of Verilis, forms part of the 18th century Pleasure Gardens at Halswell House. Restored in 1994.
www.somersite.co.uk/temple.htm
Grant Recipient/Owner: Somerset Buildings Preservation Trust
Access contact: Mr Richard Mathews
Tel: 01278 786012 **Fax:** 01278 786012
E-mail: richard.p.mathews@totalise.co.uk
Open: 1 June - end Sept: Sat & Sun 2 - 5pm, plus Easter Weekend and May Day BH. Any other day by arrangement with Mrs J Hirst, Honorary Treasurer, The Halswell Park Trust, 27 Durliegh Road, Bridgwater, Somerset TA6 7HX (tel: 01278 429342).
🅿Spaces: 4 ♿No. Guide Dogs: Yes
£Adult: £1 Child: 50p Senior: 50p

SOUTH YORKSHIRE

Hickleton Hall

Hickleton, South Yorkshire DN5 7BB
Georgian Mansion, grade II* listed, built in the 1740s to a design by James Paine with later additions. The interior is noted for its plasterwork ceilings. Set in 15 acres of formal gardens laid out in the early 1900s, the Hall is now a residential care home.
Grant Recipient/Owner: Sue Ryder Care
Access contact: Mrs A J Towriss
Tel: 01709 892070 **Fax:** 01709 890140
Open: By prior arrangement with Mrs Towriss at Sue Ryder Care, Mon - Fri 2 - 4pm.
🅿Available.
♿Wheelchair access to Hall only; no access to gardens. WC for the disabled. Guide Dogs: Yes
£No

The Lyceum Theatre

Tudor Square, Sheffield, South Yorkshire S1 1DA
Grade II* listed theatre built 1897. The only surviving example of the work of WGR Sprague outside London. Its special features include a domed corner tower, a lavish Rococo auditorium (1097 seats) and a proscenium arch with a rare open-work valance in gilded plasterwork. A notable example of a theatre of the period, with a largely unaltered interior.
www.sheffieldtheatres.co.uk
Grant Recipient/Owner: The Lyceum Theatre Trust
Access contact: The Box Office
Tel: 0114 249 6000 **Fax:** 0114 249 6003
Open: Performances throughout the year. 21 scheduled backstage tours per year. All tours commence at 10.30am. Group guided tours by arrangement. Contact the Box Office (tel:0114 249 6000) or check the website for further information.
🅿National Car Park adjacent to the theatre. Spaces: 600
♿Wheelchair access all areas except 2 private entertaining rooms. WC for the disabled. Guide Dogs: Yes
£Adult: £3 (backstage tour) Other: Charge for performances

Moated Site & Chapel

Thorpe Lane, Thorpe-in-Balne, Doncaster, South Yorks DN6 0DY
Medieval chapel, moated site and fishponds. Built 12th century with 13th, 14th, 15th and 19th century alterations. Restored and re-roofed in 1994/5. In 1452 the chapel was the scene of the forcible abduction of Joan, wife of Charles Nowel, by Edward Lancaster of Skipton in Craven, which resulted in the passing of an Act of Parliament for the redress of grievance and the better protection of females.
Grant Recipient/Owner: Mr Attey

Access contact: Mrs Attey
Tel: 01302 883160
Open: By arrangement with Mrs Attey at the Manor House, Thorpe Ln, Thorpe-in-Balne, Doncaster, South Yorks DN6 0DY.
🅿Spaces: 10
♿No. Guide Dogs: Yes
£No, but donations for charity welcomed

STAFFORDSHIRE

10 The Close

Lichfield, Staffordshire WS13 7LD
Early 15th century timber-framed house, originally one-up one-down and part of a five-dwelling range in the Vicar's Close. Notable doors and solid tread staircase remains in attic. Currently residence of assistant cathedral organist.
Grant Recipient/Owner: Dean & Chapter of Lichfield Cathedral
Access contact: Mr Alexander Mason
Tel: 01543 306201 **Fax:** 01543 306201
Open: By prior written arrangement.
🅿Public car parks nearby.
♿No. Guide Dogs: Yes
£No

Barlaston Hall

Barlaston, nr. Stoke-on-Trent, Staffordshire ST12 9AT
Mid-18th century Palladian villa attributed to Sir Robert Taylor, with public rooms containing some fine examples of 18th century plasterwork. Extensively restored during the 1990s.
Grant Recipient/Owner/Access contact: Mr James Hall
Fax: 01782 372391
Open: 9 Mar - 14 Sept: Tues 2 - 5pm. No groups.
🅿Spaces: 6 ♿No £Adult: £2.50 Child: £1.50
Other: No charge for Historic Houses Association members

Biddulph Grange Garden

Biddulph, Stoke-on-Trent, Staffordshire ST8 7SD
Garden with series of connected apartments designed to display specimens from James Bateman's extensive and wide ranging plant collection. Visitors are taken on a miniature tour of the world featuring the Egyptian court, China, a Scottish glen, as well as a pinetum and rock areas.
www.nationaltrust.org.uk
Grant Recipient/Owner: The National Trust
Access contact: Property Manager
Tel: 01782 517999 **Fax:** 01782 510624
E-mail: biddulphgrange@nationaltrust.org.uk
Open: 20 and 21 Mar: 12 noon - 6pm. 27 Mar - 31 Oct: Wed - Sun 12 noon - 6pm (High Season). 1 Nov - 19 Dec: Sat & Sun 11am - 3pm (Low Season).
🅿Spaces: 100 ♿Wheelchair access to Lime Avenue, Lake, Pinetum, Cheshire Cottage, Egypt and East Terrace. No WC for the disabled. Guide Dogs: Yes
£Adult: £4.80 (High Season), £2 (Low Season) Child: £2.40 (High Season), £1 (Low Season)
Other: £12 (family, High Season), £5 (family, Low Season)

Cheddleton Flint Mill

Cheddleton, Leek, nr. Stoke-on-Trent, Staffordshire ST13 7HL
18th century complex for grinding flint comprising two working watermills. South Mill modified in 19th century and now contains displays relating to the pottery industry.
www.ex.ac.uk/~akoutram/cheddleton-mill
Grant Recipient/Owner: Cheddleton Flint Mill Industrial Heritage Trust
Access contact: Mr E E Royle, MBE
Tel: 01782 502907
Open: Apr - Sept (including BHs), Sat - Sun 1pm - 5pm. Weekdays by arrangement (tel: 01782 502907).
🅿Spaces: 18
♿Wheelchair access to ground floor only. WC for disabled planned for 2004. Guide Dogs: No
£No

Claymills Pumping Engines

Victorian Pumping Station, The Sewage Works, Meadow Lane, Stretton, Burton-on-Trent, Staffordshire DE13 0DA
Large Victorian steam-operated sewage pumping station built in 1885. Four beam engines housed in two Italianate engine houses, two operational on

steaming weekends. Boiler house with range of five Lancashire boilers, large Victorian steam-operated workshop with blacksmith's forge, steam hammer, and steam driven machinery. 1930s dynamo house with very early D.C. generating equipment, earliest dynamo 1889 (all operational). The site houses the largest number of steam engines in Britain still working in their original state (19).
www.claymills.org.uk
Grant Recipient/Owner: Severn Trent Water Ltd
Access contact: Mr Roy Barratt
Tel: 01283 534960 **Fax:** 07092 275534
E-mail: roybarratt@yahoo.co.uk
Open: Every Thurs and Sat for static viewing. Steaming weekends 10am - 5pm: Easter 11 - 12 Apr, Early May BH 2 - 3 May, Father's Day 12 - 13 June, Aug BH 29 - 30 Aug, 18 - 19 Sept, 23 - 24 Oct, 1 - 2 Jan 2005. Admission charged for steaming weekends, donations requested on other open days. Refreshments available.
P For disabled adjacent to site. 6 coaches. Spaces: 100
♿ Wheelchair access to ground floor only (boiler house, workshop, refreshments, engine house). WC for the disabled. Guide Dogs: Yes
£ **Adult:** £3 **Child/Seniors:** £2 **Family:** £7

Clifton Hall

Clifton Campville, Staffordshire B79 0BE
Small country house built in 1705, perhaps by Francis Smith of Warwick for Sir Charles Pye. Two monumental wings flanking a courtyard, the intention being to link them with a central main building which was never constructed. This strange history explains why the Hall unusually developed out of what would have been the servants' wing.
Grant Recipient/Owner/Access contact:
Mr Richard Blunt
Tel: 01827 373681 **Fax:** 01827 373681
Open: By prior arrangement only, any weekday 9am - 5pm all year.
P Spaces: 10
♿ Yes No WC for the disabled. Guide Dogs: Yes
£ **Adult:** £4.50 **Child:** £2 **Other:** £2

Kinver Edge (Hill Fort)

nr. Stourbridge, Staffordshire
A sandstone ridge covered in woodland and heath with Iron Age hill fort with views across surrounding countryside. Famous Holy Austin Rock Houses, inhabited until 1950s, have been restored and parts are open to visitors at selected times.
www.nationaltrust.org.uk
Grant Recipient/Owner: The National Trust
Access contact: The Warden
Tel: 01384 872418
E-mail: kinveredge@nationaltrust.org.uk
Open: Kinver Edge is open at all times free of charge. Holy Austin Rock House grounds: daily, Apr - Sept 9am - 7pm, Oct - Mar 9am - 4pm. Upper Terrace: Wed, Sat & Sun, Apr - Sept 2 - 5pm, Oct - Mar 2 - 4pm. Lower Rock Houses: Mar - Nov, Sat & Sun 2 - 4pm. Other times for guided tours by arrangement with Custodian (tel:01384 872553).
P Spaces: 100 ♿ No. Guide Dogs: Yes
£ Lower Rock Houses only **Adult:** 50p **Child:** 25p

Shugborough

Milford, Stafford, Staffordshire ST17 0XB
The present house was begun c1695. Between 1760 and 1770 it was enlarged and again partly remodelled by Samuel Wyatt at end of 18th century. The interior is particularly notable for its plaster work and other decorations. Ancestral home of the Earls of Lichfield. Houses the Staffordshire County Museum, Georgian working farm and Rare Livestock Breed project.
www.staffordshire.gov.uk
Grant Recipient/Owner: The National Trust
Access contact: Property Manager
Tel: 01889 881388 **Fax:** 01889 881323
E-mail: shugborough.promotions@staffordshire.gov.uk
Open: House, county museum, farm and gardens: 27 Mar - 26 Sept, daily except Mons (but open BH Mons); Oct first four Suns only; 11am - 5pm (last adm 4.15pm). Opening times may vary, telephone to check. Tours for booked groups daily from 10.30am. Evening tours also available.
P Spaces: 600
♿ Wheelchair access to ground floor of house and museum only. WC for the disabled. Guide Dogs: Yes
£ **Adult:** £6 (House & servants' quarters), £2 (Farm) **Child:** £4 (House & servants' quarters), £1 (Farm) **Other:** £4 (House & servants' quarters), £1 (Farm)

Sinai House

Shobnall Road, Burton on Trent, Staffordshire DE14 2BB
Timber-framed E-shaped house, two-thirds derelict, on moated hill-top site, dating from the 13th century. House built variously during 15th, 16th and 17th centuries with later additions, including wall paintings and carpenters marks. 18th century bridge and plunge pool in the grounds.
Grant Recipient/Owner/Access contact: Ms C A Newton
Tel: 01283 544161/01889 561000
Fax: 01889 563258
E-mail: knewton@brookesvernons.co.uk
Open: By prior arrangement only.
P No ♿ No. Guide Dogs: Yes
£ Donations requested

South Fortification Wall

The Close, Lichfield, Staffordshire WS13 7LD
External wall comprising remaining part of medieval building. Set in grounds adjacent to Cathedral Visitors' Centre and at the rear of Cathedral Coffee shop.
www.lichfield.cathedral.org
Grant Recipient/Owner/Access contact: The Dean & Chapter of Lichfield Cathedral
Tel: 01543 306100 **Fax:** 01543 306109
E-mail: enquiries@lichfield-cathedral.org
Open: Grounds: daily 9am - 5pm.
P Public car parks nearby.
♿ Yes. WC for the disabled. Guide Dogs: Yes
£ No

Speedwell Castle

Bargate Street, Brewood, Staffordshire ST19 9BB
Grade I listed. Mid 18th century, red brick designed in the manner of Strawberry Hill. Reputed to have been built by William Rock (d.1753) from the proceeds of betting on the racehorse Speedwell.
Grant Recipient/Owner: Penk Holdings Ltd
Access contact: Mr A S Monckton
Tel: 01902 850214 **Fax:** 01902 850354
Open: The façade can be viewed from Bargate Street and Stafford Street (interior not open to the public).
P No ♿ No Guide Dogs: Yes £ No

St Mary's (Lichfield Heritage Centre)

Market Square, Lichfield, Staffordshire WS13 6LG
Grade II* medieval guild church, rebuilt 1868-70 by James Fowler. Many original features are preserved and the building is a prominent landmark in the city. Now houses a Community Centre comprising a Heritage Centre, Social Centre for senior citizens, coffee and gift shops, as well as continuing to function as the parish church.
www.lichfieldheritage.org.uk
Grant Recipient/Owner:/Access contact: The Guild of St Mary's Centre
Tel: 01543 256611
Open: Lichfield Heritage Centre: daily 10am - 5pm (last adm 4.00pm).
P Pay-&-display nearby
♿ Yes. WC for the disabled. Guide Dogs: Yes
£ **Adult:** £3.50 **Child:** £1 (age 5-14, under 5s free) **Other:** £2.50 (concessions), £8 (family)

SUFFOLK

Abbey Farm Barn

Snape, Saxmundham, Suffolk IP17 1RQ
Grade II* listed Aisled barn. Circa 1300. Built by resident monks living in adjacent Priory (no remains standing above ground). Refurbished and still used by farmer for storage.
Grant Recipient/Owner/Access contact:
Mr & Mrs Raynor
Tel: 01728 688088 **Fax:** 01728 688989
E-mail: thecartshed@onetel.net.uk
Open: By prior arrangement.
P Spaces: 1 ♿ No £ No

Aldeburgh Moot Hall

Aldeburgh, Suffolk IP15 5DS
Grade I listed 16th century woodframed building, still in use as a Town Hall. Houses the Moot Hall Museum with collections of local historical interest, and objects from the Snape Ship Burial.
Grant Recipient/Owner/Access contact: Aldeburgh Town Council
Tel: 01728 452158 (Town Hall)
Open: Apr - Oct: Town Hall: Mons and Fris 9.30am - 12.30pm, Weds 2.30 - 4.30pm. Museum: Apr and May: Sats and Suns 2.30 - 5pm; June, Sept and Oct: daily 2.30 - 5pm; July and Aug: daily 10.30am - 12.30pm and 2.30 - 5pm. School parties and tours by arrangement with the Museum (tel. 01728 454666).
P Public parking alongside building.
♿ No. Guide Dogs: Yes
£ **Adult:** £1 (museum) **Child:** Free (museum)

Christchurch Mansion

Christchurch Park, Soane Street, Ipswich, Suffolk IP4 2BD
16th century red brick mansion with some blue brick diapering, set in fine parkland in the centre of town. The Mansion and its collections trace the lives of the three wealthy families who made it their home. Paintings, English domestic furniture, kitchen and servants' area.
www.ipswich.gov.uk/tourism/guide/mansion.htm
Grant Recipient/Owner: Ipswich Borough Council
Access contact: Mr Tony Butler
Tel: 01473 433574
E-mail: tony.butler@ipswich.gov.uk
Open: Nov - Mar: Tues - Sat 10am - 4pm, Sun 2 - 4pm. Apr - Oct: Tues - Sat 10am - 5pm, Sun 2 - 4pm.
P Public parking within 400m. Spaces: 1200
♿ Wheelchair access to most of ground floor and Wolsey Art Gallery. WC for the disabled.
£ No

Culford School Iron Bridge

Culford, Bury St Edmunds, Suffolk IP28 6TX
Constructed for the second Marquis Cornwallis in the late 1790s by Samuel Wyatt, brother of James, to a design patented by Wyatt. The bridge, in Culford Park, is one of the earliest surviving bridges with an unmodified cast-iron structure, being the earliest known example with hollow ribs.
Grant Recipient/Owner: Culford Lake Restoration & Conservation Group
Access contact: Michael Wooley
Tel: 01284 729318 **Fax:** 01284 729077
E-mail: bursar@culford.co.uk
Open: Access to the iron bridge and Culford Park is available at any time throughout the year.
P Spaces: 100
♿ Disabled access may be difficult as grass and rough track. WCs only available when Culford School is open & ramps in place. Guide Dogs: Yes
£ No

Elms Farm Wallpaintings

Old Station Road, Mendlesham, Suffolk IP14 5RS
Wealden hall house dating from 1480, wallpaintings consist of 16th century floral design and Biblical texts in the upper hall and solar and 17th century armorial patterning in the parlour.
Grant Recipient/Owner/Access contact:
Mrs Pamela Gilmour
Open: By prior written arrangement.
P Spaces: 10 ♿ No £ No

Flatford Mill

Willy Lott's House & Flatford Bridge Cottage, Flatford, East Bergholt, Colchester, Suffolk CO7 6OL
Flatford watermill, 1733 datestone, incorporating possibly earlier but altered former granary range to rear and further 19th century range adjoining granary. Later alterations. The mill was in the possession of the Constable family from the mid 18th century. Willy Lott's farmhouse, late 16th century - 17th century. Grade I listing of both buildings reflects their significance in the life and work of John Constable. Both buildings are leased by the National Trust to the Field Studies Council. Flatford Bridge Cottage, 16th century thatched cottage, upstream from Flatford Mill houses an exhibition on John Constable.
www.nationaltrust.org.uk
Grant Recipient/Owner: The National Trust
Access contact: Property Manager
Tel: 01206 298260 **Fax:** 01206 299193
E-mail: flatfordbridgecottage@nationaltrust.org.uk
Open: Flatford Mill and Willy Lott's House are owned by the National Trust and leased to the Field Studies Council which runs arts-based courses for all age groups (for information on courses tel: 01206 298283). There is no general public access to these buildings, but the Field Studies Council will arrange tours for groups. Flatford Bridge Cottage is open Mar and Apr daily except Mon and Tues 11am - 5.00pm; May to end Sept daily 10am - 5.30pm; Oct daily 11am

- 4.30pm; Nov and Dec daily except Mon and Tues 11am - 3.30pm. Closed Christmas and New Year. For further information contact the Property Manager on 01206 298260.

Ⓟ Private pay car park 200 meters from Flatford Bridge Cottage. Parking near the Cottage is available for disabled visitors. Spaces: 2000

♿ Wheelchair access to tea-garden and shop. WC for disabled available in car park owned by Babergh DC, 23 metres away. Guide Dogs: Yes

£ No

Hall Farm Barn

Withersfield, Suffolk CB9 7RY

100ft long by 30ft wide thatched barn built c1400, with later alterations. Floor is split into 3 levels with the east wall having been bricked-in between the timbers and the west wall consisting of horsehair, lath and plaster. Situated in working farmyard.

Grant Recipient/Owner: Mr C R W Bradford

Access contact: Mr T Mytton-Mills

Tel: 01440 702146 **Fax:** 01440 702552

E-mail: tom@hall-farm.fsnet.co.uk

Open: By prior telephone arrangement.

Ⓟ Spaces: 12

♿ Yes. WC for the disabled. Guide Dogs: Yes £ No

Horseman's House

Boundary Farm, Framsden, Suffolk IP14 6LH

Mid 17th century brick stable. Gable ended with brick pinnacles along upper edge with panels of diaper work in dark headers below round vents/owl holes. Original three bay, two storey structure housed horseman above his charges in unusually ornate accommodation for all.

Grant Recipient/Owner/Access contact: Mr Bacon

Tel: 01728 860370 **Fax:** 01728 860370

E-mail: info@boundaryfarm.co.uk

Open: By prior arrangement with Mr Bacon.

Ⓟ Spaces: 4

♿ Wheelchair access to ground floor stable and outside of building. WC for the disabled. Guide Dogs: Yes

£ No

Ickworth House and Park

Horringer, Bury St Edmunds, Suffolk IP29 5QE

The Earl of Bristol created this eccentric house, with its central rotunda and curved corridors, in 1795 to display his collections. These include paintings by Titian, Gainsborough and Velasquez and a Georgian silver collection. The house is surrounded by an Italianate garden set in a 'Capability' Brown park with woodland walks, deer enclosure, vineyard, Georgian summerhouse and lake.

www.nationaltrust.org.uk

Grant Recipient/Owner: The National Trust

Access contact: Property Manager

Tel: 01284 735270 **Fax:** 01284 735175

E-mail: ickworth@nationaltrust.org.uk

Open: House: 19 Mar - 31 Oct: daily except Wed and Thurs 1 - 5pm (last adm 4.30pm). Closes 4.30pm in Oct. Garden: 2 Jan - 18 Mar: daily 10am - 4pm; 19 Mar - 31 Oct: daily 10am - 5pm (last adm 4.30pm); 1 Nov - 22 Dec: daily except Sat & Sun 10am - 4pm. Park open daily 7am - 7pm but closed Christmas Day.

Ⓟ Spaces: 2000

♿ Wheelchair access to House: ramped access (restricted access in House for large powered vehicles/chairs); lift to first floor; stairlift to basement (shop & restaurant) suitable for wheelchair users able to transfer; wheelchair on each floor. Garden largely accessible, some changes of level, gravel drive and paths. WC for the disabled. Guide Dogs: Yes

£ **Adult:** £6.40, £2.95 (park & garden only) **Child:** £2.90, 85p (park & garden only)

Long Shop Steam Museum

Main Street, Leiston, Suffolk IP16 4ES

Museum housed in the original Richard Garrett & Sons Ltd buildings including the Long Shop, built in 1852 as the first purpose-built flow line for the production of portable steam engines. Five exhibition halls and an education/resource centre.

www.longshop.care4free.net

Grant Recipient/Owner: Long Shop Project Trust

Access contact: Mrs A Napthine

Tel: 01728 832189 **Fax:** 01728 832189

E-mail: longshop@care4free.net

Open: 1 Apr - 31 Oct: Mon - Sat 10am - 5pm, Sun 11am - 5pm.

Ⓟ Spaces: 40

♿ Wheelchair access to 95% of site. WC for the disabled. Guide Dogs: Yes

£ **Adult:** £3.50 **Child:** £1 (under 5s free) **Senior:** £3

Somerleyton Hall & Gardens

Somerleyton, Lowestoft, Suffolk NR32 5QQ

Early Victorian stately home, built in Anglo-Italian style for Sir Morton Peto by John Thomas upon former Jacobean mansion. Contains fine furnishings, paintings, ornate carved stonework and wood carving, and state rooms. Set in twelve acres of historic gardens including a yew hedge maze.

www.somerleyton.co.uk

Grant Recipient/Owner: The Rt Hon Lord Somerleyton GCVO

Access contact: Mr Edward Knowles

Tel: 01502 730224 **Fax:** 01502 732143

E-mail: enquiries@somerleyton.co.uk

Open: 4 Apr - 31 Oct: Thurs, Sun and BHs, plus Tues and Wed in July and Aug, 11am - 5.30pm. Admission charges under review at time of publication, please check with the Hall for current information.

Ⓟ Spaces: 200 ♿ Yes. WC for the disabled. Guide Dogs: Yes

£ **Adult:** £5.80 **Child:** £2.90 **Other:** £5.50 (senior citizens), £16.40 (family)

St Bartholomew

Shipmeadow, Beccles, Suffolk NR34 8HL

Redundant medieval former parish church with 16th century tower, now converted into a house. 12th century nave and chancel in flint, later tower in brick and flint, with a variety of window styles.

Grant Recipient/Owner/Access contact: Mr Nick Caddick

Tel: 020 7404 0404 **Fax:** 020 7404 0505

E-mail: nick.caddick@talk21.com

Open: By prior arrangement with Mr Nick Caddick, 5 New Square, Lincolns Inn, London WC2A 3RJ (tel:020 7404 0404).

Ⓟ Additional parking available on verge. Spaces: 4

♿ Wheelchair access to porch & lower part of nave (subject to a low step at front door). No WC for the disabled. Guide Dogs: Yes

£ No

St John Lateran

Hengrave Hall, Hengrave, Bury St Edmunds, Suffolk IP28 6LZ

Grade I listed parish church dedicated to St John Lateran. Circular tower in coursed flint, possibly pre-Conquest. 13th century chancel with later additions. Noted for several of its monuments. Now known as the Church of Reconciliation, it reflects the present ecumenical vision of Hengrave Hall as a Christian retreat and conference centre and home of the Hengrave Community of Reconciliation.

www.hengravehallcentre.org.uk

Grant Recipient/Owner: Hengrave Hall Centre

Access contact: Mr J H Crowe

Tel: 01284 701561 **Fax:** 01284 702950

E-mail: administrator@hengravehallcentre.org.uk

Open: Church all year, although the Hall is closed to visitors 24-27 Dec. Tours of the Hall by arrangement with the Administrator.

Ⓟ Free 50 metres from Church, 25 metres from Hall. Overflow car park near Church. Spaces: 100

♿ Wheelchair access to Church and ground floor of Hall only. WC for the disabled. Guide Dogs: Yes

£ No. Donations to Church welcome

St Lawrence

Dial Lane, Ipswich, Suffolk IP1 1DL

15th century aisleless church with a 97 foot west tower, enlarged in the 19th century and recently restored. Declared redundant in 1975. Owned by Ipswich Borough Council.

Grant Recipient/Owner: Ipswich Historic Churches Trust

Access contact: Mr J S Hall

Tel: 01473 232300/406270 **Fax:** 01473 230524

E-mail: james-hall@birketts.co.uk

Open: By prior arrangement with Mr Hall (tel:01473 406270), office hours and weekdays only. At least 24 hours notice required. At other times and days subject to longer notice.

Ⓟ In town centre car parks (10 min walk).

♿ No £ No

St Peter

College Street, Ipswich, Suffolk IP4 1DD

Large medieval church near the docks, owned by Ipswich Borough Council and redundant since the 1970s. Noted for a Tournai font and adjacent to Thomas Wolsey's gateway. Empty and unused.

Grant Recipient/Owner: Ipswich Historic Churches Trust

Access contact: Mr J S Hall

Tel: 01473 232300/406270 **Fax:** 01473 230524

E-mail: james-hall@birketts.co.uk

Open: May - Nov, most Thurs 1.30 - 3.30pm (advisable to check in advance). Otherwise by arrangement with Mr Hall (tel: 01473 406270), office hours and weekdays only. 24 hours notice required. At other times and days subject to longer notice.

Ⓟ Car parks in town centre (¹/₂ mile).

♿ Wheelchair access to all of church apart from the vestry and parts of the chancel. No WC for the disabled. Guide Dogs: Yes

£ No

Theatre Royal

Westgate Street, Bury St Edmunds, Suffolk IP33 1QR

A rare example of a late Georgian playhouse. Built 1819, later used as a warehouse, but restored and re-opened as a theatre in 1965. Constructed of white brick and stucco with a slate roof.

www.theatreroyal.org

Grant Recipient/Owner: The National Trust

Access contact: The Administrator

Tel: 01284 755127 **Fax:** 01284 706035

E-mail: admin@theatreroyal.org

Open: June - end of Aug: Tues & Thurs 11am - 1pm and 2 - 4pm (tours at 11.30am and 2.30pm); Sats 11am - 1pm (tour at 11.30am). Open throughout the year for performances.

Ⓟ Limited parking in Westgate Street.

♿ Wheelchair access to front of house and wheelchair boxes only. WC for the disabled. Guide Dogs: Yes

£ No, but admission charge for performances & theatre tours

Woodbridge Lodge

Rendlesham, nr. Woodbridge, Suffolk IP12 2RA

Late 18th century small gothic folly. Originally a gatehouse to Rendlesham Hall, now part of a dwelling house.

Grant Recipient/Owner/Access contact: Dr C P Cooper

Tel: 01394 460642

Open: Exterior only by arrangement.

Ⓟ Spaces: 3 ♿ No £ No

SURREY

Carew Manor Dovecote (Beddington Park)

Church Road, Beddington, Wallington, Surrey SM6 7NH

Early 18th century large octagonal brick dovecote with c1200 interior nesting boxes and original potence (circular ladder).

www.sutton.gov.uk

Grant Recipient/Owner: London Borough of Sutton

Access contact: Ms Valary Murphy

Tel: 020 8770 4781 **Fax:** 020 8770 4777

E-mail: valary.murphy@sutton.gov.uk

Open: Open on the following Suns: 23 May, 27 June, 18 July, 26 Sept, 2 - 5pm. Guided tours of Carew Manor at 2pm and 3.30pm. Groups at other times by arrangement with Valary Murphy, The Heritage Service, Central Library, St Nicholas Way, Sutton, Surrey SM1 1EA (tel:020 8770 4781).

Ⓟ Spaces: 30 ♿ No. Guide Dogs: Yes

£ **Adult:** £3 **Child:** £1.50 **Other:** Charges for guided tours of dovecote & Carew Manor, otherwise dovecote free

Clandon Park

West Clandon, Guildford, Surrey GU4 7RQ

Palladian mansion, built c1730 by Venetian architect Giacomo Leoni with a two-storeyed Marble Hall, collection of 18th century furniture, porcelain, textiles, carpets, the Ivo Forde Meissen collection of Italian comedy figures and a series of Mortlake tapestries. Grounds contain grotto, sunken Dutch garden, Maori Meeting House & The Queen's Royal Surrey Regiment Museum.

www.nationaltrust.org.uk

Grant Recipient/Owner: The National Trust

Access contact: Mr David Brock-Doyle

Tel: 01483 222482 **Fax:** 01483 223479
E-mail: clandonpark@nationaltrust.org.uk
Open: House: 28 Mar - 31 Oct, daily except Mon, Fri and Sat (but open Good Fri, Easter Sat & BH Mons) 11am - 5pm (last adm 4.30pm). Museum: as for house 12 noon - 5pm. Garden: as house 11am - 5pm.
PSpaces: 200
♿Wheelchair access to lower ground floor and five steps to ground floor. WC for the disabled. Guide Dogs: Yes
£Adult: £6 **Child:** £3 **Family:** £15, £5 (group, Tues, Weds, Thurs & after 2pm Suns)

Great Fosters

Stroude Road, Egham, Surrey TW20 9UR
Grade II* registered garden. Laid out in 1918 by W H Romaine-Walker in partnership with G H Jenkins, incorporating earlier features. The site covers 50 acres and is associated with a late 16th century country house, converted to an hotel in 1927. The main formal garden is surrounded on three sides by a moat thought to be of medieval origin and is modelled on the pattern of a Persian carpet. Garden also includes a sunken rose garden and avenue of lime trees.
www.greatfosters.co.uk
Grant Recipient/Owner/Access contact: Mr Richard Young
Tel: 01784 433822 **Fax:** 01784 472455
E-mail: enquiries@greatfosters.co.uk
Open: At any time throughout the year.
PSpaces: 200
♿Wheelchair access to ground floor of the house and most of the gardens. WC for the disabled. Guide Dogs: Yes **£**No

Great Hall

Virginia Park, Christchurch Rd, Virginia Water, Surrey GU25 4BH
By W H Crossland for Charas Holloway and opened 1884. Built of red brick with Portland stone dressings and slate roofs in Franco-Flemish Gothic style. Formerly part of the Royal Holloway Sanatorium.
Grant Recipient/Owner: Virginia Park Management Co Ltd
Access contact: Ms Liz Adams
Tel: 01344 845276 **Fax:** 01344 842428
E-mail: virginia.park@btinternet.com
Open: Entrance Hall, Staircase and Great Hall of former Sanatorium open on the following Weds and Suns 10am - 4pm: Feb 18 & 22, Mar 24 & 28, Apr 14, 21 & 25, May 12, 19 & 23, June 16, 23 & 27, July 14, 21 & 25, Aug 11, 18 & 22, Sept 15, 22 & 26, Oct 13, 20 & 24, Nov 17, 24 & 28. At other times by prior telephone arrangement with the Estate Office.
PPublic car park nearby at Virginia Water Station.
♿Wheelchair access with help (steps into building). Downstairs entrance Hall but not Great Hall (no lift). WC for the disabled. Guide Dogs: Yes
£Adult: £3

The Old Mill

Outwood Common, nr. Redhill, Surrey RH1 5PW
England's oldest working windmill, built in 1665. Museum of bygones.
www.outwoodwindmill.co.uk
Grant Recipient/Owner: Mrs Sheila Thomas
Access contact: Mrs Sheila Thomas
Tel: 01342 843458 **Fax:** 01342 843458
E-mail: sheila@outwoodwindmill.co.uk
Open: Easter - Oct: Sun & BHs 2-6pm, parties by arrangement.
PSpaces: 12
♿Wheelchair access to ground floor of mill & museum only. WC for the disabled. Guide Dogs: Yes
£Adult: £2 **Child:** £1

Oxenford Farm

Milford Road, Elstead, Godalming, Surrey GU8 6LA
1840 Gothic-style cowshed and milking parlour by Pugin. Working farm with livestock.
Grant Recipient/Owner: Mr C F Baker
Access contact: Mr A C Baker
Tel: 01252 702109 **Fax:** 01252 702109
Open: 1 - 24 Dec: daily 9am - 5pm. At other times by prior written arrangement.
PSpaces: 10
♿Wheelchair access to cowsheds. No WC for the disabled. Guide Dogs: Yes
£No

Painshill Park

Portsmouth Road, Cobham, Surrey KT11 1JE
Restored Grade I 18th century landscape garden of 150 acres, created by Charles Hamilton between 1738 and 1773. Contains a Gothic temple, Chinese bridge, ruined abbey, Turkish tent, grotto and 14 acre serpentine lake fed by a large waterwheel. Europa Nostra medal winner for 'Exemplary Restoration'.
www.painshill.co.uk
Grant Recipient/Owner: Painshill Park Trust Ltd
Access contact: Miss Sarah AM Hallett
Tel: 01932 868113 **Fax:** 01932 868001
E-mail: info@painshill.co.uk
Open: Apr - Oct: Tues - Sun and BHs 10.30am - 6pm (last adm 4.30pm); Nov - Mar (except Christmas Day and Boxing Day): Tues - Thurs, Sat, Sun and BHs 11am - 4pm or dusk if earlier (last adm 3pm). Guided tours for groups of 10 plus by arrangement.
P8 coaches. Spaces: 400
♿Wheelchair access to most of the site, apart from the Grotto and Alpine Valley. Wheelchairs and electric buggies available on request. Book 1 week in advance. WC for the disabled. Guide Dogs: Yes
£Adult: £6 **Child:** £3.50 (under 5s free)
Other: £5.25

Queen Anne Statue

Tourist Information Office, Market House, Market Place, Kingston-upon-Thames, Surrey KT1 1JS
Francis Bird's statue of Queen Anne, cast in lead, was commissioned in 1706 and stood above the entrance to the pre-1840 Guildhall. Since then it has graced the balcony of the Grade II* Market House. Restoration work involved re-gilding and sculpting a back for the statue which was originally designed to occupy a niche.
Grant Recipient/Owner: Royal Borough of Kingston-upon-Thames
Access contact: Market House & Information Officer
Tel: 020 8547 5592 **Fax:** 020 8547 5594
E-mail: tourist.information@rbk.kingston.gov.uk
Open: The statue can be viewed at all times from street level from the public Market Place. Close inspection (rear of statue visible from first floor of Market House, but no access to balcony for safety reasons) by arrangement.
PPublic pay car parks available. ♿No wheelchair access to first floor of the Market House (ground floor accessible) the statue is fully visible from street level. WC for disabled in Market House. Guide Dogs: Yes
£No

Watts Memorial Chapel

Down Lane, Compton, Guildford, Surrey
Mortuary chapel for new cemetery, built by Mary Seton Watts and the villagers of Compton between 1896 and 1898. Greek cross plan within a circle in highly decorated brick and terracotta, Romanesque style exterior with Art Nouveau interior.
www.wattsgallery.org.uk
Grant Recipient/Owner: Compton Parish Council
Access contact: Mr Malcolm Airey
Tel: 01483 810872 **Fax:** 01483 812124
E-mail: malcolm@softhome.net
Open: All year, dawn - dusk.
PSpaces: 10
♿Yes. No WC for the disabled. Guide Dogs: Yes **£**No

SUSSEX

Brickwall House

Northiam, Rye, East Sussex TN31 6NL
Jacobean manor house containing a front hall, staircase, ceilings, drawing room and chamber room with leather panels. Previously home of the Frewen family, now a school for dyslexic boys aged 9-17.
Grant Recipient/Owner: Frewen Educational Trust
Access contact: Mr J S Field
Tel: 01797 253388 **Fax:** 01797 252567
E-mail: post@frewcoll.demon.co.uk
Open: School holidays on the following dates: Apr 7/8, 14/15; June 2/3/4; July 13/14/15, 20/21/22, 27/28/29; Aug 3/4/5, 10/11/12, 17/18/19 and 24/25/26; 2 - 5pm. Please note that the leather panels are fragile and covered during term time, on display on the above dates only.
PSpaces: 40
♿Wheelchair access to ground floor only. WC for the disabled. Guide Dogs: Yes
£Adult: £6

De La Warr Pavilion

The Marina, Bexhill-on-Sea, East Sussex TN40 1DP
The "People's Palace" built in 1935 by architects Erich Mendholson and Serge Chermayeff was the first steel-framed building in this country. Its circular staircase and sweeping sea views make it unique.
www.dlwp.com
Grant Recipient/Owner: Rother District Council
Access contact: Mr Alan Haydon
Tel: 01424 787900 **Fax:** 01424 787940
E-mail: info@dlwp.com
Open: Daily 10am - 5pm. Closed Christmas Day.
PPay car park.
♿Yes. WC for the disabled. Guide Dogs: Yes **£**No

The Dovecote

Alciston, East Sussex BN8 6NS
14th century dovecote of flint facings with green sand stone dressings on a chalk rubble core with chalk blocks and nesting boxes internally.
www.firleplace.co.uk
Grant Recipient/Owner: Trustees of the Firle Estate Settlement
Access contact: Mr Duncan Leslie
Tel: 01273 858567 **Fax:** 01273 858570
E-mail: duncan@firleplace.co.uk
Open: Access to the dovecote is by arrangement with the Estate Office.
PNo ♿No **£**No

The Flushing Inn

4 Market Street, Rye, East Sussex TN31 7LA
15th century timber-framed building, now a restaurant, with large recently restored 16th century wallpainting.
www.theflushinginn.com
Grant Recipient/Owner/Access contact: Mr Flynn
Tel: 01797 223292 **Fax:** 01797 229748
E-mail: j.e.flynn@talk21.com
Open: Restaurant open Wed - Sun for lunches and dinners, Mons lunch only and Tues closed. Closed first two weeks in Jan and Oct. Unless dining, visiting to view the Fresco is restricted to 10.30 - noon.
PParking on-street but restricted to 1 hour, otherwise public parking elsewhere in Rye.
♿Wheelchair access to Fresco with assistance (entrance steps to be negotiated). No WC for the disabled. Guide Dogs: Yes
£No

High Beeches Gardens Conservation Trust

High Beeches, Handcross, West Sussex RH17 6HQ
25 acre garden with woodland, open glades, natural wildflower meadows and water gardens. Many rare plants to be seen in all seasons. Tree trails. Tearoom/restaurant in restored Victorian farm.
www.highbeeches.com
Grant Recipient/Owner: The Trustees of High Beeches Conservation Trust
Access contact: The Hon Mrs Boscawen
Tel: 01444 400589 **Fax:** 01444 401543
E-mail: office@highbeeches.com
Open: 19 Mar - 30 June & 1 Sept - 31 Oct: 1 - 5pm (last adm 5pm), closed Weds. July & Aug: 1 - 5pm, closed Sat & Wed. All coaches & guided tours by arrangement.
PDisabled parking adjacent to tea room. Spaces: 100
♿Wheelchair access to tea room & tea garden only. WC for the disabled. Guide Dogs: Yes
£Adult: £5 **Child:** Free **Other:** Concessions for groups

Lamb House

(Coromandel Lacquer Panels), 3 Chapel Hill, Lewes, East Sussex BN7 2BB
The incised lacquer panels in the study of Lamb House are a unique surviving example of imported late 17th century Chinese lacquer work that remains as decorative wall panelling. Recently restored.
Grant Recipient/Owner/Access contact: Prof. Paul Benjamin
Tel: 01273 475657
E-mail: p.r.benjamin@sussex.ac.uk
Open: Weekends only by prior telephone or e-mail arrangement.
POn-street parking.
♿Wheelchair access to ground floor only. No WC for the disabled. Guide Dogs: No **£**No

Ouse Valley Viaduct

Balcombe, West Sussex

The most important surviving architectural feature of the original layout of the London - Brighton railway, the Grade II* Ouse Valley Viaduct has 37 circular arches, is 492 yards long and 92 feet high. Designed by John Rastrick with stonework accredited to David Mocatta, it is known for its pierced piers, ornate limestone parapets and pavilions. Built 1839-1841.

Grant Recipient/Owner: Railtrack plc (now Network Rail)

Access contact: Network Rail

Open: Public access at all times on the footpath running underneath the viaduct. It is possible to view the viaduct from Borde Hill Lane without walking across the field.

P Limited on-street parking.

♿ Wheelchair users can view viaduct from Borde Hill Lane. No WC for the disabled. Guide Dogs: Yes

£ No

Parham House

Parham Park, nr. Pulborough, West Sussex RH20 4HS

Granted to the Palmer family in 1540 by Henry VIII, the foundation stone of this grey-stone Elizabethan house was laid in 1577. From the panelled Great Hall to the Long Gallery running the length of the roof-space, the house contains a collection of paintings, furniture and needlework.

www.parhaminsussex.co.uk

Grant Recipient/Owner: Parham Park Ltd

Access contact: Ms Patricia Kennedy

Tel: 01903 742021 **Fax:** 01903 746557

E-mail: pat@parhaminsussex.co.uk

Open: 11 Apr - 30 Sept: Wed, Thurs, Sun & BH Mons & Tues & Fris during Aug (also Sats 15 May, 10 July & 4 Sept). Gardens open at 12 noon, House at 2pm with last entry at 5pm.

P For disabled close to the house. Spaces: 300

♿ Wheelchair access to ground floor only by arrangement, there is a reduced admission charge for wheelchair users and free loan of recorded tour tape. WC for the disabled. Guide Dogs: Yes

£ **Adult:** £6.25 **Child:** £2.50 (age 5-15) **Senior:** £5.50 **Family:** £15

Petworth House

Petworth, West Sussex GU28 0AE

Late 17th century mansion in 'Capability' Brown parkland. House contains the Trust's largest collection of pictures including Turners and Van Dycks, as well as sculptures, furniture and Grinling Gibbons' carvings. Servants' quarters with interesting kitchens and other service rooms. Extra rooms open at the weekend by kind permission of Lord and Lady Egremont.

www.nationaltrust.org.uk

Grant Recipient/Owner: The National Trust

Access contact: Property Manager

Tel: 01798 342207 **Fax:** 01798 342963

E-mail: petworth@nationaltrust.org.uk

Open: House and Servants' Quarters: 27 Mar - 31 Oct, daily except Thurs and Fri (but open Good Fri), 11am - 5.30pm (last adm to house 4.30pm, Servants' Quarters 5pm). Extra rooms shown weekdays (but not BH Mons) as follows: Mon: White and Gold Room and White Library; Tues & Wed: three bedrooms on first floor. Park: daily, all year, except 25 Dec & afternoons of open-air concerts in June.

P For house & park on A283, 800 yards away. Spaces: 150

♿ Wheelchair access to ground floor of house, shop and tea room. WC for the disabled. Guide Dogs: Yes

£ **Adult:** £7 **Child:** £4 **Family:** £18 £6 (booked groups 15+)

Rotunda Temple

Brightling Park, Rother, East Sussex

Built c1812 as an eyecatcher by Sir Robert Smirke for John Fuller, wealthy philanthropist and eccentric. Small circular building with colonnade and dome: the centrepiece of Brightling Park.

Grant Recipient/Owner: Mr H C Grissell

Access contact: Mr H C Grissell

Tel: 01424 838207 **Fax:** 01424 838467

Open: By arrangement only. Otherwise Temple can be viewed from public footpaths and other permitted access routes through Park.

P Parking in surrounding roads.

♿ No WC for the disabled. Guide Dogs: Yes £ No

The Royal Pavilion

Brighton, East Sussex BN1 1EE

Former seaside residence of George IV in Indian style with Chinese-inspired interiors. Originally a neo-classical villa by Henry Holland was built on the site in 1787, but this was subsequently replaced by the current John Nash building constructed between 1815-23.

www.royalpavilion.org.uk

Grant Recipient/Owner: Brighton & Hove City Council

Access contact: Ms Cara Bowen

Tel: 01273 292810 **Fax:** 01273 292871

E-mail: cara.bowen@brighton-hove.gov.uk

Open: Apr - Sept, daily 9.30am - 5.45pm (last adm 5pm); Oct - Mar, daily 10am - 5.15pm (last adm 4.30pm); closed 25 & 26 Dec. Admission charges are valid until 31 Mar 2004, for rates after that date please check the English Heritage website or with the Royal Pavilion for current information.

P NCP car park on Church Street. Parking for disabled is available in the grounds of the Pavilion by arrangement.

♿ Wheelchair access to ground floor only, reduced rate of admission is payable. WC for the disabled. Guide Dogs: Yes

£ **Adult:** £5.80 (see above), £2.20 (local residents, Oct - Feb only) **Child:** £3.40 under 16 (Oct - Feb, local residents free with paying adult) **Conc:** £4 **Family:** £15 (2 adults, 4 children), £9.20 (1 adult, 4 children)

St Hugh's Charterhouse

Henfield Road, Partridge Green, Horsham, West Sussex RH13 8EB

Large monastery covering 10 acres. One large cloister of over 100 square yards comprising 34 four-room hermitages where the monks live. The fore part is a smaller cloister about 200ft square which contains the cells of the Brothers' and their work places. There is also a large church, library, refectory, Brothers Chapel and other monastic buildings. The large quad encloses a cemetery. The spire is 203ft high and has a five-bell chime.

www.parkminster.org.uk

Grant Recipient/Owner: St Hugh's Charterhouse

Access contact: Fr John Babeau

Tel: 01403 864231 **Fax:** 01403 864231

Open: By arrangement, with due respect for the rules of the monastery. For further details please contact the monastery.

P Spaces: 20 ♿ No. Guide Dogs: Yes £ No

St Mary-in-the-Castle

Pelham Crescent, Hastings, East Sussex TN34 3AF

Built in 1828, architect Joseph Kay, it forms an integral part of the design of Pelham Crescent. The Church has a horseshoe-shaped auditorium with gallery and is now used as an arts centre.

www.1066.net/maryinthecastle

Grant Recipient/Owner: Friends of St Mary in the Castle

Access contact: Mr David Rosendale/Mr Nick Sangster

Tel: 01424 781635/01424 781122

Fax: 01424 781133

E-mail: nsangster@hastings.gov.uk

Open: Monthly open days with guided tours; 'Open House' three times a year; guided tours Tues - Sat by arrangement. Arts activities run all year. Contact the Box Office (01424 781624), the access contacts or check the website for further information.

P Pay & Display parking opposite. Spaces: 400

♿ Yes. WC for the disabled. Guide Dogs: Yes

£ **Adult:** £1 (guided tours). 'Open House' free but collection taken. Events individually priced.

Sackville College

High Street, East Grinstead, West Sussex RH19 3BX

Early Jacobean almshouse with original furniture, hall, chapel, common room, John Mason Neale study and library. Built with Sussex sandstone around a quadrangle. Founded in 1609 and still in use, providing 15 flats for elderly people together with the Warden's lodging.

Grant Recipient/Owner: The Warden & Trustees of Sackville College

Access contact: Mr Graham Gaisburgh-Watkyn

Tel: 01342 326561 **Fax:** 01342 326561

Open: 15 June-15 Sept: Wed-Sun 2 - 5pm. Groups by arrangement. Mar - Oct.

P Free. Additional parking at 'Chequer Mead' 50 yards away. Spaces: 4

♿ Yes. No WC for the disabled. Guide Dogs: Yes

£ **Adult:** £3. **Child:** £1

The Shell House

Goodwood House, Chichester, West Sussex PO18 0PX

One-room Shell House dating from 1740s. Walls and ceiling decorated with hundreds of thousands of shells in classical design, with coffering, niches and cornucopia. Floor with inset horses' teeth.

Grant Recipient/Owner: Goodwood Estate Company Ltd

Access contact: Curator's Secretary

Tel: 01243 755048 **Fax:** 01243 755005

E-mail: curator@goodwood.co.uk

Open: By prior written arrangement, usually on set Connoisseurs' Days (20 & 27 Apr, 18 May; also one day in Sept and Oct) or on Sun mornings Apr - Sept. Two weeks' notice preferred. Bookings can be made with the Curator's Secretary (tel: 01243 755048).

P 30 metres from house. Steps between car park & house. Spaces: 4

♿ WC for disabled available only when Goodwood House is open to the public. Guide Dogs: No

£ **Adult:** £3.50 (Connoisseurs' Day as part of House visit), £5(other days) **Child:** £2 (under 12s, accompanied)

Shipley Windmill

Shipley, nr. Horsham, West Sussex RH13 8PL

Grade II* listed smock mill with five floors, built 1879 and restored in 1990 to full working order. Once owned by the Sussex writer and poet, Hilaire Belloc, who lived nearby. The milling process is demonstrated on open days for the benefit of visitors.

www.shipleywindmill.org.uk

Grant Recipient/Owner: Shipley Windmill Charitable Trust

Access contact: Ms Penny Murray

Tel: 01243 777642 **Fax:** 01243 777848

E-mail: penny.murray@westsussex.gov.uk

Open: Apr - Oct: first, second and third Sun of each month, plus BH Mons. Also National Mills Day, Shipley Festival (May), Horsham and District Arts Fanfare (June) and the Sun of the Heritage Open Days weekend. Please check current opening arrangements with Ms Penny Murray, Assistant Clerk to the Trustees, Shipley Windmill Charitable Trust, County Hall, Chichester, West Sussex PO19 1RQ.

P Spaces: 10 ♿ No £ **Adult:** £2 **Child:** £1 **Seniors:** £1.50

Tithe Barn

Court Farm, East Street, Brighton, West Sussex BN1 9PB

Grade II* listed medieval tithe barn. Mainly of timber construction with thatched roof.

Grant Recipient/Owner: Brighton and Hove County Council

Access contact: Mr Richard Butler

Tel: 01273 291440 **Fax:** 01273 291467

E-mail: richard.butler@brighton-hove.gov.uk

Open: By arrangement with Richard Butler, Brighton and Hove County Council (or Beth Turner at Cluttons 01622 756000) and Eric Huxham - tenant at Court Farm (07802 453842).

P On-street parking within Falmer village.

♿ Barn within working farm so access can be muddy. Guide dogs are welcome but as a working farm care is requested. No WC for the disabled. Guide Dogs: Yes

£ No

TYNE & WEAR

21-23 Leazes Terrace

Newcastle-upon-Tyne, Tyne & Wear NE1 4LY

Elongated square of houses built 1829-34 in classical style. Owned by the University of Newcastle as halls of residence.

Grant Recipient/Owner: University of Newcastle

Access contact: Miss Helen Stonebank

Tel: 0191 222 7565

E-mail: H.J.Stonebank@ncl.cc.uk.

Open: Exterior accessible at all times, only one room of the interior can be viewed when the room is not occupied (Room 21F, which is in near original condition) by arrangement with Miss Helen Stonebank, Accommodation Manager, 10 Leazes Terrace, Newcastle-upon-Tyne.

P Metered parking around the Terrace. ♿ No £ No

Freemasons Hall

Queen Street East, Sunderland, Tyne & Wear SR1 2HT

Grade I listed oldest purpose-built Masonic meeting place in the world, c1785. Contains an ornate Lodge Room

which remains virtually unaltered with elaborate thrones from 1735. Also has a cellar is in its original condition and the last remaining example of a Donaldson organ which was specially constructed for the building in 1785.
Grant Recipient/Owner: Queen Street Masonic Temple Ltd
Access contact: Mr Colin Meddes
Tel: 0191 522 0115
E-mail: colinmeddes@hotmail.com
Open: Guided tours all year by arrangement.
P Spaces: 80
5 external steps to main entrance: guides available to assist wheelchair users. Access ramp due 2004. WC for the disabled. Guide Dogs: Yes £ No

Gibside Chapel & Column of Liberty

Gibside, nr. Rowlands Gill, Burnopfield, Tyne & Wear NE16 6BG
Palladian Chapel 1760-69; completed 1812 designed by James Paine for George Bowes, MP and coal owner, and Column of Liberty 1750-57 by Daniel Garrett until 1753; then James Paine, situated in extensive landscape. Much of the landscape is SSSI, and embracing many miles of riverside and forest walks. A forest garden is under restoration. The estate is the former home of the Queen Mother's family, the Bowes-Lyons.
www.nationaltrust.org.uk
Grant Recipient/Owner: The National Trust
Access contact: Visitor Services Manager
Tel: 01207 542255 **Fax:** 01207 542255
E-mail: gibside@nationaltrust.org.uk
Open: Grounds: 28 Mar - 31 Oct, daily except Mon (open BH Mons), 10am - 6pm (last adm 4.30pm). 2 Nov - end Mar 2005, daily except Mon (open BH Mons), 10am - 4pm (last adm 3.30pm). Chapel: 28 Mar - 31 Oct, 11am - 4.30pm. Winter by arrangement only.
P Spaces: 1000. Parking for disabled near the site.
Wheelchair access to tearoom, shop, toilets & part of grounds. Wheelchair access difficult to Chapel and the Avenue. Staff happy to assist. 2 manual wheelchairs available, booking essential. Tel Visitor Services Manager (01207 541820) in advance. WC for the disabled. Guide Dogs: Yes
£ **Adult:** £3.50 **Child:** £2 **Other:** £10 (family, 2+4), £7 (family, 1+3), £3 (groups 15+)

High Level Bridge

Gateshead, Tyne & Wear
Grade I listed railway and road bridge of ashlar and cast iron, 1849, designed by Robert Stephenson. One of the finest pieces of architectural iron work in the world.
Grant Recipient/Owner: Network Rail
Access contact: Mr Richard Bell
Tel: 01904 650232 **Fax:** 01904 650304
E-mail: richard.bell@networkrail.co.uk
Open: At all times. Best viewed from adjacent riverbanks or via access road/footpath under bridge. Also may be viewed from the footways which cross the lower deck of the bridge. No access to the upper deck of the bridge.
P On-street parking.
Footways across lower deck of bridge are accessible for wheelchairs. No WC for the disabled. Guide Dogs: Yes
£ No

Literary & Philosophical Society

23 Westgate Road, Newcastle-upon-Tyne, Tyne & Wear NE1 1SE
Grade II* listed 1825 private library and society rooms designed by John Green in Greek revival style. Extended in late 19th century. Interior shows classical stucco ornament on friezes, wrought-iron balconies and spiral stair to library gallery. The library contains over 140,000 books, many old and rare.
www.litandphil.org.uk
Grant Recipient/Owner: Literary & Philosophical Society
Access contact: Ms Kay Easson
Tel: 0191 232 0192 **Fax:** 0191 261 4494
E-mail: library@litandphil.org.uk
Open: Mon, Wed, Thurs & Fri: 9.30am - 7pm. Tues 9.30am - 8pm. Sat 9.30am - 1pm. The Society is closed on public & BHs. Visitors welcome to view the building free of charge. However, annual subscription is charged for use of the private library.
P On-street parking on Westgate Road. Spaces: 10
Stairlift in building allows wheelchair access, but no exterior ramp. No WC for the disabled. Guide Dogs: No
£ No

Old Town Hall

Market Place, South Shields, Tyne & Wear NE33 1AG
Built 1768 by the Dean and Chapter of Durham in the centre of the Market Place. Square two-storey building with an open arcaded ground floor and a central pillar on steps supporting what may have been a former market cross. Upper floor reached by a symmetrical, double branch stone staircase. Restored 1977.
Grant Recipient/Owner: South Tyneside Metropolitan Borough Council
Access contact: Executive Director Resources Asset Management & Procurement
Tel: 0191 424 7238 **Fax:** 0191 454 6794
Open: Access to ground floor at all reasonable times, first floor by arrangement with the Executive Director of Resources, Asset Management and Procurement, South Tyneside Metropolitan Borough Council, Town Hall and Civic Offices, Westoe Road, South Shields, Tyne & Wear NE33 2RL.
P Spaces: 450 Wheelchair & guide dog access to ground floor only. 24 hr automatic WC less than 200 metres from the site.
£ No

Theatre Royal

Grey Street, Newcastle-upon-Tyne, Tyne & Wear NE1 6BR
Victorian theatre opened in 1837, rebuilt in 1899 by Frank Matcham in a richly-ornamented style. Classical façade with rare Hanoverian coat of arms. Traditional 4-tier 1,294 seat auditorium hosting annual programme of touring productions and international companies.
www.theatre-royal-newcastle.co.uk
Grant Recipient/Owner: Newcastle Theatre Royal Trust Ltd
Access contact: Mr Peter Sarah
Tel: 0191 244 2514 **Fax:** 0191 261 1906
E-mail: peter.sarah@newcastle.gov.uk
Open: Regular tours available depending on production schedule, contact theatre on 0870 905 5060 or 0191 232 0997 for details.
P Public car parks in City centre.
Wheelchair access to foyer, cafe and stalls. WC for the disabled. Guide Dogs: Yes
£ **Adult/Child:** £3.50 (Tours, some free)

Washington Old Hall,

The Avenue, Washington Village, District 4, Washington, Tyne & Wear NE38 7LE
17th century manor house, incorporating the 12th century remains of the home of George Washington's ancestors. Recreated 17th century interiors and displays of 'Washingtonabilia' celebrating the close connection with the USA. Permanent exhibition on the recent tenement period of the property. Jacobean knot-garden and Nuttery.
www.nationaltrust.org.uk
Grant Recipient/Owner: The National Trust
Access contact: Property Manager
Tel: 0191 4166879 **Fax:** 0191 4192065
E-mail: washingtonoldhall@nationaltrust.org.uk
Open: 28 Mar - 31 Oct: Sun - Wed & Good Fri 11am - 5pm.
P Spaces: 10
Wheelchair access to ground floor of house and upper garden. WC for the disabled. Guide Dogs: Yes
£ **Adult:** £3.50 **Child:** £2 **Family:** £9, £3 (£1.50 child, groups 10+)

WARWICKSHIRE

The Bath House

Walton, Stratford-upon-Avon, Warwickshire LE17 5RG
Designed in 1748 by the architect Sanderson Miller. The upper room, where the bathers recovered, is decorated with dripping icicles and festoons of sea shells - the work of Mrs Delaney, better known for her flower pictures. Narrow steep staircases.
www.landmarktrust.co.uk
Grant Recipient/Owner: The Landmark Trust
Access contact: Mrs Victoria O'Keeffe
Tel: 01628 825920 **Fax:** 01628 825417
E-mail: vokeeffe@.landmarktrust.co.uk
Open: The Landmark Trust is an independent charity, which rescues small buildings of historic or architectural importance from decay or unsympathetic improvement. Landmark's aim is to promote the enjoyment of these historic buildings by making them available to stay in for holidays. The Bath House can be rented by anyone, at all times of the year, for periods ranging from a weekend to three weeks. Bookings can be made by telephoning the Booking Office on 01628 825925. As the building is in full-time use for holiday accommodation, it is not normally open to the public. However the public can view the building by arrangement by telephoning the access contact (Victoria O'Keeffe on 01628 825920) to make an appointment. Potential visitors will be asked to write to confirm the details of their visit.
P Spaces: 1 No £ No

Charlecote Park

Wellesbourne, Warwick, Warwickshire CV35 9ER
Owned by the Lucy family since 1247, Sir Thomas built the house in 1558. Now much altered, it is shown as it would have been a century ago. The balustraded formal garden gives onto a deer park landscaped by 'Capability' Brown.
www.nationaltrust.org.uk
Grant Recipient/Owner: The National Trust
Access contact: Property Manager
Tel: 01789 470277 **Fax:** 01789 470544
E-mail: charlecote.park@nationaltrust.org.uk
Open: House: 6 Mar - 30 Sept, daily except Wed and Thurs, 12 - 5pm; 1 Oct - 2 Nov, daily except Wed and Thurs, 12 - 4.30pm. Park and Garden: 6 Mar - 2 Nov, daily except Wed and Thurs, 10.30am - 6pm; 8 Nov - 20 Dec, Sat & Sun, 10.30am - 4pm.
P Spaces: 200
Wheelchair access to ground floor of house, restaurant and shop. WC for the disabled. Guide Dogs: Yes
£ **Adult:** £6.40 **Child:** £3.20 **Other:** £16 (family), £5.40 (group)

Lord Leycester Hospital

High Street, Warwick, Warwickshire CV34 4BH
14th century chantry chapel, Great Hall, galleried courtyard and Guildhall. Acquired by Robert Dudley, Earl of Leicester in 1571 as a home for his old soldiers. Still operating as a home for ex-servicemen.
Grant Recipient/Owner: Patron & Governors of Lord Leycester Hospital
Access contact: Lieut. Colonel G F Lesinski
Tel: 01926 491422 **Fax:** 01926 491422
Open: Tues - Sun 10am - 4pm (winter), 10am - 5pm (summer), plus BH Mons. Closed Good Fri and Christmas Day.
P Spaces: 15
Wheelchair access to ground floor only. WC for the disabled. Guide Dogs: Yes
£ **Adult:** £3.40 **Child:** £2.40 **Other:** £2.90

Nicholas Chamberlaine's Almshouses' Pump House

All Saints Square, Bedworth, Nuneaton, Warwickshire CV12 8NR
Built 1840 of English bond brick with sandstone dressings and stone pyramid roof in Tudor Gothic style. Contains original cast-iron pump. Stands in front of the almshouses and originally provided water for the residents, illuminated at night.
Grant Recipient/Owner: Nicholas Chamberlaine's Hospital Charity
Access contact: Mr David Dumbleton
Tel: 024 76227331 **Fax:** 024 76221293
E-mail: j.russell@rotherham-solicitors.co.uk
Open: Two sessions Sat & Sun of Heritage Open Days weekend and at other times by arrangement with Mr David Dumbleton, Clerk to the Governors, Nicholas Chamberlaine's Hospital Charity, Rotherhams and Co, 8/9 The Quadrant, Coventry, Warwickshire CV1 2EG. Exterior visible from All Saints Square at all times.
P Public car parks nearby.
Yes. WC for the disabled. Guide Dogs: Yes
£ No

Packwood House

Lapworth, Solihull, Warwickshire B94 6AT
Originally a 16th century house, Packwood has been much altered over the years and today is the vision of Graham Baron Ash who recreated a Jacobean house in the 1920s and 30s. Houses collection of 16th century textiles and furniture. Yew garden based on Sermon on the Mount.
www.nationaltrust.org.uk
Grant Recipient/Owner: The National Trust
Access contact: Property Manager
Tel: 01564 783294 **Fax:** 01564 782706
E-mail: packwood@nationaltrust.org.uk

Open: House: 3 Mar - 7 Nov, daily except Mon and Tues (but open BHs and Good Fri) 12 - 4.30pm. Gardens: as house 11am - 4.30pm in Mar, Apr, Oct and Nov, 11am - 5.30pm May - Sept. Park and woodland walks all year, daily. On busy days admission to the house may be by timed ticket.
P Spaces: 140
Wheelchair access to ground floor. Garden largely accessible. WC for the disabled. Guide Dogs: Yes
£ **Adult:** £5.60 (house & garden), £2.80 (grounds) **Child:** £2.80 (house & garden), £1.40 (grounds) **Family:** £14, discount for combined ticket to Packwood House and Baddesley Clinton

Polesworth Nunnery Gateway

22-24 High St, Polesworth, Tamworth, Warwickshire B78 1DU
Abbey gatehouse, late 14th century with later alterations. Upper floors now in residential use.
Grant Recipient/Owner: Polesworth PCC
Access contact: Mr W E Thompson
Tel: 01827 706861
E-mail: polesworthabbey@aol.com
Open: Exterior at all reasonable times, ground floor interior by arrangement with Mr W E Thompson, 46 Kiln Way, Polesworth, nr Tamworth, Warwickshire B78 1JE.
P In Abbey driveway for approx. 20 vehicles. Wheelchair access to ground floor only. No WC for the disabled. Guide Dogs: Yes
£ No

Ragley Hall

Alcester, Warwickshire B49 5NJ
Family home of the Marquess and Marioness of Hertford. Built in 1680 to a design by Robert Hooke in the Palladian style, with portico added by Wyatt in 1780. Contents include baroque plasterwork by James Gibb, family portraits by Sir Joshua Reynolds and a mural by Graham Rust completed in 1983. Surrounding park designed by 'Capability' Brown.
www.ragleyhall.com
Grant Recipient/Owner: Marquess of Hertford & Earl of Yarmouth
Access contact: Mr Alan Granger
Tel: 01789 762090 **Fax:** 01789 764791
E-mail: info@ragleyhall.com
Open: 1 Apr - 3 Oct, Thurs - Sun (& BH Mons) 11am - 6pm (last adm 4.30pm). Sat closing times may vary subject to events & functions. Park & gardens open daily in school holidays. Group (20+) rates: £5, adults & seniors, £3 child & school group.
P Spaces: 4000
Yes. Wheelchair access via lift to first floor. WC for the disabled. Guide Dogs: Yes
£ **Adult:** £6 **Child:** £4.50 (age 5-16) **Other:** £5 (seniors & Orange/Blue Badge), £22 (family). Season: £5 (family), £20 (single). £1 entry to State Rooms on First Floor

Stoneleigh Abbey

Kenilworth, Warwickshire CV8 2LF
16th century house built on site and incorporating remains of Cistercian Abbey founded in 1155. West wing designed by Francis Smith of Warwick 1714-26 and northern wing reconstructed in 19th century by Charles S Smith of Warwick. South wing c1820. West wing contains a range of State Apartments. Also restored Regency riding stables, 19th century conservatory & Humphrey Repton landscaped riverside gardens.
www.stoneleighabbey.org
Grant Recipient/Owner: Stoneleigh Abbey Preservation Trust (1996) Ltd
Access contact: Estate Office
Tel: 01926 858535 **Fax:** 01926 850274
E-mail: enquiries@stoneleighabbey.org
Open: Good Fri - end of Oct: Tues, Wed, Thurs and Sun, plus BHs. Opening arrangements may change, please check with the Preservation Trust for current information.
P Spaces: 400 Yes. WC for the disabled. Guide Dogs: Yes
£ **Adult:** £5 **Child:** £2.50 **Senior:** £3.50

WEST MIDLANDS

The Big House

44 Church Street, Oldbury, West Midlands B69 3AE
Grade II* 3-storey house dating from c1730. Originally with agricultural land and later the house and officers of a solicitor in 1857 when the land was sold. Restored and reopened in 2002 as Civic offices.
Grant Recipient/Owner: Sandwell Metropolitan Borough Council
Access contact: Civic Affairs Officer
Tel: 0121 569 3041 **Fax:** 0121 569 3050
E-mail: ann_oneill@sandwell.gov.uk
Open: By arrangement with the Mayor's office via the Civic Affairs officer (tel: 0121 569 3041). The Mayor will also hold "Open House" at various times throughout the year.
P Market Street Public Car Park (30 spaces). Disabled parking (4 spaces) adjacent.
Yes. WC for the disabled. Guide Dogs: Yes £ No

Castle Bromwich Hall Gardens

Chester Road, Castle Bromwich, West Midlands B36 9BT
18th century formal walled gardens set within 10 acres. Period plants and unusual historic vegetables, fruits and herbs, both culinary and medicinal. 19th century holly maze. Classical parterres with restored summer house and green house along holly walk. Refreshments, gifts and plants for sale.
www.cbhgt.colebridge.net
Grant Recipient/Owner: Castle Bromwich Hall Gardens Trust
Access contact: Mr R J Easton
Tel: 0121 749 4100 **Fax:** 0121 749 4100
E-mail: admin@cbhgt.colebridge.net
Open: 1 Apr - 31 Oct: Tues - Thurs 1.30 - 4.30pm. Sat, Sun and BH Mons 2 - 6pm. Closed Mon and Fri.
P Spaces: 200
Yes. WC for the disabled. Guide Dogs: Yes
£ **Adult:** £3.50 **Child:** £1.50 **Conc:** £2.50

Red House Glassworks

Wordsley, Stourbridge, West Midlands DY8 4AZ
Built around 1790, the Cone was used for the manufacture of glass until 1936 and is now one of only four left in the Country. Reaching 100ft into the sky, the Cone enclosed a furnace where glass was made for 140 years. In its 200 year history, the site has remained virtually unaltered and therefore provides an interesting insight into the history and tradition of glassmaking. Glassmaking demonstrations and exhibitions tell the story of glassmaking in the area and the history of the glassworks.
www.redhousecone.co.uk
Grant Recipient/Owner: Dudley Metropolitan Borough Council
Access contact: Ms Sarah Chapman
Tel: 01384 812752 **Fax:** 01384 812751
E-mail: sarah.chapman@dudley.gov.uk
Open: Jan - 31 Mar, daily 10am - 4pm. 1 Apr - 31 Oct, daily 10am - 5pm.
P Spaces: 40 Full wheelchair access to Cone, glassmaking area and all display areas. Lift to upper floor and galleries. Some studios are inaccessible. WC for the disabled. Guide Dogs: Yes
£ **Adult:** £3 **Child:** £1.50 **Other:** £2.50 **Family:** £9

Soho House Museum

Soho Avenue, Handsworth, Birmingham, West Midlands B18 5LB
Soho House Museum is the former home of Matthew Boulton, Birmingham industrialist, entrepreneur and partner of James Watt. Designed by James and Samuel Wyatt, the house was once a meeting place of the Lunar Society and contains period rooms and displays on Boulton's manufacturing activities. The visitor centre houses a temporary exhibition gallery.
www.bmag.org.uk
Grant Recipient/Owner: Birmingham Museums & Art Gallery
Access contact: Curator Manager
Tel: 0121 554 9122 **Fax:** 0121 554 5929
Open: 9 Apr (Good Fri) - 31 Oct, Tues - Sun 11.30am - 4pm, also open BH Mons.
P Spaces: 23 Yes. WC for the disabled. Guide Dogs: Yes £ No

St James

Great Packington, Meriden, nr. Coventry, West Midlands CV7 7HF
Red brick building with four domes topped by finials in neo-classical style. Built to celebrate the return to sanity of King George III. The organ was designed by Handel for his librettist, Charles Jennens, who was the cousin of the 4th Earl of Aylesford, who built the church.
Grant Recipient/Owner: St James Great Packington Trust
Access contact: Packington Estate Office
Tel: 01676 522020 **Fax:** 01676 523399
E-mail: jameschurch@packingtonestate.co.uk
Open: Mon - Fri 9am - 5pm: key can be obtained from the Estate Office at Packington Hall, preferably by phoning in advance (01676 522020). At other times by arrangement with Lord Guernsey (tel:01676 522274).
P Spaces: 10
Wheelchair access with assistance (entrance steps & heavy door). No WC for the disabled. Guide Dogs: Yes
£ Donations towards restoration welcomed

Wightwick Manor

Wightwick Bank, Wolverhampton, West Midlands WV6 8EE
Built 1887, the house is a notable surviving example of the Arts & Crafts Movement. Contains original William Morris wallpapers and fabrics, Pre-Raphaelite paintings, Kempe glass and de Morgan ware. 17 acre Victorian/Edwardian garden designed by Thomas Mawson.
www.nationaltrust.org.uk
Grant Recipient/Owner: The National Trust
Access contact: Property Manager
Tel: 01902 761400 (761108 info) **Fax:** 01902 764663
E-mail: wightwickmanor@nationaltrust.org.uk
Open: By guided tour only 4 Mar - 23 Dec: Thurs & Sat (also BH Sun and Mon to ground floor only) 1.30 - 5pm. Also family open days Weds in Aug 1.30 - 5pm. Admission by timed ticket issued from 11am at Visitor Reception. Other days by arrangement. Garden: Wed, Thurs, Sat & BH Sun & Mon 11am - 6pm.
P For coaches please telephone 01902 761400. Spaces: 50
Wheelchair access to ground floor only. No WC for the disabled. Guide Dogs: Yes
£ **Adult:** £5.80, £2.50 (garden only) **Child:** £2.90, children free for garden only **Other:** £2.90 (students), £14 (family)

WEST YORKSHIRE

Bolling Hall Museum

Bowling Hall Road, Bradford, West Yorkshire BD4 7LP
Furnished house, mainly 17th and 18th centuries with some earlier parts. Large stained glass window with armorial glass, fine collection of 16th century oak furniture. Now a free public museum.
www.bradford.gov.uk
Grant Recipient/Owner: Bradford Metropolitan District Council
Access contact: Mr Gavin Edwards
Tel: 01274 723057 **Fax:** 01274 726220
E-mail: bradarch@go-legend.net
Open: All year: Wed, Thurs and Fri 11am - 4pm; Sat 10am - 5pm; Sun 12 noon - 5pm. Closed on Mons (except BHs) & 25/26 Dec & Good Fri.
P Free. 100 metres from Museum. Spaces: 75
Wheelchair access to ground floor only. WC for the disabled. Guide Dogs: Yes
£ No

Bramham Park Lead Lads Temple

Wetherby, West Yorkshire LS23 6ND
Park folly, in the form of an open temple in the classical style, built in the 1750s by local craftsmen on the instructions of Harriet Benson (about a mile from the house in woodland called Black Fen, close to a public footpath). The 'Lead Lads' were classical lead figures that stood on the three small blocks at the apex and base of the front pediment, and were lost to vandals many years ago.
Grant Recipient/Owner: Trustees of the Bramham Settled Estate
Access contact: The Estate Office
Tel: 01937 846000 **Fax:** 01937 846007
E-mail: enquiries@bramhampark.co.uk
Open: Close to a public footpath and accessible most of the year except closed 7 - 14 June & 16 Aug - 4 Sept.
P No No No charge for visitors via the footpath but charge made for visitors to the house and gardens

City Varieties Music Hall

Swan Street, Leeds, West Yorkshire LS1 6LW
Music hall built in 1865. Grade II* listed. Used as the location for BBC TV's "Good Old Days".
www.cityvarieties.co.uk
Grant Recipient/Owner: Leeds Grand Theatre &

Opera House Ltd

Access contact: Mr Peter Sandeman
Tel: 0113 3917777 **Fax:** 0113 2341800
E-mail: info@cityvarieties.co.uk
Open: Heritage Open Days: organised tours. Other times by arrangement.
🅿No &No. Guide Dogs: Yes
£Charges for performances only.

Crossley Pavilion

**The People's Park, King Cross Road,
Halifax, West Yorks HX1 1EB**
Grade II* listed building, designed by Sir Joseph Paxton and constructed in 1857. Contains seating and a statue of the park's benefactor, Sir Francis Crossley (1860), by Joseph Durham. Four gargoyle fountains supply pools flanking each side of the pavilion, set on formal terrace, balustrades and steps.
www.calderdale.gov.uk/tourism/parks/peoples.html
Grant Recipient/Owner: Calderdale Metropolitan Borough Council
Access contact: People's Park Development Officer
Tel: 01422 359454 **Fax:** 01422 348301
Open: The Park: daily 8am - dusk. The Pavilion: visits by arrangement with Calderdale Metropolitan Borough Council Leisure Services, Wellesey Park, Halifax, West Yorkshire HX2 0AY. Public WCs open during park hours. Information Centre open by arrangement as above.
🅿On-street in Park Road (up to 10 spaces). Limited spaces in adjacent college.
&There is one step into the pavilion, otherwise full wheelchair access. WC for the disabled. Guide Dogs: Yes £No

Friends Meeting House

**off Bolton Road, Addingham, nr. Ilkley,
West Yorkshire LS29**
Land for burial ground purchased in 1666, followed by construction of Meeting House in 1669. A simple single cell building with rubblestone walls, mullioned windows, stone-slated roof and stone-flagged floor. Contains loose benches and an oak minister's stand of an unusual panelled design with turned balusters.
www.hct.org.uk
Grant Recipient/Owner: Historic Chapels Trust
Access contact: John Spencer
Tel: 01756 710225
Open: At all reasonable times by application to keyholders Mr & Mrs John Spencer, who live opposite the Meeting House at Cook's Cottage, 3 Farfield Cottages, Bolton Road, Addingham, nr. Ilkley, West Yorks LS29 0RQ.
🅿Spaces: 2 &No. Guide Dogs: Yes £No

Harewood House

Harewood, Leeds, West Yorkshire LS17 9LQ
Designed in neo-classical style by John Carr and completed in 1772. Contains Adam interiors, Chippendale furniture, an art collection and museum. Home of the Earl and Countess of Harewood.
www.harewood.org
Grant Recipient/Owner: Trustees of Harewood House Trust Ltd
Access contact: Mr Terence Suthers
Tel: 0113 218 1010 **Fax:** 0113 218 1002
E-mail: business@harewood.org
Open: Daily 11 Feb - 31 Oct: Grounds & Bird Garden open 10am - 4.30pm (last adm 4pm); House and Terrace Gallery 11am - 4.30pm (last adm 4pm). Grounds close at 6pm. Grounds and Bird Garden also open weekends between 6 Nov and 19 Dec. Guide dogs are not allowed in the Bird Garden but a free sound guide is available for the partially sighted & a babysitter for the dog.
🅿Unlimited overflow parking on grass. Spaces: 200
&Yes. WC for the disabled. Guide Dogs: Yes
£Adult: £10 (weekdays), £11 Suns & BHs Child: £5.50 Senior: £8.20 Family: £30.50. Season tickets & concessions for disabled groups, 50% reduction for arrivals by public transport, students free Weds

Huddersfield Station

**St George's Square, Huddersfield,
West Yorkshire HD1 1JF**
Designed by J P Pritchett of York and built by local builder Joseph Kaye using local ashlar sandstone, the station is the oldest of the seven grade I listed station buildings in use for railway passengers having opened on 3 Aug 1847. When the foundation stone was laid the year before a public holiday was declared and church bells were rung from dawn till dusk. The grandeur of the station is the result of it having been built at the joint expense of the Huddersfield & Manchester Rail & Canal Company and the Manchester & Leeds Railway Company.
Grant Recipient/Owner: Kirklees Metropolitan Council
Access contact: Head of Design & Property Service
Open: Operational building every day except Christmas Day and Boxing Day. Please note that the building may also be closed on other days specified by Railtrack plc or other railway operators.
🅿One hour stay maximum in station car park. Spaces: 20
&Full wheelchair access to main buildings. Access with assistance to inner platforms. No WC for the disabled. Guide Dogs: Yes
£No

Ledston Hall

**Hall Lane, Ledston, Castleford,
West Yorkshire WF10 2BB**
17th century mansion with some earlier work.
Grant Recipient/Owner: Mr G H H Wheler
Access contact: Mr J F T Hare
Tel: 01423 523423 **Fax:** 01423 521373
E-mail: james.hare@carterjonas.co.uk
Open: May - Aug: Mon - Fri 9am - 4pm. Other times by arrangement with Mr J F T Hare, Carter Jonas, Regent House, 13/15 Albert St, Harrogate, West Yorks HG1 1JF
🅿Spaces: 5
&Wheelchair access to majority of garden. No WCs available on site. Guide Dogs: Yes
£No

National Coal Mining Museum for England

**Caphouse Colliery, New Road, Wakefield,
West Yorkshire WF4 4RH**
A colliery complex dating back to the 18th century with an underground tour into authentic coal workings. There are two major galleries of social history and technology and most of the historic buildings are open to the public. Facilities include a research library, restaurant, shop and education services.
www.ncm.org.uk
Grant Recipient/Owner: The National Coal Mining Museum for England Trust Ltd
Access contact: Reception Staff
Tel: 01924 848806 **Fax:** 01924 840694
E-mail: info@ncm.org.uk
Open: All year, daily 10am - 5pm except 24 - 26 Dec and 1 Jan.
🅿Spaces: 120
&Wheelchair access to all galleries & historic buildings & underground (limited tour) but not the screens. WC for the disabled. Guide Dogs: Yes £No

Nostell Priory

**Doncaster Road, Nostell, Wakefield,
West Yorkshire WF4 1QE**
Country house, c1736-1750, by James Paine for Sir Rowland Winn 4th baronet. Later Robert Adam was commissioned to complete the State Rooms. On display is a collection of Chippendale furniture, designed especially for the house, an art collection with works by Pieter Breughel the Younger and Angelica Kauffmann, an 18th century dolls' house, complete with its original fittings and Chippendale furniture and an unrestored 18th century Muniments Room. Other attractions include lakeside walks, historic park, family croquet, giant chess set and open day for cabinets.
www.nationaltrust.org.uk
Grant Recipient/Owner: The National Trust
Access contact: Property Manager
Tel: 01924 863892 **Fax:** 01924 866846
E-mail: nostellpriory@nationaltrust.org.uk
Open: House: 27 Mar - 31 Oct, daily except Mon and Tues (open Good Fri & BHs) 1 - 5.00pm; 6 Nov - 19 Dec, Sat & Sun only 12 noon - 4pm. Grounds, shop and tearoom: 6 - 21 Mar, weekends only 11am - 4.00pm; 27 Mar - 31 Oct, as house: grounds 11am - 6pm, shop & tearoom 11am - 5.30pm; 6 Nov - 19 Dec, as house 11am - 4.30pm.
🅿Spaces: 120
&Wheelchair access to ground floor of house with lift to first floor, tearoom, children's playground and shop. No WC for the disabled. Guide Dogs: Yes
£Adult: £5, £2.50 (grounds only) Child: £2.50, £1.20 (grounds only) Family: £12.50 (no family ticket for grounds only)

The Roundhouse

Wellington Road, Leeds, West Yorkshire LS12 1DR
Grade II* railway roundhouse built in 1847 for the Leeds and Thirsk Railway by Thomas Granger. In full use by the North-Eastern Railway until 1904, now home to Leeds Commercial Van and Truck Hire.
Grant Recipient/Owner: Wellbridge Properties Ltd
Access contact: Mr J D Miller
Tel: 0113 2435964 **Fax:** 0113 246 1142
E-mail: sales@leedscommercial.co.uk
Open: By written arrangement with the occupiers, Leeds Commercial, who manage the property as a working garage, or call in during office hours.
🅿Free. Spaces: 100
&Yes. WC for the disabled. Guide Dogs: Yes £No

Temple Newsam House

**Leeds Museums and Galleries, Leeds,
West Yorkshire LS15 0AE**
Tudor-Jacobean mansion set in 1200 acres. Birthplace of Henry Lord Darnley, husband of Mary Queen of Scots, and later the home of the Ingram family, Viscounts Irwin. Over 30 rooms open to the public housing a fine and decorative arts museum with collections of furniture, metalwork and ceramics.
www.leeds.gov.uk/templenewsam
Grant Recipient/Owner: Leeds City Council
Access contact: Mr Anthony Wells-Cole
Tel: 0113 264 7321 **Fax:** 0113 260 2285
E-mail: tnewsamho.leeds@virgin.net
Open: Jan - Dec daily except Mon (open BH Mons) 10.30am - 5pm (4pm in winter). Last admission 45 minutes before closing.
🅿Spaces: 200
&Wheelchair access to all public areas except the first floor of the south wing. WC for the disabled. Guide Dogs: Yes
£Adult: £3 (includes Audio Tour) Child: £2 (5-16); Free (under 5) Family: £8

Theatre Royal & Opera House

Drury Lane, Wakefield, West Yorkshire WF1 2TE
A 500 seat Victorian Theatre designed by Frank Matcham. Notable for the quality of decoration in the auditorium, it provides a year-round programme of events.
www.wakefieldtheatres.co.uk
Grant Recipient/Owner: Wakefield Theatre Royal & Opera House
Access contact: Mr Murray Edwards
Tel: 01924 215531 **Fax:** 01924 215525
E-mail: murray@wakefieldtheatres.co.uk
Open: Programme of events published in Feb, July & Nov. Guided tours once a month (Sat), groups on weekdays by arrangement, contact Box Office 01924 211311 for further information.
🅿Spaces: 150
&Wheelchair access to stalls area only. WC for the disabled. Guide Dogs: Yes
£No but admission charge for performances.

WILTSHIRE

Avoncliffe Aqueduct

Kennet & Avon Canal, Westwood, Wiltshire
19th century limestone aqueduct carrying the Kennet and Avon Canal over the River Avon and the railway line. The canal towpath crosses alongside the canal providing a foot link to Bradford-on-Avon or Bath.
www.britishwaterways.co.uk
Grant Recipient/Owner: British Waterways
Access contact: Ms Sarah Lewis
Tel: 01452 318000
E-mail: sarah.lewis@britishwaterways.co.uk
Open: At all times.
🅿Spaces: 12
&Top of aqueduct is accessible for wheelchairs from the small car park beside the canal. No WC for the disabled. Guide Dogs: No £No

Barton Grange Farm West Barn

Bradford-on-Avon, Wiltshire
Part of Barton Farm, once a grange of Shaftesbury Abbey (the richest nunnery in England), which includes the adjacent 14th century Tithe Barn. The West Barn was destroyed by fire in 1982 but has subsequently been rebuilt by the Preservation Trust and is now used as an 'Interpretation Centre'.
www.bradfordheritage.co.uk/PAGES/project.htm
Grant Recipient/Owner: Bradford-on-Avon

Preservation Trust Limited
Access contact: Mr Chris Penny
Tel: 01225 866551
E-mail: chrispenny@lineone.net
Open: May - Sept, weekends and BHs 12 noon - 4pm. Also open at other times throughout the year, please check with Mr Penny for further details.
🅿 Charged (15 spaces) near site and at railway station.(200 spaces)
♿ Wheelchair access to main building but not galleries. Entrance pathways are loose gravel. WC for the disabled. Guide Dogs: Yes £No

The Cloisters

Iford Manor, Bradford-on-Avon, Wiltshire BA15 2BA
Small stone-built cloister in gardens of Manor, completed 1914 by Harold Peto and based on 13th century Italian style. Interesting early contents. Used for concerts and opera evenings during the summer.
www.ifordmanor.co.uk
Grant Recipient/Owner/Access contact: Mrs Cartwright-Hignett
Tel: 01225 863146 **Fax:** 01225 862364
Open: Gardens only: Apr - Oct, Suns and Easter Mon 2 - 5pm; May - Sept, daily (except Mons and Fris), 2 - 5pm. Children under 10 not encouraged at weekends. Coaches & groups by arrangement only outside normal opening hours.
🅿 Spaces: 100
♿ Wheelchair access by arrangement to Cloisters & part of the gardens. WC for the disabled. Guide Dogs: Yes
£Adult: £4   Child: £3.50 (10-16, under 10 free) Conc: £3.50

Dyrham Park

Dyrham, nr. Chippenham, Wiltshire SN14 8ER
17th century house set within an ancient deer park, woodlands and formal garden. The house was furnished in the Dutch style and still has many original contents including paintings, ceramics, furniture and 17th century tapestries. The Victorian domestic rooms include the kitchen, larder, bakehouse, dairy and tenants hall.
www.nationaltrust.org.uk
Grant Recipient/Owner: The National Trust
Access contact: Visitor Services Manager
Tel: 01179 372501 **Fax:** 01179 371353
E-mail: dyrhampark@nationaltrust.org.uk
Open: House: 26 Mar - 31 Oct, daily except Wed and Thurs 12 noon - 5pm (last adm to house 4.15pm). Garden: as for house 11am - 5.30pm or dusk if earlier. Park: all year (closed 25 Dec) 11am - 5.30pm or dusk if earlier.
🅿 Free shuttle bus from car park to house. Spaces: 250
♿ Wheelchair access to all but 4 upstairs rooms. A photograph album of these rooms is available. WC for the disabled. Guide Dogs: Yes
£Adult: £8.30, £3.20 (grounds only), £2.10 (park only when house & garden closed)
Child: £4.10, £1.60 (grounds only), £1 (park only when house & garden closed)
Other: £20.50 (family: house & grounds), £7.30 (family: grounds only)

Fonthill Underground Bath House

Fonthill Bishop, Salisbury, Wiltshire SP3 5SH
18th century boathouse or water temple of aisled 'basilica' plan with transepts and apsidal west end, the wet dock being the 'nave' and 'crossing' and the walkways the 'aisles'. Constructed of limestone ashlar with vaulted roof covered in earth.
Grant Recipient/Owner: Lord Margadale
Access contact: The Resident Agent
Tel: 01747 820246 **Fax:** 01747 820446
Open: 1 Mar - 31 July: by written arrangement with the Estate Office, Fonthill Bishop, Salisbury, Wiltshire SP3 5SH. Wellington boots will be required by visitors.
🅿 No ♿ No £Adult: £2.50 + VAT Child: Free

Hemingsby

56 The Close, Salisbury, Wiltshire SP1 2EL
14th century canonical residence with spacious 18th century rooms and medieval Great Hall. Contains 15th century linenfold panelling. Large and interesting garden. Home of Canon William Fideon, a Greek scholar who escaped from Constantinople in 1453, and Canon Edward Powell, advocate of Catherine of Aragon and later hanged for denying the Act of Supremacy.
Grant Recipient/Owner/Access contact: The Dean &

Chapter of Salisbury Cathedral
Tel: 01722 555100 **Fax:** 01722 555109
Open: By prior arrangement only.
🅿 No ♿ No. Guide Dogs: Yes
£No, but donations for charity gratefully received

Lacock Abbey

Lacock, nr. Chippenham, Wiltshire SN15 2LG
Founded in 1232 and converted into a county house c1540, the fine medieval cloisters, sacristy, chapter house and monastic rooms of the Abbey have survived largely intact. The handsome 16th century stable courtyard has half timbered gables, a clockhouse, brewery and bakehouse. Victorian woodland garden. Former residents include William Fox Talbot 'the father of modern photography'.
www.nationaltrust.org.uk
Grant Recipient/Owner: The National Trust
Access contact: Property Manager
Tel: 01249 730227 **Fax:** 01249 730501
Open: Abbey: 27 Mar - 31 Oct, daily 1 - 5.30pm (closed Tues and Good Fri). Museum, cloisters & garden: 1 Mar - 31 Oct, daily 11am - 5.30pm (closed Good Fri). Museum also open winter weekends, but closed 25 Dec - 2 Jan.
🅿 Spaces: 300
♿ Wheelchair access to Abbey is difficult (four sets of stairs). Garden, cloisters & museum accessible (non-wheelchair stairlift in museum). Limited parking in Abbey courtyard by arrangement. WC for the disabled. Guide Dogs: Yes
£Adult: £7 (Abbey, museum, cloisters & garden), £5.60 (Abbey & garden), £4.40 (garden, cloisters & museum)
Child: £3.50 (Abbey, museum, cloisters & garden), £2.80 (Abbey & garden), £2.20 (garden, cloisters & museum)
Other: £17.90 (family: Abbey, museum, cloisters & garden), £14.30 (family: Abbey & garden), £11.20 (family: garden, cloisters & museum). Group rates

Lady Margaret Hungerford Almshouses

Pound Pill, Corsham, Wiltshire SN13 9HT
Fine complex of Grade I listed 17th Almshouses, Schoolroom, Warden's House and Stables. Schoolroom with original 17th century furniture and Exhibition Room. Recently restored. Lady Margaret Hungerford founded the Almshouses for the care of six poor people and the schoolroom for educating poor children. Arms of the foundress are well displayed.
Grant Recipient/Owner: Trustees Of The Lady Margaret Hunderford Charity
Access contact: Mr R L Tonge
Tel: 01225 742471 **Fax:** 01225 742471
E-mail: rtonge@northwilts.gov.uk
Open: 19 Mar - 3 Oct daily (except Mon & Sun but open BHs) 11am - 4pm. 4 Oct - 18 Mar Sat 11am - 3pm. Closed Dec /Jan.
🅿 In the town within 100 yards. Spaces: 100
♿ Wheelchair access to ground floor only. WC for the disabled. Guide Dogs: Yes
£Adult: £2 Child: 50p Conc: £1.75

Larmer Tree Gardens

nr Tollard Royal, Salisbury, Wiltshire SP5 5PY
Created by General Pitt Rivers in 1880 as a pleasure grounds for 'public enlightenment and entertainment', the Larmer Tree Gardens are set high on the Cranbourne Chase providing exceptional views of the surrounding countryside. One of the most unusual gardens in England containing an extraordinary collection of colonial and oriental buildings, a Roman Temple and an Open Air Theatre.
www.larmertreegardens.co.uk
Grant Recipient/Owner/Access contact: The Personal Representatives of the late MALF Pitt-Rivers
Tel: 01725 516228 **Fax:** 01725 516449
E-mail: larmer.tree@rushmore-estate.co.uk
Open: 1 Apr - 31 Oct, daily except Sat & throughout July,11am - 6pm. Please telephone for winter opening times.
🅿 Spaces: 500
♿ Wheelchair access to the sunken dell is difficult. WC for the disabled. Guide Dogs: Yes
£Adult: £3.75 Child: £2.50 Other: £3

Lydiard Park

Lydiard Tregoze, Swindon, Wiltshire SN5 3PA
Ancestral home of the Bolingbrokes, the restored Palladian mansion contains family furnishings and portraits, plasterwork, rare 17th century painted

window and room dedicated to 18th century society artist Lady Diana Spencer.
Grant Recipient/Owner: Swindon Borough Council
Access contact: Mrs Sarah Finch-Crisp
Tel: 01793 770401 **Fax:** 01793 877909
Open: House: Mon - Sat 10am - 5pm, Sun 2 - 5pm, school summer holidays 10am - 5pm. Nov - Feb early closing 4pm. Grounds all day, closing at dusk.
🅿 Spaces: 400 ♿ Yes. WC for the disabled. Guide Dogs: Yes
£Adult: £1.50 Child: 75p Other: 75p (Swindon Card Holders)

Merchant's House

132 High Street, Marlborough, Wiltshire SN8 1HN
17th century town house built by the Bayly family, mercers between 1653 and c1700. Situated prominently in the High Street it contains a unique stripe-painted dining room c1665, painted balustrading to the oak staircase and a panelled chamber of the Commonwealth period.
www.themerchantshouse.co.uk
Grant Recipient/Owner: Merchant's House (Marlborough) Trust
Access contact: Mr Michael Gray
Tel: 01672 511491 **Fax:** 01672 511491
E-mail: manager@themerchantshouse.co.uk
Open: Easter - end Sept: Fris, Sats and Suns 11am - 4pm. Other times by arrangement with the Secretary at Merchant's House.
🅿 For disabled outside the building. Public parking in High St.
♿ No. Guide Dogs: Yes £Adult: £3 Child: 50p

Old Bishop's Palace

Salisbury Cathedral School, 1 The Close, Salisbury, Wilts SP1 2EQ
13th century building, much altered over the centuries, with 13th century undercroft, Georgian drawing room and a chapel.
Grant Recipient/Owner: Salisbury Diocesan Board of Finance
Access contact: Mr Neil Parsons
Tel: 01722 555302 **Fax:** 01722 410910
E-mail: bursar@salisburycathedralschool.com
Open: Guided tours on 10 days in July/Aug. Details can be obtained from the Visitors' Office at Salisbury Cathedral (tel: Jan Leniston: 01722 555124).
🅿 No
♿ No. WC for disabled in the cloister (100 yards). Guide Dogs: No £ Adult: £2.50

Salisbury Cathedral Education Centre (Wren Hall)

56c The Close, Salisbury, Wiltshire SP1 2EL
Originally north wing of adjacent Braybrook House, early 18th century. Former choristers' school (founded 13th century). Many of the original fixtures and fittings are still present. Items of particular interest are the teacher's and head teacher's desks, original wood panelling and various photographs and artefacts from the history of the schoolroom.
www.salisburycathedral.org.uk/education.php
Grant Recipient/Owner/Access contact: The Dean & Chapter of Salisbury Cathedral
Tel: 01722 555180 **Open:** By prior arrangement.
🅿 Close has parking arrangements for members of the public
♿ No. WC for disabled in the Close. Guide Dogs: Yes
£No, donation to work of Centre invited

Sarum College

19 The Close, Salisbury, Wiltshire SP1 2EE
Grade I listed house, c1677, attributed to Sir Christopher Wren. In the 1870s collegiate buildings were added, designed by William Butterfield. The college is an ecumenical education, training and conference centre.
www.sarum.ac.uk
Grant Recipient/Owner: Trustees of Salisbury & Wells Theological College/Sarum College
Access contact: Mrs Linda Cooper
Tel: 01722 424800 **Fax:** 01722 338508
E-mail: admin@sarum.ac.uk
Open: Daily during term-time, please check with College for details of term-times.
🅿 Spaces: 37
♿ Wheelchair access to ground floor only. WC for the disabled. Guide Dogs: Yes
£No

Opening arrangements at properties grant-aided by English Heritage ⊞

Wilton House

Wilton, Salisbury, Wiltshire SP2 0BJ

Ancestral home of the Earls of Pembroke for over 450 years, rebuilt by Inigo Jones and John Webb in the Palladian style with further alterations by James Wyatt c1801. Contains 17th century state rooms and an art collection including works by Van Dyck, Rubens, Joshua Reynolds and Brueghel. Surrounded by landscaped parkland.
www.wiltonhouse.com

Grant Recipient/Owner: Wilton House Charitable Trust

Access contact: Mr Ray Stedman

Tel: 01722 746720 **Fax:** 01722 744447

E-mail: tourism@wiltonhouse.com

Open: 2 Apr - 31 Oct: 10.30am - 5.30pm (last adm 4.30pm). House closed on Mons but grounds open. House and gardens open on BHs.

ⓅSpaces: 200

♿Yes. WC for the disabled. Guide Dogs: Yes

£**Adult:** £9.75 **Child:** £5.50 **Senior:** £8. Group rates on application

WORCESTERSHIRE

Abberley Hall Clock Tower

Great Witley, Worcester, Worcestershire, WR6 6DD

Victorian folly, built 1883-4, by J P St Aubyn in a fantastic mixture of 13th and 14th century Gothic styles. 161ft tall, it can be seen from six counties.

Grant Recipient/Owner: Abberley Hall Ltd

Access contact: Mr J G W Walker

Tel: 01299 896275 **Fax:** 01299 896875

E-mail: johnwalker@abberleyhall.co.uk

Open: Sats 24 & 31 July, at other times by arrangement.

ⓅSpaces: 20

♿No £**Adult:** £3 **Child:** £1.50

Abbey Gateway (formerly Priory Gatehouse)

Abbey Road, Malvern, Worcestershire WR14 3ES

15th century gatehouse of the Benedictine Monastery in Malvern. Extended and restored, notably during 16th and 19th centuries. Now houses the Malvern Museum, an independent voluntary-run local museum.

Grant Recipient/Owner: Malvern Museum Society Ltd

Access contact: The Curator

Tel: 01684 567811**Open:** Easter - end Oct: daily 10.30am - 5pm. Closed Weds in term time. (Opening hours are always subject to the availability of

volunteers).

Ⓟ On-street parking. Paid parking within ¼ mile.

♿Wheelchair access restricted due to narrow winding staircase. Full access to sales area only. Audio tape (50p) and information folder are available as an alternative 'tour' of displays. No WC for the disabled. Guide Dogs: Yes

£**Adult:** £1 **Child:** 20p

Hanbury Hall

Hanbury, Droitwich, Worcestershire WR9 7EA

Built in 1701, this William and Mary-style house contains painted ceilings and staircase. It has an orangery, ice house and Moorish gazebos. The re-created 18th century garden is surrounded by parkland and has a parterre, wilderness, fruit garden, open grove and bowling green pavilions.
www.nationaltrust.org.uk

Grant Recipient/Owner: The National Trust

Access contact: Property Manager

Tel: 01527 821214 **Fax:** 01527 821251

E-mail: hanburyhall@nationaltrust.org.uk

Open: 1 Mar - 31 Oct, Sat - Wed. House: 1 - 5pm, Garden 11am - 5.30pm. Hall and Gardens closed 12 - 14 Mar for the Homes and Gardens Exhibition.

ⓅSpaces: 80, 200 metres from house. For disabled near house.

♿Yes. WC for the disabled. Guide Dogs: Yes

£**Adult:** £5.40, £3.50 (garden only)

Child: £2.70, £1.80 (garden only) **Family:** £13 **Group:** £4.60

Harvington Hall

Harvington, nr. Kidderminster, Worcestershire DY10 4LR

An Elizabethan moated manor house, partly demolished and remodelled c1701. Contains one of the best known series of priests' hides in the country and extensive traces of an ambitious scheme of wall paintings of late 16th and early 17th century.
www.harvingtonhall.org.uk

Grant Recipient/Owner: Roman Catholic Diocese of Birmingham

Access contact: Mrs S Breeden

Tel: 01562 777846 **Fax:** 01562 777190

E-mail: thehall@harvington.fsbusiness.co.uk

Open: Mar - Oct: Sats and Suns 11.30am - 5pm; Apr - Sept: Wed - Sun 11.30am - 5pm. Groups and schools by arrangement at any time.

ⓅSpaces: 100

♿Wheelchair access to ground floor, gardens, tea room and shop. Video of upper floors available. WC for the disabled. Guide Dogs: Yes

£**Adult:** £4.20 **Child:** £3 **Seniors:** £3.50 **Family:** £12.50 **Garden:** £1

Hopton Court Conservatory

Cleobury Mortimer, Kidderminster, Worcestershire DY14 0EF

Grade II* listed conservatory, c1830, of cast iron with a rounded archway leading to a rear room roofed with curved glass. Two rooms either side, one housing the boiler beneath to supply heat by way of cast iron grilles running around the floor of the interior.
www.hoptoncourt.co.uk

Grant Recipient/Owner: Mr C R D Woodward

Access contact: Mr Christopher Woodward

Tel: 01299 270734 **Fax:** 01299 271132

E-mail: chris@hoptoncourt.fsnet.co.uk

Open: Weekends of 8 / 9 May and 4 / 5 Sept, 10am - 4.30pm. At other times by arrangement.

ⓅSpaces: 150

♿Yes. WC for the disabled. Guide Dogs: Yes

£**Adult:** £3.50

St Michael's Ruined Nave & West Tower

Abberley, Worcestershire

Ruins of tower, nave (both 12th century) and south aisle (c1260). Walls standing approximately 4ft high with many surviving features from Medieval church. 12th century chancel and south chapel, c1260, repaired in 1908 and still used for services.

Grant Recipient/Owner: Abberley Parochial Church Council

Access contact: Mrs M A Nott

Tel: 01299 896392

Open: At all times.

ⓅAlso parking at Manor Arms Hotel. Spaces: 7

♿Yes. Full wheelchair access to ruins but help required to visit interior of church. No WC for the disabled. Guide Dogs: Yes

£No, but donations welcome (place in Green Box)

Walker Hall

Market Square, Evesham, Worcestershire WR11 4RW

16th century timber-framed building adjoining Norman gateway, much altered. In the late 19th century the floor was removed and it became an open hall. In 1999 it was repaired and refitted to form offices (first floor) and a retail unit (ground floor).

Grant Recipient/Owner: Saggers & Rhodes

Access contact: Messrs Saggers & Rhodes

Tel: 01386 446623 **Fax:** 01386 48215

E-mail: wds@ricsonline.org

Open: Access to interior by arrangement only.

ⓅParking in town centre car parks. Spaces: 500

♿Wheelchair and guide dog access to ground floor only. WC for the disabled. Guide Dogs: Yes

£Charitable donation only

Key: Ⓟ Parking information. ♿ Disabled access. £ Admission prices.

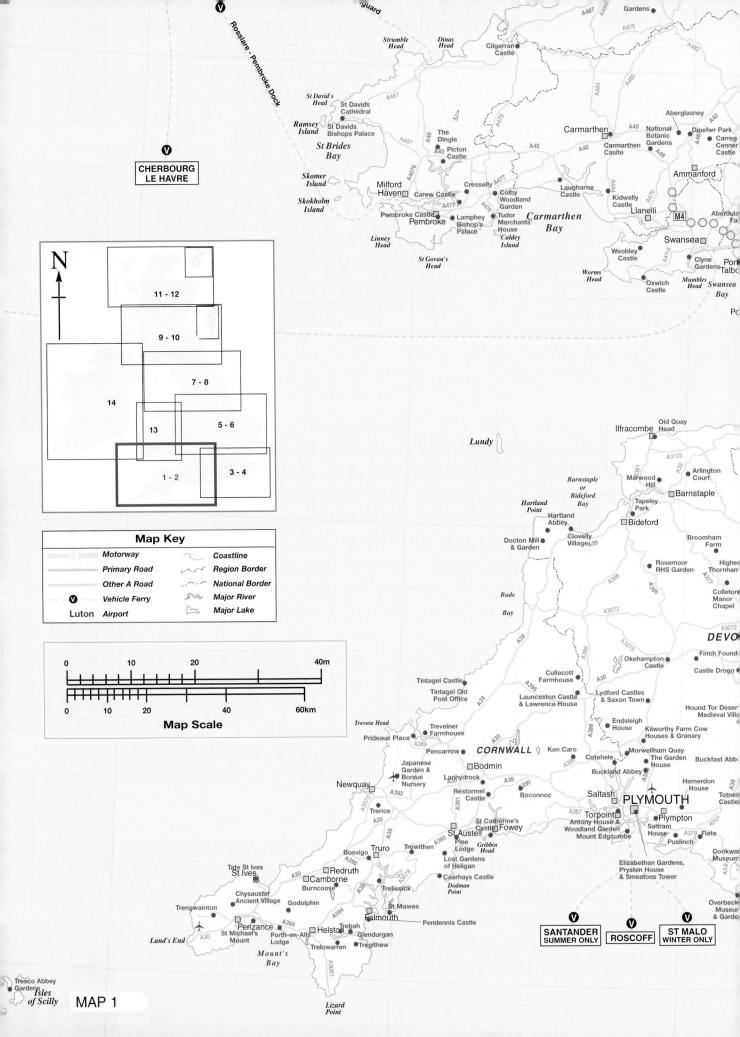

V Rossiare - Pembroke Dock

CHERBOURG LE HAVRE

N

11 - 12
9 - 10
7 - 8
14
13
5 - 6
1 - 2
3 - 4

Map Key

	Motorway		Coastline
	Primary Road		Region Border
	Other A Road		National Border
V	Vehicle Ferry		Major River
Luton	Airport		Major Lake

0   10   20   40m

0   10   20   40   60km

Map Scale

Strumble Head   Dinas Head   Cilgerran Castle

A487   Gardens

St David's Head   St Davids Cathedral

Ramsey Island   St Davids Bishops Palace

St Brides Bay   Carmarthen   National Botanic Gardens   Aberglasney   Dinefwr Park   Carreg Cennen Castle

Skomer Island   The Dingle   Picton Castle   Carmarthen Caslte   Ammanford

Skokholm Island   Milford Haven   Cresselly   Colby Woodland Garden   Laugharne Castle   Kidwelly Castle   Llanelli   Aberdula Fa

Carew Castle   Tudor Merchants House   Carmarthen Bay   Weobley Castle   Clyne Gardens   Swansea   Por Talbo

Pembroke Castle   Lamphey Bishop's Palace   Caldey Island

Pembroke   Linney Head   Caldey Island

St Govan's Head   Worms Head   Oxwich Castle   Mumbles Head   Swansea Bay

Po

Lundy   Old Quay Head   Ilfracombe   A3123

Barnstaple or Bideford Bay   Marwood Hill   Arlington Court   A39

Hartland Point   Tapeley Park   Barnstaple

Hartland Abbey   Bideford   Broomham Farm

Docton Mill & Garden   Clovelly Village A39   Rosemoor RHS Garden   Highe Thornhan

Bude Bay   A3072   Colleton Manor Chapel

A3072   DEVO

Okehampton Castle   Finch Found

Tintagel Castle   Cullacott Farmhouse   A30   Castle Drogo

Tintagel Old Post Office   Launceston Castle & Lawrence House   Lydford Castles & Saxon Town   Hound Tor Deser Medieval Villa

Trevose Head   Trevelner Farmhouse   Endsleigh House   Kilworthy Farm Cow Houses & Granary

Prideaux Place   Pencarrow   CORNWALL   Ken Caro   Cotehele   Morwellham Quay   The Garden House   Buckfast Abb

Newquay   Japanese Garden & Bonsai Nursery   Bodmin   Lanhydrock   Buckland Abbey   Hemerdon House

Trerice   Restormel Castle   Boconnoc   Saltash   PLYMOUTH   Totne Castle

Truro   Trewithen   St Catherine's Castle   Fowey   Torpoint   Plympton

Bosvigo   Pine Lodge   Gribbin Head   Antony House & Woodland Garden   Saltram House   Flete

Redruth   Lost Gardens of Heligan   Mount Edgcumbe   Puslinch

Tate St Ives   Camborne   Caerhays Castle   Elizabethan Gardens, Prysten House & Smeatons Tower   Cookwo Museum

St Ives   Burncoose   Dodman Point

Chysauster Ancient Village   Godolphin   Trelissick   Overbeck Museum & Garde

Trengwainton   Penzance   Helston   St Mawes

Land's End   St Michael's Mount   Porth-en-Alls Lodge   Trebah   Pendennis Castle

Falmouth   Glendurgan

Trelowarren   Tregithew   SANTANDER SUMMER ONLY   ROSCOFF   ST MALO WINTER ONLY

Mount's Bay

Lizard Point

Tresco Abbey Gardens   Isles of Scilly

MAP 1

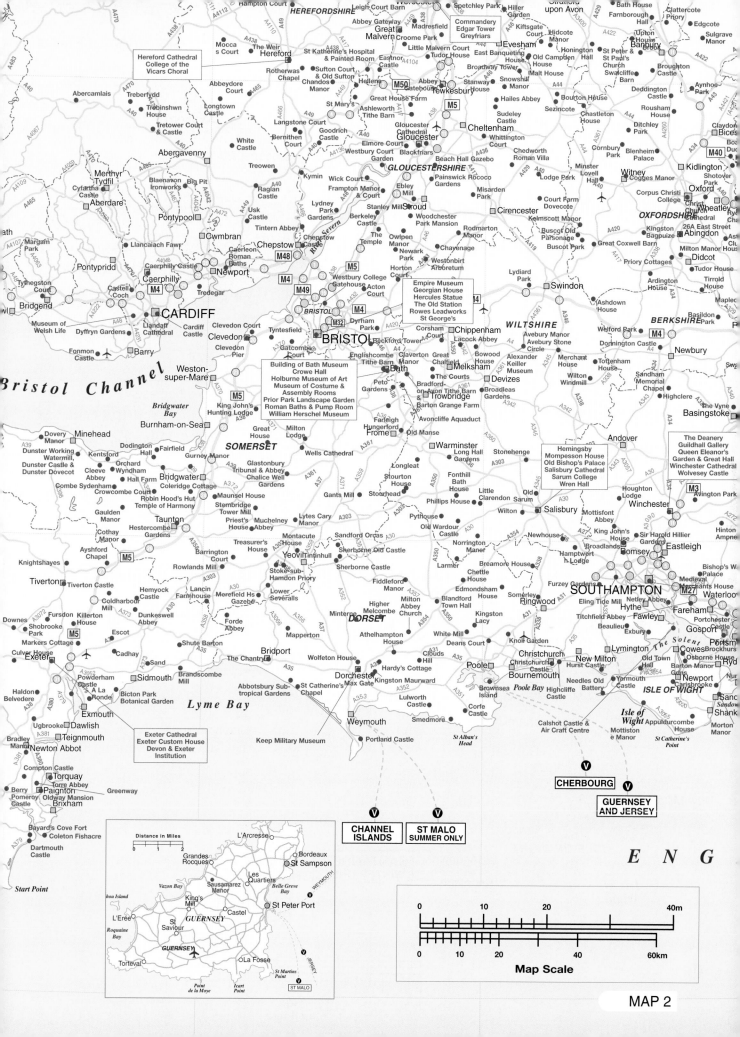

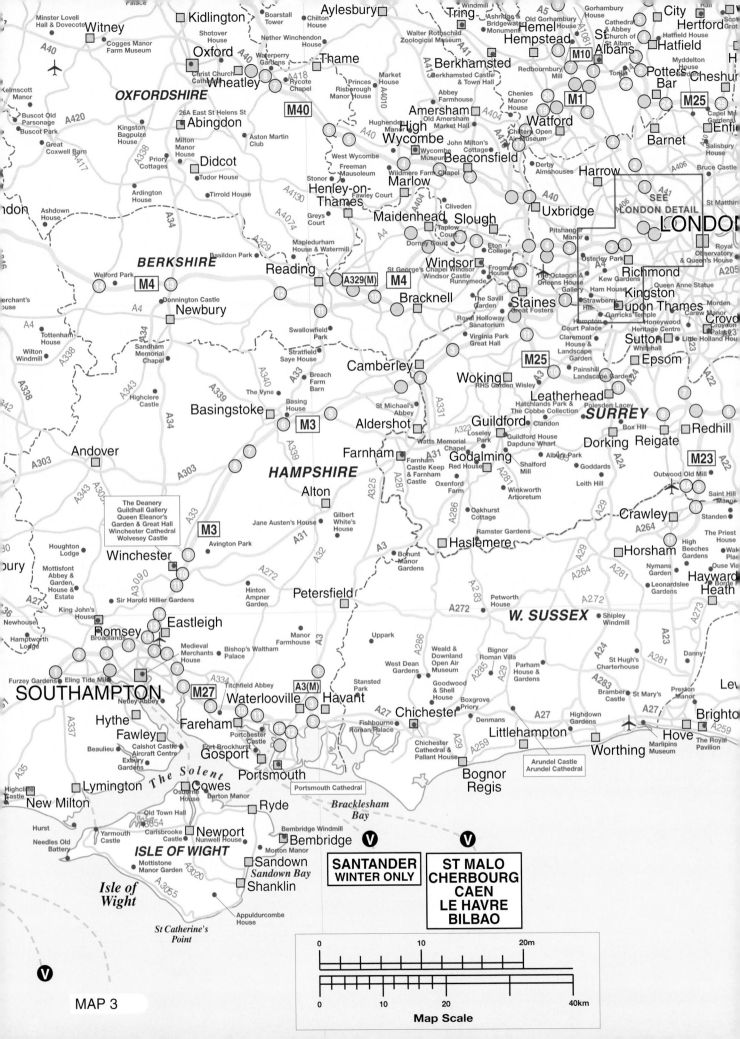

MAP 3

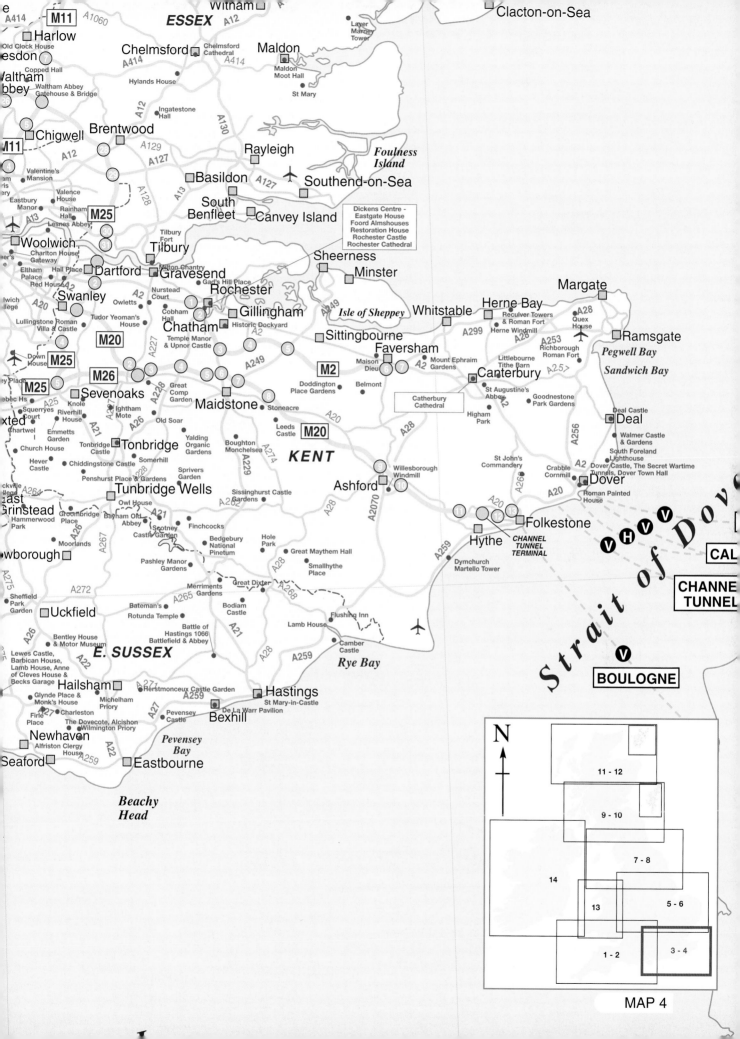

ESSEX

Clacton-on-Sea

Witham

M11 A1060

Harlow
Old Clock House
esdon
Valtham
Abbey
Waltham Abbey
Gatehouse & Bridge

Chelmsford
Chelmsford Cathedral

A414
A12

Maldon
Maldon Moot Hall
St Mary

Layer Marney Tower

Hylands House

Ingatestone Hall

Chigwell

Brentwood

A12

A129

Rayleigh

Foulness Island

M11

A127

Valentine's Mansion

Basildon

Southend-on-Sea

Eastbury Manor

Valence House

A128

A13

South Benfleet

Canvey Island

M25

Rainham Hall
Lesnes Abbey

Woolwich
Charlton House Gateway
Eltham Palace
Red House

Hall Place

Tilbury
Tilbury Fort

Dartford

Gravesend
Milton Chantry

Sheerness

Minster

Margate

Dickens Centre - Eastgate House
Foord Almshouses
Restoration House
Rochester Castle
Rochester Cathedral

Swanley
Nurstead Court
Owletts

Rochester

A249

Isle of Sheppey

Whitstable

Herne Bay
Reculver Towers & Roman Fort
Herne Windmill

Quex House

Ramsgate

Lullingstone Roman Villa & Castle

Tudor Yeoman's House

Cobham Hall

Chatham
Temple Manor & Upnor Castle
Historic Dockyard

Gillingham

A2

Sittingbourne

Faversham

A299

A28

Pegwell Bay

Sandwich Bay

Down House

M20

M25

A227

A2

A249

Maison Dieu

Mount Ephraim Gardens

A253
Richborough Roman Fort

Littlebourne
Tithe Barn

Canterbury

St Augustine's Abbey

A25

M26

Sevenoaks
Knole

Great Comp Garden

Ightham Mote

Maidstone
Stoneacre

Doddington Place Gardens

Belmont

Catherbury Cathedral

Goodnestone Park Gardens

Deal Castle

Deal

M25

Squerryes Court
Riverhill House

Old Soar

Leeds Castle

A20

Higham Park

Walmer Castle & Gardens

South Foreland Lighthouse

Emmetts Garden
Chartwell
Church House

Tonbridge
Tonbridge Castle

Somerhill

Yalding Organic Gardens

Boughton Monchelsea

A274

KENT

A28

St John's Commandery

A2

A256

Crabble Cornmill

Dover Castle, The Secret Wartime Tunnels, Dover Town Hall

Dover

Hever Castle

Chiddingstone Castle

Penshurst Place & Gardens

Sprivers Garden

Sissinghurst Castle Gardens

A229

A2070

Willesborough Windmill

Ashford

Roman Painted House

East Grinstead
Hammerwood Park

Tunbridge Wells

Owl House
Groombridge Place
Bayham Old Abbey
Scotney Castle Garden

Finchcocks

A282

A21

A28

St John's Commandery

A20

A259

Folkestone

Hythe

CHANNEL TUNNEL TERMINAL

V H V V

Strait of Dove

CAL

Moorlands

wborough

Bedgebury National Pinetum

Pashley Manor Gardens

Hole Park

Great Maytham Hall

Smallhythe Place

A28

A259

Dymchurch Martello Tower

CHANNEL TUNNEL

A275

A272

Bateman's
Rotunda Temple

Merriments Gardens

Great Dixter

A265

A268

Flushing Inn

Sheffield Park Garden

Uckfield

Bentley House & Motor Museum

Bodiam Castle

Lamb House

Battle of Hastings 1066
Battlefield & Abbey

A21

Camber Castle

Rye Bay

V

BOULOGNE

Lewes Castle,
Barbican House,
Lamb House, Anne
of Cleves House &
Becks Garage

A26

A22

E. SUSSEX

A28

A259

Newhaven

Hailsham

Glynde Place & Monk's House
Firle Place
Charleston

A271
Herstmonceux Castle Garden

A27

Michelham Priory

Pevensey Castle

The Dovecote, Alcishon
Wilmington Priory

Hastings
St Mary-in-Castle

De La Warr Pavilion

Bexhill

Pevensey Bay

Seaford

Alfriston Clergy House

A22

A259

Eastbourne

Beachy Head

N

11 - 12

9 - 10

7 - 8

14

13

5 - 6

1 - 2

3 - 4

MAP 4

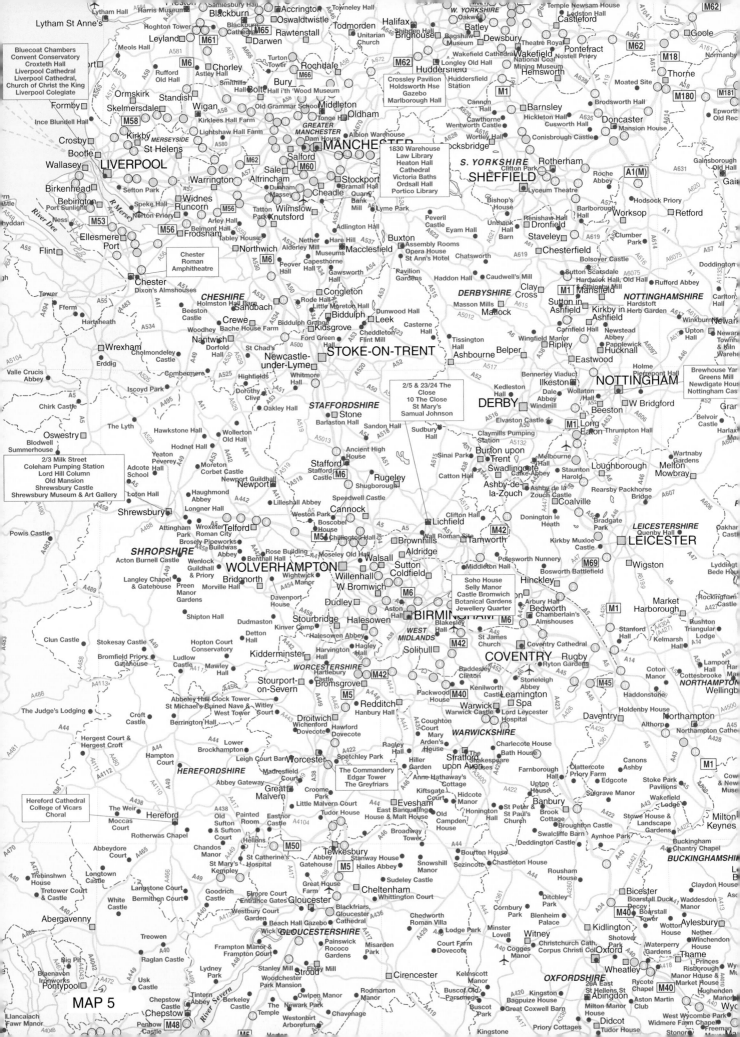

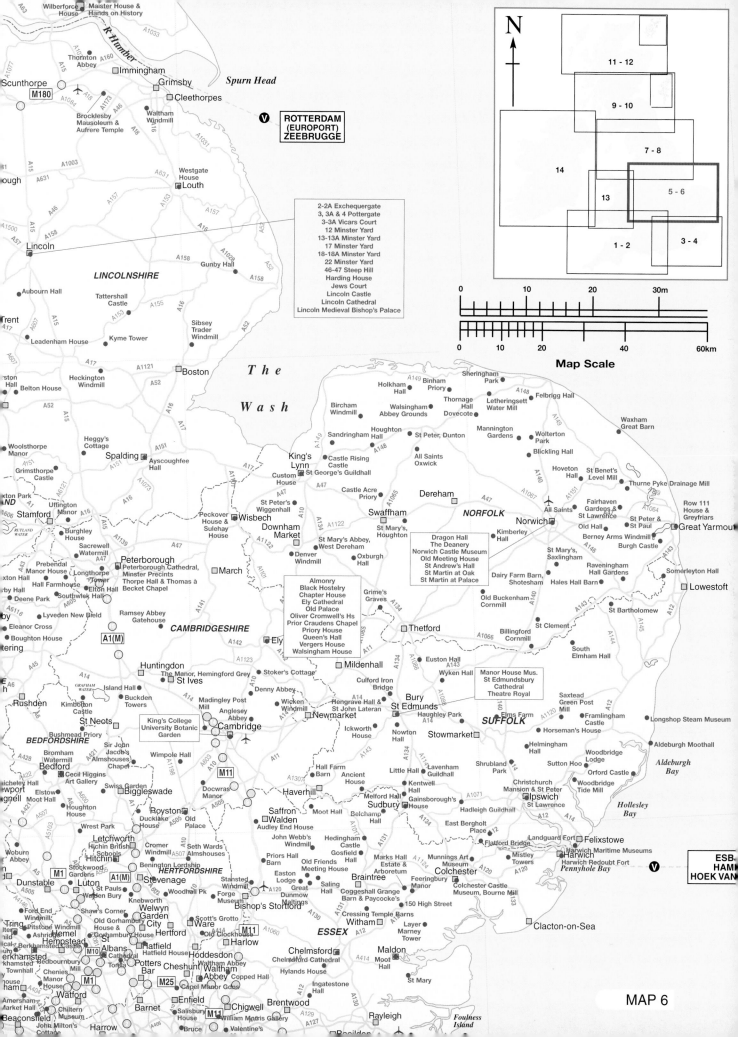

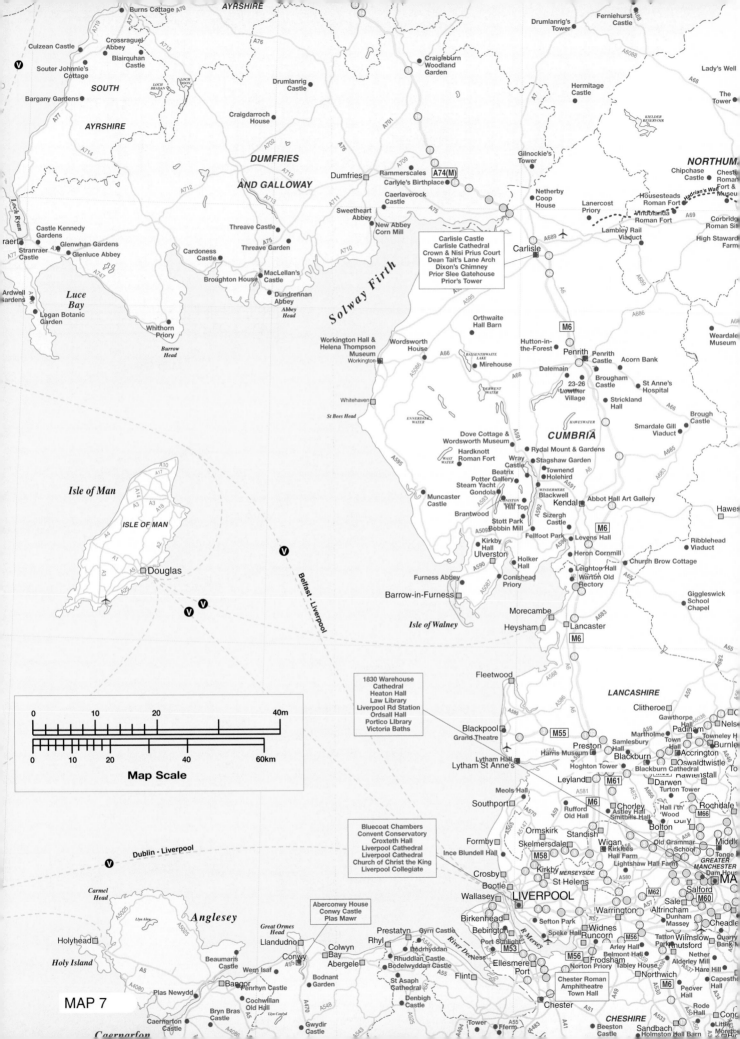

AYRSHIRE

Burns Cottage A70

Culzean Castle
Souter Johnnie's Cottage
Bargany Gardens

SOUTH

Crossraguel Abbey
Blairquhan Castle

AYRSHIRE

Craigdarroch House

Drumlanrig Castle

DUMFRIES

AND GALLOWAY

Craigieburn Woodland Garden

Drumlanrig's Tower

Fernieshurst Castle

Lady's Well

NORTHUM

Hermitage Castle

The Tower

KIELDER RESERVOIR

Dumfries
Rammerscales
Carlyle's Birthplace

A74(M)

Caerlaverock Castle

Sweetheart Abbey
New Abbey Corn Mill

Netherby Coop House

Gilnockie's Tower

Chipchase Castle

Chest Roman

Lady's Well

Lanercost Priory

Housesteads Roman Fort &

Hadrian's Wall

Mu

Carlisle

Vindolanda Roman Fort

Lambley Viaduct

A69

Corbridge Roman Sit

High Stawardi Farm

Castle Kennedy Gardens
raer
Stranraer Castle
Glenwhan Gardens
Glenluce Abbey

Ardwell Gardens
Logan Botanic Garden

Luce Bay

Threave Castle
Threave Garden

Cardoness Castle

Broughton House

MacLellan's Castle

Dundrennan Abbey

Abbey Head

Solway Firth

Whithorn Priory

Burrow Head

Workington Hall & Helena Thompson Museum
Workington

Wordsworth House

Whitehaven

St Bees Head

Carlisle Castle
Carlisle Cathedral
Crown & Nisi Prius Court
Dean Tait's Lane Arch
Dixon's Chimney
Prior Slee Gatehouse
Prior's Tower

Orthwaite Hall Barn

Hutton-in-the-Forest

M6

Penrith

Mirehouse

BASSENTHWAITE LAKE

A66

DERWENT WATER

Dalemain

Penrith Castle

Acorn Bank

23-26 Lowther Village

Brougham Castle

St Anne's Hospital

Strickland Hall

Weardale Museum

Brough Castle

Smardale Gill Viaduct

CUMBRIA

ENNERDALE WATER

WAST WATER

Dove Cottage & Wordsworth Museum

Hardknott Roman Fort

Wray Castle

Beatrix Potter Gallery
Steam Yacht Gondola

Muncaster Castle

Brantwood

Hill Top

Stott Park Bobbin Mill

Rydal Mount & Gardens
Stagshaw Garden
Townend
Holehird

Blackwell

WINDERMERE

Kendal

Sizergh Castle

Abbot Hall Art Gallery

HAWESWATER

Hawe

Ribblehead Viaduct

Kirkby Hall
Ulverston

Furness Abbey

Barrow-in-Furness

Isle of Walney

Holker Hall

Fellfoot Park

Conishead Priory

Levens Hall

Heron Cornmill

Leighton Hall
Warton Old Rectory

Church Brow Cottage

Giggleswick School Chapel

M6

Morecambe

Heysham

Lancaster

M6

Isle of Man

ISLE OF MAN

Douglas

Belfast - Liverpool

Fleetwood

1830 Warehouse
Cathedral
Heaton Hall
Law Library
Liverpool Rd Station
Ordsall Hall
Portico Library
Victoria Baths

LANCASHIRE

Clitheroe

Gawthorpe Hall

Nels

Padiham

Towneley Hall

Burnle

Blackpool
Grand Theatre

Lytham Hall
Lytham St Anne's

M55

Harris Museum
Preston

Hoghton Tower

Martholme
Samlesbury Hall

Town Hall

Blackburn

Oswaldtwistle

Accrington

Blackburn Cathedral

To

Leyland

M61

Rawtenstall

Darwen

Turton Tower

Rochdale

Map Scale

0   10   20   40m

0   10   20   40   60km

Meols Hall

Southport

Bluecoat Chambers
Convent Conservatory
Croxteth Hall
Liverpool Cathedral
Liverpool Cathedral
Church of Christ the King
Liverpool Collegiate

Dublin - Liverpool

Formby

Ormskirk

Skelmersdale

M58

Rufford Old Hall

Standish

Astley Hall

Chorley

Hall i'th' Wood

Smithills Hall

Bolton

M6

Bury

M66

Wigan

Old Grammar School

GREATER MANCHESTER

Kirklees Hall Farm
Lightshaw Hall Farm

Tonge

Dam Hou

MA

Crosby

Kirkby

MERSEYSIDE

St Helens

A580

Salford

M62

Sale

M60

Carmel Head

Anglesey

Great Ormes Head

Ince Blundell Hall

Bootle
Wallasey

LIVERPOOL

Sefton Park

Birkenhead

Speke Hall

Warrington

Altrincham

Dunham Massey

Cheadle

Holyhead

Holy Island

Llandudno

Aberconwy House
Conwy Castle
Plas Mawr

Colwyn Bay
Abergele

Prestatyn
Rhyl

Gyrn Castle

Widnes

Runcorn

Bebington

Port Sunlight

Ness

M53

Ellesmere Port

R Mersey

R Dee

Bodrhyddan

Rhuddlan Castle
Bodelwyddan Castle

St Asaph Cathedral

Flint

M56

Frodsham

Norton Priory

Tatton Park

Wilmslow
Knutsford

Arley Hall

Quarry Bank M

Alderley Mill

Nether

Tabley House

Northwich

Hare Hill

Beaumaris Castle

Wern Isaf

Bangor

Penrhyn Castle

Cochwillan Old Hall

Bryn Bras Castle

Plas Newydd

Caernarfon Castle

Gwydir Castle

Bodnant Garden

Denbigh Castle

Chester Roman Amphitheatre
Town Hall

Chester

Beeston Castle

Peover Hall

Rode Hall

CHESHIRE

Sandbach

Cong

Capesth
Hall

Holmston Hall Barn

MAP 7

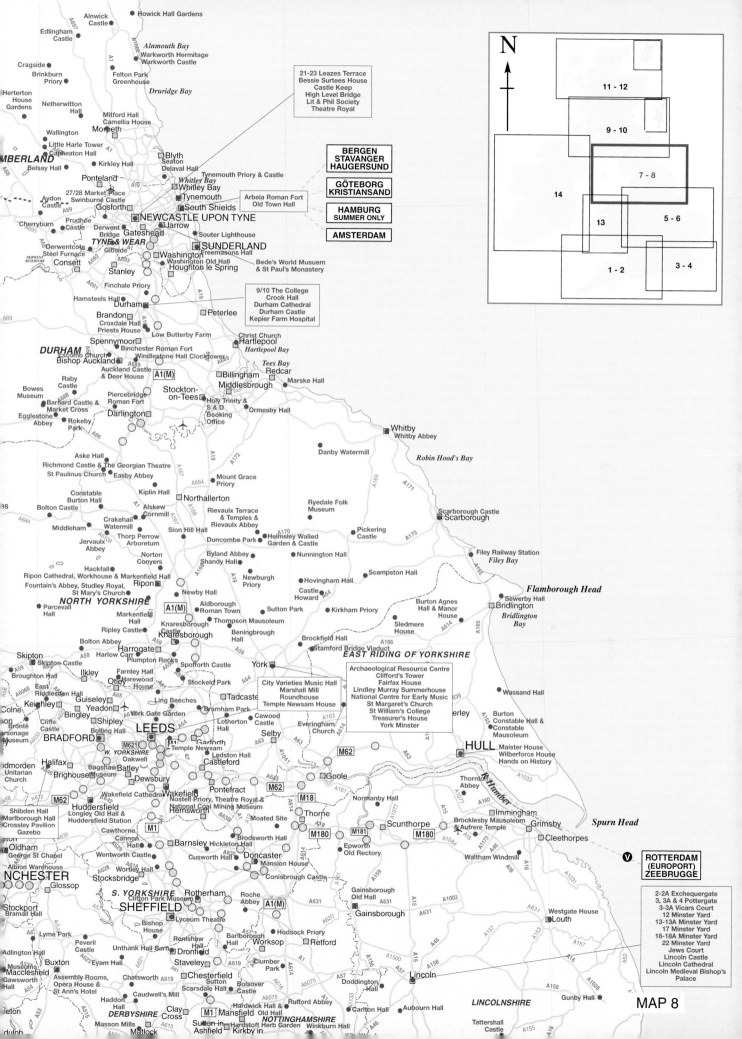

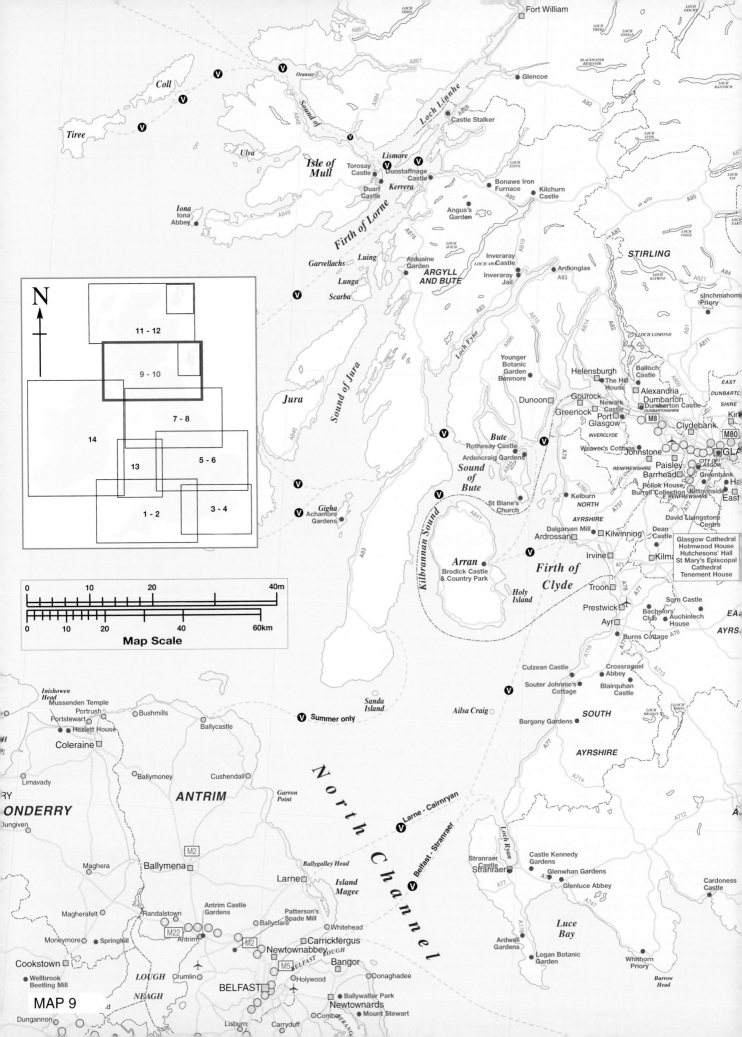

MAP 9

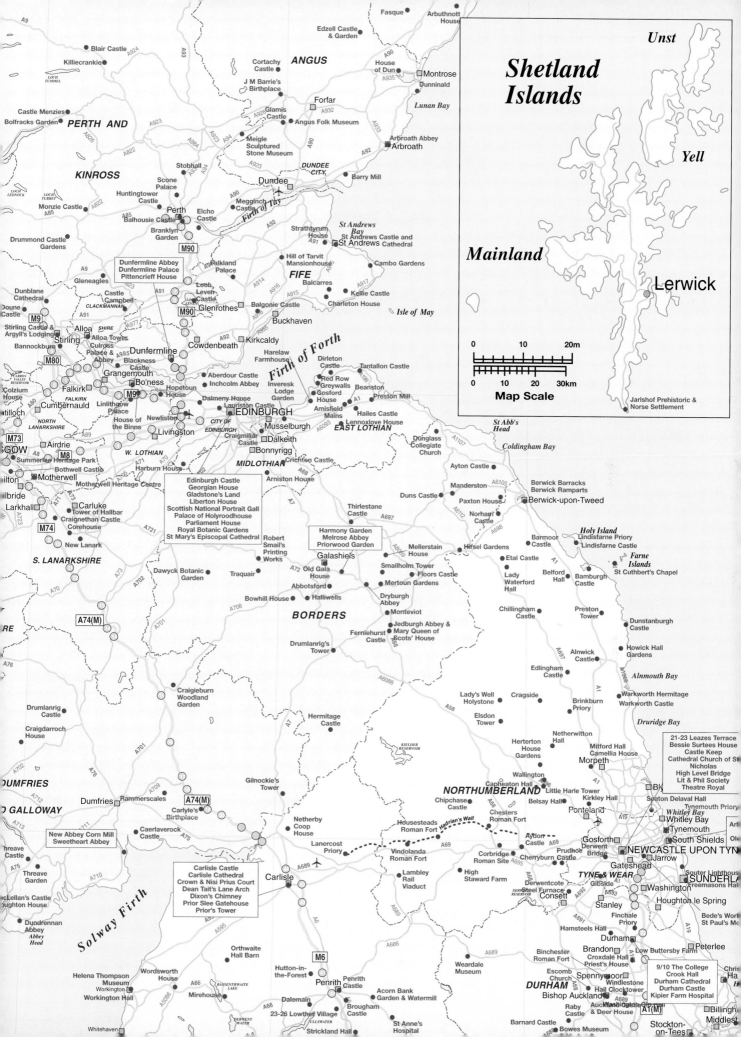

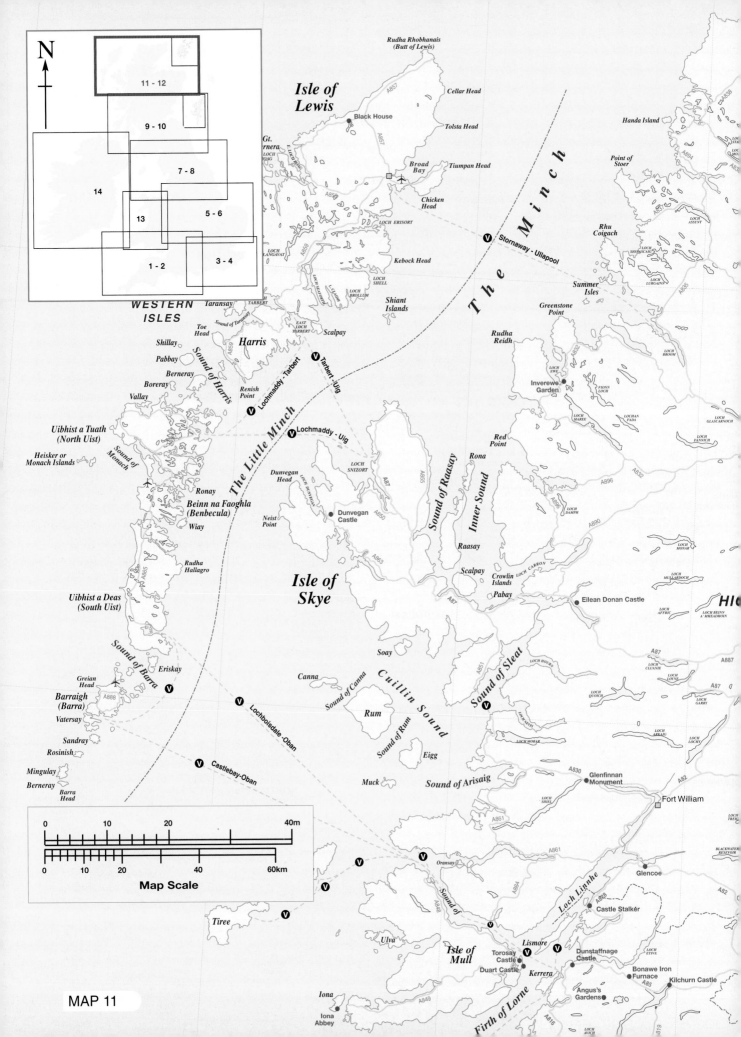

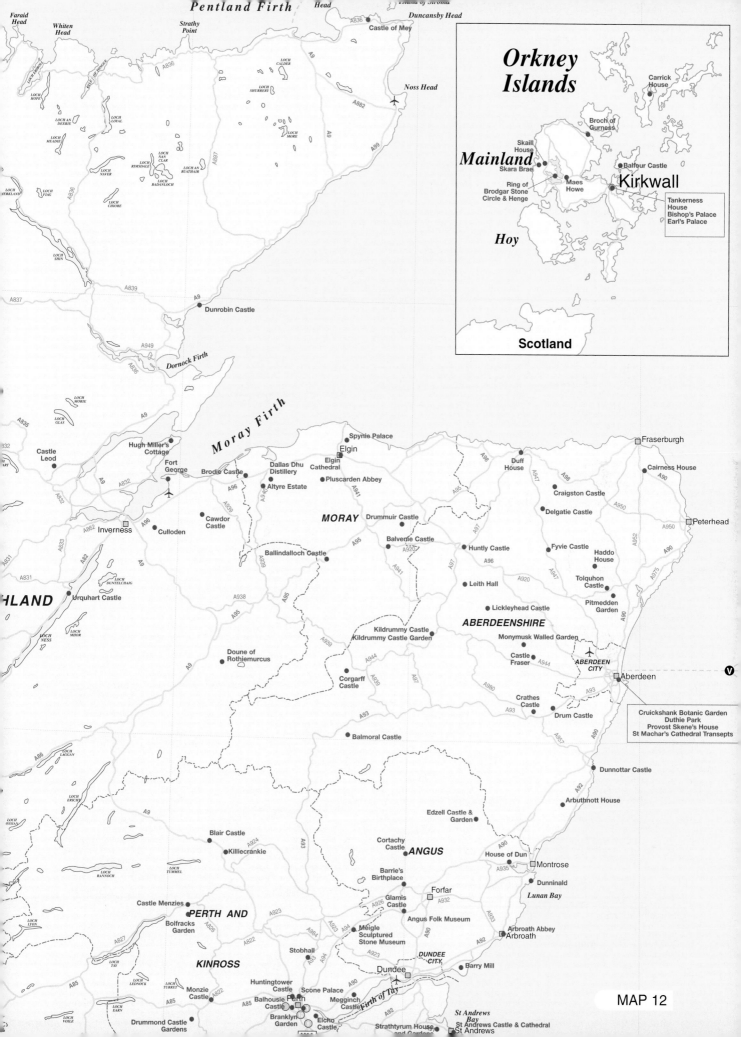

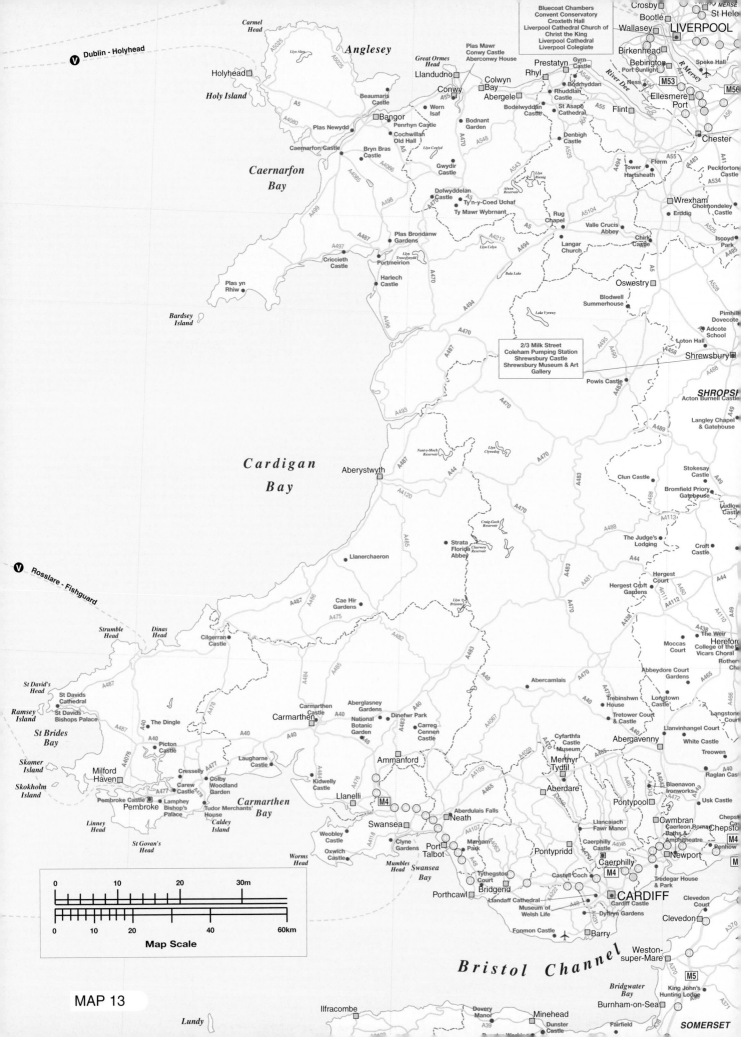

MAP 13

MAP 14

LONDON DETAIL

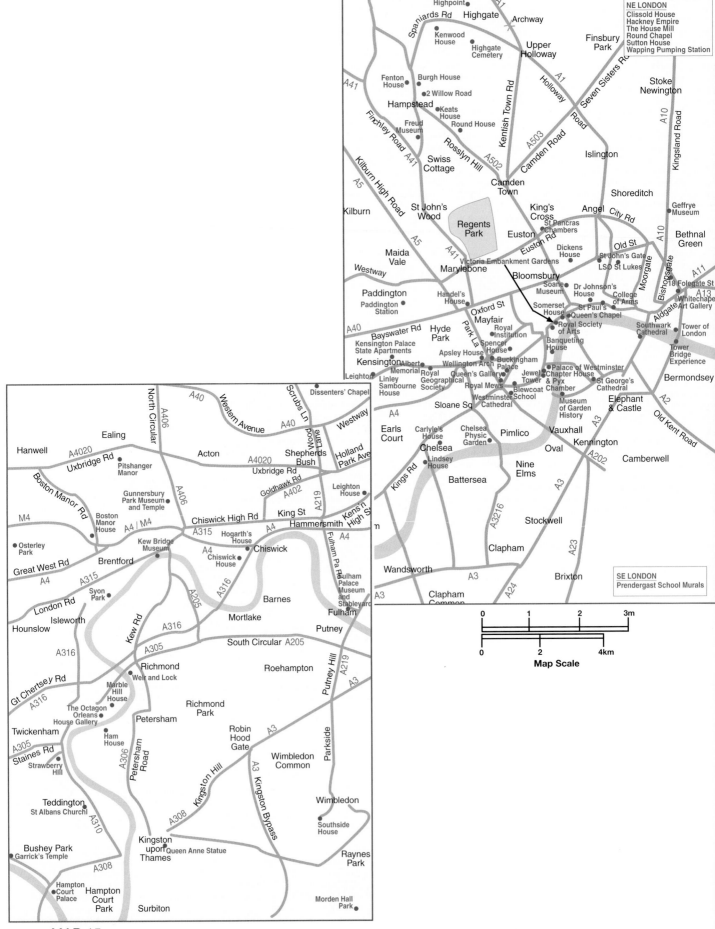

NE LONDON
Clissold House
Hackney Empire
The House Mill
Round Chapel
Sutton House
Wapping Pumping Station

SE LONDON
Prendergast School Murals

Map Scale

MAP 15

EDINBURGH & YORK DETAIL

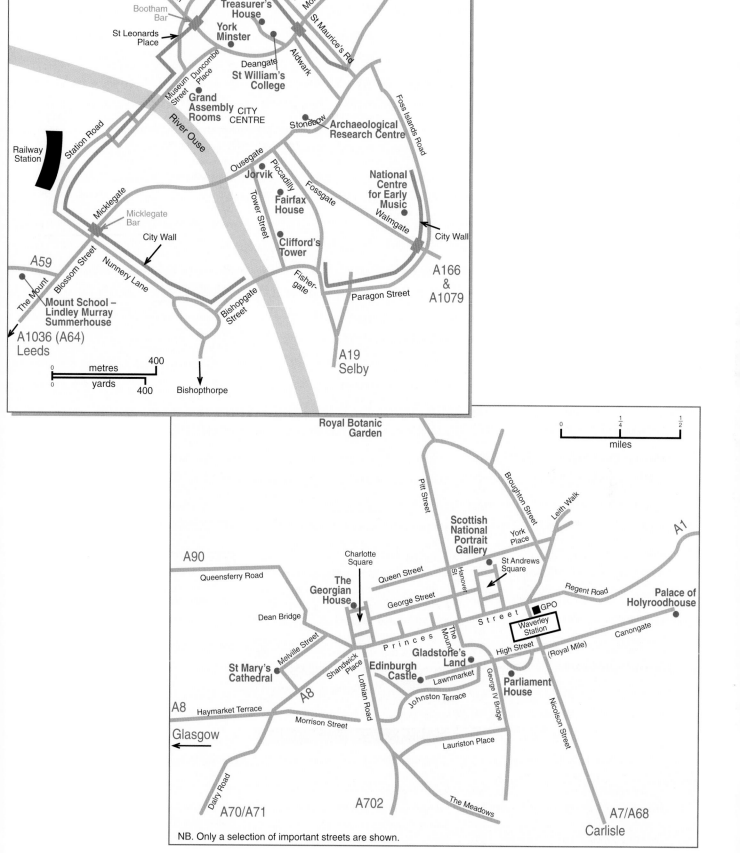

York map:

A19 Thirsk
A1036 (A64) Scarborough
Bootham
Gillygate
Lord Mayors Walk
Monkgate
Bootham Bar
St Leonards Place
St Maurice's Rd
Treasurer's House
York Minster
Deangate
St William's College
Aldwark
Museum Street
Duncombe Place
Grand Assembly Rooms
CITY CENTRE
Station Road
River Ouse
Railway Station
Stonebow
Archaeological Research Centre
Foss Islands Road
Micklegate
Micklegate Bar
City Wall
Ousegate
Jorvik
Piccadilly
Fairfax House
Fossgate
National Centre for Early Music
Walmgate
City Wall
A59
Blossom Street
Nunnery Lane
Tower Street
Clifford's Tower
A166 & A1079
The Mount
Mount School – Lindley Murray Summerhouse
Fishergate
Paragon Street
A1036 (A64) Leeds
Bishopgate Street
A19 Selby

0 ___ 400
metres
0 ___ 400
yards

Bishopthorpe

Edinburgh map:

Royal Botanic Garden
0 ¼ ½
miles
Pitt Street
Broughton Street
Leith Walk
A1
Scottish National Portrait Gallery
York Place
A90
Queensferry Road
Charlotte Square
Hanover St
St Andrews Square
Regent Road
Palace of Holyroodhouse
The Georgian House
Queen Street
George Street
Street
GPO
Waverley Station
Canongate
Dean Bridge
Melville Street
Princes
The Mound
High Street
(Royal Mile)
St Mary's Cathedral
Shandwick Place
Gladstone's Land
Edinburgh Castle
Lawnmarket
George IV Bridge
Parliament House
A8
A8 Haymarket Terrace
Lothian Road
Johnston Terrace
Nicolson Street
Morrison Street
Glasgow
Lauriston Place
Dalry Road
A70/A71
A702
The Meadows
A7/A68
Carlisle

NB. Only a selection of important streets are shown.

MAP 16

c

D

M